BANKRUPTCY
CASES AND MATERIALS

Sixth Edition

■ ■ ■

Margaret Howard
Law Alumni Association Professor of Law
Washington and Lee University

Lois R. Lupica
Maine Law Foundation Professor of Law
University of Maine School of Law

AMERICAN CASEBOOK SERIES®

WEST ACADEMIC PUBLISHING

American Casebook Series is a trademark registered in the U.S. Patent and Trademark Office.

© West, a Thomson business, 2001, 2004, 2005
© 2012 Thomson Reuters
© 2016 LEG, Inc. d/b/a West Academic
    444 Cedar Street, Suite 700
    St. Paul, MN 55101
    1-877-888-1330

West, West Academic Publishing, and West Academic are trademarks of West Publishing Corporation, used under license.

Printed in the United States of America

ISBN: 978-1-63460-252-5

To William Miller Howard, Jr.,
in memory.

M.H.

To Vincent Lupica and to
Marie Lupica, in memory

L.R.L.

Preface

Bankruptcy law has it all: a long, tough statute that leaves huge and important issues unaddressed; rich case law development; sometimes an abundance and sometimes a dearth of legislative history; intriguing policy questions that go to the heart of what the law is and ought to be doing; theory, as well as real-world practicality; economic analysis that enriches the debate on some issues and adds little on others; and even a constitutional issue or two poking around. What subject matter could be more fun to both study and practice?

The Sixth Edition of this casebook now has a new co-author, Professor Lois R. Lupica of the University of Maine School of Law. This edition, however, continues the dual emphases of earlier editions—careful case reading, and the reinforcement of concepts through problems. We continue to treat concepts common to business and consumer bankruptcies in an integrated way. We have also tried to present a balanced perspective, avoiding any one political or theoretical position.

As has been said about prior editions, we set out to write the perfect bankruptcy book. While we no doubt fell far short of that mark, this book nevertheless reflects hard thinking about the best way to present hard concepts.

M.H.
Lexington, Virginia

L.R.L.
Portland, Maine

November 2015

Acknowledgements

Andrew, Michael T., *Executory Contracts in Bankruptcy: Understanding "Rejection,"* 59 U. COLO. L.REV. 845 (1988) (p. 599).

Baird, Douglas G. & Thomas H. Jackson, *Fraudulent Conveyance Law and Its Proper Domain*, 38 VAND. L. REV. 829 (1985) (p. 392).

Blumberg, Phillip I., *Intragroup (Upstream, Cross-Stream, and Downstream) Guaranties Under the Uniform Fraudulent Transfer Act*, 9 CARDOZO L. REV. 685 (1987) (p. 394).

Browne, Dik, *Hagar the Horrible* cartoon. © Reprinted with permission of King Features Syndicate/North American Syndicate (p. 731).

Bruce, Kara J., *Rehabilitating Bankruptcy Reform*, 13 NEV. L.J. 174 (2015) (p. 606).

Clark, Robert Charles, *The Duties of the Corporate Debtor to Its Creditors*, 90 HARV. L. REV. 505 (1977) (p. 403).

Countryman, Vern, *Executory Contracts in Bankruptcy: Part I*, 57 MINN. L. REV. 439 (1973) (p. 530).

Eisenberg, Theodore, *Bankruptcy Law in Perspective*, 28 UCLA L. REV. 953 (1981) (p. 621).

Eisenberg, Theodore, *The Unsecured Creditor in Reorganizations and the Nature of Security*, 38 VAND. L. REV. 931 (1985) (p. 275).

Guisewite, Cathy. *Cathy* cartoon (two). Distributed by Universal Press Syndicate. Reprinted by permission. (p. 661).

Howard, Margaret, *A Theory of Discharge in Consumer Bankruptcy*, 48 OHIO ST. L.J. 1047 (1987) (p. 622).

Jackson, Thomas H., THE LOGIC AND LIMITS OF BANKRUPTCY LAW (1986) (p. 36).

Keating, Daniel, *Offensive Uses of the Bankruptcy Stay*, 45 VAND. L. REV. 71 (1991) (p. 146).

Robert M. Lawless, Angela K. Littwin, Katherine M. Porter, John A.E. Pottow, Deborah K. Thorne, & Elizabeth Warren, *Did Bankruptcy Reform Fail? An Empirical Study of Consumer Debtors*, 82 AM. BANK. L.J. 349 (2008) (p. 87).

Lazarus, Mell. *Miss Peach* cartoon. Creators Syndicate, Inc. Copyrighted by Mell Lazarus. (p. 326).

Ponoroff, Lawrence & F. Stephen Knippenberg, *The Implied Good Faith Filing Requirement: Sentinel of an Evolving Bankruptcy Policy*, 85 NW. U.L. REV. 919 (1991) (p. 36).

Ryan, T. K., *Tumbleweeds* cartoon (1989). © Reprinted with permission of King Features Syndicate/North American Syndicate (p. 321).

Smyser, Kathryn V., *Going Private and Going Under: Leveraged Buyouts and the Fraudulent Conveyance Problem*, 63 IND. L.J. 781 (1988) (p. 393).

Smythe, Reggie, *Andy Capp* cartoon (two). Reprinted by permission (p. 343).

Stefania Albanesi & Jaromir Nosal, INSOLVENCY AFTER THE 2005 BANKRUPTCY REFORM (Staff Report No. 725, Federal Reserve Bank of New York, April 2015) (p. 87).

Sullivan, Teresa A., Elizabeth Warren & Jay L. Westbrook, AS WE FORGIVE OUR DEBTORS: BANKRUPTCY AND CONSUMER CREDIT IN AMERICA (1989) (p. 87).

Note on Citations

The Bankruptcy Code, 11 U.S.C. § 101 et seq., is generally referred to in this casebook by section number only.

Several subsections of the Code have been renumbered since their enactment. When these subsections are cited in cases, the original numbering is omitted and the current number is indicated in brackets.

Citations in cases and quoted material are sometimes omitted without indication, but other omissions are noted with ellipses. Some citations have been moved and edited for clarity and form. Numerous references are made in the cases to the Code's legislative history, principally the House Report, H.R. Rep. No. 595, 95th Cong., 1st Sess. (1977), and to the Senate Report, S. Rep. No. 989, 95th Cong., 2nd Sess. (1978), both of which are reprinted in U.S. Code Congressional and Administrative News (1978). Almost all of those references have been edited to the following form: H.R. Rep. No. 95-595 at ___, *reprinted* in 1978 U.S.C.C.A.N. at ___; S. Rep. No. 95-989 at ___, *reprinted* in 1978 U.S.C.C.A.N. at ___.

The original numbering of footnotes found in the cases has been retained. Editorial footnotes are indicated by letters.

Summary of Contents

Table of Contents

_____

Table of Cases

Principal cases are in bold type. Cases cited or discussed in the text are in roman type. Cases cited in principal cases and within other quoted materials are not included. References are to pages.

Table of Statutes

BANKRUPTCY

CASES AND MATERIALS

Sixth Edition

Chapter 1

==

CREDITORS' RIGHTS AND REMEDIES

A. INTRODUCTION

We tend to think of obligations that debtors owe to creditors in contract terms—a loan or a purchase, each of which creates an obligation to pay that derives from the agreement between the debtor and creditor. In truth, the obligation imposed on one party (the "debtor") to pay money to another (the "creditor") may derive from many other sources. The careless driver of an automobile who plows into another car has just become a debtor. The taxpayer is a debtor, as is the parent who owes child support and the corporation that dumps toxic waste.

Debtors, whatever the source of the obligation, sometimes fail to pay. In that event, creditors can resort to collection devices made available under the contract between the parties, or under state or non-bankruptcy federal law. The nature of a particular creditor's collection choices depends upon whether that creditor is an unsecured (or general) creditor or the holder of some type of lien—that is, a collateral interest in property of the debtor. The second category includes creditors with judgment or execution liens, security interests and statutory liens—that is, liens that arise consensually, nonconsensually and by statute.

For each of these categories, we must be able to answer two important questions. First, what rights does the creditor enjoy against the debtor and the debtor's property? Second, what rights does the creditor enjoy against other creditors also seeking to be paid by this debtor? The former may be described as a question of *rights* and the latter as a question of *priority*.

1. RIGHTS

If a debtor fails to meet its obligation to a creditor, as in the case of a loan contract, or if an obligation must be established in the first instance, as in a tort case, the first step a creditor usually takes is to file a lawsuit. Successful prosecution of the suit only produces a judgment, however; it does not put money into the hands of the creditor. Here the creditor must turn to statutes that vary from state to state. These statutes are similar in broad outline, however, so we can generalize.

A debtor, of course, may choose to pay the judgment once the creditor obtains it. That happy possibility is legally uninteresting, as you might expect. Also, the debtor usually fails to pay in the first instance not because of unwillingness but because of inability. Thus, the creditor may need the resources of the state to turn the judgment into money. The two primary methods are judgment liens and execution liens.

Although a judgment lien is obtained automatically in some states when a judgment is entered, in most states a judgment must be "docketed" before a lien is created. In all but a handful of states, docketing creates a lien on any real property the debtor owns in the county in which the judgment was docketed. In three states—Alabama, Georgia and Mississippi—the judgment lien attaches to personal property as well. The judgment lien does not give the lienholder a right to immediate possession of the property. Rather, the lienholder must take whatever additional steps are required by state law, whether foreclosure or levy and sale under writ of execution.

The writ of execution, besides being the method for enforcing a judgment lien in some states, is the only method for reaching the debtor's personal property in states other than Alabama, Georgia and Mississippi. A writ of execution, which is addressed to the sheriff, directs the sheriff to seize and sell property of the debtor sufficient to satisfy the judgment creditor's claim. Levy by the sheriff creates an execution lien as of that date in most states, although in a few states the lien relates back either to the date the writ was issued by the clerk or to the date the writ was delivered to the sheriff.

Although judgment and execution liens give a creditor the right to obtain the property subject to the lien, that right may be limited by the debtor's "exemptions." Every state, by statute, lists specific items of property that are immune from the reach of creditors. These lists vary from state to state and many of them are woefully outdated, but the idea behind each state's list is the same—to provide the debtor a minimum amount of property necessary for survival. This protects both the debtor and the society upon which the debtor would otherwise become dependent. (We will examine exemptions in bankruptcy in Chapter 2, Section D of this casebook.)

2. PRIORITIES

Since a debtor often defaults on payments to more than one creditor, multiple judgments may be taken against a single debtor. These judgments are likely to result in multiple judgment liens that encumber the same property. The priority of these competing liens is determined, generally, by statute. Priority is never determined by agreement between the debtor and creditor, because such an agreement would affect the rights of third parties.

When proper execution is accomplished, the collateral is sold and the proceeds made available to the lienholders. A lien with first priority is satisfied first out of the value of the collateral. If value is left over, the next lien is satisfied, and so on down the line until value is exhausted. The creditor holding a lien that is unpaid from the value of the collateral does not lose its rights against the debtor; the debt continues in existence, but the creditor has to find another way to collect. For example, assume that the debtor's real estate, worth $60,000, is subject to two liens; the debtor owes the first lienholder $50,000 and owes the second lienholder $25,000. When the property is sold, the first lienholder will be paid in full and the second lienholder will receive $10,000. The second lienholder retains a claim for the balance ($15,000), but has no more collateral from which to seek payment.

The general priority rule is "first-in-time, first-in-right." In other words, the first lien to come into existence has first priority. (It is often referred to as a "senior" lien and liens having lower priority are "junior" liens.) A major exception to this general rule arises when some sort of public notice is required in order to "perfect" the lien. "Perfection" refers to the steps required to make a lien that is already enforceable against the debtor also enforceable against third parties, such as competing lienholders. These perfecting steps are designed to make third parties aware of the interest in the property claimed by the perfecting lienholder. If some sort of public notice is required for perfection, priority generally dates from the time the perfecting step is taken. The priority of judicial liens is normally measured from the date of docketing. Because execution liens usually arise only upon levy by the sheriff, that step accomplishes both creation of the lien and the public notice necessary to protect the executing creditor from competing claims. If the execution lien relates back to the date the writ is issued or delivered to the sheriff, however, priority problems may arise if a third party purchases the property or obtains a lien on the property before the sheriff takes possession.

A first-in-time perfected lien is not completely invulnerable. Certain types of third parties can take priority even though their interests arise later. For example, in some states a judicial lien attaches to the debtor's after-acquired real property, but that preexisting lien will be junior to a purchase money mortgagee whose loan made acquisition of the property possible.

B. CONSENSUAL LIENS

Judgment and execution liens are *nonconsensual*—that is, they arise in the absence of agreement between the debtor and creditor. The parties, however, may agree to the creation of a lien on specified items or types of the debtor's property. These *consensual* liens fall into two categories—security interests, which attach to personal property, and mortgages (including deeds of trust), which attach to real property.

1. SECURITY INTERESTS

a. Rights

A security interest is an interest in personal property, whether tangible or intangible, given to secure the performance of an obligation (typically, the repayment of a loan or the payment of the purchase price of goods). Security interests are governed by Article 9 of the Uniform Commercial Code (UCC). A security interest is enforceable between the debtor and the creditor ("secured party") when it "attaches." Attachment requires that: (1) the parties have a written "security agreement," which is the contract creating the security interest; (2) the debtor has acquired rights in the collateral subject to the security interest; and (3) the creditor has given value, as by making a loan or selling goods on credit. A written security agreement is not required if the creditor takes possession of the collateral.

A secured party has, upon the debtor's default, a cumulative assortment of remedies. Default is defined by the parties in the security agreement, rather than by Article 9, and usually includes such events as failing to make timely payments and failing to insure or otherwise properly care for collateral. Default also is often defined to include any event that increases the possibility of nonpayment, such as the filing of bankruptcy. Most security agreements accelerate the entire remaining obligation upon default.

One of the most important remedies under Article 9 is the right to take possession of the collateral without judicial process, as long as this so-called "self-help repossession" can be accomplished without a breach of the peace. After possession is obtained, whether by self-help or by judgment and execution, the collateral is sold and the proceeds applied to the expenses of sale and to the debt. The debtor is entitled to any surplus proceeds (which are as rare as the white rhino) and remains liable for any deficiency.

Collection pursuant to a security interest, unlike levy upon a writ of execution, is not limited by the debtor's exemptions. Exempt property can be collateral subject to a security interest and the exemptions statute will not insulate the debtor from the secured party's collection efforts. Because a security interest is *consensual*, the debtor is in no position to complain.

b. Priorities

In order to obtain priority against other claimants to the property of the debtor, a secured party must "perfect" its security interest. Perfection usually requires the filing of a "financing statement" in the place(s) specified in UCC § 9–501, although perfection can also be accomplished by possession in most cases. A few types of Article 9 interests, however, are automatically perfected upon attachment. The most significant example of automatic perfection is purchase money security interests in consumer goods other than automobiles. Also, a few types of Article 9 interests, such as negotiable instruments, can only be perfected by possession.

Article 9 is largely concerned with priorities. It provides rules governing the priority between competing security interests, whether perfected or unperfected, and between security interests and other types of competing claims. Article 9 generally follows the first-in-time, first-in-right rule, but as with so many other areas of law, exceptions are omnipresent and important.

One of the most significant priority provisions in Article 9, for purposes of bankruptcy law, is § 9–317(a)(2):

(a) A security interest * * * is subordinate to the rights of:

* * *

(2) except as otherwise provided in subsection (e), a person that becomes a lien creditor before the earlier of the time:

(A) the security interest * * * is perfected * * *.

Under § 9–317(a)(2), an *unperfected* security interest is subordinate (*i.e.*, junior) to a competing judicial lien. A secured party that fails to perfect its interest promptly after attachment, therefore, will be junior in priority to a creditor that obtains a judicial lien in the "gap" period before the security interest is perfected. It also follows from this subsection that a perfected security interest has priority over a judicial lien arising after the security interest was perfected.

As § 9–317(a)(2) indicates, § 9–317(e) provides a different rule:

* * * [I]f a person files a financing statement with respect to a purchase-money security interest before or within 20 days after the debtor receives delivery of the collateral, the security interest takes priority over the rights of a * * * lien creditor which arise between the time the security interest attaches and the time of filing.

Subsection (e) is a "relation back" provision. It allows a purchase money secured creditor, who files a financing statement *after* a lien creditor has acquired rights, to obtain priority nonetheless. The rule is justified by the favored position of a purchase money creditor, whose extension of value permitted the debtor to obtain the encumbered goods in the first place.

Note, too, *and remember* § 9–102(52)(C), which defines "lien creditor" to include a trustee in bankruptcy.

2. MORTGAGES

A mortgage is an interest in real estate, given to secure the performance of an obligation (usually, the repayment of a loan). As with security interests, a mortgage is effective between the debtor (mortgagor) and creditor (mortgagee) upon execution of the mortgage documents. Effectiveness against third parties is of much more concern, however, and priority requires recording. The first-in-time, first-in-right rule also applies in this context, generally dating various interests from the time that public notice is placed in the real estate records. Most real estate recording systems are not pure "race" statutes, awarding priority to the first party to file, without regard to that party's knowledge of competing interests. Real estate recording systems, rather, are either "notice" or "race-notice" systems. Under the former, a subsequent purchaser without knowledge of a prior purchaser's interest has priority, as long as the prior purchaser's interest was not recorded; no recording by the subsequent purchaser is necessary. Under the latter, a subsequent purchaser without knowledge of a prior purchaser's interest has priority, but only if the subsequent purchaser records first.

As with security interests, a mortgagee has the right to realize against the property upon default by the mortgagor. Default is defined by the mortgage documents, just as the security agreement defines default for purposes of Article 9 security interests, and usually includes failure to make timely payments of principal and interest, failure to pay taxes and insurance, and waste.

The mortgagee's remedy is foreclosure. It usually requires a judicially-approved sale, although about half the states permit foreclosure by an out-of-court sale. As with security interests, the proceeds of sale are distributed to creditors in accordance with their priority; the mortgagor is entitled to any surplus and remains liable for any deficiency.

C. STATUTORY LIENS

Statutory liens are, unsurprisingly, interests in property created by state or federal statutes. A vast array of liens fall into this category: materialmen's and mechanic's liens, which secure compensation for parties who contribute materials and labor to make improvements on land; landlord's liens, which attach to tenants' property and secure their lease obligations; artisans' liens, which secure the payment of expenses to repair personal property; environmental liens, created by both state and federal environmental statutes to secure reimbursement of amounts spent in cleaning up contaminated property; and tax liens, which need no explanation. These liens are as varied as you might imagine, so generalizations are problematic. Some of the most interesting of the priority issues surround environmental "superliens," which take priority over all others.

D. COLLECTION UNDER
NONBANKRUPTCY LAW

Bankruptcy is a creature of federal law. Before an entity (individual, corporate, or partnership) becomes the subject of a bankruptcy proceeding, state and nonbankruptcy federal law determine what a creditor must do to collect a debt. In order to appreciate bankruptcy's impact on a debtor-creditor relationship, one must first appreciate the panoply of state laws that may determine the rights of debtor and creditors before the initiation of an action in the bankruptcy court.

We have already reviewed some of these laws. Now let's consider the case of an individual who has, in fact, three legal identities as far as creditor-debtor law is concerned.

Janet Ward is a Conference Planner—a professional who attends to the details of arranging meetings for trade groups throughout the country. She is the part owner of Conferences, Inc., a corporation that typically handles logistics for meetings of more than 2,500 people at large hotels and resorts in the Eastern United States. Janet is in charge of planning, and works about 45 hours per week at that job.

Conferences, Inc. is a corporate entity, distinct from Janet Ward in the legal sense, with its own assets and liabilities. Janet owns 25% of the corporation's stock, and it has steadily increased in value as the business has grown. She is an integral part of the corporation. Without her, the corporation would not enjoy the same success and, in fact, might have to review its business plan and reduce the size of its customer base and areas of operation.

In her spare time, Janet acts as a consultant to smaller trade associations, helping them negotiate meeting space for groups of 500 or less. Janet is paid for that work at a rate of $250 per hour. She engages in that work with the knowledge and consent of the other owners of Conferences, Inc., who are happy to have her develop connections that will enhance her ability to attract new business to the corporation. Janet conducts her consulting business as a sole proprietorship, and scrupulously maintains financial records separate from her personal financial records. She uses "Janet Ward, Meeting Consultant" business cards and letterhead, and has a checking account in the name of the consulting business. All of the funds in that account are business funds and all of the checks drawn on that account are issued in payment of expenses of the sole proprietorship. She uses a business American Express card for many of the expenses of that consulting business.

Janet Ward is also, of course, an individual consumer. She never has more than $1,000 in her checking account and $2,500 in her savings account, both of which are maintained at a local credit union. She owns a car, subject to a security interest in favor of a local bank, a house, subject to a mortgage in favor of a local savings and loan, and personal effects that are unencumbered. She owes student loans and carries balances on three different Visa cards. She has a balance on her Sears card, which she recently used to purchase a new washing machine. Janet also has two retirement accounts: one funded by her employer, Conferences, Inc., and a separate Individual Retirement Account into which she has deposited $2,000 each year for the last five years.

In other words, Janet Ward is the typical young, upwardly mobile professional, living a life enhanced by relatively easy access to credit. She also has the capacity to increase her earnings as the fortunes of Conferences, Inc. improve and as she continues her private consulting business.

While it is not difficult to imagine the wealth that Janet Ward may accumulate as she grows professionally, it is also not difficult to imagine that personal and professional financial misfortunes could compromise both her current lifestyle and her future prospects. If all continues to go well, Janet will have no more than a passing interest in debtor-creditor law, state or federal. But if her financial fortunes take a turn for the worse, a panoply of laws will determine her lifestyle and prospects.

Because this book and course are concerned with the consequences of financial misfortune, focus on what can go wrong and how wrong it can all go even before the bankruptcy law is implicated.

If Janet were struck by a car and seriously injured during her daily commute, her life could change dramatically. A lengthy hospital stay followed by an extended period of rehabilitation could cost her thousands, even hundreds of thousands, of dollars. She might never recover this money, particularly if she has no insurance to cover expenses during her convalescence. Though it is not clear when her financial straits might become so dire as to make bankruptcy a (relatively) attractive option, it is clear that her personal creditors, as well as those of the corporation and of her consulting business, will take account of the rights provided them by state and federal law. Janet may have reason to learn more debtor protection law, state and federal, than she ever anticipated.

When a debtor is unable or unwilling to discharge her indebtedness (whether the debt arose in tort or contract), a creditor is generally free to pursue options designed to compel payment. So even though Janet's and her corporation's failure to pay their creditors in a timely manner was not a product of choice, creditors may pursue remedies available under state and federal law to recover on their claims.

While laws governing creditors' rights and debtors' protections vary from state to state, there is sufficient consistency to support some generalization.

1. REMEDIES AVAILABLE TO INDIVIDUAL CREDITORS

Remedies can be divided into two basic categories—provisional and post-judgment—although provisional remedies have post-judgment counterparts. Provisional remedies are available to a creditor who has not yet prosecuted its claim to judgment, but who has reason to believe that the delay involved with obtaining a judgment might compromise its ability to realize upon its claim, perhaps because the debtor is dissipating assets or presents a flight risk. Provisional remedies are designed to be temporary, to maintain the status quo pending judicial review of the claim.

Attachment: This statutory remedy (which in some states is available only to creditors with contract claims) permits a creditor to attach specific property prior to judgment if the creditor can demonstrate that its ability to collect on its claim would be in jeopardy otherwise (as, for example, if the debtor were hiding her property). The creditor generally files a complaint in a court of competent jurisdiction and an affidavit alleging the appropriate grounds of attachment. The court, after notice to the debtor and an opportunity for a hearing, will issue a writ of attachment instructing the sheriff to levy on nonexempt property of the debtor sufficient in value to satisfy the creditor's claim. From the time of levy, the creditor obtains a lien on the attached property of the debtor. That lien is perfected by entry of judgment for the plaintiff.

In the case of Janet Ward and her corporation, three different groups of creditors may use attachment if they have the statutory prerequisites. Creditors with consumer credit claims against her individually (*e.g.*, the issuer of her Visa card) and creditors of her unincorporated consulting business (*e.g.*, American Express) could attach her real and personal property. Creditors of Conferences, Inc., who failed to receive timely payments for goods and services provided to the corporation, could attach any of the corporation's property. Janet's property, of course, would be immune from the claims of corporate creditors, under principles of limited liability.

Garnishment: This is a statutory third party action addressed to an entity holding property of the debtor—typically wages or a deposit account. It instructs the third party (the garnishee) to hold the property for the garnishing creditor rather than turning it over to the debtor. Once the creditor obtains a judgment against the debtor, the creditor can recover from the property held by the garnishee. A garnishee who ignores the writ of garnishment and pays over property in its possession to the debtor will be liable to the judgment creditor. In most states, the writ of garnishment gives rise to a lien in favor of the garnishing creditor that dates from the time the writ is served on garnishee.

Personal creditors, both of Janet the consumer and Janet the consultant, could garnish her wages from Conferences, Inc. and her bank accounts. They could also garnish any other property of hers held by third parties, such as fees earned for private consulting but not yet paid.

Federal law limits the extent to which Janet's wages are subject to garnishment, however, whatever the nature of the garnishing creditor's claim. Under Title III of the Truth-in-Lending Act, the amount subject to garnishment for any "workweek" may not exceed 25% of an individual's "disposable income for that week, or the amount by which [the individual's] disposable earnings for that week exceed thirty times the federal minimum hourly wage." 15 U.S.C. § 1673(a)(1) & (2). That limitation complements, but does not restrict, state law limitations on garnishment.

The federal law restricting garnishment applies only to individuals. Thus, it does not insulate any property of the corporation, Conferences, Inc., that may be in the possession of a third party. The federal limitation also extends only to wages, and thus would not insulate any account balances that Janet maintains. Other legislation, however, may limit the rights of creditors to reach certain accounts, such as those maintained by the Social Security Administration, 42 U.S.C. § 407, or those within the scope of pension and retirement funds protections, 29 U.S.C. §§ 1003(b) & 1144(a).

A creditor may use garnishment either as a provisional or as a post-judgment remedy.

Replevin: This statutory remedy, which operates only in favor of creditors with a lien against property of the debtor, authorizes the sheriff to seize the property. When used as a provisional remedy, it enables the sheriff to hold the property pending the outcome of litigation between the debtor and the creditor claiming rights in the property, preventing the debtor from wasting the property meanwhile. The right to replevin is additional to any rights a creditor may have as a consensual secured creditor under Article 9 of the UCC.

In Janet's case, the creditor with the security interest in her car, who provided her the financing to purchase it, could replevy the car upon her default in payment. Replevin would also be available to any creditors of Conferences, Inc., who have an interest in particular property of the corporation. So if the company falls behind in the payments for its office furnishings or telephone system, for example, creditors with liens against those items could replevy them and have the sheriff hold them pending litigation on the corporation's indebtedness.

A creditor with the right to replevy may pursue that right either provisionally or after obtaining a judgment.

2. COLLECTIVE NONBANKRUPTCY REMEDIES

In addition to the collection rights available to individual creditors, state law provides a few procedures permitting creditors as a group to resolve their claims against a common debtor. Although these remedies are not used nearly as often as bankruptcy, you should appreciate these nonbankruptcy possibilities.

Receivership: A receivership *pendente lite*—a receiver appointed prior to judgment—is a device rarely invoked by the courts. More common is the post-judgment receiver, who is given the power to manage the debtor's financial affairs. The receiver will supervise (and usually liquidate and distribute) the debtor's property.

A receiver is usually appointed pursuant to the request of a creditor. The creditor obtaining the appointment, however, acquires no lien on any of the debtor's assets (although pre-existing liens are not impaired) and realizes no rights superior to those of other creditors who also benefit from the receiver's appointment.

Assignments for the Benefit of Creditors: This device enables a debtor to voluntarily liquidate its assets in order to pay creditors. The debtor conveys all nonexempt property to an assignee who liquidates it and distributes the proceeds to creditors. The device, like bankruptcy, divests the debtor of title to property in favor of an assignee who represents the interests of the debtor's creditors. Creditors often cooperate with debtors using this device, but the debtor need not obtain creditors' permission in order to make the assignment.

The remedy is generally statutory, but in states where it is not, principles of contract and trust law govern. It is generally less costly than bankruptcy, but the debtor cannot obtain a discharge of unpaid debts unless the creditors so agree as part of a composition agreement.

Composition and Extension Agreements: These are common law contractual, rather than statutory, devices that afford a debtor some debt relief without invoking the considerable, and cumbersome, power of the judiciary. Though generally utilized in the business context, they may be worthwhile devices in the consumer setting as well.

Because this device is contractual, the parties can fashion their agreement however they wish. In many instances, the agreement merely extends the time for payment, without altering the amounts owed. In other cases, the agreement is a "composition" that reduces the amount of the debtor's obligations.

The most significant obstacle to such an agreement is the necessity of obtaining the willing participation of all creditors. The possibility of "hold outs" is significant, given the lack of protections, such as the automatic stay, that are available in bankruptcy.

E. OVERVIEW OF BANKRUPTCY

Bankruptcy law is a device for the resolution of the collective interests of creditors and for the relief of overburdened debtors. It is characterized by discharge, which means that creditors are forever barred from collecting any debts remaining unpaid at the end of the bankruptcy proceeding. We saw that several state law devices, such as assignments for the benefit of creditors and compositions, may provide alternatives to bankruptcy. These devices, however, do not permit the debtor to discharge any debts remaining unpaid. The availability of discharge under bankruptcy, therefore, may be its single most distinguishing feature.

Bankruptcy law is federal law. The current Bankruptcy Code appears at 11 U.S.C. §§ 101 et seq.

1. BANKRUPTCY IN HISTORY

American bankruptcy law can be traced back through the law of England to the laws of Italian city states in the fourteenth century that derived, in turn, from Roman law. The term "bankruptcy" is said to originate from "banca rupta," which was the medieval custom of breaking the bench of a defaulting merchant.

Early bankruptcy laws were entirely creditor-oriented. They were designed to prevent the debtor from hiding assets from creditors, and were purely punitive from the debtor's point of view. They were triggered by "acts of bankruptcy" that consisted of efforts by debtors to evade responsibility to their creditors. (Not until the Eighteenth Century did bankruptcy become a procedure applicable not only to dishonest debtors, but to unfortunate debtors as well.) These early bankruptcy laws permitted only involuntary cases and did not contemplate the discharge of debts remaining unpaid at the end of the proceeding. The notion of discharge came into English law only in the last three hundred years, first appearing in the Statute of 4 Anne ch. 17 (1705). This discharge did not have a debtor-protective or humanitarian purpose, however. Rather, it was designed to encourage debtors to cooperate with their creditors, thereby enabling the creditors to obtain more information about their debtors' assets. Early bankruptcy laws were also limited to certain classes of debtors, such as merchants and traders. Even from the beginning, however, bankruptcy laws had one characteristic still present today—they were collective remedies, enabling creditors to gather and divide a debtor's assets among themselves.

These antecedents are clearly visible in the first American bankruptcy laws. Congress was given the power to enact "uniform laws on the subject of bankruptcies" by Article I, § 8, clause 4 of the United States Constitution. Congress first exercised that power in 1800. This bankruptcy statute applied only to commercial parties (merchants, bankers, brokers, and the like), permitted only involuntary petitions, and required an "act of bankruptcy." Discharge was possible, but only if a designated percentage of creditors consented. The Bankruptcy Act of 1800 was repealed in 1803.

It was followed by two other short-lived statutes, both of which were enacted in response to periods of economic crisis. The Bankruptcy Act of 1841 was very debtor-favorable; it permitted voluntary petitions, was not limited to merchants and allowed discharge (unless a majority of creditors dissented). This statute survived only 18 months.

The Bankruptcy Act of 1867 lasted longer—until 1878—but it was also unpopular.

A fourth bankruptcy statute, enacted in 1898, lasted. It was substantially revised by the Chandler Act in 1938, which added procedures for corporate reorganization and for wage-earner plans.

Gradually, the Act became hopelessly outdated and Congress began the process of reform. Congress appointed a National Bankruptcy Commission and the Commission's 1973 Report remains an important research source. Congress passed the Bankruptcy Reform Act of 1978, which became effective in October of 1979.[a] The 1978 Code is the most debtor-favorable bankruptcy law ever enacted in the United States and it immediately came under fire, chiefly from the credit industry. As a result, the Code was amended in 1984 to address some of the dissatisfactions. In addition, a new provision for family farmers was added in 1986, although it did not become a permanent part of the Bankruptcy Code for nearly twenty years. Additional amendments were passed in 1988, 1990 and 1994. The most extensive amendments since the Code was first enacted, however, came in the Bankruptcy Abuse Prevention and Consumer Protection Act of 2005 (BAPCPA).

2. PURPOSES OF BANKRUPTCY

Bankruptcy is not the source of legal obligations. It creates no rights in one party against another. Instead, rights and obligations originating from other areas of law, such as contracts and torts, are brought into bankruptcy and processed according to its special procedural and substantive rules.

One of the striking differences between bankruptcy and the state law collection devices described above is the lack of a "race of diligence" in bankruptcy. Under state law, the first creditor to obtain a judgment and to collect on it will get the first bite from the debtor's assets. This creditor will be paid in full if the debtor's assets are sufficient, but the next creditor may not be so lucky.

Traditionally, bankruptcy has stressed equality of distribution between similarly-situated creditors (although this notion is becoming increasingly eroded). Bankruptcy is also compulsory, in the sense that

---

[a] This legislation is referred to, by consensus, as the "Code," to distinguish it from the 1898 statute, which is called the "Act." These conventions will be observed in this casebook.

it presents the creditor's only chance to get paid. A creditor not paid in bankruptcy will not be paid at all, because bankruptcy offers the debtor a discharge from unpaid obligations at the end of the proceeding. The discharge is designed to facilitate the debtor's "fresh start" and is the primary reason that most individual debtors are attracted to bankruptcy. As the Supreme Court put it in *Local Loan Co. v. Hunt*, 292 U.S. 234, 244, 54 S.Ct. 695, 699, 78 L.Ed. 1230, 1235 (1934) (the most often quoted bankruptcy case ever decided), bankruptcy "gives to the honest but unfortunate debtor who surrenders for distribution the property which he owns *at the time of bankruptcy*, a new opportunity in life and a clear field for future effort, unhampered by the pressure and discouragement of preexisting debt."

In the process of accomplishing these objectives, bankruptcy is also intended to reduce overall collection costs and to preserve the estate in order to maximize the creditors' recovery. As we will see, all of these purposes cannot be achieved simultaneously.

3. STRUCTURE OF THE 1978 BANKRUPTCY CODE

The Bankruptcy Code is divided into chapters, all but one of which are odd-numbered. Chapters 1, 3 and 5 contain definitions and general provisions that apply to all bankruptcy proceedings. The remaining chapters (7, 9, 11, 12, 13 and 15) govern various types of bankruptcy proceedings. (Note that chapters are designated by Arabic numerals in the Code; the Act used Roman numerals.)

The trustee is charged with general administrative responsibility regarding the bankruptcy estate. In order to carry out that responsibility, the trustee has the power to bring back into the estate property that the debtor transferred before bankruptcy was filed. The most important of these "avoiding" powers permit recovery of fraudulent conveyances and preferences. Property recovered under one of the avoiding powers increases the size of the bankruptcy estate and becomes available for distribution to creditors holding unsecured claims. For this reason, the trustee is often described as the representative of unsecured creditors.

Two main types of bankruptcy are available—liquidation and reorganization. In liquidation, debts are paid from the value of currently owned assets. In reorganization, debtors keep their assets and pay debts out of future earnings, over the course of several years.

a. Chapter 7

Chapter 7 governs liquidation cases, also known as "straight bankruptcy." In these cases, a trustee is appointed and charged with the duty to collect the debtor's assets, reduce them to cash, and distribute the proceeds to creditors in accordance with the Code's distributional rules. The trustee learns about the debtor's financial affairs from schedules the debtor must file with the court. In addition, the debtor must appear at a meeting of creditors and answer questions under oath.

The individual debtor can keep some "exempt" property, but otherwise all assets the debtor owns at the time the case commences will be used to satisfy debts the debtor owes at that time. In "no asset" cases, nothing remains for creditors after the debtor's exemptions are set aside.

A creditor holding a valid lien will receive either the property itself or its value. That leaves only unencumbered property for unsecured creditors. This property is unlikely to be sufficient to pay all of the unsecured claims in full. Thus, under the bankruptcy policy of equality, these creditors share pro rata.

In exchange for giving up nonexempt property, the individual debtor is discharged from liability for all debts remaining unpaid. Corporate debtors do not receive a discharge in bankruptcy, but they do not need one; liquidation leaves an empty corporate shell and state law's concept of limited liability protects shareholders from the corporate creditors' unpaid claims.

b. Chapter 13

Chapter 13 is a reorganization proceeding available only to individual debtors who have a steady source of income and debts within designated limits. Under Chapter 13, the debtor proposes a plan, not exceeding five years in length, that specifies amounts to be paid to each creditor from the debtor's postpetition income. Creditors need not be fully paid, but they must get at least as much as they would get if the debtor had filed a Chapter 7 instead. Chapter 13 debtors keep all their property; payments are made to creditors out of income net of necessary living expenses.

Unlike Chapter 7, only the debtor can file a Chapter 13 petition. No involuntary petitions are permitted, although the Code may leave a particular debtor no other choice.

c. Chapter 11

Chapter 11 is also a reorganization proceeding, but it is more widely available than is Chapter 13. Chapter 11 is typically used by corporations, although it is not restricted to business use. A plan governs repayments to creditors in Chapter 11, as it does in Chapter 13, but the Code does not limit its duration to a specified number of years.

The Code provides a number of detailed requirements that a Chapter 11 plan must meet. As under Chapter 13, the plan must pay each creditor at least as much as that creditor would receive if the debtor had filed Chapter 7, unless the creditor agrees to accept less.

A Chapter 11 plan deals with similarly-situated creditors grouped together by classes. If any class of creditors refuses to accept the plan, it can nonetheless be confirmed ("crammed down") if it meets a two-part test: (1) it does not "discriminate unfairly;" and (2) it is "fair and equitable," *i.e.*, either the dissenting class is paid in full or no class of creditors with a lower priority receives anything. The latter rule, known as the "absolute priority rule," means that the creditors usually become owners of a debtor corporation at the end of the bankruptcy case. This is true because shareholders, who have a lower priority than unsecured creditors, cannot retain any ownership interest unless unsecured creditors are paid in full.

Despite these rules, Chapter 11 plans are often negotiated under which creditors agree to accept less than full payment and to allow shareholders to retain some interest in the postbankruptcy enterprise.

A trustee is not typically appointed in a Chapter 11 case. Rather, the debtor remains in control of the property of the estate as debtor-in-possession, and enjoys the powers of a trustee. The possibility that current management may retain control of a corporation may make Chapter 11 more attractive than Chapter 7. Since a liquidating plan can be proposed in Chapter 11, the liquidation/rehabilitation dichotomy is not perfect.

Corporate debtors receive a discharge as soon as the Chapter 11 plan is confirmed, so the creditors' rights in such cases are those specified in the plan. Cases involving individual debtors are treated differently. In those cases, as in Chapter 13, discharge is delayed until the debtor completes performance under the plan, unless the court orders otherwise.

Chapter 11 cases may be protracted. The Code does not regulate the length of time that may pass before a plan is proposed and confirmed, although it does grant the debtor a limited period within which only the debtor may propose a plan (the so-called "exclusivity period"). Several provisions in the Code are designed to expedite the Chapter 11 process in small business cases, by shortening the exclusivity period and setting a deadline by which the plan must be proposed.

d. Chapter 12

Chapter 12, which was added to the Code in 1986, is a reorganization provision for family farmers and fishermen with a steady source of income. Although it incorporates some aspects of Chapter 11, its roots in Chapter 13 are quite evident: only the debtor may file; eligibility is subject to debt limits (although the limits are higher in Chapter 12 than in Chapter 13); the debtor remains in possession of property of the estate; payments to creditors are determined by the terms of the plan, which only the debtor can propose; and discharge is delayed until performance under the plan is completed.

Unlike Chapter 13, the debtor's regular income must derive from a particular source—farming or fishing—whether the debtor is an individual or corporation.

Chapter 12 was originally enacted with a "sunset" provision, although Congress extended it repeatedly over the ensuing years (retroactively, when necessary). Most policy makers agreed that Chapter 12 should be permanent, but it was held hostage to efforts to pass more controversial provisions as part of broader reforms. Those efforts were successful in 2005, and Chapter 12 became a permanent part of the Bankruptcy Code.

e. Chapter 9

Chapter 9, which governs the bankruptcy of municipalities, is used only occasionally. We will not cover it in this casebook.

f. Chapter 15

The 2005 Amendments added a new Chapter 15, which applies to transnational bankruptcy cases. It is intended to encourage cooperation between the courts of the United States and foreign countries with respect to cross-border insolvency cases. We will not cover Chapter 15 in this casebook.

F. JURISDICTION AND VENUE

1. JURISDICTION

Subsections (a) and (b) of 28 U.S.C. § 1334 govern the basic grant of jurisdiction in bankruptcy cases:

> (a) Except as provided in subsection (b) of this section, the district courts shall have original and exclusive jurisdiction of all cases under title 11.

> (b) Except as provided in subsection (e)(2) and notwithstanding any Act of Congress that confers exclusive jurisdiction on a court or courts other than the district courts, the district courts shall have original but not exclusive jurisdiction of all civil proceedings arising under title 11, or arising in or related to cases under title 11.

The apparent contradiction in these subsections (one providing that jurisdiction is exclusive and the other that it is not) is explained by understanding the distinction between "cases" and "proceedings" in bankruptcy. The "case" is the entire bankruptcy that adjudicates the whole financial relationship between a debtor and all of its creditors. A "proceeding" is a subset of a case—a civil dispute that deals with particular legal issues and often involves the debtor and only an individual creditor. Each bankruptcy "case" may involve many "proceedings."

Note that the grant of jurisdiction is to district courts and not to bankruptcy courts. Bankruptcy courts originated as an administrative branch of district courts, governed by "referees." Bankruptcy judges today are Article I judges; they do not have the life tenure and protection from diminution in salary that is enjoyed by Article III judges, such as those appointed to the district and appellate courts.

This distinction was critical in *Northern Pipeline Construction Co. v. Marathon Pipe Line Co.*, 458 U.S. 50, 102 S.Ct. 2858, 73 L.Ed.2d 598 (1982), in which a debtor-in-possession brought suit in bankruptcy court for breach of a prepetition contract. The defendant asserted that the bankruptcy court lacked jurisdiction and that Congress could not authorize the bankruptcy court to hear such cases. The Supreme Court agreed, holding that the Constitution does not allow bankruptcy judges, who lack life tenure, to hear and determine cases such as the one at bar. The suit was neither directly related to the bankruptcy proceeding, nor a case in which a third party was suing the bankruptcy estate.

For practical purposes, *Marathon* voided bankruptcy court jurisdiction under the 1978 Bankruptcy Code. Congress had to amend the Code to revive the bankruptcy courts' power to hear bankruptcy cases. Simply making bankruptcy judges Article III judges—the easiest solution—was not a politically viable option. Congress, therefore, solved the *Marathon* dilemma by granting jurisdiction to the Article III judges of the district courts rather than to bankruptcy courts. Congress then provided, in 28 U.S.C. § 157(a), that district courts can delegate jurisdiction to the bankruptcy courts in "cases under" the Bankruptcy Code and in "proceedings arising under * * * or arising in or related to" the Code.

Subsection 157(b)(1) permits a bankruptcy judge to "hear and determine * * * all core proceedings arising under title 11, or arising in a case under title 11." Subsection 157(b)(2) provides a nonexclusive list of "core proceedings." The proceedings in the list, such as allowance of claims and objections to discharge, are ones that invoke substantial rights under the Code or can only arise in conjunction with a bankruptcy case. In other words, a core proceeding is "inextricably linked" to the bankruptcy case.

If a proceeding is "noncore," a bankruptcy judge may "hear and determine" it only if the parties consent. 28 U.S.C. § 157(c)(2). Otherwise, the bankruptcy judge may "hear" the matter, but cannot "determine" it; the bankruptcy judge must submit proposed findings of fact and conclusions of law to the district judge, who may enter those findings and conclusions "after consideration." The district judge must make a *de novo* review upon the record, or, if additional evidence is submitted, of any part of the bankruptcy judge's findings of fact or conclusions of law to which a party objected in accordance with Bankruptcy Rule 9033. The district judge may accept, reject, or modify the proposed findings of fact or conclusions of law, receive further evidence, or recommit the matter to the bankruptcy judge with instructions.

Congress determined that neither the district court nor the bankruptcy court should handle state law causes of action that are related to a bankruptcy case but that do not arise under title 11. Accordingly, 28 U.S.C. § 1334(c)(2) provides that a party to a proceeding based on a state law claim or cause of action may move the district court to abstain from hearing the proceeding if an action is commenced and can be timely adjudicated in an appropriate state forum. Section 1334(c) has been interpreted as a "clear congressional policy * * * to give state law claimants a right to have claims heard in state court." *Piombo Corp. v.*

Castlerock Properties (In re Castlerock Properties), 781 F.2d 159, 163 (9th Cir.1986).

Though these jurisdictional rules are perhaps not a perfect solution, they served for many years. The following case, in the portion excerpted here, addressed 28 U.S.C. § 1334.

WOOD v. WOOD (MATTER OF WOOD)

United States Court of Appeals, Fifth Circuit, 1987.
825 F.2d 90.

WISDOM, Circuit Judge.

This appeal calls upon us to decipher the jurisdictional provisions of the Bankruptcy Amendments and Federal Judgeship Act of 1984. * * *

I.

[The parties in this case were shareholders in a medical practice. After one of them filed a Chapter 11 petition, along with his wife, the other alleged that the debtor had wrongfully issued additional stock to himself, in violation of their agreement to be equal partners. The complainant sought damages and declaratory relief.]

The bankruptcy judge of the district denied the defendants' motion to dismiss for lack of subject-matter jurisdiction and held that the matter was a core proceeding. On appeal to the district court, the court held that the matter was neither a "core" proceeding, over which the bankruptcy judge had full judicial power, nor an "otherwise related" or "non-core" proceeding, over which the bankruptcy judge has limited judicial power. The court dismissed the complaint for lack of subject-matter jurisdiction. The plaintiffs appealed to this Court.

II.

The starting point in our analysis is 28 U.S.C. § 1334. *[The court quoted subsections (a) and (b).]* Section 1334 lists four types of matters over which the district court has jurisdiction:

1.   "cases under title 11,"

2.   "proceedings arising under title 11,"

3.   proceedings "arising in" a case under title 11, and

4.   proceedings "related to" a case under title 11.

The first category refers merely to the bankruptcy petition itself, over which district courts (and their bankruptcy units) have original and exclusive jurisdiction. Our concern, however, is with the other proceedings listed in subsection 1334(b), over which the district courts have original, but not exclusive, jurisdiction.

There is almost no legislative history to guide us in interpreting the 1984 Act. Subsection 1334(b), however, was taken verbatim from subsection 1471(b) of the 1978 Act. The legislative history and judicial interpretations of that Act therefore are instructive.

Legislative history indicates that the phrase "arising under title 11, or arising in or related to cases under title 11" was meant, not to distinguish between different matters, but to identify collectively a broad range of matters subject to the bankruptcy jurisdiction of federal courts. Congress was concerned with the inefficiencies of piecemeal adjudication of matters affecting the administration of bankruptcies and intended to give federal courts the power to adjudicate all matters having an effect on the bankruptcy. Courts have recognized that the grant of jurisdiction under the 1978 Act was broad.

* * * The jurisdictional provision of the 1978 Act, § 1471, accomplished two things. First, subsection (b) vested an expansive bankruptcy jurisdiction in the district courts. Second, subsection (c) conferred the power to exercise that jurisdictional grant in the bankruptcy courts.[10] The issue in *Marathon* was not the constitutionality of subsection (b), but the constitutionality of subsection (c). *Marathon* held that Congress could not vest the whole of bankruptcy jurisdiction in bankruptcy courts because the jurisdictional grant encompassed proceedings too far removed from the "core" of traditional bankruptcy powers to allow them to be adjudicated by non-Article III judges. The holding in *Marathon* suggests no concern over the constitutionality of the scope of bankruptcy jurisdiction defined by Congress; its concern is

---

[10]   Section 1471(c) of the 1978 Act read:

The bankruptcy court for the district in which a case under title 11 is commenced shall exercise all of the jurisdiction conferred by this section on the district courts.

with the *placement* of that jurisdiction in non-Article III courts. In response to *Marathon*, Congress altered the placement of bankruptcy jurisdiction by creating a statutory distinction between core and non-core proceedings and restricting the power of bankruptcy courts to adjudicate the latter. Because *Marathon* did not compel Congress to reduce the scope of bankruptcy jurisdiction, it seems plain that Congress intended no change in the scope of jurisdiction set forth in the 1978 Act when it later enacted § 1334 of the 1984 Act.

The district court expressed its concern that an overbroad interpretation of § 1334 would bring into federal court matters that should be left to state courts to decide. We have also expressed the same concern. There is no necessary reason why that concern must be met by restrictive interpretations of the statutory grant of jurisdiction under § 1334. The Act grants the district court broad power to abstain whenever appropriate "in the interest of justice, or in the interest of comity with State courts or respect for State law." The abstention provisions of the Act demonstrate the intent of Congress that concerns of comity and judicial convenience should be met, not by rigid limitations on the jurisdiction of federal courts, but by the discretionary exercise of abstention when appropriate in a particular case. Here, the possibility of abstention was not raised in the district court.

For the purpose of determining whether a particular matter falls within bankruptcy jurisdiction, it is not necessary to distinguish between proceedings "arising under," "arising in a case under," or "related to a case under," title 11. These references operate conjunctively to define the scope of jurisdiction. Therefore, it is necessary only to determine whether a matter is at least "related to" the bankruptcy. The Act does not define "related" matters. Courts have articulated various definitions of "related," but the definition of the Court of Appeals for the Third Circuit appears to have the most support: "whether the outcome of that proceeding could *conceivably* have any effect on the estate being administered in bankruptcy."[15] This definition comports with the legislative history of the statutory predecessor to § 1334. Neither *Marathon* nor general concerns of comity counsel against its use. We adopt it as our own.

Applying this test to case before us, we find that the complaint is sufficiently related to the pending bankruptcy to allow the district court to exercise jurisdiction under § 1334. The complaint against the

---

[15] *Pacor, Inc. v. Higgins*, 743 F.2d 984, 994 (3d Cir.1984) (emphasis added).

bankruptcy debtors could have a conceivable effect on their bankruptcy. The plaintiff seeks to recover stock and monies that the debtors allegedly appropriated from the clinic. They seek to resolve the disputed allocation of interest in the clinic. To the extent that the debtors' interest in the clinic, their stock holdings, or their withdrawals are now property of the estate, the complaint against them has a potential effect on their estate.

The debtors argue that the complaint raises a post-petition claim that will not affect their bankruptcy.[16] Generally, post-petition claims are not dischargeable in bankruptcy and, therefore, do not affect the estate. To fall within the court's jurisdiction, the plaintiffs' claims must affect the estate, not just the debtor. Although we acknowledge the possibility that this suit may ultimately have no effect on the bankruptcy, we cannot conclude, on the facts before us, that it will have no *conceivable* effect. First, the complaint raises a dispute over the division of ownership of the clinic. Because the debtors held their stock in the clinic before filing for bankruptcy, the disputed share is now part of the estate. Second, the complaint seeks to recover stock and cash withdrawals made after the filing of the petition. Although post-petition acquisitions of the debtor are generally not part of the estate, they may be estate property in this case if considered income from pre-petition property. We raise these possibilities, not to resolve them, for that matter is left to the district and bankruptcy courts to decide under federal law, but to illustrate the conceivable effect of the complaint on the administration of the bankruptcy.

* * *

A second question presented in *Wood* was whether, assuming that jurisdiction existed, the bankruptcy court could preside over the matter as a "core" or "non-core" proceeding. That was a matter of the "placement" of jurisdiction under 28 U.S.C. § 157, which gives bankruptcy judges the power to "hear and determine" only core proceedings (in the absence of the parties' consent). The court found that the proceeding at issue was not a "core" proceeding.

---

[16]   The complaint challenges the issuance of stock in November of 1984 and the withdrawal of money in Spring of 1985, both of which occurred after the filing of the bankruptcy petition in March of 1984.

The understanding of the *Wood* court and others as to the "placement" of jurisdiction must now be understood in light of *Stern v. Marshall*, 131 S.Ct. 2594, 180 L.Ed.2d 475 (2011), and its progeny. *Stern* had as colorful and complex a history as any case ever to have come before the Court. It all began in 1994 when Vickie Lynn Marshall, better known to the world as Anna Nicole Smith (Playboy's 1993 Playmate of the Year), married J. Howard Marshall—one of the richest men in Texas and 62 years her senior. He died a year later, leaving no provision for her in his will; rather, the beneficiary of the estate was his son, Pierce Marshall. Vickie filed suit in Texas probate court, alleging that Pierce had fraudulently induced his father not to leave Vickie half of his estate as he had intended. She then filed bankruptcy in California. Pierce filed a complaint in defamation in the bankruptcy court and also sought to bar the discharge of his claim. Vickie responded by asserting truth as a defense, and by filing a counterclaim for tortious interference with an expected gift. The bankruptcy court held that Vickie's objection to Pierce's claim, as well as her counterclaim, both qualified as "core" proceedings. The bankruptcy court granted summary judgment to Vickie on the defamation claim, and awarded substantial damages to her on the counterclaim— more than $400 million in compensatory damages, plus $25 million in punitive damages. By the time of appeal to the district court, the Texas probate court had found in Pierce's favor. Pierce had argued throughout that the federal courts lacked subject matter jurisdiction under the "probate exception." The California district court, refusing to give preclusive effect to the probate judgment, disagreed that the proceedings were "core." It undertook *de novo* review and found in Vickie's favor, but entered an award in a substantially smaller amount—$88.6 million, total, in compensatory and punitive damages. On appeal, the Ninth Circuit held that the probate exception barred federal jurisdiction, but the Supreme Court reversed. *Marshall v. Marshall*, 547 U.S. 293, 126 S.Ct. 1735, 164 L.Ed.2d 480 (2006).

On remand, the Ninth Circuit decided that a counterclaim under § 157(b)(2)(C) is a "core" proceeding "arising in a case under" the Bankruptcy Code only if the counterclaim is so closely related to the creditor's proof of claim that resolution of the counterclaim is necessary to a determination of the claim's allowance or disallowance. The court held that Vickie's counterclaim did not meet that test. Thus, the state probate judgment was first in time and should have been given preclusive effect. The Supreme Court again granted certiorari. (By the time of the Court's decision, both Vickie and Pierce were deceased. The litigation continued between their estates.)

Two issues were before the Court: whether the bankruptcy court had statutory authority under § 157(b) to issue a final judgment on Vickie's counterclaim; and, if so, whether conferring such authority is constitutional. The Court, dividing 5-4, read the statute to plainly give such authority, but held that bankruptcy courts, which are not Article III courts, cannot constitutionally determine inherently common law counterclaims. According to the Court, bankruptcy courts may enter final judgments on estate counterclaims only if "the action at issue stems from the bankruptcy itself or would necessarily be resolved in the claims allowance process."

The Court also decided that Pierce had consented to the entry of judgment on his defamation claim, but that he did not thereby consent to entry of judgment on Vickie's tortious interference counterclaim. *Stern*, therefore, adds a caveat to the usual rule that parties can consent to having the bankruptcy court hear and determine anything within its subject matter jurisdiction—namely, that the mere filing of a proof of claim does not constitute implied consent to entry of judgment on all responsive counterclaims.

It may be easier to ascertain what *Stern* does *not* mean, than what it does. *Stern* did not address the subject matter jurisdiction of bankruptcy courts—a jurisdiction that derives from § 1334 and extends as far as "related-to" jurisdiction. Instead, *Stern* dealt with ascertaining the line between core and non-core proceedings, both of which are within the bankruptcy courts' subject matter jurisdiction as long as they are related to a bankruptcy case.

The opinions in *Stern* differed as to the likely impact the decision will have on the bankruptcy system. Unsurprisingly, the majority did not believe that it had wrought a major change:

> [W]e are not convinced that the practical con-sequences of such limitations on the authority of bankruptcy courts to enter final judgments are as significant as Vickie and the dissent suggest. The dissent asserts that it is important that counterclaims such as Vickie's be resolved "in a bankruptcy court," and that, "to be effective, a single tribunal must have broad authority to restructure [debtor-creditor] relations." But the framework Congress adopted in the 1984 Act already con-templates that certain state law matters in bankruptcy cases will be resolved by judges other than those of the bankruptcy courts. Section 1334(c)(2), for example, requires that bankruptcy courts abstain from hearing specified non-core, state law claims that "can be

timely adjudicated[ ] in a State forum of appropriate jurisdiction." Section 1334(c)(1) similarly provides that bankruptcy courts may abstain from hearing any proceeding, including core matters, "in the interest of comity with State courts or respect for State law."

As described above, the current bankruptcy system also requires the district court to review *de novo* and enter final judgment on any matters that are "related to" the bankruptcy proceedings, § 157(c)(1), and permits the district court to withdraw from the bankruptcy court any referred case, proceeding, or part thereof, § 157(d). Pierce has not argued that the bankruptcy courts "are barred from 'hearing' all counterclaims" or proposing findings of fact and conclusions of law on those matters, but rather that it must be the district court that "finally decide[s]" them. We do not think the removal of counterclaims such as Vickie's from core bankruptcy jurisdiction meaningfully changes the division of labor in the current statute; we agree with the United States that the question presented here is a "narrow" one.

131 S.Ct. at 2619-20. The dissent, unsurprisingly, predicted that a major burden is in store for district courts required to make the ultimate determination in cases involving compulsory counterclaims:

The majority predicts that as a "practical matter" today's decision "does not change all that much." But I doubt that is so. * * *

Why is that a problem? Because these types of disputes arise in bankruptcy court with some frequency. Because the volume of bankruptcy cases is staggering, involving almost 1.6 million filings last year, compared to a federal district court docket of around 280,000 civil cases and 78,000 criminal cases. Because unlike the "related" non-core state law claims that bankruptcy courts must abstain from hearing, compulsory counterclaims involve the same factual disputes as the claims that may be finally adjudicated by the bankruptcy courts. Because under these circumstances, a constitutionally required game of jurisdictional ping-pong between courts would lead to inefficiency, increased cost, delay, and needless additional suffering among those faced with bankruptcy.

131 S.Ct. at 2629-30 (Breyer, J., dissenting).

Stern generated a great deal of uncertainty and consternation among bankruptcy judges, case parties and commentators regarding the scope of a bankruptcy judge's authority. Bankruptcy (and appellate) courts wrestled with fundamental and practical questions, including, first, whether bankruptcy judges are statutorily authorized under 28 U.S.C. § 157(c) to propose findings of fact and conclusions of law in core proceedings, and, second, whether Article III allows bankruptcy courts to enter final judgment on *Stern* claims with the parties' consent.

In two cases—*Executive Benefits Insurance Agency v. Arkison,* 135 S.Ct. 1932, 191 L.Ed.2d 911 (2014), and *Wellness International Network v. Sharif,* 135 S.Ct. 1932, 191 L.Ed.2d 911 (2015)—the Supreme Court dealt with some of the questions left open by *Stern*. *Arkison* addressed whether a bankruptcy court can try non-core proceedings (so-called "*Stern* claims") and submit proposed findings of fact and conclusions of law to the district court for its review. The Court held, unanimously, that when *Stern* constitutionally prohibits a bankruptcy court from entering final judgment on a bankruptcy-related claim, § 157(c) nevertheless allows that court to issue proposed findings of fact and conclusions of law for the district court's *de novo* review.

Wellness presented the question whether an Article I court may, with the parties' consent, hear and issue final judgment on a *Stern* claim—that is, one otherwise within the exclusive authority of an Article III court. In *Wellness*, a creditor argued that money in a trust, not listed on the debtor's bankruptcy petition, should be available to creditors.

The bankruptcy court held that the assets belonged to the estate and entered final judgment. The Seventh Circuit reversed, holding that, because *Stern* claims implicate structural interests inherent in Article III courts, the bankruptcy court lacked constitutional authority to issue a final judgment—without regard to the litigants' consent. A deeply divided Supreme Court reversed:

> The question here, then, is whether allowing bankruptcy courts to decide *Stern* claims by consent would "impermissibly threate[n] the institutional integrity of the Judicial Branch." [*Commodity Futures Trading Comm'n v. Schor*, 478 U.S. 833, 851 (1986)]. And that question must be decided not by "formalistic and unbending rules," but "with an eye to the practical effect that the" practice "will have on the constitutionally assigned role of the federal judiciary." *Id*. * * * The Court must weigh

the extent to which the essential attributes of judicial power are reserved to Article III courts, and, conversely, the extent to which the non-Article III forum exercises the range of jurisdiction and powers normally vested only in Article III courts, the origins and importance of the right to be adjudicated, and the concerns that drove Congress to depart from the requirements of Article III.

Id. (internal quotation marks omitted).

Applying these factors, we conclude that allowing bankruptcy litigants to waive the right to Article III adjudication of *Stern* claims does not usurp the constitutional prerogatives of Article III courts. Bankruptcy judges, like magistrate judges, "are appointed and subject to removal by Article III judges," [*Peretz* v. *United States*, 501 U.S. 923, 937 (1991)]; see 28 U.S.C. §§ 152(a)(1), (e). They "serve as judicial officers of the United States district court," § 151, and collectively "constitute a unit of the district court" for that district, § 152(a)(1). Just as "[t]he 'ultimate decision' whether to invoke [a] magistrate [judge]'s assistance is made by the district court," *Peretz*, 501 U.S. at 937, bankruptcy courts hear matters solely on a district court's reference, § 157(a), which the district court may withdraw *sua sponte* or at the request of a party, § 157(d). "[S]eparation of powers concerns are diminished" when, as here, "the decision to invoke [a non-Article III] forum is left entirely to the parties and the power of the federal judiciary to take jurisdiction" remains in place. *Schor*, 478 U.S. at 855.

Furthermore, * * * bankruptcy courts possess no free-floating authority to decide claims traditionally heard by Article III courts. Their ability to resolve such matters is limited to "a narrow class of common law claims as an incident to the [bankruptcy courts'] primary, and unchallenged, adjudicative function." *Id.* at 854. "In such circumstances, the magnitude of any intrusion on the Judicial Branch can only be termed *de minimis.*" *Id.* at 856.

Wellness, 135 S.Ct. at 1944-45. The Court then explained why this decision was not an affront to the separation of powers doctrine or the "institutional integrity" of the judiciary:

Finally, there is no indication that Congress gave bankruptcy courts the ability to decide *Stern* claims in an effort to aggrandize itself or humble the Judiciary. As in *Peretz*, "[b]ecause 'the entire process takes place under the district court's total control and jurisdiction,' there is no danger that use of the [bankruptcy court] involves a 'congressional attemp[t] "to transfer jurisdiction [to non-Article III tribunals] for the purpose of emasculating" constitutional courts.'" 501 U.S. at 937 (citation omitted) * * * .

Congress could choose to rest the full share of the Judiciary's labor on the shoulders of Article III judges. But doing so would require a substantial increase in the number of district judgeships. Instead, Congress has supplemented the capacity of district courts through the able assistance of bankruptcy judges. So long as those judges are subject to control by the Article III courts, their work poses no threat to the separation of powers.

Wellness, 135 S.Ct. 1945-46.

The Court also addressed whether consent had to be expressly given:

Nothing in the Constitution requires that consent to adjudication by a bankruptcy court be express. Nor does the relevant statute, 28 U.S.C. § 157, mandate express consent; it states only that a bankruptcy court must obtain "the consent"—consent *simpliciter*—"of all parties to the proceeding" before hearing and determining a non-core claim. § 157(c)(2). * * *

* * * [T]he key inquiry is whether "the litigant or counsel was made aware of the need for consent and the right to refuse it, and still voluntarily appeared to try the case" before the non-Article III adjudicator. [*Roell* v. *Withrow*, 538 U.S. 580, 590 (2003).]

Wellness, 135 S.Ct. at 1947-48. The Court observed in a footnote, however, that it is not only good practice for consent or nonconsent to be expressly stated, but judicial rules may require it.

In a frothy dissent, JUSTICE ROBERTS, joined by JUSTICE SCALIA and (in part) JUSTICE THOMAS, noted that the Court need not have determined whether consent to a bankruptcy court's authority can cure constitutional deficiencies because the claims at issue were not *Stern* claims. Rather, they were core matters as to which the bankruptcy court already had final constitutional authority. JUSTICE ROBERTS took issue with the majority's discussion of consent and criticized the majority for basing its opinion on "pragmatic grounds," noting that he "would not yield so fully to functionalism." *Id.* at 1950. Referring to the "sacred" separation of powers among the branches of the federal government, *id.* at 1954, JUSTICE ROBERTS predicted that allowing *Stern* claims to be finally decided by an Article I court with the parties' consent would "impermissibly threaten the institutional integrity of the Judicial Branch." *Id.* at 1957.

Hopefully this is not the last word, because questions remain. The most fundamental of them is what constitutes a *Stern* claim. Does it include fraudulent transfer actions? Preferences? Section 541 issues, including the scope of "property of the estate"?

Thus, questions of how bankruptcy courts calibrate the "core/noncore dichotomy" remain open.

2. VENUE

a. Venue of the Case

Proper venue for the entire bankruptcy *case*—that is, the court in which the petition under §§ 301, 302 or 303 should be filed—lies in the place where the debtor's domicile, residence, principal place of business or principal assets have been located for the greatest period of time in the six months preceding the filing of the petition. 28 U.S.C. § 1408. Since venue may be proper in more than one place in a given case, the party filing the bankruptcy petition may have a choice. This creates a significant potential for forum shopping.

Efforts were made, as part of the legislative process that culminated in the 2005 amendments, to curtail the ability of debtor corporations to select the venue of their bankruptcy cases. Those efforts were unsuccessful.

Other opportunities to address bankruptcy venue have similarly failed to result in reform, much to the dismay of critics of the current system. The Final Report of the American Bankruptcy Institute's Commission to Study the Reform of Chapter 11 described these issues as "some of the most difficult and divisive considered during the Commission project." Judge Steven Rhodes, however, highlighted the need for reform of the venue rules:

Venue shopping in chapter 11 cases undermines judicial legitimacy when it prevents or even impairs the meaningful participation of any of the parties. It also undermines the integrity of the adjudicative process itself.

Because the fulfillment of the judiciary's mission depends so fundamentally on its legitimacy in the eyes of the public, chapter 11 venue should be carefully restricted to maximize the participation of the parties.

Steven Rhodes, *The Baffling Rejection of Venue Reform by the Chapter 11 Reform Commission,* WALL ST. J., Bankruptcy Beat, (Feb. 9, 2015), http://blogs.wsj.com/bankruptcy/2015/02/09/the-baffling-rejection-of-venue-reform-by-the-abi-chapter-11-reform-commission/.

For a discussion of the issues implicated by forum shopping in bankruptcy see, Laura Napoli Coordes, *The Geography of Bankruptcy*, 68 VAND. L. REV. 381 (2015) (discussing bankruptcy cases filed in venues having no meaningful connection with the company, its operations, or its stakeholders, and proposing new procedures mandating rigorous standards for venue choice).

b. Venue of Proceedings

Under 28 U.S.C. § 1409(a), proper venue for a *proceeding* in a bankruptcy case lies in the district court in which the bankruptcy case is pending. In two specific instances, venue is *mandated* in the place that will prevent unfairness to third parties sued by a trustee or debtor-in-possession. First, venue lies in the district where the defendant resides if a bankruptcy trustee or debtor-in-possession attempts to collect a money judgment of less than $1,000, recover property worth less than $1,000 collect a consumer debt of less than $15,000, or collect a non-consumer debt of less than $10,000 from a noninsider. 28 U.S.C. § 1409(b). Second, if a claim arises from the debtor's business after commencement of the bankruptcy case, venue lies in the district in which a state or federal court would have had jurisdiction in the absence of bankruptcy. 28 U.S.C. § 1409(d).

If a claim arises from operation of the debtor's business after the filing and the plaintiff is the nondebtor, rather than the trustee or debtor-in-possession, then venue lies in the district court for the district in which either a state or federal court would have had jurisdiction under applicable nonbankruptcy law, or in the district in which the bankruptcy case is pending.

Finally, § 1409(c) provides an alternative venue for proceedings brought by the trustee or debtor-in-possession to claim property of the estate under § 541, or to avoid certain transfers under § 544(b). Such a proceeding can be brought in the district in which the suit could have been filed, either in state or federal court, in the absence of bankruptcy.

c. Change of Venue

Section 1412 of title 28 provides that "[a] district court may transfer a case or proceeding" in bankruptcy to another district court "in the interest of justice or for the convenience of the parties." If the original venue is proper, the party seeking a change of venue bears the burden of proving that a change of venue serves the interest of justice or eliminates inconvenience to the parties. Courts faced with a change of venue issue generally look to the following factors: (1) the economic harm to the debtor and creditors that would result from the change of venue; (2) the location of estate assets; (3) the economic administration of the estate; (4) the necessity for ancillary administration if liquidation should result; (5) the effect of the transfer on the parties' and witnesses' willingness and ability to participate in the case or proceeding; and (6) any interrelationship with another bankruptcy case involving the debtor's affiliate, general partner or partnership.

The result is much less clear if the original venue is improper. As enacted in 1978, the Code permitted the court in such a case, "in the interest of justice and for the convenience of the parties," either to retain or transfer the case or proceeding. The provision gave a court no authority to dismiss the matter. That section was repealed in 1984 and replaced by § 1412, quoted above. Section 1412 does not mention improper venue or authorize dismissal. Rule 1014(a)(2), which authorized a court to retain a case or proceeding despite improper venue, was amended in 1987. It now provides that a case "may be dismissed or transferred * * * in the interest of justice or for the convenience of the parties." Because no mention is made of retaining jurisdiction, it remains unclear whether a court can hear such a matter in the absence of waiver by the parties.

Chapter 2

===

THE FIRST CONSEQUENCES
OF BANKRUPTCY

A. INTRODUCTION

Bankruptcy law represents a balancing of interests, protecting the debtor, creditors, and the integrity of the bankruptcy court's jurisdiction. A bankruptcy proceeding, unlike state debt collection proceedings, brings together all of the debtor's creditors in a single forum, so that even the smallest creditor may participate. This, too, serves the debtor's interests. Only a proceeding that seeks to protect the interests of both debtors and creditors can achieve the Code's purpose of giving "honest but unfortunate" debtors a "fresh start."

As you read the cases and commentary throughout this chapter, keep in mind that bankruptcy policy is not only dynamic, but is also subject to ongoing debate. Professors Ponoroff and Knippenberg described two views regarding bankruptcy's purpose(s):

> "Collectivism," as we use that term, should be taken to mean the set of shared fundamental assumptions and postulates of a group of scholars writing mainly from an economics-based perspective of the law. * * *

> For the Collectivists, * * * bankruptcy serves a single purpose: it is a federal debt collection system. Accordingly, bankruptcy is properly invoked only in response to a common pool problem, a term Jackson uses to describe the situation created when a debtor's assets are insufficient to satisfy the

demands of a common pool of claimants. The purpose of bankruptcy—or, to use Jackson's term, the "first principle" of bankruptcy—is to serve as a debt collection device targeted to the common pool problem.

       * * * [In contrast, Professor Elizabeth Warren's Traditionalism proposes] that while debt collectivizing is always relevant in bankruptcy, it can be sacrificed when necessary to achieve other goals and purposes of the bankruptcy process. * * *

       By providing for the interests of non-creditors, the Traditional view recognizes that the financial collapse of a firm presents questions of loss allocation and community interest simply not implicated in individual debtor-creditor disputes. For this reason, the Traditionalist believes that the bankruptcy system is and should be designed to address a broad range of interests affected by the collapse of a debtor enterprise. This broad range should include, but not consist exclusively of, the interests of creditors with unpaid state law claims. Brought within the bankruptcy process, diverse interests can be taken into account and, perhaps, protected and accommodated collectively under the auspice of the proceeding itself.

Lawrence Ponoroff & F. Stephen Knippenberg, *The Implied Good Faith Filing Requirement: Sentinel of an Evolving Bankruptcy Policy,* 85 Nw. U.L. Rev. 919, 949–50, 959–61 (1991) (footnotes omitted).

The "common pool" problem to which Professors Ponoroff and Knippenberg referred, is an analytical analogy used to explain the purposes of bankruptcy law. It is well summarized in Thomas H. Jackson's book, The Logic and Limits of Bankruptcy Law (1986):

Imagine that you own a lake. There are fish in the lake. You are the only one who has the right to fish in that lake, and no one constrains your decision as to how much fishing to do. You have it in your power to catch all the fish this year and sell them for, say, $100,000. If you did that, however, there would be no fish in the lake next year. It might be better for you—you might maximize your total return from fishing—if you caught and sold some fish this year but left other fish in the lake so that they could multiply and you would have fish in subsequent years. Assume that, by taking this approach, you could earn (adjusting for inflation) $50,000 each year. Having this outcome is like having a perpetual annuity paying $50,000 a year. It has a present value of perhaps $500,000. Since (obviously, I hope) when all other things are equal, $500,000 is better than $100,000, you, as sole owner, would limit your fishing this year unless some other factor influenced you.

But what if you are not the only one who can fish in this lake? What if a hundred people can do so? The optimal solution has not changed: it would be preferable to leave some fish in the lake to multiply because doing so has a present value of $500,000. But in this case, unlike that where you have to control only yourself, an obstacle exists in achieving that result. If there are a hundred fishermen, you cannot be sure, by limiting *your* fishing, that there will be any more fish next year, unless you can also control the others. You may, then, have an incentive to catch as many fish as you can today because maximizing your take this year (catching, on average, $1,000 worth of fish) is better for you than holding off (catching, say, only $500 worth of fish this year) while others scramble and deplete the stock entirely. If you hold off, your aggregate return is only $500, since nothing will be left for next year or the year after. But that sort of reasoning by each of the hundred fishermen will mean that the stock of fish will be gone by the end of the first season. The fishermen will split $100,000 this year, but there will be no fish—and no money—in future years. Self-interest results in their splitting $100,000, not $500,000.

What is required is some rule that will make all hundred fishermen act as a sole owner would. That is where bankruptcy law enters the picture in a world not of fish but of credit. The grab rules of nonbankruptcy law and their allocation of assets on the basis of first-come, first-served create an incentive on the part of the individual creditors, when they sense that a debtor may have more liabilities than assets, to get in line today (by, for example, getting a sheriff to execute on the debtor's equipment), because if they do not, they run the risk of getting nothing. This decision by numerous individual creditors, however, may be the wrong decision for the creditors as a group. Even though the debtor is insolvent, they might be better off if they held the assets together. Bankruptcy provides a way to make these diverse individuals act as one, by imposing a *collective* and *compulsory* proceeding on them.

Id. at 11-13 (footnotes omitted).

B. INITIATING THE PROCEEDINGS

1. VOLUNTARY PROCEEDINGS

Section 301 of the Bankruptcy Code provides for the commencement of voluntary cases under any chapter of the Code, and § 302 governs joint cases. Under § 301, any debtor who meets the requirements of § 109 may commence a bankruptcy action by filing a petition under the appropriate chapter of the Code. Read §§ 109, 301 and 302 (remembering to consult § 101 for pertinent definitions), and answer the following Problems.

Notes and Problems

1. Under which chapter(s) of the Code could each of the following debtors file a voluntary petition?

a. Last Federal Savings and Loan, which sustained substantial losses due to improvident loan policies.

b. Imprudential Insurance Company, which insured only property in the counties hardest hit by a recent major hurricane.

c. Transylvania Railroad, whose largest customers are mines that have gradually decreased their output of highly-polluting coal.

d. Ty O'Day, an Irish actress who used to be the toast of Hollywood; her most recent pictures, however, have all too quickly become available only via download.

e. The probate estate of William Worthington Forsyth III, a publishing magnate who refused to believe that technological innovations would ever reduce the demand for in-print books and newspapers.

f. Starcrossed Partnership, which developed real estate in an overdeveloped market.

2. Consider the circumstances of each of the following debtors and determine the chapter(s) of the Code under which each could file.

a. Joe Farmer and his wife, Jill, operate a family farm that has been unable to compete with larger operations. Jill has been working in town to supplement their income, earning $70,000 a year. Their total income is $160,000. The Farmers owe the following obligations: $800,000 for the purchase of their farmland; $750,000 for construction of the house they built on their new farmland; $600,000 for various other farm-related obligations; and $1,600,000 in obligations related to a previous business venture.

ch 12

b. Beta Construction Corporation has suffered considerable losses as a result of the sharp decline in new construction projects. Beta recently defaulted on a large bank loan and is unable to pay its suppliers. Beta's debts total just over $1.8 million.

ch 11?

c. Clara Crumm is retired, with income only from Social Security. She has charged up to the limit on her thirteen credit cards, and now owes approximately $95,000 in credit card debt. Clara's other monthly expenses—rent, car payments, groceries, and the like—absorb most of her income, leaving her unable to make even the minimum payments on her credit cards.

ch 7/11?

d. Beverly Jordan works for a cleaning service occasionally, when her health permits. She has lived with David Mack for nearly 20 years, and he gives her $1,100 every month. She describes him as "family," but he has no legal obligation to support her.

ch 7?

3. Debtor, who operated a business as a sole proprietorship, had the following obligations: a mortgage for $500,000 secured by land worth $600,000; a debt of $525,000 owed to the SBA, secured by a judgment lien in the land, junior in priority to the mortgage; and debts to trade creditors totaling $150,000. All of the obligations were noncontingent and liquidated. Is Debtor eligible for Chapter 13? See § 506(a) and *Soderlund v. Cohen (In re Soderlund)*, 236 B.R. 271 (9th Cir. BAP 1999).

— If we can decide num. yes. If not know.

4. Section 109(e) sets the Chapter 13 debt limits in terms of "noncontingent, liquidated" debts. The significance of these words is illustrated by *In re Solomon*, 166 B.R. 832 (Bankr. D.Md.1994), *rev'd on other grounds*, 67 F.3d 1128 (4th Cir.1995). Several former patients brought lawsuits against Dr. Solomon alleging improper sexual conduct while the plaintiffs were in his care. The four lawsuits sought a total of $160 million in damages. Dr. Solomon filed a Chapter 13 petition that listed the claims as contingent, unliquidated and disputed, and assigned them zero value. The court held that Dr. Solomon was eligible for Chapter 13 because, as of the date of filing, the tort claims had not been reduced to judgment and the debtor had not admitted that any amount was due to those creditors. Dr. Solomon's later statement that he would not object to the claims did not retroactively liquidate the claims as of the date bankruptcy was filed. His statement merely "constituted a recognition that no interest of Debtor was served by objecting" because the tort claimants "would receive all plan payments, regardless of what was determined to be the amount of their claims, and the expense of litigation was likely to exceed what Debtor had concluded he should pay under his proposed plan." *Id*. at 838.

Does *Solomon* encourage debtors to file bankruptcy sooner rather than later? If so, is that a good thing? Is the court's interpretation of "noncontingent, liquidated" debts sound? These terms appear elsewhere in the Code; we will see them (and Dr. Solomon) again.

5. Clearly, individual debtors are eligible to file under Chapters 7 and 13, but are they also permitted to file Chapter 11 petitions? This question was addressed by the Supreme Court in *Toibb v. Radloff*, 501 U.S. 157, 111 S.Ct. 2197, 115 L.Ed.2d 145 (1991). Toibb, an out-of-work lawyer, initially filed a Chapter 7 petition. (His debts exceeded the Chapter 13 limits, which were lower at that time than they are today.) He sought to convert the case to Chapter 11 when he discovered that his major asset—shares in a company he formed with two others to produce and market electricity—was more valuable than he had realized. Precedent in the Eighth Circuit, however, limited Chapter 11 to individuals with on-going businesses. A divided Supreme Court, noting that the plain language of the Code contains no such limitation, held that individuals without on-going businesses are eligible to file Chapter 11. The Court acknowledged that some of the provisions in Chapter 11 obviously contemplate the rehabilitation of a business, but they merely reflect the expectation that Chapter 11 will be used primarily by business entities and debtors with on-going businesses; those provisions do not constitute an additional eligibility requirement. The Court dismissed the policy-based argument that consumer debtors might be able to shield more assets under Chapter 11 than Chapters 7 and 13 contemplate, because, even if so, the Code's language is plain. The Court was also unpersuaded by the argument that permitting Chapter 11s for consumer debtors would allow involuntary reorganizations, flying in the face of a congressional decision to prohibit involuntary Chapter 13 petitions because they would constitute involuntary servitude in violation of the Thirteenth Amendment. The Court noted that Chapter 11, unlike Chapter 13, did not require a debtor to pay his or her future wages to creditors. (The Code has since been amended, to add §§ 1115 and 1123(a)(8).) And, finally, the Court asserted that any concerns about a debtor's unwillingness to cooperate in an involuntary reorganization could be rectified by conversion of the case to Chapter 7.

So, we now know that individuals, even consumers, may file Chapter 11. But why they would wish to do so? Would debtors choose Chapter 11 only if they, like Toibb, have debts in excess of the Chapter 13 debt limits?

6. The 2005 Amendments added a new bankruptcy eligibility requirement in § 109(h)—that individual debtors, within 180 days before filing bankruptcy, receive a "briefing" regarding "the opportunities for available credit counseling" and assistance in "performing a related budget analysis." Approved counseling agencies must provide their services without regard to the debtor's ability to pay any fee, § 111(c)(2)(B).

This requirement is subject to several exceptions. First, a debtor need not get this prebankruptcy counseling if the United States trustee determines that adequate services are not available from approved agencies in the debtor's district, § 109(h)(2)(A). Second, the requirement can be waived in "exigent circumstances" when the debtor submits a certification, satisfactory to the court, establishing that counseling services could not be obtained within five days after they were requested, § 109(h)(3)(A). The debtor, however, is required to get that counseling within 30 days after filing, § 109(h)(3)(B). Finally, the requirement for prebankruptcy counseling does not apply to debtors who are incapacitated, disabled, or on active military service in a war zone, § 109(h)(4).

Note on the Obligations of Consumer Debtors' Attorneys

Sections 526, 527 and 528 were added by the 2005 Amendments as a result of Congress's concern that there were abuses, in need of correction, in the representation of consumer debtors. These provisions apply to "debt relief agencies," which includes "any person who provides any bankruptcy assistance to an assisted person in return for * * * payment * * *, or who is a bankruptcy petition preparer," § 101(12A). "Bankruptcy assistance" includes goods or services "provided to an assisted person with the express or implied purpose of providing information, advice, counsel, document preparation, or filing, or * * * legal representation with respect to a case or proceeding" in bankruptcy, § 101(4A). An "assisted person" is someone with limited nonexempt property whose debts are primarily consumer debts, § 101(3).

Section 526 establishes rules of professional conduct for "debt relief agencies" by imposing prohibitions that are largely consistent with existing law—failing to perform services, making false or misleading statements, and the like. Subsection 526(a)(4) goes further, however, by prohibiting a debt relief agency from advising a client to incur more debt, without regard to whether the debtor can repay the debt in bankruptcy and intends to do so. Incurring additional debt under such circumstances is legally permissible.

Section 527 mandates debt relief agencies to give certain disclosures to assisted persons. Although the details are beyond the scope of this Note, suffice it to say that the mandates are, in some instances, unclear. (For example, the replacement value of each asset must be disclosed "where requested" in "the documents filed to commence the case," § 527(a)(2)(B), but the petition commences the case and it requests no valuations.) In other instances, a debt relief agency is required to give written disclosures regarding legal questions that are—as we will see—unsettled. (For example, attorneys are required to disclose, in writing, how to do the calculations required by § 707(b)'s so-called "means test," § 527(c)(1). Keep this disclosure requirement in mind when we get to those materials.)

Section 528 requires "debt relief agencies" to identify themselves as such, and to include the following statement, or its substantial equivalent, in their advertising: "We are a debt relief agency. We help people file for bankruptcy relief under the Bankruptcy Code." §§ 528(a)(4) & (b)(2)(B).

Not unsurprisingly, attorneys chafed at these restrictions for a number of reasons, not all of which provided grounds for legal attack. For example, the fact that the additional paperwork required by these new provisions would probably raise the costs of bankruptcy cases suggests, at most, poor policy choices on the part of Congress. In addition, the demeaning tone of the legislation—perhaps what consumer attorneys resented most—gave no grounds for judicial disapproval. Other arguments, however, held more promise. First, the provisions were directed at attorneys representing consumer debtors, but poor drafting left open the possibility that attorneys representing creditors might be "debt relief agencies." Second, prohibitions against advising debtors to undertake actions that are perfectly legal arguably ran afoul of the constitutional rights of debtors and their attorneys.

These arguments reached the Supreme Court in *Milavetz, Gallop & Milavetz, P.A. v. United States*, 559 U.S. 229, 130 S.Ct. 1324, 176 L.Ed.2d 79 (2010). The Court, looking to the express language of the statute, fairly quickly dispatched the argument that attorneys do not fall within the definition of "debt relief agencies," and read the provision to apply only to attorneys representing consumer debtors. The Court then looked to the scope and validity of § 526(a)(4), and its prohibition on the giving of certain advice. The Court of Appeals for the Eighth Circuit had read § 526(a)(4) to prohibit a debt relief agency from advising an assisted person "to incur *any* additional debt when the assisted person is contemplating bankruptcy." 559 U.S. at 235. The Supreme Court characterized that reading as prohibiting "beneficial advice— even if the advice could help the assisted person avoid filing for bankruptcy altogether." *Id.* at 240. The Court of Appeals concluded that the statute was a content-based restriction on attorney-client communications that was not adequately tailored to constrain only the types of speech that the government has a substantial interest in restricting.

The Supreme Court disagreed, instead reading the statute to prohibit "a debt relief agency only from advising a debtor to incur more debt because the debtor is filing for bankruptcy, rather than for a valid purpose." *Id.* at 243. Thus, "advice to incur more debt because of bankruptcy, as prohibited by § 526(a)(4), will generally consist of advice to 'load up' on debt with the expectation of obtaining its discharge—*i.e.*, conduct that is abusive *per se*," *id.* at 244:

> * * * Congress was concerned with actions that threaten to harm debtors or creditors. Unlike the reasonable financial advice the Eighth Circuit's broad reading would proscribe, advice to incur more debt because of bankruptcy presents a substantial risk of injury to both debtors and creditors. Specifically, the incurrence of such debt stands to harm a debtor if his prepetition conduct leads a court to hold his debts nondischargeable, see § 523(a)(2), convert his case to another chapter, or dismiss it altogether, see § 707(b), thereby defeating his effort to obtain bankruptcy relief. If a debt, although manipulatively incurred, is not timely identified as abusive and therefore is

discharged, creditors will suffer harm as a result of the discharge and the consequent dilution of the bankruptcy estate. By contrast, the prudent advice that the Eighth Circuit's view of the statute forbids would likely benefit both debtors and creditors and at the very least should cause no harm. For all of these reasons, we conclude that § 526(a)(4) prohibits a debt relief agency only from advising an assisted person to incur more debt when the impelling reason for the advice is the anticipation of bankruptcy.

Id. at 245. The Court also rejected the argument that its narrow construction rendered § 526(a)(4) impermissibly vague.

Finally, the Court upheld the disclosure requirements of § 528, applying the rational basis test set forth in *Zauderer v. Office of Disciplinary Counsel*, 471 U.S. 626, 105 S.Ct. 2265, 85 L.Ed.2d 652 (1985), and concluding that "[e]vidence in the congressional record demonstrating a pattern of advertisements that hold out the promise of debt relief without alerting consumers to its potential cost is adequate to establish that the likelihood of deception in this case 'is hardly a speculative one.' " *Milavetz*, 559 U.S. at 251, quoting *Zauderer*, 471 U.S. at 652.

2. INVOLUNTARY PROCEEDINGS

Section 303 of the Code provides for involuntary cases. Such cases are surrounded by several requirements that are intended to protect debtors from possibly precipitous action by one or more disgruntled creditors. These requirements, which seem somewhat bland today, are rooted in bitter history. A taste of the hot debate that surrounded the introduction of these requirements into the law, as well as involuntary bankruptcy generally, can be found in Judge Friendly's dissent in a pre-Code case, *In re Gibraltor Amusements*, 291 F.2d 22 (2d Cir.), *cert. denied*, 368 U.S. 925, 82 S.Ct. 360, 7 L.Ed.2d 190 (1961), which discussed the history of the 1898 Bankruptcy Act:

The impulse for a new bankruptcy law came from the 200,000 business failures in the United States between the 1878 repeal of the 1867 Bankruptcy Act and 1898. Hardship had been particularly acute in the West, where a great land boom had raged from 1883 to 1889, followed by a sharp collapse. Southern and Western Populists began a crusade for at least a temporary voluntary bankruptcy law to relieve the large numbers of honest debtors from oppressive burdens and give them a fresh start in life.

Although Eastern congressmen were willing to concede that voluntary bankruptcy was a good idea, many of them were unwilling to enact a voluntary bill without accompanying involuntary features designed to insure an equitable distribution of a bankrupt's assets among his creditors, and, to that end, to abolish preferences. This the Populists opposed. They argued there was no need to infringe on state rights by creating a federal remedy for the collection of debts: state laws were adequate for the purpose. Bankruptcy was viewed as a stigma difficult to erase; it was one thing to allow a hopelessly burdened debtor to choose this disagreeable alternative as preferable to eternal debt but quite another to permit blood-thirsty creditors, with only their own interests at heart, to plunge an unwilling debtor into disgrace—the more so since in many cases the debtor reasonably might hope that the upturn in his fortunes was just around the corner, and bankruptcy would deprive him of the right to keep his business alive in the meantime. This position was summed up by Representative Lewis of Georgia, 31 Cong. Rec. 1908: "Voluntary bankruptcy is the means of the redemption of the unsuccessful and fallen debtor. Involuntary bankruptcy is a weapon in the hands of the creditor to press collections of debt harshly, to intimidate, and to destroy."[2] Thus the Populists denounced the bankruptcy bill as an "engine of oppression" (Sparkman, Fla., 31 Cong. Rec. 1851), "intended to bind hand and foot the debtors of this country and place them in the vise-like grip of the greedy cormorants of the country" (Henry, Tex., 31 Cong. Rec. 1803) * * * . Easterners countered that a properly restricted involuntary bankruptcy law was a benefit not only to creditors but to debtors as well. In the absence of such a law creditors become nervous; whenever the debtor's assets seem less than his liabilities, they are likely to grab them precipitously, thereby forcing the debtor to the wall, lest other creditors beat them to the draw and they get nothing. 31 Cong. Rec. 1789 (Henderson, Iowa), 1852 (Parker, N.J.).

The provisions of the statute with respect to involuntary bankruptcy were the resulting vector of these opposing forces, an attempt to make involuntary bankruptcy less unpalatable to the Populists by surrounding such proceedings with careful safeguards for the debtor. * * *

---

[2] Seventy years earlier, in 1827, Martin Van Buren, denouncing an attempt to provide for voluntary and involuntary bankruptcy in a single statute, had said "It is an erroneous idea * * * that this bill can be made to serve God and mammon by combining two things totally at variance." 3 Cong. Deb. 279.

Thus, the entire process that resulted in the enactment of the Act of 1898 was a pitched battle between those who wanted to give the creditor an effective remedy to assure equal distribution of a bankrupt's assets and those who were determined to protect the debtor from the harassment of ill-considered or oppressive involuntary petitions, including those by a single creditor interest. The requirement of three creditors was one of many provisions reflecting a compromise between the two opposing positions.

Id. at 27-28. These requirements are clearly serving their purpose, if the relative rarity of involuntary cases is any indication. Creditors and their attorneys need to be aware of the strategic uses of such filings, however, given that bankruptcy permits (among other things) the reversal of certain prepetition transactions. (The unwinding of particular transactions is covered in Chapter 5 of this text.) Thus, the creditor's threat of an involuntary filing provides a sort of counterbalance to the debtor's threat of a voluntary resort to bankruptcy.

Any entity that can file a voluntary petition under Chapter 7 or 11 can be the subject of an involuntary filing under that chapter, with two exceptions—farmers and not-for-profit corporations. § 303(a). Thus, no entity can be forced into a chapter under which that entity is not eligible to file voluntarily. (Here, recall § 109(b).) Involuntary petitions are not permitted under Chapters 12 and 13.

The filing of the petition automatically constitutes an "order for relief" in a voluntary proceeding under § 301. The order for relief "is tantamount to an order approving the court's exercise of jurisdiction to grant relief pursuant to the provisions of the law." Frank R. Kennedy, *The Commencement of a Case Under the New Bankruptcy Code*, 36 WASH. & LEE. L. REV. 977, 983 (1979).

The filing of the involuntary petition, in contrast, does not constitute an order for relief. Rather, a "postpetition gap" exists between the date of the filing of an involuntary petition and entry of the order for relief, giving the putative debtor an opportunity to rebut the factual premises of the filing. Thus, § 303(f) permits the debtor to conduct business and to use, acquire or dispose of property during this gap period as if the petition had not been filed. Any new debts that the debtor acquires during this period are treated as if they arose prior to the petition, § 502(f), and they are given a higher priority claim status than debts that actually did arise before the petition was filed, § 507(a)(2).

Further, the debtor may make transfers during the gap period that may not be later avoided by the bankruptcy trustee, as long as the transfers were in exchange for new value given after the petition was filed, § 549(b). A party in interest concerned that the bankruptcy estate will deteriorate during the gap period may move, pursuant to § 303(g), for appointment of an interim trustee to protect the estate until the order for relief is entered.

Section 303(b) imposes a two-part test that must be met by petitioning creditors in order to sustain the involuntary petition—a requisite number test (referred to by Judge Friendly in the excerpt above) and a requisite amount test. It also requires that the petitioning creditors hold claims that are "not contingent as to liability or the subject of a bona fide dispute." The bona fide dispute requirement in § 303 protects debtors engaged in good faith disputes with creditors from being coerced into settling by the threat of an involuntary proceeding.

The Bankruptcy Code does not permit commencement of an involuntary petition merely because a debtor's liabilities exceed its assets. Rather, § 303(h) provides that when an involuntary petition is timely disputed, a bankruptcy court may order relief against the debtor after trial only if (1) "the debtor is generally not paying such debtor's debts as such debts become due unless such debts are the subject of a bona fide dispute;" or (2) within 120 days before the petition was filed a custodian was appointed and took possession of substantially all of the debtor's property. (Compare § 101(32), defining "insolvent" in the balance sheet sense of liabilities in excess of assets, with § 303(h), which is a variant of an "equitable insolvency" test.)

Bankruptcy courts articulate what amounts to a *per se* rule that failure to satisfy liability to a single creditor is insufficient to constitute "generally not paying such debtor's debts." Under this rule, an involuntary petition filed by the only unpaid creditor is not permissible. Courts employing the doctrine, however, recognize so many exceptions that they threaten to swallow the rule—that the debtor has behaved fraudulently, or is manipulating his or her income and transferring assets in an effort to evade the debt, or that the single unpaid obligation is extraordinarily large. In *Perez v. Feinberg (In re Feinberg)*, 238 B.R. 781 (B.A.P. 8th Cir. 1999), for example, the debtor, a doctor, paid all of his obligations except one—for $2.3 million—owed to his former partners. When their efforts to collect proved fruitless, they filed an involuntary Chapter 11 petition against him. The bankruptcy court granted the debtor's motion to dismiss the petition, ruling that the creditors had failed to show that he was generally not paying his debts as they became due. The bankruptcy appellate panel reversed. It acknowledged the single creditor rule, but concluded that "the exceptions override it." The court found an exception justified by the size of the obligation and by the "debtor's actions in manipulating his and his wife's income, transferring assets, [and] attempting to hinder and delay these creditors, while living lavishly." *Id.* at 784-85.

Section 303 is the second time we have encountered the requirement that a claim be noncontingent; the first time was in § 109(e), which identifies debtors who may file Chapter 13 petitions. The court in *In re All Media Properties, Inc.*, 5 B.R. 126 (Bankr. S.D.Tex.1980), *affirmed mem.*, 646 F.2d 193 (5th Cir.1981), discussed § 303 and, in the process, stated the leading test for determining whether a claim is contingent:

> The debtors here contend that the holder of a claim which is unmatured or disputed cannot be a qualified creditor as that establishes that such claims are contingent in the sense that they are not, at the time of the filing of the petition, fixed or liquidated or now owing but rather that such claims require further proceedings or the passage of time. The debtors' contention is summed up by the following statement in their brief: "if the claim asserted by the petitioners would require proof in order to establish the merits of the claim as to the debtor's liability or the amount of this claim, then such a claim could not be considered to be not contingent as to liability."

* * *

> The court concludes that claims are contingent as to liability if the debt is one which the debtor will be called upon to pay only upon the occurrence or happening of an extrinsic event which will trigger the liability of the debtor to the alleged creditor and if such triggering event or occurrence was one reasonably contemplated by the debtor and creditor at the time the event giving rise to the claim occurred.

> Thus, in the case of the classic contingent liability of a guarantor of a promissory note executed by a third party, both the creditor and guarantor knew there would be liability only if the principal maker defaulted. No obligation arises until such default. In the case of a tort claim for negligence, the parties at the time of the alleged negligent act would be presumed to have contemplated that the alleged tortfeasor would be liable only if

it were so established by a competent tribunal. Such a tort claim is contingent as to liability until a final judgment is entered fixing the rights of the parties. On the other hand, in the ordinary debt arising from, for example, a sale of merchandise, the parties to the transaction would not at that time view the obligation as contingent. Subsequent events might lead to a dispute as to liability because of, for example, defective merchandise, but that would merely serve to render the debt a disputed one but would not make it a contingent one. A legal obligation arose at the time of the sale, although the obligation can possibly be avoided. Such a claim is disputed, but it is not contingent. A claim is contingent as to liability if the debtor's legal duty to pay does not come into existence until triggered by the occurrence of a future event and such future occurrence was within the actual or presumed contemplation of the parties at the time the original relationship of the parties was created. On the other hand, if a legal obligation to pay arose at the time of the original relationship, but that obligation is subject to being avoided by some future event or occurrence, the claim is not contingent as to liability, although it may be disputed as to liability for various reasons. Likewise, an unmatured obligation is not contingent as to liability. The obligation to pay existed from the outset; no outside event is necessary to bring the obligation into existence, but rather the obligation may be extinguished by payment. This does not render such a debt "contingent as to liability," but renders it only "unmatured."

* * *

[U]nder § 303(h)(1) of the Code the bankruptcy court shall enter an order for relief against a debtor only where "the debtor is generally not paying such debtor's debts as such debts become due." This phrase is not defined in the Code and the legislative history is not very helpful, but it seems reasonable to consider both the amount of the debt not being paid and the number of creditors not being paid in determining the answer to the issue.

During oral argument counsel for [the debtors] asserted that the term "generally" means usually or a majority of the time, and that the dividing line is one of simple mathematics. According to counsel for the alleged debtors, to be generally not paying his debts a debtor would have to be not paying at least 51% of his debts.

The court rejects this contention. The new test for involuntary petitions was adopted not to restrict and limit the involuntary process but was included to allow more flexibility. The legislative history describes § 303(h)(1) as the "most significant departure from present law concerning the present grounds for involuntary bankruptcy." Contrary to counsel's assertion at oral argument, this court believes that Congress contemplated that there would be a new and totally different approach to insolvency in involuntary cases when it passed the Code.

A hypothetical serves to illustrate the point. Consider a debtor who has 100 creditors, 15 of which hold 80% of the amount owed by the debtor. These 15 creditors also happen to be the only creditors not being paid by the debtor. Under the test suggested by [the debtors], the fact that only 15 creditors were not being paid would mean that involuntary relief would not be appropriate because a majority of the creditors were being paid. This court does not believe that Congress intended such a result. The term "generally" was not defined in order to avoid the result suggested by the mechanical test put forth by the alleged debtors and to give the bankruptcy courts enough leeway to be able to deal with the variety of situations that will arise.

Instead, the court believes that generally not paying debts includes regularly missing a significant number of payments to creditors or regularly missing payments which are significant in amount in relation to the size of the debtor's operation. Where the debtor has few creditors the number which will be significant will be fewer than where the debtor has a large number of creditors. Also, the amount of the debts not being paid is important. If the amounts of missed payments are not substantial in comparison to the magnitude of the debtor's operation, involuntary relief would be improper.

Id. at 131-32, 133, 142-43.

Questions and Problems

1. What is the difference between a *disputed* and a *contingent* claim, according to *All Media*? Give examples of each. What is the "jurisdictional" implication of concluding that a claim is noncontingent?

2. *All Media* suggested that both a prejudgment tort claim and a claim against a guarantor on a promissory note are "contingent." If so, what is the difference between a "contingent" claim and an "unliquidated" claim (which is an issue under § 109(e))?

3. Bank held a mortgage on Debtor's land, worth $25,000, securing an obligation of $50,000. Assuming that Debtor has fewer than 12 creditors and is not paying most of them, can Bank, acting alone, file an involuntary bankruptcy petition against Debtor?

4. Debtor owed Creditor $7,000 for goods sold on open account. After Creditor joined two other creditors (each of which was owed a similar amount) in filing an involuntary petition against Debtor, Debtor paid the obligation to Creditor. Debtor then argued that the involuntary petition had to be dismissed because the requisite number test was not satisfied. What result in this case?

5. State Bank, to whom Jill Debtor owed $35,000 on an unsecured obligation, filed an involuntary bankruptcy petition. Debtor's answer, contesting the validity of the filing, listed the following creditors in addition to State Bank: Visa; MasterCard; Discover Card; City Realty, Debtor's landlord; Emma Roper, Debtor's cleaning woman; Power Electric; Empire Gas; Ford Motor Credit, which held a security interest in Debtor's car; Frank's Repairs, Inc., Debtor's former employer, who caught Debtor stealing from the business six months ago, but agreed not to prosecute in exchange for monthly restitution payments; Jim Burns, Debtor's boyfriend, who loaned her the money to make the first two payments to Frank's; L.L. Bean, who issued its proprietary card to Debtor last year; Go Travel, for Debtor's beach vacation last summer; and Adelphia, Debtor's cell phone provider. Assuming that Debtor is generally not paying her debts as they become due, can State Bank, acting alone, initiate an involuntary case? If not, can the defect in the filing be cured by the postpetition addition of two more petitioners? Does the answer to that question depend on whether State Bank was aware of the defect in its petition?

6. An individual debtor who is the subject of an involuntary petition will almost certainly not have obtained prepetition credit counseling. Section 109(h), however, provides that "an individual *may not be a debtor*" in the absence of the required counseling. Does that language give individual debtors a way to controvert involuntary filings?

Note on Bad Faith Involuntary Petitions

The filing of an involuntary petition may have a devastating effect on a debtor, whether the debtor is an individual or a commercial enterprise. Congress was well aware of this reality and sought, by inclusion of § 303(i), to discourage creditors from filing involuntary petitions for improper reasons.

That § 303(i) may have considerable bite, in an appropriate case, is nowhere better illustrated than by *In re John Richards Homes Bldg. Co.*, 291 B.R. 727 (Bankr. E.D.Mich.2003). In that case, the purchaser of a luxury home, Adell, became embroiled in a construction dispute with the home's builder, JRH, and eventually filed an involuntary bankruptcy petition against JRH. The petition was dismissed because Adell's claim was the subject of a bona fide dispute. JRH then sought damages under § 303(i), asserting that the petition had been filed as part of a bad faith effort to extort a favorable settlement of the parties' dispute and, because of Adell's antipathy toward JRH's principal, to destroy JRH's business. Adell asserted that he acted out of concern for JRH's trade creditors, but the court found, on the basis of "overwhelming" evidence, that the petition had been filed in bad faith. The court pointed particularly to Adell's question, put to JRH's principal, whether the company could "take the hit to its reputation" of an involuntary petition, Adell's hiring of a public relations firm to publicize the filing, and his efforts to attract additional petitioning creditors by threatening that only those who joined would be paid. The court awarded compensatory damages of $4.1 million, punitive damages of $2 million, and attorney's fees and costs of $313,000.

3. DISMISSAL AND CONVERSION

A bankruptcy court has the power to dismiss the petition even though the eligibility requirements of § 109 (and § 303, for involuntary cases) have been met. Dismissal is permitted for "cause" under Chapters 7 and 11, §§ 707(a) & 1112(b), and debtors under those chapters do not have an absolute right to dismiss their cases. (Contrast Chapters 12 and 13 in that respect, §§ 1208(b) & 1307(b).) As you work through the following cases and materials, note the various grounds that may constitute "cause."

PHOENIX PICCADILLY, LTD. v. LIFE INSURANCE CO. OF VIRGINIA (IN RE PHOENIX PICCADILLY, LTD.)

United States Court of Appeals, Eleventh Circuit, 1988.
849 F.2d 1393.

RONEY, Chief Judge.

* * *

The critical issue on this appeal is whether the bankruptcy court gave proper consideration to whether the debtor had equity in the secured property and had a prospect of a successful reorganization, after the court had made a finding that "the petition was not filed in good faith, but rather, for the purpose of delaying and frustrating the efforts of the Secured Creditors to enforce their rights in the property." We hold, as the district court did implicitly, that the prospects of a successful reorganization do not override, as a matter of law, the finding of bad faith in this case or compel, as a matter of fact, a contrary finding. A brief examination of the case clearly reflects sufficient evidentiary support of that finding under the clearly erroneous standard of review.

The debtor, Phoenix–Piccadilly, Ltd., is a limited partnership which owns the Piccadilly Square Apartments located in Louisville, Kentucky. Legal title to the property is held by Citizens Fidelity Bank and Trust Company of Louisville, under a deed of trust.

The property is comprised of four phases known as Phases I, II, III and IV. The three secured creditors, Meritor Savings Bank, Life Insurance Company of Virginia, and Future Federal Savings Bank, separately hold first mortgage liens on all four phases. In addition, Paul A. Evola and Ronald F. Heltinger hold a note which is secured by a "wraparound"[a] mortgage encumbering the entire property.

On June 19, 1987, mortgage foreclosure proceedings were instituted by Future Federal in Jefferson County, Kentucky. On June 29, 1987, an order was entered in the state court action appointing a receiver for Phase III of the property. The debtor filed this Chapter 11 petition on November 19, 1987, the day before a hearing in the state court action to appoint a receiver for the other three phases of the property. After the automatic stay was lifted in this proceeding, a receiver was appointed for the entire property.

All three secured creditors filed motions for relief from the automatic stay provisions of the Bankruptcy Code, and subsequently filed motions to dismiss the Chapter 11 case. An automatic stay may be terminated for "cause" pursuant to § 362(d)(1) of the Bankruptcy Code if a petition was filed in bad faith. A case under Chapter 11 may be dismissed for cause pursuant to § 1112 of the Bankruptcy Code if the petition was not filed in good faith.

Although what amounts to bad faith is the same for both proceedings, there is no particular test for determining whether a debtor

---

[a] A "wraparound" mortgage is a junior mortgage with a face amount equal to the amount advanced by the junior mortgagee plus the outstanding balance on the senior mortgage. Payments on the wraparound mortgage cover both obligations, with the wraparound mortgagee responsible for making the payments to the senior mortgagee. Eds.

has filed a petition in bad faith. Instead, the courts may consider any factors which evidence "an intent to abuse the judicial process and the purposes of the reorganization provisions" or, in particular, factors which evidence that the petition was filed "to delay or frustrate the legitimate efforts of secured creditors to enforce their rights." *Albany Partners, Ltd. v. Westbrook (In re Albany Partners, Ltd.)*, 749 F.2d 670, 674 (11th Cir.1984).

The bankruptcy court's finding of bad faith is well supported by the record. The court held that many of the circumstantial factors which have been identified by the courts as evidencing a bad faith filing are present in this case:

(i)   The Debtor has only one asset, the Property, in which it does not hold legal title;

(ii)   The Debtor has few unsecured creditors whose claims are small in relation to the claims of the Secured Creditors;

(iii)   The Debtor has few employees;

(iv)   The Property is the subject of a foreclosure action as a result of arrearages on the debt;

(v)   The Debtor's financial problems involve essentially a dispute between the Debtor and the Secured Creditors which can be resolved in the pending State Court Action; and

(vi)   The timing of the Debtor's filing evidences an intent to delay or frustrate the legitimate efforts of the Debtor's secured creditors to enforce their rights.

The court held an evidentiary hearing and focused on certain evidence. Admissions of the debtor's agent, Lester N. Garripee, reveal the debtor's motive for filing its petition. In a letter to the debtor's limited partners dated July 16, 1987, Garripee detailed a plan "to fight Future Federal's foreclosure action" and, most tellingly, to posture the debtor "to make whatever legal defenses are appropriate to forestall Future Federal actions, including, if advisable, the filing of a Chapter 11 Bankruptcy Petition."

Additionally, Joey Bailey, President of Future Federal Savings Bank, testified that on July 21, 1987, another agent of the debtor,

Claude Hesse, threatened to forestall Future Federal's foreclosure action "for years" by filing a Chapter 11 case in a location "far from Louisville, Kentucky." As of the petition date, the debtor had unsecured debt of less than $250,000 and less than $50,000, if its unsecured debt to its affiliated company is excluded. The only persons employed by the debtor, other than the general partner, were the 15 persons performing maintenance and related services at the property in Kentucky under the supervision of the debtor's affiliated management company.

Finally, the venue chosen by the debtor for its Chapter 11 filing was over 700 miles from Louisville, Kentucky,[b] where the apartment complex, its employees, its secured and unsecured creditors, and the pending state court proceedings were located. Although perhaps technically proper, the choice to file the petition so far from where the property and creditors are located may itself be evidence of bad faith.

Because the bankruptcy court found that a bad faith filing had occurred, it properly did not change the consequences of that finding simply because of the debtor's possible equity in the property or potential for successful reorganization. We reject the debtor's argument that the bankruptcy court cannot ever dismiss a case for bad faith if there is equity in the property because the presence of equity indicates the potential for a successful reorganization. Rather, as this Court stated in *Natural Land Corp. v. Baker Farms, Inc. (In re Natural Land Corp.)*, 825 F.2d 296 (11th Cir.1987):

> the taint of a petition filed in bad faith must naturally extend to any subsequent reorganization proposal; thus, any proposal submitted by a debtor who filed his petition in bad faith would fail to meet § 1129's good faith requirement.

Id. at 298. The possibility of a successful reorganization cannot transform a bad faith filing into one undertaken in good faith.

AFFIRMED.

Notes and Questions

1. Is it "bad faith" to file a bankruptcy petition in order to take advantage of the automatic stay? Is that all that happened here?

---

[b] The bankruptcy petition was filed in the Middle District of Florida. Eds.

2. Can the debtor's choice of venue suggest bad faith? (Although empirical studies have found extensive evidence of forum shopping in large corporate bankruptcies—Theodore Eisenberg & Lynn M. LoPucki, *Shopping for Judges: An Empirical Analysis of Venue Choice in Large Chapter 11 Reorganizations*, 84 CORNELL L. REV. 967 (1999); Lynn M. LoPucki & William C. Whitford, *Venue Choice and Forum Shopping in the Bankruptcy Reorganization of Large, Publicly Held Companies*, 1991 WIS. L. REV. 11— recall Chapter 1's discussion of the failure of reform efforts.)

IN RE JOHNS–MANVILLE CORP.

United States Bankruptcy Court, Southern District of New York, 1984.
36 B.R. 727.

BURTON R. LIFLAND, Bankruptcy Judge.

DECISION AND ORDER ON MOTIONS TO DISMISS MANVILLE'S
CHAPTER 11 PETITION

I. Background and Issues Presented

Whether an industrial enterprise in the United States is highly successful is often gauged by its "membership" in what has come to be known as the "Fortune 500". Having attained this measure of financial achievement, Johns–Manville Corp. and its affiliated companies (collectively referred to as "Manville") were deemed a paradigm of success in corporate America by the financial community. Thus, Manville's filing for protection under Chapter 11 of Title 11 of the United States Code ("the Code or the Bankruptcy Code") on August 26, 1982 ("the filing date") was greeted with great surprise and consternation on the part of some of its creditors and other corporations that were being sued along with Manville for injuries caused by asbestos exposure. As discussed at length herein, Manville submits that the sole factor necessitating its filing is the mammoth problem of uncontrolled proliferation of asbestos health suits brought against it because of its substantial use for many years of products containing asbestos which injured those who came into contact with the dust of this lethal substance. According to Manville, this current problem of approximately 16,000 lawsuits pending as of the filing date is compounded by the crushing economic burden to be suffered by Manville over the next 20–30 years by the filing of an even more staggering number of suits by those who had been exposed but who will not manifest the asbestos-related diseases until some time during this future period ("the future asbestos claimants"). Indeed, approximately 6,000 asbestos health claims are estimated to have arisen in only the first 16 months since the filing date.

This burden is further compounded by the insurance industry's general disavowal of liability to Manville on policies written for this very purpose. Indeed, the issue of coverage has been pending for years before a state court in California ("the California Coordinated Litigation").

It is the propriety of the filing by Manville which is the subject of the instant decision. Four separate motions to dismiss the petition pursuant to § 1112(b) of the Code have been lodged before this Court * * * .

Manville has opposed all four dismissal motions and has been joined in opposition to them by the Unofficial Committee of School Creditors and the Equity Holders Committee. The Unsecured Creditors Committee has filed a brief "in response" to the motions which advocates denial of the motions.

The Asbestos Committee, which is comprised with one exception of attorneys for asbestos victims, initially moved to dismiss this case on November 8, 1982 citing Manville's alleged lack of good faith in filing this petition. However, the Asbestos Committee did not press its motion before the Court until now, more than one year later. In the interim, while engaging in plan formulation negotiations, it has vigorously pursued discovery in order to bolster its factual contention that Manville knowingly perpetrated a fraud on this Court and on all its creditors and equity holders in exaggerating the profundity of its economic distress in 1981 so as to enable it to file for reorganization in 1982. Thus, the Asbestos Committee submitted in November 1983 a multitude of volumes of materials consisting of 55 days of depositions of Manville officers in alleged support of the inference that in 1981 a small Manville group "concocted" evidence to meet the requirements for filing a Chapter 11 petition. The Asbestos Committee alleges that this group manufactured evidence of crushing economic distress so as to demonstrate falsely that pursuant to required principles of accounting * * * Manville had to book a reserve of at least $1.9 billion for asbestos health liability, and thus had no alternative but to seek Chapter 11 protection. The booking of such a reserve would, in turn, have triggered the acceleration of approximately $450 million of outstanding debt, possibly resulting in a forced liquidation of key business segments. Thus, the multitudinous submissions by the Asbestos Committee are aimed at showing their challenge to the motive, methods and data used by Manville's accounting consultants, its management and its Litigation Advisory Group ("LAG") in determining whether relief under Chapter 11 should be sought.

Mindful that there is no insolvency requirement for Chapter 11 debtor status, the issue presented for determination by this Court is whether these allegations of error by the Asbestos Committee, even egregious error, in over-calculation of Manville's financial problems are relevant to establish the kind of bad faith in the sense of an abuse of this Court's jurisdiction which will vitiate the filing of a Chapter 11 petition. This opinion will thus elucidate whether the tomes of material submitted by the Asbestos Committee defeat the essential fact that as of August 26, 1982 Manville is a real company with real debt, real creditors and a compelling need to reorganize in order to meet these obligations.

The Whitman[, GAF and Co-defendants' motions] * * * are based on the theory that because the claims of future asbestos victims are not cognizable or dischargeable in bankruptcy, the *raison d'etre* for the filing is vitiated and thus the petition should be dismissed. However, this Court must bear in mind in determining the issues raised by these movants that even if the claims of future claimants are ultimately found not dischargeable, that finding does not necessarily preclude this Court from dealing with the interests of these "parties in interest" under Code § 1109(b), especially since blinding the reorganization process to their residual interests would doom this reorganization case to ineffectiveness. If future claimants are properly represented as parties in interest, the means for the emergence of a proper plan which fairly provides for the survival and just treatment of their interests post-petition will be better assured.

As background information, it should be noted that throughout the course of the past 16 months, all parties, including the movants herein, have participated to a substantial extent in negotiations aimed at formulating a consensual plan treating all interests justly and fairly. Indeed, it is interesting to note that some of the very co-defendants which now seek to dismiss the petition, notably Owens–Illinois and Keene Corp., have previously expressed on the record before this Court their fervent desire to engraft themselves onto any plan providing for a claims-handling facility with which to deal with asbestos claimants. They have related to the Court their arduous efforts at formulating a sharing arrangement whereby all co-defendants, including Manville, may apportion their relative liabilities to the victims as a first step toward full participation in and contribution to any claims-handling Manville reorganization plan to be funded by an industry "super fund."

In addition, Keene Corp., also one of the co-defendants seeking to dismiss the petition, is the proponent of the related motion to appoint a legal representative for future asbestos claimants proposed for the purported purpose of enabling this reorganization to deal effectively with this key constituency and thereby succeed. The shifting posture of many of the co-defendants is in no small measure impelled by their continued involvement in the nonbankruptcy asbestos litigation and the filing by Manville of a plan that as yet does not provide a sharing and contribution arrangement. In any event, whether or not the co-defendants may for the purpose of the dismissal motions deem it prudent to participate in the reorganization effort and effect a global solution to the asbestos problem, Manville should have the opportunity to attempt to successfully reorganize with or without them so long as it conforms to all Code requirements.

Throughout this 16–month period, the Asbestos Committee, at considerable expense to the debtor, has engaged its own counsel and epidemiologists and, jointly with the Unsecured Creditors Committee, engaged an investment banking firm to prepare projections of future income in aid of plan formulation. It is only now that negotiations have become seemingly deadlocked that the Asbestos Committee has reverted to its original position of attacking the filing. If there was merit in the motion to dismiss on grounds of lack of good faith, it could have been fervently pressed a year ago instead of tolerating this alleged misuse of the courts. This same assertion of untimeliness can be made regarding the other co-defendant proponents of dismissal of the petition because they too may be pressing these motions as a last resort as a result of frustrations at the bargaining table. This Court must therefore bear in mind the strategical motivations underlying the pursuit of these motions at this time as well as recognize the progress toward a successful, perhaps consensual, reorganization that has already taken place. It is against this backdrop of progress and achievement accomplished by the key constituencies toward a resolution on perhaps a sweeping basis of the asbestos problem that the instant motions are now placed before me for determination.

II. Discussion of Law

A. General Eligibility Requirements for Chapter 11 Status

The motions to dismiss Manville's petition filed by the Asbestos Committee, GAF, Whitman, and the Co-defendants must be denied. Preliminarily, it must be stated that there is no question that Manville is eligible to be a debtor under the Code's statutory requirements. Section 109 of the Code contains its eligibility requirements * * * .

* * *

Moreover, it should also be noted that neither § 109 nor any other provision relating to voluntary petitions by companies contains any insolvency requirement. * * * And, with specific regard to Chapter 11, the Code eliminates the requirement contained in * * * the Act that the debtor be insolvent or unable to pay his debts as they mature. This is in striking contrast to the requirement of insolvency contained in § 303[(h)] with regard to the commencement of involuntary cases. * * *

It is only with regard to Chapter 9 (Adjustment of Debts of a Municipality) that the Code mentions insolvency or inability to meet one's debts. *See* § 109(c)(3).

Accordingly, it is abundantly clear that Manville has met all of the threshold eligibility requirements for filing a voluntary petition under the Code. This Court will now turn to the issue of whether any of the movants have demonstrated sufficient "cause" pursuant to § 1112(b) to warrant the dismissal of Manville's petition.

B. The Standard of "Cause" for Dismissal of a Chapter 11 Petition

Section 1112(b) of the Code provides for conversion or dismissal of a case for "cause." It lists nine examples of cause,[c] but the list is not exhaustive. One court has described the pertinent legislative history, declaring: "The court will be able to consider other factors as they arise, and use its equitable powers to reach an appropriate result in individual cases. What constitutes cause under § 1112(b) is subject to judicial discretion under the circumstances of each case." *In re Nancant, Inc.*, 8 B.R. 1005, 1006 (Bankr. D.Mass.1981). * * *

As is set forth in detail in part D *infra*, the interests of future claimants need not be discharged to be accounted for and fully and fairly represented in these proceedings. Indeed, under Manville's currently proposed plan, future claims would survive the Chapter 11 and would presumably be eligible to be liquidated by a claims handling facility or by another method as yet undetermined. Thus, the motions to dismiss filed by GAF, Whitman and the Codefendants premised on speculation as to the nondischargeability of future claims do not establish sufficient "cause" pursuant to § 1112(b) and must be denied in their entirety.

---

[c] The list has since expanded to sixteen. Eds.

Furthermore, much of the argument in support of all of the motions to dismiss is pitched to the confirmability of Manville's proposed plan. This argument is misplaced. * * * The essential determination here is the propriety of the filing, and whether "cause" exists to vitiate it, not the confirmability of a particular plan. If Manville is unable to effectuate a particular plan, that is not tantamount to finding that no plan can be effectuated.

C. The Motion to Dismiss Filed by The Asbestos Committee

The motion to dismiss the petition filed by the Asbestos Committee must also be denied. The Asbestos Committee premises its motion to dismiss the petition on what it contends is Manville's "bad faith" in filing for protection under Chapter 11. * * *

Because the allegations of the Asbestos Committee are not supported by concrete facts and thus do not rebut the essential fact that Manville is a real company with a substantial amount of real debt and real creditors clamoring to enforce this real debt, the Asbestos Committee has not sustained its burden of demonstrating sufficient fraud to vitiate the filing *ab initio*. * * *

Manville's Compendium [of the Factual Record On the Issue of the Propriety of the Chapter 11 Filing] relates the testimony of Manville officers and supports the inference accepted herein that these petitions were filed only after Manville undertook lengthy, careful and detailed analysis. For example, Manville commissioned and strictly scrutinized the results of studies by two separate epidemiological groups * * *. [They] corroborated each other's projections of runaway asbestos health costs within the foreseeable future.

In addition, the Compendium cites to testimony of Manville officers which details the slow and deliberate process of data commissioning and review and "soul-searching" antedating the filing, including the employment and review of results of studies * * * regarding propensity to sue. The data submitted by Manville also supports the accepted inference that the $1.9 billion projected debt figure ratified by Manville was the result of careful, conservative and perhaps understated projections.

In so doing, Manville has succeeded in rebutting in general and in specific the Asbestos Committee's allegations of fraud regarding the size of its projected debt, including those of collusion, manipulation of figures, cover-up and falsification of data. * * *

1. The Code's Policies of Open Access and Liquidation Avoidance

In determining whether to dismiss under § 1112(b), a court is not necessarily required to consider whether the debtor has filed in "good faith" because that is not a specified predicate under the Code for filing. Rather, according to § 1129(a)(3), good faith emerges as a requirement for the confirmation of a plan. The filing of a Chapter 11 case creates an estate for the benefit of all creditors and equity holders of the debtor wherein all constituencies may voice their interests and bargain for their best possible treatment. * * * It is thus logical that the good faith of the debtor be deemed a predicate primarily for emergence out of a Chapter 11 case. It is after confirmation of a concrete and immutable reorganization plan that creditors are foreclosed from advancing their distinct and parochial interests in the debtor's estate.

A "principal goal" of the Bankruptcy Code is to provide "open access" to the "bankruptcy process." Report of the Commission on the Bankruptcy Laws of the United States, H.R. Doc. No. 137, Part II, 93rd Cong., 1st Sess. 75, 79 (1973). * * * Another major goal of the Code, that of "rehabilitation of debtors," requires that relief for debtors must be "timely." *Id*. at 79. Congress declared that it is essential to both the "open access" and "rehabilitation" goals that

> [i]nitiating relief should not be a death knell. The process should encourage resort to it, by debtors and creditors, that cuts short the dissipation of assets and the accumulation of debts. Belated commencement of a case may kill an opportunity for reorganization or arrangement.

Id. at 75.

Accordingly, the drafters of the Code envisioned that a financially beleaguered debtor with real debt and real creditors should not be required to wait until the economic situation is beyond repair in order to file a reorganization petition. The "Congressional purpose" in enacting the Code was to encourage resort to the bankruptcy process. This philosophy not only comports with the elimination of an insolvency requirement, but also is a corrollary [sic] of the key aim of Chapter 11 of the Code, that of avoidance of liquidation. * * *

In the instant case, not only would liquidation be wasteful and inefficient in destroying the utility of valuable assets of the companies as well as jobs, but, more importantly, liquidation would preclude just compensation of some present asbestos victims and all future asbestos claimants. This unassailable reality represents all the more reason for this Court to adhere to this basic potential liquidation avoidance aim of Chapter 11 and deny the motions to dismiss. Manville must not be required to wait until its economic picture has deteriorated beyond salvation to file for reorganization.

* * *

Manville's purported motivation in filing to obtain a breathing spell from asbestos litigation should not conclusively establish its lack of intent to rehabilitate and justify the dismissal of its petition. On the contrary, there has been submitted no evidence that Manville has not bargained to obtain a reorganization plan in good faith.

2. Manville's "Good Faith" Filing Is Measured By The Existence Of Massive Unmanageable Real Debt Owed To Real Claimants

It is this Court's belief that there is no strict and absolute "good faith" predicate to filing a Chapter 11 petition. Earlier bankruptcy laws, for example, former Chapter X relating to corporate debtors, specifically required that the court find that the petition "had been filed in good faith." However, the present Bankruptcy Code contains no such express requirement.

This Court, along with others, has opined that the concept of good faith is an elastic one which can be read into the statute on a limited *ad hoc* basis. *In re Eden Associates*, 13 B.R. 578, 584 (Bankr. S.D.N.Y.1981). However, in *Eden* this Court also cautioned that slavish adherence to a good faith concept may redound to the detriment of those non-debtor claimants who are or may putatively be beneficiaries of the reorganization process. * * * [A] Chapter 11 filing creates a bankruptcy estate which exists for the benefit not simply of the debtor, but rather also for the benefit of all of the debtor's creditors and equity holders. The filing triggers the springing into existence of important constituencies which, along with the debtor, must be protected by a reorganization court. Accordingly, the intense focus on the debtor's motives in filing is misplaced. * * *

Moreover, courts have generally held that the concept of good faith as of the filing date may only be applied where it is demonstrated that the jurisdiction of the bankruptcy court has been abused. * * *

* * * In *Manville*, it is undeniable that there has been no sham or hoax perpetrated on the Court in that Manville is a real business with real creditors in pressing need of economic reorganization. Indeed, the Asbestos Committee has belied its own contention that Manville has no debt and no real creditors by quantifying a benchmark settlement demand approaching one billion dollars for compensation of approximately 15,500 prepetition asbestos claimants, during the course of negotiations pitched toward achieving a consensual plan. This huge asserted liability does not even take into account the estimated 6,000 new asbestos health claims which have arisen in only the first 16 months since the filing date. The number of post-filing claims increases each day as "future claims back into the present."

Moreover, asbestos related property damage claims present another substantial contingent and unliquidated liability. Prior to the filing date, various schools initiated litigation seeking compensatory and punitive damages from, *inter alia*, Manville for their unknowing use of asbestos-containing products in ceilings, walls, structural members, piping, ductwork and boilers in school buildings. * * *

Accordingly, it is clear that Manville's liability for compensatory, if not punitive, damages to school authorities is not hypothetical, but real and massive debt. A range of $500 million to $1.4 billion is the total projected amount of Manville's real debt to the school creditors.

In addition, claims of $425 million of liquidated commercial debt have been filed in this proceeding. The filing also triggered the acceleration of more than $275 million in unsecured public and institutional debt which had not been due prior to the filing. Upon a dismissal of this petition, Manville may be liable in the amount of all of the above-described real debts, plus interest. Manville's present holdings of cash and liquid assets would be insufficient to pay these obligations and, as noted above, its insurance carriers have repeatedly expressed their unwillingness to contribute to the payment of this debt. Thus, upon dismissal, Manville would become a target for economic dismemberment, liquidation, and chaos, which would benefit no one except the few winners of the race to the courthouse. The economic reality of Manville's highly precarious financial position due to massive debt sustains its eligibility and candidacy for reorganization.

In short, there was justification for Manville to elect a course contemplating a viable court-supervised rehabilitation of the real debt owed by Manville to its real creditors. Manville's filing did not in the appropriate sense abuse the jurisdiction of this Court * * *. Thus, its petition must be sustained.

3. That Tort Claims Are Dischargeable In Bankruptcy Is Further Indication That Manville Has Not Abused This Court's Jurisdiction

* * * [U]nder the Code, unlike under the predecessor Act, state court tort claims are dischargeable in bankruptcy. * * * Section 502(c) requires that the bankruptcy court estimate all unliquidated claims regardless of delay to administration of the estate with a resulting discharge of these claims. *See* §§ 502(c)(1) (claims estimation), 524 (effect of discharge) and 1141 (discharge effect of plan confirmation). * * *

Moreover, District Judge Leval of the Southern District of New York has recently recognized the appropriateness of claims estimation of these tort claims in connection with appellate review of this Court's decision denying an expansion of the automatic stay to cover Manville's tort co-defendants. He declared that "the bankruptcy judge will undoubtedly seek to design, with the cooperation of the claimants and the debtor, procedures for the adjudication or settlement of those [tort] claims in a rational consolidated fashion, whether in the bankruptcy court or elsewhere." *Keene Corp. v. Johns–Manville Corp.*, 31 B.R. 627, 628 (S.D.N.Y.1983).

Indeed, Manville has lodged a motion before this Court seeking to accomplish this very purpose. This motion coupled with Manville's currently proposed plan seeks to establish a claims-handling facility whose purpose would be to estimate asbestos-related claims in an expeditious fashion. According to the unilateral reorganization plan filed by Manville on November 21, 1983, this facility would consist, *inter alia*, of a "no fault" system where victims would submit their claims to a medical screening panel and receive a predetermined amount for the injury specified with subsequent reevaluation not precluded. Thus, Manville recognizes that these traditionally state law tort claims may be liquidated pursuant to § 502(c) as part of its first-filed reorganization plan.

Accordingly, a filing so as to substitute bankruptcy court procedures for estimation of these claims in and of itself does not constitute an abuse of the bankruptcy court's jurisdiction. Because tort claims are now dischargeable under the Code, simply because a company's economic pressures are tort-related in nature instead of more traditional financial business woes does not demonstrate an abuse of jurisdiction. * * *

In sum, Manville is a financially beseiged [sic] enterprise in desperate need of reorganization of its crushing real debt, both present and future. The reorganization provisions of the Code were drafted with the aim of liquidation avoidance by great access to Chapter 11. Accordingly, Manville's filing does not abuse the jurisdictional integrity of this Court, but rather presents * * * reasons * * * for awaiting the determination of Manville's good faith until it is considered under § 1129(a)(3) as a prerequisite to confirmation * * *.

D. The GAF, Whitman, and Co-defendants' Motions to Dismiss the Petition Must Be Denied

The GAF, Whitman and Co-defendants' motions to dismiss must be denied because future claimants, whether or not they possess dischargeable "claims," possess a cognizable interest in these proceedings. This interest must be protected. The motion filed by GAF * * * is based on the theory that because the claims of future asbestos claimants are not cognizable and dischargeable in bankruptcy, the *raison d'etre* for the filing is vitiated and thus the petition should be dismissed. * * *

It is just this concern that the [Court in a separate decision] responds to in establishing that future claimants are parties in interest to this reorganization case who must have their own legal representative to safeguard this keen and compelling interest. Because this Court finds that the claims of these asbestos-exposed claimants may survive the bankruptcy and look to be liquidated post-confirmation, the rights of these claimants will be significantly impacted by these proceedings. It is undeniable that these proceedings will result in a delivery system for Manville tort claimants, whether in the present questionably efficient tort system, a newly-created claims-estimation facility, or another form. Thus, the *raison d'etre* for the filing is not a nullity and these proceedings are not a useless exercise. * * *

The Co-defendants' motion to dismiss the petition similarly must be dismissed as it too is predicated on the theory that future claims are not dischargeable in a Chapter 11 proceeding. * * * The Equity Holders Committee's scathing criticism with regard to the Whitman motion that "only the author of Alice in Wonderland might simply declare future claims out of existence in the face of massive evidence to the contrary" applies equally to the Co-defendants' motion.

Regarding the GAF, Whitman and Co-defendants' motions, it should be noted that it is indeed possible that a liquidating plan will eventuate. As stated earlier, the type of plan which emerges, *i.e.*, whether or not it treats with future claimants fairly, if at all, is irrelevant to the threshold determination made by this Court today as to the propriety or "good faith" of Manville's filing. These pejorative considerations are more appropriately left to the decision on confirmability of a concrete plan, as applied to a plan proponent, under § 1129 of the Code.

IV. Conclusion

For the reasons set forth above * * *, all four of the motions to dismiss the Manville petition are denied in their entirety.

Notes and Questions

1. Are *Manville* and *Phoenix Piccadilly* consistent? Was Phoenix Piccadilly any less a real debtor with real debt than Manville?

2. Why did these petitioning creditors want Manville's bankruptcy petition dismissed? Was bankruptcy in the best interests of stockholders?

3. Does it make sense that insolvency not be a prerequisite for the filing of a bankruptcy petition (except, of course, under Chapter 9)?

4. Section 1112(b) allows dismissal "for cause." Is the debtor's solvency "cause" within § 1112(b)?

5. Section 1129(a)(3) requires that the plan be proposed in good faith. Does the Code require that a Chapter 11 case be *filed* in good faith? *Cf.* § 1112. *Compare* §§ 707(b)(3) and 1325(a)(7).

The court in *In re SGL Carbon Corp.*, 200 F.3d 154 (3d Cir.1999), expressly adopted a good faith filing requirement for Chapter 11, relying on four factors: the permissive language of § 1112; other circuit-level decisions, such as *Phoenix Piccadilly*, finding that lack of good faith constitutes cause for dismissing a Chapter 11 petition; bankruptcy's equitable roots; and the purpose of Chapter 11 to balance the interests of debtors and creditors, preventing abuse of the process by debtors whose overriding motive is to delay creditors. The court then found lack of good faith and dismissed the Chapter 11 petition, for lack of a valid reorganizational purpose, of a financially healthy corporation that filed in anticipation of civil antitrust liability, in an effort to pressure those plaintiffs to accept the corporation's settlement terms.

Other courts have had harsh words for the good faith filing doctrine followed by *Phoenix Piccadilly* and *SGL Carbon*, but rejected by *Manville*. In *In re Victoria Ltd. Partnership*, 187 B.R. 54 (Bankr. D.Mass.1995), the court slammed the doctrine as "in conflict with the Code, legislative history, Supreme Court precedent, and logic," even though admitting that "[g]ood faith, like apple pie, is difficult to oppose." *Id.* at 54. *Phoenix Piccadilly* came in for particular criticism: "Stripped of much of its window dressing, *Phoenix Piccadilly* stands for the startling proposition that it is an act of bad faith for a debtor to file under chapter 11 in order to prevent foreclosure upon its only asset." *Id*. at 59. The court also found deficiencies in the logic of the doctrine:

> The good faith filing doctrine * * * is a prime example of how courts should not formulate a rule of law.
>
> A rule of law should be susceptible to clear statement, so that the result of its application to particular facts can be predicted with reasonable certainty. The good faith filing doctrine fails this test miserably. Its application does not depend upon the presence of any particular circumstances the courts list as relevant. Moreover, although a filing on the eve of foreclosure is typically stated to be a factor in the doctrine, courts recognize, as they must, that invoking the automatic stay is not of itself bad faith. If that is so, it is difficult to see why filing to prevent foreclosure is an indicator of bad faith when combined with other factors. Also often stated as a factor in the doctrine is the debtor's perceived inability to reorganize. And yet, as demonstrated by *Phoenix Piccadilly*, not even this is an essential element.

* * *

> In sum, the good faith filing doctrine is an amorphous gestalt, devoid of reasoning and impenetrable to understanding.

Id. at 61-62.

As a parting shot, the court in *Victoria Ltd. Partnership* found the doctrine inconsistent with § 362(d)(3), which was added to the Code in 1994: "Congress obviously recognized the propriety of reorganization by single asset real estate debtors and their need for a reasonable period of time in which to file a plan of reorganization. The good faith filing doctrine all but bars them from reorganizing." *Id*. at 62.

The Eleventh Circuit has adhered to its views despite these arguments. A panel from that Court held, without analysis, that *Phoenix Piccadilly* was not overruled by the enactment of § 362(d)(3) and corresponding revisions to § 101. *State Street Houses, Inc. v. New York State Urban Dev. Corp. (In re State Street Houses, Inc.)*, 356 F.3d 1345 (11th Cir.2004).

6. Judge Lifland appointed a Wall Street attorney to protect the interests of future claimants in *Manville*, as an attorney would protect the interests of an unborn heir in a probate proceeding. As a result of the attorney's negotiations, Johns–Manville agreed to put certain assets, along with profits generated by them, in trust for the benefit of existing and future claimants. Though

Judge Lifland did not treat the future claimants as creditors and so did not discharge their claims against Johns–Manville, he did identify them as "parties in interest" and permanently enjoined them from making claims against *other* assets of the corporation.

In 1994, Congress amended § 524 by adding a new subsection (g) that focuses directly on the rights of the victims of asbestos-related disease. This effectively codified *Manville*'s trust device. The new provision allows a bankruptcy court to establish a trust from which future claimants may receive compensation, and it enjoins those future claimants from bringing an action against the reorganizing debtor. Although § 524(g) applies only in asbestos cases, *Manville* remains applicable, by analogy, to all mass tort cases.

Dismissal of a consumer case raises entirely different questions. Before passage of the 2005 Amendments, an individual consumer debtor's Chapter 7 case was subject to dismissal if the grant of relief would constitute a "substantial abuse" of that chapter. The statutory provision, § 707(b), gave no hint of what facts might be pertinent, so the applicable standard was left to case law development. Two approaches evolved. Under one line of authority, substantial abuse depended primarily upon the debtor's ability to repay his or her debts. Under the other, substantial abuse was determined by the "totality of the circumstances," although the most obvious and important of the pertinent "circumstances" was the debtor's ability to repay.

Critics charged that courts were too lax in exercising their power to dismiss a case as a substantial abuse under § 707(b) (and the statute did not permit creditors to initiate such actions themselves). These critics contended that a large number of debtors who file Chapter 7 could, in fact, repay a significant portion of their debts under a Chapter 13 plan. Section 707(b) became the focus of the revision process, leading to changes that are among the most controversial of the 2005 Amendments. Section 707(b) was dramatically altered, with the addition of a "means test" that is applicable to debtors whose combined family income exceeds the state median for their family size. A Chapter 7 filing that does not pass the means test is presumed to be an abuse and must be dismissed.

The means test is designed to identify debtors who are able to repay a portion of their debts, and to exclude those debtors from Chapter 7. (Such debtors will usually file Chapter 13, if they can qualify.) The means test, which is extremely complex, begins with the debtor's "current monthly income" (CMI). It is defined in § 101(10A) as the debtor's average monthly income for the six-month period preceding the date of bankruptcy filing. Income from all sources, other than Social Security, is included. (In a joint case, the income of both spouses is included.) That monthly average is then multiplied by 60— the maximum length of a Chapter 13 plan under current law—to determine the amount that the debtor(s) could repay under a Chapter 13 plan.

The definition of CMI is rigid and backward-looking, which renders it a seriously inaccurate predictive tool in many fact patterns. It does not take into account the fact that certain debtors, such as teachers, may have income that is cyclical. Nor does it take into account that a debtor may have recently lost his or her job, or may have experienced a permanent decrease in income due to illness. Similarly, it does not take into account that a debtor, such as a recent college graduate, may be about to experience an increase in income. It also does not take into account the fact that income may result from a one-time event, such as a bonus or gift. Income from such sources will not, in fact, be available in the future for repayments to creditors. Thus, the statutory rigidity and backward focus of the definition may result in a number that is unrealistically high or low, thereby distorting any conclusion as to whether the debtor could repay a reasonable amount of debt in a Chapter 13 proceeding.

This definition of CMI also permits debtors and their attorneys to time a bankruptcy filing in light of the debtor's income fluctuations, thereby manipulating the outcome of the means test. When—and whether—such strategic behavior ceases to be zealous representation and becomes an abuse of the system is an open question.

Section 707(b)(3), which we will turn to in a moment, may provide an answer to these defects in the definition of CMI. In addition, the Supreme Court's decision in *Hamilton v. Lanning*, 560 U.S. 505, 130 S.Ct. 2464, 177 L.Ed.2d 23 (2010), may also provide authority for a less rigid approach to the calculation of CMI for purposes of § 707(b). *Hamilton* was a Chapter 13 case in which the debtor had received a one-time buyout from her former employer. The question before the Court was how to interpret a phrase—"projected disposable income"—that governs the amount a Chapter 13 debtor must pay under the plan. Although the Code does not define that phrase, the term "disposable income" is defined as "current monthly income" less expenses. § 1325(b)(2). In interpreting "projected disposable income," the Court had to choose between a "mechanical" approach and the "forward-looking approach." Under the latter, a bankruptcy court can make appropriate adjustments when "significant changes in a debtor's financial circumstances are known or virtually certain." The Court adopted the forward-looking approach for purposes of Chapter 13. When we see the full case, in the next chapter of this casebook, you will be in a better position to ascertain whether it authorizes similar flexibility in Chapter 7 cases.

Once CMI is determined, various deductions are then taken. The first are derived from Standards used by the Internal Revenue Service to determine a taxpayer's ability to repay delinquent taxes. § 707(b)(2)(A)(ii)(I). These Standards are national, regional and local, depending upon the category of expense at issue.

The National Standards for living expenses, which depend upon the size of the debtor's family, include five categories: food; housekeeping supplies; apparel and services; personal care products and services; and miscellaneous expenses. The debtor's actual expenses are irrelevant, although a debtor may be able to claim up to an additional five percent of the allowance if "reasonable and necessary." The National Standards for Out-of-Pocket Health Care permit the deduction of a designated dollar amount for each member of the debtor's family. That dollar amount is higher for family members above 65 years of age.

The Local Standards cover "Housing and Utilities" and "Transportation." The Housing and Utilities Expense Standards differ by state and county, as well as by family size. These expenses fall into two categories—mortgage or rent, and nonmortgage expenses. The mortgage or rent allowance is a cap; the debtor paying more than the cap may claim no deduction at this point (although mortgage expenses are accounted for later), but a debtor actually paying less than that may claim the difference. The allowance for nonmortgage expenses covers items such as property taxes, insurance, and repair and maintenance. A debtor may deduct additional home energy costs, if they are documented to be reasonable and necessary. § 707(b)(2)(A)((ii)(V).

The Transportation Expense Standards include nationwide amounts for car ownership costs, whether through purchase or lease, and regional amounts (based on Census Region and Metropolitan Statistical Area) for operating costs. Debtors may claim allowances for no more than two cars, and a debtor without a car may claim an allowance for public transportation.

A question arose as to whether a debtor who owns a car free and clear of encumbrance may nevertheless claim the ownership allowance. Courts split on the question until the Supreme Court resolved it in the following case. The case arose under Chapter 13, but the applicable provision—§ 1325(b)(3)—looks back to § 707(b)(2). Thus, one may expect that the answer the Court reached for purposes of Chapter 13 will also apply in Chapter 7 cases.

RANSOM v. FIA CARD SERVICES, N.A.

United States Supreme Court, 2011.
562 U.S. 61, 131 S.Ct. 716, 178 L.Ed.2d 603.

JUSTICE KAGAN delivered the opinion of the Court.

Chapter 13 of the Bankruptcy Code enables an individual to obtain a discharge of his debts if he pays his creditors a portion of his monthly income in accordance with a court-approved plan. To determine how much income the debtor is capable of paying, Chapter 13 uses a statutory formula known as the "means test." §§ 707(b)(2), 1325(b)(3)(A). The means test instructs a debtor to deduct specified expenses from his current monthly income. The result is his "disposable income"—the amount he has available to reimburse creditors. § 1325(b)(2).

This case concerns the specified expense for vehicle-ownership costs. We must determine whether a debtor like petitioner Jason Ransom who owns his car outright, and so does not make loan or lease payments, may claim an allowance for car-ownership costs (thereby reducing the amount he will repay creditors). We hold that the text, context, and purpose of the statutory provision at issue preclude this result. A debtor who does not make loan or lease payments may not take the car-ownership deduction.

I

A

"Congress enacted the Bankruptcy Abuse Prevention and Consumer Protection Act of 2005 (BAPCPA or Act) to correct perceived abuses of the bankruptcy system." *Milavetz, Gallop & Milavetz, P. A.* v. *United States*, 559 U.S. 229, 231-32 (2010)). In particular, Congress adopted the means test—"[t]he heart of [BAPCPA's] consumer bankruptcy reforms," H. R. Rep. No. 109-31, pt. 1, p. 2 (2005) (hereinafter H. R. Rep.), and the home of the statutory language at issue here—to help ensure that debtors who *can* pay creditors *do* pay them.

In Chapter 13 proceedings, the means test provides a formula to calculate a debtor's disposable income, which the debtor must devote to reimbursing creditors under a court-approved plan generally lasting from three to five years. §§ 1325(b)(1)(B) and (b)(4).[1] The statute defines "disposable income" as "current monthly income" less "amounts reasonably necessary to be expended" for "maintenance or support," business expenditures, and certain charitable contributions. §§ 1325(b)(2)(A)(i) and (ii). For a debtor whose income is above the median for his State, the means test identifies which expenses qualify as "amounts reasonably necessary to be expended." The test supplants the pre-BAPCPA practice of calculating debtors' reasonable expenses on a case-by-case basis, which led to varying and often inconsistent determinations.

Under the means test, a debtor calculating his "reasonably necessary" expenses is directed to claim allowances for defined living expenses, as well as for secured and priority debt. §§ 707(b)(2)(A)(ii)-(iv). *[The Court quoted the first sentence of § 707(b)(2)(A)(ii)(I).]*

These are the principal amounts that the debtor can claim as his reasonable living expenses and thereby shield from creditors.

The National and Local Standards referenced in this provision are tables that the IRS prepares listing standardized expense amounts for basic necessities. The IRS uses the Standards to help calculate taxpayers' ability to pay overdue taxes. The IRS also prepares supplemental guidelines known as the Collection Financial Standards, which describe how to use the tables and what the amounts listed in them mean.

---

[1] Chapter 13 borrows the means test from Chapter 7, where it is used as a screening mechanism to determine whether a Chapter 7 proceeding is appropriate. Individuals who file for bankruptcy relief under Chapter 7 liquidate their non-exempt assets, rather than dedicate their future income, to repay creditors. If the debtor's Chapter 7 petition discloses that his disposable income as calculated by the means test exceeds a certain threshold, the petition is presumptively abusive. § 707(b)(2)(A)(i). If the debtor cannot rebut the presumption, the court may dismiss the case or, with the debtor's consent, convert it into a Chapter 13 proceeding. § 707(b)(1).

The Local Standards include an allowance for transportation expenses, divided into vehicle "Ownership Costs" and vehicle "Operating Costs."[3] At the time Ransom filed for bankruptcy, *[debtors were permitted an ownership cost deduction of $471 for the first car and $332 for the second car].*

The Collection Financial Standards explain that these ownership costs represent "nationwide figures for monthly loan or lease payments"; the numerical amounts listed are "base[d] * * * on the five-year average of new and used car financing data compiled by the Federal Reserve Board." The Collection Financial Standards further instruct that, in the tax-collection context, "[i]f a taxpayer has no car payment, * * * only the operating costs portion of the transportation standard is used to come up with the allowable transportation expense."

B

Ransom filed for Chapter 13 bankruptcy relief in July 2006. Among his liabilities, Ransom itemized over $82,500 in unsecured debt, including a claim held by respondent FIA Card Services, N. A. Among his assets, Ransom listed a 2004 Toyota Camry, valued at $14,000, which he owns free of any debt.

For purposes of the means test, Ransom reported income of $4,248.56 per month. He also listed monthly expenses totaling $4,038.01. In determining those expenses, Ransom claimed a car-ownership deduction of $471 for the Camry, the full amount specified in the IRS's "Ownership Costs" table. Ransom listed a separate deduction of $338 for car-operating costs. Based on these figures, Ransom had disposable income of $210.55 per month.

Ransom proposed a 5-year plan that would result in repayment of approximately 25% of his unsecured debt. FIA objected to confirmation of the plan on the ground that it did not direct all of Ransom's disposable income to unsecured creditors. In particular, FIA argued that Ransom should not have claimed the car-ownership allowance because he does not make loan or lease payments on his car. FIA noted that without this allowance, Ransom's disposable income would be $681.55—the $210.55 he reported plus the $471 he deducted

---

[3] Although both components of the transportation allowance are listed in the Local Standards, only the operating-cost expense amounts vary by geography; in contrast, the IRS provides a nationwide figure for ownership costs.

for vehicle ownership. The difference over the 60 months of the plan amounts to about $28,000.

C

The Bankruptcy Court denied confirmation of Ransom's plan. The court held that Ransom could deduct a vehicle-ownership expense only "if he is currently making loan or lease payments on that vehicle." *[The BAP and the Ninth Circuit affirmed.]*

* * *

We granted a writ of certiorari to resolve a split of authority over whether a debtor who does not make loan or lease payments on his car may claim the deduction for vehicle-ownership costs. We now affirm the Ninth Circuit's judgment.

II

Our interpretation of the Bankruptcy Code starts "where all such inquiries must begin: with the language of the statute itself." *United States* v. *Ron Pair Enterprises, Inc.*, 489 U.S. 235, 241 (1989). *[The Court quoted § 707(b)(2)(A)(ii)(I).]*

The key word in this provision is "applicable": A debtor may claim not all, but only "applicable" expense amounts listed in the Standards. Whether Ransom may claim the $471 car-ownership deduction accordingly turns on whether that expense amount is "applicable" to him.

Because the Code does not define "applicable," we look to the ordinary meaning of the term. "Applicable" means "capable of being applied: having relevance" or "fit, suitable, or right to be applied: appropriate." Webster's Third New International Dictionary 105 (2002). So an expense amount is "applicable" within the plain meaning of the statute when it is appropriate, relevant, suitable, or fit.

What makes an expense amount "applicable" in this sense (appropriate, relevant, suitable, or fit) is most naturally understood to be its correspondence to an individual debtor's financial circumstances. Rather than authorizing all debtors to take deductions in all listed categories, Congress established a filter: A debtor may claim a deduction from a National or Local Standard table (like "[Car] Ownership Costs") if but only if that deduction is appropriate for him. And a deduction is so appropriate only if the debtor has costs corresponding to the category covered by the table—that is, only if the debtor will incur that kind of expense during the life of the plan. The statute underscores the necessity of making such an individualized determination by referring to "*the debtor's* applicable monthly expense amounts," § 707(b)(2)(A)(ii)(I) (emphasis added)—in other words, the expense amounts applicable (appropriate, etc.) to each particular debtor. Identifying these amounts requires looking at the financial situation of the debtor and asking whether a National or Local Standard table is relevant to him.

If Congress had not wanted to separate in this way debtors who qualify for an allowance from those who do not, it could have omitted the term "applicable" altogether. Without that word, all debtors would be eligible to claim a deduction for each category listed in the Standards. Congress presumably included "applicable" to achieve a different result. Interpreting the statute to require a threshold determination of eligibility ensures that the term "applicable" carries meaning, as each word in a statute should.

This reading of "applicable" also draws support from the statutory context. The Code initially defines a debtor's disposable income as his "current monthly income * * * less amounts *reasonably necessary to be expended.*" § 1325(b)(2) (emphasis added). The statute then instructs that "[a]mounts reasonably necessary to be expended * * * shall be determined in accordance with" the means test. § 1325(b)(3). Because Congress intended the means test to approximate the debtor's reasonable expenditures on essential items, a debtor should be required to qualify for a deduction by actually incurring an expense in the relevant category. If a debtor will not have a particular kind of expense during his plan, an allowance to cover that cost is not "reasonably necessary" within the meaning of the statute.[5]

Finally, consideration of BAPCPA's purpose strengthens our reading of the term "applicable." Congress designed the means test to measure debtors' disposable income and, in that way, "to ensure that

---

[5] This interpretation also avoids the anomalous result of granting preferential treatment to individuals with above-median income. Because the means test does not apply to Chapter 13 debtors whose incomes are below the median, those debtors must prove on a case-by-case basis that each claimed expense is reasonably necessary. See §§ 1325(b)(2) and (3). If a below-median-income debtor cannot take a deduction for a nonexistent expense, we doubt Congress meant to provide such an allowance to an above-median-income debtor—the very kind of debtor whose perceived abuse of the bankruptcy system inspired Congress to enact the means test.

[they] repay creditors the maximum they can afford." H. R. Rep., at 2. This purpose is best achieved by interpreting the means test, consistent with the statutory text, to reflect a debtor's ability to afford repayment. Requiring a debtor to incur the kind of expenses for which he claims a means-test deduction thus advances BAPCPA's objectives.

Because we conclude that a person cannot claim an allowance for vehicle-ownership costs unless he has some expense falling within that category, the question in this case becomes: What expenses does the vehicle-ownership category cover? If it covers loan and lease payments alone, Ransom does not qualify, because he has no such expense. Only if that category also covers other costs associated with having a car would Ransom be entitled to this deduction.

The less inclusive understanding is the right one: The owner-ship category encompasses the costs of a car loan or lease and nothing more. As noted earlier, the numerical amounts listed in the "Ownership Costs" table are "base[d] * * * on the five-year average of new and used car financing data compiled by the Federal Reserve Board." In other words, the sum $471 is the average monthly payment for loans and leases nationwide; it is not intended to estimate other conceivable expenses associated with maintaining a car. The Standards do account for those additional expenses, but in a different way: They are mainly the province of the separate deduction for vehicle "Operating Costs," which include payments for "[v]ehicle insurance, * * * maintenance, fuel, state and local registration, required inspection, parking fees, tolls, [and] driver's license." Internal Revenue Manual §§ 5.15.1.7 and 5.15.1.8 (May 1, 2004). A person who owns a car free and clear is entitled to claim the "Operating Costs" deduction for all these expenses of driving—and Ransom in fact did so, to the tune of $338. But such a person is not entitled to claim the "Ownership Costs" deduction, because that allowance is for the separate costs of a car loan or lease.

The Collection Financial Standards—the IRS's explanatory guidelines to the National and Local Standards—explicitly recognize this distinction between ownership and operating costs, making clear that individuals who have a car but make no loan or lease payments may claim only the operating allowance. Although the statute does not incorporate the IRS's guidelines, courts may consult this material in interpreting the National and Local Standards; after all, the IRS uses those tables for a similar purpose—to determine how much money a delinquent taxpayer can afford to pay the Government. The guidelines of course cannot control if they are at odds with the statutory language. But here, the Collection Financial Standards' treatment of the car-ownership deduction reinforces our conclusion that, under the statute, a debtor seeking to claim this deduction must make some loan or lease payments.

Because Ransom owns his vehicle free and clear of any encumbrance, he incurs no expense in the "Ownership Costs" category of the Local Standards. Accordingly, the car-ownership expense amount is not "applicable" to him, and the Ninth Circuit correctly denied that deduction.

III

Ransom's argument to the contrary relies on a different interpretation of the key word "applicable," an objection to our view of the scope of the "Ownership Costs" category, and a criticism of the policy implications of our approach. We do not think these claims persuasive.

A

Ransom first offers another understanding of the term "applicable." A debtor, he says, determines his "applicable" deductions by locating the box in each National or Local Standard table that corresponds to his geographic location, income, family size, or number of cars. Under this approach, a debtor "consult[s] the table[s] alone" to determine his appropriate expense amounts. Because he has one car, Ransom argues that his "applicable" allowance is the sum listed in the first column of the "Ownership Costs" table ($471); if he had a second vehicle, the amount in the second column ($332) would also be "applicable." On this approach, the word "applicable" serves a function wholly internal to the tables; rather than filtering out debtors for whom a deduction is not at all suitable, the term merely directs each debtor to the correct box (and associated dollar amount of deduction) within every table.

This alternative reading of "applicable" fails to comport with the statute's text, context, or purpose. As intimated earlier, Ransom's interpretation would render the term "applicable" superfluous. Assume Congress had omitted that word and simply authorized a deduction of "the debtor's monthly expense amounts" specified in the Standards. That language, most naturally read, would direct each debtor to locate the box in every table corresponding to his location, income, family size, or number of cars and to deduct the amount stated. In other words, the language would instruct the debtor to use the exact approach Ransom urges. The word "applicable" is not necessary to accomplish that result; it is necessary only for the different purpose of dividing debtors eligible to make use of the tables from those who are not. Further, Ransom's reading of "applicable" would sever the connection between the means test and the statutory provision it is meant to implement—the authorization of an allowance for (but only for) "reasonably necessary" expenses. Expenses that are wholly fictional are not easily thought of as reasonably necessary. And finally, Ransom's interpretation would run counter to the statute's overall purpose of ensuring that debtors repay creditors to the extent they can—here, by shielding some $28,000 that he does not in fact need for loan or lease payments.

As against all this, Ransom argues that his reading is necessary to account for the means test's distinction between "applicable" and "actual" expenses—more fully stated, between the phrase "*applicable* monthly expense amounts" specified in the Standards and the phrase "*actual* monthly expenses for * * * Other Necessary Expenses." § 707(b)(2)(A)(ii)(I) (emphasis added). The latter phrase enables a debtor to deduct his actual expenses in particular categories that the IRS designates relating mainly to taxpayers' health and welfare. According to Ransom, "applicable" cannot mean the same thing as "actual." He thus concludes that "an 'applicable' expense can be claimed [under the means test] even if no 'actual' expense was incurred."

Our interpretation of the statute, however, equally avoids conflating "applicable" with "actual" costs. Although the expense amounts in the Standards apply only if the debtor incurs the relevant expense, the debtor's out-of-pocket cost may well not control the amount of the deduction. If a debtor's actual expenses exceed the amounts listed in the tables, for example, the debtor may claim an allowance only for the specified sum, rather than for his real expenditures.[8] For the Other Necessary Expense categories, by contrast, the debtor may deduct his actual expenses, no matter how high they are. Our reading of the means test thus gives full effect to "the distinction

---

[8] The parties and the Solicitor General as *amicus curiae* dispute the proper deduction for a debtor who has expenses that are *lower* than the amounts listed in the Local Standards. Ransom argues that a debtor may claim the specified expense amount in full regardless of his out-of-pocket costs. The Government concurs with this view, provided (as we require) that a debtor has *some* expense relating to the deduction. FIA, relying on the IRS's practice, contends to the contrary that a debtor may claim only his actual expenditures in this circumstance. We decline to resolve this issue. Because Ransom incurs no ownership expense at all, the car-ownership allowance is not applicable to him in the first instance. Ransom is therefore not entitled to a deduction under either approach.

between 'applicable' and 'actual' without taking a further step to conclude that 'applicable' means 'nonexistent.' "

Finally, Ransom's reading of "applicable" may not even answer the essential question: whether a debtor may claim a deduction. "[C]onsult[ing] the table[s] alone" to determine a debtor's deduction, as Ransom urges us to do, often will not be sufficient because the tables are not self-defining. This case provides a prime example. The "Ownership Costs" table features two columns labeled "First Car" and "Second Car." Standing alone, the table does not specify whether it refers to the first and second cars *owned* (as Ransom avers), or the first and second cars for which the debtor incurs *ownership costs* (as FIA maintains)—and so the table does not resolve the issue in dispute.[10] Some amount of interpretation is necessary to decide what the deduction is for and whether it is applicable to Ransom; and so we are brought back full circle to our prior analysis.

B

Ransom next argues that viewing the car-ownership deduction as covering no more than loan and lease payments is inconsistent with a separate sentence of the means test that provides: "Notwithstanding any other provision of this clause, the monthly expenses of the debtor shall not include any payments for debts." § 707(b)(2)(A)(ii)(I). The car-ownership deduction cannot comprise *only* loan and lease payments, Ransom contends, because those payments are *always* debts.

Ransom ignores that the "notwithstanding" sentence governs the full panoply of deductions under the National and Local Standards and the Other Necessary Expense categories. We hesitate to rely on that general provision to interpret the content of the car-ownership deduction because Congress did not draft the former with the latter specially in mind; any friction between the two likely reflects only a lack of attention to how an across-the-board exclusion of debt payments would correspond to a particular IRS allowance.[11] Further, the "notwithstanding" sentence by its terms functions only to exclude, and not to authorize, deductions. It cannot establish an allowance for non-loan

---

[10] The interpretive problem is not, as the dissent suggests, "whether to claim a deduction for one car or for two," but rather whether to claim a deduction for *any* car that is owned if the debtor has no ownership costs. * * *

[11] Because Ransom does not make payments on his car, we need not and do not resolve how the "notwithstanding" sentence affects the vehicle-ownership deduction when a debtor has a loan or lease expense.

or -lease ownership costs that no National or Local Standard covers. Accordingly, the "notwithstanding" sentence does nothing to alter our conclusion that the "Ownership Costs" table does not apply to a debtor whose car is not encumbered.

C

Ransom finally contends that his view of the means test is necessary to avoid senseless results not intended by Congress. At the outset, we note that the policy concerns Ransom emphasizes pale beside one his reading creates: His interpretation, as we have explained, would frustrate BAPCPA's core purpose of ensuring that debtors devote their full disposable income to repaying creditors. We nonetheless address each of Ransom's policy arguments in turn.

Ransom first points out a troubling anomaly: Under our interpretation, "[d]ebtors can time their bankruptcy filing to take place while they still have a few car payments left, thus retaining an ownership deduction which they would lose if they filed just after making their last payment." Indeed, a debtor with only a single car payment remaining, Ransom notes, is eligible to claim a monthly ownership deduction.

But this kind of oddity is the inevitable result of a standardized formula like the means test, even more under Ransom's reading than under ours. Such formulas are by their nature over- and under-inclusive. In eliminating the pre-BAPCPA case-by-case adjudication of above-median-income debtors' expenses, on the ground that it lent itself to abuse, Congress chose to tolerate the occasional peculiarity that a brighter-line test produces. And Ransom's alternative reading of the statute would spawn its own anomalies—even placing to one side the fundamental strangeness of giving a debtor an allowance for loan or lease payments when he has not a penny of loan or lease costs. On Ransom's view, for example, a debtor entering bankruptcy might purchase for a song a junkyard car—"an old, rusted pile of scrap metal [that would] si[t] on cinder blocks in his backyard"—in order to deduct the $471 car-ownership expense and reduce his payment to creditors by that amount. We do not see why Congress would have preferred that result to the one that worries Ransom. That is especially so because creditors may well be able to remedy Ransom's "one payment left" problem. If car payments cease during the life of the plan, just as if other financial circumstances change, an unsecured creditor may move to modify the plan to increase the amount the debtor must repay.

Ransom next contends that denying the ownership allowance to debtors in his position "sends entirely the wrong message, namely, that it is advantageous to be deeply in debt on motor vehicle loans, rather than to pay them off." But the choice here is not between thrifty savers and profligate borrowers, as Ransom would have it. Money is fungible: The $14,000 that Ransom spent to purchase his Camry outright was money he did not devote to paying down his credit card debt, and Congress did not express a preference for one use of these funds over the other. Further, Ransom's argument mistakes what the deductions in the means test are meant to accomplish. [Rather than effecting any broad federal policy as to saving or borrowing, the deductions serve merely to ensure that debtors in bankruptcy can afford essential items.] (The car-ownership allowance thus safeguards a debtor's ability to retain a car throughout the plan period. If the debtor already owns a car outright, he has no need for this protection.)

— Valid Point

Ransom finally argues that a debtor who owns his car free and clear may need to replace it during the life of the plan; "[g]ranting the ownership cost deduction to a vehicle that is owned outright," he states, "accords best with economic reality." In essence, Ransom seeks an emergency cushion for car owners. But nothing in the statute authorizes such a cushion, which all debtors presumably would like in the event some unexpected need arises. And a person who enters bankruptcy without any car at all may also have to buy one during the plan period; yet Ransom concedes that a person in this position cannot claim the ownership deduction. The appropriate way to account for unanticipated expenses like a new vehicle purchase is not to distort the scope of a deduction, but to use the method that the Code provides for all Chapter 13 debtors (and their creditors): modification of the plan in light of changed circumstances. See § 1329(a)(1).

IV

Based on BAPCPA's text, context, and purpose, we hold that the Local Standard expense amount for transportation "Ownership Costs" is not "applicable" to a debtor who will not incur any such costs during his bankruptcy plan. Because the "Ownership Costs" category covers only loan and lease payments and because Ransom owns his car free from any debt or obligation, he may not claim the allowance. In short, Ransom may not deduct loan or lease expenses when he does not have any. We therefore affirm the judgment of the Ninth Circuit.

It is so ordered.

Notes and Questions

1. In a dissenting opinion, JUSTICE SCALIA agreed with the debtor's view of the word "applicable," reading it to mean the number of cars owned by a debtor: "In my judgment the 'applicable monthly expense amounts' for operating costs 'specified under the * * * Local Standards,' are the amounts specified in those Standards for either one car or two cars, whichever of those is applicable." 562 U.S. at 85. He also asserted that "the Court's imagined horrible in which 'a debtor entering bankruptcy might purchase for a song a junkyard car' * * * is fairly matched by the imagined horrible that, under the Court's scheme, a debtor entering bankruptcy might purchase a junkyard car for a song plus a $10 promissory note payable over several years. He would get the full ownership expense deduction." *Id*. at 84.

Are these arguments persuasive to you? Do you believe that *Ransom* may encourage debtors to incur more debt, prepetition, by purchasing a new car or by using a car as collateral for a new loan?

2. The means test is widely understood to constitute a rigid formula, used to determine the amount a debtor can afford to repay creditors. The majority opinion seemed to understand as much, by observing that its reading would permit an ownership deduction for a debtor with only a single car payment remaining. That, the Court said "is the inevitable result of a standardized formula like the means test." Would it not, however, have been equally "the result of a standardized formula" to read the statute as the debtor (and JUSTICE SCALIA) advocated? Did the Court ignore its own observation?

3. Which is the better choice as a matter of policy—that only debtors with car payments be allowed an ownership deduction, or that such a deduction should be available even to debtors who have paid for their cars? Even if you prefer the Court's result on policy grounds, do you believe that the Court decided the case properly? Is its rationale persuasive?

A deduction for Other Necessary Expenses, permitted under the first sentence of § 707(b)(2)(A)(ii)(I), includes reasonably necessary health insurance expenses and expenses necessitated for safety from family violence. Some of the additional items in the IRS's category of Other Necessary Expenses duplicate expenses expressly covered by other subsections of the Bankruptcy Code, but with additional limitations. For example, the IRS lists "care for elderly or handicapped dependents" in the category of Other Necessary Expenses, but the Bankruptcy Code allows those expenses only if they are "reasonable and necessary" and if the dependents are unable to meet those expenses themselves. § 707(b)(2)(A)(ii)(II).

Debtors may deduct their minor children's private or public school tuition, up to the designated maximum,[d] if those expenses are "reasonable and necessary" and are not otherwise accounted for. § 707(b)(2)(A)(ii)(IV). Obviously, courts will have to decide what is "reasonable and necessary" on a case-by-case basis. The leading case, *In re Cleary*, 357 B.R. 369 (Bankr. D.S.C.2006), permitted the deduction for purposes of the debtors' Chapter 13 plan, because their children (who were "bright and need[ed] to be challenged") had attended parochial school for years, the debtors had strong religious convictions, and the debtor-wife worked outside the home—at the very school attended by her children—solely to make that education possible.

Note the third sentence of § 707(b)(2)(A)(ii)(I): "Notwithstanding any other provision of this clause, the monthly expenses of the debtor shall not include any payments for debts." That sentence means that payments for debts are deductible, if at all, only under some other subsection of § 707(b)(2). The most important of those other provisions is § 707(b)(2)(A)(iii), which authorizes deductions for the debtor's obligations to secured creditors. A debtor with monthly mortgage or car payments in excess of the allowances, who therefore cannot take deductions under the Standards, can deduct the full payments here. The statute imposes no requirement that the collateral subject to the lien be necessary for the support of the debtor and his or her dependents. This subsection codifies a discrimination against debtors who rent their homes or lease their cars; those debtors can claim the amount of the appropriate allowance and no more. In addition, the statute may invite debtors to load up on secured debt before filing, in order to increase these deductions. As before, the only answer may be found in § 707(b)(3).

Debtors who are in arrears on their mortgage or car payments may also deduct "additional payments to secured creditors" that would be required under a Chapter 13 to enable the debtors "to maintain possession" of a house, car, or other necessary property. § 707-(b)(2)(A)(iii)(II). This deduction recognizes that debtors can use Chapter 13 to catch up on arrearages, so that payments on secured obligations are back on schedule by the end of the plan.

Although charitable contributions are not listed as a deduction in § 707(b)(2), § 707(b)(1) directs that a court, in determining whether

---

[d] All of the dollar amounts set out in § 707(b) are adjusted every three years, as required by § 104(b)(1). The adjustments occur in April of the appropriate year.

to dismiss a debtor's Chapter 7 case, "not take into consideration whether a debtor has made, or continues to make, charitable contributions." Of course, the only sensible way to obey the statutory directive is to treat those contributions as a deduction, and Official Form 22A, Line 40, does just that. Interestingly, the statute does not expressly provide the types of limitations on charitable contributions—based on a percentage of the debtor's income, or the debtor's established practices—that we will see, later in the course, in other places in the Code. At least one court, however, has derived an historical limitation from the words "has made, or continues to make." *In re Bender*, 373 B.R. 25, 30 (Bankr. E.D.Mich.2007) ("[N]othing in the statute can be construed to permit a debtor to suddenly become substantially more charitable after filing for bankruptcy, especially when it is the increased charitable contributions that deprive the debtor of the income which could fund a hypothetical Chapter 13 plan.").

Once all of these deductions (and others not mentioned here) are taken, the remainder, multiplied by 60, is the amount that the debtor is supposedly able to repay to unsecured creditors over a five-year period. That amount is then subjected to the formula in § 707-(b)(2)(A)(i). This confusing language translates to something fairly straightforward: if that amount is less than the amount specified in § 707(b)(2)(A)(i)(I), then the presumption of abuse does not arise; if that amount is equal to or more than the amount specified in § 707(b)(2)(A)(i)(II), then the debtor's Chapter 7 filing is presumed to be an abuse; in between those amounts, the presumption of abuse only arises if that amount is at least 25% of the debtor's nonpriority[e] unsecured debts.

If the presumption of abuse arises, it can be rebutted only if "special circumstances" justify additional expenses sufficient to reduce the debtor's repayment ability below the threshold. § 707(b)(2)(B). Those "special circumstances" must be documented in detail.

The means test is not the only grounds for dismissal of a Chapter 7 petition. The "substantial abuse" test of old § 707(b) remains in the Code as an alternative to the means test, albeit in altered form. The word "substantial" was removed and courts may consider either of two factors: whether the petition was filed in bad faith, § 707(b)(3)(A); or, under a "totality of the circumstances," whether the debtor's financial situation is indicative of abuse, § 707(b)(3)(B). Thus, a debtor

---

[e] We will study priorities later in this chapter.

who passes the means test may nonetheless suffer the dismissal of his or her Chapter 7 petition.

Read § 707—carefully!—and answer the following Problems.

Notes and Problems

Do this tomorrow as practice

1. Greg, a salesman, and his wife, Patricia, a part-time clerk in a convenience store, live in the City of St. Louis, Missouri. They have one child, Danielle, who is 3 years old. Patricia's son, Mark, who is 12, was born to her first marriage. He lives full-time with Greg and Patricia.

Greg and Patricia have used credit cards heavily over the years, and they hardly noticed when they began to spend more than they earned. Their balance climbed slowly but relentlessly until they finally realized that they could no longer make the payments. They have come to you for bankruptcy advice and, in response to your questions, they have given you the following information regarding their income and monthly expenses.

The family has taken a nice vacation every summer, putting most of the expenses on credit cards. They also bought new furniture for the house and did some landscaping, using credit cards to pay the bills. Their credit card balance has just topped $50,000, and they have other unsecured debts of about $15,000.

They bought their home six years ago, paying $2,500 down and financing the balance of $200,000 over 30 years. Their mortgage payment is $1,460, and they have missed the last two payments.

The payment on Greg's one-year-old car is $500, and he has three years remaining on the vehicle loan. Patricia's car is a six-year-old Ford sedan that she bought three years ago for $12,000. Her monthly car payment is $300. She is scheduled to pay it off in 18 months.

Greg makes $60,600 per year ($5,050 a month), although $8,700 of that is withheld annually for Social Security and various taxes. Patricia made only $18,000 last year ($1,500 a month), taking home approximately $13,500. She spends about $242 per month for Danielle's child care.

a. Using Official Form 22A and the information from the United States Trustee website, www.usdoj.gov/ust, determine whether Greg and Patricia qualify for Chapter 7 under the means test.

b. If they are not currently eligible for Chapter 7, could they become eligible if Patricia sold her six-year-old Ford shortly before filing bankruptcy and bought a new car, incurring a monthly obligation of $650 for the next five years? If so, could you ethically advise her to do so?

No due to the earlier section

c. Assume that Patricia is entitled to receive $1,200 every month in child support payments for Mark, but that Mark's father makes payments only sporadically. What impact will that have on Greg and Patricia's eligibility for Chapter 7?

d. Assume that Patricia pays $500 per month in educational loans for a technical training course she intends to complete when Danielle is older. How are those payments accounted for in determining the couple's eligibility for Chapter 7?

e. Could Greg enhance his prospects of qualifying for Chapter 7 by quitting his job several months before filing?

f. Assume that Greg lost his job two months ago, when his employer closed its doors and filed its own bankruptcy proceeding. Would that affect the couple's current eligibility for Chapter 7 under the means test?

2. Debtors' house is encumbered by two mortgages, securing debts in excess of the value of the property. The monthly payment on the two mortgages is $4,000 and Debtors took a deduction for that amount in the process of completing the means test calculations. With that deduction, Debtors passed the means test; if the deduction had not been available, the presumption of abuse would have arisen in Debtors' Chapter 7 filing. Debtors have decided to surrender the property to the mortgage holders and walk away. Given that intention, was the deduction appropriate? See *Morse v. Rudler (In re Rudler)*, 576 F.3d 37 (1st Cir.2009).

3. After years of penury as a student, Jeremy Williams is about to get his law degree. A job with a prominent firm is waiting for him, and he will have no trouble paying the $80,000 he owes in educational loans. The only problem is that Jeremy has missed several car payments. The lender tried to repossess the car last night, but Jeremy appeared just in time and told the men to leave. He is sure they will try again very soon, and he needs the car in order to get to the bar review classes. He wonders if he can qualify for a Chapter 7 bankruptcy, in order to protect his car from repossession. Advise Jeremy.

4. For many years before she filed Chapter 7, Debtor has been making a monthly contribution to her retirement plan of several hundred dollars. Because her income exceeds the state median, she is subject to the means test. That test does not permit the deduction of such contributions and, therefore, Debtor's filing is presumed abusive. If the amount of those contributions were directed to the repayment of her creditors, she could repay nearly 50% of her obligations. Those contributions, however, are not included in disposable income for purposes of Chapter 13, § 541(b)(7), so Debtor would not be required to make any payments whatsoever to unsecured creditors under a Chapter 13 plan. In light of these facts, can the bankruptcy court permit her to remain in Chapter 7? See *In re Siler*, 426 B.R. 167 (Bankr. W.D.N.C.2010).

5. If Manville's solvency does not constitute a reason to dismiss, why should a consumer debtor's ability to make modest repayments to his or her creditors support dismissal? Whether such debtors existed in any significant numbers was doubtful from the very beginning. See Teresa A. Sullivan, Elizabeth Warren & Jay L. Westbrook, AS WE FORGIVE OUR DEBTORS: BANKRUPTCY & CONSUMER CREDIT IN AMERICA 220 (1989) (footnotes omitted) ("After an exhaustive (and exhausting) search for a sizable group of can-pay debtors, we find so few likely prospects for repayment that we conclude the effort to keep can-pay debtors out of bankruptcy or force them into Chapter 13 is a wasteful misdirection of energy. * * * We conclude that bankruptcy laws should not be shaped around the can-pay question.").

Nonetheless, BAPCPA was based on the supposition that individuals who could repay their debts, if they were but willing, were instead filing Chapter 7 cases and discharging those debts. See 151 Cong. Rec. S1856 (daily ed. Mar. 1, 2005) (statement of Sen. Grassley) ("This bill [BAPCPA] would make it harder for individuals who can repay their debt to file for bankruptcy under chapter 7 * * * ."). Congress added the "means test" now found in § 707(b)(2) to the law in 2005 to force can-pay debtors to choose between proceeding under Chapter 13 or suffering outright dismissal of their Chapter 7 bankruptcy cases.

The precipitous decline in bankruptcy filings following 2005 (by about 800,000 cases) might be taken as proof of BAPCPA's success. Empirical investigations, however, suggest that the amendments have failed to live up to their billing. Scholars involved in the Consumer Bankruptcy Project, using data from 2007, looked at the income levels of debtors in bankruptcy:

> The data indicate that those who filed in 2007 largely have the same income profile as those who filed in 2001; there has been no shift in the income levels of filers that would have occurred if 800,000 high-income abusers had been pushed from the system. These income data suggest that instead of functioning like a sieve, carefully sorting the high-income abusers from those in true need, the amendments' means test functioned more like a barricade, blocking out hundreds of thousands of struggling families indiscriminately, regardless of their individual income circumstances.

> Even worse for consumers, the new data also reveal a dark side to bankruptcy and to the American credit market. Continuing a trend begun in the early 1980s, the families in bankruptcy are much more deeply laden with debt. Their net worth, which has always been negative, sank further, and their debt-to-income ratios rose higher. In short, with each succeeding study over the past twenty-five years of the Consumer Bankruptcy Project, the data show that the families filing for bankruptcy are in ever-increasing financial distress. The 2005 amendments did nothing to halt this trend.

The data showing rising debt loads are consistent with the view that troubled families are delaying bankruptcy—struggling longer with their bills and building up bigger loads of debt before succumbing. The data also support the "sweat box" theory of consumer lending, in which lenders profit if failing customers can be persuaded to make high-interest payments for a few extra months, suggesting that the 2005 amendments delivered a very different benefit to the credit industry than its supporters claimed. By this analysis, creditors gain from BAPCPA less because of any effect on carefully targeted can-pay debtors and more because they have a stronger hand to press the debtors—all debtors, regardless of income—to struggle outside the bankruptcy system.

Robert M. Lawless, Angela K. Littwin, Katherine M. Porter, John A.E. Pottow, Deborah K. Thorne, & Elizabeth Warren, *Did Bankruptcy Reform Fail? An Empirical Study of Consumer Debtors*, 82 AM. BANK. L.J. 349, 353 (2008) (footnote omitted).

Conclusions similar to those reached by the Consumer Bankruptcy Project were reported in a Staff Report issued by the Federal Reserve Bank of New York:

Our analysis has wide-ranging implications for the design of policies regulating consumer credit and bankruptcy. First, we show that a sizable group of individuals exists that does not file for bankruptcy, but seems unable to pay off their debts. These individuals are concentrated at the bottom of the income distribution, and therefore they are the ones who would be expected to benefit most from the relief offered by personal bankruptcy. Our analysis suggests that any policies affecting the financial cost of filing for bankruptcy will impact disproportionately these individuals. Second, we show that there is a strong substitution between Chapter 7 bankruptcy and foreclosure, and hence regulating either one of these institutions is likely to impact the other in significant ways. Finally, we provide a systematic analysis of the consequences of failure to file for bankruptcy for insolvent individuals, which include lower access to credit and lower credit scores.

One of the main goals of personal bankruptcy is to provide an incentive compatible insurance scheme against streams of negative income shocks that make repayment of debts contracted in better times too onerous or impossible for the debtor. Our finding that bankruptcy filings have declined mostly for low income, possibly liquidity constrained individuals, resulting in a substantial rise in the rate and persistence of insolvency suggests that the Act may have removed this form of insurance for these households. It also suggests that the income means test that was introduced to ameliorate possible moral hazard associated with Chapter 7 bankruptcy was not effective.

Further, the fact that the decline in bankruptcy filings was associated with a rise in the foreclosure rate implies that formal default on unsecured debt has been replaced to a substantial degree by default on secured debt, possibly exacerbating the housing crisis.

* * *

Our analysis suggests that the 2005 bankruptcy reform caused a decline in bankruptcy filings, which were replaced by a sizable rise in insolvency and foreclosure. We show that insolvency is a state associated with a high degree of financial distress in comparison to bankruptcy. This consequence of BAPCPA is potentially welfare reducing for households. However, since the recovery rates for creditors from insolvent loans are higher than on bankrupt loans, this could have induced banks and credit card companies to expand access and improve conditions for personal loans. Indeed, Simkovic (2009) finds that BAPCPA reduced credit card company losses and increased their profits. However, there is little evidence that credit conditions for consumers improved. Taken together, these findings suggest the main effect of the 2005 bankruptcy reform was to shift financially stressed individuals from bankruptcy to insolvency.

Stefania Albanesi & Jaromir Nosal, INSOLVENCY AFTER THE 2005 BANKRUPTCY REFORM 5-6, 35-36 (Staff Report No. 725, Federal Reserve Bank of New York, April 2015) (footnote omitted).

6. Cases may also be dismissed for reasons other than "for cause" or abuse. Section 521(a) requires automatic dismissal on the 46th day after filing if an individual debtor fails to provide the information listed in the statute, unless the debtor obtains an extension of the deadline from the court or the trustee requests that the debtor be excused because he or she, in good faith, attempted to provide the mandated information and the creditors' best interests would be served by continuation of the case.

Section 521(a)'s "automatic dismissal" has provided a puzzle for the courts, especially given that § 521(i)(2) permits any party in interest to request dismissal. Indeed, if dismissal is automatic, a request seems superfluous. Additionally, "automatic dismissal" poses a quandary if the case has proceeded, perhaps as far as discharge, before discovery of the fact that mandated information is missing. Judge Jay Cristol, a bankruptcy judge noted for breaking into verse, commented on the statute's "unusual and confusing language" in his own inimitable way. It is a bonus that the name of the case is—really!—*Riddle*:

> I do not like dismissal automatic,
> It seems to me to be traumatic.
> I do not like it in this case,

I do not like it any place.

As a judge I am most keen
        to understand, *What does it mean?*
How can any person know
what the docket does not show?

What is the clue on the 46th day?
Is the case still here, or gone away?
And if a debtor did not do
        what the Code had told him to
        and no concerned party knew it,
Still the Code says the debtor blew it.
Well that is what it seems to say:
        the debtor's case is then *"Oy vay!"*

This kind of law is symptomatic
        of something very problematic.
For if the Trustee does not know
        then which way should the trustee go?

Should the trustee's view prismatic
        continue to search the debtor's attic
        and collect debtors' assets in his fist
        for distribution in a case that stands dismissed?
After a dismissal automatic
        would this not be a bit erratic?
The poor trustee cannot know
        the docket does not dismissal show.
What's a poor trustee to do—
        except perhaps to say, "Boo hoo!"

And if the case goes on as normal
        and debtor gets a discharge formal,
        what if a year later some fanatic
        claims the case was dismissed automatic?

Was there a case, or wasn't there one?
How do you undo what's been done?
Debtor's property is gone as if by a thief,
        and Debtor is stripped but gets no relief.
I do not like dismissal automatic.

On this point I am emphatic!
I do not wish to be dramatic,
        but I can not endure this static.
Something more in 521 is needed
        for dismissal automatic to be heeded.

Dismissal automatic is not understood.
For all concerned this is not good.
Before this problem gets too old
     it would be good if we were told:

What does automatic dismissal mean?
And by what means can it been seen?
Are we only left to guess?
Oh please Congress, fix this mess!
Until it's fixed what should I do?
How can I explain this mess to you?

If the Code required an old fashioned order,
     that would create a legal border,
     with complying debtors' cases defended
     and 521 violators' cases ended,
     from the unknown status of dismissal automatic,
     to the certainty of a status charismatic.
The dismissal automatic problem would be gone,
     and debtors, trustees and courts could move on.

As to this case, how should I proceed?
Review of the record is warranted, indeed.
A very careful record review,
     tells this Court what it should do.
Was this case dismissed automatic?
It definitely was NOT and that's emphatic.

In re Riddle, 344 B.R. 702, 702-03 (Bankr. S.D.Fla.2006).

Note on Voluntary Dismissal

What happens when debtors file for bankruptcy and then decide on their own initiative to dismiss the petition? Often such a debtor wants to dismiss in order to refile shortly thereafter, thus sweeping a postpetition obligation into the refiled proceeding. The question is whether the debtor has demonstrated "cause" for dismissal, as required by § 707(a).

Courts generally frown on debtors' attempts to dismiss in these circumstances. In *In re McCollough*, 229 B.R. 374 (Bankr. E.D. Va.1999), the debtor was concerned about potential liability for an automobile accident involving her son, but the court rejected her effort to dismiss and refile:

Case law is clear in holding that the dismissal of a voluntary bankruptcy proceeding for the purpose of refiling another case is not cause for dismissal. The Debtor's purpose, it would seem, would be to dismiss the present case in order to refile and include any creditors who may come into existence as a result of the Accident; thus, the

Debtor would be able to add creditors who came into existence following the first petition but prior to the second petition. Case law, again, is clear in holding that a debtor is not entitled to a dismissal if only for the purpose of listing post-petition creditors in a new petition.

Id. at 377 (citations omitted). See also *In re Underwood*, 7 B.R. 936 (Bankr. W.Va.1981), *aff'd*, 24 B.R. 570 (S.D.W.Va.1982).

Contrary to the rule requiring debtors to show cause for dismissal in a Chapter 7 case, Chapters 12 and 13 seem to afford debtors a virtually absolute right to dismiss the petition. Section 1307(b) gives debtors an absolute right to dismiss a Chapter 13 petition at any time before the case is converted to Chapter 7 or Chapter 11. Any waiver of that right is unenforceable. The rule does not apply, however, if the proceeding was converted to Chapter 13 from Chapters 7, 11 or 12. Similarly, § 1208(b) permits a debtor to dismiss a Chapter 12 petition at any time prior to the conversion of the case to a Chapter 7 or Chapter 11. Again, waiver of this right to dismiss is unenforceable.

Although a debtor's right to dismiss a Chapter 12 or 13 petition voluntarily seems almost absolute, a court may refuse dismissal on the basis of other Code sections. For instance, § 1208(d) allows a court to dismiss a debtor's Chapter 12 petition or convert the case to Chapter 7 upon the motion of a party in interest, if that party can show that the debtor committed fraud in connection with the Chapter 12 case. Similarly, § 1307(c) permits a court to dismiss or convert a debtor's Chapter 13 petition for cause. These provisions have led to inconsistent results when debtors have sought voluntary dismissal of Chapter 12 or 13 petitions. In *Graven v. Fink (In re Graven)*, 936 F.2d 378 (8th Cir.1991), for example, a farmer who had filed for Chapter 12 reorganization sought to have the petition dismissed pursuant to § 1208(b). Before the petition could actually be dismissed, however, one of the farmer's creditors sought conversion to Chapter 7, alleging with the support of overwhelming evidence that the farmer had fraudulently transferred all of his assets to family members and closely held corporations prior to filing the Chapter 12 petition. Notwithstanding the farmer's § 1208(b) motion to dismiss, the bankruptcy court converted the case as requested by the creditor. The district court affirmed and the farmer appealed to the Eighth Circuit, arguing that § 1208(b) requires immediate dismissal upon a debtor's request, regardless of motions filed by other parties or allegations of fraud.

The Court of Appeals recognized that the language of § 1208(b) seems to give a debtor an absolute right to dismiss a Chapter 12 petition voluntarily, and that § 1208(d) does not specifically state that a creditor's motion to convert overrides a debtor's motion to dismiss. The court concluded, however, that Congress enacted the Bankruptcy Code to provide protection for honest debtors, "not to provide a shield for those who exploit the code's protection then seek to escape judicial authority when their fraudulent schemes are exposed." *Id*. at 385. To permit § 1208(b) to give debtors an absolute right to dismiss would render meaningless a court's power under § 1208(d), which was enacted to protect against exactly the types of abuses that had occurred in the case. The court upheld conversion of the case to a Chapter 7 proceeding pursuant to § 1208(d).

Rather than being dismissed, a bankruptcy case may be converted to a different chapter than the one under which it was begun. Sections 706(a), 1112, 1208, and 1307(a) and (c) govern the conversion of cases. Creditors may seek conversion (when it is available—see, *e.g.*, § 706(c)) only "for cause." Debtors, arguably, have an absolute right to convert, given that §§ 706(a), 1208(a) and 1307(a) all state that "[t]he debtor may convert a case * * * at any time."

In the next case, the Supreme Court addressed a question that had divided the courts below—namely, whether debtors who have engaged in some sort of misconduct can convert their cases and thereby avoid some or all of the consequences of that misconduct. In the process, the Court also gave us reason to question whether the "right" to dismiss is as absolute as the statutory provisions might seem to suggest.

MARRAMA v. CITIZENS BANK OF MASSACHUSETTS

United States Supreme Court, 2007.
549 U.S. 365, 127 S.Ct. 1105, 166 L.Ed.2d 956.

JUSTICE STEVENS delivered the opinion of the Court.

* * *

An issue that has arisen with disturbing frequency is whether a debtor who acts in bad faith prior to, or in the course of, filing a Chapter 13 petition by, for example, fraudulently concealing significant assets, thereby forfeits his right to obtain Chapter 13 relief. The issue may arise at the outset of a Chapter 13 case in response to a motion by creditors or by the United States trustee either to dismiss the case or to convert it to Chapter 7, see § 1307(c). It also may arise in a Chapter 7 case when a debtor files a motion under § 706(a) to convert to Chapter 13. In the former context, despite the absence of any statutory provision specifically addressing the issue, the federal courts are virtually unanimous that prepetition bad-faith conduct may cause a forfeiture of any right to proceed with a Chapter 13 case. In the latter context, however, some courts have suggested that even a bad-faith debtor has an absolute right to convert at least one Chapter 7 proceeding into a Chapter 13 case even though the case will thereafter be dismissed or immediately returned to Chapter 7. We granted certiorari to decide whether the Code mandates that procedural anomaly.

I

On March 11, 2003, petitioner, Robert Marrama, filed a voluntary petition under Chapter 7, thereby creating an estate consisting of all his property "wherever located and by whomever held." § 541(a). Respondent Mark DeGiacomo is the trustee of that estate. Respondent Citizens Bank of Massachusetts (hereinafter Bank) is the principal creditor.

In verified schedules attached to his petition, Marrama made a number of statements about his principal asset, a house in Maine, that were misleading or inaccurate. For instance, while he disclosed that he was the sole beneficiary of the trust that owned the property, he listed its value as zero. He also denied that he had transferred any property other than in the ordinary course of business during the year preceding the filing of his petition. Neither statement was true. In fact, the Maine property had substantial value, and Marrama had transferred it into the newly created trust for no consideration seven months prior to filing his Chapter 13 petition. Marrama later admitted that the purpose of the transfer was to protect the property from his creditors.

After Marrama's examination at the meeting of creditors, see § 341, the trustee advised Marrama's counsel that he intended to recover the Maine property as an asset of the estate. Thereafter, Marrama filed a "Verified Notice of Conversion to Chapter 13." Pursuant to Federal Rule of Bankruptcy Procedure 1017(c)(2), the notice of conversion was treated as a motion to convert, to which both the trustee and the Bank filed objections. Relying primarily on Marrama's attempt to conceal the Maine property from his creditors,[3] the trustee contended

---

[3] The trustee also noted that in his original verified schedules Marrama had claimed a property in Gloucester, Mass., as a homestead exemption, but testified at the meeting of creditors that he did not reside at the property and was receiving rental income from it. Moreover, when asked at the meeting whether anyone owed him any money, Marrama responded "No," and in response to a similar question on Schedule B to his petition, which specifically requested a description of any "tax refunds," Marrama indicated that he had "none." In fact, Marrama had filed an amended tax return in July 2002 in which he claimed the right to a refund, and shortly before the hearing on the motion to convert, the Internal Revenue Service informed the trustee that Marrama was entitled to a refund of $8,745.86.

that the request to convert was made in bad faith and would constitute an abuse of the bankruptcy process. The Bank opposed the conversion on similar grounds.

At the hearing on the conversion issue, Marrama explained through counsel that his misstatements about the Maine property were attributable to "scrivener's error," that he had originally filed under Chapter 7 rather than Chapter 13 because he was then unemployed, and that he had recently become employed and was therefore eligible to proceed under Chapter 13. The Bankruptcy Judge rejected these arguments, ruling that there is no "Oops" defense to the concealment of assets and that the facts established a "bad faith" case. The judge denied the request for conversion.

Marrama's principal argument on appeal to the Bankruptcy Appellate Panel for the First Circuit was that he had an absolute right to convert his case from Chapter 7 to Chapter 13 under the plain language of § 706(a) of the Code. The panel affirmed the decision of the Bankruptcy Court. It construed § 706(a), when read in connection with other provisions of the Code and the Bankruptcy Rules, as creating a right to convert a case from Chapter 7 to Chapter 13 that "is absolute only in the absence of extreme circumstances." In concluding that the record disclosed such circumstances, the panel relied on Marrama's failure to describe the transfer of the Maine residence into the revocable trust, his attempt to obtain a homestead exemption on rental property in Massachusetts, and his nondisclosure of an anticipated tax refund.

On appeal from the panel, the Court of Appeals for the First Circuit also rejected the argument that § 706(a) gives a Chapter 7 debtor an absolute right to convert to Chapter 13. In addition to emphasizing that the statute uses the word "may" rather than "shall," the court added:

> "In construing subsection 706(a), it is important to bear in mind that the bankruptcy court has unquestioned authority to dismiss a chapter 13 petition—as distinguished from converting the case to chapter 13—based upon a showing of 'bad faith' on the part of the debtor. We can discern neither a theoretical nor a practical reason that Congress would have chosen to treat a first-time motion to convert a chapter 7 case to chapter 13 under subsection 706(a) differently from the filing of a chapter 13 petition in the first instance."

While other Courts of Appeals and bankruptcy appellate panels have refused to recognize any "bad faith" exception to the conversion right created by § 706(a), we conclude that the courts in this case correctly held that Marrama forfeited his right to proceed under Chapter 13.

II

The two provisions of the Bankruptcy Code most relevant to our resolution of the issue are subsections (a) and (d) of § 706 * * * .

Petitioner contends that subsection (a) creates an unqualified right of conversion. He seeks support from language in both the House and Senate Committee Reports on the provision. The Senate Report stated:

> "Subsection (a) of this section gives the debtor the one-time absolute right of conversion of a liquidation case to a reorganization or individual repayment plan case. If the case has already once been converted from chapter 11 or 13 to chapter 7, then the debtor does not have that right. The policy of the provision is that the debtor should always be given the opportunity to repay his debts, and a waiver of the right to convert a case is unenforceable." S. Rep. No. 95-989, p. 94 (1978); see also H.R. Rep. No. 95-595, p. 380 (1977) (using nearly identical language).

The Committee Reports' reference to an "absolute right" of conversion is more equivocal than petitioner suggests. Assuming that the described debtor's "opportunity to repay his debts" is a short-hand reference to a right to proceed under Chapter 13, the statement that he should "always" have that right is inconsistent with the earlier recognition that it is only a one-time right that does not survive a previous conversion to, or filing under, Chapter 13. More importantly, the broad description of the right as "absolute" fails to give full effect to the express limitation in subsection (d). The words "unless the debtor may be a debtor under such chapter" expressly conditioned Marrama's right to convert on his ability to qualify as a "debtor" under Chapter 13.

There are at least two possible reasons why Marrama may not qualify as such a debtor, one arising under § 109(e) of the Code, and the other turning on the construction of the word "cause" in § 1307(c). The former provision imposes a limit on the amount of indebtedness that an individual may have in order to qualify for Chapter 13 relief. More pertinently, the latter provision, § 1307(c), provides that a Chapter 13 proceeding may be either dismissed or converted to a Chapter 7 proceeding "for cause" and includes a nonexclusive list of 10 causes justifying that relief. None of the specified causes mentions prepetition bad-faith conduct (although subparagraph 10 does identify one form of Chapter 7 error—which is necessarily prepetition conduct—that would justify dismissal of a Chapter 13 case). Bankruptcy courts nevertheless routinely treat dismissal for prepetition bad-faith conduct as implicitly authorized by the words "for cause." In practical effect, a ruling that an individual's Chapter 13 case should be dismissed or converted to Chapter 7 because of prepetition bad-faith conduct, including fraudulent acts committed in an earlier Chapter 7 proceeding, is tantamount to a ruling that the individual does not qualify as a debtor under Chapter 13. That individual, in other words, is not a member of the class of "honest but unfortunate debtors" that the bankruptcy laws were enacted to protect. See *Grogan v. Garner*, 498 U.S. 279, 287 (1991). The text of § 706(d) therefore provides adequate authority for the denial of his motion to convert.

The class of honest but unfortunate debtors who do possess an absolute right to convert their cases from Chapter 7 to Chapter 13 includes the vast majority of the hundreds of thousands of individuals who file Chapter 7 petitions each year. Congress sought to give these individuals the chance to repay their debts should they acquire the means to do so. Moreover, as the Court of Appeals observed, the reference in § 706(a) to the unenforceability of a waiver of the right to convert functions "as a consumer protection provision against adhesion contracts, whereby a debtor's creditors might be precluded from attempting to prescribe a waiver of the debtor's right to convert to chapter 13 as a nonnegotiable condition of its contractual agreements."

A statutory provision protecting a borrower from waiver is not a shield against forfeiture. Nothing in the text of either § 706 or § 1307(c) (or the legislative history of either provision) limits the authority of the court to take appropriate action in response to fraudulent conduct by the atypical litigant who has demonstrated that he is not entitled to the relief available to the typical debtor.[11] On the

---

[11] We have no occasion here to articulate with precision what conduct qualifies as "bad faith" sufficient to permit a bankruptcy judge to dismiss a Chapter 13 case or to deny conversion from Chapter 7. It suffices to emphasize that the debtor's conduct must, in fact, be atypical. Limiting dismissal or denial of conversion to extraordinary cases is particularly appropriate in light of the fact that lack of good faith in proposing a Chapter 13 plan is an express statutory ground for denying plan confirmation. § 1325(a)(3) * * * .

contrary, the broad authority granted to bankruptcy judges to take any action that is necessary or appropriate "to prevent an abuse of process" described in § 105(a) of the Code, is surely adequate to authorize an immediate denial of a motion to convert filed under § 706 in lieu of a conversion order that merely postpones the allowance of equivalent relief and may provide a debtor with an opportunity to take action prejudicial to creditors.

Indeed, as the Solicitor General has argued in his brief *amicus curiae,* even if § 105(a) had not been enacted, the inherent power of every federal court to sanction "abusive litigation practices" might well provide an adequate justification for a prompt, rather than a delayed, ruling on an unmeritorious attempt to qualify as a debtor under Chapter 13.

Accordingly, the judgment of the Court of Appeals is affirmed.

It is so ordered.

[JUSTICE ALITO, joined by JUSTICE ROBERTS, JUSTICE SCALIA and JUSTICE THOMAS, dissented on the grounds that the Code does not, by its terms, condition a debtor's right to convert on his or her "good faith."]

Notes and Questions

1. The dissent charged that the majority violated the principle that statutes should be interpreted in accordance with their plain meaning. Do you agree?

2. The majority relied as an alternative ground on § 105, which is bankruptcy's "all-writs" statute. As the dissent pointed out, however, governing authorities clearly hold that courts may use their power under § 105 only to implement other express provisions of the Code. Is *Marrama* inconsistent with that interpretation of § 105? (Interestingly, JUSTICE STEVENS joined the unanimous opinion in *Norwest Bank Worthington v. Ahlers*, 485 U.S. 197 (1988), which was cited in the *Marrama* dissent and elsewhere for the proposition that a court's power under § 105 is constrained by the rest of the Code. The *Ahlers* opinion is set out in Chapter 8 of this casebook.)

3. One of the purposes of the 2005 Amendments was to curb the discretion of bankruptcy judges, and the Amendments did just that in any number of areas. Has the *Marrama* decision reinvigorated judicial discretion and expanded the equitable power of bankruptcy judges?

C. PROPERTY OF THE ESTATE

Section 541(a) provides that the filing of a bankruptcy petition creates an "estate"—a new legal entity—that is comprised, at least initially, of "all legal and equitable interests of the debtor in property" as of the time of filing. Only property of the estate is subject to bankruptcy administration, so this broadly encompassing definition enables the bankruptcy proceeding to result in a comprehensive settlement of the debtor's financial affairs. Whether particular property is included in the estate is important in Chapter 7 cases, because only estate property is liquidated and its proceeds distributed to creditors. The process is a bit different in Chapters 11, 12 and 13, given that property of the estate is not liquidated, but, as we will see later, the amount a debtor must pay to unsecured creditors under those chapters is calculated in light of the amount creditors would receive in a Chapter 7 liquidation. That, in turn, depends on the value of the property in the estate.

Generally, property that a debtor acquires postpetition does not become property of the estate. There are a few notable exceptions, however. One of the most important of these exceptions applies to the postpetition income of individual debtors in Chapters 11, 12 and 13 (but not Chapter 7). §§ 1115(a), 1207(a) & 1306(a). Five other exceptions are set out in §§ 541(a)(3) through (7).

Despite the policy favoring broad inclusiveness, some property is excluded from the estate even though it fits the definition under § 541(a). Subsections (b) through (d) of § 541 list types of property interests that never come into the estate. In addition, individual debtors are entitled to claim "exemptions," effectively removing certain property from the estate. (We will study exemptions in the next section of this chapter.)

One of the most important principles in bankruptcy—that property rights created by state law are respected in bankruptcy—derives from two important pre-Code Supreme Court cases. In *Chicago Board of Trade v. Johnson*, 264 U.S. 1, 44 S.Ct. 232, 68 L.Ed. 533 (1924), the debtor had a seat on the Board of Trade. Members could, under Board rules, transfer their memberships only if debts owed to other members were paid in full, but sale of memberships in order to pay debts could not be compelled. The debtor owed $60,000 to other members at the time bankruptcy was filed. The bankruptcy trustee wanted to sell the seat without complying with the Board's restrictions (indeed, paying the obligations to other members would have consumed the entire value of the seat) and to use the proceeds to pay unsecured creditors. He argued that the seat was property of the bankruptcy estate, even though the Supreme Court of Illinois had previously held that the memberships were not property under state law because of the transfer restrictions imposed by Board rules.

The Supreme Court nevertheless held that the seat constituted property of the estate, concluding that "when the language of Congress indicates a policy requiring a broader construction of the statute than the state decisions would give it, federal courts can not be concluded by them." 264 U.S. at 10. Thus, what constitutes property of the estate is determined under § 541.

That holding led to a second question, however—whether the property was subject to the claims of other members, as it would have been outside of bankruptcy. The Court held that the restrictions on the property were analogous to a lien that was "inherent in the property in its creation," *id*. at 15, which bankruptcy had to respect. As a result, the $60,000 owed to other members "must be satisfied before the trustee can realize anything on the transfer of the seat for the general estate." *Id*. In other words, because the debtor's interest in his seat on the Board was encumbered by an obligation to pay debts to other members before the membership could be transferred, the property in the trustee's hands was similarly encumbered. Under *Chicago Board of Trade*, therefore, what is "property" is determined by federal bankruptcy law, but the nature of the property rights (that is, the *attributes* of that property) are governed by state law.

The Court reiterated in *Butner v. United States*, 440 U.S. 48, 99 S.Ct. 914, 59 L.Ed.2d 136 (1979), that state law rights will be respected in bankruptcy unless bankruptcy policy mandates a different rule. In *Butner*, a mortgagee asserted a right to postpetition rents generated by the debtor's real property subject to the mortgage. The circuit courts had split on the question whether state or federal law should determine entitlement to rents—a question on which the Bankruptcy Act was silent. The Court of Appeals in *Butner* held, first, that state law should determine the question, and then concluded that the mortgagee had not taken the steps required by state law to create an entitlement to rents. The Supreme Court expressly declined to decide whether the Court of Appeals had applied state law correctly. Instead, the Court sought to decide the "proper approach" to such disputes—specifically, whether state law should determine entitlement to rents. The Court held that it should:

Property interests are created and defined by state law. Unless some federal interest requires a different result, there is no reason why such interests should be analyzed differently simply because an interested party is involved in a bankruptcy proceeding. Uniform treatment of property interests by both state and federal courts within a State serves to reduce uncertainty, to discourage forum shopping, and to prevent a party from receiving "a windfall merely by reason of the happenstance of bankruptcy."

440 U.S. at 55 (citation omitted).

Thus, *Chicago Board of Trade* and *Butner*, together, stand for propositions fundamental to bankruptcy law: what constitutes property of the estate under § 541 is a federal law question, but state law determines the *attributes* of that property.

Notes and Problems

For the most part, § 541(a) brings into the estate all property in which the debtor has an interest at the time bankruptcy is filed, thereby carrying out the policy that the bankruptcy trustee succeeds to all of the debtor's property rights. A few types of after-acquired property, however, are also within § 541(a).

1. Determine whether the following assets would be property of the bankruptcy estate under § 541:

    a.   Right to use the name of a company that was in business for twenty-five years before filing a petition in bankruptcy.

    b.   Copyrights owned in full by a bankrupt publisher.

    c.   Copyrights a bankrupt publisher shares with various authors.

    d.   Residential lease for a rent-controlled apartment in New York City, occupied by Debtor.

    e.   Commercial lease for warehouse space under which Debtor, a shipping company, is lessee. *Cf.* § 541(b)(2).

    f.   Lottery winnings from a drawing that occurred postpetition, on a ticket purchased prepetition.

2. Debtor owned "Adamante," a Lhasa Apso that won Best-in-Show at the Eastminster Dog Show several years ago. Adamante gave birth to a litter of six puppies shortly after Debtor filed bankruptcy. Is Adamante property of the estate? Are the puppies?

3. Debtor opened an educational savings account four years ago, in accordance with a state tuition program, to help pay for his granddaughter's college education. Because Debtor got a late start (his granddaughter was already 13 years old), he made rather sizeable contributions—$6,000 a year. When Debtor filed bankruptcy, the account had a balance of $24,000. Is the account, or any part of it, property of the estate?

4. Heavenly Hamburgers rents the small shop from which it sells the biggest, greasiest burgers in town. Sales have fallen since a local TV news story reported the cholesterol count in HH's burgers. HH filed bankruptcy with six years left to run on its lease. One of the terms of the lease provides for immediate termination upon the filing of any insolvency proceeding. Will HH's interest in the remaining lease term become property of its bankruptcy estate? See § 541(c)(1)(B).

5. Debtor was aware, first, that her financial situation would shortly compel the filing of bankruptcy, second, that her father was seriously ill and unlikely to live much longer, and third, that she stood to inherit a great deal of money under her father's will. Therefore, Debtor renounced all potential interest under the will, effectively giving the inheritance to the next legatee, Debtor's son. She then filed bankruptcy. Her father died two months later. Are the assets passing under the will property of the bankruptcy estate? See *Jones v. Atchison (In re Atchison)*, 925 F.2d 209 (7th Cir. 1991).

———————————

Congress passed the Employee Retirement Income Security Act of 1974 (ERISA), 29 U.S.C. §§ 1001 et seq., to provide nationally-uniform protection for workers' pension benefits. To be "ERISA-qualified," and thus eligible for favorable tax treatment, a plan must provide that plan benefits "may not be assigned or alienated." With such a provision, an ERISA-qualified plan appears to be excluded from the bankruptcy estate by § 541(c)(2). The legislative history, however, states that (c)(2) was intended to preserve "restrictions on transfer of a spendthrift trust" if such restrictions are enforceable under nonbankruptcy law. Under state spendthrift trust law, self-settled trusts—*i.e.*, those created by a debtor for his or her own benefit—cannot be insulated from the reach of creditors. The problem arises because a pension plan may be both ERISA-qualified and self-settled. The question became whether § 541(c)(2) excludes from the bankruptcy estate only those plans that meet the stringent requirements of state spendthrift trust law, or whether ERISA-qualified plans, with their transfer restrictions, are also covered. The circuit courts divided on the issue before the Supreme Court, in the following case, resolved it.

PATTERSON v. SHUMATE

United States Supreme Court, 1992.
504 U.S. 753, 112 S.Ct. 2242, 119 L.Ed.2d 519.

JUSTICE BLACKMUN delivered the opinion of the Court.

The Bankruptcy Code excludes from the bankruptcy estate property of the debtor that is subject to a restriction on transfer enforceable under "applicable nonbankruptcy law." § 541(c)(2). We must decide in this case whether an anti-alienation provision contained in an ERISA-qualified pension plan constitutes a restriction on transfer enforceable under "applicable nonbankruptcy law," and whether, accordingly, a debtor may exclude his interest in such a plan from the property of the bankruptcy estate.

I

Respondent Joseph B. Shumate, Jr., was employed for over 30 years by Coleman Furniture Corporation, where he ultimately attained the position of president and chairman of the board of directors. Shumate and approximately 400 other employees were participants in the Coleman Furniture Corporation Pension Plan (Plan). The Plan satisfied all applicable requirements of the Employee Retirement Income Security Act of 1974 (ERISA) and qualified for favorable tax treatment under the Internal Revenue Code. In particular, Article 16.1 of the Plan contained the anti-alienation provision required for qualification under § 206(d)(1) of ERISA, 29 U.S.C. § 1056(d)(1) ("Each pension plan shall provide that benefits provided under the plan may not be assigned or alienated"). Shumate's interest in the plan was valued at $250,000.

In 1982, Coleman Furniture filed a petition for bankruptcy under Chapter 11 of the Bankruptcy Code. The case was converted to a Chapter 7 proceeding and a trustee, Roy V. Creasy, was appointed. Shumate himself encountered financial difficulties and filed a petition for bankruptcy in 1984. His case, too, was converted to a Chapter 7 proceeding, and petitioner John R. Patterson was appointed trustee.

Creasy terminated and liquidated the Plan, providing full distributions to all participants except Shumate. Patterson then filed an adversary proceeding against Creasy in the Bankruptcy Court for the Western District of Virginia to recover Shumate's interest in the Plan for the benefit of Shumate's bankruptcy estate. Shumate in turn asked the United States District Court for the Western District of Virginia, which already had jurisdiction over a related proceeding, to compel

Creasy to pay Shumate's interest in the Plan directly to him. The bankruptcy proceeding subsequently was consolidated with the district court action.

The District Court rejected Shumate's contention that his interest in the Plan should be excluded from his bankruptcy estate. The court held that § 541(c)(2)'s reference to "nonbankruptcy law" embraced only state law, not federal law such as ERISA. Applying Virginia law, the court held that Shumate's interest in the Plan did not qualify for protection as a spendthrift trust. The District Court also rejected Shumate's alternative argument that even if his interest in the Plan could not be excluded from the bankruptcy estate under § 541(c)(2), he was entitled to an exemption under § 522(b)(2)(A), which allows a debtor to exempt from property of the estate "any property that is exempt under Federal law." The District Court ordered Creasy to pay Shumate's interest in the Plan over to his bankruptcy estate.

The Court of Appeals for the Fourth Circuit reversed. The court relied on its earlier decision in *Anderson v. Raine (In re Moore)*, 907 F.2d 1476 (1990), in which another Fourth Circuit panel was described as holding, subsequent to the District Court's decision in the instant case, that "ERISA-qualified plans, which by definition have a non-alienation provision, constitute 'applicable nonbankruptcy law' and contain enforceable restrictions on the transfer of pension interests." Thus, the Court of Appeals held that Shumate's interest in the Plan should be excluded from the bankruptcy estate under § 541(c)(2). The court then declined to consider Shumate's alternative argument that his interest in the Plan qualified for exemption under § 522(b).

We granted certiorari to resolve the conflict among the Courts of Appeals as to whether an anti-alienation provision in an ERISA-qualified pension plan constitutes a restriction on transfer enforceable under "applicable nonbankruptcy law" for purposes of the § 541(c)(2) exclusion of property from the debtor's bankruptcy estate.

II

A

In our view, the plain language of the Bankruptcy Code and ERISA is our determinant. Section 541(c)(2) provides the following exclusion from the otherwise broad definition of "property of the estate" contained in § 541(a)(1) of the Code:

> "A restriction on the transfer of a beneficial interest of the debtor in a trust that is enforceable under *applicable nonbankruptcy law* is enforceable in a case under this title" (emphasis added).

The natural reading of the provision entitles a debtor to exclude from property of the estate any interest in a plan or trust that contains a transfer restriction enforceable under any relevant nonbankruptcy law. Nothing in § 541 suggests that the phrase "applicable nonbankruptcy law" refers, as petitioner contends, exclusively to *state* law. The text contains no limitation on "applicable nonbankruptcy law" relating to the source of the law.

Reading the term "applicable nonbankruptcy law" in § 541(c)(2) to include federal as well as state law comports with other references in the Bankruptcy Code to sources of law. The Code reveals, significantly, that Congress, when it desired to do so, knew how to restrict the scope of applicable law to "state law" and did so with some frequency. See, *e.g.*, § 109(c)(2) (entity may be a debtor under chapter 9 if authorized "by State law"); § 522(b)([2]) (election of exemptions controlled by "the State law that is applicable to the debtor"); § 523(a)(5) (a debt for alimony, maintenance, or support determined "in accordance with State or territorial law"[f] is not dischargeable); § 903(1) ("a State law prescribing a method of composition of indebtedness" of municipalities is not binding on nonconsenting creditors); see also §§ 362(b)(12) and 1145(a). Congress' decision to use the broader phrase "applicable nonbankruptcy law" in § 541(c)(2) strongly suggests that it did not intend to restrict the provision in the manner that petitioner contends.

The text of § 541(c)(2) does not support petitioner's contention that "applicable nonbankruptcy law" is limited to state law. Plainly read, the provision encompasses any relevant nonbankruptcy law, including federal law such as ERISA. We must enforce the statute according to its terms.

B

Having concluded that "applicable nonbankruptcy law" is not limited to state law, we next determine whether the anti-alienation provision contained in the ERISA-qualified plan at issue here satisfies the literal terms of § 541(c)(2).

---

[f] This provision was reworded in 2005. Eds.

[The Court found that the plan, by its terms, satisfied the requirement of ERISA's § 206(d)(1) that "[e]ach pension plan shall provide that benefits provided under the plan may not be assigned or alienated." The restriction was also "enforceable."]

The anti-alienation provision required for ERISA qualification and contained in the Plan at issue in this case thus constitutes an enforceable transfer restriction for purposes of § 541(c)(2)'s exclusion of property from the bankruptcy estate.

III

Petitioner raises several challenges to this conclusion. Given the clarity of the statutory text, however, he bears an "exceptionally heavy" burden of persuading us that Congress intended to limit the § 541(c)(2) exclusion to restrictions on transfer that are enforceable only under state spendthrift trust law. *Union Bank v. Wolas*, 112 S.Ct. 527, 530 (1991).

A

Petitioner first contends that contemporaneous legislative materials demonstrate that § 541(c)(2)'s exclusion of property from the bankruptcy estate should not extend to a debtor's interest in an ERISA-qualified pension plan. Although courts "appropriately may refer to a statute's legislative history to resolve statutory ambiguity," *Toibb v. Radloff*, 501 U.S. 157, 162 (1991), the clarity of the statutory language at issue in this case obviates the need for any such inquiry.

Even were we to consider the legislative materials to which petitioner refers, however, we could discern no "clearly expressed legislative intention" contrary to the result reached above. In his brief, petitioner quotes from House and Senate reports accompanying the Bankruptcy Reform Act of 1978 that purportedly reflect "unmistakable" congressional intent to limit § 541(c)(2)'s exclusion to pension plans that qualify under state law as spendthrift trusts. Those reports contain only the briefest of discussions addressing § 541(c)(2). The House Report states: "Paragraph (2) of subsection (c) * * * preserves restrictions on transfer of a spendthrift trust to the extent that the restriction is enforceable under applicable nonbankruptcy law." H.R. Rep. No. 95–595 at 369, *reprinted in* 1978 U.S.C.C.A.N. at 6325. A general introductory section to the House Report contains the additional statement that the new law "continues over the exclusion from property of the estate of the debtor's interest in a spendthrift trust to the extent the trust is protected from creditors under applicable State law." *Id.* at 176, *reprinted* *in* 1978 U.S.C.C.A.N. at 6136. These meager excerpts reflect at best congressional intent to *include* state spendthrift trust law within the meaning of "applicable nonbankruptcy law." By no means do they provide a sufficient basis for concluding, in derogation of the statute's clear language, that Congress intended to *exclude* other state and federal law from the provision's scope.

B

Petitioner next contends that our construction of § 541(c)(2), pursuant to which a debtor may exclude his interest in an ERISA-qualified pension plan from the bankruptcy estate, renders § 522(d)(10)(E) of the Bankruptcy Code superfluous. Under § 522(d)(10)(E), a debtor who elects the federal exemptions set forth in § 522(d) may exempt from the bankruptcy estate his right to receive "a payment under a stock bonus, pension, profitsharing, annuity, or similar plan or contract * * *, to the extent reasonably necessary for the support of the debtor and any dependent of the debtor." If a debtor's interest in a pension plan could be *excluded* in full from the bankruptcy estate, the argument goes, then there would have been no reason for Congress to create a limited *exemption* for such interests elsewhere in the statute.

Petitioner's surplusage argument fails, however, for the reason that § 522(d)(10)(E) exempts from the bankruptcy estate a much broader category of interests than § 541(c)(2) excludes. For example, pension plans established by governmental entities and churches need not comply with Subchapter I of ERISA, including the anti-alienation requirement of § 206(d)(1). So, too, pension plans that qualify for preferential tax treatment under 26 U.S.C. § 408 (individual retirement accounts) are specifically excepted from ERISA's anti-alienation requirement. Although a debtor's interest in these plans could not be excluded under § 541(c)(2) because the plans lack transfer restrictions enforceable under "applicable nonbankruptcy law," that interest nevertheless could be exempted under § 522(d)(10)(E). Once petitioner concedes that § 522(d)(10)(E)'s exemption applies to more than ERISA-qualified plans containing anti-alienation provisions, his argument that our reading of § 541(c)(2) renders the exemption provision superfluous must collapse.

C

Finally, petitioner contends that our holding frustrates the Bankruptcy Code's policy of ensuring a broad inclusion of assets in the bankruptcy estate. As an initial matter, we think that petitioner mistakes an admittedly broad definition of includable property for a "policy" underlying the Code as a whole. In any event, to the extent that policy considerations are even relevant where the language of the statute is so clear, we believe that our construction of § 541(c)(2) is preferable to the one petitioner urges upon us.

First, our decision today ensures that the treatment of pension benefits will not vary based on the beneficiary's bankruptcy status. See *Butner v. United States*, 440 U.S. 48, 55 (1978) (observing that "[u]niform treatment of property interests" prevents "a party from 'receiving a windfall merely by reason of the happenstance of bankruptcy,' " quoting *Lewis v. Manufacturers National Bank*, 364 U.S. 603, 609 (1961)). We previously have declined to recognize any exceptions to ERISA's anti-alienation provision outside the bankruptcy context. Declining to recognize any exceptions to that provision *within* the bankruptcy context minimizes the possibility that creditors will engage in strategic manipulation of the bankruptcy laws in order to gain access to otherwise inaccessible funds.

Our holding also gives full and appropriate effect to ERISA's goal of protecting pension benefits. This Court has described that goal as one of ensuring that "if a worker has been promised a defined pension benefit upon retirement—and if he has fulfilled whatever conditions are required to obtain a vested benefit—he actually will receive it." *Nachman Corp. v. Pension Benefit Guaranty Corp.*, 446 U.S. 359, 375 (1980). In furtherance of these principles, we recently declined in *Guidry v. Sheet Metal Workers Pension Fund*, 493 U.S. 365 (1990), notwithstanding strong equitable considerations to the contrary, to recognize an implied exception to ERISA's anti-alienation provision that would have allowed a labor union to impose a constructive trust on the pension benefits of a corrupt union official. We explained:

> "Section 206(d) reflects a considered congressional policy choice, a decision to safeguard a stream of income for pensioners (and their dependents, who may be, and perhaps usually are, blameless), even if that decision prevents others from securing relief for the wrongs done them. If exceptions to this policy are to be made, it is for Congress to undertake that task." *Id*. at 376.

These considerations apply with equal, if not greater, force in the present context.

Finally, our holding furthers another important policy underlying ERISA: uniform national treatment of pension benefits. Construing "applicable nonbankruptcy law" to include federal law ensures that the security of a debtor's pension benefits will be governed by ERISA, not left to the vagaries of state spendthrift trust law.

* * *

The judgment of the Court of Appeals is affirmed.

It is so ordered.

JUSTICE SCALIA, concurring.

The Court's opinion today, which I join, prompts several observations.

When the phrase "applicable nonbankruptcy law" is considered in isolation, the phenomenon that three Courts of Appeals could have thought it a synonym for "state law" is mystifying. When the phrase is considered together with the rest of the Bankruptcy Code (in which Congress chose to refer to state law as, logically enough, "state law"), the phenomenon calls into question whether our legal culture has so far departed from attention to text, or is so lacking in agreed-upon methodology for creating and interpreting text, that it any longer makes sense to talk of "a government of laws, not of men."

Speaking of agreed-upon methodology: It is good that the Court's analysis today proceeds on the assumption that use of the phrases "state law" and "applicable nonbankruptcy law" in *other* provisions of the Bankruptcy Code is highly relevant to whether "applicable nonbankruptcy law" means "state law" in § 541(c)(2), since consistency of usage within the same statute is to be presumed. This application of a normal and obvious principle of statutory construction would not merit comment, except that we explicitly rejected it, in favor of a one-subsection-at-a-time approach, when interpreting another provision of this very statute earlier this Term. See *Dewsnup v. Timm*, 502 U.S. 410, 415-17 (1992). "[W]e express no opinion," our decision said, "as to whether the words [at issue] have different meaning in other provisions of the Bankruptcy Code." *Id*. at 417 n.3. I trust that in our search for a neutral and rational interpretive methodology we have now come to rest, so that the symbol of our profession may remain the scales, not the see-saw.

Notes and Questions

1. What policy is suggested by the language in § 541(c)(2) and the Court's construction of it? Who are the ultimate winners and losers? (In particular, who gets the $250,000?)

2. How do state spendthrift trusts differ from ERISA? Is there any reasoned basis to distinguish between federal and state law as "otherwise applicable nonbankruptcy law"? In any context?

3. Assume that a debtor makes voluntary after-tax contributions to the plan and, because the restriction on alienation required by ERISA only affects third parties, the debtor has immediate access to those funds. Are those amounts property of the estate notwithstanding § 541(c)(2) and *Patterson*? See *Barkley v. Conner (In re Conner)*, 73 F.3d 258 (9th Cir.), *cert. denied*, 519 U.S. 817, 117 S.Ct. 68, 136 L.Ed.2d 29 (1996).

4. The 2005 Amendments added § 541(b)(7) to the Code. Does it moot *Patterson* in whole or in part? Is it important to know that ERISA-qualified plans include contributions made by employers as well as employees? Does § 541(b)(7) operate to exclude the entire plan from the estate? Does it apply only to amounts withheld or contributed postpetition?

The following Notes and Problems serve to illustrate some of the many fact patterns that can raise questions as to what constitutes property of the estate under § 541.

Notes and Problems

1. Bruce Clark, a football player for the New Orleans Saints, signed three one-year contracts on the form in use by all NFL teams. Under the 1988–89 contract, his salary of $575,000 was payable in sixteen equal installments over the course of the regular season. The contract contained the following clauses: a "skill guarantee," effective upon passing the club physical, providing that the full salary would be paid despite unsatisfactory performance; a clause providing for incremental forgiveness of a $725,000 loan, over the course of the season, conditional on Clark's "fulfilling his contractual obligations by playing or being available to play"; and clauses requiring Clark to report promptly and participate, to devote his best efforts, to maintain his physical condition, and to permit examinations by the club doctor. Clark filed a Chapter 7 petition after seven of the sixteen games had been played. Is his salary for the next nine games property of the bankruptcy estate? See *Clark v. First City Bank (Matter of Clark)*, 891 F.2d 111 (5th Cir.1989).

2. Vera Rash was overwhelmed by her credit card obligations and filed bankruptcy on August 1. Her case was still pending in May of the next year when she received a $600 tax refund from the IRS, relating to the prior tax year. Is any or all of the refund property of the estate? See *In re Meyers*, 616 F.3d 626 (7th Cir.2010).

3. Debtor, who is a prolific writer, published a popular antitrust casebook. Unfortunately, Debtor is also a prolific spender and he had to file bankruptcy the very next year. He received a royalty check for $1,000 three months after his bankruptcy filing, for sales of his antitrust book. Is any or all of the $1,000 property of the estate?

4. Debtor retired after a career as an insurance agent. During his career, he was paid solely by commissions on the policies he sold. He received a commission whenever one of his policies was renewed, even after retirement. Are those commissions property of his bankruptcy estate? See *In re Braddy*, 226 B.R. 479 (Bankr. N.D.Fla.1998).

5. Debtor owned season tickets to the Phoenix Suns' games. Tickets ordinarily carry rights to annual renewal, but the Suns routinely send annual notices to season ticket holders stating that the renewal opportunity is a privilege that can be withdrawn in the Suns' discretion. When Debtor's bankruptcy trustee decided to sell the tickets, the Suns objected. What result? See *Abele v. Phoenix Suns Ltd. Partnership (In re Harrell)*, 73 F.3d 218 (9th Cir.1996).

6. Debtor was an attorney, specializing in personal injury cases. One of those cases was ongoing when he filed a Chapter 7 bankruptcy petition. Debtor continued to work on the case, which settled six months after his bankruptcy filing. Debtor received one-third of the settlement proceeds, as his contingent-fee contract with his client provided. Is all or any part of that fee property of his bankruptcy estate? See *Jess v. Carey (In re Jess)*, 169 F.3d 1204 (9th Cir.1999).

7. Several years before filing bankruptcy, Debtor registered a domain name for the Internet website through which she conducted a small mail-order business. Although the business was successful, other financial dealings forced Debtor to file a bankruptcy petition. The trustee in Debtor's case realized that the domain name was valuable. Therefore, he argued that it was property of the estate and subject to sale. Is he correct? See *Paige v. Jubber (In re Paige)*, 443 B.R. 878 (D. Utah 2011).

8. Liquor licenses have created interesting difficulties under § 541(a). In *In re Nejberger*, 934 F.2d 1300 (3d Cir.1991), the issue was whether a debtor's right to seek renewal of his liquor license was property of his estate. The state Liquor Control Board rejected debtor's renewal application, pursuant to state law, for failure to pay certain state taxes, but granted debtor a one-year

grace period in which to pay the taxes and to reapply. Debtor filed Chapter 11 during the grace period. At the end of the period, the Board issued a final termination of debtor's license because debtor had failed to satisfy his tax obligation.

Debtor sought to compel the Board to renew his application, arguing that the tax liability was stayed automatically by his Chapter 11 petition. The bankruptcy court concluded that debtor's expectation of renewal was property of the estate and that nonrenewal was based solely on debtor's failure to pay taxes that constituted prepetition claims. Thus, the bankruptcy court ordered the Board to renew debtor's license. The district court agreed that the expectation created by the renewal grace period was property of the estate, but found that reasons other than nonpayment of taxes might have influenced the decision not to renew. The district court, therefore, ordered debtor to reapply for the license and directed the Board to consider the application without regard to the unpaid taxes.

The Third Circuit affirmed, agreeing that the expectation of consideration for renewal constituted property of the estate and that the bankruptcy court's order was too much of an intrusion on the Board's authority under state law. Therefore, the court ordered that the Board make an appropriate decision regarding debtor's renewal application, based on any factors—other than nonpayment of taxes—that state law allowed the Board to consider.

9. Generally, whatever the debtor owns at the moment a Chapter 7 petition is filed becomes property of the estate and is used to satisfy obligations that the debtor owes as of the same moment. Section 541(a)(5), however, includes certain property that the debtor acquires within six months after the filing—specifically, property obtained by inheritance, through a property settlement, or as beneficiary of a life insurance policy. Chapter 13, in contrast, includes all property the debtor acquires after the filing. § 1306.

These distinctions created difficulties when a Chapter 13 case was converted to a Chapter 7, as often happens. Before the 1994 Amendments, some courts held that the Chapter 7 estate included all property acquired after the filing, even though it would not have been property of the estate if Chapter 7 had been filed initially; other courts held that the converted case consisted of property held at the time of the original bankruptcy filing. The 1994 Amendments added § 348(f), which adopts the latter view.

Courts have struggled with the proper treatment of Social Security benefits that a debtor is entitled to receive on an ongoing basis. Resolution of this question requires consideration of two major federal statutes—the Bankruptcy Code as well as the Social Security Act. The following case discusses the issue and also serves as a bridge to our next topic—exemptions.

CARPENTER v. RIES (IN RE CARPENTER)

United States Court of Appeals, Eighth Circuit, 2010.
614 F.3d 930.

RILEY, Chief Judge.

Todd Carpenter received a lump sum payment from the Social Security Administration (SSA). Shortly thereafter, Carpenter filed for bankruptcy relief under Chapter 7. Carpenter claimed the social security payment was exempt and should not be included in his bankruptcy estate, relying on 42 U.S.C. § 407 ("[N]one of the moneys paid * * * under this [Social Security Act] shall be subject to * * * the operation of any bankruptcy or insolvency law."). The bankruptcy Trustee, Charles W. Ries (Trustee), objected to the exemption, and the bankruptcy court sustained the Trustee's objection, finding the social security proceeds were property of the estate pursuant to § 541 (including "all legal or equitable interests of the debtor in property as of the commencement of the case," and not excluding social security payments). The United States Bankruptcy Appellate Panel for the Eighth Circuit (BAP) reversed, finding the social security payment was excluded from the Chapter 7 bankruptcy estate pursuant to 42 U.S.C. § 407. We agree with the BAP and reverse the bankruptcy court.

I. BACKGROUND

In March 2006, the SSA determined Carpenter was disabled. In September 2007, the SSA sent Carpenter a lump sum payment in the amount of $17,165 for retroactive benefits due for September 2006 through August 2007. Carpenter deposited the check into a bank account on November 6, 2007, and kept the funds segregated. On April 3, 2008, Carpenter filed for relief under Chapter 7 of the Bankruptcy Code. Shortly before filing for bankruptcy, Carpenter withdrew the social security funds in the form of a cashier's check, dated January 31, 2008.

When a debtor files for bankruptcy, a bankruptcy estate is established. See § 541(a). The bankruptcy estate is generally deemed to include all of the debtor's legal or equitable interests in property at the time of filing. The Bankruptcy Code, however, permits the debtor to exempt certain property from the estate. There are two separate exemption schemes. § 522(b)(1). Debtors may choose to take either (1) the exemptions listed in the Bankruptcy Code at § 522(d); or (2) the exemptions found in applicable state law and federal law other than § 522(d). The debtor may choose only one of these options, to the exclusion of the other, and may not combine the two.

Carpenter elected the federal bankruptcy exemptions listed in § 522(d). One of the listed exemptions under § 522(d) exempts "[t]he debtor's right to receive * * *. a social security benefit, unemployment compensation, or a local public assistance benefit." § 522(d)(10)(A). Carpenter claimed his social security proceeds were exempt under this provision. * * * Carpenter also generally asserted his social security proceeds were protected by 42 U.S.C. § 407, which provides, in pertinent part:

> **(a)** The right of any person to any future payment under this subchapter shall not be transferable or assignable, at law or in equity, and ***none of the moneys paid*** or payable or rights existing ***under this subchapter shall be subject to*** execution, levy, attachment, garnishment, or other legal process, or to *the operation of any bankruptcy or insolvency law.*

> **(b)** *No other provision of law*, enacted before, on, or after April 20, 1983, *may be construed to limit*, supersede, or otherwise modify *the provisions of this section except to the extent that it does so by express reference to this section.*

(Emphasis added).

The bankruptcy court * * * declared, "[t]he ultimate question here is whether the amendment to [42 U.S.C.] § 407 adding paragraph (b) serves to completely exempt Carpenter's Social Security disability proceeds even though he voluntarily elected the federal exemptions and claimed the proceeds exempt under § 522(d)(10)(A)." The bankruptcy court concluded "§ 407 has no application in light of the debtor's claim of exemptions under §§ 522(b)(2) and (d)."

Carpenter appealed the bankruptcy court's adverse finding to the BAP. The BAP agreed with the bankruptcy court's position that Carpenter's social security proceeds were not exempt under § 522(d)(10)(A), because "the cashier's check held by Carpenter does not constitute 'the right to receive' a social security benefit, but instead represents funds which were previously paid as such a benefit." The BAP determined "the ultimate question in this appeal is whether [42

U.S.C.] § 407 excludes social security proceeds from the recipient's bankruptcy estate altogether. If so, a court need not reach the question of whether such debtor is entitled to exempt them from that estate under another statute such as § 522(d)(10)(A)." The BAP conducted an analysis of the impact of 42 U.S.C. § 407 on the Bankruptcy Code, and held,

> since no provision in the Bankruptcy Code makes express reference to § 407, and, without such express reference, that statute renders social security benefits, paid or payable, free from the operation of any bankruptcy law, a bankruptcy trustee has no authority to administer, as property of the bankruptcy estate, moneys paid to a debtor as social security benefits.

408 B.R. 244, 248 (8th Cir. BAP 2009). The BAP concluded Carpenter's social security proceeds must be excluded from the bankruptcy estate pursuant to 42 U.S.C. § 407 and may be retained by the debtor. The Trustee appeals the BAP's decision.

II. DISCUSSION

* * *

B. Relevant Statutes

"Title II of the Social Security Act of 1935 established a social insurance program for wage earners and their dependents, to be paid out of a trust funded by the payroll taxes of wage earners and their employers." *Hildebrand v. SSA (In re Buren)*, 725 F.2d 1080, 1084 (6th Cir.1984). Section 207 of the Social Security Act protected these social security payments, stating, in part, "none of the moneys paid * * * under this subchapter shall be subject to * * * the operation of any bankruptcy or insolvency law." 42 U.S.C. § 407. Congress amended Title XVI of the Social Security Act in 1972, and expanded several existing programs to establish a welfare program for "individuals who have attained the age of 65 or are blind or disabled." When Congress amended Title XVI, it explicitly incorporated § 407 to protect the added social security beneficiaries.

Congress later enacted the Bankruptcy Reform Act of 1978. In doing so, Congress reformulated the classes of persons who may qualify as a "debtor" for purposes of Title 11. The Bankruptcy Reform Act did not significantly change the previous law as to who was eligible for liquidation under Chapter 7; however, it did broaden the class of persons who were eligible for relief under Chapter 13. H.R. Rep. No.

95-595, at 118-19 (1977), *reprinted in* 1978 U.S.C.C.A.N. 5963, 6080 (noting under the previous law, only a "wage earner" could file a Chapter 13 case, and by extending eligibility to any "individual with regular income," the Act would permit "even individuals whose primary income is from investments, pensions, social security, or welfare [to] use Chapter 13 if their income is sufficiently stable and regular"). Congress also expanded the definition of "property of the estate," declaring, as relevant here, that the bankruptcy estate is comprised of "all legal or equitable interests of the debtor in property as of the commencement of the case."

Despite this broad definition of "property of the estate," the Bankruptcy Code contains several provisions which *exclude* specific property interests from the estate. See § 541(b)(1)-(9). * * * [T]he Bankruptcy Code also permits debtors to *exempt* certain property from the estate. Pursuant to § 522(b)(1), a debtor may elect to exempt the property listed under § 522(b)(2), or the property listed under § 522(b)(3), unless of course, the state opts out of the federal bankruptcy scheme. If the debtor elects to exempt the property listed under § 522(b)(2), the debtor may exempt from the estate all the property specified under § 522(d). One of the exemptions listed under § 522(d) includes "[t]he debtor's right to receive * * * a social security benefit, unemployment compensation, or a local public assistance benefit." § 522(d)(10)(A). On the other hand, if the debtor elects to exempt the property set forth in § 522(b)(3), the debtor generally may exempt "any property that is exempt under Federal law, other than subsection (d) of this section, or State and local law that is applicable on the date of the filing." § 522(b)(3)(A). None of the relevant Bankruptcy Code provisions mention 42 U.S.C. § 407, nor do they specify whether past and future social security proceeds are *excluded* from property of the bankruptcy estate altogether, or whether such proceeds may only be *exempted* under either § 522(b)(2) or § 522(b)(3).

C. Conflicting Statutes

The conflict between the applicable bankruptcy statutes and 42 U.S.C. § 407 is readily apparent. Section 407, in its original form, expressly declared, "none of the moneys paid or payable * * * shall be subject to * * * the operation of any bankruptcy or insolvency law." In contrast, under the Bankruptcy Code, "all legal or equitable interests of the debtor in property" are deemed to be property of the bankruptcy estate. § 541(a)(1). The Bankruptcy Code does not expressly reference § 407 or exclude social security income from property of the estate, but instead provides certain exemptions, which may, or may not, permit the debtor to exempt social security proceeds. The inconsistency between § 407 and the Bankruptcy Code is most transparent under Chapter 13 of the Bankruptcy Code, which was designed, in part, to expand relief under the Bankruptcy Code to social security recipients. See *United States v. Devall*, 704 F.2d 1513, 1516 (11th Cir.1983) (reasoning, "[b]ecause it is evident that Congress anticipated social security recipients could use Chapter 13, it follows that social security benefits are properly included in the debtor's Chapter 13 estate"); *Toson v. United States*, 18 B.R. 371, 373-75 (Bankr. N.D.Ga.1982) (recognizing the "conflict between Chapter 13 of the Bankruptcy Code and the Social Security Act," distinguishing Chapter 13 cases from bankruptcy filings under other chapters, and concluding "enactment of the Bankruptcy Code partially repealed the anti-assignment provisions" of the Social Security Act, 42 U.S.C. § 407). Chapter 13 also invests bankruptcy courts with the power to "order any entity from whom the debtor receives income to pay all or any part of such income to the trustees." § 1325(c). This provision also conflicts with § 407 under circumstances where a court orders the SSA to send a debtor's social security payments to the bankruptcy trustee.

Due to these inconsistent provisions, courts have struggled to determine when social security proceeds should be included in a debtor's bankruptcy estate. Some courts have held Congress implicitly repealed 42 U.S.C. § 407 by enacting the Bankruptcy Reform Act of 1978. See *Devall*, 704 F.2d at 1518; *Toson*, 18 B.R. at 373 (listing cases). The Eleventh Circuit determined, in *Walker v. Treadwell (In re Treadwell)*, 699 F.2d 1050 (11th Cir.1983), that § 407 is merely an exemption provision which the debtor must affirmatively claim. As a consequence, debtors who elect the state and federal exemptions other than those set forth in § 522(d) may use 42 U.S.C. § 407 to preclude both past and future social security payments. Under the Eleventh Circuit's interpretation, § 407 is inapplicable to those debtors who elect the exemptions set forth under § 522(d). This creates an unusual result because debtors choosing the exemptions listed in § 522(d) may exempt future social security payments under § 522(d)(10)(A), but no protection is provided to social security payments which have already been received by the debtor.

In 1983, Congress reacted to court decisions limiting the scope of the Social Security Act by *[adding subsection (b).]*[2] * * * This

---

[2] We need not consider the legislative history behind the amendment because the language of the statute is unambiguous and clear on its face. However, at least some members of Congress were concerned bankruptcy courts had ordered the

amendment did little to clarify the interplay between § 407 and the Bankruptcy Code, and courts have failed to interpret the applicable provisions consistently.

D. Proper Resolution

The Sixth Circuit, in *Buren*, conducted a thorough analysis of the impact of § 407 on the Bankruptcy Code. *Buren* involved seven consolidated cases in which debtors receiving social security disability payments filed voluntary petitions under Chapter 13. In each case, the debtor informed the bankruptcy court the social security benefits constituted regular income, as required to qualify for Chapter 13. The bankruptcy court ordered the government to send the social security benefits directly to the trustee, and on appeal, the district court affirmed. The Sixth Circuit reversed, concluding § 407 "specifically prevents judicial intrusion into the benefit payment process," and "Chapter 13 was never intended to allow bankruptcy courts to compel the [SSA] to pay debtor's social security benefits directly to the trustee." 725 F.2d at 1086, 1087. The Sixth Circuit noted the Bankruptcy Code explicitly repealed and modified numerous statutory provisions, yet failed to include § 407 in the list of those provisions. The Sixth Circuit criticized the district court's finding that to interpret § 407 to prohibit the taking of social security proceeds would "[r]emove [] social security recipients from the purview of Chapter 13." *Id.* at 1085. The appellate court reasoned that § 407 "leaves unimpaired Congress' desire to open Chapter 13 to social security recipients," because, "[a]s a practical matter, a willing debtor can simply sign his check over to the trustee." *Id.* at 1086; see also *Combustion Fed. Credit Union v. Barron (In re Barron)*, 85 B.R. 603, 607 (Bankr. N.D.Ala.1988) ("The removal of the court's power to enforce a benefits deduction order against the [SSA] does not prevent a debtor from consummating a successful plan of reorganization under [Chapter 13], under which the debtor would make payments to the trustee.").

SSA to send debtors' social security payments directly to trustees. See H.R. Rep. No. 98-25, pt. 1, at 82-83 (1983), reprinted in 1983 U.S.C.C.A.N. 219, 302 ("Based on the legislative history of the Bankruptcy Reform Act of 1978, some bankruptcy courts have considered social security and SSI benefits listed by the debtor to be income for purposes of a Chapter XIII bankruptcy and have ordered SSA in several hundred cases to send all or part of a debtor's benefit check to the trustee in bankruptcy. Your committee's bill specifically provides that social security and SSI benefits may not be assigned notwithstanding any other provisions of law, including * * * the 'Bankruptcy Reform Act of 1978.' ").

Although Carpenter's case here involves a Chapter 7 bankruptcy, as opposed to a Chapter 13 bankruptcy, we believe *Buren* is instructive. As recognized by the Sixth Circuit, § 407 does not contain any qualifying language. It explicitly demands that no past or future social security payments may be subject to the operation of any bankruptcy law. Section 407 also instructs that it is not to be limited by any other provision of law, without express reference to § 407. If we were to hold, as the bankruptcy court did in this case, that § 407 is a mere exemption which may not be claimed if the debtor instead elects the exemptions set forth in § 522(d), then we would also be interpreting § 407 contrary to the express language of § 407, saying the scope of § 407's protection is limited. "This interpretation of the intent of Congress is untenable because the language of the statute expresses an intent that social security benefits are to be encapsulated with a total shield from the bankruptcy laws." *In re Barron*, 85 B.R. at 606.

We therefore hold, in accord with the BAP's decision, that § 407 operates as a complete bar to the forced inclusion of past and future social security proceeds in the bankruptcy estate. See also *In re Buren*, 725 F.2d at 1086 (noting "social security payments only become part of a debtor's estate if he chooses to include them"). We conclude § 407 must be read as an exclusion provision, which automatically and completely excludes social security proceeds from the bankruptcy estate, and not as an exemption provision which must be claimed by the debtor.[3] See 4 Alan N. Resnick & Henry J. Sommer, Collier on Bankruptcy ¶ 522.09[10][a] n.76 (16th ed. 2010) ("Congress amended

---

[3] We recognize it is not easy to reconcile our interpretation of § 407 with the provision in the Bankruptcy Code which states that a debtor may elect to exempt "[t]he debtor's right to receive * * * a social security benefit, unemployment compensation, or a local public assistance benefit." § 522(d)(10)(A). As discussed above, there is no way to construe § 407 in a manner which would not conflict with the Bankruptcy Code. The bankruptcy court in *In re Barron*, 85 B.R. at 606, dismissed the discrepancy, reasoning "the addition of subsection (b) to the anti-assignment statute (42 U.S.C. § 407) by the 1983 amendment, is the later expression of the will of Congress." The Sixth Circuit observed "§§ 522(b)(2)(A) and 522(d)(10) are hortatory reaffirmations of the uncontested fact that social security payments only become part of a debtor's estate if [the debtor] chooses to include them." *In re Buren*, 725 F.2d at 1086. Further, the Supreme Court has found these exemptions should not be deemed "surplusage" if the exemption provision excludes a broader category of interests than those which are excluded from the bankruptcy estate altogether. See *Patterson v. Shumate*, 504 U.S. 753, 762-63 (1992). Section 522(d)(10)(A) clearly exempts more than just social security payments from the SSA, and therefore, is not necessarily inconsistent with our interpretation of the proper application of the statutes.

42 U.S.C. § 407 to clarify that the inalienability of Social Security benefits was not repealed by the Bankruptcy Code, so that such benefits should not even become part of the bankruptcy estate.").[4]

* * *

Questions

1. The Court, in essence, decided that the Social Security Act trumps the Bankruptcy Code. Do you agree? Did the Court give satisfactory reasons?

2. The Court did not mention § 101(10A)(B), which expressly excludes Social Security benefits from the definition of "current monthly income." Although that definition was not directly pertinent to the case, do you think it provides some degree of support for the Court's conclusion?

D. EXEMPTIONS

"Exempt" property cannot be reached by creditors through judicial enforcement proceedings. Thus, such property is retained by the debtor free from the claims of creditors (except as otherwise provided by § 522(c)). Exemptions, which are available only to individual debtors, are intended to prevent a debtor from falling into financial ruin and to provide an opportunity for a "fresh start."

Exemptions are not unique to bankruptcy. Every state permits obligors, whether bankruptcy debtors or not, to hold certain property free from the claims of creditors. These state provisions are enormously variable both as to the types of property that can be exempted and the dollar values of that property. The state provisions are also, in some instances, quite archaic.

Section 522 of the Bankruptcy Code governs exemptions. Subsection (b) gives a debtor a choice of law regarding exemptions. The debtor may choose the exemptions provided by the law of his or her domicile (as well as exemptions provided by certain nonbankruptcy federal law), or the exemptions provided in § 522(d). Once property is claimed as exempt, it no longer constitutes property of the estate.

State schemes frequently benefit debtors who own real property more than those who do not, because the "homestead" exemption is often the most generous in amount and is generally available only to

_____

[4] Such a holding does not deny social security recipients the opportunity to file for relief under Chapter 13 of the Bankruptcy Code.

owners of residential real property. The federal scheme was designed with an eye toward equality for persons who do not own real property (although it got only half-way there). Section 522(d)(5) allows debtors who do not use the full amount of the homestead exemption provided by § 522(d)(1) to apply a portion of the unused amount to other property. Section 522(d)(5) also allows debtors to exempt up to a few hundred dollars of any property, without regard to whether it is otherwise exemptable. Thus, this catch-all provision (typically called the "wild card") enables debtors who do not own real property or do not use their entire homestead exemption to protect additional property from the reach of creditors. Section 104(b), which was added in 1994, requires that all of the dollar amounts in the federal exemptions (and a few other places in the Code, as we have seen) be adjusted every three years.

The choice between the federal scheme and a state scheme is not available to many debtors, however. Section 522(b)(2) allows the individual states to "opt out" of the federal scheme. In other words, states may require their residents who file bankruptcy to use only the state exemption scheme. Over two-thirds of the states have opted out of the federal scheme.

Notes and Problems

1. Many of the federal exemptions provided by § 522(d), like their state counterparts, are subject to specific dollar maximums. Section 522(a) defines "value" to mean fair market value as of the date of the petition, but it will not surprise you to learn that the parties often disagree about the value of particular items of property. If enough dollars are at stake, the bankruptcy court will hold a valuation hearing; if not, the only reasonable course is for the parties to settle their dispute. In the somewhat unrealistic setting of a casebook, values are often simply given to you. Be aware, however, that valuation is a pervasive problem in bankruptcy; we will return to it, in varying contexts, several times.

2. Consider the circumstances of the following debtors. Which assets may each exempt under the federal scheme set out in § 522(d)?

> a. Anna, who is single and has no dependents, rents an apartment. Her material possessions are comprised of the following: jewelry worth approximately $4,000 (including her great-grandmother's engagement ring); furniture for which she paid $6,000 two years ago; vacuum cleaners and other equipment worth approximately $3,000 that she uses in her housecleaning business; and an eight-year-old automobile on which she still owes $6,000. The car is

subject to a security interest held by Bank and is currently worth $7,000.

b. Bernie and his wife Beth have filed for bankruptcy jointly. They own their condominium, worth $85,000, all of the furniture in their home, a painting appraised at $50,000 (which has been in Beth's family for over a century), a ten-year-old pickup truck, which they own free and clear, and a late model sports car on which they owe $14,000. Both Bernie and Beth are retired and receive Social Security. They raise exotic birds as pets, although they sometimes sell them to local pet stores. Bernie and Beth disagree as to which exemption scheme benefits them most. What federal exemptions may they claim? May Bernie opt for the federal exemptions, while Beth uses the state exemptions?

c. Clara lives in a home, worth $200,000, that she inherited from her parents. The home is fully furnished, although the valuable antiques were inherited by Clara's brother, who is merely storing them in Clara's home while he is out of the country. Clara has insured her life for $250,000 and her brother is the beneficiary of the policy. Clara has a car that she uses to get to and from work. It is worth $9,500, and she still owes $4,000 on it. The car is subject to a security interest held by AutoBank.

d. Douglas receives monthly alimony payments from his former wife of $800 and child support payments of $400 per month, which he uses to raise his daughter. Douglas is an independent contractor and owns a truck worth $8,000 that he uses in his business; he also owns business tools worth $3,000. When Douglas obtained a loan several years ago, the bank took a security interest in his business tools. He still owes the bank $2,000. He also owns a home, worth $95,000, that is subject to a first mortgage of $80,000 and a second mortgage of $25,000.

3. The Pattersons, who are dairy farmers, want to exempt their breeding bulls under their state's $5,000 exemption for tools of the trade. May they do so? Would it affect your answer if the state also provided a separate exemption for "one cow, two goats, 10 sheep, 10 chickens, and feed sufficient to keep the specified livestock through one winter"? Compare *Matter of Patterson*, 825 F.2d 1140 (7th Cir.1987), with *Parrotte v. Sensenich (In re Parrotte)*, 22 F.3d 472 (2d Cir.1994).

4. Debtor was injured in three separate prepetition accidents. She reached settlements entitling her to more than $20,000 for each accident. How much can she claim as exempt under § 522(d)(11)(D)? See *Christo v. Yellin (In re Christo)*, 192 F.3d 36 (1st Cir.1999).

5. Section 522(d)(10)(E) exempts from a debtor's bankruptcy estate "a payment under a stock bonus, pension, profitsharing, annuity, or similar plan or contract on account of illness, disability, death, age, or length of service, to the extent reasonably necessary for the support of the debtor." For several reasons, this exemption is of less and less significance.

On the one hand, property to which the exemption might otherwise apply may be excluded from the estate in one of three ways. First, as we have seen, the Supreme Court decided in *Patterson v. Shumate* that ERISA-qualified pension plans are not property of the estate under § 541(c)(2). (Recall the trustee's argument in *Patterson* that the Court's interpretation of § 541(c)(2) rendered § 522(d)(10)(E) "superfluous.") Second, plans that qualify as state spendthrift trusts will also be excluded from the estate under § 541(c)(2). And third, the 2005 Amendments added § 541(b)(7), which excludes amounts withheld from an employee's wages for, or received as contributions to, an ERISA-qualified plan or other designated types of plans.

On the other hand, new exemptions may largely supplant § 522-(d)(10(E). The 2005 Amendments added §§ 522(b)(3)(C) and 522(d)(12), which permit the exemption of certain tax-qualified retirement plans, whether the debtor elects state or federal exemptions. In addition, § 522(n) imposes a generous cap—subject to adjustment every three years—that is not limited by reasonableness or necessity, as is § 522(d)(10(E). In addition, those amounts "may be increased if the interests of justice so require." These differences make the new exemptions much more attractive.

Section 522(d)(10)(E) is not completely gutted, however. It remains applicable to pension plans that are not tax-qualified and that do not qualify as spendthrift trusts because, as is usually the case, they are self-settled or the debtor exercises too much control.

6. Debtor received payments of $10,000 per month, under his private disability income insurance policy, for a disabling medical condition. After filing bankruptcy, he claimed that the payments were completely exempt under § 522(d)(10)(C). The trustee, on the other hand, argued that the payments were exempt only to the extent reasonably necessary for support under § 522(d)(10)(E). Which of them is correct? See *Sheehan v. Morehead (In re Morehead)*, 283 F.3d 199 (4th Cir.2002).

7. When Debtor was transferred from Texas to Florida, he sold his house in Dallas and bought another lovely home in Miami. Just over two years later, his company dissolved and Debtor lost his job. He soon had to file bankruptcy. Texas and Florida both provide for a homestead exemption with an acreage limit (not exceeded in Debtor's case), but with no limit as to value. Can Debtor keep his house, which is now worth $2.5 million?

8. When Debtor's closely-held corporation failed, the company's creditors sought to collect on his personal guarantees of the corporation's debts. Last month, Debtor filed a personal Chapter 7 proceeding and claimed

a homestead exemption in the full value of his Dallas residence. He had purchased it nearly five years before for $500,000, but it had appreciated dramatically; at the time of filing, it was worth $1,200,000. The trustee argued that, under § 522(p), Debtor could exempt only $130,000, which was the amount of appreciation attributable to the 1,215 days before filing. Is the trustee correct? See *In re Blair*, 334 B.R. 374 (Bankr. N.D.Tex.2005).

9. Debtor was CEO of a mega-corporation, based in Houston, that collapsed in spectacular fashion in the wake of revelations of securities fraud and serious accounting irregularities. Although Debtor has proclaimed his ignorance of those activities, most observers are doubtful that he was truly unaware. If Debtor files bankruptcy, will he be able to keep the beautiful $7 million home that he has owned for many years?

10. Debtor inherited her mother's IRA several years before filing bankruptcy. At the time of bankruptcy, the fund had a balance of $300,000. May Debtor exempt the inherited IRA under § 522(b)(3)(C) as "retirement funds"? See *Clark v. Ramaker*, 573 U.S. ___, 134 S. Ct. 2242 (2014).

11. In reorganization, unlike liquidation, the debtor keeps his or her property and pays creditors out of future income. What, then, is the relevance of exemptions in Chapter 13s and individual Chapter 11s?

The following case deals with a debtor who was, to say the least, quite badly behaved in the course of his bankruptcy proceeding. The trustee incurred substantial expenses as a result, and naturally sought some sort of recovery. In the process of dealing with the trustee's efforts, the Supreme Court addressed some fundamental questions about the nature and purpose of exemptions.

LAW v. SIEGEL

United States Supreme Court, 2014.
571 U.S. ___, 134 S.Ct. 1188, 188 L.Ed.2d 146.

JUSTICE SCALIA delivered the opinion for a unanimous Court.

The Bankruptcy Code provides that a debtor may exempt certain assets from the bankruptcy estate. It further provides that exempt assets generally are not liable for any expenses associated with administering the estate. In this case, we consider whether a bankruptcy court nonetheless may order that a debtor's exempt assets be used to pay administrative expenses incurred as a result of the debtor's misconduct.

I. Background

* * *

B

Petitioner, Stephen Law, filed for Chapter 7 bankruptcy in 2004, and respondent, Alfred H. Siegel, was appointed to serve as trustee. The estate's only significant asset was Law's house in Hacienda Heights, California. On a schedule filed with the Bankruptcy Court, Law valued the house at $363,348 and claimed that $75,000 of its value was covered by California's homestead exemption. He also reported that the house was subject to two voluntary liens: a note and deed of trust for $147,156.52 in favor of Washington Mutual Bank, and a second note and deed of trust for $156,929.04 in favor of "Lin's Mortgage & Associates." Law thus represented that there was no equity in the house that could be recovered for his other creditors, because the sum of the two liens exceeded the house's nonexempt value.

If Law's representations had been accurate, he presumably would have been able to retain the house, since Siegel would have had no reason to pursue its sale. Instead, a few months after Law's petition was filed, Siegel initiated an adversary proceeding alleging that the lien in favor of "Lin's Mortgage & Associates" was fraudulent. The deed of trust supporting that lien had been recorded by Law in 1999 and reflected a debt to someone named "Lili Lin." Not one but two individuals claiming to be Lili Lin ultimately responded to Siegel's complaint. One, Lili Lin of Artesia, California, was a former acquaintance of Law's who denied ever having loaned him money and described his repeated efforts to involve her in various sham transactions relating to the disputed deed of trust. *That* Lili Lin promptly entered into a stipulated judgment disclaiming any interest in the house. But that was not the end of the matter, because the second "Lili Lin" claimed to be the true beneficiary of the disputed deed of trust. Over the next five years, *this* "Lili Lin" managed—despite supposedly living in China and speaking no English—to engage in extensive and costly litigation, including several appeals, contesting the avoidance of the deed of trust and Siegel's subsequent sale of the house.

Finally, in 2009, the Bankruptcy Court entered an order concluding that "no person named Lili Lin ever made a loan to [Law] in exchange for the disputed deed of trust." The court found that "the loan was a fiction, meant to preserve [Law's] equity in his residence beyond what he was entitled to exempt" by perpetrating "a fraud on his creditors and the court." With regard to the second "Lili Lin," the court declared itself "unpersuaded that Lili Lin of China signed or approved any declaration or pleading purporting to come from her." Rather, it said, the "most plausible conclusion" was that Law himself had "authored, signed, and filed some or all of these papers." It also found that Law had submitted false evidence "in an effort to persuade the court that Lili Lin of China—rather than Lili Lin of Artesia—was the true holder of the lien on his residence." The court determined that Siegel had incurred more than $500,000 in attorney's fees overcoming Law's fraudulent misrepresentations. It therefore granted Siegel's motion to "surcharge" the entirety of Law's $75,000 homestead exemption, making those funds available to defray Siegel's attorney's fees.

The Ninth Circuit Bankruptcy Appellate Panel affirmed. * * *

The Ninth Circuit affirmed. It held that the surcharge was proper because it was "calculated to compensate the estate for the actual monetary costs imposed by the debtor's misconduct, and was warranted to protect the integrity of the bankruptcy process." We granted certiorari.

II. Analysis

A

A bankruptcy court has statutory authority to "issue any order, process, or judgment that is necessary or appropriate to carry out the provisions of" the Bankruptcy Code. § 105(a). And it may also possess "inherent power * * * to sanction 'abusive litigation practices.'" *Marrama* v. *Citizens Bank of Mass.*, 549 U.S. 365, 375-376 (2007). But in exercising those statutory and inherent powers, a bankruptcy court may not contravene specific statutory provisions. It is hornbook law that § 105(a) "does not allow the bankruptcy court to override explicit mandates of other sections of the Bankruptcy Code." 2 COLLIER ON BANKRUPTCY ¶ 105.01[2], p. 105-6 (16th ed. 2013). Section 105(a) confers authority to "carry out" the provisions of the Code, but it is quite impossible to do that by taking action that the Code prohibits. That is simply an application of the axiom that a statute's general permission to take actions of a certain type must yield to a specific prohibition found elsewhere. Courts' inherent sanctioning powers are likewise subordinate to valid statutory directives and prohibitions. We have long held that "whatever equitable powers remain in the bankruptcy courts must and can only be exercised within the confines of" the Bankruptcy Code. *Norwest Bank Worthington* v. *Ahlers*, 485 U.S. 197, 206 (1988).

Thus, the Bankruptcy Court's "surcharge" was unauthorized if it contravened a specific provision of the Code. We conclude that it did. Section 522 (by reference to California law) entitled Law to exempt $75,000 of equity in his home from the bankruptcy estate. § 522(b)(3)(A). And it made that $75,000 "not liable for payment of any administrative expense." § 522(k).[2] The reasonable attorney's fees Siegel incurred defeating the "Lili Lin" lien were indubitably an administrative expense * * * . Siegel argues that even though attorney's fees incurred responding to a debtor's fraud qualify as "administrative expenses" for purposes of determining the trustee's right to reimbursement under § 503(b), they do not so qualify for purposes of § 522(k); but he gives us no reason to depart from the "normal rule of statutory construction" that words repeated in different parts of the same statute generally have the same meaning.

The Bankruptcy Court thus violated § 522's express terms when it ordered that the $75,000 protected by Law's homestead exemption be made available to pay Siegel's attorney's fees, an administrative expense. In doing so, the court exceeded the limits of its authority under § 105(a) and its inherent powers.

B

Siegel does not dispute the premise that a bankruptcy court's § 105(a) and inherent powers may not be exercised in contravention of the Code. Instead, his main argument is that the Bankruptcy Court's surcharge did not contravene § 522. That statute, Siegel contends, "establish[es] the procedure by which a debtor may seek to claim exemptions" but "contains no directive requiring [courts] to allow [an exemption] regardless of the circumstances." Thus, he says, recognition of an equitable power in the Bankruptcy Court to deny an exemption by "surcharging" the exempt property in response to the debtor's misconduct can coexist comfortably with § 522. * * *

But * * * § 522 does not give courts discretion to grant or withhold exemptions based on whatever considerations they deem appropriate. Rather, the statute exhaustively specifies the criteria that will

---

[2] The statute's general rule that exempt assets are not liable for administrative expenses is subject to two narrow exceptions, both pertaining to the use of exempt assets to pay expenses associated with the avoidance of certain voidable transfers of exempt property. § 522(k)(1)–(2). Neither of those exceptions is relevant here.

render property exempt. Siegel insists that because § 522(b) says that the debtor "may exempt" certain property, rather than that he "*shall* be entitled" to do so, the court retains discretion to grant or deny exemptions even when the statutory criteria are met. But the subject of "may exempt" in § 522(b) is the debtor, not the court, so it is the debtor in whom the statute vests discretion. A debtor need not invoke an exemption to which the statute entitles him; but if he does, the court may not refuse to honor the exemption absent a valid statutory basis for doing so.

Moreover, § 522 sets forth a number of carefully calibrated exceptions and limitations, some of which relate to the debtor's misconduct. For example, § 522(c) makes exempt property liable for certain kinds of prepetition debts, including debts arising from tax fraud, fraud in connection with student loans, and other specified types of wrongdoing. Section 522(*o*) prevents a debtor from claiming a homestead exemption to the extent he acquired the homestead with nonexempt property in the previous 10 years "with the intent to hinder, delay, or defraud a creditor." And § 522(q) caps a debtor's homestead exemption at approximately $150,000 (but does not eliminate it entirely) where the debtor has been convicted of a felony that shows "that the filing of the case was an abuse of the provisions of " the Code, or where the debtor owes a debt arising from specified wrongful acts— such as securities fraud, civil violations of the Racketeer Influenced and Corrupt Organizations Act, or "any criminal act, intentional tort, or willful or reckless misconduct that caused serious physical injury or death to another individual in the preceding 5 years." § 522(q). The Code's meticulous—not to say mind-numbingly detailed—enumeration of exemptions and exceptions to those exemptions confirms that courts are not authorized to create additional exceptions.

Siegel points out that a handful of courts have claimed authority to disallow an exemption (or to bar a debtor from amending his schedules to claim an exemption, which is much the same thing) based on the debtor's fraudulent concealment of the asset alleged to be exempt. He suggests that those decisions reflect a general, equitable power in bankruptcy courts to deny exemptions based on a debtor's bad-faith conduct. For the reasons we have given, the Bankruptcy Code admits no such power. It is of course true that when a debtor claims a *state-created* exemption, the exemption's scope is determined by state law, which may provide that certain types of debtor misconduct warrant denial of the exemption. Some of the early decisions on which Siegel relies, * * * are instances in which federal courts applied state law to disallow state-created exemptions. But *federal law* provides no authority for bankruptcy courts to deny an exemption on a ground not specified in the Code.

C

Our decision in *Marrama* v. *Citizens Bank*, 549 U.S. 365 (2007), on which Siegel and the United States heavily rely, does not point toward a different result. The question there was whether a debtor's bad-faith conduct was a valid basis for a bankruptcy court to refuse to convert the debtor's bankruptcy from a liquidation under Chapter 7 to a reorganization under Chapter 13. Although § 706(a) of the Code gave the debtor a right to convert the case, § 706(d) "expressly conditioned" that right on the debtor's "ability to qualify as a 'debtor' under Chapter 13." 549 U. S. at 372. And § 1307(c) provided that a proceeding under Chapter 13 could be dismissed or converted to a Chapter 7 proceeding "for cause," which the Court interpreted to authorize dismissal or conversion for bad-faith conduct. In light of § 1307(c), the Court held that the debtor's bad faith could stop him from qualifying as a debtor under Chapter 13, thus preventing him from satisfying § 706(d)'s *express condition* on conversion. That holding has no relevance here, since no one suggests that Law failed to satisfy any express statutory condition on his claiming of the homestead exemption. True, the Court in *Marrama* also opined that the Bankruptcy Court's refusal to convert the case was authorized under § 105(a) and might have been authorized under the court's inherent powers. But even that dictum does not support Siegel's position. In *Marrama*, the Court reasoned that if the case had been converted to Chapter 13, § 1307(c) would have required it to be either dismissed or reconverted to Chapter 7 in light of the debtor's bad faith. Therefore, the Court suggested, even if the Bankruptcy Court's refusal to convert the case had not been expressly authorized by § 706(d), that action could have been justified as a way of providing a "prompt, rather than a delayed, ruling on [the debtor's] unmeritorious attempt to qualify" under § 1307(c). *Id.* at 376. At most, *Marrama*'s dictum suggests that in some circumstances a bankruptcy court may be authorized to dispense with futile procedural niceties in order to reach more expeditiously an end result required by the Code. *Marrama* most certainly did not endorse, even in dictum, the view that equitable considerations permit a bankruptcy court to contravene express provisions of the Code.

D

We acknowledge that our ruling forces Siegel to shoulder a heavy financial burden resulting from Law's egregious misconduct, and that it may produce inequitable results for trustees and creditors in other cases. We have recognized, however, that in crafting the provisions of § 522, "Congress balanced the difficult choices that exemption limits impose on debtors with the economic harm that exemptions visit on creditors." *Schwab* v. *Reilly*, 560 U. S. 770, 791 (2010). The same can be said of the limits imposed on recovery of administrative expenses by trustees. For the reasons we have explained, it is not for courts to alter the balance struck by the statute.

* * *

Our decision today does not denude bankruptcy courts of the essential "authority to respond to debtor misconduct with meaningful sanctions." Brief for United States as *Amicus Curiae* 17. There is ample authority to deny the dishonest debtor a discharge. See § 727-(a)(2)–(6). (That sanction lacks bite here, since by reason of a post-petition settlement between Siegel and Law's major creditor, Law has no debts left to discharge; but that will not often be the case.) In addition, Federal Rule of Bankruptcy Procedure 9011—bankruptcy's analogue to Civil Rule 11—authorizes the court to impose sanctions for bad-faith litigation conduct, which may include "an order directing payment * * * of some or all of the reasonable attorneys' fees and other expenses incurred as a direct result of the violation." Fed. Rule Bkrtcy. Proc. 9011(c)(2). The court may also possess further sanctioning authority under either § 105(a) or its inherent powers. And because it arises postpetition, a bankruptcy court's monetary sanction survives the bankruptcy case and is thereafter enforceable through the normal pro-cedures for collecting money judgments. See § 727(b). Fraudulent conduct in a bankruptcy case may also subject a debtor to criminal prosecution under 18 U.S.C. § 152, which carries a maximum penalty of five years' imprisonment.

But whatever other sanctions a bankruptcy court may impose on a dishonest debtor, it may not contravene express provisions of the Bankruptcy Code by ordering that the debtor's exempt property be used to pay debts and expenses for which that property is not liable under the Code.

The judgment of the Court of Appeals is reversed, and the case is remanded for further proceedings consistent with this opinion.

It is so ordered.

Notes and Questions

1. The maximum value to the bankruptcy estate of proving the claimed lien a fabrication was $160,000, but the trustee spent $450,000 in doing so. Does that make sense? For what reasons might the trustee and his lawyer have pursued this case once it became clear that doing so would not produce a positive monetary result?

2. Did the Court cut back on *Marrama*'s suggestion that bankruptcy courts have expansive equitable powers? If so, how is *Marrama* to be understood now?

3. *Law v. Siegel* involved an exemption claim that was indisputably legitimate. Does the Court's decision nonetheless apply when a debtor makes a fraudulent exemption claim? See Rule 4003(b)(2); *Ellmann v. Baker*, 791 F.3d 677 (6th Cir.2015).

4. *Law* may have profoundly altered the balance of power between debtors and their bankruptcy trustees. If all of the debtor's property is subject to exemptions, trustees may not be able to fund legal battles with the debtor. That creates a disincentive for trustees to pursue debtors for their bad faith misconduct, and simultaneously encourages the dishonest debtor to attempt to conceal assets; if the concealment is discovered, the debtor can simply claim the exemption.

Denial of discharge may be an appropriate sanction in many cases, although, as the Court recognized, it was not as far as Stephen Law was concerned. (In Chapter 7 of this casebook, you will encounter the statutory grounds for denial of discharge, § 727(a).) Is bankruptcy law truly impotent in dealing with as bad an actor as this debtor?

Property is exempt, and therefore removed from the estate, only if the debtor properly claims it. But what if the debtor attempts to exempt property to which he or she is not entitled? Such an effort by the debtor would provide grounds for a successful objection by the trustee. The Bankruptcy Rules, however, require any such objection to be filed within 30 days, Rule 4003(b). The Supreme Court held, in *Taylor v. Freeland & Kronz*, 503 U.S. 638, 112 S.Ct. 1644, 118 L.Ed.2d 280 (1992), that a trustee's failure to timely object to an exemption, even one without legal basis, meant that the debtor got the claimed property. Then along came the next case. It may be an understatement to suggest that the result surprised many bankruptcy specialists.

SCHWAB v. REILLY

United States Supreme Court, 2010.
130 S.Ct. 2652, 177 L.Ed.2d 234.

JUSTICE THOMAS delivered the opinion of the Court.

* * *

This case presents an opportunity for us to resolve a disagreement among the Courts of Appeals about what constitutes a claim of exemption to which an interested party must object under § 522(*l*). The issue is whether an interested party must object to a claimed exemption where, as here, the Code defines the property the debtor is authorized to exempt as an interest, the value of which may not exceed a certain dollar amount, in a particular type of asset, and the debtor's schedule of exempt property accurately describes the asset and declares the "value of [the] claimed exemption" in that asset to be an amount within the limits that the Code prescribes. Fed. Rule Bankr. Proc. Official Form 6, Schedule C (1991) (hereinafter Schedule C). We hold that, in cases such as this, an interested party need not object to an exemption claimed in this manner in order to preserve the estate's ability to recover value in the asset beyond the dollar value the debtor expressly declared exempt.

I

Respondent Nadejda Reilly filed for Chapter 7 bankruptcy when her catering business failed. She supported her petition with various schedules and statements, two of which are relevant here: Schedule B, on which the Bankruptcy Rules require debtors to list their assets (most of which become property of the estate), and Schedule C, on which the Rules require debtors to list the property they wish to reclaim as exempt. The assets Reilly listed on Schedule B included an itemized list of cooking and other kitchen equipment that she described as "business equipment," and to which she assigned an estimated market value of $10,718.

On Schedule C, Reilly claimed two exempt interests in this equipment pursuant to different sections of the Code. Reilly claimed a "tool[s] of the trade" exemption of $1,850 in the equipment under § 522(d)(6), which permits a debtor to exempt his "aggregate interest, not to exceed $1,850 in value, in any implements, professional books, or tools, of [his] trade." And she claimed a miscellaneous exemption of

$8,868 in the equipment under § 522(d)(5), which, at the time she filed for bankruptcy, permitted a debtor to take a "wildcard" exemption equal to the "debtor's aggregate interest in any property, not to exceed" $10,225 "in value."[1] The total value of these claimed exemptions ($10,718) equaled the value Reilly separately listed on Schedules B and C as the equipment's estimated market value.

Subject to exceptions not relevant here, the Federal Rules of Bankruptcy Procedure require interested parties to object to a debtor's claimed exemptions within 30 days after the conclusion of the creditors' meeting held pursuant to Rule 2003(a). See Rule 4003(b). If an interested party fails to object within the time allowed, a claimed exemption will exclude the subject property from the estate even if the exemption's value exceeds what the Code permits. See, *e.g.*, § 522(*l*); *Taylor* v. *Freeland & Kronz*, 503 U.S. 638, 642-643 (1992).

Petitioner William G. Schwab, the trustee of Reilly's bankruptcy estate, did not object to Reilly's claimed exemptions in her business equipment because the dollar value Reilly assigned each exemption fell within the limits that §§ 522(d)(5) and (6) prescribe. But because an appraisal revealed that the total market value of Reilly's business equipment could be as much as $17,200,[2] Schwab moved the Bankruptcy Court for permission to auction the equipment so Reilly could receive the $10,718 she claimed as exempt, and the estate could distribute the equipment's remaining value (approximately $6,500) to Reilly's creditors.

Reilly opposed Schwab's motion. She argued that by equating on Schedule C the total value of the exemptions she claimed in the equipment with the equipment's estimated market value, she had put Schwab and her creditors on notice that she intended to exempt the equipment's full value, even if that amount turned out to be more than the dollar amount she declared, and more than the Code allowed. Citing § 522(*l*), Reilly asserted that because her Schedule C notified Schwab of her intent to exempt the full value of her business equipment, he was obliged to object if he wished to preserve the

---

[1] * * * In 2004, pursuant to § 104(b)(2), the Judicial Conference of the United States published notice that § 522(d)(5) would impose the $975 and $9,250 ($10,225 total) limits that governed Reilly's April 2005 petition. In 2007 and 2010 the limits were again increased.

[2] Schwab concedes that the appraisal occurred before Rule 4003(b)'s 30-day window for objecting to the claimed exemptions had passed.

estate's right to retain any value in the equipment in excess of the $10,718 she estimated. Because Schwab did not object within the time prescribed by Rule 4003(b), Reilly asserted that the estate forfeited its claim to such value. Reilly further informed the Bankruptcy Court that exempting her business equipment from the estate was so important to her that she would dismiss her bankruptcy case if doing so was the only way to avoid the equipment's sale at auction.[3]

The Bankruptcy Court denied both Schwab's motion to auction the equipment and Reilly's conditional motion to dismiss her case. Schwab sought relief from the District Court, arguing that neither the Code nor Rule 4003(b) requires a trustee to object to a claimed exemption where the amount the debtor declares as the "value of [the debtor's] claimed exemption" in certain property is an amount within the limits the Code prescribes. The District Court rejected Schwab's argument, and the Court of Appeals affirmed. See *In re Reilly*, 534 F.3d 173 (3d Cir.2008).

The Court of Appeals agreed with the Bankruptcy Court that by equating on Schedule C the total value of her exemptions in her business equipment with the equipment's market value, Reilly "indicate[d] the intent" to exempt the equipment's full value. In reaching this conclusion, the Court of Appeals relied on our decision in *Taylor*:

> [W]e believe this case to be controlled by *Taylor*. Just as we perceive it was important to the *Taylor* Court that the debtor meant to exempt the full amount of the property by listing 'unknown' as both the value of the property and the value of the exemption, it is important to us that Reilly valued the business equipment at $10,718 and claimed an exemption in the same amount. Such an identical listing put Schwab on notice that Reilly intended to exempt the property fully.

* * *

---

[3] Reilly's desire to avoid the equipment's auction is understandable because the equipment, which Reilly's parents purchased for her despite their own financial difficulties, has "extraordinary sentimental value." But the sentimental value of the property cannot drive our decision in this case, because sentimental value is not a basis for construing the Bankruptcy Code. Because the Code imposes limits on exemptions, many debtors who seek to take advantage of the Code are, no doubt, put to the similarly difficult choice of parting with property of "extraordinary sentimental value."

> "[A]n unstated premise" of *Taylor* was that a debtor who exempts the entire reported value of an asset is claiming the "full amount," whatever it turns out to be.

534 F.3d at 178-179. Relying on this "unstated premise," the Court of Appeals held that Schwab's failure to object to Reilly's claimed exemptions entitled Reilly to the equivalent of an in-kind interest in her business equipment, even though the value of that exemption exceeded the amount that Reilly declared on Schedule C and the amount that the Code allowed her to withdraw from the bankruptcy estate.

As noted, the Court of Appeals' decision adds to disagreement among the Circuits about what constitutes a claim of exemption to which an interested party must object under § 522(*l*). We granted certiorari to resolve this conflict. We conclude that the Court of Appeals' approach fails to account for the text of the relevant Code provisions and misinterprets our decision in *Taylor*. Accordingly, we reverse.

II

The starting point for our analysis is the proper interpretation of Reilly's Schedule C. If we read the Schedule Reilly's way, she claimed exemptions in her business equipment that could exceed statutory limits, and thus claimed exemptions to which Schwab should have objected if he wished to enforce those limits for the benefit of the estate. If we read Schedule C Schwab's way, Reilly claimed valid exemptions to which Schwab had no duty to object. The Court of Appeals construed Schedule C Reilly's way and interpreted her claimed exemptions as improper, and therefore objectionable, even though their declared value was facially within the applicable Code limits. In so doing, the Court of Appeals held that trustees evaluating the validity of exemptions in cases like this cannot take a debtor's claim at face value, and specifically cannot rely on the fact that the amount the debtor declares as the "value of [the] claimed exemption" is within statutory limits. Instead, the trustee's duty to object turns on whether the inter-play of various schedule entries supports an inference that the debtor "intended" to exempt a dollar value different than the one she wrote on the form. This complicated view of the trustee's statutory obligation, and the strained reading of Schedule C on which it rests, is inconsistent with the Code.

The parties agree that this case is governed by § 522(*l*), which states that a Chapter 7 debtor must "file a list of property that the debtor claims as exempt under subsection (b) of this section," and further states that "[u]nless a party in interest objects, the property claimed as exempt on such list is exempt." The parties further agree that the "list" to which § 522(*l*) refers is the "list of property * * * claim[ed] as exempt" currently known as "Schedule C." The parties, like the Courts of Appeals, disagree about what information on Schedule C defines the "property claimed as exempt" for purposes of evaluating an exemption's propriety under § 522(*l*). Reilly asserts that the "property claimed as exempt" is defined by reference to all the information on Schedule C, including the estimated market value of each asset in which the debtor claims an exempt interest. Schwab and the United States as *amicus curiae* argue that the Code specifically defines the "property claimed as exempt" as an interest, the value of which may not exceed a certain dollar amount, in a particular asset, *not* as the asset itself. Accordingly, they argue that the value of the property claimed exempt, *i.e.*, the value of the debtor's exempt interest in the asset, should be judged on the value the debtor assigns the interest, *not* on the value the debtor assigns the asset. * * *

According to Reilly, Schwab was required to treat the estimate of market value * * * as part of her claimed exemption in identifying the "property claimed as exempt" under § 522(*l*). Relying on this premise, Reilly argues that where, as here, a debtor equates the total value of her claimed exemptions in a certain asset * * * with her estimate of the asset's market value * * *, she establishes the "property claimed as exempt" as the full value of the asset, whatever that turns out to be. Accordingly, Reilly argues that her Schedule C clearly put Schwab on notice that she "intended" to claim an exemption for the full value of her business equipment, and that Schwab's failure to oppose the exemption in a timely manner placed the full value of the equipment outside the estate's reach.

Schwab does not dispute that [Schedule C] apprised him that Reilly equated the total value of her claimed exemptions in the equipment ($1,850 plus $8,868) with the equipment's market value ($10,718). He simply disagrees with Reilly that this "identical listing put [him] on notice that Reilly intended to exempt the property fully," regardless whether its value exceeded the exemption limits the Code prescribes. Schwab and *amicus* United States instead contend that the Code defines the "property" Reilly claimed as exempt under § 522(*l*) as an "interest" whose value cannot exceed a certain dollar amount. Construing Reilly's Schedule C in light of this statutory definition, they contend that Reilly's claimed exemption was facially unobjectionable because the "property claimed as exempt" (*i.e.*, two interests in her business equipment worth $8,868 and $1,850, respectively) is property Reilly was clearly entitled to exclude from her estate * * *. Accordingly, Schwab and the United States conclude that Schwab had no obligation to object to the exemption in order to preserve for the estate any value in Reilly's business equipment beyond the total amount ($10,718) Reilly properly claimed as exempt.

We agree. The portion of § 522(*l*) that resolves this case is not, as Reilly asserts, the provision stating that the "property claimed as exempt on [Schedule C] is exempt" unless an interested party objects. Rather, it is the portion of § 522(*l*) that defines the target of the objection, namely, the portion that says Schwab has a duty to object to the "list of property that the debtor claims as exempt *under subsection (b)*." (Emphasis added.) That subsection, § 522(b), does *not* define the "property claimed as exempt" by reference to the estimated market value on which Reilly and the Court of Appeals rely. Section 522(b) refers only to property defined in § 522(d), which in turn lists 12 categories of property that a debtor may claim as exempt. As we have recognized, most of these categories (and all of the categories applicable to Reilly's exemptions) define the "property" a debtor may "clai[m] as exempt" as the debtor's "interest"—up to a specified dollar amount—in the assets described in the category, *not* as the assets themselves. §§ 522(d)(5)-(6); see also §§ 522(d)(1)-(4), (8). Viewing Reilly's form entries in light of this definition, we agree with Schwab and the United States that Schwab had no duty to object to the property Reilly claimed as exempt (two interests in her business equipment worth $1,850 and $8,868) because the stated value of each interest, and thus of the "property claimed as exempt," was within the limits the Code allows.[7]

Reilly's contrary view of Schwab's obligations under § 522(*l*) does not withstand scrutiny because it defines the target of a trustee's objection—the "property claimed as exempt"—based on language in Schedule C and dictionary definitions of "property" that the definition in the Code itself overrides. Although we may look to dictionaries and the Bankruptcy Rules to determine the meaning of words the Code does

---

[7] Schwab's statutory duty to object to the exemptions in this case turns solely on whether the value of the property claimed as exempt exceeds statutory limits because the parties agree that Schwab had no cause to object to Reilly's attempt to claim exemptions in the equipment at issue, or to the applicability of the Code provisions Reilly cited in support of her exemptions.

not define, the Code's definition of the "property claimed as exempt" in this case is clear. As noted above, §§ 522(d)(5) and (6) define the "property claimed as exempt" as an "interest" in Reilly's business equipment, *not* as the equipment *per se*. Sections 522(d)(5) and (6) further and plainly state that claims to exempt such interests are statutorily permissible, and thus unobjectionable, if the value of the claimed interest is below a particular dollar amount. That is the case here, and Schwab was entitled to rely upon these provisions in evaluating whether Reilly's exemptions were objectionable under the Code. The Court of Appeals' contrary holding not only fails to account for the Code's definition of the "property claimed as exempt." It also fails to account for the provisions in § 522(d) that permit debtors to exempt certain property in kind or in full regardless of value. See, *e.g.*, §§ 522(d)(9) (professionally prescribed health aids), (10)(C) (disability benefits), (7) (unmatured life insurance contracts). We decline to construe Reilly's claimed exemptions in a manner that elides the distinction between these provisions and provisions such as §§ 522(d)(5) and (6), particularly based upon an entry on Schedule C— Reilly's estimate of her equipment's market value—to which the Code does not refer in defining the "property claimed as exempt."

For all of these reasons, we conclude that Schwab was entitled to evaluate the propriety of the claimed exemptions based on three, and only three, entries on Reilly's Schedule C: the description of the business equipment in which Reilly claimed the exempt interests; the Code provisions governing the claimed exemptions; and the amounts Reilly listed in the column titled "value of claimed exemption." In reaching this conclusion, we do not render the market value estimate on Reilly's Schedule C superfluous. We simply confine the estimate to its proper role: aiding the trustee in administering the estate by helping him identify assets that may have value beyond the dollar amount the debtor claims as exempt, or whose full value may not be available for exemption because a portion of the interest is, for example, encumbered by an unavoidable lien. As noted, most assets become property of the estate upon commencement of a bankruptcy case, see § 541, and exemptions represent the debtor's attempt to reclaim those assets or, more often, certain interests in those assets, to the creditors' detriment. Accordingly, it is at least useful for a trustee to be able to compare the value of the claimed exemption (which typically represents the debtor's interest in a particular asset) with the asset's estimated market value (which belongs to the estate subject to any valid exemption) without having to consult separate schedules.

* * *

III

The Court of Appeals erred in holding that our decision in *Taylor* dictates a contrary conclusion. *Taylor* does not rest on what the debtor "meant" to exempt. Rather, *Taylor* applies to the face of a debtor's claimed exemption the Code provisions that compel reversal here.

The debtor in *Taylor*, like the debtor here, filed a schedule of exemptions with the Bankruptcy Court on which the debtor described the property subject to the claimed exemption, identified the Code provision supporting the exemption, and listed the dollar value of the exemption. Critically, however, the debtor in *Taylor* did *not*, like the debtor here, state the value of the claimed exemption as a specific dollar amount at or below the limits the Code allows. Instead, the debtor in *Taylor* listed the value of the exemption itself as "$ *unknown*" * * * .

The interested parties in *Taylor* agreed that this entry rendered the debtor's claimed exemption objectionable on its face because the exemption concerned an asset (lawsuit proceeds) that the Code did not permit the debtor to exempt beyond a specific dollar amount. Accordingly, although this case and *Taylor* both concern the consequences of a trustee's failure to object to a claimed exemption within the time specified by Rule 4003, the question arose in *Taylor* on starkly different facts. In *Taylor*, the question concerned a trustee's obligation to object to the debtor's entry of a "value claimed exempt" that was *not* plainly within the limits the Code allows. In this case, the opposite is true. The amounts Reilly listed in the Schedule C column titled "Value of Claimed Exemption" *are* facially within the limits the Code prescribes and raise no warning flags that warranted an objection.

Taylor supports this conclusion. In holding otherwise, the Court of Appeals focused on what it described as *Taylor*'s "unstated premise" that "a debtor who exempts the entire reported value of an asset is claiming the 'full amount,' whatever it turns out to be." But *Taylor* does not rest on this premise. It establishes and applies the straightforward proposition that an interested party must object to a claimed exemption if the amount the debtor lists as the "value claimed exempt" is not within statutory limits, a test the value ($ *unknown*) in *Taylor* failed, and the values ($8,868 and $1,850) in this case pass.

We adhere to this test. Doing otherwise would not only depart from *Taylor* and ignore the presumption that parties act lawfully and with knowledge of the law; it would also require us to expand the statutory definition of "property claimed as exempt" and the universe of information an interested party must consider in evaluating the validity of a claimed exemption. Even if the Code allowed such expansions, they would be ill advised. As evidenced by the differences between Reilly's Schedule C and the schedule in *Taylor*, preprinted bankruptcy schedules change over time. Basing the definition of the "property claimed as exempt," and thus an interested party's obligation to object under § 522(*l*), on inferences that party must draw from evolving forms, rather than on the facial validity of the value the debtor assigns the "property claimed as exempt" as defined by the Code, would undermine the predictability the statute is designed to provide. For all of these reasons, we take Reilly's exemptions at face value and find them unobjectionable under the Code, so the objection deadline we enforced in *Taylor* is inapplicable here.

IV

In a final effort to defend the Court of Appeals' judgment, Reilly asserts that her approach to § 522(*l*) is necessary to vindicate the Code's goal of giving debtors a fresh start, and to further its policy of discouraging trustees and creditors from sleeping on their rights. Although none of Reilly's policy arguments can overcome the Code provisions or the aspects of *Taylor* that govern this case, our decision fully accords with all of the policies she identifies. We agree that "exemptions in bankruptcy cases are part and parcel of the fundamental bankruptcy concept of a 'fresh start.' " We disagree that this policy required Schwab to object to a facially valid claim of exemption on pain of forfeiting his ability to preserve for the estate any value in Reilly's business equipment beyond the value of the interest she declared exempt. This approach threatens to convert a fresh start into a free pass.

* * *

Reilly nonetheless contends that our approach creates perverse incentives for trustees and creditors to sleep on their rights. Again, we disagree. Where a debtor intends to exempt nothing more than an interest worth a specified dollar amount in an asset that is not subject to an unlimited or in-kind exemption under the Code, our approach will ensure clear and efficient resolution of competing claims to the asset's value. If an interested party does not object to the claimed interest by the time the Rule 4003 period expires, title to the asset will remain with the estate pursuant to § 541, and the debtor will be guaranteed a payment in the dollar amount of the exemption. If an interested party timely objects, the court will rule on the objection and, if it is improper, allow the debtor to make appropriate adjustments.

Where, as here, it is important to the debtor to exempt the full market value of the asset or the asset itself, our decision will encourage the debtor to declare the value of her claimed exemption in a manner that makes the scope of the exemption clear, for example, by listing the exempt value as "full fair market value (FMV)" or "100% of FMV." Such a declaration will encourage the trustee to object promptly to the exemption if he wishes to challenge it and preserve for the estate any value in the asset beyond relevant statutory limits.[20] If the trustee fails to object, or if the trustee objects and the objection is overruled, the debtor will be entitled to exclude the full value of the asset. If the trustee objects and the objection is sustained, the debtor will be required either to forfeit the portion of the exemption that exceeds the statutory allowance, or to revise other exemptions or arrangements with her creditors to permit the exemption. See Rule 1009(a). Either result will facilitate the expeditious and final disposition of assets * * * .

For all of these reasons, the policy considerations Reilly cites support our approach. * * * Accordingly, we hold that Schwab was not required to object to Reilly's claimed exemptions in her business equipment in order to preserve the estate's right to retain any value in the equipment beyond the value of the exempt interest. In reaching this conclusion, we express no judgment on the merits of, and do not foreclose the courts from entertaining on remand, procedural or other measures that may allow Reilly to avoid auction of her business equipment.

* * *

We reverse the judgment of the Court of Appeals for the Third Circuit and remand this case for further proceedings consistent with this opinion.

It is so ordered.

---

[20] A trustee will not always file an objection. As the United States observes, Schwab did not do so in this case with respect to certain assets (perishable foodstuffs from Reilly's commercial kitchen) that could not be readily sold. See Brief for United States as *Amicus Curiae* (explaining that Schwab could have objected to Reilly's claim of a wildcard exemption for an interest in the food totaling $2,036 because this claim, combined with her wildcard claims for an interest of $8,868 in her business equipment and interests totaling $26 in her bank accounts, placed the total value of the interests she claimed exempt under the wildcard provision $975 above then-applicable limits).

Notes and Questions

1.   The Court acknowledged that the trustee had the equipment appraised before the 30-day period expired and, therefore, knew that the value exceeded $10,718. Why was the trustee's failure to act on that information, in a timely manner, not a factor in the Court's decision? Should it have been?

2.   The majority made much of the distinction between "interest" and "property," as those words are used in § 522, and concluded that the words used on the debtor's Schedule C were inconsistent with the Code. The Court's solution for a debtor like Reilly was to use language like "100% FMV" on the schedule. Does the Court's own suggestion comport with the statutory language?

3.   In a dissenting opinion joined by CHIEF JUSTICE ROBERTS and JUSTICE BREYER, JUSTICE GINSBURG argued that the Court's decision "drastically reduce[d] Rule 4003's governance" and "expose[d] debtors to protracted uncertainty concerning their right to retain exempt property." Setting aside the interesting—perhaps even strange—line-up of judicial bedfellows in this case, later cases suggest the dissent's prescience as far as uncertainty is concerned.

One positive result of *Schwab*, supposedly, was the majority's tutorial regarding how debtors should express an exemption claim when they want to claim the full value of the asset or the asset itself—namely, by listing the exemption as "full fair market value" or "100% of FMV." Not unexpectedly, competent debtors' attorneys began doing just that. This supposed safe-harbor has not turned out to be safe after all, however, because courts (some of them from the same district, no less) have divided on the efficacy of such an exemption claim. Compare *In re Moore*, 442 B.R. 865 (Bankr. N.D.Tex.2010) (rejecting the trustee's argument that debtors, by claiming "100% FMV," sought "to game the system"; rather "[t]he Supreme Court offered direction to debtors seeking to force the issue of whether exemption of an interest in an asset covered the entire asset" and these debtors "have here done no more than follow the Court's direction"), with *In re Salazar*, 449 B.R. 890 (Bankr. N.D.Tex.2011) (holding that *Schwab* makes an exemption claim of "100% of FMV" valid only when a timely objection is *not* filed; a filed objection will be sustained "[u]nless the debtor cures the exemption claim by amending it to place it within the statutory limit.")

Additional ramifications of *Schwab* are illustrated by *Gebhart v. Gaughan (In re Gebhart)*, 621 F.3d 1206 (9th Cir.2010), which was decided three months after *Schwab*. In *Gebhart*, Debtor claimed a homestead exemption in the amount of the equity in his home, which was less than the maximum amount of the applicable exemption. The trustee filed no objection. Debtor received a discharge, continued making payments to the mortgagee, and even refinanced the mortgage. The bankruptcy estate was not closed, however, and the trustee—three years later—sought to sell the house in order to realize the amount by which the property had appreciated since the filing of the case. The court relied on *Schwab* in ruling for the trustee, finding *Schwab*'s mandate "clear": "[T]he fact that the value of the claimed exemption plus the amount of the encumbrances on the debtor's residence was * * * equal to the market value of the residence at the time of filing the petition did *not* remove the entire asset from the estate." *Id.* at 1210. The court was not unaware of the implications of its decision:

> The debtors argue that the result we reach today will lead to uncertainty about the status of exempt property and abuses by trustees. The facts * * * suggest that some of these concerns are legitimate. Gebhart remained in his home for five years after filing for bankruptcy, paying his mortgage and believing that his bankruptcy was finished when he received his discharge. Gebhart may have been mistaken in this belief, but his misapprehension was shared by his mortgage lender, which refinanced his home, apparently unaware of any claims on the property by the Trustee. A Chapter 7 debtor will not be certain about the status of a homestead property until the case is closed (something that may not happen for several years after bankruptcy filing) or the trustee abandons the property.

Id. at 1211-12. What can debtors' attorneys do to deal with the risk that a trustee will sit back and wait for property to appreciate?

Note on Choice of Law

Although the debtor may—or must—choose exemptions available under state law, an additional question may be which state's law is applicable. This becomes an issue when the debtor has moved shortly before filing bankruptcy. Before 2005, the Code provided that the applicable state was the one in which the debtor was domiciled for 180 days prepetition, or for the longer portion of the 180-day period—*i.e.*, 91 days. Debtors who had moved within 90 days of bankruptcy were required by that rule to choose exemptions under the laws of a state in which they no longer resided and in which they may no longer have owned property. This raised questions about the extraterritorial application of state exemptions laws. In *In re Drenttel*, 403 F.3d 611 (8th Cir.2005), for example, the debtors moved from Minnesota to Arizona less than 90 days before they filed bankruptcy—in Minnesota, as the venue provisions required. They sought to claim their Arizona homestead, worth $181,000, exempt under the Minnesota homestead exemption, which had a value limit of $200,000. Because the Minnesota statute was silent about its extraterritorial effect, the Eighth Circuit approved the exemption.

Other debtors were not so lucky. When state exemptions statutes expressly limited their application to in-state property (or when the state courts had so interpreted the statutes) and the state had opted out, a debtor would be left with no exemption at all. See, e.g., *In re Ginther*, 282 B.R. 16 (Bankr. D.Kan.2002).

Congress was concerned that debtors might engage in so-called "exemption planning" by moving to a state with generous exemptions, waiting 91 days, and then filing bankruptcy. Thus, new language, now found in § 522(a)(3), was added to the Code in 2005. The new rules bring some impressive complexity. Now, debtors cannot claim exemptions under the law of the state to which they have moved unless they have lived there for the entire 730 days—two years—before filing, and not just for the longer portion of that period. If a debtor was not domiciled in the new state for that entire period, then the applicable exemptions law is that of the state in which the debtor was domiciled during the 180-day period preceding that two-year period—that is, the six-month period ending two years before bankruptcy. If the debtor was domiciled in more than one state during that six-month period, then the applicable state is the one in which the debtor was domiciled for the greater portion of that six-month period.

Interestingly, although these rules were designed to curb exemption planning, the debtor's actual motives in moving are irrelevant under the statute's language.

The new rules also address the problem, discussed above, of a debtor who is left with no exemptions at all. A debtor caught in such a situation is now able to claim the federal exemptions. In *In re West*, 352 B.R. 905 (Bankr. M.D.Fla.2006), for example, the debtor moved from Indiana to Florida before filing bankruptcy. He could not use the Florida exemptions because he had not resided there for 730 days, and he could not use the Indiana exemptions because they were available only to debtors residing there on the date of the bankruptcy filing. Thus, the court held that the last sentence of § 522(b)(3) permitted the debtor to claim the federal exemptions.

Problems

1. Because Debtor moved from Florida to Texas less than two years before filing bankruptcy, Florida was the state whose law was applicable under § 522(b)(3)(A). Florida's opt-out statute provides as follows:

> In accordance with the provisions of [§ 522(b)], residents of this state shall not be entitled to the federal exemptions provided in [§ 522(d)]. Nothing herein shall affect the exemptions given to residents of this state by the State Constitution and the Florida Statutes.

May Debtor choose the federal exemptions, if he wishes to do so? See *Camp v. Ingalls (In re Camp)*, 631 F.3d 757 (5th Cir. 2011).

2. Assume that the state from which Debtor moved, shortly before filing bankruptcy, had opted out and, in addition, that its exemptions statute expressly provides that the listed exemptions are only available to "residents."

Can Debtor nonetheless claim the state exemptions? See *In re Garrett*, 435 B.R. 434 (Bankr. S.D.Tex.2010).

3. A number of states have enacted exemptions statutes that apply only to debtors in bankruptcy. Are such statutes inconsistent with the Code's provisions regarding the distribution of assets and, therefore, unconstitutional under the Supremacy Clause? Compare *Kanter v. Moneymaker (In re Kanter)*, 505 F.2d 228 (9th Cir.1974) (California), with *Sheehan v. Peveich (In re Peveich)*, 574 F.3d 248 (4th Cir.2009) (West Virginia). Are such statutes unconstitutional because inconsistent with the uniformity requirement of the Bankruptcy Clause (art. I, § 8, cl. 4)? Compare *Richardson v. Schafer (In re Schafer)*, 2011 WL 650545 (6th Cir.BAP) (Michigan), with *Sticka v. Applebaum (In re Applebaum)*, 422 B.R. 684 (9th Cir.BAP 2009) (California).

E. AUTOMATIC STAY

1. SCOPE OF THE STAY

Section 362 of the Code provides for an "automatic stay" that suspends nearly all activities of almost all creditors regarding any financial obligations of the debtor. The stay is a self-executing injunction; it operates at the moment a voluntary or involuntary petition is filed, without the need for notice or for a formal court order. Any action a creditor takes in violation of the automatic stay is ineffective, even though the creditor is unaware of the bankruptcy filing and, thus, of the stay's existence.

The stay is primarily a protection for debtors, as the legislative history to the 1978 Code explained:

> The automatic stay is one of the fundamental debtor protections provided by the bankruptcy laws. It gives the debtor a breathing spell from his creditors. It stops all collection efforts, all harassment, and all foreclosure actions. It permits the debtor to attempt a repayment or reorganization plan, or simply to be relieved of the financial pressures that drove him into bankruptcy.

HR. Rep. No. 95-595 at 340, *reprinted in* 1978 U.S.C.C.A.N. at 54-55. Thus, the stay provides an opportunity to assess the debtor's financial situation and to prepare a reorganization or distribution plan without interference or harassment from creditors. The stay also fixes the relationship of each creditor to the debtor, as of the date of the filing of the bankruptcy petition. In this sense, the stay protects creditors as well as the debtor, by preventing individual creditors from pursuing their own remedies at the expense of other creditors.

Exceptions to the stay are listed in § 362(b) and include activities such as collection of alimony or child support, and continuation of a criminal proceeding against the debtor. When one of the exceptions applies, the affected creditor may continue otherwise-prohibited activity without first obtaining relief from the stay, just as if the debtor had never filed for bankruptcy. The list of exceptions in subsection (b) seems ever-expanding, as special interests catch the ear of their representatives in Congress and as Congress seeks to codify evolving policy preferences. As to the former, see §§ 362(b)(22) and (23). As to the latter, see §§ 362(b)(20) and (d)(4)(B), which attempt to curb abusive serial filings.

The automatic stay does not destroy creditors' claims; it merely suspends them. Secured creditors do not lose their right to collect against their collateral even after discharge of the debtor's obligations. In addition, these creditors can obtain relief from the stay if their claim against the property is jeopardized.

Most courts regard the stay as a "shield" that protects debtors from creditor pressure during a bankruptcy proceeding or from a creditors' collection efforts. For example, a debtor whose sole asset is an overencumbered residence can file bankruptcy the day before a fore-closure proceeding is scheduled, in order to prevent dispossession. Debtors can use the stay even more aggressively, however, as Professor Keating noted:

> In a number of important and recurring cases courts regularly are allowing both individual and corporate debtors to use the stay offensively as a means of extracting a future benefit from a nondebtor party to whom the debtor owes a prepetition debt. The dangers of this trend are subtle but significant. With an increase in use of the stay as a weapon will come a decrease in the willingness of nondebtor parties to extend credit to financially troubled corporations and individuals.

Daniel Keating, *Offensive Uses of the Automatic Stay*, 45 VAND. L. REV. 71, 73 (1991) (footnote omitted). You should be alert in studying the materials that follow for so-called "offensive" or "strategic" uses of the automatic stay. Does such an "offensive" use of bankruptcy constitute a bad faith filing? (Recall *Phoenix Piccadilly* and the debate over the good faith filing requirement in Chapter 11.)

Problems

1. Determine whether the following actions, taken postpetition, violate the automatic stay of § 362(a):

  a. Prior to bankruptcy, Debtor obtained a $15,000 loan from Bank, at which Debtor maintains a checking account. Since Debtor's loan is in default, Bank applies the $2,500 balance in Debtor's account to the amount Debtor owes Bank on the loan.

  b. A representative of Charge Card Company to which Debtor owes $750, calls Debtor at work and suggests that Debtor get a cash advance from another credit card in order to pay the debt to Charge Card Company.

  c. Secured Creditor repossesses Debtor's car after the trustee determines that the car is of no value to the estate and abandons it. (See § 554.)

  d. Local Electric shuts off Debtor's power because Debtor failed to pay for service used in the three months before the petition was filed. Would a different result be reached as to electric power used postpetition? See § 366.

  e. An account creditor sends Debtor a very polite letter stating the amount of the debt and that "prompt payment would be very much appreciated."

  f. An accident victim attempts to collect from Debtor's insurance company on a prepetition judgment against Debtor, arising from an automobile accident that occurred two years before bankruptcy.

  g. Lender attempts to collect payment from Debtor's parents, who are guarantors on the loan. See §§ 1201 and 1301.

2. John and Jill Smith filed Chapter 7. Eleven days later, Southwest Auto Finance, which held a security interest in the Smiths' two cars, repossessed one of them. Southwest had no knowledge of the Smiths' bankruptcy petition at the time of the repossession, but still refused to return the car even after it learned the facts from the Smiths' attorney. Has Southwest violated the automatic stay? If so, can the Smiths recover damages and attorney's fees under § 362(k)?

3. Debtor, an information services company that provided internet access to customers across the world, depended upon dedicated internet services it purchased from Creditor. For more than a year, the parties had been engaged in a sometimes-acrimonious dispute regarding the amount Debtor owed Creditor. Debtor had often threatened to file bankruptcy and Creditor

frequently countered with threats to terminate service. Debtor ultimately did file bankruptcy and its attorney so informed Creditor, sending a letter written on law firm letterhead that including a filing number. Creditor decided it was merely another threat and terminated Debtor's service. As a result, Debtor's business was brought to a halt until it could locate a new supplier. Can Debtor recover both compensatory and punitive damages? If so, what is the source of the court's authority to enter such an order? See *In re WVF Acquisition, LLC*, 420 B.R. 902 (Bankr. S.D.Fla.2009).

4. Sportfame, a sporting goods retailer, fell behind on payments to its primary supplier, Wilson Sporting Goods. Consequently, Wilson ceased shipping inventory to Sportfame. After filing for reorganization under Chapter 11, Sportfame attempted to have inventory shipments resumed by offering to pay cash for all goods shipped. Wilson refused to supply any additional inventory until Sportfame brought its accounts current or made arrangements to pay 100% of the arrearage. Has Wilson violated the automatic stay? See *Sportfame of Ohio, Inc. v. Wilson Sporting Goods Co. (In re Sportfame of Ohio, Inc.)*, 40 B.R. 47 (Bankr. N.D.Ohio 1984).

5. Debtor filed a petition in bankruptcy, listing on the schedules filed with the bankruptcy court two debts owed to Creditor. One of the debts was a $4,000 car loan secured by Debtor's car; the other was a $2,500 unsecured loan. Debtor sought to reaffirm the car loan so that she could retain possession of the car. Creditor refused to allow Debtor to reaffirm the car loan without also reaffirming the unsecured loan. Has Creditor violated the automatic stay? What if Creditor threatened repossession of the car if Debtor did not reaffirm the unsecured debt? See *Jamo v. Katahdin Federal Credit Union (In re Jamo)*, 283 F.3d 392 (1st Cir.2002).

6. When Debtor defaulted on her obligations under a car lease, Creditor obtained a judgment and began garnishment of Debtor's wages. Under the garnishment statute, creditors only had to deliver the proper paperwork to the sheriff one time; after that, the sheriff would collect from the debtor's employer and send monthly checks to the creditor until the appropriate amount of money had been recovered. Debtor filed bankruptcy and her attorney sent a letter to Creditor asking that the postpetition garnishment be discontinued. Creditor responded that Debtor had to make that request directly to the sheriff. Has Creditor violated the stay? If so, was the violation willful? See *Sucre v. MIC Leasing Corp. (In re Sucre)*, 226 B.R. 340 (Bankr. S.D.N.Y.1998).

7. Sears sent a letter to Debtor's attorney offering to give Debtor a modest amount of postpetition credit if he chose to reaffirm the debt. Sears sent a copy of the letter to Debtor, marked "for information purposes only." Has Sears violated the stay? See *Matter of Duke*, 79 F.3d 43 (7th Cir.1996).

8. Prepetition, Debtor purchased a car from Creditor on which a "PayTeck" device had been installed. The device requires the driver to punch in a new code every 30 days, in order to start the car. Each month's code is

provided by Creditor upon receipt of that month's payment. After Debtor fell behind on her payments and filed bankruptcy, she repeatedly had trouble with the codes provided to her, and even the correct codes worked for less than 30 days. Has Creditor violated the automatic stay? If so, was the violation willful if, as Creditor argued, any incorrect codes were the result of accident or oversight? See *Hampton v. Yam's Choice Plus Autos, Inc. (In re Hampton)*, 319 B.R. 163 (Bankr. E.D. Ark.2005).

9. Debtor, whose business was the management of a commercial office building, owed Bank $4 million on a note secured by a mortgage on the building. Following a default, the parties negotiated a modification agreement under which Bank extended the due date on the note and Debtor agreed that it would not object to any motion to lift stay filed by Bank in any subsequent bankruptcy proceeding. Debtor filed a Chapter 11 petition a year later and Bank sought relief from the stay. Is Debtor's agreement not to contest such a motion enforceable? Does it matter what other creditors may think? See *In re Atrium High Point Ltd. Partnership*, 189 B.R. 599 (Bankr. M.D.N.C.1995).

2. EXCEPTIONS TO THE STAY

The automatic stay appears to bar *any* action of *any* character, by *any* party, against the debtor, the debtor's property, or property of the estate. As with many rules, however, the mandate of § 362(a)'s automatic stay has exceptions, set out in § 362(b). The subsections of § 362 strike a balance between aiding the debtor's rehabilitation and allowing socially desirable actions against the debtor to proceed—or, at least, that is the theory. In fact, each successive set of amendments may reflect nothing more lofty than the pressure of interest groups on willing legislators.

Notes and Problems

1. Determine whether the following actions, taken postpetition, violate the automatic stay under § 362(a) and, if they do, whether they are excepted under § 362(b):

a. The Supreme Court of Debtor's state initiates disbarment proceedings against Debtor.

b. Manufacturing Co. files a financing statement two days after Debtor, Inc.'s bankruptcy filing, in order to perfect its security interest in a machine Debtor, Inc. bought the week before.

c. The state tax department sends Debtor a notice of property tax due on Debtor's car.

d. Debtor's ex-wife files a garnishment proceeding to collect on a judgment, obtained prepetition, for unpaid child support. (Does it matter whether Debtor filed under Chapter 7 or under Chapter 13?)

2. After Debtor filed a bankruptcy petition, his ex-wife filed a criminal complaint with the local district attorney regarding unpaid prepetition child support, and the district attorney initiated criminal proceedings. Is the district attorney's action excepted from the automatic stay under § 362(b)(1)? Does the answer depend on whether payment is a complete defense under the criminal statute?

In cases like this, arguably, the criminal law is being used for the purpose of collecting debts. The applicability of § 362(b)(1), however, does not depend upon whether collection is at the heart of the criminal proceeding. See *Gruntz v. County of Los Angeles*, 202 F.3d 1074 (9th Cir.2000) (en banc). Debtor-defendants have a fall-back position, however—§ 105, which is the "all writs" provision in Code. The argument is that § 362(b)(1) simply prevents an injunction from arising automatically upon the filing of the case; nevertheless, an injunction may issue under § 105 in an appropriate case, which is determined on a case-by-case basis. Although this argument finds support in the legislative history, requests for injunctive relief under § 105 are rarely granted in criminal cases.

The Supreme Court addressed whether state criminal actions may be stayed by federal injunction in *Younger v. Harris*, 401 U.S. 37, 91 S.Ct. 746, 27 L.Ed.2d 669 (1971). The *Younger* doctrine generally limits federal injunctive relief against state criminal prosecutions to rare cases in which a threat of great and immediate irreparable injury exists that is related to "federally protected rights" and that "cannot be eliminated by * * * defense in a single criminal prosecution." 401 U.S. at 46. The usual prerequisites for a finding of irreparable harm are "bad faith or harassment" in the prosecution. *Id*. at 50.

In determining whether bad faith exists, most courts rely on the "principal motivation test," which looks to the creditor's main reason for pursuing the criminal action, regardless of whether the action was initiated in good faith. Courts applying the principal motivation test attempt to determine whether a state criminal prosecution is being used to "vindicate the public good" or whether it is "to collect the debt for one of its residents." *Brinkman v. City of Edina (In re Brinkman)*, 123 B.R. 318, 322 (Bankr. D.Minn.1991). The problem with this approach is, of course, that a prosecution motivated by debt collection is not necessarily brought in bad faith, which may explain why the approach has enjoyed more success in the bankruptcy courts than it has at the appellate level.

We first saw § 105 in connection with *Marrama*, and we will see it repeatedly as the course progresses. Be alert to the various contexts in which it is applied.

One of the most important stay exceptions is found in § 362(b)(4). It permits a "governmental unit" to enforce its "police and regulatory power," including the enforcement of a non-money judgment obtained in such an action. This exception is intended to protect the health, safety and welfare of the public. It permits governmental actions undertaken to prevent or stop violation of laws regulating fraud, environmental protection, consumer protection, safety, and the like, as well as actions to fix damages for violations of such laws. In such cases, the government is not functioning as a creditor; rather, it is carrying out its appropriate regulatory duties.

The exception does not apply when the governmental unit is functioning as a creditor. The following case addresses § 362(b)(4) and the "exception to the exception" prohibiting governmental efforts to enforce a "money judgment." As the case explains, § 362(b)(4) is the product of a 1998 amendment that combined former subsections (b)(4) and (b)(5). The remaining subsections of § 362(b) were not renumbered.

SEC v. BRENNAN

United States Court of Appeals, Second Circuit, 2000.
230 F.3d 65.

CABRANES, Circuit Judge.

This appeal requires us to interpret the automatic stay provision of the Bankruptcy Code, an exception to that provision, and an exception to that exception. Specifically, the question presented, as a matter of first impression, is whether an order obtained by the Securities and Exchange Commission * * * requiring defendant Robert E. Brennan, a debtor in bankruptcy, to repatriate the assets of an offshore asset protection trust violates the automatic stay provision. The SEC argues that the order fits within an exception to the automatic stay provision for any "action or proceeding by a governmental unit * * * to enforce such governmental unit's * * * police and regulatory power." § 362(b)(4). Brennan contends that the order violates the automatic stay provision because it fits within an exception to this "governmental unit" exception for any effort to enforce a money judgment. * * *

I.

[The SEC brought suit in New York against Brennan for violations of federal securities laws. During the pendency of the proceedings, Brennan established an offshore asset protection trust—the Cardinal Trust—in Gibraltar and funded it with $5 million in securities.

Thereafter, in July 1995, the district court entered judgment against Brennan, finding him liable in fraud and ordering him to disgorge $75 million in illegal profits. Brennan filed Chapter 11 in New Jersey the following month, and valued his interest in the trust at $0.

The bankruptcy court appointed a trustee. The trustee and the SEC believed that Brennan controlled the Cardinal Trust because he enjoyed a "lavish, globetrotting lifestyle" despite the fact that his assets were tied up in bankruptcy. Thus, the trustee and the SEC, working together, made several attempts to force Brennan to repatriate the Cardinal Trust's assets. During these efforts the Trust was moved, first to Mauritius and then to Nevis, pursuant to a "flight clause." The clause required relocation upon the occurrence of efforts anywhere in the world to control trust assets or to restrict free disposal of trust property.

The trustee first sought a bankruptcy court order requiring repatriation, but the court denied the application. The trustee then brought suit in Nevis, but the action was dismissed for failure to state a claim under Nevis law. Finally, the SEC moved the district court in New York for an order to show cause why Brennan should not be held in contempt of the 1995 disgorgement judgment, and for repatriation of the Trust. The SEC asserted that it was not seeking to collect; rather, it was seeking to preserve the assets for the benefit of all bankruptcy claimants, subject to the orders of the bankruptcy court. The district court issued the Repatriation Order and Brennan appealed.]

II.

On appeal, Brennan challenges the [Repatriation Order] * * * because it violates § 362(a) * * * . We agree * * * .

"The general policy behind [§ 362(a)] is to grant complete, immediate, albeit temporary relief to the debtor from creditors, and also to prevent dissipation of the debtor's assets before orderly distribution to creditors can be effected." *Penn Terra Ltd. v. Department of Envtl. Resources*, 733 F.2d 267, 271 (3d Cir.1984). In addition, the automatic stay provision is intended "to allow the bankruptcy court to centralize all disputes concerning property of the debtor's estate so that reorganization can proceed efficiently, unimpeded by uncoordinated proceedings in other arenas." *In re United States Lines, Inc.*, 197 F.3d 631, 640 (2d Cir.1999) (internal quotation marks omitted).

Section 362(b) establishes several exceptions to the automatic stay. One of these exceptions, set forth in subsection (b)(4), is at the heart of the dispute in this case. * * * [T]he purpose of this exception is to prevent a debtor from "frustrating necessary governmental functions by seeking refuge in bankruptcy court." *City of New York v. Exxon Corp.*, 932 F.2d 1020, 1024 (2d Cir.1991) (internal quotation marks omitted). Thus, "where a governmental unit is suing a debtor to prevent or stop violation of fraud, environmental protection, consumer protection, safety, or similar police or regulatory laws, or attempting to fix damages for violation of such a law, the action or proceeding is not stayed under the automatic stay." H.R. Rep. No. 95-595, at 343.

In the present case, Brennan concedes that the SEC obtained the Repatriation Order in a proceeding to enforce its "police and regulatory power." Nevertheless, Brennan argues that the "governmental unit" exception of § 362(b)(4) is inapplicable because the Repatriation Order is part of an effort by the SEC to enforce a money judgment—namely, the July 1995 Judgment * * * .

Although the question is a close one, we agree with Brennan that the Repatriation Order fits within the exception to the governmental unit exception and that the order therefore violates the automatic stay. It is well established that the governmental unit exception of § 362(b)(4) permits the *entry* of a money judgment against a debtor so long as the proceeding in which such a judgment is entered is one to enforce the governmental unit's police or regulatory power. *See, e.g., EEOC v. Rath Packing Co.*, 787 F.2d 318, 326-27 (8th Cir.1986); *Penn Terra*, 733 F.2d at 275. However, these and other cases hold that *anything beyond the mere entry of a money judgment* against a debtor is prohibited by the automatic stay. *See, e.g., EEOC v. McLean Trucking Co.*, 834 F.2d 398, 402 (4th Cir.1987) (holding that the Equal Employment Opportunity Commission's suit was "exempt from the automatic stay *until its prayer for monetary relief is reduced to judgment.*" (emphasis added); *NLRB v. Edward Cooper Painting, Inc.*, 804 F.2d 934, 942-43 (6th Cir.1986) ("Once proceedings are excepted from the stay by section 362(b)(4), courts have allowed governmental units to fix the amount of penalties, *up to and including entry of a money judgment.*" (Emphasis added.)

* * *

It is not, as the dissent suggests, out of mere obeisance to each other's "side remarks," that various circuits have insisted that the line between "police or regulatory power" on the one hand, and "enforcement of a * * * money judgment" on the other, be drawn at entry of judgment. Rather, courts have drawn the line there because that is the most logical place for it. When the government seeks to impose financial liability on a party, it is plainly acting in its police or regulatory capacity—it is attempting to curb certain behavior (such as defrauding investors, or polluting groundwater) by making the behavior that much more expensive. * * * However, once liability is fixed and a money judgment has been entered, the government necessarily acts only to vindicate its own interest in collecting its judgment. Except in an indirect and attenuated manner, it is no longer attempting to deter wrongful conduct. It is therefore no longer acting in its "police or regulatory" capacity, and the exception to the exception does not apply.[3]

In the present case, it is plain that the District Court went beyond the mere entry of a money judgment in entering the Repatriation Order since the money judgment obtained by the SEC against Brennan was entered in July 1995. To be sure, the SEC asserts that it is not seeking to collect the July 1995 Judgment, but only to prevent Brennan from concealing or dissipating the assets of the Cardinal Trust. In addition, the SEC acknowledges that it may be entitled to no more than its pro rata share of any assets obtained. However, as the *Rath Packing* Court held, the "exception to the exception" for enforcement of a money judgment does not depend on a governmental unit's profession of good faith. Moreover, notwithstanding the SEC's assertions to the contrary, the record makes clear that the SEC *is* seeking repatriation of the Cardinal Trust for the purposes of enforcing the July 1995 Judgment—even if it does not claim an exclusive entitlement to the trust assets. * * *

---

[3] The dissent argues that "enforcement of a * * * money judgment" within the meaning of § 362(b)(4) occurs "when the government's action with respect to the judgment would have the effect of benefitting itself at the expense of other creditors." But the exception to the exception cannot be interpreted as being animated *solely* by a concern with the government benefitting itself at others' expense. If § 362(b)(4) were so interpreted, the government could collect on its judgments in any court of competent jurisdiction so long as it bound itself *ex ante* to distribute the proceeds thus collected to other creditors on a *pro rata* basis * * * . But such an arrangement, which follows from the dissent's approach to § 362, would badly undermine one of the key purposes of that provision—namely, the centralization of adjudication so that "reorganization can proceed efficiently, unimpeded by uncoordinated proceedings in other arenas." *In re United States Lines, Inc.*, 197 F.3d at 640. Moreover, such an arrangement would confer on the government a significant "benefit[]" that other creditors do not and should not have—a right to shop for a forum, a right to chose *where* it will seek to collect on its judgment.

We are unpersuaded by the SEC's arguments against application of the "exception to the exception" for enforcement of money judgments in this case. First, the SEC places heavy reliance on the amendments to the governmental unit exception enacted by Congress in 1998. Prior to those amendments, the governmental unit exception was embodied in two subsections of § 362(b), which provided that the filing of a bankruptcy petition does not operate as a stay:

> (4) under subsection (a)(1) of this section, of the commencement or continuation of an action or proceeding by a governmental unit to enforce such governmental unit's police or regulatory power;

> (5) under subsection (a)(2) of this section, of the enforcement of a judgment, other than a money judgment, obtained in an action or proceeding by a governmental unit to enforce such governmental unit's police or regulatory power * * * .

The Chemical Weapons Convention Implementation Act of 1998, part of the Omnibus Consolidated Emergency Supplemental Appropriations Act of 1999, amended the exception by, *inter alia*, combining subsections (b)(4) and (b)(5) into one subsection (b)(4) and expanding the scope of the exception to cover proceedings "to obtain possession of property of the estate * * * or to exercise control over property of the estate" otherwise stayed by § 362(a)(3).

The SEC's argument that these amendments are material to this case is belied by the fact that Congress maintained the "exception to the exception" for enforcement of money judgments. The SEC would have us interpret the expansion of the governmental unit exception to cover proceedings otherwise stayed by § 362(a)(3) to mean that a governmental unit has "unqualified" authority to seek custody of estate property outside the bankruptcy proceedings. However, this proposed "exception to the exception to the exception" would virtually swallow whole the exception to the exception for enforcement of money judgments. Moreover, it would run contrary to the limited legislative history of the 1998 amendments, which provides in relevant part that the amendments "should not be read to expand the exceptions to the automatic stay to cases where governmental units are merely seeking to exercise control of a debtor's property to satisfy debt." 143 Cong. Rec. E2305 (1998) (statement of Rep. Conyers, Ranking Member of the Judiciary Committee); *cf.* 3 COLLIER ON BANKRUPTCY § 362.05[5][b], at 362-60 to 61 (5th ed. 2000) ("The addition of the introductory references to subsection (a)(3) * * * may have affected the operation of the second phrase, derived from former subsection (b)(5). Thus, acts to obtain possession or exercise control over property of [an] estate * * * would not be stayed. This expansion of the exception to stay should be read, however, * * * so that the expansion covers only the enforcement of *nonmoney* judgments. This would be consistent with the purpose of the amendment * * * and with the limited legislative history of the amendment." (Emphasis added).

Second, the SEC argues that * * * while the purpose of the "exception to the exception" for money judgments is to prevent the Government from gaining "preferential treatment" in bankruptcy proceedings "to the detriment of all other creditors," S. Rep. No. 95-989, at 52 (1978); *accord* H.R. Rep. No. 95-595, at 343 (1978), its actions in seeking the Repatriation Order are intended to, and will, benefit all other creditors. However, nothing in the legislative history suggests, let alone shows, that the "preferential treatment" rationale was Congress's sole purpose in enacting the "exception to the exception." To the contrary, the "exception to the exception" is also designed to reinforce the scheme of priorities set forth in § 507 and to preserve the benefits to a debtor of discharge, both of which could be undermined by allowing governmental units to initiate proceedings like the present one. Moreover, at bottom, the SEC's argument that it is not seeking "preferential treatment" depends on its assertion that it is not seeking to collect the July 1995 Judgment. As we stated above, however, the "exception to the exception" for enforcement of a money judgment does not depend on a governmental unit's profession of good faith.

In the final analysis, the policies behind § 362 as a whole weigh strongly in favor of applying the automatic stay in these circumstances. * * * Section 362(b)(4) carves out a limited exception to these policies, in order to prevent a debtor from "frustrating necessary governmental functions by seeking refuge in bankruptcy court." *Exxon Corp.*, 932 F.2d at 1024 (internal quotation marks omitted). Here, however, it is undisputed that the type of relief sought by the SEC is available through the Bankruptcy Court; indeed, the bankruptcy trustee (with the support of the SEC) tried, but failed, to obtain an order from the Bankruptcy Court requiring repatriation of the Cardinal Trust in 1998. Thus, it is hard, if not impossible, to argue that Brennan is "seeking refuge in bankruptcy court." * * *

III.

* * * [I]f the bankruptcy trustee and its ally, the SEC, were aggrieved by the Bankruptcy Court's ruling on the * * * application for

repatriation, their proper recourse was to appeal that ruling to the United States District Court for the District of New Jersey, not to bring a new motion for the same relief in the United States District Court for the Southern District of New York.

The order of the District Court is vacated.

CALABRESI, Circuit Judge, dissenting:

* * *

The majority, incorrectly in my view, concludes that the Commission's repatriation order constitutes the enforcement of a money judgment. It notes that several "cases hold that *anything beyond the mere entry of a money judgment* against a debtor is prohibited by the automatic stay." But, in fact, none of the cases that the majority cites is in any way binding on us, and only one of them can be said actually to stand for that proposition. The only case the majority cites that actually holds that anything beyond the entry of a money judgment is automatically stayed—the Eighth Circuit's decision in *EEOC v. Rath Packing Co.*, 787 F.2d 318, 326 (8th Cir.1986)—is, moreover, not at all apposite to the instant case. The judgment against Rath Packing called for the transfer of funds *directly* to the EEOC. And the only reassurance the court had that the EEOC would not "attempt to actually obtain execution of the judgment," during the pendency of the bankruptcy proceedings was the EEOC's own unsupported promise. Here, in contrast, preventing the actual transfer of funds to the governmental creditor is in no way dependent upon the "promise" of the governmental unit. The trust's assets, were they to be repatriated, would remain in the district court's registry. Moreover, the Commission would have no access to them *except through bankruptcy proceedings*. * * *

* * * I do not doubt that the *collection* of a judgment would in the ordinary course constitute the enforcement of a money judgment. In asking the *court* to seize the assets of the Cardinal Trust through repatriation, however, the Commission in this case does not seek to satisfy, or collect on, its 1995 judgment. Rather, the Commission aims to have the assets brought back in order to place them at the disposal of the bankruptcy court. That * * * collection would be stayed under § 362(b)(4) therefore provides no guidance as to governmental actions that, like the repatriation order before us, fall somewhere in between the entry of a judgment and its collection.

The majority's prohibition of any governmental action beyond the entry of a money judgment thus fails to find adequate support in the existing case law. It also finds none in the language of § 362(b)(4). For the "enforcement" of a money judgment that is forbidden can as readily refer only to those moves that are meant to favor the governmental action in relation to other creditors as it can to any step that is taken beyond the entry of the judgment.

Because neither language nor authority suffices to justify the majority's restrictions on the government's power to regulate this trust, we must look to the section's purpose, to the "mischief" it was designed to avoid in order to determine its meaning. This is the same as examining the majority's underlying concerns for a persuasive justification for its decision. Once again, however, such an inquiry fails to support the majority's result.

The majority emphasizes, rightly, that the policy behind the automatic stay, its function, is "'to grant complete, immediate, albeit temporary relief to the debtor from creditors, and also to prevent dissipation of the debtor's assets before orderly distribution to creditors can be effected.'" (quoting *Penn Terra Ltd. v. Department of Envtl. Resources*, 733 F.2d 267, 271 (3d Cir.1984)). But this principle does not, as the majority holds, imply that any governmental action is automatically stayed if it requires either the outlay of debtor assets during bankruptcy proceedings or the third-party control of those assets. It only means that the bankruptcy court's power over the ultimate distribution of the assets and their allocation among creditors must remain unhampered by such governmental steps. Indeed, to hold otherwise contravenes considerable precedent and undermines the very goal the majority's holding purports to effectuate.

* * *

Because affirming the district court's order in this case would have furthered the majority's stated goals of preventing the favoring of particular creditors and the dissipation of a debtor's assets, it is hard to understand the majority's opinion unless that opinion is more concerned with the Commission's *motives* in pursuing the repatriation of the trust's assets rather than with the ultimate *effect* of such repatriation. * * * I do not dispute that the Commission's goal was ultimately to obtain part of the disgorgement judgment, and indeed to protect its interests in that judgment from dissipation by Brennan. I dispute the relevance of this fact.

The majority seems to assume that the combination of detriment to the debtor and the governmental unit's goal of receiving some of the assets at some later date converts the repatriation order into an enforcement of a money judgment. But the same combination—detriment to the debtor and desire to protect one's interest—was present in the government's, concededly valid, seeking of the entry of the 1995 judgment against Brennan in the first place. And the majority's leap from the Commission's goal (of ultimately collecting on its judgment) to the conclusion that the district court's order actually constituted the enforcement of a money judgment is as unwarranted as it is unexplained. I believe, rather, that the proper inquiry must focus on the objective result of the district court's order, which in this case is to place additional assets at the bankruptcy court's disposal. For, as the majority opinion itself notes, the purpose of excluding the enforcement of money judgments from the governmental exception to the automatic stay is simply "to prevent the Government from gaining 'preferential treatment' in bankruptcy proceedings 'to the detriment of other creditors.'"[4]

* * *

This would seem to settle the matter, since the majority itself identifies no such harm. But the majority appears to deem the Commission's very right to appeal to a forum other than the bankruptcy court for the repatriation of Brennan's assets to be a measure of preferential treatment and hence to be forbidden. Yet, in enacting § 362, that was precisely what Congress intended. Congress explicitly excepted the government when it is acting pursuant to its regulatory powers from the automatic stay in order to prevent debtors from "frustrating necessary governmental functions by seeking refuge in bankruptcy court." *City of New York v. Exxon Corp.*, 932 F.2d 1020, 1024 (2d Cir.1991) (quotation marks omitted). And to effectuate this exception and its purposes, Congress granted both the bankruptcy court and the district court jurisdiction to determine when the governmental exception to the automatic stay applies. It follows that seeking relief in the federal district court cannot constitute prohibited preferential treatment.

* * *

Once we recognize that the crucial question in this case, and in the application of § 362(b)(4) generally, is whether the government's

---

[4] Although the majority claims that "the 'preferential treatment' rationale" was not the "sole" purpose in enacting § 362(b)(4), it finds no support for that proposition in either the Bankruptcy Code itself or in the Code's legislative history.

action enables the government to enrich itself at the expense of non-governmental creditors, we can see how unduly restrictive on governmental regulatory authority the majority's decision is. * * * Indeed, as the bankruptcy trustee's support of the Commission's action in this case indicates, Brennan's creditors, not simply the Commission, would be better off if Brennan were made to repatriate the Cardinal Trust. Only "wrongdoer" Brennan, who I fear has successfully manipulated this court into providing him with a "haven" in bankruptcy, would suffer any possible loss at all.

For all these reasons, I would affirm the district court and hold that its order was excepted from the automatic stay under § 362(b)(4).

Notes and Questions

1. Which of the opinions in *Brennan* is right—the majority or the dissent? Why?

2. What are the purposes of the automatic stay? Which, if any, of those purposes would be undermined by permitting the SEC to force repatriation of the Cardinal Trust's assets? How does that fit within the exception provided by § 362(b)(4)?

3. The majority in *Brennan* draws a bright line at the entry of judgment, reasoning that anything occurring thereafter constitutes "enforcement." What are the advantages of such an approach? The disadvantages?

4. Brennan ran a brokerage firm, First Jersey Securities, specializing in so-called "penny" stocks. He made millions of dollars in the 1970s and 1980s, but spent many of the ensuing years fighting both civil and criminal charges. He was convicted of money laundering and bankruptcy fraud, in the Third Circuit, in 2001. *United States v. Brennan*, 326 F.3d 176 (3d Cir. 2003), *cert. denied*, 540 U.S. 898, 124 S.Ct. 248, 157 L.Ed.2d 178 (2003). He was also held in civil contempt of the $75 million disgorgement order—the obligation involved in the principal case—and, later, held in criminal contempt of an order freezing assets, both in the Second Circuit. He pleaded guilty to the criminal charge, but appealed his sentence, including the order that his contempt and bankruptcy fraud sentences run consecutively. The appeal was mostly unsuccessful, *United States v. Brennan*, 395 F.3d 59 (2d Cir.2005), *as amended*, 406 F.3d 113 (2d Cir.2005).

An interviewer who talked with Brennan in 2006, in prison, said that he "reveals himself to be mostly the same persuasive, mysterious, intense and mischievous person he was while making tens of millions of dollars, only to be forced to relinquish it to his creditors. He also remains defiant." Greg Saitz,

Behind Bars with Brennan, STAR-LEDGER (Newark, N.J.), February 5, 2006, at 1.

5. Before 1998, as the case explained, the stay exception for certain actions by governmental units was found in two separate sections: § 362(b)(4) provided an exception to § 362(a)(1); and § 362(b)(5) constituted an exception to § 362(a)(2). One of the changes made by the Amendments was to add exceptions to §§ 362(a)(3) and (a)(6). Although neither the majority nor the dissent found it significant, does this aspect of the 1998 Amendment support one viewpoint more than the other?

6. Any unit of government, including the United States, a state, a municipality, a public agency or a foreign state, can benefit from the stay exceptions for "governmental units" enumerated in § 362(b)(4). See § 101(27). The term is limited, however, to "actual governmental groups" and does not include "organizations acting in a governmental capacity." See *In re Colin, Hochstin Co.*, 41 B.R. 322, 324-25 (Bankr. S.D.N.Y.1984) (holding that § 362(b)(4) does not apply to the New York Stock Exchange).

Environmental cases raise several important problems in bankruptcy. One of them is the proper interpretation of the exception for actions by governmental units. The following case, which deals with this issue, was decided before the 1998 amendments consolidated §§ 362(b)(4) and (b)(5).

IN RE COMMERCE OIL CO.

United States Court of Appeals, Sixth Circuit, 1988.
847 F.2d 291.

JOHNSTONE, Chief District Judge, sitting by designation.

This appeal concerns a ruling of the bankruptcy court for the Eastern District of Tennessee which held that proceedings by the state of Tennessee to fix civil fines and penalties under the Tennessee Water Quality Control Act of 1977, Tenn. Code Ann. § 69-3-101 et seq., are stayed under § 362.

Facts

[In November 1984, Tennessee's Commissioner of Health and Environment issued a complaint against Commerce Oil for allegedly violating the Tennessee Water Quality Control Act, and ordered Commerce to cease illegal discharges of brine into a creek and to

repair certain wells. The complaint assessed damages at $1,235.37 and civil penalties at $15,000. Commerce appealed to the Water Quality Board in December and, a week later, filed Chapter 11. The state filed a proof of claim for $16,235.37 in fines and penalties.

At the hearing before the Board, Commerce's lawyer argued that § 362(a) applied to stay that hearing. He threatened to file a contempt petition in the bankruptcy court unless the state ceased its proceedings. The state thereupon ceased proceedings and asked the bankruptcy court to determine whether the "police power" exception to the automatic stay found in § 362(b)(4) applied to the state's proceedings to fix liability for civil penalties and damages.]

The bankruptcy court held that the state's consideration of *remedial measures* and *injunctive relief* was not stayed because such matters were within the "police power" exception to the automatic stay. However, it also held that the state's review and determination of civil fines and penalties was an action on a claim against the debtor's estate and was stayed under § 362. The state appealed. The district court affirmed, holding that Tennessee is precluded from assessing and/or collecting money damages from the debtor under § 362, but remains free to exercise injunctive relief and to order remedial steps for the protection and safety of its citizens under § 362(b)(4).

* * *

II. The Police Power Exception

The courts below ruled that the state's *review* of the assessment against Commerce was an action on a claim stayed by § 362(a)(1), but that the state's *consideration of remedial measures and injunctive relief* was within the "police power" exception to the automatic stay. We disagree with the lower courts' views for several reasons.

First, although the provisions of the automatic stay contained in § 362 are quite broad, the automatic stay is not all-encompassing. In particular, §§ 362(b)(4) and 362(b)(5) of the automatic stay except both "the commencement or continuation of an action or proceeding" and "the enforcement of a judgment, other than a money judgment, obtained in an action or proceeding by a governmental unit to enforce such governmental unit's police or regulatory powers" from the automatic stay. Sections 362(b)(4) and (5) comprise the so-called "police power" exception to the automatic stay.

Congress clearly intended for the police power exception to allow governmental agencies to remain unfettered by the bankruptcy code in the exercise of their regulatory powers. As explained in the House Report on §§ 362(b)(4) and (5):

> Paragraph (4) excepts commencement or continuation of actions and proceedings by governmental units to enforce police or regulatory power. Thus, where a governmental unit is suing a debtor to prevent or stop violation of fraud, *environmental protection*, safety, or similar police or regulatory laws, or *attempting to fix damages for violation of such a law*, the action or proceeding is not stayed under the automatic stay. Paragraph (5) makes clear that the exception extends to permit an injunction and enforcement of an injunction, *and to permit the entry of a money judgment*, but does not extend to permit enforcement of a money judgment.

H.R. Rep. No. 95-595, 95th Cong., 1st Sess. 343 (1977), *reprinted in* [1978] U.S.C.C.A.N. 5963, 6299 (emphasis added). Taking cognizance of the clearly expressed legislative intent of Congress, we have recognized that damages for civil liability may be assessed under § 362(b)(4) for violation of state and federal laws.

Second, we find that the actions of the state in this case were regulatory in nature and therefore fall within the police power exception to the automatic stay. * * * [T]here are two tests for determining whether an action by a governmental unit falls within the automatic stay or is excepted under the "police power" exception: the pecuniary purpose test and the public policy test. Under the pecuniary purpose test, reviewing courts focus on whether the governmental proceeding relates primarily to the protection of the government's pecuniary interest in the debtor's property, and not to matters of public safety. Those proceedings which relate primarily to matters of public safety are excepted from the stay. Under the public policy test, reviewing courts must distinguish between proceedings that adjudicate private rights and those that effectuate public policy. Those proceedings that effectuate a public policy are excepted from the stay. Under either test, the state's actions should have been stayed under § 362 if the state was seeking a monetary sum merely as collection of a debt or as compensation for reclamation it had already performed.

The state's actions in this case have not been undertaken for primarily pecuniary purposes. Neither the initial assessment, nor the administrative review of the assessment was primarily an adjudication of private rights or interests in the debtor's estate. The statute under which Tennessee assessed penalties here is primarily remedial in nature. The express purpose of the Act is

> to abate existing pollution of the waters of Tennessee, to re-claim polluted waters, to prevent the future pollution of the waters, and to plan for the future use of the waters so that the water resources of Tennessee might be used and enjoyed to the fullest extent consistent with the maintenance of unpolluted waters.

Tenn. Code Ann. § 69-3-102(b). Under § 69-3-116(c) damages may be assessed for violation of the Act to cover the costs involved in investigating and enforcing the law and in removing, correcting or terminating any pollution. Under § 69-3-115(a)(2)(D), penalties for violation of the Act may be assessed in light of such factors as whether the penalty imposed will be a substantial economic deterrent to the illegal activity, the amount of damage to the environment and costs of rectifying such damage, the cost of enforcing the law, the severity of the discharge, the effect of the discharge on the receiving waters, the technical and economic reasonableness of reducing or eliminating the discharge and the social and economic value of the discharge source.

We do not find the rationale, policy and factors expressed in the Tennessee Water Quality Control Act to be based upon the state's ownership of or pecuniary interest in the natural resources of Tennessee. Punishing wrongdoers, deterring illegal activity, recovering remedial costs of damage to the environment, providing for the costs of administration and weighing the social and economic value of a discharge source are exercises of the state's regulatory power to effectuate public policy and are not actions based upon the state's property interests. Likewise removing, correcting or terminating pollution and determining the severity and effect of discharges on the receiving waters are actions to protect the public health and safety, and are not grounded upon the state's property interests.

The proprietary or pecuniary reward in assessing penalties under the Act is apparently of only secondary importance to the state. In this regard, although the state contends that it may *fix* civil liability under § 362(b)(4), it concedes that it may not *collect* any penalties assessed or any judgment entered by the Board. The state likewise concedes that even if it had been allowed to fix fines and penalties in this case, that it still would have to pursue its claim subject to the jurisdiction of the bankruptcy court. Furthermore, the state points out that any money eventually collected from Commerce for violation of the Act must be placed in a special fund used only for administration of the act and restoration and maintenance of the environment. Given the state's position, it is difficult to see what pecuniary advantage the state sought to gain in the debtor's estate or what pecuniary purpose would be served by assessing civil liability against Commerce.

We find nothing in the state's review of the Commissioner's assessments which would convert the state's proceedings into an action primarily designed to protect a pecuniary interest. The state proceeding concerned here was an adjudicatory review of the damages and penalties assessed against Commerce by the Commissioner under [Tennessee law]. The primary purpose of the hearing was to determine whether and to what extent the Tennessee Water Quality Control Act was violated and to review the damages and penalties assessed by the Commissioner in light of those violations. This was a regulatory action in the purest sense. We conclude therefore that both the state's initial assessment and the state's review of the assessment were actions to "enforce" Tennessee law within the meaning of § 362(b)(4).

Finally, Commerce warns us that if we hold assessment proceedings within the police power exception to the automatic stay, we will cause needless and unintended expenditure of estate resources because debtors will have the burden of petitioning the bankruptcy court for a stay of the proceedings under § 105(a) to protect the estate. We do not agree with Commerce that requiring the debtor to use § 105 to protect the bankrupt estate from state administrative proceedings imposes any unintended or undue burden on the estate. *See* H.R. Rep. No. 95-595, *supra*, at 342, *reprinted in* [1978] U.S.C.C.A.N. at 6298 ("By excepting an act or action from the automatic stay, the bill simply requires that the trustee move the court into action, rather than requiring the stayed party to request relief from the stay."). Moreover, we decline to adopt Commerce's premise that preservation of the debtor's estate is of greater priority in the statutory scheme set forth by Congress in Title 11 than is the enforcement of environmental protection laws explicitly intended to be excepted from the automatic stay. The plain meaning, the structure and the policy behind § 362(b) all indicate otherwise.

For the foregoing reasons, we hold that the Tennessee Water Quality Control Board's proceedings to fix civil liability under the Tennessee Water Quality Control Act of 1977 are within the § 362(b)(4) exception to the automatic stay in bankruptcy. We hereby reverse and vacate the lower courts' rulings.

Notes and Questions

1. The court in *Commerce Oil* sets out the usual tests for ascertaining whether governmental action falls within the automatic stay exception. Do those tests seem markedly different from each other? Do you suppose that different results are likely to follow, depending upon which test a court applies?

2. *Commerce Oil* presents one of the standard fact patterns raised by environmental cases—namely, whether, under the police power exception, an action to assess damages may proceed against a debtor in bankruptcy. The line is drawn at collection of any damages, and, as the court noted, the State of Tennessee conceded that it could not attempt to collect.

Another fact pattern involves a state's effort to obtain injunctive relief. An environmental injunction typically takes one of two forms (if not both): an order to cease polluting; and an order to clean up the effects of past pollution. Both types of orders must be understood in light of 28 U.S.C. § 959(b), which requires a debtor-in-possession or trustee, in the operation of a business, to "manage and operate the property in his possession according to the requirements of the valid laws of the State." Under that provision, an order to cease polluting seems clearly to fall within the automatic stay exception. The order to clean up past pollution is a bit more difficult, since it will undoubtedly require the expenditure of estate funds. If the environmental authority undertook the remedial work itself, it would have a claim against the debtor for reimbursement. That claim, typically unsecured, should be paid pro rata along with all the other unsecured claims. Requiring instead that the debtor do the work effectively gives environmental authorities a nonstatutory priority over other unsecured creditors. Nevertheless, courts routinely find such orders within the police power exception to the automatic stay. See *In re Commerce Oil Refining Co.*, 805 F.2d 1175 (5th Cir. 1986), *cert. denied sub nom. Commonwealth Oil Refining Co. v. United States EPA*, 483 U.S. 1005, 107 S.Ct. 3228, 97 L.Ed.2d 734 (1987).

3. As we saw in *Brennan*, it is not enough that the state is seeking to enforce its police and regulatory powers; the action also must not constitute "the enforcement of a money judgment." That provision was determinative in a prominent environmental case—*Penn Terra Ltd. v. Department of Environmental Resources*, 733 F.2d 267 (3d Cir. 1984)—that also presented a slightly different fact pattern. In *Penn Terra*, the debtor was liquidating rather than continuing in business, so 28 U.S.C. § 959(b) did not come into play. The state sought to enforce a prepetition order requiring the debtor to remediate pollution caused by its operation of surface coal mines. The cost of doing so exceeded the debtor's available assets, however, so application of the automatic stay exception would leave nothing for other creditors.

The Third Circuit found that the environmental authority's actions were clearly an exercise of police power, so the dispositive question was whether the injunction fell within the "exception to the exception" as an effort to enforce a money judgment. The Court held that it did not because the order did not constitute a "money judgment" in the first place:

> In common understanding, a money judgment * * * need consist of only two elements: (1) an identification of the parties for and against whom judgment is being entered, and (2) a *definite* and *certain* designation of the amount which plaintiff is owed by defendant. It need not, and generally does not, contain provisions for its enforcement. As the legislative history explicitly notes, the mere *entry* of a money judgment by a governmental unit is not affected by the automatic stay, provided of course that such proceedings are related to that government's police or regulatory powers.

> Quite separate from the entry of a money judgment, however, is a proceeding to *enforce* that money judgment. The paradigm for such a proceeding is when, having obtained a judgment for a sum certain, a plaintiff attempts to seize property of the defendant in order to satisfy that judgment. It is this seizure of a defendant-debtor's property, to satisfy the judgment obtained by a plaintiff-creditor, which is proscribed by subsection 362(b)(5).

> At least as a matter of form, it is clear to us that the proceeding initiated by DER in Commonwealth Court was not to enforce a money judgment. Indeed, it could not have resulted even in the mere entry of a money judgment. DER brought its action in equity to compel the performance of certain remedial acts by Penn Terra. It did not seek the payment of compensation to the Commonwealth's coffers, and the injunction actually issued by the Commonwealth Court did not direct such payment. This proceeding, therefore, could never have resulted in the adjudication of liability for a sum certain, an essential element of a money judgment. Since this action was in form and substance * * * not one to obtain a money judgment, it follows that it could not be one to *enforce* the payment of such a judgment.

Id. at 275 (footnotes omitted).

Do you agree? Should "money judgment" be construed to focus on enforcement or on impairment of the estate's ability to pay creditors? If the latter, when would governmental action *not* constitute "enforcement of a money judgment"? What is the object of drawing a distinction between past and future harm?

Against *Penn Terra*, one should contrast the statement in *In re Kovacs*, 681 F.2d 454 (6th Cir.1982), *vacated & remanded*, 459 U.S. 1167, 103 S.Ct. 810, 74 L.Ed.2d 1010 (1983), that there was "very little in substance to distinguish" the order at issue—requiring the debtor to turn over all of his nonexempt assets to a receiver who was authorized to collect any sums payable to the debtor in the future—from a "money judgment."

4. According to the courts, the 1998 amendment to former §§ 362-(b)(4) and (b)(5) made three changes: (1) the two subsections were combined into one; (2) language was added to make the exception applicable to §§ 362-(a)(1), (2), (3) and (6), rather than only to (a)(1) (to which former (b)(4) applied) and to (a)(2) (to which former (b)(5) applied); and (3) organizations exercising authority under the Chemical Weapons Convention were given the benefit of the exception. See, e.g., *In re Nelson*, 240 B.R. 802 (Bankr. D.Me.1999).

Are the courts correct? Do you see another possible interpretation, based on the language of revised § 362(b)(4)? See *In re PMI–DVW Real Estate Holdings, L.L.P.*, 240 B.R. 24 (Bankr. D.Ariz.1999).

3. RELIEF FROM, AND TERMINATION OF, THE STAY

As we have seen, the automatic stay's pervasiveness is ameliorated by the existence of numerous exceptions. A creditor interested in continuing an activity subject to the stay, but not covered by an exception, has two other alternatives—to obtain relief or await termination of the stay under the Code. Relief from the stay is primarily governed by § 362(d). Subsection (d)(1), which deals with relief from the stay for cause, provides one example of what constitutes cause—lack of adequate protection. That is most often applicable in the context of a secured claim and we will save those issues for Chapter 4 of this text, where the focus is on the rights of secured creditors. Subsection (d)(1) does not otherwise define "cause."

The second alternative for a creditor affected by the stay is to await its automatic termination under the Code. The stay expires as to property of the estate when it ceases to be such property, § 362(c)(1), although that does not necessarily invite a creditor merrily to proceed against the property. (Recall the distinction between §§ 362(a)(4) and (a)(5), but also note § 362(h)(1).) The stay also expires when the case is closed or dismissed, or when a discharge is either granted or denied. § 362(c)(2). Here, again, the creditor may not be able to proceed with efforts to get paid. If the debtor received a discharge, the automatic stay is replaced with a discharge injunction that prohibits efforts to collect obligations covered by the discharge, § 524(a).

Section 362(c) also covers a type of debtor misconduct— repeated filings intended solely to take advantage of the automatic stay. This is an "offensive" use of the stay addressed by Professor Keating in the excerpt quoted at the beginning of this section. This strategy was most often used in order to frustrate efforts by secured creditors to fore-close on their collateral. In many of these instances, debtors never submitted the required schedules of assets or, in Chapter 13 cases, proposed a plan. The Code has always included provisions that police certain types of misbehavior: § 707(b), permitting dismissal of abusive petitions; §§ 1112(b), 1208(c) and 1307(c), authorizing dismissal of petitions for cause; §§ 1129(a)(3) and 1325(a)(3), requiring plans to be proposed in good faith; and § 727(a)(8) and (9), barring repeated dis-charges. None of these provisions address the problem of serial filings head-on, however. Nor do they provide a solution to the perceived reluctance of bankruptcy judges—whether imagined or real—to crack down on debtors who repeatedly file.

In 1984, Congress made an effort to address abusive serial filers by enacting § 109(g). That subsection makes individuals ineligible if an earlier case was dismissed under specified circumstances, but it did not solve all the problems. (For one thing, it addresses only court-ordered dismissals, yet dismissal under Chapters 12 and 13 may be at the debtor's initiative.) The 2005 Amendments remedied that by adding §§ 362(c)(3) and (4) to the Code. Those subsections are directed toward the automatic stay, providing that it quickly terminates or never arises in circumstances of second and third (or more!) filings within a year. While not phrased as stay exceptions, these provisions operate as such. See also § 362(b)(21).

Subsection (c)(3) seems particularly obtuse. The question it raises is whether the phrase "shall terminate with respect to the debtor" is limited to the debtor and his or her property, or also terminates the stay with respect to property of the estate. Most courts take the former view. *Jumpp v. Chase Home Finance, LLC (In re Jumpp)*, 356 B.R. 789 (1st Cir. BAP 2006). Courts taking the minority view assert that such a reading largely eviscerates § 362(c)(3)(B); an individual debtor would rarely need to seek an extension of the stay because his or her property is almost always property of the estate and, under the majority view, it would remain protected without an extension of the stay. See *In re Jupiter*, 344 B.R. 754 (Bankr. D.S.C.2006).

Obviously, §§ 362(c)(3) and (c)(4) may place debtors in sub-stantial jeopardy, even though dismissal of their prior case (or cases) came about for fairly innocent reasons—usually, failure to obtain the prepetition credit counseling mandated by § 109(h). One strategy adopted by bankruptcy courts to avoid these adverse consequences is to find that the stay never arises when a debtor is ineligible under

§ 109(h), because no case is commenced by such a filing. This approach relies on language in § 301 to the effect that a case is commenced by "an entity that *may be a debtor*" under a particular chapter and, of course, an individual who has not received credit counseling "may not be a debtor," § 109(h)(1). The proper response in such a case, according to the court in *In re Elmendorf*, 345 B.R. 486 (Bankr. S.D.N.Y.2006), is to strike the petition rather than dismissing it. In a consolidated appeal, however, the Second Circuit disagreed. In *Adams v. Zarnel (In re Zarnel)*, 619 F.3d 156 (2d Cir.2010), the Court found that § 301, in conjunction with §§ 302 and 303,

> define the prerequisites for relief under particular chapters of the Bankruptcy Code, rather than the existence in a jurisdictional sense of a voluntary, joint, or involuntary case. * * *
>
> Each of the three parallel sections implicated here contains limiting language indicating that it is referencing a particular type of case, whether voluntary, joint, or involuntary, that in turn is treated in a separate chapter of the Bankruptcy Code. * * * This limiting language in all three sections suggests that the sections are not concerned with determining the existence of a "case" in the broader sense * * * . Rather, they clarify that, when a debtor commences a case, the debtor is not eligible for relief under a particular chapter of the Bankruptcy Code unless it meets the requirements to be a debtor under that chapter.

Id. at 166. Thus, the Court concluded that a case is commenced, and the automatic stay is triggered, even though the petition was filed by an ineligible entity. The debtors were not completely out of luck, however, because the Court did not find that dismissal is the only option in such a case. Instead, it remanded that question to the bankruptcy court:

> The bankruptcy court's determination that its equitable powers included striking the petitions was premised on the belief that there were no cases to dismiss. While we note that we are unaware of any case similar to this one in which a court has determined that a case has commenced and yet taken an action other than dismissal, the bankruptcy court did not address whether other actions, including striking a petition, might be appropriate in these circumstances. We thus conclude that this is a question for the bankruptcy court to address initially.

Id. at 171-72.

Read § 362(c) and (d) and answer the following Problems.

Problems

1. Debtor, acting as the trustee of a trust created under a decedent's will, was making inadvisable investment decisions—or so the trust beneficiaries believe. They want to file suit alleging breach of fiduciary duty, but Debtor has recently filed personal bankruptcy. Can they get relief from the stay for "cause"?

2. After Debtor was disbarred, the state Disciplinary Board obtained a judgment against Debtor for costs of the proceeding, as permitted by the Board's rules. Assuming that the judgment is nondischargeable, does that, without more, give the Board "cause" for relief from the stay? See *Disciplinary Board v. Feingold (In re Feingold)*, 730 F.3d 1268 (11th Cir.2013).

3. Debtor's Chapter 7 petition was dismissed under § 707(b)'s means test. Two months later, Debtor filed a Chapter 13 petition. Can his mortgage lender, frustrated in its efforts to foreclose, wait 30 days and then proceed against Debtor's home under § 362(c), without seeking relief from the stay?

4. Debtor filed a Chapter 13 bankruptcy petition in order to stop the imminent foreclosure of her home, but the case was dismissed three months later because Debtor failed to file her recent tax returns as required by § 521(e)(2)(A). Her mortgage lender did not get around to resuming its foreclosure efforts until ten months after dismissal of the Chapter 13 case, but Debtor filed a Chapter 7 petition as soon as the lender sent the first notice. Can the lender wait 30 days and then continue its foreclosure efforts under § 362(c)? Would it matter if Debtor had provided her tax returns to her attorney, but the attorney had failed to file them on time due to a family crisis?

5. Debtor filed two Chapter 13 cases during the past year in an effort to prevent the foreclosure of his home, but both cases were dismissed for failure to file a viable plan. Debtor's mortgage lender promptly began foreclosure proceedings, and was on the verge of selling the property. Debtor's other creditors viewed that sale with alarm, because they were aware that foreclosure sales bring a much smaller price than can be obtained through a bankruptcy sale. They also knew that the house was Debtor's major asset; they would receive little or nothing unless the house could be sold for the best possible price. Thus, three of Debtor's unsecured creditors filed an involuntary Chapter 7 petition against Debtor. Does that filing trigger the automatic stay?

Chapter 3

==

UNSECURED CLAIMS IN BANKRUPTCY

A. INTRODUCTION

Bankruptcy law, as we will see, draws few distinctions among different types of creditors. All of them, regardless of the source of the debtor's obligation, are holders of claims. The source of the obligation can be important, however. A contract creditor is in a position to plan for possible default and to take precautions that will minimize the risk upon default. The creditor can assess the debtor's creditworthiness and adjust the terms of the contract on that basis. The parties can, and usually do, agree on terms defining default, accelerating the loan upon default and requiring the payment of collection costs. Nonconsensual creditors, such as tort victims, do not choose to become holders of claims owed by a particular debtor, and are not in a position to protect themselves from the risk of default. Bankruptcy, as a matter of policy, generally ignores these distinctions; all of these creditors are merely holders of claims.

Because bankruptcy revolves around the disposition of "claims" held by the debtor's various creditors, the question of what constitutes a claim is fundamental. This question arises in at least four important contexts. First, it is critical to a determination of the scope of the automatic stay, which bars, inter alia, any action "to recover a claim against the debtor that arose before" bankruptcy. § 362(a)(1). Second, it affects discharge, which covers "all debts" arising "before the date of the order for relief." § 727(b). A "debt," in turn, is defined in § 101(12) as "liability on a claim." Third, only "claims" are entitled to receive payment in bankruptcy, regardless of the chapter under which the case is filed. §§ 726(a), 1123(a)(1)-(4), 1325(a)(4)-(5). And finally, only

172

creditors with allowed claims (as well as the shareholders of a corporate debtor) are entitled to vote on a Chapter 11 plan. § 1126(a).

A claim must be "allowed" if its holder is to receive a payment from the bankruptcy estate. Allowance, which is governed by § 502, simply means that the claim is valid. Because most claims are not disputed, a claim is "deemed allowed" by § 502 if it is filed (see § 501) and no objection to it is raised. Section 1111(a), which applies only to Chapter 11 cases, states that no proof of claim need be filed as long as the claim is included in the debtor's schedules and the debtor does not list it as disputed, contingent or unliquidated.

The Bankruptcy Rules impose fairly strict deadlines on the filing of claims, but permit late filings in instances of "excusable neglect." The Supreme Court held in *Pioneer Investment Services Co. v. Brunswick Associates Limited Partnership*, 507 U.S. 380, 113 S.Ct. 1489, 123 L.Ed.2d 74 (1993), that "excusable neglect" is not limited to intervening circumstances beyond a party's control, but also includes cases in which the failure to file on time is due to carelessness, inadvertence or mistake. The Court did not open the safety net widely, however, because notice of the bar date had been given in an unusual manner in *Pioneer Investment*, and neither the debtor nor efficient judicial administration was prejudiced by allowing the tardy claim.

If a party in interest objects to a claim, the court must determine if the claim falls into one of the categories of claims not allowable in bankruptcy. These categories are listed in § 502(b). Chief among the reasons why a claim might be disallowed in bankruptcy is that the claim is unenforceable against the debtor under nonbankruptcy law (see § 502(b)(1)). Sensibly, such a claim is not magically transformed into an enforceable claim by the filing of a bankruptcy petition. Another frequently-encountered reason for disallowing a claim in bankruptcy is that the claim is for unmatured interest (see § 502(b)(2)).

The universe of claims breaks down into two rough categories—secured and unsecured. Holders of secured claims have a legally recognized property interest in collateral of the debtor; holders of unsecured claims have a legally recognized right to payment by the debtor, but no property interests to support the debtor's obligation.

Section 506(a)(1) determines an important category of unsecured claims. Under that subsection, a creditor with collateral worth less than the amount of the debt is treated as the holder of two claims—

a secured claim, measured by the value of the collateral; and an unsecured claim, measured by the difference between the value of the collateral and the debt. For example, a creditor owed $125,000 that has a security interest in property worth $100,000 has a secured claim of $100,000 and an unsecured claim of $25,000. This concept, known as "bifurcation," is basic to bankruptcy and will appear again and again throughout the course.

The identity of holders of claims comes from the schedule of assets and liabilities that debtors must file as part of the bankruptcy petition. The list of liabilities will include the names and addresses of creditors.

Read §§ 502(a) and (b) and answer the following Problems.

Problems and Questions

1. Debtor Corp. borrowed $120,000 from Bank on August 1, at an interest rate of 10%. Debtor Corp. signed a note promising to pay $11,000 on the first of every month (representing $10,000 in principal and $1,000 in interest), beginning on September 1, for one year. The note included the following acceleration clause:

> In the event of nonpayment of any installment due under the terms of this Note, Bank may, at its discretion and without prior notice to Borrower, declare the entire obligation hereunder due and payable.

Debtor Corp. failed to make any payments under the note and filed bankruptcy on October 10. What is the amount of Bank's allowable claim? Does the answer depend upon whether Bank has exercised its right to accelerate the loan? Would your answer change if the note did not include an acceleration clause?

2. Assume the same facts as in the prior Problem, except that Debtor made two payments of $11,000 each before filing bankruptcy. What is the amount of Bank's allowable claim? If Bank is not paid by the trustee until April of the next year, can Bank claim an additional $6,000 in interest?

3. Debtor Corp. borrowed $120,000 from Bank on August 1, at an interest rate of 10%. Debtor Corp. signed a note that obligated it to pay $1,000 in interest on the first of every month, beginning September 1, for one year, at which time principal was payable in full. Debtor made two interest payments and, on October 10, filed bankruptcy. What is the amount of Bank's allowable claim?

4. The purchasing agent for Buyer Company telephoned Seller, Inc. and ordered 100 cases of widgets at $15 per case, for delivery in three weeks. Seller, Inc. confirmed the order over the phone, but did not mail an acknowledgment of the sale. A week after the call, Buyer Company repudiated the deal and filed bankruptcy. What is the amount of Seller, Inc.'s allowable claim?

5. Debtor bought a VCR from Electronics Galore on credit for $400. The VCR was, in fact, assembled without several necessary parts. Debtor, however, was distracted by his deteriorating financial situation and he never got around to returning the VCR or asserting a warranty claim. Instead, he simply did not pay. Debtor then filed bankruptcy and Electronics Galore filed a proof of claim for $400. No one objected to the claim. Unsecured creditors will get a 10% dividend in this case. Is Electronics Galore entitled to $40?

6. In an effort to avoid having to file bankruptcy, Debtor sought help from Consumer Credit Counseling Services. CCCS drew up a repayment plan that required Debtor to cut up his Visa card and to repay three-quarters of his credit card balance over the next six months. When Debtor's CCCS counselor called Visa to try to settle the debt for 75¢ on the dollar, no one at Visa would even discuss it. Debtor was forced to file bankruptcy a month later and Visa filed a claim for the full balance. Can Debtor contest all or part of Visa's claim? See § 502(k).

7. Debtor owes an obligation to Creditor that is not dischargeable in bankruptcy. Does Creditor have any reason to file a proof of claim? If Creditor does not file a proof of claim, does Debtor have any reason to do so? (See § 501(c), which allows a debtor to file a proof of claim if the creditor does not.)

The following case deals with § 502(b)(6), which places a cap on claims of a particular type—specifically, those resulting from the termination of real property leases. Note that this provision places a ceiling on the amount of the lessor's claim; it does not entitle a lessor to a claim in that amount in every instance. A lessor whose actual damages are lower, when computed in accordance with nonbankruptcy law, may assert a claim only in the amount of its actual damages. And, as always, the right to file the claim is a far cry from being paid.

Later in the course, when we study the assumption and rejection of executory contracts and unexpired leases, we will see additional rules that affect the amount of a lessor's claim.

SADDLEBACK VALLEY COMMUNITY CHURCH v. EL TORO MATERIALS CO. (IN RE EL TORO MATERIALS CO.)

United States Court of Appeals, Ninth Circuit, 2007.
504 F.3d 978, *cert. denied*, 552 U.S. 1311, 128 S.Ct. 1875, 170 L.Ed.2d 746 (2008).

KOZINSKI, Circuit Judge.

Bankruptcy presents a unique challenge: How should a paucity of resources be allocated to cover a multiplicity of claims? Distributing money to satisfy claims is, in most cases, a zero-sum game: Every dollar given to one creditor is a dollar unavailable to satisfy the debt owed to others. For Paul to be paid in full, Peter must be short-changed. Congress sought to balance the interests of competing creditors through an extensive set of rules organizing, prioritizing and structuring claims against the estate.

The bankruptcy estate of mining company El Toro Materials hopes to use one of these rules—a cap on damages "resulting from the termination of a lease of real property," *id.* § 502(b)(6)—to limit its liability for allegedly leaving one million tons of its wet clay "goo," mining equipment and other materials on Saddleback Community Church's property after rejecting its lease.[1] Saddleback brought an adversary proceeding against El Toro claiming $ 23 million in damages for the alleged cost of removing the mess, under theories of waste, nuisance, trespass and breach of contract. The bankruptcy court, on a motion for partial summary judgment, found that Saddleback's recovery would not be limited by the § 502(b)(6) cap. On certified cross-appeal the Bankruptcy Appellate Panel (BAP) reversed, holding that any damages would be capped. Saddleback appeals.

Claims made by landlords against their bankrupt tenants for lost rent have always been treated differently than other unsecured claims. Prior to 1934, landlords could not recover at all for the loss of rental income they suffered when a bankrupt tenant rejected a long-term lease agreement; future lease payments were considered contingent and thus not provable debts in bankruptcy.

The Great Depression created pressure to reform the system: A wave of bankruptcies left many landlords with broken long-term leases,

---

[1] The parties entered into a stipulation that the lease would be rejected under § 365(a) (allowing bankrupt tenants to reject the remaining term of leases).

buildings sitting empty and no way to recover from the estates of their former tenants. On the one hand, allowing landlords to make a claim for lost rental income would reduce the harm done to them by a tenant's breach of a long-term lease, especially in a down market when it was difficult or impossible to re-lease the premises. On the other hand, "extravagant claims for * * * unearned rent" could quickly deplete the estate, to the detriment of other creditors. *In re Best Prods. Co.*, 229 B.R. 673, 676 (Bankr. E.D.Va.1998). The solution was a compromise in the Bankruptcy Act of 1934 allowing a claim against the bankruptcy estate for back rent to the date of abandonment, plus damages no greater than one year of future rent.

Congress dramatically overhauled bankruptcy law when it passed the Bankruptcy Reform Act of 1978. However, § 502(b)(6) of the 1978 Act was intended to carry forward existing law allowing limited damages for lost rental income. Only the method of calculating the cap was changed. Under the current Act, the cap limits damages "resulting from the termination of a lease of real property" to "the greater of one year, or 15 percent, not to exceed three years, of the remaining term of such lease." § 502(b)(6). The damages cap was "designed to compensate the landlord for his loss while not permitting a claim so large (based on a long-term lease) as to prevent other general unsecured creditors from recovering a dividend from the estate." S. Rep. No. 95-989, at 63.

The structure of the cap—measured as a fraction of the remaining term—suggests that damages other than those based on a loss of future rental income are not subject to the cap. It makes sense to cap damages for lost rental income based on the amount of expected rent: Landlords may have the ability to mitigate their damages by re-leasing or selling the premises, but will suffer injury in proportion to the value of their lost rent in the meantime. In contrast, collateral damages are likely to bear only a weak correlation to the amount of rent: A tenant may cause a lot of damage to a premises leased cheaply, or cause little damage to premises underlying an expensive leasehold.[2]

One major purpose of bankruptcy law is to allow creditors to receive an aliquot share of the estate to settle their debts. Metering these collateral damages by the amount of the rent would be inconsistent with the goal of providing compensation to each creditor in propor-

---

[2] Here, El Toro is alleged to have caused $23 million of damage to a property that it leased for only $28,000 per month.

tion with what it is owed. Landlords in future cases may have significant claims for both lost rental income and for breach of other provisions of the lease. To limit their recovery for collateral damages only to a portion of their lost rent would leave landlords in a materially worse position than other creditors. In contrast, capping rent claims but allowing uncapped claims for collateral damage to the rented premises will follow congressional intent by preventing a potentially overwhelming claim for lost rent from draining the estate,[3] while putting landlords on equal footing with other creditors for their collateral claims.

The statutory language supports this interpretation. The cap applies to damages "resulting from" the rejection of the lease. Saddleback's claims for waste, nuisance and trespass do not result from the rejection of the lease—they result from the pile of dirt allegedly left on the property. Rejection of the lease may or may not have triggered Saddleback's ability to sue for the alleged damages. But the harm to Saddleback's property existed whether or not the lease was rejected. A simple test reveals whether the damages result from the rejection of the lease: Assuming all other conditions remain constant, would the landlord have the same claim against the tenant if the tenant were to assume the lease rather than rejecting it? Here, Saddleback would still have the same claim it brings today had El Toro accepted the lease and committed to finish its term: The pile of dirt would still be allegedly trespassing on Saddleback's land and Saddleback still would have the same basis for its theories of nuisance, waste and breach of contract. The million-ton heap of dirt was not put there by the rejection of the lease—it was put there by the actions and inactions of El Toro in preparing to turn over the site.

Interpreting the § 502(b)(6) cap to include damage collateral to the lease would also create a perverse incentive for tenants to reject their lease in bankruptcy instead of running it out: Rejecting the lease would allow the tenant to cap its liability for any collateral damage to the premises and thus reduce its overall liability, even if staying on the property would otherwise be desirable and preserve the operating value of the business. Bankrupt tenants—especially those who have damaged the property and thus may face liability upon expiration of the lease—

---

[3] The structure of the cap suggests congressional concern about damages from long-term leases spanning many years: The cap maxes out at 15 or 20 years, or 3 years' rent. A claim for lost rent for a full 20 years would in many cases overwhelm any other claims against the estate.

would pack up their wares[6] and reject otherwise desirable leases in order to gain the benefit of capping unrelated damages. This would both reduce the operating value of the business and deny recovery to a creditor—a lose-lose situation counter to bankruptcy policy. An incentive to sacrifice efficiency in order to exploit a loophole in the liability-capping provisions would be plainly counter to congressional intent to maximize the value of the estate to creditors.

Further, extending the cap to cover any collateral damage to the premises would allow a post-petition but pre-rejection tenant to cause any amount of damage to the premises—either negligently or intentionally—without fear of liability beyond the cap. If the tenant's debt to the landlord already exceeded the cap then there would be no deterrence against even the most flagrant acts in violation of the lease, possibly even to the point of the tenant burning down the property in a fit of pique. Absent clear statutory language supporting such an absurd result, we cannot suppose that Congress intended it.

The BAP reached a contrary conclusion because it considered itself bound by its precedent in *Kuske* v. *McSheridan (In re McSheridan)*, 184 B.R. 91 (BAP 9th Cir.1995), and therefore held that Saddleback's recovery against El Toro would be capped under § 502(b)(6). To the extent that *McSheridan* holds § 502(b)(6) to be a limit on tort claims other than those based on lost rent, rent-like payments or other damages directly arising from a tenant's failure to complete a lease term, it is overruled.

* * *

Reversed and remanded.

Questions and Problems

1. This case clearly involved highly unusual—and sympathetic— facts. Do you think they influenced the outcome?

2. Undoubtedly, the mining company's failure to remove its "goo" from the church's property was a breach of a lease covenant, which gives the offense a breach of contract flavor. Yet, the court overruled *McSheridan* to the extent that it held the cap "a limit on tort claims other than those based on lost rent, rent-like payments or other damages directly arising from a tenant's failure to complete a lease term." Is the court drawing a tort-contract

---

[6] Or fail to pack them up at all, as is alleged here.

distinction? Is the outcome consistent with the statute's language? With its purpose?

3. Whether § 502(b)(6) should be read narrowly, as did the court in *El Toro*, or expansively, as did *McSheridan*, has been a subject of much debate and continues to divide the courts. See, e.g., *In re Foamex Int'l, Inc.*, 368 B.R. 383 (Bankr. D.Del.2007) (holding a landlord's claim for $769,400 in repair obligations limited by § 502(b)(6)).

4. Debtor leased commercial premises from Landlord. Five years remained in the lease term at the time Debtor filed bankruptcy and vacated the premises. Rent was $1,000 per month. Landlord has been unable to relet the premises despite its best efforts to do so. What is the amount of Landlord's allowable claim? See § 502(b)(6). *12,000* *54,00*

5. Assume the same facts as in the prior Problem, except that ten years remained in the lease term. What is the amount of Landlord's allowable claim? Does the result change in either Problem if Landlord is able to relet the premises for the remaining term for $500 per month?

B. WHAT CONSTITUTES A "CLAIM" IN BANKRUPTCY

A number of important bankruptcy cases have addressed whether a particular party holds a "claim" against the debtor. These cases involve different contexts, such as the automatic stay or discharge, but they are unified by the need to address the same ultimate issue of what constitutes a "claim."

Two distinct problems have arisen regarding the definition of "claim." The first is a timing problem, which is presented whenever some of the factual events pertinent to the claim occur after the bankruptcy filing. Two of the introductory Problems in Section A illustrate a straightforward timing question—the treatment of unmatured debts. More difficult timing questions are presented, however, when some period of time has passed between the debtor's conduct and the claim-holder's injury. This happens primarily in tort cases. Claims are determined as of the date the petition is filed, § 502(b), but the debtor's tortious prepetition conduct may not produce cognizable consequences for some time. In addition, the nature of the connection between the debtor and the tort victim varies; the more attenuated that connection, the more difficult it becomes for a court to find that the tort victim has a claim in the debtor's bankruptcy.

The second problem is determining when a right to an equitable remedy gives rise to a claim. This problem is encountered most often in the context of environmental injunctions, but it also arises when the creditor seeks to enforce other types of equitable remedies, such as covenants not to compete. The next two cases discuss these problems in turn.

JELD-WEN, INC. v. VAN BRUNT (IN RE GROSSMAN'S, INC.)

United States Court of Appeals, Third Circuit, 2010 (en banc).
607 F.3d 114.

SLOVITER, Circuit Judge.

* * *

In the appeal before us, the Bankruptcy Court, affirmed by the District Court, followed our precedent in *Avellino & Bienes v. M. Frenville Co. (Matter of M. Frenville Co.)*, 744 F.2d 332 (3d Cir.1984) ("*Frenville*"), to hold that a plan of reorganization did not discharge asbestos-related tort claims filed by Mary Van Brunt and her husband Gordon (the "Van Brunts") against Grossman's Inc. The underlying asbestos exposure occurred pre-petition but the injury manifested itself post-petition. The Appellant, JELD-WEN, Inc., successor to defendant Grossman's Inc. and its affiliates (hereafter "Grossman's"), asks us to overrule the holding of *Frenville*.

I.

Background

[In 1977, Mary Van Brunt bought products containing asbestos for a home renovation project from Grossman's. The company filed Chapter 11 in 1997 and the court confirmed a plan purporting to discharge all prepetition claims.

Mary had no symptoms of illness until 2006. In March 2007, she was diagnosed with mesothelioma, which is a type of cancer linked to asbestos exposure. She and her husband filed a tort suit against JELD-WEN, Grossman's successor-in-interest, in New York state court, and the parties conceded that New York law governed. JELD-WEN moved to reopen the bankruptcy case, which had been filed in Delaware, and sought a determination that the Van Brunts' claims were discharged by the plan. After Mary's death in 2008, her husband was substituted as the representative of her estate. The state court proceeding was informally stayed pending this appeal.]

The Bankruptcy Court concluded that the 1997 Plan of Reorganization did not discharge the Van Brunts' asbestos-related claims because they arose after the effective date of the Plan. In so holding, the Bankruptcy Court relied on our decisions in *Frenville* and its progeny. *Frenville* held that a "claim," as that term is defined by the Bankruptcy Code, arises when the underlying state law cause of action accrues. The applicable New York law provides that a cause of action for asbestos-related injury does not accrue until the injury manifests itself. The Bankruptcy Court therefore reasoned that the Van Brunts had no "claim" subject to discharge in 1997 because Ms. Van Brunt did not manifest symptoms of mesothelioma—and thus the New York cause of action did not accrue—until 2006. The Bankruptcy Court entered judgment for the Van Brunts and against JELD-WEN, effectively allowing the Van Brunts to proceed with their claims in the New York state court.

The District Court affirmed * * * .

* * *

III.

Discussion

A. The *Frenville* Accrual Test

In 1980, M. Frenville Co. was the subject of an involuntary petition for bankruptcy filed in New Jersey under Chapter 7 of the Bankruptcy Reform Act of 1978. Thereafter, involuntary petitions under Chapter 7 of the Code were filed against two principals of the company.

Later that year, four banks filed a lawsuit in a New York state court against the company's former accountants, Avellino & Bienes ("A & B"), alleging that A & B negligently and recklessly prepared the company's pre-petition financial statements and seeking damages for their alleged losses exceeding five million dollars. A & B filed a complaint in the bankruptcy court in New Jersey seeking relief from the automatic stay in order to implead Frenville as a third-party defendant in order to obtain indemnification or contribution under New York law.

The bankruptcy court, affirmed by the district court, held that the automatic stay barred A & B's action. A & B appealed.

We reversed, holding that because the automatic stay applied only to claims that arose pre-petition, under New York law A & B did not have a right to payment for its claim for indemnification or contribution from Frenville until after the banks filed their suit against A & B. It followed that A & B's claim against Frenville arose post-petition even though the conduct upon which A & B's liability was predicated (negligent preparation of Frenville's financial statements) occurred pre-petition. It followed that the automatic stay was inapplicable. We emphasized that the "crucial issue" was when the "right to payment" arose as determined by reference to the New York law that governed the indemnification claim.

This court subsequently summarized *Frenville* as holding that "the existence of a valid claim depends on: (1) whether the claimant possessed a right to payment; and (2) when that right arose" as determined by reference to the relevant non-bankruptcy law. *Kilbarr Corp. v. Gen. Servs. Admin., Office of Supply & Servs. (In re Remington Rand Corp.)*, 836 F.2d 825, 830 (3d Cir.1988). The *Frenville* test for determining when a claim arises has been referred to as the "accrual test."

In the case before us, the District Court and Bankruptcy Court correctly applied the accrual test * * * .

The question remains, however, whether we should continue to follow *Frenville* and its accrual test. * * * The courts of appeals that have considered *Frenville* have uniformly declined to follow it. At least one bankruptcy court has stated that *Frenville* "may be fairly characterized as one of the most criticized and least followed precedents decided under the current Bankruptcy Code." *Firearms Imp. & Exp. Corp. v. United Capital Ins. Co. (In re Firearms Imp. & Exp. Corp.)*, 131 B.R. 1009, 1015 (Bankr. S.D.Fla.1991).

* * *

Notwithstanding what appears to be universal disapproval, we decide cases before us based on our own examination of the issue, not on the views of other jurisdictions. Nevertheless, those widely held views impel us to consider whether the reasoning applied by our colleagues elsewhere is persuasive.

* * *

The *Frenville* court focused on the "right to payment" language in § 101(5) and, according to some courts, "impos[ed] too narrow an interpretation on the term claim," *Epstein v. Official Comm. of Unsecured Creditors of the Estate of Piper Aircraft Corp. (In re Piper Aircraft, Corp.)*, 58 F.3d 1573, 1576 n.2 (11th Cir.1995), by failing to give sufficient weight to the words modifying it: "contingent," "unmatured," and "unliquidated." The accrual test in *Frenville* does not account for the fact that a "claim" can exist under the Code before a right to payment exists under state law.

We are persuaded that the widespread criticism of *Frenville's* accrual test is justified, as it imposes too narrow an interpretation of a "claim" under the Bankruptcy Code. Accordingly, the *Frenville* accrual test should be and now is overruled.

B. When a Claim Arises

Our decision to overrule *Frenville* leaves a void in our jurisprudence as to when a claim arises. That decision has various implications. * * *

Principal among the effects of the determination when a claim arises is the effect on the dischargeability of a claim. Under § 1141-(d)(1)(A) of the Code, the confirmation of a plan of reorganization "discharges the debtor from any debt that arose before the date of such confirmation * * * ." A "debt" is defined as liability on a "claim," § 101(12), which in turn is defined as a "right to payment," § 101(5). This is consistent with Congress' intent to provide debtors with a fresh start * * * . On the other hand, a broad discharge may disadvantage potential claimants, such as tort claimants, whose injuries were allegedly caused by the debtor but which have not yet manifested and who therefore had no reason to file claims in the bankruptcy. These competing considerations have not been resolved consistently by the cases decided to date.

Moreover, the determination when a claim arises has significant due process implications. If potential future tort claimants have not filed claims because they are unaware of their injuries, they might challenge the effectiveness of any purported notice of the claims bar date. Discharge of such claims without providing adequate notice raises questions under the Fourteenth Amendment.

The courts have generally divided into two groups on the decision as to when a claim arises for purposes of the Code, with numerous variations. One group has applied the conduct test and the other has applied what has been termed the pre-petition relationship test. Illustrative of the cases that have adopted the conduct test is the decision of the Fourth Circuit in *Grady v. A.H. Robins Co.*, 839 F.2d 198 (4th Cir.1988).

In *Grady*, the plaintiff had inserted a Dalkon Shield intrauterine contraceptive device several years before the manufacturer filed a petition for Chapter 11 bankruptcy. The plaintiff alleged that she experienced injuries from the Dalkon Shield, including the need for a hysterectomy. The district court, which did not refer the case to the bankruptcy court, determined that the plaintiff's claim arose "when the acts giving rise to [the defendant's] liability were performed, not when the harm caused by those acts was manifested." The court of appeals affirmed, finding that the plaintiff held a contingent claim that arose before the commencement of the bankruptcy case. The court cautioned that it was not deciding whether Grady's claim "or those of [future tort claimants] are dischargeable in this case." *Id.* at 203. It held only that because the Dalkon Shield was inserted in the claimant before the filing of the bankruptcy petition, it constituted a claim within the meaning of the automatic stay, § 362(a)(1), *i.e.*, a pre-petition claim.

In contrast, the Eleventh Circuit criticized a conduct test that would enable individuals to hold a claim against a debtor by virtue of their potential future exposure to "the debtor's product," regardless of whether the claimant had any relationship or contact with the debtor. *Piper*, 58 F.3d at 1577. It stated that approach would define a "claim" too broadly in certain circumstances and would "stretch the scope of § 101(5)" too far. Similarly, a commentator observed that under the conduct test, "[c]laimants who did not use or have any exposure to the dangerous product until long after the bankruptcy case has concluded would nonetheless be subject to the terms of a preexisting confirmed Chapter 11 plan." Alan N. Resnick, *Bankruptcy as a Vehicle for Resolving Enterprise-Threatening Mass Tort Liability*, 148 U. PA. L. REV. 2045, 2071 (2000). "These claimants may be unidentifiable because of their lack of contact with the debtor or the product and, accordingly, may not have had the benefit of notice and an opportunity to participate in the bankruptcy case." *Id.*

Some of the courts concerned that the conduct test may be too broad have adopted what has been referred to as a pre-petition relation-ship test. Under this test, a claim arises from a debtor's pre-petition tortious conduct where there is also some pre-petition relationship between the debtor and the claimant, such as a purchase, use, operation of, or exposure to the debtor's product. One commentator opined that "[t]he 'pre-petition relationship test' ameliorates the problem often attributed to the 'conduct test'—that a bankruptcy proceeding cannot identify and afford due process to claimants." Barbara J. Houser, *Chapter 11 as a Mass Tort Solution*, 31 LOY. L.A. L. REV. 451, 465 (1998).

In *Lemelle v. Univ. Mfg. Corp.*, 18 F.3d 1268, 1277 (5th Cir.1994), the plaintiff brought a wrongful death action against the successor corporation of a mobile home manufacturer that had emerged from Chapter 11 proceedings. The plaintiff alleged that the decedent's death was caused by the manufacturer's defective mobile home design and construction. The decedent died in a fire allegedly caused by the manufacturing defect about two years after the debtor's plan of reorganization was confirmed and approximately fifteen years after the design and manufacture of the mobile home. The district court determined that the plan of reorganization discharged all of the debtor's obligations, including the liability on the tort claim.

The Fifth Circuit reversed, noting that in order for the plaintiff's wrongful death claim to have been discharged in the debtor's bankruptcy, "at a minimum, there must be evidence that would permit the debtor to identify, during the course of the bankruptcy proceedings, potential victims and thereby permit notice to these potential victims of the pendency of the proceedings." The court found that the record was "devoid of any evidence of any pre-petition contact, privity, or other relationship between [the debtor], on the one hand, and [the plaintiff] or the decedents, on the other." The court concluded that absent any such evidence, the district court could not find "that the claims asserted by [the plaintiff] were discharged in [the debtor's] bankruptcy proceedings." The court reasoned that "even the broad definition of 'claim' cannot be extended to include * * * claimants whom the record indicates were completely unknown and unidentified at the time [the debtor] filed its petition and whose rights depended entirely on the fortuity of future occurrences." *Id.* at 1277.

The Second Circuit followed a similar approach in an environmental regulatory context. In *In re Chateaugay Corp.*, 944 F.2d 997 (2d Cir.1991), the court held that the EPA's post-confirmation costs of responding to a release of hazardous waste, even if not yet incurred at the time of bankruptcy, involved "claims" under § 101(5). The court reasoned that "[t]he relationship between environmental regulating agencies and those subject to regulation provides sufficient 'contemplation' of contingencies to bring most ultimately maturing payment obligations based on pre-petition conduct within the definition of 'claims' [under the Bankruptcy Code]." *Id*. at 1005.

A somewhat modified approach was taken by the Eleventh Circuit in a case involving the bankruptcy of Piper Aircraft, Inc., a manufacturer of general aviation aircraft and spare aircraft parts. The bankruptcy court, affirmed by the district court, held that a class of future claimants who might assert, after confirmation of the debtor's plan of reorganization, personal injury or property damage claims against Piper based on its aircraft products that were manufactured or sold before the confirmation date, did not have claims under § 101(5). The bankruptcy and district courts had adopted the pre-petition relationship test which, according to the court of appeals, requires "some pre-petition relationship, such as contact, exposure, impact, or privity, between the debtor's pre-petition conduct and the claimant in order for the claimant to have a § 101(5) claim."

The court of appeals agreed that the pre-petition relationship test was generally superior to either our test in *Frenville* or the "conduct test" adopted by other courts of appeals. It also held that claimants having contact with the debtor's product post-petition, but prior to confirmation, also could be identified during the course of the bankruptcy procedure. It thus framed what it chose to denominate as the "*Piper*" test as follows:

> [A]n individual has a § 101(5) claim against a debtor manufacturer if (i) events occurring before confirmation create a relationship, such as contact, exposure, impact, or privity, between the claimant and the debtor's product; and (ii) the basis for liability is the debtor's prepetition conduct in designing, manufacturing and selling the allegedly defective or dangerous product.

58 F.3d at 1577. The court stated that "[t]he debtor's prepetition conduct gives rise to a claim to be administered in a case only if there is a relationship established before confirmation between an identifiable claimant or group of claimants and that prepetition conduct." *Id*.

* * *

The pre-petition relationship test in *Piper* has been criticized for narrowing the definition of "claim" under § 101(5). * * * In a final report issued in 1997, the National Bankruptcy Review Commission proposed a definition of "claim" that incorporated the conduct test, albeit with some limitations, rather than the prepetition relationship test. *See* Nat'l Bankr. Rev. Comm'n, *Bankruptcy*: *The Next Twenty Years*, National Bankruptcy Review Commission Final Report at 326 (Oct. 20, 1997).

* * *

Irrespective of the title used, there seems to be something approaching a consensus among the courts that a prerequisite for recognizing a "claim" is that the claimant's exposure to a product giving rise to the "claim" occurred pre-petition, even though the injury manifested after the reorganization. We agree and hold that a "claim" arises when an individual is exposed pre-petition to a product or other conduct giving rise to an injury, which underlies a "right to payment" under the Bankruptcy Code. Applied to the Van Brunts, it means that their claims arose sometime in 1977, the date Mary Van Brunt alleged that Grossman's product exposed her to asbestos.

That does not necessarily mean that the Van Brunts' claims were discharged by the Plan of Reorganization. Any application of the test to be applied cannot be divorced from fundamental principles of due process.[11] Notice is "[a]n elementary and fundamental requirement of due process in any proceeding which is to be accorded finality." *Mullane v. Cent. Hanover Bank & Trust Co.*, 339 U.S. 306, 314 (1950). Without notice of a bankruptcy claim, the claimant will not have a meaningful opportunity to protect his or her claim. Inadequate notice therefore "precludes discharge of a claim in bankruptcy." This issue has arisen starkly in the situation presented by persons with asbestos injuries that are not manifested until years or even decades after exposure.

The most innovative approach yet to the asbestos problem was adopted by the New York bankruptcy court as part of the Manville plan of reorganization. *See In the Matter of Johns-Manville Corp.*, 68 B.R. 618 (Bankr. S.D.N.Y.1986). In an effort "to grapple with a social, economic and legal crisis of national importance within the statutory framework of [C]hapter 11," the bankruptcy court oversaw the "largely consensual plan" leading to the establishment of a trust out of which all asbestos health-related claims were to be paid. The trust was "designed to satisfy the claims of all victims, whenever their disease manifest[ed]," (the "Manville Trust"). Manville agreed to fund the trust in an amount that, over time, was "in excess of approximately $2.5

---

[11] Because we have before us an asbestos case, we do not decide when a "claim" arises in the context of an environmental cleanup case involving conflicting statutory frameworks.

billion." *Id*. at 621. The Manville Trust was the basis for Congress' effort to deal with the problem of asbestos claims on a national basis, which it did by enacting § 524(g) of the Bankruptcy Code as part of the Bankruptcy Reform Act of 1994. * * *

It is apparent from the legislative history of § 524(g) that Congress was concerned that future claims by presently unknown claimants could cripple the debtor's reorganization. Senator Graham stated during floor debate on the bill that § 524(g) "provides companies who are seeking to fairly address the burden of thousands of current asbestos injury claims *and unknown future claims* * * * a method to pay their current asbestos claims and provide for equitable treatment of future asbestos claims." 140 Cong. Rec. S4523 (Apr. 20, 1994) (emphasis added). The House of Representatives Committee on the Judiciary wrote in its report that § 524(g) was included in the bill "to offer similar certitude to other asbestos trust/injunction mechanisms that meet the same kind of high standards with respect to regard for the rights of claimants, present and future, as displayed in [*Johns-Manville* and a case following it, *In re UNR Indus., Inc.*, 71 B.R. 467, 473 (Bankr. N.D.Ill.1987)]." H.R. Rep. No. 103-835, at 41 (1994), *reprinted in* 1994 U.S.C.C.A.N. 3349.

By enacting § 524(g), Congress took account of the due process implications of discharging future claims of individuals whose injuries were not manifest at the time of the bankruptcy petition. * * *

The due process safeguards in § 524(g) are of no help to the Van Brunts as Grossman's Plan of Reorganization did not provide for a channeling injunction or trust under that provision.[13] A court therefore must decide whether discharge of the Van Brunts' claims would comport with due process, which may invite inquiry into the adequacy of the notice of the claims bar date. The only open matter before the District Court is JELD-WEN's request for a declaration that the Van Brunts' claims had been discharged.

Whether a particular claim has been discharged by a plan of reorganization depends on factors applicable to the particular case and is best determined by the appropriate bankruptcy court or the district court. In determining whether an asbestos claim has been discharged, the court may wish to consider, *inter alia*, the circumstances of the initial exposure to asbestos, whether and/or when the claimants were aware of their vulnerability to asbestos, whether the notice of the claims

---

[13] Nor could it have done so, as § 524(g) applies only to companies that have been sued for damages before the date of the bankruptcy petition. § 524(g)(2)(B)(i)(I).

bar date came to their attention, whether the claimants were known or unknown creditors, whether the claimants had a colorable claim at the time of the bar date, and other circumstances specific to the parties, including whether it was reasonable or possible for the debtor to establish a trust for future claimants as provided by § 524(g).

[The court reversed and remanded the case.]

Notes and Questions

1. The Court in *Grossman's* began by overruling its earlier decision in *Frenville*. Do you see why *Frenville* has been so reviled?

2. After overruling *Frenville*, the Court reviewed the alternative tests utilized by other jurisdictions to determine when a claim arises. Although there are variations, as the Court noted, the primary alternatives are the "conduct test" and the "prepetition relationship" test. Each of those alternatives has drawn criticism from the courts. Perhaps the most cogent critique of the conduct test was expressed by the court in *Chateaugay*, discussed in *Grossman's*, through its well-known "bridge hypothetical":

> Defining claims to include any ultimate right to payment arising from pre-petition conduct by the debtor * * * yields questionable results. Consider, for example, a company that builds bridges around the world. It can estimate that of 10,000 bridges it builds, one will fail, causing 10 deaths. Having built 10,000 bridges, it becomes insolvent and files a petition in bankruptcy. Is there a "claim" on behalf of the 10 people who will be killed when they drive across the one bridge that will fail someday in the future? If the only test is whether the ultimate right to payment will arise out of the debtor's pre-petition conduct, the future victims have a "claim." Yet it must be obvious that enormous practical and perhaps constitutional problems would arise from recognition of such a claim. The potential victims are not only unidentified, but there is no way to identify them. Sheer fortuity will determine who will be on that one bridge when it crashes. What notice is to be given to these potential "claimants"? Or would it suffice to designate a representative for future victims and authorize the representative to negotiate terms of a binding reorganization plan?

In re Chateaugay Corp., 944 F.2d 997, 1003 (2d Cir.1991). Are these difficulties sufficiently addressed by the prepetition relationship test, or is it equally impossible under both tests to identify future victims of the debtor's defective product?

3. What test for whether a claim exists did the Third Circuit adopt? What is the role of due process in this determination? Do you see a realistic possibility that, on remand, the lower court will find the Van Brunts had a claim that was discharged?

4. What does it mean to be "exposed" to a product? How would *Chauteaugay*'s bridge hypothetical come out under *Grossman's* test? Would it matter whether the victim injured by collapse of the bridge had crossed it every day for years, or was on it for the first time?

5. In *Wright v. Owens Corning*, 679 F.3d 101 (3d Cir.2012), the Court extended *Grossman's* to include claims arising preconfirmation. Two individuals bought roofing shingles manufactured by Debtor. One of them, Wright, made the purchase before Debtor's bankruptcy filing. The other, West, purchased and installed the shingles afterwards. Both roofs cracked and began leaking after passage of the claims bar date. In response to the purchasers' class action lawsuit, Debtor argued that both purchasers held "claims" that were discharged under the reasoning of *Grossman's*.

The Court first reviewed *Grossman's*, describing it as "an amalgam of the two tests that other Courts of Appeals generally follow—the conduct test and the pre-petition relationship test." *Id.* at 106. *Wright* identified an evolving consensus among courts, reflected in the test adopted by *Grossman's*, that a claimant must have suffered prepetition exposure to the debtor's product or conduct. Under that approach, Wright clearly held a claim. West, however, bought the shingles postpetition, but preconfirmation—a factual scenario not present in *Grossman's*. Citing *Piper*, the Court in *Wright* held that *Grossman's* test should be extended:

> Not extending our test to post-petition, but pre-confirmation, exposure would unnecessarily restrict the Bankruptcy Code's expansive treatment of "claims" that we recognized in *Grossman's*. It also would separate artificially individuals who are affected by a debtor's products or conduct pre-petition from those who are affected after the debtor's filing of its bankruptcy petition but before confirmation of a plan. We thus restate the test announced in *Grossman's* to include such exposure and hold that a claim arises when an individual is exposed *pre-confirmation* to a product or other conduct giving rise to an injury that underlies a "right to payment" under the Code. As West's exposure to Owens Corning's shingles occurred pre-confirmation, he also held a claim.

Id. at 107. The Court then pointed out, however, that discharging these claims might raise due process problems, despite the extensive publication notice that was given in Owens Corning's bankruptcy case:

> Though the Debtors' notices were sufficient as to most unknown claimants, the Plaintiffs' situation differed significantly from that of the typical unknown claimant. At the time the Plaintiffs received their notices, *Frenville* was the law in our Circuit (though we refrain from saying "good" law). As noted, under the *Frenville* test the Plaintiffs did not hold "claims" under the Bankruptcy Code. On reading the notices, the Plaintiffs could only understand that their rights would not be affected in any way by the referenced pro-

ceedings, and thus, correctly, would not have taken any action to ensure that their interests were represented. Not until we overturned *Frenville* and established our new test for determining when a claim exists under the Code did the Plaintiffs unexpectedly hold "claims" that arguably could be discharged in the proceedings addressed in the notices. By that time, however, the bar date had passed, the Confirmation Order had been entered, and the Confirmation Date had occurred, each of which affected the Plaintiffs' newfound claim status without an opportunity for them to be heard. Due process affords a re-do in these special situations to be sure all claimants have equal rights. We thus hold that, for persons who have "claims" under the Bankruptcy Code based solely on the retroactive effect of the rule announced in *Grossman's*, those claims are not discharged when the notice given to those persons was with the understanding that they did not hold claims.

Id. (footnote omitted).

6. How can future debtors deal with possible future tort liabilities, and the claims they will generate, without destroying the feasibility either of reorganization or of a sale of assets to a successor-in-interest? *Chateaugay*, in the excerpt above, questioned whether a representative could be appointed. (This is done in other contexts, such as probate matters, of course.) Could such a representative supervise the creation of a trust, similar to that in *Manville*, and thereby solve the problems of both feasibility and due process? Is the Court in *Grossman's* suggesting as much by its reference to § 524(g)—a provision it knew to be inapplicable to the case?

A judgment for money damages is not the only remedy available to an aggrieved party. Injunctions are often sought as a way to force a debtor to conform its conduct to some particular standard. It is sometimes difficult, however, for courts to determine when a right to an equitable remedy gives rise to a claim. The next case discusses one type of equitable remedy—the covenant not to compete.

MAIDS INTERNATIONAL, INC. v. WARD (IN RE WARD)

United States Bankruptcy Court, District of Massachusetts, 1996.
194 B.R. 703.

JAMES F. QUEENAN, JR., Bankruptcy Judge.

Seeking to enforce a noncompetition clause in its franchise agreement, The Maids International, Inc. ("Maids") has brought this complaint to enjoin Michael E. Ward and Angela L. Ward (the "Debt-ors") from owning or operating a maintenance and cleaning service within a fifty mile radius of the franchised territory. Maids contends neither the Debtors' bankruptcy filing nor rejection of their covenant not to compete affects its right to an injunction against the Debtors' competition. I am thus faced with the question of whether Maids' right to injunctive relief is a "claim" within the meaning of the Bankruptcy Code and hence subject to being discharged. At the hearing on Maids' motion for a temporary restraining order, I ruled its right to an injunc-tion is a claim. I therefore dismissed the complaint and ordered Maids to file a proof of claim, reserving jurisdiction to issue the present opinion. Set forth here are my findings of fact and conclusions of law in support of the order of dismissal.

I. FACTS

The facts are not in dispute. Maids has developed a system for establishing and operating a household maintenance and cleaning service. Having a principal office in Omaha, Nebraska, Maids fran-chises its rights in the system to numerous parties throughout the United States.

On April 10, 1989, Maids signed a franchise agreement with a corporation owned and operated by the Debtors named Award Services, Inc. ("Award"). In addition to signing on behalf of Award, the Debtors signed the agreement personally as guarantors of Award's performance thereunder. The agreement also includes the Debtors within the meaning of the term "Franchise," thereby making them jointly respon-sible with Award. Under the agreement, Maids gave Award the exclu-sive right to use its system and the name "Maids" in Concord, Massa-chusetts and in several nearby towns. In return, Award paid Maids $15,900 and obligated itself (and the Debtors) to pay Maids a royalty based on a percentage of its gross sales at rates which range from 4.5% to 7%, depending upon the amount of weekly gross sales. The agree-ment was for an initial term of five years.

* * *

The franchisee agreement expired on April 9, 1994, the end of its five year term. Thereafter, the Debtors commenced operation of a cleaning service within the franchised territory. They operate the business under the name "Mops" and do not hold themselves out as operating a franchise of Maids.

Maids responded to this competition with a series of legal actions. It first commenced an arbitration proceeding in Omaha with the American Arbitration Association. This was uncontested by the Debtors. On March 31, 1995, the arbitrator awarded Maids damages (including interest) of $29,232. He also ordered the Debtors to cease and desist the ownership or operation of a maintenance and cleaning service until April 9, 1996, within a radius of fifty miles from the franchised area or within a radius of fifty miles from any Maids franchise existing on April 9, 1994. Maids then brought suit in the District Court of Douglas County, Nebraska. On July 20, 1995, that court entered a default judgment against the Debtors in the sum of $61,056. Apparently this was in part a confirmation of the arbitration award. At no time has any court entered an injunction against the Debtors competing, in confirmation of the arbitration award or otherwise. Maids next brought its attack closer to home. On November 1, 1995, it filed suit on the judgment in the District Court of Concord, Massachusetts. That court authorized attachments of the Debtors' residence and bank accounts.

Shortly thereafter, on November 13, 1995, the Debtors filed a petition with this court requesting entry of an order for relief under chapter 7 of the Bankruptcy Code. Undeterred, Maids on January 25, 1996 filed its complaint commencing the present adversary proceeding. In its complaint Maids requested an injunction against the Debtors owning or operating a maintenance and cleaning establishment within a fifty mile radius of the franchised territory. At the same time, Maids filed a motion for a temporary restraining order and asked for an emergency hearing. At the hearing on February 5, 1996, I denied the motion, dismissed the complaint and ordered Maids to file a proof of claim. Maids thereafter filed a proof of claim within the permissible filing period.

* * *

III. MAIDS' INJUNCTIVE RIGHTS AS A "CLAIM"

The Debtors are clearly in breach of their covenant not to compete. Breach of the ordinary contract gives rise only to a claim for damages. Maids, however, has the additional right under state law to obtain an injunction against the Debtors' competition, without regard to the provision in the agreement permitting such relief. * * * [B]reach of a covenant not to compete presents a question which has proven difficult for the courts: Do the nondebtor's injunctive rights constitute a "claim" so as to be subject to discharge? The Debtors' discharge hinges upon this issue. A discharge in bankruptcy releases a debtor only as to liability on a "debt," which is defined as "liability on a claim."

[*The court quoted § 101(5)*].

Maids unquestionably has a "right to an equitable remedy" for breach of the Debtors' covenant. But does the breach also give rise to a "right to payment" within the meaning of the statute? That question is not answered by Maids having obtained a damage judgment. As shall be explained, the damages available for breach of the covenant must be an alternative to an equitable remedy if "a right to payment" is to be present. For all we know, the arbitration award and default judgment Maids obtained were only for damages accrued to the date of the hearings, and did not include the future damages that are an alternative to equitable relief.

The only order issued against the Debtors competing is the arbitrator's cease and desist order. No court has entered an injunction against the competition. Even if one had, it would make no difference on the claim issue. The inclusion of an equitable remedy within the definition of "claim" applies "whether or not such right to an equitable remedy is reduced to judgment."

The Supreme Court's decision in *Ohio v. Kovacs* did not involve a covenant not to compete, but it deals with the meaning of the phrase "right to payment" in the context of paragraph (B) of the claim definition. *Kovacs* has been influential in cases involving covenants not to compete. * * *

* * *

Kovacs bears close study. The Court made no attempt to analyze the statutory definition of claim, except to note that the phrases "equitable remedy," "breach of performance" and "right to payment" are undefined.[14] For an equitable remedy to be a claim, the definition requires only that the breach giving rise to the equitable remedy also give rise to a "right" to payment. It imposes no requirement that the claimant exercise his right to payment or show an intent to exercise it. Yet, without pointing to statutory language, the Court saw significance

---

[14]   Of these phrases, only the meaning of "breach of performance" was contested. The Court held this phrase encompassed breach of an obligation imposed by law as well as by private contract. *Id*. at 279.

in the State's intention to seek reimbursement for cleanup costs. Nor does the statute say compliance with a court decree granting the equitable remedy must involve an expenditure of money. The Court nevertheless quotes with apparent approval from the opinion of the bankruptcy court requiring such linkage. Indeed, the Court took pains to tie its opinion to all the various views of the lower courts. This makes the decision vague. The Court also seemed intent on confining its rationale to the particular facts before it. It apparently took this approach because of the inherent difficulty in meshing the compelling environmental concerns before it with a Bankruptcy Code which promotes a fresh start and gives no priority to prepetition environmental claims. The reasoning employed in *Kovacs* should therefore not be binding in cases involving covenants not to compete.

opt ①

Some courts nevertheless rely upon *Kovacs* or its progeny in cases dealing with covenants. They hold that a right to injunctive relief against the debtor's competition is not a claim, and hence is not dischargeable, because compliance with the injunction involves no monetary expenditure.

opt ②

There is also case law rejecting application of the *Kovacs* reasoning to these covenants. In *In re Kilpatrick*,[17] before the bankruptcy filing a state court had enjoined the debtor from breaching his covenant not to compete. In discussing *Kovacs*, the court observed that the statutory definition of "claim" speaks only of a "right" to payment, without imposing any requirement that the claimant pursue that right or disavow the equitable remedy. Because under state law the beneficiary of a covenant can elect to receive either damages or an injunction, the court held injunctive rights are a claim.

* * *

opt ③

Focusing more on the statutory definition, some courts hold the nondebtor party's injunctive right is not a claim because it is present only if the remedy at law is "inadequate," or only if the threatened harm is "irreparable," concluding from this that the nondebtor has no right to payment within the meaning of the statutory definition. Although these courts are correct in ruling a right to payment must exist under nonbankruptcy law, their holding that there is no right to payment for breach of a covenant not to compete conflicts with the damage rights of the beneficiary of a covenant as well as with the general standard

---

[17]   160 B.R. 560 (Bankr. E.D.Mich.1993).

employed by courts in determining whether a party's remedy at law is adequate. This requires some explanation.

An injunction against breach of the covenant is a grant of specific performance. As a result of the historical separation of courts of law and equity, such an equitable remedy is available only if the remedy at law, typically damages, is "inadequate." Courts take into account a number of factors in determining whether damages are inadequate. Principal among them are difficulty in proving the existence and amount of damages with reasonable certainty, difficulty in collecting a monetary judgment, and uncertainty that the benefits of a monetary judgment would be equivalent to the promised performance. * * *

Courts thus compare the remedies at law and equity to see which is more effective in serving the ends of justice. Difficulty in fixing damages is only one factor in that equation. In any event, damages need only be difficult, not impossible, to prove for equitable relief to be available. Comparison of the two remedies usually leads to the grant of equitable relief. Doubts as to the adequacy of the remedy at law are resolved in favor of granting equitable relief. In sum, courts look quite favorably upon equitable relief. This has led one author to conclude that the adequate remedy rule is essentially dead.[30]

Loss of future profits is typically a principal element of damages for breach of a covenant not to compete. The evidentiary problems here for Maids and other covenant beneficiaries are obvious. The proof involves futuristic projections which are especially subject to contest. Courts therefore readily grant an injunction for breach of a covenant not to compete. Indeed, the injured party invariably requests injunctive relief because an injunction gives strong assurance he will receive precisely what was bargained for. This avoids the trauma of future injury, the need to prove damages, and problems in collecting a money judgment. The request for equitable relief has historically been regarded as the election of a preferred remedy.

If the beneficiary of a covenant not to compete elects to receive damages for loss of future profits, he gets the lost profits. Lost profits are a proper element of damages for any breach of contract so long as at the time of the contract the breaching party had reason to know they would be the probable result of breach. The Debtors certainly had that knowledge. The purpose of their covenant was to protect Maids' busi-

---

[30] Douglas Laycock, *The Death of the Irreparable Injury Rule*, 103 HARV. L. REV. 688 (1990).

ness. Although damages must be established with reasonable certainty, an approximation rather than mathematical accuracy is all that is required. The perceived difficulty in proving lost profits is less present today because of the receptive attitude of modern courts toward proof of sophisticated financial data through expert testimony. The award of damages for lost future profits is now a commonplace remedy for breach of all kinds of contracts.

Maids therefore has the right to obtain either damages for the Debtors' future competition or an injunction against the competition. As a result, in the words of the statute, Maids has a "right to an equitable remedy for breach of performance * * * [which] breach gives rise to a right to payment." As an alternative remedy, this right to payment permits a dollar sign to be placed on the equitable remedy, as is done with other claims. Including equitable remedies within the statute's definition of "claim" is therefore supported by a strong bankruptcy policy—equal treatment of similar rights. And because a "claim" is subject to discharge, another important bankruptcy policy is promoted—the policy favoring a debtor's fresh start, unencumbered by past commitments.

In *In re Udell*,[42] the Seventh Circuit came to the opposite conclusion, and in the process added greatly to the confusion in this troubled area of the law. The debtor there had signed an agreement not to compete with his former employer, Standard Carpetland USA, Inc. The covenant was for three years, commencing on termination of employment, and covered a fifty mile radius from the store where the debtor worked. It further provided: "In the event of [the debtor's] actual or threatened breach of the [covenant], Carpetland shall be entitled to an injunction restraining [the debtor] as well as reimbursement for reasonably [sic] attorneys fees incurred in securing said judgment and stipulated damages in the sum of $25,000." Soon after leaving his employment, the debtor purchased a carpet store which he claimed did not compete in the same market as Carpetland's. He sued Carpetland in state court, seeking past due commissions and other compensation. Contending the debtor had breached his agreement not to compete, Carpetland counterclaimed for damages and an injunction against the debtor operating his new store. The state court issued the requested preliminary injunction. The debtor appealed and then filed a chapter 13 petition. Carpetland moved for relief from the automatic stay in order to pursue the state court litigation.

---

[42]   18 F.3d 403 (7th Cir.1994).

In approving relief from stay as a proper exercise of discretion, the Seventh Circuit in *Udell* held Carpetland's injunctive rights were not a "claim" and hence were not dischargeable in bankruptcy.[43] Although not finding the statutory definition of claim ambiguous, the court nevertheless looked to the legislative history that accompanied the final version of the definition, which reconciled differences in the House and Senate bills. It saw significance in the following statement made on the floors of both houses of Congress:

> Section [101(5)(B)] represents a modification of the House-passed bill to include [sic] the definition of "claim" a right to an equitable remedy for breach of performance if such breach gives rise to a right to payment. This is intended to cause the liquidation or estimation of contingent rights of payment for which there may be an alternative equitable remedy with the result that the equitable remedy will be susceptible to being discharged in bankruptcy. For example, in some States, a judgment for specific performance may be satisfied by an alternative right to payment, in the event performance is refused; in that event the creditor entitled to specific performance would have a "claim" for purposes of proceeding under title 11.

> On the other hand, rights to an equitable remedy for breach of performance with respect to which such breach does not give rise to a right to payment are not "claims" and would therefore not be susceptible to discharge in bankruptcy.[46]

The *Udell* court constructed a confusing alternative test from this floor statement. It seized on the awkward phrase "with respect to

---

[43]   In so holding, the Seventh Circuit reversed the district court, which had ruled Carpetland's injunctive rights constituted a claim because the $25,000 liquidated damage clause gave it a "right to payment" within the meaning of the statutory definition of "claim." To qualify as the grant of a right to payment within the meaning of the statute, the district court reasoned, the liquidated damage clause must provide compensation for both past and future damage and hence be the monetary equivalent of an injunction. It concluded the clause qualified because it was stated to be compensation for "actual or threatened harm." This is questionable. There is no reason to require that the clause provide compensation for both past and future damages. The parties apparently intended liquidated damages to be compensation for past damages and an injunction to be protection against incurring future damages.

[46]   124 Cong. Rec. H11090 (daily ed. Sept. 28, 1978); S17406 (daily ed. Oct. 6, 1978) (statements of Rep. Edwards and Sen. DeConcini).

which such breach does not give rise to a right to payment" appearing in the last sentence. Because the phrase arguably modifies "equitable remedy" rather than "breach of performance," the court concluded equitable rights are a claim if payment arises from their exercise. This is opposed to the wording of the statute, which clearly requires that the breach, not the equitable remedy, give rise to a right to payment. And the test makes no sense because equitable remedies are typically designed to provide nonmonetary relief. Having thus created a virtually unpassable test, the court ruled it was flunked by the facts before it because the right to obtain liquidated damages arose from the contract, not from an equitable remedy under it.

The *Udell* court also fashioned another test which, if passed, would make an equitable remedy a claim. It here focused on the reference in the floor statement to a right to payment being an "alternative" to the equitable remedy. From this the court concluded *all* right to payment must be an alternative to the equitable remedy. Because state courts would enforce the parties' agreement by granting both damages and an injunction, the court ruled an alternative right to payment was not present, so Carpetland's rights failed this test as well. This reasoning ignores Carpetland's right to damages for future loss, which *is* an alternative to its equitable remedy. The floor statement's reference to a right to payment being an alternative to equitable relief is understandable because the claim for future loss is the monetary equivalent to the right to an injunction against further competition. Nor is there any reason to believe Congress intended that this alternative right to payment be the only right to payment. The statute does not say so. The injured party is obviously entitled to compensation for damages already incurred by the time of trial, as well as to an injunction against future competition. The liquidated damage clause before the court was presumably designed to provide this compensation because the parties also agreed upon an injunction to prevent future loss. *Udell* thus commits the double sin of elevating legislative history above the statute's plain wording and then misunderstanding the legislative history.

The real basis for the *Udell* court's holding emerges from the concurring opinion of Judge Raum. He thought the majority opinion "dodges this statute's plain language in an effort to reach a sensible result." To Judge Raum, and one suspects to the other panel members, discharge in bankruptcy of an injunction against competition is like a bankruptcy discharge of an injunction against trespassing, polluting, stalking or battering. Because he thought the debtor's discharge would have similar "patently absurd consequences," Judge Raum believed the plain language of the statute should not be followed.

Judge Raum's reasoning leaves much to be desired as well, quite apart from his willingness to elide what he admits to be the statute's plain wording. The case concerned breach of contract, not trespass, pollution, stalking or battery. Moreover, trespass and the like is prohibited by law, without regard to the existence of an injunction. So a bankruptcy discharge does not terminate the obligation to refrain from such conduct. In the final analysis, the decision in *Udell* comes down to this: The court could not bring itself to equate an injunction against breach of contract with a monetary judgment for breach of contract which is routinely discharged in bankruptcy.

IV. CONCLUSION

In summary, although the decisions are in disarray, Maids' alternative right to damages from the Debtors' future competition in breach of their covenant not to compete is a "right to payment" within the meaning of the statutory definition of an equitable claim. Hence, under the definition, Maids' injunctive rights constitute a claim. That state courts consider damages inadequate when compared to the equitable remedy of an injunction is beside the point. Although damages for breach of the covenant, particularly damages for lost future profits, are difficult to fix, courts are perfectly capable of doing so. This alternative right to damages fits into the statutory definition of an equitable claim very well. The same breach, a debtor's competition and threat of further competition, "gives rise" to both a damage claim and injunctive rights. The definition imposes no requirement that the claimant elect to receive a monetary payment, that compliance with the injunction require an expenditure of funds, or that the equitable remedy, as opposed to the breach, give rise to a right to payment. Following the statute's plain meaning promotes two fundamental policies of the Bankruptcy Code—the policy favoring a debtor's fresh start and the policy favoring equality among holders of similar rights.

Notes and Questions

1. Has *Maids* gutted the distinction between an injunctive remedy and a damages remedy?

2. It is fair to say that the disagreement among the courts, discussed in *Maids*, has not been resolved. See, e.g., *Kennedy v. Medicap Pharmacies, Inc.*, 267 F.3d 493 (6th Cir.2001) (following *Udell* and holding an injunction, which protects "against the future realization of a threatened breach of the covenant not to compete," not a claim and, thus, not dischargeable).

C. PAYMENT OF UNSECURED CLAIMS
IN CHAPTER 7

Chapter 7 is conceptually simple. The trustee collects the debtor's assets, liquidates them, and distributes the proceeds in accordance with the Code's directions. See §§ 704(1) & 726. Nonexempt assets owned on the date of filing are used to pay the debts owed on that date. For example, assume that after the trustee collects and liquidates the debtor's assets (and the expenses of doing so are deducted), $5,000 remain. If twenty unsecured creditors are owed $500 each, a total of $10,000 in claims is being asserted against an estate worth half that amount. Each claim will receive 50 cents on the dollar.

Reality is slightly more complicated (isn't it always?), because certain distributions are made from property of the estate ahead of unsecured creditors. Some of the debtor's assets may be subject to valid liens. The lienholder, who is the holder of a secured claim, is entitled to the property that is collateral for its lien (§ 725), thus removing it from the pot of assets available to unsecured creditors. In addition, the debtor may exempt certain types of property, again removing those assets from the reach of creditors. Finally, certain claims, although unsecured, enjoy priority status and are entitled to be paid before general unsecured claims are satisfied. We examined exemptions in Chapter 2 of this text. Priorities are examined later in this Chapter. The rights of secured creditors are the subject of the next Chapter.

D. PAYMENT OF UNSECURED CLAIMS
IN CHAPTERS 12 AND 13

In Chapter 7, payments to holders of general unsecured claims are determined by the amount remaining in the estate after secured claims, estate expenses, exemptions and priorities are satisfied. In Chapters 12 and 13, payments to holders of unsecured claims are determined by the plan proposed by the debtor. Sections 1225(a)(4) and 1325(a)(4) set a floor, however. They require that the plan provide an amount "not less than the amount that would be paid on such claim if the estate of the debtor were liquidated under chapter 7." This "best interests" test necessitates a hypothetical Chapter 7 calculation.

Since unsecured creditors receive nothing in many Chapter 7 cases (generally referred to as "no asset" cases), the best interests test frequently does not provide an effective floor for payments to unsecured creditors in Chapter 13 cases. Courts troubled by this result often seized upon § 1325(a)(3)'s "good faith" requirement, reading it to mandate minimum payment amounts. After Congress added § 1325(b) to the Code in 1984, with its disposable income test, most courts held that a plan meeting the minimum payment requirements of § 1325(b) could not be attacked on the grounds that low payments indicated a lack of good faith. See, e.g., *In re Greer*, 60 B.R. 547 (Bankr. C.D.Cal. 1986). The 2005 Amendments substantially revised § 1325(b) by importing the means test of § 707(b) under certain circumstances.

If the trustee or an unsecured creditor objects to the debtor's plan, § 1325(b)(1)(B) requires that the debtor devote all "projected disposable income" to payments under the plan for the "applicable commitment period." "Disposable income" is defined in § 1325(b)(2) as "current monthly income," § 101(10A), less amounts "reasonably necessary to be expended" for the support of the debtor and his or her family. If the debtor's income is above the state median, amounts "reasonably necessary to be expended" for support must be calculated in accordance with § 707(b)'s means test. The "applicable commitment period" is three years, unless, again, the debtor's income is above the state median. If so, the "applicable commitment period" is five years. § 1325(b)(4).

Application of these provisions requires two determinations: what is to be counted as income, and what expenses are reasonably necessary. The issue of what is included in the disposable income calculation has not always been clear. For example, in *Solomon v. Cosby (In re Solomon)*, 67 F.3d 1128 (4th Cir.1995)—a case involving a debtor we encountered in the Notes and Problems at the beginning of Chapter 2, Section B)—the court had to decide whether the debtor's disposable income (the amount he was required to pay creditors under his Chapter 13 plan) must include funds held in retirement accounts. The Court of Appeals held no:

> Solomon's IRAs are not "income" under the clear terms of this section. Both the statutory definition of "disposable income" as income that is received by the debtor as well as the requirement that projected income must be calculated over the life of the plan contemplate income that a debtor is actually receiving at the time of confirmation. Projected disposable income typically is calculated by multiplying a debtor's monthly income at the time of confirmation by 36 months, the normal duration of a Chapter 13 plan, then determining the portion of that income which is "disposable" according to the statutory definition. It is undisputed that, at the time of the confirmation hearing on Solomon's plan, he was not actually

receiving any disbursements from his IRAs; he further insisted that he had no intention of withdrawing funds from the IRAs during the life of the plan.

> On these facts, we cannot sanction the bankruptcy court's inclusion of some hypothetical amount of income from the IRAs in the calculation of disposable income. "[R]ather than engaging in hopeless speculation about the future," a court should determine projected disposable income by calculating a debtor's "present monthly income and expenditures" and extending those amounts over the life of the plan. *In re Crompton*, 73 B.R. 800, 808 (Bankr. E.D.Pa.1987). Solomon's present, regular monthly income does not include distributions from his IRAs, and the bankruptcy court's imputation of amounts from such speculative distributions in its calculation of disposable income is contrary to the plain terms of the statutory definition.

Id. at 1132. Although the debtor's IRAs were assets of the bankruptcy estate, they were exempt under state law. Therefore, they were not available to creditors for purposes of the "best interests" test under § 1325(a)(4), which requires that unsecured creditors receive no less in Chapter 13 than they would in a Chapter 7 liquidation:

> Because the IRAs would be unavailable to creditors in a Chapter 7 proceeding by virtue of the state law exemption, creditors would receive nothing from those accounts if Solomon's non-exempt assets were to be liquidated. Thus, preserving the IRAs from the claims of Solomon's creditors in this Chapter 13 proceeding is both logically sound and in keeping with the Code. In fact, in a Chapter 7 proceeding, Solomon's creditors would be entitled to the proceeds from liquidation of non-exempt assets worth approximately $40,000. The $45,000 he proposes to pay the creditors under his Chapter 13 plan thus appears to satisfy the "best interests of creditors" prerequisite for confirmation. The Supreme Court has emphasized that the mere happenstance of bankruptcy should not result in a windfall to creditors. *Patterson v. Shumate*, 504 U.S. 753 (1992). Nor, we think, should a debtor's choice to proceed under Chapter 13 invariably entitle creditors to more than they would receive in Chapter 7, contrary to the mandate of the Bankruptcy Code.

Id. at 1133. The court remanded the case for a determination of whether the debtor proposed his plan in good faith under § 1325(a)(3), given that the only creditors were former patients and a patient's spouse who had sued him for alleged sexual misconduct during the course of their medical treatment. As the court observed, good faith is a

> totality-of-the-circumstances inquiry [that] focuses on such factors as the percentage of proposed repayment to creditors, the debtor's financial situation, the period of time over which creditors will be paid, the debtor's employment history and prospects, the nature and amount of unsecured claims, the debtor's past bankruptcy filings, the debtor's honesty in representing the facts of the case, the nature of the debtor's prepetition conduct that gave rise to the debts, whether the debts would be dischargeable in a Chapter 7 proceeding, and any other unusual or exceptional problems the debtor faces. On remand, the bankruptcy court should consider relevant factors in its § 1325(a)(3) analysis of Solomon's plan, mindful of the fact that the good faith inquiry is intended to prevent abuse of the provisions, purpose, or spirit of Chapter 13.

Id. at 1134.

Questions and Problems

1. If you were the judge on remand, how would you decide *In re Solomon*?

2. What is the relationship between the best interests test of § 1325-(a)(4) and the disposable income test of § 1325(b)(2)?

3. Debtor has equity in her residence of $105,000 and is entitled to an exemption of $45,000 under state law. Debtor proposed a plan requiring payment of all her excess disposable income to the trustee for the requisite period of time, but a total of only $14,000 would be paid to unsecured creditors. One of them argued that unsecured creditors should receive at least $60,000—that is, the difference between the equity in her residence and the amount of the permissible exemption. Debtor countered with the argument that if the property were sold in a Chapter 7, capital gains taxes and costs of sale would consume $46,000 and, therefore, that § 1325(a)(4) is satisfied by her plan. Assuming that Debtor's numbers are correct, who wins? See *In re Card*, 114 B.R. 226 (Bankr. N.D.Cal.1990). *Cf.* § 506(a)(2).

Before the 2005 Amendments, a Chapter 13 debtor's "projected disposable income" was determined by actual income and expenses, derived from information set out in the debtor's schedules. In 2005, BAPCPA redefined "disposable income" as "current monthly income received by the debtor," excluding money reasonably necessary for the debtor's support and maintenance, as well as certain business expenses and charitable contributions. Section 101(10A) defines "current monthly income" as "the average monthly income from all sources that the debtor receives" for the last six months before the bankruptcy filing, excluding Social Security benefits. For five years, bankruptcy courts grappled with the question whether the "disposable income" definition, altered by BAPCPA, should be based on an individual debtor's "current disposable income," or on § 101(10A)'s look back at the prior six months. In 2010, the Supreme Court answered this question.

HAMILTON v. LANNING

United States Supreme Court, 2010.
560 U.S. 505, 130 S.Ct. 2464, 177 L.Ed.2d 23.

JUSTICE ALITO delivered the opinion of the Court.

* * *

We granted certiorari to decide how a bankruptcy court should calculate a debtor's "projected disposable income." Some lower courts have taken what the parties term the "mechanical approach," while most have adopted what has been called the "forward-looking approach." We hold that the "forward-looking approach" is correct.

I

* * * [Section] 1325 provides that if a trustee or an unsecured creditor objects to a Chapter 13 debtor's plan, a bankruptcy court may not approve the plan unless it provides for the full repayment of unsecured claims or "provides that all of the debtor's projected disposable income to be received" over the duration of the plan "will be applied to make payments" in accordance with the terms of the plan. Before the enactment of the Bankruptcy Abuse Prevention and Consumer Protection Act of 2005 (BAPCPA), the Bankruptcy Code (Code) loosely defined "disposable income" as "income which is received by the debtor and which is not reasonably necessary to be expended" for the "maintenance or support of the debtor," for qualifying charitable contributions, or for business expenditures. § 1325(b)(2)(A), (B).

The Code did not define the term "projected disposable income," and in most cases, bankruptcy courts used a mechanical approach in calculating projected disposable income. That is, they first multiplied monthly income by the number of months in the plan and then determined what portion of the result was "excess" or "disposable." See 2 K. Lundin, Chapter 13 Bankruptcy § 164.1, p. 164-1, and n. 4 (3d ed. 2000) (hereinafter Lundin (2000 ed.)) (citing cases).

In exceptional cases, however, bankruptcy courts took into account foreseeable changes in a debtor's income or expenses. 1 Lundin § 35.10, at 35-14 (2000 ed.) ("The debtor should take some care to project estimated future income on Schedule I to include anticipated increases or decreases [in income] so that the schedule will be consistent with any evidence of income the debtor would offer at a contested confirmation hearing").

BAPCPA left the term "projected disposable income" undefined but specified in some detail how "disposable income" is to be calculated. "Disposable income" is now defined as "current monthly income received by the debtor" less "amounts reasonably necessary to be expended" for the debtor's maintenance and support, for qualifying charitable contributions, and for business expenditures. § 1325-(b)(2)(A)(i) and (ii) (2006 ed.). "Current monthly income," in turn, is calculated by averaging the debtor's monthly income during what the parties refer to as the 6-month look-back period, which generally consists of the six full months preceding the filing of the bankruptcy petition. See § 101(10A)(A)(i). The phrase "amounts reasonably necessary to be expended" in § 1325(b)(2) is also newly defined. For a debtor whose income is below the median for his or her State, the phrase includes the full amount needed for "maintenance or support," see § 1325(b)(2)(A)(i), but for a debtor with income that exceeds the state median, only certain specified expenses are included, see §§ 707(b)(2), 1325(b)(3)(A).

II

A

Respondent had $36,793.36 in unsecured debt when she filed for Chapter 13 bankruptcy protection in October 2006. In the six months before her filing, she received a one-time buyout from her former employer, and this payment greatly inflated her gross income for April 2006 (to $11,990.03) and for May 2006 (to $15,356.42). As a result of these payments, respondent's current monthly income, as averaged from April through October 2006, was $5,343.70—a figure that exceeds the median income for a family of one in Kansas. Respondent's monthly expenses, calculated pursuant to § 707(b)(2), were $4,228.71. She reported a monthly "disposable income" of $1,114.98 on Form 22C.

On the form used for reporting monthly income (Schedule I), she reported income from her new job of $1,922 per month—which is below the state median. On the form used for reporting monthly expenses (Schedule J), she reported actual monthly expenses of $1,772.97. Subtracting the Schedule J figure from the Schedule I figure resulted in monthly disposable income of $149.03.

Respondent filed a plan that would have required her to pay $144 per month for 36 months. Petitioner, a private Chapter 13 trustee, objected to confirmation of the plan because the amount respondent proposed to pay was less than the full amount of the claims against her, see § 1325(b)(1)(A), and because, in petitioner's view, respondent was not committing all of her "projected disposable income" to the repayment of creditors, see § 1325(b)(1)(B). According to petitioner, the proper way to calculate projected disposable income was simply to multiply disposable income, as calculated on Form 22C, by the number of months in the commitment period. Employing this mechanical approach, petitioner calculated that creditors would be paid in full if respondent made monthly payments of $756 for a period of 60 months. There is no dispute that respondent's actual income was insufficient to make payments in that amount.

B

The Bankruptcy Court endorsed respondent's proposed monthly payment of $144 but required a 60-month plan period. The court agreed with the majority view that the word "projected" in § 1325-(b)(1)(B) requires courts "to consider at confirmation the debtor's *actual* income as it was reported on Schedule I." (Emphasis added). This conclusion was warranted by the text of § 1325(b)(1), the Bankruptcy Court reasoned, and was necessary to avoid the absurd result of denying bankruptcy protection to individuals with deteriorating finances in the six months before filing.

Petitioner appealed to the Tenth Circuit Bankruptcy Appellate Panel, which affirmed. The Panel noted that, although Congress redefined "disposable income" in 2005, it chose not to alter the pre-existing term "projected disposable income." Thus, the Panel concluded, there was no reason to believe that Congress intended to alter the pre-BAPCPA practice under which bankruptcy courts determined projected disposable income by reference to Schedules I and J but considered other evidence when there was reason to believe that the schedules did not reflect a debtor's actual ability to pay.

The Tenth Circuit affirmed. According to the Tenth Circuit, a court, in calculating "projected disposable income," should begin with the "presumption" that the figure yielded by the mechanical approach is correct, but the Court concluded that this figure may be rebutted by evidence of a substantial change in the debtor's circumstances.

This petition followed, and we granted certiorari.

III

A

The parties differ sharply in their interpretation of § 1325's reference to "projected disposable income." Petitioner, advocating the mechanical approach, contends that "projected disposable income" means past average monthly disposable income multiplied by the number of months in a debtor's plan. Respondent, who favors the forward-looking approach, agrees that the method outlined by petitioner should be determinative in most cases, but she argues that in exceptional cases, where significant changes in a debtor's financial circumstances are known or virtually certain, a bankruptcy court has discretion to make an appropriate adjustment. Respondent has the stronger argument.

First, respondent's argument is supported by the ordinary meaning of the term "projected." * * * [I]n ordinary usage future occurrences are not "projected" based on the assumption that the past will necessarily repeat itself. For example, * * * sports analysts do not project that a team's winning percentage at the end of a new season will be the same as the team's winning percentage last year or the team's winning percentage at the end of the first month of competition. While a projection takes past events into account, adjustments are often made based on other factors that may affect the final outcome.

Second, the word "projected" appears in many federal statutes, yet Congress rarely has used it to mean simple multiplication. * * *

By contrast, we need look no further than the Bankruptcy Code to see that when Congress wishes to mandate simple multiplication, it does so unambiguously—most commonly by using the term "multiplied." See, *e.g.*, § 1325(b)(3) ("current monthly income, when multiplied by 12"); §§ 704(b)(2), 707(b)(6), (7)(A) (same); § 707-(b)(2)(A)(i), (B)(iv) ("multiplied by 60"). Accord, 2 U.S.C. § 58(b)(1)(B) ("multiplied by the number of months in such year"); 5 U.S.C. § 8415(a) ("multiplied by such individual's total service"); 42 U.S.C. § 403(f)(3) ("multiplied by the number of months in such year").

Third, pre-BAPCPA case law points in favor of the "forward-looking" approach. Prior to BAPCPA, the general rule was that courts would multiply a debtor's current monthly income by the number of months in the commitment period as the first step in determining projected disposable income. See 2 Lundin § 164.1, at 164-1 (2000 ed.) ("Most courts focus on the debtor's current income and extend current income (and expenditures) over the life of the plan to calculate projected disposable income"). But courts also had discretion to account for known or virtually certain changes in the debtor's income.[4] This judicial discretion was well documented in contemporary bankruptcy treatises. See 8 Collier on Bankruptcy ¶ 1325.08[4][a], p. 1325-50 (15th ed. rev. 2004) (hereinafter Collier) ("As a practical matter, *unless there are changes which can be clearly foreseen*, the court must simply multiply the debtor's known monthly income by 36 and determine whether the amount to be paid under the plan equals or exceeds that amount" (emphasis added)); 2 Lundin § 164.1, at 164-28 to 164-31 (2000 ed.) (describing how reported decisions treated anticipated changes in income, particularly where such changes were "too speculative to be projected"). Indeed, petitioner concedes that courts possessed this discretion prior to BAPCPA.

Pre-BAPCPA bankruptcy practice is telling because we " 'will not read the Bankruptcy Code to erode past bankruptcy practice absent a clear indication that Congress intended such a departure.' " *Travelers Casualty & Surety Co. of America* v. *Pacific Gas & Elec. Co.*, 549 U.S. 443, 454 (2007). Congress did not amend the term "projected disposable income" in 2005, and pre-BAPCPA bankruptcy practice reflected a

---

[4] When pre-BAPCPA courts declined to make adjustments based on possible changes in a debtor's future income or expenses, they did so because the changes were not sufficiently foreseeable, not because they concluded that they lacked discretion to depart from a strictly mechanical approach. In *In re Solomon*, 67 F.3d 1128 (4th Cir.1995), for example, the Fourth Circuit refused to make such an adjustment because it deemed disbursements from an individual retirement account during the plan period to be "speculative" and "hypothetical." *Id*. at 1132. There is no reason to assume that the result would have been the same if future disbursements had been more assured. * * *

widely acknowledged and well-documented view that courts may take into account known or virtually certain changes to debtors' income or expenses when projecting disposable income. In light of this historical practice, we would expect that, had Congress intended for "projected" to carry a specialized—and indeed, unusual—meaning in Chapter 13, Congress would have said so expressly.

B

The mechanical approach also clashes repeatedly with the terms of § 1325.

First, § 1325(b)(1)(B)'s reference to projected disposable income "to be received in the applicable commitment period" strongly favors the forward-looking approach. There is no dispute that respondent would in fact receive far less than $756 per month in disposable income during the plan period, so petitioner's projection does not accurately reflect "income to be received" during that period. The mechanical approach effectively reads this phrase out of the statute when a debtor's current disposable income is substantially higher than the income that the debtor predictably will receive during the plan period.

Second, § 1325(b)(1) directs courts to determine projected disposable income "as of the effective date of the plan," which is the date on which the plan is confirmed and becomes binding, § 1327(a). Had Congress intended for projected disposable income to be nothing more than a multiple of disposable income in all cases, we see no reason why Congress would not have required courts to determine that value as of the *filing* date of the plan. In the very next section of the Code, for example, Congress specified that a debtor shall commence payments "not later than 30 days after the *date of the filing of the plan*." § 1326(a)(1) (emphasis added). Congress' decision to require courts to measure projected disposable income "as of the *effective* date of the plan" is more consistent with the view that Congress expected courts to consider postfiling information about the debtor's financial circumstances.

Third, the requirement that projected disposable income "will be applied to make payments" is most naturally read to contemplate that the debtor will actually pay creditors in the calculated monthly amounts. § 1325(b)(1)(B). But when, as of the effective date of a plan, the debtor lacks the means to do so, this language is rendered a hollow command.

C

The arguments advanced in favor of the mechanical approach are unpersuasive. Noting that the Code now provides a detailed and precise definition of "disposable income," proponents of the mechanical approach maintain that any departure from this method leaves that definition " 'with no apparent purpose.' " *In re Kagenveama*, 541 F.3d 868, 873 (9th Cir.2008). This argument overlooks the important role that the statutory formula for calculating "disposable income" plays under the forward-looking approach. As the Tenth Circuit recognized in this case, a court taking the forward-looking approach should begin by calculating disposable income, and in most cases, nothing more is required. It is only in unusual cases that a court may go further and take into account other known or virtually certain information about the debtor's future income or expenses.

Petitioner faults the Tenth Circuit for referring to a rebuttable "presumption" that the figure produced by the mechanical approach accurately represents a debtor's "projected disposable income." Petitioner notes that the Code makes no reference to any such presumption but that related Code provisions expressly create other rebuttable presumptions. See §§ 707(b)(2)(A)(i) and (B)(i). He thus suggests that the Tenth Circuit improperly supplemented the text of the Code.

The Tenth Circuit's analysis, however, simply heeds the ordinary meaning of the term "projected." As noted, a person making a projection uses past occurrences as a starting point, and that is precisely what the Tenth Circuit prescribed.

Petitioner argues that only the mechanical approach is consistent with § 1129(a)(15)(B), which refers to "projected disposable income of the debtor (as defined in section 1325(b)(2))." This cross-reference, petitioner argues, shows that Congress intended for the term "projected disposable income" to incorporate, presumably in all contexts, the defined term "disposable income." It is evident that § 1129-(a)(15)(B) refers to the defined term "disposable income," see § 1325-(b)(2), but that fact offers no insight into the meaning of the word "projected" in §§ 1129(a)(15)(B) and 1325(b)(1)(B). We fail to see how that word acquires a specialized meaning as a result of this cross-reference—particularly where both §§ 1129(a)(15)(B) and 1325-(b)(1)(B) refer to projected disposable income "to be received" during the relevant period.

Petitioner also notes that § 707 allows courts to take "special circumstances" into consideration, but that § 1325(b)(3) incorporates § 707 only with respect to calculating expenses. Thus, he argues, a "special circumstances" exception should not be inferred with respect to the debtor's income. We decline to infer from § 1325's incorporation of § 707 that Congress intended to eliminate, *sub silentio*, the discretion that courts previously exercised when projecting disposable income to account for known or virtually certain changes.

D

In cases in which a debtor's disposable income during the 6-month look-back period is either substantially lower or higher than the debtor's disposable income during the plan period, the mechanical approach would produce senseless results that we do not think Congress intended. In cases in which the debtor's disposable income is higher during the plan period, the mechanical approach would deny creditors payments that the debtor could easily make. And where, as in the present case, the debtor's disposable income during the plan period is substantially lower, the mechanical approach would deny the protection of Chapter 13 to debtors who meet the chapter's main eligibility requirements. Here, for example, respondent is an "individual whose income is sufficiently stable and regular" to allow her "to make payments under a plan," § 101(30), and her debts fall below the limits set out in § 109(e). But if the mechanical approach were used, she could not file a confirmable plan. Under § 1325(a)(6), a plan cannot be confirmed unless "the debtor will be able to make all payments under the plan and comply with the plan." And as petitioner concedes, respondent could not possibly make the payments that the mechanical approach prescribes.

In order to avoid or at least to mitigate the harsh results that the mechanical approach may produce for debtors, petitioner advances several possible escape strategies. He proposes no comparable strategies for creditors harmed by the mechanical approach, and in any event none of the maneuvers that he proposes for debtors is satisfactory.

1

Petitioner first suggests that a debtor may delay filing a petition so as to place any extraordinary income outside the 6-month look-back period. We see at least two problems with this proposal.

First, delay is often not a viable option for a debtor sliding into bankruptcy.

Potential Chapter 13 debtors typically find a lawyer's office when they are one step from financial Armageddon: There is a foreclosure sale of the debtor's home the next day; the debtor's only car was mysteriously repossessed in the dark of last night; a garnishment has reduced the debtor's take-home pay below the ordinary requirements of food and rent. Instantaneous relief is expected, if not necessary."

K. Lundin & W. Brown, CHAPTER 13 BANKRUPTCY § 3.1[2] (4th ed. rev. 2009).

Second, even when a debtor is able to delay filing a petition, such delay could be risky if it gives the appearance of bad faith. See § 1325(a)(7) (requiring, as a condition of confirmation, that "the action of the debtor in filing the petition was in good faith").

2

Petitioner next argues that a debtor with unusually high income during the 6 months prior to the filing of a petition, could seek leave to delay filing a schedule of current income (Schedule I) and then ask the bankruptcy court to exercise its authority under § 101(10A)(A)(ii) to select a 6-month period that is more representative of the debtor's future disposable income. We see little merit in this convoluted strategy. If the Code required the use of the mechanical approach in all cases, this strategy would improperly undermine what the Code demands. And if, as we believe, the Code does not insist upon rigid adherence to the mechanical approach in all cases, this strategy is not needed. In any event, even if this strategy were allowed, it would not help all debtors whose disposable income during the plan period is sharply lower than their previous disposable income.[6]

3

Petitioner suggests that a debtor can dismiss the petition and refile at a later, more favorable date. But petitioner offers only the tepid assurance that courts "generally" do not find this practice to be abusive. This questionable stratagem plainly circumvents the statutory limits on

---

[6] Under § 521(i)(3), a debtor seeking additional time to file a schedule of income must submit the request within 45 days after filing the petition, and the court may not grant an extension of more than 45 days.

a court's ability to shift the look-back period, and should give debtors pause.[7]

4

Petitioner argues that respondent might have been able to obtain relief by filing under Chapter 7 or by converting her Chapter 13 petition to one under Chapter 7. The availability of Chapter 7 to debtors like respondent who have above-median incomes is limited. In respondent's case, a presumption of abuse would attach under § 707(b)(2)(A)(i) because her disposable income, "multiplied by 60," exceeds the amounts specified in subclauses (I) and (II). Nevertheless, petitioner argues, respondent might have been able to overcome this presumption by claiming that her case involves "special circumstances" within the meaning of § 707(b)(2)(B)(i). Section 707 identifies as examples of "special circumstances" a "serious medical condition or a call or order to active duty in the Armed Forces," and petitioner directs us to no authority for the proposition that a prepetition decline in income would qualify as a "special circumstance." In any event, the "special circumstances" exception is available only to the extent that "there is no reasonable alternative," a proposition we reject with our interpretation of § 1325(b)(1) today.

In sum, each of the strategies that petitioner identifies for mitigating the anomalous effects of the mechanical approach is flawed. There is no reason to think that Congress meant for any of these strategies to operate as a safety valve for the mechanical approach.

IV

We find petitioner's remaining arguments unpersuasive. Consistent with the text of § 1325 and pre-BAPCPA practice, we hold that when a bankruptcy court calculates a debtor's projected disposable income, the court may account for changes in the debtor's income or expenses that are known or virtually certain at the time of confirmation. We therefore affirm the decision of the Court of Appeals.

It is so ordered.

---

[7] For example, a debtor otherwise eligible for Chapter 13 protection may become ineligible if "at any time in the preceding 180 days" "the case was dismissed by the court for willful failure of the debtor to abide by orders of the court, or to appear before the court in proper prosecution of the case," or "the debtor requested and obtained the voluntary dismissal of the case following the filing of a request for relief from the automatic stay provided by section 362 of this title." § 109(g).

Notes and Questions

1. In a dissenting opinion, JUSTICE SCALIA argued that the majority's conclusion was inconsistent with the Code's text. The Court's "interpretation runs aground because it either renders superfluous text Congress included or requires adding text Congress did not. It would be pointless to define disposable income in such detail, based on data during a specific 6-month period, if a court were free to set the resulting figure aside whenever it appears to be a poor predictor." JUSTICE SCALIA agreed that "[t]he word "projected" * * * most sensibly refers to a calculation, prediction, or estimation of future events. But one assuredly can calculate, predict, or estimate future figures based on the past." He was dismissive of the Court's gambling and football analogies:

> Such analogies do not establish that carrying current monthly income forward to determine a debtor's future ability to pay is not a "projection." They show only that relying exclusively on past data for the projection may be a bad idea. One who is asked to predict future results, but is armed with no other information than prior performance, can still make a projection; it may simply be off the mark.

560 U.S. at 528.

2. Factually, *Lanning* involved a one-time spike in the debtor's income, rather than a fluctuation in expenses. Does the case also apply to a one-time expense incurred by the debtor? Apparently, the majority thought so; it lumped income and expenses together in holding that a bankruptcy court "may account for changes in the debtor's income *or expenses* that are known or virtually certain at the time of confirmation." Technically, any references to expenses were merely dicta. Interestingly, however, JUSTICE SCALIA seemed to think that the case presented an appropriate opportunity to discuss expenses; he clearly believed that the expense side of the calculation permits a flexibility not available, statutorily, as to income:

> While under my reading a court must determine the *income* half of the "projected disposable income" equation by multiplying a fixed number, that is not necessarily true of the *expenses* excludable under § 1325(b)(2)(A) and (B). Unlike the debtor's current monthly income, none of the three types of expenses—payments for the support of the debtor and his dependents, charitable contributions, and expenses to keep an existing business above water—is explicitly defined in terms of historical figures (at least for debtors with incomes below the state median).

Id. at 529.

3. The Court said that a mechanical approach in facts like these "would produce senseless results that we do not think Congress intended." Do you agree? Is it not equally possible that Congress wanted a mechanical

approach for other reasons—for example, as a way of reducing the discretion of bankruptcy judges, which was also a goal of the 2005 Amendments—and that Congress would have been willing to accept "senseless" results in a few cases, presenting unusual facts, in order to accomplish those other goals? The Court, apparently, thought not; it "decline[d] to infer from § 1325's incorporation of § 707 that Congress intended to eliminate, *sub silentio*, the discretion that courts previously exercised when projecting disposable income to account for known or virtually certain changes."

4. Recall *Ransom*, which we encountered in Chapter 2, Section B.3, of this casebook. It was decided by the Supreme Court seven months before *Lanning*. Together, those two cases give some insight into how lower courts should approach the myriad interpretive problems raised by the 2005 Amendments. "The common thread that can be derived from the Supreme Court's decisions in *Lanning* and *Ransom* is that the means test must be applied in light of the debtor's actual circumstances * * * to give effect to its purpose—that is, that debtors who can afford to pay their creditors should pay their creditors." *In re Johnson*, 454 B.R. 882, 889 (Bankr. M.D.Fla.2011).

5. Assume that Debtor is making payments on a secured debt at the time of bankruptcy filing, but intends to surrender the collateral to the secured creditor in the near future. Is *Lanning* relevant to the question whether Debtor can deduct the amount of the payment in making the means test calculation, even though that obligation will soon cease? See *Darrohn v. Hildebrand (In re Darrohn)*, 615 F.3d 470 (6th Cir.2010).

Once the bankruptcy court has assessed income, it must next determine the *expenses* that are appropriately deducted from income. Before passage of the 2005 Amendments, a Chapter 13 debtor's expenses were derived from information set out in the debtor's schedules. Courts were left to determine what sorts of expenses might qualify, and what expenditures constituted "excessive spending." See *In re Woodman*, 287 B.R. 589 (Bankr. D. Me.2003) (discussing whether the cost of two packs of cigarettes a day is reasonable), and *In re Ploegert*, 93 B.R. 641 (Bankr. N.D. Ind.1988) (addressing whether $840 per month for recreation and entertainment, which included $35 for cable television and "dining out on a weekly basis," was reasonable for a single debtor). Now, § 1325(b)(3) requires that reasonably necessary expenses be determined in accordance with § 707(b)(2)—the means test—if the debtor's income exceeds the state median for a household of the same size. In such a case, the plan cannot be for less than five years, unless it pays 100% of unsecured claims over a shorter period of time.

A debtor is also required, as a condition of plan confirmation, to have paid all domestic support obligations, § 1325(a)(8), and to have filed all prepetition tax returns, § 1325(a)(9). Filing a return, of course, is not the same thing as paying the taxes.

Finally, the Code requires that the debtor both file the petition in good faith, § 1325(a)(7), and propose the plan in good faith, § 1325-(a)(3). (Recall the court's discussion in *In re Solomon*.) The former requirement is new, but the latter has been a part of the Code since its inception.

Problems

1. Debtor embezzled $57,000 from her employer, Corporation One, and was placed in a pretrial diversion program that required restitution. Debtor obtained employment with Corporation Two and embezzled $105,000, using part of the proceeds to repay Corporation One. Debtor was caught again and this time sentenced to jail. Upon her release, Debtor found a job (!) but never offered or attempted to repay Corporation Two. Instead, when Corporation Two began collection proceedings, Debtor filed Chapter 13. She listed three creditors: 1) Bank, with an $8,000 secured claim in Debtor's car; 2) Visa, with a $1,000 unsecured claim; and 3) Corporation Two, with an unsecured claim of $105,000. Debtor's three-year plan proposed to pay 100% to Bank and 3% to the unsecured creditors. Does the plan meet the good faith requirement of § 1325(a)(3)? See *In re Zelnar*, 91 B.R. 448 (Bankr. N.D. Ohio 1988).

2. Debtor, who had been a homemaker for 19 years, filed for an automobile dealer's license "in order to put food on the table" when her husband lost his license for rolling back odometers. Debtor knew nothing about the business, but her husband promised that he would help her and that he would not do anything dishonest. Despite those promises, he altered odometers and bribed state officials. Debtor was held civilly liable under agency principles for $200,000. She filed Chapter 13 in an effort to discharge that debt. Does Debtor's plan lack § 1325(a)(3) good faith? See *In re Hughes*, 98 B.R. 784 (Bankr. S.D. Ohio 1989).

E. PAYMENT OF UNSECURED CLAIMS
IN CHAPTER 11

Payments to unsecured creditors in Chapter 11 are governed by the plan, as they are in Chapter 13. Classes of creditors in Chapter 11 get to vote on the plan, with each creditor in the class voting in proportion to the dollar amount of debt owed to that creditor. (A case later in this Chapter, *Kane v. Johns–Manville Corp.*, discusses Chapter

11's voting requirements in further detail.) Any treatment under the plan is permissible if the affected creditors agree to it. If a creditor votes against the plan, however, Chapter 11 imposes a "best interests" test much like the one in Chapter 13—the plan must pay the individual dissenting creditor as much as that creditor would have received in a Chapter 7. See § 1129(a)(7)(A)(ii). The Code also permits the debtor to confirm a plan over the objection of certain *classes* of creditors; when the dissenting class is unsecured, the "absolute priority rule" requires the debtor either to pay those claims in full or leave shareholders with nothing. (Chapter 8 of this casebook covers these provisions in detail, in the context of corporate reorganizations.)

Chapter 11 imposes a disposable income test in cases filed by individual debtors, if an unsecured creditor objects to confirmation of the proposed plan. Section 1129(a)(15) imports the disposable income test of § 1325(b)(2): "current monthly income" reduced by "reasonably necessary" expenses. As you recall, reasonably necessary expenses are determined in accordance with the means test of § 707(b)(2) if the debtor's income is above the state median for a family of equivalent size.

F. PRIORITIES

Despite bankruptcy's equality principle, some creditors are more equal than others. We already know that secured creditors are paid first, leaving unsecured creditors to share whatever is left. But some unsecured creditors are paid before the rest. These favored creditors are "priority" creditors. Bankruptcy's priorities are listed in § 507.

Under § 507, each level of claims is paid in full before any payment is made to the next lower priority level, as long as funds are sufficient. When funds are insufficient to pay all of the claims at a particular priority level, those claims are paid pro rata. Any claims at a lower priority level, as well as general unsecured claims having no priority, will get nothing.

In Chapter 11, priority claims in the second and third levels must be paid in full and in cash on the effective date of the plan, unless the individual claimholder waives this requirement. The remaining priority claims (except those taxes having an eighth priority) must also be paid in full in cash on the plan's effective date unless the class of claimholders votes to accept payment over time. Priority tax claims can be paid in installments, over a period not exceeding five years. § 1129(a)(9). In Chapter 13, priority claims must be paid in full, although payment can be made over time unless the claimholder agrees to different treatment. § 1322(a)(2). Claims for domestic support obligations owed to governmental units, however, can receive less than full payment if all of the debtor's projected disposable income for the next five years is devoted to plan payments. § 1322(a)(4).

Domestic support obligations are entitled to first priority under the Code, having been promoted from seventh-level priority by the 2005 Amendments. These claims have always enjoyed special status in bankruptcy, due to the particular vulnerability of the claimants, and this change was only one of several ways in which they have been favored. Be alert to these provisions as we progress through these materials.

Administrative expenses, *i.e.*, expenses of bankruptcy itself, had first priority until enactment of the 2005 Amendments. Now, those claims have been demoted to second under § 507(a). You should not be surprised to learn that fees for the trustee and for attorneys enjoy such a high priority. Given the favorable relative position administrative expenses enjoy, creditors with a possible entitlement to that status have a strong incentive to press their argument. That incentive might have been reduced by the 2005 Amendments, but it certainly was not eliminated.

The following case explores the scope of the administrative expense priority, relying on the seminal Supreme Court case on the issue, *Reading Co. v. Brown*, 391 U.S. 471, 88 S.Ct 1759, 20 L.Ed.2d 751 (1968).

ALABAMA SURFACE MINING COMM'N v. N.P. MINING CO. (IN RE N.P. MINING CO.)

United States Court of Appeals, Eleventh Circuit, 1992.
963 F.2d 1449.

KRAVITCH, Circuit Judge.

The Alabama Surface Mining Commission ("ASMC" or "Commission") appeals from a decision of the bankruptcy court, affirmed by the district court, holding that under the facts of this case, punitive civil penalties assessed after the debtor filed a voluntary petition for protection under chapter 11 and before the case was converted to chapter 7 liquidation proceedings were not entitled to administrative-expense priority under § 503(b). We reverse, and remand the case for further factfinding by the bankruptcy court consistent with our opinion.

BACKGROUND

The ASMC is responsible for administering and enforcing the Alabama Surface Mining Control and Reclamation Act ("Alabama SMCRA"). Debtor N.P. Mining Co. ("N.P."), licensed under the Alabama SMCRA, was engaged in the business of harvesting and brokering coal gathered by surface mining, which is also known as strip mining.

Surface mining is a practice that is heavily regulated in the State of Alabama. State law requires that a licensed operator purchase non-cancelable reclamation bonds that ensure that the land it mines will be environmentally reclaimed even if the company becomes insolvent. This scheme apparently worked here as expected: After N.P. became insolvent, its insurer, American Resources, honored the bonds, paying the State of Alabama more than two million dollars to repair the actual damage done to the land. The actual costs of reclaiming the land are not at issue in this suit.

* * * [T]he Commission cited and fined N.P. for numerous violations of the Alabama SMCRA. These fines are solely punitive; that is, they are completely unrelated to the actual costs of correcting harm to the environment. The amount of the fines is figured based on a formula in the Alabama Code. The fines were assessed both before and after N.P. filed its voluntary petition for protection under chapter 11 of the Bankruptcy Code, but we are here concerned only with those fines assessed postpetition. * * * Eventually, the postpetition penalties totalled $2,349,000, the great majority of which was assessed when the estate was no longer in a position to abate the violations and thereby avoid the fines. * * *

The Commission seeks administrative-expense priority for these punitive postpetition penalties under § 503(b). * * *

[The ASMC assessed $399,700 in fines during the period that N.P. operated as debtor in possession, and $1,949,400 after a Chapter 11 trustee was appointed and mining operations ceased.]

On April 14, 1989, the case was converted to chapter 7 liquidation proceedings * * * . Presently, there appears to be between $400,000 to $500,000 in assets remaining in the estate. * * *

N.P. and the chapter 7 trustee * * * argued that the penalties should not be raised to the level of first-priority administrative expenses ahead of the unsecured creditors. The bankruptcy court agreed, * * * holding that these punitive, postpetition, civil penalties did not constitute an administrative expense under § 503(b)(1)(A), largely because they did not serve to benefit the estate in any way. The district court affirmed this decision.

DISCUSSION

* * * Whether and when postpetition, punitive, non-tax penalties can be accorded administrative-expense status under § 503(b) is an issue of first impression in this circuit. * * * No circuit has addressed precisely this question.

* * *

* * * [T]he postpetition penalties for which the ASMC is seeking administrative-expense status are not compensatory. They will not reimburse innocent victims of tortious conduct by a trustee or debtor in possession, nor will they be used to repair environmental damage. Further, there is no evidence that any of the violations pose an imminent health hazard. If we grant administrative-expense status to these noncompensatory penalties, we will create a new category of postpetition costs entitled to first priority.

The ASMC presents an argument, consisting of three separate but related components, for according the penalties here administrative-expense status. The first part of the argument relies on *Reading Co. v. Brown*, 391 U.S. 471 (1968), which, interpreting the former Bankruptcy Code, held that tort claims against a bankruptcy trustee were payable as administrative expenses even though they were not beneficial to the estate. The ASMC argues that the logic of *Reading*—that costs "normally incident to operation of a business" can be administrative expenses—applies to the penalties here in question. The ASMC next contends, relying on cases holding that a bankruptcy trustee cannot circumvent environmental protection laws and that the actual costs of environmental cleanup can be administrative expenses, that a Bankruptcy Code policy in favor of environmental protection mandates that punitive environmental fines should be treated the same as compensatory environmental fines. The ASMC finally argues that a federal policy mandating trustees' compliance with state law requires that all postpetition civil penalties receive administrative-expense status as "actual, necessary" costs of preserving the estate.

Although not convinced by all of the ASMC's arguments, we find that punitive, civil penalties assessed for postpetition mining activities qualify as an administrative expense under § 503(b)(1)(A). We do not base our decision on the Bankruptcy Code policies—such as fairness to claimholders or environmental protection—relied on by other courts that have granted administrative-expense status to costs that do not benefit the bankruptcy estate. Rather, we base our decision on the federal policy, embodied in 28 U.S.C. § 959(b), that trustees "operate" an estate in compliance with state law. In accordance with this policy, we hold that the penalties in question receive first priority, but only to the extent that they were incurred as a consequence of mining operations after the bankruptcy petition was filed and while the business was still "operating."

* * *

A. Reading *and Administrative-Expense Priority for "Costs Ordinarily Incident to Operation of a Business"*

Appellant cites *Reading* and a line of cases employing its reasoning. In these cases, courts have created categories of costs that are entitled to administrative-expense status as "actual, necessary" costs of preserving the estate even though these costs do not confer an actual benefit on the estate. * * *

One policy behind [§ 503(b)] is "to facilitate the rehabilitation of insolvent businesses by encouraging third parties to provide those businesses with necessary goods and services." *United Trucking Serv., Inc. v. Trailer Rental Co., Inc. (In re United Trucking Serv., Inc.)*, 851 F.2d 159, 161 (6th Cir.1988). Obviously, without a guarantee of first-priority payment, third parties would not deal with a business in chapter 11 reorganization, and the goal of rehabilitation could not be achieved. Another "overriding concern in the [Bankruptcy] Act [is] with keeping fees and administrative expenses at a minimum so as to preserve as much of the estate as possible for the creditors." *Otte v. United States*, 419 U.S. 43, 53 (1974). Thus, some courts have interpreted § 503-(b)(1)(A) narrowly to apply only to those costs that either help to rehabilitate the business or to preserve the estate's assets, in other words, only to those costs that benefit the estate in some way.

* * *

Such a reading, however, ignores that there are other policies also involved in § 503(b). The Supreme Court has not construed the meaning of administrative expense s narrowly. Interpreting * * * the predecessor to § 503(b), the Court, holding that tort claims were "actual and necessary" costs, stated:

> [D]ecisions in analogous cases suggest that "actual and necessary costs" should include *costs ordinarily incident to operation of a business,* and not be limited to costs without which rehabilitation would be impossible. It has long been the rule of equity receiverships that torts of the receivership create claims against the receivership itself; in those cases the statutory limitation to "actual and necessary costs" is not involved, but the explicit recognition extended to tort claims in those cases weighs heavily in favor of considering them within the general category of costs and expenses.

> In *some cases* arising under Chapter XI it has been recognized that "actual and necessary costs" are not limited to those claims which the business must be able to pay in full if it is to be able to deal at all. *For example, state and federal taxes accruing during a receivership have been held to be actual and necessary costs of an arrangement.* The United States, recognizing and supporting these holdings, agrees with petitioner that costs that form "an integral and essential element of the continuation of the business" are necessary expenses even though priority is not necessary *to* [emphasis in original] the continuation of the business. * * * We hold that damages resulting from the negligence of a receiver acting within the scope of his authority as receiver give rise to "actual and necessary costs" of a Chapter XI arrangement.

Reading Co., 391 U.S. at 484-85 (emphasis added except where noted) (footnote omitted).

If postpetition costs "ordinarily incident to operation of a business" that do not confer a benefit on the estate can indeed qualify as "actual, necessary" expenses of preserving the estate, then a strong case can be made that when a licensed business operates in the regulated atmosphere of strip mining in Alabama, incurring regulatory penalties is a cost ordinarily incident to operation of a business and should be accorded administrative-expense priority. * * *

The *Reading* Court did not hold, however, that in *all cases* costs normally incident to operation of a business are administrative expenses. Only in "*some cases*," the Court stated, do they merit such status. * * *

B.   Must Reading's Interpretation of the Former Code Be Followed in Interpreting the Current Code?

[The court rejected appellees' argument that Reading *was in-applicable because it arose under the Bankruptcy Act; § 503(b)(1)(A) is substantially like the subsection at issue in* Reading, *and both iterations of the statute use the word "including." That indicates Congress's intent to include claims other than those serving to preserve the estate.]*

C.   Administrative-Expense Status for Compensation of Innocent Victims of the Estate's Actions

According to the *Reading* Court, administrative-expense status may sometimes be given to postpetition costs ordinarily incident to the operation of a business that do not benefit the estate. The Court held that the statutory objective of "fairness to all persons having claims against an insolvent," mandated that those injured by a trustee's negligence be entitled to first priority. The Court reasoned that postpetition tort claims should be treated as actual and necessary expenses because, in part:

> in considering whether those injured by the operation of the business during an arrangement should share equally with, or recover ahead of, those for whose benefit the business is carried on, the latter seems more natural and just. Existing creditors are, to be sure, in a dilemma not of their own making, but there is no obvious reason why they should be allowed to attempt to escape that dilemma at the risk of imposing it on others equally innocent.

391 U.S. at 482-83. This concern does not apply in the instant case, however, because the ASMC fines do not represent compensation for any injury. A policy of fairness to persons injured by the estate, therefore, does not dictate that the postpetition penalties levied by the ASMC

receive first priority. In fact, fairness is the reason that punitive penalties have historically been disfavored in the Code.[4]

The *Reading* Court also justified giving tort claims first priority by reasoning that such a holding would encourage receivers to insure adequately the businesses they operate. Here, the equivalent of insurance was the reclamation bonds, the premiums of which were in fact paid by the chapter 11 trustee. Because the ASMC penalties had no connection to the actual cost of land reclamation, their status as a first-priority administrative expense would neither encourage nor discourage the purchase of reclamation bonds.

* * *

D.   Administrative-Expense Status for Environmental Cleanup

Appellant puts forward another policy supporting granting of administrative-expense status here: environmental protection. In *Midlantic National Bank v. New Jersey Department of Environmental Protection*, 474 U.S. 494 (1986), the Supreme Court held that a bankruptcy trustee could not abandon a debtor's contaminated property in contravention of a state statute designed to protect the public health or safety from an identified hazard. The Court partly based its decision on "repeated congressional emphasis on its 'goal of protecting the environment against toxic pollution.'" The Court also described this policy as "Congress' undisputed concern over the risks of the improper storage and disposal of hazardous and toxic substances." The Court held:

> Where the Bankruptcy Code has conferred special powers upon the trustee and where there was no common-law limitation on that power, Congress has expressly provided that *the efforts of the trustee to marshall and distribute the assets of the estate must yield to governmental interest in public health and safety.*

Id. at 502 (emphasis added).

* * *

None of these factors is present in the instant case. Here, there is no threat to public health or safety. Nor will the fines pay for environmental cleanup. Further, the mining sites—which N.P. leased and

---

[4] Prepetition punitive penalties receive a lower level of priority than prepetition compensatory penalties in chapter 7 distribution. See § 726(a)(2) & (4). * * *

did not own—are not part of the bankruptcy estate, so abating violations there does not even provide an indirect benefit to the estate by
bringing the property into compliance. Because these punitive penalties
will not be used to abate any identified environmental hazard caused by
the estate, they should more properly be thought of simply as civil
penalties no different from penalties for violating antitrust or securities
laws. In short, although this case involves environmental penalties, no
policy in favor of environmental protection justifies giving these penalties administrative-expense priority.

E.   Compliance with State Law as an Administrative Expense

     Appellant raises another federal policy, one that we hold does
justify giving first priority to punitive penalties that are ordinarily
incident to operation of a business. The ASMC points to 28 U.S.C.
§ 959(b) * * *.

     The Alabama SMCRA requires that operators avoid violating
specified environmental rules, abate violations when they do occur, and
pay fines for noncompliance. Because an operator outside the
protection of the bankruptcy laws would be bound to pay these fines,
the policy of § 959(b) that state law govern the actions of a trustee
mandates that these fines be paid. * * *

     We find that a policy of ensuring compliance by trustees with
state law is sufficient justification to place civil penalties assessed for
postpetition mining operations in the category of the "some cases" in
which "costs ordinarily incident to operation of a business" are accorded administrative-expense priority. * * * Even though these civil
penalties are not compensatory, it makes sense that when a trustee or
debtor in possession operates a bankruptcy estate, compliance with state
law should be considered an administrative expense. Otherwise, the
bankruptcy estate would have an unfair advantage over nonbankrupt
competitors. A mining operation could, under the protection of chapter
11, cut costs by ignoring safety and environmental violations.

     However, although we are mindful that the Alabama statute
requires mining operators to abate past violations and that penalties are
assessed for a failure to abate, we exclude from consideration as an
administrative expense any penalty assessed postpetition for the failure
of the debtor in possession or the trustee to abate a prepetition violation
of the statute. A requirement that a debtor in possession or a trustee
expend funds in the bankruptcy estate for the purpose of abating prior
mining violations would deprive the estate of its "new day" beginning

and frustrate the purpose of the bankruptcy statute. The ASMC has as one of its remedies the right to secure an administrative or court order mandating cessation of the operation of a mine by an operator who violates any of the provisions of the mining act and regulations. If prior to bankruptcy the Commission has not sought abatement of certain practices of a mining operator we deem those violations not to be of such consequence as to require the bankruptcy estate liable for penalties assessed for failure to abate after the filing of a petition.

We hold that under the reasoning of *Reading* and the policy of § 959(b), punitive civil penalties assessed as a consequence of the operation of a bankruptcy estate's business are "actual, necessary costs and expenses of preserving the estate" under § 503(b)(1)(A).

* * *

G. Was the Trustee "Managing or Operating the Property" When the Fines Were Incurred?

Appellees argue that the great majority of the fines should not be allowed because they were assessed after the business had essentially ceased all operations upon the appointment of the chapter 11 trustee. All mining operations had ceased and the trustee's only duty was to keep alive a coal-brokering contract: therefore, the trustee was not "operating" the estate and hence neither the policy of § 959(b) that a trustee "manage and operate a property" in compliance with state law nor the language of *Reading* that "costs incident to operation of a business" is implicated.

A number of courts have held that § 959(b) does not apply when a business's operations have ceased and its assets are being liquidated. * * * Interpreting * * * the predecessor to § 959, Judge Learned Hand stated, "Merely to hold matters in the status quo; to mark time, as it were; to do only what is necessary to hold the assets intact; such activities are not a continuance of the business." *Vass v. Conron Bros. Co.*, 59 F.2d 969, 971 (2d Cir.1932). For the same reasons, penalties incurred when a trustee is merely maintaining an estate for later distribution of assets cannot be considered "costs ordinarily incident to operation of a business." Therefore, they also cannot be "actual, necessary costs or expenses of preserving the estate" and administrative expenses under § 503(b)(1)(A).

The chapter 11 trustee administered the estate for approximately ten months. Within five weeks of taking control, however, he determined that rehabilitation would be impossible and he filed a motion to have the case converted to chapter 7. * * * Although N.P. under the trustee's administration was not entirely inactive, it appears that the trustee engaged in coal brokering merely to protect an asset of the estate and that the trustee was essentially holding matters in status quo. Because the business was not being administered for the purpose of continuing operations after the trustee took control, the policy of § 959(b) applies only with respect to those fines assessed for mining operations after the petition was filed and before the chapter 11 trustee took control.

Further, because the mining operations had ceased completely, the estate was not able to gain an unfair advantage over competitors by cutting costs in its surface mining operation by ignoring the ASMC fines. We hold, therefore, that the penalties incurred by the estate after the appointment of the chapter 11 trustee, which in this particular case marked the ceasing of the business's operations, are not entitled to administrative-expense priority.

* * *

CONCLUSION

In conclusion, we hold the following with respect to coal mining penalties assessed by the ASMC in the context of bankruptcy proceedings: (1) Penalties assessed prior to and subsequent to the filing of a bankruptcy petition for mining violations that occur prior to the filing of a petition shall not be given administrative expense status; (2) penalties assessed for mining violations that are sustained during the operation of a mine by the debtor in possession or the trustee shall be given administrative expense status * * * .

Notes and Questions

1. N.P. Mining's bankruptcy estate had assets of less than $500,000, and the State of Alabama's claim totaled more than $2 million. Thus, none of N.P. Mining's other unsecured creditors would have received a dime if the State had gotten administrative expense priority for its entire claim.

2. The court in *N.P. Mining* relied on the Supreme Court's pre-Code decision in *Reading*. In *Reading*, a postpetition fire, caused by the negligence of the trustee's employee, destroyed the debtor's only asset—an eight-story industrial building in Philadelphia. The fire also destroyed the property of 147 others, generating claims in excess of $3,500,000. Granting administrative expense status to those claims would have wiped out the entire estate, leaving

nothing for any other claimant. The United States, which held a lower priority tax claim, argued that the fire claims were not entitled to administrative expense status. The Supreme Court held otherwise, as *N.P. Mining* explained.

Based on *Reading*, can the phrase "actual, necessary costs and expenses of preserving the estate" in § 503(b)(1) be read as a requirement of *benefit* to the estate?

3. *Reading* spoke of "fairness to all persons having claims against an insolvent." What did the Supreme Court mean by "fairness"? Which way does "fairness" cut in this case?

4. The court in *N.P. Mining* also relied on the Supreme Court's decision in *Midlantic*, but that case dealt with the trustee's power to abandon property under § 554. What is the relevance of *Midlantic* to the question of administrative expense priority?

———————

As we noted, the first priority for domestic support obligations is justifiable on the grounds that those claimants are particularly, even uniquely, deserving. The remaining priorities cover an assortment of different claims and reflect varying types of congressional concerns. Some of them (such as the sixth-level priority for grain producers and fishermen) are most likely the result of political influence. As you work through the following materials, see if you can discern what public policy (if any!) is served by the particular priority at issue.

Problems

1. Joe Debtor, who practiced law as a professional corporation, had one employee who earned $72,000 per year. When Debtor, P.C. filed Chapter 11, it owed $12,000 in wages to the employee for work performed in the two months immediately preceding the filing. How much, if any, of the wage claim is entitled to a priority?

2. Assume that the employee from the prior Problem continued to work for Debtor, P.C. for two months after bankruptcy was filed, but that the employee then quit in disgust because no wages were paid. What priority, if any, will the employee's claim for $12,000 in post-petition wages enjoy?

3. Debtor loved to take his Cigarette boat out on the lake, and to run full-throttle across the water. Unfortunately, he took the boat out one evening after an all-day barbeque that had involved more beer than food, and did not notice several swimmers in the water. One of the swimmers drowned in the wake. Her parents filed suit and won a substantial judgment, and they were

outraged when Debtor immediately file bankruptcy. Will they have to settle for a pro rata portion of Debtor's estate, or can they assert a priority claim?

4. Customer ordered a custom-made sofa for his den from Furniture Manufacturer, Inc. The price of the sofa was $2,200 and Customer paid 50% down. Before the sofa was delivered, FMI filed Chapter 7. Customer received neither refund nor sofa. What priority, if any, will Customer's claim enjoy in FMI's bankruptcy?

5. Wooden Furniture Warehouse, Inc. sold a large number of gift certificates as holiday presents. Before any of them could be redeemed, however, WFW filed a Chapter 11 petition. WFW proposed a plan that treated the holders of the gift certificates as general unsecured creditors. Should those creditors be treated, instead, as having seventh priority claims? See *In re WW Warehouse, Inc.*, 313 B.R. 588 (Bankr. D.Del.2004).

6. Debtor owed federal income taxes for the tax years 2011, 2012, 2013 and 2014. The taxes for each year were due on April 15th of the next year. Debtor received no extensions and the IRS filed no notice of tax lien. What priority, if any, will the tax claims enjoy if Debtor files bankruptcy on April 10, 2016? Does it matter whether Debtor filed no returns at all, or filed returns but included no checks?

The next case involves the question whether premiums for workers' compensation benefits are entitled to priority under § 507(a)(5). It was a question that sharply divided the circuit courts, until the Supreme Court resolved it.

HOWARD DELIVERY SERVICE, INC. v. ZURICH AMERICAN INSURANCE CO.

United States Supreme Court, 2006.
547 U.S. 651, 126 S.Ct. 2105, 165 L.Ed.2d 110.

JUSTICE GINSBURG delivered the opinion of the Court.

The Bankruptcy Code accords a priority, among unsecured creditors' claims, for unpaid "wages, salaries, or commissions," § 507-(a)(4)(A), and for unpaid contributions to "an employee benefit plan," § 507(a)(5). It is uncontested here that § 507(a)(5) covers fringe benefits that complete a pay package—typically pension plans, and group health, life, and disability insurance—whether unilaterally provided by an employer or the result of collective bargaining. This case presents the question whether the § 507(a)(5) priority also encompasses claims for unpaid premiums on a policy purchased by an employer to cover its workers' compensation liability. We hold that premiums owed by an employer to a workers' compensation carrier do not fit within § 507(a)(5).

Workers' compensation laws assure that workers will be compensated for work-related injuries whether or not negligence of the employer contributed to the injury. To that extent, arrangements for the payment of compensation awards might be typed "employee benefit plan[s]." On the other hand, statutorily prescribed workers' compensation regimes do not run exclusively to the employees' benefit. In this regard, they differ from privately ordered, employer-funded pension and welfare plans that, together with wages, remunerate employees for services rendered. Employers, too, gain from workers' compensation prescriptions. In exchange for no-fault liability, employers gain immunity from tort actions that might yield damages many times higher than awards payable under workers' compensation schedules. Although the question is close, we conclude that premiums paid for workers' compensation insurance are more appropriately bracketed with premiums paid for other liability insurance, *e.g.*, motor vehicle, fire, or theft insurance, than with contributions made to secure employee retirement, health, and disability benefits.

In holding that claims for workers' compensation insurance premiums do not qualify for § 507(a)(5) priority, we are mindful that the Bankruptcy Code aims, in the main, to secure equal distribution among creditors. We take into account, as well, the complementary principle that preferential treatment of a class of creditors is in order only when clearly authorized by Congress.

I

[Howard Delivery Service operated a freight business, employing 480 people. Each of the dozen states in which it operated mandated workers' compensation coverage, which Howard obtained from Zurich. At the time of Howard's Chapter 11 filing, it owed Zurich $400,000 in unpaid premiums. Zurich asserted that its claim was entitled to priority under § 507(a)(5). The bankruptcy court denied priority and the district court affirmed.]

The Court of Appeals for the Fourth Circuit reversed 2 to 1 in a *per curiam* opinion. The judges in the majority, however, disagreed on the rationale. Judge King concluded that § 507(a)(5) unambiguously accorded priority status to claims for unpaid workers' compensation premiums. Judge Shedd, concurring in the judgment, found the § 507(a)(5) phrase "employee benefit plan" ambiguous. Looking to legislative history, he concluded that Congress likely intended to give past due workers' compensation premiums priority status. In dissent, Judge Niemeyer, like Judge King, relied on the "plain meaning" of § 507(a)(5), but read the provision unequivocally to deny priority status to an insurer's claim for unpaid workers' compensation premiums

We granted certiorari to resolve a split among the Circuits concerning the priority status of premiums owed by a bankrupt employer to a workers' compensation carrier.

II

Adjoining subsections of the Bankruptcy Code, §§ 507(a)(4) and (5), are centrally involved in this case. * * *

Two decisions of this Court, *United States v. Embassy Restaurant, Inc.*, 359 U.S. 29 (1959), and *Joint Industry Bd. of Elec. Industry v. United States*, 391 U.S. 224 (1968), prompted the enactment of § 507(a)(5). *Embassy Restaurant* concerned a provision of the 1898 Bankruptcy Act that granted priority status to "wages" but said nothing of "employee benefits plans" or anything similar. We held that a debtor's unpaid contributions to a union welfare plan—which provided life insurance, weekly sick benefits, hospital and surgical benefits, and other advantages—did not qualify within the priority for unpaid "wages." In *Joint Industry Bd.*, we followed *Embassy Restaurant* and held that an employer's bargained-for contributions to an employees' annuity plan did not qualify as "wages" entitled to priority status.

To provide a priority for fringe benefits of the kind at issue in *Embassy Restaurant* and *Joint Industry Bd.*, Congress added what is now § 507(a)(5) when it amended the Bankruptcy Act in 1978. Notably, Congress did not enlarge the "wages, salaries, [and] commissions" priority, § 507(a)(4), to include fringe benefits. Instead, Congress created a new priority for such benefits, one step lower than the wage priority. The new provision, currently contained in § 507(a)(5), allows the provider of an employee benefit plan to recover unpaid premiums—albeit only after the employees' claims for "wages, salaries, or commissions" have been paid.

Beyond genuine debate, the main office of § 507(a)(5) is to capture portions of employee compensation for services rendered not covered by § 507(a)(4). The current Code's juxtaposition of the wages and employee benefit plan priorities manifests Congress' comprehension that fringe benefits generally complement, or "substitute" for, hourly pay. See H.R. Rep. No. 95-595, p. 357 (noting "the realities of labor contract negotiations, under which wage demands are often reduced if adequate fringe benefits are substituted"); *id.,* at 187 ("[T]o ignore the reality of collective bargaining that often trades wage dollars for fringe benefits does a severe disservice to those working for a failing enterprise.").

Congress tightened the linkage of (a)(4) and (a)(5) by imposing a combined cap on the two priorities, currently set at $10,000 per employee. See § 507(a)(5)(B). Because (a)(4) has a higher priority status, all claims for wages are paid first, up to the $10,000 limit; claims under (a)(5) for contributions to employee benefit plans can be recovered next up to the remainder of the $10,000 ceiling. No other subsections of § 507 are joined together by a common cap in this way.

Putting aside the clues provided by *Embassy Restaurant, Joint Industry Bd.,* and the textual ties binding § 507(a)(4) and (5), we recognize that Congress left undefined the § 507(a)(5) terms: "*contributions* to an *employee benefit plan* * * * arising from *services rendered* within 180 days before the date of the filing of the [bankruptcy] petition." (Emphases added.) Maintaining that subsection (a)(5) covers more than wage substitutes of the kind at issue in *Embassy Restaurant* and *Joint Industry Bd.,* Zurich urges the Court to borrow the encompassing definition of employee benefit plan contained in the Employee Retirement Income Security Act of 1974 (ERISA), 29 U.S.C. § 1001 et seq. * * *

Federal courts have questioned whether ERISA is appropriately used to fill in blanks in a Bankruptcy Code provision, and the panel below parted ways on this issue. * * *

ERISA's omnibus definition does show, at least, that the term "employee welfare benefit plan" is susceptible of a construction that would include workers' compensation plans. That Act's signals are mixed, however, for 29 U.S.C. § 1003(b)(3) specifically exempts from ERISA's coverage the genre of plan here at issue, *i.e.,* one "maintained solely for the purpose of complying with applicable work[ers'] compensation laws." The § 1003(b)(3) exemption strengthens our resistance to Zurich's argument. We follow the lead of an earlier decision, *United States v. Reorganized CF&I Fabricators of Utah, Inc.,* 518 U.S. 213, 219-220 (1996), in noting that "[h]ere and there in the Bankruptcy Code Congress has included specific directions that establish the significance for bankruptcy law of a term used elsewhere in the federal statutes."

No such directions are contained in § 507(a)(5), and we have no warrant to write them into the text.

This case turns, we hold, not on a definition borrowed from a statute designed without bankruptcy in mind, but on the essential character of workers' compensation regimes. Unlike pension provisions or group life, health, and disability insurance plans—negotiated or granted as pay supplements or substitutes—workers' compensation prescriptions have a dominant employer-oriented thrust: They modify, or substitute for, the common-law tort liability to which employers were exposed for work-related accidents. As typically explained:

> "The invention of workers compensation as it has existed in this country since about 1910 involves a classic social trade-off or, to use a Latin term, a *quid pro quo.* * * * What is given to the injured employee is the right to receive certain limited benefits regardless of fault, that is, even in cases in which the employee is partially or entirely at fault, or when there is no fault on anyone's part. What is taken away is the employee's right to recover full tort damages, including damages for pain and suffering, in cases in which there is fault on the employer's part." P. Lencsis, WORKERS COMPENSATION: A REFERENCE & GUIDE 9 (1998) (hereinafter Lencsis).

Workers' compensation regimes thus provide something for employees—they assure limited fixed payments for on-the-job injuries—and something for employers—they remove the risk of large judgments and heavy costs generated by tort litigation. No such trade-off is involved in fringe benefit plans that augment each covered worker's hourly pay.[6]

Employer-sponsored pension plans, and group health or life insurance plans, characteristically insure the employee (or his survivor) only. In contrast, workers' compensation insurance, in common with

---

. [6] Providing health care to workers fosters a healthy and happy workforce, and a contented workforce benefits employers. The dissent suggests this as a reason to rank workers' compensation insurance with health and pension plans for bankruptcy priority purposes. But the benefit employers gain from providing health and pension plans for their employees is of a secondary order; indeed, under the dissent's logic, wages could be said to "benefit" the employer because they ensure that employees come to work, can afford transportation to the job site, etc. These benefits redound to the employer reflexively, as a consequence of the benefit to the employee. Workers' compensation insurance, by contrast, directly benefits insured employers by eliminating their tort liability for workplace accidents.

other liability insurance in this regard, *e.g.,* fire, theft, and motor vehicle insurance, shield the insured enterprise: Workers' compensation policies both protect the employer-policyholder from liability in tort, and cover its obligation to pay workers' compensation benefits. When an employer fails to secure workers' compensation coverage, or loses coverage for nonpayment of premiums, an affected employee's remedy would not lie in a suit for premiums that should have been paid to a compensation carrier. Instead, employees who sustain work-related injuries would commonly have recourse to a state-maintained fund. Or, in lieu of the limited benefits obtainable from a state fund under workers' compensation schedules, the injured employee might be authorized to pursue the larger recoveries successful tort litigation ordinarily yields.

Further distancing workers' compensation arrangements from bargained-for or voluntarily accorded fringe benefits, nearly all States, with limited exceptions, require employers to participate in their workers' compensation systems. An employer who fails to secure the mandatory coverage is subject to substantial penalties, even criminal liability. We do not suggest, as the dissent hypothesizes, that a compensation carrier would gain § 507(a)(5) priority for unpaid premiums in States where workers' compensation coverage is elective. Nor do we suggest that wage surrogates or supplements, *e.g.,* pension and health benefits plans, would lose protection under § 507(a)(5) if a State were to mandate them. We simply count it a factor relevant to our assessment that States overwhelmingly prescribe and regulate insurance coverage for on-the-job accidents, while commonly leaving pension, health, and life insurance plans to private ordering.

* * *

Zurich argues that according its claim an (a)(5) priority will give workers' compensation carriers an incentive to continue coverage of a failing enterprise, thus promoting rehabilitation of the business. It may be doubted whether the projected incentive would outweigh competing financial pressure to pull the plug swiftly on an insolvent policyholder, and thereby contain potential losses. An insurer undertakes to pay the scheduled benefits to workers injured on the job while the policy is in effect. In the case of serious injuries, however, benefits may remain payable years after termination of coverage. While cancellation relieves the insurer from responsibility for future injuries, the insurer cannot escape the obligation to continue paying benefits for enduring maladies or disabilities, even though no premiums are paid by the former policyholder. An insurer would likely weigh in the balance the risk of incurring fresh obligations of long duration were it to continue insuring employers unable to pay currently for coverage. That consideration might well be controlling even with an assurance of priority status, for there is no guarantee that creditors accorded preferred positions will in fact be paid.

Rather than speculating on how workers' compensation insurers might react were they to be granted an (a)(5) priority, we are guided in reaching our decision by the equal distribution objective underlying the Bankruptcy Code, and the corollary principle that provisions allowing preferences must be tightly construed.

Every claim granted priority status reduces the funds available to general unsecured creditors and may diminish the recovery of other claimants qualifying for equal or lesser priorities. Cases like Zurich's are illustrative. The Bankruptcy Code caps the amount recoverable for contributions to employee benefit plans. Opening the (a)(5) priority to workers' compensation carriers could shrink the amount available to cover unpaid contributions to plans paradigmatically qualifying as wage surrogates, prime among them, pension and health benefit plans.

In sum, we find it far from clear that an employer's liability to provide workers' compensation coverage fits the § 507(a)(5) category "contributions to an employee benefit plan * * * arising from services rendered." Weighing against such categorization, workers' compensation does not compensate employees for work performed, but instead, for on-the-job injuries incurred; workers' compensation regimes substitute not for wage payments, but for tort liability. Any doubt concerning the appropriate characterization, we conclude, is best resolved in accord with the Bankruptcy Code's equal distribution aim. We therefore reject the expanded interpretation Zurich invites. Unless and until Congress otherwise directs, we hold that carriers' claims for unpaid workers' compensation premiums remain outside the priority allowed by § 507(a)(5).

* * *

For the reasons stated, the judgment of the United States Court of Appeals for the Fourth Circuit is reversed, and the case is remanded for further proceedings consistent with this opinion.

It is so ordered.

Questions and Problems

1. In a dissenting opinion, JUSTICE KENNEDY, joined by JUSTICES SOUTER and ALITO, noted that the Court did not seem to dispute that the payments were "contributions" that "aris[e] from services rendered." The disagreement among the justices centered on the third statutory requirement—that workers' compensation insurance constitute an "employee benefit plan."

2. The Court said that workers' compensation cannot be an "employee benefit plan" largely because it also benefits employers. Is it not also true, however, that pension, health, and disability plans—all of which the Court acknowledged to be within § 507(a)(5)—benefit employers in substantially similar ways?

3. Empirical studies, cited by the dissent, have found that employers pass the cost of workers' compensation on to employees in the form of reduced wages. If, as the Court acknowledged, the (a)(5) priority is intended to cover "wage substitutes," do these empirical studies provide support for a different outcome?

4. The Court said that it was guided "by the equal distribution objective underlying the Bankruptcy Code." Did the Court rely on that broad objective at the expense of the Code's plain language?

5. Is there any risk that workers' compensation coverage will be jeopardized by this holding, either for the period before the debtor-corporation's bankruptcy filing or during reorganization? Whatever the answer to that question, should it matter to the outcome of the case?

6. Several employees of Debtor, Inc. cashed their payroll checks at Brooks Supermarket. None of the checks was for more than $10,000. Debtor, Inc. filed bankruptcy and the checks were dishonored for insufficient funds when Brooks presented them. Brooks filed a claim in Debtor, Inc.'s bank-ruptcy and now seeks priority for its claim under § 507(a)(4). Given § 507(d), is the claim entitled to priority? See *Wilson v. Brooks Supermarket, Inc. (In re Missionary Baptist Foundation of America, Inc.)*, 667 F.2d 1244 (5th Cir.1982); *In re All American Manufacturing Corp.*, 185 B.R. 79 (Bankr. S.D. Fla.1995).

7. Debtor Corp. had 20 employees who were covered by two benefit plans—a retirement plan and a medical plan. At the time bankruptcy was filed, Debtor Corp. owed a total of $50,000 in back wages for work performed by its employees in the three months before filing. Debtor Corp. also owed $80,000 in contributions to the retirement plan and $120,000 to the medical plan, based on work performed during the same period. What priority, if any, can the retirement and medical plans enjoy?

G. ESTIMATION OF UNLIQUIDATED AND CONTINGENT CLAIMS

Although the Code defines "claim" broadly, to include obligations that are "contingent" and "unliquidated," it does not define these terms. Consider a lawsuit brought against the debtor that has not been resolved by the time bankruptcy is filed. Because the debtor's obligation to the creditor, if any, has not been fixed, the claim is "unliquidated." Some obligations depend upon the happening of a future event. For example, the debtor may have endorsed a promissory note as an accommodation party; liability does not arise unless the maker fails to pay. Because the debtor's liability arises only if a condition precedent occurs, the holder of the note has a "contingent" claim. (We have already seen the requirement that a claim be non-contingent in connection with Chapter 13 eligibility, § 109(e), and in connection with the filing of involuntary petitions, § 303(b)(1).)

Under pre-Code law, courts excluded most claims that were not fixed and undisputed. The holders of such claims could not share in the distribution of the debtor's assets, although they could pursue their rights against the debtor after the case was closed. This result was unfair to both debtors and creditors. A corporation that successfully reorganized, or an individual with post-bankruptcy assets, would be forced to pay the creditor 100% of its claim after the case, rather than the pro rata share the creditor would have received in bankruptcy. That jeopardized the fresh start Congress intended bankruptcy to provide. On the other hand, if the debtor was a corporation that liquidated or an individual with no post-bankruptcy assets, then the creditor at issue would receive no pro rata share during the case and nothing thereafter, and other creditors in the case would receive a dividend undiminished by the additional claim.

The Code drafters responded with § 101(5), which we have already seen, and with § 502(c), which directs the bankruptcy court to estimate contingent or unliquidated claims for the purpose of allowance if fixing or liquidating such claims would unduly delay administration of the case. The major practical effect of allowing a claim in Chapter 11 is to permit the creditor to vote on confirmation of the debtor's Chapter 11 reorganization plan and to receive payments under the confirmed plan. Once a plan is confirmed in a corporate reorganization, debts that arose before bankruptcy are discharged under § 1141(d). (In an individual's Chapter 11, discharge will usually be delayed until completion of the plan, § 1141(d)(5).) Estimation under § 502(c), therefore, appears to constitute a final adjudication of the claim in a corporate case.

Courts have consistently asserted otherwise, however, stating that estimation does not fix ultimate liability:

> At an estimation hearing, the bankruptcy court would not decide liability or assign a permanently fixed value for the claim. Rather, [the court] would estimate the *likelihood* of liability and the *probable* value of that liability. The estimated amount would be the amount that claimants would be entitled to vote for or against confirmation of [the debtor's] reorganization plan. If the plan is confirmed the estimated amount would be set aside pending the determination of liability and the liquidation of the claim, which would not occur in a bankruptcy court. If liability is ultimately found, claimants would then be able to receive payment up to the amount of the judgment or the estimated value, whichever is lower.

In re Baldwin–United Corp., 57 B.R. 751, 758 (S.D. Ohio 1985). Although the court in *Baldwin–United* suggested that the estimated value may provide a *ceiling* on the claim, estimation may be for the purposes of confirmation and voting, but not for the purposes of distribution.

Another issue is the method a bankruptcy court should use to estimate a contingent or unliquidated claim. In *Baldwin–United*, the court held a two-day hearing and allowed one witness per party, even though it was dealing with complex indemnity and contribution claims involving hundreds of millions of dollars.

Obviously, estimation is anything but simple. The following cases address the two issues most often raised under § 502(c)—the procedure a bankruptcy court should use to estimate contingent and unliquidated claims, and the purposes for which a claim is estimated.

BITTNER v. BORNE CHEMICAL CO.

United States Court of Appeals, Third Circuit, 1982.
691 F.2d 134.

GIBBONS, Circuit Judge.

Stockholders of The Rolfite Company appeal from the judgment of the district court, affirming the decision of the bankruptcy court to assign a zero value to their claims in the reorganization proceedings of Borne Chemical Company, Inc. (Borne) under Chapter 11 of the Bankruptcy Code (Code). Since the bankruptcy court neither abused its discretionary authority to estimate the value of the claims pursuant to § 502(c)(1) nor relied on clearly erroneous findings of fact, we affirm.

I.

Prior to filing its voluntary petition under Chapter 11 of the Code, Borne commenced a state court action against Rolfite for the alleged pirating of trade secrets and proprietary information from Borne. The Rolfite Company filed a counterclaim, alleging, *inter alia*, that Borne had tortiously interfered with a proposed merger between Rolfite and the Quaker Chemical Corporation (Quaker) by unilaterally terminating a contract to manufacture Rolfite products and by bringing its suit. Sometime after Borne filed its Chapter 11 petition, the Rolfite stockholders sought relief from the automatic stay so that the state court proceedings might be continued. Borne then filed a motion to disallow temporarily the Rolfite claims until they were finally liquidated in the state court. The bankruptcy court lifted the automatic stay but also granted Borne's motion to disallow temporarily the claims, extending the time within which such claims could be filed and allowed if they should be eventually liquidated.

Upon denial of their motion to stay the hearing on confirmation of Borne's reorganization plan, the Rolfite stockholders appealed to the district court, which vacated the temporary disallowance order and directed the bankruptcy court to hold an estimation hearing. The parties agreed to establish guidelines for the submission of evidence at the hearing, and, in accordance with this agreement, the bankruptcy court relied on the parties' choice of relevant pleadings and other documents related to the state court litigation, and on briefs and oral argument. After weighing the evidence, the court assigned a zero value to the Rolfite claims and reinstated its earlier order to disallow temporarily the claims until such time as they might be liquidated in the state court, in effect requiring a waiver of discharge of the Rolfite claims from Borne. Upon appeal, the district court affirmed.

II.

Section 502(c) of the Code * * * [and] the Rules of Bankruptcy Procedure * * * are silent as to the manner in which contingent or un-liquidated claims are to be estimated. Despite the lack of express direction on the matter, we are persuaded that Congress intended the procedure to be undertaken initially by the bankruptcy judges, using whatever method is best suited to the particular contingencies at issue. The principal consideration must be an accommodation to the underlying purposes of the Code. It is conceivable that in rare and unusual cases arbitration or even a jury trial on all or some of the issues may be necessary to obtain a reasonably accurate evaluation of the claims. Such methods, however, usually will run counter to the efficient administration of the bankrupt's estate and where there is sufficient evidence on which to base a reasonable estimate of the claim, the bankruptcy judge should determine the value. In so doing, the court is bound by the legal rules which may govern the ultimate value of the claim. For example, when the claim is based on an alleged breach of contract, the court must estimate its worth in accordance with accepted contract law. However, there are no other limitations on the court's authority to evaluate the claim save those general principles which should inform all decisions made pursuant to the Code.

* * *

According to the Rolfite stockholders, the estimate which § 502(c)(1) requires is the present value of the probability that appellants will be successful in their state court action. Thus, if the bankruptcy court should determine as of this date that the Rolfite stockholders' case is not supported by a preponderance or 51% of the evidence but merely by 40%, they apparently would be entitled to have 40% of their claims allowed during the reorganization proceedings, subject to modification if and when the claims are liquidated in state court. The Rolfite stockholders contend that instead of estimating their claims in this manner, the bankruptcy court assessed the ultimate merits and, believing that they could not establish their case by a preponderance of the evidence, valued the claims at zero.

We note first that the bankruptcy court did not explicitly draw the distinction that the Rolfite stockholders make. Assuming however that the bankruptcy court did estimate their claims according to their ultimate merits rather than the present value of the probability that they would succeed in their state court action, we cannot find that such a valuation method is an abuse of the discretion conferred by § 502(c)(1).

The validity of this estimation must be determined in light of the policy underlying reorganization proceedings. In Chapter 11 of the Code, Congress addressed the complex issues which are raised when a corporation faces mounting financial problems.

The modern corporation is a complex and multi-faceted entity. Most corporations do not have a significant market share of the lines of business in which they compete. The success, and even the survival, of a corporation in contemporary markets depends on three elements: First, the ability to attract and hold skilled management; second, the ability to obtain credit; and third, the corporation's ability to project to the public an image of vitality.
* * *

One cannot overemphasize the advantages of speed and simplicity to both creditors and debtors. Chapter XI allows a debtor to negotiate a plan outside of court and, having reached a settlement with a majority in number and amount of each class of creditors, permits the debtor to bind all unsecured creditors to the terms of the arrangement. From the perspective of creditors, early confirmation of a plan of arrangement: first, generally reduces administrative expenses which have priority over the claims of unsecured creditors; second, permits creditors to receive prompt distributions on their claims with respect to which interest does not accrue after the filing date; and third, increases the ultimate recovery on creditor claims by minimizing the adverse effect on the business which often accompanies efforts to operate an enterprise under the protection of the Bankruptcy Act.

124 Cong. Rec. H 11101–H 11102 (daily ed. Sept. 28, 1978) (statement of Rep. D. Edwards of California, floor manager for bankruptcy legislation in the House of Representatives). Thus, in order to realize the goals of Chapter 11, a reorganization must be accomplished quickly and efficiently.

If the bankruptcy court estimated the value of the Rolfite stockholders' claims according to the ultimate merits of their state court action, such a valuation method is not inconsistent with the principles which imbue Chapter 11. Those claims are contingent[5] and unliquidated. According to the bankruptcy court's findings of fact, the Rolfite stockholders' chances of ultimately succeeding in the state court action are uncertain at best. Yet, if the court had valued the Rolfite stockholders' claims according to the present probability of success, the

---

[5] The Rolfite stockholders assert that the claims are not contingent since they are not dependent on some future event which may never occur. In as much as the very existence of the claims in the reorganization proceeding is dependent on a favorable decision by the state court, the Rolfite stockholders are clearly mistaken.

Rolfite stockholders might well have acquired a significant, if not controlling, voice in the reorganization proceedings. The interests of those creditors with liquidated claims would have been subject to the Rolfite interests, despite the fact that the state court might ultimately decide against those interests after the reorganization. The bankruptcy court may well have decided that such a situation would at best unduly complicate the reorganization proceedings and at worst undermine Borne's attempts to rehabilitate its business and preserve its assets for the benefit of its creditors and employees.[7] By valuing the ultimate merits of the Rolfite stockholders' claims at zero, and temporarily disallowing them until the final resolution of the state action, the bankruptcy court avoided the possibility of a protracted and inequitable reorganization proceeding while ensuring that Borne will be responsible to pay a dividend on the claims in the event that the state court decides in the Rolfite stockholders' favor. Such a solution is consistent with the Chapter 11 concerns of speed and simplicity but does not deprive the Rolfite stockholders of the right to recover on their contingent claims against Borne.

III.

* * *

[T]he Rolfite counterclaim in the state action lacked legal merit. Faced with only the remote possibility that the state court would find otherwise, the bankruptcy court correctly valued the claims at zero. On the basis of the court's subsidiary findings, such an estimation was consistent both with the claims' present value and with the court's assessment of the ultimate merits.

* * *

Questions

1. What sort of procedure does *Bittner* contemplate for purposes of estimation?

2. Is the court correct, as it asserted in footnote 5, that a claim is contingent if it has not yet been ruled upon favorably by a state court?

---

[7] Certainly this consideration played a role in the bankruptcy court's initial decision to disallow the claims. According to the court, "[T]o allow the hotly disputed claims, both present and prospective, herein referenced, would be for all practical purposes to doom Borne's rehabilitation efforts, now nearing their final stages, defeating the very purpose of reorganization."

3. Do you agree that a claim should be disallowed if, in the bankruptcy court's judgment, the creditor has only a 49% chance of winning the state court suit? Did the court, in attempting to avoid giving the claimants "a significant, if not controlling, voice in the reorganization proceedings," end up giving them too little voice?

4. For what purpose(s) did the court value the claims at zero? Did the court disallow the claims forever and for all purposes? What if the creditors obtained relief from the stay and later won the state suit? After this ruling, would the creditors have any reason to continue prosecution of the state suit?

The task of claims estimation is particularly acute in mega-tort cases, because the number of unliquidated claims is often quite large. The following case was one of the first ever to address this issue, and it charted the way for the cases that followed.

KANE v. JOHNS–MANVILLE CORP.

United States Court of Appeals, Second Circuit, 1988.
843 F.2d 636.

JON O. NEWMAN, Circuit Judge.

This appeal challenges the lawfulness of the reorganization plan of the Johns–Manville Corporation ("Manville"), a debtor in one of the nation's most significant Chapter 11 bankruptcy proceedings. Lawrence Kane, on behalf of himself and a group of other personal injury claimants, appeals from an order of the District Court for the Southern District of New York (Whitman Knapp, Judge) affirming an order of the Bankruptcy Court (Burton R. Lifland, Chief Judge) that confirmed a Second Amended Plan of Reorganization (the "Plan"). Kane and the group of 765 individuals he represents (collectively "Kane") are persons with asbestos-related disease who had filed personal injury suits against Manville prior to Manville's Chapter 11 petition. The suits were stayed, and Kane and other claimants presently afflicted with asbestos-related disease were designated as Class–4 creditors in the reorganization proceedings. Kane now objects to confirmation of the reorganization Plan on [the grounds that] the voting procedures used in approving the Plan violated the Bankruptcy Code and due process requirements * * *. [W]e reject on the merits * * *. The order of the District Court affirming the Bankruptcy Court's confirmation of the Plan is affirmed.

BACKGROUND

* * *

Because future asbestos-related liability was the *raison d'etre* of the Manville reorganization, an important question at the initial stages of the proceedings concerned the representation and treatment of what were termed "future asbestos health claimants" ("future claimants"). The future claimants were persons who had been exposed to Manville's asbestos prior to the August 1982 petition date but had not yet shown any signs of disease at that time. Since the future claimants were not yet ill at the time the Chapter 11 proceedings were commenced, none had filed claims against Manville, and their identities were unknown. An Asbestos Health Committee was appointed to represent all personal injury claimants, but the Committee took the position that it represented the interests only of "present claimants," persons who, prior to the petition date, had been exposed to Manville asbestos and had already developed an asbestos-related disease. The Committee declined to represent the future claimants. Other parties in the proceedings, recognizing that an effective reorganization would have to account for the future asbestos victims as well as the present ones, moved the Bankruptcy Court to appoint a legal guardian for the future claimants. The Bankruptcy Court granted the motion, reasoning that regardless of whether the future claimants technically had "claims" cognizable in bankruptcy proceedings, *see* [§ 101(5)], they were at least "parties in interest" under § 1109(b) of the Code and were therefore entitled to a voice in the proceedings. The Court appointed a Legal Representative to participate on behalf of the future claimants. Additionally, the Court invited any person who had been exposed to Manville's asbestos but had not developed an illness to participate in the proceedings, and two such persons appeared.

The Second Amended Plan of Reorganization resulted from more than four years of negotiations among Manville, the Asbestos Health Committee, the Legal Representative, the Equity Security Holders' Committee, and other groups interested in the estate. The cornerstone of the Plan is the Asbestos Health Trust (the "Trust"), a mechanism designed to satisfy the claims of all asbestos health victims, both present and future. The Trust is funded with the proceeds from Manville's settlements with its insurers; certain cash, receivables, and stock of the reorganized Manville Corporation; long term notes; and the right to receive up to 20% of Manville's yearly profits for as long as it takes to satisfy all health claims. According to the terms of the Trust, individuals with asbestos-related disease must first try to settle their claims by a mandatory exchange of settlement offers with Trust representatives. If a settlement cannot be reached, the claimant may elect mediation, binding arbitration, or traditional tort litigation. The claimant may collect from the Trust the full amount of whatever compensatory damages he is awarded. The only restriction on recovery is that the claimant may not obtain punitive damages.

The purpose of the Trust is to provide a means of satisfying Manville's ongoing personal injury liability while allowing Manville to maximize its value by continuing as an ongoing concern. To fulfill this purpose, the Plan seeks to ensure that health claims can be asserted only against the Trust and that Manville's operating entities will be protected from an onslaught of crippling lawsuits that could jeopardize the entire reorganization effort. To this end, the parties agreed that as a condition precedent to confirmation of the Plan, the Bankruptcy Court would issue an injunction channeling all asbestos-related personal injury claims to the Trust (the "Injunction"). The Injunction provides that asbestos health claimants may proceed only against the Trust to satisfy their claims and may not sue Manville, its other operating entities, and certain other specified parties, including Manville's insurers. Significantly, the Injunction applies to all health claimants, both present and future, regardless of whether they technically have dischargeable "claims" under the Code. The Injunction applies to any suit to recover "on or with respect to any Claim, Interest or Other Asbestos Obligation." "Claim" covers the present claimants, who are categorized as Class–4 unsecured creditors under the Plan and who have dischargeable "claims" within the meaning of [§ 101(5)]. The future claimants are subject to the Injunction under the rubric of "Other Asbestos Obligation," which is defined by the Plan as asbestos-related health liability caused by pre-petition exposure to Manville asbestos, regardless of when the individual develops clinically observable symptoms. Thus, while the future claimants are not given creditor status under the Plan, they are nevertheless treated identically to the present claimants by virtue of the Injunction, which channels all claims to the Trust.

The Plan was submitted to the Bankruptcy Court for voting in June of 1986. At that time relatively few present asbestos health claimants had appeared in the reorganization proceedings. Approximately 6,400 proofs of claims had been filed for personal injuries, which accounted for less than half of the more than 16,000 persons who had filed pre-petition personal injury suits against Manville. Moreover, Manville estimated that there were tens of thousands of additional present asbestos victims who had neither filed suits nor presented proofs of claims. Manville and the creditor constituencies agreed that as many present claimants as possible should be brought into the proceedings so that they could vote on the Plan. However, the parties were reluctant to embark on the standard Code procedure of establishing a bar date, soliciting proofs of claims, resolving all disputed claims on notice and hearing, and then weighting the votes by the amounts of the claims, as such a process could delay the reorganization for many years. To avoid this delay, the Bankruptcy Court adopted special voting procedures for Class 4. Manville was directed to undertake a comprehensive multi-media notice campaign to inform persons with present health claims of the pendency of the reorganization and their opportunity to participate. Potential health claimants who responded to the campaign were given a combined proof-of-claim-and-voting form in which each could present a medical diagnosis of his asbestos-related disease and vote to accept or reject the Plan. For voting purposes only, each claim was valued in the amount of one dollar. Claimants were informed that the proof-of-claim-and-voting form would be used only for voting and that to collect from the Trust, they would have to execute an additional proof of claim establishing the actual value of their damages.

The notice campaign produced a large number of present asbestos claimants. In all, 52,440 such claimants submitted proof-of-claim-and-voting forms. Of these, 50,275 or 95.8% approved the Plan, while 2,165 or 4.2% opposed it. In addition to these Class–4 claimants, all other classes of creditors also approved the Plan. Class 8, the common stockholders, opposed the Plan.

A confirmation hearing was held on December 16, 1986, at which Manville presented evidence regarding the feasibility and fairness of the Plan. Objections to confirmation were filed by several parties, including Kane. On December 18, 1986, the Bankruptcy Court issued a Determination of Confirmation Issues in which it rejected all objections to confirmation. With respect to Kane's challenge to the Injunction and the voting procedures, the Court relied primarily on its broad equitable powers to achieve reorganizations. * * * The Court entered an order confirming the Plan on December 22, 1986. Kane and others appealed. By order dated July 15, 1987, the District Court affirmed the Bankruptcy Court's confirmation order "for substantially the reasons set forth" in the Bankruptcy Judge's Determination of Confirmation Issues. This appeal followed.

DISCUSSION

* * *

B. Voting Procedures

Consideration of Kane's challenge to the voting procedures requires a brief outline of pertinent provisions of the Bankruptcy Code. A plan of reorganization must either be accepted by each impaired class of claims or interests, § 1129(a)(8), or meet certain rigid requirements with respect to each non-accepting class, § 1129(b) (so-called "cram down" provision). A class of creditors has accepted a plan under the Code "if such plan has been accepted by creditors * * * that hold at least two-thirds in amount and more than one-half in number of the allowed claims of such class held by creditors * * * that have accepted or rejected such plan." § 1126(c). Claims are "allowed" in the amount filed unless they are objected to by a party in interest, including the debtor or another creditor. § 502(a). * * *

Kane contends that the special Class–4 voting procedures adopted by the Bankruptcy Court violated his rights under the Code in several ways. First, since proofs of claims and votes were simultaneously solicited from present claimants in a combined mailing form, no creditor had an opportunity to object to the Class–4 members' claims before their votes were cast. Kane argues that this lack of opportunity to object prejudiced him because some of the claims might have been invalid and counting votes of those with invalid claims diluted his own vote. Second, Kane argues that the Bankruptcy Court improperly "allowed" claims for voting purposes in the arbitrary amount of one dollar, thereby depriving him of the opportunity to vote his claim weighted in the amount indicated in his proof of claim. By weighting all Class–4 votes equally, the Bankruptcy Court, in Kane's view, failed to adhere to the Code's voting scheme whereby a minority of class members with just over one third of the value of the total claims may reject a plan. Finally, Kane suggests that by assigning the one dollar value to all of the claims, the Bankruptcy Court might have discouraged Plan opponents with large claims from casting their votes since such opponents might have believed that, without the benefit of weighted voting, their opposition to the Plan would be futile.

Appellees respond that the Code is sufficiently flexible to accommodate the creative voting scheme used in this case. They argue primarily that the Code evinces a strong preference for facilitating reorganizations and that strict adherence to a weighted voting scheme would have been impractical in this case. Appellees point out that either the reorganization would have been delayed for years while the dollar value of every disputed health claim was determined or the vote would have been taken without contacting present health claimants other than the few who had voluntarily submitted proofs of claims, leaving a large group of important creditors disenfranchised. * * *

We need not decide whether the special Class–4 voting procedures violate the Code because, in view of the outcome of the vote, the alleged irregularities were at most harmless error. * * *

None of the procedures that Kane contends were required would have changed the outcome of the vote. With respect to denial of the opportunity to object to the Class–4 claims before they were voted, no substantial rights were impaired because Kane is unable to show that, had he been afforded a chance to object, any of the present health claims would have been excluded. The only objection Kane contends that he would have asserted is that the combined proof-of-claim-and-voting form approved by the Bankruptcy Court permitted a filing supported only by a written medical diagnosis of an asbestos-related condition without evidence that the claimant was exposed to Manville's product, as opposed to the product of some other company. However, it is clear from the record that this objection would have been unavailing. The combined proof-of-claim-and-voting form required anyone who had not already filed a lawsuit against Manville to submit a diagnosis of his disease *and* to represent that he had been exposed to Manville's product. Such a representation would have sufficed to warrant accepting the claim for voting purposes, especially in the absence of any particularized contrary evidence from Kane. In any event, since 95.8% of those Class–4 members who voted approved the Plan, the result would not have been different unless more than 90% of those who voted in favor had invalid claims, an improbable circumstance.

Similarly, Kane was not prejudiced by the assignment of a one dollar value to each claim. If we make the reasonable assumption that the percentage of claims that are valid is the same for "yes" votes and "no" votes, then the "no" votes would have to be at least ten times larger, on average, than the "yes" votes in order to change the result from what occurred with equal weighting of each vote. Nothing in the record gives any indication that such a large variation in claims existed, much less that the "no" votes were the larger claims. Indeed, it is safe to assume that if the procedures insisted upon by Kane had been used, all the votes would have still been weighted roughly the same since significant variations would not likely occur in the damages sustained by similar groups of people from similar kinds of injuries. Even if Kane is correct that some Plan opponents with larger claims were discouraged from voting, no prejudice occurred. Even if we make the unlikely assumption, favorable to Kane, that Plan opponents in Class 4, on average, had claims twice the size of the claims of Plan proponents, the number of "no" votes in this class would have had to increase nearly six times, from 2,165 to 12,569, in order to change the result. If there really were 12,569 Class–4 claimants opposed to the Plan, it is highly unlikely that 10,404 or 83% of them would have been discouraged from voting.

* * *

MINER, Circuit Judge, concurring.

* * *

By the time of the June 23, 1986 hearing held to consider the Disclosure Statement and the Second Amended and Restated Plan of Reorganization filed by the debtors, approximately 6,400 proofs of claim had been submitted by asbestos health claimants for personal injuries. It was apparent at that juncture in the proceedings that the administration of the case would be delayed unduly if each of those unliquidated claims were to be considered separately for allowance purposes. Referring to the number of actual lawsuits then pending on behalf of asbestos health claimants, the bankruptcy judge observed that more than 16,500 hearings would be necessary "to treat each individual claim discretely." In the words of the debtors' attorney, "the practical effect of having to value each and every claim individually would * * * be delay[ ] beyond anybody's reasonable expectations and probably lifetime." The problem of delay was even more apparent at the conclusion of the notice campaign, when proof-of-claim-and-voting forms had been received from 52,440 claimants.

Under the circumstances, the bankruptcy judge properly exercised his authority to estimate each of the claims at $1.00. The asbestos health claims were especially suited to estimation because of the uncertain nature of both liability and damages. Moreover, the very purpose of the reorganization would be defeated if each claim were to be considered separately for purposes of allowance and voting. Indeed, the delay entailed by such an approach would not only be fatal to the entire plan but might very well be fatal to any recovery for the claimants. Section 502(c)(1) is designed to forestall these types of consequences.

In any event, the assignment of a value of $1.00 per claim is merely the temporary allowance contemplated by Rule 3018(a), with the right reserved to each claimant to seek actual damages from the Asbestos Health Trust. Although the Rule calls for objections to the claims, followed by notice and hearing, before temporary allowances for voting purposes are made, there was substantial compliance with this requirement here. * * *

Notes and Problems

1. For what purpose(s) did the court set asbestosis victims' claims at $1.00? Is the court holding that the claims cannot be paid more than that? Is the court opening the door to trumped-up claims filed by people never exposed to asbestos?

2. Estimation under § 502(c) is mandatory only if liquidation in the usual way—by trial in an appropriate forum—would unduly delay the bankruptcy case. If resolution outside of bankruptcy is imminent, the bankruptcy court will almost certainly lift the stay so that the nonbankruptcy court can complete its adjudication. See *Apex Oil Co. v. Stinnes Interoil, Inc. (In re Apex Oil Co.),* 107 B.R. 189 (E.D.Mo.1989).

3. The procedural rules granting bankruptcy judges jurisdiction over core proceedings arguably permit estimation of claims for purposes of distribution as well as allowance. The explicit prohibition against estimating personal injury tort and wrongful death claims for purposes of distribution, found in 28 U.S.C. § 157(b)(5), may be an implicit acknowledgement of jurisdiction to estimate all other claims for purposes of distribution. See *Matter of Poole Funeral Chapel, Inc.,* 63 B.R. 527, 533 (Bankr. N.D.Ala.1986).

4. *Kane* highlights the conflict between the rights of future claimants and the continued viability of a company, created by a bankruptcy reorganization plan that binds all creditors with claims against the company. While binding future claimants to a Chapter 11 reorganization plan raises significant due process issues, the alternative may have far graver consequences. For example, if not included within a reorganization plan, future claimants may be shut off from recovery due to a lack of assets on the part of the debtor. On the other hand, a debtor whose assets are not depleted could be subjected to ongoing and unlimited liability far into the future. The experience of Johns–Manville, with 130,000 claimants filing suit against it by 1990 and an estimated liability of $8.8 billion, makes the former possibility far more likely than the latter. *Kane* describes the trust device, along with the channeling injunction, created to deal with the debtor's mass tort liabilities. These innovations alone would have made *Manville* one of the most important bankruptcy cases ever filed.

Congress recognized the creativity and utility of the *Manville* trust device. The 1994 Amendments adopted the trust device in § 524(g), which applies only to asbestos cases. The trust device remains available in other types of cases, however, through reasoned extensions of *Manville*.

5. Bank made an unsecured loan of $100,000 to Debtor Corporation. Paula Prez, the president and sole shareholder of Debtor Corporation, guaranteed payment of the debt. Debtor Corporation defaulted on the obligation and filed a Chapter 7 case. It has assets sufficient to pay 25% of unsecured claims. Answer the following questions, using §§ 502(e) and 509.

a.   Bank has been paid nothing on the debt and files a claim for $100,000 in Debtor Corporation's bankruptcy. Paula also files a claim for $100,000. How are the claims handled?

b.   Paula paid Bank in full before Debtor Corporation's bankruptcy filing. Which of them has an allowable claim in bankruptcy and for how much?

c.   Paula paid Bank only $50,000 before Debtor Corporation's bankruptcy filing. Which of them has an allowable claim in bankruptcy and for how much?

H. CLASSIFICATION OF CLAIMS IN REORGANIZATION CASES

As noted above, payments to unsecured creditors in Chapters 11 and 13 depend to a large degree on the provisions in the plan. The statute provides minimum payment amounts, but does not otherwise dictate a rigid distribution scheme.

Payments in reorganization cases are made to *classes* of creditors and, in Chapter 11, voting is by classes. Thus, how the plan classifies a claim is crucial. The relevant statutory provisions are §§ 1122, 1123(a), 1222(b)(1) and 1322(b)(1).

Section 1123(a)(1) requires a Chapter 11 plan to designate classes of claims (with certain exceptions we can ignore for now) and requires that the designation comport with § 1122. Section 1122(a), in turn, provides that "a plan may place a claim or an interest in a particular class only if such claim or interest is substantially similar to the other claims or interests of such class." In other words, only like claims can be classified together.

Section 1322(b)(1) provides, in pertinent part, that a Chapter 13 plan may designate classes "as provided in section 1122 of this title, but may not discriminate unfairly against any class so designated." By the cross-reference to § 1122, Chapter 13 also requires that only "substantially similar" claims be classified together. *See also* § 1222(b)(1).

None of these statutory provisions addresses the attributes that make claims similar, or whether similar claims can be classified separately.

1. CLASSIFICATION IN CHAPTER 13

BENTLEY v. BOYAJIAN (IN RE BENTLEY)

Bankruptcy Appellate Panel, First Circuit, 2001.
266 B.R. 229.

PER CURIAM.

I. Introduction

In their Chapter 13 plan, the Debtors proposed to pay their nondischargeable student loan obligations in full but to pay all other nonpriority unsecured claims all of which were eligible to be discharged upon completion of the plan payments a dividend of only three percent. The Debtors argued that such disparate treatment was justified by their desire to emerge from bankruptcy free of all prepetition debt. Upon objection by the Chapter 13 Trustee, the bankruptcy court disagreed and denied confirmation of the plan on the basis that it discriminated unfairly between the two classes of unsecured claims, in contravention of § 1322(b)(1). For the reasons set forth below, we affirm.

II. Background

The Debtors, William and Kara Bentley, who filed a joint petition for relief under Chapter 13 of the Bankruptcy Code on December 1, 2000, filed a Chapter 13 plan that, in relevant part, divided nonpriority unsecured creditors into two classes and proposed to treat them quite differently. The first of the two classes was comprised solely of creditors holding student loan obligations that, by operation of § 1328(a)(2) of the Bankruptcy Code, would be excepted from discharge in Chapter 13. The claims in this class totaled $57,727.95, and the plan proposed to pay them in full over the life of the plan. The second class consisted of all other unsecured claims, totaling (according to the Debtors' schedules) approximately $55,000. The plan proposed to pay creditors in this class a total of $2,000, to be shared among them on a *pro rata* basis, yielding a dividend of 3.6 percent. The plan proposed to fund these and all other dividends with monthly payments from their future earnings over a period of sixty months.

The Chapter 13 Trustee, John Boyajian, objected to the plan on two grounds: that the plan did not provide for all the Debtors' projected disposable income received in the three-year period following confirmation to be paid into the plan, as required by § 1325(b)(1)(B); and that the plan unfairly discriminated against the class of general unsecured creditors in contravention of § 1322(b)(1). *[The parties settled the first objection, but the bankruptcy court denied confirmation on the grounds of unfair discrimination.]*

In its memorandum of decision, the bankruptcy court * * * [held] that the nondischargeability of student loans does not justify the preferential treatment of student loans over other unsecured debt; such disparity of treatment is unfair and violates both the letter and spirit of § 1322(b)(1). *[The debtors promptly appealed.]*

* * *

VI. Unfair Discrimination

A. *The Chapter 13 Context*

In the normal course of a case under Chapter 13 of the Bankruptcy Code, a debtor obtains confirmation of, and then follows through on, a plan under which he or she makes payments over three to five years from disposable income on his or her prepetition debts. Though priority claims must be paid in full over the life of the plan, § 1322(a)(2), plan payments usually need not and do not pay the non-priority, unsecured debt in full. A plan can be confirmed despite its failure to pay all nonpriority unsecured claims in full if "the plan provides that all of the debtor's projected disposable income to be received in the three-year period beginning on the date that the first payment is due under the plan will be applied to make payments under the plan." § 1325(b)(1)(B). So generally, upon completion of the plan payments, a balance remains owing on the debts paid through the plan, and as to this balance "the court shall grant the debtor a discharge." § 1328(a).

However, this Chapter 13 discharge is subject to exceptions— that is, some debts are excepted from discharge—and the exceptions create the dynamic that gives rise to this appeal. Nothing in the Bankruptcy Code requires that a nondischargeable debt, as such, be paid in full through a Chapter 13 plan. Rather, the only consequence of nondischargeability is that, to the extent the debt is not paid through the Chapter 13 plan, it must be paid after completion of the plan, or at least from a source other than the funds devoted to the plan. Debtors therefore have incentive to direct their plan payments toward those debts that, to the extent not paid in bankruptcy, would survive it: the nondischargeable debts. By doing so they can minimize the total they must pay to free themselves, whether by discharge or by satisfaction, from the universe of prepetition debt. The strategy of many debtors will accordingly be to channel their plan payments first to the nondischargeable debt, to the extent necessary to pay it off, and to leave only the remainder, by comparison a much smaller dividend, for the dischargeable debt.

With respect to those nondischargeable obligations that also happen to be priority debts, the Bankruptcy Code requires that a Chapter 13 plan provide for exactly that treatment. This is because § 1322(a)(2) of the Code requires, as a condition of confirmation, that the plan provide for full payment of all claims entitled to priority. § 1322(a)(2). But nondischargeability is not the same as priority. Priority gives a claim a better right to estate assets or plan payments— *i.e.*, to the funds distributed through bankruptcy—than is enjoyed by other unsecured claims. Nondischargeability, on the other hand, confers no priority as to estate assets; it merely causes a debt to survive the discharge, such that its holder can continue to collect it despite the discharge. Certain nondischargeable debts also happen to be priority claims, but only because the same debts appear on two lists: thus, in Chapter 13, spousal and child support obligations appear both on the list of priority claims, at § 507(a)(7), and on the list of debts excepted from discharge, at §§ 523(a)(5) and 1328(a)(2). But priority does not *per se* confer or entail nondischargeability; and nondischargeability does not *per se* confer or entail priority.

The nondischargeable debts at issue in this case, student loan obligations of the kind set forth in § 523(a)(8), are not priority claims. Though the Code excepts debts of this kind from discharge in Chapter 13, the Code neither grants them priority over other unsecured claims nor requires that they be paid in full. Hence the question now presented: may debtors nonetheless structure their Chapter 13 plans to prefer these debts over other unsecured debts, to provide that they be paid in full while other unsecureds get less or nothing at all?

Chapter 13 of the Bankruptcy Code answers this question with § 1322(b)(1): "the plan may designate a class or classes of unsecured claims, as provided in section 1122 of this title, but may not discriminate unfairly against any class so designated." This section deals first with classification and then with discrimination among classes.

Classification is simply the grouping together of claims with respect to which the plan proposes a common treatment. § 1322(a)(3) (if the plan classifies claims, it "shall provide the same treatment for each claim within a particular class"). Section 1322(b)(1) first permits a plan to designate "a class or classes of unsecured claims." It thus permits the debtor to separate unsecured claims into different classes and, except as provided in § 1122, places no limits on the debtor's ability to do so.

Discrimination among classes of creditors, on the other hand, *is* subject to limitation. The plan "may not discriminate unfairly against any class so designated." § 1322(b)(1). Before determining what this phrase prohibits, we note first that it tacitly *permits* some measure of discrimination between different classes. In prohibiting only such discrimination as is unfair against any class, § 1322(b)(1) signals that a plan may, to an extent, treat different classes differently. So a plan may discriminate, but not unfairly.

We come now to the terms at the heart of this appeal. What does § 1322(b)(1) mean by "discriminate unfairly" against a class? Neither the phrase nor its component terms is defined in the Bankruptcy Code, the legislative history offers no insight into their meaning, and the Court of Appeals for this circuit has not addressed the issue.

B. *"Discriminate"*

Because § 1322(b)(1) distinguishes between discrimination that is unfair and discrimination that is not, we understand "discriminate" to have no pejorative connotation here. "To discriminate," in its broadest sense, is to make a distinction or to note a difference between two things. Derivatively, it is to treat two things differently on account of a distinction between them. Accordingly, in § 1322(b)(1), to discriminate is simply to treat two classes differently on the basis of a difference between them; the difference in treatment need not be unfair, wrongful, or even adverse to a class in order to constitute discrimination within the meaning of this statute. The treatment need only be different.[12]

C. *"Unfairly"*

Section 1322(b)(1) prohibits only such discrimination as is unfair to any class of unsecured claims and, conversely, sanctions such

---

[12] Accordingly we reject any suggestion that, by virtue of the fact that it authorizes discrimination between classes, § 1322(b)(1) necessarily authorizes treatment that prefers one class over another. It may merely authorize differences that nonetheless result in equal treatment.

differences in treatment as are fair. The operative term here is fair. Like good, just, and right, however, "fair" in the abstract is too indefinite, and therefore prohibitively difficult, to define and apply. The world is full of competing theories and perspectives from which to determine what is fair, and the word "fair," standing alone, does not specify which of them to apply. This problem has left the courts casting about for a definite standard of its meaning in this statute.

Among the many courts that have addressed the fairness of discrimination in favor of student loan creditors in Chapter 13 plans, most have seized upon a four part test adopted by the Eighth Circuit Court of Appeals in *In re Leser,* 939 F.2d 669 (8th Cir.1991): discrimination against a class of unsecured creditors is fair if (1) it has a "reasonable basis," which has come to mean simply that the discrimination furthers a legitimate interest of the debtor; (2) the debtor cannot carry out a plan without it; (3) the discrimination is proposed in good faith; and (4) the degree of discrimination is directly related to the basis or rationale for the discrimination. *Id.* at 672. This test has been used in many cases, but in very different ways and with wildly disparate results. It has been criticized for numerous shortcomings, not least of which is that, insofar as the test relies upon abstract, undefined notions of "reasonableness," "legitimacy," and "good faith," it fails to direct the court's analysis and instead creates a vacuum that the court itself must fill. The test prescribes no baseline from which to assess what is owing to a particular class, what departures are justified, and what compensation is owing (if any) on account of a particular departure. It offers no real direction for determining the fairness of discrimination in any given instance. Moreover, the test appears to be designed only to minimize discrimination—permitting only so much as is necessary to advance a debtor's interests—not, as § 1322(b)(1) requires, to identify and prevent such discrimination as is unfair.[15] For these and the reasons catalogued more fully in *McCullough v. Brown (In re Brown),* 162 B.R. 506, 509-15, *Leser* is not a useful starting point.

Based in part on these criticisms, some courts opted for an alternate test under which discrimination would be deemed fair if it furthered a legitimate interest of the debtor. The most elaborate defense of this position is articulated by Bankruptcy Judge Wedoff in his opinion in *In re Brown,* 152 B.R. 232, 244 (Bankr. N.D.Ill.1993), *rev'd* 162 B.R. 506 (N.D.Ill.1993). As he summarizes the position:

---

[15] This is not to say that courts employing the test have not decided their cases on the basis of considerations germane to fairness and to § 1322(b)(1). Our point is that they arrived at their considerations despite the test, not because of it.

debtors should be allowed to make preferential classifications when the resulting discrimination rationally furthers a legitimate interest of the debtors. In the cases now before the court, the debtors have a legitimate interest in paying their nondischargeable student loans in full through their Chapter 13 plans, so that they may complete their plans free of debt. Accordingly, their plans do not unfairly discriminate by providing for full payment of student loans and proportionately smaller payments of other unsecured claims.

In re Brown, 152 B.R. at 244. Though *Brown* was reversed on appeal, it is precisely this position that the Debtors now urge us to adopt.

We decline to do so. By asking whether a plan provision "rationally furthers a legitimate interest of the debtor," one determines only whether the provision is prudent, not whether it is fair. Fairness, in the sense plainly intended by § 1322(b)(1), is a matter of balancing correctly the interests *of two or more parties*. This is all the more evident when "unfairly" modifies "discriminate," an act that, of necessity, involves three parties: the debtor, the class preferred, and the class discriminated against. Lest there be any doubt that the affected classes should figure into this analysis, § 1322(b)(1) makes explicit that the plan "may not discriminate unfairly *against any class so designated*." § 1322(b)(1) (emphasis added); *In re Brown,* 162 B.R. at 512-13 ("[t]he normal meaning of 'unfairly against any class' measures the unfairness of the difference in treatment * * * in terms of unfairness to the victim ('against any class'), rather than unfairness to the person who elects to impose the discriminatory treatment."). Thus fairness in § 1322(b)(1) requires consideration not solely of the debtor's interest but also of the interests of the affected classes. The standard of fairness that the Debtors now advocate fails to take account of the very interest that the statute expressly protects, and so we reject that standard, too, as the measure of fairness.[17]

Instead, we prefer the approach adopted in *In re Colfer,* 159 B.R. 602 (Bankr. D.Me.1993), in the appellate decision in *Brown,* and less explicitly in many other decisions, which is to look to Chapter 13 itself

---

[17] Because we reject the proposition that discrimination is fair if it advances a legitimate interest of the debtor, we need not address the Debtors' further contention that a debtor's interest in emerging from bankruptcy free of nondischargeable student loan obligations, and thus with a fresh start, is "legitimate." However, as the discussion below should make clear, we do not view this interest as justifying unequal treatment in the circumstances of this case.

for what is normative, the baseline from which departures can be discerned, measured, and evaluated for fairness. This approach is based on the supposition that, in using the standard of "fairness" that is implicit in § 1322(b)(1), Congress did not intend to leave courts with a notion so abstract as to supply no definite content or real guidance or to require each judge to define fairness according to his or her own lights: in effect, to improvise individual standards. Congress cannot have intended such a wholesale assignment to individual judges of a legislative function. Rather, we understand § 1322(b)(1) as mandating the standard of fairness that is implicit in Chapter 13, the context in which that term is used. *Colfer,* 159 B.R. at 608 & n. 20 (fairness of proposed discrimination requires analysis of "the impact of the discrimination on Congress' chosen statutory definition of the legitimate interests and expectations of parties-in-interest to Chapter 13 proceedings," including distributional priorities, fresh start, expressly permitted classifications, availability of subordination, extent of the estate, and amounts available for distribution under the plan).

Accordingly, for the baseline against which to evaluate discriminatory provisions for fairness, we look to the principles and structure of Chapter 13 itself. * * * When a plan prescribes different treatment for two classes but, despite the differences, offers to each class benefits and burdens that are equivalent to those it would receive at the baseline, then the discrimination is fair. On the other hand, when the discrimination alters the allocation of benefits and burdens to the detriment of one class, the discrimination is unfair and prohibited. In this instance, the guiding provisions and principles of Chapter 13 are four.

1. *Equality of Distribution*

The first is equality of distribution: absent an express grant of priority (as under § 507(a)) or cause for subordination under § 510(c), unsecured creditors should share equally in any dividend. * * *

2. *Nonpriority of Student Loans*

Second, the Debtors' student loan obligations are not debts to which the Code grants priority. Student loan obligations do not appear in the list of claims granted priority in § 507(a). They are indeed excepted from discharge, but, as we explained above, nondischargeability is not, and does not entail, priority as to any distribution in or through bankruptcy; it merely permits the holder to continue to enforce the debt after bankruptcy. Nor do the Debtors suggest that these claims are entitled priority, or payment in full, by virtue of any other provision of Chapter 13. Accordingly, as far as the Code is concerned, nothing in the nature of the claims at issue here warrants or justifies treating the student loans more favorably than the others.

3. *Contributions: Mandatory v. Optional*

Third, as a condition of plan confirmation, Chapter 13 requires that, if a debtor's plan does not propose to pay the full amount of each allowed unsecured claim, then the debtor must devote at least a certain quantum of property to the plan: an amount equal to "all of the debtor's projected disposable income to be received in the three-year period beginning on the date that the first payment is due under the plan." § 1325(b)(1). Debtors may, in their discretion, devote more value to their plans, but they must devote at least this minimum, and, in fact, the Debtors in this case have proposed to submit only the minimum. For those unsecured creditors whose claims are dischargeable, this minimum represents the only assured source of satisfaction for their claims. As to this minimum, fairness clearly gives these unsecured creditors an especially strong claim to an equal—which is to say *pro rata*—share. Sharing on a *pro rata* basis is fair as between the debtor and each unsecured creditor whose debt is dischargeable, because the creditor's *pro rata* share in the debtor's three years' of disposable income is, in the Chapter 13 scheme, the *quid pro quo* that the debtor must pay for the discharge of the balance of the creditor's claim. And sharing on a *pro rata* basis is fair as between those creditors whose debts are dischargeable and those whose are not, because, as we stated above, their claims are of equal priority. In fact, even with *pro rata* sharing, the nondischargeable claims still are treated better than the dischargeables because, by virtue of nondischargeability, they retain the right to collect their debts after bankruptcy, an advantage the discharge-ables do not share. An insistence on *pro rata* sharing does not cure this disparity but at least prevents the disparity from being further exacerbated. Certainly the fact that their claims are nondischargeable is not cause, as a matter of fairness between the two classes, to give them still more at the expense of those who begin with less.

4. *The Fresh Start*

Do the Debtors have an interest that might trump the creditors' strong claim to a *pro rata* sharing? The question brings us to the "fresh start" and its limits. The Debtors argue that discrimination in favor of student loan claims is justified by the purpose it would serve: to enable them to pay their student loans in full through the plan and then to emerge from bankruptcy free of those obligations, with a fresh start.

Without question, affording debtors a fresh start is one of the fundamental purposes of Chapter 13 and of the Bankruptcy Code in general. However, the fresh start is effectuated principally through the discharge of prepetition debt, and the discharge is not available as to all debt. More to the point, the student loans from which the present machinations are intended to provide a fresh start are debts that, except in instances of undue hardship, *Chapter 13 expressly excepts from discharge* (and this despite the fact that its exceptions from discharge are considerably fewer than in Chapter 7). §§ 523(a)(8), 1328(a), and 727(b). In other words, Chapter 13 does not contemplate that a debtor will necessarily emerge from Chapter 13 entirely free of student loan obligations. See *Colfer,* 159 B.R. at 607-08 ("Reliance on idealized notions of 'fresh start,' divorced from the very statute that provides the fresh start, is inappropriate."); *McDonald v. Sperna (In re Sperna),* 173 B.R. 654, 659 (B.A.P. 9th Cir.1994) ("[T]here is nothing in the code or case law that defines 'fresh start' as the emergence from bankruptcy completely free of all debt.").

D. *Conclusion*

When this exception from discharge is viewed with the other significant features of Chapter 13—the expectation that nonpriority unsecured creditors will share equally in the required plan contributions, and the fact that student loans are not accorded priority—what emerges is a clear expectation in Chapter 13 that the balance due on nondischargeable student loans after bankruptcy (that is, after the student loan claims have shared on a *pro rata* basis with other general unsecured claims in the distribution funded by the Chapter 13 plan) must be paid by debtors out of assets that they need not contribute to the plan. In the balance of burdens and benefits that the Code establishes as a baseline, the post-bankruptcy balance due on student loans should be paid by the Debtors out of assets that they are not required to commit to the plan, not by general unsecured creditors out of their share of the Debtor's minimum contribution. The Debtors' interest in a fresh start, in the sense of emerging from Chapter 13 without further obligation on their student loans, does not justify the discrimination here proposed, which, in essence, would foist upon the unsecured creditors a burden that Chapter 13 places on the Debtors themselves.

Where a plan redistributes benefits and burdens to the debtor's benefit and the unsecured creditors' detriment, as this one does, it can remain fair only if the debtor "places something material onto the scales to show a correlative benefit to the other unsecured creditors." *McCullough v. Brown,* 162 B.R. at 517-18. This plan offers no correlative benefit. It arrogates the unsecured creditors' dividend for the Debtors' benefit without compensation of equivalent value (or any compensation at all). Therefore, we conclude that the plan discriminates unfairly[26] and AFFIRM the order denying its confirmation.

Questions

1. Consider the following statement from *In re Young*, 102 B.R. 1022 (Bankr. W.D.Mo.1989):

> [This Court concludes] that while the amendments to Chapter 13 allow certain latitude in discriminating between some claims that latitude is circumscribed still by the measurements of equity and fairness. Neither allow[s] totally different treatment of *identical* claims. One unsecured, cosigned, consumer claim must be treated comparably to another unsecured, cosigned, consumer claim. To rule otherwise is to undermine the entire structure and concept of equal treatment. A debtor has never been allowed, in bankruptcy, to pick and choose between his creditors—the statute instead outlines any priority to be afforded his creditors.

Id. at 1023. Is *Young* correct? Is it not plain that the Code permits some differences in treatment of classes under the plan?

2. Debtor cosigned a loan for her son, so that he could buy a car. May Debtor separately classify the loan in her Chapter 13 plan and propose to pay it 50% if her other unsecured claims are to receive 5%?

3. Debtor was convicted of a crime and, as a condition of probation, was required to pay $1,000. That obligation is not dischargeable. Debtor filed a Chapter 13 petition and proposed a three-year plan under which $100 a month would be paid on the restitution obligation, for the first ten months of the plan. Other unsecured creditors were to receive a total of 5% of their claims over the remaining term of the plan. Is that difference in treatment permissible? See *In re Williams*, 231 B.R. 280 (Bankr. S.D.Ohio 1999).

---

[26] Because the first 36 months' disposable income is mandatory but further plan contributions are not, at least one court would prohibit discrimination in distribution of the first 36 months' disposable income but permit discrimination in favor of nondischargeable student loans with respect to any further contributions. *In re Strickland*, 181 B.R. 598 (Bankr. N.D.Ala.1995), whose holding is endorsed by Judge Lundin. See Keith M. Lundin, CHAPTER 13 BANKRUPTCY, at 153-9 to 153-11, and § 159.1 (3d ed.2000) * * * . Like the court in *Strickland*, we attach importance to the fact that the discrimination here involved the disposition of mandatory contributions. However, because this case involves no contributions beyond the mandatory minimum, we express no opinion on when and whether a plan may discriminate in the distribution of optional contributions.

2. CLASSIFICATION IN CHAPTER 11

Section 1129(a) imposes two apparently inconsistent requirements that must be met before a plan can be confirmed—each impaired class must accept the plan, § 1129(a)(8), and at least one impaired class must accept the plan, § 1129(a)(10). The apparent inconsistency melts away when § 1129(b) is consulted—a plan can be confirmed despite its failure to win acceptance by each impaired class as required by (a)(8) if the requirements of § 1129(b) (having to do with minimum payments and the order of payments) are satisfied. This is "cram down." It permits a debtor to impose a plan on dissenting creditors, as long as certain payment requirements are met. But cram down cannot be attempted unless all the requirements of § 1129(a) other than (a)(8) are satisfied. Among those requirements of § 1129(a) that must still be met is (a)(10)—at least one impaired class must accept the plan. In other words, at least one impaired class must vote for the plan before it can be crammed down the throats of the others.

You should now be able to guess that a substantial number of Chapter 11 classification cases involve the debtor's attempt to gerrymander classes so as to obtain the one vote necessary to satisfy § 1129-(a)(10). This issue is treated in more detail in Chapter 8 of this text.

I. EQUITABLE SUBORDINATION

The Bankruptcy Code authorizes several types of subordination. For example, a claim will not take its usual place in the bankruptcy distribution line if the claimholder has agreed to subordinate its position to another creditor. Such contracts are enforced in bankruptcy, under § 510(a), thus preventing a creditor from avoiding in bankruptcy an agreement that would govern outside of bankruptcy. Similarly, claims arising from securities fraud are subordinated under § 510(b), which serves to place the risk of the debtor's illegal securities sale on the purchasers of those securities rather than on other creditors.

Other claims may not take their usual distributive position for reasons of fairness or equity. Section 510(c) recognizes the inherent equitable power of the bankruptcy court to subordinate a claim, which is almost always based on some type of misbehavior by the claimholder. This is a codification of the equitable subordination doctrine articulated in *Pepper v. Litton*, 308 U.S. 295, 60 S.Ct. 238, 84 L.Ed. 281 (1939). In *Pepper*, a corporation's dominant shareholder caused the corporation to confess judgment, prepetition, on a dormant wage claim held by the shareholder. JUSTICE DOUGLAS, writing for the Court, noted that the shareholder had manipulated the corporation's affairs in such a way that unsecured creditors would receive nothing. JUSTICE DOUGLAS concluded that the transaction did not carry "the earmarks of an arm's length bargain," *id*. at 306–07, 60 S.Ct. at 245, 84 L.Ed. at 289, and approved subordination in priority of the shareholder's claim relative to the claims of other creditors.

The Code does not specify the standards that bankruptcy courts should apply in deciding equitable subordination issues. Rather, the legislative history states that § 510(c) was intended to codify existing case law, such as *Pepper*, and was "not intended to limit the court's power in any way." H.R. Rep. No. 95–595 at 359, *reprinted in* 1978 U.S.C.C.A.N. at 6315. Courts are especially vigilant when an insider is involved, as was true in *Pepper*.

The next case, which does not involve an insider, is one of the leading decisions dealing with the circumstances under which a secured creditor's claim might be subordinated.

SMITH v. ASSOCIATES COMMERCIAL CORP. (IN RE CLARK PIPE & SUPPLY CO.)

United States Court of Appeals, Fifth Circuit, 1990.
893 F.2d 693.

E. GRADY JOLLY, Circuit Judge.

Treating the suggestion for rehearing en banc filed in this case by Associates Commercial Corporation ("Associates"), as a petition for panel rehearing, we hereby grant the petition for rehearing. After re-examining the evidence in this case and the applicable law, we conclude that our prior opinion was in error. We therefore withdraw our prior opinion[a] and substitute the following:

In this bankruptcy case we are presented with two issues arising out of the conduct of the bankrupt's lender during the ninety days prior to the bankrupt's filing for protection from creditors. * * * [T]he second question is whether the lender engaged in such inequitable conduct that would justify subordination of the lender's claims to the extent that the conduct harmed other creditors. * * *

---

[a] 870 F.2d 1022 (5th Cir.1989). Eds.

I

Clark Pipe and Supply Company, Inc., ("Clark") was in the business of buying and selling steel pipe used in the fabrication of off-shore drilling platforms. In September 1980, Associates and Clark executed various agreements under which Associates would make revolving loans secured by an assignment of accounts receivable and an inventory mortgage. Under the agreements, Clark was required to deposit all collections from the accounts receivable in a bank account belonging to Associates. The amount that Associates would lend was determined by a formula, i.e., a certain percentage of the amount of eligible accounts receivable plus a certain percentage of the cost of inventory. The agreements provided that Associates could reduce the percentage advance rates at any time at its discretion.

When bad times hit the oil fields in late 1981, Clark's business slumped. In February 1982 Associates began reducing the percentage advance rates so that Clark would have just enough cash to pay its direct operating expenses. Clark used the advances to keep its doors open and to sell inventory, the proceeds of which were used to pay off the past advances from Associates. Associates did not expressly dictate to Clark which bills to pay. Neither did it direct Clark not to pay vendors or threaten Clark with a cut-off of advances if it did pay vendors. But Clark had no funds left over from the advances to pay vendors or other creditors whose services were not essential to keeping its doors open.

One of Clark's vendors, going unpaid, initiated foreclosure proceedings in February and seized the pipe it had sold Clark. Another attempted to do so in March. The resulting priority dispute was resolved only in litigation. ([Five vendors] had valid vendors' privileges in the goods they had sold Clark that, under Louisiana law, primed Associates' inventory mortgage). When a third unpaid creditor initiated foreclosure proceedings in May, Clark sought protection from creditors by filing for reorganization under Chapter 11 of the Bankruptcy Code.

The case was converted to a Chapter 7 liquidation on August 31, 1982, and a trustee was appointed. In 1983, the trustee brought this adversary proceeding against Clark's lender, Associates. The trustee sought * * * equitable subordination of Associates' claims. Following a one-day trial on August 28, 1986, the bankruptcy court entered judgment on April 10, 1987, and an amended judgment on June 9, 1987.

The court * * * subordinated Associates' claims. The district court affirmed on May 24, 1988.

* * *

III

The second issue before us is whether the bankruptcy court was justified in equitably subordinating Associates' claims. This court has enunciated a three-pronged test to determine whether and to what extent a claim should be equitably subordinated: (1) the claimant must have engaged in some type of inequitable conduct, (2) the misconduct must have resulted in injury to the creditors of the bankrupt or conferred an unfair advantage on the claimant, and (3) equitable subordination of the claim must not be inconsistent with the provisions of the Bankruptcy Code. Three general categories of conduct have been recognized as sufficient to satisfy the first prong of the three-part test: (1) fraud, illegality or breach of fiduciary duties; (2) undercapitalization; and (3) a claimant's use of the debtor as a mere instrumentality or alter ego.

In essence, the bankruptcy court found that once Associates realized Clark's desperate financial condition, Associates asserted total control and used Clark as a mere instrumentality to liquidate Associates' unpaid loans. Moreover, it did so, the trustee argues, to the detriment of the rights of Clark's other creditors.

Associates contends that its control over Clark was far from total. Associates says that it did no more than determine the percentage of advances as expressly permitted in the loan agreement; it never made or dictated decisions as to which creditors were paid. Thus, argues Associates, it never had the "actual, participatory, total control of the debtor" required to make Clark its instrumentality * * *. If it did not use Clark as an instrumentality or engage in any other type of inequitable conduct * * *, argues Associates, then it cannot be equitably subordinated.

A

We first consider whether Associates asserted such control over the activities of Clark that we should consider that it was using Clark as its mere instrumentality. In our prior opinion, we agreed with the district court and the bankruptcy court that, as a practical matter, Associates asserted total control over Clark's liquidation, and that it used its control in a manner detrimental to the unsecured creditors. Upon reconsideration, we have concluded that we cannot say that the sort of control Associates asserted over Clark's financial affairs rises to the level of unconscionable conduct necessary to justify the application of the doctrine of equitable subordination. We have reached our revised conclusion primarily because we cannot escape the salient fact that, pursuant to its loan agreement with Clark, Associates had the right to reduce funding, just as it did, as Clark's sales slowed. We now conclude that there is no evidence that Associates exceeded its authority under the loan agreement, or that Associates acted inequitably in exercising its rights under that agreement.

We think it is important to note at the outset that the loan and security agreements between Associates and Clark, which are at issue here, were executed in 1980, at the inception of their relationship. There is no evidence that Clark was insolvent at the time the agreements were entered into. Clark was represented by counsel during the negotiations, and there is no evidence that the loan documents were negotiated at anything other than arm's length or that they are atypical of loan documents used in similar asset-based financings.

The loan agreement between Associates and Clark established a line of credit varying from $2.2 million to approximately $2.7 million over the life of the loan. The amount that Associates would lend was determined by a formula: 85% of the amount of eligible accounts receivables plus 60% of the cost of inventory. Under the agreement, Clark was required to deposit all collections from the accounts receivable in a bank account belonging to Associates. Associates would, in turn, re-advance the agreed-upon portion of those funds to Clark on a revolving basis. The agreement provided that Associates could reduce the percentage advance rates at any time in its discretion.

When Clark's business began to decline, along with that of the oil patch generally, Associates advised Clark that it would reduce the advance ratio for the inventory loan by 5% per month beginning in January 1982. After that time, the company stopped buying new inventory and, according to the Trustee's expert witness, Clark's monthly sales revenues amounted to less than one-fifth of the company's outstanding accounts payable. Clark prepared a budget at Associates' request that indicated the disbursements necessary to keep the company operating. The budget did not include payment to vendors for previously shipped goods. Associates' former loan officer, Fred Slice, testified as to what he had in mind:

If he [the comptroller of Clark] had had the availability [of funds to pay a vendor or other trade creditor] that particular day, I would have said, "Are you sure you've got that much availability, Jim," because he shouldn't have that much. The way I had structured it, he wouldn't have any money to pay his suppliers.

* * *

But you know, the possibility that—this is all hypothetical. I had it structured so that there was no—there was barely enough money—there was enough money, if I did it right, enough money to keep the doors open. Clark could continue to operate, sell the inventory, turn it into receivables, collect the cash, transfer that cash to me, and reduce my loans.

And, if he had ever had availability for other things, that meant I had done something wrong, and I would have been surprised. To ask me what I would have done is purely hypothetical[;] I don't think it would happen. I think it's so unrealistic, I don't know.

Despite Associates' motive, which was, according to Slice, "to get in the best position I can prior to the bankruptcy, i.e., I want to get the absolute amount of dollars as low as I can by hook or crook," the evidence shows that the amount of its advances continued to be based on the applicable funding formulas. Slice testified that the lender did not appreciably alter its original credit procedures when Clark fell into financial difficulty.

In our original opinion, we failed to focus sufficiently on the loan agreement, which gave Associates the right to conduct its affairs with Clark in the manner in which it did. In addition, we think that in our previous opinion we were overly influenced by the negative and inculpatory tone of Slice's testimony. Given the agreement he was working under, his testimony was hardly more than fanfaronading about the power that the agreement afforded him over the financial affairs of Clark. Although his talk was crass (e.g., "I want to get the absolute dollars as low as I can, by hook or crook"), our careful examination of the record does not reveal any conduct on his part that was inconsistent with the loan agreement, irrespective of what his personal motive may have been.

Through its loan agreement, every lender effectively exercises "control" over its borrower to some degree. A lender in Associates' position will usually possess "control" in the sense that it can foreclose or drastically reduce the debtor's financing. The purpose of equitable subordination is to distinguish between the unilateral remedies that a creditor may properly enforce pursuant to its agreements with the debtor and other inequitable conduct such as fraud, misrepresentation, or the exercise of such total control over the debtor as to have essentially replaced its decision-making capacity with that of the lender. The crucial distinction between what is inequitable and what a lender can reasonably and legitimately do to protect its interests is the distinction between the existence of "control" and the exercise of that "control" to direct the activities of the debtor. As the Supreme Court stated in *Comstock v. Group of Institutional Investors*, 335 U.S. 211, 229 (1948): "It is not mere existence of an opportunity to do wrong that brings the rule into play; it is the unconscionable use of the opportunity afforded by the domination to advantage itself at the injury of the subsidiary that deprives the wrongdoer of the fruits of his wrong."

In our prior opinion, we drew support from *In re American Lumber Co.*, 5 B.R. 470 (D.Minn.1980), to reach our conclusion that Associates' claims should be equitably subordinated. Upon reconsideration, however, we find that the facts of that case are significantly more egregious than we have here. In that case, the court equitably subordinated the claims of a bank because the bank "controlled" the debtor through its right to a controlling interest in the debtor's stock. The bank forced the debtor to convey security interests in its remaining unencumbered assets to the bank after the borrower defaulted on an existing debt. Immediately thereafter, the bank foreclosed on the borrower's accounts receivable, terminated the borrower's employees, hired its own skeleton crew to conduct a liquidation, and selectively honored the debtor's payables to improve its own position. The bank began receiving and opening all incoming mail at the borrower's office, and it established a bank account into which all amounts received by the borrower were deposited and over which the bank had sole control. The bankruptcy court found that the bank exercised control over all aspects of the debtor's finances and operation including: payments of payables and wages, collection and use of accounts receivable and contract rights, purchase and use of supplies and materials, inventory sales, a lumber yard, the salaries of the principals, the employment of employees, and the receipt of payments for sales and accounts receivable.

Despite its decision to prohibit further advances to the debtor, its declaration that the debtor was in default of its loans, and its decisions to use all available funds of the company to offset the company's obligations to it, the bank in *American Lumber* made two specific representations to the American Lumbermen's Credit Association that the debtor was not in a bankruptcy situation and that current contracts would be fulfilled. Two days after this second reassurance, the bank gave notice of foreclosure of its security interests in the company's inventory and equipment. Approximately two weeks later the bank sold equipment and inventory of the debtor amounting to roughly $450,000, applying all of the proceeds to the debtor's indebtedness to the bank.

Associates exercised significantly less "control" over the activities of Clark than did the lender in *American Lumber*. Associates did not own any stock of Clark, much less a controlling block. Nor did Associates interfere with the operations of the borrower to an extent even roughly commensurate with the degree of interference exercised by the bank in *American Lumber*. Associates made no management decisions for Clark, such as deciding which creditors to prefer with the diminishing amount of funds available. At no time did Associates place any of its employees as either a director or officer of Clark. Associates never influenced the removal from office of any Clark personnel, nor did Associates ever request Clark to take any particular action at a shareholders meeting. Associates did not expressly dictate to Clark which bills to pay, nor did it direct Clark not to pay vendors or threaten a cut-off of advances if it did pay vendors. Clark handled its own daily operations. The same basic procedures with respect to the reporting of collateral, the calculation of availability of funds, and the procedures for the advancement of funds were followed throughout the relationship between Clark and Associates. Unlike the lender in *American Lumber*, Associates did not mislead creditors to continue supplying Clark. Perhaps the most important fact that distinguishes this case from *American Lumber* is that Associates did not coerce Clark into executing the security agreements after Clark became insolvent. Instead, the loan and security agreements between Clark and Associates were entered into at arm's length prior to Clark's insolvency, and all of Associates' activities were conducted pursuant to those agreements.

Associates' control over Clark's finances, admittedly powerful and ultimately severe, was based solely on the exercise of powers found in the loan agreement. Associates' close watch over Clark's affairs does not, by itself, however, amount to such control as would justify equitable subordination. "There is nothing inherently wrong with a creditor carefully monitoring his debtor's financial situation or with suggesting what course of action the debtor ought to follow." *In re Teltronics Services, Inc.*, 29 B.R. 139, 172 (Bankr. E.D.N.Y.1983) (citations omitted). Although the terms of the agreement did give

Associates potent leverage over Clark, that agreement did not give Associates total control over Clark's activities. At all material times Clark had the power to act autonomously and, if it chose, to disregard the advice of Associates; for example, Clark was free to shut its doors at any time it chose to do so and to file for bankruptcy.

Finally, on reconsideration, we are persuaded that the rationale of *In re W.T. Grant Co.*, 699 F.2d 599 (2d Cir.1983), should control the case before us. In that case, the Second Circuit recognized that

> a creditor is under no fiduciary obligation to its debtor or to other creditors of the debtor in the collection of its claim. The permissible parameters of a creditor's efforts to seek collection from a debtor are generally those with respect to voidable preferences and fraudulent conveyances proscribed by the Bankruptcy Act; apart from these there is generally no objection to a creditor's using his bargaining position, including his ability to refuse to make further loans needed by the debtor, to improve the status of his existing claims.

699 F.2d at 609–10. Associates was not a fiduciary of Clark, it did not exert improper control over Clark's financial affairs, and it did not act inequitably in exercising its rights under its loan agreement with Clark.

* * *

We therefore conclude that the district court erred in affirming the bankruptcy court's decision to subordinate Associates' claims.

* * *

Questions

1. Why was it so important that the contract between Associates and Clark provided for the actions Associates took?

2. A transferee cannot escape responsibility for a fraudulent conveyance by pointing to a contract clause permitting such actions. Is the court suggesting that a creditor can escape the subordination of its claim by relying on contractual terms?

3. Assume that the contract authorized Associates to require additional collateral in the event of Clark's default, to foreclose on it immediately, to conduct a liquidation sale using its own employees, and to decide whether

purchases would be made or other creditors paid. If Associates took those authorized actions, would its claim be equitably subordinated?

4. Will a creditor escape subordination as long as the debtor has retained control over the decision to remain open or to shut its doors?

5. The legislative history to § 510(c) states that "a claim is generally subordinated only if [the] holder of such claim is guilty of inequitable conduct, *or the claim itself is of a status susceptible to subordination, such as a penalty* * * * ." 124 Cong. Rec. 32398 (1978) (statement of Rep. Edwards); *id.* at 33998 (statement of Sen. DeConcini) (emphasis added). Relying on this language, a number of courts equitably subordinated tax penalties, which do not represent pecuniary losses, to secured and unsecured claims held by creditors who extended value to the debtor. The Supreme Court put a stop to this in *United States v. Noland*, 517 U.S. 535, 116 S.Ct. 1524, 134 L.Ed.2d 748 (1996). The government's priority claim had been subordinated not because of inequitable conduct, but solely because of status. The Court stated that if § 510(c)

> authorized a court to conclude on a general, categorical level that tax penalties should not be treated as administrative expenses to be paid first, it would empower a court to modify the operation of the priority statute at the same level at which Congress operated when it made its characteristically general judgment to establish the hierarchy of claims in the first place. That is, the distinction between characteristic legislative and trial court functions would simply be swept away, and the statute would delegate legislative revision, not authorize equitable exception.

Id. at 540, 116 S.Ct. at 1527, 134 L.Ed.2d at 755. Because the Court held categorical subordination inappropriate, it found no need to decide "whether a bankruptcy court must always find creditor misconduct before a claim may be equitably subordinated." *Id.* at 543. See also *United States v. Reorganized CF&I Fabricators of Utah, Inc.*, 518 U.S. 213 (1996) (holding *Noland* applicable to subordination of a tax penalty not entitled to priority).

Chapter 4

==

SECURED CLAIMS IN BANKRUPTCY

A. INTRODUCTION

According to § 506(a)(1), as we have seen, a claim "secured by a lien on property in which the estate has an interest * * * is a secured claim to the extent of the value of such creditor's interest in the estate's interest in such property." It "is an unsecured claim to the extent that the value of such creditor's interest * * * is less than the amount of such allowed claim."

Although one might wish that the plain-English school of legal writing had enlightened the Code's drafters, § 506(a)(1) is fairly straightforward. Consider two fact patterns. First, assume that Debtor, Inc. borrows $100,000 from Bank and grants a mortgage on its factory to secure repayment of the obligation. Assume in addition that the property is worth $130,000 at the time Debtor, Inc.'s Chapter 7 bankruptcy is filed. Under § 506(a)(1), Bank has a secured claim in the amount of $100,000. If Debtor, Inc. liquidates, the property will be sold and Bank will be paid $100,000 from the proceeds. The excess value of the property ($30,000) will remain in the estate to be distributed to unsecured creditors.

Assume, however, that the property is worth only $80,000 when bankruptcy is filed. Under § 506(a)(1), Bank's security interest is measured by the value of the property. Because only $80,000 in value is available from the property, Bank's secured claim is only $80,000. Bank also has an unsecured claim of $20,000. This is known as "bifurcation" of an undersecured claim. The undersecured creditor is treated as the holder of two claims, one secured and one unsecured.

Because no value is available to the bankruptcy estate from overencumbered property, the creditor should readily obtain relief from the stay under § 362(d)(2) in a liquidation case. (Reorganizations are different, as we will see, because the property may be necessary to the reorganization effort.) The trustee, however, usually abandons property that has no economic value to the estate. § 554. (In addition, § 725 requires the trustee to dispose of property in which another party holds an interest, before the estate is distributed under § 726.) Once property is abandoned it reverts to the debtor and those provisions of the automatic stay prohibiting acts to collect prepetition debts from property of the estate no longer apply, § 362(c)(1). The creditor will have to seek relief from the stay nonetheless, because § 362(a)(5) also stays efforts to enforce prepetition obligations against property of the debtor.

Note that *by definition* assets are available to pay holders of secured claims.

A secured claim is one secured by a "lien." Section 101(37) defines lien as a "charge against or interest in property to secure payment of a debt or performance of an obligation." This includes in the single category of secured claims many types of interests distinct under state law—security interests, mortgages, tax liens, judicial liens and statutory liens.

One of bankruptcy's fundamental policy decisions is that property rights created under nonbankruptcy law will be respected in bankruptcy. The Code's drafters believed this to be constitutionally necessary, although that premise is debatable. See James Steven Rogers, *The Impairment of Secured Creditors' Rights in Reorganization: A Study of the Relationship Between the Fifth Amendment and the Bankruptcy Clause*, 96 HARV. L. REV. 973 (1983). Acceptance of the premise that lienholders' rights are respected in bankruptcy does not require, however, that the rights themselves be recognized. Professor Theodore Eisenberg's "alternative, scaled-down view of the nature of a secured creditor's right in bankruptcy" describes the concept around which the 1978 Code was originally structured. Under Professor Eisenberg's view, the *value* of a secured creditor's rights is respected rather than the *in rem* rights themselves. The significance of secured status, therefore, is the priority afforded its holder:

> This view translates secured status into a priority claim equal to the value of the creditor's collateral, which alone is the measure of the value of the creditor's secured status in bankruptcy.

Under the priority approach, secured creditors have merely a right to be paid ahead of other creditors to the extent of the value of the secured creditors' collateral. They have no right to force surrender of specific property.

Theodore Eisenberg, *The Undersecured Creditor in Reorganizations and the Nature of Security*, 38 VAND. L. REV. 931, 952 (1985).

This tension between the value of rights and the rights themselves has been pervasive in bankruptcy. The 2005 Amendments, however, have reduced the tension by imposing rules requiring debtors to make payments measured not by the value of repossessed collateral in the hands of the creditor, but by either replacement cost or by the amount of the debt. These rules, without exception, apply only to individual debtors. Be alert, throughout our study of secured claims, to provisions that prescribe the value of such claims or that mandate the payments debtors must make to secured creditors in order to retain property.

Problems

1. Debtor's house, which she purchased three years ago, is subject to two purchase money mortgages. The first mortgage is for $100,000 and the second is for $50,000. If the house is worth $175,000, what claims are held by the first and second mortgagees?

2. Assume the same facts as in the prior Problem, except that the house is only worth $130,000. What claims are held by the two mortgagees?

3. Assume the same first and second mortgagees as above and that the house is worth $130,000. Assume also that another creditor, to whom Debtor owes $45,000, obtains a third-priority judicial lien against the house. What claims are held by the two mortgagees and by the judicial lienholder?

B. RELIEF FROM THE STAY AND ADEQUATE PROTECTION

The 2005 Amendments added some new exceptions to the automatic stay, directed toward secured claims. One of the new provisions, § 362(b)(21), excepts enforcement actions against real estate from the automatic stay in cases involving certain instances of repeated filings. (Another—§ 521(a)(6)—is a "stealth" exception, because it does not appear in § 362.)

Without the benefit of an exception to the stay, creditors are subject to its mandate. The automatic stay applies in all types of bankruptcy cases and to all claims, as we know. The impact of the stay is very different under the various chapters, however. In a Chapter 11, for example, the debtor is operating the business while formulating and negotiating the plan. The debtor must use property of the estate while holding off creditors who have interests in that property. Those creditors assume an increased risk of loss while the debtor tries to reorganize. If the reorganization fails (and most never culminate in a confirmed plan) and the case is converted to a liquidation, secured creditors may suffer damage as a result of depreciation in the value of their collateral during the reorganization effort. The Code provides that, if creditors are subjected to this risk, they are entitled to "adequate protection" of their interests. § 363(e).

A secured creditor facing the risk of deterioration in the value of its collateral is likely to want to obtain relief from the stay in order to take the collateral immediately. Section 362(d) applies to a creditor's effort to obtain relief from the stay. Its four subsections state alternative grounds for that relief.

Relief is granted under § 362(d)(1) "for cause, including the lack of adequate protection." Although the Code provides no definition, courts have found cause if the debtor abuses the bankruptcy process (for example, by repeated filings in order to stave off a foreclosure) or if the debtor defaults under a plan. Subsection (d)(4), which was added in 2005, may be viewed as a codification of two types of "cause," both involving "a scheme to hinder, delay and defraud" a secured creditor with an interest in real estate. Note also, the postamble to § 362(d)(4), which echoes the exception to the automatic stay found in § 362(b)(20).

Relief is granted under § 362(d)(2) if property is fully encumbered and is not needed in the reorganization effort. Subsection (2) applies in a case like the hypothetical presented above, in which collateral worth $80,000 secures a debt of $100,000 and the debtor files a Chapter 7.

Subsection (d)(3), which was added in 1994, provides for the lifting of the stay in a single asset real estate case if, within the designated time period, the debtor fails to file a feasible reorganization plan or to begin making monthly payments at the contract rate to the creditor holding an interest in the real estate. (Notice that both of the principal cases in this section are, apparently, single asset real estate cases. Such cases are treated in more detail in Chapter 8 of this casebook.)

Section 362(e) puts a short fuse on motions for relief from the automatic stay.

BANKERS LIFE INSURANCE COMPANY OF NEBRASKA v. ALYUCAN INTERSTATE CORP. (IN RE ALYUCAN INTERSTATE CORP.)

United States Bankruptcy Court, District of Utah, 1981.
12 B.R. 803.

RALPH R. MABEY, Bankruptcy Judge.

INTRODUCTION AND BACKGROUND

This case raises the question whether an "equity cushion" is necessary to provide adequate protection under § 362(d)(1). This Court concludes that it is not.

On January 14, 1981, Alyucan Interstate Corporation (debtor), a construction and real estate development firm, filed a petition under Chapter 11 of the Code. On May 4, Bankers Life Insurance Company of Nebraska (Bankers Life), holder of a trust deed on realty owned by debtor, brought this action for relief from the automatic stay under § 362(d). The complaint alleges that the realty secures a debt in the principal amount of $1,220,000 and that Bankers Life is not adequately protected. On May 20, the preliminary hearing contemplated by § 362(e) was held. After receiving evidence, the Court fixed the value of the realty on the date of the petition at $1,425,000 and found that there had been no erosion in that value as of the hearing. The debt owing was $1,297,226 as of the petition, and with interest accruing at roughly $8,000 per month, had increased to $1,330,761 as of the hearing.[a] Thus, there was an "equity cushion" of $127,774 or approximately nine percent of the value of the collateral, as of the petition, which had decreased to $94,239, or approximately six and one half percent of the value of the collateral, as of the hearing. As interest accumulates, and if no payments are made, this cushion will dissipate within a year.

---

[a] See § 506(b). Eds.

THE MEANING OF ADEQUATE PROTECTION

Section 362(d)(1) mandates relief, in some form, from the stay "for cause, including the lack of adequate protection of an interest in property." The only cause asserted in this proceeding is a lack of adequate protection.

Adequate protection is not defined in the Code. This omission was probably deliberate. Congress was aware of the turbulent rivalry of interests in reorganization. It needed a concept which would mediate polarities. But a carefully calibrated concept, subject to a brittle construction, could not accommodate the "infinite number of variations possible in dealings between debtors and creditors." H.R. Rep. No. 95–595 at 339, *reprinted in* 1978 U.S.C.C.A.N. at 6295. This problem required, not a formula, but a calculus, open-textured, pliant, and versatile, adaptable to "new ideas" which are "continually being implemented in this field" and to "varying circumstances and changing modes of financing." *Id.* Adequate protection was requisitioned to meet these needs. Its meaning, therefore, is born afresh out of the "reflective equilibrium"[2] of each decision, understood through analysis of the reorganization context and the language of § 362(d).

A. The Reorganization Context

Relief from the stay cannot be viewed in isolation from the reorganization process. Bankruptcy in general and Chapter 11 in particular are "procedural devices" for the rehabilitation of financially embarrassed enterprises. The process presupposes dynamic rather than static uses of property and denouement in a plan which accommodates the many, not just the few.

The automatic stay, within this framework, is designed "to prevent a chaotic and uncontrolled scramble for the debtor's assets in a variety of uncoordinated proceedings in different courts." *Fidelity Mortgage Investors v. Camelia Builders, Inc.*, 550 F.2d 47, 55 (2d Cir.1976). It grants a "breathing spell" for debtors to regroup. It shields creditors from one another by replacing "race" and other preferential systems of debt collection with a more equitable and orderly distribution of assets. It encourages rehabilitation: debtors may seek its asylum while recovery is possible rather than coasting to the point of no

---

[2]   This phrase is coined in J. Rawls, A THEORY OF JUSTICE 20–21 (1971), to describe a hypothetical deliberative process.

return; creditors, realizing that foreclosure is useless, may rechannel energies toward more therapeutic ends.

Although self-help and other unilateral recourse against debtors are forbidden, creditors are not left remediless. They may act through committees with professional assistance, often at the expense of the estate, or by seeking appointment of a trustee or examiner. Conversion to Chapter 7 and dismissal are options. Within certain time constraints, they may file a plan.

In short, the adequate protection vouchsafed creditors in Chapter 11 is interim protection, designed not as a purgative of all creditor ailments, but as a palliative of the worst: reorganization, dismissal, or liquidation will provide the final relief. During this interim, the policies favoring rehabilitation and the benefits derived from the stay should not be lightly discarded. Alternative remedies are available to creditors. Indeed, even relief from the stay need not mean termination of the stay. Section 362(d) provides for relief, *such as* "terminating, annulling, modifying, or conditioning" the stay. Thus, relief may be fashioned to suit the exigencies of the case.

B. The Language of § 362(d)

Turning from Chapter 11 at large to § 362(d) in specific, several issues must be addressed. First, what is the "interest in property" being protected? Second, what aspects of the "interest in property" require protection? Third, from what is the "interest in property" being protected? Fourth, what is the method of protection?

(1) What is the "interest in property" being protected? The legislative history mentions only "the interest of a secured creditor or co-owner of property with the debtor" in connection with adequate protection. H.R. Rep. No. 95–595 at 338. Within these classes of creditors, however, "the interests of which the court may provide protection * * * include equitable as well as legal interests. For example, a right to redeem under a pledge or a right to recover property under a consignment are both interests that are entitled to protection." *Id.* This classification is important because adequate protection depends upon the interest *and* property involved. Protection afforded a lessor, for example, may be different from that afforded a secured creditor. Treatment of a secured creditor who faces turnover may be different from treatment of a secured creditor who has not repossessed. Treatment of a senior lienholder may be different from treatment of a junior lienholder. Similarly, protection may vary if the property is real or per-

sonal, tangible or intangible, perdurable or perishable, or if its value is constant, depreciating, or subject to sudden or extreme fluctuations. Also relevant is the proposed use or idleness of the property.

(2) What aspects of the "interest in property" require protection? Adequate protection is concerned with the value of the interest in property. The legislative commentary to § 361 underscores this point: "Though the creditor might not receive his bargain in kind, the purpose of the section is to insure that the secured creditor receives *in value* essentially what he bargained for." *Id.* at 339 (emphasis supplied). The legislative history reemphasizes this point by noting that adequate protection is "derived from the fifth amendment protection of property interests," *id.*, citing *Wright v. Union Central Insurance Co.*, 311 U.S. 273 (1940), and *Louisville Bank v. Radford*, 295 U.S. 555 (1935). In *Wright*, Justice Douglas held that the bank received "the value of the [interest in] property" and that "there is no constitutional claim of a creditor to more than that." 311 U.S. at 278. Debtors were allowed to redeem the property at its appraised price, despite an obligation which exceeded the value of the collateral by $10,000. Thus, the "interest in property" entitled to protection is not measured by the amount of the debt but by the value of the lien. A mushrooming debt, through accrual of interest or otherwise, may be immaterial, if the amount of the lien is not thereby increased, while vicissitudes in the market, loss of insurance or other factors affecting the value of the lien are relevant to adequate protection. The purpose of adequate protection is to assure the recoverability of this value during the hiatus between petition and plan, or in the event the reorganization is stillborn, between petition and dismissal.[11]

---

[11] Some cases have interpreted adequate protection more in terms of contractual benefits than economic values. They have focused on language in the legislative history suggesting that secured creditors must receive the "benefit of their bargain." H.R. Rep. No. 95–595 at 339. Congress, however, was not referring to the *contractual* bargain between creditors and debtors because the next portion of the House Report acknowledges "there may be situations in bankruptcy where giving a secured creditor an absolute right to his bargain may be impossible or seriously detrimental to the bankruptcy laws. Thus, this section [§ 361] recognizes the availability of alternate means of protecting a secured creditor's interest. Though the creditor might not receive his bargain in kind, the purpose of the section is to insure that the secured creditor receives in value essentially what he bargained for." *Id.* Whether and to what extent noncontractual or business elements of a bargain may be factored into the adequate protection equation is problematical. Some courts, employing an equity cushion analysis (discussed below), insist that a ratio of debt to collateral is "bargained for" between debtor and creditor and must be considered in determining adequate protection. The stream of inquiry along this path, however, may be difficult to contain. Many

(3) From what is the "interest in property" being protected?
The short answer is from any impairment in value attributable to the
stay. The stay does not cause, but it may forestall a creditor from preventing or mitigating, a decline in value. Some harm to collateral,
however, may be unavoidable with or without the stay. Likewise,
creditors may acquiesce in some harm to collateral for business or other
reasons notwithstanding the stay. In these situations, and others which
may arise, any impairment in value may not be attributable to the stay.
Hence, not every decline in value must be recompensed, only those
which, but for the stay, could be and probably would be prevented or
mitigated.

(4) What is the method of protection? The method of affording
adequate protection, as noted above, will vary with the interest in property to be protected. In some cases, the debtor need do nothing, either
because the value of the interest in property is not declining or because
the decline in value is not attributable to the stay. If the stay is
responsible for a decline in value, § 361 states three illustrative methods
for providing adequate protection. Some courts, however, have not
looked beyond its trilogy of alternatives. Others have insisted on a
showing of indubitable equivalence. These approaches miss the mark:
they violate the nonprescriptive character of § 361, and may simply
exchange one imponderable for another. Indubitable equivalence is not
a method; nor does it have substantive content. Indeed, something
"indubitable" is more than "adequate;" "equivalent" is more than
"protection;" hence, the illustration may eclipse the concept. At best, it
is a semantic substitute for adequate protection and one with dubious,
not indubitable, application to the question of relief from the stay.

C. Application to This Proceeding

In this proceeding, the "interest in property" is the lien of
Bankers Life on the realty of debtor. It is a trust deed and therefore

---

business motives, which may or may not be expressed in the documents
memorializing a transaction, could then become relevant to adequate protection.
As a practical matter, for example, foreclosure may not be an attractive prospect
for some lenders who are, after all, in the business of loaning money not managing
properties. Hence, their bargain is primarily for payment with interest and, as a
last resort, for liquidation with its burdens of custodial care and costs. Foreclosure
may likewise pose regulatory complications. Banks and insurance companies are
traditionally limited in the amount of illiquid assets, such as realty, which they can
carry at any given time in their portfolio.

may be peremptorily foreclosed. It is a first lien with ample collateral to protect Bankers Life. The collateral and therefore the lien are not declining or subject to sudden depreciation in value. Bankers Life is suffering no pain cognizable under § 362 as a result of the stay, and relief from the stay is therefore, at this juncture, unnecessary.

Moreover, this property is essential to the reorganization of the debtor. Foreclosure and liquidation of the property would run counter to this need and would deprive debtor and other creditors of its going concern value. If liquidation is allowed, it should occur under the aegis of the Court and in the interests of all. Bankers Life is no better qualified to handle this liquidation than the debtor or the trustee. Indeed, Bankers Life may be ill-equipped to undertake this task, both because its interests are parochial and because, for regulatory or other reasons, it may be a reluctant caretaker. *See* discussion *supra* note 11. In any event, Bankers Life has other remedies under the Code. A trustee has been appointed. It may work with him or with creditor committees to negotiate a sale of the property. It can seek dismissal or conversion to Chapter 7. It can propose a plan of liquidation. In short, the application of adequate protection to the facts of this case avoids the trauma of relief from the stay and maintains the equilibrium of interests in this reorganization.

THE EQUITY CUSHION ANALYSIS

In contrast to these principles, there is a trend toward defining adequate protection in terms of an "equity cushion": the difference between outstanding debt and the value of the property against which the creditor desires to act. Where the difference is substantial, a cushion is said to exist, adequately protecting the creditor. As interest accrues, or depreciation advances, and the margin declines, the cushion weakens and the stay may be lifted. Naturally, courts disagree on what is an acceptable margin. The emerging view, however, may be that the stay should be terminated when the cushion will be absorbed through interest, commissions, and other costs of resale. The cushion analysis enjoys practical appeal and ease of application.

This Court rejects a cushion analysis upon four grounds: (1) It is inconsistent with the purpose of adequate protection. (2) It is inconsistent with the illustrations of adequate protection found in § 361. (3) It is inconsistent with the statutory scheme of § 362(d). (4) It has no basis in the historical development of relief from stay proceedings.

(1) The cushion analysis, by focusing on the ratio of debt to collateral, obscures the purpose of adequate protection, *viz.*, to guard against impairment of a lien. This blurring of objectives may produce improper results. If Bankers Life had been undersecured at the petition, for example, the absence of cushion would have dictated relief from the stay, even though the stay did not impair its lien and notwithstanding the usual appreciation in the value of realty.

(2) Since the thrust of adequate protection is to assure maintenance of the value of the lien, it is largely compensatory. Sections 361(1) and (2) therefore speak not in terms of preserving equity but in terms of compensating for any "decrease in the value of [an] interest in property." Moreover, the cushion analysis, because it is confined to the relationship between debt and collateral in a specific property, ignores the recoverability of value, not only from the property at stake but also from other sources. Sections 361(1) and (2), which provide for interim payments and replacement liens, contemplate that value from other assets held by debtors may be appropriated to supply any needed protection. Indeed, the legislative history to § 361 suggests the use of sureties or guarantors for this purpose. Even if the debtor has no other assets, it is nevertheless conceivable that an enterprise valuation, which approaches value in terms of capitalized earnings, could show an income potential sufficient to meet the adequate protection standard.

(3) Under § 362(d)(2) a lack of equity, absent a further showing that the property is unnecessary to an effective reorganization, does not warrant relief from the stay. This statutory provision expresses a legislative judgment, first, that it is the *absence* of equity rather than any particular cushion which is the criterion for relief from stay, and second, that the absence of equity is not alone dispositive—the court must still weigh the necessity of the property to an effective reorganization. The cushion analysis is inconsistent with this judgment. It makes surplusage out of § 362(d)(2) which speaks in terms of equity *and* reorganization. Indeed, this dual requirement emphasizes the role of equity, when present, not as a cushion, but to underwrite, through sale or credit, the rehabilitation of debtors.

(4) The cushion analysis is alien to the development of stay litigation. The stay provisions in Chapter proceedings in the Act * * * allowed relief "for cause shown." This was interpreted to require consideration of a number of factors, including the presence of equity, the likelihood of harm to the creditor, prospects for reorganization, and essentiality of the property in the operation of the estate. *See*, *e.g.*, Peitzman and Smith, "The Secured Creditor's Complaint: Relief from

the Automatic Stays in Bankruptcy Proceedings," 65 CAL. L. REV. 1216, 1226 (1977).

Although the "idea of equity" became "something of a totem for courts," *id*. at 1227, it was equity in the sense contemplated under § 362(d)(2), not an equity cushion. Thus, it was acknowledged that "deciding whether to continue or vacate the stay solely on the ground of the debtor's equity in the property may produce an unjust result," for example where "the encumbered property is so vital to the operation of debtor's business that foreclosure will simply not be allowed." *Id*.

* * *

CONCLUSION

Adequate protection is a concept designed to balance the rights of creditors and debtors in the preliminary stages of reorganization. It is, in each case, *ad hoc*. For this reason the cushion analysis, which may be helpful in general, falls short in the particular. It is not fully alert to the legislative directive that "the facts," in each hearing under § 362(d), "will determine whether relief is appropriate under the circumstances." H.R. Rep. No. 95–595 at 344. The facts of each case, thoughtfully weighed, not formularized, define adequate protection.

Questions and Problems

1. According to *Alyucan*, exactly what property interests of the secured creditor are entitled to adequate protection? — *Value of the liens*

2. The court asserted that "[a] mushrooming debt, through accrual of interest or otherwise, may be immaterial, if the amount of the lien is not thereby increased." When, factually, will that occur?

3. Loan agreements frequently require a debt-to-equity ratio of a designated percentage. This means that the debt cannot exceed that percentage of the value of the collateral, and assures the creditor of a continuous equity cushion. What if such an agreement had been present in *Alyucan*?

4. Assume the same facts as in *Alyucan*, except that the collateral is depreciating at the rate of $200 per month rather than holding its value. What rights to adequate protection would the secured creditor have?

5. Debtor owned an apartment building worth $300,000. It was subject to a first purchase money mortgage of $150,000 and a second purchase money mortgage of $50,000. Debtor later gave a third lien on the property to

a bank, in exchange for a loan of $70,000, and a fourth priority judgment lien for $130,000 was taken by a previously unsecured creditor. Debtor filed bankruptcy and the holder of the first mortgage sought relief from the stay under § 362(d)(2). Debtor argued that the requirements of (d)(2)(A) were not satisfied because the property had a value of $150,000 in excess of the movant's lien. Movant argued that "equity" is the difference between the property's value and the total amount of liens encumbering it. Who prevails? See *Nantucket Investors II v. California Federal Bank (In re Indian Palms Assocs., Ltd.)*, 61 F.3d 197, 206-08 (3d Cir.1995).

UNITED SAVINGS ASSOCIATION OF TEXAS v. TIMBERS OF INWOOD FOREST ASSOCIATES, LTD.

United States Supreme Court, 1988.
484 U.S. 365, 108 S.Ct. 626, 98 L.Ed.2d 740.

JUSTICE SCALIA delivered the opinion of the Court.

Petitioner United Savings Association of Texas seeks review of an en banc decision of the United States Court of Appeals for the Fifth Circuit, holding that petitioner was not entitled to receive from respondent debtor, which is undergoing reorganization in bankruptcy, monthly payments for the use value of the loan collateral which the bankruptcy stay prevented it from possessing. We granted certiorari to resolve a conflict in the Courts of Appeals regarding application of §§ 361 and 362(d)(1) of the Bankruptcy Code.

I

On June 29, 1982, respondent Timbers of Inwood Forest Associates, Ltd., executed a note in the principal amount of $4,100,000. Petitioner is the holder of the note as well as of a security interest created the same day in an apartment project owned by respondent in Houston, Texas. The security interest included an assignment of rents from the project. On March 4, 1985, respondent filed a voluntary petition under Chapter 11 of the Bankruptcy Code in the United States Bankruptcy Court for the Southern District of Texas.

On March 18, 1985, petitioner moved for relief from the automatic stay of enforcement of liens triggered by the petition, see § 362(a), on the ground that there was lack of "adequate protection" of its interest within the meaning of § 362(d)(1). At a hearing before the Bankruptcy Court, it was established that respondent owed petitioner

$4,366,388.77, and evidence was presented that the value of the collateral was somewhere between $2,650,000 and $4,250,000. The collateral was appreciating in value, but only very slightly. It was therefore undisputed that petitioner was an undersecured creditor. Respondent had agreed to pay petitioner the postpetition rents from the apartment project (covered by the after-acquired property clause in the security agreement), minus operating expenses. Petitioner contended, however, that it was entitled to additional compensation. The Bankruptcy Court agreed and on April 19, 1985, it conditioned continuance of the stay on monthly payments by respondent, at the market rate of 12% per annum, on the estimated amount realizable on foreclosure, $4,250,000—commencing six months after the filing of the bankruptcy petition, to reflect the normal foreclosure delays. The court held that the postpetition rents could be applied to these payments. Respondent appealed to the District Court and petitioner cross-appealed on the amount of the adequate protection payments. The District Court affirmed but the Fifth Circuit en banc reversed.

We granted certiorari to determine whether undersecured creditors are entitled to compensation under § 362(d)(1) for the delay caused by the automatic stay in foreclosing on their collateral.

II

When a bankruptcy petition is filed, § 362(a) of the Bankruptcy Code provides an automatic stay of, among other things, actions taken to realize the value of collateral given by the debtor. The provision of the Code central to the decision of this case is § 362(d) * * *. The phrase "adequate protection" in paragraph (1) of [§ 362(d)] is given further content by § 361 of the Code * * *.

It is common ground that the "interest in property" referred to by § 362(d)(1) includes the right of a secured creditor to have the security applied in payment of the debt upon completion of the reorganization; and that that interest is not adequately protected if the security is depreciating during the term of the stay. Thus, it is agreed that if the apartment project in this case had been declining in value petitioner would have been entitled, under § 362(d)(1), to cash payments or additional security in the amount of the decline, as § 361 describes. The crux of the present dispute is that petitioner asserts, and respondent denies, that the phrase "interest in property" also includes the secured party's right (suspended by the stay) to take immediate possession of the defaulted security, and apply it in payment of the debt. If that right is embraced by the term, it is obviously not adequately protected unless the secured party is reimbursed for the use of the proceeds he is deprived of during the term of the stay.

The term "interest in property" certainly summons up such concepts as "fee ownership," "life estate," "co-ownership," and "security interest" more readily than it does the notion of "right to immediate foreclosure." Nonetheless, viewed in the isolated context of § 362-(d)(1), the phrase could reasonably be given the meaning petitioner asserts. Statutory construction, however, is a holistic endeavor. A provision that may seem ambiguous in isolation is often clarified by the remainder of the statutory scheme—because the same terminology is used elsewhere in a context that makes its meaning clear or because only one of the permissible meanings produces a substantive effect that is compatible with the rest of the law. That is the case here. Section 362(d)(1) is only one of a series of provisions in the Bankruptcy Code dealing with the rights of secured creditors. The language in those other provisions, and the substantive dispositions that they effect, persuade us that the "interest in property" protected by § 362(d)(1) does not include a secured party's right to immediate foreclosure.

Section 506 of the Code defines the amount of the secured creditor's allowed secured claim and the conditions of his receiving postpetition interest. * * * In subsection (a)[(1)] of this provision the creditor's "interest in property" obviously means his security interest without taking account of his right to immediate possession of the collateral on default. If the latter were included, the "value of such creditor's interest" would increase, and the proportions of the claim that are secured and unsecured would alter, as the stay continues—since the value of the entitlement to use the collateral from the date of bankruptcy would rise with the passage of time. No one suggests this was intended. The phrase "value of such creditor's interest" in § 506-(a)[(1)] means "the value of the collateral." H.R. Rep. No. 95–595 at 181, 356. We think the phrase "value of such entity's interest" in § 361(1) and (2), when applied to secured creditors, means the same.

Even more important for our purposes than § 506's use of terminology is its substantive effect of denying undersecured creditors postpetition interest on their claims—just as it denies *over* secured creditors postpetition interest to the extent that such interest, when added to the principal amount of the claim, will exceed the value of the collateral. Section 506(b) provides that "*[t]o the extent that* an allowed secured claim is secured by property the value of which * * * is greater than the amount of such claim, there shall be allowed to the holder of such claim, interest on such claim." (Emphasis added.) Since this provision permits postpetition interest to be paid only out of the "security cushion," the undersecured creditor, who has no such cushion, falls within the general rule disallowing postpetition interest. See § 502-(b)(2). If the Code had meant to give the undersecured creditor, who is thus denied interest on his *claim*, interest on the value of his *collateral*, surely this is where that disposition would have been set forth, and not obscured within the "adequate protection" provision of § 362(d)(1). Instead of the intricate phraseology set forth above, § 506(b) would simply have said that the secured creditor is entitled to interest "on his allowed claim, or on the value of the property securing his allowed claim, whichever is lesser." Petitioner's interpretation of § 362(d)(1) must be regarded as contradicting the carefully drawn disposition of § 506(b).

Petitioner seeks to avoid this conclusion by characterizing § 506(b) as merely an alternative method for compensating oversecured creditors, which does not imply that no compensation is available to undersecured creditors. This theory of duplicate protection for oversecured creditors is implausible even in the abstract, but even more so in light of the historical principles of bankruptcy law. Section 506(b)'s denial of postpetition interest to undersecured creditors merely codified pre-Code bankruptcy law, in which that denial was part of the conscious allocation of reorganization benefits and losses between undersecured and unsecured creditors. "To allow a secured creditor interest where his security was worth less than the value of his debt was thought to be inequitable to unsecured creditors." *Vanston Bond-holders Protective Committee v. Green*, 329 U.S. 156, 164 (1946). It was considered unfair to allow an undersecured creditor to recover interest from the estate's unencumbered assets before unsecured creditors had recovered any principal. We think it unlikely that § 506(b) codified the pre-Code rule with the intent, not of achieving the principal purpose and function of that rule, but of providing oversecured creditors an alternative method of compensation. Moreover, it is incomprehensible why Congress would want to favor undersecured creditors with interest if they move for it under § 362(d)(1) at the inception of the reorganization process—thereby probably pushing the estate into liquidation—but not if they forbear and seek it only at the completion of the reorganization.

Second, petitioner's interpretation of § 362(d)(1) is structurally inconsistent with § 552. Section 552(a) states the general rule that a prepetition security interest does not reach property acquired by the estate or debtor postpetition. Section 552(b) sets forth an exception, allowing postpetition "proceeds, product, offspring, rents, or profits" of the collateral to be covered only if the security agreement expressly provides for an interest in such property, and the interest has been perfected under "applicable nonbankruptcy law."[b] Section 552(b) therefore makes possession of a perfected security interest in postpetition rents or profits from collateral a condition of having them applied to satisfying the claim of the secured creditor ahead of the claims of unsecured creditors. Under petitioner's interpretation, however, the undersecured creditor who lacks such a perfected security interest in effect achieves the same result by demanding the "use value" of his collateral under § 362. It is true that § 506(b) gives the *over* secured creditor, despite lack of compliance with the conditions of § 552, a similar priority over unsecured creditors; but that does not compromise the principle of § 552, since the interest payments come only out of the "cushion" in which the oversecured creditor *does have* a perfected security interest.

Third, petitioner's interpretation of § 362(d)(1) makes nonsense of § 362(d)(2). On petitioner's theory, the undersecured creditor's inability to take immediate possession of his collateral is always "cause" for conditioning the stay (upon the payment of market rate interest) under § 362(d)(1), since there is, within the meaning of that paragraph, "lack of adequate protection of an interest in property." But § 362(d)(2) expressly provides a different standard for relief from a stay "of an act against property," which of course includes taking possession of collateral. It provides that the court shall grant relief "if * * * (A) the debtor does not have an equity in such property [*i.e.*, the creditor is undersecured]; *and* (B) such property is not necessary to an effective reorganization." (Emphasis added.) By applying the "adequate protection of an interest in property" provision of § 362(d)(1) to the alleged "interest" in the earning power of collateral, petitioner creates the strange consequence that § 362 entitles the secured creditor to relief from the stay (1) if he is undersecured (and thus not eligible for interest under § 506(b)), *or* (2) if he is undersecured *and* his collateral "is not necessary to an effective reorganization." This renders § 362(d)(2) a practical nullity and a theoretical absurdity. If § 362(d)(1) is interpreted in this fashion, an undersecured creditor would seek relief under § 362(d)(2) only if his collateral was not depreciating (or he was being compensated for depreciation) and it was receiving market rate interest on his collateral, but nonetheless wanted to foreclose. Petitioner offers

---

[b]   In 1994, § 552(b) was renumbered § 552(b)(1), the reference to "rents" was deleted, and § 552(b)(2) was added. The new subsection now treats rents separately. Eds.

no reason why Congress would want to provide relief for such an obstreperous and thoroughly unharmed creditor.

Section 362(d)(2) also belies petitioner's contention that undersecured creditors will face inordinate and extortionate delay if they are denied compensation for interest lost during the stay as part of "adequate protection" under § 362(d)(1). Once the movant under § 362-(d)(2) establishes that he is an undersecured creditor, it is the burden of the *debtor* to establish that the collateral at issue is "necessary to an effective reorganization." See § 362(g). What this requires is not merely a showing that if there is conceivably to be an effective reorganization, this property will be needed for it; but that the property is essential for an effective reorganization *that is in prospect*. This means, as many lower courts, including the en banc court in this case, have properly said, that there must be "a reasonable possibility of a successful reorganization within a reasonable time." The cases are numerous in which § 362(d)(2) relief has been provided within less than a year from the filing of the bankruptcy petition. And while the bankruptcy courts demand less detailed showings during the four months in which the debtor is given the exclusive right to put together a plan, see §§ 1121(b), (c)(2), even within that period lack of any realistic prospect of effective reorganization will require § 362(d)(2) relief.

III

A

Petitioner contends that denying it compensation under § 362-(d)(1) is inconsistent with sections of the Code other than those just discussed. Petitioner principally relies on the phrase "indubitable equivalent" in § 361(3), which also appears in § 1129(b)(2)(A)(iii). Petitioner contends that in the latter context, which sets forth the standards for confirming a reorganization plan, the phrase has developed a well-settled meaning connoting the right of a secured creditor to receive present value of his security—thus requiring interest if the claim is to be paid over time. It is true that under § 1129(b) a secured claimant has a right to receive under a plan the present value of his collateral. This entitlement arises, however, not from the phrase "indubitable equivalent" in § 1129(b)(2)(A)(iii), but from the provision of § 1129-(b)(2)(A)(i)(II) that guarantees the secured creditor "deferred cash payments * * * of a value, *as of the effective date of the plan*, of at least the value of such [secured claimant's] interest in the estate's interest in such property." (Emphasis added.) Under this formulation, even though the undersecured creditor's "interest" is regarded (properly) as solely the value of the collateral, he must be rendered payments that assure him that value *as of the effective date of the plan*. In § 361(3), by contrast, the relief pending the stay need only be such *"as will result in the realization * * * of the indubitable equivalent"* of the collateral. (Emphasis added.) It is obvious (since §§ 361 and 362(d)(1) do not entitle the secured creditor to immediate payment of the principal of his collateral) that this "realization" is to "result" not at once, but only upon completion of the reorganization. It is *then* that he must be assured "realization * * * of the indubitable equivalent" of his collateral. To put the point differently: similarity of outcome between § 361(3) and § 1129 would be demanded only if the former read "such other relief * * * as will give such entity, *as of the date of the relief*, the indubitable equivalent of such entity's interest in such property."

Nor is there merit in petitioner's suggestion that "indubitable equivalent" in § 361(3) connotes reimbursement for the use value of collateral because the phrase is derived from *In re Murel Holding Corp.*, 75 F.2d 941 (2d Cir.1935), where it bore that meaning. *Murel* involved a proposed reorganization plan that gave the secured creditor interest on his collateral for 10 years, with full payment of the secured principal due at the end of that term; the plan made no provision, however, for amortization of principal or maintenance of the collateral's value during the term. In rejecting the plan, *Murel* used the words "indubitable equivalence" with specific reference not to interest (which was assured), but to the jeopardized principal of the loan:

> "Interest is indeed the common measure of the difference [between payment now and payment 10 years hence], but a creditor who fears the safety of his principal will scarcely be content with that; he wishes to get his money or at least the property. We see no reason to suppose that the statute was intended to deprive him of that in the interest of junior holders, unless by a substitute of the most indubitable equivalence." *Id*. at 942.

Of course *Murel*, like § 1129, proceeds from the premise that in the confirmation context the secured creditor is entitled to present value. But no more from *Murel* than from § 1129 can it be inferred that a similar requirement exists as of the time of the bankruptcy stay. The reorganized debtor is supposed to stand on his own two feet. The debtor in process of reorganization, by contrast, is given many temporary protections against the normal operation of the law.

Petitioner also contends that the Code embodies a principle that secured creditors do not bear the costs of reorganization. It derives this from the rule that general administrative expenses do not have priority over secured claims. See §§ 506(c), 507(a). But the general principle does not follow from the particular rule. That secured creditors do not bear one kind of reorganization cost hardly means that they bear none of them. The Code rule on administrative expenses merely continues pre-Code law. But it was also pre-Code law that undersecured creditors were not entitled to postpetition interest as compensation for the delay of reorganization. Congress could hardly have understood that the readoption of the rule on administrative expenses would work a change in the rule on postpetition interest, which it also readopted.

Finally, petitioner contends that failure to interpret § 362(d)(1) to require compensation of undersecured creditors for delay will create an inconsistency in the Code in the (admittedly rare) case when the debtor proves solvent. When that occurs, § 726(a)(5) provides that postpetition interest is allowed on unsecured claims. Petitioner contends it would be absurd to allow postpetition interest on unsecured claims but not on the secured portion of undersecured creditors' claims. It would be disingenuous to deny that this is an apparent anomaly, but it will occur so rarely that it is more likely the product of inadvertence than are the blatant inconsistencies petitioner's interpretation would produce. Its inequitable effects, moreover, are entirely avoidable, since an undersecured creditor is entitled to "surrender or waive his security and prove his entire claim as an unsecured one." *United States Nat'l Bank v. Chase Nat'l Bank*, 331 U.S. 28, 34 (1947). Section 726(a)(5) therefore requires no more than that undersecured creditors receive postpetition interest from a solvent debtor on equal terms with unsecured creditors rather than ahead of them—which, where the debtor is solvent, involves no hardship.

B

Petitioner contends that its interpretation is supported by the legislative history of §§ 361 and 362(d)(1), relying almost entirely on statements that "[s]ecured creditors should not be deprived of the benefit of their bargain." H.R. Rep. No. 95–595 at 339, *reprinted in* 1978 U.S.C.C.A.N. at 6295; S. Rep. No. 95–989 at 53, *reprinted in* 1978 U.S.C.C.A.N. at 5839. Such generalizations are inadequate to overcome the plain textual indication in §§ 506 and 362(d)(2) of the Code that Congress did not wish the undersecured creditor to receive interest on his collateral during the term of the stay. If it is at all relevant, the legislative history tends to subvert rather than support petitioner's thesis, since it contains not a hint that § 362(d)(1) entitles the undersecured creditor to postpetition interest. Such a major change in the existing rules would not likely have been made without specific provision in the text of the statute; it is most improbable that it would have been made without even any mention in the legislative history.

* * *

The Fifth Circuit correctly held that the undersecured petitioner is not entitled to interest on its collateral during the stay to assure adequate protection under § 362(d)(1). Petitioner has never sought relief from the stay under § 362(d)(2) or on any ground other than lack of adequate protection. Accordingly, the judgment of the Fifth Circuit is

Affirmed.

Notes and Questions

1. Are *Alyucan* and *Timbers* consistent?

2. What would be the practical impact of a contrary result in *Timbers*?

3. Outside of bankruptcy, the secured creditor could have foreclosed on the collateral, sold it, and reinvested the proceeds. Doesn't the result in *Timbers* essentially force the creditor to make an interest-free loan to the debtor for the duration of the bankruptcy case? Does the Court give sufficient consideration to the rights of the creditor under state law?

4. Does *Timbers* give the debtor and junior creditors an incentive to procrastinate? Would that incentive have been removed by a contrary decision?

5. The Court's answer to "inordinate and extortionate delay" is § 362(d)(2), which requires that relief from the stay be granted if the collateral is not necessary to an effective reorganization. According to the Court, this means a "reorganization *that is in prospect.*" Do you think this protection is really reassuring to an undersecured creditor?

6. If the debtor anticipates a liquidating plan in Chapter 11, is the property still "necessary to an effective reorganization" within § 362(d)(2)?

7. Section 1205(a) makes § 361 inapplicable in a Chapter 12 case. Congress included § 1205(a) because several circuit-level cases had held that an undersecured creditor's lost opportunity costs were an interest entitled to adequate protection under § 361. Now that *Timbers* has overruled those cases, the reason for § 1205(a) has been eliminated.

8. In 1994, Congress added § 362(d)(3), providing relief to secured creditors in single asset real estate cases. In many instances, the secured lender is the only creditor of any significance, so these cases do not present the "common pool problem" addressed by Professor Jackson in the excerpt at the beginning of Chapter 2 of these materials. Note the parallel between § 362-(d)(3)(A) and the language in *Timbers*.

Under (d)(3), the debtor must either file a feasible plan or begin making monthly interest payments within the designated time period. That effectively reverses *Timbers* for cases to which (d)(3) applies—namely, "single asset real estate" cases, as defined in § 101(51B). Would § 362(d)(3) have been helpful to United Savings Association?

9. Apex purchased a gas station from Robert and Susan Neier, paying $165,000 in cash and giving a note for the $450,000 balance. The note was fully secured by a mortgage on the property. When Apex filed Chapter 11, it stopped making payments on the note. The Neiers sought relief from the stay, on the grounds that the monthly payments on the note were their primary source of income and were needed in order to support their family. (They had two children with special needs and were responsible for three elderly aunts.) Does the creditor's neediness constitute "cause" under § 362(d)(1)? See *Neier v. Clark Oil & Refining Corp. (In re Apex Oil)*, 85 B.R. 538 (Bankr. E.D.Mo.1988).

C. RIGHTS OF SECURED CREDITORS TO POSTPETITION INTEREST

The secured creditor's claim in *Alyucan* was increasing after the filing of bankruptcy because § 506(b) allows postpetition interest to oversecured creditors. In *Alyucan*, the creditor's claim arose out of a prepetition contract with the debtor. But what of the nonconsensual secured creditor, whose rights against the debtor arise by operation of law? Does such a creditor also have a right to postpetition interest under § 506(b)?

UNITED STATES v. RON PAIR ENTERPRISES, INC.

United States Supreme Court, 1989.
489 U.S. 235, 109 S.Ct. 1026, 103 L.Ed.2d 290.

JUSTICE BLACKMUN delivered the opinion of the Court.

In this case we must decide the narrow statutory issue whether § 506(b) of the Bankruptcy Code of 1978 entitles a creditor to receive postpetition interest on a nonconsensual oversecured claim allowed in a bankruptcy proceeding. We conclude that it does, and we therefore reverse the judgment of the Court of Appeals.

I

Respondent Ron Pair Enterprises, Inc. filed a petition for reorganization under Chapter 11 of the Bankruptcy Code on May 1, 1984, in the United States Bankruptcy Court for the Eastern District of Michigan. The Government filed timely proof of a prepetition claim of $52,277.93, comprised of assessments for unpaid withholding and Social Security taxes, penalties, and prepetition interest. The claim was perfected through a tax lien on property owned by respondent. Respondent's First Amended Plan of Reorganization, filed October 1, 1985, provided for full payment of the prepetition claim, but did not provide for postpetition interest on that claim. The Government filed a timely objection, claiming that § 506(b) allowed recovery of postpetition interest, since the property securing the claim had a value greater than the amount of the principal debt. At the Bankruptcy Court hearing, the parties stipulated that the claim was oversecured, but the court subsequently overruled the Government's objection. The Government appealed to the United States District Court for the Eastern District of Michigan. That court reversed the Bankruptcy Court's judgment, concluding that the plain language of § 506(b) entitled the Government to postpetition interest.

The United States Court of Appeals for the Sixth Circuit, in its turn, reversed the District Court. While not directly ruling that the language of § 506(b) was ambiguous, the court reasoned that reference to pre-Code law was appropriate "in order to better understand the context in which the provision was drafted and therefore the language itself." The court went on to note that under pre-Code law the general rule was that postpetition interest on an oversecured prepetition claim was allowable only where the lien was consensual in nature. In light of this practice, and of the lack of any legislative history evincing an intent to change the standard, the court held that § 506(b) codified the preexisting standard, and that postpetition interest was allowable only on consensual claims. Because this result was in direct conflict with the view of the Court of Appeals for the Fourth Circuit, see *Best Repair Co. v. United States*, 789 F.2d 1080 (1986), and with the views of other courts, we granted certiorari to resolve the conflict.

II

Section 506, enacted as part of the extensive 1978 revision of the bankruptcy laws, governs the definition and treatment of secured claims, *i.e.*, claims by creditors against the estate that are secured by a lien on property in which the estate has an interest. Subsection (a) of § 506 provides that a claim is secured only to the extent of the value of the property on which the lien is fixed; the remainder of that claim is considered unsecured. Subsection (b) is concerned specifically with oversecured claims, that is, any claim that is for an amount less than the value of the property securing it. Thus, if a $50,000 claim were secured by a lien on property having a value of $75,000, the claim would be oversecured, provided the trustee's costs of preserving or disposing of the property were less than $25,000. Section 506(b) allows a holder of an oversecured claim to recover, in addition to the prepetition amount of the claim, "interest on such claim, and any reasonable fees, costs, or charges provided for under the agreement under which such claim arose."

The question before us today arises because there are two types of secured claims: (1) voluntary (or consensual) secured claims, each created by agreement between the debtor and the creditor and called a "security interest" by the Code, [§ 101(51)], and (2) involuntary secured claims, such as a judicial or statutory lien, see [§§ 101(36) and (53)], which are fixed by operation of law and do not require the consent of the debtor. The claim against respondent's estate was of this latter kind. Prior to the passage of the 1978 Code, some Courts of Appeals drew a distinction between the two types for purposes of determining postpetition interest. The question we must answer is whether the 1978 Code recognizes and enforces this distinction, or whether Congress intended that all oversecured claims be treated the same way for purposes of postpetition interest.

III

Initially, it is worth recalling that Congress worked on the formulation of the Code for nearly a decade. It was intended to modernize the bankruptcy laws, see H.R. Rep. No. 95–595 at 3, *reprinted in* 1978 U.S.C.C.A.N. at 5965 (Report), and as a result made significant changes in both the substantive and procedural laws of bankruptcy. In particular, Congress intended "significant changes from current law in * * * the treatment of secured creditors and secured claims." Report at 180. In such a substantial overhaul of the system, it is not appropriate or realistic to expect Congress to have explained with particularity each step it took. Rather, as long as the statutory scheme is coherent and consistent, there generally is no need for a court to inquire beyond the plain language of the statute.

A

The task of resolving the dispute over the meaning of § 506(b) begins where all such inquiries must begin: with the language of the statute itself. In this case it is also where the inquiry should end, for where, as here, the statute's language is plain, "the sole function of the courts is to enforce it according to its terms." *Caminetti v. United States*, 242 U.S. 470, 485 (1917). The language before us expresses Congress' intent—that postpetition interest be available—with sufficient precision so that reference to legislative history and to pre-Code practice is hardly necessary.

The relevant phrase in § 506(b) is: "[t]here shall be allowed to the holder of such claim, interest on such claim, and any reasonable fees, costs, or charges provided for under the agreement under which such claim arose." "Such claim" refers to an oversecured claim. The natural reading of the phrase entitles the holder of an oversecured claim to postpetition interest and, in addition, gives one having a secured claim created pursuant to an agreement the right to reasonable fees, costs, and charges provided for in that agreement. Recovery of postpetition interest is unqualified. Recovery of fees, costs, and charges, however, is allowed only if they are reasonable and provided for in the agreement under which the claim arose. Therefore, in the absence of an agreement, postpetition interest is the only added recovery available.

This reading is also mandated by the grammatical structure of the statute. The phrase "interest on such claim" is set aside by commas, and separated from the reference to fees, costs, and charges by the conjunctive words "and any." As a result, the phrase "interest on such claim" stands independent of the language that follows. "[I]nterest on such claim" is not part of the list made up of "fees, costs, or charges," nor is it joined to the following clause so that the final "provided for under the agreement" modifies it as well. The language and punctuation Congress used cannot be read in any other way. By the plain language of the statute, the two types of recovery are distinct.[5]

---

[5] It seems to us that the interpretation adopted by the Court of Appeals in this case not only requires that the statutory language be read in an unnatural way, but that it is inconsistent with the remainder of § 506 and with terminology used throughout the Code. Adopting the Court of Appeals' view would mean that § 506(b) is

B

The plain meaning of legislation should be conclusive, except in the "rare cases [in which] the literal application of a statute will produce a result demonstrably at odds with the intentions of its drafters." *Griffin v. Oceanic Contractors, Inc.*, 458 U.S. 564, 571 (1982). In such cases, the intention of the drafters, rather than the strict language, controls. It is clear that allowing postpetition interest on nonconsensual oversecured liens does not contravene the intent of the framers of the Code. Allowing such interest does not conflict with any other section of the Code, or with any important state or federal interest; nor is a contrary view suggested by the legislative history. Respondent has not articulated, nor can we discern, any significant reason why Congress would have intended, or any policy reason would compel, that the two types of secured claims be treated differently in allowing postpetition interest.

C

Respondent urges that pre-Code practice drew a distinction between consensual and nonconsensual liens for the purpose of determining entitlement to postpetition interest, and that Congress' failure to repudiate that distinction requires us to enforce it. It is respondent's view, as it was the view of the Court of Appeals, that *Midlantic National Bank v. New Jersey Dept. of Environmental Protection*, 474 U.S. 494 (1986), and *Kelly v. Robinson*, 479 U.S. 36 (1986), so require. We disagree.

In *Midlantic* we held that § 554(a) of the Code, which provides that "the trustee may abandon any property of the estate that is burdensome to the estate," does not give a trustee the authority to violate state health and safety laws by abandoning property containing hazardous wastes. In reaching that conclusion, we noted that according to pre-

---

operative only in regard to consensual liens, *i.e.*, that only a holder of an oversecured claim arising from an agreement is entitled to any added recovery. But the other portions of § 506 make no distinction between consensual and nonconsensual liens. Moreover, had Congress intended § 506(b) to apply only to consensual liens, it would have clarified its intent by using the specific phrase, "security interest," which the Code employs to refer to liens created by agreement. [§ 101(51).] When Congress wanted to restrict the application of a particular provision of the Code to such liens, it used the term "security interest." See, *e.g.*, §§ 362(b)(12) and (13), 363(a), 547(c)(3), (5), 552, 752(c), 1110(a), 1168(a), 1322(b)(2).

Code doctrine the trustee's authority to dispose of property could be limited in order "to protect legitimate state or federal interests." 474 U.S. at 500. But we did not rest solely, or even primarily, on a presumption of continuity with pre-Code practice. Rather, we concluded that a contrary result would render abandonment doctrine inconsistent with other provisions of the Code itself, which embody the principle that "the trustee is not to have *carte blanche* to ignore nonbankruptcy law." *Id.* at 502. We also recognized that the outcome sought would be not only a departure from pre-Code practice, but also "an extraordinary exemption from nonbankruptcy law," *id.* at 501, requiring some clearer expression of congressional intent. We relied as well on Congress' repeated emphasis in environmental legislation "on its 'goal of protecting the environment against toxic pollution.'" *Id.* at 505, quoting *Chemical Manufacturers Assn. v. Natural Resources Defense Council, Inc.*, 470 U.S. 116, 143 (1985). To put it simply, we looked to pre-Code practice for interpretive assistance, because it appeared that a literal application of the statute would be "demonstrably at odds with the intentions of its drafters." *Griffin v. Oceanic Contractors, Inc.*, 458 U.S. at 571.

A similar issue presented itself in *Kelly v. Robinson*, where we held that a restitution obligation, imposed as part of a state criminal sentence, was not dischargeable in bankruptcy. We reached this conclusion by interpreting § 523(a)(7) of the Code as "preserv[ing] from discharge any condition a state criminal court imposes as part of a criminal sentence." 479 U.S. at 50. We noted that the Code provision was "subject to interpretation" and considered both legislative history and pre-Code practice in aid of that interpretation. But in determining that Congress had not intended to depart from pre-Code practice in this regard, we did not rely on a pale presumption to that effect. We concluded that the pre-Code practice had been animated by "a deep conviction that federal bankruptcy courts should not invalidate the results of state criminal proceedings," *id.* at 47, which has its source in the basic principle of our federalism that "the States' interest in administering their criminal justice systems free from federal interference is one of the most powerful of the considerations that should influence a court considering equitable types of relief." *Id.* at 49. In *Kelly*, as in *Midlantic*, pre-Code practice was significant because it reflected policy considerations of great longevity and importance.

Kelly and *Midlantic* make clear that, in an appropriate case, a court must determine whether Congress has expressed an intent to change the interpretation of a judicially created concept in enacting the Code. But *Midlantic* and *Kelly* suggest that there are limits to what may constitute an appropriate case. Both decisions concerned statutory language which, at least to some degree, was open to interpretation. Each involved a situation where bankruptcy law, under the proposed interpretation, was in clear conflict with state or federal laws of great importance. In the present case, in contrast, the language in question is clearer than the language at issue in *Midlantic* and *Kelly*: as written it directs that postpetition interest be paid on all oversecured claims. In addition, this natural interpretation of the statutory language does not conflict with any significant state or federal interest, nor with any other aspect of the Code. Although the payment of postpetition interest is arguably somewhat in tension with the desirability of paying all creditors as uniformly as practicable, Congress expressly chose to create that alleged tension. There is no reason to suspect that Congress did not mean what the language of the statute says.

D

But even if we saw the need to turn to pre-Code practice in this case, it would be of little assistance. The practice of denying postpetition interest to the holders of nonconsensual liens, while allowing it to holders of consensual liens, was an exception to an exception, recognized by only a few courts and often dependent on particular circumstances. It was certainly not the type of "rule" that we assume Congress was aware of when enacting the Code; nor was it of such significance that Congress would have taken steps other than enacting statutory language to the contrary.

There was, indeed, a pre-Code rule that the running of interest ceased when a bankruptcy petition was filed. Two exceptions to this rule had been recognized under pre-Code practice. The first allowed postpetition interest when the debtor ultimately proved to be solvent; the second allowed dividends and interest earned by securities held by the creditor as collateral to be applied to postpetition interest. Neither of these exceptions would be relevant to this case. A third exception was of more doubtful provenance: an exception for oversecured claims. At least one Court of Appeals refused to apply this exception, and there was some uncertainty among courts which did recognize it as to whether this Court ever had done so.

What is at issue in this case is not the oversecured claim exception *per se*, but an exception to that exception. Several Courts of Appeals refused to apply the oversecured claim exception to an oversecured federal tax claim. It is this refusal to apply the exception that the Court of Appeals thought constituted a well-established judicially created rule.

The fact that this Court never clearly has acknowledged or relied upon this limitation on the oversecured-claim exception counsels against concluding that the limitation was well recognized. Also arguing against considering this limitation a clear rule is the fact that all the cases that limited the third exception were tax-lien cases. Each gave weight to *City of New York v. Saper*, 336 U.S. 328 (1949), where this Court had ruled that postpetition interest was not available on *unsecured* tax claims, and reasoned that the broad language of that case denied it for all tax claims. The rule articulated in these cases never was extended to other forms of nonconsensual liens. Obviously, there is no way to read § 506(b) as allowing postpetition interest on all over-secured claims except claims based on unpaid taxes. For this reason, the statute Congress wrote is simply not subject to a reading that would harmonize it with the supposed pre-Code rule.

More importantly, this "rule," in the few cases where it was recognized, was only a guide to the trustee's exercise of his powers in the particular circumstances of the case. We have noted that "the touchstone of each decision on allowance of interest in bankruptcy * * * has been a balance of equities between creditor and creditor or between creditors and the debtor." *Vanston Bondholders Protective Committee v. Green*, 329 U.S. 156, 165 (1946). All the exceptions to the denial of postpetition interest "are not rigid doctrinal categories. Rather, they are flexible guidelines which have been developed by the courts in the exercise of their equitable powers in insolvency proceedings." *In re Boston & Maine Corp.*, 719 F.2d 493, 496 (1st Cir.1983), cert. denied *sub nom. City of Cambridge v. Meserve*, 466 U.S. 938 (1984). None of the cases cited by the Court of Appeals states that the doctrine does anything more than provide a bankruptcy court with guidance in the exercise of its equitable powers. As such, there is no reason to think that Congress, in enacting a contrary standard, would have felt the need expressly to repudiate it. The contrary view, which is the view we adopt today, is more consistent with Congress' stated intent, in enacting the Code, to "codif[y] creditors' rights *more clearly than the case law* * * * by defin[ing] the protections to which a secured creditor is entitled, and the means through which the court may grant that protection." Report at 4–5 (emphasis added). Whether or not Congress took notice of the pre-Code standard, it acted with sufficient clarity in enacting the statute.

* * *

[Justice O'CONNOR dissented, in an opinion joined by JUSTICES BRENNAN, MARSHALL and STEVENS. She took issue with the Court's reliance on the comma: "Without this 'capricious' bit of punctuation, In re Newbury Cafe, Inc., 841 F.2d 20, 22 (1st Cir.1988), the * * * phrase 'interest on such claim' would be qualified by the phrase 'provided for under the agreement under which such claim arose,' and nonconsensual liens would not accrue postpetition interest." The dissenters also took issue with the majority's interpretation of Midlantic *and* Kelly, *and the application of those precedents to the situation before the Court.]*

Questions and Problems

1. In grammatical terms, what is the issue in *Ron Pair*? Do you find it disingenuous for a majority of the Court to assert that statutory language is "plain" when four of its members read the statute differently?

2. If the IRS is entitled to interest as the holder of an oversecured nonconsensual lien, from whose pocket does the money come? Does that make good sense as a matter of bankruptcy policy?

3. *Ron Pair* has now settled the question whether the holder of a nonconsensual, oversecured lien is entitled to interest. But we have no contract setting the rate. What rate is appropriate in these circumstances?

4. Debtor's property, Blackacre, was encumbered by a first lien of $600,000 and a second lien of $150,000. Blackacre was worth $700,000. Debtor defaulted on both obligations and filed Chapter 11. When the first lienholder sought postpetition interest, the second lienholder objected, arguing that the interest would come directly out of its pocket. Which creditor prevails?

5. Debtor's home, which was worth $150,000, was encumbered by a purchase money mortgage. The mortgage documents permitted Bank to accelerate the obligation if Debtor missed a payment, but neither the documents nor state law provided for interest on arrearages. When the debt was $120,000, Debtor missed several payments (totaling $2,750) and Bank accelerated. Debtor filed Chapter 13 before Bank could begin foreclosure proceedings. Under Debtor's proposed plan, Debtor would make regular monthly payments in accordance with the loan documents and pay the arrearage over the life of the plan. The plan did not provide for interest, either before or after confirmation, on the $2,750 arrearage. Bank argued it was entitled to pre- and postconfirmation interest, under § 506(b) and *Ron Pair,* because it was oversecured. What result? See § 1322(e).

D. TURNOVER OF COLLATERAL REPOSSESSED BEFORE FILING

Debtors sliding into financial crisis almost always default on one or more of their obligations to various creditors. A secured creditor who finds itself among the ranks of the unpaid is likely to respond by repossessing or seizing the property subject to its lien. Such a repossession or seizure may spell financial doom if the debtor is a business enterprise that needs the property in order to continue operating. Can such a debtor find some strategic help in the Bankruptcy Code?

UNITED STATES v. WHITING POOLS, INC.

United States Supreme Court, 1983.
462 U.S. 198, 103 S.Ct. 2309, 76 L.Ed.2d 515.

JUSTICE BLACKMUN delivered the opinion of the Court.

Promptly after the Internal Revenue Service (IRS or Service) seized respondent's property to satisfy a tax lien, respondent filed a petition for reorganization under the Bankruptcy Reform Act of 1978, hereinafter referred to as the "Bankruptcy Code." The issue before us is whether § 542(a) of that Code authorized the Bankruptcy Court to subject the IRS to a turnover order with respect to the seized property.

I

A

Respondent Whiting Pools, Inc., a corporation, sells, installs, and services swimming pools and related equipment and supplies. As of January 1981, Whiting owed approximately $92,000 in Federal Insurance Contribution Act taxes and federal taxes withheld from its employees, but had failed to respond to assessments and demands for payment by the IRS. As a consequence, a tax lien in that amount attached to all of Whiting's property.

On January 14, 1981, the Service seized Whiting's tangible personal property—equipment, vehicles, inventory, and office supplies—pursuant to the levy and distraint provision of the Internal Revenue Code of 1954. According to uncontroverted findings, the estimated liquidation value of the property seized was, at most, $35,000, but its estimated going-concern value in Whiting's hands was $162,876. The very next day, January 15, Whiting filed a petition for reorganization, under the Bankruptcy Code's Chapter 11 in the United States Bankruptcy Court for the Western District of New York. Whiting was continued as debtor-in-possession.

The United States, intending to proceed with a tax sale of the property, moved in the Bankruptcy Court for a declaration that the automatic stay provision of the Bankruptcy Code, § 362(a), is inapplicable to the IRS or, in the alternative, for relief from the stay. Whiting counterclaimed for an order requiring the Service to turn the seized property over to the bankruptcy estate pursuant to § 542(a) of the Bankruptcy Code. Whiting intended to use the property in its reorganized business.

B

The Bankruptcy Court determined that the IRS was bound by the automatic stay provision. Because it found that the seized property was essential to Whiting's reorganization effort, it refused to lift the stay. Acting under § 543(b)(1) of the Bankruptcy Code, rather than under § 542(a), the court directed the IRS to turn the property over to Whiting on the condition that Whiting provide the Service with specified protection for its interests.[7]

The United States District Court reversed, holding that a turnover order against the Service was not authorized by either § 542(a) or § 543(b)(1). The United States Court of Appeals for the Second Circuit, in turn, reversed the District Court. It held that a turnover order could issue against the Service under § 542(a), and it remanded the case for reconsideration of the adequacy of the Bankruptcy Court's protection conditions. The Court of Appeals acknowledged that its ruling was contrary to that reached by the United States Court of Appeals for the Fourth Circuit in *Cross Electric Co. v. United States*, 664 F.2d 1218 (1981), and noted confusion on the issue among bankruptcy and district courts. We granted certiorari to resolve this conflict in an important area of the law under the new Bankruptcy Code.

---

[7]   * * * Pursuant to [§ 363(e)], the Bankruptcy Court set the following conditions to protect the tax lien: Whiting was to pay the Service $20,000 before the turnover occurred; Whiting also was to pay $1,000 a month until the taxes were satisfied; the IRS was to retain its lien during this period; and if Whiting failed to make the payments, the stay was to be lifted.

II

By virtue of its tax lien, the Service holds a secured interest in Whiting's property. We first examine whether § 542(a) of the Bankruptcy Code generally authorizes the turnover of a debtor's property seized by a secured creditor prior to the commencement of reorganization proceedings. Section 542(a) requires an entity in possession of "property that the trustee may use, sell, or lease under § 363" to deliver that property to the trustee. Subsections (b) and (c) of § 363 authorize the trustee to use, sell, or lease any "property of the estate," subject to certain conditions for the protection of creditors with an interest in the property. Section 541(a)(1) defines the "estate" as "comprised of all the following property, wherever located: * * * all legal or equitable interests of the debtor in property as of the commencement of the case." Although these statutes could be read to limit the estate to those "interests of the debtor in property" at the time of the filing of the petition, we view them as a definition of what is included in the estate, rather than as a limitation.

A

In proceedings under the reorganization provisions of the Bankruptcy Code, a troubled enterprise may be restructured to enable it to operate successfully in the future. Until the business can be reorganized pursuant to a plan under §§ 1121–1129, the trustee or debtor-in-possession is authorized to manage the property of the estate and to continue the operation of the business. See § 1108. By permitting reorganization, Congress anticipated that the business would continue to provide jobs, to satisfy creditors' claims, and to produce a return for its owners. H.R. Rep. No. 95–595 at 220, *reprinted in* 1978 U.S.C.C.A.N. at 5787. Congress presumed that the assets of the debtor would be more valuable if used in a rehabilitated business than if "sold for scrap." The reorganization effort would have small chance of success, however, if property essential to running the business were excluded from the estate. Thus, to facilitate the rehabilitation of the debtor's business, all the debtor's property must be included in the reorganization estate.

This authorization extends even to property of the estate in which a creditor has a secured interest. §§ 363(b) and (c); see H.R. Rep. No. 95–595 at 182. Although Congress might have safeguarded the interests of secured creditors outright by excluding from the estate any property subject to a secured interest, it chose instead to include such property in the estate and to provide secured creditors with "adequate protection" for their interests. § 363(e). At the secured creditor's insistence, the bankruptcy court must place such limits or conditions on the trustee's power to sell, use, or lease property as are necessary to protect the creditor. The creditor with a secured interest in property included in the estate must look to this provision for protection, rather than to the nonbankruptcy remedy of possession.

Both the congressional goal of encouraging reorganizations and Congress' choice of methods to protect secured creditors suggest that Congress intended a broad range of property to be included in the estate.

B

The statutory language reflects this view of the scope of the estate. * * * The House and Senate Reports on the Bankruptcy Code indicate that § 541(a)(1)'s scope is broad. Most important, in the context of this case, § 541(a)(1) is intended to include in the estate any property made available to the estate by other provisions of the Bankruptcy Code. Several of these provisions bring into the estate property in which the debtor did not have a possessory interest at the time the bankruptcy proceedings commenced.[10]

Section 542(a) is such a provision. It requires an entity (other than a custodian) holding any property of the debtor that the trustee can use under § 363 to turn that property over to the trustee. Given the broad scope of the reorganization estate, property of the debtor repossessed by a secured creditor falls within this rule, and therefore may be drawn into the estate. While there are explicit limitations on the reach of § 542(a), none requires that the debtor hold a possessory interest in the property at the commencement of the reorganization proceedings.

As does all bankruptcy law, § 542(a) modifies the procedural rights available to creditors to protect and satisfy their liens.[14] In effect, § 542(a) grants to the estate a possessory interest in certain property of the debtor that was not held by the debtor at the commencement of

---

[10] See, *e.g.*, §§ 543, 547, and 548. These sections permit the trustee to demand the turnover of property that is in the possession of others if that possession is due to a custodial arrangement, § 543, to a preferential transfer, § 547, or to a fraudulent transfer, § 548. * * *

[14] One of the procedural rights the law of secured transactions grants a secured creditor to enforce its lien is the right to take possession of the secured property upon the debtor's default. Uniform Commercial Code § [9–609]. * * *

reorganization proceedings. The Bankruptcy Code provides secured creditors various rights, including the right to adequate protection, and these rights replace the protection afforded by possession.

C

This interpretation of § 542(a) is supported by the section's legislative history. Although the legislative reports are silent on the precise issue before us, the House and Senate hearings from which § 542(a) emerged provide guidance. Several witnesses at those hearings noted, without contradiction, the need for a provision authorizing the turnover of property of the debtor in the possession of secured creditors. Section 542(a) first appeared in the proposed legislation shortly after these hearings. The section remained unchanged through subsequent versions of the legislation.

Moreover, this interpretation of § 542 in the reorganization context is consistent with judicial precedent predating the Bankruptcy Code. * * * Nothing in the legislative history evinces a congressional intent to depart from that practice. Any other interpretation of § 542(a) would deprive the bankruptcy estate of the assets and property essential to its rehabilitation effort and thereby would frustrate the congressional purpose behind the reorganization provisions.[17]

We conclude that the reorganization estate includes property of the debtor that has been seized by a creditor prior to the filing of a petition for reorganization.

III

A

We see no reason why a different result should obtain when the IRS is the creditor. The Service is bound by § 542(a) to the same extent as any other secured creditor. The Bankruptcy Code expressly states that the term "entity," used in § 542(a), includes a governmental unit.

---

[17] Section 542(a) also governs turnovers in liquidation and individual adjustment of debt proceedings under Chapters 7 and 13 of the Bankruptcy Code. See § 103(a). Our analysis in this case depends in part on the reorganization context in which the turnover order is sought. We express no view on the issue whether § 542(a) has the same broad effect in liquidation or adjustment of debt proceedings.

[§ 101(15)]. Moreover, Congress carefully considered the effect of the new Bankruptcy Code on tax collection, see generally S. Rep. No. 95–1106 (1978) (Report of Senate Finance Committee), and decided to provide protection to tax collectors, such as the IRS, through grants of enhanced priorities for unsecured tax claims, [§ 507(a)(8)], and by the nondischarge of tax liabilities, § 523(a)(1). S. Rep. No. 95–989 at 14–15. Tax collectors also enjoy the generally applicable right under § 363(e) to adequate protection for property subject to their liens. Nothing in the Bankruptcy Code or its legislative history indicates that Congress intended a special exception for the tax collector in the form of an exclusion from the estate of property seized to satisfy a tax lien.

B

Of course, if a tax levy or seizure transfers to the IRS ownership of the property seized, § 542(a) may not apply. The enforcement provisions of the Internal Revenue Code of 1954 do grant to the Service powers to enforce its tax liens that are greater than those possessed by private secured creditors under state law. But those provisions do not transfer ownership of the property to the IRS.

The Service's interest in seized property is its lien on that property. The Internal Revenue Code's levy and seizure provisions are special procedural devices available to the IRS to protect and satisfy its liens and are analogous to the remedies available to private secured creditors. See Uniform Commercial Code § [9–609]. * * * Ownership of the property is transferred only when the property is sold to a bona fide purchaser at a tax sale. In fact, the tax sale provision itself refers to the debtor as the owner of the property after the seizure but prior to the sale. Until such a sale takes place, the property remains the debtor's and thus is subject to the turnover requirement of § 542(a).

IV

When property seized prior to the filing of a petition is drawn into the Chapter 11 reorganization estate, the Service's tax lien is not dissolved; nor is its status as a secured creditor destroyed. The IRS, under § 363(e), remains entitled to adequate protection for its interests, to other rights enjoyed by secured creditors, and to the specific privileges accorded tax collectors. Section 542(a) simply requires the Service to seek protection of its interest according to the congressionally established bankruptcy procedures, rather than by withholding the seized property from the debtor's efforts to reorganize.

The judgment of the Court of Appeals is affirmed.

It is so ordered.

Notes and Questions

1. Section 342(g)(2), which was added to the Code by the 2005 Amendments, provides that a monetary penalty cannot be imposed upon a creditor for violation of the automatic stay, or for failure to comply with §§ 542 or 543, unless the creditor has received effective notice of the bankruptcy filing. Damages could not have been imposed on the IRS under § 362(k) for violation of the stay, because that subsection applies only when the debtor is an "individual." But what about damages for failure to comply with § 542 (once notice has been received, of course)? What provision of the Code authorizes the imposition of such damages? Does § 342(g)(2)'s reference to such damages imply the existence of the requisite authority?

2. The Court did not decide whether its analysis applies in a Chapter 7 or a Chapter 13 case. Does it? Should it?

3. The IRS, forced to give up possession, gets "adequate protection" in return. Is that sufficient recompense?

4. Does *Whiting Pools* apply when the collateral is real estate upon which the creditor has foreclosed?

5. At what point is it too late for the debtor to file bankruptcy in order to force the return of repossessed and foreclosed collateral? See § 1322(c)(1); *Homeside Lending, Inc. v. Denny (In re Denny)*, 242 B.R. 593 (Bankr. D.Md. 1999).

6. To the extent that § 542 and *Whiting Pools* apply, they provide a powerful tool for debtors seeking to undo collection actions taken by creditors. Debtors have no other way, short of paying the full debt, of forcing creditors to return collateral seized through levy, foreclosure or repossession. Once you understand this, you will see why the threat of bankruptcy may be a persuasive negotiating strategy for obligors.

E. CHARGES AGAINST A SECURED CREDITOR'S COLLATERAL

Section 506(c) permits expenses of preserving or disposing of property subject to a lien to be charged against the property. For example, assume that a reorganizing debtor has a fleet of trucks that is both subject to a security interest and also necessary to the reorganization. The trustee must spend money for maintenance and insurance in order to keep the trucks on the road. These expenditures are of benefit to the secured creditor also, since they protect the value of the collateral. Thus, § 506(c) permits the trustee to "surcharge" the collateral in order to reimburse the estate for these expenses.

That is an easy, prototypical § 506(c) case. But what if the estate has enjoyed the value of goods and services for which payment has not been made? These claims enjoy an administrative expense priority—a status that is of little comfort when the estate is administratively insolvent. Can the claimant look to § 506(c)?

HARTFORD UNDERWRITERS INSURANCE CO. v. UNION PLANTERS BANK, N. A.

United States Supreme Court, 2000.
530 U.S. 1, 120 S.Ct. 1942, 147 L.Ed.2d 1.

JUSTICE SCALIA delivered the opinion of the Court.

In this case, we consider whether § 506(c) allows an administrative claimant of a bankruptcy estate to seek payment of its claim from property encumbered by a secured creditor's lien.

I

This case arises out of the bankruptcy proceedings of Hen House Interstate, Inc., which at one time owned or operated several restaurants and service stations, as well as an outdoor-advertising firm. On September 5, 1991, Hen House filed a voluntary petition under Chapter 11 of the Bankruptcy Code in the United States Bankruptcy Court for the Eastern District of Missouri. As a Chapter 11 debtor-in-possession, Hen House retained possession of its assets and continued operating its business.

Respondent had been Hen House's primary lender. At the time the Chapter 11 petition was filed, it held a security interest in essentially all of Hen House's real and personal property, securing an indebtedness of over $4 million. After the Chapter 11 proceedings were commenced, it agreed to lend Hen House an additional $300,000 to help finance the reorganization. The Bankruptcy Court entered a financing order approving the loan agreement and authorizing Hen House to use loan proceeds and cash collateral to pay expenses, including workers' compensation expenses.

During the attempted reorganization, Hen House obtained workers' compensation insurance from petitioner Hartford Underwriters (which was unaware of the bankruptcy proceedings). Although the policy required monthly premium payments, Hen House repeatedly failed to make them; Hartford continued to provide insurance nonetheless. The reorganization ultimately failed, and on January 20, 1993, the Bankruptcy Court converted the case to a liquidation proceeding under Chapter 7 and appointed a trustee. At the time of the conversion, Hen House owed Hartford more than $50,000 in unpaid premiums. Hartford learned of Hen House's bankruptcy proceedings after the conversion, in March 1993.

Recognizing that the estate lacked unencumbered funds to pay the premiums, Hartford attempted to charge the premiums to respondent, the secured creditor, by filing with the Bankruptcy Court an "Application for Allowance of Administrative Expense, Pursuant to § 503 and Charge Against Collateral, Pursuant to § 506(c)." The Bankruptcy Court ruled in favor of Hartford, and the District Court and an Eighth Circuit panel affirmed. The Eighth Circuit subsequently granted en banc review, however, and reversed, concluding that § 506(c) could not be invoked by an administrative claimant. We granted certiorari.

II

Petitioner's effort to recover the unpaid premiums involves two provisions, §§ 503(b) and 506(c). Section 503(b) provides that "the actual, necessary costs and expenses of preserving the estate, including wages, salaries, or commissions for services rendered after the commencement of the case" are treated as administrative expenses, which are, as a rule, entitled to priority over prepetition unsecured claims, see §§ 507(a)[(2)], 726(a)(1), 1129(a)(9)(A). Respondent does not dispute that the cost of the workers' compensation insurance Hen House purchased from petitioner is an administrative expense within the meaning of this provision. Administrative expenses, however, do not have priority over secured claims, and because respondent held a security interest in essentially all of the estate's assets, there were no unencumbered funds available to pay even administrative claimants.

Petitioner therefore looked to § 506(c), which constitutes an important exception to the rule that secured claims are superior to administrative claims. *[The Court quoted § 506(c).]* Petitioner argued that this provision entitled it to recover from the property subject to respondent's security interest the unpaid premiums owed by Hen

House, since its furnishing of workers' compensation insurance benefited respondent by allowing continued operation of Hen House's business, thereby preserving the value of respondent's collateral; or alternatively, that such benefit could be presumed from respondent's consent to the postpetition financing order. Although it was contested below whether, under either theory, the workers' compensation insurance constituted a "benefit to the holder" within the meaning of § 506(c), that issue is not before us here; we assume for purposes of this decision that it did, and consider only whether petitioner—an administrative claimant—is a proper party to seek recovery under § 506(c).

In answering this question, we begin with the understanding that Congress "says in a statute what it means and means in a statute what it says there," *Connecticut Nat. Bank* v. *Germain,* 503 U.S. 249, 254 (1992). * * * Here, the statute appears quite plain in specifying who may use § 506(c)—"[t]he trustee." It is true, however, as petitioner notes, that all this actually "says" is that the trustee may seek recovery under the section, not that others may not. The question thus becomes whether it is a proper inference that the trustee is the only party empowered to invoke the provision.[3] We have little difficulty answering yes.

Several contextual features here support the conclusion that exclusivity is intended. First, a situation in which a statute authorizes specific action and designates a particular party empowered to take it is surely among the least appropriate in which to presume nonexclusivity. * * * Second, the fact that the sole party named—the trustee—has a unique role in bankruptcy proceedings makes it entirely plausible that Congress would provide a power to him and not to others. * * * It is thus far more sensible to view the provision as answering the question "Who may use the provision?" with "only the trustee" than to view it as simply answering the question "May the trustee use the provision?" with "yes."

Nor can it be argued that the point of the provision was simply to establish that certain costs may be recovered from collateral, and not to say anything about who may recover them. Had * * * Congress intended the provision to be broadly available, it could simply have said so, as it did in describing the parties who could act under other sections

---

[3] Debtors-in-possession may also use the section, as they are expressly given the rights and powers of a trustee by § 1107.

of the Code. Section 502(a), for example, provides that a claim is allowed unless "a party in interest" objects, and § 503(b)(4) allows "an entity" to file a request for payment of an administrative expense. The broad phrasing of these sections, when contrasted with the use of "the trustee" in § 506(c), supports the conclusion that entities other than the trustee are not entitled to use § 506(c).

Petitioner's primary argument from the text of § 506(c) is that "what matters is that § 506(c) does not say that 'only' a trustee may enforce its provisions." To bolster this argument, petitioner cites other provisions of the Bankruptcy Code that do use "only" or other expressly restrictive language in specifying the parties at issue. See, *e.g.*, § 109(a) ("[O]nly a person that resides or has a domicile, a place of business, or property in the United States, or a municipality, may be a debtor under this title"); § 707(b) (providing that a case may be dismissed for substantial abuse by "the court, on its own motion or on a motion by the United States trustee, but not at the request or suggestion of any party in interest").[c] Petitioner argues that in the absence of such restrictive language, no party in interest is excluded. This theory—that the expression of one thing indicates the inclusion of others unless exclusion is made explicit—is contrary to common sense and common usage. Many provisions of the Bankruptcy Code that do not contain an express exclusion cannot sensibly be read to extend to all parties in interest. See, *e.g.*, § 363(b)(1) (providing that "[t]he trustee, after notice and a hearing, may use, sell, or lease * * * property of the estate"); § 364(a) (providing that "the trustee" may incur debt on behalf of the bankruptcy estate); § 554(a) (giving "the trustee" power to abandon property of the bankruptcy estate).

* * *

III

Because we believe that by far the most natural reading of § 506(c) is that it extends only to the trustee, petitioner's burden of persuading us that the section must be read to allow its use by other parties is "'exceptionally heavy.'" *Patterson* v. *Shumate,* 504 U.S. 753, 760 (1992) (quoting *Union Bank* v. *Wolas,* 502 U.S. 151, 156 (1991)). To support its proffered reading, petitioner advances arguments based on pre-Code practice and policy considerations. We address these arguments in turn.

---

[c] Section 707(b) was substantially amended in 2005. Eds.

A

Section 506(c)'s provision for the charge of certain administrative expenses against lienholders continues a practice that existed under the Bankruptcy Act of 1898. It was not to be found in the text of the Act, but traced its origin to early cases establishing an equitable principle that where a court has custody of property, costs of administering and preserving the property are a dominant charge. It was the norm that recovery of costs from a secured creditor would be sought by the trustee. Petitioner cites a number of lower court cases, however, in which—without meaningful discussion of the point—parties other than the trustee were permitted to pursue such charges under the Act, sometimes simultaneously with the trustee's pursuit of his own expenses. * * *

It is questionable whether these precedents establish a bankruptcy practice sufficiently widespread and well recognized to justify the conclusion of implicit adoption by the Code. We have no confidence that the allowance of recovery from collateral by nontrustees is "the type of 'rule' that * * * Congress was aware of when enacting the Code." *United States* v. *Ron Pair Enterprises, Inc., 489 U.S. 235, 246 (1989). In any event, while pre-Code practice "informs our understanding of the language of the Code," *Kelly* v. *Robinson,* 479 U.S. 36, 44 (1986), it cannot overcome that language. It is a tool of construction, not an extratextual supplement. We have applied it to the construction of provisions which were "subject to interpretation," *id.,* at 50, or contained "ambiguity in the text," *Dewsnup* v. *Timm,* 502 U.S. 410, 417 (1992). * * *

In this case, we think the language of the Code leaves no room for clarification by pre-Code practice. If § 506(c) provided only that certain costs and expenses could be recovered from property securing a secured claim, without specifying any particular party by whom the recovery could be pursued, the case would be akin to those in which we used prior practice to fill in the details of a pre-Code concept that the Code had adopted without elaboration. See, *e.g., United States* v. *Noland,* 517 U.S. 535, 539 (1996) (looking to pre-Code practice in interpreting Code's reference to "principles of equitable subordination"); *Midlantic Nat. Bank* v. *New Jersey Dept. of Environmental Protection,* 474 U.S. 494, 501 (1986) (codification of trustee's abandonment power held to incorporate established exceptions). Here, however, it is not the unelaborated concept but only a specifically narrowed one that has been adopted: a rule allowing the charge of costs to secured assets *by the trustee*. Pre-Code practice cannot transform § 506(c)'s reference to "the trustee" to "the trustee and other parties in interest."

B

Finally, petitioner argues that its reading is necessary as a matter of policy, since in some cases the trustee may lack an incentive to pursue payment. Section 506(c) must be open to nontrustees, petitioner asserts, lest secured creditors enjoy the benefit of services without paying for them. Moreover, ensuring that administrative claimants are compensated may also serve purposes beyond the avoidance of unjust enrichment. To the extent that there are circumstances in which the trustee will not use the section although an individual creditor would, allowing suits by nontrustees could encourage the provision of postpetition services to debtors on more favorable terms, which would in turn further bankruptcy's goals.

Although these concerns may be valid, it is far from clear that the policy implications favor petitioner's position. The class of cases in which § 506(c) would lie dormant without nontrustee use is limited by the fact that the trustee is obliged to seek recovery under the section whenever his fiduciary duties so require. And limiting § 506(c) to the trustee does not leave those who provide goods or services that benefit secured interests without other means of protecting themselves as against other creditors: They may insist on cash payment, or contract directly with the secured creditor, and may be able to obtain superpriority under § 364(c)(1) or a security interest under §§ 364(c)(2), (3) or § 364(d). And of course postpetition creditors can avoid unnecessary losses simply by paying attention to the status of their accounts, a protection which, by all appearances, petitioner neglected here.

On the other side of the ledger, petitioner's reading would itself lead to results that seem undesirable as a matter of policy. In particular, expanding the number of parties who could use § 506(c) would create the possibility of multiple administrative claimants seeking recovery under the section. Each such claim would require inquiry into the necessity of the services at issue and the degree of benefit to the secured creditor. Allowing recovery to be sought at the behest of parties other than the trustee could therefore impair the ability of the bankruptcy court to coordinate proceedings, as well as the ability of the trustee to manage the estate. Indeed, if administrative claimants were free to seek recovery on their own, they could proceed even where the trustee himself planned to do so.[5] Further, where unencumbered assets were scarce, creditors might attempt to use § 506(c) even though their claim to have benefited the secured creditor was quite weak. The possibility of being targeted for such claims by various administrative claimants could make secured creditors less willing to provide post-petition financing.

In any event, we do not sit to assess the relative merits of different approaches to various bankruptcy problems. It suffices that the natural reading of the text produces the result we announce. Achieving a better policy outcome—if what petitioner urges is that—is a task for Congress, not the courts.

* * *

We have considered the other points urged by petitioner and find them to be without merit. We conclude that § 506(c) does not provide an administrative claimant an independent right to use the section to seek payment of its claim. The judgment of the Eighth Circuit is affirmed.

Notes and Questions

1. Is it relevant that the Bank, although undersecured, had a security interest in everything Debtor owned, so that the benefits of Debtor's reorganization effort, had there been any, would have flowed first and foremost to the Bank?

2. Was Hartford lax in looking after its own interests, as the Court suggested?

3. The Court observed, in footnote 5, that the case did not involve a derivative action, undertaken with approval from the bankruptcy court. The

---

[5] We do not address whether a bankruptcy court can allow other interested parties to act in the trustee's stead in pursuing recovery under § 506(c). *Amici* American Insurance Association and National Union Fire Insurance Co. draw our attention to the practice of some courts of allowing creditors or creditors' committees a derivative right to bring avoidance actions when the trustee refuses to do so, even though the applicable Code provisions, see §§ 544, 545, 547(b), 548(a), 549(a), mention only the trustee. Whatever the validity of that practice, it has no analogous application here, since petitioner did not ask the trustee to pursue payment under § 506(c) and did not seek permission from the Bankruptcy Court to take such action in the trustee's stead. Petitioner asserted an independent right to use § 506(c), which is what we reject today.

question whether *Hartford* prevents a bankruptcy court from authorizing someone other than the trustee to pursue avoidance actions arose in *Official Committee of Unsecured Creditors ex rel. Cybergenics v. Chinery*, 330 F.3d 548 (3d Cir.) (en banc), *cert. dismissed sub nom. Lincolnshire Mgmt., Inc. v. Official Committee of Unsecured Creditors*, 540 U.S. 1001, 124 S.Ct. 530, 157 L.Ed.2d 406 (2003). In *Cybergenics*, the bankruptcy court had authorized the creditors' committee to pursue a fraudulent conveyance action. The target of the action, not unsurprisingly, argued that only the debtor-in-possession could bring such an action, but the court disagreed. First, it distinguished *Hartford*:

> The situation at bar is markedly different. When the Committee discovered that certain transfers made by Cybergenics were potentially avoidable as fraudulent, it first petitioned the Cybergenics management to file an avoidance action under § 544(b). But management refused to file that action, claiming that the costs would likely outweigh the benefits, and it maintained this position even after the Committee volunteered to bear all litigation costs. The Committee, finding management's stance unreasonable, petitioned the bankruptcy court for permission to prosecute a § 544(b) avoidance action in Cybergenics's name and on its behalf—any recovery would go not to the Committee, but to the estate itself. The Bankruptcy Court concluded that the fraud claims were colorable, and that the Committee's offer to bear the litigation costs insulated the estate from risk. Noting that the debtor-in-possession has a duty to maximize the value of the estate, the court concluded that management's refusal to act was unreasonable even given the usual judicial deference to business judgment, and it authorized the Committee to sue in Cybergenics's name.

Id. at 558-59. The court then found authority in the Code for such derivative actions:

> The Code clearly demonstrates that Congress approved of derivative standing, but none of the three sections discussed—§§ 1109(b), 1103-(c)(5), or 503(b)(3)(B)—seems directly to *authorize* such standing. Section 503 comes closest, but read fairly, that provision merely empowers bankruptcy courts to reimburse creditors' committees for the expenses they incur while suing derivatively. It does not authorize derivative actions in the first instance. To be sure, that section would be meaningless unless authority existed, but such reasoning by negative implication is less than satisfying. We believe that the missing link is supplied by bankruptcy courts' equitable power to craft flexible remedies in situations where the Code's causes of action fail to achieve their intended purpose.

Id. at 567. Finally, the court concluded that derivative actions are important in achieving Congress's policy goals:

In Chapter 11 cases where no trustee is appointed, § 1107(a) provides that the debtor-in-possession, *i.e.*, the debtor's management, enjoys the powers that would otherwise vest in the bankruptcy trustee. Along with those powers, of course, comes the trustee's fiduciary duty to maximize the value of the bankruptcy estate.

This situation immediately gives rise to the proverbial problem of the fox guarding the henhouse. If no trustee is appointed, the debtor—really, the debtor's management—bears a fiduciary duty to avoid fraudulent transfers that it itself made. One suspects that if managers can devise any opportunity to avoid bringing a claim that would amount to reputational self-immolation, they will seize it. * * * For example, a debtor may be unwilling to pursue claims against individuals or businesses, such as critical suppliers, with whom it has an ongoing relationship that it fears damaging. Finally, even if a bankrupt debtor is willing to bring an avoidance action, it might be too financially weakened to advocate vigorously for itself. In any of these situations, the real losers are the unsecured creditors whose interests avoidance actions are designed to protect.

The possibility of a derivative suit by a creditors' committee provides a critical safeguard against lax pursuit of avoidance actions.

Id. at 573. Do you agree that *Hartford* does not foreclose bankruptcy court authorization of derivative actions? (Four of the eleven judges on the Third Circuit, relying heavily on *Hartford*, dissented in *Cybergenics*.)

F. TREATMENT OF SECURED CLAIMS IN REORGANIZATIONS

1. GENERALLY

As you recall, the theory of Chapter 7 is that debtors exchange all nonexempt property owned at the time of filing for a discharge of debts owed at that time. The theory of Chapter 13, on the other hand, is that debtors keep their property and creditors are paid out of the debtors' future earnings. Debtors frequently choose Chapter 13 because it may allow them to keep their homes and cars. Similarly, in Chapter 11 debtors may retain their property as long as creditors are paid the minimum amounts required by the Code.

A plan under either Chapter 11 or Chapter 13 may deal with a secured creditor in one of three ways. First, the debtor may obtain the creditor's acceptance of its treatment under the plan; anything is permissible, as long as the affected creditor agrees. §§ 1129(a)(7)(A)(i);

1325(a)(5)(A). A creditor's decision to accept the plan's treatment of its claim is formed against a background of the remaining two alternatives—that is, what can be imposed on an unwilling creditor.

Second, a debtor not in need of encumbered assets may satisfy the secured claim either by surrendering the collateral to the creditor or by selling it and remitting the proceeds. Although only Chapter 13 specifically permits surrender, § 1325(a)(5)(C), the legislative history makes clear that surrender gives the Chapter 11 creditor the "indubitable equivalent" of its claim, within § 1129(b)(2)(A)(iii). 124 Cong. Rec. S17,421 (daily ed. Oct 6, 1978) (remarks of Sen. DeConcini). In addition, the Chapter 11 debtor may sell the collateral free and clear of encumbrances, with the secured creditor's lien to attach to the proceeds, § 1129(b)(2)(A)(ii).

The third option is the most important, because it allows the debtor to retain the collateral. Under this option, known as "cram down," the Chapter 13 plan must provide that the secured creditor retain its lien and that "the value, as of the effective date of the plan, of property to be distributed under the plan on account of such claim is not less than the allowed amount of such claim." § 1325(a)(5)(B)(ii). This "present value" requirement also appears in § 1129(b)(2)(A)(i). It requires that the creditor retain its lien and receive a stream of payments meeting a two-part test: 1) "deferred cash payments totaling at least the allowed amount of such claim" (a "principal amount" test); and 2) "of a value, as of the effective date of the plan, of at least the value of such holder's interest in the estate's interest in such property" (a "present value" test).

The concept of "present value" reflects the time value of money—that is, the fact that a particular amount of money is worth more today than the same amount is worth at some future date. Assume, for example, that Debtor owes Creditor $15,000 and that the obligation is secured by a lien on collateral worth $10,000. (Obviously, Creditor's allowed secured claim, under § 506(a), is $10,000.) Debtor proposes a plan providing that Creditor will retain its lien and receive payments of $917 per month for 12 months. The "principal amount" test requires that the stream of payments total at least as much as the secured claim—$10,000. The payments proposed here total $11,004, so the principal amount test is met. Under the "present value" test, the right to receive $917 a month for 12 months must have a present value of $10,000. The test is met if the appropriate discount rate is 10% or less. Or one could say that, in order to satisfy an obligation of $10,000 at 10% interest, a one-year plan must pay at least $11,000. If the court finds that a higher discount rate should be used, however, the present value test is not met and the plan cannot be confirmed. (These requirements are treated in more detail in Chapter 8 of this casebook.)

2. VALUATION

Two determinations must be made for purposes of cram down under §§ 1129(b)(2)(A)(i) and 1325(a)(5)(B)—the value of the collateral (which determines the amount of the secured claim, at least for claims not covered by § 1325(a)'s postamble) and the proper discount rate. We will postpone the second of those issues for a moment and begin with valuation.

Valuation of collateral is crucial legally but uncertain factually. Lower courts were deeply divided on the proper approach to this issue, before the Supreme Court agreed to hear *Associates Commercial Corp. v. Rash*, 520 U.S. 953, 117 S.Ct. 1879, 138 L.Ed.2d 148 (1997).

The debtors in *Rash* filed Chapter 13 and proposed a plan under which they would keep the truck the husband used in his freight hauling business. At the time of filing, they still owed $41,171 to the secured creditor. The debtors argued that the truck's value, and thus the amount that they had to pay under the plan in order to comply with § 1325(a)(5)(B)(ii), should be measured by the amount that the creditor could obtain in a foreclosure sale. In this case, that was $31,875. The creditor, on the other hand, argued that replacement value should be used—here, $41,000. The Fifth Circuit agreed with the debtors, but the Supreme Court reversed:

> Rejecting this replacement-value standard, and selecting instead the typically lower foreclosure-value standard, the Fifth Circuit trained its attention on the first sentence of § 506-(a)[(1)]. In particular, the Fifth Circuit relied on these first sentence words: a claim is secured "to the extent of the value of such *creditor's interest* in the estate's interest in such property." (Emphasis added.) The Fifth Circuit read this phrase to instruct that the "starting point for the valuation [is] what the creditor could realize if it sold the estate's interest in the property according to the security agreement," namely, through "repossessing and selling the collateral."

> We do not find in the § 506(a)[(1)] first sentence words—"the creditor's interest in the estate's interest in such property"—the foreclosure-value meaning advanced by the Fifth Circuit. Even read in isolation, the phrase imparts no valuation standard: A direction simply to consider the "value of such creditor's interest" does not expressly reveal *how* that interest is to be valued.

> Reading the first sentence of § 506(a)[(1)] as a whole, we are satisfied that the phrase the Fifth Circuit considered key is not an instruction to equate a "creditor's interest" with the net value a creditor could realize through a foreclosure sale. The first sentence, in its entirety, tells us that a secured creditor's claim is to be divided into secured and unsecured portions, with the secured portion of the claim limited to the value of the collateral. To separate the secured from the unsecured portion of a

claim, a court must compare the creditor's claim to the value of "such property," *i.e.*, the collateral. That comparison is sometimes complicated. A debtor may own only a part interest in the property pledged as collateral, in which case the court will be required to ascertain the "estate's interest" in the collateral. Or, a creditor may hold a junior or subordinate lien, which would require the court to ascertain the creditor's interest in the collateral. The § 506(a)[(1)] phrase referring to the "creditor's interest in the estate's interest in such property" thus recognizes that a court may encounter, and in such instances must evaluate, limited or partial interests in collateral. The full first sentence of § 506(a)[(1)], in short, tells a court what it must evaluate, but it does not say more; it is not enlightening on how to value collateral.

The second sentence of § 506(a)[(1)] does speak to the *how* question. "Such value," that sentence provides, "shall be determined in light of the purpose of the valuation and of the proposed disposition or use of such property." By deriving a foreclosure-value standard from § 506(a)[(1)]'s first sentence, the Fifth Circuit rendered inconsequential the sentence that expressly addresses how "value shall be determined."

As we comprehend § 506(a)[(1)], the "proposed disposition or use" of the collateral is of paramount importance to the valuation question. If a secured creditor does not accept a debtor's Chapter 13 plan, the debtor has two options for handling allowed secured claims: surrender the collateral to the creditor, § 1325(a)(5)(C); or, under the cram down option, keep the collateral over the creditor's objection and provide the creditor, over the life of the plan, with the equivalent of the present value of the collateral, § 1325(a)(5)(B). The "disposition or use" of the collateral thus turns on the alternative the debtor chooses—in one case the collateral will be surrendered to the creditor, and in the other, the collateral will be retained and used by the debtor. Applying a foreclosure-value standard when the cram down option is invoked attributes no significance to the different consequences of the debtor's choice to surrender the property or retain it. A replacement-value standard, on the other hand, distinguishes retention from surrender and renders meaningful the key words "disposition or use."

Tying valuation to the actual "disposition or use" of the property points away from a foreclosure-value standard when a

Chapter 13 debtor, invoking cram down power, retains and uses the property. Under that option, foreclosure is averted by the debtor's choice and over the creditor's objection. From the creditor's perspective as well as the debtor's, surrender and retention are not equivalent acts.

* * *

The Fifth Circuit considered the replacement-value standard disrespectful of state law, which permits the secured creditor to sell the collateral, thereby obtaining its net foreclosure value "and nothing more." In allowing Chapter 13 debtors to retain and use collateral over the objection of secured creditors, however, the Bankruptcy Code has reshaped debtor and creditor rights in marked departure from state law. The Code's cram down option displaces a secured creditor's state-law right to obtain immediate foreclosure upon a debtor's default. That change, ordered by federal law, is attended by a direction that courts look to the "proposed disposition or use" of the collateral in determining its value. It no more disrupts state law to make "disposition or use" the guide for valuation than to authorize the rearrangement of rights the cram down power entails.

Id. at 960-62, 964, 117 S.Ct. at 1884-85, 1886, 138 L.Ed.2d at 157-58, 159. Having settled on replacement value as the appropriate measure of the amount that a Chapter 13 debtor must pay in order to satisfy § 1325(a)(5)(B)(ii), the Court cast immediate doubt on how to measure that value, in its infamous footnote 6:

Our recognition that the replacement-value standard, not the foreclosure-value standard, governs in cram down cases leaves to bankruptcy courts, as triers of fact, identification of the best way of ascertaining replacement value on the basis of the evidence presented. Whether replacement value is the equivalent of retail value, wholesale value, or some other value will depend on the type of debtor and the nature of the property. We note, however, that replacement value, in this context, should not include certain items. For example, where the proper measure of the replacement value of a vehicle is its retail value, an adjustment to that value may be necessary: A creditor should not receive portions of the retail price, if any, that reflect the value of items the debtor does not receive when he retains his vehicle, items such as warranties, inventory storage, and reconditioning. Nor should the creditor gain from modifications to the property—*e.g.*, the addition of accessories to a vehicle—to which a creditor's lien would not extend under state law.

Id. at 965 n.6, 117 S.Ct. at 1886 n.6, 138 L.Ed.2d at 160 n.6. The problem created by footnote 6 is that deduction of those amounts could very well reduce replacement value back to a number closely resembling foreclosure value. Judge Easterbrook explained this in a case, arising out of another context, in which a Bank held a security interest in the inventory of a debtor furniture store:

> [W]holesale and retail goods are different things. A furniture store, a supermarket, or the manufacturer of a product (the three situations are identical) uses raw materials purchased at wholesale to produce a new item. In the retailing business the difference between the wholesale price and the retail price is the "value added" of the business. It is the amount contributed by storing, inspecting, displaying, hawking, collecting for, delivering, and handling warranty claims on the goods. This difference covers the employees' wages, rent and utilities of the premises, interest on the cost of goods, bad debts, repairs, the value of entrepreneurial talent, and so on. The increment of price is attributable to this investment of time and other resources. The Bank does not have a security interest in these labors. It has an interest only in its merchandise and cash on hand. The value of its interest depends on what the Bank could do, outside of bankruptcy, to realize on its security. What it could do is seize and sell the inventory. It would get at most the wholesale price—maybe less because the Bank would sell the goods "as is" and would not offer the wholesaler's usual services to its customer. The Bank does not operate its own furniture store, and if it did it would still incur all the costs of retailing the goods, costs that would have to be subtracted from the retail price to determine the "value" of the inventory on the day the Bank seized it.

Samson v. Alton Banking & Trust Co. (In re Ebbler Furniture & Appliances, Inc.), 804 F.2d 87, 92 (7th Cir.1986) (Easterbrook, J., concurring) (footnote omitted).

Section 506(a)(2) was added to the Code in 2005, after *Rash* was decided. It mandates the use of replacement value, without deduction for costs of sale or marketing, for personal property in cases filed by individuals under Chapters 7 and 13.

The impact of § 506(a)(2) extends beyond §§ 1129(b)(2)(A)(i) and 1325(a)(5)(B), to some issues that might not occur to you at first glance. In *Brown & Co. Securities Corp. v. Balbus (In re Balbus)*, 933 F.2d 246 (4th Cir.1991), for instance, the question was whether the debtor met § 109(e)'s eligibility requirements for filing a Chapter 13 petition. The debtor listed secured and unsecured obligations in amounts within Chapter 13's debt limits, but several of the secured claims were undersecured. Addition of the postbifurcation unsecured claims to the pre-existing ones took the total of unsecured claims very close to the ceiling under § 109(e), but not over it. An unsecured creditor then argued, however, that the value of the collateral supporting the debtor's secured claims should be reduced by 6% to account for the costs of selling it. Doing so would increase the postbifurcation unsecured claims even further, putting the debtor over § 109(e)'s debt limit for unsecured claims. The debtor resisted this argument because he intended to keep the property and no costs of sale would be incurred. (Interestingly, the debtor argued that the secured claim was *higher* in amount than the undersecured creditor asserted. Does this make sense in light of § 1325(a)(5)(B)?)

The statutory issue in *Balbus* was the same as in *Rash*—namely, how to interpret "value" within § 506(a)(1) when the debtor intends to keep the collateral. Although the court in *Balbus* declined to deduct hypothetical costs, in part because doing so would read the second sentence out of § 506(a)(1), authority for that result will now be found in § 506(a)(2).

Subsection 506(a)(2) does not apply to Chapter 11 cases or to valuations involving real property. While *Rash* might fit uncomfortably in the context of real estate, the case may have some viability in Chapter 11s. After all, § 1129(b)(2)(A)(i) is worded much like § 1325-(a)(5)(B)(ii)—the provision at issue in *Rash*.

MISS PEACH

3. DETERMINING THE APPROPRIATE INTEREST RATE

The second of the determinations required for purposes of cram down under §§ 1129(b)(2)(A)(i) and 1325(a)(5)(B)—the proper discount rate—was at issue in the following case. As you will see, the Court was deeply divided.

TILL v. SCS CREDIT CORP.

United States Supreme Court, 2004.
541 U.S. 465, 124 S. Ct. 1951, 158 L.Ed.2d 787.

JUSTICE STEVENS announced the judgment of the Court and delivered an opinion, in which JUSTICE SOUTER, JUSTICE GINSBURG, and JUSTICE BREYER join.

To qualify for court approval under Chapter 13 of the Bankruptcy Code, an individual debtor's proposed debt adjustment plan must accommodate each allowed, secured creditor in one of three ways: (1) by obtaining the creditor's acceptance of the plan; (2) by surrendering the property securing the claim; or (3) by providing the creditor both a lien securing the claim and a promise of future property distributions (such as deferred cash payments) whose total "value, as of the effective date of the plan, * * * is not less than the allowed amount of such claim."[1] The third alternative is commonly known as the "cram down option" because it may be enforced over a claim holder's objection.

Plans that invoke the cram down power often provide for installment payments over a period of years rather than a single payment. In such circumstances, the amount of each installment must be calibrated to ensure that, over time, the creditor receives disbursements whose total present value[4] equals or exceeds that of the allowed claim.
* * *

I

[In October 1998, Debtors bought a used truck for $6,395 plus $330.75 in fees and taxes. They paid $300 down and signed a retail

---

[1] § 1325(a)(5).

[4] In the remainder of the opinion, we use the term "present value" to refer to the value as of the effective date of the bankruptcy plan.

installment contract, granting a security interest in the truck and promising to pay the balance of $6,425.75, plus a finance charge of 21%, over 136 weeks. They filed bankruptcy a year later, after defaulting on the note. At the time of filing, they owed $4,894.89 on the truck. It was then worth $4,000.]

The proposed plan also provided that petitioners would pay interest on the secured portion of respondent's claim at a rate of 9.5% per year. Petitioners arrived at this "prime-plus" or "formula rate" by augmenting the national prime rate of approximately 8% (applied by banks when making low-risk loans) to account for the risk of nonpayment posed by borrowers in their financial position. Respondent objected to the proposed rate, contending that the company was "entitled to interest at the rate of 21%, which is the rate * * * it would obtain if it could foreclose on the vehicle and reinvest the proceeds in loans of equivalent duration and risk as the loan" originally made to petitioners.

At the hearing on its objection, respondent presented expert testimony establishing that it uniformly charges 21% interest on so-called "subprime" loans, or loans to borrowers with poor credit ratings, and that other lenders in the subprime market also charge that rate. Petitioners countered with the testimony of an Indiana University-Purdue University Indianapolis economics professor, who * * * described the 9.5% formula rate as "very reasonable" given that Chapter 13 plans are "supposed to be financially feasible."[8] * * * The bankruptcy trustee also filed comments supporting the formula rate as, among other things, easily ascertainable, closely tied to the "condition of the financial market," and independent of the financial circumstances of any particular lender. Accepting petitioners' evidence, the Bankruptcy Court overruled respondent's objection and confirmed the proposed plan.

The District Court reversed. It understood Seventh Circuit precedent to require that bankruptcy courts set cram down interest rates at the level the creditor could have obtained if it had foreclosed on the loan, sold the collateral, and reinvested the proceeds in loans of equivalent duration and risk. * * *

On appeal, the Seventh Circuit endorsed a slightly modified version of the District Court's "coerced" or "forced loan" approach. * * * The court recognized, however, that using the contract rate would not "duplicate precisely * * * the present value of the collateral to the creditor" because loans to bankrupt, court-supervised debtors "involve

---

[8] The requirement of financial feasibility derives from § 1325(a)(6) * * * .

some risks that would not be incurred in a new loan to a debtor not in default" and also produce "some economies." To correct for these inaccuracies, the majority held that the original contract rate should "serve as a presumptive [cram down] rate," which either the creditor or the debtor could challenge with evidence that a higher or lower rate should apply. Accordingly, the court remanded the case to the Bankruptcy Court to afford petitioners and respondent an opportunity to rebut the presumptive 21% rate.

Dissenting, Judge Rovner argued that the majority's presumptive contract rate approach overcompensates secured creditors because it fails to account for costs a creditor would have to incur in issuing a new loan. Rather than focusing on the market for comparable loans, Judge Rovner advocated either the Bankruptcy Court's formula approach or a "straightforward * * * cost of funds" approach that would simply ask "what it would cost the creditor to obtain the cash equivalent of the collateral from an alternative source." * * * We granted certiorari and now reverse.

II

The Bankruptcy Code provides little guidance as to which of the rates of interest advocated by the four opinions in this case—the formula rate, the coerced loan rate, the presumptive contract rate, or the cost of funds rate—Congress had in mind when it adopted the cram down provision. That provision, § 1325(a)(5)(B), does not mention the term "discount rate" or the word "interest." Rather, it simply requires bankruptcy courts to ensure that the property to be distributed to a particular secured creditor over the life of a bankruptcy plan has a total "value, as of the effective date of the plan," that equals or exceeds the value of the creditor's allowed secured claim—in this case, $4,000.

That command is easily satisfied when the plan provides for a lump-sum payment to the creditor. Matters are not so simple, however, when the debt is to be discharged by a series of payments over time. A debtor's promise of future payments is worth less than an immediate payment of the same total amount because the creditor cannot use the money right away, inflation may cause the value of the dollar to decline before the debtor pays, and there is always some risk of nonpayment. The challenge for bankruptcy courts reviewing such repayment schemes, therefore, is to choose an interest rate sufficient to compensate the creditor for these concerns.

Three important considerations govern that choice. First, the Bankruptcy Code includes numerous provisions that, like the cram down provision, require a court to "discount * * * [a] stream of deferred payments back to their present dollar value," *Rake v. Wade*, 508 U.S. 464, 472 (1993),[10] to ensure that a creditor receives at least the value of its claim. We think it likely that Congress intended bankruptcy judges and trustees to follow essentially the same approach when choosing an appropriate interest rate under any of these provisions. Moreover, we think Congress would favor an approach that is familiar in the financial community and that minimizes the need for expensive evidentiary proceedings.

Second, Chapter 13 expressly authorizes a bankruptcy court to modify the rights of any creditor whose claim is secured by an interest in anything other than "real property that is the debtor's principal residence." § 1322(b)(2). * * * Further, the potential need to modify the loan terms to account for intervening changes in circumstances is also clear: On the one hand, the fact of the bankruptcy establishes that the debtor is overextended and thus poses a significant risk of default; on the other hand, the postbankruptcy obligor is no longer the individual debtor but the court-supervised estate, and the risk of default is thus somewhat reduced.[12]

Third, from the point of view of a creditor, the cram down provision mandates an objective rather than a subjective inquiry. That is, although § 1325(a)(5)(B) entitles the creditor to property whose present value objectively equals or exceeds the value of the collateral, it does

[10] See § 1129(a)(7)(A)(ii) (requiring payment of property whose "value, as of the effective date of the plan" equals or exceeds the value of the creditor's claim); §§ 1129(a)(7)(B), 1129(a)(9)(B)(i), 1129(a)(9)(C), 1129(b)(2)(A)[(i)(II)], 1129-(b)(2)(B)(i), 1129(b)(2)(C)(i), 1173(a)(2), 1225(a)(4), 1225(a)(5)(B)(ii), 1228(b)(2), 1325(a)(4), 1228(b)(2) (same).

[12] Several factors contribute to this reduction in risk. First, as noted below, a court may only approve a cram down loan (and the debt adjustment plan of which the loan is a part) if it believes the debtor will be able to make all of the required payments. Thus, such loans will only be approved for debtors that the court deems creditworthy. Second, Chapter 13 plans must "provide for the submission" to the trustee "of all or such portion of [the debtor's] future * * * income * * as is necessary for the execution of the plan," § 1322(a)(1), so the possibility of nonpayment is greatly reduced. Third, the Bankruptcy Code's extensive disclosure requirements reduce the risk that the debtor has significant undisclosed obligations. Fourth, as a practical matter, the public nature of the bankruptcy proceeding is likely to reduce the debtor's opportunities to take on additional debt.

not require that the terms of the cram down loan match the terms to which the debtor and creditor agreed prebankruptcy, nor does it require that the cram down terms make the creditor subjectively indifferent between present foreclosure and future payment. Indeed, the very idea of a "cram down" loan *precludes* the latter result: By definition, a creditor forced to accept such a loan would prefer instead to foreclose.[14] Thus, a court choosing a cram down interest rate need not consider the creditor's individual circumstances, such as its prebankruptcy dealings with the debtor or the alternative loans it could make if permitted to foreclose. Rather, the court should aim to treat similarly situated creditors similarly, and to ensure that an objective economic analysis would suggest the debtor's interest payments will adequately compensate all such creditors for the time value of their money and the risk of default.

III

These considerations lead us to reject the coerced loan, presumptive contract rate, and cost of funds approaches. Each of these approaches is complicated, imposes significant evidentiary costs, and aims to make each individual creditor whole rather than to ensure the debtor's payments have the required present value. For example, the coerced loan approach requires bankruptcy courts to consider evidence about the market for comparable loans to similar (though nonbankrupt) debtors—an inquiry far removed from such courts' usual task of evaluating debtors' financial circumstances and the feasibility of their debt adjustment plans. In addition, the approach overcompensates creditors because the market lending rate must be high enough to cover factors, like lenders' transaction costs and overall profits, that are no longer relevant in the context of court-administered and court-supervised cram down loans.

Like the coerced loan approach, the presumptive contract rate approach improperly focuses on the creditor's potential use of the proceeds of a foreclosure sale. In addition, * * * the approach produces absurd results, entitling "inefficient, poorly managed lenders" with

---

[14] This fact helps to explain why there is no readily apparent Chapter 13 "cram down market rate of interest": Because every cram down loan is imposed by a court over the objection of the secured creditor, there is no free market of willing cram down lenders. Interestingly, the same is *not* true in the Chapter 11 context, as numerous lenders advertise financing for Chapter 11 debtors in possession. Thus, when picking a cram down rate in a Chapter 11 case, it might make sense to ask what rate an efficient market would produce. In the Chapter 13 context, by contrast, the absence of any such market obligates courts to look to first principles and ask only what rate will fairly compensate a creditor for its exposure.

lower profit margins to obtain higher cram down rates than "well managed, better capitalized lenders." 2 K. Lundin, Chapter 13 Bankruptcy § 112.1, p. 112-8 (3d ed. 2000). Finally, because the approach relies heavily on a creditor's prior dealings with the debtor, similarly situated creditors may end up with vastly different cram down rates.

The cost of funds approach, too, is improperly aimed. Although it rightly disregards the now-irrelevant terms of the parties' original contract, it mistakenly focuses on the creditworthiness of the *creditor* rather than the debtor. In addition, the approach has many of the other flaws of the coerced loan and presumptive contract rate approaches. For example, like the presumptive contract rate approach, the cost of funds approach imposes a significant evidentiary burden, as a debtor seeking to rebut a creditor's asserted cost of borrowing must introduce expert testimony about the creditor's financial condition. Also, under this approach, a creditworthy lender with a low cost of borrowing may obtain a lower cram down rate than a financially unsound, fly-by-night lender.

IV

The formula approach has none of these defects. Taking its cue from ordinary lending practices, the approach begins by looking to the national prime rate, reported daily in the press, which reflects the financial market's estimate of the amount a commercial bank should charge a creditworthy commercial borrower to compensate for the opportunity costs of the loan, the risk of inflation, and the relatively slight risk of default. Because bankrupt debtors typically pose a greater risk of nonpayment than solvent commercial borrowers, the approach then requires a bankruptcy court to adjust the prime rate accordingly. The appropriate size of that risk adjustment depends, of course, on such factors as the circumstances of the estate, the nature of the security, and the duration and feasibility of the reorganization plan. The court must therefore hold a hearing at which the debtor and any creditors may present evidence about the appropriate risk adjustment. Some of this evidence will be included in the debtor's bankruptcy filings, however, so the debtor and creditors may not incur significant additional expense. Moreover, starting from a concededly *low* estimate and adjusting *upward* places the evidentiary burden squarely on the creditors, who are likely to have readier access to any information absent from the debtor's filing (such as evidence about the "liquidity of the collateral market," (SCALIA, J., dissenting)). Finally, many of the factors relevant to the adjustment fall squarely within the bankruptcy court's area of expertise.

Thus, unlike the coerced loan, presumptive contract rate, and cost of funds approaches, the formula approach entails a straightforward, familiar, and objective inquiry, and minimizes the need for potentially costly additional evidentiary proceedings. Moreover, the resulting "prime-plus" rate of interest depends only on the state of financial markets, the circumstances of the bankruptcy estate, and the characteristics of the loan, not on the creditor's circumstances or its prior interactions with the debtor. For these reasons, the prime-plus or formula rate best comports with the purposes of the Bankruptcy Code.

We do not decide the proper scale for the risk adjustment, as the issue is not before us. The Bankruptcy Court in this case approved a risk adjustment of 1.5%, and other courts have generally approved adjustments of 1% to 3%. Respondent's core argument is that a risk adjustment in this range is entirely inadequate to compensate a creditor for the real risk that the plan will fail. * * * We need not resolve that dispute. It is sufficient for our purposes to note that, under § 1325(a)(6), a court may not approve a plan unless, after considering all creditors' objections and receiving the advice of the trustee, the judge is persuaded that "the debtor will be able to make all payments under the plan and to comply with the plan." Together with the cram down provision, this requirement obligates the court to select a rate high enough to compensate the creditor for its risk but not so high as to doom the plan. If the court determines that the likelihood of default is so high as to necessitate an "eye-popping" interest rate, the plan probably should not be confirmed.

V

The dissent's endorsement of the presumptive contract rate approach rests on two assumptions: (1) "subprime lending markets are competitive and therefore largely efficient"; and (2) the risk of default in Chapter 13 is normally no less than the risk of default at the time of the original loan. Although the Bankruptcy Code provides little guidance on the question, we think it highly unlikely that Congress would endorse either premise.

First, the dissent assumes that subprime loans are negotiated between fully informed buyers and sellers in a classic free market. But there is no basis for concluding that Congress relied on this assumption when it enacted Chapter 13. Moreover, several considerations suggest that the subprime market is not, in fact, perfectly competitive. To begin with, used vehicles are regularly sold by means of tie-in transactions, in which the price of the vehicle is the subject of negotiation, while the terms of the financing are dictated by the seller. In addition, there is extensive federal and state regulation of subprime lending, which not only itself distorts the market, but also evinces regulators' belief that unregulated subprime lenders would exploit borrowers' ignorance and charge rates above what a competitive market would allow.[23] * * *

Second, the dissent apparently believes that the debtor's pre-bankruptcy default—on a loan made in a market in which creditors commonly charge the maximum rate of interest allowed by law, and in which neither creditors nor debtors have the protections afforded by Chapter 13—translates into a high probability that the same debtor's confirmed Chapter 13 plan will fail. In our view, however, Congress intended to create a program under which plans that qualify for confirmation have a high probability of success. Perhaps bankruptcy judges currently confirm too many risky plans, but the solution is to confirm fewer such plans, not to set default cram down rates at absurdly high levels, thereby increasing the risk of default.

* * *

JUSTICE SCALIA identifies four "relevant factors bearing on risk premium[:] (1) the probability of plan failure; (2) the rate of collateral depreciation; (3) the liquidity of the collateral market; and (4) the administrative expenses of enforcement." In our view, any information debtors have about any of these factors is likely to be included in their bankruptcy filings, while the remaining information will be far more accessible to creditors (who must collect information about their lending markets to remain competitive) than to individual debtors (whose only experience with those markets might be the single loan at issue in the case). Thus, the formula approach, which begins with a concededly low estimate of the appropriate interest rate and requires the creditor to present evidence supporting a higher rate, places the evidentiary burden on the more knowledgeable party, thereby facilitating more accurate calculation of the appropriate interest rate.

If the rather sketchy data uncovered by the dissent support an argument that Chapter 13 of the Bankruptcy Code should mandate ap-

---

[23] Lending practices in Mississippi, "where there currently is no legal usury rate," support this conclusion: in that State, subprime lenders charge rates "as high as 30 to 40%"—well above the rates that apparently suffice to support the industry in States like Indiana. Norberg, *Consumer Bankruptcy's New Clothes: An Empirical Study of Discharge and Debt Collection in Chapter 13,* 7 Am. BANKR. INST. L. REV. 415, 438-439 (1999).

plication of the presumptive contract rate approach (rather than merely an argument that bankruptcy judges should exercise greater caution before approving debt adjustment plans), those data should be forwarded to Congress. We are not persuaded, however, that the data undermine our interpretation of the statutory scheme Congress has enacted.

The judgment of the Court of Appeals is reversed, and the case is remanded with instructions to remand the case to the Bankruptcy Court for further proceedings consistent with this opinion.

It is so ordered.

JUSTICE SCALIA, with whom THE CHIEF JUSTICE, JUSTICE O'CONNOR, and JUSTICE KENNEDY join, dissenting.

My areas of agreement with the plurality are substantial. We agree that, although all confirmed Chapter 13 plans have been deemed feasible by a bankruptcy judge, some nevertheless fail. We agree that any deferred payments to a secured creditor must fully compensate it for the risk that such a failure will occur. Finally, we agree that adequate compensation may sometimes require an "eye-popping" interest rate, and that, if the rate is too high for the plan to succeed, the appropriate course is not to reduce it to a more palatable level, but to refuse to confirm the plan.

Our only disagreement is over what procedure will more often produce accurate estimates of the appropriate interest rate. The plurality would use the prime lending rate—a rate we *know* is too low—and require the judge in every case to determine an amount by which to increase it. I believe that, in practice, this approach will systematically undercompensate secured creditors for the true risks of default. I would instead adopt the contract rate—*i.e.*, the rate at which the creditor actually loaned funds to the debtor—as a presumption that the bankruptcy judge could revise on motion of either party. Since that rate is generally a good indicator of actual risk, disputes should be infrequent, and it will provide a quick and reasonably accurate standard.

I

The contract-rate approach makes two assumptions, both of which are reasonable. First, it assumes that subprime lending markets are competitive and therefore largely efficient. If so, the high interest rates lenders charge reflect not extortionate profits or excessive costs, but the actual risks of default that subprime borrowers present. Lenders with excessive rates would be undercut by their competitors, and inefficient ones would be priced out of the market. * * * By relying on the prime rate, the plurality implicitly assumes that the *prime* lending market is efficient; I see no reason not to make a similar assumption about the *sub*prime lending market.

The second assumption is that the expected costs of default in Chapter 13 are normally no less than those at the time of lending. This assumption is also reasonable. Chapter 13 plans often fail. * * * The failure rate [petitioners] offer—which we may take to be a conservative estimate, as it is doubtless the lowest one they could find—is 37%. See Girth, *The Role of Empirical Data in Developing Bankruptcy Legislation for Individuals*, 65 IND. L.J. 17, 40-42 (1989) (reporting a 63.1% success rate).[1] In every one of the failed plans making up that 37%, a bankruptcy judge had found that "the debtor will be able to make all payments under the plan," § 1325(a)(6), and a trustee had supervised the debtor's compliance, § 1302. That so many nonetheless failed proves that bankruptcy judges are not oracles and that trustees cannot draw blood from a stone.

While court and trustee oversight may provide some marginal benefit to the creditor, it seems obviously outweighed by the fact that (1) an already-bankrupt borrower has demonstrated a financial instability and a proclivity to seek legal protection that other subprime borrowers have not, and (2) the costs of foreclosure are substantially higher in bankruptcy because the automatic stay bars repossession without judicial permission. * * * The better assumption is that bankrupt debtors are riskier than other subprime debtors—or, at the very least, not systematically *less* risky.

The first of the two assumptions means that the contract rate reasonably reflects actual risk at the time of borrowing. The second means that this risk persists when the debtor files for Chapter 13. It

---

[1] The true rate of plan failure is almost certainly much higher. * * * [O]ne study * * * finds 32% of filings successful, 18% dismissed without confirmation of a plan, and 49% dismissed after confirmation, for a postconfirmation failure rate of 60% (*i.e.*, 49%/(32% + 49%)). See Norberg, *Consumer Bankruptcy's New Clothes: An Empirical Study of Discharge and Debt Collection in Chapter 13*, 7 AM. BANKR. INST. L. REV. 415, 440-41 (1999). This 60% failure rate is far higher than the 37% reported by Girth.

follows that the contract rate is a decent estimate, or at least the lower bound, for the appropriate interest rate in cramdown.[2]

The plurality disputes these two assumptions. It argues that subprime lending markets are not competitive because "vehicles are regularly sold by means of tie-in transactions, in which the price of the vehicle is the subject of negotiation, while the terms of the financing are dictated by the seller."[3] * * * The force of the plurality's argument depends entirely on its claim that "the terms of the financing are dictated by the seller." This unsubstantiated assertion is contrary to common experience. Car sellers routinely advertise their interest rates, offer promotions like "zero-percent financing," and engage in other behavior that plainly assumes customers are sensitive to interest rates and not just price.[4]

The plurality also points to state and federal regulation of lending markets. It claims that state usury laws evince a belief that subprime lending markets are noncompetitive. While that is one *conceivable* explanation for such laws, there are countless others. * * *

* * *

As to the second assumption (that the expected costs of default in Chapter 13 are normally no less than those at the time of lending), the plurality responds, not that Chapter 13 *as currently administered* is less risky than subprime lending generally, but that it *would* be less risky, if only bankruptcy courts would confirm fewer risky plans. Of

---

[2] The contract rate is only a presumption, however, and either party remains free to prove that a higher or lower rate is appropriate in a particular case. * * *

[3] To the extent the plurality argues that subprime lending markets are not "*perfectly* competitive," (emphasis added), I agree. But there is no reason to doubt they are *reasonably* competitive, so that pricing in those markets is *reasonably* efficient.

[4] I confess that this is "nonresponsive" to the argument made in the plurality's footnote (that the contract interest rate may not accurately reflect risk when set jointly with a car's sale price); it is in response to the quite different argument made in the plurality's text (that joint pricing shows that the subprime lending market is not competitive). As to the *former* issue, the plurality's footnote makes a fair point. When the seller provides financing itself, there is a possibility that the contract interest rate might not reflect actual risk because a higher contract interest rate can be traded off for a lower sale price and vice versa. Nonetheless, this fact is not likely to bias the contract-rate approach in favor of creditors to any significant degree. * * *

course, it is often quite difficult to predict which plans will fail. But even assuming the high failure rate primarily reflects judicial dereliction rather than unavoidable uncertainty, the plurality's argument fails for want of any reason to believe the dereliction will abate. While full compensation can be attained either by low-risk plans and low interest rates, or by high-risk plans and high interest rates, it cannot be attained by *high*-risk plans and *low* interest rates, which, absent cause to anticipate a change in confirmation practices, is precisely what the formula approach would yield.

The plurality also claims that the contract rate overcompensates creditors because it includes "transaction costs and overall profits." But the same is true of the rate the plurality prescribes: The prime lending rate includes banks' overhead and profits. These are necessary components of *any* commercial lending rate, since creditors will not lend money if they cannot cover their costs and return a level of profit sufficient to prevent their investors from going elsewhere. The plurality's criticism might have force if there were reason to believe sub-prime lenders made exorbitant profits while banks did not—but, again, the data suggest otherwise.[6]

Finally, the plurality objects that similarly situated creditors might not be treated alike. But the contract rate is only a presumption. If a judge thinks it necessary to modify the rate to avoid unjustified disparity, he can do so. * * * The plurality's argument might be valid against an approach that *irrebuttably* presumes the contract rate, but that is not what I propose.

II

The defects of the formula approach far outweigh those of the contract-rate approach. The formula approach starts with the prime lending rate—a number that, while objective and easily ascertainable, is indisputably too low. It then adjusts by adding a risk premium that, unlike the prime rate, is neither objective nor easily ascertainable. If the risk premium is typically small relative to the prime rate—as the 1.5% premium added to the 8% prime rate by the court below would lead one to believe—then this subjective element of the computation might be forgiven. But in fact risk premiums, if properly computed,

---

[6] Some transaction costs are avoided by the creditor in bankruptcy—for example, loan-origination costs such as advertising. But these are likely only a minor component of the interest rate. * * * Any transaction costs the creditor avoids in bankruptcy are thus far less than the additional ones he incurs.

would typically be substantial. For example, if the 21% contract rate is an accurate reflection of risk in this case, the risk premium would be 13%—nearly two-thirds of the total interest rate. When the risk premium is the greater part of the overall rate, the formula approach no longer depends on objective and easily ascertainable numbers. The prime rate becomes the objective tail wagging a dog of unknown size.

As I explain below, the most relevant factors bearing on risk premium are (1) the probability of plan failure; (2) the rate of collateral depreciation; (3) the liquidity of the collateral market; and (4) the administrative expenses of enforcement. Under the formula approach, a risk premium must be computed in every case, so judges will invariably grapple with these imponderables. Under the contract-rate approach, by contrast, the task of assessing all these risk factors is entrusted to the entity most capable of undertaking it: the market. All the risk factors are reflected (assuming market efficiency) in the debtor's contract rate—a number readily found in the loan document. If neither party disputes it, the bankruptcy judge's task is at an end. There are straightforward ways a debtor *could* dispute it—for example, by showing that the creditor is now substantially oversecured, or that some other lender is willing to extend credit at a lower rate. But unlike the formula approach, which requires difficult estimation in every case, the contract-rate approach requires it only when the parties choose to contest the issue.

The plurality defends the formula approach on the ground that creditors have better access to the relevant information. But this is not a case where we must choose between one initial estimate that is too low and another that is too high. Rather, the choice is between one that is far too low and another that is generally reasonably accurate (or, if anything, a bit too low). In these circumstances, consciously choosing the less accurate estimate merely because creditors have better information smacks more of policymaking than of faithful adherence to the statutory command that the secured creditor receive property worth "*not less than* the allowed amount" of its claim, § 1325(a)(5)(B)(ii) (emphasis added). Moreover, the plurality's argument assumes it is plausible—and desirable—that the issue will be litigated in most cases. But the costs of conducting a detailed risk analysis and defending it in court are prohibitively high in relation to the amount at stake in most consumer loan cases. Whatever approach we prescribe, the norm should be—and undoubtedly will be—that the issue is not litigated because it is not worth litigating. Given this reality, it is far more important that the initial estimate be accurate than that the burden of proving inaccuracy fall on the better informed party.

* * *

Based on even a rudimentary financial analysis of the facts of this case, the 1.5% figure is obviously wrong—not just off by a couple percent, but probably by roughly an order of magnitude. For a risk premium to be adequate, a hypothetical, rational creditor must be indifferent between accepting (1) the proposed risky stream of payments over time and (2) immediate payment of its present value in a lump sum. Whether he is indifferent—*i.e.*, whether the risk premium added to the prime rate is adequate—can be gauged by comparing benefits and costs: on the one hand, the expected value of the extra interest, and on the other, the expected costs of default.

Respondent was offered a risk premium of 1.5% on top of the prime rate of 8%. If that premium were fully paid as the plan contemplated, it would yield about $60. If the debtor defaulted, all or part of that interest would not be paid, so the expected value is only about $50.[9] The prime rate itself already includes some compensation for risk; as it turns out, about the same amount, yielding another $50.[10] Given the 1.5% risk premium, then, the total expected benefit to respondent was about $100. Against this we must weigh the expected costs of default. While precise calculations are impossible, rough estimates convey a sense of their scale.

The first cost of default involves depreciation. If the debtor defaults, the creditor can eventually repossess and sell the collateral, but by then it may be substantially less valuable than the remaining balance due—and the debtor may stop paying long before the creditor receives permission to repossess. When petitioners purchased their truck in this case, its value was almost equal to the principal balance on the loan. By the time the plan was confirmed, however, the truck was worth only $4,000, while the balance on the loan was $4,895. If petitioners were to

---

[9] Assuming a 37% rate of default that results on average in only half the interest's being paid, the expected value is $60 x (1 − 37%/2), or about $50.

[10] According to the record in this case, the prime rate at the time of filing was 2% higher than the risk-free treasury rate, and the difference represented "mostly * * * risk [and] to some extent transaction costs." If "mostly" means about three-quarters of 2%, then the risk compensation included in the prime rate is 1.5%. Because this figure happens to be the same as the risk premium over prime, the expected value is similarly $50.

default on their Chapter 13 payments and if respondent suffered the same relative loss from depreciation, it would amount to about $ 550.[12]

The second cost of default involves liquidation. The $4,000 to which respondent would be entitled if paid in a lump sum reflects the *replacement* value of the vehicle, *i.e.*, the amount it would cost the debtor to purchase a similar used truck. If the debtor defaults, the creditor cannot sell the truck for that amount; it receives only a lesser *foreclosure* value because collateral markets are not perfectly liquid and there is thus a spread between what a buyer will pay and what a seller will demand. The foreclosure value of petitioners' truck is not in the record, but, using the relative liquidity figures in *Associates Commercial Corp. v. Rash*, 520 U.S. 953 (1997), as a rough guide, respondent would suffer a further loss of about $450.[13]

The third cost of default consists of the administrative expenses of foreclosure. While a Chapter 13 plan is in effect, the automatic stay prevents secured creditors from repossessing their collateral, even if the debtor fails to pay. The creditor's attorney must move the bankruptcy court to lift the stay. In the District where this case arose, the filing fee for such motions is now $150. And the standard attorney's fee for such motions, according to one survey, is $350 in Indiana and as high as $875 in other States. Moreover, bankruptcy judges will often excuse first offenses, so foreclosure may require multiple trips to court. The total expected administrative expenses in the event of default could reasonably be estimated at $600 or more.

I have omitted several other costs of default, but the point is already adequately made. The three figures above total $1,600. Even accepting petitioners' low estimate of the plan failure rate, a creditor choosing the stream of future payments instead of the immediate lump sum would be selecting an alternative with an expected cost of about $590 ($1,600 multiplied by 37%, the chance of failure) and an expected benefit of about $100 (as computed above). No rational creditor would

---

[12] On the original loan, depreciation ($6,395 − $4,000, or $2,395) exceeded loan repayment ($6,426 − $4,895, or $1,531) by $864, *i.e.*, 14% of the original truck value of $6,395. Applying the same percentage to the new $4,000 truck value yields approximately $550.

[13] The truck in *Rash* had a replacement value of $41,000 and a foreclosure value of $31,875, *i.e.*, 22% less. If the market in this case had similar liquidity and the truck were repossessed after losing half its remaining value, the loss would be 22% of $2,000, or about $450.

make such a choice. The risk premium over prime necessary to make these costs and benefits equal is in the neighborhood of 16%, for a total interest rate of 24%.

Of course, many of the estimates I have made can be disputed. Perhaps the truck will depreciate more slowly now than at first, perhaps the collateral market is more liquid than the one in *Rash*, perhaps respondent can economize on attorney's fees, and perhaps there is some reason (other than judicial optimism) to think the Tills were unlikely to default. I have made some liberal assumptions,[15] but also some conservative ones.[16] When a risk premium is off by an order of magnitude, one's estimates need not be very precise to show that it cannot possibly be correct.

* * *

III

* * *

There are very good reasons for Congress to prescribe full risk compensation for creditors. Every action in the free market has a reaction somewhere. If subprime lenders are systematically undercompensated in bankruptcy, they will charge higher rates or, if they already charge the legal maximum under state law, lend to fewer of the riskiest borrowers. As a result, some marginal but deserving borrowers will be denied vehicle loans in the first place. Congress evidently concluded that widespread access to credit is worth preserving, even if it means being ungenerous to sympathetic debtors.

* * * Because I read the statute to require full risk compensation, and because I would adopt a valuation method that has a realistic prospect of enforcing that directive, I respectfully dissent.

---

[15] For example, by ignoring the possibility that the creditor might recover some of its undersecurity as an unsecured claimant, that the plan might fail only after full repayment of secured claims, or that an oversecured creditor might recover some of its expenses under § 506(b).

[16] For example, by assuming a failure rate of 37%, and by ignoring all costs of default other than the three mentioned.

Notes and Questions

1. In a separate concurring opinion, JUSTICE THOMAS noted that the plurality and dissent agreed that "the proper interest rate must also reflect the risk of nonpayment." JUSTICE THOMAS, however, found "no such requirement" in the language of § 1325(a)(5)(B)(ii). The plurality responded to that argument somewhat dismissively: "[W]e think it too late in the day to endorse that approach now."

2. What are the four approaches to present value? How do they differ?

3. The plurality endorsed the "formula" approach, while the dissent supported the "contract rate" approach. Which seems more appropriate?

4. Does the plurality's approach require a hearing in every case? That such hearings are not economically feasible, as the dissent argued, seems beyond debate. How, then, is the formula approach to be determined in a particular case?

5. What is the appropriate rate of interest for a nonconsensual lien, such as a judgment lien?

6. Does *Till* apply in Chapter 11 cases? The Court seems to have been inconsistent on this point: on the one hand, the plurality said, in the text at footnote 10, that Congress probably intended the same approach to be used across the Code; on the other hand, footnote 14 states that the market rate might be appropriate in Chapter 11 cases because there is in fact a market.

Later decisions have grappled with this apparent inconsistency, but few cases have reached the circuit courts. If the decisions so far are any guide, however, *Till* may not be readily extended to Chapter 11 cases. In one of the decisions, *Drive Financial Services, L.P v. Jordan*, 521 F.3d 343 (5th Cir.2008), the Fifth Circuit pointed to the lack of a Supreme Court majority as a reason why courts still have latitude. Similarly, the Sixth Circuit in *Bank of Montreal v. Committee of Unsecured Creditors (In re American Homepatient, Inc.)*, 420 F.3d 559 (6th Cir.2005), pointed to conflicting authority and declined to blindly adopt *Till*'s endorsement of the formula approach for Chapter 13 cases in the Chapter 11 context. Rather, we opt to take our cue from Footnote 14 of the opinion * * * . This means that the market rate should be applied in Chapter 11 cases where there exists an efficient market. But where no efficient market exists for a Chapter 11 debtor, then the bankruptcy court should employ the formula approach endorsed by the *Till* plurality. This nuanced approach should obviate the concern of commentators who argue that, even in the Chapter 11 context, there are instances where no efficient market exists.

Id. at 568. Meanwhile, a substantial body of authority is building at the bankruptcy-court level.

4. RETENTION OF LIENS

A secured creditor who is forced to accept payment over time is entitled to retain its lien, §§ 1129(b)(2)(A)(i)(I) & 1325(a)(5)(B)(i)(I), and a plan should so provide. If it does not, an objection to confirmation, raised by the affected creditor, should result in addition of the missing provision. A plan confirmation order has preclusive effect once it becomes final, however; later attacks on the plan's provisions are barred by res judicata, even if the plan contains an illegal provision. Thus, a creditor must object to confirmation and, if not satisfied with the bankruptcy court's response to that objection, appeal the confirmation order. A creditor who is not paying attention and who fails to raise the matter before confirmation may find itself without a lien. See *Matter of Penrod*, 50 F.3d 459 (7th Cir.1995). (Can a lawyer knowingly draft such a plan—leaving out provisions that are required to be included, or including provisions that are patently inconsistent with the Code—without violating the rules of ethics?)

It works both ways, of course. A debtor displeased by something—such as the amount of a creditor's claim, perhaps—is similarly barred once the plan has been confirmed.

G. RETENTION OF COLLATERAL BY THE DEBTOR

Since the early days of the Code, Chapter 13 has been understood to provide a way for debtors to keep their homes and cars. (How effectively the Code serves those goals today is a question you should keep in mind as you study these materials.) One of the early questions was how Chapter 13 would operate with respect to a mortgage that had been accelerated, in accordance with its terms and with state law, before the date of filing. That was the fact pattern in *Di Pierro v. Taddeo (In re Taddeo)*, 685 F.2d 24 (2d Cir.1982). After Debtors defaulted on their residential mortgage, the mortgagee accelerated in accordance with state law and began foreclosure proceedings. Debtors filed Chapter 13 before the mortgagee could obtain a final judgment of foreclosure and sale. Debtors proposed to cure the default and to reinstate the mortgage under § 1322(b)(5). The mortgagee objected to the plan, arguing that once the mortgage was accelerated, the debtors had to pay the full amount in accordance with state law. The mortgagee sought relief from the stay in order to continue foreclosure. The court rejected the mortgagee's arguments and held that debtors can use Chapter 13 to "de-accelerate" residential mortgages:

> When Congress empowered Chapter 13 debtors to "cure defaults," we think Congress intended to allow mortgagors to "de-accelerate" their mortgage and reinstate its original payment schedule. We so hold for two reasons. First, we think that the power to cure must comprehend the power to "de-accelerate." This follows from the concept of "curing a default." A default is an event in the debtor-creditor relationship which triggers certain consequences—here, acceleration. Curing a default commonly means taking care of the triggering event and returning to pre-default conditions. The consequences are thus nullified. This is the concept of "cure" used throughout the Bankruptcy Code. * * *

> Policy considerations strongly support this reading of the statute. Conditioning a debtor's right to cure on its having filed a Chapter 13 petition prior to acceleration would prompt unseemly and wasteful races to the courthouse. Worse, these would be races in which mortgagees possess an unwarranted and likely insurmountable advantage: wage earners seldom will possess the sophistication in bankruptcy matters that financial institutions do, and often will not have retained counsel in time for counsel to do much good. In contrast, permitting debtors in the Taddeos' position to de-accelerate by payment of the arrearages will encourage parties to negotiate in good faith rather than having to fear that the mortgagee will tip the balance irrevocably by accelerating or that the debtor may prevent or at least long postpone this by filing a Chapter 13 petition.

> Secondly, we believe that the power to "cure any default" granted in § 1322(b)(3) and (b)(5) is not limited by the ban against "modifying" home mortgages in § 1322(b)(2)

because we do not read "curing defaults" under (b)(3) or "curing defaults and maintaining payments" under (b)(5) to be *modifications* of claims.

It is true that § 1322(b)(5)'s preface, "notwithstanding paragraph (2)," seems to treat the power to cure in (b)(5) as a subset of the power to modify set forth in (b)(2), but that superficial reading of the statute must fall in the light of legislative history and legislative purpose. The "notwithstanding" clause was added to § 1322(b)(5) to emphasize that defaults in mortgages could be cured notwithstanding § 1322(b)(2). But the clause was not necessary. The Senate protected home mortgages from *modification* in its last bill; it evinced no intent to protect these mortgages from *cure*.

Id. at 26–28. Under the authority of *Taddeo*, Chapter 13 is an attractive alternative for debtors faced with the loss of their residences. (We will see a case later in these materials that deals with the interpretation of § 1322(b)(2). Be alert to whether that case—*Nobelman*—requires a reassessment of *Taddeo*.)

Chapter 7 operates differently. If the value of collateral exceeds the total amount owed to creditors with liens against the collateral, the Chapter 7 trustee will sell the property, pay secured claims in full from the proceeds, give the debtor the value of any permissible exemption, and put the remaining equity in the pot to be divided among unsecured claims. If the value of collateral is entirely consumed by the claims of creditors with liens against the collateral, the trustee will abandon the property (recall § 554) and leave the creditors to fight it out among themselves under state law.

More difficult questions arise when a Chapter 7 debtor wants to keep the collateral. Necessarily, something has to be done about the lien. One possibility is redemption under § 722. Redemption requires a lump sum payment, however; installment payments are not an option. Although postpetition earnings are not property of the Chapter 7 estate, the debtor may not have accumulated sufficient funds to make such a payment. Another possibility is reaffirmation under § 524(c), which contemplates the signing of a new contract by the debtor and creditor. That requires the consent of both parties, and creditors are often unwilling to continue dealing with a borrower who has filed bankruptcy. It will also almost always require the debtor's agreement to repay the *entire* debt, since creditors are unlikely to accept anything less. (Reaffirmations are not limited to secured obligations. Thus, we will return to them in Chapter 7, Section E of this casebook.)

One other strategy, known as "ride through," was often used by Chapter 7 debtors to keep their cars. The debtor would not reaffirm the debt or redeem the collateral; rather, he or she would simply keep the car and continue making payments in accordance with the contract. The Courts of Appeal were deeply divided on the question whether this strategy was a permissible "fourth option" under what is now § 521(a)(2)(A), or whether that subsection gave debtors a choice among only reaffirmation, redemption or surrender of the collateral. The 2005 Amendments definitively answered the question by adding subsection (6) to § 521(a), as well as § 521(d) and, for good measure, § 362(h).

Read §§ 506(a)(2), 521 and 722, and answer these Problems.

Problems

1. Debtor owned a car that was financed by Bank and subject to Bank's secured claim. Debtor filed a Chapter 7 petition, still owing $12,000 on the car. According to information published by the National Automobile Dealers' Association, a car like Debtor's had the following values: a low retail value of $8,200; an average retail value of $9,100; a high retail value of $9,500; a wholesale value of $5,500; and a loan value of $5,000. Can Debtor redeem the car? If so, for how much?

2. A year before filing Chapter 7, Debtor bought a new plasma screen television set for her den, giving the dealer a purchase money security interest in the TV. The TV has a replacement value of $3,000, and Debtor still owes $1,900. She used all of her available exemptions on other items, but she really wants to keep the new TV. Can Debtor redeem the TV? If so, for how much?

3. Although Debtor filed a Chapter 7 petition on March 1, he needed to keep his car in order to get to work. He did not want to turn it over to Bank, which held an undersecured claim and was famous for demanding possession as soon as a trustee would abandon. Thus, on March 28, Debtor filed a statement indicating his intent to redeem the car. He was unable to scrape the necessary funds together, unfortunately, and Bank refused to discuss a reaffirmation. Instead, Bank repossessed the car on May 25. Was Bank entitled to do that?

4. Cases permitting the so-called "fourth option" usually involved oversecured claims and facts suggesting that repayment was fairly certain. Given that, would automobile lenders prefer ride-through or repossession? If a debtor wants to continue paying in accordance with the contract, why would an oversecured creditor not be satisfied? If the creditor were undersecured,

would it be willing to reaffirm the debt?   Why would a debtor not seek reaffirmation in either event?

H. STRIP DOWN OF LIENS

Section 722's requirement of a lump-sum payment may make redemption unavailable in many cases. Some debtors have access to funds, however, often through the generosity of family or friends. These debtors may want to keep property by paying off the amount of the secured claim and requiring the creditor to release the lien. If the property falls within § 722, there is no problem. But what if it does not? The following case, which deals with debtors' efforts to keep property not within § 722, rests on a widely-criticized decision rendered 22 years before.

BANK OF AMERICA, N. A. v. CAULKETT

United States Supreme Court, 2015.
135 S. Ct. 1995, 192 L. Ed. 2d 52.

JUSTICE THOMAS delivered the opinion of the Court. JUSTICE KENNEDY, JUSTICE BREYER, and JUSTICE SOTOMAYOR join this opinion, except as to the footnote.

Section 506(d) of the Bankruptcy Code allows a debtor to void a lien on his property "[t]o the extent that [the] lien secures a claim against the debtor that is not an allowed secured claim." § 506(d). These consolidated cases present the question whether a debtor in a Chapter 7 bankruptcy proceeding may void a junior mortgage under § 506(d) when the debt owed on a senior mortgage exceeds the present value of the property. We hold that a debtor may not, and we therefore reverse the judgments of the Court of Appeals.

I

The facts in these consolidated cases are largely the same. The debtors * * * each have two mortgage liens on their respective houses. Petitioner Bank of America (Bank) holds the junior mortgage lien—*i.e.*, the mortgage lien subordinate to the other mortgage lien—on each home. The amount owed on each debtor's senior mortgage lien is greater than each home's current market value. The Bank's junior mortgage liens are thus wholly underwater: because each home is worth less than the amount the debtor owes on the senior mortgage, the Bank would receive nothing if the properties were sold today.

In 2013, the debtors each filed for Chapter 7 bankruptcy. In their respective bankruptcy proceedings, they moved to "strip off"—or void—the junior mortgage liens under § 506(d) of the Bankruptcy Code. In each case, the Bankruptcy Court granted the motion, and both the District Court and the Court of Appeals for the Eleventh Circuit affirmed. The Eleventh Circuit explained that it was bound by Circuit precedent holding that § 506(d) allows debtors to void a wholly underwater mortgage lien.

We granted certiorari and now reverse the judgments of the Eleventh Circuit.

II

* * * [Section] 506(d) permits the debtors here to strip off the Bank's junior mortgages only if the Bank's "claim"—generally, its right to repayment from the debtors, §101(5)—is "not an allowed secured claim." Subject to some exceptions not relevant here, a claim filed by a creditor is deemed "allowed" under § 502 if no interested party objects or if, in the case of an objection, the Bankruptcy Court determines that the claim should be allowed under the Code. §§ 502(a)-(b). The parties agree that the Bank's claims meet this requirement. They disagree, however, over whether the Bank's claims are "secured" within the meaning of § 506(d).

The Code suggests that the Bank's claims are not secured. Section 506(a)(1) provides that "[a]n allowed claim of a creditor secured by a lien on property * * * is a *secured claim* to the extent of the value of such creditor's interest in * * * such property," and "an *unsecured claim* to the extent that the value of such creditor's interest * * * is less than the amount of such allowed claim." (Emphasis added.) In other words, if the value of a creditor's interest in the property is zero—as is the case here—his claim cannot be a "secured claim" within the meaning of § 506(a). And given that these identical words are later used in the same section of the same Act—§ 506(d)—one would think this "presents a classic case for application of the normal rule of statutory construction that identical words used in different parts of the same act are intended to have the same meaning." *Desert Palace, Inc.* v. *Costa*, 539 U. S. 90, 101 (2003) (internal quotation marks omitted). Under that straightforward reading of the statute, the debtors would be able to void the Bank's claims.

Unfortunately for the debtors, this Court has already adopted a construction of the term "secured claim" in § 506(d) that forecloses this textual analysis. See *Dewsnup* v. *Timm*, 502 U.S. 410 (1992). In *Dewsnup*, the Court confronted a situation in which a Chapter 7 debtor wanted to "strip down"—or reduce—a partially underwater lien under § 506(d) to the value of the collateral. Specifically, she sought, under § 506(d), to reduce her debt of approximately $120,000 to the value of the collateral securing her debt at that time ($39,000). Relying on the statutory definition of "allowed secured claim" in § 506(a), she contended that her creditors' claim was "secured only to the extent of the judicially determined value of the real property on which the lien [wa]s fixed." *Id*. at 414.

The Court rejected her argument. Rather than apply the statutory definition of "secured claim" in § 506(a), the Court reasoned that the term "secured" in § 506(d) contained an ambiguity because the self-interested parties before it disagreed over the term's meaning. Relying on policy considerations and its understanding of pre-Code practice, the Court concluded that if a claim "has been 'allowed' pursuant to § 502 of the Code and is secured by a lien with recourse to the underlying collateral, it does not come within the scope of § 506(d)." *Id*. at 415. It therefore held that the debtor could not strip down the creditors' lien to the value of the property under § 506(d) "because [the creditors'] claim [wa]s secured by a lien and ha[d] been fully allowed pursuant to § 502." *Id*. at 417. In other words, *Dewsnup* defined the term "secured claim" in § 506(d) to mean a claim supported by a security interest in property, regardless of whether the value of that property would be sufficient to cover the claim. Under this definition, § 506(d)'s function is reduced to "voiding a lien whenever a claim secured by the lien itself has not been allowed." *Id*. at 416.

Dewsnup's construction of "secured claim" resolves the question presented here. *Dewsnup* construed the term "secured claim" in § 506(d) to include any claim "secured by a lien and * * * fully allowed pursuant to § 502." *Id*. at 417. Because the Bank's claims here are both secured by liens and allowed under § 502, they cannot be voided under the definition given to the term "allowed secured claim" by *Dewsnup*.

III

The debtors do not ask us to overrule *Dewsnup*,[+] but instead request that we limit that decision to partially—as opposed to wholly—

[+] From its inception, *Dewsnup v. Timm*, 502 U.S. 410 (1992), has been the target of criticism. See, *e.g., id.*, at 420-436 (Scalia, J., dissenting); *In re Woolsey*, 696 F.3d 1266, 1273-1274, 1278 (10th Cir. 2012); *In re Dever*, 164 B.R. 132, 138,

underwater liens. We decline to adopt this distinction. The debtors offer several reasons why we should cabin *Dewsnup* in this manner, but none of them is compelling.

To start, the debtors rely on language in *Dewsnup* stating that the Court was not addressing "all possible fact situations," but was instead "allow[ing] other facts to await their legal resolution on another day." *Id.* at 416-417. But this disclaimer provides an insufficient foundation for the debtors' proposed distinction. *Dewsnup* considered several possible definitions of the term "secured claim" in § 506(d). The definition it settled on—that a claim is "secured" if it is "secured by a lien" and "has been fully allowed pursuant to § 502," *id.*, at 417— does not depend on whether a lien is partially or wholly underwater. Whatever the Court's hedging language meant, it does not provide a reason to limit *Dewsnup* in the manner the debtors propose.

The debtors next contend that the term "secured claim" in § 506(d) could be redefined as any claim that is backed by collateral with *some* value. Embracing this reading of § 506(d), however, would give the term "allowed secured claim" in § 506(d) a different meaning than its statutory definition in § 506(a). We refuse to adopt this artificial definition.

Nor do we think *Nobelman* v. *American Savings Bank*, 508 U.S. 324 (1993), supports the debtors' proposed distinction. *Nobelman* said nothing about the meaning of the term "secured claim" in § 506(d). Instead, it addressed the interaction between the meaning of the term "secured claim" in § 506(a) and an entirely separate provision, § 1322(b)(2). *Nobelman* offers no guidance on the question presented in these cases because the Court in *Dewsnup* already declined to apply the definition in § 506(a) to the phrase "secured claim" in § 506(d).

The debtors alternatively urge us to limit *Dewsnup*'s definition to the facts of that case because the historical and policy concerns that

---

145 (Bankr. C.D. Cal.1994); Carlson, *Bifurcation of Undersecured Claims in Bankruptcy*, 70 AM. BANKR. L.J. 1, 12-20 (1996); Ponoroff & Knippenberg, *The Immovable Object Versus the Irresistible Force: Rethinking the Relationship Between Secured Credit and Bankruptcy Policy*, 95 MICH. L. REV. 2234, 2305-2307 (1997); see also *Bank of America Nat. Trust & Sav. Ass'n v. 203 North LaSalle Street P'ship,* 526 U.S. 434, 463, and n.3 (1999) (THOMAS, J., concurring in judgment) (collecting cases and observing that "[t]he methodological confusion created by *Dewsnup* has enshrouded both the Courts of Appeals and * * * Bankruptcy Courts"). Despite this criticism, the debtors have repeatedly insisted that they are not asking us to overrule *Dewsnup.*

motivated the Court do not apply in the context of wholly underwater liens. Whether or not that proposition is true, it is an insufficient justification for giving the term "secured claim" in § 506(d) a different definition depending on the value of the collateral. We are generally reluctant to give the "same words a different meaning" when construing statutes, *Pasquantino* v. *U.S.*, 544 U. S. 349, 358 (2005) (internal quotation marks omitted), and we decline to do so here based on policy arguments.

Ultimately, embracing the debtors' distinction would not vindicate § 506(d)'s original meaning, and it would leave an odd statutory framework in its place. Under the debtors' approach, if a court valued the collateral at one dollar more than the amount of a senior lien, the debtor could not strip down a junior lien under *Dewsnup*, but if it valued the property at one dollar less, the debtor could strip off the entire junior lien. Given the constantly shifting value of real property, this reading could lead to arbitrary results. To be sure, the Code engages in line-drawing elsewhere, and sometimes a dollar's difference will have a significant impact on bankruptcy proceedings. See, *e.g.*, § 707(b)(2)(A)(i) (presumption of abuse of provisions of Chapter 7 triggered if debtor's projected disposable income over the next five years is $12,475). But these lines were set by Congress, not this Court. There is scant support for the view that § 506(d) applies differently depending on whether a lien was partially or wholly underwater. Even if *Dewsnup* were deemed not to reflect the correct meaning of § 506(d), the debtors' solution would not either.

* * *

The reasoning of *Dewsnup* dictates that a debtor in a Chapter 7 bankruptcy proceeding may not void a junior mortgage lien under § 506(d) when the debt owed on a senior mortgage lien exceeds the current value of the collateral. The debtors here have not asked us to overrule *Dewsnup*, and we decline to adopt the artificial distinction they propose instead. We therefore reverse the judgments of the Court of Appeals and remand the cases for further proceedings consistent with this opinion.

It is so ordered.

Notes and Questions

1. Why do you suppose three justices refused to support the Court's footnote?

2. Caulkett bought his home in June 2006 for $249,500, financing 100 percent of the purchase price with a first mortgage of $199,600 (80%) and a second mortgage of $49,900 (20%). At the time of his bankruptcy filing in 2013, his home was worth $98,000. The outstanding balances on his first and second mortgages were $183,264 and $47,855, respectively, for a total of $231,119. Thus, the balance on his first mortgage alone was almost twice the value of the home (187%), and the two mortgages had a combined loan-to-value ratio of 235.8%. (The facts presented by the consolidated case were quite similar.)

One must expect that Caulkett would be unwilling or unable to pay more than twice the value of his home in order to keep it. The house, therefore, will likely be sold by the first mortgagee, perhaps in a foreclosure proceeding. Under state law, Bank of America will receive nothing in such a sale and its lien will be terminated. Given that Bank of American had nothing to gain from its mortgage, why did it pursue this case all the way to the Supreme Court?

3. As the Court acknowledged, its opinion in *Dewsnup* has been heavily criticized. To begin with, its statutory methodology was deeply flawed because the Court read each of the three statutory words—"allowed," "secured" and "claim"—separately, ultimately interpreting the subsection to apply to any claim that is supported by some amount of collateral. That gave the phrase a different meaning in § 506(d) than it carries in § 506(a).

The Court bolstered this interpretation with policy arguments that do not hold up under scrutiny. First, the *Dewsnup* Court believed its interpretation was necessary in order to protect a creditor's right to any post-petition appreciation in the value of the property. The Court failed to realize, however, that Chapter 7 cases move rapidly enough that appreciation is seldom seen. Furthermore, any increase that does occur is fully captured by valuation as of the time the debtor pays off the creditor's interest, thereby satisfying the lien. Second, *Dewsnup* erroneously believed that the maxim "liens pass through bankruptcy unaffected" provides a correct statement of the law. In fact, numerous provisions of the Bankruptcy Code may affect liens, and they survive bankruptcy unaffected only if none of those bankruptcy powers come into play. Third, the *Dewsnup* Court misread its own precedents regarding the treatment of liens in bankruptcy. The Court read *Louisville Joint Stock Land Bank v. Radford*, 295 U.S. 555, 55 S.Ct. 854; 79 L.Ed. 1593 (1935), to suggest that stripping a lien down to its supporting value raises constitutional concerns. It failed to note a line of later cases to the contrary, at least one of which specifically asserted that a bankruptcy statute permitting the debtor to purchase encumbered property by paying its current value does not violate the mortgagee's constitutionally-protected rights: "Safeguards were provided to protect the rights of secured creditors, throughout the proceedings, to the extent of the value of the property. * * * There is no constitutional claim of the creditor to more than that." *Wright v. Union Central Life Ins. Co.*, 311 U.S. 273, 278, 61 S.Ct. 196, 199-200; 85 L.Ed. 184, 187 (1940). Finally,

Dewsnup failed to recognize that the drafters of the 1978 Bankruptcy Code adopted a statutory structure under which secured creditors are assured the value of their collateral, but not *in rem* rights to that specific piece of property.

Given these flaws in the controlling precedent, why was the Court unwilling to overrule *Dewsnup* in the course of deciding *Caulkett*? Could it not have done so, despite respondents' effort to distinguish *Dewsnup* rather than attack that case head-on? (Perhaps it helps here to know that respondents' amici did ask the Court to do just that.) And why did respondents not call for overruling *Dewsnup*?

Although *Dewsnup* dealt with § 506(a)—a provision applicable to cases under all chapters of the Code—later cases have agreed that the holding is limited to Chapter 7. See, e.g., *Dever v. Internal Revenue Serv. (In re Dever)*, 164 B.R. 132 (Bankr. C.D.Cal.1994). Whether *Caulkett* will be similarly limited is a question that awaits further case law development.

Specialized provisions in the reorganization chapters make it clear that those chapters, generally, follow the approach we saw at the beginning of this chapter of the text. That is, undersecured claims are to be bifurcated and the holders of those claims are entitled to receive an amount equal to the value of their collateral (plus interest, if payments under the plan are made over time), §§ 1129(b)(2)(A) & 1325(a)(5)(B), plus the appropriate dividend on the unsecured deficiency. Indeed, if the rule were otherwise, effective reorganizations would be unlikely.

Two provisions in Chapter 13 alter the general approach just described. The first of them is § 1322(b)(2), which applies only to home mortgages. It was the focus of the dispute in the next case, which was cited in *Caulkett*.

NOBELMAN v. AMERICAN SAVINGS BANK

United States Supreme Court, 1993.
508 U.S. 324, 113 S.Ct. 2106, 124 L.Ed.2d 228.

Justice Thomas delivered the opinion of the Court.

This case focuses on the interplay between two provisions of the Bankruptcy Code. The question is whether § 1322(b)(2) prohibits a Chapter 13 debtor from relying on § 506(a)[(1)] to reduce an undersecured homestead mortgage to the fair market value of the mortgaged residence. We conclude that it does and therefore affirm the judgment of the Court of Appeals.

I

In 1984, respondent American Savings Bank loaned petitioners Leonard and Harriet Nobelman $68,250 for the purchase of their principal residence, a condominium in Dallas, Texas. In exchange, petitioners executed an adjustable rate note payable to the bank and secured by a deed of trust on the residence. In 1990, after falling behind in their mortgage payments, petitioners sought relief under Chapter 13 of the Bankruptcy Code. The bank filed a proof of claim with the Bankruptcy Court for $71,335 in principal, interest, and fees owed on the note. Petitioners' modified Chapter 13 plan valued the residence at a mere $23,500—an uncontroverted valuation—and proposed to make payments pursuant to the mortgage contract only up to that amount (plus prepetition arrearages). Relying on § 506(a)[(1)] of the Bankruptcy Code, petitioners proposed to treat the remainder of the bank's claim as unsecured. Under the plan, unsecured creditors would receive nothing.

The bank and the Chapter 13 trustee, also a respondent here, objected to petitioners' plan. They argued that the proposed bifurcation of the bank's claim into a secured claim for $23,500 and an effectively worthless unsecured claim modified the bank's rights as a homestead mortgagee, in violation of § 1322(b)(2). The Bankruptcy Court agreed with respondents and denied confirmation of the plan. The District Court affirmed, as did the Court of Appeals. We granted certiorari to resolve a conflict among the Courts of Appeals.

II

Under Chapter 13 of the Bankruptcy Code, individual debtors may obtain adjustment of their indebtedness through a flexible repayment plan approved by a bankruptcy court. Section 1322 sets forth the elements of a confirmable Chapter 13 plan. The plan must provide, *inter alia*, for the submission of a portion of the debtor's future earnings and income to the control of a trustee and for supervised payments to creditors over a period not exceeding five years. See §§ 1322(a)(1) and 1322[(d)]. Section 1322(b)(2), the provision at issue here, allows modification of the rights of both secured and unsecured creditors, subject to special protection for creditors whose claims are secured only by a lien on the debtor's home. * * *

The parties agree that the "other than" exception in § 1322-(b)(2) proscribes modification of the rights of a homestead mortgagee. Petitioners maintain, however, that their Chapter 13 plan proposes no such modification. They argue that the protection of § 1322(b)(2) applies only to the extent the mortgagee holds a "secured claim" in the debtor's residence and that we must look first to § 506(a)[(1)] to determine the value of the mortgagee's "secured claim." Section 506(a)[(1)] provides that an allowed claim secured by a lien on the debtor's property "is a secured claim to the extent of the value of [the] property"; to the extent the claim exceeds the value of the property, it "is an unsecured claim." Petitioners contend that the valuation provided for in § 506(a)[(1)] operates automatically to adjust downward the amount of a lender's undersecured home mortgage before any disposition proposed in the debtor's Chapter 13 plan. Under this view, the bank is the holder of a "secured claim" only in the amount of $23,500 — the value of the collateral property. Because the plan proposes to make $23,500 worth of payments pursuant to the monthly payment terms of the mortgage contract, petitioners argue, the plan effects no alteration of the bank's rights as the holder of that claim. Section 1322(b)(2), they assert, allows unconditional modification of the bank's leftover "unsecured claim."

This interpretation fails to take adequate account of § 1322-(b)(2)'s focus on "rights." That provision does not state that a plan may modify "claims" or that the plan may not modify "a claim secured only by" a home mortgage. Rather, it focuses on the modification of the *"rights of holders"* of such claims. By virtue of its mortgage contract with petitioners, the bank is indisputably the holder of a claim secured by a lien on petitioners' home. Petitioners were correct in looking to § 506(a)[(1)] for a judicial valuation of the collateral to determine the status of the bank's secured claim. It was permissible for petitioners to seek a valuation in proposing their Chapter 13 plan, since § 506(a) states that "[s]uch value shall be determined * * * in conjunction with any hearing * * * on a plan affecting such creditor's interest." But even if we accept petitioners' valuation, the bank is still the "holder" of a "secured claim," because petitioners' home retains $23,500 of value as collateral. The portion of the bank's claim that exceeds $23,500 is an "unsecured claim componen[t]" under § 506(a), *United States v. Ron Pair Enterprises, Inc.*, 489 U.S. 235, 239 n.3 (1989) (internal quotation marks omitted); however, that determination does not necessarily mean that the "rights" the bank enjoys as a mortgagee, which are protected by § 1322(b)(2), are limited by the valuation of its secured claim.

The term "rights" is nowhere defined in the Bankruptcy Code. In the absence of a controlling federal rule, we generally assume that Congress has "left the determination of property rights in the assets of a bankrupt's estate to state law," since such "[p]roperty interests are created and defined by state law." *Butner v. United States*, 440 U.S. 48, 54–55 (1979). Moreover, we have specifically recognized that "[t]he justifications for application of state law are not limited to ownership interests," but "apply with equal force to security interests, including the interest of a mortgagee." *Id.* at 55. The bank's "rights," therefore, are reflected in the relevant mortgage instruments, which are enforceable under Texas law. They include the right to repayment of the principal in monthly installments over a fixed term at specified adjustable rates of interest, the right to retain the lien until the debt is paid off, the right to accelerate the loan upon default and to proceed against petitioners' residence by foreclosure and public sale, and the right to bring an action to recover any deficiency remaining after foreclosure. These are the rights that were "bargained for by the mortgagor and the mortgagee," *Dewsnup v. Timm*, 112 S.Ct. 773, 778 (1992), and are rights protected from modification by § 1322(b)(2).

This is not to say, of course, that the contractual rights of a home mortgage lender are unaffected by the mortgagor's Chapter 13 bankruptcy. The lender's power to enforce its rights—and, in particular, its right to foreclose on the property in the event of default—is checked by the Bankruptcy Code's automatic stay provision. § 362. In addition, § 1322(b)(5) permits the debtor to cure prepetition defaults on a home mortgage by paying off arrearages over the life of the plan "notwithstanding" the exception in § 1322(b)(2). These statutory limitations on the lender's rights, however, are independent of the debtor's plan or otherwise outside § 1322(b)(2)'s prohibition.

Petitioners urge us to apply the so-called "rule of the last antecedent," which has been relied upon by some Courts of Appeals to interpret § 1322(b)(2) the way petitioners favor. According to this argument, the operative clause "other than a claim secured only by a security interest in * * * the debtor's principal residence" must be read to refer to and modify its immediate antecedent, "secured claims." Thus, § 1322(b)(2)'s protection would then apply only to that subset of allowed "secured claims," determined by application of § 506(a)[(1)], that are secured by a lien on the debtor's home—including, with respect to the mortgage involved here, the bank's secured claim for $23,500. We acknowledge that this reading of the clause is quite sensible as a matter of grammar. But it is not compelled. Congress chose to use the phrase "claim secured * * * by" in § 1322(b)(2)'s exception, rather than repeating the term of art "secured claim." The unqualified word "claim" is broadly defined under the Code to encompass any "right to payment, whether * * * secure[d] or unsecured" or any "right to an equitable remedy for breach of performance if such breach gives rise to a right to payment, whether * * * secure[d] or unsecured." § 101(5). It is also plausible, therefore, to read "a claim secured only by a [homestead lien]" as referring to the lienholder's entire claim, including both the secured and the unsecured components of the claim. Indeed, § 506(a)[(1)] itself uses the phrase "claim * * * secured by a lien" to encompass both portions of an undersecured claim.

This latter interpretation is the more reasonable one, since we cannot discern how § 1322(b)(2) could be administered under petitioners' interpretation. Petitioners propose to reduce the outstanding mortgage principal to the fair market value of the collateral, and, at the same time, they insist that they can do so without modifying the bank's rights "as to interest rates, payment amounts, and [other] contract terms." That appears to be impossible. The bank's contractual rights are contained in a unitary note that applies at once to the bank's overall claim, including both the secured and unsecured components. Petitioners cannot modify the payment and interest terms for the unsecured component, as they propose to do, without also modifying the terms of the secured component. Thus, to preserve the interest rate and the amount of each monthly payment specified in the note after having reduced the principal to $23,500, the plan would also have to reduce the term of the note dramatically. That would be a significant modification of a contractual right. Furthermore, the bank holds an adjustable rate mortgage, and the principal and interest payments on the loan must be recalculated with each adjustment in the interest rate. There is nothing in the mortgage contract or the Code that suggests any basis for recalculating the amortization schedule—whether by reference to the face value of the remaining principal or by reference to the unamortized value of the collateral. This conundrum alone indicates that § 1322(b)(2) cannot operate in combination with § 506(a)[(1)] in the manner theorized by petitioners.

In other words, to give effect to § 506(a)[(1)]'s valuation and bifurcation of secured claims through a Chapter 13 plan in the manner petitioners propose would require a modification of the rights of the holder of the security interest. Section 1322(b)(2) prohibits such a modification where, as here, the lender's claim is secured only by a lien on the debtor's principal residence.

The judgment of the Court of Appeals is therefore affirmed.

It is so ordered.

JUSTICE STEVENS, concurring.

At first blush it seems somewhat strange that the Bankruptcy Code should provide less protection to an individual's interest in retaining possession of his or her home than of other assets. The anomaly is, however, explained by the legislative history indicating that favorable treatment of residential mortgagees was intended to encourage the flow of capital into the home lending market. It therefore seems quite clear that the Court's literal reading of the text of the statute is faithful to the intent of Congress. Accordingly, I join its opinion and judgment.

Notes and Questions

1. Subsection 1123(b)(5), which was added by the 1994 Amendments, provides protections for the residential mortgagee in Chapter 11 that parallel § 1322(b)(2). This has effectively extended *Nobelman* to individual Chapter 11 cases.

2. Does § 1322(b)(2), as interpreted by *Nobelman*, prohibit bifurcation and strip down when the creditor holds collateral in addition to the debtor's home? See *Hammond v. Commonwealth Mortgage Corp. of America (In re Hammond)*, 27 F.3d 52 (3d Cir. 1994). What if the property is a multi-unit dwelling, with debtor living in one unit and renting out the others? Compare *Lomas Mortgage, Inc. v. Louis*, 82 F.3d 1 (1st Cir.1996), with *Brunson v. Wendover Funding, Inc. (In re Brunson)*, 201 B.R. 351 (Bankr. W.D.N.Y.1996).

3. If the debtor is unable to confirm a plan that pays the full amount of the debt and, instead, gives the undersecured creditor the keys to the house, is the deficiency discharged?

4. Debtor owed Bank $22,000 on a note secured by a mobile home, in which Debtor lived, worth $15,000. The note is due in three years. Debtor filed a Chapter 13 petition this year and proposed a five-year plan. Under the plan, Bank will be paid $15,000 in 60 monthly installments, with appropriate interest. The balance of Bank's obligation is treated as unsecured. Bank objected to confirmation of the plan, citing § 1322(b)(2). Debtor countered by pointing to § 1322(c)(2), which was added to the Code after *Nobelman* was decided. Does § 1322(c)(2) apply in this case and, if so, does it affect *Nobelman*? See *Witt v. United Companies Lending Corp. (In re Witt)*, 113 F.3d 508 (4th Cir.1997).

5. Recall our discussion of *Taddeo* in Section G of this chapter. Does anything in *Nobelman* affect *Taddeo*? Is that court's distinction between modification and cure still persuasive?

6. Now that you have read *Nobelman* and *Caulkett*, consider a case in which a Chapter 13 debtor owns a house that is encumbered by a partially secured first mortgage and an underwater second. Can the debtor accomplish in Chapter 13 what a debtor in Chapter 7 cannot—namely, complete avoidance of the second mortgage? Courts were somewhat divided on this question before the Supreme Court's decision in *Caulkett*. See, e.g., *First Mariner Bank v. Johnson*, 411 B.R. 221 (D. Md.2009), *aff'd mem. sub nom. First Mariner Bank v. Johnson (In re Johnson)*, 407 Fed.Appx. 713 (4th Cir.2011) (holding that *Nobelman*'s result depended on the existence of some value to support the lien, and permitting stripoff). Does *Caulkett* affect this analysis?

In addition to § 1322(b)(2), another provision of Chapter 13 also alters the usual approach to undersecured claims. This is the unnumbered paragraph that was added to the Code in 2005 and codified at the end of § 1325(a). Known as the "hanging paragraph," it states that § 506(a) "shall not apply" to a purchase money secured claim in a motor vehicle acquired for personal use within 910 days (roughly 2-½ years) before bankruptcy, or to a debt, secured by any other thing of value, incurred within the year preceding bankruptcy. The provision is clearly intended to prohibit bifurcation. The debtor must pay the full amount of an undersecured "910 claim," in order to keep the collateral and cram down the plan (although it is not much of a "cram down" when the creditor receives 100% of the debt).

The hanging paragraph's meaning is not so clear, however, when the debtor chooses to give overencumbered collateral back to the creditor, as § 1325(a)(5)(C) permits. The question is whether surrender of the vehicle constitutes full satisfaction, leaving the creditor without an unsecured claim for the deficiency. Debtors argued that if the claim is treated as fully secured when the car is retained, then it should be treated as fully satisfied when the car is surrendered. The hanging paragraph unambiguously precludes application of § 506 and, by precluding bifurcation, creates the fiction that a "910 vehicle" is worth the same amount as the claim asserted by the creditor—namely, the amount of the debt.

The first cases to deal with this question generally agreed with the debtors. Then the Seventh Circuit decided *Wright*—the first circuit-level opinion on this issue. *Wright* adopted the then-minority view, and turned the tide of the decisions.

IN RE WRIGHT

United States Court of Appeals, Seventh Circuit, 2007.
492 F.3d 829.

EASTERBROOK, Chief Judge.

Bankruptcy judges across the nation have divided over the effect of the unnumbered hanging paragraph that the Bankruptcy Abuse Prevention and Consumer Protection Act of 2005 added to § 1325(a) of the Bankruptcy Code. Section 1325, part of Chapter 13, specifies the circumstances under which a consumer's plan of repayment can be confirmed. The hanging paragraph says that, for the purpose of a Chapter 13 plan, § 506 of the Code does not apply to certain secured loans.

Section 506(a) divides loans into secured and unsecured portions; the unsecured portion is the amount by which the debt exceeds the current value of the collateral. In a Chapter 13 bankruptcy, consumers may retain the collateral (despite contractual provisions entitling creditors to repossess) by making monthly payments that the judge deems equal to the market value of the asset, with a rate of interest that the judge will set (rather than the contractual rate). See *Associates Commercial Corp. v. Rash*, 520 U.S. 953 (1997); *Till v. SCS Credit Corp.*, 541 U.S. 465 (2004). This procedure is known as a "cramdown"—the court crams down the creditor's throat the substitution of money for the collateral, a situation that creditors usually oppose because the court may underestimate the collateral's market value and the appropriate interest rate, and the debtor may fail to make all promised payments, so that the payment stream falls short of the collateral's full value. (The effect is asymmetric: if a judge overestimates the collateral's value or the interest rate, the debtor will surrender the asset and the creditor will realize no more than the market price. When the judge errs in the debtor's favor, however, the debtor keeps the asset and pays at the reduced rate. Creditors systematically lose from this asymmetry—and in the long run solvent borrowers must pay extra to make up for creditors' anticipated loss in bankruptcy.)

The question we must decide is what happens when, as a result of the hanging paragraph, § 506 vanishes from the picture. The majority view among bankruptcy judges is that, with § 506(a) gone, creditors cannot divide their loans into secured and unsecured components. Because § 1325(a)(5)(C) allows a debtor to surrender the collateral to the lender, it follows (on this view) that surrender fully satisfies the borrower's obligations. If this is so, then many secured loans have been rendered nonrecourse, no matter what the contract provides. The minority view is that Article 9 of the Uniform Commercial Code plus the law of contracts entitle the creditor to an unsecured deficiency judgment after surrender of the collateral, unless the contract itself provides that the loan is without recourse against the borrower. That unsecured balance must be treated the same as other unsecured debts under the Chapter 13 plan.

* * * [D]ebtors in this proceeding owe more on their purchase-money automobile loan than the car is worth. Because the purchase occurred within 910 days of the bankruptcy's commencement, the hanging paragraph in § 1325(a)(5) applies. * * * Debtors proposed a plan that would surrender the car to the creditor and pay nothing on account of the difference between the loan's balance and the collateral's market value. After taking the minority position on the effect of bypassing § 506, the bankruptcy judge declined to approve the Chapter 13 plan, because debtors did not propose to pay any portion of the shortfall.

[The bankruptcy judge certified the case for direct appeal to the circuit court, under 28 U.S.C. § 158(d)(2)(A).] A motions panel of this court accepted the appeal because the issue not only has divided the bankruptcy courts but also arises in a large fraction of all consumer bankruptcy proceedings. A clear answer is needed—yet this issue appears to be "stuck" in the bankruptcy courts. No court of appeals has addressed the subject, and few district judges have done so. Lower litigation costs for thousands of debtors and creditors may be achieved by expediting appellate consideration of this case.

Like the bankruptcy court, we think that, by knocking out § 506, the hanging paragraph leaves the parties to their contractual entitlements. True enough, § 506(a) divides claims into secured and unsecured components. * * * Yet it is a mistake to assume, as the majority of bankruptcy courts have done, that § 506 is the *only* source of authority for a deficiency judgment when the collateral is insufficient. The Supreme Court held in *Butner v. United States*, 440 U.S. 48 (1979), that state law determines rights and obligations when the Code does not supply a federal rule.

The contract between the Wrights and their lender is explicit: If the debt is not paid, the collateral may be seized and sold. Creditor "must account to Buyer for any surplus. Buyer shall be liable for any deficiency." In other words, the contract creates an ordinary secured loan with recourse against the borrower. Just in case there were doubt, the contract provides that the parties enjoy all of their rights under the Uniform Commercial Code. Section 9-615(d)(2) of the UCC provides that the obligor must satisfy any deficiency if the collateral's value is insufficient to cover the amount due.

If the Wrights had surrendered their car the day before filing for bankruptcy, the creditor would have been entitled to treat any shortfall in the collateral's value as an unsecured debt. It is hard to see why the result should be different if the debtors surrender the collateral the day after filing for bankruptcy when, given the hanging paragraph, no operative section of the Bankruptcy Code contains any contrary rule. Section 306(b) of the 2005 Act, which enacted the hanging paragraph, is captioned "Restoring the Foundation for Secured Credit." This implies replacing a contract-defeating provision such as § 506 (which allows judges rather than the market to value the collateral and set an interest rate, and may prevent creditors from repossessing) with the agreement freely negotiated between debtor and creditor. Debtors do not offer any argument that "the Foundation for Secured Credit" could be "restored" by making all purchase-money secured loans non-recourse; they do not argue that nonrecourse lending is common in consumer transactions, and it is hard to imagine that Congress took such an indirect means of making nonrecourse lending *compulsory*.

Appearing as *amicus curiae*, the National Association of Consumer Bankruptcy Attorneys makes the bold argument that loans covered by the hanging paragraph cannot be treated as secured in any respect. Only § 506 provides for an "allowed secured claim," *amicus* insists, so the entire debt must be unsecured. This also would imply that a lender is not entitled to any postpetition interest. *Amicus* recognizes that § 502 rather than § 506 determines whether a claim should be "allowed" but insists that only § 506 permits an "allowed" claim to be a "secured" one.

This line of argument makes the same basic mistake as the debtors' position: it supposes that contracts and state law are irrelevant unless specifically implemented by the Bankruptcy Code. *Butner* holds that the presumption runs the other way: rights under state law count in bankruptcy unless the Code says otherwise. Creditors don't need § 506 to create, allow, or recognize security interests, which rest on contracts (and the UCC) rather than federal law. Section 502 tells bankruptcy courts to allow claims that stem from contractual debts; nothing in § 502 disfavors or curtails secured claims. Limitations, if any, depend on § 506, which the hanging paragraph makes inapplicable to purchase-money interests in personal motor vehicles granted during the 910 days preceding bankruptcy (and in other assets during the year before bankruptcy).

Both the debtors and the *amicus curiae* observe that many decisions, of which *United States v. Ron Pair Enterprises, Inc.*, 489 U.S. 235, 238-39 (1989), is a good example, state that § 506 governs the treatment of secured claims in bankruptcy. No one doubts this, but the question at hand is what happens when § 506 does not apply. The fallback under *Butner* is the parties' contract (to the extent the deal is enforceable under state law), rather than nonrecourse secured debt (the Wrights' position) or no security interest (the *amicus curiae*'s position). And there is no debate about how the parties' contract works: the secured lender is entitled to an (unsecured) deficiency judgment for the difference between the value of the collateral and the balance on the loan.

By surrendering the car, debtors gave their creditor the full market value of the collateral. Any shortfall must be treated as an unsecured debt. It need not be paid in full, any more than the Wrights' other unsecured debts, but it can't be written off *in toto* while other unsecured creditors are paid some fraction of their entitlements.

Affirmed.

Notes and Questions

1. As indicated in the text preceding *Wright*, a majority of the early cases held that the hanging paragraph precludes a creditor from asserting a deficiency claim when the debtor surrenders 910 collateral. Every circuit-level opinion to date, however, has agreed with *Wright*. *Tidewater Fin. Co. v. Kenney*, 531 F.3d 312 (4th Cir.2008); *DaimlerChrysler Fin. Serv. Americas LLC v. Ballard (In re Ballard)*, 526 F.3d 634 (10th Cir.2008); *AmeriCredit Fin. Servs., Inc. v. Long (In re Long)*, 519 F.3d 288 (6th Cir.2008); *Americredit Fin. Servs., Inc. v. Moore*, 517 F.3d 987 (8th Cir.2008); *Capital One Auto Fin. v. Osborn*, 515 F.3d 817 (8th Cir.2008).

Courts on both sides of the issue have found the statute "plain." Which side has the better argument under the language of the Code?

2. Judge Easterbrook asserted that no provision in the Bankruptcy Code changes the state law rules permitting an undersecured creditor to assert a deficiency claim, but he did not discuss § 1325(a)(5)—a section that has played a central role in other courts' analysis. Under § 1325(a)(5), a debtor has two alternatives for dealing with a nonconsenting secured creditor: the debtor may retain the collateral in accordance with § 1325(a)(5)(B); or the debtor may surrender the collateral to the creditor under § 1325(a)(5)(C). All courts agree that the hanging paragraph requires a debtor choosing to retain 910 collateral under § 1325(a)(5)(B) to pay the full amount of the debt. In other words, the hanging paragraph makes the creditor fully secured for purposes of § 1325(a)(5)(B). Some courts have concluded that the hanging paragraph prevents § 506(a)'s application to the entirety of § 1325(a)(5), however, making the creditor similarly fully secured when the debtor surrenders the collateral under § 1325(a)(5)(C). See, e.g., *In re Ezell*, 338 B.R. 330, 340 (Bankr. E.D. Tenn.2006) (concluding that "[i]t only stands to reason that the same analysis" applies to surrender under § 1325(a)(5)(C) as to retention under § 1325(a)(5)(B)); *Daimler Chrysler Fin. Serv. Americas LLC v. Quick (In re Quick)*, 371 B.R. 459, 463 (B.A.P. 10th Cir.2007), *rev'd & remanded sub nom. DaimlerChrysler Fin. Serv. Americas LLC v. Ballard (In re Ballard)*, 526 F.3d 634 (10th Cir.2008) ("Congress easily could have specified that the hanging paragraph applies only to § 1325(a)(5)(B), but it did not.").

The court in *Capital One Auto Finance v. Osborn*, 515 F.3d 817 (8th Cir.2008), did discuss the role of § 1325(a)(5) and found no such symmetry:

"[N]othing in § 1325(a)(5) says that [the] 'allowed secured claim' is satisfied by the debtor choosing the surrender option in subparagraph (C)." *In re Hoffman*, 359 B.R. 163, 166 (Bankr. E.D. Mich.2006). Unlike the retention option in § 1325(a)(5)(B), the surrender option in § 1325(a)(5)(C) does not speak to satisfaction of a claim. Section 1325(a)(5)(C) states that if the debtor chooses to surrender the vehicle, the plan should be confirmed—even if the creditor does not prefer the surrender option. "Unambiguously, it means nothing more than this." *Hoffman*, 359 B.R. at 166.

The [debtors] invoke the core rationale of the majority position: "If a 910-claim is fully secured under § 1325(a)(5)(B)(ii) and bifurcation is prohibited, as the majority of courts have thus far held, there is no logic in saying that a 910-claim may still be bifurcated if the debtor chooses instead to surrender the collateral pursuant to Section 1325(a)(5)(C)." *See AmeriCredit Fin. Servs., Inc. v. Moore*, 363 B.R. 91, 94 (Bankr. W.D. Ark.2006). This assumes that the bankruptcy code prohibits bifurcation. This is not true; the hanging paragraph simply removes the bankruptcy code's method of bifurcation. The hanging paragraph has no effect on state-law rights. Moreover, retention and surrender are treated differently in the bankruptcy code. *Compare* §§ 1325(a)(5)(B)(ii) (requiring full payment of the secured claim when the debtor retains the collateral), *with* 1325(a)(5)(C) (not discussing payment requirements when the debtor surrenders the collateral).

Id. at 821-22. Which interpretation of § 1325(a) is more persuasive?

3. *Wright*, as well as other opinions in accord, relied on *Butner* for the proposition that state law applies in the absence of a federal rule to the contrary. *Butner*, however, expressly recognized that state law must give way when "some federal interest requires a different result." *Butner v. United States*, 440 U.S. 48, 55 (1979). Is there such a federal interest here?

4. *Wright* read the hanging paragraph to *preclude* bifurcation when the debtor keeps the car, thus mandating payment of the debt in full, and *not* to preclude bifurcation when the debtor surrenders the car, thus giving the creditor a claim for the deficiency. Is such a "win-win" for creditors with 910 claims sensible?

5. The hanging paragraph applies only to "a purchase money security interest." Although the concept is relevant here and elsewhere (specifically, §§ 547(c)(3) and 522(f)(1)(B), both of which we will study later in the course), the Code includes no definition. Most bankruptcy courts look to § 9-103(a)(2) of the Uniform Commercial Code, which defines a "purchase money obligation" as one "incurred as all or part of the price of the collateral," despite the warning in Official Comment 8 to § 9-103 that state law does not control this federal issue.

A recurring question is whether purchase money status is lost, thereby rendering the hanging paragraph inapplicable, when the debtor refinances an obligation or trades in an overencumbered automobile as part of the purchase price of a new car, rolling the old balance into the principal of the new loan. Courts have differed on the outcome in the latter fact pattern, although the circuit-level decisions overwhelmingly hold that a loan does not lose its purchase money status by the financing of this "negative equity." For a case going the other way, see *Americredit Financial Servs. v. Penrod*, 611 F.3d 1158 (9th Cir.2010), and 636 F.3d 1175, 1176 (9th Cir. 2011) (dissent from denial of rehearing *en banc*, lamenting that the Court found itself "on the wrong end of an eight to one circuit split.").

Chapter 5

AVOIDING POWERS

A. INTRODUCTION

Transfers of the debtor's property that occur pre- or postpetition may make the goals of bankruptcy—equality of distribution for creditors and a fresh start for the debtor—more difficult to achieve. These transfers may take out of the estate property that should be available to all the creditors or to the debtor. In order to reverse these effects, the Code gives the trustee (and, in limited circumstances, the debtor) the power to *avoid* or undo certain transfers.

"Transfer" is defined in § 101(54) to include "each mode * * * of disposing of or parting with * * * property" or "an interest in property," as well as "the creation of a lien." When an outright disposition (such as a gift or sale) is avoided, the property is recovered from the transferee and, under § 541(a)(3), becomes property of the bankruptcy estate. When a lien is avoided, the property is freed from encumbrance. The secured creditor whose lien is avoided becomes an unsecured creditor. Because involuntary as well as voluntary transfers are included, avoiding powers apply equally to judicial liens and to security interests.

Existence of the avoiding powers serves to regulate the conduct of parties operating in the shadow of bankruptcy. Because certain transfers can be undone in bankruptcy, the threat of a bankruptcy filing can be a powerful negotiating tool.

Although benefit to the debtor is occasionally the purpose of avoidance, the benefit most often goes to creditors because property is pulled back into the estate and into the pot of assets divided among holders of unsecured claims. For that reason, the trustee is often referred to as the representative of unsecured creditors.

This chapter deals with a number of avoiding powers, including fraudulent conveyances, preferences and the "strong-arm" power.

B. FRAUDULENT CONVEYANCES

1. INTRODUCTION

To avoid having property seized by creditors, a debtor might transfer it to a friend or relative in exchange for little or no consideration. Or the debtor might transfer title to the property, with the understanding that the debtor will continue to have the use and benefit of the property. Such attempts to insulate property from creditors' claims are generally rendered ineffective by fraudulent conveyances law.

Fraudulent conveyances law, which draws upon state law as well as the Bankruptcy Code, covers two types of transfers—those intended to delay or defraud creditors and those made for inadequate consideration by an insolvent transferor. The clearest example of the former is my decision to hide my personal assets, in order to keep my creditors from getting them. The second branch of fraudulent conveyances law, which prevents an insolvent person from making gifts, is summed up in the maxim that a debtor must be "just before generous." Transfers covered by the second branch of fraudulent conveyances law are "constructively fraudulent."

Modern fraudulent conveyances law is rooted in the Statute of 13 Elizabeth, enacted in 1570, which provided for the avoidance of fraudulent transfers made by debtors with actual intent to hinder, delay or defraud creditors. *Twyne's Case*, 3 Coke 80b, 76 Eng. Rep. 809 (Star Chamber 1601), decided under the Statute, is the basis of contemporary fraudulent dispositions law. The debtor in *Twyne's Case*, Pierce, was indebted to Twyne for four hundred pounds and to C for two hundred pounds. C brought an action against Pierce to recover the debt. While the action was pending, Pierce secretly conveyed all of his property, worth three hundred pounds, to Twyne by a deed of gift. Despite the "gift," Pierce kept some sheep in his possession and treated them as his own. After C obtained a judgment against Pierce, the sheriff sought to levy on the sheep; he was prevented from doing so by friends of Pierce, who asserted that the sheep actually belonged to Twyne. C sued Twyne to set aside the conveyance.

The court held that the transfer to Twyne was in fact fraudulent and enumerated "badges of fraud" to support its holding. These "badges of fraud"—circumstances indicative of an intent to defraud— were used to meet the Statute's requirement of proof of "intent to delay, hinder or defraud." *Twyne's Case* involved the following badges of fraud: (1) the conveyance consisted of all of Pierce's property, (2) the property remained in Pierce's possession and he treated it as his own, (3) the conveyance was made while a suit was pending against Pierce, (4) the transaction was secret, and (5) Twyne held the property in trust for Pierce. Contemporary courts use similar indicia of an intent to defraud creditors.

Although the Statute of Elizabeth was recognized in many American jurisdictions as part of the common law inherited from England, most states have enacted their own statutory provisions. Many states adopted the Uniform Fraudulent Conveyance Act (UFCA), adopted the Uniform Fraudulent Transfer Act (UFTA), or based their fraudulent conveyance statutes, at least in part, on one of the uniform laws. The UFCA was officially withdrawn in 1984 by the National Conference of Commissioners on Uniform State Laws in favor of the UFTA. Like the Statute of Elizabeth, both model statutes condemn transfers that are *actually* fraudulent because the debtor had an actual, subjective intent to hinder, defraud or delay creditors. See UFCA § 7; UFTA § 4(a)(1). In addition, the uniform statutes deem *constructively* fraudulent certain transfers that prejudice creditors because of circumstances existing at the time of the transfer, regardless of the debtor's intent.

The Bankruptcy Code contains its own fraudulent conveyance provision, § 548, after which the UFTA was patterned. Section 548 authorizes the trustee to avoid any transfer of the debtor's property that was fraudulently made or any obligation of the debtor that was fraudulently incurred. The two branches of fraudulent conveyances law are found in subsections (a)(1)(A) and (a)(1)(B). For a transfer to be deemed actually "fraudulent," § 548(a)(1)(A) requires the trustee to show that (1) an interest in the debtor's property was transferred, (2) the transfer was made with actual intent to hinder, delay or defraud a creditor, and (3) the transfer occurred within two years before the bankruptcy petition was filed. Obviously, a debtor will rarely admit fraudulent intent, so meeting the requirements of subsection (a)(1)(A) is no simple task.

The trustee may avoid a transfer as constructively fraudulent under § 548(a)(1)(B) if the trustee can show that (1) an interest in the debtor's property was transferred, (2) the transfer occurred within two years before the bankruptcy petition was filed, (3) the debtor received less than reasonably equivalent value in exchange for the transfer, and (4) the debtor was insolvent at the time of the transfer or became insolvent as a result of it. Because proving the elements of subsection (a)(1)(B) is easier than proving those of (a)(1)(A), (a)(1)(B) is more often asserted. The trustee usually invokes subsection (a)(1)(A) only if insolvency, as required by subsection (a)(1)(B), cannot be established.

The Bankruptcy Code also enables the trustee to use *state* fraudulent conveyances law. This alternative, found in § 544(b), allows the trustee to avoid any transfer that an unsecured creditor of the debtor could avoid under applicable nonbankruptcy law. This route is particularly useful when the targeted transfer occurred more than two years before the bankruptcy petition was filed, because state statutes of limitation tend to be longer than two years. In order for the trustee to use § 544(b), however, an unsecured creditor with power to avoid the transfer *actually must exist*. The trustee, in essence, is subrogated to the actual creditor's nonbankruptcy avoiding power.

Section 544(b) follows the rule in *Moore v. Bay*, 284 U.S. 4, 52 S.Ct. 3, 76 L.Ed. 133 (1931), that a transfer is entirely avoidable by a trustee regardless of the amount of the creditor's claim relied upon by the trustee. The effect of this rule is illustrated by the following hypothetical: Debtor made a $500 gift to Friend when Debtor was insolvent. Trustee cannot avoid it under § 548 because the gift was made more than a year before Debtor filed bankruptcy. Creditor has a $25 unsecured claim against Debtor that would allow Creditor to avoid the gift, under state law, to the extent necessary to repay Creditor—$25. Trustee is subrogated to Creditor's avoiding power under § 544(b) and, under the rule in *Moore v. Bay*, may avoid the entire $500 transfer. Trustee is not limited to the recovery of $25; it is irrelevant that Creditor's claim, asserted by Trustee, is considerably smaller than the amount of the transfer. In addition, Creditor shares equally with the other unsecured creditors in bankruptcy, despite the fact that Creditor's state law avoiding power was used by Trustee to avoid the transfer in the first place.

2. CONSTRUCTIVELY FRAUDULENT DISPOSITIONS

Problems

Assume the following transactions take place within two years of the date the debtor files a bankruptcy petition. Determine whether the transactions are constructively fraudulent and avoidable under § 548(a)(1)(B):

1. Aunt Nellie transferred her home, worth approximately $150,000, to her nephew, Joe, in exchange for Joe's promise to care for Aunt Nellie for the rest of her life. At the time of the transfer, Aunt Nellie owed Mercy Hospital $5,000 and had credit card debts totaling $45,000. Aunt Nellie's home was her only significant asset.

2. Steve owed his grocer $1,000, not including interest, as a result of the grocer's allowing Steve to charge his groceries to his account while Steve was between jobs. Steve's debts increased steadily while he was without an income, and he failed to pay many of his bills. After Steve had been out of work for many months, he gave the grocer his stereo system, worth about $1,100, in exchange for cancellation of his debt.

3. Tom, who was entitled to a tax refund by reason of overpayment of his 2011 taxes, opted to have the overpayment applied to his 2012 estimated tax. Tom figured that this would provide him a greater benefit than accepting the refund, since the amount of the refund would not be enough to pay most of the debts he owed to various creditors.

4. Corporation decided to pay its president a large bonus at the end of its fiscal year. Corporation's board of directors felt that the president deserved the bonus for his hard work, despite the fact that Corporation was no longer able to pay its suppliers and had not paid its shareholders a dividend in five years.

5. Corporation's Board was concerned that key employees would look for other jobs, rather than stick it out during Corporation's mounting financial crisis. The Board, therefore, offered two-year employment contracts to its top-level managers. The contracts promised large "retention bonuses" to these individuals for each six-month period they remained with the company, both before and after any bankruptcy filing. Corporation ultimately filed a Chapter 11 petition. In the two years before filing, Corporation paid $2.5 million in retention bonuses under the terms of the contracts.

6. When Mary finished her medical residency four years ago, she decided to open her own practice. She was worried that future malpractice suits might ruin her financially, not because she lacked confidence in her abilities, but because she had heard so many stories about bogus claims. To protect her current and future assets, Mary created a trust into which all of her current assets were placed and into which most of her earnings from the practice were directed over the years. She and her immediate family were the beneficiaries. This year, Mary suffered severe financial losses from unwise investment decisions and she was forced to file bankruptcy. She has no significant assets other than the trust.

7. Father was very proud of his daughter for graduating from medical school and so, as a graduation gift, he paid off her $50,000 loan balance.

Father also thought of the payment as a good investment, as he was sure that his daughter would be willing to return the favor when she started making a good salary. Unfortunately, by paying off the medical school debt, Father became unable to pay his own bills.

8. Debtor, who had a gross income of $44,000, made a first-time contribution of $10,000 to his college. The gift rendered Debtor unable to meet his obligations to his creditors. See *Murray v. Louisiana State University Foundation (In re Zohdi)*, 234 B.R. 371 (Bankr. M.D.La.1999).

9. Debtor's sister, Lacey, founded a new company to manufacture and market kumquat jam, made from her own recipe. The company needed $150,000 to get started, but Lacey had few assets to her name. She went to Bank for a loan, but encountered a great deal of reluctance (the Bank's loan officer had never even heard of kumquats). Thus, Lacey turned to her brother. Debtor agreed to personally guarantee the loan, although he was only marginally solvent at the time. Lacey's venture ultimately proved unsuccessful and her company folded, leaving the obligation to Bank unpaid. It sought to collect on the guarantee, but Debtor had encountered financial problems of his own.

The following case addresses, in a somewhat unusual setting, a trustee's allegations that a transfer was constructively fraudulent.

ALLARD v. FLAMINGO HILTON (IN RE CHOMAKOS)

United States Court of Appeals, Sixth Circuit, 1995.
69 F.3d 769.

DAVID A. NELSON, Circuit Judge.

This is a bankruptcy case in which the trustee sought to recover pre-petition gambling losses from the operator of a state-regulated casino. The casino operator contended that the opportunity for the debtors to win more than the sums they bet, coupled with the entertainment value that the casino provided its customers, constituted "reasonably equivalent value" and "fair consideration" for the bets at issue. The bankruptcy court accepted this contention and held that the bets were not voidable under the Bankruptcy Code or under the Uniform Fraudulent Conveyance Act. The district court affirmed the bankruptcy court's decision on appeal. We shall affirm the affirmance.

I

The debtors, George and Nikki Chomakos of Rochester, Michigan, filed a bankruptcy petition on August 2, 1990, after having lost several thousand dollars at a casino operated by Flamingo Hilton Corporation in Las Vegas, Nevada. The petition sought relief under Chapter 11 of the Bankruptcy Code, but the matter was soon converted into a Chapter 7 case. The trustee in bankruptcy subsequently commenced an adversary proceeding against Flamingo in the United States Bankruptcy Court for the Eastern District of Michigan.

The trustee's complaint alleged that Mr. and Mrs. Chomakos had been insolvent for six years prior to the filing of the petition; that during this time Nikki Chomakos transferred various sums to Flamingo for the purpose of gambling; that she made some of these transfers during the year preceding the filing; and that she did not receive a reasonably equivalent value or fair consideration in exchange. The complaint was subsequently amended to allege that George Chomakos had also made losing bets at the casino while insolvent. Invoking § 548(a), the trustee sought to recover under that section losses incurred during the year[a] preceding the bankruptcy filing. Under Mich. Comp. Laws 566.11 et seq., Michigan's version of the Uniform Fraudulent Conveyance Act, the trustee sought to recover losses incurred throughout the entire six-year period in which Mr. and Mrs. Chomakos were alleged to have been insolvent.

The case went to trial, and the bankruptcy court found that the debtors should be deemed to have been insolvent from and after January of 1988; that at various times in June and September of 1989 Nikki Chomakos won a total of $9,000 playing slot machines at the Flamingo casino, while losing a total of $14,000; and that George Chomakos lost a net amount of $2,710 at the casino after January of 1988 and before the filing of the petition. The combined net losses of the two debtors during the period when they were insolvent came to $7,710.

* * * [T]he bankruptcy court (Shapero, J.) held that the relief requested by the trustee should be denied because defendant Flamingo gave reasonably equivalent value in exchange for the debtors' money. The order denying relief was appealed to the district court. That court

---

[a] Section 548(a), as enacted in 1978, reached transfers that occurred within a year before bankruptcy. The reach-back period was extended to two years by the 2005 Amendments. Eds.

affirmed the decision on the basis of Judge Shapero's opinion, and the trustee filed a timely notice of appeal.

II

[The court quoted §§ 548(a)(2)(A) and (B), and 548(d)(2).]

Under Michigan's Uniform Fraudulent Conveyance Act, to which Flamingo does not deny it is subject, a conveyance made by one who is insolvent is fraudulent as to creditors if made without a fair consideration. Mich. Comp. Laws 566.14. "Fair consideration" is given for property, Mich. Comp. Laws 566.13 provides, "when in exchange for such property * * * as a fair equivalent therefor, and in good faith, property is conveyed or an antecedent debt is satisfied." The Michigan statute does not have a time limit corresponding to that in the Bankruptcy Code; the two provisions are substantially the same otherwise.

The point in time as of which we must determine whether Mr. and Mrs. Chomakos received property of reasonably equivalent value in exchange for the money they wagered at the casino is the point at which their bets were placed. See *In re Morris Communications NC, Inc.*, 914 F.2d 458, 466 (4th Cir. 1990), quoting *Collier on Bankruptcy* § 548.09 at p. 116 (15th ed. 1984) as follows:

> The critical time is when the transfer is 'made.' Neither subsequent depreciation in nor appreciation in value of the consideration affects the * * * question whether reasonable [sic] equivalent value was given.

Where gambling is lawful, as it was in the case at bar, the placing of a bet gives rise to legally enforceable contract rights. These contract rights constitute "property," of course, and at the time which Collier identifies as "critical"—a time before anyone can know whether the bet will be successful—the property has economic value. The property is not unlike futures contracts purchased on margin. The investor in futures may win big, or his position may be wiped out, but the contractual right to a payoff if the market happens to move the right way at the right time constitutes a value reasonably equivalent to the money at risk.

The trustee's brief takes the bankruptcy court to task for making the suggestion—a suggestion characterized by the trustee as "incredible"—that gambling is arguably "an 'investment' that can have economic value." But the trustee looks at the picture only as of the time when Mr. and Mrs. Chomakos left the casino "with nothing in exchange for the monies they gambled away." The time that counts is not the time when the bet is won or lost, but the time when the bet is placed. The "investment" may turn out badly, but unless and until it does, the contractual right to receive payment in the event that it turns out well is obviously worth something.

Morris Communications illustrates the point nicely. At issue there was the valuation of the debtor's interest in a corporation ("C-PACT") that had only one asset—an application pending before the Federal Communications Commission for a cellular telephone license. Licenses were to be awarded at a future date under a lottery procedure. C-PACT had a chance of winning a license, but it also had a chance of losing. If the license were won, C-PACT stock would have substantial value; if the license were lost, the stock would be worthless. Before the lottery took place, the debtor sold its C-PACT stock for a price negotiated at arm's length. Rejecting a claim that the price was too low, the court of appeals held that the debtor's transfer of the stock was not voidable under § 548(a)(2)(A) and (B).

The games of chance in which Mr. and Mrs. Chomakos participated (slot machine games and blackjack) were not FCC lotteries, of course, and a casino gambler is not kept waiting for months to learn whether a particular bet is successful. The principle, however, is the same in both cases. Take blackjack, for instance. The trial record shows that a person who bets $2 at the blackjack table where Mr. Chomakos did his gambling will win $3 if he receives a black jack. At the point in time when Mr. Chomakos placed a $2 bet, his chance of winning $3 had an economic value no less real in nature than the economic value of C-PACT's chance of winning a cellular telephone license.

The existence of an economic value may be immaterial, however, if the dollar value of the gambler's chance of winning—augmented, perhaps, by an element of entertainment value—is not "reasonably equivalent" to the amount of money wagered. We believe that the evidence presented by Flamingo showed a reasonable equivalency here, and the trustee presented no evidence to the contrary.

The casino's evidence showed, among other things, that the gambling business in Nevada is closely regulated by the state; that this regulation extends to payout ratios for both slot machines and table games; that casinos depend on repeat business, which is encouraged by customers winning; and that competition among casinos is intense. The evidence further showed that a three dollar slot machine bet could produce a jackpot of over a million dollars, which would be paid on the spot; that in a single year, Flamingo slot machine players had more than 9,500 jackpots of $1,200 or more, in addition to many lesser jackpots; that for all the dollars deposited in all Flamingo slot machines over the course of a year, Flamingo paid out 94 percent in winnings; and that the payout ratio for the particular machines played by Mrs. Chomakos was even higher, ranging from 95.73 percent to 97.43 percent. The customer enjoys better odds at the blackjack table, moreover. Assuming the blackjack player has a fair knowledge of the game and uses good basic strategy, the evidence showed that the house advantage is only one percent or less.

The trustee disputes none of these facts and does not seriously challenge Flamingo's good faith. Looking at the situation from the standpoint of creditors, however, the trustee argues that the very existence of a house advantage, coupled with the fact that Mr. and Mrs. Chomakos ultimately lost more than they won, means that there was no reasonably equivalent economic benefit. And citing *In re Young*, 148 Bankr. 886 (Bankr. D. Minn. 1992), *aff'd*, 152 Bankr. 939 (D. Minn. 1993), where church contributions made by an insolvent donor were held to be fraudulent conveyances, the trustee maintains that it would be anomalous for gambling losses not to be treated as fraudulent conveyances too.

As far as church contributions are concerned, the cases are in conflict. While the *Young* donor was held not to have received reasonably equivalent value, bankruptcy courts reached a contrary result in *In re Missionary Baptist Foundation of America, Inc.*, 24 B.R. 973 (Bankr. N.D. Tex 1982), and *In re Moses*, 59 B.R. 815 (Bankr. N.D. Ga. 1986). There is no need for us to take sides in the church contribution controversy, however. Looking at the matter from the standpoint of creditors, as the trustee urges us to do, it seems reasonably clear that the intangible property rights accruing to Mr. and Mrs. Chomakos when they placed their bets differed significantly from the benefits accruing to the donors in the church contribution cases.

A debtor who contributes to a church may receive spiritual and social returns of great value to the debtor, but such returns are not likely to be of much benefit to creditors. A debtor who places a bet in a fair and lawful game of chance, on the other hand, may receive hard cash in return. On one of the days when Mrs. Chomakos played Flamingo's slot machines, for example, she had winnings of $5,000. Suppose she had won a $5,000 jackpot at the start of her visit to the casino and had stopped playing as soon as she won; the return on her "investment" would obviously have benefited her creditors.

It is true that gambling odds always favor the house, and that Mrs. Chomakos would have been almost certain to lose her $5,000 jackpot—and more—if she continued playing long enough. On the record before us, however, we cannot say that the existence of a modest house advantage means that unsuccessful bets are fraudulent conveyances.

The trustee argues that Mr. and Mrs. Chomakos did not occupy a bargaining position equal to Flamingo's, and the gambling transactions were therefore not at arm's length. But this argument overlooks the governmental and business forces by which Flamingo was constrained. Flamingo was subject to state regulations designed to create a reasonably level playing field, and Flamingo had to compete with nearby casinos to which Mr. and Mrs. Chomakos and all other customers were free to take their business. Without reasonably generous payouts and competitive odds, Flamingo could not hope to attract the repeat customers on whom, according to the evidence, Flamingo and other casino operators depend for survival. "The *quid pro quo*," as the bankruptcy court observed, "was established in the context of a state regulated business, existing in an open competitive marketplace responding and responsive to desires of legitimate tourists pursuing and engaging in a legal and legitimate pursuit."

As far as federal law is concerned, moreover, we are not persuaded that we ought to evaluate the transactions at issue here solely from the standpoint of creditors. Casino patrons receive what the bankruptcy court called "psychic and other intangible values," just as patrons of a fine restaurant do, for example. If, instead of gambling, Mr. and Mrs. Chomakos had spent $7,710 on expensive dinners, the creditors would have been no better off than they are now. Yet the trustee concedes that the restaurateur would not be liable for return of the money—and when asked at oral argument how money spent at a blackjack table differs from money spent at a dinner table, the trustee had no satisfactory answer.

The judgment affirming the decision of the bankruptcy court is AFFIRMED.

Questions

1. What were the trustee's grounds for arguing that the debtors had not received reasonably equivalent value, within § 548(a)(2), or fair consideration, as required by the UFTA?

2. Were you persuaded by the court's reasoning? Even if some sort of value is received by a gambler, is it "reasonably equivalent" to the amount of the bet?

3. Apparently, the trustee could not distinguish an expensive dinner from money spent at a blackjack table. Can you?

Note on Real Property Foreclosures

Sales prices are notoriously low in the context of real property foreclosures, although sales are not set aside on that ground under state law unless the price is so low as to "shock the conscience." But what of fraudulent conveyances law? Is the requirement of "reasonably equivalent value" satisfied in such cases?

The Fifth Circuit stunned property lawyers when, in *Durrett v. Washington National Insurance Co.*, 621 F.2d 201 (5th Cir.1980), it invalidated a regularly-conducted foreclosure sale that yielded 57% of the property's fair market value. The court held, first, that fraudulent conveyances law may apply to such sales, despite the involuntary nature of the transfer, and then found the price inadequate. The court, in dicta, suggested that a sale for less than 70% of fair market value constitutes a fraudulent conveyance. This "*Durrett* rule" caused near panic because virtually all foreclosure sales would be vulnerable.

Shortly thereafter, the Ninth Circuit came to the opposite conclusion. In *Madrid v. Lawyers Title Insurance Corp. (In re Madrid)*, 725 F.2d 1197 (9th Cir.1984), the court held that the "transfer" occurred when the encumbrance was created. Since that was more than a year before bankruptcy, under the facts of the case, § 548 did not apply. *Madrid* also disagreed with *Durrett* on the question of fraudulent conveyance law's applicability to involuntary transfers, such as foreclosure sales. The court expressed concern that *Durrett*'s approach would create de facto redemption rights that would frustrate the operation of foreclosure law and upset the balance of debtors' and creditors' rights reflected in state law.

A deeply divided Supreme Court resolved the question in *BFP v. Resolution Trust Corp.*, 511 U.S. 531, 114 S.Ct. 1757, 128 L.Ed.2d 556 (1994). BFP, a partnership, took title to a house subject to a deed of trust in favor of Imperial Savings Association. Upon BFP's default, Imperial conducted a foreclosure sale in accordance with state procedures. Osborne purchased the house for $433,000. BFP then filed a Chapter 11 petition and sought to set aside the sale to Osborne as a fraudulent transfer, claiming the house was actually worth $725,000 at the time of sale. The bankruptcy court found that the sale complied with California law and was neither collusive nor fraudulent. It granted summary judgment in favor of Imperial. (RTC was receiver for Imperial.) The district court, BAP and Ninth Circuit all affirmed. Ultimately, the Supreme Court did, too.

According to the Court, "reasonably equivalent value" does not necessarily connote a strictly economic or dollar-for-dollar analysis. "One must suspect the language means that fair market value cannot—or at least cannot always—be the benchmark" for determining reasonably equivalent value. The Court held that the price received at a mortgage foreclosure sale conclusively establishes the "reasonably equivalent value" of the mortgaged property when state foreclosure requirements are met. "Reasonably equivalent value" under § 548 is not to be equated with fair market value, in the context of mortgage foreclosure sales. "Reasonably equivalent value" is the price in fact received at a foreclosure sale. Section 548 does not use the phrase "fair market value." Moreover, market value is inapplicable in the foreclosure sale context because property that must be sold at distress is, simply, worth less.

The Court also expressed concerns based on federalism: "Fraudulent transfer law and foreclosure law enjoyed over 400 years of peaceful coexistence in Anglo-American jurisprudence until the Fifth Circuit's unprecedented 1980 decision in *Durrett*." *Id*. at 542, 114 S.Ct. at 1764. The Court believed that Congress would have used language clearer than "reasonably equivalent value" if it had intended "to disrupt the ancient harmony that foreclosure law and fraudulent-conveyance law, those two pillars of debtor-creditor jurisprudence, have heretofore enjoyed." *Id*. at 543, 114 S.Ct. at 1764.

The majority, as the dissent noted, did not consider the federal bankruptcy policy of maximizing the value of the estate for the benefit of creditors. Thus, in *BFP*, Osborne kept $292,000 ($725,000 – $433,000) that, otherwise, would have become property of the estate, to be shared by BFP's creditors.

3. CORPORATE CONTEXTS

a. Leveraged Buyouts

The following case deals with a leveraged buyout ("LBO"), and explains why such transactions raise fraudulent transfer concerns. Provisions in the statute at issue, the UFTA, parallel the Bankruptcy Code's two branches of fraud. Because the bankruptcy trustee can use state law through § 544(b), decisions involving the UFTA are persuasive bankruptcy precedents.

BAY PLASTICS, INC. v. BT COMMERCIAL CORP. (IN RE BAY PLASTICS, INC.)

United States Bankruptcy Court, Central District of California, 1995.
187 B.R. 315.

SAMUEL L. BUFFORD, Bankruptcy Judge

I. INTRODUCTION

The debtor has brought this adversary proceeding against the selling shareholders of a leveraged buyout ("LBO") to recover the funds that they received in the buyout transaction. * * * The Court grants summary judgment to the debtor on the undisputed facts.

The Court holds that the transaction may be avoided as a constructive fraudulent transfer under the California version of the Uniform Fraudulent Transfer Act ("UFTA"), on which the debtor relies pursuant to Bankruptcy Code § 544(b), and that in consequence the debtor is entitled to recover against the selling shareholders. The Court finds that the transaction rendered the debtor insolvent, and that the sellers did not act in good faith.

II. FACTS

The Court finds that the following facts are undisputed. Defendants Bob Younger, Abner Smith and Paul Dodson ("the selling shareholders") formed debtor Bay Plastics, Inc. ("Bay Plastics") in 1979 to manufacture polyvinyl chloride ("PVC") plastic pipe for water well casings and turf irrigation. Bay Plastics filed this bankruptcy case on January 25, 1990.

A. The Buyout

Because they were nearing retirement, on October 31, 1988 (fifteen months before this bankruptcy filing) the selling shareholders sold their Bay Plastics stock to Milhous Corporation ("Milhous") for $3.5 million in cash plus $1.8 million in deferred payments. Milhous did not acquire the Bay Plastics stock directly. Instead, it caused its subsidiary Nicole Plastics to form its own subsidiary, BPI Acquisition Corp. ("BPI"), to take ownership of the Bay Plastics stock. Formally, the parties to the stock sale transaction were ultimately BPI and the selling shareholders.

The sale was unexceptional. The difficulty lay in the financing of the purchase. Milhous put no money of its own, or even any money that it borrowed, into this transaction. Instead, it caused Bay Plastics to borrow approximately $3.95 million from defendant BT Commercial Corp. ("BT") (a subsidiary of Bankers Trust), and then caused Bay Plastics to direct that $3.5 million of the loan be disbursed to BPI. BPI in turn directed that the $3.5 million be paid directly to the selling shareholders in substantial payment for their stock. Thus, at the closing, $3.5 million of the funds paid into escrow by BT went directly to the selling shareholders.

As security for its $3.95 million loan, BT received a first priority security interest in essentially all of the assets of Bay Plastics. In consequence, BT has received all of the proceeds of debtor's assets in this bankruptcy case, and nothing is left for unsecured or even for administrative creditors.

The financing also provided a revolving credit facility for working capital, in addition to the payment for the LBO, up to a total loan of $7 million. A total of just over $4 million was owing to BT at the time of the bankruptcy filing, according to the debtor's schedules. Thus most of the debt (all but approximately $500,000) owing to BT at the time of the filing resulted from the LBO.

The selling shareholders were not in the dark about the financing. On October 25, 1988 they and their attorney met with Milhous representatives in Los Angeles to finalize the deal. While the Milhous representatives provided rather little information about the Milhous finances, they did disclose the details of the BT secured loan to Bay Plastics to finance the stock purchase. In addition, the selling shareholders received a projected post-transaction balance sheet, which showed a balance of $250,000 in equity only because of the addition to the asset side of the ledger the sum of $2,259,270 in goodwill. Both the selling shareholders and their attorney were experienced in LBOs, and the selling shareholders discussed this feature of the transaction, and their exposure on a fraudulent transfer claim, with their attorney on that date. With this information in hand, Younger, Smith and Dodson approved the terms of the sale.

In contrast to the selling shareholders, the industry did not know about the LBO character of the transaction until a number of months later. Shintech Corp., a creditor at the time of the transaction (and continuously thereafter), did not learn of it until ten months later, in August, 1989.

B. The Shintech Debt

Some three months before the LBO, on July 22, 1988, Bay Plastics entered into a requirements contract with Shintech to supply PVC resin. Shintech agreed under the contract to supply up to 2.6 million pounds of PVC resin per month on payment terms of 30 days after shipment. To induce Shintech to enter into this contract, Bay Plastics granted Shintech a security interest in all its assets, and the shareholders gave personal guaranties. This arrangement stood in the way of the BT transaction.

In consequence, the selling shareholders, their attorney, and Milhous representatives met with Shintech in late October, 1988 (after Milhous had disclosed to the selling shareholders the terms of the LBO), to arrange a new deal with Shintech. The parties to the LBO persuaded Shintech of Milhous' good credit, and induced Shintech to release both its security interest and the guaranties.[5] However, they did not disclose the LBO character of the transaction, and Shintech did not learn of this until ten months later.

The impact of this transaction on the balance sheet of Bay Plastics was dramatic. Immediately after the transaction, its balance sheet showed tangible assets of approximately $7 million, and liabilities of approximately $9 million. Only the addition of almost $2.26 million in goodwill, which had not appeared on prior balance sheets, and for which no explanation has been provided, permitted the balance sheet to show a modest shareholder equity of $250,000. But for the newly discovered goodwill, there would have been a net deficiency of some $2 million. In contrast, immediately before the transaction Bay Plastics had assets of $6.7 million and liabilities of $5.6 million, and a net equity of $1.1 million.

Bay Plastics was unable to service this overload of debt, and filed its bankruptcy petition fifteen months later. According to the debtor's schedules, at the time of filing its two principal creditors were BT and Shintech: it owed approximately $4 million in secured debt to BT, and $3.5 million in unsecured debt to Shintech. No other creditor was owed more than $20,000.

---

[5] In consequence of giving up its security and its guaranties, Shintech now holds more than 99% of the unsecured debt in this case.

III. DISCUSSION

* * *

The basic structure of an LBO involves a transfer of corporate ownership financed primarily by the assets of the corporation itself.[11] Typically the corporation borrows the funds, secured by the assets of the corporation, and advances them to the purchasers, who use the funds to pay the purchase price to the selling shareholders. LBOs have two essential features:

> First, the purchaser acquires the funds necessary for the acquisition through borrowings secured directly or indirectly by the assets of the company being acquired. Second, the lender who provides such funds is looking primarily to the future operating earnings of the acquired company and/or to the proceeds from future sales of assets of the company, rather than to any other assets of the purchasers, to repay the borrowings used to effect the acquisition.

Kathryn V. Smyser, *Going Private and Going Under: Leveraged Buyouts and the Fraudulent Conveyance Problem*, 63 IND. L.J. 781, 785 (1988). LBO investors thus generally consider cash flow, the money available for working capital and debt service, as the most important factor in assessing a potential buyout candidate.

The application of fraudulent transfer law to LBOs has generated considerable debate among courts and commentators. LBOs were a popular form of consensual corporate takeover in the 1980's. They fell into disuse at the end of that decade for economic reasons. However, the use of the LBO as an acquisition device has recently become popular again.

The LBO dates back long before the 1980's. In earlier years, it was known as a "bootstrap acquisition." Some of these transactions were invalidated as fraudulent conveyances.

* * *

---

[11] While LBOs have frequently been used by management to buy out existing shareholders and take over the ownership of a business, management is not an essential party to an LBO. Indeed, in this case the purchaser was an outside third party.

B. Trustee's Prima Facie Case

* * *

The Court notes at the outset that this case is not determined by the Ninth Circuit case law as set forth in [*Lippi v. City Bank*, 955 F.2d 599 (9th Cir.1992), and *Kupetz v. Wolf*, 845 F.2d 842 at 843 (9th Cir.1988)]. Those cases both involved a fraudulent transfer attack on behalf of subsequent creditors. This case, in contrast, is brought for the principal benefit of a creditor existing at the time of the transaction, which holds more than 99% of the outstanding unsecured debt.

We begin with the elements of the cause of action under the UFTA § 5, as adopted in California, for a constructive fraudulent transfer rendering the debtor insolvent. The elements of a cause of action under this statute are as follows: the debtor (1) made a transfer or incurred an obligation, (2) without receiving a reasonably equivalent value in exchange, (3) which rendered the debtor insolvent (or the debtor was already insolvent), and (4) which is attacked by a pre-transaction creditor.

1. Transfer or Obligation

The selling shareholders do not dispute that, in making the BT loan, the debtor made a transfer or incurred an obligation. In fact, the debtor did both. The debtor undertook the $3.95 million obligation to BT, it transferred a security interest in essentially all of its assets to BT, and it transferred $3.5 million ultimately to the selling shareholders. Thus the first element of the cause of action is satisfied.

2. Lack of Reasonably Equivalent Value

The selling shareholders likewise do not contest whether the debtor received reasonably equivalent value for the BT loan. However, this element is not apparent on its face.

Nominally, BT's transaction was only with Bay Plastics. It lent the $3.95 million to the debtor, the debtor promised to repay the loan, and the debtor gave a first priority security interest in essentially all of its assets to secure the repayment. If this were the transaction, creditors likely would have no grounds for complaint, and it would not be vulnerable to fraudulent transfer attack.

However, the foregoing structure obscures the reality of the transaction. The selling shareholders' transaction was formally with Milhous, and eventually with BPI, the new owner of Bay Plastics. BPI purchased their stock, and arranged for their payment with funds that Bay Plastics borrowed from BT. Before Bay Plastics received the funds, it directed that $3.5 million be transferred to its incoming parent, BPI, and BPI in turn directed that the funds be paid out for the stock purchase. Thus in substance $3.5 million of the funds that Bay Plastics borrowed from BT went to pay for the stock of the selling shareholders, rather than to Bay Plastics.

This raises the question whether the Court should collapse the various transactions in this case into one integrated transaction. Under *Lippi* this turns on whether, from the perspective of the selling shareholders, the transaction appeared to be a straight sale without an LBO. If, in contrast, there is evidence that the parties knew or should have known that the transaction would deplete the assets of the company, the Court should look beyond the formal structure. In *Kupetz* the Ninth Circuit found it improper to collapse the transactions where the selling shareholders had no knowledge of the LBO character of the transaction, and there were no pre-transaction creditors.

In this case, in contrast, the selling shareholders had full knowledge that this was an LBO. * * *

This knowledge of the selling shareholders distinguishes this case from both *Kupetz* (where the selling shareholders did not know or have reason to know of the LBO) and from *Lippi* (where the evidence was disputed). Instead, this case is like [others] where the transaction was collapsed because of the knowledge of the selling shareholders.

In addition, because Shintech qualifies as a pre-transaction creditor, the Court does not need to reach the issue of the knowledge of the LBO feature of the transaction by the selling shareholders: this is material to whether the transaction's various parts should be collapsed only when challenged by post-transaction creditors.

Thus, in this case the Court finds it appropriate to collapse the various pieces of this transaction into one integral transaction, in which the funds went to the selling shareholders, not to Bay Plastics or to its new parent BPI. The loan obligation, in contrast, was undertaken by Bay Plastics, which also provided the security for the loan.

Bay Plastics received no reasonably equivalent value for the security interest in all of its assets that it gave to BT in exchange for BT's funding of the stock sale. Under California law, reasonable equivalence must be determined from the standpoint of creditors. Payment of funds to a parent corporation prevents a transaction from satisfying the "reasonably equivalent value" requirement. A financially healthy entity may give away its assets as it pleases so long as there remains enough to pay its debts. A financially distressed donor, however, may not be so generous.

From the debtor's perspective, it is apparent that the $450,000 that Bay Plastics presumably received (the $3.95 million loan less the $3.5 million paid to the selling shareholders) is not reasonably equivalent to the $3.95 million obligation that it undertook. Thus Bay Plastics did not receive reasonably equivalent value for the loan obligation and security interest that it granted to BT.

3. Insolvency of the Debtor

The third element of the fraudulent transfer cause of action at issue in this litigation is that the transaction rendered the debtor insolvent, if it was not so already. In this case the Court finds the evidence undisputed that the LBO rendered the debtor insolvent.

[UFTA § 2(a) adopts] the balance sheet test for insolvency: a debtor is insolvent if the liabilities exceed the assets.

* * *

The valuation of assets for insolvency purposes is based on "a fair valuation." This differs from a balance sheet, where most assets apart from publicly traded stocks and bonds are carried at historic cost, rather than current market value. The values of assets must be updated in light of subsequent use and market conditions: in accounting parlance, they must be "marked to market."

In addition, a balance sheet may include intangible assets such as goodwill[24] that may have no liquidation or going concern value, and

---

[24] Goodwill is generally understood to represent the value of intangible factors that are expected to translate into greater than normal earning power. In addition to the advantageous relationship that a business enjoys with its customers, goodwill also includes advantageous relationships with employees, suppliers, lenders and others.

which thus must be deleted in evaluating the solvency of an entity. Goodwill cannot be sold to satisfy a creditor's claim. Thus, in a liquidation bankruptcy case it must be disregarded in determining solvency of the debtor at the time of an LBO.

Nominally, Bay Plastic's corporate balance sheet showed the debtor to be solvent after the LBO. But this resulted only from the addition of $2.26 million of goodwill to the asset side of the balance sheet. Bay Plastics had not previously carried any goodwill on its balance sheets.

* * *

The Court finds that the balance sheet must be adjusted by deleting the unamortized goodwill of $2.26 million. It was not carried on the balance sheet before the LBO, and in any case it could not be sold to satisfy a creditor's claim. This is a liquidation case, where goodwill has no other value. This downward adjustment left Bay Plastics with a negative net worth of approximately $2 million immediately after the LBO. For fraudulent transfer purposes, it was rendered insolvent by the transaction.

Indeed, this is exactly the type of transaction that poses the extreme risk of an LBO. No Milhous entity put any funds or assets at risk in the investment at all. In consequence of the structure of the transaction, all of the risks of the enterprise were placed on its creditors. Milhous retained only the right to reap the benefits if the business was sufficiently profitable to avoid bankruptcy.[25]

4. Attack by a Pre-Transaction Creditor

The final element of the cause of action for fraudulent transfer rendering a debtor insolvent is that the transaction must be attacked by a pre-transaction creditor. This element is satisfied in this case.

Because goodwill has no independent market or liquidation value, generally accepted accounting principles require that goodwill be written off over a period of time. In acquisition accounting, going concern value in excess of asset value is treated as goodwill. * * *

[25] In such a transaction there is a danger that the selling shareholders will be paid more than their stock is worth. With nothing at risk if the business is not sufficiently profitable, the purchaser has less incentive to make sure that the price is not excessive. Absent fraudulent transfer law, there is nothing to deter the buyers, sellers and bank from imposing all of the risks of loss on the creditors, as they did in this case.

* * *

The selling shareholders make [two] arguments against considering Shintech a qualifying pre-transaction creditor. First, they argue that Shintech's account was current at the time of the LBO, and that in consequence all of its debt comes from a later date. Second, they argue that Shintech had an opportunity at the pre-closing meeting, where it agreed to release its security interest and guaranties, to ask any questions that it wanted, and it declared that it was satisfied with the information provided to it. * * * The Court finds all of these arguments unpersuasive.

a. Shintech as Creditor

First, the Court finds that Shintech is a pre-transaction creditor of Bay Plastics, even if the account was current at the time of the LBO. Just three months earlier Shintech had entered into a massive contract with Bay Plastics to provide all of its requirements of PVC, which were monumental—up to 2.6 million pounds (1,300 tons) per month. Under this contract Bay Plastics owed a duty to Shintech to buy its PVC from Shintech for the duration of the contract, whether or not the account was current on any particular day. The contract was in place on the day of the LBO, and remained in force until after the bankruptcy filing.

* * *

Shintech's contract rights under its requirements contract to provide PVC were certainly not valueless, even if payments were current at the time of the LBO. If Bay Plastics had repudiated the contract on the day after the LBO, it would have owed massive damages to Shintech. * * * The Court finds that this right satisfied the definitional requirements to make it a creditor holding a claim * * * .

b. Investigation of the Transaction

Second, the selling shareholders argue that Shintech, the largest supplier of PVC resin in the industry, had every opportunity to investigate the nature of the LBO transaction, and cannot now be heard to complain about it. The Court finds this is irrelevant to the cause of action for a fraudulent transfer that renders a debtor insolvent.

* * *

The shareholders assert that the sale notice sent to 25 suppliers of the debtor (presumably a bulk sale notice under UCC Article 6) gave sufficient notice of the LBO. This notice, however, did not state that the transaction was an LBO or that the transaction would render the debtor insolvent. Furthermore, a public LBO only puts subsequent creditors on notice of possible financial problems. They may decide not to do business with the debtor, and avoid becoming creditors. Existing creditors, on the other hand, are already locked in, and subsequent notice does not do them any good.

* * *

C. Application of Fraudulent Transfer Law to LBOs

The Court finds it appropriate to apply fraudulent transfer law to an LBO. An LBO is different, not just in degree, but in character from the ordinary business and investment transactions engaged in by a corporation's management. An LBO is not a routine business transaction that should normally be given deference by the courts. It is not a corporate investment in a new venture, new equipment or property. Indeed, an LBO normally does not affect the business of the corporation at all: it only changes the ownership and adds a large layer of secured debt. Rather, an LBO is an investment of corporate assets, by borrowing against them, for the personal benefit of both old and new equity owners. Thus, the application of fraudulent transfer law to LBOs does not limit corporate entrepreneurial decisions.

Since an LBO reduces the availability of unencumbered assets, the buyout depletes estate assets available to pay creditors' claims. * * * An LBO is attractive to the sellers, the buyers and the lender because it shifts most of the risk of loss to other creditors of the corporation. The acquired corporation receives little or nothing in exchange for the debt that it incurs.

From a creditor's point of view, an LBO is indistinguishable from a distribution or a gift to shareholders. The harm is quite like the harm imposed on creditors by donative transfers to third parties, which is one of the most traditional kinds of fraudulent transfers. If the value of the security interest given by the corporation does not exceed the shareholders' equity as shown on the balance sheet (after suitable revisions to mark the assets to market and to eliminate intangible assets of dubious value), there is usually no substantial harm to creditors. Indeed, typical corporate distribution statutes permit the payment of dividends in such circumstances, to the extent of the balance sheet equity. If the price paid to selling shareholders is higher, however, there may be insufficient assets remaining to satisfy creditors.

The vice of an LBO lies in the fact that the selling shareholders are paid indirectly with assets from the corporation itself, rather than by the purchasers. In effect, in an LBO the shareholders are paid with a corporate dividend or distribution. An LBO enables the selling shareholders to liquidate their equity interests, which are otherwise subordinate to general unsecured claims, without first paying creditors, which a normal liquidation would require. The selling shareholders in the transaction in effect disregard the status of the corporation as a separate entity for their benefit, but insist on respect of the corporation's separate status when it comes to creditors' claims (apart from those of the lender providing the funds for the transaction).

The possible detriment to creditors is exacerbated if the corporation's cash flow is not sufficient to service the loan. The bank eventually proceeds to foreclose on the corporation's assets and sells them at foreclosure prices, and leaves nothing for other creditors. Such foreclosure is frequently interrupted by the filing of a bankruptcy case. So it happened in this case.

* * *

Should all LBO's be exposed to fraudulent transfer challenge? Certainly not. Under this Court's analysis, two kinds of LBO's ordinarily escape fraudulent transfer attack. This includes many, if not most, LBOs.

First, in a legitimate LBO, in which the assets mortgaged by a corporation to support an LBO do not exceed the net equity of the business (after appropriate adjustments), the transaction will not make the corporation insolvent, at least according to the balance sheet test.[34] If in addition it has sufficient projected cash flow to pay its debts as they come due, the cash flow solvency test is met, also. This leaves an

---

[34] It makes sense to limit legitimate LBOs to transactions that do not leave a corporation insolvent. In a perfect world (as typically assumed by economists), an LBO would never run afoul of this rule, because the price paid for the stock would be the net equity in the firm. Such an LBO would place the corporation on the verge of insolvency, but not beyond. In the real world, some LBOs leave corporations insolvent, perhaps because of imperfect information about the value of the corporation's stock.

LBO exposed to fraudulent transfer attack only if the margin of equity is too thin to support the corporation's business.

A second kind of LBO also escapes fraudulent transfer attack, even though it leaves the subject corporation insolvent. If the cash flow is sufficient to make the debt payments, the transaction also is unassailable. This ordinarily turns on two factors: the degree of risk of default undertaken in the first instance, and the degree to which projected economic developments impacting the business are not overly optimistic. These LBOs escape fraudulent transfer attack either because of good financial projections or because of good luck: either factor is sufficient.

The Court's view of the proper application of fraudulent transfer law to LBO's does not make the selling shareholders the guarantors of the success of the LBO. A legitimate LBO shifts the risk of failure off their shoulders. As to subsequent creditors, they should not be required to shoulder the risk if the failure is caused by outside forces not reasonably foreseeable at the time of the transaction.

However, an LBO that is leveraged beyond the net worth of the business is a gamble. A highly leveraged business is much less able to weather temporary financial storms, because debt demands are less flexible than equity interest. The risks of this gamble should rest on the shoulders of the shareholders (old and new), not those of the creditors: the shareholders enjoy the benefits if the gamble is successful, and they should bear the burdens if it is not. This, after all, is the role of equity owners of a corporation. The application of fraudulent transfer law to LBOs shifts the risks of an LBO transaction from the creditors, who are not parties to the transaction, back to the old and new shareholders who bring about such transactions.

How long should selling shareholders be exposed to the risk that an LBO will go bad? There is a traditional answer to this question: until the statute of limitations runs. Perhaps there should be a shorter statute of limitations for LBOs than the four to seven years that is common under the UFTA. This is a decision for the legislature to make.

The Court perceives no unfairness in imposing the risks of an overleveraged LBO on the old and new shareholders who undertake the risks, rather on the creditors who do not intend to do so. Indeed, it is the selling shareholders who are ordinarily least worthy of sympathy in an LBO. As Epstein states:

In the beginning of the transaction they are below existing creditors. In the end, they "cash out" and march off over the heads of the existing creditors. It is a neat trick of legal magic that allow the shareholders to subordinate, unilaterally, the creditors' claims.

2 David G. Epstein et al., Bankruptcy § 6-52 at 74 (1992).

* * *

Notes

1. Perhaps the most influential argument against the general application of fraudulent conveyance law to leveraged buyouts was made by Professors Baird and Jackson, Douglas G. Baird & Thomas H. Jackson, *Fraudulent Conveyance Law and Its Proper Domain*, 38 VAND. L. REV. 829, 850-54 (1985):

An important conceptual question is whether a leveraged buyout in fact presents fraudulent conveyance problems or comes under a per se rule that turns out to be overbroad as applied to this particular case. A firm that incurs obligations in the course of a buyout does not seem at all like the Elizabethan deadbeat who sells his sheep to his brother for a pittance.

The question, in other words, is whether a corporate debtor that incurs additional debt in a leveraged buyout can be presumed either to be engaging in a manipulation by which it (or its shareholders) will profit at its creditors' expense or in some other transfer that its creditors would almost always want to ban. At one level, the answer to this question is straightforward. This transaction does hinder the general creditors of Firm. After the transaction, the general creditors are less likely to be paid. * * *

It thus might seem a good thing that these transactions appear to trigger sections of existing fraudulent conveyance statutes. But we doubt this is the case. These transactions do not seem to be clearly to the detriment of creditors, nor did we always see creditors treating such transactions as events of default in their loan agreements, even before the issue was moved to the domain of fraudulent conveyance law. With the buyout may come more streamlined and more effective management. Among other things, a going-private transaction may save the costs of complying with relevant federal securities statutes.

* * *

Ultimately, it is the inability of parties to opt out of fraudulent conveyance law that leads us to think that its reach should be limited. Fraudulent conveyance law should never apply to arms-length transactions, even if it appears after the fact that the debtor's actions injured the creditors. A broader rule than this one might pick up more cases of fraudulent behavior by debtors and might allow fewer transactions that creditors would want to prohibit, but it would do so only at the cost of preventing some desirable transactions from taking place. A broader rule subjects parties who bargain noncollusively and in good faith to the risk that a court later will find that the buyer paid too little. The uncertainty such a rule imposes makes debtors and creditors as a group worse off.

Id. at 852-55.

Professor Smyser, in the article quoted in *Bay Plastics*, criticized Professors Baird and Jackson for failing "to comprehend fully the distinctive potential for harm to creditors in those leveraged buyout transactions occurring under circumstances which trigger the application of fraudulent conveyance statutes." Kathryn V. Smyser, *Going Private and Going Under: Leveraged Buyouts and the Fraudulent Conveyance Problem,* 63 IND. L.J. 781, 784 (1988). Professor Smyser argued that the use of fraudulent conveyance law in the context of leveraged buyouts is "consistent with the policies underlying traditional applications of fraudulent conveyance statutes and is both necessary and appropriate to afford creditors protection against transactions which are the fundamental equivalent of transactions generally prohibited under state corporation laws." *Id.* She concluded that leveraged buyouts are within the "proper domain" of fraudulent conveyance law:

Where corporate debtors are concerned, the application of fraudulent conveyance laws to leveraged buyouts serves as an essential complement to the statutory protections afforded to corporate creditors by restrictions on shareholder distributions contained in the corporation laws. Unless one is prepared to argue for the abolition of statutory restrictions to shareholders as inconsistent with creditors' desires and best interests, there is no reason to believe that creditors do not consistently and rationally desire to limit leveraged buyouts of insolvent or nearly insolvent companies. Whatever the evidence may ultimately indicate concerning the economic benefit of leveraged buyouts generally, the limited marginal categories of buyouts involving financially ailing ventures, and of buyouts of otherwise healthy companies which are so highly leveraged in the course of the buyout as to threaten the company's solvency are probably not so beneficial that the traditional policies of creditor protection embodied in the fraudulent conveyance laws should be sacrificed.

Id. at 824.

3. In one of the precedent cases dealt with in *Bay Plastics*, *Kupetz v. Continental Illinois National Bank & Trust Co.*, 77 B.R. 754 (Bankr. C.D.Cal.1987), *aff'd sub nom. Kupetz v. Wolf*, 845 F.2d 842 (9th Cir.1988), the court was swayed by Baird and Jackson's argument that application of fraudulent conveyance law to leveraged buyouts is not in the best interests of creditors. In *Kupetz*, the owners of a company that manufactured mannequins decided to sell the company in order to finance their retirement. Purchase of the company was financed by a $1.1 million loan secured by the company's assets. Unable to service its debts, the company filed bankruptcy two and one-half years later. The bankruptcy trustee attempted to set aside the purchase agreement as a fraudulent conveyance because the way the purchase was financed left the company's creditors without a chance of collecting their debts. The district court found that the owners did not know the buyer intended to secure repayment of acquisition financing by causing the acquired company to grant the bank a collateral interest in its real and personal property. The district court noted "the broader questions posed by Baird and Jackson of whether the fraudulent conveyance laws should be applied to buyouts entered in the ordinary course." 77 B.R. at 760 n.5.

4. Which side of this debate has the better argument? *Should* fraudulent transfer law apply to LBOs?

b. Intragroup Transactions

Corporate enterprises made up of affiliated companies operate to promote the welfare of the enterprise as a whole, rather than as separate unrelated corporations. Frequently, one member of the corporate group guarantees the obligations of another. The guaranty by a parent of a subsidiary's obligations is known as a "downstream" guaranty. The opposite, a guaranty by a subsidiary of a parent's obligations, is an "upstream" guaranty. When one subsidiary guarantees the obligations of another, it is a "cross-stream" guaranty. Because a guarantor incurs an obligation, the undertaking may constitute a fraudulent conveyance. (As you recall, § 548 applies to "any obligation * * * incurred by the debtor," as well as to "any transfer * * * of an interest of the debtor in property.")

Professor Blumberg maintained that the provisions of the Bankruptcy Code and the Uniform Fraudulent Transfer Act reflect the trend toward viewing corporate affiliates within a group as a single entity rather than viewing affiliates as separate entities:

> Upstream and cross-stream guaranties occupy an important place in the process. They represent the inevitable response of lenders and corporate groups in fashioning group financing to harness the economic strength of a group to support the

financing which will effectuate the objectives of the group, although it may not affect all constituent companies, or even all guarantor-constituents, to the same degree. It is important that this process be encouraged in order to permit the more effective functioning of the economic system. It is equally important to provide equivalent protection for creditors dealing with group constituents against insider manipulation to their detriment as well as against economic consequences from legal rules contrary to their expectations. This is a continuing challenge to the law. The UFTA and the changes it incorporates with respect to insider transactions are, notwithstanding minor areas of disagreement, a considerable step forward in helping meet that challenge.

Phillip I. Blumberg, *Intragroup (Upstream, Cross–Stream, and Down–stream) Guaranties Under the Uniform Fraudulent Transfer Act,* 9 CARDOZO L. REV. 685, 728 (1987).

The following case explores the problem of reasonably equivalent value in the context of a cross-stream guaranty.

LEIBOWITZ v. PARKWAY BANK & TRUST CO. (IN RE IMAGE WORLDWIDE, LTD.)

United States Court of Appeals, Seventh Circuit, 1998.
139 F.3d 574.

ESCHBACH, Circuit Judge.

Image Worldwide, Ltd. guaranteed loans paid to an affiliate corporation, Image Marketing, Ltd. Both corporations were owned by the same person, but only Image Marketing received funds from the loan. The Image Worldwide's bankruptcy trustee filed suit to avoid the guarantees as a fraudulent transfer, alleging that the guarantees made Image Worldwide insolvent, and that Image Worldwide did not receive reasonably equivalent value in exchange for its guarantees. The bankruptcy and district courts found in favor of the trustee. This bankruptcy appeal presents the issue of when a corporation receives reasonably equivalent value for its guarantee of an affiliate's debts. The bankruptcy court held that a guarantor must receive direct economic benefits in exchange for its guarantee in order to have received reasonably equivalent value for its guarantee. While the bankruptcy court applied an overly narrow interpretation of what may constitute reasonably equivalent value for a guarantee, the bankruptcy court did not clearly err in finding that Image Worldwide did not receive reasonably equivalent value for its guarantees. We affirm.

I. Facts

Richard Steinberg was the sole shareholder, sole officer, and sole director of Image Marketing, Ltd. (IM), an Illinois corporation incorporated in June 1991. IM was in the commercial printing business, primarily dealing in wholesale sales of music and sports merchandise. IM leased space from FCL Graphics, a printing company that did all of the printing for IM.

In 1992, IM obtained a line of credit from Parkway Bank secured by a first lien against substantially all of IM's assets (IM loan). The line of credit allowed IM to borrow against up to 70% of its eligible accounts receivable, and required IM to reduce its indebtedness to 70% of its accounts receivable in the event that its eligible accounts receivable declined. By June 1993, IM had borrowed $300,000 on its line of credit.

At the end of 1993, IM was several hundred thousand dollars in debt to trade creditors. So in December 1993, Steinberg incorporated a new Illinois corporation, Image Worldwide, Ltd. (IW). Steinberg was the sole shareholder, officer, and director of IW as well. IW leased the same space from FCL as IM, used the same suppliers, and had many of the same customers. In early 1994, Steinberg liquidated IM. Parkway knew of and cooperated in the liquidation of IM. Instead of demanding that IM pay off its loan under the terms of the agreement, however, Parkway allowed Steinberg to use the money obtained from the liquidation of IM to pay down IM's trade debts. Parkway never required IM to pay off its loan, even when its accounts receivable declined to zero in 1994.

Instead, Parkway demanded that IW guarantee IM's $ 300,000 debt. IW executed the guarantee on May 27, 1994. The guarantee was secured by a first lien on substantially all of IW's assets. IW never borrowed any money from Parkway on its own. Parkway's consideration for the guarantee was its allowing IW to stay in business. Between May 27, 1994 and when IW was forced into bankruptcy, IW paid principal and interest on the loan as it became due.

Even after IM was wound down, IM still owed $200,000 to FCL Graphics. Parkway lent $200,000 to Steinberg to pay this debt (Steinberg loan). The bank paid the proceeds from this loan directly to

FCL.[1] The loan was secured by all of IW's accounts receivable. As of the date of its bankruptcy, IW had paid down $72,076.49 in principal and $26,863.45 in interest on the loan.

IW was no more successful than IM. At trial, Parkway stipulated that the guarantees made IW insolvent. In August 1995, FCL stopped doing work for IW, and filed an involuntary chapter 7 petition for bankruptcy against IW. David Leibowitz was appointed as the trustee of IW's bankruptcy estate. * * *

The trustee instituted this adversarial proceeding in July 1996 to recover the amounts transferred to Parkway. Pursuant to § 544(b), the trustee charged that the transfers to Parkway were fraudulent transfers in violation of the Uniform Fraudulent Transfer Act (UFTA), because IW never received reasonably equivalent value for its guarantees to Parkway. The bankruptcy court found in favor of the trustee, and ordered Parkway to disgorge the amounts it received from IW. The district court affirmed. Parkway now appeals to this court * * * .

III. Analysis

* * * [T]he key issue in this case is whether IW, as guarantor, received reasonably equivalent value for its guarantee when the direct benefits of the transaction were received by a third party, IM. Parkway argues that its allowing IW to stay in business constituted reasonably equivalent value for IW's guarantee of IM's debt. * * *

The bankruptcy court determined as a matter of law that "a conveyance by a corporation for the benefit of an affiliate is not regarded as given [sic] fair consideration to the creditors of the conveying corporations," citing *Rubin v. Manufacturers Hanover Trust Co.*, 661 F.2d 979 (2d Cir. 1981). This determination is an overly narrow statement of law, and misreads the holding of *Rubin*. Nevertheless, under the appropriate law, the bankruptcy court did not clearly err in ruling that the guarantees were fraudulent transfers.

* * *

Intercorporate guarantees are a routine business practice, and their potential voidability creates a risk for unwary lenders. Intercorpo-

---

[1] The Bankruptcy Court found that "FCL Graphics was an important customer of Parkway Bank and its sole shareholder, Frank Calabrese, was also a shareholder of Parkway Bank."

rate guarantees are common because they benefit both the creditor and debtor in a loan transaction. Within a corporate group, some units will often have better credit ratings than others. The units which are perceived as credit risks by lenders will be either unable to obtain loans, or able to obtain a loan only at a higher interest rate. However, when the corporate group exploits the units with good credit ratings by having them guarantee the debt of the weaker unit, the weaker unit will benefit from either obtaining the loan, or getting the loan at a better rate. The creditor benefits from greater security in repayment. So between creditor and debtor, the guarantee is a win-win situation.

However, the creditors of the guarantor making a cross-stream guarantee can sometimes lose out in the transaction, because the guaranteeing corporation may not receive a direct economic benefit from the guarantee. Should the guarantee push the guarantor into insolvency, these transactions will be scrutinized under a fraudulent transfer analysis. Fraudulent transfer law seeks to preserve assets of the estate for creditors. Some courts applying traditional fraudulent transfer rules to intercorporate guarantees therefore found that the guarantor had not received reasonably equivalent value for the guarantee, because from the standpoint of the unsecured creditor, the guarantor had received no consideration for the guarantee.

However, requiring a direct flow of capital to a cross-guarantor to avoid a finding of a fraudulent transfer "is inhibitory of contemporary financing practices, which recognize that cross-guarantees are often needed because of the unequal abilities of interrelated corporate entities to collateralize loans." *TeleFest, Inc. v. Vu-TV, Inc.*, 591 F.Supp. 1368, 1379 (D.N.J. 1984). Often, these guarantees are legitimate business transactions, and not made to frustrate creditors. In recognition of this economic reality, courts have loosened the old rule that transfers primarily for the benefit of a third party invariably give no consideration to the transferor. Thus, even when there has been no direct economic benefit to a guarantor, courts performing a fraudulent transfer analysis have been increasingly willing to look at whether a guarantor received indirect benefits from the guarantee if there has been an indirect benefit. "One theme permeates the authorities upholding guaranty obligations: that the guaranty at issue was the result of arm's length negotiations at a time when the common enterprise was commercially viable." Jack F. Williams, *The Fallacies of Contemporary Fraudulent Transfer Models as Applied to Intercorporate Guaranties: Fraudulent Transfer Law as a Fuzzy System*, 15 CARDOZO L. REV. 1403, 1438 (1994).

Generally, a court will not recognize an indirect benefit unless it is "fairly concrete." The most straightforward indirect benefit is when the guarantor receives from the debtor some of the consideration paid to it. But courts have found other economic benefits to qualify as indirect benefits. For example, in *Mellon Bank, N.A. v. Metro Communications, Inc.*, 945 F.2d 635, 646-48 (3d Cir.1991), the court found reasonably equivalent value for a debtor corporation's guarantee of an affiliate's debt when the loan strengthened the corporate group as a whole, so that the guarantor corporation would benefit from "synergy" within the corporate group. The *Mellon* court stated that indirect benefits included intangibles such as goodwill, and an increased ability to borrow working capital. *TeleFest, Inc. v. Vu-TV Inc.*, 591 F. Supp. 1368 (D.N.J. 1984), indicated that indirect benefits to a guarantor exist when "the transaction of which the guaranty is a part may safeguard an important source of supply, or an important customer for the guarantor. Or substantial indirect benefits may result from the general relationship" between affiliates. *Id.* at 1380-81. In *In re Xonics Photochem., Inc.*, 841 F.2d 198, 202 (7th Cir. 1988), we recognized the ability of a smaller company to use the distribution system of a larger affiliate as an indirect benefit as well.

* * *

However, in order to prevail, Parkway must show that the bankruptcy court clearly erred in finding that no consideration or reasonably equivalent value were given in exchange for the guarantee. Parkway argues that its allowing IW to stay in business constituted reasonably equivalent value for the guarantee. The trustee, relying on *Leonard v. Norman Vinitsky Residuary Trust (In re Jolly's Inc.)*, 188 B.R. 832 (Bankr. D. Minn. 1995), counters that allowing the guarantor to stay in business can never be reasonably equivalent value for the guarantee of a third party's debt. *Jolly's* does not support this broad proposition.

Jolly's involved the guarantee by a wholly owned subsidiary of its parent company's debt. The parent company (SEI) acquired Jolly's in a leveraged buyout (LBO). The debt SEI incurred in the acquisition of Jolly's was secured by the stock of Jolly's, as well as substantially all the assets of Jolly's. When Jolly's was involuntarily forced into bankruptcy, the defendants argued that the reasonably equivalent value for this guarantee was "the opportunity to continue to carry on business, relieved of the immediate threat of foreclosure by [the secured creditor]." While the *Jolly's* court did find that this was inadequate value in that case, its analysis does not extend beyond the LBO context. Indeed, other courts have noted the uniqueness of the LBO:

The effect of an LBO is that a corporation's shareholders are replaced by secured creditors. Put simply, stockholders' equity is supplanted by corporate debt. The level of risk facing the newly structured corporation rises significantly due to the increased debt to equity ratio. This added risk is borne primarily by the unsecured creditors, those who will most likely not be paid in the event of bankruptcy.

Mellon Bank, 945 F.2d at 645-46.

* * *

Even so, Parkway fails to show that IW received reasonably equivalent value for the IM loan. We agree with the bankruptcy court that there was no consideration for the guarantee of the IM loan. In this case, prior to IW's signing the guarantee to repay [the] IM loan, Parkway had no claim against IW because IW had never dealt with Parkway. Parkway might have had a claim against IM or Steinberg (though this is questionable, given that uncontroverted testimony at trial showed that Parkway was aware of and cooperated in the liquidation of IM), but Parkway could not have attacked IW for the winding down of IM. While Parkway might have decided not to exercise its rights against IM under the IM loan, under Illinois law, forbearance is sufficient consideration for a guarantee only when it is pursuant to an agreement to forbear. While an agreement to forbear need not be express, the bank did not allege that such an agreement existed. Even if it had, reasonably equivalent value is something more than consideration to support a contract, and in the absence of countervailing factors, such an agreement would not likely meet the higher standard.

* * *

The Steinberg loan presents a much closer case, because IW may have received an indirect benefit from this guarantee. FCL Graphics was IW's printer, and thus its most important supplier. FCL also allowed IM and IW to operate their business on FCL's premises. * * * If the Steinberg loan had not been made to pay off IM's debt to FCL, FCL Graphics clearly posed a substantial threat to IW because of its ability to evict IW and discontinue providing services to IW. *TeleFest* states that:

[Some courts have] rationalized upholding various transfers against fraudulent conveyance challenges by finding that sufficient consideration passed to the transferor because an opportunity had been given to it to avoid bankruptcy through the strengthening of an affiliated corporation that received the benefit of the transfer. Such an approach seems indisputably proper when a weak but still solvent entity is rendered insolvent only because of the inclusion of the guaranty on the liability side of the balance sheet. This permits the analysis to focus upon economic reality in the appropriate factual context without rewarding legal laxity or inflexibly ignoring real benefits merely because they have no place on the company's balance sheet.

TeleFest, 591 F. Supp. at 1379. Under the broad reading of the indirect benefit doctrine laid down in cases like *TeleFest*, IW received an indirect benefit from the payment of the Steinberg loan because the loan kept FCL Graphics from kicking Steinberg and his companies off of FCL's property, and from refusing to do business with Steinberg. True, the balance sheet showed that IW was insolvent after taking on the IM loan and the Steinberg loan, but IW was not finished as a going concern, as IW was able to remain in business for 17 months after guaranteeing the Steinberg loan.

On the other hand, the circumstances of this case do not fit the circumstances when indirect benefits from a guarantee are found to constitute reasonably equivalent value. As indicated above, courts that uphold cross-stream guarantees generally do so when the transaction strengthens the viability of the corporate group. In this case, though, there were not two functioning corporations that benefitted mutually from the loan. By the time IW guaranteed the Steinberg loan, IM had been wound down. Even though it was not officially dissolved, the company had been liquidated and was inactive. IW became insolvent to pay an inactive affiliate's debts. Indeed, while IW was able to timely pay the bank pursuant to the loans for a time after guaranteeing the loans, IW eventually fell behind in payments to trade creditors just like IM had. In effect, by paying off IM's debts, IW kept IM out of bankruptcy by bankrupting itself. This shift of risk from the creditors of the debtor to the creditors of the guarantor is exactly the situation that fraudulent transfer law seeks to avoid when applied to guarantees. Thus, while IW received an indirect benefit from the transaction, it did not receive reasonably equivalent value.

* * *

We therefore hold that indirect benefits to a guarantor may be considered when determining whether a corporation receives reasonably equivalent value for a guarantee. However, we do not believe that the bankruptcy court clearly erred when it found that IW did not receive reasonably equivalent value for its guarantees. * * *

Notes and Problems

1. The court recognized that indirect benefits may figure into a determination of reasonably equivalent value, but found no error in the bankruptcy court's conclusion that the debtor did not receive reasonably equivalent value in this case. In what situations might a debtor receive reasonably equivalent value as a result of an intercorporate guarantee?

2. Corporation-A sought a loan of $5,000,000 from Bank. Despite Corporation-A's strong financial position, Bank required Corporation-A to obtain a guaranty from its affiliate, Corporation-D, as a condition of loan approval. Corporation-D's product line had fallen out of fashion with the public and it was not as strong financially as Corporation-A, having net assets at the time of the transaction of only $2,500,000. Nonetheless, the guaranty was given and Bank made the loan. Within a few months, Corporation-D's business collapsed and it filed a bankruptcy petition. Is Corporation-D's guaranty avoidable as a fraudulent conveyance? Can you think of an argument that it is not? Cf. *Matter of Xonics Photochemical, Inc.*, 841 F.2d 198 (7th Cir.1988).

C. PREFERENCES

1. INTRODUCTION

Unlike state law's condemnation of fraudulent transfers, state law generally does not condemn preferences (with one exception[b]). A debtor may treat some creditors more favorably than others. In other words, if Debtor has $1,000 in assets and owes $500 to each of five creditors, state law allows Debtor to pay two of them in full and not to pay the remaining three anything at all. The Bankruptcy Code, however, does not allow such preferred treatment of creditors. The objects of preference law are to assure that all those with claims against the debtor share in an equitable fashion, as determined by the nature of their claims, and that creditors do not rush in on a shaky debtor, thus propelling the debtor into bankruptcy. While a solvent debtor is free to

[b] The exception is found in § 5(b) of the UFTA. Under that provision, a transfer made by an insolvent debtor to an insider for an antecedent debt is a fraudulent transfer, as to an existing creditor, if the insider had reasonable cause to believe that the debtor was insolvent when the transfer was made. Transfers to insiders attract special attention—here, as well as in the Bankruptcy Code's preference provision—because insiders are in a unique position to protect themselves at the expense of other creditors.

pay creditors in any order whatever, preference law assures that the insolvent debtor does not favor one creditor over another. Preference law constitutes a conclusion that each of Debtor's five creditors should realize $200, rather than two receiving the full $500 owed them and the other three receiving nothing. Preferences are an important part of bankruptcy law. "Probably none of [the trustee's avoiding] powers is of more concern to pre-bankruptcy transferees than the trustee's power to avoid preferential transfers." Vern Countryman, *The Concept of a Voidable Preference in Bankruptcy*, 38 VAND. L. REV. 713, 713 (1985).

Fraudulent transfers and preferences may appear to be distinct transactions in commercial insolvency law. For a transfer to be fraudulent, the debtor must either receive less than reasonably equivalent value while insolvent, or the transfer must have been infected with an actual intent to hinder, delay or defraud creditors. Neither of those circumstances is necessarily the case when the debtor prefers one creditor over another. The two avoiding powers, however, may apply to the same transaction. Indeed, the most noteworthy case in the fraudulent conveyance jurisprudence, *Twyne's Case*, actually involved a preference: Pierce preferred Twyne as a creditor over C and did so with an intent to hinder his other creditors. Preferences and fraudulent transfers also share a policy affinity, as Dean Robert Clark recognized:

> The law of fraudulent conveyances, together with the law of voidable preferences, implicates a coherent set of conceptually distinct moral principles that should govern the conduct of debtors toward their creditors. These principles of Truth, Respect and Evenhandedness, which may be grouped under the more general duty of Nonhindrance, are so related to one another in practice and under the standard "rules" of fraudulent conveyance actions that courts understandably have trouble, at times, distinguishing fraudulent conveyances from preferences.

Robert Charles Clark, *The Duties of the Corporate Debtor to Its Creditors*, 90 HARV. L. REV. 505, 560–61 (1977).

The conclusion that no creditor should be preferred is not unassailable, as a matter of policy. Arguably, the insolvent debtor should be just as free as the solvent debtor to prefer some creditors over others—by preferring one to another the debtor may be compensating the preferred creditor for some favor or relationship that was of greater value to the debtor (and, more or less directly, to the other creditors) than was the value extended to the debtor by creditors who were not preferred. Even if preferences are allowed, however, a potential fraud problem remains: the law cannot be certain that the preferred creditor has not engaged in some type of overreaching inimical to the object of debtor-creditor law. At that juncture, an affinity between constructively fraudulent transfers and preference principles is manifest.

2. ELEMENTS OF A PREFERENCE

The elements of a preference are found in § 547(b). (Exceptions, to which we will turn shortly, are listed in § 547(c).) In order to find a preference, *every single one* of the elements must be satisfied.

Problems

Read §§ 547(b), (e) and (f) and decide which of the following fact patterns present preferences. In each case, assume that unsecured creditors will be paid less than 100% of their claims out of the bankruptcy estate.

1. Debtor borrowed $25,000 from Bank on May 1 on an unsecured basis. Debtor repaid the loan on June 15 and filed bankruptcy on September 1. Can the trustee avoid the payment as a preference?

2. Would your answer to Problem # 1 change if Debtor filed bankruptcy on October 1?

3. Paul made an unsecured loan of $15,000 to Corporation on February 1. Because Paul was president of Corporation, he was aware that Corporation was encountering financial problems. Corporation repaid Paul's loan on April 20 and filed bankruptcy on November 1. Can the trustee avoid the payment as a preference?

4. Creditor obtained a judgment against Debtor on June 5 for $6,000 and docketed it in the county where Debtor lived. Debtor's house, which was worth $100,000, was already encumbered by a mortgage of $70,000 and a prior judgment lien of $15,000. Debtor filed bankruptcy on September 1. Has a preferential transfer occurred?

5. Debtor borrowed $20,000 from Bank on October 1 and signed a security agreement granting Bank a security interest in equipment Debtor already owned, which was worth $10,000, to secure repayment of the loan. Bank did not file the financing statement until October 8. Debtor filed bankruptcy on January 5 of the next year. Has a preferential transfer occurred?

6. Would your answer to Problem # 5 change if Bank filed its financing statement on November 3? If Bank never filed the financing statement?

7. Debtor borrowed $20,000 from Bank, in order to purchase a luxury car; Bank perfected a security interest in the car immediately. When Debtor

filed bankruptcy 18 months later, the car was worth $12,000 and Debtor still owed $15,000 to Bank. In the 90 days before bankruptcy, Debtor paid Bank three loan installments of $350 each. Are the payments preferential transfers?

8. Would your answer to Problem # 7 change if the car were worth $18,000?

9. Debtor Corp. borrowed $50,000 from Bank. The loan was guaranteed by Debtor Corp.'s president, who had substantial personal assets. Debtor Corp. made a $20,000 payment to Bank and filed bankruptcy 10 days later. Can the trustee avoid the payment as a preference?

Note on Avoidability of Payments by Check

One of the preference requirements, found in § 547(b)(4), is that the transfer occur (in noninsider cases) within the 90 days preceding bankruptcy. A debtor who pays a creditor by check may unwittingly enter the preference period. The debtor may draw a check and deliver it to the creditor several days before the 90–day period. The creditor then deposits the check, but a few days pass before the check reaches the debtor's bank and is honored. If the check is honored within the preference period, the question is whether the operative transfer for preference purposes occurred when the check was delivered to the payee or when the drawee bank honored it.

In *Barnhill v. Johnson*, 503 U.S. 393, 112 S.Ct. 1386, 118 L.Ed.2d 39 (1992), the trustee argued that the transfer occurred on the date the bank honored the check. The creditor, on the other hand, argued for a "date of delivery" rule. The bankruptcy court agreed with the creditor, but the Tenth Circuit reversed. The Supreme Court then affirmed.

The Supreme Court looked to commercial paper law, which gives the holder of a checking account a claim against the bank in an amount equal to the account balance. The check is an order to the drawee bank to pay, but it gives the recipient of the check no rights against the drawee bank if the bank refuses to honor the check. See UCC § 3–408. The disappointed recipient may sue the drawer either on the check or on the underlying obligation for which the check was given, but the recipient may not sue the bank. The Court concluded, in light of these state law rules, "that no transfer of any part of the debtor's claim against the bank occurred until the bank honored the check." 503 U.S. at 399.

The creditor then made an argument based on the definition of "transfer" found in § 101(54):

Petitioner urges that rather than viewing the transaction as involving two distinct actions—delivery of the check, with no interest in property thereby being transferred, and honoring of the check, with an interest being transferred—that we instead should view delivery of the check as a "conditional" transfer. We acknowledge that § 101(54) adopts an expansive definition of transfer, one that includes "every mode * * * absolute or conditional * * * of disposing of or parting with property or with an interest in property." There is thus some force in petitioner's claim that he did, in fact, gain something when he received the check. But at most, what petitioner gained was a chose in action against the debtor. Such a right, however, cannot fairly be characterized as a conditional right to "property or an interest in property," § 101(54), where the property in this case is the account maintained with the drawee bank. For as noted above, until the moment of honor the debtor retains full control over disposition of the account and the account remains subject to a variety of actions by third parties. To treat petitioner's nebulous right to bring suit as a "conditional transfer" of the property would accomplish a near-limitless expansion of the term "conditional." In the absence of any right against the bank or the account, we think the fairer description is that petitioner had received no interest in debtor's property, not that his interest was "conditional."

Finally, we note that our conclusion that no transfer of property occurs until the time of honor is consistent with § 547(e)(2)(A). That section provides that a transfer occurs at the time the transfer "takes effect between the transferor and the transferee." For the reasons given above, and in particular because the debtor in this case retained the ability to stop payment on the check until the very last, we do not think that the transfer of funds in this case can be said to have "taken effect between the debtor and petitioner" until the moment of honor.

Id. at 400-01. The creditor also argued that the legislative history calls for a date-of-delivery rule, but the Court disagreed:

[The legislative history applies] only to § 547(c), not § 547(b). Section 547(c), in turn, establishes various exceptions to § 547(b)'s general rule permitting recovery of preferential transfers. Subsection (c)(1) provides an exception for transfers that are part of a contemporaneous exchange of new value between a debtor and creditor; subsection (c)(2) provides an exception for transfers made from debtor to creditor in the ordinary course of business. These sections are designed to encourage creditors to continue to deal with troubled debtors on normal business terms by obviating any worry that a subsequent bankruptcy filing might require the creditor to disgorge as a preference an earlier received payment. But given this specialized purpose, we see no basis for concluding that the legislative history, particularly legislative history explicitly confined by its own terms to § 547(c), should cause us to adopt a "date of delivery" rule for purposes of § 547(b).

Id. at 402. Because the drawer's underlying obligation on a check is suspended pro tanto under UCC § 3–310(b), the two dissenters concluded that delivery was the operative event for preference purposes.

The Court's holding leaves open the possibility that a date-of-honor rule might apply for purposes of determining whether a preference occurred, but that a date-of-delivery rule might govern the preference exceptions.

We often speak of the five elements of a preference, referring to §§ 547(b)(1) through (b)(5). The preamble to (b)(1), however, contains two additional requirements—that there be a "transfer" and that the transfer be "of an interest of the debtor in property." The following case required the court to identify what constituted the "transfer," but resolution of that question also determined whether the 90-day requirement was satisfied.

FREEDOM GROUP, INC. v. LAPHAM-HICKEY STEEL CORP. (IN RE FREEDOM GROUP, INC.)

United States Court of Appeals, Seventh Circuit, 1995.
50 F.3d 408.

POSNER, Chief Judge.

Freedom Group, a bankrupt, filed an adversary proceeding against Lapham–Hickey, seeking to undo what it claimed had been a preferential transfer resulting from a judicial seizure of Freedom Group's bank account. The bankruptcy judge agreed with Freedom Group and ordered Lapham–Hickey to return the money, but the district court reversed, so the case comes to us on Freedom Group's appeal.

The facts were stipulated. On June 2 Lapham–Hickey obtained a judgment for $7,335.49 (plus interest and costs) against Freedom Group in an Indiana state court. Ten days later, the court entered an order called a "notice of garnishment" in favor of Lapham–Hickey, and on June 15 Lapham–Hickey served the order on Freedom Group's bank. The balance in Freedom Group's bank account that day was only $108.25. But on the next day Freedom Group deposited $18,000 in the account. On the following day—June 17, 1992—the state court entered a final order of attachment (= garnishment), directing the bank to pay any and all money in Freedom Group's account up to the limit of the judgment. In compliance with this order, the bank cut a check to Lapham–Hickey for $7,743.11 (the difference between that amount and the amount of the judgment representing, we assume, interest). Freedom Group declared bankruptcy on September 14, 1992. The sequence, then, was: judgment; notice of garnishment issued; notice of garnishment served on bank; bank account augmented by large deposit; final order of attachment (equivalently, of garnishment) entered; bank pays creditor, pursuant to that final order; debtor declares bankruptcy.

June 15, the day the notice of garnishment was served on the bank, was the ninety-first day before the declaration of bankruptcy. June 16, the day the $18,000 was deposited in Freedom Group's bank account, was the ninetieth day before the bankruptcy. June 17, the day the final order of attachment was issued, was the eighty-ninth day before the bankruptcy. If the transfer of the $7,743.11 occurred within 90 days of the bankruptcy—that is, occurred anytime after June 15—it is avoidable; otherwise not. A preferential transfer is avoidable only if made within 90 days before bankruptcy was declared. § 547(b)(4)(A).

The Bankruptcy Code defines "transfer" broadly, as "every mode, direct or indirect, absolute or conditional, voluntary or involuntary, of disposing of or parting with property or with an interest in property," § 101(54),[c] and provides, so far as bears on this case, that a preferential transfer "is made * * * at the time such transfer takes effect between the transferor and the transferee, if such transfer is perfected at, or within 10 days after, such time." § 547(e)(2)(A). But although the Code defines transfer and specifies when a transfer is made—thus making whether and when a transfer occurs issues of federal law, *Barnhill v. Johnson*, 503 U.S. 393, 112 S.Ct. 1386 (1992)—it looks to state law for the definition of "property" and "interest in property." Under Indiana law a notice of garnishment not only prevents the debtor from withdrawing the funds in his bank account but also gives the judgment creditor who procured the notice a lien against the funds up to the amount of the judgment. A lien is a property interest, and it was acquired by Lapham–Hickey. The funds themselves were not transferred to Lapham–Hickey. They were merely frozen, until the final order of attachment was issued and complied with—and if the transfer did not occur until then, it came too late for Lapham–Hickey to avert a finding of preferential transfer. Lapham–Hickey argues, however, that a "transfer" within the meaning of the Bankruptcy Code is any mode of

---

[c] This section was reconfigured in 2005. Eds.

disposing of an interest in property; a lien—a right to satisfy a judgment out of specific property (here, Freedom Group's bank account)—is an interest in that property; that right was "disposed of" to Lapham–Hickey by the notice of garnishment; therefore the transfer occurred before the ninety-day portcullis descended. It is a nice, tidy, "logical" argument but so manifestly contrary to the purpose of the statute as to incite grave doubts, at least in judges who are not in thrall to the syllogistic style of legal reasoning.

The purpose of allowing preferential transfers to be set aside is to prevent debtors who are tottering toward bankruptcy from playing favorites among their creditors, trying to keep alive a little longer by placating the most importunate ones. The reason for worrying about this favoritism is that the possibility of it makes creditors less likely to forbear—more likely to insist on immediate payment—and, if immediate payment is not forthcoming, to sue and obtain judgments, thus increasing the costs to all creditors, retarding an orderly liquidation, and hurrying the debtor into bankruptcy faster than if creditors did not have to fear each other. The statute reduces the debtor's ability to play favorites, and hence the anxiety of creditors, and hence the costly melee that such anxiety can engender, by telling the favored creditor that if the debtor goes broke within ninety days after the transfer, the transfer will be undone and the favored creditor tossed back in the pool with the rest of the creditors.

The position for which Lapham–Hickey contends undermines this policy in two ways. The first has to do with the continuing character of the notice of garnishment. The notice does not freeze just the amount of money in the garnished bank account on the date of the notice. It freezes any increments up until the service of the final order of attachment. When that order is served, the judgment creditor becomes entitled to whatever money has accumulated in the account, up to the level of the judgment. How much that shall be is within the debtor's discretion to decide. Freedom Group did not have to deposit $18,000—or 1 cent—in its bank account after the notice of garnishment was issued. That was a decision made (or effectuated) by Freedom Group within ninety days of declaring bankruptcy, and thus during the period of avoidable preferences. The effect was to put one of its creditors, the one that had succeeded in garnishing its bank account, ahead of the others—and that is just the sort of thing that the preferential-transfer statute is intended to prevent.

Lapham–Hickey argues that even though it did not pocket the $18,000 until after the ninety-day countdown to bankruptcy began, the transfer relates back to the ninety-first day, the day of the notice of garnishment, because the notice "perfected" Lapham–Hickey's claim to the contents of Freedom Group's bank account. But perfection and transfer are distinct concepts, as is plain from the provision of the Code that we quoted earlier on the timing of a preferential transfer. "Perfection" refers to the priority of rights among creditors. The notice of garnishment perfected Lapham–Hickey's lien in the sense of putting that lien ahead of any other lien that a creditor of Freedom Group's might attempt to assert against the bank account; first in time, first in right—and the relevant time is when the notice of garnishment is served. The preference-avoidance provision of the Bankruptcy Code is not concerned with the order of liens on Freedom Group's bank account. It is concerned with preventing the debtor from picking and choosing among creditors. Freedom Group picked and chose within the preference period when it decided to deposit money in an account controlled by one of its creditors.

The second way in which Lapham–Hickey's position undermines the purposes of preference avoidance arises from the tentative nature of a notice of garnishment, and shows that Lapham–Hickey is not entitled to keep even the $108.25 that was in the bank account when the notice was served. The notice of garnishment is like a preliminary injunction. It seeks to protect a creditor against the irreparable harm that will ensue if the debtor dissipates funds needed to pay the creditor. It does this by freezing funds owed to the debtor (as by the bank that was the garnishee in this case), so that they will be available to the creditor if and when he establishes his right to them. But the notice does not itself establish that right. It merely gives him a breathing space in which to establish it. In this case, that did not take long—just two days. But until the two days were up, there was some chance that the creditor, Lapham–Hickey, would not get the funds after all. There might be another creditor ahead of it; there might be some serious defect in the judgment; the judgment might not be against this debtor; the garnishee might not be holding funds owed to the debtor; and so forth. Suppose the debtor wanted this creditor to get his money. The debtor might decide not to interpose valid defenses to the garnishment. This decision might come, or take effect, well into the preference period. The effect would be, within that period, to favor one creditor over another.

We are mindful of the flock of cases which equate perfection to transfer for purposes of applying the preference-avoidance provision—indeed which hold specifically that a transfer occurs within the meaning of the Code when a notice of garnishment is served. All but one of these cases, however, were decided before the Supreme Court's decision in *Barnhill v. Johnson, supra,* and in our view do not survive that decision. The issue in *Barnhill* was whether a transfer within the meaning of the preferential-transfer provision of the Code—the provision at issue in our case, as well as in the cases we have just cited—occurred when the debtor delivered his check to the creditor or not until the bank on which the check was drawn honored the check; and the Court held that it was the latter, because "myriad events can intervene between delivery and presentment of the check that would result in the check being dishonored." 112 S.Ct. at 1390. The same thing is true here. Between the service of the notice of garnishment, corresponding to the delivery of a check, and the final order of attachment, corresponding to the bank's decision to honor (pay) the check, all sorts of events might intervene that would prevent the creditor from obtaining payment.

Many of the cases rely on § 547(e)(2)(B), which provides, as an alternative time at which a preferential transfer occurs, "the time such transfer is perfected, if such transfer is perfected after 10 days."[d] But this provision is intended for the case in which the transfer occurs first, and is later perfected. Here we had perfection, but no transfer until the right of the favored creditor to the money was determined, which took place within the 90-day preference period.

Naturally we are given pause by the Sixth Circuit's decision in *In re Battery One-Stop Ltd.*, 36 F.3d 493, 494-98 (6th Cir. 1994), because it was decided after *Barnhill*. But it failed even to cite, let alone attempt to distinguish, *Barnhill*, and it does not discuss, let alone alleviate, our concern that treating the service of the notice of garnishment as the transfer would undermine the policy behind the preference-avoidance provision. It does not discuss that policy.

We conclude that a garnishment or attachment does not transfer money or other property to a creditor, for purposes of determining whether the transfer is an avoidable preference, until a final order of garnishment or attachment is issued. Until then, the transfer is tentative, its amount uncertain, and control or influence retained by the debtor to be used possibly to play favorites among his creditors. The judgment is therefore reversed with instructions to grant judgment to Freedom Group.

* * *

---

[d] The 2005 Amendments changed "10 days" to "30 days." Eds.

Questions

1. What was the "transfer" that the trustee was trying to avoid in this case? Was it Lapham–Hickey's garnishment lien, or was it the payment to Lapham–Hickey of $7,743.11 out of the debtor's bank account? Is there a difference?

2. The garnishment lien attached to the debtor's account and became perfected on June 15, did it not? The account had a balance of $108 at that time. Why, then, was Lapham–Hickey not entitled to keep $108?

3. Was the court appropriately concerned that the debtor might be trying to favor Lapham–Hickey, in violation of preference policy? Are there facts suggesting that no such favoritism was at play?

4. Was the court so caught up in preference policy that it ignored the language of the Code?

The second of the additional preference requirements found in the preamble to (b)(1) is that the transfer be "of an interest of the debtor in property." This requirement parallels § 541(a)(1), which determines property of the estate. Thus, cases dealing with this language in § 547-(b)(1)'s preamble may be, in reality, decisions about what constitutes property of the estate.

In *Begier v. Internal Revenue Service*, 496 U.S. 53, 110 S.Ct. 2258, 110 L.Ed.2d 46 (1990), for example, the trustee sought to recover payments of withholding and excise taxes—so-called "trust fund" taxes—that the debtor made to the IRS from its general bank account in the 90 days before its bankruptcy filing. The Court looked to § 541, which "serves as the postpetition analog to § 547(b)'s 'property of the debtor.'" *Id.* at 59. Under § 541(d), property in which the debtor has no equitable interest is not property of the estate and, therefore, is not "property of the debtor" for purposes of § 547(b). Thus the issue, according to the Court, was whether the funds paid from the general bank account were funds held in trust for the IRS.

The Court first found that the Internal Revenue Code does not require segregation of funds in a special account in order to create a trust. Rather, the trust was created when the payments were made to the IRS.

That did not solve the question "whether the *particular dollars* that [the debtor] paid to the IRS from its general operating accounts were 'property of the debtor,' " however. *Id.* at 62. In the absence of statutory guidance, the Court turned to legislative history:

> A payment of withholding taxes constitutes a payment of money held in trust under Internal Revenue Code § 7501(a), and thus will not be a preference because the beneficiary of the trust, the taxing authority, is in a separate class with respect to those taxes, if they have been properly held for payment, as they will have been if the debtor is able to make the payments.

H.R. Rep. No. 95–595 at 373, *reprinted in* 1978 U.S.C.C.A.N. at 6329. Under a "literal reading" of this excerpt, according to the Court, "the bankruptcy trustee could not avoid *any* voluntary prepetition payment of trust-fund taxes, regardless of the source of the funds." *Id.* at 66. "The debtor's act of voluntarily paying its trust-fund tax obligation therefore is alone sufficient to establish the required nexus between the 'amount' held in trust and the funds paid." *Id.* at 66-67.

JUSTICE SCALIA, concurring, unsurprisingly took great exception to the Court's "scouring [of] the legislative history for some scrap that is on point (and therefore *ipso facto* relevant, no matter how unlikely a source of congressional reliance or attention)." *Id.* at 70. And even though "[a] trust without a res can no more be created by legislative decree than can a pink rock-candy mountain," *id.*, he concluded

> that one must at least give this effect to § 7501's clearly expressed but sometimes ineffectual intent to create an *immediate* trust: If and when the trust res is identified from otherwise unencumbered assets, the trust should be deemed to have been in existence from the time of the collection or withholding. Thus, the designation of res does not constitute a preference, and the funds paid were not part of the debtor's estate.

Id. at 71.

Another aspect of § 547(b)'s requirement that the transfer be "of an interest of the debtor in property" arose in the next case. Here we encounter a judicially-created gloss on the Code, known as the "earmarking" doctrine.

PARKS v. FIA CARD SERVICES, N.A.
(IN RE MARSHALL)

United States Court of Appeals, Tenth Circuit, 2008.
550 F.3d 1251, *cert. denied*, 557 U.S. 937, 129 S.Ct. 2871, 174 L.Ed.2d 579 (2009).

O'BRIEN, Circuit Judge.

* * *

[Debtors had two credit card accounts with MBNA and two with Capital One. During the 90 days before they filed Chapter 7, Debtors used two balance transfer orders (one for each account) directing Capital One to pay a total of $38,000 to the two MBNA accounts. The bankruptcy trustee sought to recover the transfers from MBNA's successor-in-interest, FIA Card Services, as preferences.]

I. BACKGROUND

* * *

The bankruptcy court determined Debtors' payments to MBNA were not preferential transfers because they did not constitute transfers of an interest of Debtors in property as required by § 547(b):

> [T]he funds paid to * * * MBNA were assets of Capit[a]l One in which the Debtors did not have an interest for purposes of § 547. Debtors merely exercised an offer to transfer credit card balances; this offer, if not exercised as of the date of filing, would have added no value to the estate. The transfer was a mere substitution of creditors which had no impact on either the property of the estate or the value of the claims asserted against the estate.

Parks appealed to the district court.

The district court affirmed the bankruptcy court's decision but analyzed the case under the earmarking doctrine which, in its broadest terms, exempts a debtor's use of borrowed funds from the Trustee's avoidance powers when those funds are lent for the purpose of paying a specific debt. In doing so, it looked to the amount of control Debtors exercised over the payments to MBNA and whether the transfer of those payments diminished the bankruptcy estate. It thought Debtors lacked the requisite control over the payments for them to constitute interests of Debtors in property:

> It is undisputed that the debtors never possessed a check or proceeds of a loan. Capital One was under no obligation to cooperate with the debtors' request. The debtor[s] could not compel Capital One to make a payment. Nonetheless, Capital One chose to make a payment directly and specifically to MBNA on the debtors' behalf and essentially substituted itself as the debtors' creditor for the MBNA debt under the terms agreed [to] through the balance transfer agreement. The Court finds this to be a bank to bank transfer resulting in a substitution of the debtors' creditors.

The district court also concluded that because there was never a transfer of assets, only credit, the bankruptcy estate was not diminished.

II. DISCUSSION

* * *

Only the threshold requirement of § 574(b) is at issue here, *i.e.*, whether the payments made to Debtors' MBNA credit card accounts from their Capital One credit card accounts constitute transfers of "an interest of the debtor in property." This is a legal issue we review de novo.

The Bankruptcy Code does not define "an interest of the debtor in property." However, in *Begier v. IRS*, 496 U.S. 53 (1990), the Supreme Court said:

> Because the purpose of the avoidance provision is to preserve the property includable within the bankruptcy estate—the property available for distribution to creditors—"property of the debtor" subject to the preferential transfer provision is best understood as that property that would have been part of the estate had it not been transferred before the commencement of bankruptcy proceedings. For guidance, then, we must turn to § 541, which delineates the scope of "property of the estate" and serves as the postpetition analog to § 547(b)'s "property of the debtor."

Id. at 58-59.[2] Section 541(a)(1) provides that the property of the estate includes "all legal or equitable interests of the debtor in property as of the commencement of the [bankruptcy] case" wherever located and by whomever held. "[T]he scope of [§] 541 is broad and should be generously construed[;] * * * an interest may be property of the estate even if it is novel or contingent." *Baer v. Jones (In re Montgomery)*, 224 F.3d 1193, 1194 (10th Cir.2000) (quotations omitted).

* * * We have uncovered no Kansas authority specifically addressing the issue presented here but, in general, the right to use an item or to control its use is a property interest.

Courts have used this dominion/control test to determine whether a transfer of property was a transfer of "an interest of the debtor in property." *See, e.g., McLemore v. Third Nat'l Bank in Nashville (In re Montgomery)*, 983 F.2d 1389, 1395 (6th Cir.1993). Under this test, a transfer of property will be a transfer of "an interest of the debtor in property" if the debtor exercised dominion or control over the transferred property.

Other courts have applied a diminution of the estate test. *See, e.g., Southmark Corp. v. Grosz (In re Southmark Corp.)*, 49 F.3d 1111, 1116-17 (5th Cir.1995). Under this analysis, a debtor's transfer of property constitutes a transfer of "an interest of the debtor in property" if it deprives the bankruptcy estate of resources which would otherwise have been used to satisfy the claims of creditors. "[I]f the debtor transfers property that would not have been available for distribution to his creditors in a bankruptcy proceeding, the policy behind the avoidance power is not implicated." *Begier*, 496 U.S. at 58.

As both the district court and bankruptcy court acknowledged, their conclusion that the credit card payments in this case were not transfers of "an interest of [Debtors] in property" represents the minority view. The majority of courts to address the issue have gone the other way. *See, e.g., Meoli v. MBNA Am. Bank, N.A. (In re Wells)*, 382 B.R. 355 (B.A.P. 6th Cir.2008). These courts reason that the debtor, even if never in actual possession of the loaned proceeds, exercises dominion or control over them as evidenced by an ability to direct their

---

[2] In *Begier*, the Court analyzed the meaning of the phrase "property of the debtor" which was the language used in the pre-1984 version of § 547(b). Nevertheless, because the amendment of that phrase to the current phrase ("interest of the debtor in property") was only a "clarifying change," the Court said both phrases were coextensive with property of the estate as defined in § 541(a)(1).

distribution. They also conclude such transactions deplete the bankruptcy estate—when a debtor converts an offer of credit into loan proceeds and uses those proceeds to pay another creditor, the debtor deprives the bankruptcy estate of those proceeds.

We agree with the majority view. Technology masks the processes involved here. Separating them into constituent elements reveals a sequence of events, not just one: Debtors drew on their Capital One line of credit; that draw converted available credit into a loan; Debtors directed Capital One to use the loan proceeds to pay MBNA; and Capital One complied. It is essentially the same as if Debtors had drawn on their Capital One line of credit, deposited the proceeds into an account within their control, and then wrote [*sic*] a check to MBNA. The latter is clearly a preference. That [a] case involved constructive[4] rather than physical possession and took place electronically rather than mechanically (through deposit slips and checks) is of no moment. In both scenarios, debtors obtained an interest in the loan proceeds even if the interest was only fleeting. An ability to control, made manifest, must equate to physical control. *See Yoppolo v. Greenwood Trust (In re Spitler)*, 213 B.R. 995, 999 (Bankr. N.D. Ohio 1997) (stating it is "the substance of the transfer, not its form, [which] is dispositive" as to whether a debtor has the ability to control the distribution of credit proceeds) (quotations omitted). The Debtors' exercise of their ability to control the disposition of the loan proceeds is the essence of this case.

Contrary to the district court's conclusion, there is no evidence Capital One could have stopped the payments to MBNA once it honored Debtors' draw. The payments were a debtor's discretionary use of borrowed funds to pay another debt. Such transactions are

---

[4] At bottom constructive possession is a convenient way to describe a right or ability to control personal property or an interest in it.

> Constructive possession of personal property by its owner exists where the owner has [i]ntentionally given the [a]ctual possession— namely, the direct physical control—of the property to another for the purpose of having him do some act [f]or the owner to or with the property; that is to say, constructive possession exists wholly in contemplation of law without possession in fact. If the controlling reason or primary purpose for which the surrender of possession is made belongs to the owner, he retains constructive possession. Where the owner retains constructive possession, the party to whom bare physical control of the property has been entrusted for the owner's purpose does not have possession but only custody.

Jacobson v. Aetna Cas. & Sur. Co., 46 N.W.2d 868, 871 (Minn.1951).

generally considered preferential transfers. The only exception to this rule is the earmarking doctrine, which the district court incorrectly applied.

Earmarking, even if extended beyond the codebtor context,[5] only applies when the lender requires the funds be used to pay a specific debt. Here, Capital One placed no conditions on Debtors' use of the funds, it only honored their instructions. The earmarking doctrine is inapplicable.

And Debtors' exercise of control of the loan proceeds also distinguishes this case from a bank-to-bank transfer of consumer debt, in which one bank simply agrees to purchase consumer debt from another bank. A debtor is not directly involved, let alone in control—a notice comes to the debtor redirecting required payments to the acquiring institution. Moreover, there was no agreement between Capital One and MBNA for the purchase of Debtors' paper.

We also consider whether Debtors' transfer of the Capital One loan proceeds to MBNA diminished the bankruptcy estate. It did. The net value of the estate did not change because the Capital One infusion of loan proceeds was totally offset by additional debt to Capital One. But that is not the relevant test. We must ask whether the loan proceeds "would have been part of the estate had [they] not been transferred before the commencement of bankruptcy proceedings." *Begier*, 496 U.S. at 58. The Capital One loan proceeds were an asset of the estate

---

[5] The judicially-created earmarking doctrine was originally limited to codebtor cases, *i.e.*, cases in which the lender who provides the funds to the debtor to pay off the creditor was also obligated to the creditor either as a guarantor or surety. *Manchester v. First Bank & Trust Co. (In re Moses)*, 256 B.R. 641, 645 (B.A.P. 10th Cir.2000). In such cases, there were three rationales for why such payments were not voidable by the Trustee: (1) the lender's payment to the creditor did not constitute a transfer of the debtor's property; (2) no diminution of the debtor's estate occurred since the debtor's new obligation to the lender was equal to the amount the debtor had owed to the creditor; and (3) to prevent unfairness to the lender—if its payment to the creditor was avoided and the money was recaptured for the bankruptcy estate, the lender, as guarantor, would forfeit that money but remain obligated to the creditor. *Id.* at 646. Eventually this doctrine was extended to cases in which the lender was not a guarantor or surety but rather provided funds to the debtor for the purpose of paying a specific indebtedness. *Id.*

In *In re Moses*, the Tenth Circuit Bankruptcy Appellate Panel concluded the earmarking doctrine should not have been extended beyond the codebtor context. *Id.* at 651. We need not resolve the issue here because even if so extended, it does not apply in this case.

for at least an instant before they were preferentially transferred to MBNA.[6] The preferential transfer look back is not time sensitive—the issue is whether any asset, regardless of how fleeting its presence in the bankrupt's estate during the relevant period of time, should be ratably apportioned among qualified creditors or permitted to benefit only a preferred creditor. The answer is as clear as the statute itself—all preferential transfers of estate assets during the ninety-day look back are subject to recapture.

In reaching the opposite conclusion, the district court and bankruptcy court mistakenly characterized the transferred property as untapped credit. In their view untapped credit cannot be used to satisfy creditors and, thus, no diminution of the estate occurred. But this case does not involve untapped credit. A transfer of loan proceeds (an asset) diminishes the bankrupt's estate.

Treating the payments to MBNA as avoidable preferential transfers furthers § 547(b)'s policy of equality of distribution between similarly situated creditors. Recapture allows all qualifying creditors, including Capital One and FIA, to ratably share in a $38,000 estate asset.

We reverse and remand to the district court for further proceedings consistent with this opinion.

Notes and Questions

1. What are the elements of the earmarking doctrine?

2. What are the policy justifications for the doctrine?

3. Do you agree with the result reached in *Marshall*? Why is it not relevant that the funds would never have been available to creditors other than

---

[6] The moment Capital One honored Debtors' draw on their line of credit those proceeds (the newly loaned funds) became an asset of Debtors' estate. A short time (perhaps only a nanosecond) later the assets were dissipated by the transfers to MBNA. The loan proceeds, like all preferential transfers, were not in the hands of Debtors when the bankruptcy petition was filed. But because of the preferential transfer statute, we must determine whether the proceeds were part of Debtors' estate at any time during the ninety-day look back. They were part of the bankruptcy estate immediately before being transferred to MBNA. The additional debt which accompanied the Capital One transactions is not relevant to our preference analysis, which concerns only assets.

MBNA because the debtors would not have drawn funds from Capital One except to pay MBNA?

4. Can the earmarking doctrine apply when the creditor making the new loan takes security for it? Later, we will see a case in which that occurred.

3. PREFERENCE EXCEPTIONS

As you work through the following materials on the preference exceptions, keep in mind the commercial policies that underlie preference law. Are the "exceptions" really exceptional or do they, rather, clarify the preference elements? That is, do the excepted transfers compromise preference principles in any way?

a. Contemporaneous Exchanges for New Value—§ 547(c)(1)

We saw, in the Note relating to payments by check, that delay between the moment the debt arose and the time of the debtor's payment may occur even when the parties are intending an entirely unsuspicious cash-for-goods transaction. Delay is even more typical when debtors grant security interests and mortgages; the Problems at the beginning of this section illustrated that a delay in recording can create preference problems even when the parties did not intend to create a "secret lien." The first preference exception, § 547(c)(1), recognizes that preference policies are not implicated in all cases in which a transfer is made for an antecedent debt.

Subsection (c)(1) requires, first, that the parties intended a contemporaneous exchange for new value and, second, that the transfer was in fact such an exchange. The first of these requirements derives from the Supreme Court's decision in *National City Bank v. Hotchkiss*, 231 U.S. 50, 34 S.Ct. 20, 58 L.Ed.115 (1913). In *Hotchkiss*, a creditor made an unsecured loan in the morning to a borrower who was a stockbroker. The market fell later in the day and the debtor was suspended by the stock exchange. When the creditor learned of these events in the afternoon, it demanded and received collateral for its loan. An involuntary bankruptcy petition was filed against the borrower later that day and the bankruptcy trustee sought to avoid the transfer. The Court held that the transfer of security was avoidable. Section § 547(c)(1)(A) leads to the same outcome by requiring that the parties have intended a substantially contemporaneous exchange, even when the transfer quickly follows creation of the debt.

The second of these requirements derives from *Dean v. Davis*, 242 U.S. 438, 37 S.Ct. 130, 61 L.Ed. 419 (1917). In *Dean*, an individual, Jones, negotiated promissory notes to a bank. The bank decided that the notes were forged and demanded that Jones pay their face amount. In order to avoid arrest, Jones borrowed $1,600 from his brother-in-law, Dean, and secured the obligation with a mortgage on all of his property. The mortgage instrument was dated September 3rd, executed September 10th, and recorded September 11th. The obligation was payable in four installments—seven, thirty, sixty and ninety days after the date of the mortgage—and included an acceleration clause. The first installment was overdue by the time the mortgage was recorded, so the entire obligation was due. Dean took possession of Jones's property two days after the mortgage was recorded. Jones was thrust into bankruptcy and the mortgaged property was sold. It brought only $1,634, which would leave nothing for his unsecured creditors if the mortgage were valid. Davis, the bankruptcy trustee, sought to set the mortgage aside as, *inter alia*, a preference. The Supreme Court found none: "The mortgage was given to secure Dean for a substantially contemporary advance. The bank, not Dean, was preferred." *Id.* at 443, 37 S.Ct. at 131, 61 L.Ed. at 421.[e] The case survives today in § 547(c)(1)'s requirement that the transfer be, in fact, "substantially contemporaneous."

The following case deals with subsection (c)(1) in an unexpected context—criminal law.

---

[e] The trustee's effort to avoid the mortgage on fraudulent conveyance grounds met with more success:

> Making a mortgage to secure an advance with which the insolvent debtor intends to pay a preexisting debt does not necessarily imply an intent to hinder, delay or defraud creditors. The mortgage may be made in the expectation that thereby the debtor will extricate himself from a particular difficulty and be enabled to promote the interest of all other creditors by continuing his business. The lender who makes an advance for that purpose with full knowledge of the facts may be acting in perfect "good faith." But where the advance is made to enable the debtor to make a preferential payment with bankruptcy in contemplation, the transaction presents an element upon which fraud may be predicated. The fact that the money advanced is actually used to pay a debt does not necessarily establish good faith. It is a question of fact in each case what the intent was with which the loan was sought and made.

242 U.S. at 444. The Court then concluded that the lower courts were within their discretion in finding that the mortgage was given with the intent to hinder, delay or defraud Jones's creditors.

LIBERTY MUTUAL INSURANCE CO. v. NEW YORK (IN RE CITRON)

United States Bankruptcy Court, Eastern District of New York, 2010.
428 B.R. 562.

ALAN S. TRUST, United States Bankruptcy Judge.

* * *

[Debtors Jeffrey and Lynn Citron were both indicted for multiple felony charges for defrauding Liberty Mutual Insurance Company. Jeffrey pleaded guilty to five felonies and received an indeterminate sentence of one and two-thirds to five years, along with a $75,000 fine to be paid by the sentencing date. Lynn pleaded guilty to a misdemeanor in exchange for which she was sentenced to three years' probation. In lieu of fines totaling $175,000, she agreed to pay $5,000 by her sentencing date, and an additional $4,722 per month over the duration of her probation. Both were sentenced on December 19, 2007 and Lynn paid $5,000 on that date. With permission from the criminal court, Jeffrey paid his entire fine on March 25, 2008 and Lynn paid an additional $9,000 on that date. They filed Chapter 13 two days later. Lynn never made any further payments and the state, in accordance with the parties' agreement, executed its lien on Debtors' house. Liberty Mutual, acting as fiduciary for the bankruptcy estate, sought to recover, from the state, the payments made by Debtors in March. New York conceded that the March payments were preferences.]

* * * This case presents the possibly anomalous result that a debtor could plead guilty, avoid jail, pay his or her monetary penalties, then file bankruptcy and have the federal, state or local sovereign stripped of the benefit of its bargain, with no ability to restore the criminal proceeding. However, the issue before this Court is not whether that possible result should flow from the Bankruptcy Code; the question for this Court is what result does derive from the Bankruptcy Code.

NY rests its entire preference defense on Section 547(c)(1) * * * . *[The court quoted §§ 547(c)(1) and (a)(2).]* As the *Tower* court noted, criminal restitution payments which are not fraudulent transfers may be preferences. *In re Tower Environmental, Inc.*, 260 B.R. 213, 223 (M.D.Fla.1998). NY has conceded that the March 2008 Payments satisfy each of the preference elements.

The analysis of the new value defense is different for Lynn Citron than for Jeffrey Citron. Jeffrey Citron made one payment contemporaneous with his sentencing on March 25, 2008, which was his only transfer. Lynn Citron, however, made one $5,000.00 payment contemporaneous with her sentencing on December 19, 2007, which was outside the preference window, and one payment of $9,000.00 on March 25, 2008. To the extent Lynn Citron received new value in exchange for agreeing to plead guilty, she received that value on December 19, 2007, when her plea was accepted and her sentence imposed. NY conceded that Lynn Citron's sentencing date had to be adjourned on several occasions because she claimed she did not have the funds available to pay the initial $5,000.00 installment, which she ultimately paid on December 19, 2007, when she was sentenced. However, the new value defense requires not only new value be received, but that the exchange of the new value for the transfer be intended to be and be in fact a substantially contemporaneous exchange.

NY argues that the sentencing of Lynn Citron resulted in a credit transaction, and that the new value defense still shelters the payments she was to make subsequent to sentencing, as these were due on a regular schedule. Even if this Court were to accept that argument, however, the undisputed facts here are that Lynn Citron did not pay according to the agreed schedule. The $9,000.00 payment she made on March 25, 2008, represented past due payments for the payments due for January and February 2008, which were supposed to be monthly payments of $4,722.22 over the term of her thirty-six months of probation.

Thus, NY cannot prevail on its claim as a matter of law that Lynn Citron's $9,000.00 payment on March 25, 2008, four (4) months after she was sentenced and received the benefit of her plea agreement, and well after the dates she agreed to make payments, was in fact a substantially contemporaneous exchange for new value for the December 19, 2007, plea agreement for purposes of § 547(c)(1)(B). Therefore, Liberty Mutual is entitled to recovery of the $9,000.00 paid by Lynn Citron on March 25, 2008.

The question as to Jeffrey Citron is more difficult. Neither side has provided briefing on whether agreeing to a prison sentence shorter than what the charged offenses could provide and/or reduced fines of less than what the charged offenses could provide constitutes money or money's worth transferred by NY for purposes of § 547(c)(2) [*sic*]. Further, no summary judgment evidence is before this Court as to the quantitative value of the reduced prison term and/or reduced fines from which this Court could determine the extent to which NY provided new value, if any. This Court does conclude, however, that if new value was provided under § 547(a)(2) incident to Jeffrey Citron's plea agreement, the $75,000.00 he paid was intended to be a contemporaneous exchange and was in fact a contemporaneous exchange for purposes of § 547(c)(1).

Further, neither side has cited the line of cases addressing whether restitution payments are subject to preference recovery. Several courts have held that payments made pursuant to criminal restitution obligations are subject to recovery through chapter 5 avoidance actions.

In *Smith v. Rogers (In re Castelhano)*, 2009 WL 1870956, 2009 Bankr. LEXIS 1805 (Bankr. D.N.H. June 24, 2009), a chapter 7 trustee sought to recover certain pre- and post-petition restitution payments made by the debtor to the victim of his criminal conduct. In support of the victim's motion for summary judgment, the debtor asserted that avoidance of the restitution payments would lead to an inequitable and unfair result for the debtor. The court took a contrary view, and stated that "excepting restitution obligations from avoidance actions takes money away from the estate and other unsecured creditors. The consequence would leave the unsecured creditors paying for the Debtor's criminal actions."

Again, the issue here is not whether to except criminal fines, penalties and forfeitures from the strictures of the preference provisions of the Bankruptcy Code. That is a legislative function for Congress to undertake in the crafting of the Bankruptcy Code. For example, Congress made a policy determination to except certain domestic support obligation payments from avoidance recovery by enacting § 547(c)(7), which provides an affirmative defense for preferential payments made to the extent such payments were bona fide payments for a domestic support obligation. No similar exception has been made for criminal fines or restitution.

Similarly, the issue is not whether allowing NY to keep a preferential payment would upset the bargain the State of New York made with Debtors. That, too, is a legislative function for Congress.

This Court's analysis should not, however, be read as being without regard for Judge Vaughan's comments in *Castelhano*—that excluding restitution payments from avoidance recovery "would leave the unsecured creditors paying for the Debtor's criminal actions." As noted, this is not an action to avoid restitution payments.

Similarly, the issue before this Court is not whether avoiding any of the Transfers would have the effect of rewriting the plea agreements, and converting fines and forfeiture paid to NY into restitution paid to Liberty Mutual. As the parties here have agreed, Liberty Mutual was one of the parties defrauded, resulting in the indictment being brought in the first place. The plea agreements were, in part, to vindicate the wrong done to Liberty Mutual. Liberty Mutual has adduced evidence that it holds in excess of 95% of the filed unsecured claims in this case. Had the plea agreements been structured to provide direct restitution to Liberty Mutual rather than fines or forfeitures paid to NY, and this litigation commenced against Liberty Mutual, a similar avoidance analysis would have to have been conducted.

Thus, a trial is required to determine what the potential maximum prison sentences and monetary fines would have likely been had Jeffrey Citron not pleaded guilty, and the quantitative value of avoiding these potential terms of incarceration and fines, in order to determine what money or money's worth in goods, services, or new credit Jeffrey Citron received in exchange for his plea agreement for §§ 547(c)(1) and 547(c)(2) [*sic*] purposes.

* * *

Questions

1. The parties conceded that the payments were preferences within § 547(b), so the court did not discuss that issue. Are you surprised that criminal fines can be avoidable preferences? How would you argue for a contrary result?

2. The *Citron* court drew a distinction between the facts before it and an action to avoid restitution payments. Should the result be different in the latter situation? The court cited one case on point—*Castelhano*. For another, discussing whether restitution payments may constitute preferences and deciding in the affirmative, see *State Compensation Insurance Fund v. Zamora (In re Silverman)*, 616 F.3d 1001 (9th Cir.2010).

3. How does one put a value on a reduced prison sentence? Is a reduced fine valued at the amount of the reduction?

4. Is the state's deal with the debtors voided upon recovery of the fines as preferential transfers? Will Lynn's probation be revoked? Will

Jeffrey now have to serve a longer prison sentence? Clearly, the bankruptcy court did not think so. Do you agree?

5. The second requirement of § 547(c)(1)—that the transfer was in fact substantially contemporaneous—has presented problems for the courts, especially in cases involving delay in perfecting a lien. Use of the term "substantially" makes it clear that some delay is permissible, but how much? Subsection 547(e)(2) provides a grace period in such cases that was, before the 2005 Amendments, 10 days. The First and Sixth Circuits adopted a "bright line" rule, "borrowing" (e)(2)'s time limit for purposes of (c)(1) and holding that the transfer of a security interest could not be substantially contemporaneous unless it occurred within the 10-day grace period. *Collins v. Greater Atlantic Mortgage Corp. (In re Lazarus)*, 478 F.3d 12 (1st Cir.2007); *Ray v. Security Mutual Finance Corp. (In re Arnett)*, 731 F.2d 358 (6th Cir.1984). A majority of the circuits however, took a more flexible, case-by-case approach. *Gordon v. Novastar Mortgage, Inc. (In re Sharma)*, 524 F.3d 1175 (11th Cir.2008); *Lindquist v. Dorholt, Inc. (In re Dorholt, Inc.)*, 224 F.3d 871 (8th Cir.2000); *Pine Top Insurance Co. v. Bank of America Nat'l Trust & Savings Ass'n*, 969 F.2d 321 (7th Cir.1992); *Dye v. Rivera (In re Marino)*, 193 B.R. 907 (9th Cir. BAP 1996). Now that the grace period under (e)(2) is 30 days, the question is whether that subsection will continue to inform decisions under (c)(1).

b. Transfers in Ordinary Course—§ 547(c)(2)

Preference law is not intended to interfere with the ordinary, everyday payments commonly made by every individual or business entity. Thus, Congress included an "ordinary course" preference exception in § 547(c)(2):

> The purpose of the exception is to leave undisturbed normal financial relations, because it does not detract from the general policy of the preference section to discourage unusual action by either the debtor or his creditors during the debtor's slide into bankruptcy.

H.R. Rep. No. 95-595, 95th Cong., 1st Sess., 373 (1977), *reprinted in* 1978 U.S.C.C.A.N. 5963, 6329. This is by far the most significant of the preference exceptions, both in terms of the frequency with which it is raised and the extent to which it undermines bankruptcy's equality principle.

As enacted in 1978, § 547(c)(2) protected only transfers made within 45 days of the time the debtor incurred the debt. Thus, long-term debts were plainly outside of the exception. When Congress removed the 45-day rule, the question was whether long-term debts remained outside the exclusion's reach. The Supreme Court answered that question in the following case.

UNION BANK v. WOLAS

United States Supreme Court, 1991.
502 U.S. 151, 112 S.Ct. 527, 116 L.Ed.2d 514.

JUSTICE STEVENS delivered the opinion of the Court.

Section 547(b) of the Bankruptcy Code authorizes a trustee to avoid certain property transfers made by a debtor within 90 days before bankruptcy. The Code makes an exception, however, for transfers made in the ordinary course of business, § 547(c)(2). The question presented is whether payments on long-term debt may qualify for that exception.

On December 17, 1986, ZZZZ Best Co., Inc. (Debtor) borrowed seven million dollars from petitioner, Union Bank (Bank). On July 8, 1987, the Debtor filed a voluntary petition under Chapter 7 of the Bankruptcy Code. During the preceding 90–day period, the Debtor had made two interest payments totalling approximately $100,000 and had paid a loan commitment fee of about $2,500 to the Bank. After his appointment as trustee of the Debtor's estate, respondent filed a complaint against the Bank to recover those payments pursuant to § 547(b).

The Bankruptcy Court found that the loans had been made "in the ordinary course of business or financial affairs" of both the Debtor and the Bank, and that both interest payments as well as the payment of the loan commitment fee had been made according to ordinary business terms and in the ordinary course of business. As a matter of law, the Bankruptcy Court concluded that the payments satisfied the requirements of § 547(c)(2) and therefore were not avoidable by the trustee. The District Court affirmed the Bankruptcy Court's summary judgment in favor of the Bank.

Shortly thereafter, in another case, the Court of Appeals held that the ordinary course of business exception to avoidance of preferential transfers was not available to long-term creditors. *In re CHG International, Inc.*, 897 F.2d 1479 (9th Cir.1990). In reaching that conclusion, the Court of Appeals relied primarily on the policies underlying the voidable preference provisions and the state of the law prior to the enactment of the 1978 Bankruptcy Code and its amendment in 1984.

Thus, the Ninth Circuit concluded, its holding in *CHG International, Inc.* dictated a reversal in this case. The importance of the question of law decided by the Ninth Circuit, coupled with the fact that the Sixth Circuit had interpreted § 547(c)(2) in a contrary manner, *In re Finn*, 909 F.2d 903 (1990), persuaded us to grant the Bank's petition for certiorari.

I

We shall discuss the history and policy of § 547 after examining its text. In subsection (b), Congress broadly authorized bankruptcy trustees to "avoid any transfer of an interest of the debtor in property" *if* five conditions are satisfied and *unless* one of seven exceptions defined in subsection (c) is applicable. * * * In this case, it is undisputed that * * * the interest and loan commitment fee payments were voidable preferences unless excepted by subsection (c)(2).

The most significant feature of subsection (c)(2) that is relevant to this case is the absence of any language distinguishing between long-term debt and short-term debt.[7] That subsection provides:

"The trustee may not avoid under this section a transfer—

* * *

"(2) to the extent that such transfer was—

"(A) in payment of a debt incurred by the debtor in the ordinary course of business or financial affairs of the debtor and the transferee;

"(B) made in the ordinary course of business or financial affairs of the debtor and the transferee; and
"(C) made according to ordinary business terms."

Instead of focusing on the term of the debt for which the transfer was made, subsection (c)(2) focuses on whether the debt was in-

---

[7] Nor does the definitional section of the Bankruptcy Code, which defines the term "debt" broadly as a "liability on a claim," [§ 101(12)], distinguish between short-term debt and long-term debt.

curred, and payment made, in the "ordinary course of business or financial affairs" of the debtor and transferee. Thus, the text provides no support for respondent's contention that § 547(c)(2)'s coverage is limited to short-term debt, such as commercial paper or trade debt. Given the clarity of the statutory text, respondent's burden of persuading us that Congress intended to create or to preserve a special rule for long-term debt is exceptionally heavy. As did the Ninth Circuit, respondent relies on the history and the policies underlying the preference provision.

II

The relevant history of § 547 contains two chapters, one of which clearly supports, and the second of which is not inconsistent with, the Bank's literal reading of the statute. Section 547 was enacted in 1978 when Congress overhauled the Nation's bankruptcy laws. The section was amended in 1984. For purposes of the question presented in this case, the original version of § 547 differed in one significant respect from the current version: it contained a provision that the ordinary course of business exception did not apply unless the payment was made within 45 days of the date the debt was incurred.[8] That provision presumably excluded most payments on long-term debt from the exception.[9] In 1984 Congress repealed the 45–day limitation but did not substitute a comparable limitation.

---

[8] As enacted in 1978, § 547(c) provided, in relevant part:

"The trustee may not avoid under this section a transfer—

* * *

"(2) to the extent that such transfer was—

"(A) in payment of a debt incurred in the ordinary course of business or financial affairs of the debtor and the transferee;

"(B) *made not later than 45 days after such debt was incurred*;

"(C) made in the ordinary course of business or financial affairs of the debtor and the transferee; and

"(D) made according to ordinary business terms." (Emphasis added.)

[9] We use the term "presumably" because it is not necessary in this case to decide whether monthly interest payments on long-term debt were protected by the initial version of § 547(c)(2). Cf. *In re Iowa Premium Service Co., Inc.*, 695 F.2d 1109

Respondent contends that this amendment was intended to satisfy complaints by issuers of commercial paper and by trade creditors that regularly extended credit for periods of more than 45 days. Furthermore, respondent continues, there is no evidence in the legislative history that Congress intended to make the ordinary course of business exception available to conventional long-term lenders. Therefore, respondent argues, we should follow the analysis of the Ninth Circuit and read § 547(c)(2) as protecting only short-term debt payments.

We need not dispute the accuracy of respondent's description of the legislative history of the 1984 amendment in order to reject his conclusion. For even if Congress adopted the 1984 amendment to redress particular problems of specific short-term creditors, it remains true that Congress redressed those problems by entirely deleting the time limitation in § 547(c)(2). The fact that Congress may not have foreseen all of the consequences of a statutory enactment is not a sufficient reason for refusing to give effect to its plain meaning.

Respondent also relies on the history of voidable preferences prior to the enactment of the 1978 Bankruptcy Code. The text of the preference provision in the earlier Bankruptcy Act did not specifically include an exception for payments made in the ordinary course of business. The courts had, however, developed what is sometimes described as the "current expense" rule to cover situations in which a debtor's payments on the eve of bankruptcy did not diminish the net estate because tangible assets were obtained in exchange for the payment. Without such an exception, trade creditors and other suppliers of necessary goods and services might have been reluctant to extend even short-term credit and might have required advance payment instead, thus making it difficult for many companies in temporary distress to have remained in business. Respondent argues that Congress enacted § 547(c)(2) in 1978 to codify that exception, and therefore the Court should construe § 547(c)(2) as limited to the confines of the current expense rule.

This argument is not compelling for several reasons. First, it is by no means clear that § 547(c)(2) should be construed as the statutory

---

(8th Cir.1982) (en banc) (holding that interest obligations are "incurred" when they become due, rather than when the promissory note is signed). We refer to "most" instead of "all" long-term debt payments because of the possibility that a debtor's otherwise avoidable payment was made within 45 days of the date the long-term loan was made.

analogue of the judicially crafted current expense rule because there are other exceptions in § 547(c) that explicitly cover contemporaneous exchanges for new value.[13] Those provisions occupy some (if not all) of the territory previously covered by the current expense rule. Nor has respondent directed our attention to any extrinsic evidence suggesting that Congress intended to codify the current expense rule in § 547(c)(2).[14]

The current expense rule developed when the statutory preference provision was significantly narrower than it is today. To establish a preference under the Bankruptcy Act, the trustee had to prove that the challenged payment was made at a time when the creditor had "reasonable cause to believe that the debtor [was] insolvent." When Congress rewrote the preference provision in the 1978 Bankruptcy Code, it substantially enlarged the trustee's power to avoid preferential transfers by eliminating the reasonable cause to believe requirement for transfers made within 90 days of bankruptcy and creating a presumption of insolvency during that period. At the same time, Congress created a new exception for transfers made in the ordinary course of business, § 547(c)(2). This exception was intended to "leave undisturbed normal financial relations, because it does not detract from the general policy of the preference section to discourage unusual action by either the debtor or his creditors during the debtor's slide into bankruptcy." H.R. Rep. No. 95–595 at 373, *reprinted in* 1978 U.S.C.C.A.N. at 6329.

In light of these substantial changes in the preference provision, there is no reason to assume that the justification for narrowly confining the "current expense" exception to trade creditors before 1978 should apply to the ordinary course of business exception under the 1978 Code. Instead, the fact that Congress carefully reexamined and entirely rewrote the preference provision in 1978 supports the conclusion that the text of § 547(c)(2) as enacted reflects the deliberate choice of Congress.

---

[13] Thus, for example, § 547(c)(1) exempts a transfer to the extent that it was a "contemporaneous exchange for new value given to the debtor," and § 547(c)(4) exempts a transfer to a creditor "to the extent that, after such transfer, such creditor gave new value to or for the benefit of the debtor."

[14] In fact, the legislative history apparently does not even mention the current expense rule. See Broome, *Payments on Long–Term Debt as Voidable Preferences: The Impact of the 1984 Bankruptcy Amendments*, 1987 DUKE L.J. 78, 97.

III

The Bank and the trustee agree that § 547 is intended to serve two basic policies that are fairly described in the House Committee Report. The Committee explained:

> "A preference is a transfer that enables a creditor to receive payment of a greater percentage of his claim against the debtor than he would have received if the transfer had not been made and he had participated in the distribution of the assets of the bankrupt estate. The purpose of the preference section is two-fold. First, by permitting the trustee to avoid prebankruptcy transfers that occur within a short period before bankruptcy, creditors are discouraged from racing to the courthouse to dismember the debtor during his slide into bankruptcy. The protection thus afforded the debtor often enables him to work his way out of a difficult financial situation through cooperation with all of his creditors. Second, and more important, the preference provisions facilitate the prime bankruptcy policy of equality of distribution among creditors of the debtor. Any creditor that received a greater payment than others of his class is required to disgorge so that all may share equally. The operation of the preference section to deter 'the race of diligence' of creditors to dismember the debtor before bankruptcy furthers the second goal of the preference section—that of equality of distribution." *Id*. at 177–78, *reprinted in* 1978 U.S.C.C.A.N. at 6138.

As this comment demonstrates, the two policies are not entirely independent. On the one hand, any exception for a payment on account of an antecedent debt tends to favor the payee over other creditors and therefore may conflict with the policy of equal treatment. On the other hand, the ordinary course of business exception may benefit all creditors by deterring the "race to the courthouse" and enabling the struggling debtor to continue operating its business.

Respondent places primary emphasis, as did the Court of Appeals, on the interest in equal distribution. When a debtor is insolvent, a transfer to one creditor necessarily impairs the claims of the debtor's other unsecured and undersecured creditors. By authorizing the avoidance of such preferential transfers, § 547(b) empowers the trustee to restore equal status to all creditors. Respondent thus contends that the ordinary course of business exception should be limited to short-term debt so the trustee may order that preferential long-term debt payments be returned to the estate to be distributed among all of the creditors.

But the statutory text—which makes no distinction between short-term debt and long-term debt—precludes an analysis that divorces the policy of favoring equal distribution from the policy of discouraging creditors from racing to the courthouse to dismember the debtor. Long-term creditors, as well as trade creditors, may seek a head start in that race. Thus, even if we accept the Court of Appeals' conclusion that the availability of the ordinary business exception to long-term creditors does not directly further the policy of equal treatment, we must recognize that it does further the policy of deterring the race to the courthouse and, as the House Report recognized, may indirectly further the goal of equal distribution as well. Whether Congress has wisely balanced the sometimes conflicting policies underlying § 547 is not a question that we are authorized to decide.

IV

In sum, we hold that payments on long-term debt, as well as payments on short-term debt, may qualify for the ordinary course of business exception to the trustee's power to avoid preferential transfers. We express no opinion, however, on the question whether the Bankruptcy Court correctly concluded that the Debtor's payments of interest and the loan commitment fee qualify for the ordinary course of business exception, § 547(c)(2). In particular, we do not decide whether the loan involved in this case was incurred in the ordinary course of the Debtor's business and of the Bank's business, whether the payments were made in the ordinary course of business, or whether the payments were made according to ordinary business terms. These questions remain open for the Court of Appeals on remand.

The judgment of the Court of Appeals is reversed and the case is remanded for further proceedings consistent with this opinion.

It is so ordered.

JUSTICE SCALIA, concurring.

I join the opinion of the Court, including Parts II and III, which respond persuasively to legislative-history and policy arguments made by respondent. It is regrettable that we have a legal culture in which such arguments have to be addressed (and are indeed credited by a Court of Appeals), with respect to a statute utterly devoid of language that could remotely be thought to distinguish between long-term and short-term debt. Since there was here no contention of a "scrivener's error" producing an absurd result, the plain text of the statute should have made this litigation unnecessary and unmaintainable.

Notes and Problems

1. The debtor in *Wolas*, ZZZZ Best Co., was a carpet cleaning and disaster restoration company begun by Barry Minkow when he was 16 years old. It became one of the most sensational frauds in Southern California history, raking in $100 million on the basis of almost totally fabricated paper profits. The fraud was uncovered in 1987, soon after publication of Minkow's ghost-written autobiography, "Making It in America." (A book about the scheme, entitled "Faking It in America," was written by Joe Domanick.)

Minkow was sentenced in 1989, at the age of 23, to a 25-year prison sentence. At his sentencing he said, "Today is a great day for this country. The system works. * * * They got the right guy." District Judge Tevrizian, who sentenced him, was unimpressed: "El toro poo-poo, that's what I'm hearing. * * * Is he trying to clean my carpet or what?"

Minkow served 7½ years, during which he earned a degree from Liberty University and started a prison Bible-study group called "Barry's Boys." When he got out of prison, he began a "Consumer Hotline" radio show, with profits going toward the $26 million he owed to his victims. He also wrote "Cleaning Up: One Man's Redemptive Journey Through the Seductive World of Corporate Crime." He became the pastor of a church in San Diego and founder of Fraud Discovery Institute, which worked with investigators, auditors, underwriters and bankers to detect ongoing fraud. With his help, the FBI uncovered frauds totaling $1.1 billion in 2004 alone. Minkow's restitution order was lifted in 2002, but for many years he did not miss a payment on the $7 million he owed Union Bank.

Unfortunately, Minkow's redemption came to an end in 2009 when he was charged with securities fraud for disseminating false information about a home builder, Lennar Corp., that drove down the price of its stock. He pleaded guilty and, in July 2011, was sentenced to five years in prison. He was also ordered to pay nearly $600,000 in restitution. Additionally, in 2014, Minkow pleaded guilty to embezzling more than $3 million from his church. He received the maximum sentence under his plea bargaining agreement, and can be released from prison no earlier than 2019.

2. The Court believed that its reading of (c)(2), to encompass payments on long-term debt, was consistent with the underlying policies of preference law: to discourage creditors from racing to dismember the debtor; and to treat similarly-situated creditors equally. Is that true? Why would a creditor desist from taking steps to collect just because payments (*if* the debtor chooses to make any) would be avoidable? If payments are generally avoidable, at

least when voluntarily made by the debtor, then why would creditors not be *more* likely to find ways to get paid, rather than *less*?

3. JUSTICE STEVENS referred to the "current expense" rule, which was used before the ordinary course of business exception came into existence. The current expense rule, according to JUSTICE STEVENS, covered "situations in which a debtor's payments on the eve of bankruptcy did not diminish the net estate because tangible assets were obtained in exchange for the payment." Recall the discussion of such a "no harm, no foul" approach in reference to the earmarking doctrine.

4. The Court did not hold that these payments were in the ordinary course, within § 547(c)(2). Rather, it held that payments on long-term debt do not suffer a per se exclusion from (c)(2).

The 2005 Amendments significantly reconfigured § 547(c)(2). Previously, in order to gain the benefit of the ordinary course defense under (c)(2), a creditor had to establish three elements: that the debt had been incurred in the ordinary course of the business of both the debtor and the creditor; that the payment, too, had been made and received in the ordinary course of their businesses; and that the payment had been made according to ordinary business terms. The meaning of the third element was at issue in *Matter of Tolona Pizza Products Corp.*, 3 F.3d 1029 (7th Cir.1993), in which the debtor-in-possession—a pizza maker—sought to recover payments made during the preference period to Rose, its sausage supplier. The Seventh Circuit's interpretation of what it means for a payment to have been "made according to ordinary business terms" has become the seminal ruling on the issue:

> It may seem odd that paying a debt late would ever be regarded as a preference to the creditor thus paid belatedly. But it is all relative. A debtor who has entered the preference period—who is therefore only 90 days, or fewer, away from plunging into bankruptcy—is typically unable to pay all his outstanding debts in full as they come due. If he pays one and not the others, as happened here, the payment though late is still a preference to that creditor, and is avoidable unless the conditions of § 547(c)(2) are met. One condition is that payment be in the ordinary course of both the debtor's and the creditor's business. A late payment normally will not be. It will therefore be an avoidable preference.

This is not a dryly syllogistic conclusion. The purpose of the preference statute is to prevent the debtor during his slide toward bankruptcy from trying to stave off the evil day by giving preferential treatment to his most importunate creditors, who may sometimes be those who have been waiting longest to be paid. Unless the favoring of particular creditors is outlawed, the mass of creditors of a shaky firm will be nervous, fearing that one or a few of their number are going to walk away with all the firm's assets; and this fear may precipitate debtors into bankruptcy earlier than is socially desirable.

From this standpoint, however, the most important thing is not that the dealings between the debtor and the allegedly favored creditor conform to some industry norm but that they conform to the norm established by the debtor and the creditor in the period before, preferably well before, the preference period. That condition is satisfied here—if anything, Rose treated Tolona more favorably (and hence Tolona treated Rose less preferentially) before the preference period than during it.

But if this is all that the third subsection of 547(c)(2) requires, it might seem to add nothing to the first two subsections, which require that both the debt and the payment be within the ordinary course of business of both the debtor and the creditor. For, provided these conditions are fulfilled, a "late" payment really isn't late if the parties have established a practice that deviates from the strict terms of their written contract. But we hesitate to conclude that the third subsection, requiring conformity to "ordinary business terms," has no function in the statute. We can think of two functions that it might have. One is evidentiary. If the debtor and creditor dealt on terms that the creditor testifies were normal for them but that are wholly unknown in the industry, this casts some doubt on his (self-serving) testimony. Preferences are disfavored, and [this subsection] makes them more difficult to prove. The second possible function of the subsection is to allay the concerns of creditors that one or more of their number may have worked out a special deal with the debtor, before the preference period, designed to put that creditor ahead of the others in the event of bankruptcy. It may seem odd that allowing late payments from a debtor would be a way for a creditor to make himself more rather than less assured of repayment. But such a creditor does have an advantage during the preference period, because he can receive late payments then and they will still be in the ordinary course of business for him and his debtor.

The functions that we have identified, combined with a natural reluctance to cut out and throw away one-third of an important provision of the Bankruptcy Code, persuade us that the creditor must show that the payment he received was made in accordance with the ordinary business terms in the industry. But this does not mean that the creditor must establish the existence of some single, uniform set of business terms, as Tolona argues. Not only is it difficult to identify the industry whose norm shall govern (is it, here, the sale of sausages to makers of pizza? The sale of sausages to anyone? The sale of anything to makers of pizza?), but there can be great variance in billing practices within an industry. Apparently there is in this industry, whatever exactly "this industry" is; for while it is plain that neither Rose nor its competitors enforce payment within seven days, it is unclear that there is a standard outer limit of forbearance. It seems that 21 days is a goal but that payment as late as 30 days is generally tolerated and that for good customers even longer delays are allowed. * * *

We conclude that "ordinary business terms" refers to the *range* of terms that encompasses the practices in which firms similar in some general way to the creditor in question engage, and that only dealings so idiosyncratic as to fall outside that broad range should be deemed extraordinary and therefore outside the scope of [this subsection].

Id. at 1032-33.

Subsection (c)(2) was rewritten in 2005 to make the second and third elements alternatives to each other. Thus, once a creditor establishes that the debt was incurred in the ordinary course of both parties' business, the creditor may prevail by establishing *either* that payment was made in the ordinary course of their dealings with each other *or* that payment was made in accordance with terms ordinary in the industry. Because evidence regarding the first of these alternatives may be more readily available, the second alternative may not often be utilized.

Problems

1. Debtor Corp. hired Attorney to represent an employee of Debtor. Debtor's usual practice was to send payment at least a month after Debtor

received Attorney's bill for services. Later, Attorney demanded assurance of payment *before* he would proceed with a deposition. Consequently, Debtor sent payment less than a week after Attorney billed it. Debtor Corp. filed bankruptcy a month later and the trustee sought to recover the payment made for the deposition. Attorney maintained that the payment was made in the ordinary course of business and was therefore not avoidable as a preference. Who wins? See *Boone v. Marlatt (In re Day Telecommunications, Inc.)*, 70 B.R. 904 (Bankr. E.D.N.C.1987).

2. Debtor, a distributor of televisions and computers imported from Asia, borrowed $2 million from Lender, but—in an effort to mislead another creditor—reflected the funds on its books as a receipt from Insight Corp. for goods it purchased. In fact, there was no such entity as Insight. During the preference period, Debtor repaid Lender a total of $400,000. An involuntary bankruptcy petition was filed against Debtor, and the trustee sought to recover the payments as preferences. Lender admitted that the elements of § 547(b) were satisfied, but argued that the (c)(2) exception was applicable. The trustee countered on two grounds: that Lender and Debtor had never dealt together before, so they had established no "ordinary course"; and that Debtor's fraud precluded application of the section. Are these good arguments? See *Computer World Solution, Inc. v. Apple Fund, LP*, 427 B.R. 680 (Bankr. N.D.Ill.2010).

c. "Enabling Loans"—§ 547(c)(3)

Section 547(c)(3) sets forth the so-called "enabling loan" exception. It applies to extensions of credit that enable a debtor to purchase property that then serves as collateral for its own purchase price. This is the Bankruptcy Code version of the "purchase money security interest" that may be familiar to you from UCC § 9–103(a)(2). That provision defines purchase money security interests to include those created in favor of the seller of goods on credit, as well as those given to lenders who make loans for the purpose of permitting the borrower to buy goods, as long as the loan funds are "in fact so used." Clearly, these same concepts are imbedded in § 547(c)(3), despite differences in wording.

This preference exception is designed to mesh with state-law provisions giving priority to purchase money secured parties who perfect their interests within a few days of the time the debtor takes possession of the encumbered property. UCC § 9–317(e) provides that secured parties who perfect within 20 days after the debtor gets possession of the property have priority over competing claimants who obtained rights in the debtor's property before the secured party's perfection. Section 547(c)(3)(B) mimics these state law grace periods, albeit with a 30-day rule.

d. Subsequent Advances of New Value—§ 547(c)(4)

In revolving credit arrangements, such as the "open account," the debtor's payments are not necessarily coordinated with the creditor's extensions of new credit (*e.g.,* accomplished by the shipment of additional goods). Payments during the 90–day period will be preferences and, if the new value is not given in exchange for the preferential transfer, the preferences will not be saved by § 547(c)(1). Another exception—§ 547(c)(4)—may apply in these cases.

Read § 547(c)(4) and apply it to the following Problems.

Problems

1. Creditor made an unsecured $10,000 loan to Debtor on August 1. Debtor paid Creditor $2,500 on September 15 and borrowed an additional $1,000 on October 1. Debtor filed a bankruptcy petition on November 15.

2. Creditor made an unsecured $10,000 loan to Debtor on August 1 and loaned an additional $1,000 on September 15. Debtor paid Creditor $2,500 on October 1 and filed a bankruptcy petition on November 15.

3. Creditor made an unsecured $10,000 loan to Debtor on August 1. Debtor paid Creditor $2,500 on September 15. Debtor sought an additional $1,000 from Creditor on October 1, but Creditor refused to lend without security. In exchange for the additional funds, therefore, Debtor gave Creditor a security interest in personal property worth $5,000 to secure the new loan. Creditor filed a financing statement immediately. Debtor filed a bankruptcy petition on November 15.

4. Does your answer to Problem # 3 change if Creditor failed to file a financing statement?

5. Creditor sold Debtor $10,000 worth of widgets on open account on July1, with payment due in 30 days. Debtor paid only $2,500 and paid it late—on September 1. Ten days later, Debtor ordered $1,000 worth of thingamajigs. Creditor demanded, and got, Debtor's promise to pay on 15-day terms. Creditor shipped the thingamajigs on September 15, but again Debtor did not pay on time. Ultimately—on October 12—Debtor issued a check. Creditor received the check on October 16 and Debtor's bank honored it on October 20. Debtor filed bankruptcy on November 15.

e. "Floating Liens"—§ 547(c)(5)

A so-called "floating lien" is one that attaches to types of collateral, such as inventory and accounts receivable, that constantly turn over. Such liens normally secure lines of credit, which consist of numerous extensions of value over time, rather than one-shot loans. Thus, the collateral needs to be replenished in order to protect the creditor. The solution is an after-acquired property clause that enables the lien to "float" over the collateral and to attach to new items as soon as the debtor acquires an interest in them. This will occur long after value was first extended and the security interest first attached and was perfected.

The floating lien raises special problems in bankruptcy. If the security interest in the newly-acquired property arises within the 90 days before bankruptcy, it looks suspiciously like a preference.

Arguments concerning the treatment of floating liens under the 1898 Act centered around § 60a(2):

> [A] transfer of property other than real property shall be deemed to have been made or suffered at the time when it became so far perfected that no subsequent lien upon such property obtainable by legal or equitable proceedings on a simple contract could become superior to the rights of the transferee.

Trustees made a straightforward argument based on § 60a(2): First, a security interest has priority over a lien creditor only when the security interest is perfected; second, a security interest must attach before it can be perfected; third, a security interest cannot attach until the debtor has rights in the collateral; fourth, the debtor does not have rights in inventory and accounts until inventory is received and accounts come into existence. Therefore, the transfer is deemed made for preference purposes at the time inventory is received or accounts arise.

Two important cases decided in 1969 rejected this reasoning and held that floating liens do not create preferences. The court in *DuBay v. Williams*, 417 F.2d 1277 (9th Cir.1969), held that a "transfer" occurs for bankruptcy purposes when the secured creditor will take priority over lien creditors under state law, and not when the security interest attaches to the newly-acquired inventory or accounts. Thus, the "transfer" occurs when the financing statement is first filed.

The court in *Grain Merchants v. Union Bank & Savings Co.*, 408 F.2d 209 (7th Cir.), *cert. denied sub nom. France v. Union Bank & Savings Co.*, 396 U.S. 827, 90 S.Ct. 75, 24 L.Ed.2d 78 (1969), agreed with *DuBay*'s time-of-transfer theory and advanced two others. First, a floating lien is not taken in individual components of accounts or inventory, but in the entity as a whole. The analogy is to a river that retains its identity even though the water constantly changes. Under this "entity theory," the transfer occurred when the interest in the entity was transferred—*i.e.*, when the financing statement was originally filed. Second, the interest in new components of accounts or inventory is merely a substitute for the old accounts that are collected or items of inventory that are sold. Floating liens, therefore, fit within the long-standing substitution-of-collateral exception to preferences.

Section 547(e)(3) was included in the 1978 Code in order to eliminate the time-of-transfer argument adopted by *DuBay* and *Grain Merchants*. According to the legislative history, "[t]his provision, more than any other in the section, overrules *DuBay* and *Grain Merchants*." H.R. Rep. No. 95–595 at 374, *reprinted in* 1978 U.S.C.C.A.N. at 6330. Now, a transfer for preference purposes cannot occur until the debtor has rights in the collateral—that is, when new shipments of inventory are received or when new accounts arise.

The drafters also included a new preference exception in § 547(c)(5) that imposes a "two-point net improvement test." It applies only to inventory and accounts—the types of collateral that turn over—and avoids as a preference only those transfers that improve the creditor's position during the preference period.

Although § 547(c)(5) appears nightmarish upon first reading, it is not really so bad. It requires determining the amount by which the creditor's position has improved from one point in time to another. The later of those two points in time is always the time the petition was filed. The earlier one varies from case to case. For most cases, it is 90 days before the filing. In an insider case, it is one year before the filing. If, however, the creditor first extended value to the debtor after whichever of those dates is otherwise applicable, then the earlier point in time is the date on which the creditor first gave value.

You must, for each of the two points in time, determine the amount by which the creditor was undersecured—that is, the "amount by which the debt secured by such security interest exceeded the value of all security interests for such debt." The amount by which the creditor's position has improved between the two points in time—that is, the "reduction" of the creditor's undersecurity—is the amount of the preference.

Section 547(c)(5) is intended to prevent build-up of the creditor's collateral at the expense of the estate. Improvements in the creditor's position just before bankruptcy are often due to illicit, but disguised, overreaching by the benefited creditor. These improvements in position will be undone by § 547(c)(5).

Read § 547(c)(5) and determine the amount of the avoidable preference in each of the following fact patterns.

Problems

1. Debtor owes Creditor $200,000 90 days before bankruptcy. Creditor has a security interest in inventory worth $150,000 at that time. When the bankruptcy petition is filed, the debt is still $200,000 but the inventory is worth $175,000.

2. Debtor owes Creditor $200,000 90 days before bankruptcy. Creditor has a security interest in inventory worth $150,000 at that time. When the bankruptcy petition is filed, the debt is $175,000 and the inventory is worth $100,000.

3. Debtor owes Creditor $30,000 90 days before bankruptcy. Creditor has a security interest in Debtor's inventory of baseball cards, which is worth $15,000 at that time. Although Debtor does not acquire any new cards before bankruptcy, the value of the cards in Debtor's inventory increases to $20,000 by the time the bankruptcy petition is filed. Debtor still owes Creditor $30,000.

4. Debtor borrowed $15,000 from Bank and gave Bank a security interest in accounts worth $25,000 at that time. Under their security agreement, the accounts were collateral for "any and all obligations of Debtor to Bank, whenever arising." A month later, when bankruptcy appeared imminent, Bank bought an unsecured debt from Trade Creditor to whom Debtor owed $5,000. Trade Creditor, who expected to get nothing in bankruptcy, received $1,000 from Bank for the claim. Debtor filed a bankruptcy petition two weeks later, and Bank filed a secured claim of $20,000.

D. RECOVERY OF AVOIDED TRANSFERS

Section 550 specifies from whom property that was the subject of an avoidable transfer may be recovered. Under § 550(a), a trustee may recover property from the initial transferee or beneficiary of the transfer, or from any immediate or mediate transferee of the initial transferee. Consider the following example: Debtor transfers property, prepetition, to X, and the trustee of Debtor's estate avoids the transfer under one of the avoiding powers—§§ 544, 545, 547, 548, 549, 553(b) or 724(a). X, who still possesses the property, is liable under § 550(a)(1) as the initial transferee. A debtor's initial transferee is always, and any succeeding transferee is typically, held accountable to the trustee. Section 550(b), however, prevents the trustee from recovering from any succeeding good faith transferee who takes for value and without knowledge of the voidability of the transfer.

Add some facts to the previous example: Assume that after X received the property from Debtor, X sold it to Y, who subsequently transferred the property to Z. Nothing has happened to affect X 's liability. Y is now liable, under § 550(a)(2), as the immediate transferee, and Z also is liable as the mediate transferee. Y and Z, however, have the defense of § 550(b) available to them. If Y gave X value in good faith for the property, and Y was unaware that the initial transfer was voidable, Y will be protected from liability by § 550(b)(1). If Y is protected, then so too is Z, under § 550(b)(2), if Z took the property in good faith.

Section 550 further provides that a good faith transferee from whom the trustee recovers is entitled to a lien on the recovered property in the lesser of (1) the amounts expended to improve the property, or (2) the increase in value of the transferred property due to such improvements. Assume in the above examples that X acted in good faith, but was liable for recovery as an initial transferee. If X made repairs to the property after receiving it from Debtor, then X has a claim against Debtor's estate for the amount the property increased in value due to the repairs. If the cost of making the repairs was less than the increase in the property's value, then X is only entitled to a claim in the amount he spent to make the repairs.

The following cases and notes deal with the appropriate target of the trustee's recovery powers. Although they arise under different avoiding powers, each of them involves the proper interpretation of § 550.

BONDED FINANCIAL SERVICES, INC. v. EUROPEAN AMERICAN BANK

United States Court of Appeals, Seventh Circuit, 1988.
838 F.2d 890.

EASTERBROOK, Circuit Judge.

Michael Ryan controlled a number of currency exchanges in Illinois. He also owned quite a few horses, doing business as Shamrock Hill Farm. Ryan had borrowed $655,000 from European American Bank to run this business. One of the currency exchanges, Bonded Financial Services, put $200,000 at Ryan's disposal in January 1983.

Bonded sent the Bank a check payable to the Bank's order on January 21 with a note directing the Bank to "deposit this check into Mike [Ryan]'s account." The Bank did this. On January 31 Ryan instructed the Bank to debit the account $200,000 in order to reduce the outstanding balance of the Shamrock loan. The Bank did this. Ryan paid off the loan in two more installments, on February 11 and 14, 1983. The Bank released its security interest in the horses.

The currency exchanges and Ryan paid visits to the judicial system. Bonded filed a petition in bankruptcy on February 10, 1983, along with about 65 other entities that Ryan controlled. Creditors later filed involuntary proceedings against Ryan. Ryan was convicted of mail fraud on account of his irregular administration of the currency exchanges (Bonded was not, for starters) and is in prison. The transfer of $200,000 out of Bonded on January 21, 1983, was a fraudulent conveyance, see § 548(a), and the trustee may recover for the benefit of creditors the value of such a conveyance. The trustee seeks to recover from the Bank, which unlike Ryan is solvent.

The right of recovery depends on § 550 * * *. Bonded's trustee contends in this adversary proceeding that the Bank is the "initial transferee" under § 550(a)(1) because it was the payee of the check it received on January 21; that the Bank is in any event the "entity for whose benefit such transfer was made" because Ryan intended to pay off the loan when he caused Bonded to write the check; that if the Bank is a subsequent transferee under § 550(a)(2) it did not give "value" under § 550(b)(1) because Bonded received nothing; and that the Bank loses even if it gave value because it should have known that something was amiss, given the substantial sum Bonded was transferring to a corporate officer. The bankruptcy court granted summary judgment to the Bank without explicitly discussing § 550. The district court affirmed on appeal under 28 U.S.C. § 158(a). It held that the Bank handled the check of January 21 as a "mere conduit" and so was not the initial transferee; that Ryan was the person "for whose benefit the transfer was made" because he got the benefit of the reduction in the balance of the loan; that the Bank's giving value to Ryan satisfied § 550(b)(1); and that because the trustee presented no evidence that the Bank knew or should have known of Bonded's impending collapse, the Bank took in good faith. * * *

I

If the note accompanying Bonded's check had said: "use this check to reduce Ryan's loan" instead of "deposit this check into

[Ryan]'s account," § 550(a)(1) would provide a ready answer. The Bank would be the "initial transferee" and Ryan would be the "entity for whose benefit [the] transfer was made." The trustee could recover the $200,000 from the Bank, Ryan, or both, subject to the rule of [§ 550(d)] that there may be but one recovery. The trustee contends that the apparently formal difference—depositing the check in Ryan's account and then debiting that account—should not affect the outcome. In either case the Bank is the payee of the check and ends up with the money, while Ryan gets the horses free of liens and Bonded is left holding the bag. From a larger perspective, however, the two cases are different.

Fraudulent conveyance law protects creditors from last-minute diminutions of the pool of assets in which they have interests. They accordingly need not monitor debtors so closely, and the savings in monitoring costs make businesses more productive. See Douglas G. Baird & Thomas H. Jackson, *Fraudulent Conveyance Law and its Proper Domain*, 38 VAND. L. REV. 829 (1985); Robert Charles Clark, *The Duties of the Corporate Debtor to its Creditors*, 90 HARV. L. REV. 505, 554–60 (1977). The original rule, in 13 Eliz. ch. 5 (1571), dealt with debtors who transferred property to their relatives, while the debtors themselves sought sanctuary from creditors. The family enjoyed the value of the assets, which the debtor might reclaim if the creditors stopped pursuing him. In the last 400 years the principle has been generalized to address transfers without either sufficient consideration or bad intent, for they, no less than gifts, reduce the value of the debtor's estate and thus the net return to creditors as a group.[1] The trustee reverses, for the benefit of all creditors, un- or under-compensated conveyances within a specified period before the bankruptcy.

There have always been limits on the pursuit of transfers. If the recipient of a fraudulent conveyance uses the money to buy a Rolls Royce, the auto dealer need not return the money to the bankrupt even if the trustee can identify the serial numbers on the bills. The misfortune of the firm's creditors is not a good reason to mulct the dealer, who gave value for the money and was in no position to monitor the debtor. Some monitoring is both inevitable and desirable, and the creditors are in a better position to carry out this task than are auto dealers and the

---

[1] The fraudulent conveyance must be distinguished from a preferential transfer to a creditor, which does not diminish the total payoff for the group, but which may be undone to reduce the incentive individual creditors have to rush to dismember the debtor before rival creditors can do so. The collective bankruptcy proceeding solves the common pool problem, which otherwise may produce a reduction in the value of the productive assets taken jointly.

many others with whom the firm's transferees may deal. The considerations behind the holder in due course rule for commercial paper, Uniform Commercial Code § 3–302, and the bona fide purchaser rule for chattels, UCC § 2–403(1)—the waste that would be created if people either had to inquire how their transferors obtained their property or to accept a risk that a commercial deal would be reversed for no reason they could perceive at the time—also apply to subsequent holders of assets fraudulently conveyed out of bankrupts. Just as the holder in due course rule requires the transferor of commercial paper to bear the risk and burden of inquiry, increasing the liquidity of paper, so § 550(b) leaves with the initial transferee the burden of inquiry and the risk if the conveyance is fraudulent. The initial transferee is the best monitor; subsequent transferees usually do not know where the assets came from and would be ineffectual monitors if they did.

The potential costs of monitoring and residual risk are evident when the transferees include banks and other financial intermediaries. The check-clearing system processes more than 100 million instruments every day; most pass through several banks as part of the collection process; each bank may be an owner of the instrument or agent for purposes of collecting at a given moment. Some of these instruments represent funds fraudulently conveyed out of bankrupts, yet the cost of checking back on the earlier transferors would be staggering. Bonded's trustee dismisses financial intermediaries on the ground that they obviously are not initial transferees, but this is not so clear. Hundreds of thousands of wire transfers occur every day. The sender of money on a wire transfer tells its bank to send instructions to the Federal Reserve System (for a Fedwire transfer) or to a correspondent bank to make money or credit available through still another bank. The Fed or the receiving bank could be called the "initial transferee" of the funds if we disregarded the function of fraudulent conveyance law. Similarly, an armored car company might be called the "initial transferee" if the bankrupt gave it valuables or specie to carry. Exposing financial intermediaries and couriers to the risk of disgorging a "fraudulent conveyance" in such circumstances would lead them to take precautions, the costs of which would fall on solvent customers without significantly increasing the protection of creditors.

The functions of fraudulent conveyance law lead us to conclude that the Bank was not the "initial transferee" of Bonded's check even though it was the payee. The Bank acted as a financial intermediary. It received no benefit. Ryan's loan was fully secured and not in arrears, so the Bank did not even acquire a valuable right to offset its loan against the funds in Ryan's account. Under the law of contracts, the

Bank had to follow the instructions that came with the check. The Uniform Commercial Code treats such instructions as binding to the extent any contract binds (see UCC § [3–117]). The Bank therefore was no different from a courier or an intermediary on a wire transfer; it held the check only for the purpose of fulfilling an instruction to make the funds available to someone else.

Although the Bankruptcy Code does not define "transferee," and there is no legislative history on the point, we think the minimum requirement of status as a "transferee" is dominion over the money or other asset, the right to put the money to one's own purposes. When A gives a check to B as agent for C, then C is the "initial transferee"; the agent may be disregarded. This perspective had impressive support under the 1898 Code and has been employed under the 1978 Code as well.

As the Bank saw the transaction on January 21, it was Ryan's agent for the purpose of collecting a check from Bonded's bank. Cf. UCC § 4–201([a]) (giving a collecting bank a presumption of agency status unless "a contrary intent clearly appears"). It received nothing from Bonded that it could call its own; the Bank was not Bonded's creditor, and Ryan owed the Bank as much as ever. The Bank had no dominion over the $200,000 until January 31, when Ryan instructed the Bank to debit the account to reduce the loan; in the interim, so far as the Bank was concerned, Ryan was free to invest the whole $200,000 in lottery tickets or uranium stocks. As the Bank saw things on January 31, it was getting Ryan's money. It would be at risk if Ryan were defrauding his other creditors or preferring the Bank, but the Bank would perceive no reason to investigate Bonded or sequester the money for the benefit of Bonded's creditors. So the two-step transaction is indeed different from the one-step transaction we hypothesized at the beginning of this discussion.

We are aware that some courts say that an agent (or a bank in a case like ours) is an "initial transferee" but that courts may excuse the transferee from repaying using equitable powers. This is misleading. "Transferee" is not a self-defining term; it must mean something different from "possessor" or "holder" or "agent." To treat "transferee" as "anyone who touches the money" and then to escape the absurd results that follow is to introduce useless steps; we slice these off with Occam's Razor and leave a more functional rule.

There is a related, and more nettlesome, question about the use of equitable powers under § 550(a). Genuine transferees can be caught in a time warp as a result of the special treatment of inside guarantors. Suppose Firm borrows money from Lender, with Guarantor as surety. When Firm pays off the debt, Lender is the "initial transferee" and Guarantor is an "entity for whose benefit [the] transfer was made." The payment of a debt benefits the guarantor. Each may have received a preference voidable under § 547 (and therefore recoverable under § 550). If Guarantor is a stranger to Firm, the trustee may recover only preferences within 90 days of the petition. § 547(b)(4)(A). If Guarantor is an "insider" at the time of the transfer, the preference period lasts a year. § 547(b)(4)(B). Section 547(b)(4) distinguishes according to the status of Guarantor, but § 550 does not. It says that if a transfer is recoverable by the trustee, it may be recovered from *either* the "initial transferee" (Lender) or the "entity for whose benefit such transfer was made" (Guarantor). This creates a situation that several courts have perceived to be "inequitable": Lender must satisfy the trustee (if Firm goes bankrupt between 91 days and a year after the preference) when Guarantor is an insider, but not when Guarantor is a stranger, yet, it seems, this has nothing to do with any proper theory of Lender's liability. Most bankruptcy courts that have addressed this question conclude that "equity" will relieve Lender from a literal construction of § 550. Commentators, whose articles collect and discuss the cases, are divided. We have serious doubts both about the amount of equity in Lender's position (for Firm may have paid Lender preferentially only to assist Guarantor, the insider, and Lender is in a good position to monitor the performance of its debtor; if Firm collects from Lender, Lender may collect in turn from Guarantor, bearing the risk of Firm's insolvency it planned to bear all along) and about the propriety of judges' declining to enforce statutes that produce inequitable results. Bankruptcy statutes are not special cases. We mention the problem not to resolve it (for it is not before us) but to show that this appeal to "equity"—to deny recovery against an "initial transferee" within the statute—is different in source and scope from the way in which we have employed considerations of policy to *define* "transferee" under § 550(a)(1). Doubts about this use of equity do not imply that courts should take "transferee" for all it could be worth rather than for what a sensible policy implies it is worth.

II

If the Bank is not the "initial transferee," the trustee insists, it is at least the "entity for whose benefit such transfer was made." The Bank ultimately was paid and therefore, one might think, it got the "benefit" of the transfer—though the Bank cancelled the note and gave up a security interest in horses that, the trustee concedes, was sufficient to cover the balance. Kenneth Kortas, Bonded's day-to-day manager, filed an affidavit stating that he prepared the check in question at Ryan's request as part of Ryan's program "to put the horse business in a position where it could function and sustain itself for at least several months even if his other business ventures ran into financial difficulty. * * * At the request of Ryan, I routinely prepared checks payable to banks where Ryan had personal accounts and loan accounts to finance his horse business." This may show that Ryan intended all along to wash the $200,000 through his personal account and pay the Bank; at a minimum, the argument would run, questions of intent prevent summary judgment.

The Bank responds that *it* did not "intend" to be the beneficiary of the transfer; it was not in cahoots with Ryan or Bonded and did not know of their plans. Moreover, the Bank insists that it did not receive a "benefit" because it gave value for the $200,000. The only beneficiary on this view was Ryan, who increased his equity position in Shamrock Hill Farm and obtained clear title to the horses. As both initial transferee and ultimate beneficiary, Ryan is the only person covered by § 550(a)(1), the Bank insists. The distinction is important, because entities covered by § 550(a)(1) cannot use the value-and-good-faith defense provided by § 550(b).

This exchange seems to raise difficult questions. To what extent does "intent" matter under § 550(a)(1)? If intent matters, whose? To what extent must courts find the true economic benefits of a transaction? If the Bank were undersecured, would the transfer make the Bank the beneficiary by the amount of the difference between the loan and the security? Suppose Ryan planned to, and did, buy a Rolls Royce with the money; would the dealer be the beneficiary by the difference between the wholesale and retail price of the car? How are bankruptcy courts to determine "intent" and compute the benefit in transactions of this nature?

These questions need not be answered, because a subsequent transferee cannot be the "entity for whose benefit" the initial transfer was made. The structure of the statute separates initial transferees and beneficiaries, on the one hand, from "immediate or mediate transferee[s]," on the other. The implication is that the "entity for whose benefit" is different from a transferee, "immediate" or otherwise. The paradigm "entity for whose benefit such transfer was made" is a guarantor or debtor—someone who receives the benefit but not the money. In the Firm–Guarantor–Lender example at the end of Part I, when Firm pays the loan, Lender is the initial transferee and Guarantor, which no longer is exposed to liability, is the "entity for whose benefit." If Bonded had sent a check to the Bank with instructions to reduce Ryan's loan, the Bank would have been the initial transferee and Ryan the "entity for whose benefit." Section 550(a)(1) recognizes that debtors often pay money to A for the benefit of B; that B may indeed have arranged for the payment (likely so if B is an insider of the payor); that but for the payment B may have had to make good on the guarantee or pay off his own debt; and accordingly that B should be treated the same way initial recipients are treated. If B gave value to the bankrupt for the benefit, B will receive credit in the bankruptcy, see § 547-(c)(1)(A), § 548(c), and if not, B should be subject to recovery to the same extent as A—sometimes ahead of A, although § 550 does not make this distinction. Someone who receives the money later on is not an "entity for whose benefit such transfer was made"; only a person who receives a benefit from the initial transfer is within this language.

The legislative history of § 550(a) might show that a transferee also could be an "entity for whose benefit"—but it does not. There is no legislative history concerning the "entity for whose benefit" language and little legislative history for the rest of § 550. The section was extensively revised after the bill had been reported by the committees in both houses of Congress. Senator DiConcini and Representative Edwards read into the Congressional Record identical statements about the effect of the amendment, 124 Cong. Rec. 32400 (1978) (Edwards), 124 Cong. Rec. 34000 (DiConcini):

> Section 550(a)(1) of the House amendment has been modified in order to permit recovery from an entity for whose benefit an avoided transfer is made in addition to a recovery from the initial transferee of the transfer. Section [550(d)] would still apply, and the trustee is entitled only to a single satisfaction. The liability of a transferee under § 550(a) applies only "to the extent that a transfer is avoided." This means that liability is not imposed on a transferee to the extent that a transferee is protected under a provision such as § 548(c) which grants a good faith transferee for value of a transfer that is avoided only as a fraudulent transfer, a lien on the property transferred to the extent of value given.

This is the only discussion of the enacted version of § 550(a) in the legislative history of the 1978 Code, and it does not address the problems our case presents. We are left with the inference from structure: § 550 distinguishes transferees (those who receive the money or other property) from entities that get a benefit because someone else received the money or property.

To say that the categories "transferee" and "entity for whose benefit such transfer was made" are mutually exclusive does not necessarily make it easy to determine in which category a given entity falls. The method we employed in Part I of this opinion to decide that the Bank was not an "initial" transferee governs the question whether entities are subsequent transferees, too. The answer is not difficult in this case, however. The Bank did not obtain a benefit from the transfer to Ryan on January 21; it obtained dominion over the funds on January 31. The Bank is a transferee.

III

A trustee may not recover from a subsequent transferee who "takes for value, including satisfaction * * * of a present or antecedent debt, in good faith, and without knowledge of the voidability of the transfer avoided," § 550(b)(1). The Bank took for value on January 31. It had extended $655,000 in credit to Ryan, and the payment satisfied $200,000 of this debt; the Bank also released a share of its security interest. Bonded's trustee contends, however, that a subsequent transferee must give value to the debtor; the Bank gave value only to Ryan.

The statute does not say "value to the debtor"; it says "value." A natural reading looks to what the transferee gave up rather than what the debtor received. Other portions of the Code require value to the debtor. Section 548(c), for example, gives the initial recipient of a fraudulent conveyance a lien against any assets it hands back, "to the extent that such transferee * * * gave value to the debtor in exchange for such transfer." The difference between "value" in § 550(b)(1) and "value to the debtor" in § 548(c) makes sense. Section 550(b)(1) implements a system well known in commercial law, in which a transferee of commercial paper or chattels acquires an interest to the extent he purchased the items without knowledge of a defect in the chain. These recipients receive protection because monitoring of earlier stages is impractical, and exposing them to risk on account of earlier delicts would make commerce harder to conduct. Benefits to the commercial economy, and not to the initial transferors (who may be victims of fraud), justify this approach.

Transferees and other purchasers generally deal only with the previous person in line; they give value, if at all, to their transferors (or the transferors' designees). The statute emulates the pattern of other rules protecting good faith purchasers. All of the courts that have considered this question have held or implied that value to the transferor is sufficient. We agree with these cases. * * *

IV

The final question is whether the Bank received the $200,000 "in good faith, and without knowledge of the voidability of the transfer avoided." The trustee does not contend that the Bank knew of Bonded's precarious condition or Ryan's plan to use Bonded's money to pay his personal debts. He does not say that the Bank acted in bad faith—or even that there is a difference between "good faith" and "without knowledge of the voidability of the transfer." See Lawrence P. King, 4 *Collier on Bankruptcy* ¶ 550.03[1] p. 550–10 (15th ed. 1987) (treating the two as redundant). (We need not decide whether there is a difference.) And the trustee does not try to show that this transaction satisfies the test suggested by the legislative history of § 550(b)(1):

> The phrase "good faith" in [§ 550(b)] is intended to prevent a transferee from whom the trustee could recover from transferring the recoverable property to an innocent transferee, and receiving a retransfer from him, that is, "washing" the transaction through an innocent third party. In order for the transferee to be excepted from liability * * * he himself must be a good faith transferee.

H.R. Rep. No. 95–595 at 376, *reprinted in* 1978 U.S.C.C.A.N. at 6332; S. Rep. No. 95–989 at 90, *reprinted in* 1978 U.S.C.C.A.N. at 5876. The trustee contends, instead, that the Bank should have known about Bonded's distress and Ryan's chicanery; had it investigated the deposit on January 21, it would have found out; and because it should have known, this is as good as knowledge.

Imputed knowledge is an old idea, employed even in the criminal law. Venerable authority has it that the recipient of a voidable transfer may lack good faith if he possessed enough knowledge of the events to induce a reasonable person to investigate. No one supposes that "knowledge of voidability" means complete understanding of the facts and receipt of a lawyer's opinion that such a transfer is voidable; some lesser knowledge will do. Some facts strongly suggest the presence of others; a recipient that closes its eyes to the remaining facts may not deny knowledge. But this is not the same as a duty to investigate, to be a monitor for creditors' benefit when nothing known so far suggests that there is a fraudulent conveyance in the chain. "Knowledge" is a stronger term than "notice." A transferee that lacks the information necessary to support an inference of knowledge need not start investigating on his own.

Nothing in the record of this case suggests that the Bank knew of Bonded's financial peril or Ryan's plan. Bonded was not the Bank's customer. The transfer from Ryan to the Bank on January 31 was innocuous. The Bank thought it got Ryan's money; its loan was fully secured; it perceived Ryan as a well-heeled horse breeder, with a balance sheet in the millions, current on his loan payments.

The transfer from Bonded to Ryan on January 21 was only slightly more problematic from the Bank's perspective. A corporation was transferring $200,000 to one of its executives. This does not hint at a fraudulent conveyance by a firm on the brink of insolvency; for all the Bank knew, Bonded had plenty more where the $200,000 came from. Banks frequently receive large checks from corporations to their officers; think of the annual bonus checks General Motors issues, or the check to repurchase a bloc of shares. A $200,000 check is not a plausible bonus for a currency exchange, however. It could hint at embezzlement. Several Illinois cases say that a bank should inquire when a firm's employee signs a large check with himself as payee.

Since those cases were decided, Illinois adopted the Uniform Fiduciaries Act, which relieves banks of such a duty to inquire into the authority of the fiduciary signing the check on the maker's behalf. At all events, the Bank had no reason to think Ryan an embezzler. The check was accompanied by a memorandum from Kenneth Kortas, Bonded's manager, demonstrating that Ryan was not keeping other corporate officers in the dark. The Kortas memorandum would have led a reasonable bank to conclude that Bonded as a corporate entity wanted to make the transfer—and a bank drawing that inference here would have been right. Had the Bank called Kortas (or anyone else at Bonded) to inquire about the check, the Bank would have learned that the instrument was authorized by the appropriate corporate officials. Since the inquiry would have turned up nothing pertinent to voidability, the Bank's failure to make it does not permit a court to attribute to it the necessary knowledge.

The Bank is a subsequent transferee covered by § 550(b)(1). It took for value and without knowledge of the voidability of the initial transaction.

AFFIRMED.

Notes and Questions

1. This case would have turned out differently, according to the court, if the note accompanying Bonded's check had said "use this check to reduce Ryan's loan" instead of "deposit this check into [Ryan]'s account." Did the court promote form over substance, despite its protestation to the contrary? If not, what is the substantive difference between the two? Does the court's conclusion give bad actors like Michael Ryan too much flexibility to structure transfers so that effective recovery is precluded?

2. *Bonded Financial*'s "dominion and control" test for determining whether an entity is an "initial transferee" under § 550 has been widely adopted. See *Taunt v. Hurtado (In re Hurtado)*, 342 F.3d 528 (6th Cir.2003). The same widespread acceptance has not greeted some other aspects of *Bonded Financial*'s analysis, however. For example, the court in *Meoli v. Huntington National Bank (In re Teleservices Group, Inc.)*, 469 B.R. 713 (Bankr. W.D. Mich.2012), disagreed with *Bonded Financial*'s conclusion that the bank did not become a subsequent transferee until it exercised its setoff rights pursuant to its depositor's order. The court in *Meoli* found that a depositary bank's "rights arising from the account relationship itself also permits for the type of domination that *Bonded Financial* speaks of." *Id*. at 736. The court pointed to the fact that banks take title to deposited funds; as far as the bank-depositor relationship is concerned, the accountholder is the creditor and the bank is the debtor. A bank has an unrestricted right to use deposited funds as it will, subject to its contractual obligation to follow an accountholder's payment directions.

Other courts also disagree with the conclusion, reached by the Seventh Circuit in *Bonded Financial*, that a subsequent transferee cannot be an "entity for whose benefit" the transfer was made. See e.g. *Max Sugarman Funeral Home, Inc. v. A.D.B. Investors*, 926 F.2d 1248, 1256-57 (1st Cir.1991).

Was the court in *Bonded Financial* so influenced by the "functions of fraudulent conveyance law" that it disregarded the plain meaning of the statute?

3. In *Bonded Financial*, Judge Easterbrook anticipated a fact pattern in which Firm pays all or part of its debt to Lender more than 90 days but less than a year before filing bankruptcy. If the debt is guaranteed by a noninsider, the payment is not recoverable. If Guarantor is an insider, however, Lender remains the "initial transferee" under § 550(a), but Guarantor is an "entity for whose benefit [the] transfer was made." That may allow recovery from Lender.

That very fact pattern came before Judge Easterbrook the next year in *Levit v. Ingersoll Rand Financial Corp. (In re V.N. Deprizio Construction Corp.)*, 874 F.2d 1186 (7th Cir.1989) (which is often referred to as the

Deprizio case). In that case, V.N. Deprizio Construction Corp. borrowed money from a number of lenders, including Ingersoll Rand Financial. The loans were guaranteed by the Deprizio brothers, all of whom were insiders of the corporation. After the corporation filed bankruptcy, the trustee sought to recover from the lenders, as preferences, payments made in the year before the filing, including those made more than 90 days previously.

The court held the payments recoverable, using reasoning based on a multitude of Code sections. An "insider" (§ 101(21)(B)(ii)) Guarantor has a "claim" (§ 101(5)(A)), because he or she has a contingent right to payment, and is therefore a "creditor" of the debtor Firm (§ 101(10)). Every payment made by Firm to Lender is a "transfer" (§ 101(54)) that is "for the benefit of a creditor" (§ 547(b)(1)), Guarantor, because it reduces the amount Guarantor might be called upon to pay in the event of Firm's default. That makes the transfer avoidable under § 547(b)(4)(B). Once a transfer is found avoidable under § 547, § 550 determines from whom recovery can be obtained. Section 547 distinguishes insiders from noninsiders, but § 550 does not. It permits recovery from either the "initial transferee," Lender, or from the "entity for whose benefit such transfer was made," Guarantor. Thus, Lender may be required to repay the preferential transfer even though it is not an insider.

Deprizio caused a substantial negative reaction in the lending community, which saw itself made *more* vulnerable in its borrowers' bankruptcies, due to the presence of guarantors, rather than less. Congress responded by passing § 550(c) in 1994; it provides that, in fact patterns like *Deprizio*, the trustee may not recover from the non-insider.

Section 550(c) did not completely eviscerate *Deprizio*, however. Consider a case in which a lender perfects a security interest long enough after attachment that the perfection constitutes a preference, and that the lender takes this perfecting step less than a year, but more than 90 days, before the debtor files bankruptcy. In addition, assume that the security interest secures a debt that is guaranteed by debtor's insider. Facts much like these arose in *Roost v. Associates Home Equity Services, Inc. (In re Williams)*, 234 B.R. 801 (Bankr. D.Ore.1999). The trustee sought to avoid the security interest as a preference, arguing that § 550(c) was inapplicable because no "recovery" was necessary. The court agreed, holding that when

> the property is already property of the estate pursuant to § 541 and the property has not been transferred to the creditor or some other third party prior to the filing of the bankruptcy, the trustee has no need for "recovery." In such a case, where the trustee seeks merely to avoid a security interest, the security interest is avoided and automatically preserved for the benefit of the estate pursuant to § 551.

Id. at 805. Congress tried again in 2005 to eliminate the line of reasoning used in *Deprizio*, this time by adding § 547(i) to the Code. That seems to have done the job. Now, under the *Deprizio* fact pattern, a preference is avoided only as to the insider-guarantor and not as to the bank.

The distinction between "avoidance" and "recovery," drawn by the court in *Williams*, has other implications, however. For example, is a creditor who has suffered the avoidance of its security interest entitled to claim the benefit of § 550(e)? See *Suhar v. Burns (In re Burns)*, 322 F.3d 421 (6th Cir. 2003).

4. In *Bonded Financial*, the Seventh Circuit talked about the "common pool" problem. Recall the description of it, from Thomas H. Jackson's book, THE LOGIC AND LIMITS OF BANKRUPTCY LAW (1986), set out in Chapter 2, Section A of this casebook.

The following case involves a letter of credit, which can serve either as a payment device or as a credit enhancer. A "payment" or "commercial" letter is often used in situations in which the parties are not well-acquainted, such as international sales, or when goods are to be sent so far that recovery would be inconvenient if not impossible. The seller may not be willing to ship on credit without first learning a great deal about the buyer's creditworthiness, but doing the necessary investigation may be expensive and time-consuming. Prepayment would be financially risky from the buyer's point of view, however. The solution is a payment letter of credit. The buyer obtains a letter of credit from a reputable bank, the "issuer," which represents the bank's promise to pay upon receipt of specified documents—typically, an invoice, a bill of lading showing shipment, and an inspection certificate or certificate of insurance. With a payment letter, the seller can be assured that shipment of conforming goods will result in payment, and the buyer knows that payment will not be forthcoming until conforming goods are shipped.

A "standby" letter is a type of credit enhancer. It represents a promise by the letter's issuer to pay a designated party—the "beneficiary"—if some sort of default occurs. The creditor-beneficiary is on financially firm ground when payment is promised by a reputable institution, such as the debtor's bank, and the debtor's bank is in a position to judge the debtor's creditworthiness or to obtain collateral.

The following case deals with a standby letter of credit, which did not end up providing the creditor—here, a seller of oil—the expected protection from the risk of the debtor's bankruptcy.

KELLOGG v. BLUE QUAIL ENERGY, INC.
(MATTER OF COMPTON CORP.)

United States Court of Appeals, Fifth Circuit, 1987.
831 F.2d 586.

JERRE S. WILLIAMS, Circuit Judge.

This is a bankruptcy preference case in which a bankruptcy trustee seeks to recover a transfer made via a letter of credit for the benefit of one of the debtor's unsecured creditors on the eve of bankruptcy. The bankruptcy court and the district court found there to be no voidable preference. We reverse.

I. FACTUAL BACKGROUND

In March 1982, Blue Quail Energy, Inc., delivered a shipment of oil to debtor Compton Corporation. Payment of $585,443.85 for this shipment of oil was due on or about April 20, 1982. Compton failed to make timely payment. Compton induced Abilene National Bank (now MBank–Abilene) to issue an irrevocable standby letter of credit in Blue Quail's favor on May 6, 1982. Under the terms of the letter of credit, payment of up to $585,443.85 was due Blue Quail if Compton failed to pay Blue Quail this amount by June 22, 1982. Compton paid MBank $1,463.61 to issue the letter of credit. MBank also received a promissory note payable on demand for $585,443.85. MBank did not need a security agreement to cover the letter of credit transaction because a prior 1980 security agreement between the bank and Compton had a future advances provision.[1] This 1980 security agreement had been perfected as to a variety of Compton's assets through the filing of several financing statements. The most recent financing statement had been filed a year before, May 7, 1981. The letter of credit on its face noted that it was for an antecedent debt due Blue Quail.

On May 7, 1982, the day after MBank issued the letter of credit in Blue Quail's favor, several of Compton's creditors filed an involuntary bankruptcy petition against Compton. On June 22, 1982, MBank paid Blue Quail $569,932.03 on the letter of credit after Compton failed to pay Blue Quail.

---

[1] A future advances clause in a security agreement subjects the specified collateral to any future loan made by the creditor in addition to the current loans.

In the ensuing bankruptcy proceeding, MBank's aggregate secured claims against Compton, including the letter of credit payment to Blue Quail, were paid in full from the liquidation of Compton's assets which served as the bank's collateral. Walter Kellogg, bankruptcy trustee for Compton, did not contest the validity of MBank's secured claim against Compton's assets for the amount drawn under the letter of credit by Blue Quail. Instead, on June 14, 1983, trustee Kellogg filed a complaint in the bankruptcy court against Blue Quail asserting that Blue Quail had received a preferential transfer under § 547 through the letter of credit transaction. The trustee sought to recover $585,443.85 from Blue Quail pursuant to § 550.

Blue Quail answered and filed a third party complaint against MBank. On June 16, 1986, Blue Quail filed a motion for summary judgment asserting that the trustee could not recover any preference from Blue Quail because Blue Quail had been paid from MBank's funds under the letter of credit and therefore had not received any of Compton's property. On August 27, 1986, the bankruptcy court granted Blue Quail's motion, agreeing that the payment under the letter of credit did not constitute a transfer of debtor Compton's property but rather was a transfer of the bank's property. The bankruptcy court entered judgment on the motion on September 10, 1986. Trustee Kellogg appealed this decision to the district court. On December 11, 1986, the district court affirmed the bankruptcy court ruling, holding that the trustee did not establish two necessary elements of a voidable transfer under § 547. The district court agreed with Blue Quail and the bankruptcy court that the trustee could not establish that the funds transferred to Blue Quail were ever property of Compton. Furthermore, the district court held that the transfer of the increased security interest to MBank was a transfer of the debtor's property for the sole benefit of the bank and in no way benefitted Blue Quail. The district court therefore found no voidable preference as to Blue Quail. The trustee is appealing the decision to this Court.

II. THE LETTER OF CREDIT

It is well established that a letter of credit and the proceeds therefrom are not property of the debtor's estate under § 541. When the issuer honors a proper draft under a letter of credit, it does so from its own assets and not from the assets of its customer who caused the letter of credit to be issued. As a result, a bankruptcy trustee is not entitled to enjoin a post petition payment of funds under a letter of credit from the issuer to the beneficiary, because such a payment is not a transfer of debtor's property (a threshold requirement under § 547(b)). A case apparently holding otherwise, *In re Twist Cap, Inc.*, 1 B.R. 284 (Bankr. D.Fla.1979), has been roundly criticized and otherwise ignored by courts and commentators alike.

Recognizing these characteristics of a letter of credit in a bankruptcy case is necessary in order to maintain the independence principle, the cornerstone of letter of credit law. Under the independence principle, an issuer's obligation to the letter of credit's beneficiary is independent from any obligation between the beneficiary and the issuer's customer. All a beneficiary has to do to receive payment under a letter of credit is to show that it has performed all the duties required by the letter of credit. Any disputes between the beneficiary and the customer do not affect the issuer's obligation to the beneficiary to pay under the letter of credit.

Letters of credit are most commonly arranged by a party who benefits from the provision of goods or services. The party will request a bank to issue a letter of credit which names the provider of the goods or services as the beneficiary. Under a standby letter of credit, the bank becomes primarily liable to the beneficiary upon the default of the bank's customer to pay for the goods or services. The bank charges a fee to issue a letter of credit and to undertake this liability. The shifting of liability to the bank rather than to the services or goods provider is the main purpose of the letter of credit. After all, the bank is in a much better position to assess the risk of its customer's insolvency than is the service or goods provider. It should be noted, however, that it is the risk of the debtor's insolvency and not the risk of a preference attack that a bank assumes under a letter of credit transaction. Overall, the independence principle is necessary to insure "the certainty of payments for services or goods rendered regardless of any intervening misfortune which may befall the other contracting party." *In re North Shore & Central Ill. Freight Co.*, 30 B.R. 377, 378 (Bankr. N.D.Ill.1983).

The trustee in this case accepts this analysis and does not ask us to upset it. The trustee is not attempting to set aside the post petition payments by MBank to Blue Quail under the letter of credit as a preference; nor does the trustee claim the letter of credit itself constitutes debtor's property. The trustee is instead challenging the earlier transfer in which Compton granted MBank an increased security interest in its assets to obtain the letter of credit for the benefit of Blue Quail. Collateral which has been pledged by a debtor as security for a letter of credit is property of the debtor's estate. The trustee claims that the direct transfer to MBank of the increased security interest on May 6, 1982, also constituted an indirect transfer to Blue Quail which occurred one day prior to the filing of the involuntary bankruptcy petition and is voidable as a preference under § 547. This assertion of a preferential transfer is evaluated in Parts III and IV of this opinion.

It is important to note that the irrevocable standby letter of credit in the case at bar was not arranged in connection with Blue Quail's initial decision to sell oil to Compton on credit. Compton arranged for the letter of credit after Blue Quail had shipped the oil and after Compton had defaulted in payment. The letter of credit in this case did not serve its usual function of backing up a contemporaneous credit decision, but instead served as a back up payment guarantee on an extension of credit already in jeopardy. The letter of credit was issued to pay off an antecedent unsecured debt. This fact was clearly noted on the face of the letter of credit. Blue Quail, the beneficiary of the letter of credit, did not give new value for the issuance of the letter of credit by MBank on May 6, 1982, or for the resulting increased security interest held by MBank. MBank, however, did give new value for the increased security interest it obtained in Compton's collateral: the bank issued the letter of credit.

When a debtor pledges its assets to secure a letter of credit, a transfer of debtor's property has occurred under the provisions of § 547. By subjecting its assets to MBank's reimbursement claim in the event MBank had to pay on the letter of credit, Compton made a transfer of its property. The broad definition of "transfer" under [§ 101(54)] is clearly designed to cover such a transfer. Overall, the letter of credit itself and the payments thereunder may not be property of debtor, but the collateral pledged as a security interest for the letter of credit is.

Furthermore, in a secured letter of credit transaction, the transfer of debtor's property takes place at the time the letter of credit is issued (when the security interest is granted) and received by the beneficiary, not at the time the issuer pays on the letter of credit.

The transfer to MBank of the increased security interest was a direct transfer which occurred on May 6, 1982, when the bank issued the letter of credit. Under § 547(e)(2)(A), however, such a transfer is deemed to have taken place for purposes of § 547 at the time such transfer "takes effect" between the transferor and transferee if such transfer is perfected within 10 days. The phrase "takes effect" is undefined in the Bankruptcy Code, but under Uniform Commercial Code Article 9 law, a transfer of a security interest "takes effect" when the security interest attaches. Because of the future advances clause in MBank's 1980 security agreement with Compton, the attachment of the

MBank's security interest relates back to May 9, 1980, the date the security agreement went into effect. The bottom line is that the direct transfer of the increased security interest to MBank is artifically [sic] deemed to have occurred at least by May 7, 1981, the date MBank filed its final financing statement, for purposes of a preference attack against the bank. This date is well before the 90 day window of § 547-(b)(4)(A). This would protect the bank from a preference attack by the trustee even if the bank had not given new value at the time it received the increased security interest. MBank is therefore protected from a preference attack by the trustee for the increased security interest transfer under either of two theories: under § 547(c)(1) because it gave new value and under the operation of the relation back provision of § 547-(e)(2)(A). The bank is also protected from any claims of reimbursement by Blue Quail because the bank received no voidable preference.

The relation back provision of § 547(e)(2)(A), however, applies only to the direct transfer of the increased security interest to MBank. The indirect transfer to Blue Quail that allegedly resulted from the direct transfer to MBank occurred on May 6, 1982, the date of issuance of the letter of credit. The relation back principle of § 547(e)(2)(A) does not apply to this indirect transfer to Blue Quail. Blue Quail was not a party to the security agreement between MBank and Compton. So it will not be able to utilize the relation back provision if it is deemed to have received an indirect transfer resulting from the direct transfer of the increased security interest to MBank. Blue Quail, therefore, cannot assert either of the two defenses to a preference attack which MBank can claim. Blue Quail did not give new value under § 547(c)(1), and it received a transfer within 90 days of the filing of Compton's bankruptcy petition.

III. DIRECT/INDIRECT TRANSFER DOCTRINE

The federal courts have long recognized that "[t]o constitute a preference, it is not necessary that the transfer be made directly to the creditor." *National Bank of Newport v. National Herkimer County Bank*, 225 U.S. 178, 184 (1912). "If the bankrupt has made a transfer of his property, the *effect* of which is to enable one of his creditors to obtain a greater percentage of his debt than another creditor of the same class, circuity of arrangement will not avail to save it." *Id*. (Emphasis added.) To combat such circuity, the courts have broken down certain transfers into two transfers, one direct and one indirect. The direct transfer to the third party may be valid and not subject to a preference attack. The indirect transfer, arising from the same action by the debtor, however, may constitute a voidable preference as to the creditor who indirectly benefitted from the direct transfer to the third party.

This is the situation presented in the case before us. The term "transfer" as used in the various bankruptcy statutes through the years has always been broad enough to cover such indirect transfers and to catch various circuitous arrangements. The new Bankruptcy Code implicitly adopts this doctrine through its broad definition of "transfer." Examining the case law that has developed since the *National Bank of Newport* case yields an understanding of what types of transfers the direct/indirect doctrine is meant to cover.

In *Palmer v. Radio Corporation of America*, 453 F.2d 1133 (5th Cir.1971), a third party purchased from the debtor a television station for $40,000 cash and the assumption of certain liabilities of the debtor, including unsecured claims by creditor RCA. This Court found the direct transfer from the debtor to the third party purchaser constituted an indirect preferential transfer to creditor RCA. We found that the assumption by the third party purchaser of the debt owed by the debtor to RCA and the subsequent payments made thereunder constituted a voidable transfer as to RCA. The court noted that such indirect transfers as this had long been held to constitute voidable preferences under bankruptcy laws.

Although the *Palmer* court did not elaborate its reasoning behind this holding, such reasoning is self evident. A secured creditor was essentially substituted for an unsecured creditor through the transfer of the television station to the third party purchaser and the assumption of the unsecured debt by the purchaser. The third party purchaser was in effect secured because it had the television station. Creditor RCA would receive payments directly from the solvent third party without having to worry about its original debtor's financial condition. The original debtor's other unsecured creditors were harmed because a valuable asset of the debtor, the television station, was removed from the debtor's estate. The end result of the *Palmer* case was that the third party's payments on the RCA debt were to be made to the debtor's estate instead of to RCA. RCA would then recover the same percentage of its unsecured claim from the estate as the other unsecured creditors.

* * *

In *Virginia National Bank v. Woodson*, 329 F.2d 836 (4th Cir.1964), the debtor had several overdrawn accounts with his bank.[8] The debtor talked his sister into paying off $8,000 of the overdrafts in exchange for an $8,000 promissory note and an assignment of some collateral as security. The debtor's sister made the $8,000 payment directly to the bank. The $8,000 technically was never part of the debtor's estate. The court, however, held that the payment of the $8,000 by the sister to the bank was a preference as to the bank to the extent of the value of the collateral held by the sister. The court noted that the measure of the value of a voidable preference is diminution of the debtor's estate and not the value of the transfer to the creditor.

In the *Woodson* case the sister was secured only to the extent the pledged collateral had value; the remainder of her loan to her brother was unsecured. Swapping one unsecured creditor for another unsecured creditor does not create any kind of preference. The court held that a preference in such a transaction arises only when a secured creditor is swapped for an unsecured creditor. Only then is the pool of assets available for distribution to the general unsecured creditors depleted because the secured creditor has priorty [sic] over the unsecured creditors. Furthermore, the court held that the bank and not the sister had received the voidable preference and had to pay back to the trustee an amount equal to the value of the collateral.

* * *

IV. THE DIRECT/INDIRECT DOCTRINE IN THE CONTEXT OF A LETTER OF CREDIT TRANSACTION

The case at bar differs from the cases discussed in Part III *supra* only by the presence of the letter of credit as the mechanism for paying off the unsecured creditor. Blue Quail's attempt to otherwise distinguish the case from the direct/indirect transfer cases does not withstand scrutiny.

In the letter of credit cases discussed in Part II *supra*, the letters of credit were issued contemporaneously with the initial extension of credit by the beneficiaries of the letters. In those cases the letters of credit effectively served as security devices for the benefit of the creditor beneficiaries and took the place of formal security interests. The courts in those cases properly found there had been no voidable transfers, direct or indirect, in the letter of credit transactions involved. New value was given contemporaneously with the issuance of the letters of

---

[8] Unsecured antecedent debts.

credit in the form of the extensions of credit by the beneficiaries of the letters. As a result, the § 547(c)(1) preference exception was applicable.

The case at bar differs from these other letter of credit cases by one very important fact: the letter of credit in this case was issued to secure an antecedent unsecured debt due the beneficiary of the letter of credit. The unsecured creditor beneficiary gave no new value upon the issuance of the letter of credit. When the issuer paid off the letter of credit and foreclosed on the collateral securing the letter of credit, a preferential transfer had occurred. An unsecured creditor was paid in full and a secured creditor was substituted in its place.

The district court upheld the bankruptcy court in maintaining the validity of the letter of credit issued to cover the antecedent debt. The district court held that MBank, the issuer of the letter of credit, could pay off the letter of credit and foreclose on the collateral securing it. We are in full agreement. But we also look to the impact of the transaction as it affects the situation of Blue Quail in the bankrupt estate. We hold that the bankruptcy trustee can recover from Blue Quail, the beneficiary of the letter of credit, because Blue Quail received an indirect preference. This result preserves the sanctity of letter of credit and carries out the purposes of the Bankruptcy Code by avoiding a preferential transfer. MBank, the issuer of the letter of credit, being just the intermediary through which the preferential transfer was accomplished, completely falls out of the picture and is not involved in this particular legal proceeding.

MBank did not receive any preferential transfer—it gave new value for the security interest. Furthermore, because the direct and indirect transfers are separate and independent, the trustee does not even need to challenge the direct transfer of the increased security interest to MBank, or seek any relief at all from MBank, in order to attack the indirect transfer and recover under § 550 from the indirect transferee Blue Quail.

We hold that a creditor cannot secure payment of an unsecured antecedent debt through a letter of credit transaction when it could not do so through any other type of transaction. The purpose of the letter of credit transaction in this case was to secure payment of an unsecured antecedent debt for the benefit of an unsecured creditor. This is the only proper way to look at such letters of credit in the bankruptcy context. The promised transfer of pledged collateral induced the bank to issue the letter of credit in favor of the creditor. The increased security interest held by the bank clearly benefitted the creditor because the bank would not have issued the letter of credit without this security. A secured creditor was substituted for an unsecured creditor to the detriment of the other unsecured creditors.

We also hold, therefore, that the trustee can recover under § 550(a)(1) the value of the transferred property from "the entity for whose benefit such transfer was made." In the case at bar, this entity was the creditor beneficiary, not the issuer, of the letter of credit even though the issuer received the direct transfer from the debtor. The entire purpose of the direct/indirect doctrine is to look through the form of a transaction and determine which entity actually benefitted from the transfer.

The fact that there was a prior security agreement between the issuing bank and the debtor containing the future advances clause does not alter this conclusion. As we pointed out in Part II *supra*, this prior security agreement gave MBank an additional shield from preferential attack because of the relation back mechanism of § 547(e)(2)(A). Section 547(e)(2)(A), however, does not avail Blue Quail to shield it from a preferential attack for the indirect transfer. The indirect transfer to Blue Quail occurred on May 6, 1982, when the letter of credit was issued and the increased security interest was pledged. This was the day before the involuntary bankruptcy petition was filed. For purposes of § 547, a transfer of Compton's property for the benefit of Blue Quail did occur within 90 days of the bankruptcy filing. The bankruptcy and district courts erred in failing to analyze properly the transfer of debtor's property that occurred when Compton pledged its assets to obtain the letter of credit. This transfer consisted of two aspects: the direct transfer to MBank which is not a voidable preference for various reasons and the indirect transfer to Blue Quail which is a voidable preference.

All of the requirements of § 547(b) have been satisfied in the trustee's preferential attack against Blue Quail. * * * The net effect of the indirect transfer to Blue Quail was to remove $585,443.85 from the pool of assets available to Compton's unsecured creditors and substitute in its place a secured claim for the same amount.

The precise holding in this case needs to be emphasized. We do not hold that payment under a letter of credit, or even a letter of credit itself, constitute preferential transfers under § 547(b) or property of a debtor under § 541. The holding of this case fully allows the letter of credit to function. We preserve its sanctity and the underlying independence doctrine. We do not, however, allow an unsecured creditor to avoid a preference attack by utilizing a letter of credit to secure payment of an antecedent debt. Otherwise the unsecured creditor would receive an indirect preferential transfer from the granting of the security for the letter of credit to the extent of the value of that security. Our holding does not affect the strength of or the proper use of letters of credit. When a letter of credit is issued contemporaneously with a new extension of credit, the creditor beneficiary will not be subject to a preferential attack under the direct/indirect doctrine elaborated in this case because the creditor will have given new value in exchange for the indirect benefit of the secured letter of credit. Only when a creditor receives a secured letter of credit to cover an unsecured antecedent debt will it be subject to a preferential attack under § 547(b).

* * *

VI. CONCLUSION

Blue Quail Energy received an indirect preferential transfer from Compton Corporation on May 6, 1982, one day prior to the filing of Compton's bankruptcy petition. We reverse the district court and render judgment in favor of Trustee Kellogg against Blue Quail Energy, Inc. in the amount of $585,443.85 plus interest to be fixed by the district court pursuant to §§ 547, 550. The district court's dismissal of Blue Quail's claim against MBank for reimbursement is affirmed.

Notes and Questions

1. Not all courts accept the two-transfer analysis utilized in *Blue Quail*. In *Deprizio*, for example, the Seventh Circuit criticized this approach because it equates "transfer" with "benefit received." But the Code's preference and recovery provisions, at issue in that case, refer only to transfers vis-à-vis the debtor, not the transferee:

> Sections 547 and 550 both speak of a transfer being avoided; avoidability is an attribute of the transfer rather than of the creditor. While the lenders want to define transfer from the recipients' perspectives, the Code consistently defines it from the debtor's. A single payment therefore is one "transfer," no matter how many persons gain thereby.

874 F.2d at 1195-96 (footnote omitted). Does the fact that *Deprizio* arose in a different context affect the appropriateness of a two-transfer approach?

2. Recall Problem # 4 on page 442, in the materials on § 547(c)(5). Does *Blue Quail* suggest an argument the trustee could use in an effort to avoid the transfer under those facts?

3. Look again at *Dean v. Davis*, which is discussed in Section C.3 of this chapter. Now that you have read *Blue Quail*, do you see a preference in *Dean v. Davis* despite the Supreme Court's conclusion to the contrary?

Note on Recovery From Governmental Units

As we have seen, the avoiding powers are designed to further several of bankruptcy's fundamental principles—namely, that creditors should be discouraged from "rushing in" and hastening a shaky debtor's economic demise, and that similarly situated creditors should be treated equally. States and other governmental units are often among those creditors in bankruptcy cases who have taken avoidable transfers before bankruptcy filing. They may also have violated the automatic stay with postpetition efforts to collect, in contravention of the principle that debtors should be afforded a "breathing space." Until a few years ago, trustees simply relied on § 106—a broadly-worded abrogation of sovereign immunity—to hold states accountable in such situations.

All of that began to change with *Seminole Tribe v. Florida*, 517 U.S. 44, 116 S.Ct. 1114, 134 L.Ed.2d 252 (1996). The case dealt with the Indian Gaming Regulatory Act, which permits an Indian tribe to conduct certain gaming activities within a state if the tribe and the state have first agreed on conditions governing the conduct of those activities. The Seminole Tribe sued Florida in federal court, asserting that the State failed to negotiate such an agreement in good faith. The State sought dismissal on the grounds of sovereign immunity. The Supreme Court agreed with the State, holding that Congress cannot abrogate a state's immunity under the Eleventh Amendment by enacting legislation pursuant to powers enumerated in Article I of the Constitution.

Language in *Seminole Tribe* suggested that the same result would apply in bankruptcy, although the case did not involve the Constitution's Bankruptcy Clause, and the case was understood to prevent trustees from hauling states into bankruptcy court to account for avoidable transfers or violations of the stay. The primary option remaining for trustees seeking to call states to account under the Bankruptcy Code, however, was to bring suit in state court. While state courts are not as attractive to trustees as bankruptcy courts for a number of reasons, *Seminole* did not foreclose that alternative.

Then, in June of 1999, that door seemed to slam shut with the decision in the Supreme Court of three more sovereign immunity cases. Although none of them involved bankruptcy, their applicability is evident and they cast serious doubt on the power of trustees to demand state compliance with the mandates of the Bankruptcy Code. In *Alden v. Maine*, 527 U.S. 706, 119 S.Ct. 2240, 144 L.Ed.2d 636 (1999), the Court held that states may assert sovereign immunity as a defense to suits brought in state court to enforce legislation enacted under Article I of the Constitution. The Court held in *Florida Prepaid Postsecondary Education Expense Board v. College Savings Bank*, 527 U.S. 627, 119 S.Ct. 2199, 144 L.Ed.2d 575 (1999), that a federal statute authorizing patent infringement suits against states was unconstitutional. And, in *College Savings Bank v. Florida Prepaid Postsecondary Education Expense Board*, 527 U.S. 666, 119 S.Ct. 2219, 144 L.Ed.2d 605 (1999), the Court invalidated the doctrine of constructive waiver of sovereign immunity. Taken together, these cases leave trustees very little power to rectify abuse of the bankruptcy process by states.

The Supreme Court granted certiorari in a sovereign immunity case that arose in bankruptcy, *Tennessee Student Assistance Corp. v. Hood*, 541 U.S. 440, 124 S.Ct. 1905, 158 L.Ed.2d 764 (2004), in order to resolve the question whether the Bankruptcy Clause granted Congress the authority to abrogate sovereign immunity, but the Court ultimately left that question undecided. The debtor in *Hood* owed student loans to a state entity. Student loans are not discharged in bankruptcy unless a debtor establishes "undue hardship," so Hood served the state entity with a complaint, as required by the Bankruptcy Rules, to obtain a determination of dischargeability. The State argued that § 106(a) violated its sovereign immunity under the Eleventh Amendment. The Court held, however, that a bankruptcy court has *in rem* jurisdiction over the estate and the debtor's discharge. That jurisdiction permits the court to bind States, whether they choose to participate in the bankruptcy proceedings or not, just as other creditors are bound. Although the Bankruptcy Rules require debtors to proceed by summons and complaint, which is normally an indignity to a State's sovereignty, in this circumstance the summons has the same effect as a motion, which does not raise constitutional concern. The Court distinguished this from an adversary proceeding in which a bankruptcy trustee tries to recover property in the State's hands as an avoidable preference. The Court did not decide whether a bankruptcy court's exercise of personal jurisdiction over a State would be valid under the Eleventh Amendment.

Thus, the Court left open the two most troubling questions in bankruptcy, as far as sovereign immunity is concerned—whether a bankruptcy court can call states to account when they violate the automatic stay or when they have taken preferential transfers. By distinguishing preference recoveries, *Hood* clearly suggested that such cases will require a different outcome. The automatic stay question, however, falls in between preference cases and the discharge issue involved in *Hood*. A trustee seeking to recover property taken in violation of the automatic stay is vindicating the bankruptcy court's *in rem* jurisdiction. That seems clearly permissible under *Hood*. But that effort will necessitate affirmative relief against a state, which *Hood* suggested is problematic under the Eleventh Amendment.

The Court again granted certiorari to decide whether Congress may use the Bankruptcy Clause to abrogate a state's sovereign immunity and, in

Central Virginia Community College v. Katz, 546 U.S. 356, 126 S.Ct. 990, 163 L.Ed.2d 945 (2006), came much closer to resolving the question. In *Katz*, the trustee of a corporation that operated a chain of college bookstores sought to recover preferential transfers made by the debtor to four state educational institutions, only one of which had filed a claim in the bankruptcy case. Those state entities resisted on sovereign immunity grounds. The Court framed the issue as "whether Congress' attempt to abrogate state sovereign immunity in § 106(a) is valid," but never actually reached the question of congressional abrogation. Rather, after examining the history of the Constitutional Convention in great detail, the Court found that it was the "plan of the Convention" that states, by ratifying the Constitution, agreed to surrender their sovereign immunity in regard to matters, such as recovery of preferential transfers, that are ancillary to the bankruptcy courts' *in rem* jurisdiction. The Court dismissed statements to the contrary, made in *Seminole Tribe*, as dicta.

The Court cautioned, however, that this abrogation of sovereign immunity is "limited," and pointed out that it was not suggesting "that every law labeled a 'bankruptcy' law could, consistent with the Bankruptcy Clause, properly impinge upon state sovereign immunity." 546 U.S. at 378, n.15. Thus, the constitutionality of § 106 in connection with issues less clearly related to the bankruptcy courts' *in rem* jurisdiction—as for example, when a bankruptcy court exercises its "related to" jurisdiction under 28 U.S.C. § 1334(b) and hears a nonbankruptcy issue—remains uncertain. For a critical analysis of *Katz*, see Martin H. Redish & Daniel M. Greenfield, *Bankruptcy, Sovereign Immunity and the Dilemma of Principled Decision Making: The Curious Case of* Central Virginia Community College, v. Katz, 15 AM. BANKR. INST. L. REV. 13 (2007).

Meanwhile, express waiver remains a viable doctrine, because the Eleventh Amendment prohibits suits against unconsenting states only. Thus, §§ 106(b) and (c) can be constitutionally applied to some counterclaims and setoffs asserted against state entities that file proofs of claim in bankruptcy cases. See, *e.g.*, *Arecibo Community Health Care, Inc. v. Puerto Rico*, 270 F.3d 17 (1st Cir.2001) (holding that Puerto Rico waived its sovereign immunity by filing a claim for breach of contract in the amount of $1.65 million, thus exposing itself to the debtor's compulsory counterclaim, arising out of the same contract, for $8.2 million, plus interest, fees and costs). Second, Eleventh Amendment protection extends only to states and their instrumentalities. Other governmental units, such as local jurisdictions, are not protected. Finally, suits against state officials under the doctrine of *Ex parte Young*, 209 U.S. 123, 28 S.Ct. 441, 52 L.Ed. 714 (1908), remain a possibility. Under *Young*, a federal judge can issue a prospective injunction to enjoin continuing violations of the Bankruptcy Code. Such injunctions, however, will not be effective in recovering avoided transfers or in remedying violations of the automatic stay.

E. THE "STRONG ARM" POWER

Section 544(a), which is known as the "strong arm clause," is designed primarily to permit avoidance of unrecorded security interests and mortgages. Under § 544(a)(1), the trustee has the rights of a judicial lien creditor. Those rights, as far as unrecorded security interests are concerned, are specified in Article 9 of the Uniform Commercial Code. Under UCC § 9–317(a)(2), "[a] security interest * * * is subordinate to the rights of * * * a person that becomes a lien creditor before the earlier of the time the security interest * * * is perfected or a financing statement covering the collateral is filed." In other words, a judicial lien creditor has priority over an unperfected security interest. The trustee, therefore, can avoid an unperfected security interest under § 544(a)(1).

In most states, an unrecorded mortgage has priority over judicial lien creditors, but not over subsequent bona fide purchasers. Because § 544(a)(3) gives the trustee the power of a bfp, the trustee can also avoid an unrecorded mortgage under the strong arm clause.

Subsection 544(a)(2) is less often invoked than the other two. It will be useful if state law gives unsatisfied execution creditors greater rights than those enjoyed by judicial lien creditors.

The key to § 544(a) is the avoiding power of specified entities—judicial lien creditors, judgment lien creditors and bona fide purchasers—under state law. We hypothesize such an entity as of the moment bankruptcy is filed. The trustee has, under § 544(a), whatever avoiding power that hypothetical entity would have under state law.

Problems

1. Debtor bought residential real estate on May 1, giving Creditor a mortgage on the property to secure the purchase money loan of $120,000. Creditor failed to record its interest and Debtor filed a Chapter 7 petition on October 15. Can the trustee avoid the mortgage under § 544(a)?

2. Does your answer to Problem # 1 change if Creditor properly recorded its interest in the real estate records on October 13?

3. Debtor obtained a loan of $20,000 on May 1, giving Creditor a security interest in Debtor's equipment. Creditor failed to file a financing statement and Debtor filed a Chapter 7 petition on October 15. Can the trustee avoid the security interest under § 544(a)?

4. Debtor Corp. was wholly owned by Peter President, who also served as CEO. President, on behalf of Debtor Corp., borrowed $100,000 from Bank and gave a mortgage on Debtor Corp.'s real estate to secure the loan. As President well knew, Bank failed to record the mortgage before Debtor Corp. filed a Chapter 11 petition. Under state law, an unrecorded mortgage is effective against a bona fide purchaser for value who has knowledge of the unrecorded instrument. Can Debtor Corp., acting as debtor in possession, avoid the mortgage under § 544(a)?

5. Debtor sold a parcel of real estate to Buyer, who failed to record the deed prior to Debtor's filing of a Chapter 7 petition. Can the trustee bring the property into the bankruptcy estate under § 544(a)(3)? Would your answer change if Buyer took open possession of the land after the purchase and before Debtor's bankruptcy filing?

As you have no doubt begun to realize, § 544(a) depends on provisions of local law. The following case illustrates that point and discusses the conflict some courts have perceived between §§ 544(a) and 541(d).

COMMONWEALTH LAND TITLE INSURANCE CO. v. MILLER (IN RE PROJECT HOMESTEAD, INC.)

United States Bankruptcy Court, Middle District of North Carolina, 2007.
374 B.R. 193.

WILLIAM L. STOCKS, United States Bankruptcy Judge.

* * *

BACKGROUND

Prior to ceasing operations during the latter part of 2003, the Debtor, a North Carolina non-profit corporation, was engaged in the business of developing and selling affordable housing to low and moderate income purchasers in North Carolina. Each of these six adversary proceedings involves a residence that the Debtor purportedly sold to a purchaser in 2003 (the "Properties"). The plaintiffs in these proceedings are Commonwealth Land Title Insurance Company ("Commonwealth") and various lenders who hold promissory notes and deeds of trust from the individuals who purchased the residences from the Debtor (the "Lenders"). Commonwealth issued Closing Protection Letters when the residences were purchased. The defendants in these proceedings are William P. Miller, the Chapter 7 trustee for the Debtor (the "Trustee"), and the individuals who purchased the residences (the "Purchasers").

Although each of these proceedings arises out of a separate transaction, the fact patterns involved in the transactions are very similar. In each case, the Purchasers entered into purchase contracts with the Debtor and obtained loans in order to finance the purchase of their homes. Closings, or what the parties understood to be closings, were scheduled in early 2003 and held in each case in order to consummate the purchases. The closing attorney for each of the closings was an attorney named Armina Swittenberg. Prior to the closings, the Lenders who had extended loans to the Purchasers wired the loan proceeds to Ms. Swittenberg's trust account. At each closing, one or more representatives of the Debtor and the respective Purchasers were present. At each closing, the Debtor received the purchase price of the property, including the portion that was paid from the loan proceeds that had been wired to Ms. Swittenberg, and a duly executed deed from the Debtor was delivered to the Purchasers that purportedly conveyed the property to the Purchasers. At each closing, the Purchasers executed a promissory note in favor of the Lender, along with a deed of trust purportedly granting the Lender a lien on the property being purchased to secure the promissory note. The deed from the Debtor and the deed of trust from the Purchasers were left with Ms. Swittenberg so that she could record the deed and deed of trust. Each of the properties involved in the six closings was encumbered by a pre-existing deed of trust from the Debtor and in each case Ms. Swittenberg retained a sufficient amount of funds at the closing to payoff the indebtedness secured by the pre-existing deed of trust. In each instance, Ms. Swittenberg, in fact, did pay off the indebtedness secured by the pre-existing deed of trust. However, Ms. Swittenberg failed to record either the deeds from the Debtor or the deeds of trust from the Purchasers to their Lender and none of the deeds or the deeds of trust had been recorded when the Debtor filed its Chapter 7 petition on January 24, 2004.

These adversary proceedings were filed on November 4, 2005. The plaintiffs allege a controversy with the Trustee regarding whether the bankruptcy estate has any beneficial interest in the properties and seek declaratory relief that would establish the Purchasers as the owners of the properties in question and establish a first lien in favor of the Lenders securing the indebtedness due under the promissory notes that were executed by the Purchasers. The Trustee denies that the plaintiffs are entitled to the relief sought in these proceedings and has asserted a counterclaim against the plaintiffs and a cross-claim against the Purchasers seeking an adjudication that as bankruptcy trustee, he holds title to the properties in question free and clear of all unrecorded interests, including any claims or interests of the plaintiffs or the Purchasers. The plaintiffs and the Trustee both assert that there are no material issues of fact and seek summary judgment in their favor.

* * *

ANALYSIS OF CLAIMS

* * *

In their second claim, the plaintiffs seek a declaratory judgment that: (a) a constructive trust was created in favor of the Purchasers as of dates prior to the petition date; (b) that on the petition date, only the bare legal title to the properties came into the Debtor's estate; and (c) that the Trustee be ordered to transfer the legal title to the properties to the Purchasers.

Plaintiffs base their claim upon state law regarding the imposition of constructive trusts and § 541(d) of the Bankruptcy Code. Plaintiffs argue that under applicable North Carolina law, the Purchasers are entitled to have a constructive trust imposed with respect to the Properties and that under North Carolina law such constructive trusts relate back to the conduct giving rise to such constructive trusts which, in each case, was prior to the petition date. As a result of the constructive trust, plaintiffs maintain that on the petition date the Purchasers held equitable title, the Debtor held only bare legal title and § 541(d) therefore operates to exclude the properties from the bankruptcy estate and place the properties beyond the reach of the Trustee's powers under § 544(a)(3).

While not conceding that the Purchasers are entitled to a constructive trust, the Trustee argues that even if a constructive trust were imposed, the Trustee's rights under § 544(a)(3) are not subordinate to a constructive trust and that as a bona fide purchaser for value under § 544(a)(3), he is entitled to prevail over any rights of the Purchasers under a constructive trust.

The issue thus presented is whether § 541(d) trumps the Trustee's rights and powers under § 544(a)(3). As noted by both parties, there is a split of authority regarding the issue. The decisions cited by the parties to support their respective positions unfortunately do not include a dispositive decision from the Court of Appeals for the

Fourth Circuit and none apparently exists at this time. Having carefully reviewed the authorities cited by both sides, including this court's earlier decisions, this court agrees with the reasoning and conclusion of the court in *Mayer v. United States (In re Reasonover)*, 236 B.R. 219 (Bankr. E.D.Va.1999), that § 541(d) does not trump the trustee's rights and powers under § 544(a)(3).

As pointed out in *Reasonover*, most of the decisions reaching a contrary result do not discuss or take into account the 1984 amendments to § 541(d). Prior to those amendments, § 541(d) referred to property that became property of the estate under "subsection (a)." The 1984 amendments significantly modified the language of § 541(d) by deleting "subsection (a)" and replacing it with "subsection (a)(1) or (2)." This court agrees with the conclusion that "[b]y excluding from the operation of § 541(d) those portions of § 541(a) other than subsections (a)(1) and (a)(2), Congress clearly signaled its intention that the trustee's avoidance powers would trump claims based solely on the debtor's lack of equitable title." *Id.* at 227-28.

The decision in *Reasonover* also supports the Trustee's argument that under § 544(a)(3) no transfer is required in order for a bankruptcy trustee to have the rights and powers of a bona fide purchaser of real property. As pointed out in *Reasonover*, the text of § 544(a)(3) not only does not limit the trustee's avoidance powers to transfers "by" the debtor, it is not even limited to "transfers." What § 544(a)(3) says is that the trustee has "the *rights and powers of,* or may avoid any transfer of property of the debtor * * * that is avoidable by * * * a bona fide purchaser of real property." (Emphasis added.) The fact that this preamble is phrased in the disjunctive, is a strong indication that the trustee may exercise any "rights and powers" of a bona fide purchaser even in the absence of a transfer. "In other words, the trustee occupies the position of a bona fide purchaser and takes real property free and clear of any unperfected liens or interests." *Id.* at 228. This means that in these proceedings, if a bona fide purchaser of the Properties from the Debtor would have acquired a superior right and title as against the Purchasers or entities claiming through the Purchasers, then so does the Trustee.

While a bankruptcy trustee's rights and powers as a bona fide purchaser of real property are created or conferred by federal bankruptcy law, the extent of the trustee's rights as a bona fide purchaser are measured by applicable state law.

The Trustee argues that under North Carolina law, even if the Purchasers were granted a constructive trust, his rights as a bona fide purchaser of real property are superior to the rights of the Purchasers as the beneficiaries of the constructive trust. The Trustee's argument is fully supported by North Carolina law under which the interests of a bona fide purchaser of real property without notice of the trust are superior to the rights of a beneficiary of an unrecorded equitable trust. *See In re Creech,* 350 B.R. 24, 29 (Bankr. M.D.N.C.2006); *Bank of Vance v. Crowder,* 139 S.E. 601, 602-03 (N.C.1927) ("Equity makes use of the machinery of a trust for the purpose of affording redress in cases of fraud, and will follow the property obtained by a fraud in order to remedy the wrong, and only stops the pursuit when the means of ascertainment fails or the rights of bona fide purchasers for value, without notice of the fraud or trust, have intervened."). Thus, as a matter of law, the rights of the Trustee, as a hypothetical bona fide purchaser of the Properties, are superior to any rights that the plaintiffs or the Purchasers could acquire under a constructive trust. It follows that the Trustee is entitled to summary judgment with respect to the plaintiffs' constructive trust claims.

* * *

Notes and Questions

1. What is the nature of the "conflict" between §§ 544(a) and 541? Did *Project Homestead* address that issue persuasively?

2. Another approach to the issue of constructive trusts in bankruptcy was taken by the court in *XL/Datacomp, Inc. v. Wilson (In re Omegas Group, Inc.),* 16 F.3d 1443 (6th Cir.1994). Creditors in *Omegas* made an argument, similar to the one made by the plaintiffs in *Project Homestead,* that their rights as beneficiaries under a constructive trust trumped the trustee's avoiding powers:

> The problem with the * * * analyses of the vast majority of courts which have addressed bankruptcy claims based on constructive trust, is that a constructive trust is not really a trust. A constructive trust is a legal fiction, a common-law remedy in equity that may only exist by the grace of judicial action. As Professor Sherwin writes,

>> the constructive trust remedy developed in equity, by analogy to the express trust arrangements in which one person holds legal title to property for the benefit of another. The same concept of separate legal and beneficial interests in property suggested a remedy for unjust enrichment: if, under principles of unjust enrichment, the defendant holds title to property that ought to belong to the plaintiff, the court will treat the defendant as a trustee, holding title for the plaintiff's benefit.

At that point, however, the analogy to an express trust ends. The result of a constructive trust is a judicial decree ordering the defendant to convey the property to the plaintiff * * * . A constructive trust is merely a means by which the court can say that the defendant must relinquish to the plaintiff property that represents an unjust enrichment.

Emily L. Sherwin, *Constructive Trusts in Bankruptcy*, 1989 U. ILL. L. REV. 297, 301 (1989). The distribution of assets in a bankruptcy case is based on an identification of what assets and liabilities the debtor has "as of the commencement of the case," this being the exact moment the debtor files. A debtor that served prior to bankruptcy as trustee of an express trust generally has no right to the assets kept in trust, and the trustee in bankruptcy must fork them over to the beneficiary. However, a claim filed in bankruptcy court asserting rights to certain assets "held" in "constructive trust" for the claimant is nothing more than that: a claim. Unless a court has already impressed a constructive trust upon certain assets or a legislature has created a specific statutory right to have particular kinds of funds held as if in trust, the claimant cannot properly represent to the bankruptcy court that he was, at the time of the commencement of the case, a beneficiary of a constructive trust held by the debtor.

Thus, the essence of the argument put forth by [such] claimants goes as follows: "Judge, due to debtor's fraud (or whatever), our property rights as beneficiaries of the constructive trust arose prepetition. Therefore, we stand not in the position of unsecured creditors, nor even equal to the trustee in the position of judgment creditors, but as the rightful owner of the *res* held in trust. Oh, and by the way, would you mind conferring on us these ownership rights and declaring that they arose prepetition?" This may seem silly phrased in this manner, but it is exactly the argument that most courts have accepted in holding that, due to some prepetition breach or bad act by the debtor, the claimed property or money is subject to a constructive trust and therefore "did not come into the bankruptcy estate and must be returned to the [debtor]."

* * * We think that § 541(d) simply does not permit a claimant * * * to persuade the bankruptcy court to impose the remedy of constructive trust for alleged fraud committed against it by the debtor in the course of their business dealings, and thus to take ahead of all creditors, and indeed, ahead of the trustee. Because a constructive trust, unlike an express trust, is a remedy, it does not exist until a plaintiff obtains a judicial decision finding him to be entitled to a judgment "impressing" defendant's property or assets with a constructive trust. Therefore, a creditor's claim of entitlement to a constructive trust is not an "equitable interest" in the debtor's estate existing prepetition, excluded from the estate under § 541(d).

16 F.3d at 1449-51. Is this analysis preferable to that set out in *Project Homestead*?

3. Although the purchasers in *Project Homestead* were nominally defendants, they were surely aligned with the plaintiffs, who sought to have the purchasers' interests recognized as superior to the trustee's. Although the outcome here might have led to the purchasers' loss of their homes, the parties in the case entered into a global settlement under which the title insurance company paid a lump sum to the estate, the nondefaulting purchasers executed documents properly reflecting the liens on their homes, and the trustee issued quitclaim deeds to the purchasers. The lawyer whose neglect created the problem was disbarred and ultimately filed her own bankruptcy proceeding.

F. DELAYED RECORDING

Nonbankruptcy law requires that certain types of property interests, both real and personal, be publicly recorded. These requirements are based generally on the notion that an unrecorded interest can be misleading to other creditors who are not aware that the common debtor's property is subject to someone else's preexisting claims. This is an "ostensible ownership" problem, because the appearance that assets are unencumbered might lead others to extend credit in reliance on those assets. Nonbankruptcy law, therefore, protects certain categories of creditors from the perils of "secret liens."

The bankruptcy trustee has the power to avoid liens that are either never recorded or not recorded in a timely fashion. The avoiding powers that apply to these fact patterns are ones that we have seen before, so this section of the casebook can serve as a review. The unifying theme here is the fact pattern of delayed (or nonexistent) recording.

Problems

Determine whether the following can be avoided by a trustee using §§ 544(a) or 547. Does § 544(b) provide any help to the trustee?

1. Debtor Corp. obtained a $50,000 loan from Bank, giving Bank a security interest in equipment as collateral for the obligation. Debtor Corp. made regular loan payments right up to the moment it filed a Chapter 7 petition, including payments totaling $4,000 in the 90 days before bankruptcy. Bank never filed a financing statement. See UCC § 9–317(a)(2).

2. Debtor obtained a $50,000 loan from Bank that is secured by a mortgage on Debtor's home. Debtor began making regular loan payments, but

soon fell behind. Debtor filed a petition in bankruptcy one month after making a payment of $1,000. At the time the petition was filed, Bank had not yet recorded the mortgage. Under the law of the state, an unrecorded conveyance of real property is void against a good faith purchaser.

3. Tortfeasor filed a petition in bankruptcy with a state law suit pending against her. As a result of the pending lawsuit, Victim secured an attachment lien on Tortfeasor's property. Victim cannot enforce the lien unless he wins the lawsuit, but state law provides that an attachment lien has priority over a subsequent judicial lien.

4. Debtor obtained a $200,000 loan from Bank on July 1, signing a security agreement giving a security interest in property Debtor already owned. On July 25, Trade Creditor shipped Debtor $50,000 in goods on open account. Bank filed its financing statement in the appropriate place on August 2. Debtor filed a bankruptcy petition on December 1.

5. Debtor obtained a $20,000 loan from Creditor on October 10 to buy equipment, giving Creditor a security interest in the purchased equipment. Debtor took delivery of the equipment that day. Debtor filed a bankruptcy petition on October 15 and Creditor filed its financing statement on October 17. Is the security interest avoidable under § 544(a)? § 547(b)? See § 546(b) and UCC § 9–317(a)(2) & (e). Does your answer change if the security interest is not purchase money?

6. Debtor obtained a $20,000 loan from Creditor on October 10 to buy equipment, giving Creditor a security interest in the purchased equipment. Debtor took delivery of the equipment that day. Debtor filed a bankruptcy petition on October 15 and Creditor filed its financing statement on November 5. Is the security interest avoidable under § 544(a)? § 547(b)? Does your answer change if the security interest is not purchase money?

7. Have the creditors in the above Problems violated the automatic stay by filing financing statements after commencement of the bankruptcy cases? See § 362(b)(3). Does your answer depend on whether the security interest is purchase money?

G. AVOIDING POWERS INTENDED TO PROTECT EXEMPTIONS

By the time a bankruptcy petition is filed, any property the debtor owns is likely to be encumbered by one or more liens. Real estate may have been purchased with borrowed funds and therefore be subject to a purchase money mortgage. Disappointed creditors may have sued to judgment and taken judgment liens that attach to real estate. In addition, personalty may be covered by security interests, both purchase money and not. Inevitably, these liens will encumber property that Congress or the debtor's state legislature deemed important to a fresh start. (Remember § 522(c).)

Section 522(f) is intended to protect that fresh start. Subsection (f)(1)(B) allows the debtor to avoid nonpossessory, nonpurchase money security interests on designated categories of property. That subsection was intended to prevent creditor overreaching:

> Frequently, creditors lending money to a consumer debtor take a security interest in all of the debtor's belongings, and obtain a waiver by the debtor of his exemptions. In most of these cases, the debtor is unaware of the consequences of the forms he signs. The creditor's experience provides him with a substantial advantage. If the debtor encounters financial difficulty, creditors often use threats of repossession of all the debtor's household goods as a means of obtaining payment.
>
> In fact, were the creditor to carry through on his threat and foreclose on the property, he would receive little, for household goods have little resale value. They are far more valuable to the creditor in the debtor's hands, for they provide a credible basis for the threat, because the replacement costs of the goods are generally high. Thus, creditors rarely repossess, and the debtors, ignorant of the creditors' true intentions, are coerced into payments they simply cannot afford to make.
>
> The exemption provision allows the debtor, after bankruptcy has been filed, and creditor collection techniques have been stayed, to undo the consequences of a contract of adhesion, signed in ignorance, by permitting the invalidation of nonpurchase money security interests in household goods. Such security interests have too often been used by over-reaching creditors. The bill eliminates any unfair advantage creditors have.

H.R. Rep. No. 95–595 at 127, *reprinted in* 1978 U.S.C.C.A.N. at 6088 (footnote omitted).

The justification for subsection (f)(1)(A), which permits the debtor to avoid judicial liens, is more difficult to identify. The legislative history says that the subsection allows the debtor to undo the actions of creditors that bring legal action against the debtor shortly before bankruptcy. Bankruptcy exists to provide relief for an overburdened debtor. If a creditor beats the debtor into court, the debtor is nevertheless entitled to his exemptions.

Id. at 126–27, *reprinted in* 1978 U.S.C.C.A.N. at 6087-88. This justification overlooks § 547, which already serves the function of avoiding judicial liens taken within the preference period. Section 522(f)(1)(A) is hardly needed to undo a judicial lien taken by a creditor who "shortly before bankruptcy * * * beats the debtor into court." Perhaps the policy behind § 522(f)(1)(A) looks to the nature of the creditor—one who initially dealt with the debtor on an unsecured basis, not bargaining for security on the front end and not relying on the availability of particular assets from which to seek repayment. This may not be the sort of creditor who should be protected from the debtor's power to claim exemptions.

Read § 522(f) and review § 522(d). In answering the following Problems, assume that the debtor selects the federal exemptions.

Problems

1. Debtors' home is subject to two liens—a first priority mortgage for $50,000 and a second priority judgment lien of $10,000. The property is worth $70,000. Debtors file a joint Chapter 7 petition. Is either lien avoidable? If so, in what amount? What is the amount of the exemption Debtors can claim in the property?

2. Assume the same facts as in Problem # 1, except that the property is worth $55,000. Is either lien avoidable? If so, in what amount? What is the amount of the exemption Debtors can claim in the property?

3. Debtor obtained a loan from Consumer Finance, giving a security interest in a pearl-studded brooch she purchased several years ago from the craftsperson who made it. The brooch was appraised for $875 at the time Debtor filed bankruptcy. She wants to avoid the security interest and exempt the brooch. Can she do so?

4. Debtor bought a piano and a stereo from a music store in early December, using proceeds of a $3,000 loan from Consumer Finance. Debtor granted Consumer Finance a security interest in all of Debtor's household goods, including the piano and stereo, to secure repayment of the loan. Debtor filed a bankruptcy petition in May of the next year. Can Debtor avoid all or part of the security interest in the piano? The stereo? Debtor's remaining

household goods (assuming that their aggregate value does not exceed the cap under § 522(d)(3))?

5. Assume the same facts as in Problem # 4, except that Debtor did not file a bankruptcy petition in May. Rather, when Debtor had trouble making the payments on the loan, Debtor and Consumer Finance refinanced it. Consumer Finance made a new loan and used its proceeds to pay off the old loan, to pay additional finance charges and insurance, and to give Debtor $60 in cash. The new loan was for a longer period than the old loan, and required smaller monthly payments. Debtor eventually was unable to pay this loan, too, and filed a bankruptcy petition in October. Can Debtor avoid all or part of the security interest in the piano? The stereo? Debtor's remaining household goods? See *Matthews v. Transamerica Financial Services* (*In re Matthews*), 724 F.2d 798 (9th Cir.1984).

As originally enacted, § 522(f)(1) referred only to judicial liens and (f)(2) dealt with nonpossessory, nonpurchase money security interests. These subsections were redesignated (f)(1)(A) and (f)(1)(B), respectively, in 1994, and a formula for determining impairment was added as § 522(f)(2). As the following case indicates, the formula has not produced the hoped-for certainty.

KOLICH v. ANTIOCH LAUREL VETERINARY HOSPITAL (IN RE KOLICH)

United States Court of Appeals, Eighth Circuit, 2003.
328 F.3d 406.

LOKEN, Chief Judge.

Section 522(f)(1) of the Bankruptcy Code provides that the debtor may avoid most judicial liens "to the extent that such lien impairs an exemption to which the debtor would have been entitled." In this case, Chapter 7 debtors Dean and Michelle Kolich moved to avoid a judicial lien on their homestead held by Antioch Laurel Veterinary Hospital ("Antioch"). Applying the formula for determining when a lien impairs an exemption in § 522(f)(2)(A), the Eighth Circuit Bankruptcy Appellate Panel ("BAP") concluded that the homestead exemption was impaired and avoided Antioch's lien in its entirety. Antioch appeals, arguing that the BAP's "mechanical application" of the statutory formula produces an absurd result and an unjust windfall to a junior secured creditor and the bankruptcy debtors. * * * We affirm.

Section 522(f) was enacted when Congress rewrote the Code's exemption provisions in the Bankruptcy Reform Act of 1978. * * * Initially, § 522(f) did not define when a judicial lien impairs an exemption, which led to a variety of inconsistent judicial interpretations. In 1994, Congress added the formula in § 522(f)(2)(A), intending to bring order out of the prior chaos. Unfortunately, as this case illustrates, the formula has itself generated inconsistent judicial interpretations.

The relevant facts are undisputed and may be quickly summarized. (For convenience, we round all values to the nearest $1,000.) The Kolichs purchased their homestead in 1998, borrowing much of the purchase price and giving the World Savings Bank ("WSB") a first mortgage on the home as security for its loan. In the fall of 2000, Antioch obtained a $134,000 judgment against the Kolichs and recorded the judgment as a judicial lien against their homestead. In December 2000, the Kolichs borrowed $80,000 from Norbank, giving Norbank a second mortgage on their homestead to secure its loan. Under state law, as between these secured creditors, WSB had the first priority interest in the homestead, Antioch's judicial lien had the second priority interest, and Norbank's junior lien had the third priority interest. When Antioch began proceedings to collect its judicial lien in the spring of 2001, the Kolichs commenced this Chapter 7 proceeding. At that time, the homestead's fair market value was $275,000, the WSB loan had an outstanding balance of $219,000, and both Antioch's judgment and the Norbank loan were unpaid. Missouri allows a homestead exemption of $8,000.

After filing their Chapter 7 petition, the Kolichs moved to avoid Antioch's judicial lien under § 522(f)(1), arguing that the lien impairs their homestead exemption. That motion turns on the proper application of the formula defining an impairment set forth in § 522(f)(2)(A) * * * .

Applying the formula to this case, if the term "all other liens" in subsection (f)(2)(A)(ii) is construed literally, as the BAP concluded, then Antioch's entire judicial lien must be avoided because the impairment exceeds the value of its lien. That is, the sum of the judicial lien ($134,000), the two mortgage liens ($299,000), and the homestead exemption ($8,000) is $441,000, which exceeds the Kolichs' $275,000 interest in the property in the absence of any liens by $166,000, more than the total value of the judicial lien. On the other hand, the bankruptcy court concluded that Norbank's lien should be excluded in applying the formula because it is junior to Antioch's lien under state law. Excluding the Norbank lien reduces the impairment from $166,000 to $86,000, which means that only $86,000 of Antioch's judicial lien is avoided, while the remaining $48,000 remains an unavoided lien on the Kolichs' homestead. On appeal, Antioch urges us to adopt the bankruptcy court's interpretation of § 522(f)(2)(A) rather than the BAP's.

As this is a statutory formula, we begin, as we must, with the language of the statute. Antioch concedes that the BAP's ruling is consistent with a literal application of the statutory formula. We agree with Antioch's reading of the statute's plain meaning.[3] But the concession leaves Antioch with a decidedly uphill battle. "The plain meaning of legislation should be conclusive, except in the rare cases in which the literal application of a statute will produce a result demonstrably at odds with the intentions of its drafters." *United States v. Ron Pair Enters., Inc.*, 489 U.S. 235, 242 (1989).

Antioch's contention becomes more tenable when we take into account that a number of courts have declined to apply the statutory formula literally in another frequently litigated context. When a debtor has only a fifty percent interest in exempt property—usually, a homestead jointly owned with a spouse who did not join in the bankruptcy petition—but one or more of the outstanding liens apply to the entire property, the statutory formula produces an unreasonably high impairment that has the effect of *creating* additional equity for the debtor at the expense of the lienholder whose lien is thereby avoided. Most courts faced with this situation have refused to apply the formula literally, instead refashioning it to achieve a more realistic computation of the impairment. As the First Circuit said after concluding that the formula literally applied would produce an unintended measure of lien avoidance, "courts are not required to follow literal language where it would produce an outcome at odds with the purpose of Congress and where the result stems merely from an unintended quirk in drafting." *Nelson v. Scala*, 192 F.3d 32, 35 (1st Cir.1999); accord *In re Lehman*, 205 F.3d 1255 (11th Cir.2000).

On appeal, Antioch cites *Nelson* and *Lehman* and urges us to apply their reasoning to this case. But the issues are dissimilar. Here,

---

[3] The bankruptcy court reasoned that the word "liens" in § 522(f)(2)(A)(ii) should not include junior liens on over-encumbered property that are wholly "under water" because, "in bankruptcy parlance, a lien which is secured by no value at all is considered to be an unsecured claim, and not a lien at all." But that parlance is not reflected in the Code's definition of a lien: " 'lien' means charge against or interest in property to secure payment of a debt or performance of an obligation." § 101(37). We find no indication that Congress intended a different definition of "liens" in § 522(f)(2)(A)(ii).

the problem is not created by the formula's mathematical progression, as it was in those cases. Rather, the issue is whether "all other liens" in subsection 522(f)(2)(A)(ii) includes consensual liens junior to the judicial lien at issue. Or, to state the issue more broadly, the question is whether Congress intended that this statutory formula disrupt lien priorities created by state law, for if Antioch's second priority lien is avoided, the primary beneficiary is Norbank, whose third priority consensual lien was junior to Antioch's lien under state law but may not be avoided under § 522(f). This problem may not be dismissed as a mere "quirk in drafting," because it would have been relatively easy to draft § 522-(f)(2)(A)(ii) to exclude such junior consensual liens from the phrase "all other liens on the property." To our knowledge, no circuit court has considered this issue. The few bankruptcy courts to consider the issue have reached inconsistent decisions.

Having carefully considered these conflicting precedents, we find no sufficient basis for concluding that the statutory formula produces, in this situation, a result "demonstrably at odds with the intentions of its drafters." To be sure, the Bankruptcy Code usually looks to state law to define the property rights and priorities of creditors, including secured creditors. But § 522(f) is an exception to that policy. It was enacted to permit the avoidance of judicial liens that can interfere with the debtor's post-petition fresh start. This selective avoidance gives an advantage under federal law to secured creditors holding consensual liens, typically, residential mortgage lenders. But Congress intended to treat consensual lienholders more favorably, because their contractual relationships with the bankruptcy debtor typically allow the debtor to acquire equity in the exempt property by making post-petition mortgage payments. The 1994 amendment creating the statutory formula here at issue was expressly aimed at overruling prior judicial decisions compromising that intent.

We are not entirely comfortable with the equities of literally applying the statutory formula in this situation. It may give a debtor contemplating bankruptcy the ability to wipe out judicial liens by persuading a lender to take an otherwise junior consensual lien that renders the exempt property over-encumbered and therefore ripe for impairment. One would expect lenders to refuse to make such high-risk loans, but there may be times when self-interest or hard-to-detect collusion will lead to an abuse of § 522(f). On the other hand, refusing to apply the statutory formula as written may result in denying deserving debtors the fresh-start advantage § 522(f) was enacted to provide—for example, if a drop in market value has left exempt property over-encumbered by a judicial lien and a junior consensual lien, and the judicial lienholder insists upon foreclosure. With the competing equities both hard to weigh and finely balanced, our task is simply to apply § 522(f)(2)(A) as Congress wrote it.

Accordingly, the judgment of the BAP is affirmed.

Notes and Questions

1. A standard maxim of statutory construction is that the language of a statute should be given its plain meaning unless that leads to an "absurd" result. The lienholder in this case argued on appeal that a literal reading in this case would be absurd and would constitute an unjust windfall to the debtors and to the junior secured creditor. Why did the Eighth Circuit reject that argument?

2. Clearly, one of bankruptcy's policies is not to interfere with state law's determination of lien priority. The outcome in this case does just that, however, does it not? Is that justifiable in this situation?

3. The obligation in this case arose from a contract for sale of the business—just in case you are curious as to how one becomes indebted to a veterinary hospital for more than $134,000.

Subsection 522(f)(1), which was added in 1994, permits a debtor to "avoid the fixing of a [judicial] lien on an interest of the debtor in property" if the lien impairs an exemption. This provision came to be used in possibly unanticipated ways in domestic relations cases. Divorce courts often permit one spouse to keep the couple's house, and require that spouse to make payments to the other in order to even up the value of the divided assets. The obligation to make the stream of payments is usually secured by a lien on the retained property. In a number of cases, obligor spouses later filed bankruptcy and argued that the lien was a judicial lien, avoidable under § 522(f). Courts divided on the question whether avoidance was permissible in that fact pattern, and many commentators lamented the misuse of bankruptcy when the strategy met with success. The Supreme Court decided the issue in the next case. (Remember that subsection (f)(1) was amended in 2005, after the date of this decision. The subsection was renumbered (f)(1)(A) and language regarding domestic support obligations was added. After you understand the Court's holding, we will look at the statutory changes.)

FARREY v. SANDERFOOT

United States Supreme Court, 1991.
500 U.S. 291, 111 S.Ct. 1825, 114 L.Ed.2d 337.

JUSTICE WHITE delivered the opinion of the Court.

In this case we consider whether § 522(f) of the Bankruptcy Code allows a debtor to avoid the fixing of a lien on a homestead, where the lien is granted to the debtor's former spouse under a divorce decree that extinguishes all previous interests the parties had in the property, and in no event secures more than the value of the non-debtor spouse's former interest. We hold that it does not.

I

Petitioner Jeanne Farrey and respondent Gerald Sanderfoot were married on August 12, 1966. The couple eventually built a home on 27 acres of land in Hortonville, Wisconsin, where they raised their three children. On September 12, 1986, the Wisconsin Circuit Court for Outagamie County entered a bench decision granting a judgment of divorce and property division that resolved all contested issues and terminated the marriage. A written decree followed on February 5, 1987.

The decision awarded each party one-half of their net $60,600.68 marital estate. This division reflected Wisconsin's statutory presumption that the marital estate "be divided equally between the parties." The decree granted Sanderfoot sole title to all the real estate and the family house, which was subject to a mortgage and which was valued at $104,000, and most of the personal property. For her share, Farrey received the remaining items of personal property and the proceeds from a court-ordered auction of the furniture from the home. The judgment also allocated the couple's liabilities. Under this preliminary calculation of assets and debts, Sanderfoot stood to receive a net award of $59,508.79, while Farrey's award would otherwise have been $1,091.90. To insure that the division of the estate was equal, the court ordered Sanderfoot to pay Farrey $29,208.44, half the difference in the value of their net assets. Sanderfoot was to pay this amount in two installments: half by January 10, 1987, and the remaining half by April 10, 1987. To secure this award, the decree provided that Farrey "shall have a lien against the real estate property of [Sanderfoot] for the total amount of money due her pursuant to this Order of the Court, *i.e.* $29,208.44, and the lien shall remain attached to the real estate property * * * until the total amount of money is paid in full."

Sanderfoot never made the required payments nor complied with any other order of the state court. Instead, on May 4, 1987, he voluntarily filed for Chapter 7 bankruptcy. Sanderfoot listed the marital home and real estate on the schedule of assets with his bankruptcy petition and listed it as exempt homestead property. Exercising his option to invoke the state rather than the federal homestead exemption, § 522(b)(2)(A), Sanderfoot claimed the property as exempt "to the amount of $40,000." * * * He also filed a motion to avoid Farrey's lien under the provision in dispute, § 522(f)(1), claiming that Farrey possessed a judicial lien that impaired his homestead exemption. Farrey objected to the motion, claiming that § 522(f)(1) could not divest her of her interest in the marital home. The Bankruptcy Court denied Sanderfoot's motion, holding that the lien could not be avoided because it protected Farrey's pre-existing interest in the marital property. The District Court reversed, concluding that the lien was avoidable because it "is fixed on an interest of the debtor in the property."

A divided panel of the Court of Appeals affirmed. The court reasoned that the divorce proceeding dissolved any pre-existing interest Farrey had in the homestead and that her new interest, "created in the dissolution order and evidenced by her lien, attached to Mr. Sanderfoot's interest in the property." Noting that the issue had caused a split among the Courts of Appeals, the court expressly relied on those decisions that it termed more "faithful to the plain language of § 522(f)."

Judge Posner, in dissent, argued that to avoid a lien under § 522(f), a debtor must have an interest in the property at the time the court places the lien on that interest. Judge Posner concluded that because the same decree that gave the entire property to Sanderfoot simultaneously created the lien in favor of Farrey, the lien did not attach to a pre-existing interest of the husband. * * *

We granted certiorari to resolve the conflict of authority. We now reverse the Court of Appeals' judgment and remand.

II

* * *

Section 522(f)(1) provides in relevant part:

"Notwithstanding any waiver of exemptions, the debtor may avoid the fixing of a lien on an interest of the debtor in property to the extent that such lien impairs an exemption to which the debtor would have been entitled under subsection (b) of this section, if such lien is—

"(1) a judicial lien * * * ."

The provision establishes several conditions for a lien to be avoided, only one of which is at issue. Farrey does not challenge the Court of Appeals' determination that her lien was a judicial lien, nor do we address that question here. The Court of Appeals also determined that Farrey had waived any challenge as to whether Sanderfoot was otherwise entitled to a homestead exemption under state law and we agree. The sole question presented in this case is whether § 522(f)(1) permits Sanderfoot to avoid the fixing of Farrey's lien on the property interest that he obtained in the divorce decree.

The key portion of § 522(f) states that "the debtor may avoid the fixing of a lien on an interest in * * * property." Sanderfoot, following several Courts of Appeals, suggests that this phrase means that a lien may be avoided so long as it is currently fixed on a debtor's interest. Farrey, following Judge Posner's lead, reads the text as permitting the avoidance of a lien only where the lien attached to the debtor's interest at some point after the debtor obtained the interest.

We agree with Farrey. No one asserts that the two verbs underlying the provision possess anything other than their standard legal meaning: "avoid" meaning "annul" or "undo," see Black's Law Dictionary 136 (6th ed. 1990); H.R. Rep. No. 95–595 at 126–27, *reprinted in* U.S.C.C.A.N. at 6087–88, and "fix" meaning to "fasten a liability upon," see Black's Law Dictionary, *supra*, at 637. The statute does not say that the debtor may undo a lien on an interest in property. Rather, the statute expressly states that the debtor may avoid "the fixing" of a lien on the debtor's interest in property. The gerund "fixing" refers to a temporal event. That event—the fastening of a liability—presupposes an object onto which the liability can fasten. The statute defines this pre-existing object as "an interest of the debtor in property." Therefore, unless the debtor had the property interest to which the lien attached at some point *before* the lien attached to that interest, he or she cannot avoid the fixing of the lien under the terms of § 522(f)(1).

This reading fully comports with the provision's purpose and history. Congress enacted § 522(f) with the broad purpose of protecting the debtor's exempt property. Ordinarily, liens and other secured interests survive bankruptcy. In particular, it was well settled when § 522(f) was enacted that valid liens obtained before bankruptcy could be enforced on exempt property, see *Louisville Joint Stock Land Bank* v. *Radford*, 295 U.S. 555, 582–83 (1935), including otherwise exempt homestead property, *Long* v. *Bullard*, 117 U.S. 617, 620–21 (1886). Congress generally preserved this principle when it comprehensively revised bankruptcy law with the Bankruptcy Reform Act of 1978. But Congress also revised the law to permit the debtor to avoid the fixing of some liens. See, *e.g.*, § 545 (statutory liens).

Section 522(f)(1), by its terms, extends this protection to cases involving the fixing of judicial liens onto exempt property. What specific legislative history exists suggests that a principal reason Congress singled out judicial liens was because they are a device commonly used by creditors to defeat the protection bankruptcy law accords exempt property against debts. As the House Report stated:

> "The first right [§ 522(f)(1)] allows the debtor to undo the actions of creditors that bring legal action against the debtor shortly before bankruptcy. Bankruptcy exists to provide relief for an overburdened debtor. If a creditor beats the debtor into court, the debtor is nevertheless entitled to his exemptions." H.R. Rep. No. 95–595 at 126–27, *reprinted in* 1978 U.S.C.C.A.N. at 6087–88.

One factor supporting the view that Congress intended § 522(f)(1) to thwart a rush to the courthouse is Congress' contemporaneous elimination of § 67 of the 1898 Bankruptcy Act. Prior to its repeal, § 67(a) invalidated any lien obtained on an exempt interest of an insolvent debtor within four months of the bankruptcy filing. The Bankruptcy Reform Act eliminated the insolvency and timing requirements. It is possible that Congress simply decided to leave exemptions exposed despite its longstanding policy against doing so. But given the legislative history's express concern over protecting exemptions, it follows instead that § 522(f)(1) was intended as a new device to handle the old provision's job by "giv[ing] the debtor certain rights not available under current law with respect to exempt property." H.R. Rep. No. 95–595 at 126-27, *reprinted in* 1978 U.S.C.C.A.N. at 6087.

Conversely, the text, history, and purpose of § 522(f)(1) also indicate what the provision is *not* concerned with. It cannot be concerned with liens that fixed on an interest before the debtor acquired that interest. Neither party contends otherwise. Section 522(f)(1) does not state that any fixing of a lien may be avoided; instead, it permits avoidance of the "fixing of a lien on an interest of the debtor." If the fixing took place before the debtor acquired that interest, the "fixing" by definition was not on the debtor's interest. Nor could the statute apply given its purpose of preventing a creditor from beating the debtor to the courthouse, since the debtor at no point possessed the interest without the judicial lien. There would be no fixing to avoid since the lien was already there. To permit lien avoidance in these circumstances, in fact, would be to allow judicial lienholders to be defrauded through the conveyance of an encumbered interest to a prospective debtor. For these reasons, it is settled that a debtor cannot use § 522(f)(1) to avoid a lien on an interest acquired after the lien attached. As before, the critical inquiry remains whether the debtor ever possessed the interest to which the lien fixed, before it fixed. If he or she did not, § 522(f)(1) does not permit the debtor to avoid the fixing of the lien on that interest.

III

We turn to the application of § 522(f)(1) to this case.

Whether Sanderfoot ever possessed an interest to which the lien fixed, before it fixed, is a question of state law. Farrey contends that prior to the divorce judgment, she and her husband held title to the real estate in joint tenancy, each possessing an undivided one-half interest. She further asserts that the divorce decree extinguished these previous interests. At the same time and in the same transaction, she concludes, the decree created new interests in place of the old: for Sanderfoot, ownership in fee simple of the house and real estate; for Farrey, various assets and a debt of $29,208.44 secured by a lien on Sanderfoot's new fee simple interest. Both in his briefs and at oral argument, Sanderfoot agreed on each point.

On the assumption that the parties characterize Wisconsin law correctly, Sanderfoot must lose. Under their view, the lien could not have fixed on Sanderfoot's pre-existing undivided half interest because the divorce decree extinguished it. Instead, the only interest that the lien encumbers is debtor's wholly new fee simple interest. The same decree that awarded Sanderfoot his fee simple interest simultaneously granted the lien to Farrey. As the judgment stated, he acquired the property "free and clear" of any claim "except as expressly provided in this [decree]." Sanderfoot took the interest and the lien together, as if he had purchased an already encumbered estate from a third party. Since Sanderfoot never possessed his new fee simple interest before the lien "fixed", § 522(f)(1) is not available to void the lien.

The same result follows even if the divorce decree did not extinguish the couple's pre-existing interests but instead merely reordered them. The parties' current position notwithstanding, it may be that under Wisconsin law the divorce decree augmented Sanderfoot's previous interest by adding to it Farrey's prior interest. If the court in exchange sought to protect Farrey's previous interest with a lien, § 522(f)(1) could be used to undo the encumbrance to the extent the lien fastened to any portion of Sanderfoot's previous surviving interest. This follows because Sanderfoot would have possessed the interest to which that part of the lien fixed, before it fixed. But in this case, the divorce court did not purport to encumber any part of Sanderfoot's previous interest even on the assumption that state law would deem that interest to have survived. The decree instead transferred Farrey's previous interest to Sanderfoot and, again simultaneously, granted a lien equal to that interest minus the small amount of personal property she retained. Sanderfoot thus would still be unable to avoid the lien in this case since it fastened only to what had been Farrey's pre-existing interest, and this interest Sanderfoot would never have possessed without the lien already having fixed.[4]

The result, on either theory, accords with the provision's main purpose. As noted, the legislative history suggests that Congress primarily intended § 522(f)(1) as a device to thwart creditors who, sensing an impending bankruptcy, rush to court to obtain a judgment to defeat the debtor's exemptions. That is not what occurs in a divorce proceeding such as this. Farrey obtained the lien not to defeat Sanderfoot's pre-existing interest in the homestead but to protect her own pre-existing interest in the homestead that was fully equal to that of her spouse. The divorce court awarded the lien to secure an obligation the court imposed on the husband in exchange for the court's simultaneous award of the wife's homestead interest to the husband. We agree with Judge Posner that to permit a debtor in these circumstances to use the Code to deprive a spouse of this protection would neither follow the language of the statute nor serve the main goal it was designed to address.

IV

We hold that § 522(f)(1) of the Bankruptcy Code requires a debtor to have possessed an interest to which a lien attached, before it attached, to avoid the fixing of the lien on that interest. Accordingly, the judgment of the Court of Appeals is reversed, and the case is remanded for further proceedings consistent with this opinion.

It is so ordered.

---

[4] Justice Scalia does not join in this paragraph.

[In a concurring opinion, JUSTICE KENNEDY, joined by JUSTICE SOUTER noted the debtor's concession—"fatal to the argument" he had to make in order to prevail—that his prior interest in the property had been extinguished and new rights put in place. JUSTICE KENNEDY also noted that the result might have been different if, under state law or the parties' agreement, the debtor had retained his original half interest in the home, Farrey's half interest had been conveyed to him, and then the court had given Farrey a lien on the entire property. JUSTICE KENNEDY suggested that congressional action might be necessary to prevent this result in another case.]

Notes and Questions

1. *Farrey* was decided before the 1994 Amendments created § 522-(f)(1)(A), which protects liens securing support obligations. The legislative history indicates that the new subsection was intended to "supplement the reach of *Farrey*." In what way does it "supplement" *Farrey*? Would it have controlled the result in *Farrey* if it had been in effect when the case arose?

That part of the statute was redrafted in 2005 to cross-reference § 523(a)(5), but it was not substantively changed.

2. Note the Court's reliance on § 522's "purpose and history" and its assertion that "Congress enacted § 522(f) with the broad purpose of protecting the debtor's exempt property." Note also that the Court used dictionary definitions to guide its construction of the statute.

3. The concurrence acknowledged that the majority's opinion is consistent "with fairness and common sense," but recognized as well that the decision was dependent on Sanderfoot's stipulation regarding the effect of the family court's order. Would the concurrence be comfortable with the 1994 amendment creating § 522(f)(1)(A)?

4. If Sanderfoot's concessions were fatal to his case, as the concurring opinion noted, why were they made?

5. Judgment lienholders typically are nonreliance creditors, having first dealt with the debtor on an unsecured basis. Does the lien at issue in *Farrey* more nearly resemble a judgment lien or a purchase money mortgage?

6. Shortly after passage of the Bankruptcy Code, a number of states attempted to circumvent debtors' avoiding power under § 522(f) by redefining state exemptions. If an exemption were available only in the debtor's "equity" or only to the extent of a debtor's "interest" in property, then by definition the exemption could not be impaired by a lien. See, e.g., *McManus v. Avco Fin. Servs., Inc. (In re McManus)*, 681 F.2d 353 (5th Cir.1982). The Supreme Court put a stop to this practice (albeit on different facts) in a case decided the

same day as *Farrey*. In *Owen v. Owen*, 500 U.S. 305, 111 S.Ct. 1833, 114 L.Ed.2d 350 (1991), the Court held that § 522(f)

> establishes as the baseline, against which impairment is to be measured, not an exemption to which the debtor "*is* entitled," but one to which he "*would have been* entitled." The latter phrase denotes a state of affairs that is conceived or hypothetical, rather than actual, and requires the reader to disregard some element of reality. "Would have been" *but for what*? The answer given, with respect to the federal exemptions, has been *but for the lien at issue*, and that seems to us correct.

> * * *

> We have no doubt, then, that the lower courts' unanimously agreed-upon manner of applying § 522(f) to federal exemptions—ask first whether avoiding the lien would entitle the debtor to an exemption, and if it would, then avoid and recover the lien—is correct. The question then becomes whether a different interpretation should be adopted for state exemptions. We do not see how that could be possible.

Id. at 311-13, 111 S.Ct. at 1837-38, 114 L.Ed.2d at 359-60.

Several subsections of § 522 enable the debtor, in certain circumstances, to exempt property recovered by virtue of the trustee's avoiding powers, or to exercise the avoiding powers, if the trustee does not, when exemptable property could be recovered thereby. These provisions, although a bit complicated, are intended to protect the debtor's exemptions.

Begin with a straightforward case. Assume that a previously unsecured creditor obtains a judgment for $25,000 and a judicial lien against the debtor's residence. The home, which is worth $100,000, was already encumbered by a first priority mortgage of $75,000. A month after the judgment lien attaches, the debtor files bankruptcy. The trustee avoids the judicial lien as a preference under § 547, thus freeing the property from encumbrance. Under § 522(g), the debtor can take the homestead exemption out of the $25,000 in value brought into the estate; the transfer was not voluntary and the debtor did not conceal the property. If any amount remains after satisfaction of the homestead exemption, it goes into the estate, to be distributed to general unsecured creditors.

Assume, however, that the trustee fails to avoid the judicial lien, deciding that the remainder for the estate is not worth the trouble. Sections 522(h) and (i) allow the debtor to exercise the avoiding power so that the exemption will not be lost. Ordinarily, avoided liens are preserved for the benefit of the estate, § 551. Subsection 522(i)(2) allows the debtor, rather than the estate, to enjoy the benefit of the avoided lien when exemptions are at stake.

Read §§ 522(g), (h) and (i) and apply them to the following Problems.

Problems

1. Debtor owed $30,000 on a signature loan obtained from First National Bank. When Debtor defaulted, First National sued to judgment and obtained a judgment lien on Debtor's house. A month after the lien attached, Debtor filed bankruptcy. The house is worth $100,000 and is also subject to a first mortgage (which is senior to the judgment lien) of $80,000. The trustee avoided First National's interest as a preference. Can Debtor claim a homestead exemption out of the value that avoidance brought into the estate? See § 522(g).

2. Last year, Debtor borrowed $4,500 from Finance Company to pay some medical bills and granted a security interest in Debtor's car. Finance Company failed to perfect its interest until two weeks before Debtor filed a bankruptcy petition, but the trustee has made no move to avoid the security interest because the car is only worth $2,000. Can Debtor avoid the security interest and then claim an exemption in the car?

H. SETOFFS

Assume that Borrower obtains an unsecured loan from Bank for $10,000 and that Borrower also maintains a checking account there. On the loan transaction, Borrower is the debtor and Bank is the creditor. A checking account, however, represents a bank's obligation to its account holder. As far as the checking account is concerned, Borrower is the creditor and Bank is the debtor. Borrower and Bank owe each other mutual debts. If Borrower fails to pay the loan when it is due, Bank has the right under state law to set off the account against the loan balance. If the account has a balance of $7,500, then the loan balance is reduced to $2,500 and the account balance is reduced to zero. If the account has a balance of $12,000, then the loan balance is reduced to zero and the account balance is reduced to $2,000. As the Code recognizes, the right of setoff is, from the creditor's vantage point, akin to having collateral for a loan. See § 506(a)(1) ("An allowed claim of a creditor * * * that is subject to setoff under § 553 * * * is a secured claim * * * .").

Bankruptcy law does not create the right of setoff, but recognizes it. Section 553(a) provides that bankruptcy "does not affect" a creditor's right to set off mutual prepetition debts. The Code, however, limits the exercise of setoff. Setoff can be either pre- or postpetition, but the latter is subject to the automatic stay. See § 362(a)(7).

Subsections (a)(1), (a)(2) and (a)(3) of § 553, which apply to both pre- and postpetition setoffs, provide circumstances under which setoff will be denied. Subsection (a)(1) prohibits setoff when the creditor's claim against the debtor is not allowed, thus preventing indirect recovery of claims that cannot be recovered directly.

Subsections (a)(2) and (a)(3) prevent efforts to increase the right to setoff during the 90 days preceding bankruptcy. Subsection (a)(2) prevents a creditor from amassing claims against the debtor for the purpose of exercising setoff rights. It prohibits the setoff of claims obtained from another creditor after bankruptcy was filed, or shortly before filing, if the debtor was insolvent at the time. (And the debtor is presumed to have been insolvent during that period, § 553(c).)

Subsection (a)(3) applies when the creditor incurs a debt to the bankruptcy debtor, rather than acquiring a claim against the debtor. It would apply if Bank in the hypothetical above, knowing that bankruptcy was imminent and that any payment would be a preference, "encouraged" Borrower to build up the checking account balance instead of making a direct payment on the loan.

A fourth limitation on setoff in bankruptcy, found in § 553(b), applies only to prepetition setoffs. It imposes an improvement-in-position test patterned after § 547(c)(5). The kinship between setoff and preferences is clear (hence the placement of setoff in this casebook's chapter on avoiding powers), and Congress was concerned that creditors in a position to exercise the right of setoff would "rush in" on faltering debtors by decreasing the amount of their "insufficiency." See § 553(b)(2). Thus, § 553(b) prohibits setoff to the extent it reduces the "insufficiency." This improvement-in-position test applies only to setoffs that occur during the 90 days before bankruptcy; the reason for the rule is not implicated if the creditor waits until after the petition is filed and then seeks relief from the stay in order to exercise its right of setoff.

The 1994 Amendments added a specialized sort of setoff by creating § 546(h). It allows a buyer to return goods shipped before bankruptcy, subject to the rights of secured parties, if the seller consents and if return would be in the best interests of the estate. The buyer can then set off the price of the unsold goods against the seller's claim. Return of goods under § 546(h) requires a motion by the trustee (which, of course, includes the debtor in possession), made within 120 days of the filing, and approval by the court.

Read § 553 and solve the following Problems.

Problems

1. Debtor was a trial lawyer who, despite some success, could not maintain her extravagant lifestyle. Debtor won a large verdict for a client and deposited defendant's payment on the judgment in her trust account at Bank, pending distribution to her client. Before Debtor could send her client a check, Bank seized the proceeds of Debtor's trust account in order to satisfy Debtor's overdue loan obligation. Debtor immediately filed bankruptcy and argued that Bank's setoff was improper. What result?

2. Debtor, who was in the business of buying and selling antiques, frequently dealt with Joe Byer. At the time of Debtor's bankruptcy filing, Byer owed him $80,000 for a shipment of English furniture received in the preceding month. Because Debtor owed Byer $55,000 for several paintings purchased last year, Byer tendered only $25,000 to the estate. Debtor, however, claims that one of the paintings, valued at $20,000, was a forgery, and he has some convincing evidence to support that claim. Does that affect Byer's setoff rights?

3. Debtor Corp. maintained its general checking account at Bank, to which it was obligated on an overdue $15,000 loan. The account balance often fluctuated, sometimes to large amounts, despite Debtor Corp.'s continuing financial problems. When another of Bank's customers mentioned its difficulties in getting payment from Debtor Corp. on its $8,500 unsecured trade debt, and its suspicion that bankruptcy was imminent, Bank's manager had a brainstorm. Bank offered to buy the unsecured debt for 25¢ on the dollar— several times what the trade creditor would get in a bankruptcy. The creditor agreed and Bank bought the claim. At that time, the account balance was $12,000. When Debtor filed bankruptcy two weeks later, the account balance was $30,000. Bank sought relief from the stay in order to set off $23,500. What argument should the trustee make in response?

4. Bank's Investment Department often bought unsecured obligations from creditors who did not wish to spend resources on accounting and billing, as long as the obligors were financially solid. One such debt, for $18,500, was owed to Trade Creditor by one of Bank's customers, Debtor Corp., a start-up

manufacturer of baby products. Debtor Corp. was not yet profitable, but its prospects seemed sufficiently positive that Bank decided to buy the debt. Bank paid $16,650, which reflected the usual 10% discount. Two months later, three babies were permanently paralyzed when their necks were caught in a crib made by Debtor Corp. Multi-million dollar lawsuits were filed and Debtor Corp.'s business dried up overnight. It filed bankruptcy immediately. At that time, Debtor Corp.'s account at Bank had a balance of over $20,000, so Bank sought relief from the stay in order to set off $18,500. What result?

5. Debtor Corp. owed Bank $125,000 on an unsecured loan. Bank's manager, aware that Debtor Corp. was in serious financial difficulty, called Debtor Corp's president. She reminded him of his other business ventures that were supported by Bank, and asked him to "do something" about Debtor Corp.'s loan. He offered to make a large payment, but she suggested that, instead, he make a deposit to Debtor Corp.'s account at Bank. He added $100,000 to the existing $20,000 balance. Debtor Corp. filed bankruptcy six weeks later. Bank then sought relief from the stay in order to setoff $120,000 against the balance on its loan. What result?

6. Bank made Corporation an unsecured loan of $125,000 and Corporation's President personally guaranteed repayment. When Corporation began to experience financial problems, President made several deposits of corporate funds in Corporation's checking account at Bank, increasing the balance from $10,000 to $100,000 during the 90 days before bankruptcy. Bank sought relief from the stay in order to set off the checking account against the loan. Is set-off proper?

7. Corporation owed Bank $100,000 on the 90th day before bankruptcy. At that time, Corporation's checking account at Bank had a balance of $40,000. When Bank exercised its right of setoff two days before filing, the balance in the account was $50,000. The loan balance was unchanged. How much, if anything, can the trustee recover under § 553?

8. Corporation owed Bank $30,000 throughout the 90 days before bankruptcy. The amounts in Corporation's checking account at Bank fluctuated during that period as follows: $30,000 on the 90th day; $20,000 on the 85th day; $15,000 on the 80th day; and $29,000 on the 25th day, which was the day of setoff. How much, if anything, can the trustee recover under § 553?

9. Assume the same facts as in Problem # 8, except that the amount in Corporation's checking account on the 90th day is $29,998. Does your answer change?

Setoff is often described as a "legalized preference," because it allows the creditor to receive more than it would receive without the setoff. The first requirement for a preference is a "transfer," as we have seen, and the definition of "transfer," § 101(54), omits any reference to setoffs. According to the legislative history, this omission was intentional, so that setoffs cannot be treated as preferences. To further drive home the point, § 553(a) states that nothing in "this title"—that is, bankruptcy—affects the right of setoff.

Even though setoffs are not subject to avoidance as a preference, the kinship between §§ 553(a)(2), (a)(3) and (b), on the one hand, and § 547, on the other, is nevertheless clear. Those subsections of § 553 are designed to prevent a creditor's use of setoff to gain an advantage over others, thereby undermining bankruptcy's equality principle—a goal that is entirely compatible with what preference law is designed to achieve.

The following case illustrates this affinity between setoff and preference law.

DURHAM v. SMI INDUSTRIES CORP.

United States Court of Appeals, Fourth Circuit, 1989.
882 F.2d 881.

WILKINS, Circuit Judge.

SMI Industries, Inc., a creditor of Continental Commodities, Inc., appeals from the district court judgment affirming a bankruptcy court ruling that its receipt of a check as part of a check exchange by the two companies constituted an avoidable preferential transfer under the Bankruptcy Code, § 547(b). We reverse and remand.

I.

SMI and Continental are scrap metal dealers that until November 1983 engaged in a substantial amount of business with each other, selling each other materials on open account. Although the total dollar figures of the open account invoices often grew quite large, the net balance due either party at any one time was relatively small. Periodically, in order to reduce these account debts, SMI and Continental would either make mutual accounting entries cancelling corresponding debts and credits, or they would exchange checks for the outstanding balances. The check exchanges were carefully coordinated to allow simultaneous deposits in their respective bank accounts to ensure that the checks would clear.

In late August 1983 SMI and Continental made such a check exchange. Continental sent SMI 17 checks totalling $273,137.62 from August 25 to August 26, representing amounts it owed SMI for invoiced deliveries from September 3, 1982 to June 28, 1983. On August 29 SMI sent Continental its check for $271,967.20 for invoiced deliveries by Continental from February 22, 1983 through August 16, 1983. Both parties deposited the checks into their bank accounts on August 30.

On November 18, 1983, less than 90 days later, Continental filed a petition in bankruptcy under Chapter 7. In November 1985 Continental's Trustee filed an adversary action against SMI seeking to recover $273,137.62, which represented the total amount of the checks Continental had sent SMI as part of the check exchange. The bankruptcy court held in favor of the Trustee, finding that Continental's remittance of the checks to SMI constituted avoidable preferential transfers, § 547(b), that were not part of a valid setoff under § 553. * * *

The district court affirmed, finding that SMI's payment constituted a transfer under the Code, which defines "transfer" very broadly in [§ 101(54)], and was a preference under § 547. * * *

II.

Section 547(b) provides that a trustee may avoid, and proceed to seek recovery of, any transfer made by a debtor to a creditor within 90 days prior to filing for bankruptcy that has the effect of enabling that creditor to receive more than it would in the bankruptcy proceeding had the transfer not been made. However, under § 553(b), a valid setoff executed within 90 days of the date of the filing of a bankruptcy petition is nonetheless protected from avoidance under § 547, except for any insufficiency. Where a pre-petition setoff is asserted in defense to a proceeding brought by a trustee the court must first determine whether the setoff is valid under § 553. Only if the court finds the setoff invalid, and further concludes that no right of setoff exists in bankruptcy, is § 547 applied. We hold that the lower courts erred by attempting to resolve this case under § 547 after SMI asserted that it and Continental had completed a pre-petition setoff of their mutual debts.

* * *

B.

Section 553(b)(1) provides, in pertinent part, that except as to circumstances not relevant here:[4]

> [I]f a creditor offsets a mutual debt owing to the debtor against a claim against the debtor on or within 90 days before the date of the filing of the petition, then the trustee may recover from such creditor the amount so offset to the extent [of] any insufficiency on the date of such setoff. * * *

"Insufficiency" is defined in § 553(b)(2) as the amount by which a party's credit against the debtor exceeded its mutual debt to the debtor at the time the setoff was effected. Where there is no improvement in position found, a setoff within 90 days of the filing of a bankruptcy petition as to mutual debts incurred more than 90 days prior to the filing of the petition is effective as between the impending bankrupt debtor and a creditor except to the extent that the creditor receives more in the setoff than it pays.

Section 553 does not create a right of setoff or prescribe the means by which a setoff must be executed in order to be effective. It merely preserves any right of setoff accorded by state law, subject to certain limitations. North Carolina has long recognized the right of setoff where mutual debts exist between parties. North Carolina has not, however, prescribed any method by which a setoff must be executed to be valid.

The United States Supreme Court, applying the former Bankruptcy Act, recognized that a pre-petition setoff may be effected where parties with mutual debts have "themselves given checks, charged notes, made book entries, or stated an account whereby the smaller

---

[4] The right of pre-petition setoff is further limited by the "improvement-in-position" test designed to ensure that a creditor will not improve its position during the 90–day period before bankruptcy and then protect its position by completing a setoff prior to the debtor's filing of a petition. This improvement-in-position test is "in essence, a miniature preference provision akin to § 547(d)(5) [sic]." *In re Balducci Oil Co.*, 33 B.R. 847, 852 (Bankr. D.Colo.1983).

Since the mutual debts Continental and SMI extinguished by the check swap represented only shipments delivered more than 90 days before Continental filed its petition, and there has been no allegation that SMI improved its position as to these debts prior to completing the setoff, the improvement-in-position test does not limit this setoff.

obligation is applied on the larger." *Studley v. Boylston Nat'l Bank*, 229 U.S. 523, 528 (1913). The Trustee concedes that had the parties executed this setoff by corresponding accounting entries it would have been valid, but he argues that a setoff may not be effected by exchanging checks. We see no reason to distinguish between the two practices. Indeed, the exchange of checks, with the resulting endorsements each made on the other's checks before depositing them, provided better documentation of satisfaction of the debt than mere book entries. We hold that the check exchange constituted an effective exercise of setoff pursuant to North Carolina law and § 553(b).

The lower courts used "hypothetical facts" to ignore the intent of the parties at the time of the check exchange and to view each party's act of sending a check as the independent payment of a valid debt. Under these "facts," the Trustee argues, SMI should be seen as merely having decided to pay a valid debt without a cognizable expectation that its corresponding debt from Continental would be paid. If SMI and Continental's payments of their unrelated debts could be seen as unrelated occurrences that just happened to coincide, then Continental's payment could be found to be a preference avoidable under § 547.

However, the clear intent of the parties, as expressed through their overt acts, may not be so readily ignored. As part of their general and longstanding business practice SMI and Continental customarily accrued and then set off, sometimes by accounting entries and sometimes by check exchange, debts to the other. In the check exchange in question SMI and Continental took every step possible to ensure that their checks would cross in the collection process since neither had funds sufficient to cover their checks. As neither intended a substantial amount of money to change hands, there was no need to have sufficient funds on hand, apart from the coordinated deposits of the other's check, to ensure that their own check would clear. Although checks were used, in essence the exchange constituted an accounting exercise to clear their books of mutual debts.

SMI would have been entitled to assert its right of setoff under § 553(a) post-petition if the check exchange had not been executed before Continental's petition was filed since both debts were incurred pre-petition. Where a creditor fails "to exercise its right of setoff prior to the filing of the petition" it does not lose the right, but must "proceed in the bankruptcy court by means of a complaint to lift the automatic stay so as to be allowed to exercise its already existing right to offset." *In re Compton Corp.,* 22 B.R. 276, 278 (Bankr.N.D.Tex.1982). And, as the Trustee concedes, there is no evidence that the debt SMI extinguished in the setoff was incurred either fraudulently or " 'for the purpose of obtaining a right of setoff against the debtor.' " *In re Southern Indus. Banking Corp.*, 809 F.2d 329, 332 (6th Cir.1987) (quoting § 553(a)(3)(C)). It would be inequitable to construe § 553(b) to prevent "the parties from voluntarily doing, before the petition is filed, what the law itself requires to be done after proceedings in bankruptcy are instituted." *Studley*, 229 U.S. at 528–29.

III.

Since the debts the two parties eliminated with the setoff were not exactly the same, the resulting checks were not equal. The check exchange was a proper setoff only up to the amount that SMI and Continental owed each other equivalent amounts. Since SMI sent Continental $271,967.20 while receiving from Continental $273,137.62, an insufficiency of $1,170.42, recoverable from SMI, was created pursuant to §§ 553(b)(1) and (b)(2). SMI must return this insufficiency to Continental's estate. The district court judgment is reversed, and the case is remanded for entry of an appropriate judgment in favor of the estate consistent with this opinion.

Notes and Questions

1. The court stated that "a valid setoff executed within 90 days of the date of the filing of a bankruptcy petition is nonetheless protected from avoidance under § 547." Does the text of the Code support this assertion?

2. To what extent was the intent of the parties pertinent to the *Durham* court's application of § 553? Does the court suggest that intent determines whether § 553 or § 547 is applicable?

3. In footnote 4, the court asserted that § 553(b)(1) is "a miniature preference provision akin to" § 547(c)(5). While that is true, the two provisions have differences that may lead to very different results. Consider the following example:

> Ninety days before bankruptcy, Debtor owes Creditor $10,000, repayment of which is fully secured by a floating lien on inventory and receivables. Forty-five days before bankruptcy, the outstanding debt is still $10,000, but the collateral has decreased in value to $6,000. On the day before bankruptcy, the outstanding indebtedness still has not changed, but the collateral has increased in value to $9,000.
>
> Assume that Creditor sets off Debtor's loan against the collateral on the day before bankruptcy. Under § 553(b)(1), the trustee may

recover $3,000 from Creditor, as Day 45 was the first date on which there was an insufficiency and the insufficiency on the setoff day had decreased by $3,000.

The trustee, however, could not avoid Creditor's security interest under § 547(c)(5)'s improvement of position test; Creditor was fully secured and could not improve its position.

Section 553 requires "mutuality," which means that the obligations (one a "claim" and the other a "debt") must be between the same parties, acting in the same capacity. The illustration with which this section began—a loan made by the bank at which the debtor maintains an account—is a simple case, presenting no mutuality issue. As the following case illustrates, however, many fact patterns are much more complicated.

MATTER OF ELCONA HOMES CORP.

United States Court of Appeals, Seventh Circuit, 1988.
863 F.2d 483.

POSNER, Circuit Judge.

This appeal requires us to examine the Bankruptcy Code's provision on set offs, which states that the Code "does not affect any right of a creditor to offset a [prebankruptcy] mutual debt owing by such creditor to the debtor * * * against a [prebankruptcy] claim of such creditor against the debtor." § 553(a). The debtor, Elcona Homes Corporation, was (and still is, for this is a reorganization case) a manufacturer of mobile homes. Shortly before it went broke, Linda Markle had ordered a mobile home from one of its dealers, Monro Homes, Inc. The price was $36,700. Markle paid $14,000 down, and Elcona agreed to sell the home to Monro for $22,700. This was, of course, the difference between the retail price and the amount of the down payment; so the latter amount represented Monro's profit.

Payment of the balance was to be due when Monro delivered the home to Markle and set it up for her. Green Tree Acceptance, Inc., the creditor in the case, agreed to finance Markle's purchase by giving Monro $22,700 in exchange for an assignment of the installment contract that Monro had signed with Markle. So instead of making her monthly payments to Monro, Markle would make them to Green Tree, and Green Tree's profit would come from the interest it charged Markle. Upon receipt of the $22,700 from Green Tree, Monro would remit an equal amount to Elcona to pay for the mobile home. The parties refer to the type of arrangement by which Green Tree financed Monro's business as "retail proceeds" financing. It bears a family resemblance to the more common "floor-planning" system of dealer financing, but there the lender takes a security interest in the goods before the dealer sells them and here it was afterward.

This was not the first time that Green Tree had financed Monro's sales of Elcona homes; and a practice had developed of Green Tree's paying Elcona directly rather than paying Monro for remittance to Elcona. This meant that instead of Green Tree's paying Monro $22,700 for the installment contract and Monro's then turning around and paying Elcona $22,700 for the mobile home, Green Tree would be expected simply to pay $22,700 to Elcona. Elcona preferred this arrangement, since it protected it (how far we shall see) against the risk of Monro's defaulting. This was not only the practice between the parties but also, they have stipulated, the practice generally followed in the mobile home industry.

Elcona's bankruptcy occurred after the sale to Markle but before Green Tree had paid Elcona. Now it happened that Elcona owed Green Tree $16,000 (more or less) on an earlier transaction. Green Tree decided to set off this debt against the $22,700 that normally it would have sent directly to Elcona, and therefore sent Elcona only the difference between $22,700 and $16,000 (actually somewhat less, but like the exact amount owed Green Tree in the earlier transaction, that is a detail of no importance to this appeal). The bankruptcy judge did not consider this a proper set off. Since the $22,700 was not a debt that Green Tree owed Elcona but a debt it owed Monro, there was no mutual indebtedness between Elcona and Green Tree, as the statute requires. (Elcona adds that Green Tree was really just an escrow agent of Monro, Elcona's real debtor.) The district judge * * * reversed the bankruptcy judge. He thought the evidence showed "a mutuality of obligations between Green Tree and Elcona and vice versa because it was both the industry practice and the practice between the parties for the lender (Green Tree) to pay the manufacturer (Elcona) directly the amount due the manufacturer from the dealer. That being the case, Green Tree was entitled to setoff the debt owed it by Elcona." Elcona appeals.

The set-off provision in the Bankruptcy Code seems at first glance inconsistent with the usual result in bankruptcy, which is that all unsecured creditors are treated alike ("equity is equality"). But it is no more than the usual result precisely because the principle that unsecured creditors shall be treated alike is riddled with exceptions. There are all sorts of preferences (for the Internal Revenue Service, for employees having wage claims, for persons who extend credit to the debtor after the petition for bankruptcy is filed, etc.) and discriminations (e.g., against creditors treated preferentially on the eve of bankruptcy). And it might be more accurate to say not that there is a principle (however qualified) of equal treatment among creditors but that bankruptcy provides a mechanism for enforcing pre-bankruptcy entitlements given by state or federal law, with some exceptions. But the idea of equal treatment is a useful as well as persistent one. An important purpose of bankruptcy law is to prevent individual creditors from starting a "run" on the debtor by assuring them that they will be treated equally if the debtor is precipitated into bankruptcy, rather than being given either preferential treatment for having jumped the gun or disadvantageous treatment for having hung back.

The principle is not absolute, as we have stressed, but its exceptions generally are intelligible; and we will be helped in determining the scope of the set-off exception—which on its face is arbitrary—if we can understand its rationale, too.

Set-offs outside of bankruptcy are in no wise anomalous or problematic; no third party's rights comparable to those of unsecured creditors in bankruptcy are affected, and circuitous proceedings are avoided. But in bankruptcy an unsecured creditor fortunate enough to owe his debtor as much as or more than the debtor owes him can, by setting off his debt against the debtor's, in effect receive 100 cents on the dollar, while the other unsecured creditors, who have nothing to set off against the debtor, might be lucky to collect 10 cents on the dollar. The difference in treatment seems based on a fortuitous difference among the unsecured creditors, and therefore arbitrary. Let us inquire further.

Although the right of set off has been a part of Anglo–American bankruptcy law since 1705, see Act of 4 Anne, ch. 17, § 11, its rationale has never been made clear. To say that it "recognize[s] the possible injustice in compelling a creditor to file its claim in full and accepting possible dividends thereon, while at the same time paying in full its indebtedness to the estate," 4 Collier on Bankruptcy ¶ 553.02, at p. 553–10 (King 15th ed. 1988) (footnote omitted), is to say very little; for why is it not an equal or greater injustice to advance one unsecured creditor over another merely because the first happens also to owe money to their common debtor? Nor is it helpful to point out that "it is only the balance which is the real and just sum owing by or to the bankrupt," *Prudential Ins. Co. v. Nelson*, 101 F.2d 441, 443 (6th Cir.1939), for if the set off is allowed, the other unsecured creditors will not receive "the real and just sum owing" to them.

The only sense we can make of the rule is that it recognizes that the creditor who owes his debtor money is like a secured creditor; indeed, the mutual debts, to the extent equal, secure each party against the other's default. This reasoning figured in Congress's decision to retain the right of set off in the 1978 overhaul of bankruptcy law. The reasoning may seem circular, however, for it is only by virtue of the Bankruptcy Code's preserving the right of set off that the creditor has, in the event of his debtor's bankruptcy, a form of security for the debt he is owed. (But of course not all defaulting debtors are bankrupt.) And one might suppose that if the theory of the set off is that it provides the creditor with security, the creditor would have to prove that the parties had intended a right of set off as a means of securing the creditor—that is, would have to prove that the creditor had been counting on the right in extending credit to the debtor on the terms he did. But such proof is not in fact required.

Banks argue that the right to set off deposits (a bank deposit is a debt of the bank to the depositor) against the depositor's debts to the bank facilitates the provision of bank credit and lowers the rate of interest, by giving the bank security in the event of the depositor's going broke. But the more secure the bank is, the less secure the depositor's other creditors will be, so they will charge higher interest rates. This, however, is a general characteristic of secured lending. The secured lender faces a lower risk of loss in the event of default and therefore will lend at a lower interest rate, but unsecured lenders, facing a higher risk of loss because fewer assets will be available to satisfy their claims in the event of default, will charge higher interest rates. Nevertheless secured financing is so firmly established a commercial practice that it is hard to believe it does not serve important commercial purposes, and it is apparent what they might be: lenders differ in their ability to monitor their borrowers (in order to prevent the borrower from increasing the riskiness of its activities) and to bear risk, and thus a combination of secured and unsecured financing enables a borrower to appeal to the different capabilities and preferences of different lenders.

Yet if deposits are intended to secure the bank's loans, why not treat the bank as a secured creditor rather than creating a general right in all creditors to set off their debts against the bankrupt's debts to them? Maybe the answer is simply that set offs are just another form of secured financing that the Bankruptcy Code has decided to recognize, though under a different name and with different restrictions. But the underlying rights of creditors which are asserted in bankruptcy proceedings are the creation of state law, not of the Bankruptcy Code. * * * Maybe the right question to ask, therefore, is not why the Code allows set offs (for it also allows secured creditors to withdraw their collateral from the pool available to other creditors), but why it places restrictions on them. Against this view of set offs as a species of secured financing, however, it can be argued that, apart perhaps from such special situations as that of banks dealing with their depositor-borrowers, set offs are recognized in state law for their procedural convenience—the consolidation of offsetting claims in the same suit—and that this convenience should receive little weight in bankruptcy. Professor Gilmore thought the express exemption of set offs from the filing requirements in Article 9 (secured financing) of the Uniform Commercial Code, see § 9–104(i), absurd: "Of course a right of setoff is not a security interest and has never been confused with one: the statute might as appropriately exclude fan dancing." 1 Gilmore, Security Interests in Personal Property § 10.7, at pp. 315–16 (1965). This view seems extreme and has been questioned, but certainly there is no evidence here that the existence of mutual debts (if that is what they were) between Elcona and Green Tree reflected a desire by the parties to secure each other's obligations; it appears to have been an accident.

But we need not resolve these questions, or press our inquiry into the rationale for the Bankruptcy Code's treatment of set offs further, in order to decide this case. Whether that treatment reflects a felt tension between the right of set off and the normal practice in bankruptcy of treating unsecured creditors equally, or whether one denies the tension, points out that the recognition by state law of a right of set off makes the set off a form of secured financing, and argues (contrary to our earlier point) that there really is no policy of treating unsecured creditors in bankruptcy equally, the statute itself speaks of "a *mutual* debt" (emphasis ours) and therefore precludes "triangular" set offs. See, e.g., *In re Berger Steel Co.*, 327 F.2d 401 (7th Cir.1964); *Depositors Trust Co. v. Frati Enterprises, Inc.*, 590 F.2d 377, 379 (1st Cir.1979).

Two recurrent cases should be noted. In the first and easier, illustrated by *In re Southern Industrial Banking Corp.*, 809 F.2d 329 (6th Cir.1987), the creditor of a bankrupt buys a debt owed by someone else to the debtor in order to offset the debt that the bankrupt debtor owes him and so gain an advantage over the other unsecured creditors.

This is plainly evasive and easily rebuffed. Indeed, it will normally violate § 553(a)(3), which was added in 1978 to close a loophole that had allowed preferences in the form of set offs, and which forbids a set off where the debt was incurred within 90 days before bankruptcy, while the debtor was insolvent, and for the purpose of obtaining a set off against him.

In the second case, illustrated by both *Berger Steel* and *Depositors Trust*, a subsidiary or other affiliate of the creditor owes money to the bankrupt and the two affiliates ask that they be treated as a single entity. This is rebuffed by pointing out that, save in exceptional circumstances, corporate and commercial law treat affiliated corporations as separate enterprises.

Our case follows neither of these familiar patterns. It is neither a transaction in contemplation of bankruptcy (the timing suggests it may be but Elcona does not argue the point, and it is therefore waived) nor an attempt by affiliated corporations to lift the corporate veil that separates them. Nevertheless there can be no set off unless the $22,700 was in fact a debt owed by Green Tree to Elcona.

The district court's opinion does not deal satisfactorily with this issue. The court inferred the existence of a mutual debt from the practice of the parties and of the industry; indeed, he equated obligation to practice. He said, "there was a mutuality of obligation between Green Tree and Elcona and vice versa *because* it was both the industry practice and the practice between the parties for the lender (Green Tree) to pay the manufacturer (Elcona) directly the amount due the manufacturer from the dealer. *That being the case*, Green Tree was entitled to setoff the debt owed it by Elcona." (Emphasis added.) In other words, a practice equals or creates an obligation. It does not. Suppose the practice of a landlord is to accept late payment from his tenant. That practice does not entitle the tenant to pay late; it does not modify the contract. If every forbearance to enforce a contract to its hilt operated to modify the contract against the party exercising forbearance, such forbearance would become rare; promisees would always insist on exact performance of the promisor's obligation, and defaults and litigation would become more frequent. A practice may be evidence of an obligation, may give meaning to vague terms, and so on; but it is not the equivalent of it.

The question can be put this way: if, instead of remitting $22,700 directly to Elcona, Green Tree had remitted the money to Monro, and Monro had absconded with the money without paying

Elcona, could Elcona have sued Green Tree? Possibly so, since as we said the practice of Green Tree in remitting directly to Elcona provided both parties with security against a default by the dealer, and the security would be less if the contract were interpreted to allow either party to disregard the practice. Maybe, then, the practice was also an implied term of the contract. If so—and if, therefore, Elcona could have sued Green Tree (and won) in our hypothetical case—this would show that Green Tree was indeed indebted to Elcona, and then the debts were mutual and could be offset. The case must be remanded for a determination whether there was not only a practice of direct payment from the finance company to the manufacturer but an obligation to make such payments.

* * *

The decision of the district court is vacated and the case remanded for further proceedings consistent with this opinion.

[The dissenting opinion of Senior District Judge Will, sitting by designation, is omitted. The district court, in Judge Will's view, had already determined that Green Tree was obligated to pay Elcona directly. Thus, Judge Will would have affirmed, rather than remanded.]

Questions and Problems

1. Green Tree's obligation to Elcona (if such it was) arose within 90 days before bankruptcy. Why, then, did § 553(a)(3) not control this case?

2. This sort of "triangular" relationship generally falls outside of § 553 because of the lack of mutuality. The district court (reversing the bankruptcy court) found mutuality because the parties acted in accordance with industry practice and their own course of dealing. The Seventh Circuit, on the other hand, believed that mutuality requires legal obligation. Will the industry practice be relevant on remand?

3. Debtor, a farmer, owed $320,000 on a loan received from the Farmers Home Administration. He participated in a crop reduction program run by the Commodity Credit Commission, which owed him $250,000 for not planting cotton last year. When Debtor filed bankruptcy, the CCC sought to set off the FHA loan against its obligation to the estate. Is such a setoff permissible?

_____

As we previously noted, setoff often arises in the context of loans made by banks to their depositors. The amount in the deposit account can be set off against the loan balance if the depositor-borrower fails to pay. That is all well and good, but how does the bank protect its setoff rights if the depositor-borrower files a bankruptcy petition and then attempts to clean out the account? Can the bank refuse to permit the withdrawal or refuse to honor checks as they are presented? If it does, has it violated the automatic stay? These questions sharply divided the Courts of Appeal until the Supreme Court decided the issue in the following case.

CITIZENS BANK OF MARYLAND v. STRUMPF

United States Supreme Court, 1995.
516 U.S. 16, 116 S.Ct. 286, 133 L.Ed.2d 258.

JUSTICE SCALIA delivered the opinion of the Court.

We must decide whether the creditor of a debtor in bankruptcy may, in order to protect its setoff rights, temporarily withhold payment of a debt that it owes to the debtor in bankruptcy without violating the automatic stay imposed by § 362(a).

I

On January 25, 1991, when respondent filed for relief under Chapter 13 of the Bankruptcy Code, he had a checking account with petitioner, a bank conducting business in the State of Maryland. He also was in default on the remaining balance of a loan of $5,068.75 from the bank. Under § 362(a), respondent's bankruptcy filing gave rise to an automatic stay of various types of activity by his creditors, including "the setoff of any debt owing to the debtor that arose before the commencement of the [bankruptcy case] against any claim against the debtor." § 362(a)(7).

On October 2, 1991, petitioner placed what it termed an "administrative hold" on so much of respondent's account as it claimed was subject to setoff—that is, the bank refused to pay withdrawals from the account that would reduce the balance below the sum that it claimed was due on respondent's loan. Five days later, petitioner filed in the Bankruptcy Court, under § 362(d), a "Motion for Relief from Automatic Stay and for Setoff." Respondent then filed a motion to hold petitioner in contempt, claiming that petitioner's administrative hold violated the automatic stay established by § 362(a).

The Bankruptcy Court ruled on respondent's contempt motion first. It concluded that petitioner's "administrative hold" constituted a "setoff" in violation of § 362(a)(7) and sanctioned petitioner. Several weeks later, the Bankruptcy Court granted petitioner's motion for relief from the stay and authorized petitioner to set off respondent's remaining checking account balance against the unpaid loan. By that time, however, respondent had reduced the checking account balance to zero, so there was nothing to set off.

The District Court reversed the judgment that petitioner had violated the automatic stay, concluding that the administrative hold was not a violation of § 362(a). The Court of Appeals reversed. "An administrative hold," it said, "is tantamount to the exercise of a right of setoff and thus violates the automatic stay of § 362(a)(7)." We granted certiorari.

II

The right of setoff (also called "offset") allows entities that owe each other money to apply their mutual debts against each other, thereby avoiding "the absurdity of making A pay B when B owes A." *Studley v. Boylston Nat. Bank*, 229 U.S. 523, 528 (1913). Although no federal right of setoff is created by the Bankruptcy Code, § 553(a) provides that, with certain exceptions, whatever right of setoff otherwise exists is preserved in bankruptcy. Here it is undisputed that, prior to the bankruptcy filing, petitioner had the right under Maryland law to set off the defaulted loan against the balance in the checking account. It is also undisputed that under § 362(a) respondent's bankruptcy filing stayed any exercise of that right by petitioner. The principal question for decision is whether petitioner's refusal to pay its debt to respondent upon the latter's demand constituted an exercise of the setoff right and hence violated the stay.

In our view, petitioner's action was not a setoff within the meaning of § 362(a)(7). Petitioner refused to pay its debt, not permanently and absolutely, but only while it sought relief under § 362(d) from the automatic stay. Whether that temporary refusal was otherwise wrongful is a separate matter—we do not consider, for example, respondent's contention that the portion of the account subjected to the "administrative hold" exceeded the amount properly subject to setoff. All that concerns us here is whether the refusal *was a setoff*. We think it was not, because—as evidenced by petitioner's "Motion for Relief from Automatic Stay and for Setoff"—petitioner did not purport permanently to reduce respondent's account balance by the amount of the defaulted loan. A requirement of such an intent is implicit in the rule followed by a majority of jurisdictions addressing the question, that a setoff has not occurred until three steps have been taken: (i) a decision to effectuate a setoff, (ii) some action accomplishing the setoff, and (iii) a recording of the setoff. But even if state law were different, the question whether a setoff *under § 362(a)(7)* has occurred is a matter of federal law, and other provisions of the Bankruptcy Code would lead us to embrace the same requirement of an intent permanently to settle accounts.

Section 542(b) of the Code, which concerns turnover of property to the estate, requires a bankrupt's debtors to "pay" to the trustee (or on his order) any "debt that is property of the estate and that is matured, payable on demand, or payable on order * * * *except to the extent that such debt may be offset under § 553 of this title against a claim against the debtor*." § 542(b) (emphasis added). Section 553(a), in turn, sets forth a general rule, with certain exceptions, that any right of setoff that a creditor possessed prior to the debtor's filing for bankruptcy is not affected by the Bankruptcy Code. It would be an odd construction of § 362(a)(7) that required a creditor with a right of setoff to do immediately that which § 542(b) specifically excuses it from doing as a general matter: pay a claim to which a defense of setoff applies.

Nor is our assessment of these provisions changed by the fact that § 553(a), in generally providing that nothing in the Bankruptcy Code affects creditors' prebankruptcy setoff rights, qualifies this rule with the phrase "except as otherwise provided in this section and in sections 362 and 363." This undoubtedly refers to § 362(a)(7), but we think it is most naturally read as merely recognizing that provision's restriction upon *when* an *actual setoff* may be effected—which is to say, not during the automatic stay. When this perfectly reasonable reading is available, it would be foolish to take the § 553(a) "except" clause as indicating that § 362(a)(7) requires immediate payment of a debt subject to setoff. That would render § 553(a)'s general rule that the Bankruptcy Code does not affect the right of setoff meaningless, for by forcing the creditor to pay *its* debt immediately, it would divest the creditor of the very thing that supports the right of setoff. Furthermore, it would, as we have stated, eviscerate § 542(b)'s exception to the duty to pay debts. It is an elementary rule of construction that "the act cannot be held to destroy itself." *Texas & Pacific R. Co. v. Abilene Cotton Oil Co.*, 204 U.S. 426, 446 (1907).

Finally, we are unpersuaded by respondent's additional contentions that the administrative hold violated §§ 362(a)(3) and 362(a)(6). Under these sections, a bankruptcy filing automatically stays "any act to obtain possession of property of the estate or of property from the estate or to exercise control over property of the estate," § 362(a)(3), and "any act to collect, assess, or recover a claim against the debtor that arose before the commencement of the case under this title," § 362(a)(6). Respondent's reliance on these provisions rests on the false premise that petitioner's administrative hold took something from respondent, or exercised dominion over property that belonged to respondent. That view of things might be arguable if a bank account consisted of money belonging to the depositor and held by the bank. In fact, however, it consists of nothing more or less than a promise to pay, from the bank to the depositor, and petitioner's temporary refusal to pay was neither a taking of possession of respondent's property nor an exercising of control over it, but merely a refusal to perform its promise. In any event, we will not give § 362(a)(3) or § 362(a)(6) an interpretation that would proscribe what § 542(b)'s "exception" and § 553(a)'s general rule were plainly intended to permit: the temporary refusal of a creditor to pay a debt that is subject to setoff against a debt owed by the bankrupt.

The judgment of the Court of Appeals for the Fourth Circuit is reversed.

It is so ordered.

Questions and Problems

1. The Court stressed that the bank's administrative hold was temporary. How long is "temporary"? Is it necessary that a bank using an administrative hold also immediately seek relief from the automatic stay?

2. When Debtor Corp. filed its bankruptcy petition, its checking account at Bank had a balance of $75,000. Trustee sought a turnover order compelling Bank to remit the funds to the estate. Bank wants to fight the trustee's efforts because Debtor Corp. is obligated to Bank on an unsecured $70,000 loan. Look at §§ 506(a), 363(c)(2) and 363(e), and formulate Bank's argument. Could these provisions have helped Citizens Bank in *Strumpf?*

I. STATUTORY LIENS

Section 545 enables the trustee to avoid statutory liens—that is, involuntary liens that arise solely by statute, without the necessity for legal or equitable proceedings. Its reach is limited.

Subsection (1) avoids liens that arise only upon the happening of one of the events listed, all of which relate to the debtor's financial condition. It was enacted to prevent states from circumventing bankruptcy priorities by creating statutory liens for favored creditors that would arise only when a debtor filed bankruptcy or suffered a similar financial indignity. States have gotten the message, so § 545(1) will seldom apply.

Subsection (2) avoids liens that are vulnerable to a bona fide purchaser because of nonrecording. This provision overlaps to some extent with § 544(a)'s strong arm power, and will seldom apply because most statutory liens are enforceable against bfps.

Subsection (3) avoids liens for rent, and will apply even if the lien is invulnerable under § 544(a) (because perfected) and under § 547(b) (because outside the 90–day period).

Subsection (4) applies to a lien of distress for rent, which is actually a common law lien rather than statutory. It is treated for bankruptcy purposes as a statutory lien, however.

Any statutory lien not within the preceding categories is invulnerable to the trustee under § 545. It may, however, be vulnerable under one of the other avoiding powers, with one exception—§ 547. One of the preference exceptions, § 547(c)(6), protects a statutory lien from avoidance as a preference as long as it is not avoidable under § 545.

J. POSTPETITION TRANSFERS

All of the avoiding powers that we have seen so far are applicable to *prepetition* transfers of an interest in the debtor's property. (Please never make the mistake, on a bankruptcy exam or in front of a judge, of thinking that a transfer made after the filing of the petition is possibly a preference!) Once the petition is filed, all of the debtor's property becomes property of the estate and its disposition should be in accordance with the Code's directions.

The debtor does not lose possession and control of estate property in a Chapter 11, however, and it takes time to put a trustee in place in a Chapter 7 or 13 case. Thus, the debtor will have the opportunity, though not the right, to transfer estate property.

   Section 549 governs postpetition transfers. That the trustee can avoid unauthorized postpetition transfers, § 549(a)(2)(B), should come as no surprise. But the trustee can, under § 549(a)(2)(A), avoid certain *authorized* transfers as well—those authorized *only* under § 303(f) or § 542(c). Since § 549(a) is subject to §§ 549(b) and (c), avoidance of these transfers under (a) has the effect of testing them under (b) and (c). Section 303(f) permits the debtor to continue to operate its business during the "involuntary gap period" (that is, the time between the filing of an involuntary petition and the hearing under § 303(h)). Section 542(c) protects an entity who, without knowledge of the bankruptcy, transfers property of the estate or pays a debt owed to the debtor to someone other than the trustee. The legislative history to § 542(c) indicates that it codifies *Bank of Marin v. England*, 385 U.S. 99, 87 S.Ct. 274, 14 L.Ed.2d 197 (1966), which held that a drawee bank is not liable for honoring a debtor's checks postpetition unless the bank knew of the bankruptcy. But § 542(c) only protects the bank; the payee will be tested under § 549(b).

   Read § 549 and answer the following:

Questions and Problems

   1. A few days after filing a bankruptcy petition, Debtor sold her car to Neighbor for the amount listed in the National Automobile Dealer Association's "Blue Book" as the car's wholesale value. Neighbor knew that Debtor was in bankruptcy. Can the trustee recover the car?

   2. Would it matter under the facts of Problem # 1 if the car had been sold for its listed retail value?

   3. Would it matter under the facts of Problem # 1 if Neighbor had been unaware of the bankruptcy?

   4. A few days after filing a bankruptcy petition, Debtor sold a lot on which she had hoped to build a vacation home to Purchaser for $45,000—its fair market value. No notice of the bankruptcy had been filed in Distant County, where the lot was located, and Purchaser was unaware of Debtor's bankruptcy case. Is the transfer avoidable? What is the relationship between §§ 362(a) and 549(c)? See *Glendenning v. Third Federal Savings Bank (In re Glendenning)*, 243 B.R. 629 (Bankr. E.D.Pa.2000).

   5. Debtor, a wholesaler of women's clothing, received an order for evening dresses from one of its regular customers a few days after filing a

petition under Chapter 11. Debtor sent the dresses to its customer with payment due in 15 days. Bank, to which Debtor owes a large unsecured obligation, wants to use § 549 to recover the shipment of dresses. Assuming Bank can get the court's permission to pursue this action, will it succeed? See § 363(c)(1).

6. In *Harris v. McCauley* (*In re McCauley*), 814 F.2d 1350 (9th Cir.1987), Debtor and his parents each owned real estate. Debtor's parents owned the Susanville property, which they had bought in 1979 for $16,500. Debtor owned the Truckee property, which he had bought in 1981 and in which he had equity of $35,000. In October of 1981, Debtor quit-claimed the Truckee property to his parents; they quitclaimed the Susanville property to him, as consideration for conveyance of the Truckee property, in February of 1982. Debtor filed bankruptcy in June of 1982. Four days later, the parties quitclaimed the properties back to each other, on advice of counsel, believing that the original exchange would be avoided "due to lack of consideration."

The court held the postpetition transfer of the Susanville property avoidable under § 549(a). The court rejected the parents' argument that this gave the trustee more than a single satisfaction, contrary to § 550(d), because the trustee would keep both parcels. If the parents had been good faith purchasers for value, without knowledge of the bankruptcy, either the transfer would not have been avoided or they would have had a lien on the property. They knew of the bankruptcy, however, and voluntarily transferred the Truckee property back to the estate, accepting an avoidable transfer in return. Thus, *both* parcels came into the hands of the bankruptcy trustee.

Could this debtor and his parents have traded parcels immediately before bankruptcy and prevented this result?

7. Debtor owned a house worth $640,000. He owed $463,000 to the mortgagee and $3,850 in dues to his homeowner's association. Purchaser bought the house for the amount of the delinquent dues at a foreclosure sale initiated by the homeowner's association. The sale was held shortly after Debtor's bankruptcy filing, but Purchaser was unaware of the bankruptcy and no notice had been filed in the appropriate real estate office. The trustee sought to set aside the sale, arguing that the purchase price did not constitute "present fair equivalent value." Purchaser cited *BFP v. Resolution Trust Corp.*, 511 U.S. 531 (1994) (which is discussed in Section B of this chapter), and pointed out that the foreclosure sale was conducted in accordance with state law. Does *BFP*'s holding—that whatever is received at a noncollusive, regularly-conducted prepetition foreclosure sale constitutes "reasonably equivalent value" for purposes of § 548—also apply to postpetition sales for purposes of § 549(c)? Should it? Compare *T.F. Stone Co. v. Harper*, 72 F.3d 466 (5th Cir.1995), with *Miller v. NLVK, LLC*, 454 F.3d 899 (8th Cir.2006).

The next case, which deals with recovery of postpetition transfers in the context of a Chapter 11 reorganization, illustrates the tension between § 549 and other provisions of the Code. The result the court reached has caused considerable consternation both to reorganizing debtors and to those who deal with them in the ordinary course of business.

MARATHON PETROLEUM CO. v. COHEN (IN RE DELCO OIL, INC.)

United States Court of Appeals, Eleventh Circuit, 2010.
599 F.3d 1255.

BALDOCK, Circuit Judge.

* * * The issue presented to this Court is whether a bankruptcy trustee may avoid post-petition payments by a debtor under §§ 549(a) and 363(c)(2) as unauthorized transfers of cash collateral. * * * [W]e conclude in this case the trustee may avoid the debtor's unauthorized post-petition transfers of cash collateral. We, therefore, affirm the district court's decision affirming the bankruptcy court's entry of summary judgment in favor of Cohen.

I.

Delco Oil, Inc. (Debtor) is a distributor of motor fuel and associated products. Debtor began purchasing petroleum products from Marathon in 2003 pursuant to a sales agreement. Debtor also entered into a financing agreement with CapitalSource Finance in April 2006, in which CapitalSource agreed to provide financing to Debtor in exchange for Debtor's pledge of all rights to Debtor's personal property, including collections, cash payments, and inventory.

On October 17, 2006, Debtor filed for Chapter 11 bankruptcy protection and filed an emergency motion with the bankruptcy court requesting authorization to use cash collateral to continue its operations. CapitalSource objected. The following day, the bankruptcy court authorized Debtor to continue its business as a debtor-in-possession. On November 6, 2006 the bankruptcy court denied Debtor's request to use its cash collateral (later reduced to a written order). Between October 18 and November 6, however, Debtor distributed over $1.9 million in cash to Marathon in exchange for petroleum products pursuant to its sales agreement.

In December 2006, Debtor voluntarily converted its bankruptcy to a Chapter 7 proceeding and the bankruptcy court appointed Cohen as trustee. Cohen filed an adversary proceeding against Marathon to avoid the post-petition cash transfers and ultimately filed the motion for summary judgment that is the subject of this appeal. The bankruptcy court granted summary judgment in favor of Cohen and entered a judgment for $1,960,088.91 against Marathon, concluding Debtor used Capital-Source's cash collateral to pay Marathon without authorization. On appeal, the district court affirmed the bankruptcy court's entry of summary judgment in favor of Cohen.

* * *

III.

[*The Court quoted § 363(a)*.] The Bankruptcy Code prohibits the post-petition use of cash collateral by a trustee or a debtor-in-possession, unless the secured party or the bankruptcy court after notice and a hearing authorizes the use of cash collateral upon a finding that the secured party's interest in the cash is adequately protected. See §§ 363(c)(2) and (e). Section 363(c)(2) balances competing interests in a Chapter 11 reorganization. As we have explained, a debtor reorganizing his business has a compelling need to use cash collateral in order to meet its daily operating expenses and rehabilitate its business. *In re George Ruggiere Chrysler-Plymouth, Inc.*, 727 F.2d 1017 (11th Cir.1984). At the same time, however, unhindered use of cash collateral, *i.e.*, "secured 'property' may result in the dissipation of the estate." *Id.* at 1019. Section 363(c)(2) resolves this tension between a debtor and a secured creditor by only allowing the debtor to use cash collateral after it has procured either the secured creditor's or the bankruptcy court's permission upon a showing that the secured creditor's interest is adequately protected.

Section 549(a) of the Bankruptcy Code authorizes a trustee to recover unauthorized post-petition transfers of estate property. To avoid a transfer under § 549(a) a trustee need only demonstrate: (1) a post-petition transfer (2) of estate property (3) which was not authorized by the Bankruptcy Code or the court.

IV.

Marathon asserts the bankruptcy and district courts erred because a material issue of fact remains regarding whether the funds it received from Debtor actually constituted CapitalSource's cash collateral. *[Marathon relied on Florida's version of UCC § 9–332(b), which provides that a transferee of funds from a deposit account takes free of a security interest in the account, in the absence of collusion. Thus, according to Marathon, the funds were freed of CapitalSource's security interest upon receipt, and could not constitute cash collateral. The Court thought this point was not dispositive of the case.]*

Lest any confusion exist, Cohen may avoid and recover from Marathon the funds Debtor transferred to it not because CapitalSource continued to have a security interest in the funds once they were in the hands of Marathon, but because Debtor was not authorized to transfer the funds to anyone post-petition without the permission of Capital-Source or the bankruptcy court. We agree with Marathon that under Florida law, CapitalSource did not have a security interest in the funds *after* Debtor transferred them to Marathon. But that is beside the point. To ascertain whether Debtor could lawfully transfer the funds in its deposit accounts to a third party without permission from CapitalSource or the bankruptcy court, we first determine whether those funds were cash collateral. To determine whether the funds constitute cash collateral, we examine the status of the funds while they were in Debtor's hands before the disputed transfer, not at the moment the bankruptcy petition was filed and certainly not at the moment after the funds left Debtor's control. Otherwise, a debtor could circumvent § 363(c)(2)'s prohibition on the use of cash collateral without the secured creditor's or bankruptcy court's permission by distributing cash proceeds it knows are subject to a security interest as it likes, knowing that once distributed the proceeds would not be defined as cash collateral under § 363(a) and, therefore, the transfer would not violate § 363(c). Such an outcome would render § 363(c) virtually meaningless, leaving a debtor generally free to transfer cash or its equivalent that is subject to a security interest. Cohen, therefore, retains the power to avoid and recover these funds because *before* Debtor transferred them they constituted the proceeds of CapitalSource's perfected security interest in all of Debtor's personal property and, therefore, they constituted cash collateral which § 363 prohibited Debtor from transferring to anyone without CapitalSource's or the court's permission.

* * *

V.

In addition, Marathon also argues assuming that the funds constituted cash collateral Cohen may not avoid the payments because any violation of § 363(c)(2) caused no harm to CapitalSource or the estate.

Marathon asserts it gave equivalent value in inventory for the funds transferred to it by Debtor through a series of ordinary course transactions. Because CapitalSource admittedly had a perfected security interest in all of Debtor's personal property, Marathon claims CapitalSource's interests were not diminished when Debtor received equivalent value in petroleum products from Marathon in exchange for the funds.

But a "harmless" exception to a trustee's § 549(a) avoiding powers does not exist. * * * Section 549 does not require any analysis of the adequacy of protection of secured creditors' interests nor does it provide a harmless error exception. * * *

Finally, Marathon argues that as a matter of policy an implicit defense exists under § 549 for ordinary course transfers and for innocent vendors who deal with a debtor-in-possession. These arguments do not persuade us. Section 363(c)(1) allows a debtor-in-possession acting as a trustee to "enter into transactions, including the sale or lease of property of the estate, in the ordinary course of business, without notice or a hearing." Subsection (c)(2), however, forbids a debtor-in-possession from using "cash collateral under paragraph (1) of this subsection *unless*—(A) each entity that has an interest in such cash collateral consents; or (B) the court, after notice and a hearing, authorizes such use." (Emphasis added.) Congress's prohibition on the use of cash collateral in (c)(2) is a specific limitation on the express ability provided in (c)(1) to use estate property in the ordinary course of business. Congress evidently did not intend to allow the use of cash collateral without the permission of the interested secured creditor or the bankruptcy court, even if used in the ordinary course of business.

As to Marathon's status as an "innocent vendor," §§ 549(a) and 550(a) by their terms contain no reference to, let alone an actual defense based on, the transferee's status (vendor, purchaser, etc.) or upon its state of mind (innocent, culpable, etc.). Congress knew how to create exceptions based on [a] transferee's status and culpability. But it chose not to do so when it came to initial transferees of post-petition transfers of cash collateral. We will not create such exceptions in Congress's absence.

VI.

Having admitted CapitalSource had a perfected security interest in all of Debtor's inventory, collections, and cash payments, Marathon has provided nothing more than mere speculation to support its claim that the over $1.9 million it received from Debtor did not constitute CapitalSource's cash collateral as defined in § 363(a). We, therefore, agree with the bankruptcy and district courts that no genuine issue of fact exists as to whether the disputed payments to Marathon constituted unauthorized transfers of cash collateral, which are avoidable under § 549(a). Furthermore, we conclude no exception exists to prevent Cohen from avoiding these transfers pursuant to § 549(a) and recovering the funds from Marathon pursuant to § 550(a). Consequently, the judgment of the district court is AFFIRMED.

Notes and Questions

1. Before this decision, many vendors probably assumed that they could "safely" deal with debtors in bankruptcy on a cash-on-delivery basis. In fact, other provisions of the Code may prevent vendors from *not* continuing to do so. You may recall *Sportfame of Ohio, Inc. v. Wilson Sporting Goods Co. (In re Sportfame of Ohio, Inc.)*, 40 B.R. 47 (Bankr. N.D.Ohio 1984), which was noted in one of the problems dealing with the automatic stay, Chapter 2, Section E, and the court's conclusion that the vendor violated the automatic stay when it stopped selling to a debtor who offered cash terms. Also, as you will see in the next chapter of these materials, a party to an executory contract may not be able simply to stop doing business once its contract partner files bankruptcy. Now, *Delco Oil* puts vendors in a "damned-if-you-do, damned-if-you-don't" position. How do you advise your vendor-clients?

2. Inevitably, the decision in *Delco Oil* poses problems for vendors who are willing to deal with debtors in bankruptcy, as well as for the debtors themselves. Vendors will have to determine the source of funds that a debtor is using for its payments and, if those funds are subject to a security interest, that the debtor has obtained the requisite approval for their use, either from the affected creditor or from the court. The debtor, meanwhile, may not be able to obtain necessary goods and services without detrimental delay. And note that *Delco Oil* imposed this burden and delay despite very vendor-favorable facts: the transactions were in the ordinary course of business; the debtor received goods equivalent in value to the amount it paid; and the vendor acted in good faith and without knowledge that the debtor's use of the funds was unauthorized.

3. Given that § 363(c)(1) permits a debtor to operate in the ordinary course of business without first seeking authority from the court, it is odd that the bankruptcy court had authorized the debtor to continue its business as debtor-in-possession. Such an order is completely unnecessary. Nonetheless, could the existence of the order have provided an argument for the vendor in this case?

4. The Court focused on the need to prevent misbehavior by debtors, reasoning that, if recovery were not permitted, a debtor could use cash

collateral and render § 363(c) "virtually meaningless." Other tools are available to courts to police debtor behavior, however. For example, Chapter 11 debtors are required to be represented by counsel and those lawyers, as officers of the court, should be advising against the use of cash collateral without proper authority. In addition, certain violations of the Code may lead to dismissal or conversion of the case, or to the appointment of a trustee. Finally, some courts have imposed sanctions on the individuals in control of a debtor corporation that used cash collateral without authority. Are these alternatives sufficient to police debtors' use of cash collateral?

K. RECLAMATION

An unpaid seller of goods to the debtor has only an unsecured claim. The seller cannot take back the goods, except to the extent permitted by state law. The governing state law rules are found in §§ 2–702(2) and (3) of the UCC, which give sellers, under certain circumstances, a right to reclaim goods:

> (2) Where the seller discovers that the buyer has received goods on credit while insolvent he may reclaim the goods upon demand made within ten days after the receipt, but if misrepresentation of solvency has been made to the particular seller in writing within three months before delivery the ten day limitation does not apply. Except as provided in this subsection the seller may not base a right to reclaim goods on the buyer's fraudulent or innocent misrepresentation of solvency or of intent to pay.

> (3) The seller's right to reclaim under subsection (2) is subject to the rights of a buyer in ordinary course or other good faith purchaser under this Article (§ 2-403). Successful reclamation of goods excludes all other remedies with respect to them.

A right of reclamation is akin to a lien, since the seller can recover the goods and apply their value to the unpaid purchase price.

The Bankruptcy Code contains its own reclamation provision— § 546(c). That section, however, imposes requirements that do not exactly track those of UCC § 2–702.

Read UCC § 2–702(2) and § 546(c), and then answer the following Problems.

Problems

1. Neighbor sold her used lawnmower to Debtor when Neighbor bought a new one. She agreed to accept payment in 30 days. Five days after the sale, however, one of Debtor's other creditors knocked on Neighbor's door while looking for Debtor and told Neighbor a tale of default, pursuit and evasion. Neighbor telephoned Debtor that evening and demanded return of the lawnmower. Debtor filed a bankruptcy petition the next day. Is Neighbor entitled to reclaim the lawnmower?

2. Debtor, a farmer, sought to purchase goods on credit from Seller, a retailer of farm equipment. Debtor provided Seller a financial statement reflecting marginal solvency. Seller, relying on that information, sold Debtor $18,000 worth of equipment. Debtor never paid for the goods and, four months later, Seller learned that the financial statement was inaccurate — Debtor had been hopelessly insolvent all along. Seller sent a written reclamation demand immediately thereafter and, a week later, Debtor filed bankruptcy. What are Seller's rights under § 546(c)?

3. Seller was a manufacturer of tow tractors, used to haul cargo to and from airplanes. Seller delivered three tow tractors to Debtor less than a week before Debtor filed Chapter 11. The price for the tow tractors was $86,000 each. Seller learned of Debtor's bankruptcy the day it was filed and immediately sent a written reclamation demand. Debtor refused to turn over the tow tractors, asserting that they were needed in the reorganization effort. Seller filed a reclamation action in the bankruptcy court. What result?

4. Trade Creditor delivered inventory to Debtor two weeks before Debtor filed Chapter 11. Trade Creditor learned of Debtor's bankruptcy the day it was filed and immediately phoned Debtor, demanding return of the goods. Debtor refused and Trade Creditor filed a reclamation action in the bankruptcy court. Debtor defended on the grounds that Trade Creditor's reclamation demand was not in writing. You represent Trade Creditor. Do you have a fall-back position?

5. Trade Creditor delivered inventory to Debtor two weeks before Debtor filed Chapter 11, but Trade Creditor did not learn of Debtor's bankruptcy until three weeks after it was filed. Is it too late to send a reclamation demand?

6. Have the sellers in these Problems violated the automatic stay by making post-petition reclamation demands?

7. Retailer received a shipment of hairdryers from Wholesaler on September 1, with payment due in 60 days. Wholesaler learned in early October that Retailer was insolvent and had been for quite some time, although Wholesaler had not inquired. Wholesaler sent a written reclamation demand on

October 10, but Retailer filed a bankruptcy petition the next day. Is Wholesaler entitled to reclaim the goods?

One of the fundamental principles governing reclamation in bankruptcy has been that state law and the Bankruptcy Code impose independent sets of requirements regarding reclamation, both of which must be met. This principle was based on the language "any statutory or common law right of a seller of goods," which appeared in § 546(c) until it was amended in 2005. The provision now merely refers to "the right" of a seller to reclaim goods.

Difficulties arise when a seller has satisfied all of the requirements of § 546(c), but not those of UCC § 2–702(2). The question is whether the changes wrought by the 2005 Amendments have altered our prior understanding and instituted a federal right of reclamation, available even when the state requirements are not satisfied. If state and federal law conflict (for example, as to time periods, evidenced by the last Problem above), then surely federal law must control. In other respects, however, the revised version of § 546(c) is silent as to some matters (such as the rights of a buyer in ordinary course) covered by UCC § 2–702. The next case grappled with these issues.

IN RE DANA CORP.

United States Bankruptcy Court, Southern District of New York, 2007.
367 B.R. 409.

BURTON R. LIFLAND, Bankruptcy Judge.

[Debtors were part of a large family of corporations that manufactured equipment used in the automotive industry. After they filed bankruptcy, they received over 450 reclamation demands totaling nearly $300,000,000. The claimants argued, inter alia, that § 546(c), as amended in 2005, created a new federal right of reclamation that is not subject to case law interpretations of the previous version.]

* * *

As this Court observed more than 23 years ago in an early interpretation of § 546(c), reclamation is actually "a misnomer, as seldom if ever is property actually returned or reclaimed in a reorganization case in lieu of other available relief." *Crown Quilt Corp. v. HRT Industries,*

Inc. (In re HRT Industries, Inc.), 29 B.R. 861, 862 (Bankr. S.D.N.Y. 1983). The passage of time has validated this observation. From its enactment it was commonly understood that former § 546(c) was not the source of a right of reclamation, but simply allowed a seller to exercise a right of reclamation existing under non-bankruptcy law, subject to certain limitations.

The right to reclamation is codified, in most states, in § 2-702 of the Uniform Commercial Code. Former § 546(c) also established certain additional requirements the seller needed to follow that were not otherwise required under state law.

Under BAPCPA, amended § 546(c) expands the reclamation reach-back period in two different ways. First, the look-back period before bankruptcy during which goods may be subject to reclamation is expanded from 10 days to 45 days. Second, the grace period, which gives a seller additional time after a bankruptcy filing during which to file its notice of reclamation, is expanded from 10 days to 20 days. The seller is also given up to 20 days after the bankruptcy filing to send its reclamation demand where the 45-day reclamation demand period expires after the bankruptcy filing.

In addition, amended § 546(c) provides for an administrative claim: "If a seller of goods fails to provide notice in the manner described in paragraph (1), the seller still may assert the rights contained in section 503(b)(9)." New § 503(b)(9) in turn allows the seller an administrative expense claim equal to "the value of any goods received by the debtor within 20 days before the date of commencement of a case under this title in which the goods have been sold to the debtor in the ordinary course of such debtor's business." There is no shortage of commentary on the interplay of §§ 503(b)(9) and 546(c).[5]

---

[5] With the introduction of § 503(b)(9) priority, reclamation claims under amended § 546(c) have decreased importance because goods delivered to a debtor in the 20 days prior to bankruptcy will have automatic priority. Thus, reclamation rights are now mainly beneficial for goods delivered in the 21 to 45 days prior to the bankruptcy filing under amended § 546(c). However, with the expansion of the reclamation period, the likelihood of early administrative insolvency will increase, and debtor companies will need greater financial resources to reorganize.

The provision of an administrative claim under § 503(b)(9) also resolves a conflict among the courts concerning whether a reclaiming seller may be granted an administrative claim or a lien on property of the debtor's estate pursuant to former § 546(c) even where there existed a lienholder with a superior interest.

Section 546(c) was also modified to remove the reference to the "statutory or common law right" of the seller. Instead, amended § 546(c) provides that reclamation rights are "subject to the prior rights of a holder of a security interest in such goods." Congress provided no explanation in the legislative history of § 546(c) for what it intended by this deletion.[7] The Reclamation Claimants contend that the deletion of the reference to state law in the amended § 546(c) no longer incorporates the state law right of reclamation, and instead creates a brand new federal bankruptcy law right. I disagree.

Former § 546 was entitled "Limitations on avoiding powers," and provided that if a seller followed the procedures set forth in § 546(c), the trustee could not avoid the reclamation right. Amended § 546(c) remains a "Limitation on avoiding powers." It is not a section dedicated to granting an independent federal right of reclamation nor does it create a coherent comprehensive federal scheme for reclamation. First, Congress did not use the language of creation—Congress did not say that "a seller may reclaim goods when * * * ." Moreover, if amended § 546(c) was a new federal reclamation right arising under the Bankruptcy Code, it would not be subject to the avoiding powers.

Importantly, "[w]hen Congress amends the bankruptcy laws, it does not write 'on a clean slate.' * * * [T]his Court has been reluctant to accept arguments that would interpret the Code * * * to effect a major change in pre-Code practice that is not the subject of at least some discussion in the legislative history." *Dewsnup v. Timm*, 502 U.S. 410, 419 (1992). As recently reminded by the Second Circuit Court of Appeals, "we must not be guided by a single sentence or member of a sentence, but look to the provisions of the whole law." *See Northwest*

---

[7] Several possible explanations have been suggested. One is that Congress sought to resolve the issue of whether a secured creditor was a "good faith purchaser" under the U.C.C. *See In re Reliable Drug Stores, Inc.*, 70 F.3d 948, 949 (7th Cir. 1995) (Court of Appeals, in *dicta*, noted that there was room for debate as to whether a party with a security interest qualified as a good faith purchaser.); *In re Arlco, Inc.*, 239 B.R. at 266-67 (stating that "[m]ost courts have treated a holder of a prior perfected, floating lien on inventory * * * as a good faith purchaser with rights superior to those of a reclaiming seller" and collecting cases demonstrating the majority rule); *In re Victory Markets Inc.*, 212 B.R. 738, 742 (Bankr. N.D.N.Y. 1997) (same). Another explanation is that amended "§ 546(c) codifies the subordination of a reclaiming seller's rights to those of a lender secured by a floating lien in the same goods, although § 546(c) has to date applied nonbankruptcy law to the same effect." 2005 Norton Ann. Surv. of Bankr. Law Part I § 15 (Sept. 2006).

Airlines Corp. v. Assoc. of Flight Attendants-CWA, (In re Northwest Airlines Corp.), 483 F.3d 160 (2d Cir.2007).

In addition, the limitation that the reclamation claimant's right is "subject to the prior rights of a holder of a security interest in such goods or the proceeds thereof" does not deal with the rights of other "purchasers" or "buyers" of goods whereas the U.C.C. specifically makes a seller's reclamation right "subject to the rights of a buyer in ordinary course or other good faith purchaser." If amended § 546(c) created an independent federal reclamation right that replaced state law, then in bankruptcy a reclaiming seller would conceivably have broad rights superior to those of buyers in the ordinary course of business, lien creditors or good faith purchasers other than a holder of a prior security interest. Clearly, Congress could not have intended to permit reclamation of goods that have been sold to consumers or other good faith purchasers. *See, e.g., In re Incredible Auto Sales LLC,* 2007 Bankr. LEXIS 1024 (Bankr. D.Mont.2007) ("It may be a mistake to assume that the amended § 546(c) was intended to provide an entirely new and self-contained body of reclamation law, because it fails to recognize the rights of buyers in the ordinary course, other good faith purchasers and lien creditors, who were always protected under the U.C.C. Perhaps the intent was to incorporate and expand on the U.C.C. reclamation rights, rather than to supplant them entirely, in which case some U.C.C. analysis may continue to be relevant in interpreting and applying the new § 546(c).").

Moreover, without reference to state law, it is not clear if a seller could reclaim goods already paid for, as there is no requirement that the "sold goods" be on credit terms. *Cf.* U.C.C. § 2–702(2). Further, amended § 546(c) does not provide a limitation on when the seller discovers the buyer's insolvency when the historic purpose underlying the right to reclamation was to protect the seller from the buyer's fraud with respect to insolvency. In addition, under former § 546(c), goods must be identifiable and in the possession of the debtor on the day of demand. Courts did not allow reclamation of goods that had been commingled with other goods or were not identifiable. It is unlikely that Congress intended to remove these defenses as well.

Moreover, as the reclaiming seller possesses certain rights "subject to the prior rights of a holder of a security interest in such goods" and the Bankruptcy Code otherwise gives no indication of what those "prior rights" might be, the only available referent for such "prior rights" is nonbankruptcy law. And the use of the definite article "the" to replace "any statutory or common law" indicates that "the right" already exists—particularly where there is no discussion in the legislative history that Congress intended to create a new independent right.

Finally, it is contrary to the purpose of the Bankruptcy Code to enhance the rights of one set of creditors at the expense of other creditors simply because a bankruptcy petition has been filed. *See Butner v. United States,* 440 U.S. 48, 54-55 (1979) ("Property interests are defined by state law. Unless some federal interest requires a different result, there is no reason why such interest should be analyzed differently simply because an interested party is involved in a bankruptcy proceeding.").

Based upon the foregoing, I find that the amended § 546(c) does not create a new "federal right of reclamation."

* * *

Notes and Questions

1. *Dana* has not been without its critics, but the sharpest retort has been aimed at a different part of the opinion than the portion set out above— namely, the court's conclusion, regarding the so-called "prior lien defense," that reclamation claims are valueless if they are smaller than the claims of holders of prepetition liens. *See, e.g.,* Lisa Gretchko, *Seller Beware! Is your Reclamation Claim as Strong as you Think it Is?* 22 AM. BANKR. INST. J. 20, 50 (2003).

2. Although congressional intent is unclear, what purpose could have been served by deleting the phrase "any statutory or common law right of a seller of goods," and replacing it with a reference to "the right of a seller of goods," other than divorcing reclamation under state law from reclamation in bankruptcy?

Chapter 6

==

EXECUTORY CONTRACTS AND
UNEXPIRED LEASES

A. INTRODUCTION

Section 365 of the Code provides special treatment for the debtor's executory contracts and unexpired leases (which are, after all, just a species of executory contract), carrying rights and powers not available to the debtor outside of bankruptcy. Determining when § 365 applies is important because of its special rules. To help focus you on the types of transactions that are of concern, consider the following fact patterns:

1. Debtor ordered a case of widgets from Seller that is delivered on Day 1. A case of widgets costs $500, but Debtor has not yet paid. Debtor files a bankruptcy petition on Day 10.

2. Debtor ordered a case of widgets from Seller on Day 1 and included a check for $500 along with the order. Debtor files a bankruptcy petition on Day 10 and the widgets have not yet been delivered.

3. Debtor ordered a case of widgets from Seller on Day 1, which is to be delivered and paid for on Day 15. Debtor files a bankruptcy petition on Day 10.

What are the bankruptcy consequences of each of these fact patterns? Do you see what sets an executory contract apart from other contracts?

What to do with these contracts, on which some future performance is due, is a question of considerable importance in bankruptcy. It is particularly important in reorganization cases, in which the debtor needs to retain the benefits of favorable bargains and to escape the burdens of unfavorable ones.

B. TRANSACTIONS TO WHICH § 365 APPLIES

The first question is to determine what transactions fall within the category of "executory contracts and unexpired leases." The most-cited authority on this question is an article written by Professor Vern Countryman before the Code was enacted:

VERN COUNTRYMAN, EXECUTORY CONTRACTS IN BANKRUPTCY: PART I

57 MINN. L. REV. 439, 450-52, 456-61 (1973) (most footnotes omitted).

II. WHAT IS AN EXECUTORY CONTRACT?

As Professor Williston has said, "All contracts to a greater or less extent are executory. When they cease to be so, they cease to be contracts." But that expansive meaning can hardly be given to the term as used in the Bankruptcy Act or even to the Act's occasional alternative reference to contracts "executory in whole or in part." The concept of the "executory contract" in bankruptcy should be defined in the light of the purpose for which the trustee is given the option to assume or reject. Similar to his general power to abandon or accept other property, this is an option to be exercised when it will benefit the estate. A fortiori, it should not extend to situations where the only effect of its exercise would be to prejudice other creditors of the estate.

A. Contracts Performed by the Nonbankrupt

Executory contracts, in the sense in which Professor Williston spoke, abound in a bankruptcy proceeding. One example is the contract under which the nonbankrupt party has fully rendered the performance to which the bankrupt is entitled, but which the bankrupt has performed only partially or not at all. Such a contract will give the nonbankrupt party a provable claim in the bankruptcy proceeding, whether it is liquidated or unliquidated and whether it is absolute or contingent as to liability. The trustee's option to assume or reject should not extend to such contracts. The estate has whatever benefit it can obtain from the other party's performance and the trustee's rejection would neither add to nor detract from the creditor's claim or the estate's liability. His assumption, on the other hand, would in no way benefit the estate and would only have the effect of converting the claim into a first priority expense of administration and thus of preferring it over all claims not assumed—a prerogative which the Bankruptcy Act has never been supposed to have vested in either the trustee or the court.

* * *

It seems clear, therefore, that a contract which is executory only in the sense that it provides the fully performed nonbankrupt party with a claim against the bankrupt estate is not one which may be assumed or rejected. * * * Of course, the nonbankrupt party who has fully performed may have provided an asset which comes into the bankrupt estate and which the trustee will have the option to abandon or accept, quite apart from the bankrupt's liability with respect to it. But if the trustee does accept the property, he accepts it *cum onere*, taking its burdens with its benefits, whether the burden be a liability imposed upon the owner by law solely by virtue of his ownership, a condition to full enjoyment imposed by a contract valid against the trustee, or a lien which the trustee cannot avoid. But the trustee's acceptance of such property should not amount to assumption of a contract of sale so as to elevate an unsecured obligation for the purchase price to the level of a first priority administration expense. Nor should his abandonment of the property, or even his mistaken attempt to reject the contract of sale, have any effect on a seller's unsecured claim for the price.

Of course, to speak of a contract under which the nonbankrupt party has "fully performed" is to draw an extremely fine line, one which would include among the executory contracts which the trustee can accept or reject some which should be excluded. What of the nonbankrupt building contractor who has fully performed save that he has failed to connect the water or has made a defective connection? Such a failure, even if not cured, would entitle the bankrupt to damages but would not be sufficiently material to permit him to refuse to accept the building or to excuse his performance. The trustee's rejection of such a contract would neither add to nor detract from the estate's benefits or its liabilities; his assumption of it, which likewise would not benefit the estate, should therefore not convert the contractor's claim into a first priority administration expense. Hence, a contract so nearly performed by the nonbankrupt party that failure to complete performance would not be sufficiently material to excuse performance by the bankrupt should not be treated as an executory contract in bankruptcy.

B. Contracts Performed by the Bankrupt

Another example of a contract executory in the Willistonian sense which should not be treated as an executory contract within the meaning of the Bankruptcy Act is a contract which the bankrupt has fully performed, but which the nonbankrupt party has performed only partially or not at all. The bankrupt's claim to further performance under such a contract obviously is an asset which in most instances will pass to the trustee * * *.

Since the bankrupt's claim against the other party is an asset which will pass to the trustee, it is one which the trustee can accept or abandon just as he can accept or abandon noncontractual claims. But his acceptance of the asset merely leaves the other party's liability where § 70a of the Act[a] has already transferred it, while his abandonment of it merely leaves the other party liable to the bankrupt as he was before bankruptcy.

Indeed, this is the manner in which the Act and the courts have treated such contracts when questions have arisen as to the treatment of actions on them which the bankrupt had pending at bankruptcy. Section 11c of the Act provides that the trustee may, with approval of the court, prosecute any suit commenced by the bankrupt prior to adjudication.[b] This section has been construed by the courts, which follow the statute in making no distinction between suits based on contract and others, as meaning that the trustee has three choices: (1) he may take over the bankrupt's suit; (2) he may allow the bankrupt to continue it for the benefit of the estate; or (3) he may abandon the claim to the bankrupt.

Here again, the concept of a nonexecutory contract should accommodate the contract so nearly performed by the bankrupt that his failure to complete performance would not constitute a material breach which would excuse performance by the nonbankrupt party. Rejection of such a contract by the trustee should not be treated as a material breach excusing the other party's performance. Nor should the trustee's assumption of such a contract require either that performance of the

---

[a]   Section 541 of the Code, which governs property of the estate, is the successor to § 70a of the Act. Eds.

[b]   Section 11c of the Act was not carried over into the Code. Eds.

bankrupt's obligation be completed at the expense of the estate or that the nonbankrupt party's damage claim be elevated to a first priority expense of administration.

C. Contracts Unperformed on Both Sides

Thus, by a process similar to one method of sculpting an elephant,[85] we approach a definition of executory contract within the meaning of the Bankruptcy Act: a contract under which the obligation of both the bankrupt and the other party to the contract are so far unperformed that the failure of either to complete performance would constitute a material breach excusing the performance of the other.

Such a contract, similar to the contract under which the other party has fully performed but the bankrupt has not, represents a claim against the estate. But here that claim may be reduced or totally eliminated if the trustee rejects the contract, because the other party is required to mitigate damages by an amount approximating the value of the performance he is spared by the trustee's rejection. In addition, such a contract, like the one under which the bankrupt has fully performed but the other party has not, represents an asset of the estate to the extent that it carries the unperformed obligation of the other party. But if the trustee elects to assume the contract, as when he accepts other assets to which he takes the title of the bankrupt under § 70a, he takes it *cum onere* and must render that performance which the bankrupt had contracted to perform as a condition to receiving the benefits of the contract. Whether in a given case the trustee will assume or reject depends, presumably, on his comparative appraisal of the value of the remaining performance by the other party and the cost to the estate of the unperformed obligation of the bankrupt, although the Act is silent on that point.

Notes

Undoubtedly, the Countryman test is the most widely used in determining what constitutes an executory contract. Even so, it is not the only approach. One case, *In re Jolly*, 574 F.2d 349, 351 (6th Cir.1978), *cert. denied sub nom. Still v. Chattanooga Memorial Park*, 439 U.S. 929, 99 S.Ct. 316, 58 L.Ed.2d 322 (1978), seems to call unabashedly for a result-oriented approach to the determination of executoriness:

---

[85]   Obtain a large piece of stone. Take hammer and chisel and knock off everything that doesn't look like an elephant.

> [S]uch definitions [as the Countryman test] are helpful, but do not resolve this problem. The key, it seems, to deciphering the meaning of the executory contract rejection provisions, is to work backward, proceeding from an examination of the purposes rejection is expected to accomplish. If those objectives have already been accomplished, or if they can't be accomplished through rejection, then the contract is not executory within the meaning of the Bankruptcy Act.

Id. at 351. Although *Jolly* was decided under the Act, its statement was approved in a Code case, *Martin Bros. Toolmakers, Inc. v. Industrial Development Board (In re Martin Bros. Toolmakers, Inc.),* 796 F.2d 1435, 1439 (11th Cir.1986).

Another case, *In re Booth*, 19 B.R. 53 (Bankr. D. Utah 1982), was one of the first to raise questions about the Countryman test, and remains one of the most prominent. The question in *Booth* was whether a land sales contract under which the debtor is the buyer is an executory contract. The court reviewed precedent cases, legislative history, and bankruptcy policies before concluding that a land sale contract should be treated as a secured transaction, rather than an executory contract, when the debtor is the buyer:

> [I]n the final analysis, executory contracts are measured not by a mutuality of commitments but by the nature of the parties and the goals of reorganization. A debtor as vendee is free from the constraints of § 365, and is thereby afforded flexibility in proposing a plan, but meanwhile must provide, upon request, adequate protection to vendors. A debtor as vendor may use § 365 as a springboard to rehabilitation but not at the expense of vendees. Thus, it is the consequences of applying § 365 to a party, especially in terms of benefit to the estate and the protection of creditors, not the form of contract between vendor and vendee, which controls. * * *

> The contract for deed, where debtor is vendee, benefits the estate more when viewed as a lien than as an executory contract. This is because treatment of the contract for deed as a lien enlarges the value of the estate and furthers the rehabilitation of the debtor. This treatment likewise makes adequate protection available to creditors.

* * *

> The upshot is that nondebtor vendees, by virtue of §§ 365(i) and 365(j), may receive more favorable treatment in bankruptcy than debtor vendees. And debtor vendors, because of other policies and provisions in the Code, may fare better than debtor vendees. It may be argued that this disparity in treatment is warranted because of the risk of default when debtor is vendor, or because the nondebtor, in each instance, is an innocent victim. But this argument admits that the reasons for calling a contract "executory" may have less to do

with the terms of the "paper" than with the status of the parties and their interests in light of bankruptcy policies.

Id. at 56-57, 63-64. The court in *Booth* recognized that its approach could be "criticized for being result oriented." The court, however, was undeterred: "Result-orientation, however, is endemic to the policymaking which has determined what is an executory contract and when it is rejectable within the scope of §§ 365 and 70(b) [of the Act]. Indeed, the Countryman test, which is predicated on the policy of benefit to the estate, is result oriented." *Id.* at 57, n.6.

The court's prediction has proved accurate. Professor Westbrook described *Booth* as a case that "leave[s] bankruptcy law too unbounded and too greatly unsettle[s] the commercial world that bankruptcy serves." Jay Lawrence Westbrook, *A Functional Analysis of Executory Contracts*, 74 MINN. L. REV. 227, 337 (1989). In addition, Professors Baird and Jackson cited *Booth* after asserting that "[t]oo many [judges and scholars] seem to think that a bankruptcy proceeding provides, in the main, an essentially unlimited opportunity to do what appears at the moment to be good, just or fair without regard to the reasons for having a system of bankruptcy laws in the first place." Douglas G. Baird & Thomas H. Jackson, *Corporate Reorganizations and the Treatment of Diverse Ownership Interests: A Comment On Adequate Protection of Secured Creditors in Bankruptcy,* 51 U. CHI. L. REV. 97, 97 (1984).

Courts have struggled long and hard to determine whether a particular transaction constitutes a lease or a disguised security interest. This question is important in bankruptcy as well as out. The governing law is UCC § 1–203 (formerly § 1–201(37)), which focuses on the functional characteristics of a transaction. It looks particularly at whether an economically meaningful residual remains at the end of the lease term.

If a transaction is a disguised security interest rather than a lease, the nondebtor party is a secured creditor. If that party failed to perfect its security interest, then it will be rendered an unsecured creditor (after the trustee finishes wielding the avoiding powers) rather than a party to an executory contract entitled to performance according to the contract terms. That's a long way to fall.

Even if the nondebtor party is at no risk of suffering from an exercise of the trustee's avoiding powers, the question whether the transaction created a lease or a secured interest remains a critically important one. The next case reviews the governing law and explains the consequences of that determination.

UNITED AIRLINES, INC. v. HSBC BANK USA, N.A.

United States Court of Appeals, Seventh Circuit, 2005.
416 F.3d 609, *cert. denied sub nom. HSBC Bank USA v. United Air Lines, Inc.*,
547 U.S. 1003, 126 S.Ct. 1465, 164 L.Ed.2d 247 (2006).

EASTERBROOK, Circuit Judge.

What is a "lease" in federal bankruptcy law? Businesses that do not pay up front for assets may acquire them via unsecured debt, secured debt, or lease; in each event the business pays over time. Similar economic function implies the ability to draft leases that work like security agreements, and secured loans that work like leases. Yet the Bankruptcy Code of 1978 distinguishes among these devices. A lessee must either assume the lease and fully perform all of its obligations, or surrender the property. § 365. A borrower that has given security, by contrast, may retain the property without paying the full agreed price. The borrower must pay enough to give the lender the economic value of the security interest; if this is less than the balance due on the loan, the difference is an unsecured debt. See § 506(a) and § 1129(b)(2)(A). There are other ways in which the Code treats leases differently from security interests, but they don't matter to today's dispute.

During the 1990s United Air Lines entered into complex transactions to obtain money to build or improve premises at four airports— San Francisco, Los Angeles, Denver, and John F. Kennedy in New York. For each airport, a public body issued bonds that, because of the issuer's status as a unit of state government, paid interest that is free of federal taxation. The public bodies turned this money over to United against its promise to retire the bonds and reimburse administrative costs. At each airport, United entered into a lease giving the body that had issued the bonds the right to evict United from operational facilities if it did not pay.

When United entered bankruptcy in 2002, however, it took the position that none of these transactions is a "lease" for purposes of § 365. United proposed to treat each transaction as a secured loan, so that it could continue using the airport facilities while paying only a fraction of the promised "rent." Chief Bankruptcy Judge Wedoff concluded that the word "lease" in § 365—a term not defined anywhere in the Bankruptcy Code—includes "true leases" but not transactions where the form of a lease is used but the substance is that of a security interest. Applying this approach as a matter of federal law, Judge Wedoff concluded that the Denver transaction is a true lease but that the other three are not. This meant that United had to cure the default and resume full payments on its Denver deal but could reduce its payments on the other transactions and treat the difference as unsecured debt.

Everyone appealed. The district judge issued four opinions, one for each airport, and held that all four transactions are "true leases." Relying principally on *Butner v. United States*, 440 U.S. 48 (1979), and *In re Powers*, 983 F.2d 88 (7th Cir.1993), Judge Darrah first concluded that state rather than federal law controls the distinction between security interests and leases. Then, applying California, Colorado, and New York law, he held that each transaction must be treated as a "lease." * * * The San Francisco dispute has been fully briefed; the other appeals are being held for the disposition of this one. * * *

Since 1973 United has been the lessee of 128 acres, used for a maintenance base, at San Francisco International Airport. The lease will end in 2013 unless the parties negotiate an extension; rent depends on an independent party's estimate of the property's market value. In 1997 the California Statewide Communities Development Authority (CSCDA) issued $155 million in bonds for United's benefit. United received the proceeds for use in improving its facilities at the Airport—though not at the maintenance base. The transaction was accomplished through four documents.

The sublease. United subleases 20 acres of the 128-acre maintenance base to the CSCDA for 36 years. This term matches the debt-repayment schedule rather than United's lease with the Airport. The total rent CSCDA pays is $1.

The leaseback. The CSCDA leases the 20 acres back to United for a rent (paid to HBSC Bank as the Indenture Trustee) equal to interest on the bonds plus an administrative fee. The lease has a $155 million balloon payment in 2033 to retire the principal. United may postpone final payment until 2038; if it does, the sublease also is extended. United also is entitled to prepay; if it does, the sublease and leaseback terminate. If United does not pay as agreed, the CSCDA may evict it from the 20 acres. The leaseback includes a "hell or high water" clause: United must pay the promised rent even if its lease from the Airport ends before 2033, the property is submerged in an earthquake (the Airport abuts San Francisco Bay), or some other physical or legal event deprives United of the use or economic benefit of the maintenance base.

The trust indenture. The CSCDA issues the bonds, turns the $155 million over to United against the promises made in the sublease, and arranges for the Trustee to receive United's payments for distribution to the bondholders. The bonds are without recourse against the CSCDA.

The guaranty. United commits its corporate treasury to repayment of the bonds.

That the sublease and leaseback have the form of "leases" is unquestioned. But does § 365 use form, or substance, to distinguish "leases" from secured credit?

Although the statute does not answer that question in so many words, every appellate court that has considered the issue holds, and the parties agree, that substance controls and that only a "true lease" counts as a "lease" under § 365. We'll return to what a "true lease" might be; that term is no more self-defining than the bare word "lease." Before fleshing out the definition, we explain why we agree with these decisions, because the reasons for preferring substance over form affect *which* substantive features of the transactions matter.

Whether the word "lease" in a federal statute has a formal or a substantive connotation is a question of federal law; it could not be otherwise. (Whether federal law incorporates state law to answer the questions that result from this choice is a different issue, to which we turn later). The Bankruptcy Code specifies different consequences for leases and secured loans. If these were formally distinct—in the way that mergers and asset sales in corporate law are distinct—then the statutory reference might best be understood as adopting the established forms. But "lease" is a label rather than a form. A transaction by which A sells a widget to B in exchange for periodic payments, with B to own the asset after the last payment, could be structured as an installment sale, a loan secured by the asset, or a lease, with only a few changes in verbiage and none in substance. It is unlikely that the Code makes big economic effects turn on the parties' choice of language rather than the substance of their transaction; why bother to distinguish transactions if these distinctions can be obliterated at the drafters' will?

Many provisions in the Code, particularly those that deal with the treatment of secured credit, are designed to distinguish financial from economic distress. A firm that cannot meet its debts as they come due, but has a positive cash flow from current operations, is in financial but not economic distress. It is carrying too much debt, which can be written down in a reorganization. A firm with a negative cash flow, by contrast, is in economic distress, and liquidation may be the best option. In order to distinguish financial from economic distress, the Code effectively treats the date on which the bankruptcy begins as the creation of a new firm, unburdened by the debts of its predecessor. The new firm must cover all new expenses, while debt attributable to former operations is adjusted. Section 365, which deals with leases, classifies payments for retaining airplanes and occupying business premises as new expenses, just like payments for labor and jet fuel. The rules for credit, by contrast, treat debt service as an "old" expense to be adjusted to deal with financial distress.

This works nicely when rent under a lease really *does* pay for new inputs: each monthly payment on an airplane lease covers another month's use of a productive asset, just as payments for jet fuel do. But "rent" that represents the cost of funds for capital assets or past operations rather than ongoing inputs into production has the quality of debt, and to require such obligations to be assumed under § 365 to retain an asset would permit financial distress from past operations to shut down a firm that has a positive cash flow from current operations. * * * To separate financial from economic distress it would be essential to separate the loan components of that "lease" from the current-consumption components. The cost of capital hired before the bankruptcy could be written down while the expenses of current operations continued to be met.

When Congress enacted the Bankruptcy Code in 1978, the legal system afforded rules that facilitated the disentangling of credit and consumption components of leases. Since 1939 this had been routine in tax law. During the 1940s and 1950s much state law on the subject was summed up and codified in the Uniform Commercial Code. Section 1–201(37) of the 1958 Official Text separates credit components, in which the asset serves as security, from consumption components this way:

Unless a lease * * * is intended as security, reservation of title thereunder is not a "security interest" * * * . Whether a lease is intended as security is to be determined by the facts of each case; however, (a) the inclusion of an option to purchase does not of itself make the lease one intended for security, and (b) an agreement that upon compliance with the terms of the lease the lessee shall become or has the option to become the owner of the property for no additional consideration or for a nominal consideration does make the lease one intended for security.[c]

A lease in which the consumption component dominates often is called a "true lease," while one in which the asset serves as security for an extension of credit is treated as a security agreement governed by the UCC's Article 9.

No legally sophisticated person writing in 1978 could have thought that the word "lease" in a text that distinguishes between current consumption (which must be paid for in full) and secured debt (which may be written down to ease financial distress) means any transaction in the form of a lease. The need to look through form to substance would be apparent not only from the structure of the statute but also from the fact that many of the leased assets would be covered directly by the UCC. Section 365 in particular deals with leases of both personal and real property; it would not be sensible to read the same word as referring to substance when dealing with personal property and form when dealing with real property. The statute thus must refer to substance throughout § 365. Nothing else respects both the structure of the Bankruptcy Code and the way the legal community understood the distinction between leases and security agreements in the 1970s.

Because the parties have made so much of the legislative history, we add that the understanding that § 365 deals with substance rather than form is reflected in many of the documents that precede the Code's enactment. The passage to which the litigants pay the most attention reads:

> The phrase "lease of real property" applies only to a "true" or "bona fide" lease and does not apply to financing leases of real property or interests therein, or to leases of such property which are intended as security.

> In a true lease of real property, the lessor retains all risk and benefits as to the value of the real estate at the termination of the lease * * * .

> Whether a "lease" is [a] true or bona fide lease or, in the alternative, a financing "lease" or a lease intended as security, depends upon the circumstances of each case. The distinction between a true lease and a financing transaction is based upon

---

[c] Equivalent language is currently found in UCC § 1–203. Eds.

the economic substance of the transaction and not, for example, upon the locus of title, the form of the transaction or the fact that the transaction is denominated as a "lease." The fact that the lessee, upon compliance with the terms of the lease, becomes or has the option to become the owner of the leased property for no additional consideration or for nominal consideration indicates that the transaction is a financing lease or lease intended as security. In such cases, the lessor has no substantial interest in the leased property at the expiration of the lease term. In addition, the fact that the lessee assumes and discharges substantially all the risks and obligations ordinarily attributed to the outright ownership of the property is more indicative of a financing transaction than of a true lease. The rental payments in such cases are in substance payments of principal and interest either on a loan secured by the leased real property or on the purchase of the leased real property.

S. Rep. No. 989, 95th Cong., 2d Sess. 64 (1978). This passage is interesting because it illustrates how the legal community thought in 1978 about the roles of form versus substance in dealing with a word such as "lease." It would be a mistake to find rules of decision in this unenacted passage, but it does show that Congress shared the legal community's understanding that some transactions with the form of a lease are best treated as security agreements.

     To say that substance prevails over form as a matter of federal law is not to resolve all issues of detail—or for that matter to imply that federal law supplies the details. Which *aspects* of substance matter? The Senate Report does not supply the answer. * * * Reports are not enacted and do not create rules independent of the text in the United States Code. Anyway, this report sounds like a reminder to be sensible rather than a formulary.

     Because nothing in the Bankruptcy Code says which economic features of a transaction have what consequences, we turn to state law. All of the states have devoted substantial efforts to differentiating leases from secured credit in commercial and banking law. Leases are state-law instruments, after all, and the norm in bankruptcy law is that contracts (of which leases are a species) and property rights in general have the same force they would have in state court, unless the Code overrides the state entitlement. See *Butner v. United States*, 440 U.S. 48 (1979). A state law that identified a "lease" in a formal rather than a functional manner would conflict with the Code, because it would disrupt the federal system of separating financial from economic distress; a state approach that gives a little more or a little less weight to one of several "factors" does not conflict with any federal rule, because there is none with which it *could* conflict.

United contends that the second and ninth circuits have held that federal law supplies the definition of a "lease" in addition to establishing a functional approach to the inquiry. Perhaps some language in *In re PCH Associates*, 804 F.2d 193 (2d Cir.1986), and *In re Moreggia & Sons, Inc.*, 852 F.2d 1179 (9th Cir.1988), could be read that way, though we think it more likely that both courts were concerned with the first question (whether the word "lease" in § 365 has a formal or functional scope), which is a matter of federal law, than with the second— what body of law identifies a "true lease" under the functional approach? Neither opinion cites *Butner* or any of the Supreme Court's other decisions specifying that state law must be used whenever possible to define the interests on which the Code operates. If either the second or the ninth circuits believes that federal law answers *all* questions concerning the operation of § 365, then we disagree; for the reasons we have given, the third circuit (which in *In re Continental Airlines, Inc.*, 932 F.2d 282 (3d Cir. 1991), and *Duke Energy Royal, LLC v. Pillowtex Corp. (In re Pillowtex, Inc.)*, 349 F.3d 711 (3d Cir. 2003), used state definitions) got this right. Indeed, we held exactly this in *Powers*, a decision under § 365 that the bankruptcy judge did not mention. *Powers* involves the choice between lease and installment sales contract for personal property; we cannot imagine any reason why state law would define a "true lease" for personal property while federal law would supply the definition for real property.

So what does California law provide? The district judge thought that California allows form to control, and because United and the CSCDA chose the form of a lease United is stuck with that characterization under § 365. If indeed California identifies leases in such a mechanical fashion, then its law must yield, but we do not understand it to distinguish leases from secured credit in this way. * * *

Like the district judge, the parties in this court seek to find California's law in the decisions of federal bankruptcy judges sitting in California, and they debate the significance of what these judges have said about the subject. Yet federal judges are not the source of state law or even its oracles. To find state law we must examine California's statute books and the decisions of its judiciary. California has enacted the UCC; there can be no doubt that it uses a functional approach to separating leases from secured credit with respect to personal property. California takes a similar approach for real property as a matter of common law. *Burr v. Capital Reserve Corp.*, 71 Cal.2d 983, 458 P.2d 185, 80 Cal.Rptr. 345 (1969), and *Beeler v. American Trust Co.*, 24 Cal.2d 1, 147 P.2d 583 (1944), are especially revealing.

Beeler arose from a sale and leaseback of real property. When the tenant stopped paying, the court had to decide whether he could be evicted under landlord-tenant law, with the landlord retaining the fee title to the property, or whether instead the tenant retained an equity of redemption under the law of mortgage loans, so that any payments in excess of the market rental value would redound to the tenant's benefit. The Supreme Court of California characterized the transaction as an equitable mortgage despite the fact that the papers cast it as an absolute deed plus a lease. It relied not only on the fact that the landlord was a financial institution but also on the fact that the rent was equal to the sum needed to pay off a loan and the fact that the lessee would become an owner after some years. (This is the UCC's *per se* rule: If the lessee has an option to acquire ownership at the end of the term for no or a nominal payment, then the transaction must be treated as secured credit.) The yearly rent was $3,000, substantially less than the going rate for similar property but exactly equal to the amount needed to amortize a $60,000 extension of credit—and the $60,000 for which the property had been "sold" initially was less than the market price of equivalent real estate. The state court thought that this deal had all the hallmarks of a mortgage loan except the form—and the form had to yield. This was not a "true lease" as the court saw it.

Burr posed the question whether a lease of personal property should be treated as a loan; the answer mattered because at the time California's usury law set a 10% maximum interest rate on loans, but there was no price control on leases. Burr needed money to expand his business. He obtained cash by selling some of the existing business's property to a bank and immediately leasing it back at a rental designed to amortize the extension of credit. The Supreme Court of California held that this form must be pierced to get at the substance: Burr had borrowed money on security of the property subject to the lease, and as the interest rate in one of the parties' three transactions exceeded 10% the bank could not collect the full agreed payment.

* * *

The transaction between United and the CSCDA is not a "true lease" under California law. (i) The "rent" is measured not by the market value of 20 acres within the maintenance base but by the amount United borrowed. The hell or high water clause demonstrates the lack of connection between the maintenance base's rental value and

United's financial obligation. (ii) At the end of the lease, the CSCDA has no remaining interest. The CSCDA stresses that United will not "own" anything as of 2033; it still would be the Airport's tenant. But its full tenancy interest reverts to it for no additional charge. Reversion without additional payment is the UCC's *per se* rule for identifying secured credit. (iii) The balloon payment has no parallel in a true lease, though it is a common feature of secured credit. (iv) If United prepays, the lease and sublease terminate immediately; in a true lease, by contrast, prepayment would secure the tenant's right to occupy the property for an additional period. The parties have not cited *any* case from *any* state deeming an arrangement of this kind to be a "true lease."

We do not doubt that many financing devices are true leases; the lessor owns the property and thus finances its acquisition, relieving the lessee of the need to raise funds itself, and net leases may measure rent by the lessor's financial commitments. United acquired many of its airplanes that way. But in such a transaction the lessee acquires an asset; from the lessee's perspective, it is engaged in securing assets with current value, and it can escape the rental obligation by surrendering the asset. United did not obtain the maintenance base from CSCDA; it already had the base under its lease from the Airport, and could not end the obligation to the CSCDA by vacating the maintenance base. What United did was use an asset (its leasehold interest in the maintenance base) to secure an extension of credit, just as the business did in *Burr*, and as in *Beeler* it agreed to pay "rent" equal to the price of that credit rather than any element of value in the "leased" premises.

* * *

The transaction between United and the CSCDA at San Francisco Airport is a secured loan and not a lease for the purpose of § 365. The judgment of the district court is reversed, and the case is remanded for further proceedings consistent with this opinion.

Notes and Questions

1. "Recharacterization" of a transaction nominally a lease into a secured transaction has the effect of denying the protections of § 365 to the nondebtor. A great many cases have dealt with the recharacterization of equipment leases, given the application of UCC Article 9 to personal property. *United Airlines*, however, is one of the few cases to have addressed recharacterization in a real property context. Does it make sense to follow the personal property approach in a real property context?

2. As the court indicated, the San Francisco case was tried first and was expected to serve as authority for the transactions in other cities. When

the Los Angeles transaction was tried, the court also found it to be a financing agreement. *United Air Lines, Inc. v. U.S. Bank Nat'l Assoc., Inc.*, 447 F.3d 504 (7th Cir.2006). The Denver transaction came out differently, however, largely because the parties had "cemented their deal into one document." *United Air Lines, Inc. v. HSBC Bank USA*, 453 F.3d 463, 467 (7th Cir.2006). The leasehold was connected with the bond transaction to improve the premises, and that "cemented" contract could not be severed under state law.

3. Judge Easterbrook's "old firm/new firm" approach in *United Airlines* echoed one of his earlier opinions, *Boston & Maine Corp. v. Chicago Pacific Corp.*, 785 F.2d 562 (7th Cir.1986): "Bankruptcy draws a line between the existing claims to a firm's assets and newly-arising claims. * * * If there are not enough assets to go around, some [existing] claims may be written down or extinguished. The ongoing operations of the business are treated entirely differently; new claims are paid in full as they arise. It is as if the bankruptcy process creates two separate firms—the pre-bankruptcy firm that pays off old claims against pre-bankruptcy assets, and the post-bankruptcy firm that acts as a brand new venture." *Id.* at 565.

Is that the right approach in a positive sense? That approach seems to sit uneasily with the structure of § 365, given that the Code does not in fact distinguish past-due lease payments from current and future obligations. Rather, the Code requires the trustee to pay all of those obligations, in full, in order to assume the lease. In addition, Judge Easterbrook's analytical approach is inconsistent with the Supreme Court's statements in *NLRB v. Bildisco & Bildisco*, 465 U.S. 513, 104 S.Ct. 1188; 79 L.Ed.2d 482 (1984): "Much effort has been expended by the parties on the question of whether the debtor is more properly characterized as an 'alter ego' or a 'successor employer' of the prebankruptcy debtor, as those terms have been used in our labor decisions. We see no profit in an exhaustive effort to identify which, if either, of these terms represents the closest analogy to the debtor-in-possession. Obviously if the latter were a wholly 'new entity,' it would be unnecessary for the Bankruptcy Code to allow it to reject executory contracts, since it would not be bound by such contracts in the first place. For our purposes, it is sensible to view the debtor-in-possession as the same 'entity' which existed before the filing of the bankruptcy petition, but empowered by virtue of the Bankruptcy Code to deal with its contracts and property in a manner it could not have employed absent the bankruptcy filing." *Id.* at 527-28.

Even if Judge Easterbrook's old firm/new firm analysis is flawed in a positive sense, is it nonetheless normatively persuasive?

C. ASSUMPTION AND ASSIGNMENT

1. GENERAL RULES

Section 365 gives a trustee (or, often, a debtor-in-possession) three choices regarding an executory contract or lease—to assume and retain, to assume and assign, or to reject. Assumption turns the debtor's obligations under the agreement into obligations of the estate, entitled to administrative expense priority. Rejection of the agreement is treated as a breach of contract, and the nondebtor party acquires a claim for damages that is treated as if it arose before the petition. We will return to rejection in a moment, after we explore the meaning and consequences of assumption, as well as of assignment.

As you have already seen, if a contract is assumed it is assumed *cum onere*—with all its benefits and burdens. Thus, a debtor should assume only those executory contracts on which the benefits outweigh the burdens. Remember, a favorable contract can be assumed even if the debtor does not itself have any use for the benefits of the deal (because, for example, it is liquidating or streamlining its business in order to reorganize). In such a case, the debtor will realize the benefits of the favorable deal by assigning the contract to another party. For example, if the price of premises has risen above the lease price, the debtor will assume the lease and sell (assign) it at the higher market rate to a third party; the nondebtor lessor will receive the lease price and the debtor will retain the appreciation.

Subsections (a) and (b) of § 365 set out the requirements for assumption. Section 365(f)(2)(A) makes assumption a prerequisite for assignment. Read §§ 365(a) and (b) and solve the following Problems.

Problems

1. Debtor, Inc. filed a Chapter 11 petition on July 15 and wants to assume the lease of the premises on which its retail store is located. Debtor, however, has not paid any rent since April. Is the arrearage an impediment to assumption of the lease?

2. Debtor, Inc.'s lease contains a so-called "ipso facto" clause, which provides that the filing of bankruptcy is a default under the lease that terminates the lease automatically. Debtor filed bankruptcy and sought to assume the lease. Lessor argued that no lease existed because of the termination provision. Can Debtor assume?

3. Debtor operated an automobile dealership on leased premises. Both the franchise agreement and the lease had seven-day "going dark" clauses—*i.e.*, provisions permitting termination for failure to operate the business for a stated period. Debtor encountered such serious financial problems that the dealership closed for a couple of weeks, but Debtor then filed a Chapter 11 petition in an effort to reopen and resurrect the business. Debtor sought to assume both the lease and the franchise agreement. The lessor and the franchisor argued that Debtor had committed noncurable

defaults and thus could not meet the requirements for assumption. Debtor countered that such a default need not be cured under § 365(b). What result?

— Ask on Monday!

4. Gardinier, Inc. contracted to sell land for over $5 million and to pay a 10% commission for brokerage services to the real estate agent who located the buyer. After a buyer was located, Gardinier filed a Chapter 11 petition and sought to assume the contract. Some of Gardinier's creditors objected to payment of the brokerage fee. If Gardinier assumes the contract, must it pay the fee? See *Byrd v. Gardinier, Inc. (In re Gardinier, Inc.)*, 831 F.2d 974 (11th Cir.1987), *cert. denied*, 488 U.S. 853, 109 S.Ct. 140, 102 L.Ed.2d 112 (1988).

One of the requirements for assumption is that the debtor give "adequate assurance of future performance." § 365(b)(1)(C). Similarly, a requirement for assignment is that the nondebtor party get "adequate assurance of future performance by the assignee." § 365(f)(2)(B). Courts look to the same factors, whether adequate assurance is of the debtor's or of an assignee's future performance. The following case deals with adequate assurance when the assignee will violate a use provision in a lease.

MATTER OF U.L. RADIO CORP.

United States Bankruptcy Court, Southern District of New York, 1982.
19 B.R. 537.

JOHN J. GALGAY, Bankruptcy Judge.

Debtor, U.L. Radio Corp., has moved for an order, pursuant to Bankruptcy Code § 365(f), authorizing it to assume its lease ("Lease") with Jemrock Realty Company ("Jemrock"), the landlord, and authorizing U.L. Radio to assign the Lease to Just Heaven Restaurant, Ltd. ("Just Heaven"). U.L. Radio operates the leasehold as a television sales and service store. Just Heaven, the prospective assignee, will operate the premises as a small bistro. Jemrock opposes such an assignment, citing a use clause in the Lease which provides that the lessee shall use the premises only for television service and sale of electrical appliances. Jemrock asserts that the assignment of the Lease to Just Heaven would unlawfully modify the Lease by violating the use clause. Such modification, Jemrock avers, is not permitted under § 365 without the landlord's consent, which consent Jemrock withholds.

* * * The Court grants debtor's motion to assume and assign the Lease to Just Heaven.

I. BACKGROUND

On September 17, 1979, the debtor entered into the Lease with Jemrock for a store located at 2656 Broadway, New York, New York. The store is located in a building which is also occupied by a grocery store, a Chinese restaurant, a liquor store, and 170 apartments. The term of the Lease is for ten years. The rent required to be paid is as follows: $9600 per year from November 1, 1979, to October 31, 1982; $10,800 from November 1, 1982, to October 31, 1985; and $12,000 from November 1, 1985 to October 31, 1989. Paragraph 43 of the Rider to the Lease provides that the tenant may assign the Lease with the written consent of the Landlord, which consent is not to be unreasonably withheld.

On May 20, 1981, the debtor filed an original petition under Chapter 11 of the Bankruptcy Code and continues to operate its business as debtor in possession. No creditors' committee has been formed. The debtor intends to propose a liquidation plan of reorganization. The debtor is current in the payment of rent and related charges required by the terms of the Lease and is not in default of any of the Lease terms.

In furtherance of its intention to liquidate all of its assets and to propose a plan of reorganization, the debtor, subject to the approval of this Court, entered into an assignment of the Lease to Just Heaven. The proposed assignment provides, *inter alia*, that Just Heaven will pay to the Debtor as consideration for the assignment as follows: for the period commencing three months after this Court's approval of the assignment to October 31, 1988, the sum of $2000 per month. Such payments will fund a plan paying unsecured creditors 100 percent of their claims. Rockwell International, the largest creditor, recommends the assignment.

The president of Just Heaven has executed a personal guarantee for the payment of rent in favor of the landlord for the first two years of the assignment, together with a statement that her net worth exceeds $50,000.

The Lease provides in paragraph 45 of the rider to the Lease that "any noise emanating from said premises shall be deemed a breach of the terms and conditions of this Lease." Just Heaven has allocated

$20,000 for construction, including soundproofing. David Humpal St. James, Vice President and Secretary as well as a director and a share-holder of Just Heaven, is a noted interior designer including the design of commercial restaurants. His design work has involved sound-proofing.

II. ISSUES

Two issues confront this Court:

(1) Have the provisions of § 365, regarding assumption and assignment of leases, been satisfied?

(2) Can deviation from a use clause prevent the assignment of a lease, when the assumption and assignment otherwise comport with the requirements of § 365?

III. ASSUMPTION AND ASSIGNMENT UNDER § 365

Code § 365 governs the assumption and assignment of execu-tory contracts, providing broad authority to a trustee or debtor in pos-session to assume and assign an unexpired lease. The aim of this statutory authority to assume a lease is to "assist in the debtor's rehabi-litation or liquidation." H.R. Rep. No. 95–595 at 348, *reprinted in* 1978 U.S.C.C.A.N. at 6304.

Assignment of a lease, which is at issue here, must comply with § 365(f) * * *.

Subsection (f)(1) "partially invalidates restrictions on assign-ment of contracts or leases by the trustee to a third party." H.R. Rep. No. 95–595 at 349, *reprinted in* 1978 U.S.C.C.A.N. at 6305. Subsec-tion (f)(2) "imposes two restrictions on assignment by the trustee: (1) he must first assume the contract or lease, subject to all the restrictions found in the section; and (2) adequate assurance of future performance must be provided to the other contracting party." *Id.* at 349, *reprinted in* 1978 U.S.C.C.A.N. at 6305.[2] Finally, subsection (f)(3) "invalidates contractual provisions that permit termination or modification in the

---

[2]   Code § 365(f) does not state which party must provide assurance. However, since Code § 365(k) relieves the debtor-assignor of liability under the lease after assignment, it is sensible that the assignee must provide the assurance of performance.

event of an assignment, as contrary to the policy of this subsection." *Id.* at 349, *reprinted in* 1978 U.S.C.C.A.N. at 6305.

A. Requirements of Assumption

The first requirement of assignment under § 365(f)(2) is proper assumption under § 365. § 365(f)(2)(A). The broad authority of a trustee or debtor in possession to assume is limited in Code § 365 by sub-sections (b), (c), and (d).

Section[s] 365(b)(1) and (2) prescribe conditions to assumption of a lease if a default has occurred. "Subsection (b) requires the [debtor] to cure any default in the * * * lease and to provide adequate assurance of future performance * * * before he may assume." H.R. Rep. No. 95–595 at 347, *reprinted in* 1978 U.S.C.C.A.N. at 6304. No default exists under the Lease before this Court; therefore, the subsection (b) requirements for assignment are not applicable.

Section 365(c) prohibits a debtor from assuming a lease if applicable nonbankruptcy law "independent of any language in the contract or Lease itself" excuses the other party from giving performance to or receiving performance from someone other than the debtor. H.R. Rep. No. 95–595 at 348, *reprinted in* 1978 U.S.C.C.A.N. at 6304. Such "nondelegable" and, therefore, nonassumable contracts and leases include those for unique personal services, as well as those to extend credit, to make loans, and to issue securities. The Lease before this Court does not fall under the prohibition of § 365(c).

Section 365(d) sets time limits on the assumption of unexpired leases. The time requirements of subsection (d) have been met and are not at issue.

B. Adequate Assurance of Future Performance

The second requirement of assignment under § 365(f)(2) is adequate assurance of future performance. § 365(f)(2)(B). Adequate assurance also appears in § 365(b) as a requirement of assumption if an executory contract is in default. § 365(b)(1)(C). The phrase "adequate assurance of future performance" is not found in the Bankruptcy Act.

Adequate assurance is not defined in § 365(f) nor in the legislative history of § 365(f), but "[t]he definition should generally be the same as in § 365(b)." Fogel, *Executory Contracts and Unexpired Leases in the Bankruptcy Code*, 64 MINN. L. REV. 341, 362 (1980). In the legislative history of § 365(b), Congress while discussing assumption under § 365(b) and the bankruptcy clause under § 365(f), provided this explanation of adequate assurance:

> If a trustee is to assume a contract or lease, the courts will have to insure that the trustee's performance under the contract or lease gives the other contracting party the full benefit of the bargain.

H.R. Rep. No. 95–595 at 348, *reprinted in* 1978 U.S.C.C.A.N. at 6304-05.

Beyond equating adequate assurance with the full benefit of the bargain, Congress offers no definition of adequate assurance except in the case of real property leases in shopping centers. The Lease at issue here is not located in a shopping center. Congress described a shopping center as "often a carefully planned enterprise, and though it consists of numerous individual tenants, the center is planned as a single unit, often subject to a master lease or financing agreement." *Id.* at 348, *reprinted in* 1978 U.S.C.C.A.N. at 6305. The building in which U.L. Radio is located is primarily a residential apartment building, with a liquor store, a grocery store, a restaurant, and U.L. Radio on the first floor. Thus the specific provisions of adequate assurance in the shopping center case do not apply to the assignment at issue here.

Apart from shopping center leases, Congress "entrusted the courts with the definition of adequate assurance of the performance of contracts and other leases." Fogel, *Executory Contracts* at 359. Adequate assurance of future performance are not words of art, but are to be given practical, pragmatic construction. What constitutes "adequate assurance" is to be determined by factual conditions. The broad authorization of the trustee or debtor to assume or assign unexpired leases, notwithstanding anti-assignment or bankruptcy clauses, prompted the admonition from Congress that the courts must "be sensitive to the rights of the nondebtor party to * * * unexpired leases." H.R. Rep. No. 95–595 at 348, *reprinted in* 1978 U.S.C.C.A.N. at 6304.

The phrase "adequate assurance of future performance" was adopted from Uniform Commercial Code § 2–609. U.C.C. § 2–609 provides that a party with reasonable grounds for insecurity regarding another party's performance may demand "adequate assurance." Official Comment 4 to § 2–609 * * * indicates that "adequate assurance" focuses on the financial condition of a contracting party and his ability to meet his financial obligations. Regarding adequate assurance under an assignment pursuant to § 365(f)(2), the Court in *In re Lafayette Radio Electronics* stated, "[T]he Court's primary focus will be on the ability of [the assignee] to comply with the financial obligations under the agreement." 9 B.R. 993, 998 (Bankr. E.D.N.Y.1981).[6]

In *In re Pin Oaks Apartments*, 7 B.R. 364 (Bankr. S.D.Tex. 1980), the Court found that changes in financial provisions of a lease, a percentage rental clause and a sublease provision which protected that rental clause, precluded a finding that adequate assurance had been provided because of the drastic effect the changes would have on rentals received.

Thus, the primary focus of adequate assurance is the assignee's ability to satisfy financial obligations under the lease. In this case, the president of the assignee has executed a personal guarantee of the payment of rent in favor of the landlord for the first two years of the assignment, together with a statement that her net worth exceeds $50,000. The assignee has budgeted $20,000 for construction, enhancing the chances of success of the assignee's enterprise. The assignee will have operating capital of an additional $30,000. Upon these facts, the Court rules that adequate assurance of future financial performance has been provided by the assignee.

IV. USE CLAUSE

However, adequate assurance of future financial performance is not the complete statutory requirement; adequate assurance of future performance is. The financial capability of an assignee may be sufficient for a finding of adequate assurance under an executory sales contract or a similar commercial transaction. In a landlord-tenant relationship, more than an assignee's ability to comply with the financial provisions of a lease may be required. More particularly, will compliance with a use clause be required in order to provide adequate assurance?

Congress indicates that adequate assurance will give the landlord the full benefit of his bargain. H.R. Rep. No. 95–595 at 348. In its case-by-case determination of those factors, beyond financial assurance,

---

[6] The *Lafayette Radio* Court found that the agreement in that case was a sublease not an assignment. Thus, the Court's inquiry was the debtor's ability to fulfill the financial obligations of the lease. Nonetheless, *financial* wherewithal is the key component of adequate assurance.

which constitute the landlord's bargain, the Court will generally consider the provisions of the lease to be assigned.

However, it is equally clear that, by requiring provision of adequate assurance under § 365, i.e., "the lessor's receipt of the 'full benefit of his bargain'," Congress did not require the Court to assure "literal fulfillment by the lessee of each and every term of the bargain." Simpson, *Leases and the Bankruptcy Code: The Protean Concept of Adequate Assurance of Future Performance* at 35 (unpublished draft in Bankruptcy Court, S.D.N.Y.).[d] Section 365, by its own terms, empowers the court to render unenforceable bankruptcy clauses and anti-assignment clauses which permit modification or termination of a lease for filing in bankruptcy or assignment of the lease. § 365(e), (f)(3). Section 365(k) relieves the estate of liability for future breaches of a lease after assignment, notwithstanding lease provisions to the contrary.

The Court in *In re Pin Oaks Apartments* argued that court authority to abrogate lease provisions extends only to those provisions expressly stated by Congress:

> If Congress intended to give this Court or the trustee the power to abrogate any contractual rights between a debtor and nondebtor contracting party other than anti-assignment and "ipso facto" [*i.e.* bankruptcy] clauses, it would have expressly done so.

7 B.R. at 367.

Such a narrow view of court authority is not supported by the statute or the legislative history. First, such a narrow view would frustrate the express policy of Congress favoring assignment. Under the *Pin Oaks* reasoning, lessors could employ very specific use clauses to prevent assignment and thus circumvent the Code. Section 365(f), in broad language, empowers the Court to authorize assignment of an unexpired lease and invalidate any lease provision which would terminate or modify the lease because of the assignment of that lease. § 365(f)(1), (3). Any lease provision, not merely one entitled "anti-assignment clause," would be subject to the court's scrutiny regarding its anti-assignment effect. The court could render unenforceable any provision whose sole effect is to restrict assignment, "as contrary to the policy of [subsection (f)(3)]." H.R. Rep. No. 95–595 at 349.

---

[d]   This article was published at 56 AM. BANKR. L.J. 233 (1982). Eds.

Further, when Congress intended that all terms and provisions of an agreement remain unaltered, it expressly stated such an intent. Section 1124 sets down stringent requirements to define unimpaired claims, requiring the cure of defaults and the unaltered maintenance of legal, equitable, and contractual rights. § 1124(2)(D). As one commentator points out, these expressed, stringent requirements for unimpaired claims differ from the requirement that Congress mandated under § 365—mere provision of adequate assurance. Simpson, *Leases* at 40–41. Under both §§ 1124 and 365, Congress expressly stated the requirements. Under § 365, literal compliance with all lease terms was not required. Even under the tightly drawn definition of adequate assurance in the shopping center case, Congress did not envision literal compliance with all lease provisions; insubstantial disruptions in, *inter alia*, tenant mix and insubstantial breaches in other leases or agreements were contemplated and allowed. § 365(b)(3)(C), (D).

Thus, provision of adequate assurance of future performance does not require an assignee's literal compliance with each and every term of the lease. The court may permit deviations from strict enforcement of any provision including a use clause.

One commentator suggested that the court render completely invalid any use clause in a nonshopping center lease because: (1) "the lessor is seeking to protect his tenant mix with the lease provision, and the Code does not require the court to provide such protection"; and (2) a use clause "invalidly conditions assignment." Fogel, *Executory Contracts* at 364 (footnote omitted). The Court rejects this "*per se* unenforceable" reading of a use clause.

However, the Court will not go to the other extreme and adopt the "insubstantial" breach or disruption standard for non-shopping center cases that is applicable only to shopping center leases. The insubstantial breaches and disruptions language of § 365(b)(3) "clearly reflects an attempt to limit the effects of what was understood—and feared—to be the more expansive authority conferred by the balance of § 365(a)." Simpson, *Leases* at 37–38. The Court's authority to waive strict enforcement of lease provisions in the non-shopping center cases will permit deviations which would exceed those permitted in the shopping center cases.

Within the range between unenforceability of a use clause and insubstantial breaches of a use clause, the Code provides no specific standard by which to measure permissible deviations in use. Whatever standard is applied must serve the policy aims of Congress.

Section 365 expresses a clear Congressional policy favoring assumption and assignment. Such a policy will insure that potential valuable assets will not be lost by a debtor who is reorganizing his affairs or liquidating assets for distribution to creditors. This policy parallels case law which disfavors forfeiture. To prevent an assignment of an unexpired lease by demanding strict enforcement of a use clause, and thereby contradict clear Congressional policy, a landlord or lessor must show that actual and substantial detriment would be incurred by him if the deviation in use was permitted.

In this case, the contemplated deviation in use is from an appliance store to a small bistro. The building in which the unexpired leasehold is located already contains a restaurant, a laundry, and a liquor store. The landlord has failed to demonstrate any actual and substantial detriment which he would incur if the proposed deviation in use is permitted. The Court also notes that the contemplated use, along with the planned soundproofing, will have no adverse effect on other tenants in the building. Thus, this Court rules that the use clause may not be enforced so as to block assignment of this lease to Just Heaven. The fact that Jemrock withholds its consent to the proposed assignment will not prevent the assignment. Consent is required only in leases governed by § 365(c). The lease here is not subject to § 365(c).

* * *

Congress, in § 365, has stated a general policy favoring assignment. Balanced against this general policy is the requirement that the non-debtor contracting party receive the full benefit of his bargain. Jemrock Realty will receive the full benefit of its bargain under the proposed assignment of the leasehold from U.L. Radio to Just Heaven. No defaults exist under the lease. The lease has properly been assumed and Just Heaven has provided adequate assurance of future performance. The landlord has shown no actual or substantial detriment to him from the proposed assignment. The statutory requirements have been satisfied. The assignment is authorized.

Notes and Problems

1. Standor Jewelers operated several retail jewelry stores. When bankruptcy became necessary, Standor decided to streamline its operation. It sought to assign the lease of one of its stores. A provision in the lease required the lessor's consent as a condition to assignment and, as a condition to consent, Standor was required to pay 75% of the appreciation in value of the premises to the lessor. Is Standor required to make that payment in order to

assign the lease? See *South Coast Plaza v. Standor Jewelers W., Inc. (In re Standor Jewelers W., Inc.)*, 129 B.R. 200 (9th Cir. BAP 1991).

2. Debtor, Fashions by Evelyn, leased premises on Park Avenue in New York City where it sold high-fashion women's clothing. Fashions by Evelyn sought to assign the lease to Labels for Less, a discounter of designer dresses. The lease provided that "tenant shall use the premises for the sale of fine women's clothing and for no other purpose" and that "tenant shall conduct its business in a high grade and reputable manner." Lessor objected to assignment because Labels for Less appoints its stores with track lighting and chrome fixtures, rather than as a "salon" decorated like the living room of a home. Lessor argued that Labels for Less is just not "elegant." Will that argument suffice to prevent assignment? See *In re Evelyn Byrnes, Inc.*, 32 B.R. 825 (Bankr. S.D.N.Y.1983).

3. John's Adult Discotheque, Inc. operated under a lease limiting use to operation of a "lounge bar and discotheque." The lease also prohibited "any practices that may be a nuisance or objectionable to other local merchants." After filing a bankruptcy petition, John realized that he could attract a new audience because of Monday Night Football. Thus, John's Adult Discotheque began male striptease shows "for women only" on Monday nights. The dancers performed only after 10 p.m. and the shows were not advertised. A number of local merchants complained, but others said that their traffic increased because of the shows. If the lessor objects to assumption of the lease, will that objection succeed? See *In re Johns*, 5 B.C.D. 1074 (Bankr. D.Nev.1979).

4. As we have seen debtors often use Chapter 13 to save their houses and cars. But what of debtors who rent? If a debtor's lease of residential property is unexpired, then assumption under § 365 is a possibility (although it comes at the cost of curing arrearages and providing adequate assurance). An entirely different scenario arises if the landlord has acquired a judgment for possession before the date of filing. That triggers two automatic stay exceptions relevant to residential real property leases—§ 362(b)(22), which permits continuation (subject to § 362(*l*)) of eviction proceedings; and § 362(b)(23), which permits (subject to § 362(m)) an eviction proceeding when the tenant has endangered the premises or illegally used controlled substances on the property.

2. SPECIAL RULES FOR SHOPPING CENTERS

Congress was concerned with the special problems faced by shopping center lessors, as well as other tenants, when lessees of space in shopping centers go into bankruptcy. In these cases, the economic interests of a number of nonbankrupt parties are implicated. Thus, Congress included § 365(b)(3), which governs adequate assurance of future performance when leased premises are in a shopping center. In such cases, a court has less latitude than it has in other cases to permit the debtor or an assignee to deviate from strict performance of lease provisions. It is important to determine, therefore, whether the premises are in a shopping center. Because the Code does not define "shopping center," courts have undertaken the task.

The following case deals with the definition of "shopping center" and with the heightened requirements for "adequate assurance" when a shopping center is involved.

IN RE JOSHUA SLOCUM, LTD.

United States Court of Appeals, Third Circuit, 1990.
922 F.2d 1081.

A. LEON HIGGINBOTHAM, JR., Chief Judge.

This case concerns the power of the bankruptcy court to excise a paragraph from a shopping center lease. On November 21, 1988 (the "Filing Date"), Joshua Slocum, Ltd., a Pennsylvania corporation (the "Debtor"), filed a voluntary petition for relief under chapter 11 of the United States Code with the bankruptcy court. On February 16, 1989, the bankruptcy court appointed Melvin Lashner (the "Trustee") to act as trustee in the case pursuant to § 1104. Appellant George Denney ("Denney") contends that the bankruptcy court erred in entering its orders excising paragraph 20 of the lease in question, and then authorizing the assumption and assignment of that lease, without paragraph 20, over his objections. He also maintains that the district court erred in affirming the bankruptcy court's decision. We agree with the appellant and therefore will reverse the district court's summary affirmance of the bankruptcy court's judgment.

I. FACTS AND PROCEDURAL HISTORY

The Debtor, Joshua Slocum, Ltd., d/b/a JS. Acquisition Corporation, began its relationship with Landlord, George Denney, in May of 1983 when Debtor signed a ten year lease for retail space at the Denney Block in Freeport, Maine. The Denney Block, which consisted of three buildings containing seven stores, was developed in two phases commencing in 1982 and completed in 1983. The first phase was undertaken by Cole Haan, a manufacturer and retailer of fine men's and women's shoes, of which Denney is the President. Cole Haan purchased and renovated a building on Main Street in Freeport, Maine, and gave Denney the option to purchase the building in the event that the stock of Cole Haan was acquired by a third person. When the capital stock of Cole Haan was purchased by Nike, George Denney exercised his option to purchase the Cole Haan building.

Shortly thereafter, Denney purchased the building immediately adjoining the Cole Haan building and a third building separated from the second building by a courtyard. Architectural plans to develop the two new buildings in a manner consistent with the Cole Haan building as a common scheme were commissioned by Denney and presented to the Freeport, Maine planning board for approval.

The buildings comprising Denney Block front on Main Street and are part of the downtown shopping district in Freeport. The shopping district consists of a number of streets lined with stores. In addition to the Landlord's three buildings, the Denney Block has a courtyard located between two of its buildings and a parking lot behind the stores. George Denney owns the parking lot which is primarily for the use of patrons of the Denney Block, although according to local ordinance it is also open to the public (thus, it can be used by all persons who shop in the stores along Main Street, Freeport).

Debtor's lease, signed in 1983, along with the leases of some or all of the other Denney Block tenants, contains an average sales clause. This clause allows for Debtor or Landlord to terminate the lease if, after six years, Debtor's average yearly sales are below $711,245. A similar option also existed after the third year of the lease. At that point, either party held the power to terminate the lease if the tenant's average yearly sales were below $602,750.

The lease also contains a percentage rent clause. For the years currently remaining in the lease, this clause requires the tenant to pay additional rent in the amount of four percent of gross sales in excess of $1,175,362. Otherwise, the base rent due in the final five years of the lease is $3,917.88 per month. The leases also require the tenants to provide Landlord with financial information concerning their business so that these lease provisions can be implemented.

Joshua Slocum, Ltd. filed a voluntary petition for relief under chapter 11 of the United States Bankruptcy Code with the bankruptcy court. By application to the bankruptcy court dated February 2, 1989 (the "Application"), the Trustee requested authorization to assume and assign the Lease pursuant to § 365. In March 1989, Denney filed written objections and a memorandum of law in opposition to the application with the bankruptcy court.

By opinion (the "opinion") and order both dated March 29, 1989 (the "interim order"), the bankruptcy court granted the relief requested in the Application and authorized the Trustee to assume and assign the Lease to European Collections, Inc. (the "assignee"). The bankruptcy court entered another Order on April 11, 1989 (the "final order"), setting forth fully the rights and obligations of the parties. In the opinion and the final order, the bankruptcy court held unenforceable and excised paragraph 20 of the Lease ("paragraph 20"), which provides that "in the event that Tenant's gross sales for the first six (6) lease-years of the term of this Lease do not average Seven Hundred Eleven Thousand Two Hundred Forty Five and 00/100 Dollars ($711,245.00) per lease-year either Landlord or Tenant may elect to terminate this Lease."

The court approved the assignment of the lease without paragraph 20 to European Collections. European Collection[s] has begun occupancy and operation of a store in George Denney's premises in Freeport, Maine. Denney's consolidated appeals followed.

On May 31, 1989, the Trustee filed a motion to dismiss George Denney's appeal as moot. By Order dated December 21, 1989 the district court affirmed without opinion the bankruptcy court's opinion and final order and denied Trustee's motion to dismiss. On January 22, 1990, Denney appealed the district court order.

II. DISCUSSION

* * *

B. Shopping Center

The Bankruptcy Code imposes heightened restrictions on the assumption and assignment of leases for shopping centers. * * *

George Denney, the landlord of the Denney Block, wishes to take advantage of these heightened restrictions in order to block the assignment of the lease to European Collections. Thus, appellant Denney contends that the Denney Block is a "shopping center" within the meaning of § 365(b)(3). We agree.

However, the bankruptcy court agreed with the appellee, Trustee, and found that Denney Block was not a "shopping center" within the meaning of § 365(b)(3). The court looked to *Collier on Bankruptcy* and two cases addressing the question of whether a particular arrangement of stores constitutes a "shopping center" for purposes of § 365(b)(3). *See In re Goldblatt Bros., Inc.*, 766 F.2d 1136, 1140–41 (7th Cir.1985); *In re 905 Int'l Stores, Inc.*, 57 B.R. 786, 788–89 (E.D. Mo.1985). Both of these appellate decisions affirm bankruptcy court determinations that the respective premises in question were not in "shopping centers."

In *Goldblatt*, although the court found the common ownership of contiguous parcels, the presence of an "anchor tenant" (Goldblatt) and joint off street parking adjacent to all stores was significant in deciding whether the arrangement at issue was a shopping center, those factors were not determinative. The court was persuaded by the absence of other typical indicia of shopping centers, i.e., a master lease, fixed hours during which the stores are all open, common areas and joint advertising, and particularly whether the stores were developed to be a shopping center.

In *905 Int'l*, the court, in finding that the arrangement at issue in that case was not a "shopping center," was impressed with "the absence of contractual interdependence among tenants." 57 B.R. at 788. That case, like *Goldblatt*, also sets out several objective criteria in determining whether an arrangement is a "shopping center." In addition to contractual interdependence, these factors include the existence of percentage rent clauses, anchor tenant clauses, joint contribution to trash and maintenance needs, contiguous grouping of stores, a tenant mix, and restrictive clauses. Relying on the indicia pointed to in *Goldblatt*, the court found that only one of the four, joint advertising, was satisfied, and concluded the stores did not comprise a shopping center.

The bankruptcy court utilized the correct criteria for determining what constitutes a "shopping center." The court's focus on the physical attributes of the Denney Block, however, i.e., the fact that it was located on a typical "Main St." in a downtown district, is not a factor laid out as dispositive in the Bankruptcy Code, Collier's treatise, or either of the above cited cases. Nor is there any intrinsic sense to the bankruptcy court's conclusion that the Denney Block's location makes it fall outside the purview of the definition of "shopping center." The court noted that "a shopping center brings to mind a configuration of stores which are not freestanding or detached in the sense that stores appear in a typical 'Main St.' downtown shopping district. Such a downtown shopping district is usually considered in many communities, as the *alternative* (emphasis in original) to the archetypal 'shopping center,' i.e., the large enclosed shopping mall." While it is true that the mall *is* the archetypal "shopping center," all shopping centers do not necessarily take the form of shopping malls.

Location is only one element in the determination of whether a group of stores can properly be described as a "shopping center." However, more significant are the following criteria sketched in Collier, *Goldblatt* and *905 Int'l*:

(a)   A combination of leases;

(b)   All leases held by a single landlord;

(c)   All tenants engaged in the commercial retail distribution of goods;

(d)   The presence of a common parking area;

(e)   The purposeful development of the premises as a shopping center;

(f)   The existence of a master lease;

(g)   The existence of fixed hours during which all stores are open;

(h)   The existence of joint advertising;

(j)   Contractual interdependence of the tenants as evidenced by restrictive use provisions in their leases;

(k)   The existence of percentage rent provisions in the leases;

(*l*)   The right of the tenants to terminate their leases if the anchor tenant terminates its lease;

(m)   Joint participation by tenants in trash removal and other maintenance;

(n)   The existence of a tenant mix; and

(*o*)   The contiguity of the stores.

We do not think that the bankruptcy court gave adequate consideration to all of the factors described above and gave undue weight to the testimony that the Denney Block does not look like a shopping center. The bankruptcy court placed what it termed "the physical configuration" of the Denney Block at the center of its analysis: "we find that the physical characteristics of the Denney Block *preclude* its characterization as a 'shopping center.'" We are not convinced that the physical configuration of the property plays such a prominent role. Indeed, Collier notes that "the most important characteristic will be a combination of leases held by a single landlord, leased to commercial retail distributors of goods, with the presence of a common parking area." 2 *Collier on Bankruptcy* ¶ 365.04[3]. Except for contiguity of stores criterion listed above, the appearance of premises or their location within a downtown shopping district has not been cited as a factor in the determination of whether a group of stores is a "shopping center." All of the stores of Denney Block, except to the extent that they are separated by common areas, are contiguous.

Moreover, George Denney is the sole landlord of all the stores in the Denney Block. Those stores share and provide support for the maintenance of common areas. The stores are all retail distributors of goods subject to substantially similar leases which include both percentage rent provisions and clauses for the benefit of other tenants that restrict the type of goods that a tenant may sell. There is a mix of tenants at Denney Block. Cole Haan primarily sells footwear, Laura Ashley sells a variety of goods including clothing, wall paper and linens, Jones New York sells men's and women's clothing, Benneton sells sports wear, Class Perfume sells perfume and Christmas Magic sells Christmas decorations and ornaments. The plot plan for Denney Block was presented to the Freeport planning board as a common scheme.

The bankruptcy court found that there was no common parking because customers of stores other than those shops in the Denney Block also use [the] parking lot located directly behind it. That common parking is available at the Denney Block is not obviated by the fact that according to local ordinance the public must also have access to that lot. Hence, the Denney Block satisfies, with the exception of joint advertising, the existence of a master lease and the right of a tenant to terminate the lease if the anchor tenant does so, all of the criteria for determining what constitutes a "shopping center," and all of the "most important" characteristics listed by Collier. Because the bankruptcy court did not adequately consider each of the factors enumerated above its reading of the Act was overly restrictive.

The provisions of § 365 are intended to remedy three "serious problems caused shopping centers and their solvent tenants by the administration of the bankruptcy code." 130 Cong. Rec. S8891 (statement by the Hon. Orrin G. Hatch, a ranking majority member of the Senate Committee on the Judiciary and a Senate conferee), *reprinted in* 1984 U.S.C.C.A.N. 590, 598. Congress wished to alleviate the hardship caused landlord and tenant resulting from vacancy or partial operation of the debtor's space in the shopping center. Section 365 also insures that the landlord will continue to receive payments due under the lease. Finally, the statute guarantees to the landlord and remaining tenants that the tenant mix will not be substantially disrupted. Each of these serious problems was faced by Denney and the remaining shops after Joshua Slocum, Ltd. went bankrupt. We conclude that in light of the harms § 365 was intended to remedy, and after application of all relevant criteria, denying Denney and his tenants the protections of § 365 would not further the congressional will.

Additionally, the legislative history of the Bankruptcy Reform Act of 1978 briefly addresses the definition of a "shopping center."

> A shopping center is often a carefully planned enterprise, and though it consists of numerous individual tenants, the center is planned as a single unit, *often* subject to a master lease or financing agreement. Under these agreements, the tenant mix in a shopping center may be as important to the lessor as the actual promised rental payments, because certain mixes will attract higher patronage of the stores in the center, and thus, a higher rental for the landlord from those stores that are subject to a percentage of gross receipts rental agreement.

H.R. Rep. No. 95–595 at 348, *reprinted in* 1978 U.S.C.C.A.N. at 6305 (emphasis added).

We think that the Denney Block fits within Congress' conceptualization of a shopping center. The use of the term "often" in the above quoted passage indicates that the existence of a master lease should not be determinative in this court's analysis. We also note that a "single unit" as described above does not have to be an enclosed mall as the bankruptcy court would have it, but rather could be properly conceived of as a cluster of three relatively contiguous buildings as with the Denney Block.

We conclude that Denney Block is a "shopping center" within the meaning of § 365(b)(3) and should be entitled to its special protections.

C. Bankruptcy Court's Power to Excise Paragraph 20 of the Lease

The bankruptcy court, in considering the motion of the Trustee, Melvin Lashner to allow the Debtor, Joshua Slocum, Ltd. to assume and assign its store lease with the Denney Block, held that the average sales clause in paragraph 20 of that lease [is] unenforceable because it is not material or economically significant to the landlord and/or landlord's other tenants. The bankruptcy court granted Trustee's motion to assume and assign the lease and deleted the average sales clause. Appellant, George Denney takes issue with the court's authority to excise paragraph 20 of his leasehold with Joshua Slocum, Ltd. We shall defer the issue of whether that clause was material until later in our discussion. However, we now turn our attention to the question of the bankruptcy court's authority to delete paragraph 20.

Paragraph 20 of Joshua Slocum, Ltd.'s lease at the Denney Block provides as follows:

Paragraph 20 ("average sales"):

> *Option to Terminate.* In the event that Tenant's gross sales for the first three (3) lease-years of the term of this Lease do not average at lease [sic] Six Hundred Thousand Seven Hundred Fifty and 009/100 Dollars ($602,750.00) [sic] per lease-year, either Landlord or Tenant may elect to terminate this Lease; and in the event that Tenant's gross sales for the first six (6) lease-years of the term of this lease do not average Seven Hundred Eleven Thousand Two Hundred Forty Five Dollars and 00/100 Dollars ($711,245.00) per lease-year, either Landlord or Tenant may elect to terminate this Lease. Such election must be made, if at all, by written notice to the other party received within thirty (30) days from the date of receipt by Landlord of the accountant's statement described in Paragraph 4(b) hereinabove; and termination shall become effective ninety (90) days after receipt of such notice. * * *

The bankruptcy court viewed this average sales provision as a cleverly disguised anti-assignment clause. The court stated:

Perhaps the most novel issue raised by this motion is the enforceability of the "minimum sales" provision which, if enforced, would probably allow Denney to terminate the Lease in July, 1989. If this provision were enforced, with EC having to incorporate the Debtor's sales record through February 20, 1989, the value of the Lease would obviously be nominal. EC's offer to pay $77,000 for the right to obtain an assignment of the Lessee was expressly predicated on its receiving the right to utilize the Debtor's former Freeport store for at least the remaining four years of the lease. It is certainly questionable whether, in the short time before EC could open the store and July, 1989, it could attain a sales volume, when combined with the Debtor's interrupted sales record, sufficient to meet that required as the minimum in the first six lease-years of the Debtor's lease.

Working from the premise that Denney Block is not a "shopping center," the bankruptcy court held that the heightened protection accorded to non-debtor contractual rights under § 365(b)(3) of the Bankruptcy Code does not apply and turned its attention to § 365(f) dealing with assumptions and assignments of lease in non-shopping center cases. However, as discussed above, Denney Block is a "shopping center" and thus, § 365(f) does not apply.

The bankruptcy court does have some latitude in waiving contractual provisions when authorizing a trustee to assume and assign an unexpired lease. Section 365(b)(2) on its face permits the court to ignore so-called *ipso facto* and forfeiture clauses. However, the court's authority to waive the strict enforcement of lease provisions in the context of shopping center cases like this one is further qualified by § 365(b)(3) of the Bankruptcy Code. Even under the tightly drawn definition of "adequate assurance" in the shopping center context, Congress did not envision literal compliance with all lease provisions; insubstantial disruptions in, *inter alia*, tenant mix, and insubstantial breaches in other leases or agreements were contemplated and allowed. § 365(b)(3)(C), (D).

In this case, however, the bankruptcy court did not have the authority to excise paragraph 20 of the shopping center lease which addresses the landlord and/or tenant's option to terminate dependent upon the average sales generated by the tenant. We note that even if the Denney Block were not a shopping center, the bankruptcy court's authority to excise paragraph 20 of the lease is questionable. That paragraph must be read in conjunction with paragraph 4, the percent rent clause of the lease which provides a formula requiring Joshua Slocum, Ltd. to pay a percentage of the lease as specified on any amount in excess of the designated gross sales threshold for a given lease-year. These two clauses taken together clearly indicate that a bargained for element in this contract was that tenant, Joshua Slocum, Ltd., average a certain volume of sales as specified in paragraph 20 of the lease so that the Landlord could accurately calculate the minimum total rent expected pursuant to paragraph 4 of the lease. Even standing alone, paragraph 20 is an essential bargained for element of this lease agreement because it governs occupancy. We also note that paragraph 20 of the lease falls within the statutory meaning of "other consideration due"[9] under the lease, and without this clause the trustee could not give adequate assurance as to its future performance.

Congress has suggested that the modification of a contracting party's rights is not to be taken lightly. Rather, a bankruptcy court in authorizing assumptions and assignment of unexpired leases must be sensitive to the rights of the non-debtor contracting party (here, George Denney) and the policy requiring that the non-debtor receive the full benefit of his or her bargain. Congress' solicitous attitudes toward shopping centers is reflected in the legislative history regarding § 365(b)(3), which states:

> A shopping center is often a carefully planned enterprise, and though it consists of numerous individual tenants, the center is planned as a single unit, often subject to a master lease or financing agreement. Under these agreements, the tenant mix in a shopping center may be as important to the lessor as the actual promised rental payments, because certain mixes will attract higher patronage of the stores in the center, and thus a higher rental for the landlord from those stores that are subject to a percentage of gross receipts rental agreement. Thus, in order to assure a landlord of his bargained for exchange, the court would have to consider such factors as the nature of the business to be conducted by the trustee or his assignee, whether that business complies with the requirements of any master agreement, whether the kind of business proposed will generate gross sales in an amount such that the percentage rent specified in the lease is substantially the same as what would have been provided by the debtor, and whether the business proposed to be conducted would result in a breach of other causes [sic] in master agreements relating, for example to tenant mix and location.

---

[9] *See* § 365(b)(3)(A).

H.R. Rep. No. 95–595 at 348–49, *reprinted in* 1978 U.S.C.C.A.N. 5963, 6305; *see also* S. Rep. No. 95–989, *reprinted in id*. at 5787, 5845.

In excising paragraph 20, the bankruptcy court undermined both the Congressional policy and the statutory requirement under § 365-(b)(3)(A) that the trustee give adequate assurance of "other consideration due" under an unexpired lease. We find that the bankruptcy court did not have the authority to excise paragraph 20 of the lease.

D. *Materiality*

Appellant takes issue with the bankruptcy court's conclusion that paragraph 20 of the lease at issue, allowing for the termination of the lease by either the landlord, Denney or the debtor-tenant, Joshua Slocum, Ltd., if certain minimum sales figure were not realized, was not enforceable. Central to the bankruptcy court's view was the notion that unless the landlord establishes that a leasehold is in a "shopping center," such a restrictive clause is only enforceable if the landlord is able to establish that such terms are material and jeopardize the economic position of the landlord and/or the landlord's other tenants. The bankruptcy court, working from the premise that the Denney Block is not a "shopping center," looked to case law interpreting § 365 of the Bankruptcy Code and distilled the concepts of "materiality and economic significance." Those cases state that "the [bankruptcy] court does retain some discretion in determining that lease provisions * * * may still be refused enforcement in a bankruptcy context in which there is no substantial economic detriment to the landlord shown, and in which enforcement would preclude the bankruptcy estate from realizing the intrinsic value of its assets." *In re Mr. Grocer, Inc.*, 77 B.R. 349, 354 (Bankr. D.N.H.1987).

[The bankruptcy court] was incorrect in finding that on these facts, paragraph 20 of the lease, addressing the right of the parties to terminate the leasehold is not "material or economically significant." That conclusion flies in the face of logic and simple common sense. * * *

We find that the average sales provision of paragraph 20 was not merely inserted as an escape hatch in the event that the location became unprofitable for the protection of the tenant. But rather, that particular clause is of financial import to the landlord in insuring occupancy by high volume sales, viable businesses, thus increasing the rent received under the percentage rent clause. The combination of paragraph 4 and paragraph 20 acts as a minimum income guarantee for the landlord. Certainly nothing could be as material or economically significant to landlords as some minimal assurance that there will be a positive return on their investments. The clause is also significant to landlord as well as the other tenants because customers will be attracted to stores where business is perceived as booming. We conclude, therefore, paragraph 20 is a material and economically significant clause in the leasehold at issue.

III. CONCLUSION

* * * [W]e hold that the Denney Block, a contiguous grouping of stores, is subject to the heightened restrictions on the assumption and assignment of leases of real property in shopping centers. We find that the district court erred in affirming the bankruptcy court's approval of the assignment of the leasehold at issue without paragraph 20, an average sales clause, to European Collections. The bankruptcy court did not have authority to excise paragraph 20, a material provision governing the terms of occupancy under the lease. Therefore, we will vacate the judgment of the district court and remand to the district court for further proceedings consistent with this opinion.

Questions

1. Did George Denney face the kinds of risks about which Congress was concerned when it enacted the special provisions in § 365 for shopping centers?

2. How many of the characteristics of a shopping center, listed by the court, were present in the Denney Block? What minimum is necessary?

3. Are physical characteristics, such as contiguity, or contractual characteristics, such as a master lease, more important in the court's view? Why?

4. Does *Joshua Slocum* effectively resurrect ipso facto clauses, as far as shopping centers are concerned?

3. NONASSIGNABLE CONTRACTS

Contract law prohibits assignments that might jeopardize the justifiable expectations of a party. If, for example, one party's obligations depend upon the discretion of the other party, substitution of an assignee for the other party might significantly change the obligor's duties. Or an assignment might increase the risk a party faces. Under circumstances such as these, contract law holds assignments ineffective.

Congress understood the policy reasons behind nonassignability, but also recognized that bankruptcy policies can be undermined if nondebtor contracting parties are able to stand aloof. (Evidence of the latter was readily available, since ipso facto clauses were enforceable under the Act.) Congress, therefore, sought to balance these competing considerations in § 365. The following case may help you evaluate the success of that effort.

RIESER v. DAYTON COUNTRY CLUB CO. (IN RE MAGNESS)

United States Court of Appeals, Sixth Circuit, 1992.
972 F.2d 689.

CHARLES W. JOINER, Senior District Judge.

In this case we are asked to review an order barring a trustee in bankruptcy under Chapter 7 from assuming and assigning a golf membership in a country club as an executory contract, pursuant to § 365 of the Bankruptcy Code.

I.

The Dayton Country Club is an organization, in the form of a corporation, consisting of several hundred individuals who have joined together for recreation and entertainment. Its shares of stock may be held only by the members of the club and may not be accumulated in any substantial amount by one member.

The club offers social events, dining facilities, tennis courts, a swimming pool, and a golf course. It became apparent over a period of time that each of these diverse programs could be enjoyed to full advantage by a different number of members. For example, since there was only one 18-hole golf course available, and because of the nature of the game, the maximum number of members eligible to play golf needed to be limited in order to make the playing of the game enjoyable to those playing. There was no need to so limit the number of members who could use the tennis courts, the pool, the restaurants, or who could enjoy the social events of the club. The club developed within its membership a special membership category for those who had full golfing privileges. This category was limited to 375 members. Detailed rules, procedures, and practices were developed to ensure the fair selection of golfing members. These rules, procedures, and practices define how this additional privilege is allocated, how the number of members is maintained at 375, how vacancies occur, how they are filled, and what additional fees are charged.

The record reflects that members of the club are entitled to play, eat, and socialize in all activities of the club except golf. If, in addition to these activities, a member desires to play golf, he or she asks to become a golfing member in one of several golf membership categories. When he or she makes this request, an additional substantial fee is paid to the club and the individual is placed on a waiting list. At the time the record was made in this case, there were about 70 persons on that list. When a vacancy occurs because of a failure to pay dues or a resignation, the first person on the waiting list is given the option to become a golfing member by paying an additional substantial fee. Upon becoming a golfing member, the monthly dues also increase substantially. If the person at the top of the waiting list declines the membership, then that person is placed at the bottom of the list and the next person on the list is given the opportunity to become a golfing member. There is no provision for any person to assign or sell the golf membership to any other person or for any person to become a golfing member in any other way except in two intimate and personal situations dealt with in discrete ways. When the death of a golfing member occurs, a spouse (who had been enjoying the hospitality of the club) may take the deceased member's place. If a divorce occurs, the member may designate his or her spouse as the golfing member. The club also has a program to encourage the younger generation of member families to become golfing members. Golfing members are permitted also to invite guests. Through its membership committee, the club makes the rules and establishes the procedures to describe whom among its larger membership list may be golfing members.

The nature of the golf membership within the overall club membership is the heart of this case. We are not dealing with the right to be a member of the club and there is nothing in this case relating to laws and social policies against discrimination. The issues in this case relate solely to the rights, duties, and privileges of the club and its members arising from the club's effort to provide golfing privileges to some but not all of its members, and the effect of the bankruptcy laws upon that effort.

This matter involves appeals from separate orders entered in the bankruptcies of debtors Magness and Redman, both of whom were golfing members of the Dayton Country Club. The trustee in bankruptcy sought to assume and assign, through sale, the rights under these memberships to (1) members on the waiting list, (2) other club members, or (3) the general public, provided that the purchaser first obtains membership in the Dayton Country Club. In other words, the trustee seeks to increase the value of the bankruptcy estate by taking value for and assigning to others a relationship between the bankrupt and the club. The assignment would be to the detriment of other club members who had paid for and acquired the right to become golfing members in due course. The question is whether the trustee has the right to make the assignment.

* * *

Not only is it appropriate to cast these complex relationships in terms of both executed and executory contracts, it is not inappropriate to think of these contracts as creating a type of property interest. The full golf membership and the rights that come from that relationship with the club can be described as a property right of that member, the parameters of which are defined by the rules, procedures, and practices of the club. These rules, procedures, and practices, and therefore the extent of the members' property interest, do not extend to any right on the members' part to pass on the membership to others, except in the two situations described above (death or divorce). The persons on the waiting list also can be described as having a type of property interest in the relationships described in their contracts with the club. Theirs is a lesser interest than that of the full golfing members, but a real one nonetheless. They have paid the club for the right to be considered in the numbered order on the list to become full golfing members as vacancies occur. They, like the full golfing members, have a status defined by the various rules, procedures, and practices pertaining to filling the membership roster.

The bankruptcy courts found, and the district court affirmed, that the full golf memberships are executory contracts under § 365 of the Bankruptcy Code. Section 365(f)(1) of the Bankruptcy Code provides that executory contracts may be assigned notwithstanding non-assignment provisions in the contract or the law. *[The court quoted (f)(1).]* Section 365(c)(1) contains an exception to § 365(f)'s bar to enforcement of non-assignment provisions. *[The court quoted (c)(1).]*

The bankruptcy courts found that the trustee was barred from assigning the full golf memberships by Ohio law under § 365(c). The courts concluded that the club's rules were, in effect, anti-assignment provisions, and that Ohio law excused the club from accepting performance by others. * * *

The district court affirmed the order barring assignment of Magness' full golf membership on the basis of the bankruptcy court's reasoning, and observed as well that the case did not involve "the legal equivalent of a long-term commercial lease" but rather "a non-commercial dispute over the possession of a valuable membership in a recreational and social club."

* * * We now affirm.

* * *

III.

The trustee asserts that what is involved is simply an executory contract between the bankrupt and the club permitting the bankrupt to play golf on the club course. As such, the trustee asserts that this executory contract can be sold and assigned, and the estate of the bankrupt is entitled to the value that can be realized from such an assignment and sale.

* * *

Section 365(a) of the Bankruptcy Code specifically permits the trustee to assume an executory contract. Sections 365(f) and (c) also permit the assignment of such a contract, albeit with some limitations.

* * *

The Court of Appeals for the First Circuit attempted to harmonize §§ 365(f) and (c) in the case of *In re Pioneer Ford Sales, Inc.*, 729 F.2d 27 (1st Cir. 1984). That court also held that no personal service contract limitation appeared in the language of § 365(c). In attempting to reach a rational explanation of the interplay of §§ 365(f) and (c), however, the court proceeded to read additional language into § 365(f):

> As a matter of logic * * * we see no conflict, for (c)(1)(A) refers to state laws that prohibit assignment "whether or not" the contract is silent, while (f)(1) contains no such limitation. Apparently (f)(1) includes state laws that prohibit assignment only when the contract is *not* silent about assignment; that is to say, state laws that enforce contract provisions prohibiting assignment.

Id. at 29 (emphasis in original). There is simply nothing in the language of § 365(f) which supports the limitation read into it by that court. In addition, it is at least equally as plausible that the phrase "whether or not such contract * * * prohibits * * * assignment" in § 365(c) was intended merely to emphasize that § 365(c) should not be construed to apply only to applicable law barring assignment, irrespective of the contract's provisions (as opposed to applicable law enforcing anti-assignment provisions in certain contracts), a construction which might otherwise seem logical in light of § 365(f)'s explicit override of contractual anti-assignment provisions. Neither *Pioneer Ford* nor any other decision to date provides a defensible explication of the parameters of the § 365(c) exception.

We must read §§ 365(f) and (c) together. At first, it might seem that they are not consistent, but a careful parsing of the provisions suggests that § 365(f) contains the broad rule and § 365(c) contains a carefully crafted exception to the broad rule made necessary by general principles of the common law and our constitutions.

The parameters of subsections (f) and (c) are revealed through a straightforward reading of those subsections. Subsection (f) states that although the contract or applicable law prohibits assignment, these provisions do not diminish the broad power to assume and assign executory contracts granted the trustee by § 365(a). In other words, a general prohibition against the assignment of executory contracts, *i.e.*, by contract or "applicable law," is ineffective against the trustee. In this case the complex nature of the arrangements by the parties for filling vacancies in the full golf membership category is a clear statement that by virtue of these arrangements the parties may not assign these memberships. However, subsection (f), by specific reference to subsection (c), allows one specific circumstance in which the power of the trustee may be diminished. Subsection (c) states that if the attempted assignment by the trustee will impact upon the rights of a non-debtor third party, then any applicable law protecting the right of such party to refuse to accept from or render performance to an assignee will prohibit assignment by the trustee. While subsections (f) and (c) appear contradictory by referring to "applicable law" and commanding opposite results, a careful reading reveals that each subsection recognizes an "applicable law" of markedly different scope.

Thus, in application to this case, § 365(f) permits the executory contract between the plaintiffs and the club regarding full golf membership to be assigned by the trustee even though the arrangements between the club and its members clearly do not permit them to assign such contracts, unless there is something in § 365(c) that indicates to the contrary. Section 365(c) requires us to look at the rights and duties of the club as the other party to the contract and the "applicable law" regarding whether the club must accept performance from the assignee member chosen by the trustee or render performance to that member. As required in § 365(c), the applicable law of controlling significance to the solution of this problem addresses the interests of the non-debtor third parties, rather than law relating to general prohibitions or restrictions on assignment of executory contracts covered by § 365(f).

This leads us to a careful examination of Ohio law in light of the nature of the contract. We must determine whether Ohio law excuses the club, as "a party other than the debtor," from accepting as a full golfing member a person chosen by the trustee to be that member.

IV.

As stated earlier in this opinion, the contracts involve complex issues and multiple parties: the members of the club, in having an orderly procedure for the selection of full golfing members; the club itself, in demonstrating to all who would become members that there is a predictable and orderly method of filling vacancies in the golfing roster; and more particularly, persons on the waiting list who have deposited substantial sums of money based on an expectation and a developed procedure that in due course they, in turn, would become full golfing members.

If the trustee is permitted to assume and assign the full golf membership, the club would be required to breach its agreement with the persons on the waiting list, each of whom has contractual rights with the club. It would require the club to accept performance from and render performance to a person other than the debtor. Section 365(c)(1)(A) is directly implicated if Ohio law excuses such performance.

* * *

The contracts creating the complex relationships among the parties and others are not in any way commercial. They create personal relationships among individuals who play golf, who are waiting to play golf, who eat together, swim and play together. They are personal contracts and Ohio law does not permit the assignment of personal contracts. * * *

The claim that the assignment will be made only to those who are already members of the club is not relevant. "Nor would the fact that a particular person it attempted to designate [assign] was personally unexceptionable affect the nature of the contract." *Starchroom Publishing Co. v. Threlkeld Eng'g Co.*, 13 Ohio App. 281, 282 (1920).

Therefore, we believe that the trustee's motion to assign the full golf membership should be denied. We reach this conclusion because the arrangements for filling vacancies proscribe assignment, the club did not consent to the assignment and sale, and applicable law excuses the club from accepting performance from or rendering performance to a person other than the debtor.

* * *

RALPH B. GUY, JR., Circuit Judge, concurring in result.

Although I agree with the result reached by the court, I arrive at the result by different reasoning. For me, the entire case turns on the meaning of the term "applicable law" appearing in the two relevant portions of § 365 of the Bankruptcy Code, which governs the trustee's assumption (or rejection) of executory contracts within the debtor's estate. Section 365(f) is considered the "general rule" and, by nullifying anti-assignment provisions in private contracts and in "applicable law," embodies the policy favoring the alienability of executory contracts. *[The opinion quoted § 365(f)(1), emphasizing "applicable law."]* The confusion lies in the fact that § 365(c), the recognized exception to § 365(f), appears at first to resuscitate in full the very anti-assignment "applicable law" which § 365(f) nullifies. (Anti-assignment clauses in the contracts themselves remain non-dispositive, however.) *[The opinion quoted § 365(c)(1), emphasizing "applicable law."]* If these two apparently contrary provisions are to be reconciled, "applicable law" saved by § 365(c) must either mean something completely different from the "applicable law" trumped by § 365(f), or it must refer only to a discrete subpart of the law encompassed by § 365(f). All agree, however, that "applicable law" refers to non-bankruptcy law.

The district court, adopting the reasoning of the bankruptcy judges, found that the "applicable law" saved under § 365(c) was Ohio case law recognizing that the members of voluntary associations are subject to the associations' regulations which are immune from judicial review absent fraud, arbitrariness, or collusion. Since the regulations at issue here permitted transfer to spouses only upon death or divorce, that was the end of the matter.

The trustee argues that the applicable law to be heeded by § 365(c) is broader than the voluntary association jurisprudence, and should also encompass—as far more pertinent to the issue—Ohio jurisprudence which, like its federal counterpart, favors the assignability of executory contracts. No one disputes that Ohio, in general, encourages such alienation unless the contract itself prohibits assignment or "is one for personal services, or involves a relationship of personal confidence * * * [where] the personality of one of the parties is material." 6 Ohio Jur. 3d *Assignments* § 11 (1990).

* * *

On appeal, the club and Mr. Magness's former wife—to whom his membership was transferred by court order—reassert the district court's reasoning that "applicable law" here refers to Ohio law regarding the sanctity of private clubs' self-governance. The defendants also insist that the membership agreement, even if it is to be termed an executory contract, is a "personal" contract such that Ohio law would "excuse" the club from accepting performance from anyone other than Mr. Magness or his former wife.

There is little authority on the scope of the "applicable law" to be heeded under § 365(c). * * *

Similarly unhelpful is the First Circuit's interpretation of the interplay between §§ 365(c) and 365(f).

> [W]e see no conflict, for (c)(1)(A) refers to state laws that prohibit assignment "whether or not" the contract is silent, while (f)(1) contains no such limitation. Apparently (f)(1) includes state laws that prohibit assignment only when the contract is *not* silent about assignment; that is to say, state laws that enforce contract provisions prohibiting assignment. These state laws are to be ignored. The section specifically excepts (c)(1)(A)'s state laws that forbid assignment even when the contract *is* silent; they are to be heeded.

In re Pioneer Ford Sales, Inc., 729 F.2d 27, 29 (1st Cir.1984) (citation omitted). This dense passage appears to be founded on the erroneous belief that § 365(f) applies only when the bar to assignment is in a (legally-enforceable) contractual provision. Section 365(f), however, specifically includes within its scope situations in which the bar to assignment is not contractual but purely a product of the law.

I need not resolve the problem, however, nor fully articulate my perception that the two sections refer to completely different legal concerns, with § 365(f) covering "applicable law" (and contractual clauses) prohibiting or restricting assignments as such, and § 365(c) embracing legal excuses for refusing to render or accept performance, regardless of the contract's status as "assignable" according to state law or its own terms. According to this understanding, the executory contract's apparent prohibition against assignment in this case is plainly immaterial under § 365(f). Prohibiting assignment by concluding that the "applicable law" under § 365(c) is Ohio's deference to the rules of voluntary associations would be to breathe life back into that nullified anti-assignment clause. Unlike the district and bankruptcy courts, I turn instead to the longstanding Ohio rule which excuses a contracting party from rendering performance to, or accepting performance from, a third person or entity where the identity of the original contacting party was material. Such contracts are considered non-assignable precisely because of this right of refusal. In my view, this recognition of the right to refuse is the very sort of "applicable law" saved by § 365(c). And, in compliance with § 365(f), I do not rest my analysis on the fact that Ohio law makes such contracts non-assignable, but rather on the reason behind that legal conclusion.

Ohio courts have long recognized that

> so-called personal contracts, or contracts in which the personality of one of the parties is material, are not assignable. Whether the personality of one or both parties is material depends upon the intention of the parties, as shown by the language which they have used, and upon the nature of the contract.

Starchroom Publishing Co. v. Threlkeld Engraving Co., 13 Ohio App. 281, 283 (1920). Given that the club is a voluntary association, the identity of its members is surely "material" to the membership agreements. The club's objection to the proposed assignment is the resulting interference with its ability to confer the full golf privileges on those members by the method of its choice.

* * *

Questions and Problems

1. What is the "conflict" between §§ 365(c)(1)(A) and (f)(1)? How did the two opinions in *Magness* resolve this "conflict"? According to the court in *Ford Motor Co. v. Claremont Acquisition Corp. (In re Claremont*

Acquisition Corp.), 186 B.R. 977, 982 (C.D. Cal.1995), *aff'd sub nom. Worthington v. GMC (In re Claremont Acquisition Corp.),* 113 F.3d 1029 (9th Cir.1997), "[b]oth opinions in *Magness* resolve the conflict between the two subsections by narrowing the scope of (c)(1), as opposed to the *Pioneer Ford* court's narrowing of (f)(1)." Do you agree? How does *Pioneer Ford*'s resolution differ from that in the two *Magness* opinions? Which of the three is most persuasive?

2. One generally applicable principle of statutory interpretation is that identical language used in two places in a statute should be read to mean the same thing in both places. Did the court in *Magness* depart from this principle? If so, was it justified in doing so?

3. The court in *Murray v. Franke–Misal Technologies Group, LLC (In re Supernatural Foods, LLC),* 268 B.R. 759 (Bankr. M.D. La.2001), in an exhaustive opinion, took issue with the Sixth Circuit's reading of §§ 365-(c)(1)(A) and (f)(1). According to *Murray, Magness* and cases following it

> purport to offer an interpretation that is not limited to personal service contracts, when it really is. *Magness* and [its progeny] require that a generally applicable restriction or prohibition on transfer or assignment of contractual rights contained within "applicable law" must be examined to determine whether personality is at the heart of the law; it is only contracts concerned with the personality or identity of the contracting parties that are covered by § 365(c)(1)(A). Any other law is merely a general proscription against assignment and is dealt with (and nullified) under § 365(f)(1).
>
> What [those courts] miss, however, is that ***every law of general application to a certain set of contracts, that is, a law not dependent upon the terms of the contract itself, which prohibits or restricts transfers is by definition making the identity of the parties to the contract material.*** In effect, a law of general application which states that certain forms of contracts are not transferable, makes that contract a personal contract. A law which states that certain forms of contracts cannot be assigned is inherently concerned with the identity of the parties to the contract. * * *
>
> The point of the foregoing discussion is to highlight that the statutory distinction so clearly perceived in *Magness* is not, regardless of the words of the Ninth Circuit, credible. Any law which states a generally applicable prohibition on assignment transmutes the nature of such contract from impersonal or heritable to a personal contract. The fact that all generally applicable laws speaking to the subject of non-assignability are laws concerned with the identity of the parties denotes a fundamental flaw in the *Magness* court's attempt to discredit the reasoning of *Pioneer Ford.*

Id. at 781-82. *Murray* agreed with the result reached in *Magness*—namely, that "[a]pplicable state law prohibited assignment of the ownership without consent of the club, whether or not the agreement contained a restriction or transfer." *Id.* at 783. The problem was the reasoning producing that result:

> By finding a distinction of nature between prohibitions on assignment and the right to refuse performance by an assignee, the court constructed a camouflaged return to the old personal services limitation, while simultaneously denouncing it. * * * [T]he error lies in these courts' initial perception that what is actually described by § 365(c)(1) cannot be found there because it is also found in § 365-(f)(1), which eradicates it. Interpreting the reference in § 365(f)(1) to "applicable law" as referring to those laws which make a general prohibition against assignments, sets up the interpretation that § 365-(c)(1) must refer to "applicable law" of lesser scope than that outlined in § 365(f)(1). These courts, however, have ignored the fact that § 365(f)(1) describes a larger universe of "applicable law" than general restrictions on assignment, and can only have effect after the laws enforceable through § 365(c) are excluded from its effect.

Id. at 784, 788. *Murray* then offered its own interpretation of these provisions, substantially agreeing with *Pioneer Ford*:

> The only limitation imposed on the applicability of § 365(c)(1) is that the "applicable law" restrict or prohibit assignment, *i.e.,* excuse performance, independent of the contract ("***whether or not such contract or lease prohibits or restricts assignment of rights or delegation of duties***"). Through this language, § 365(c)(1) decrees the requirement that the applicable law be independent of and not relate to the enforceability of prohibitions on assignment or restrictions upon delegation on duties within the language of the contract itself. If the law acts as a general prohibition on assignment, which, as has been discussed, is nothing more than a legal excuse for one party to refuse to perform or accept performance, and the law acts independent of any provision in the contract calling for a restriction on transfer, the law should be enforced against the trustee via § 365(c)(1).
>
> This requirement of independence from restrictions within the contract is the crucial distinction between laws which are encompassed by § 365(c)(1), and those which are not excepted from § 365-(f)(1) pursuant to the introductory clause of that subsection ("Except as provided in subsection (c) of this section") and are therefore nullified by that section. "Applicable law" referenced in § 365(f)(1) includes, without limitation, all laws that prohibit, restrict, or condition assignment. However, specifically excepted are laws covered under § 365(c)(1). As has been discussed, § 365(c)(1) covers all laws which, regardless of a provision in a contract, act to bar assignment. What, then, is left for § 365(f)(1)? As recognized by the First

Circuit in *Pioneer Ford,* in addition to covering generally applicable prohibitions on assignment, § 365(f)(1) also applies to specially applicable anti-assignment laws—laws which operate to bar assignment, but which are dependent in application upon provisions contained within the contracts themselves. This is the only cogent interpretation of the interplay between §§ 365(c)(1) and (f)(1).

* * *

Our analysis reads §§ 365(c) and 365(f)(1) to be cohesive, without conflict. Section 365(c) deals with a certain type of contract right. If the rights and obligations are covered by § 365(c), they are not included in the types of contract rights and obligations included in § 365(f). Section 365(f)(1), simply, deals with what is left.

Id. at 789, 792 (footnotes omitted).

Do you agree with *Pioneer Ford* and *Murray,* or does *Magness* more accurately interpret §§ 365(c)(1)(A) and (f)(1)?

4. West Electronics had a contract with the federal government to supply missile launchers to the Air Force. When West missed delivery deadlines, the government served an administrative notice on West to show cause why the contract should not be terminated. West promptly filed for bankruptcy protection and moved to assume the contract. The government objected to assumption, citing 41 U.S.C. § 15, which provides that "no [government] contract * * * shall be transferred by the party to whom such contract * * * is given to any other party, and any such transfer shall cause the annulment of the contract." Can West assume the contract in the absence of the government's consent? See *Matter of West Electronics Inc.,* 852 F.2d 79 (3d Cir.1988).

5. May a debtor assume a contract that is not assumable under nonbankruptcy law, such as a license to use a patent, if the debtor has no plans to assign the contract? Under that circumstance the licensor would not be subjected to substitute performance—the risk § 365(c)(1) guards against. Does that provide a reason for a court to find the bar against assumption inapplicable?

This question has sharply divided the courts. One line of authority follows *Perlman v. Catapult Entertainment, Inc. (In re Catapult Entertainment, Inc.),* 165 F.3d 747 (9th Cir. 1999), which adopted a "hypothetical test" for § 365(c)(1). Under that test, a debtor-in-possession may not assume an executory contract over the nondebtor's objection if applicable law would bar assignment to a hypothetical third party, even when the debtor-in-possession has no intention of assigning the contract. The other line of authority follows the "actual" test set out in *Institut Pasteur v. Cambridge Biotech Corp.,* 104 F.3d 489, 117 S.Ct. 2511, 138 L.Ed.2d 1014 (1st Cir.), *cert. denied,* 521 U.S.

1120 (1997). Under that test, the court must make a case-by-case inquiry to determine whether the nondebtor party is actually being forced to accept performance under an executory contract from someone other than the now-debtor with which it originally contracted.

This division of authority led JUSTICE BREYER to make the following comment upon the denial of certiorari in *N.C.P. Marketing Group, Inc. v. Blanks (In re N.C.P. Marketing Group, Inc.)*, 337 B.R. 230 (D. Nev.2005), *aff'd*, 279 Fed. Appx. 561 (9th Cir.2008)—a case in which the court had barred the debtor from assuming a license to use trademarks, in the absence of the licensor's consent, even though the debtor did not intend to assign the license:

> The hypothetical test is not, however, without its detractors. One arguable criticism of the hypothetical approach is that it purchases fidelity to the Bankruptcy Code's text by sacrificing sound bankruptcy policy. For one thing, the hypothetical test may prevent debtors-in-possession from continuing to exercise their rights under nonassignable contracts, such as patent and copyright licenses. Without these contracts, some debtors-in-possession may be unable to effect the successful reorganization that Chapter 11 was designed to promote. For another thing, the hypothetical test provides a windfall to nondebtor parties to valuable executory contracts: If the debtor is outside of bankruptcy, then the nondebtor does not have the option to renege on its agreement; but if the debtor seeks bankruptcy protecttion, then the nondebtor obtains the power to reclaim—and resell at the prevailing, potentially higher market rate—the rights it sold to the debtor.

> To prevent § 365(c) from engendering unwise policy, one Court of Appeals, and a number of Bankruptcy Courts, reject the hypothetical test in favor of an 'actual test,' under which a Chapter 11 debtor-in-possession may assume an executory contract provided it has no actual intent to assign the contract to a third party. [Citing *Institut Pasteur* and *Catapult*, which collected cases.] Of course, the actual test may present problems of its own. It may be argued, for instance, that the actual test aligns § 365(c) with sound bankruptcy policy only at the cost of departing from at least one interpretation of the plain text of the law.

> The division in the courts over the meaning of § 365(c)(1) is an important one to resolve for Bankruptcy Courts and for businesses that seek reorganization. This petition for certiorari, however, is not the most suitable case for our resolution of the conflict. Addressing the issue here might first require us to resolve issues that may turn on the correct interpretation of antecedent questions under state law and trademark-protection principles. For those and other reasons, I reluctantly agree with the Court's decision to deny certiorari. In a different

case the Court should consider granting certiorari on this significant question."

N.C.P. Marketing Group, Inc. v. BG Star Productions, Inc., 556 U.S. 1145, 129 S.Ct. 1577, 173 L.Ed.2d 1028 (2009) (BREYER, J., concurring).

D. REJECTION

1. GENERAL RULES

As we have noted, a trustee or debtor-in-possession will reject an agreement if its burdens outweigh its benefits. For example, if the debtor has a contract for the purchase of computer equipment for $5,000, but the market price of such equipment has fallen to $4,000, then the debtor-in-possession will reject the contract and negotiate a new contract at the lower market price. Rejection, however, constitutes a breach by the debtor-in-possession under § 365(g). Although it is a postpetition event, the breach is treated as if it occurred "immediately before the date of the filing of the petition," in order to give the non-debtor party an unsecured claim in the bankruptcy. See § 502(g).

Thus, in our hypothetical, the lessor will have a $1,000 claim. But where is the advantage of rejection if rejection creates a new claim against the estate in an amount equal to the estate's savings? The answer lies in the fact that the nondebtor-seller's claim is unsecured; it will be paid in "bankruptcy dollars," which are not worth 100¢.

The power to reject executory contracts and unexpired leases is one of the most important aspects of bankruptcy, and may be in itself a reason for filing. For example, a large corporation may have substantial obligations, often negotiated with unions representing its employees, to fund health and pension plans. The obligations reflected in that collective bargaining agreement—an executory contract—are enforceable under nonbankruptcy law. Bankruptcy, however, provides an escape. The Supreme Court in *NLRB v. Bildisco & Bildisco*, 465 U.S. 513, 526, 104 S.Ct. 1188, 1196 79 L.Ed.2d 482, 495 (1984), held that rejection is permissible "if the debtor can show that the collective-bargaining agreement burdens the estate, and that after careful scrutiny, the equities balance in favor of rejecting the labor contract." Congress responded by enacting § 1113, which imposes largely procedural restrictions on the rejection of a collective bargaining agreement, but does not make substantive changes to the employer's ability to reject.

A more recent example of the power of § 365—here, outside of the collective bargaining context—is found in *Old Carco LLC (f/k/a/*

Chrysler LLC) v. Kroger (In re Old Carco LLC (f/k/a/ Chrysler LLC)), 442 B.R. 196 (S.D.N.Y.2010). The debtors entered into a purchase agreement under which New Chrysler would acquire all of Old Chrysler's assets and liabilities for $2 billion. The purchased assets included dealer agreements that were assumed and assigned, but other dealer agreements were rejected. The attorneys general of several states objected, arguing that state laws intended to protect vehicle dealers did not allow for rejection. The district court affirmed a bankruptcy court order approving rejection on the grounds of the debtors' "persuasive showing" that rejection of existing dealer contracts would benefit the estate and was the product of sound business judgment. While those state laws may have been adopted in the public interest, they did not account for the national interest embodied in federal bankruptcy laws, and were not designed to protect the states' citizens from imminent threats to health or safety. Thus, application of the state statutes would obstruct federal bankruptcy adjudication, especially the bankruptcy court's power to reject executory contracts under § 365. The court held those statutes preempted.

The *power* of rejection is clear, but the *effect* of rejection, at least in some fact patterns, is a matter of considerable debate. The Code provides an answer in a limited group of cases—when the debtor is a lessor or seller of certain real estate interests, or a licensor of rights to certain types of intellectual property. In those cases, §§ 365(h), (i), (j) and (n) protect the nondebtor party. In addition, § 365(o) provides special protection for certain governmental agencies, such as the FDIC, that are creditors in bankruptcy cases. The Code, however, leaves open the question of the effect of rejection when those subsections are inapplicable. The following cases present this issue in several contexts.

IN RE CARRERE

United States Bankruptcy Court, Central District of California, 1986.
64 B.R. 156.

GERALDINE MUND, Bankruptcy Judge.

STATEMENT OF FACTS

In August, 1985, Tia Carrere ("Carrere") entered into a personal services contract with American Broadcasting Company ("ABC") whereby she agreed to perform in the television series "General Hospital" from that time until August, 1988 ("ABC Contract"). Under the terms of the contract, Carrere was guaranteed employment on the average of 1½ performances per week. She was to be paid between $600 and $700 for each 60-minute program in which she performed.

While the contract with ABC was still in effect, Carrere agreed to make an appearance on the show "A Team." Under the terms of her agreement with Steven J. Cannell Productions ("A Team Contract"), if she became a regular on A Team, she would make considerably more money over the life of the contract than if she remained on General Hospital.

Although a state court suit was filed by ABC against Carrere for breach of contract due to her agreement with A Team, it appears that no actual breach of the ABC contract will take place until the option in the A Team Contract has been exercised.

On March 4, 1986, Carrere filed her voluntary petition under Chapter 11. The next day she filed a Notice of Rejection of Executory Contract, seeking to reject the ABC Contract. A motion to reject the ABC Contract was filed by the debtor and the matter was set for hearing.

In her declaration in support of the motion to reject, Carrere makes it clear that her primary motivation in seeking the protection of this Court was to reject the contract with ABC so as to enter into the more lucrative contract with A Team. In fact, she claims she did not enter into the contract with A Team until she had obtained advice that the bankruptcy would allow her to reject the contract with ABC. In her schedules she claims unsecured debt only. Her stated liabilities are $76,575 and her assets are $13,191. The amount of debts is disputed by ABC.

ABC vigorously opposed the rejection of its contract and has sought extensive discovery concerning Carrere's liabilities and motivations in filing this bankruptcy. ABC also brought a motion to dismiss the Chapter 11 proceeding on the grounds that it was filed in bad faith.

ANALYSIS

The key issue to be determined by this Court is whether a debtor, who is a performer under a personal services contract, is entitled to reject the contract by virtue of the provisions of § 365.[1] If so, what criteria must be applied?

*A Personal Services Contract is not Property of the Estate
in Chapters 7 or 11*

* * *

Section 541(a)(6) states that property of the estate does not include "earnings from services performed by an individual debtor after the commencement of the case." This is limited to cases under Chapter 7 or 11, as post-petition earnings of the debtor become property of the estate in Chapter 13 cases (§ 1306). The post-petition earnings from personal services contracts are thus excluded from the Chapter 7 or Chapter 11 estate. Does this exclude the contract itself?

* * * The language of § 541(a)(6), which excludes post-petition proceeds from property of the estate, is an enactment of case law which specified that where an executory contract between the debtor and another is based upon the personal service or skill of the debtor, the Trustee does not take title to the debtor's rights in the contract.

Under the Code, it has been held that a contract for personal services is excluded from the estate pursuant to both § 541(a)(6) and § 365(c). The foremost recent opinion on this matter is *In re Noonan*, 17 B.R. 793 (Bankr. S.D.N.Y.1982), which is cited by both sides in support of their respective positions. While *Noonan* is usually cited for the proposition that a debtor may not be forced to assume a personal services contract, it also deals with the personal services contract as property of the estate.

In *Noonan* the debtor was also a performer. He had entered into a personal services contract with a recording company, which wished to exercise its option and require him to record new albums. Noonan, a debtor-in-possession, sought to reject the contract. When the recording company vigorously opposed Noonan's motion, Noonan converted to Chapter 7, knowing that the trustee could not assume the contract, nor could he force the debtor to perform. Therefore the contract would be automatically rejected.

---

[1] The practical issue raised here is whether Carrere may deprive ABC of a cause of action for a negative injunction if she seeks further employment under the A Team Contract.

The recording company moved to reconvert to Chapter 11 and to be allowed to confirm a creditor's plan requiring Noonan to assume the contract and perform under it. The Court denied the motion. Among the grounds for denial was the holding that a personal services contract is not property of the estate.

The *Noonan* case did not deal with the issue of rejection of a personal services contract, for the debtor's motion to reject was never heard. But the case clearly held that a personal services contract is not property of the estate. The Court finds this line of reasoning to be persuasive.

Since the trustee has no interest in the contract, he has no standing to act at all under § 365. Therefore, he cannot assume or reject the contract.

The Rights of a Debtor-in-Possession are No Greater Than Those of a Trustee

An argument might be made that the debtor-in-possession, by virtue of the fact that she is also the individual who can perform the contract, has greater rights than the trustee and therefore can assume or reject the contract. The Court does not agree with this.

Upon the filing of a Chapter 11, Ms. Carrere created a new entity called a debtor-in-possession. That debtor-in-possession is not identical to the debtor herself. She is granted the rights and duties of a trustee (§ 323). Therefore while the debtor (Tia Carrere) may have duties under the ABC contract and may wish to reject those duties, the debtor-in-possession (who represents the estate of Tia Carrere) has no rights or duties whatsoever in the contract and therefore is a stranger to it.

In her role as debtor-in-possession, she has no interest in the proceeds of the personal services contract, nor in the contract itself. The contract never comes under the jurisdiction of the Bankruptcy Court. The Court has no interest, the estate has no interest, and even if the debtor-in-possession were allowed by consent of all parties to assume the contract under § 365, the assumption would not create an asset of the estate, for the proceeds would not be an asset of the estate, nor would the contract be assignable. Therefore, no rights of assumption are vested in the debtor-in-possession.

The only one who has rights or duties under the contract is the debtor herself. But the statutory scheme of § 365(d)(1) does not allow the debtor to reject an executory contract. It only allows the trustee to do so.

Therefore this Court finds that § 365 concerning assumption or rejection of a contract does not apply to a personal services contract in a bankruptcy case under Chapter 7 or 11, whether or not a trustee has been appointed.[4]

It Would be Inequitable to Allow the Contract to Be Rejected

Beyond the legal arguments described above, the Court is concerned about the good faith issue of allowing a debtor to file for the primary purpose of rejecting a personal services contract. A personal services contract is unique and money damages will often not make the employer whole. In weighing the rights of the employer to require performance against the rights of the performer to refuse to perform, California courts have allowed the employer to seek an injunction against the performer so that she could not breach the negative promises not to compete. It is this very remedy that Carrere seeks to avoid.

The Bankruptcy Court is a court of equity, as well as a court of law. It would be inequitable to allow a greedy debtor to seek the equitable protection of this Court when her major motivation is to cut off the equitable remedies of her employer.

For that reason this Court finds that there is not "cause" to reject this contract, if the major motivation of the debtor in filing the case was to be able to perform under the more lucrative A Team contract. It is clear that for Carrere this is the major motivation, even if it is not the sole motivation. Therefore, rejection is denied for lack of cause.

---

[4]   The Court has no need at this time to deal with rejection of a contract under Chapter 13. Unlike Chapter 7 or 11, post-petition earnings from a personal services contract do become property of the estate under Chapter 13. Therefore the theories set forth to this point in the opinion are not applicable to Chapter 13. However, the Court does question the equity of allowing a Chapter 13 trustee to reject the contract, while denying the Chapter 13 [sic] trustee the power to assume it.

The issues of good faith, equity, and effect of rejection as described in the balance of this opinion apply equally to cases under all chapters.

Rejection Would Not Relieve the Debtor of a Possible
Negative Injunction

There is yet another issue that arises and impacts on the ultimate outcome of such cases: if rejection were permitted, what would be its effect on the creditor's right to seek a negative injunction against the debtor?

Rejection of an executory contract constitutes a breach, which is deemed to have occurred immediately before the date of the filing of the petition (§ 365(g)(1)). The claim for monetary damages thus becomes a claim in the estate (§ 502(g)).

But a rejection under the Bankruptcy Code only affects the monetary rights of the creditor. It does not disturb equitable, nonmonetary rights that the creditor may have against the debtor because of the breach of contract.

This issue was raised in *In re Mercury Homes Development Co.*, 4 B.C.D. 837 (Bankr. N.D.Cal.1978). The debtor/vendor of a condominium rejected the land sale contract. The buyer requested specific performance; the trustee argued that the only remedy left to the buyer was his unsecured claim for monetary damages. The court rejected the trustee's argument and held that the buyer was entitled to enforce the equitable remedies given to it by state law.

While the *Mercury Homes* case does not differentiate between the equitable rights that the aggrieved party has against the debtor and those that he has against the trustee, the Court finds no reason in this situation to make any such distinction. California law has given ABC an equitable remedy: to seek a negative injunction against Carrere and thereby prevent her from performing elsewhere. Rejection of the ABC contract would not interfere with ABC's rights to seek that equitable remedy. Rejection would merely categorize any claim for monetary damages as a pre-petition debt. Therefore, whether this Court were to allow rejection or not, Carrere cannot use the Bankruptcy Code to protect her from whatever nonmonetary remedies are enforceable under state law.

On both the legal and equitable grounds set forth above, Carrere's Motion to Reject this contract is denied.

Notes and Questions

1. What about the debtor's fresh start? Should the court have given some weight to that consideration?

2. In *Delightful Music Ltd. v. Taylor (In re Taylor)*, 913 F.2d 102 (3d Cir.1990), singer James Taylor sought to reject a recording contract. (The debtor was not Sweet Baby James; he was J.T., lead singer in "Kool and the Gang.") The recording company's arguments seemed straight out of *Carrere*:

> This appeal presents an issue which has not previously been addressed in any reported appellate decision, namely, whether executory contracts for the personal services of the debtor may be rejected under § 365 of the Bankruptcy Code. Appellant argues that personal-service contracts are not, and cannot become, part of the estate being dealt with in the bankruptcy court, and therefore cannot be rejected or otherwise affected in a Chapter 11 proceeding. Alternatively, appellant argues that rejection should not have been permitted in this case because it was not sought in good faith and would not benefit the estate. * * *

> On its face, the statute places no restrictions on a trustee's right to reject a personal services contract. This is not in the least surprising, since, as we read the statute, it implicitly provides that any executory contract which is not assumed—either in the course of the proceedings, or in the reorganization plan approved by the court—is automatically rejected. *See* § 365(g)(1).

> Appellant argues that this straightforward reading of the plain language of § 365 is inappropriate, because it does not take into account other provisions of the Bankruptcy Code, most notably § 541(a)(6) which, in defining "property of the estate," makes clear that the proceeds of the debtor's post-petition personal services are excluded from the estate. Since an executory contract for the debtor's personal services is not part of the estate, the argument continues, such a contract is not within the "jurisdiction" of the trustee, and the trustee simply has no power to deal with such a contract. This line of argument rests upon some fundamental misconceptions.

> To the extent that money is due the debtor for pre-petition services under a personal services contract, the debtor's claim for those sums is undoubtedly an asset of the estate which passes to the trustee/debtor-in-possession. And this is so regardless of whether the trustee later affirms or rejects the contract. Stated otherwise, the issue of affirmance or rejection relates only to those aspects of the contract which remained unfulfilled as of the date the petition was filed. It serves no useful purpose to speak generally about whether "the contract" becomes part of "the estate." The real question is the status of

the reciprocal rights and obligations of the contracting parties arising after the petition was filed. As to these, the "assume or reject" dichotomy means simply that if the trustee wishes to obtain for the estate the future benefits of the executory portion of the contract, the trustee must also assume the burdens of that contract, as an expense of bankruptcy administration (*i.e.*, having priority over all pre-bankruptcy claims of creditors).

It is simply a *non sequitur* to suggest that a trustee may not reject an executory contract because it is not property of the estate. It is the trustee's decision (whether to assume or reject) that determines whether the benefits of an executory contract will or will not become property of the estate. And that decision is obviously within the power ("jurisdiction") of the trustee.

Personal services contracts differ from other executory contracts only in that the consent of the parties is required before the trustee has authority to assume them—a qualification which reflects the peculiar nature of such contracts and the widespread distaste for involuntary servitude. On the other hand, the trustee's authority to reject extends to all executory contracts—including personal-services contracts.

Id. at 103, 106–07. Do you agree with this critique of *Carrere*'s reasoning?

3. *Carrere* and *Taylor* both arose in the context of Chapter 11 cases. If those debtors had filed Chapter 7 petitions, § 707(b)(3) would have been applicable. Would either or both of the cases have been dismissed on the grounds of abuse, based on the facts you know?

Similarly, Chapter 13 plans could not have been confirmed unless the filings were in good faith, § 1325(a)(7). Would either or both of these debtors have had difficulty passing that requirement?

The next case deals with the effect of rejection on a covenant not to compete. We saw a similar issue in *Maids International, Inc. v. Ward (In re Ward)*, in Chapter 3, Section B of this casebook. There, the issue was whether a right to enjoin a debtor from competing is a "claim" in bankruptcy. In an omitted footnote, *Ward* declined to "waste ink and trees going through the usual protracted exercise for a determination of whether a covenant not to compete is an 'executory contract' within the meaning of § 365 of the Code." As the next case shows, another way of looking at the issue is to ask whether the covenant not to compete survives rejection.

SILK PLANTS, ETC. FRANCHISE SYSTEMS, INC. v. REGISTER (IN RE REGISTER)

United States Bankruptcy Court, Middle District of Tennessee, 1989.
95 B.R. 73, *affirmed* 100 B.R. 360 (M.D.Tenn.1989).

GEORGE C. PAINE, II, Chief Judge.

The issue presented is whether a covenant-not-to-compete contained in a franchise agreement is still enforceable after the debtors-franchisees rejected the executory franchise agreement. The plaintiff, Silk Plants, Etc. Franchise Systems, Inc., is seeking to enjoin the debtors from operating a business in apparent violation of the covenant-not-to-compete. * * *

On March 8, 1986, the Registers executed a franchise agreement with the plaintiff granting the Registers a franchise to operate a Silk Plants, Etc. specialty retail store offering artificial flowers, plants and related items. Under part of the franchise agreement the debtors covenanted not to engage in any capacity in a business offering to sell or selling merchandise or products similar to those sold in the Silk Plants, Etc. Systems business for a period of two years after the termination of the franchise agreement. The covenant-not-to-compete was also limited to business activities within a ten-mile radius of the Register's Silk Plants, Etc. store.

On March 15, 1988, the Registers filed their Chapter 13 bankruptcy petition. On May 18, 1988, the Registers rejected the franchise agreement through an agreed order with Silk Plants, Etc. Since then the Registers have operated a business very similar to their former Silk Plants, Etc. franchise. The plaintiffs then filed this adversary proceeding to enjoin the Registers from operating that store arguing that such activities violated the covenant-not-to-compete contained in the original franchise agreement.

Debtors in a bankruptcy proceeding may accept or reject executory contracts. The primary purposes behind allowing debtors to reject executory contracts are (1) to relieve the estate from burdensome obligations while the debtor is trying to recover financially, and (2) to effect a breach of contract allowing the injured party to file a claim.

Both of these goals are furthered by permitting debtors to reject covenants-not-to-compete with the rest of the executory contract. In fact, equitably enforcing such clauses in contracts that have been rejected would directly frustrate the purposes of relieving debtors from burdens that would hinder rehabilitation. For these reasons the debtor should be able to reject the covenant-not-to-compete along with the rest of the executory contract; Silk Plants, Etc. should then be able to file a claim for the injury resulting from that breach of contract under § 502(g) of the Bankruptcy Code. This is also consistent with the general rule that executory contracts must be accepted or rejected as a whole. The franchise agreement here clearly is an executory contract and as such may be rejected as it was in this case.

Silk Plants, Etc., however, argues that the covenant-not-to-compete was not executory and so cannot be rejected. According to Silk Plants, the covenant was severable from the executory parts of this contract and was based on a separate consideration which Silk Plants, Etc. had fully provided. This separate consideration according to Silk Plants, Etc. was the provision of training and information at the beginning of the franchise relationship. Silk Plants argues that it fully performed its portion of this severable agreement when it provided the promised training and information to the debtors.

The franchise agreement, when taken as a whole, however, shows that the debtors and Silk Plants Etc. contemplated that the covenant-not-to-compete would only be enforceable if Silk Plants performed on the entire franchise agreement, not just the sections requiring it to provide special training to the debtors. If Silk Plants had rejected the contract in a bankruptcy proceeding or had otherwise breached the franchising agreement the debtors clearly would not have had to honor the covenant-not-to-compete.

Silk Plants' reliance on *Leasing Service Corp. v. First Tennessee Bank, N.A.*, 826 F.2d 434 (6th Cir.1987), is misplaced. The question there was whether the granting and perfecting of a security interest was severable from the rest of a lease. A security interest is far different from a covenant-not-to-compete. Once perfected the security interest is a present interest in property; it establishes the priority of the holder of the security interest; and the existence of the security interest is not dependent on the holders' performance of the rest of the contract. For example, in *Leasing Service Corp.* if the lessor had breached, it would have been liable to the tenant for damages. If the lessor had some valid claim against the tenant, however, the security interest would have been available to satisfy that claim regardless of the lessor's breach. Here, however, the franchisor's ability to enforce the covenant-not-to-compete is totally dependent on his faithful performance of the entire agreement. Thus the covenant-not-to-compete is not severable from the rest of the executory contract.

Silk Plants, Etc. next argues that a covenant-not-to-compete is enforced by an injunction and other equitable relief and not by a suit for money damages. Therefore the breach of this covenant does not give rise to a claim as defined by [§ 101(5)]. Silk Plants, Etc.'s right to equitable relief then should not be affected by the bankruptcy.

In support of this claim Silk Plants, Etc. cites *In re Noco, Inc.*, 76 B.R. 839 (Bankr. N.D.Fla.1987), and *In re Carrere*, 64 B.R. 156 (Bankr. C.D.Cal.1986). Both of these cases may be distinguished from the instant case because in both cases the filing of bankruptcy had elements of bad faith. The bankruptcies seemed to have been filed solely for the purpose of avoiding the covenants not to compete. Such is not the case here. * * *

To the extent that these cases support Silk Plants, Etc.'s position, this court declines to follow them. For purposes of [§ 101(5)], the principle issue is whether this court is capable of reducing the injury that Silk Plant[s] incurs as a result of the breach of this covenant to a dollar amount. If it can, then Silk Plants has a claim under §§ [101(5)] and 502(g). Although state courts have ruled that they cannot put a value on the injury incurred for breach of these covenants this Court believes that it can. As the court in *In re Norquist*, 43 B.R. 224, 231 (Bankr. E.D.Wash.1984), noted, "The equitable configuration of this court may very well permit a just determination and treatment of [a breach of a covenant-not-to-compete] which would not be accomplished under the rigid application of evidentiary rules in state court." This approach furthers the underlying goals of § 365 by relieving the debtor completely of the burden of this executory contract and by granting the creditor a claim for the injury incurred.

The court holds that the covenant-not-to-compete terminated when the contract was rejected and that Silk Plants may file a claim for the breach of the entire franchise agreement, including the covenant-not-to-compete, under § 502(g).

———————————

The case law on post-rejection enforceability of covenants not to compete is deeply divided. See *In re Printronics, Inc.*, 189 B.R. 995 (Bankr. N.D.Fla.1995). Much of the disagreement stems from evolving concepts about the effect of rejection.

In one of the most well-known, if not one of the most infamous, cases dealing with § 365, *Lubrizol Enterprises, Inc. v. Richmond Metal Finishers, Inc.,* 756 F.2d 1043 (4th Cir.1985), the debtor, Richmond Metal Finishers (RMF), entered into a non-exclusive license agreement with Lubrizol, granting Lubrizol a license to use a metal coating technology. When RMF filed for bankruptcy, it rejected this agreement as executory. The bankruptcy court approved the rejection, but the district court reversed. Upon appeal, the Court of Appeals for the Fourth Circuit held, in turn, reversed:

> Under § 365(g), Lubrizol would be entitled to treat rejection as a breach and seek a money damages remedy; however, it could not seek to retain its contract rights in the technology by specific performance even if that remedy would ordinarily be available upon breach of this type of contract. Even though § 365(g) treats rejection as a breach, the legislative history of § 365(g) makes clear that the purpose of the provision is to provide only a damages remedy for the non-bankrupt party. H.Rep. No. 95-595, 95th Cong., 2d Sess. 349, *reprinted in* 1978 U.S.C.C.A.N. 5963, 6305. For the same reason, Lubrizol cannot rely on provisions within its agreement with RMF for continued use of the technology by Lubrizol upon breach by RMF. Here again, the statutory "breach" contemplated by § 365(g) controls, and provides only a money damages remedy for the non-bankrupt party. Allowing specific performance would obviously undercut the core purpose of rejection under. § 365(a), and that consequence cannot therefore be read into congressional intent.

Id. at 1048. When the debtor rejected the agreement, Lubrizol, as licensee, lost its rights under the contract.

A number of cases—including those dealing with covenants not to compete, such as *Register*—have followed *Lubrizol*'s analysis. *Lubrizol*, however, has generated volumes of commentary and, to say the least, the case has not been the subject of universal acclaim. Largely in response to *Lubrizol*, Congress added § 365(n) to the Bankruptcy Code in 1988. That subsection applies to agreements governing certain types of intellectual property—but not trademarks—and reverses the specific result in *Lubrizol* for the types of property covered. In the following case, the Seventh Circuit repudiated *Lubrizol* and held that trademark licensees also enjoy protections against the risk of rejection.

SUNBEAM PRODUCTS, INC. v. CHICAGO AMERICAN MANUFACTURING, LLC

United States Court of Appeals, Seventh Circuit, 2012.
686 F.3d 372.

EASTERBROOK, Chief Judge.

Lakewood Engineering & Manufacturing Co. made and sold a variety of consumer products, which were covered by its patents and trademarks. In 2008, losing money on every box fan, Lakewood contracted their manufacture to Chicago American Manufacturing (CAM). The contract authorized CAM to practice Lakewood's patents and put its trademarks on the completed fans. Lakewood was to take orders from retailers such as Sears, Walmart, and Ace Hardware; CAM would ship directly to these customers on Lakewood's instructions. Because Lakewood was in financial distress, CAM was reluctant to invest the money necessary to gear up for production—and to make about 1.2 million fans that Lakewood estimated it would require during the 2009 cooling season—without assured payment. Lakewood provided that assurance by authorizing CAM to sell the 2009 run of box fans for its own account if Lakewood did not purchase them.

In February 2009, three months into the contract, several of Lakewood's creditors filed an involuntary bankruptcy petition against it. The court appointed a trustee, who decided to sell Lakewood's business. Sunbeam Products, doing business as Jarden Consumer Solutions, bought the assets, including Lakewood's patents and trademarks. Jarden did not want the Lakewood-branded fans CAM had in inventory, nor did it want CAM to sell those fans in competition with Jarden's products. Lakewood's trustee rejected the executory portion of the CAM contract under § 365(a). When CAM continued to make and sell Lakewood-branded fans, Jarden filed this adversary action. It will receive 75% of any recovery and the trustee the other 25% for the benefit of Lakewood's creditors.

The bankruptcy judge held a trial. After determining that the Lakewood–CAM contract is ambiguous, the judge relied on extrinsic evidence to conclude that CAM was entitled to make as many fans as Lakewood estimated it would need for the entire 2009 selling season and sell them bearing Lakewood's marks. Jarden contends in this court * * * that CAM had to stop making and selling fans once Lakewood stopped having requirements for them. The bankruptcy court did not err in reading the contract as it did, but the effect of the trustee's rejection remains to be determined.

   Lubrizol Enterprises, Inc. v. Richmond Metal Finishers, Inc., 756 F.2d 1043 (4th Cir.1985), holds that, when an intellectual-property license is rejected in bankruptcy, the licensee loses the ability to use any licensed copyrights, trademarks, and patents. Three years after *Lubrizol*, Congress added § 365(n) to the Bankruptcy Code. It allows licensees to continue using the intellectual property after rejection, provided they meet certain conditions. The bankruptcy judge held that § 365(n) allowed CAM to practice Lakewood's patents when making box fans for the 2009 season. That ruling is no longer contested. But "intellec-tual property" is a defined term in the Bankruptcy Code: § 101(35A) provides that "intellectual property" includes patents, copyrights, and trade secrets. It does not mention trademarks. Some bankruptcy judges have inferred from the omission that Congress codified *Lubrizol* with respect to trademarks, but an omission is just an omission. The limited definition in § 101(35A) means that § 365(n) does not affect trademarks one way or the other. According to the Senate committee report on the bill that included § 365(n), the omission was designed to allow more time for study, not to approve *Lubrizol*. See S. Rep. No. 100-505, 100th Cong., 2d Sess. 5 (1988). See also *In re Exide Technologies*, 607 F.3d 957, 966-67 (3d Cir.2010) (Ambro, J., concurring) (concluding that § 365(n) neither codifies nor disapproves *Lubrizol* as applied to trademarks). The subject seems to have fallen off the legislative agenda, but this does not change the effect of what Congress did in 1988.

   The bankruptcy judge in this case agreed with Judge Ambro that § 365(n) and § 101(35A) leave open the question whether rejection of an intellectual-property license ends the licensee's right to use trade-marks. Without deciding whether a contract's rejection under § 365(a) ends the licensee's right to use the trademarks, the judge stated that she would allow CAM, which invested substantial resources in making Lakewood-branded box fans, to continue using the Lakewood marks "on equitable grounds." This led to the entry of judgment in CAM's favor, and Jarden has appealed.

   What the Bankruptcy Code provides, a judge cannot override by declaring that enforcement would be "inequitable." There are hundreds of bankruptcy judges, who have many different ideas about what is equitable in any given situation. Some may think that equity favors licensees' reliance interests; others may believe that equity favors the creditors, who can realize more of their claims if the debtor can terminate IP licenses. Rights depend, however, on what the Code provides rather than on notions of equity. Recently the Supreme Court emphasized that arguments based on views about the purposes behind the Code, and wise public policy, cannot be used to supersede the Code's provisions. It remarked: "The Bankruptcy Code standardizes an expansive (and sometimes unruly) area of law, and it is our obligation to interpret the Code clearly and predictably using well established principles of statutory construction." *RadLAX Gateway Hotel, LLC v. Amalgamated Bank*, 132 S.Ct. 2065, 2073 (2012).

Although the bankruptcy judge's ground of decision is untenable, that does not necessarily require reversal. We need to determine whether *Lubrizol* correctly understood § 365(g), which specifies the consequences of a rejection under § 365(a). No other court of appeals has agreed with *Lubrizol*—or for that matter disagreed with it. *Exide*, the only other appellate case in which the subject came up, was resolved on the ground that the contract was not executory and therefore could not be rejected. (*Lubrizol* has been cited in other appellate opinions, none of which concerns the effect of rejection on intellectual-property licenses.) Judge Ambro, who filed a concurring opinion in *Exide*, concluded that, had the contract been eligible for rejection under § 365(a), the licensee could have continued using the trademarks. Like Judge Ambro, we too think *Lubrizol* mistaken.

* * *

* * * For our purpose, [the relevant language of § 365(g)] * * * is the opening proposition: that rejection "constitutes a breach of such contract."

Outside of bankruptcy, a licensor's breach does not terminate a licensee's right to use intellectual property. Lakewood had two principal obligations under its contract with CAM: to provide CAM with motors and cord sets (CAM was to build the rest of the fan) and to pay for the completed fans that CAM drop-shipped to retailers. Suppose that, before the bankruptcy began, Lakewood had broken its promise by failing to provide the motors. CAM might have elected to treat that breach as ending its own obligations, see Uniform Commercial Code § 2–711(1), but it also could have covered in the market by purchasing motors and billed Lakewood for the extra cost. UCC § 2–712. CAM had bargained for the security of being able to sell Lakewood-branded fans for its own account if Lakewood defaulted; outside of bankruptcy, Lakewood could not have ended CAM's right to sell the box fans by failing to perform its own duties, any more than a borrower could end the lender's right to collect just by declaring that the debt will not be paid.

What § 365(g) does by classifying rejection as breach is establish that in bankruptcy, as outside of it, the other party's rights remain in place. After rejecting a contract, a debtor is not subject to an order of specific performance. The debtor's unfulfilled obligations are converted to damages; when a debtor does not assume the contract before rejecting it, these damages are treated as a pre-petition obligation, which may be written down in common with other debts of the same class. But nothing about this process implies that any rights of the other contracting party have been vaporized. Consider how rejection works for leases. A lessee that enters bankruptcy may reject the lease and pay damages for abandoning the premises, but rejection does not abrogate the lease (which would absolve the debtor of the need to pay damages). Similarly a lessor that enters bankruptcy could not, by rejecting the lease, end the tenant's right to possession and thus reacquire premises that might be rented out for a higher price. The bankrupt lessor might substitute damages for an obligation to make repairs, but not rescind the lease altogether.

Bankruptcy law does provide means for eliminating rights under some contracts. For example, contracts that entitle creditors to preferential transfers (that is, to payments exceeding the value of goods and services provided to the debtor) can be avoided under § 547, and recent payments can be recouped. A trustee has several avoiding powers. See §§ 544–51. But Lakewood's trustee has never contended that Lakewood's contract with CAM is subject to rescission. The trustee used § 365(a) rather than any of the avoiding powers—and rejection is not "the functional equivalent of a rescission, rendering void the contract and requiring that the parties be put back in the positions they occupied before the contract was formed." *Thompkins v. Lil' Joe Records, Inc.*, 476 F.3d 1294, 1306 (11th Cir.2007). It "merely frees the estate from the obligation to perform" and "has absolutely no effect upon the contract's continued existence." *Id.* (internal citations omitted).

Scholars uniformly criticize *Lubrizol*, concluding that it confuses rejection with the use of an avoiding power. See, e.g., Douglas G. Baird, ELEMENTS OF BANKRUPTCY 130-40 & n.10 (4th ed.2006); Michael T. Andrew, *Executory Contracts in Bankruptcy: Understanding "Rejection,"* 59 U. COLO. L. REV. 845, 916-19 (1988); Jay Lawrence Westbrook, *The Commission's Recommendations Concerning the Treatment of Bankruptcy Contracts*, 5 A.B.I. L. REV. 463,

470-72 (1997). *Lubrizol* itself devoted scant attention to the question whether rejection cancels a contract, worrying instead about the right way to identify executory contracts to which the rejection power applies.

Lubrizol does not persuade us. * * * Because the trustee's rejection of Lakewood's contract with CAM did not abrogate CAM's contractual rights, this adversary proceeding properly ended with a judgment in CAM's favor.

Notes and Questions

1. According to the court, what consequences follow from rejection of an executory contract under § 365(a)?

2. The standard for rejection stated in *Lubrizol*—the "business judgment rule"—is widely accepted as the correct approach. (It is a deferential standard, but not toothless. Cf. *In re Premier Concrete, LLC*, 2010 Bankr. LEXIS 1475, 2010 WL 1780046 (Bankr. D.N.M. May 3, 2010).) Is that the standard used by the court in *Sunbeam*?

3.. Debtor entered into a 20–year licensing agreement under which Nondebtor, Inc. was given the exclusive right to manufacture and sell Debtor's inventions in Canada. Debtor filed Chapter 11 and sought to reject the agreement. Nondebtor, Inc. resisted the motion to reject, arguing that it was incorporated for the purpose of enjoying rights under the agreement and all of its business and income was based on the agreement. Should rejection be permitted when it will totally destroy Nondebtor, Inc.'s business? See *In re Petur U.S.A. Instrument Co.*, 35 B.R. 561 (Bankr. W.D.Wash.1983).

The following article, which was cited in *Sunbeam*, describes the issues courts have considered while grappling with the thorny issue of "rejection."

MICHAEL T. ANDREW, EXECUTORY CONTRACTS IN BANKRUPTCY: UNDERSTANDING "REJECTION"

59 U. Colo. L. Rev. 845, 848-49, 883-84, 901-02, 916-18, 920-22 (1988) (footnotes omitted).

In this article I suggest that much of the jurisprudence of "rejection" is profoundly confused, and that the strikingly simple concept embodied in that term has been all but lost in the confusion. As will be seen, rejection is not the revocation or repudiation or cancellation of a contract or lease, nor does it affect contract or lease liabilities. It is simply a bankruptcy estate's decision not to assume, because the contract or lease does not represent a favorable or appropriate investment of the estate's resources. Rejection does not change the substantive rights of the parties to the contract or lease, but merely means that the bankruptcy estate itself will not become a party to it. Simply put, the election to "assume or reject" is the election to assume or not assume; "rejection" is the name for the latter alternative.

Far from benign, the confusion over rejection has yielded wasteful litigation, absurd results, and dramatic distortions in bankruptcy law. Understanding that rejection does not affect contract liabilities demonstrates, for example, that litigation over whether rejection will be permitted is largely a pointless exercise. The understanding also makes clear that terminating rights in or to property arising under contracts that happen to be "executory" is fundamentally contrary to general bankruptcy principles, to the history and purpose of executory contracts doctrine itself, and to common sense. The most serious consequence of the confusion over rejection is that it has diverted attention away from important questions of bankruptcy policy, focusing it instead on the generally meaningless question of what constitutes an "executory" contract.

* * *

"Assumption" aptly describes what occurs when a bankruptcy estate elects to take on the obligations of a contract or lease as the price of obtaining the benefit of the non-debtor party's performance. By contrast, "rejection" is a particularly inapt term to describe the election *not* to assume. The reason: it suggests, misleadingly, that the trustee or debtor in possession is somehow rejecting (cancelling? repudiating? renouncing? rescinding?) *liabilities*. In fact, what the estate's representative is rejecting is the contract or lease *asset*, which conceivably could carry continuing obligations with it into the estate on an administrative basis. Rejection simply prevents the *estate* from unadvisedly stepping into such liabilities. The liabilities are not repudiated; to the contrary, as the rejection-as-breach doctrine is designed to insure, the contract or lease liabilities remain intact after rejection and give the non-debtor party a claim in the distribution of the estate.

The doctrinal labelling of rejection as a "breach" is also unfortunate, though, for two reasons. First, it undoubtedly exacerbates the confused view of rejection as a cancellation or repudiation of liabilities.

A superficial reading of the doctrine can suggest the upside-down conclusion that bankruptcy law confers on bankruptcy trustees and debtors in possession a special "power" to breach contracts. That confused restatement of the doctrine at least implies that a trustee or debtor in possession can make obligations simply disappear, or can in some other way impair the rights of the non-debtor party, *just because the contract is "executory."* In fact, rejection-as-breach doctrine exists for precisely the opposite reason: It assures non-debtor parties to executory contracts and leases that, for purposes of the bankruptcy distribution, they will not be treated differently than other claimants and the obligations owed to them will *not* disappear.

Second, the use of "breach" terminology (particularly when coupled to rejection rather than bankruptcy itself) suggests that there is some discontinuity between the treatment of "executory" contracts and other liabilities. In fact, "breach" was used as an indirect way of saying that there is *no* discontinuity: For executory contracts, as for all other obligations, claims will be determined based upon the presumption that the debtor will not perform. To say that an executory contract is "breached" is merely to say what is already presumed to be true with respect to all other obligations. Again, it must be emphasized that the "breach" here is a presumed pre-bankruptcy breach *by the debtor*.

Much confusion would have been averted had the election to "assume or reject" been called, more comprehensibly but to identical effect, the election to "assume or decline" or, as in *Copeland* [*v. Stephens*, 106 Eng.Rep. (K.B. 1818)], the election to "accept or refuse." Similarly, the "breach" rule would have been eminently more understandable described as what it is: a presumption of the debtor's non-performance for claims allowance purposes.

* * *

Another more significant result of confusion about "rejection" has been the creation of a distinct doctrine—"avoiding-power" rejection, as I call it—only spuriously related to basic executory contracts doctrine. That separate doctrine, like bankruptcy's explicit avoiding powers, terminates the rights of third parties in or to property in which the debtor had an interest. It does so, however, without any of the justifications of the avoiding powers, but instead only because the third party's rights arise under a contract that happens to be "executory" when the bankruptcy commences.

* * *

The case that illustrates perhaps better than any other what is wrong with avoiding-power rejection, and how the Countryman test of an "executory" contract fuels it, is the Fourth Circuit's decision in *Lubrizol Enterprises, Inc. v. Richmond Metal Finishers, Inc.* There the debtor had licensed certain technology to Lubrizol non-exclusively, and sought in its chapter 11 case to reject the license and terminate Lubrizol's rights to the technology. The key issue, thought the court, was the hunt for mutual "executoriness."

Addressing first the debtor-licensor's side of the agreement, the court found executory aspects in the "continuing duties of notifying Lubrizol of further licensing of the process and of reducing Lubrizol's royalty rate to meet any more favorable rates granted to subsequent licensees." In addition, the debtor had the "additional contingent duties of notifying [Lubrizol] of suits, defending suits and indemnifying it for certain losses."

The "executoriness" of Lubrizol's side of the arrangement was more difficult, because the court thought the mutual performance test required remaining duties other than merely the payment of money. But the necessary "executory" obligations were found, as the court explained in this remarkable passage:

> [I]f Lubrizol had owed [the debtor] nothing more than a duty to make fixed payments or cancel specified indebtedness under the agreement, the agreement would not be executory as to Lubrizol. However, the promise to account for and pay royalties *required that Lubrizol deliver written quarterly sales reports and keep books of account subject to inspection by an independent Certified Public Accountant.* This promise goes beyond a mere debt, or promise to pay money, and was at the critical time executory.

The court went on to approve rejection of the license and termination of the licensee's interest, relying in part on the absence of any special protection for licensees in § 365.

The passage just quoted is one of the most noteworthy in the annals of avoiding-power rejection. Lubrizol had what everyone apparently believed was a perfectly valid license. Nothing suggests that the license was in any way subject to termination by any creditor of, or purchaser from, the debtor under non-bankruptcy law, or that it was in any other way avoidable under bankruptcy law. It also seems quite clear that if the license had been found to have been non-"executory," the court would have enforced it. *Lubrizol lost its right to the technology because it had the duty to "deliver written quarterly sales reports and keep books of account subject to inspection."*

The court did not pause to ask why the happenstance of "executoriness" should control an issue so important as the licensee's continued ability to use the technology. Its only real attempt at an explanation of the result was to observe that the "clear" purpose of § 365(g), the rejection-as-breach rule, "is to provide only a damages remedy for the non-bankrupt party" * * *.

* * *

Whether the debtor is a licensor, lessor, vendor, or mortgagor, or any other owner of real or personal property in or to which a third party has rights under a contract, the analysis should be the same. Rejection of the contract by the estate—the estate's decision not to assume—is not a rescission or cancellation of the contract. It is merely the estate's decision not to become obligated on it. Thus, rejection of the *contract* does not enhance the estate's rights to the *underlying asset*. The estate acquires that asset, like all other assets, in the "same plight and condition that the [debtor] himself held it, and subject to all the equities impressed upon it in the hands of the [debtor]," even though clearly the estate is not itself bound by the contract.

As a starting premise, therefore, the position of the estate is no different from that of any other ordinary transferee acquiring the under-lying asset from the debtor without assuming the debtor's contract obligations. The proper inquiry is what the position of such a nonassuming transferee would be vis-à-vis the non-debtor party. To the extent that the non-debtor could enforce its rights as against such a transferee of the underlying asset—by specific performance, other injunctive relief, replevin, or some other remedy—it should be able to do so as against the estate despite the rejection of the contract. It is for precisely that reason that a lessee is entitled to remain in possession of property despite rejection of a lease by the lessor's bankruptcy estate.

It must be clearly understood, though, that this analysis does not somehow elevate the non-debtor party over other claimants. The non-debtor's right to the property or to some use of it, like any other right in or to property in bankruptcy, is good against the estate only if it survives the true avoiding powers. To that extent, the estate has *better* rights in the asset than would an ordinary transferee from the debtor. That means, among other things, that a right to property not good against a lien creditor of the debtor (or a bona fide purchaser of real property from the debtor) under state law would not be good as against the estate. Thus, the contract right in or to the property is enforced in bankruptcy only to the extent that it was a right *good against other claimants in the first place*.

That point also makes clear the error in arguing that recognition of the non-debtor's rights in or to property will somehow defeat a fundamental purpose of rejection—to insure that parties to executory contracts are treated the same as other claimants. Bankruptcy law distinguishes between *other* claimants on the basis of rights in or to property. Nothing in executory contracts doctrine remotely suggests a design to treat all parties to unassumed executory contracts as unsecured creditors, any more than bankruptcy law generally treats all other claimants as unsecured creditors, which it plainly does not. Rather, the design of executory contracts doctrine is to eliminate "executoriness" as a factor in determining the non-debtor party's rights when a contract is not assumed.

2. SPECIAL RULES FOR CERTAIN REAL ESTATE INTERESTS

The Code contains special protections when the party in bankruptcy is the lessor, the seller under a real estate sales contract, or the seller of a timeshare interest. Congress believed that the nondebtor party to these types of contracts is particularly vulnerable and in need of protection.

Read §§ 365(h), (i) and (j) and solve the following Problems.

Problems

1. Debtor Corp. owns an office building and leases space to Law Firm. The lease, which runs for 10 more years, requires Law Firm to pay $10,000 per month in rent. It also requires Debtor Corp. to heat and cool the building, to keep the building clean and to provide elevator service. The demand for office space has risen in the last year and Debtor Corp. wants to reject Law Firm's lease and relet the premises for more money. Can Debtor Corp. reject the lease? If so, can it dispossess Law Firm following rejection? What are Law Firm's options? See § 365(h).

2. Flowers-by-Florence leased space in Downtown Mall, which was owned by Debtor, Inc. Florence chose to remain in place when Debtor, Inc. filed bankruptcy and rejected the lease, but Florence later decided to close the shop and assign the balance of the lease term to Wilma's Wines. The lease

provides that no more than one specialty store of any type can occupy premises in the Mall. Both Debtor, Inc. and Fred's Fine Wines, which is located on the other end of Downtown Mall, object to the assignment. What result? See § 365(h).

3. Debtor Corp. owned an apartment complex. Two years ago, facing severe financial problems, Debtor Corp. decided to convert the premises to condominiums. Mary Occupant agreed to purchase her unit and signed a contract requiring payments over a 10–year period, with title remaining in Debtor Corp. until payment of the last installment. Debtor Corp. filed Chapter 11 last month and notified Mary that it intended to reject her purchase contract. What are Mary's options? See § 365(i).

4. Developer sold a beachfront lot to Greg Greene under an installment sales contract requiring the payment of $7,500 per year for five years. Title was to remain in Developer until completion of payments. After Greg made two annual payments, Developer filed bankruptcy and sought to reject the contract. Greg had looked forward to building a get-away cottage on the lot as soon as he could afford to, and he is very upset. What are Greg's options? See §§ 365(i) and (j).

5. Developer owned a tract of land on which Bank held a purchase money mortgage for $400,000. Developer contracted with Joe and Jane Homeowner to build them a house on the lot for $520,000. The Homeowners gave Developer a down payment of $60,000, which Developer used to pay for labor and materials. At the time Developer stopped work and filed bankruptcy, $50,000 remained owing to materials suppliers. The land and unfinished house were sold for $430,000. Claims against the proceeds were asserted by Bank, the materials suppliers and the Homeowners. How should the proceeds be distributed? See *Thompson Designs, Inc. v. Treasurer of Hamilton County (In re Thompson Designs, Inc.)*, 213 B.R. 725 (Bankr. S.D. Ind.1997).

3. REJECTION OF PREVIOUSLY ASSUMED CONTRACTS AND LEASES

As we have seen, assumption turns the debtor's obligations under an executory contract or lease into obligations of the estate that enjoy administrative expense priority. A trustee or debtor-in-possession should assume only after determining that the lease or contract will benefit the estate enough to merit burdening the estate with the obligations that will flow from assumption. But what if those beneficial projections prove to have been overly optimistic, as happens all too often, and the lease or contract is later rejected? What is the status of the obligations under the contract or lease—do all of the remaining obligations enjoy administrative expense priority? And what about the cap on a long-term lessor's claim under § 502(b)(6)?

Section 503(b)(7), which was added in 2005, now answers these questions for leases of nonresidential real property. It gives two years' worth of administrative expenses status to the monetary obligations under the lease, and subjects the remaining obligations to § 502(b)(6)'s cap. For fact patterns not covered by § 503(b)(7), cases that struggled with these questions before 2005 may remain persuasive. See, e.g., *Nostas Associates v. Costich (In re Klein Sleep Products, Inc.)*, 78 F.3d 18 (2d Cir.1996).

E. TIME LIMITS FOR DECIDING WHETHER TO ASSUME OR REJECT

Because the interests of the nondebtor party to a lease or executory contract can be seriously and adversely affected by delay, § 365 imposes time limits within which the trustee or debtor-in-possession must decide whether to assume or reject.

The applicable time period depends, in the case of real estate leases, upon whether the premises are residential or nonresidential. The applicable time period also depends upon the chapter under which bankruptcy was filed.

Section 365(d)(4) limits the amount of time available to commercial debtors to assume or reject a nonresidential lease. The following excerpt discusses the economic implications of this subsection, as amended by the Bankruptcy Abuse Prevention and Consumer Protection Act of 2005 ("BAPCPA").

KARA J. BRUCE, REHABILITATING BANKRUPTCY REFORM

13 Nev. L. J. 174, 202-07 (2012) (footnotes omitted).

Section 365 of the Bankruptcy Code affords debtors the opportunity to either assume or reject executory contracts or unexpired leases. Grounded in the "fresh start" principle of reorganization, this provision allows a debtor "to use valuable property of the estate and to 'renounce title to and abandon burdensome property.'" As part of the debtor's power to assume contracts, the debtor may assign them to third parties, avoiding anti-assignment clauses and other limiting provisions in the contracts. Companies operating in multiple locations have historically used § 365 to reject above-market leases, close underperforming locations, and sell below-market leases to willing buyers. In this way, § 365(d)(4) allows debtors to both cut operating costs and bring value to the estate.

Before BAPCPA, a debtor faced a sixty-day window to assume or reject non-residential real property leases, such as store, plant, or office leases. That window could be extended by the bankruptcy court for "cause." Courts routinely granted debtors' requests for extensions and, over time, debtors and lenders relied on the ability to obtain as many extensions as needed to make reasoned lease decisions. Commercial landlords, frustrated with the long delays, lobbied forcefully for an amendment that would "remove the bankruptcy judge's discretion to grant extensions of the time."

Section 365(d)(4) now provides the debtor an initial 120 days after the petition date to assume or reject non-residential real property leases. This time frame is subject to only one ninety-day extension, resulting in a maximum 210-day window to make lease determinations.

If the debtor needs additional time to evaluate its leases, the debtor must obtain each landlord's written consent for a further extension. If the debtor fails to elect assumption or rejection and cannot obtain the landlord's written consent to a further extension, then the lease is deemed rejected. This new time limit has proved challenging for large retailers, who can have thousands of retail leases to evaluate. * * *

* * * Revised § 365(d)(4) gives landlords a great deal of leverage, particularly over larger debtors who may be in greater need of additional time. Landlords may, for example, exact fees or other concessions as a condition to any extensions beyond the outside window of 210 days. Requiring individual negotiations with each landlord also imposes a potentially significant communications burden on a debtor that already faces a truncated bankruptcy process.

This change has seriously impacted the ability of retailers to secure meaningful debtor-in-possession ("DIP") financing. Debtors entering Chapter 11 bankruptcy need liquidity to stabilize trade credit, pay their lawyers and financial advisors, meet general operating costs, and avoid a premature liquidation of the business. As companies facing bankruptcy are frequently in a tight cash position, they may rely on DIP financing to meet these obligations. The reduced time frames presented by § 365(d)(4), coupled with debtors' increased cash demands, make a retail bankruptcy case a much less attractive investment for DIP lenders than it was before BAPCPA.

To understand § 365(d)(4)'s impact, it is important to note that a DIP financer's willingness to lend to a retailer has historically relied on the debtor's ability to market the debtor's commercial leases. Before BAPCPA, retail debtors frequently assigned their below-market leases to third parties, generating significant value for the bankruptcy estate. Likewise, the sale of "designation rights" allowed the debtor to obtain immediate liquidity early in a bankruptcy case. Designation rights are the rights to direct the debtors to assume and assign unexpired leases to qualifying third parties. Designation-rights sales have been especially helpful to large retail bankruptcies because they allow the debtor to quickly monetize the value of the leases while shifting the administrative burden of assigning individual leases to a willing buyer. Due to the reduction of the time periods for assigning leases under BAPCPA, the time to market commercial leases and designation rights packages is starkly reduced.

Moreover, a DIP lender generally relies on the value of a retailer's inventory to secure its loan. The debtor's inventory is most valuable to a lender if it remains on the store shelves, available to customers. If the debtor must liquidate, lenders will frequently demand that the liquidation proceed while existing stores remain open. Thus, a lender's agreement to provide bankruptcy financing will likely require the debtor to make lease decisions nine to twelve weeks in advance of the lease decision deadline to allow for sufficient time to conduct a going-out-of-business sale on site. In effect, this truncates the retailer's reorganization process to no more than a five-month window.

E. Taking Stock of BAPCPA: Impact on the Retail Industry

In recent years, retail bankruptcy cases have largely followed a predictable pattern: when the retailer enters bankruptcy, the case is either filed as a liquidation from the outset, or its lenders allow a one-shot attempt to complete an internal reorganization or locate a going-concern buyer. If the debtor fails to do so within five months of filing, the retailer will be liquidated before the lease rejection window has closed. This rushed and mechanical process affords little opportunity for market participants to determine the best use for the debtor's assets, or to negotiate an alternate course.

An increased prevalence of liquidations harms a number of parties, from employees to nearby retailers, as well as other businesses in the supply chain. Ironically, several of the purported beneficiaries of BAPCPA's amendments have found themselves in a worse position following the recent spate of retail liquidations. Large real estate conglomerates, which lease much of the U.S. retail space, have sustained major losses from the liquidation of numerous national retail chains. Indeed, in the wake of widespread retail liquidations and plunging real estate values, the nation's second-largest shopping mall operator filed for bankruptcy relief. Additionally, utility companies and twenty-day claimants lose continuing business relationships when their customers liquidate. Twenty-day claims will be subordinated to Chapter 7 administrative expenses if a bankruptcy case converts to a Chapter 7 liquidation. Thus, in the wake of rampant retail liquidations, many retail creditors may find the benefits promised by BAPCPA to be illusory.

* * *

The retail story is one of unintended consequences resulting from BAPCPA's emphasis on crystalline rules. BAPCPA's expansion of interest-group benefits and reduction of the judicial role have made reorganization more costly and time-pressured and have incentivized many creditors to favor the debtor's liquidation.

The rise of retail liquidations under BAPCPA suggests that the structure of BAPCPA's reforms has undermined their substance, upsetting both foundational bankruptcy policies and BAPCPA's normative goals.

Read § 365(d) and answer the following Problems.

Problems

1. Dan Debtor filed Chapter 7, largely as a result of bad financial management. Dan leased a beautiful apartment overlooking a river and the trustee thought the apartment might be worth a lot more than Dan was paying. How long does the trustee have to decide whether to assume or reject? Does the trustee have to keep paying rent while deciding?

2. Would your answers to Problem # 1 change if Dan filed under Chapter 13 instead?

3. Accounting Firm leased its premises from Landlord and all of its office machines from Supplier, Inc. If Accounting Firm files a Chapter 11 petition, how long does it have to decide whether to assume or reject the real estate lease? The lease of office equipment?

4. Dorothy Debtor operated a restaurant as a sole proprietorship, using furniture and kitchen equipment leased from Restaurant Supply Services. Dorothy had never run a business before and her poor management skills were obvious. She started taking a financial management course, but it was too late to avoid bankruptcy. She filed Chapter 7 and made plans to revive her business. She needs to keep the furniture and kitchen equipment, but the trustee refuses to do anything about the lease. Bankruptcy was filed 59 days ago. Is Dorothy out of luck? See § 365(p).

5. Darryl Debtor leased his dream car—a classic Thunderbird—from Car Classics, Inc. Darryl's Chapter 7 trustee did nothing about the lease and Darryl assumed that he could keep the car as long as he remained current on the payments. Two months after Darryl's bankruptcy filing, however, Car Classics repossessed the car. When Darryl sought damages for violation of the stay, Car Classics point to the parties' lease agreement and a clause that terminated the lease upon the filing of a bankruptcy petition. Was Car Classics within its rights, or did it violate the stay? See §§ 362(h), 521(a)(6) and 521(d).

6. Larry Lippman leased three apartments in the same building. He lived in one of them with his daughter and sublet the other two. Larry filed a Chapter 11 petition, but made no move to assume or reject any of the leases. Sixty-five days after bankruptcy was filed and before Larry had proposed a plan of reorganization, Lessor moved for relief from the stay on the grounds that the leases were deemed rejected. What result? See *In re Lippman*, 122 B.R. 206 (Bankr.S.D.N.Y.1990).

F. PRE–DECISION OBLIGATIONS OF THE PARTIES

A "gap period" necessarily occurs between the filing of bankruptcy and a debtor's decision whether to assume or reject a lease or executory contract. Because these agreements involve mutual obligations, determination of the rights and responsibilities of both the debtor and nondebtor during this period is vitally important.

Section 365 addresses the nondebtor's obligation to continue performance during the gap period only in § 365(b)(4), which excuses a nondebtor from providing services and supplies, without compensation, under a lease that is in default. The negative implication is that the lessor is not otherwise excused, and must not interfere with the debtor's right to continue its occupancy or use of goods. (And, of course, that negative implication is consistent with § 362(a)(3)'s prohibition against interference with property of the estate.)

The Code is much more direct as far as the debtor's obligations are concerned. Subsection 365(d)(3), which was added in 1984, requires the trustee (almost always a Chapter 11 debtor-in-possession) to perform under a lease of nonresidential real property while deciding whether to assume or reject the lease. This obligation applies regardless of the chapter under which bankruptcy was filed. Subsection 365(d)(5) was added in 1994 (and renumbered in 2005); it imposes similar requirements for nonconsumer personal property leases, but only in Chapter 11.

Problems

1. Accounting Firm leased its premises from Landlord and all of its office machines from Supplier, Inc. If Accounting Firm files a Chapter 11 petition, does it have to keep paying Supplier, Inc. and Landlord while deciding whether to assume or reject the two leases?

2. Debtor operated several retail locations on leased premises. Each of the leases required payment in advance, on the first of each month. Debtor filed a Chapter 11 petition on September 15 without having paid any of the rental obligations for that month. Although Debtor has not yet decided whether to assume or reject any of the leases, the lessors assert that § 365(d)(3) entitles them to immediate payment of the portion of September rents due postpetition—the so-called "stub" period. Debtor asserts that no rent is due under § 365(d)(3) until October 1. Which argument is correct? See *In re HQ Global Holdings, Inc.*, 282 B.R. 169 (Bankr. D.Del.2002).

3. Debtor, Inc. was tenant under a lease requiring it to pay all property taxes on the premises. Debtor filed bankruptcy on October 1 and had not yet decided whether to assume or reject the lease when the bill for that year's property taxes came due. The lessor argued that debtor was required to pay the entire tax obligation under § 365(d)(3). Debtor countered that only the portion of taxes due postpetition and prerejection would be payable under § 365(d)(3). Which argument is correct? Compare *Centerpoint Properties v. Montgomery Ward Holding Corp. (In re Montgomery Ward Holding Corp.)*, 268 F.3d 205 (3d Cir.2003), with *In re Handy Andy Home Improvement Centers, Inc.*, 144 F.3d 1125 (7th Cir.1998).

4. Whitcomb & Keller, Inc. is a mortgage banker that is also in the business of servicing mortgage accounts for investors. W & K contracted with Data–Link for the computer services necessary to maintain its customer accounts. The contract provided that, upon termination, W & K would pay any outstanding balance in full and Data–Link would return all master files to

W & K. W & K filed Chapter 11, owing Data–Link $13,000 for prepetition computer services. While W & K was looking for a buyer for its mortgage account servicing operation, and before it decided whether to assume or reject the contract, Data–Link terminated its services. That paralyzed W & K's operation. Can W & K obtain a court order forcing Data–Link to resume performance on this contract? See *Data-Link Systems, Inc. v. Whitcomb & Keller Mortgage Co. (Matter of Whitcomb & Keller Mortgage Co.)*, 715 F.2d 375 (7th Cir.1983).

5. Debtor leased several gas station and convenience store locations from Lessor. The leases, which had an initial term of ten years, permitted renewal for an additional ten-year term, but the option to renew could not be exercised if any lease was in default. Debtor filed a Chapter 11 petition six months before expiration of the original term and obtained an extension of time within which to assume or reject the leases. Debtor sought to exercise the renewal option during that period, but Lessor objected because Debtor's prepetition defaults had not been cured. Can Debtor renew the leases, without first deciding whether to assume or reject and without curing the defaults? See *Coleman Oil Co. v. Circle K Corp. (In re Circle K Corp.)*, 127 F.3d 904 (9th Cir.1997), *cert. denied*, 522 U.S. 1148, 118 S.Ct. 1166, 140 L.Ed.2d 176 (1998).

The following case raises an interpretive problem under § 365(d)(3). A similar question may also be encountered under § 365(d)(5).

IN RE PYXSYS CORP.

United States Bankruptcy Court, District of Massachusetts, 2003.
288 B.R. 309.

HENRY J. BOROFF, United States Bankruptcy Judge.

[Cummings Properties, LLC (CPL) leased nonresidential real estate to Debtor, Pyxsys Corp. An involuntary Chapter 7 petition was filed against Debtor on January 18, 2002 and the court entered an order for relief on February 5, 2002. CPL moved for immediate payment of $26,673.13 pursuant to §§ 365(d)(3) and 503(b)(1). That amount represented rent due from the date the order of relief was entered through the 60-day period until the lease was deemed automatically rejected, plus use and occupancy charges ending on the date the premises were vacated.]

I. FACTS AND TRAVEL OF THE CASE

At case commencement, the Debtor was in the business of developing high performance, intelligent computer network storage solutions. * * *

Under the Lease, monthly rent for calendar year 2002 was set at $8,891.05, due in advance on the first day of each month. In this case, the Trustee did not make any postpetition rental payments nor did he formally assume or reject the Lease. Consequently, pursuant to § 365(d)(4), the Lease was deemed automatically rejected on April 6, 2002. Notwithstanding rejection of the Lease, certain assets remained stored at the Property until they were sold by the Trustee for approximately $65,000.00. The Property was then fully vacated on May 6, 2002.

CPL * * * requests allowance and prompt payment of the total claim amount of $26,673.15, consisting of $17,782.10 in postpetition, pre-rejection rent (the "Rent Claim") and $8,891.05 in use and occupancy charges for storing estate assets during the post-rejection period, ending when the Property was vacated (the "Use Claim"). The Trustee filed a Limited Objection, countering that, pursuant to §§ 507(a) and 503(b)(1), CPL is not entitled to immediate payment on its claims. The Trustee contends that payment should be withheld until a final determination of estate solvency is made and that disbursement should then follow pro rata for like claims. * * *

II. POSITIONS OF THE PARTIES

CPL contends that this Court should order the Trustee to pay the claims immediately. In support of its argument, CPL points to § 365(d)(3), which requires a trustee to timely perform all obligations under a lease until assumed or rejected. CPL asserts that the Trustee has failed to timely perform the Lease obligations by not paying the Rent Claim. CPL asserts further that the Court should order the Trustee to immediately pay the Use Claim as well. In support, CPL argues that, by permitting estate assets to be stored at the Property until liquidation by the Trustee, CPL suffered a loss preserving the estate, compensable under § 503(b)(1)(A). CPL contends that payment on its postpetition claims should not be conditioned upon future estate solvency nor subject to subsequent disgorgement in the event of estate insolvency.

The Trustee maintains that, pursuant to the priority scheme established under § 507(a)(1), the Rent and Use Claims are not subject to immediate payment, but rather, payment should await final administration of the estate or a determination that the Trustee has sufficient funds to pay all administrative creditors in full. The Trustee argues that recent case law has withdrawn from the stance that § 365(d)(3) mandates superpriority status for rents to commercial landlords unpaid during the postpetition, pre-rejection period. * * * In support, the Trustee maintains that under the Bankruptcy Code priorities are strictly construed in order to adhere to the distribution scheme established under §§ 726 and 507. On that basis, the Trustee urges the Court to refrain from invoking its equitable powers under § 105(a) to grant payment of either of the claims at this time. In the alternative, the Trustee argues that any claims now paid be subject to recapture in case of administrative insolvency. * * *

III. DISCUSSION

A. Non-residential postpetition, pre-rejection rents under § 365(d)(3).

Section 365(d)(3) of the Code provides the framework for how estate representatives shall handle unexpired, non-residential leases. This section was added to the Bankruptcy Code by 1984 amendment (the "BAFJA Amendments"). Prior to the BAFJA Amendments, estate representatives were not required to make rental payments during the postpetition, pre-rejection period. In effect, a commercial landlord was forced to lease property rent free to the bankruptcy estate postpetition while awaiting a decision from the estate representative on lease assumption or rejection. These "administrative rent" claims were then subject to adjustment, in abrogation of the lease terms, to reflect the reasonable value of the estate's use and occupancy, and, if paid at all, were eventually paid with other administrative claimants on a pro rata basis.

The legislative history of the BAFJA Amendments suggests that Congress adopted § 365(d)(3) as an attempt to alleviate the unique financial strains the Code placed upon the commercial lessor.[3] How-

---

[3] Senator Hatch's floor comments at the time of the BAFJA Amendments identified: the commercial lessor as uniquely burdened among bankruptcy creditors; the financial consequences the pre-amended Code imposed upon such lessors; and the curative potential of the amendments:

ever, notwithstanding the command of § 365(d)(3) that the estate representative make timely payments due under a lease not yet assumed or rejected, the Code provides no specific consequences for non-payment. In essence, it has been observed that § 365(d)(3) provides a right but no remedy. *In re Brennick*, 178 B.R. 305, 308 (Bankr. D. Mass. 1995). It is, perhaps, this absence of an enforcement provision in the face of estate representative default that has led courts to such divergent conclusions about the array of rights and obligations under § 365(d)(3).

* * * [T]here is at least general agreement on three changes to the treatment of these claims wrought by § 365(d)(3). First, there is little dispute that the clause "notwithstanding section 503(b)(1) of this title" eliminates the requirement for an order expressly authorizing payment of an administrative rent claim. § 365(d)(3). Second, many courts have held that same clause to eliminate the "benefits test" of § 503(b)(1) and view § 365(d)(3) as having no threshold requirement that administrative rent claims reflect an objective benefit to the estate.

A second and related problem is that during the time the debtor has vacated space but has not yet decided whether to assume or reject the lease, the trustee has stopped making payments due under the lease. These payments include rent due the landlord and common area charges which are paid by all the tenants according to the amount of space they lease. In this situation, the landlord is forced to provide current services—without current payment. No other creditor is put in this position. In addition, the other tenants often must increase their common area charge payments to compensate for the trustee's failure to make the required payments for the debtor.

The bill would lessen these problems by requiring the trustee to perform all the obligations of the debtor under the lease of nonresidential property at the time required in the lease. This timely performance requirement will insure that debtor-tenants pay their rent, common area, and other charges on time pending the trustee's assumption or rejection of the lease * * * . At the end of this period, the amounts due during the first 60 days would be required to be paid, and thereafter, all obligations must be performed on time. This permissible 60-day grace period is intended to give the trustee time to determine what lease obligations the debtor has and to locate the cash to make the required payments in exceptionally large or complicated cases. The bill does not require the performance of obligations specified in § 365(b)(2), which relate to solvency and financial conditions. The performance by the trustee of the debtor's obligations has no effect under subsections (b) or (f) of § 365. The acceptance by the lessor of any payments made by the trustee as required by this subsection does not constitute a waiver or relinquishment of the lessor's rights under such lease or under the bankruptcy code.

130 Cong. Rec. S8, 994-95 (daily ed. June 29, 1984) (statement of Sen. Hatch).

Third, most courts have agreed that the clause has the further and corollary effect of allowing landlords to assert claims under § 365(d)(3) valued according to the lease terms and not according to a reasonable value based upon benefit to the estate.

The published decisions regarding the actual payment of claims brought under § 365(d)(3) fall into two main camps. The majority view is that since § 365(d)(3) contains no explicit authority for the payment of administrative rent claims as a priority to the derogation of other claims against the insolvent estate, these claims are not entitled to superpriority status. *Towers v. Chickering & Gregory (In re Pacific-Atlantic Trading Co.)*, 27 F.3d 401 (9th Cir.1994); *Pudgie's Development of NY, Inc.*, 239 B.R. 688, 692 (Bankr. S.D.N.Y.1999); *In re J.T. Rapps, Inc.*, 225 B.R. 257, 260 (Bankr. D.Mass.1998). As this Court noted in *In re J.T. Rapps,* there are only three sections of the Code in which Congress made an explicit provision for "a blanket priority over another class of claims," and, notably, § 365(d)(3) is not among them. 225 B.R. at 263 (citing §§ 726(b), 364(c)(1), & 507(b)). Those espousing this view reason that providing superpriority status to post-petition, pre-rejection rent claims would disturb the distribution scheme envisioned by Congress and, as the *Pudgie's Development* court admonished, "the Bankruptcy Court cannot reorder the priority scheme established for claims by Congress." 239 B.R. at 692; see *United States v. Noland*, 517 U.S. 535, 542 (1996) (holding that the bankruptcy court could not invoke its equitable powers to subordinate claims in abrogation of the scheme established by Congress).

The line of cases in the minority view hold that, given the legis-lative history of § 365(d)(3), the conscripted position of the landlord creditor, and the "clear command that the trustee 'shall timely perform' the debtor's obligation to pay rent," immediate payment of postpetition, pre-rejection rents is the only appropriate remedy. *Brennick*, 178 B.R. at 307-08; see *In re Telesphere Communications, Inc.*, 148 B.R. 525 (Bankr. N.D. Ill. 1992). As Judge Queenan noted in *Brennick*, 178 B.R. at 308, §§ 365(d)(3) and 365(d)(10) are the only sections of the entire Code "requiring the estate to perform the debtor's obligations at all, much less in a 'timely' manner."

Within the minority line of cases there is a further split of authority. Some courts authorize payment of § 365(d)(3) claims subject to later disgorgement in the event of administrative insolvency. *In re Tel-Central Communications, Inc.*, 212 B.R. 342 (Bankr. W.D. Mo.1997). Presumably, while those courts view § 365(d)(3) as mandating immediate payment, they do not view the statute as conferring any additional priority over other administrative claimants.

Other courts hold that the plain meaning of the statute requires payment of these claims as a so-called superpriority, subject to neither the current administrative solvency of the estate nor subsequent disgorgement in the event of future estate insolvency. *In re Rare Coin Galleries of America, Inc.*, 72 B.R. 415 (D. Mass. 1987).

Here, CPL holds a postpetition, pre-rejection Rent Claim of $17,782.10. The Trustee has stated that the estate has approximately $75,000 in assets and less than $30,000 in current administrative expenses, not including the asserted claims of CPL. In the case law, on either side of the issue, estate solvency has been the linchpin of the analysis; relatively few courts disregarded estate solvency altogether. Compare *In re Tel-Central Communications, Inc.*, 212 B.R. 342 (Bankr. W.D. Mo. 1997) (holding that the likelihood of administrative solvency weighed heavily on the decision to grant immediate payment of § 365(d)(3) rent claim); *In re Buyer's Club Markets, Inc.*, 115 B.R. 700 (Bankr. D. Colo. 1990) (holding that recapture of § 365(d)(3) claim payment was necessary if administrative insolvency occurred); with *In re Rare Coin Galleries of America, Inc.*, 72 B.R. 415 (D. Mass. 1987) (ordering immediate payment of § 365(d)(3) claim despite administrative insolvency); *In re Brennick*, 178 B.R. 305 (Bankr. D. Mass. 1995) (holding for payment of § 365(d)(3) claim regardless of estate solvency to further Congressional intent to aid commercial lessors).

Since the Debtor's estate is administratively solvent, payment of the Rent Claim at this time would not result in a derogation of either payment of like claims or the congressionally mandated distribution scheme. Nor would immediate payment of the Rent Claim be at variance with this Court's holding in *J.T. Rapps*. In *J.T. Rapps*, this Court followed those who have held that § 365(d)(3) does not grant automatic superpriority status to a commercial lessor's postpetition, pre-rejection claims. Notably, however, in *J.T. Rapps*, the estate was administratively insolvent.

Accordingly, *J.T. Rapps* is easily distinguishable from the scenario presented here—but for one important similarity. Even in *J.T. Rapps*, this Court noted that a court *could* grant superpriority status to a commercial lessor's postpetition, pre-rejection claim where necessary to adequately protect payment of an accruing claim, in lieu of granting other relief (such as an order rejecting the lease, granting relief from the automatic stay, or converting the case to Chapter 7). Logically, payment resulting from such an order should not be subject to disgorgement. However, here, as in *J.T. Rapps*, CPL waited until all the dust settled before seeking court relief. CPL's rights do not emanate from an order attempting to adequately protect an accruing claim; rather, the Rent Claim of CPL is a garden variety administrative claim for services already rendered and should be granted early payment (but no special status) on account of § 365(d)(3). Therefore, in the unlikely event of future administrative insolvency of the estate, the payment made to CPL at this time may be subject to disgorgement.

The Trustee argues further that payment of the Rent Claim should wait because insolvency *may* result from the costs incurred by the Trustee in litigation against former officers of the Debtor. The Trustee's stated purpose in the litigation is to return assets to the estate. The Trustee's argument utilizes the prospective litigation as both carrot and stick; that is, all creditors will be paid in full if the litigation is successful, but, if not, the estate will likely become insolvent on account of the litigation expense. Yet the Trustee cites no statutory provision or case law, nor can this Court locate any, to support his contention that an administratively solvent estate may delay payment of a § 365(d)(3) claim for such a reason. Where a trustee seeks to defer such payment, the trustee must demonstrate a reasonable likelihood of future estate insolvency. See *In re Four Star Pizza, Inc.*, 135 B.R. 498, 500 (Bankr. W.D. Pa. 1992) (requiring a showing of substantial doubt as to estate solvency for a trustee to withhold payment of administrative expense claims). Here, the Trustee, in reference to the two litigation efforts being undertaken and the other anticipated expenses associated with winding-up the estate, states only that "the cost of prosecution of the two open matters is unknown, as is the remaining cost of administration of the bankruptcy estate." Those comments, without more, do not meet the standard required to create a reasonable doubt of estate solvency.

* * *

CPL is allowed a claim of $17,782.10 for postpetition, prerejection rent, pursuant to § 365(d)(3). Similarly, CPL is allowed an administrative use and occupancy claim in the amount of $8,891.05, pursuant to § 503(b)(1)(A), for use and occupancy during the period following rejection of the Lease. Payment should be made at this time inasmuch as there is no persuasive evidence of future estate administrative insolvency. Nevertheless, disgorgement is possible, subject to the Court's discretion, should circumstances change. * * *

Notes and Questions

1. The court in *Pyxsys* cited *Telesphere*, which reached the opposite outcome regarding payment of § 365(d)(3) obligations when the estate is or is likely to be administratively insolvent. The court in *Telesphere* relied in part on an "operational payments" reasoning:

> The Bankruptcy Code contains two distinct procedures for the payment of administrative expenses. One of these procedures—the one that involves § 503(b)(1)—is supervised by the court, and requires application, notice and hearing. The court supervised procedure requires pro rata payment of administrative claims, pursuant to § 726(b), unless the claim involved is given an express superpriority.

> The other procedure for payment of administrative expenses does not involve § 503(b)(1) or any court supervision. Section 1108 of the Code authorizes the trustee (and hence the debtor in possession under § 1107) to operate the business of a Chapter 11 debtor unless otherwise ordered by the court. Section 363(c)(1) allows a trustee or debtor in possession, authorized to operate the debtor's business, to "use property of the estate in the ordinary course of business without notice or a hearing." Thus, a trustee or debtor in possession may expend unencumbered cash (property of the estate), in the ordinary course of the debtor's business, to pay providers of goods and services to the estate. This alternative to court supervised payment of administrative expenses may be referred to as "operational payment."

> In contrast to payments made pursuant to the court supervised procedure, there is no requirement that operational payments be made pro rata with other administrative expenses; operational payments are final. * * * Although it appears that no other decision to date has addressed the question, vendors who receive payments from the trustee or debtor in possession, for value in the ordinary course of business under § 363(c)(1), need not fear that the money they receive is subject to disgorgement. Thus, operational payments, by their nature, enjoy a de facto priority over other administrative expenses, without any express provision for superpriority.

> Given this structure of the Code, the language of § 365(d)(3) should be read as requiring that rental payments be made according to the procedure for operational payments under § 363(c)(1). There is nothing in the language of § 365(d)(3) suggesting that it involves any of the procedures for court supervised payment. To the contrary, § 365(d)(3) provides that its terms apply "notwithstanding § 503(b)(1)"—the section providing a right to court supervised payment—and it requires the trustee or debtor in possession to act without application and without court review. Consequently, and contrary to the reasoning of the majority decisions, there would have been no

reason for Congress to have provided any express grant of super-priority for § 365(d)(3) rent payments—such a "superpriority" is implicit in the direction that the debtor make the payments without court involvement. The absence of an express grant of superpriority cannot, then, be a basis for disregarding the plain language of § 365(d)(3).

148 B.R. at 530-31. *Telesphere* reasoned that the rental payments at issue were "administrative expenses," but they were not paid pursuant to § 503-(b)(1). Rather, they were "operational payments" pursuant to § 363(c)(1). Therefore, the rents were payable despite potential administrative insolvency. Is this reasoning supported by the phrase in § 365(d)(3) "notwithstanding § 503(b)(1)"? Could that phrase be referring to something else entirely? (Hint: What if the rents had not been an actual cost of preserving the estate because the debtor had not used the leased premises postpetition?)

     2. Which court, *Pyxsys* or *Telesphere*, has the better statutory argument? Which viewpoint reflects the better bankruptcy policy?

Chapter 7

===

DISCHARGE

A. INTRODUCTION

Discharge, which effectuates the "fresh start," is the reason most individual debtors file bankruptcy. The Code as enacted in 1978 contained the most liberal discharge provisions ever enacted in American bankruptcy law. Ever since that time, lobbying efforts have been directed toward retrenchment. These efforts have met with some success, as we will see; numerous amendments, beginning in 1984, have cut back the generosity of discharge. Political support for curtailment has come primarily from the credit industry lobby. Theoretical justification for curtailment has come largely from economically-oriented bankruptcy analysts who argue that liberal discharge results in the pass-along of increased credit costs to debtors:

> [I]f one assumes that by increasing interest rates lenders are economically as well placed as debtors to bear the added risk inherent in a discharge system that prevents access to future wages, * * * the existing discharge system can be said to have a questionable interdebtor effect. Those debtors who pay their debts bear the assumed increased credit costs. Nonpaying debtors, to whose defaults the increased cost of credit is attributable, do not fully share in that increased cost. Liberal discharge provisions thus increase the extent to which those who repay their debts subsidize those who do not.

Theodore Eisenberg, *Bankruptcy Law in Perspective*, 28 UCLA L. REV. 953, 983 (1981). Does this make sense to you? Read the following excerpt and see if you still agree.

MARGARET HOWARD, A THEORY OF DISCHARGE IN CONSUMER BANKRUPTCY

48 OHIO ST. L.J. 1047, 1066-68 (1987) (footnotes omitted).

The concern with which we should greet this potential pass-along of costs depends in part on its likelihood. That, in turn, depends upon the elasticity of the supply of funds available for lending. If the supply is perfectly elastic, increased costs will be borne completely by borrowers; if the supply is not perfectly elastic, creditors will bear part of these increased costs. "But only if the elasticity of supply is zero * * * will the full costs of increases in bad-debt losses be borne entirely by creditors, and only then will the wealth transfer be entirely from creditors to debtors."

Empirical evidence, such as it is, suggests that the supply of credit funds is not perfectly elastic. First, bad-debt losses may be taken as a tax deduction (which is, in effect, a pass-along to each of us), so only the loss not recouped through the reduced tax is passed to borrowers. Second, other legal changes, akin to changes in discharge availability, that should have increased lenders' costs have had little or no measurable effect on consumer credit. For example, more liberal state exemption laws are not associated with increased cost or reduced availability of consumer credit; states that prohibit wage garnishment do not experience increased cost or reduced availability of consumer credit; and states that permit debtors to waive their right to exemptions do not experience decreased cost or increased availability of consumer credit. Thus, even if we are prepared to concede that the costs of some credit losses are passed along, "we simply do not know" if these additional costs are significant.

Commentators who assert that more liberal bankruptcy discharge raises the cost of borrowing for those who repay their debts argue that this increased cost of borrowing forces some potential borrowers out of the credit market entirely, either because of increased interest rates or more stringent credit screenings. This argument made sense in the mid–1970s when it was advanced in opposition to passage of more liberalized discharge provisions. Today, however, when the effort is to restrict rather than liberalize discharge, the argument necessarily implies that some debtors who are *not* now in the credit market, should be—*i.e.*, that restriction of discharge will lower credit costs in the future, thus including in the credit market persons not currently able to borrow. One problem with this argument is that no empirical support exists for the proposition that persons (obviously of high risk) are currently excluded from the credit market who should not be. Furthermore, the argument is hard to square with the commonly held belief that credit is too easy to get. Finally, entry of these high risk borrowers into the credit market would surely result in an increased incidence of default and discharge in bankruptcy, thus compounding the problem of nonrepayment that troubles opponents of liberalized discharge.

The concern with which we should greet the potential pass-along of costs also depends on whether it is viewed as inappropriate. One way of viewing the added cost is as an insurance premium, paid by all users of credit to insure their own access to bankruptcy relief in the event of financial disaster. Viewed in this way, the "bankruptcy premium" is no more an undesirable deadweight economic loss than is insurance generally. In addition, empirical evidence about the relationship between bankruptcy discharge and bad debts generally would have to be adduced to determine whether the availability of discharge has any effect on the amount or distribution of this "insurance premium."

Last, the concern with which we should greet this potential pass-along of costs depends in part on the group to whom costs will be passed. Commentators who argue that this cost will be passed on in the form of increased costs for borrowers who repay their debts do not agree as to the category of borrowers to whom these costs will be passed. The outcome turns on whether lenders are able to, and do, stratify borrowers into various risk groups. If lenders are able to isolate the group of borrowers that poses the highest risk of bankruptcy, lenders will pass increased costs attributable to more liberal bankruptcy discharge on to that group. The result would be to place the cost of the system on those who use it. Unless the consequence would be exclusion of those persons from the credit market altogether, which does not seem to be the case, this outcome seems perfectly acceptable both economically and ethically.

Commentators engaged in the debate about the group to which costs will be passed assume, apparently, that these costs will be passed, in the form of higher interest rates, only to borrowers—either solely to those who default, or to both those who default and those who repay. None of the commentators has discussed the possibility that costs may be spread even more broadly—that is, to all purchasers, whether for cash or on credit—in the form of increased prices of goods and services. At least two factors suggest this possibility. First, putting aside certain gasoline stations that offer "discounts" for cash, sellers typically do not price products differently for users of credit than for users of cash. Second, credit sellers do not typically carry their own notes; rather, they discount their commercial paper to institutional lenders. The discount rate must be accounted for by the seller in setting the price of his goods and services. Since the discount rate reflects, in part, the risk that the obligation will not be repaid, setting prices to account for the discount automatically passes on the cost of default by some credit purchasers to all buyers, including those who pay cash.

If this broader pass-along of costs in fact occurs, then it reduces the extent to which any one group bears the cost and, therefore, reduces the force of the argument that some borrowers will be forced out of the credit market. A broader pass-along also invites the argument that increased costs for cash purchasers, attributable to defaults by credit buyers, will exclude cash buyers from the market by raising the prices of goods and services to levels these cash buyers can no longer afford to pay on a cash basis. (Whether they will then become credit buyers is another issue.) In the absence of empirical evidence to the contrary (and there are, apparently, no empirical data for any of this), one can only speculate that any such price increase would be spread so broadly that the incremental difference would not be sufficiently great to affect any decision to purchase.

Before tinkering with bankruptcy rules in the name of economic efficiency, we should admit our limitations. First, if costs are passed along when creditors bear the risk, so that paying debtors subsidize nonpayers, this pass-along will occur without regard to the rules in bankruptcy. Those who pay subsidize those who *default*, not just those who default and obtain a discharge in bankruptcy. A change in the rules of discharge to reach a debtor's future income would make a difference in this pass-along of costs only to the extent that consumer debtors end up in bankruptcy, are able to pay out of future income and in fact pay through the vehicle of mandatory 13. Second, economic analysis requires a great many assumptions. Before we make major changes in the scope of bankruptcy in order to benefit commercial lenders and sellers, we need substantially more empirical data.[a]

---

[a] Cf. Adam J. Levitin, *Resolving the Foreclosure Crisis: Modification of Mortgages in Bankruptcy*, 2009 WIS. L. REV. 565, 647 ("A wide range of empirical data shows that permitting bankruptcy modification of all mortgages would have little or no impact on mortgage credit cost or availability. * * * This finding neuters the hitherto untested policy assumption underlying the special protection for mortgages in Chapter 13, namely that permitting modification would result in mortgage credit constriction.")

As you work through the materials in this chapter, think about why we allow discharge of debts at all, and about whether the benefits of granting discharge outweigh the costs to creditors who remain unpaid and, perhaps, the costs to society as a whole. Should debtors be able to escape full liability for their actions through the vehicle of bankruptcy? If not, is some measure of "fresh start" appropriate? How much of a fresh start? When has a fresh start become a head start?

Finally, consider whether some obligations are based on conduct so egregious that discharge should not be permissible. If so, ask whether the Code identifies that conduct appropriately.

B. DEBTORS ENTITLED TO DISCHARGE

1. IN GENERAL

The Bankruptcy Code distinguishes denial of discharge from exceptions to discharge. If discharge is denied, all of the debtor's obligations remain fully due and owing after the bankruptcy case is over. Section 727, which governs denial of discharge, is applicable primarily in Chapter 7 cases (except to the limited extent that § 1141(d)(3) imports it into Chapter 11). Thus, when discharge is denied, the Chapter 7 debtor's nonexempt property will be gone and the debts will not—in most cases, a decidedly unhappy outcome. Exceptions to discharge, on the other hand, are governed primarily by § 523 (which is imported into Chapter 13 by § 1328(a) and into Chapter 11 by § 1141(d)(2)).

Objections to discharge under § 523 must be raised, under Rule 4004(a), within 60 days of the meeting of creditors that is required by § 341. In *Kontrick v. Ryan*, 540 U.S. 443, 124 S.Ct. 906, 157 L.Ed.2d 867 (2004), the creditor's objection was tardy, but the debtor did not raise that issue until after the objection was adjudicated on the merits and (of course) he lost. In seeking reconsideration, the debtor asserted that the time limits are "jurisdictional," in the sense that they can be raised at any point in the proceedings. The bankruptcy, district and circuit courts all disagreed with that contention, as did the Supreme Court. The Court held that Rule 4004(a) is a claims-processing rule, and its benefits can be forfeited if a party waits too long. The Court assumed for the sake of argument, citing *Taylor v. Freeland & Kronz* (discussed in *Schwab v. Reilly*, which is set out in Chapter 2, Section D of this casebook), that the debtor would have prevailed if his timeliness objection had itself been timely.

We will hold our discussions about discharge exceptions for Section C of this Chapter. We begin here by considering circumstances under which discharge might be denied altogether. Read §§ 727(a), 1141(d) and 1328(b)–(h), and answer the following Problems.

Problems

1. Debtor Corp. filed a Chapter 7 bankruptcy petition. Is it entitled to discharge?

2. Joe Smith filed a Chapter 7 bankruptcy petition in 2007 and received a discharge in June of 2009. If Joe files another Chapter 7 in February of 2016, can he receive a discharge?

3. Assume that Joe Smith's Chapter 7 filing was in 2009, rather than 2007. If he files another Chapter 7 in February of 2016, can he receive a discharge? Does your answer change if Joe's second bankruptcy petition is necessitated by catastrophic, uninsured medical expenses? Does your answer change if Joe's creditors file the second petition?

4. Bob Brown filed a Chapter 7 bankruptcy petition in April of 2012 and received a discharge. If Bob files a Chapter 13 petition in February of 2016, confirms a three-year plan and fully performs it, will he be entitled to a discharge in 2019?

5. Jane Jones filed a Chapter 13 bankruptcy petition six years ago. At that time, she owed $75,000 to secured creditors (primarily, the mortgagee on her house) and $140,000 to unsecured creditors (mainly credit card issuers). Her three-year plan, which was confirmed in June of the next year, proposed 100% repayment on all debts. Jane encountered some health problems a couple of years later, and she was unable to complete the plan. By the end of three years, she had paid just under $100,000 to her unsecured creditors. (She paid her mortgagee in full, however, in order to prevent foreclosure.) She received a discharge two years ago because the court found that she failed to complete the plan for reasons beyond her control and that modification of the plan was not feasible. If Jane files a Chapter 7 petition in January of this year, can she receive a discharge?

6. Mike Moore had a good job and substantial savings, but he was addicted to gambling. He loved Las Vegas and made several trips there every year. Mike hit an unlucky streak, lost everything he owned, and filed Chapter 7. Assuming that he reveals his losses on his bankruptcy schedules, can he receive a discharge?

7. Assume that Mike Moore's gambling habit runs toward betting on sporting events, which is illegal in Mike's state. How can Mike get the benefit of a bankruptcy discharge without exposing himself to criminal sanctions?

8. Deborah Cox, a school teacher with a master's degree, stopped working when her first child was born. Her husband, Stephen, whose business ventures included diamond and bullion trading, became the family's sole breadwinner. Deborah was a nominal participant in his ventures, however, and she signed whatever documents he put in front of her. She did not read them, nor did she ask any questions. Ultimately, the ventures collapsed and angry creditors began pursuing the couple. Stephen became a fugitive and Deborah was left to face an involuntary bankruptcy petition. When creditors learned that Deborah had no records regarding the business activities, they objected to her discharge. What result? See *Lansdowne v. Cox (In re Cox)*, 41 F.3d 1294 (9th Cir.1994).

9. Joe Baker filed a Chapter 13 petition five years ago, confirmed a plan, and faithfully performed it. Believing that he is now entitled to discharge, he consulted his lawyer in order to schedule the discharge hearing. His lawyer said he was not eligible for discharge until he completed a financial management course. Joe argued that he had already gotten financial counseling, before filing bankruptcy in the first place. Will that suffice? Compare §§ 109(h) and 1328(g).

10. Easterly Airlines, Inc., which filed a Chapter 11 petition, tried to confirm a plan to reorganize the company. When that proved impossible, Easterly proposed a plan under which all of its assets will be sold for the benefit of its creditors, shareholders will receive nothing, and its operations will shut down. Will Easterly receive a discharge upon confirmation of this plan?

11. Second Time, Inc. filed a Chapter 11 case in June of 2009 and confirmed its plan of reorganization in August of 2010. The plan provided for payments over five years, but Second Time was unable to meet all of the payments during the last year of the plan. Thus, Second Time filed another Chapter 11 petition in January of 2016. It proposed a reorganization plan under which its obligations would be paid over a longer period of time. If Second Time is able to propose a confirmable plan, will confirmation of that plan discharge Second Time's debts?

12. Ken Ray was CEO of a large corporation that collapsed after revelation of major violations of the securities laws. Ken is being pursued personally by investors who blame him, in part, for their losses. Ken wants to know whether he can escape these contingent obligations by filing bankruptcy. Can he? Would the result change if Ken had a child facing substantial uninsured medical expenses?

13. When, if ever, is it in a creditor's interest to file an objection to a debtor's discharge?

We have already seen that transfers are avoidable under both state law and § 548(a)(1)(A) if they are made by the debtor with an intent to hinder, delay or defraud creditors. Such transfers may carry an addition consequence, however—they may lead to loss of the discharge under § 727(a)(2). This is, of course, a very serious outcome from the debtor's point of view; all nonexempt property will be gone and all obligations will remain due and owing. The following case involves such a fact pattern.

DAVIS v. DAVIS (IN RE DAVIS)

United States Court of Appeals, Eleventh Circuit, 1990.
911 F.2d 560.

PER CURIAM.

This is an appeal from the district court's order affirming the bankruptcy court's order which denied the Debtor/Appellant's discharge. We affirm.

In 1983, the Appellee, Roe Davis, and the Debtor/Appellant, Don Davis, opened a pharmacy business. Roe Davis owned fifty-one percent of the stock, while Don Davis owned the remaining forty-nine percent. Both Roe and Don Davis, who are unrelated, individually signed promissory notes for the money they borrowed to operate the business. The business failed and was closed in October 1985. The final bank loan used to finance the pharmacy was payable in October 1986. Two days after the due date, the Debtor/Appellant discussed with his attorney his inability to pay this note and his concern about possibly losing his home. At the suggestion of his attorney, the Debtor/Appellant deeded his one-half interest in his home to his wife. Shortly thereafter, in November 1986, Appellee Roe Davis paid off the outstanding balance on the bank note, amounting to $118,395.24.

Appellee Roe Davis sued the Debtor/Appellant for contribution and obtained a default judgment for $58,694.24. Two days after obtaining this judgment, the Appellee filed a fraudulent conveyance action against the Debtor/Appellant seeking to set aside the transfer of the Debtor's interest in his home to his wife. Upon service of this complaint, the Debtor/Appellant consulted his attorney, who advised him to see a bankruptcy lawyer. The Debtor/Appellant did so, and was advised to reverse the transfer of his home to his wife. The necessary deed was prepared, executed and recorded. The day following recordation, the Debtor/Appellant filed for bankruptcy protection under Chapter 7 of the Bankruptcy Code.

In his bankruptcy schedules, the Debtor/Appellant disclosed the existence of these transfers, which had taken place within one year of the bankruptcy filing. In April 1987, the Appellee filed an adversary proceeding seeking to deny the Debtor/Appellant's discharge under § 727(a)(2)(A) of the Code. * * *

The matter was tried in December 1987. The bankruptcy court found that the transfer of property of the Debtor/Appellant to his wife was made with the intent to hinder, delay or defraud a creditor as proscribed by § 727(a)(2)(A), notwithstanding retransfer of the property completed the day before the petition was filed. The Debtor/Appellant contended that discharge should not be denied under § 727(a)(2)(A), since the transfer in question did not in fact diminish the assets available to creditors. In a subsequent memorandum opinion, the bankruptcy court rejected this argument, relying chiefly on *Future Time, Inc. v. Yates*, 26 B.R. 1006 (M.D.Ga.), *aff'd mem.*, 712 F.2d 1417 (11th Cir.1983), and denied the Debtor/Appellant a discharge. Debtor/Appellant Davis appealed this order to the district court, which affirmed.

In his appeal to this court, the Debtor/Appellant identifies two issues. First, the Debtor/Appellant argues the district court erred in affirming the denial of discharge in light of the fact that the Debtor/Appellant's transfer of property to his wife did not in fact reduce the assets available to creditors. We disagree in light of *Future Time*. In *Future Time*, the district court affirmed the denial of the debtor's discharge under § 727(a)(2)(A) despite the fact that mortgages and tax liens on the property transferred exceeded its fair market value so that, even without the transfer, the creditors were deprived of no assets since the debtor had no equity in the property.[2] That court reasoned:

> When appellant transferred his interest in the residence to his wife, he obviously intended to shield what he thought was valuable property from the claims of his creditors. To hold now that there occurred no transfer of property with the intent to hinder creditors merely because the debts on the residence exceeded its

---

[2] * * * We point out that in cases such as this one, the creditor is harmed whether or not any equity exists in the property transferred that may come into the estate. The creditor presumably incurred legal fees and expenses when he brought an action challenging the fraudulent transfer.

estimated fair market value would be to reward appellant for his wrongdoing, which the court refuses to do.

26 B.R. at 1009.

The Debtor/Appellant next argues the district court erred in affirming the denial of the Debtor/Appellant's discharge under § 727(a)(2)(A) since the property fraudulently conveyed to his wife was recovered prior to his filing bankruptcy. The Debtor/Appellant relies principally on *In re Adeeb*, 787 F.2d 1339 (9th Cir.1986), for the proposition that, as used in § 727(a)(2)(A), the word "transferred" should be read to mean "transferred and remained transferred" at the time a debtor files his bankruptcy petition. Despite the clear, unambiguous language used in the statute, the *Adeeb* court reasoned that its reading of "transferred" was "most consistent with the legislative purpose of the section." *Id*. at 1344. The court wrote that such a reading would "encourage honest debtors to recover property they have transferred during the year preceding bankruptcy" and serve to facilitate "the equitable distribution of assets among creditors by ensuring that the trustee has possession of all of the debtor's assets." *Id*. at 1345. The court added that this readily allowed the "honest debtor to undo his mistakes and receive his discharge." *Id*. Finally, the court noted its reliance on the practical aspects of such a situation:

> It is not uncommon for an uncounseled or poorly counseled debtor faced with mounting debts and pressure from his creditors to attempt to protect his property by transferring it to others. Upon later reflection or upon obtaining advice from experienced bankruptcy counsel, the debtor may realize that his original transfer of the property was a mistake. If the debtor is informed that his mistake bars him from a discharge in bankruptcy, he will have no incentive to attempt to recover the property or to reveal its existence to his creditors. Rather, he will have a strong incentive to continue to hide his assets.

Id.[3]

Normally, a court should interpret a statute in a manner consistent with the plain meaning of the language used in the statute.

---

[3] Even among courts that follow *Adeeb*, and indeed in that case itself, it has been held that reliance on an attorney's bad advice to transfer assets to avoid losing them to creditors can be asserted to avoid denial of discharge only when that advice is sought in good faith.

The statutory language of § 727(a)(2)(A) is plain and unambiguous. Congress certainly was capable of drafting a statute which would deny a discharge only when assets were fraudulently transferred and remained transferred at the time of filing of bankruptcy proceedings, but it did not. We are a court and not a legislative body; therefore, we are not free to create by interpretation an exception in a statute which is plain on its face. We therefore reject the approach initiated by the Ninth Circuit in *Adeeb*. We recognize that our holding may work hardship in some cases, perhaps this one, but we are compelled to apply statutory law as enacted by Congress.

AFFIRMED.

Questions

1. The Code defines "transfer" as "disposing of or parting with" property," § 101(54)(D). If property has been reacquired, are these requirements satisfied?

2. Apart from § 727(a)(2), the Code's "cure" for a fraudulent conveyance is recovery of the property or its value from the transferee. In *Davis*, the debtor "cured" the fraudulent conveyance by recovering the property before filing bankruptcy. Why was that not sufficient? Which is better bankruptcy policy—the result reached by *Davis* or by *Adeeb*?

3. In response to Don Davis's argument that creditors were not harmed because the property was returned, the court pointed to Roe Davis's litigation costs. Would it have made more sense for the court to have required Don to reimburse Roe for his expenses, rather than denying Don a discharge? Does a bankruptcy court have the power to require such reimbursement under the Code?

4. Do you have any reactions to the quality of the advice given to Don Davis in October of 1986 by his first attorney? Does Davis have a malpractice action? If so, is it an asset of the estate? What is the value of that asset?

5. Is a Chapter 13 filing a possible solution for the debtor in *Davis v. Davis*?

6. The First Circuit decided a similar issue in *Martin v. Bajgar (In re Bajgar)*, 104 F.3d 495 (1st Cir.1997). In *Bajgar*, the debtor conveyed his interest in real estate to his wife as a belated engagement gift—delayed by 23 years—receiving "love and affection" in exchange. He was facing several foreclosures and a collection action at the time. Less than a year later, he filed a Chapter 7 petition and disclosed the transfer. He and his wife volunteered at the creditors' meeting to reconvey the property. They did so three months

later, after a creditor filed an objection to discharge. The court distinguished *Adeeb*, which involved an involuntary bankruptcy petition and a prepetition reconveyance, denying the debtor a discharge under § 727(a)(2)(A).

2. EXEMPTION PLANNING AS ACTUAL FRAUD

A debtor, particularly one living in a state with generous exemptions, is understandably interested in taking maximum advantage of those exemptions. The debtor's assets might not be configured in a way that permits enjoyment of the maximum dollar value of the allowable exemptions, however. In that situation, the debtor may want to convert nonexempt assets into exempt assets before filing the bankruptcy petition. As the following case indicates, such prebankruptcy planning seems to be permitted by the Code's legislative history. The problem is that such a conversion of assets may be difficult to distinguish from an "intent to hinder, delay or defraud" creditors, which carries two rather unpleasant consequences: it renders a transfer avoidable as a fraudulent conveyance under either state law, via § 544(b), or § 548(a)(1)(A); and it provides grounds for denial of discharge under § 727(a)(2). It is the latter consequence with which we are presently concerned. And keep in mind that entitlement to an exemption may be governed by state law, but federal law always determines whether a discharge will be granted.

NORWEST BANK NEBRASKA, N.A. v. TVETEN (IN RE TVETEN)

United States Court of Appeals, Eighth Circuit, 1988.
848 F.2d 871.

TIMBERS, Circuit Judge.

Appellant Omar A. Tveten, a physician who owed creditors almost $19,000,000, mostly in the form of personal guaranties on a number of investments whose value had deteriorated greatly, petitioned for Chapter 11 bankruptcy. He had converted almost all of his nonexempt property, with a value of about $700,000, into exempt property that could not be reached by his creditors. The bankruptcy court, on the basis of its findings of fact and conclusions of law, entered an order on February 27, 1987, denying a discharge in view of its finding that Tveten intended to defraud, delay, and hinder his creditors. The district court, in an order entered July 10, 1987 in the District of Minnesota, Diana E. Murphy, *District Judge*, affirmed the bankruptcy court's order. On appeal, Tveten asserts that his transfers merely constituted astute pre-bankruptcy planning. We hold that the bankruptcy court was not clearly erroneous in inferring fraudulent intent on the part of Tveten. We affirm.

I.

We shall summarize only those facts and prior proceedings believed necessary to an understanding of the issues raised on appeal.

Tveten is a 59 year old physician in general practice. He is the sole shareholder of Omar A. Tveten, P.A., a professional corporation. He has no dependents. He began investing in various real estate developments. These investments initially were quite successful. Various physician friends of Tveten joined him in organizing a corporation to invest in these ventures. These investments were highly leveraged. The physicians, including Tveten, personally had guaranteed the debt arising out of these investments. In mid–1985, Tveten's investments began to sour. He became personally liable for an amount close to $19,000,000—well beyond his ability to pay. Appellees Norwest Bank Nebraska, N.A. ("Norwest Bank"), Business Development Corporation of Nebraska ("Business Development"), and Harold J. Panuska ("Panuska") as trustee of the Harold J. Panuska Profit Sharing Trust and the Harold J. Panuska Employee Trust Fund, became creditors of Tveten as a result of his various investment ventures.

Tveten filed a Chapter 11 petition on January 7, 1986. Meanwhile, several creditors already had commenced lawsuits against him. Panuska had obtained a $139,657 judgment against him on October 9, 1985. Norwest Bank and Business Development had commenced an action against him but had not obtained judgment when Tveten filed for bankruptcy. On the date the Chapter 11 petition was filed, Tveten owed his creditors close to $19,000,000.

Before filing for bankruptcy, Tveten consulted counsel. As part of his pre-bankruptcy planning, he liquidated almost all of his non-exempt property, converting it into exempt property worth approximately $700,000. This was accomplished through some seventeen separate transfers. The non-exempt property he liquidated included land sold to his parents and his brother, respectively, for $70,000 and $75,732 in cash; life insurance policies and annuities with a for-profit company with cash values totalling $96,307.58; his net salary and bonuses of $27,820.91; his KEOGH plan and individual retirement fund of $20,487.35; his corporation's profit-sharing plan worth

$325,774.51; and a home sold for $50,000.[1] All of the liquidated property was converted into life insurance or annuity contracts with the Lutheran Brotherhood, a fraternal benefit association, which, under Minnesota law, cannot be attached by creditors. Tveten concedes that the purpose of these transfers was to shield his assets from creditors. Minnesota law provides that creditors cannot attach *any* money or other benefits payable by a fraternal benefit association. Unlike most exemption provisions in other states, the Minnesota exemption has no monetary limit. Indeed, under this exemption, Tveten attempted to place $700,000 worth of his property out of his creditors' reach.

Tveten sought a discharge with respect to $18,920,000 of his debts. Appellees objected to Tveten's discharge. In its order of February 27, 1987, the bankruptcy court concluded that, although Tveten's conversion of non-exempt property to exempt property just before petitioning for bankruptcy, standing alone, would not justify denial of a discharge, his inferred intent to defraud would. The bankruptcy court held that, even if the exemptions were permissible, Tveten had abused the protections permitted a debtor under the Bankruptcy Code (the "Code"). His awareness of Panuska's judgment against him and of several pending lawsuits, his rapidly deteriorating business investments, and his exposure to extensive liability well beyond his ability to pay, all were cited by the court in its description of the circumstances under which Tveten converted his property. Moreover, the court concluded that Tveten intended to hinder and delay his creditors. Accordingly, the bankruptcy court denied Tveten a discharge.

Tveten appealed from the bankruptcy court order to the federal district court. In a memorandum opinion and order entered July 10, 1987, the district court affirmed the denial of a discharge, concluding that the bankruptcy court's finding as to Tveten's intent was not clearly erroneous.

The instant appeal followed. Basically, Tveten asserts on appeal that as a matter of law we should reject the factors relied on by the bankruptcy court to infer that Tveten intended to delay, hinder and defraud creditors. We disagree. We affirm.

II.

The sole issue on appeal is whether Tveten properly was denied a discharge in view of the transfers alleged to have been in fraud of creditors.

---

[1] There were no claims that these transfers were for less than market value.

At the outset, it is necessary to distinguish between (1) a debtor's right to exempt certain property from the claims of his creditors and (2) his right to a discharge of his debts. The Code permits a debtor to exempt property either pursuant to the provisions of the Code if not forbidden by state law, § 522(b) & (d), or pursuant to the provisions of state law and federal law other than the minimum allowances in the Code. § 522(b)(2). When the debtor claims a state-created exemption, the scope of the claim is determined by state law. It is well established that under the Code the conversion of non-exempt to exempt property for the purpose of placing the property out of the reach of creditors, without more, will not deprive the debtor of the exemption to which he otherwise would be entitled. Both the House and Senate Reports regarding the debtor's right to claim exemptions state:

> As under current law, the debtor will be permitted to convert nonexempt property into exempt property before filing a bankruptcy petition. The practice is not fraudulent as to creditors, and permits the debtor to make full use of the exemptions to which he is entitled under the law.

H.R. Rep. No. 95–595 at 361, *reprinted in* 1978 U.S.C.C.A.N. at 6317; S. Rep. No. 95–989 at 76, *reprinted in* 1978 U.S.C.C.A.N. at 5862. The rationale behind this policy is that "[t]he result which would obtain if debtors were not allowed to convert property into allowable exempt property would be extremely harsh, especially in those jurisdictions where the exemption allowance is minimal." 3 Collier on Bankruptcy, ¶ 522.08[4], at 40 (15th ed. 1984). This blanket approval of conversion is qualified, however, by denial of discharge if there was extrinsic evidence of the debtor's intent to defraud creditors.

A debtor's right to a discharge, however, unlike his right to an exemption, is determined by *federal*, not state, law. The Code provides that a debtor may be denied a discharge under Chapter 7 if, among other things, he has transferred property "with intent to hinder, delay, or defraud a creditor" within one year before the date of the filing of the petition. § 727(a)(2). Although Tveten filed for bankruptcy under Chapter 11, the proscription against discharging a debtor with fraudulent intent in a Chapter 7 proceeding is equally applicable against a debtor applying for a Chapter 11 discharge. The reason for this is that the Code provides that confirmation of a plan does not discharge a Chapter 11 debtor if "the debtor would be denied a discharge under § 727(a) of this title if the case were a case under chapter 7 of this title." § 1141(d)(3)(C).

Although the determination as to whether a discharge should be granted or denied is governed by federal law, the standard applied consistently by the courts is the same as that used to determine whether an exemption is permissible, i.e. absent extrinsic evidence of fraud, mere conversion of non-exempt property to exempt property is not fraudulent as to creditors even if the motivation behind the conversion is to place those assets beyond the reach of creditors.

As the bankruptcy court correctly found here, therefore, the issue in the instant case revolves around whether there was extrinsic evidence to demonstrate that Tveten transferred his property on the eve of bankruptcy with intent to defraud his creditors. The bankruptcy court's finding that there was such intent to defraud may be reversed by us only if clearly erroneous.

There are a number of cases in which the debtor converted non-exempt property to exempt property on the eve of bankruptcy and was granted a discharge because there was no extrinsic evidence of the debtor's intent to defraud. In *Forsberg v. Security State Bank*, 15 F.2d 499 (8th Cir.1926), an old decision of our Court, a debtor was granted a discharge despite his trade of non-exempt cattle for exempt hogs while insolvent and in contemplation of bankruptcy. Although we found that the trade was effected so that the debtor could increase his exemptions, the debtor "should [not] be penalized for merely doing what the law allows him to do." *Id.* at 501. We concluded that "before the existence of such fraudulent purpose can be properly found, there must appear in evidence some facts or circumstances which are extrinsic to the mere facts of conversion of nonexempt assets into exempt and which are indicative of such fraudulent purpose." *Id.* at 502.

There also are a number of cases, however, in which the courts have denied discharges after concluding that there was extrinsic evidence of the debtor's fraudulent intent. In *Ford v. Poston*, 773 F.2d 52 (4th Cir.1985), the debtor had executed a deed of correction transferring a tract of land to himself and his wife as tenants by the entirety. The debtor had testified that his parents originally had conveyed the land to the debtor alone, and that this was a mistake that he corrected by executing a deed of correction. Under relevant state law, the debtor's action removed the property from the reach of his creditors who were not also creditors of his wife. The Fourth Circuit, in upholding the denial of a discharge, found significant the fact that this "mistake" in the original transfer of the property was "corrected" the day after an unsecured creditor obtained judgment against the debtor. *Id.* at 55. The Fourth Circuit held that the bankruptcy court, in denying a discharge, was not clearly erroneous in finding the requisite intent to defraud, after "[h]aving heard * * * [the debtor's] testimony at trial and having considered the circumstances surrounding the transfer." *Id*. In *In re Reed*, 700 F.2d 986 (5th Cir.1983), shortly after the debtor had arranged with his creditors to be free from the payment obligations until the following year, he rapidly had converted non-exempt assets to extinguish one home mortgage and to reduce another four months before bankruptcy, and had diverted receipts from his business into an account not divulged to his creditors. The Fifth Circuit concluded that the debtor's "whole pattern of conduct evinces that intent." *Id*. at 991. The court went further and stated:

> It would constitute a perversion of the purposes of the Bankruptcy Code to permit a debtor earning $180,000 a year to convert every one of his major nonexempt assets into sheltered property on the eve of bankruptcy with actual intent to defraud his creditors and then emerge washed clean of future obligation by carefully concocted immersion in bankruptcy waters.

Id. at 992.

In most, if not all, cases determining whether discharge was properly granted or denied to a debtor who practiced "pre-bankruptcy planning", the point of reference has been the state exemptions if the debtor was claiming under them. Although discharge was not denied if the debtor merely converted his non-exempt property into exempt property as permitted under state law, the exemptions involved in these cases comported with federal policy to give the debtor a "fresh start" — by limiting the monetary value of the exemptions. This policy has been explicit, or at least implicit, in these cases. In *Forsberg*, for example, we stated that it is not fraudulent for an individual who knows he is insolvent to convert non-exempt property into exempt property, thereby placing the property out of the reach of creditors

> because the statutes granting exemptions have made no such exceptions, and because the policy of such statutes is to favor the debtors, at the expense of the creditors, *in the limited amounts allowed to them, by preventing the forced loss of the home and of the necessities of subsistence*, and because such statutes are construed liberally in favor of the exemption.

15 F.2d at 501 (emphasis added). * * *

In the instant case, however, the state exemption relied on by Tveten was unlimited, with the potential for unlimited abuse. Indeed, this case presents a situation in which the debtor liquidated almost his entire net worth of $700,000 and converted it to non-exempt [sic] property in seventeen transfers on the eve of bankruptcy while his creditors, to whom he owed close to $19,000,000, would be left to divide the little that remained in his estate. Borrowing the phrase used by another court, Tveten "did not want a mere *fresh* start, he wanted a *head* start." *In re Zouhar*, 10 B.R. 154, 156 (Bankr. D.N.M.1981) (emphasis in original). His attempt to shield property worth approximately $700,000 goes well beyond the purpose for which exemptions are permitted. Tveten's reliance on his attorney's advice does not protect him here, since that protection applies only to the extent that the reliance was reasonable.

The bankruptcy court, as affirmed by the district court, examined Tveten's entire pattern of conduct and found that he had demonstrated fraudulent intent. We agree. While state law governs the legitimacy of Tveten's exemptions, it is federal law that governs his discharge. Permitting Tveten, who earns over $60,000 annually, to convert all of his major non-exempt assets into sheltered property on the eve of bankruptcy with actual intent to defraud his creditors "would constitute a perversion of the purposes of the Bankruptcy Code". *In re Reed*, 700 F.2d at 992. Tveten still is entitled to retain, free from creditors' claims, property rightfully exempt under relevant state law.

We distinguish our decision in *Hanson v. First National Bank*, 848 F.2d 866 (8th Cir.1988), decided today. *Hanson* involves a creditor's objection to two of the debtors' claimed exemptions under South Dakota law, a matter governed by state law. The complaint centered on the Hansons' sale, while insolvent, of non-exempt property to family members for fair market value and their use of the proceeds to prepay their preexisting mortgage and to purchase life insurance policies in the limited amounts permissible under relevant state law. The bankruptcy court found no extrinsic evidence of fraud. The district court, in a memorandum opinion and order entered June 15, 1987, affirmed. We also affirmed, concluding that the case fell within the myriad of cases which have permitted such a conversion on the eve of bankruptcy.

III.

To summarize:

We hold that the bankruptcy court was not clearly erroneous in inferring fraudulent intent on the part of the debtor, rather than astute pre-bankruptcy planning, with respect to his transfers on the eve of bankruptcy which were intended to defraud, delay and hinder his creditors.

Affirmed.

ARNOLD, Circuit Judge, dissenting.

The Court reaches a result that appeals to one's general sense of righteousness. I believe, however, that it is contrary to clearly established law, and I therefore respectfully dissent.

Dr. Tveten has never made any bones about what he is doing, or trying to do, in this case. He deliberately set out to convert as much property as possible into a form exempt from attachment by creditors under Minnesota law. Such a design necessarily involves an attempt to delay or hinder creditors, in the ordinary, non-legal sense of those words, but, under long-standing principles embodied both in judicial decisions and in statute, such a purpose is not unlawful. The governing authority in this Court is *Forsberg v. Security State Bank*, 15 F.2d 499 (8th Cir.1926). There we said:

> It is well settled that it is not a fraudulent act by an individual who knows he is insolvent to convert a part of his property which is not exempt into property which is exempt, for the purpose of claiming his exemptions therein, and of thereby placing it out of the reach of his creditors.

Id. at 501. Thus, under the controlling law of this Circuit, someone who is insolvent may convert property into exempt form for the very purpose of placing that property beyond the reach of his creditors.

A debtor's right to make full use of statutory exemptions is fundamental to bankruptcy law. To unsecured creditors, a debtor's conversion of his assets into exempt categories of property will always appear unfair, but this apparent unfairness is simply a consequence of the existence of exemptions under the jurisdiction's bankruptcy law. In an early case in this Circuit, Judge Walter H. Sanborn, one of the patriarchs of this Court, explained:

> An insolvent debtor may use with impunity any of his property
> that is free from the liens and equitable interests of his creditors

to purchase a homestead. * * * If he takes property that is not exempt from judicial sale and applies it to this purpose, he merely avails himself of a plain provision of the constitution or the statute enacted for [his] benefit. * * * He takes nothing from the creditors by this action in which they have any vested right. The constitution or statute exempting the homestead from the judgments of creditors is in force when they extend the credit to him, and they do so in the face of the fact that he has this right. *Nor can the use of property that is not exempt from execution to procure a homestead be held to be a fraud upon the creditors * * *, because that which the law expressly sanctions and permits cannot be a legal fraud.*

First National Bank of Humboldt v. Glass, 79 F. 706, 707 (8th Cir.1897) (emphasis added).

The same principle was confirmed by Congress when it enacted the Bankruptcy Code of 1978. The report of the House Judiciary Committee states as follows:

As under current law, the debtor will be permitted to convert nonexempt property into exempt property before filing a bankruptcy petition. The practice is not fraudulent as to creditors, and permits the debtor to make full use of the exemptions to which he is entitled under the law.

H.R. Rep. No. 95–595 at 361, *reprinted in* 1978 U.S.C.C.A.N. at 6317. The same language appears in S. Rep. No. 95–989 at 76, *reprinted in* 1978 U.S.C.C.A.N. at 5862. In the hearings referred to in the House Committee Report, two federal judges, concerned about the "outrageous" implications of existing law, specifically urged Congress to incorporate provisions in the new Bankruptcy Code which would make pre-bankruptcy conversion of assets fraudulent as a matter of federal law. The fact that Congress declined to change existing law, when presented with the same objections to the propriety of debtor tactics like Tveten's that the Court now expresses, indicates that Congress did not intend § 727(a)(2) to proscribe such conduct. The House Report's language plainly says that debtors may convert nonexempt property into exempt property, that doing so is not fraudulent, and that debtors may make "full use" of any applicable exemption. Recent cases in our Court have reiterated this principle.

To be sure, if there is extrinsic evidence of fraud, or of a purpose to hinder or delay creditors, discharge may and should be denied, but "extrinsic," in this context, must mean something beyond the mere conversion of assets into exempt form for the purpose of putting them out of the reach of one's creditors. If Tveten had lied to his creditors, like the debtor in *McCormick v. Security State Bank*, 822 F.2d 806 (8th Cir.1987), or misled them in some way, like the debtor in *In re Reed*, 700 F.2d 986 (5th Cir.1983), or transferred property for less than fair value to a third party, like the debtor in *Ford v. Poston*, 773 F.2d 52 (4th Cir.1985), we would have a very different case. There is absolutely no evidence of that sort of misconduct in this record, and the Court's opinion filed today cites none.

One is tempted to speculate what the result would have been in this case if the amount of assets converted had been $7,000, instead of $700,000. Indeed, the large amount of money involved is the only difference I can see between this case and *Forsberg*. It is true that the *Forsberg* opinion referred to "the limited amounts allowed to" debtors by exemptions, but whether exemptions are limited in amount is a legislative question ordinarily to be decided by the people's elected representatives, in this case the Minnesota Legislature. Where courts punish debtors simply for claiming exemptions within statutory limits, troubling problems arise in separating judicial from legislative power. * * *

If there ought to be a dollar limit, and I am inclined to think that there should be, and if practices such as those engaged in by the debtor here can become abusive, and I admit that they can, the problem is simply not one susceptible of a judicial solution according to manageable objective standards. A good statement of the kind of judicial reasoning that must underlie the result the Court reaches today appears in *In re Zouhar*, 10 B.R. 154 (Bankr. D.N.M.1981), where the amount of assets converted was $130,000. The Bankruptcy Court denied discharge, stating, among other things, that "'there is a principle of too much; phrased colloquially, when a pig becomes a hog it is slaughtered.'" *Id.* at 157. If I were a member of the Minnesota Legislature, I might well vote in favor of a bill to place an over-all dollar maximum on any exemption. But sitting as a judge, by what criteria do I determine when this pig becomes a hog? If $700,000 is too much, what about $70,000? Would it matter if the debtor were a farmer, as in *Forsberg*, rather than a physician? (I ask the question because the appellee creditor's brief mentions the debtor's profession, which ought to be legally irrelevant, several times.)

Debtors deserve more definite answers to these questions than the Court's opinion provides. In effect, the Court today leaves the distinction between permissible and impermissible claims of exemption to each bankruptcy judge's own sense of proportion. As a result, debtors will be unable to know in advance how far the federal courts will allow them to exercise their rights under state law.

Where state law creates an unlimited exemption, the result may be that wealthy debtors like Tveten enjoy a windfall that appears unconscionable, and contrary to the policy of the bankruptcy law. I fully agree with Judge Kishel, however, that

> [this] result * * * cannot be laid at [the] Debtor's feet; it must be laid at the feet of the state legislature. Debtor did nothing more than exercise a prerogative that was fully his under law. It cannot be said that his actions have so tainted him or his bankruptcy petition as to merit denial of discharge.

In re Johnson, 80 B.R. 953, 963 (Bankr. D.Minn.1987) (footnote omitted). I submit that Tveten did nothing more fraudulent than seek to take advantage of a state law of which the federal courts disapprove.

I would reverse this judgment and hold that the debtor's actions in converting property into exempt form do not bar a discharge in bankruptcy.

Notes and Questions

1. Can you distinguish between an intent to enjoy the full benefit of available exemptions and an intent to "hinder" or "delay" creditors?

2. The irreconcilability of cases on this issue is nowhere better illustrated than by *Tveten* and two other decisions of the Eighth Circuit—*Hanson v. First National Bank*, 848 F.2d 866 (8th Cir.1988), and *Panuska v. Johnson (In re Johnson)*, 880 F.2d 78 (8th Cir.1989). (The dissent in *Tveten* quoted the bankruptcy judge's opinion in *Johnson*.)

Hanson was heard by the same three-judge panel of the Eighth Circuit and decided on the same day as *Tveten*. Hanson was a farmer rather than a doctor, and he tried to shelter $34,000 rather than $700,000. Hanson and his wife did not sell everything they owned, unlike Dr. Tveten, and the life insurance policies they bought were exemptable only up to $20,000 under state law. The bankruptcy court found no fraud and the Eighth Circuit affirmed.

Judge Arnold, who dissented in *Tveten*, wrote a concurring opinion in *Hanson*, in which he reiterated his disagreement with the *Tveten* majority:

> The Court is entirely correct in holding that there is no extrinsic fraud here. The money placed into exempt property was not

borrowed, the cash received from the sales was accounted for, and the property was sold for fair market value. The fact that the sale was to family members, "standing on its own, does not establish extrinsic evidence of fraud."

With all of this I agree completely, but exactly the same statements can be made, just as accurately, with respect to Dr. Tveten's case. So far as I can tell, there are only three differences between Dr. Tveten and the Hansons, and all of them are legally irrelevant: (1) Dr. Tveten is a physician, and the Hansons are farmers; (2) Dr. Tveten attempted to claim exempt status for about $700,000 worth of property, while the Hansons are claiming it for about $31,000 worth of property; and (3) the Minnesota exemption statute whose shelter Dr. Tveten sought had no dollar limit, while the South Dakota statute exempting the proceeds of life-insurance policies is limited to $20,000. The first of these three differences—the occupation of the parties—is plainly immaterial, and no one contends otherwise. The second—the amounts of money involved—is also irrelevant, in my view, because the relevant statute contains no dollar limit, and for judges to set one involves essentially a legislative decision not suitable for the judicial branch. The relevant statute for present purposes is § 522(b)(2)(A), which authorizes debtors to claim exemptions available under "State or local law," and says nothing about any dollar limitations, by contrast to § 522(d), the federal schedule of exemptions, which contains a number of dollar limitations. The third difference—that between the Minnesota and South Dakota statutes—is also legally immaterial, and for a closely related reason. The federal exemption statute, just referred to, simply incorporates state and local exemption laws without regard to whether those laws contain dollar limitations of their own.

The Court attempts to reconcile the results in the two cases by characterizing the question presented as one of fact—whether the conversion was undertaken with fraudulent intent, or with an intent to delay or hinder creditors. In *Tveten*, the Bankruptcy Court found fraudulent intent, whereas in *Hanson* it did not. Neither finding is clearly erroneous, the Court says, so both judgments are affirmed. This analysis collapses upon examination. For in *Tveten* the major indicium of fraudulent intent relied on by the Bankruptcy Court was Dr. Tveten's avowed purpose to place the assets in question out of the reach of his creditors, a purpose that, as a matter of law, cannot amount to fraudulent intent, as the Court's opinion in *Hanson* explicitly states. The result, in practice, appears to be this: a debtor will be allowed to convert property into exempt form, or not, depending on findings of fact made in the court of first instance, the Bankruptcy Court, and these findings will turn on whether the Bankruptcy Court regards the amount of money involved as too much. With all deference, that is not a rule of law. It is simply a license to make distinctions among debtors based on subjective considerations that will vary more widely than the length of the chancellor's foot.

848 F.2d at 870-71.

Dr. Johnson was involved in the same real estate investments that brought financial doom to Dr. Tveten. He also owed his creditors $19 million and sold nonexempt assets in order to purchase annuities and life insurance from a fraternal benefit organization. Each of these debtors employed the same lawyer, faced the same opposing counsel, and admitted to attempting to put their assets beyond the reach of their creditors (although Dr. Johnson sought to shelter $400,000, rather than $700,000). Dr. Johnson's asset conversions were found permissible by the bankruptcy court, however, and Dr. Tveten's were not. The Eighth Circuit affirmed both bankruptcy court decisions. (*Johnson* was remanded, however, because the bankruptcy court believed—erroneously, as the Eighth Circuit concluded—that fraudulent intent could never as a matter of law be established by the size of the exemption. On remand, the bankruptcy court found fraudulent intent on the basis of several facts: first, that the debtor, who had no dependents and already had term life insurance coverage, bought whole life coverage with a cash surrender value below the maximum exemptable amount and surrendered it soon after bankruptcy was filed; and second, that the debtor traded nonexempt assets for an exempt harpsichord and grand piano when he could not play, one instrument remained in storage, and his live-in girlfriend did not know the other was in the house.)

What explains the outcomes in exemption planning cases? The openness or lack thereof with which the debtor acted? (If so, why is it fraudulent to conceal something that is not itself fraudulent?) The amount of money involved? (Did you notice that the majority mentioned the amount of Dr. Tveten's debt five times in the course of its opinion?) Use of an exemption with an unlimited dollar amount? Prior consultation with a bankruptcy attorney? The result reached by the bankruptcy court? Would it matter if property were converted from nonexempt into exempt form just as a judgment creditor is preparing to execute?

3. Remember, conversion is particularly attractive in states with generous exemptions. If a court disapproves of conversion, is the court disturbed by the conversion itself or is the court really expressing dissatisfaction with the generosity of state exemptions? If the latter, is the draconian remedy of denial of discharge appropriate, in light of Congress's decision to adopt state exemption schemes in bankruptcy?

4. What is the impact of Dr. Tveten's conduct on his exemptions? Is he still entitled to claim the full value of the otherwise-available exemption under state law? See § 522(o).

5. The court in *In re Schwarb*, 150 B.R. 470 (Bankr. M.D.Fla.1992), gave a different view of the passage in the legislative history, cited in *Tveten* and elsewhere, that seems to approve of pre-bankruptcy planning:

> [T]he "Hearings" referred to in the Committee Report consist of a letter from Bankruptcy Judge Phelps and comments on same by Committee Members and witnesses, condemning bankruptcy planning in the strongest terms. Judge Phelps' letter states that case law on the subject of bankruptcy planning "is in a state of utter confusion;" notes "that the conversion of non-exempt assets into exempt assets on the eve of bankruptcy is not, standing alone, fraudulent," and "that the payment of regular monthly payments on a debtor's homestead * * * or various such payments in the usual manner of living of the bankrupt, are perfectly appropriate;" but damns "the deliberate enlargement of exemptions out of the usual and customary manner of living and in contemplation of bankruptcy" as "cheating" which "shocks one's conscience" and "bring[s] the whole bankruptcy process into disrepute."

> Judge Phelps observed, "To have the bankrupt form the decision that he will file * * * bankruptcy proceedings and thereafter, with guidance from his attorney, to convert his salable assets into cash and then use that cash in such a way to hide it from his creditors, even while his attorney is busy typing up the bankruptcy schedules, appears to me to be fraudulent." Judge Phelps used the word "hide" to mean "shelter," not "conceal"; for he offered an example illustrated by a debtor's own statement of affairs. Former Bankruptcy Judge Cyr, now Judge of the First Circuit Court of Appeals, agreed that such conduct by debtors is "outrageous" and especially will be more prevalent as exemptions become more generous.

> Thus, there is scant, if any support for the notion that bankruptcy planning was approved without reservation by Congress. In fact, the Committee Report often cited seems to have been merely an artless paraphrase of Judge Phelps' letter; and the real sense of the Committee should be found in Judge Phelps' letter, rather than the oft-sited [sic] quote seemingly giving a carte blanche approval of pre-bankruptcy planning. Judge Phelps' letter also made it clear that advice of counsel is no excuse for such conduct, but rather may be considered part of the very essence of the offensive conduct.

Id. at 471–72. Do you agree with this view? If so, what makes bankruptcy planning improper, while tax planning remains the great American pastime?

6. How would you advise a client, contemplating bankruptcy, whose assets are not presently configured so as to take maximum advantage of available exemptions? Do you have to outline the possibilities for pre-bankruptcy planning in order to represent your client zealously? When has an attorney

gone too far? *Cf. United States v. Zimmerman*, 943 F.2d 1204 (10th Cir.1991); *United States v. Brown*, 943 F.2d 1246 (10th Cir.1991).

C. DEBTS EXCEPTED FROM DISCHARGE

Section 727(a) bars any discharge at all and applies only in Chapter 7 *unless* incorporated into other chapters by specific provisions. See § 1141(d)(3)(C). Section 523(a), on the other hand, excepts particular debts from discharge and applies in cases under all chapters *unless* specific provisions in those chapters provide to the contrary. Chapters 11 and 12 do not have any provisions to the contrary; rather, they expressly incorporate § 523. See §§ 1141(d)(2) (applicable only to individual debtors) and 1228(a). Chapter 13 is a bit different, because it incorporates most of the provisions of § 523(a), but not all of them. See §§ 1328(a)–(c).

The types of debts excepted from discharge by § 523 vary. Some of the exceptions, such as those for taxes and support obligations, depend upon the nature of the debt and Congress's view that these sorts of obligations have a special "deservingness." Other exceptions, such as those for debts incurred by fraud or breach of fiduciary duty, depend upon the debtor's misconduct. (And, of course, some of the exceptions can be explained by nothing loftier than an ability to influence the political process enough to get a special-interest provision passed.)

1. SECTION 523(a)(1)—TAX OBLIGATIONS

Section 523(a)(1), which excepts certain tax debts from discharge, requires a little patience because of its cross references to § 507(a) (dealing with priorities) and its use of tax law terms of art. The simplest and perhaps most important rule is that a tax claim entitled to priority under § 507(a)(8) is also not dischargeable under § 523-(a)(1)(A). That simple statement, however, is merely the tip of the iceberg.

Section 523(a)(1) excepts four categories of tax obligations from discharge: those of the kind and for the period specified in § 507(a)(8), which extends an eighth-level priority to certain tax claims; those for which a required return was not filed; those for which a return was filed late and after two years before bankruptcy; and those regarding which the debtor filed a fraudulent return or sought to evade or defeat the obligation. These rules continue pre-Code policies of coordinating tax obligations with rules governing priority and discharge, and of giving taxing authorities a superior position only for non-stale tax claims. The latter policy reflects a concern that giving superiority for stale claims might burden general unsecured creditors who extended credit to the debtor after the tax obligations arose.

Problems

1. Debtor filed a Chapter 7 petition on January 22, 2016. Debtor never filed income tax returns for the 2012 and 2013 tax years. Which, if any, of those tax obligations are nondischargeable?

2. Debtor filed income tax returns for the 2012 and 2013 tax years on January 20, 2016, but did not enclose a check, and then filed a bankruptcy petition two days later. Which, if any, of these tax obligations are nondischargeable?

3. Debtor obtained an extension for filing her 2012 federal income tax return to October 15, 2013. She filed the return on October 7, 2013, but did not enclose a check. She filed Chapter 7 on October 10, 2016. Is this tax obligation dischargeable?

4. Debtor is the president and sole shareholder of Corporation. When they both went into bankruptcy, Corporation owed $150,000 to the federal government for amounts withheld from its employees' wages for social security and federal income taxes. Most of this amount related to the three years before Corporation's bankruptcy was filed, but $25,000 of it was for obligations five years old. Debtor is worried because he is a "responsible person" who is liable for these taxes. What amount, if any, of these tax obligations is nondischargeable in Debtor's bankruptcy?

5. Debtor filed a timely return for the 2012 tax year and included a check for the amount he believed was due. The IRS audited the return and sent Debtor a letter in September 2015 claiming a deficiency. Two months later the IRS sent Debtor Form 3552, claiming that he owed $33,000 in additional taxes, $5,000 in penalties and $12,000 in interest. Debtor filed a bankruptcy petition in June of 2016. Which, if any, of these amounts are nondischargeable? See *Hartman v. United States (In re Hartman)*, 110 B.R. 951 (Bankr. D.Kan.1990).

6. Debtor owed $6,000 in federal income taxes for the 2015 tax year, but did not have the money to pay when April 15, 2016 rolled around. So, a few days before the return was due, Debtor obtained a $6,000 cash advance on her American Express card and used the funds to pay her taxes. She filed a Chapter 7 petition in late July, 2016 and had no assets available to pay unsecured creditors, such as American Express. Can American Express prevent the discharge of its debt? See § 523(a)(14).

2. SECTION 523(a)(2)—OBLIGATIONS INCURRED BY FRAUD

Fraud is the most important of the exceptions to discharge, in part because it is the most litigated. Subsection 523(a)(2)(A) applies to value obtained by a false representation or by fraud *other than* a financial statement regarding the debtor. Subsection 523(a)(2)(B) applies to the use of false written financial statements on which the creditor reasonably relied.

Subsection (a)(2)(C) provides a presumption, for purposes of subsection (a)(2)(A) *only*, that certain categories of debts are nondischargeable—consumer debts for "luxury goods or services," over the designated amount, owed to one creditor and incurred in the 90 days before bankruptcy; and cash advances exceeding the designated amount obtained within 70 days before bankruptcy under open-ended consumer credit plans. (These dollar amounts are subject to adjustment every three years, under § 104(b).)

Some commentators feared that (a)(2)(C) would be interpreted to support the dischargeability of any debt not within its categories—that is, that nondischargeability under (a)(2)(A) would be limited to the categories of debts listed in (a)(2)(C). That fear has proved unfounded. Any credit obtained without an intention of repaying and in contemplation of bankruptcy may be nondischargeable under § 523(a)(2)(A). The only difference is that, for fact patterns not within (a)(2)(C), no presumption helps the creditor establish nondischargeability.

Problems

1. Debtor purchased a Chevy Lumina from Creditor, on credit, two weeks before filing a Chapter 7 petition. The car is equipped with air conditioning, power brakes, power windows, power steering, power door locks, cruise control and a sunroof. Is this obligation nondischargeable under § 523(a)(2)? Does it matter whether Debtor intended to pay for the car at the time of purchase? See *GMAC v. McDonald (In re McDonald)*, 129 B.R. 279 (Bankr. M.D.Fla.1991).

2. Debtor obtained a loan from his mother-in-law, but did not mention that he was about to divorce her daughter. Is this obligation nondischargeable under § 523(a)(2) in Debtor's Chapter 7 bankruptcy? See *Caspers v. Van Horne (In re Van Horne)*, 823 F.2d 1285 (8th Cir.1987).

3. Josephine Jones obtained a loan from Bank by intentionally misstating the value of her assets on the loan application form. When Bank

discovered what happened, it accelerated the loan and threatened her with an immediate lawsuit if she did not pay the balance at once. She does not have the money to do so. Josephine is a friend of Sheldon Toibb and knows that individuals can file Chapter 11. Can she discharge her debt to Bank by filing a bankruptcy petition under Chapter 11? See § 1141(d).

4. In his application for a $15,000 loan from Creditor, Debtor omitted reference on his financial statement to substantial obligations on an out-of-state land development deal because Debtor knew that the information would lead Creditor to reject the application. Creditor did the usual credit checks, learned nothing untoward, and made the loan. Debtor later applied for a second loan, submitting a similarly-false application. Since Debtor's interest payments on the first loan were current, Creditor filed the second loan application without reading it and loaned an additional $12,000. Debtor defaulted and Creditor agreed to forebear if Debtor would give Creditor a mortgage to secure both obligations. Debtor did so. Six months later Debtor defaulted again; Creditor foreclosed and sold the property for $12,300. Debtor filed a bankruptcy petition and Creditor objected to discharge of the remaining obligation ($14,700). How much, if any, is nondischargeable? See *Jennen v. Hunter (In re Hunter)*, 771 F.2d 1126 (8th Cir.1985).

5. Debtor owed Creditor $5,700 on an obligation that had been outstanding for a couple of years. Needing additional credit, she submitted an application that omitted several other debts. Creditor agreed to refinance by lending Debtor an additional $9,200. From that amount, $5,700 was credited to the existing loan and $3,500 was given to Debtor. Debtor later filed a Chapter 7 petition and Creditor proved that it had relied on her fraudulent application. What amount is nondischargeable—$3,500 or $9,200? See *Matter of McFarland*, 84 F.3d 943 (7th Cir.), *cert. denied sub nom. South Div. Credit Union v. McFarland*, 519 U.S. 931, 117 S.Ct. 302, 136 L.Ed.2d 220 (1996).

6. Debtor was a partner in a stock brokerage firm. Partner A, without the knowledge of her partners, misused authority granted by one of the firm's clients. She sold securities from the client's account, appropriated the proceeds, and generated false reports to cover up her misconduct. When Debtor and the other partners discovered these facts, they alerted the client and dismissed Partner A from the business. They also did not contest their vicarious liability in the client's ensuing lawsuit. The partnership was unable to pay the judgment taken against it, and Debtor filed bankruptcy. The client filed a claim against Debtor in the amount of the judgment, and argued that it was nondischargeable under § 523(a)(2)(A). What result? Does it matter whether Debtor received any benefit from Partner A's misconduct? Does it matter whether Debtor should have known of the misconduct? See *Deodati v. M.M. Winkler & Assocs. (In re M.M. Winkler & Assocs.)*, 239 F.3d 746 (5th Cir.2001).

Credit card cases are among the most difficult—and frequently litigated—under § 523(a)(2), primarily because of the difficulty of fitting the fact patterns within the standards for common law fraud. The following case not only reviews the legal approaches taken by courts faced with this issue; it also describes how the system works—information that may surprise you.

AT&T UNIVERSAL CARD SERVICES v. ELLINGSWORTH (IN RE ELLINGSWORTH)

United States Bankruptcy Court, Western District of Missouri, 1997.
212 B.R. 326.

ARTHUR B. FEDERMAN, Bankruptcy Judge.

AT&T Universal Card Services (UCS) filed this adversary proceeding to determine the dischargeability of its debt against Chapter 7 debtor Deborah Ann Ellingsworth. * * * For the reasons set forth below, I find the debt to be dischargeable in part and nondischargeable in part.

FACTUAL BACKGROUND

Ms. Ellingsworth and her husband filed their joint bankruptcy petition on November 25, 1996. According to their bankruptcy schedules Ms. Ellingsworth was indebted to UCS for the sum of $4,038.11 at the time of filing. UCS issued a pre-approved credit card to Ms. Ellingsworth on October 19, 1995, with a credit limit of $4000. * * *

* * *

Don Carter, an employee, testified on behalf of UCS. He admitted that UCS contacted Ms. Ellingsworth in 1995 and informed her that she had been pre-approved for a card. She responded by telephone and was sent a credit card and a Universal Bank Credit Agreement (the Agreement). She never filled out an application for the card. Apparently she only verified by phone her income and employment. She was not asked about other liabilities. According to her bankruptcy schedules and the credit bureau report admitted at the trial, Ms. Ellingsworth and her husband already possessed at least 16 credit cards when she was offered the UCS card. Mr. Carter stated that UCS pre-approved Ms. Ellingsworth for its card based upon a credit score it obtained from a credit bureau. He stated that UCS obtained a Fair, Issacs Credit Bureau Score (a FICO score) of 759 on Ms. Ellingsworth prior to issuing her the card, and that any score above 680 merits consideration for a pre-approved card. He stated that UCS has developed some internal indicators that it uses in addition to the FICO score, but he was not certain of how the internal analysis is performed. And, other than the FICO score and the information provided by the customer as to her income and employment, it appears UCS had no other information available to it prior to issuing the card. According to Mr. Carter, once a card is issued to a customer, it is UCS policy to obtain a FICO score not less than every quarter, and to consider raising or lowering the credit limit or revoking the card, based on any changes. He said full credit bureau reports are not obtained prior to issuing cards because analyzing the credit bureau report itself would be too time consuming.

Mr. Carter testified that a full credit bureau report was generated on Ms. Ellingsworth on July 2, 1997, in preparation for this trial. That report showed her various obligations in detail. A casual reading of the report indicates that Ms. Ellingsworth is insolvent and unable to meet her obligations. UCS did not present any evidence that a quarterly credit score had been obtained on Ms. Ellingsworth between October of 1995, when she received the card, and July 2, 1997, when the credit bureau report was obtained.

UCS claims that Ms. Ellingsworth represented with each purchase and cash advance that she had the ability and the intent to repay her obligation to UCS. It also claims that any cash advances she took within 60[b] days of the bankruptcy filing aggregating more than $1000 are presumed nondischargeable.

DISCUSSION

A. *Introduction*

The dischargeability of credit card debt is but one small piece in the puzzle that represents unsecured lending today because the use of credit cards is, in fact, a form of unsecured lending. The following scenario illustrates this point. Assume you are a loan officer for a large metropolitan bank. A woman walks in one day and says she wants to borrow $60,000 on her signature. She willingly fills out a financial statement which shows that she already has $300,000 in unsecured debt, but she needs these additional funds for a business trip. She also shows one asset, a heavily encumbered apartment building that is being foreclosed. Of course, she promises to repay the loan if one is made to

---

[b] Section 523(a)(2)(C) had a 60-day period at the time this case was decided. It was extended to 70 days by the 2005 Amendments, and the dollar figure was reduced. Eds.

her. Would a bank that makes such a loan be found to have justifiably relied on her promise? Of course not. But, what if, instead, the bank made the loan without bothering to ask her basic information about assets, liabilities, and income? And what if she did not make an express promise to repay the loan? Should this bank be allowed to claim that it justifiably relied on her implied promises to pay? One would think not. However, those are the very facts of a recent bankruptcy opinion, except that rather than a face to face encounter with a bank officer, the debt was incurred through use of a credit card.[1] In *In re Hashemi* the debtor used his American Express Card to run up over $60,000 in debt while vacationing in France with his family. Dr. Hashemi then came home and filed for bankruptcy protection. The Ninth Circuit held that the debt was nondischargeable. The opinion pays scant attention to whether American Express acted justifiably in relying on debtor's promise to pay, whether express or implied. The Court found only that when Dr. Hashemi began his spending spree his account balance was $227.00, and that he had often repaid balances in excess of $60,000 in the past. Nonetheless, surely if American Express had been aware of Dr. Hashemi's current situation, it would not have extended the credit. And, if it was not aware that Dr. Hashemi was insolvent, then it should have taken some steps to find out before extending such a large amount of credit. If no lender would have made that loan in a face to face transaction, why are American Express' unreasonable lending practices afforded special protection under the Bankruptcy Code? Is there something in the Bankruptcy Code that treats credit card loans differently from face to face loans? Congress has created certain presumptions of nondischargeability as to credit card debt.[3] To the extent those presumptions are applicable, a portion of Ms. Ellingsworth's debt is nondischargeable. However, to the extent there is not a presumption of nondischargeability, the conduct of UCS in making credit available to her is a significant factor, which renders that portion of her debt dischargeable. * * *

B. *The Growth of Credit Card Use*

In 1995 2.7 billion unrequested solicitations for credit cards were mailed to American consumers. That amounts to about 17 offers per adult. The average card has a spending limit of $6007, therefore, if

---

[1] *American Express Travel Related Services Co., Inc. v. Hashemi (In re Hashemi)*, 104 F.3d 1122 (9th Cir.), *cert. denied*, 520 U.S. 1230, 117 S.Ct. 1824, 137 L.Ed.2d 1031 (1997).

[3] § 523(a)(2)(C).

a consumer accepted every offer, she would end up with a potential credit line of $102,119. And, while the industry average for charging off credit card debt is 6 percent, bank profits have hit the highest levels in more than half a century, thanks primarily to the profits from credit cards. The average household carries about $4000 a month in card debt, a total of $367 billion, and banks earned approximately $35 billion in interest on this total in 1995. Since credit cards are so profitable, and the profits derive from having a very large customer base, issuers such as UCS may choose to ignore the usual standards of credit worthiness. Additionally, the creditors actively seek out undisciplined spenders who carry large unpaid balances from month to month. They dangle large credit lines in front of these consumers, and offer come-ons like lower interest rates for the first few months, as well as pre-printed cash advance checks. Some banks have even started to penalize consumers who pay their accounts in full each month. In their eagerness to capture market share, banks spend little time gathering financial information about their potential credit card customers. Prior to a mass mailing, creditors such as UCS obtain lists from credit bureaus with the names of candidates and a "credit score" for each person on the list. These scores relate generally to past card use, whether the candidate pays the minimum monthly balance on current cards, and whether there are any delinquencies or bankruptcies on record. Car loans, medical bills, and mortgages are not included in the credit score, nor are income, job history, marital status, and assets.

The credit score, which can range from 450 to 850, is a supposedly scientific way of assessing the likelihood that a debtor will repay a loan. The computer credit model upon which most lenders rely today was developed by Fair, Issacs, and Company in California. The score is based on all credit-related data in a credit bureau report, but it is not a measure of a borrower's income, assets, or bank accounts. Fair Issacs, which is the service that UCS uses, identifies credit patterns, each of which corresponds to the probability that a lender [sic] will make payments. * * * In other words, as long as you use a credit card instead of a financial statement to obtain an unsecured loan, you do not have to indicate any form of credit-worthiness, other than the fact that, until now, you have paid your bills on time. Unfortunately, this tactic guarantees that borrowers who are encouraged to use credit cards until they acquire unsecured debt that far exceeds their income will ultimately not be able to pay their bills on time.

Banks use other techniques as well to encourage consumers to keep large balances on their credit cards. For example, VISA and MASTERCARD issuer Citibank offer credit cards that give a 2 percent interest rate break to customers who keep a balance of more than $2,500. UCS, the plaintiff here, rewards customers with bonus points if they carry a large balance. More disturbing, credit card companies flood college campuses with sign-up tables to hook customers early in adulthood. It is not unusual for college students with no income at all to accumulate 10 to 15 cards while in college. Why do the credit card companies solicit college students who have no regular job, little income, and no credit history? Because market research indicates that consumers are likely to hang onto the first credit card they obtain and use it long after graduation. Moreover, they will make 77 percent of their monthly purchases with that card.

* * *

C. Section 523(a)(2)(A)

* * * The United States Supreme Court recently held that § 523(a)(2)(A) encompasses common law misrepresentation or actual fraud.[37] This approach confirms * * * that the three torts [false pretenses, false representations and actual fraud] are all subject to the single action test of actual fraud. To prove actual or common law fraud, a creditor must prove the following:

(1)   the debtor made a false representation;

(2)   at the time the representation was made the debtor knew it was false;

(3)   debtor subjectively intended to deceive the creditor at the time he made the representation;

(4)   the creditor justifiably relied upon the representation; and

(5)   [the] creditor was damaged.

While case law makes much of these five elements, most cases turn on whether debtor's use of a credit card is an actual representation that she intends to repay the money borrowed, and whether the creditor justifiably relied on debtor's representation that she intended to repay. * * *

* * * In the past, courts have held that a debtor makes an implied representation with each use of a credit card that she has both the ability and intent to repay the debt. But, fraud can be based on any type

---

[37]   *Field v. Mans*, 516 U.S. 59, 116 S.Ct. 437, 444, 133 L.Ed.2d 351 (1995).

of conduct calculated to convey a misleading impression, thus, it is not relevant whether the representation is express or implied. The Court in *Chevy Chase Bank v. Briese (In re Briese)* found that "debtors do not commit fraud just by using their credit cards, even when they are heavily in debt. * * * To permit credit card plaintiffs to benefit from 'implications' is to engage in impermissible burden-shifting."[44]

The implied representation theory developed due to the unique nature of credit card transactions. Since a debtor presents a credit card to a third party merchant when making a purchase, not the issuer, courts held that there could be no direct representation or contemporaneous reliance with each use of the card. Courts, therefore, held that with each use of the card, a debtor made an implied representation that she had the ability and intent to repay the debt. With the advent of electronic transmission of credit card transactions, creditors are now instantly aware when a debtor uses its card. Therefore, debtors make an express representation to the issuer each time they use the card that they intend to repay the debt. It is not clear if debtors ever made a representation of an ability to repay. However, as was recently pointed out by the Honorable Leif M. Clark, in the real world very few people who use credit cards represent a present ability to pay.[50] They are using a credit card instead of cash precisely because they do not have the present ability to pay. It is this condition that allows card issuers to charge the interest and finance charges that make the credit card business so profitable. Judge Clark noted, ironically, that "an ability to repay is inferred to protect an industry that purposefully solicits customers who generally lack such ability."

A minority of Courts hold that the credit card company assumes the risk of non-payment with the use of the card, unless the issuer told the debtor to stop using its card.[53] Both the assumption of the risk theory and the implied representation theory were developed at a time when there was a significant lag between the time the card was used and the transaction was actually recorded with the issuer. Neither theory is as relevant today when most credit transactions are automatically recorded electronically at the instant the card is used. The

---

[44]   196 B.R. 440, 449 (Bankr. W.D.Wis.1996).

[50]   *Sears, Roebuck and Co. v. Hernandez (In re Hernandez)*, 208 B.R. 872, 880 (Bankr. W.D.Tex.1997).

[53]   *See, e.g., First Nat'l Bank of Mobile v. Roddenberry (In re Roddenberry)*, 701 F.2d 927, 932-33 (11th Cir.1983).

issuer has the technology to refuse to accept the transaction before the merchant completes the sale. In fact, most merchants today will not complete the sale until they receive a code accepting the card. Likewise, if an issuer wishes to terminate the use of a card it can do so automatically. It does not have to inform the debtor to stop using the card, and then wait for it to be mailed back. I, therefore, find that debtors make [an] express representation that they intend to repay the obligation each time they use a credit card.

With these fictional theories removed from the analysis, I must decide two things. Did Ms. Ellingsworth falsely represent to UCS that she intended to repay her obligation to UCS at the time she used the credit card, and did UCS justifiably rely on that representation.

Direct proof of an individual's actual intention and purpose is nearly impossible to find. Therefore, case law has developed a list of circumstantial factors which a creditor might use to infer intent.[55] These objective or circumstantial factors, much like the "badges of fraud," are:

1.　　　The length of time between the charges made and the filing of bankruptcy;

2.　　　Whether or not an attorney has been consulted concerning the filing of bankruptcy before the charges were made;

3.　　　The number of charges made;

4.　　　The amount of the charges;

5.　　　The financial condition of the debtor at the time the charges are made;

6.　　　Whether the charges were above the credit limit of the account;

7.　　　Did the debtor make multiple charges on the same day;

8.　　　Whether or not the debtor was employed;

---

[55] *Citibank South Dakota N.A. v. Dougherty (In re Dougherty)*, 84 B.R. 653, 657 (B.A.P. 9th Cir.1988).

9.   The debtor's prospects for employment;

10.   The debtor's financial sophistication;

11.   Whether there was a sudden change in the debtor's buying habits; and

12.   Whether the purchases were made for luxuries or necessities.

The goal in applying these factors is not to determine whether a reasonable debtor should have known that she was in over her head, and would not be able to pay her obligations. Instead, these factors are an aid in determining whether this debtor knew she would actually be unable to repay this debt. If so, the debtor incurred the debt with the intent not to repay it.

Here, the Ellingsworths filed their Chapter 7 petition within 75 days of using the credit card for the first time. The majority of the cash advances were taken within 60 days of the filing. Between September 11, 1996, and October 15, 1996, Ms. Ellingsworth made 16 cash advances and 8 purchases totaling approximately $4000. According to the bankruptcy schedules, the debtors had over $70,000 in unsecured debt at the time of filing. Ms. Ellingsworth testified that all of the other credit cards were "maxed out" when she began to use the UCS card, therefore, she and her husband had at least $65,000 in debt when the charges were made. Ms. Ellingsworth testified that she did not contact an attorney until she stopped using the UCS card. She did, however, state that she realized on October 15, 1996, that they could not go on using credit cards to meet their expenses, and that they needed credit counseling. She stated she and Mr. Ellingsworth made an appointment with Consumer Credit Counseling on October 18, 1996. The counselor at Consumer Credit Counseling told the debtors that they could not cut their expenses enough to service their debt, and that they should consider filing bankruptcy. According to the worksheet prepared by debtors and the counselor, debtors had net income of $4180 and minimum living expenses of $3383 leaving disposable income of $797. They needed $1465 a month to pay the minimum on their credit cards. Ms. Ellingsworth testified that she voluntarily ceased using the UCS card before she went to credit counseling. I note, however, that she stopped using the card when she reached the credit limit. I also note that Mr. Ellingsworth testified that he contacted Consumer Credit Counseling long enough before their appointment to allow debtors to fill out all the financial information and return it to the counselor five days before their appointment. It appears, therefore, that debtors had determined they at least needed professional advice before they ceased using the UCS card.

Debtor's employment is not at issue here, as she has been employed as a school teacher for 18 years. Though both Mr. and Mrs. Ellingsworth claim that Mr. Ellingsworth's job change was the straw that broke their financial backs, they did not well substantiate that claim. Mr. Ellingsworth claimed he took a decrease in salary, but the decrease seems to be related to the loss of a potential bonus he may have received as a buyer. He also made up for some of the decrease in pay by eliminating a voluntary contribution he was making to a 401(k) plan in the amount of $175.50 a month. Mr. Ellingsworth stated his employer had provided him with a car when he was a buyer, and now he had to provide his own transportation. The car expense represented the largest increased expense after this job change. Ms. Ellingsworth testified that they pay $187 a month for the car plus car insurance and gasoline. His job change was effective in August of 1997. They both insisted at trial that all of the charges were made for necessities. But, Ms. Ellingsworth could not explain a charge in the amount of $63.46 at Dave's Guns in Pataskala, Ohio, nor could she explain a charge in the amount of $217.23 at Golf Discount Campbell in Springfield, Missouri. Ms. Ellingsworth attempted to explain the medical expenses she encounters with three children, but she again failed to document these expenses. She admitted that they have health insurance that pays 80 percent of their health costs, and she did not refer to any specific illness that accounted for some of the funds she obtained with the UCS card.

Finally, I note that the debtors are intelligent and articulate people. They were not convincing when they said that, even though they had over $70,000 in unsecured debt, a second mortgage on their home, and had been using credit cards for six years to make ends meet, they didn't realize the extent of their financial difficulty until they went to client counseling. I especially note that the charges on the UCS card were made over a very short period of time and debtors stopped using the card as soon as the limit was reached. I, therefore, find that when Ms. Ellingsworth used the UCS card she knew that she would be unable to ever repay the debt, and she, therefore, did not intend to repay the debt.

A determination of intent, however, deals only with the debtor's conduct. I turn next to whether UCS proved that it justifiably relied upon Ms. Ellingsworth's representation of her intent to repay. The Supreme Court attempted to distinguish reasonable and justifiable reliance in *Field v. Mans* as follows. Reliance may be justifiable even if it does not conform to the standard of a reasonable man. For example, a creditor may justifiably rely on a debtor's statement that his house is free and clear of liens, without going to the recorder of deeds office to check for itself. On the other hand, a creditor is "required to use his senses, and cannot recover if he blindly relies upon a misrepresentation the falsity of which would be patent to him if he had utilized his opportunity to make a cursory examination or investigation."[64] For example, the Supreme Court stated, if a seller represents that a horse is sound when it is apparent that it has one eye, the buyer cannot be said to have justifiably relied upon the representation. This clarification is not always apparent in the credit card context. The **Restatement (Second) of Torts** does instruct, however, that "justification is a matter of the qualities and characteristics of a particular plaintiff, and the circumstances of a particular case, rather than of the application of a community standard of conduct in all cases." * * * [I]t becomes clear that UCS had access to much of the same information emphasized in the *Dougherty* factors that is now available to this Court. Credit card issuers have come to rely on these factors when determining whether to object to the discharge of their debt after someone files for bankruptcy relief. Interestingly, rarely do creditors consider these factors prior issuing a card. * * *

Credit card issuers are very sophisticated creditors. They have instant electronic access each time a credit card is used now. They know the number of charges made in a given day, they know the amount of those charges, and they know when a customer exceeds his credit limit. While they do not know with each use whether a debtor is employed, the issuers could, and often choose not to, obtain updated information about debtor's employment status. Moreover, the issuers elect not to obtain any other financial information, including assets and liabilities, about potential customers at the time a pre-approved card is issued. Often the reaction of a creditor at the time a user exceeds the credit limit on his account is to increase the limit. * * *

* * * [Issuers] make their decisions to offer customers credit cards not out of some altruistic notion of helping society, but because credit cards are very profitable. They carefully solicit customers who are most likely to use their services in a manner that increases those profits. They don't seek out or want customers who demonstrate an ability to pay by paying their other accounts in full each month. Judge

---

[64] 516 U.S. at 71 (*quoting* Restatement (Second) of Torts, § 541A, Comment a (1976)).

Clark noted in *In re Hernandez* that one large credit card company (not UCS) makes $318 a year on the typical customer who carries a balance, while it loses $30 a year on customers who pay their monthly balance each month.[76] A credit score demonstrates a likelihood a debtor will not default. It is not based upon an analysis of one's assets, secured liabilities, and living expenses. Mr. Carter admitted that credit scoring will not eliminate potential customers who are insolvent. In fact, Ms. Ellingsworth received a credit score, which was acceptable to UCS, at a time when, according to her bankruptcy schedules, the credit bureau report, and the information sheet from Consumer Client Counseling, her expenses exceeded her income by at least $500.00 a month.

* * * Offering this customer a pre-approved card, without making any individual inquiry into her financial status, is the equivalent of buying a horse with one eye. If the credit card issuers choose to continue this profitable technique to increase their customer base, they cannot claim that they justifiably relied upon any representation the customer made at the time the card was issued. * * * Moreover, if UCS did not justifiably rely upon Ms. Ellingsworth's representations at the time the card was issued, reliance cannot then attach when the card is used. I find, therefore, that the credit in this case was extended to Ms. Ellingsworth without justifiable consideration of her ability to repay. If UCS did not consider her ability to repay, it certainly cannot now claim that it relied on her intent. Indeed, to hold otherwise only encourages creditors to continue to act irresponsibly. * * *

D. *Section 523(a)(2)(C)*

Section 523(a)(2)(C) presumes the nondischargeability of cash advances exceeding a total of $1000 taken within 60 days of filing: *[the court quoted the subsection]*.

* * * Congress adopted this provision to address what it considered an especially egregious form of behavior referred to as "loading up."[83] Loading up is defined as "going on a buying spree in contemplation of bankruptcy." The Court in *In re Cox* found that the presumption in § 523(a)(2)(C) is the exclusive remedy against loading up.[85] * * * The legislative history indicates that the presumption shifts the burden

---

[76] 208 B.R. 872, 879 (Bankr. W.D.Tex.1997).

[83] S. Rep. No. 65, 98th Cong., 1st Sess. 58 (1985).

[85] *GM Card v. Cox (In re Cox)*, 182 B.R. 626, 635 (Bankr. D.Mass.1995).

to the debtor to prove the dischargeability of a debt, as opposed to the burden resting squarely on the creditor to prove the nondischargeability of a debt incurred outside the presumption period. This shift of the burden means "the reliance element inherent in § 523(a)(2)(A) is not relevant in the context of subsection 523(a)(2)(C)."[89] Thus, if the debt is subject to the presumption, Congress has determined that it is the debtor's intent alone, and not the creditor's conduct, which determines dischargeability.

> [The court held the amount of cash advances taken within 60 days of filing—a total of $2,058—nondischargeable.]

* * *

Questions and Problems

1. Could you not interpret Ms. Ellingsworth's actions in going to credit counseling, and not using her cards anymore, as a demonstration of responsibility? Why, then, did the court interpret these actions as indicative of a fraudulent intent not to repay?

2. Is the court's analysis of how credit card issuers conduct their business correct, when measured against the requirement of justifiable reliance?

---

[89]   *Sears Roebuck and Co. v. Hernandez (In re Hernandez)*, 208 B.R. 872, 881 n.17 (Bankr. W.D.Tex.1997).

Or is the court inappropriately curbing the ability of credit card issuers to function in the marketplace?

Note on Dischargeability of Punitive Damages

Given the broad definition of "claim" in § 101(4), a debtor may be liable for obligations that are noncompensatory. Damages in tort cases are only the most obvious example; others include treble damages permitted under various statutes, such as RICO, 18 U.S.C. § 1964(c), and antitrust, 15 U.S.C. § 15. The Code recognizes that payment of such claims would come out of the pockets of other creditors, serving to diminish their pro rata portions. Thus, § 726(a)(4) subordinates payments on claims for "any fine, penalty, or forfeiture, or for multiple, exemplary, or punitive damages." As a result, such claims are very unlikely to be paid in bankruptcy.

Are those claims dischargeable? Courts were divided on the question until the Supreme Court resolved it in *Cohen v. De La Cruz*, 523 U.S. 213, 118 S.Ct. 1212, 140 L.Ed.2d 341 (1998). The debtor violated rent control laws and was ordered to refund $31,382 in rental overcharges. He filed bankruptcy without paying, and the tenants sought to bar discharge of the treble damages to which they were entitled under the state consumer fraud statute. The debtor argued that § 523(a)(2)(A) excepts from discharge only the portion of damages corresponding to the amount obtained by fraud—here, $31,382. The bankruptcy court held for the tenants, however, finding all obligations arising from fraudulent conduct, including both punitive and compensatory damages, nondischargeable. The Third Circuit affirmed in a divided opinion. The Supreme Court also affirmed, holding that both compensatory and punitive damages flowing from fraudulent conduct are nondischargeable under § 523(a)(2)(A).

The Court reasoned that § 523(a)(2)(A) bars discharge of "any debt" for money incurred through fraud, which plainly includes treble damages awards. The phrase "to the extent obtained by" does not support a conclusion that treble damages are outside § 523(a)(2)(A). It modifies "money, property, services, or * * * credit," and not "any debt." Thus, "any debt" that arises from money, etc., obtained by fraud is excepted from discharge. In this case, $31,382 was obtained by fraud and the full liability traceable to that sum—$94,147 plus attorney's fees and costs—fell within the exception.

The history of the fraud exception, in the Court's view, reinforces this reading. Debtor's reading, limiting the exception to the value of money or property fraudulently obtained by a debtor, would lead to inappropriate consequences when the injury to the creditor exceeds the value of money, etc., the debtor obtained.

Debtors charged with fraudulent conduct may choose to settle rather than litigate. What happens if the debtor files bankruptcy without meeting the terms of the settlement agreement? Is the creditor able to assert the fraud in order to except the debt from discharge? Does the answer depend upon whether the settlement agreement contains a general release? The Supreme Court addressed these questions in the following case.

ARCHER v. WARNER

United States Supreme Court, 2003.
538 U.S. 314, 123 S.Ct. 1462, 155 L.Ed.2d 454.

JUSTICE BREYER delivered the opinion of the Court.

The Bankruptcy Code provides that a debt shall not be dischargeable in bankruptcy "to the extent" it is "for money * * * obtained by * * * false pretenses, a false representation, or actual fraud." § 523-(a)(2)(A). Can this language cover a debt embodied in a settlement agreement that settled a creditor's earlier claim "for money * * * obtained by * * * fraud"? In our view, the statute can cover such a debt, and we reverse a lower court judgment to the contrary.

I

This case arises out of circumstances that we outline as follows:
(1) *A* sues *B* seeking money that (*A* says) *B* obtained through fraud; (2) the parties settle the lawsuit and release related claims; (3) the settlement agreement does not resolve the issue of fraud, but provides that *B* will pay *A* a fixed sum; (4) *B* does not pay the fixed sum; (5) *B* enters bankruptcy; and (6) *A* claims that *B*'s obligation to pay the fixed settlement sum is nondischargeable because, like the original debt, it is for "money * * * obtained by * * * fraud."

This outline summarizes the following circumstances: In late 1991, Leonard and Arlene Warner bought the Warner Manufacturing Company for $250,000. About six months later they sold the company to Elliott and Carol Archer for $610,000. A few months after that the Archers sued the Warners in North Carolina state court for (among other things) fraud connected with the sale.

In May 1995, the parties settled the lawsuit. The settlement agreement specified that the Warners would pay the Archers "$300,000.00 less legal and accounting expenses" "as compensation for emotional distress/personal injury type damages." It added that the Archers would "execute releases to any and all claims * * * arising out of this litigation, except as to amounts set forth in [the] Settlement

Agreement." The Warners paid the Archers $200,000 and executed a promissory note for the remaining $100,000. The Archers executed releases "discharging" the Warners "from any and every right, claim, or demand" that the Archers "now have or might otherwise hereafter have against" them, "excepting only obligations under" the promissory note and related instruments. The releases, signed by all parties, added that the parties did not "admit any liability or wrongdoing," that the settlement was "the compromise of disputed claims, and that payment [was] not to be construed as an admission of liability." A few days later the Archers voluntarily dismissed the state-court lawsuit with prejudice.

In November 1995, the Warners failed to make the first payment on the $100,000 promissory note. The Archers sued for the payment in state court. The Warners filed for bankruptcy. The Bankruptcy Court ordered liquidation under Chapter 7 of the Bankruptcy Code. And the Archers brought the present claim, asking the Bankruptcy Court to find the $100,000 debt nondischargeable, and to order the Warners to pay the $100,000. Leonard Warner agreed to a consent order holding his debt nondischargeable. Arlene Warner contested nondischargeability. The Archers argued that Arlene Warner's promissory note debt was nondischargeable because it was for "money * * * obtained by * * * fraud."

The Bankruptcy Court, finding the promissory note debt dischargeable, denied the Archers' claim. The District Court affirmed the Bankruptcy Court. And the Court of Appeals for the Fourth Circuit, dividing two to one, affirmed the District Court. The majority reasoned that the settlement agreement, releases, and promissory note had worked a kind of "novation." This novation replaced (1) an original potential debt to the Archers for money obtained by fraud with (2) a new debt. The new debt was not for money obtained by fraud. It was for money promised in a settlement contract. And it was consequently dischargeable in bankruptcy.

We granted the Archers' petition for certiorari because different Circuits have come to different conclusions about this matter.

II

We agree with the Court of Appeals and the dissent that "the settlement agreement and promissory note here, coupled with the broad language of the release, completely addressed and released each and every underlying state law claim." That agreement left only one relevant debt: a debt for money promised in the settlement agreement itself. To recognize that fact, however, does not end our inquiry. We must decide whether that same debt can *also* amount to a debt for *money obtained by fraud*, within the terms of the nondischargeability statute. Given this Court's precedent, we believe that it can.

Brown v. Felsen, 442 U.S. 127 (1979), governs the outcome here. The circumstances there were the following: (1) Brown sued Felsen in state court seeking money that (Brown said) Felsen had obtained through fraud; (2) the state court entered a consent decree embodying a stipulation providing that Felsen would pay Brown a certain amount; (3) neither the decree nor the stipulation indicated the payment was for fraud; (4) Felsen did not pay; (5) Felsen entered bankruptcy; and (6) Brown asked the Bankruptcy Court to look behind the decree and stipulation and to hold that the debt was nondischargeable because it was a debt for money obtained by fraud.

The lower courts had held against Brown. They pointed out that the relevant debt was for money owed pursuant to a consent judgment; they noted that the relevant judgment-related documents did not refer to fraud; they added that the doctrine of res judicata prevented the Bankruptcy Court from looking behind those documents to uncover the nature of the claim that had led to their creation; and they consequently concluded that the relevant debt could not be characterized as one for money obtained by fraud.

This Court unanimously rejected the lower court's reasoning. The Court conceded that the state law of claim preclusion would bar Brown from making any claim " 'based on the same cause of action' " that Brown had brought in state court. *Id.* at 131. Indeed, this aspect of res judicata would prevent Brown from litigating "all grounds for * * * recovery" previously available to Brown, whether or not Brown had previously "asserted" those grounds in the prior state court "proceeding." But all this, the Court held, was beside the point. Claim preclusion did not prevent the Bankruptcy Court from looking beyond the record of the state-court proceeding and the documents that terminated that proceeding (the stipulation and consent judgment) in order to decide whether the debt at issue (namely, the debt embodied in the consent decree and stipulation) was a debt for money obtained by fraud

As a matter of logic, *Brown*'s holding means that the Fourth Circuit's novation theory cannot be right. The reduction of Brown's state-court fraud claim to a stipulation (embodied in a consent decree) worked the same kind of novation as the "novation" at issue here. (Despite the dissent's suggestions to the contrary, it did so by an agreement of the parties that would seem to have "severed the causal relationship" between liquidated debt and underlying fraud no more and no less than did the settlement and releases at issue here.) Yet, in *Brown*, this Court held that the Bankruptcy Court should look behind that stipulation to determine whether it reflected settlement of a valid claim for fraud. If the Fourth Circuit's view were correct—if reducing a fraud claim to settlement definitively changed the nature of the debt for dischargeability purposes—the nature of the debt in *Brown* would have changed similarly, thereby rendering the debt dischargeable. This Court's instruction that the Bankruptcy Court could "weigh all the evidence" would have been pointless. There would have been nothing for the Bankruptcy Court to examine.

Moreover, the Court's language in *Brown* strongly favors the Archers' position here. The Court said that "the mere fact that a conscientious creditor has previously reduced his claim to judgment should not bar further inquiry into the true nature of the debt." If we substitute the word "settlement" for the word "judgment," the Court's statement describes this case.

Finally, the Court's basic reasoning in *Brown* applies here. The Court pointed out that the Bankruptcy Code's nondischargeability provision had originally covered "only 'judgments' sounding in fraud." Congress later changed the language so that it covered all such "liabilities. " This change indicated that "Congress intended the fullest possible inquiry" to ensure that "all debts arising out of" fraud are "excepted from discharge," no matter what their form. See also § 523(a) (current "any debt" language). Congress also intended to allow the relevant determination (whether a debt arises out of fraud) to take place in bankruptcy court, not to force it to occur earlier in state court at a time when nondischargeability concerns "are not directly in issue and neither party has a full incentive to litigate them."

The only difference we can find between *Brown* and the present case consists of the fact that the relevant debt here is embodied in a settlement, not in a stipulation and consent judgment. But we do not see how that difference could prove determinative. The dischargeability provision applies to all debts that "arise out of" fraud. A debt embodied in the settlement of a fraud case "arises" no less "out of" the underlying fraud than a debt embodied in a stipulation and consent decree. Policies that favor the settlement of disputes, like those that favor "repose," are neither any more nor any less at issue here than in *Brown*. In *Brown*, the doctrine of res judicata itself ensured "a blanket release" of the underlying claim of fraud, just as the contractual releases did here.

Despite the dissent's protests to the contrary, what has *not* been established here, as in *Brown,* is that the parties meant to resolve the *issue* of fraud or, more narrowly, to resolve that issue for purposes of a later claim of nondischargeability in bankruptcy. In a word, we can find no significant difference between *Brown* and the case now before us.

Arlene Warner argues that we should affirm the Court of Appeals' decision on alternative grounds. She says that the settlement agreement and releases not only worked a novation by converting potential tort liabilities into a contract debt, but also included a promise that the Archers would not make the present claim of nondischargeability for fraud. * * *

Without suggesting that these additional arguments are meritorious, we note that the Court of Appeals did not determine the merits of either argument, both of which are, in any event, outside the scope of the question presented and insufficiently addressed below. * * * The Court of Appeals remains free, on remand, to determine whether such questions were properly raised or preserved, and, if so, to decide them.

We conclude that the Archers' settlement agreement and releases may have worked a kind of novation, but that fact does not bar the Archers from showing that the settlement debt arose out of "false pretenses, a false representation, or actual fraud," and consequently is nondischargeable, § 523(a)(2)(A). We reverse the Court of Appeals' judgment to the contrary. And we remand this case for further proceedings consistent with this opinion.

It is so ordered.

Justice Thomas, with whom Justice Stevens joins, dissenting.

[The opinion quoted § 523(a)(2)(A), emphasizing "obtained by."] The Court holds that a debt owed under a settlement agreement was "obtained by" fraud even though the debt resulted from a contractual arrangement pursuant to which the parties agreed, using the broadest language possible, to release one another from "any and every right, claim, or demand * * * arising out of" a fraud action filed by petitioners in North Carolina state court. Because the Court's conclusion is supported neither by the text of the Bankruptcy Code nor by any of the agreements executed by the parties, I respectfully dissent.

The Court begins its description of this case with the observation that "the settlement agreement does not *resolve* the issue of fraud, but provides that *B* will pay *A* a fixed sum" (emphasis added). Based on that erroneous premise, the Court goes on to find that there is "no significant difference between *Brown* and [this case]." The only distinction, the Court explains, is that "the relevant debt here is embodied in a settlement, not in a stipulation and consent judgment" as in *Brown v. Felsen*, 442 U.S. 127 (1979).

Remarkably, however, the Court fails to address the critical difference between this case and *Brown:* The parties here executed a blanket release, rather than entered into a consent judgment. And, in my view, "if it is shown that [a] note was given and received as payment or waiver of the original debt and the parties agreed that the note was to substitute a new obligation for the old, the note fully discharges the original debt, and the nondischargeability of the original debt does not affect the dischargeability of the obligation under the note." *In re West*, 22 F.3d 775, 778 (7th Cir.1994). That is the case before us, and, accordingly, *Brown* does not control our disposition of this matter.

In *Brown*, * * * [t]he Court held that principles of res judicata did not bar the Bankruptcy Court from looking behind the consent judgment and stipulation to determine the extent to which the debt was "obtained by" fraud. The Court concluded that it would upset the policy of the Bankruptcy Code for "state courts to decide [questions of nondischargeability] at a stage when they are not directly in issue and neither party has a full incentive to litigate them." *Brown* did not, however, address the question presented in this case—whether a creditor may, *without the participation of the state court*, completely release a debtor from "any and every right, claim, or demand * * * relating to" a state-court fraud action.

Based on the sweeping language of the general release, it is inaccurate for the Court to say that the parties did not "resolve the issue of fraud." To be sure, as in *Brown*, there is no legally controlling document stating that respondent did (or did not) commit fraud. But, unlike in *Brown*, where it was not clear which claims were being resolved by the consent judgment, the release in this case clearly demonstrates that the parties intended to resolve conclusively not only the issue of fraud, but also any other "rights, claims, or demands" related to the state-court litigation, "excepting only obligations under [the] Note and deeds of trust."

The fact that the parties intended, by the language of the general release, to replace an "old" fraud debt with a "new" contract debt is an important distinction from *Brown*, for the text of the Bankruptcy Code prohibits discharge of any debt "to the extent *obtained by*" fraud. § 523(a)(2) (emphasis added). In interpreting this provision, the Court has recognized that, in order for a creditor to establish that a debt is not dischargeable, he must demonstrate that there is a causal nexus between the fraud and the debt. Indeed, petitioners conceded at oral argument that the "obtained by" language of § 523(a)(2) requires a creditor to prove that a debtor's fraud is the proximate cause of the debt.

* * * While the concept of proximate cause is somewhat amorphous, the common law is clear that certain intervening events—otherwise called "superseding causes"—are sufficient to sever the causal nexus and cut off all liability.

In this case, we are faced with the novel situation where the parties have, by agreement, attempted to sever the causal relationship between the debtor's fraudulent conduct and the debt. In my view, the "intervening" settlement and release create the equivalent of a superseding cause, no different from the intervening negligent acts of a third party in a negligence action. In this case, the parties have made clear their intent to replace the old "fraud" debt with a new "contract" debt. Accordingly, the only debt that remains intact for bankruptcy purposes is the one "obtained by" voluntary agreement of the parties, not by fraud.

Petitioners' own actions in the course of this litigation support this conclusion. Throughout the proceedings below and continuing in this Court, petitioners have sought to recover only the amount of the debt set forth in the settlement agreement, which is lower than the total damages they allegedly suffered as a result of respondent's alleged fraud. See Brief for Petitioners 21 ("The nondischargeability action was brought solely in order to enforce the agreement to pay [the amount in the settlement agreement]"). This crucial fact demonstrates that petitioners seek to recover a debt based only in contract, not in fraud.

The Court concludes otherwise. The Court, however, does not explain why it permits petitioners to look at the settlement agreement for the amount of the debt they seek to recover but not for the character of that debt. Neither this Court's precedents nor the text of the Bankruptcy Code permits such a selective implementation of a valid agreement between the parties.

The Court today ignores the plain intent of the parties, as evidenced by a properly executed settlement agreement and general release, holding that a debt owed by respondent under a contract was "obtained by" fraud. Because I find no support for the Court's conclusion in the text of the Bankruptcy Code, or in the agreements of the parties, I respectfully dissent.

Questions

1. The Court said that the intent of the parties is determinative. Why was the release not sufficient to indicate the parties' intent that a new, non-fraudulent obligation on a promissory note was completely to supplant the pre-existing, fraud-tainted obligation? If the creditors did not understand that a general release would bar future proceedings based on the debtors' fraud, should their remedy—if they had any—have sounded in malpractice against their lawyers?

2. What about the converse case? Assume that, before filing bankruptcy, the debtor signed a settlement agreement containing language admitting fraudulent conduct. Can the debtor nonetheless contest the factual predicate of the creditor's nondischargeability action in the bankruptcy court?

3. If a future defendant has the negotiating power to persuade the plaintiff to accept a novation, giving up all rights based on alleged fraud, what language should be included in the settlement agreement in order to escape the fate suffered by the Warners?

4. What effect do you expect this case to have on the willingness of parties to settle such claims in the future?

3. SECTION 523(a)(3)—UNSCHEDULED DEBTS

Section 523(a)(3) is designed primarily to protect the interests of creditors who have not received adequate notice that their rights are being affected by a bankruptcy filing.

This subsection may become a trap for the unwary debtor, as *Duerkop v. Jongquist (In re Jongquist)*, 125 B.R. 558 (Bankr. D.Minn. 1991), illustrates. In that case, debtors' Chapter 7 was originally noticed as a no-asset case and creditors were instructed not to file claims. The trustee later found $390 and sent notice to scheduled creditors to file claims. The $390 was applied as follows: $212 to reimburse the trustee for expenses; $58.50 for the trustee's fees; and $65.50 for court costs. Only $54 was available for distribution to unsecured creditors. Duerkop, who was owed $29,999, was omitted from debtors' schedules and received no notice. The court held that § 523(a)(3) protects a creditor's right to file a timely claim and makes no distinction between minimal asset cases and those in which substantial distributions are made to creditors. The entire debt was held nondischargeable despite the fact that Duerkop would have received only a few dollars if he had received proper notice and had filed a timely claim.

4. SECTION 523(a)(4)—BREACH OF FIDUCIARY DUTY

Section 523(a)(4) excepts from discharge debts procured by fraud or defalcation while the debtor was acting in a fiduciary capacity, and debts that arose from embezzlement or larceny.

Several cases have discussed the requirements for finding that the debtor was acting in a fiduciary capacity—a concept ordinarily associated with trust relationships. In *Matter of Marchiando*, 13 F.3d 1111 (7th Cir.), *cert. denied sub nom. Illinois Dep't of the Lottery v. Marchiando*, 512 U.S. 1205, 114 S.Ct. 2675, 129 L.Ed.2d 810 (1994), debtor owned a convenience store that sold lottery tickets. State law provided that the proceeds of ticket sales "shall constitute a trust fund until paid to the Department." When debtor filed her bankruptcy petition, she owed the state $17,000 in proceeds that she had used in an effort to keep the business afloat. The state argued that the debt was nondischargeable under § 523(a)(4), but the Seventh Circuit disagreed:

> [E]xtension of the fiduciary concept—the use of the concept of "constructive trust" (where "constructive" bears its usual legal meaning of "no") to impose the fiduciary duty of a trustee on a person who is not a trustee—has been held not to come within the reach of § 523(a)(4). * * * To complicate the picture further, the cases are divided over the question whether a statute that, as in our case, deems a debtor a fiduciary in order to enlarge the remedies for default makes the debtor a "fiduciary" for purposes of § 523(a)(4). * * *

> The key to knitting the cases into a harmonious whole is the distinction * * * between a trust or other fiduciary relation that has an existence independent of the debtor's wrong and a trust or other fiduciary relation that has no existence before the wrong is committed. A lawyer's fiduciary duty to his client, or a director's duty to his corporation's shareholders, pre-exists any breach of the duty, while in the case of a constructive or resulting trust there is no fiduciary duty until a wrong is committed. The intermediate case, but closer we think to the constructive or resulting trust pole, is that of a trust that has a

purely nominal existence until the wrong is committed. Technically, Marchiando became a trustee as soon as she received her license to sell lottery tickets. Realistically, the trust did not begin until she failed to remit ticket receipts. For until then she had no duties of a fiduciary character toward the Department of Lottery or anything or anyone else. Until then, she was just a ticket agent. The state, afraid that she might be a disloyal agent, required her to keep the proceeds of her ticket sales separate from her other funds and threatened her with criminal punishment if she did not. These were devices by which the state sought to establish and enforce a lien in the proceeds, the better to collect them securely. * * *

If we probe more deeply the distinction between the fiduciary relation that imposes real duties in advance of the breach and the fiduciary relation that does not we find that the first group of cases involve a difference in knowledge or power between fiduciary and principal which * * * gives the former a position of ascendancy over the latter. * * *

* * *

If * * * a fiduciary is anyone whom a state calls a fiduciary—the only principle on which the discharge of Marchiando's debt could be refused—states will have it in their power to deny a fresh start to their debtors by declaring all contractual relations fiduciary. * * * Libertarians may smile approvingly at the state's equating its bureaucracies to the children and other incompetents who are the classic trust beneficiaries, but we do not think Congress would. The convenience-store keeper who commingles the proceeds of her lottery ticket sales with her other receipts is at a considerable remove from the lawyer who converts money in his clients' escrow accounts or the bank trust department that invests someone's retirement fund recklessly.

Marchiando, moreover, is playing a risky game, which makes it unlikely that our decision will endanger legitimate state interests. By successfully challenging the state's effort to prevent her from discharging her debt to it, she invites it to bring a criminal proceeding against her, since any fine levied in such a proceeding would be nondischargeable. § 523(a)(7). * * * The possibility of criminal prosecution of disloyal ticket agents is the lawful alternative, denied most creditors, to the

State of Illinois' foredoomed effort to squeeze its lottery law into the nondischarge provision.

Id. at 1115–17.

Another issue that divided the Courts of Appeal concerned the level of scienter—if any—required for application of § 523(a)(4). Three standards emerged. Under one view, adopted by three circuits (the Fourth, Eighth and Ninth), negligent conduct, or even an entirely innocent mistake, was sufficient to constitute defalcation within the meaning of subsection (a)(4). These courts merely pointed to the definition of the term—failure to account for money or property received—and found no limitation to intentional conduct. A second viewpoint, requiring a showing of recklessness, was adopted in four of the circuits (the Fifth, Sixth, Seventh and Eleventh). The third viewpoint, adopted in two circuits (the First and Second), required "extreme recklessness"—a standard that was apparently just shy of full-blown intent. Thus, all of the circuits, with the sole exception of the Third, had decided the issue and disagreed sharply. That rendered the question fully ripe for determination by the Supreme Court.

BULLOCK v. BANKCHAMPAIGN, N.A.

United States Supreme Court, 2013.
569 U.S. ___, 133 S.Ct. 1754, 185 L.Ed.2d 922.

JUSTICE BREYER delivered the opinion for a unanimous Court.

Section 523(a)(4) of the Federal Bankruptcy Code provides that an individual cannot obtain a bankruptcy discharge from a debt "for fraud or defalcation while acting in a fiduciary capacity, embezzlement, or larceny." We here consider the scope of the term "defalcation." We hold that it includes a culpable state of mind requirement akin to that which accompanies application of the other terms in the same statutory phrase. We describe that state of mind as one involving knowledge of, or gross recklessness in respect to, the improper nature of the relevant fiduciary behavior.

I

In 1978, the father of petitioner Randy Bullock established a trust for the benefit of his five children. He made petitioner the (non-professional) trustee; and he transferred to the trust a single asset, an insurance policy on his life. The trust instrument permitted the trustee to borrow funds from the insurer against the policy's value (which, in practice, was available at an insurance-company-determined 6% interest rate).

In 1981, petitioner, at his father's request, borrowed money from the trust, paying the funds to his mother who used them to repay a debt to the father's business. In 1984, petitioner again borrowed funds from the trust, this time using the funds to pay for certificates of deposit, which he and his mother used to buy a mill. In 1990, petitioner once again borrowed funds, this time using the money to buy real property for himself and his mother. Petitioner saw that all of the borrowed funds were repaid to the trust along with 6% interest.

In 1999, petitioner's brothers sued petitioner in Illinois state court. The state court held that petitioner had committed a breach of fiduciary duty. It explained that petitioner "does not appear to have had a malicious motive in borrowing funds from the trust" but nonetheless "was clearly involved in self-dealing." It ordered petitioner to pay the trust "the benefits he received from his breaches" (along with costs and attorney's fees). The court imposed constructive trusts on petitioner's interests in the mill and the original trust, in order to secure petitioner's payment of its judgment, with respondent BankChampaign serving as trustee for all of the trusts. After petitioner tried unsuccessfully to liquidate his interests in the mill and other constructive trust assets to obtain funds to make the court-ordered payment, petitioner filed for bankruptcy in federal court.

BankChampaign opposed petitioner's efforts to obtain a bankruptcy discharge of his state-court-imposed debts to the trust. And the Bankruptcy Court granted summary judgment in the bank's favor. It held that the debts fell within § 523(a)(4)'s exception "as a debt for defalcation while acting in a fiduciary capacity." Hence, they were not dischargeable.

[The district court affirmed, as did the Court of Appeals. The Eleventh Circuit held that "defalcation requires a known breach of a fiduciary duty, such that the conduct can be characterized as objectively reckless," and found that petitioner's conduct met that standard.] Petitioner sought certiorari. In effect he has asked us to decide whether the bankruptcy term "defalcation" applies "in the absence of any specific finding of ill intent or evidence of an ultimate loss of trust principal." The lower courts have long disagreed about whether "defalcation" includes a scienter requirement and, if so, what kind of scienter it requires. * * * In light of that disagreement, we granted the petition.

II

A

Congress first included the term "defalcation" as an exception to discharge in a federal bankruptcy statute in 1867. And legal authorities have disagreed about its meaning almost ever since. Dictionary definitions of "defalcation" are not particularly helpful. On the one hand, a law dictionary in use in 1867 defines the word "defalcation" as "the act of a defaulter," which, in turn, it defines broadly as one "who is deficient in his accounts, or fails in making his accounts correct." 1 J. Bouvier, Law Dictionary 387, 388 (4th ed. 1852). * * *

On the other hand, an 1842 bankruptcy treatise warns that fiduciaries "are not supposed to commit defalcation in the matter of their trust, without * * * at least such criminal negligence as admits of no excuse." G. Bicknell, Commentary on the Bankrupt Law of 1841, Showing Its Operation and Effect 12 (2d ed. 1842). Modern dictionaries often accompany their broad definitions with illustrative terms such as "embezzle," American Heritage Dictionary, *supra*, at 474, or "fraudulent deficiency," 4 Oxford English Dictionary, *supra*, at 369. And the editor of Black's Law Dictionary has written that the term should be read as limited to deficiencies that are "fraudulent" and which are "*the fault* of someone put in trust of the money." B. Garner, Modern American Usage 232 (3d ed.2009) (emphasis added).

Similarly, courts of appeals have long disagreed about the mental state that must accompany the bankruptcy-related definition of "defalcation." Many years ago Judge Augustus Hand wrote that "the misappropriation must be due to a known breach of the duty, and not to mere negligence or mistake." *In re Bernard*, 87 F.2d 705, 707 (2d Cir.1937). But Judge Learned Hand suggested that the term "*may* have included innocent defaults." *Central Hanover Bank & Trust Co.* v. *Herbst*, 93 F.2d 510, 511 (2d Cir.1937) (emphasis added). A more modern treatise on trusts ends its discussion of the subject with a question mark. 4 A. Scott, W. Fratcher, & M. Ascher, Scott and Ascher on Trusts §24.26 p. 1797 (5th ed. 2007).

In resolving these differences, we note that this longstanding disagreement concerns state of mind, not whether "defalcation" can cover a trustee's failure (as here) to make a trust more than whole. We consequently shall assume without deciding that the statutory term is broad enough to cover the latter type of conduct and answer only the "state of mind" question.

B

1

We base our approach and our answer upon one of this Court's precedents. In 1878, this Court interpreted the related statutory term "fraud" in the portion of the Bankruptcy Code laying out exceptions to discharge. Justice Harlan wrote for the Court:

> "[D]ebts created by 'fraud' are associated directly with debts created by 'embezzlement.' Such association justifies, if it does not imperatively require, the conclusion that the 'fraud' referred to in that section means positive fraud, or fraud in fact, involving moral turpitude or intentional wrong, as does embezzlement; and not implied fraud, or fraud in law, which may exist without the imputation of bad faith or immorality." *Neal* v. *Clark*, 95 U.S. 704, 709, 24 L.Ed. 586 (1878).

We believe that the statutory term "defalcation" should be treated similarly.

Thus, where the conduct at issue does not involve bad faith, moral turpitude, or other immoral conduct, the term requires an intentional wrong. We include as intentional not only conduct that the fiduciary knows is improper but also reckless conduct of the kind that the criminal law often treats as the equivalent. Thus, we include reckless conduct of the kind set forth in the Model Penal Code. Where actual knowledge of wrongdoing is lacking, we consider conduct as equivalent if the fiduciary "consciously disregards" (or is willfully blind to) "a substantial and unjustifiable risk" that his conduct will turn out to violate a fiduciary duty. ALI, Model Penal Code § 2.02(2)(c), p. 226 (1985). See *id.*, § 2.02 Comment 9, at 248 (explaining that the Model Penal Code's definition of "knowledge" was designed to include "'willful blindness'"). That risk "must be of such a nature and degree that, considering the nature and purpose of the actor's conduct and the circumstances known to him, its disregard involves *a gross deviation* from the standard of conduct that a law-abiding person would observe in the actor's situation." *Id.* § 2.02(2)(c), at 226 (emphasis added). Cf. *Ernst & Ernst* v. *Hochfelder*, 425 U.S. 185, 194, n.12 (1976) (defining scienter for securities law purposes as "a mental state embracing intent to deceive, manipulate, or defraud").

2

Several considerations lead us to interpret the statutory term "defalcation" in this way. First, as Justice Harlan pointed out in *Neal*, statutory context strongly favors this interpretation. Applying the canon of interpretation *noscitur a sociis*, the Court there looked to fraud's linguistic neighbor, "embezzlement." It found that both terms refer to different forms of generally similar conduct. It wrote that both are "'*ejusdem generis*,'" of the same kind, and that both are "'referable to the same subject-matter.'" 95 U.S. at 709. Moreover, embezzlement requires a showing of wrongful intent. *Id.* (noting that embezzlement "involv[es] moral turpitude or intentional wrong"). Hence, the Court concluded, "fraud" must require an equivalent showing. *Neal*, *supra*, at 709. *Neal* has been the law for more than a century. And here, the additional neighbors ("larceny" and, as defined in *Neal*, "fraud") mean that the canon *noscitur a sociis* argues even more strongly for similarly interpreting the similar statutory term "defalcation."

Second, this interpretation does not make the word identical to its statutory neighbors. As commonly used, "embezzlement" requires conversion, and "larceny" requires taking and carrying away another's property. See LaFave, Criminal Law §§ 19.2, 19.5 (larceny); *id.*, § 19.6 (embezzlement). "Fraud" typically requires a false statement or omission. "Defalcation," as commonly used (hence as Congress might have understood it), can encompass a breach of fiduciary obligation that involves neither conversion, nor taking and carrying away another's property, nor falsity.

Nor are embezzlement, larceny, and fiduciary fraud simply special cases of defalcation as so defined. The statutory provision makes clear that the first two terms apply outside of the fiduciary context; and "defalcation," unlike "fraud," may be used to refer to *nonfraudulent* breaches of fiduciary duty. Black's 479.

Third, the interpretation is consistent with the long-standing principle that "exceptions to discharge 'should be confined to those plainly expressed.'" *Kawaauhau* v. *Geiger*, 523 U.S. 57, 62 (1998) (quoting *Gleason* v. *Thaw*, 236 U.S. 558, 562 (1915)). It is also consistent with a set of statutory exceptions that Congress normally confines to circumstances where strong, special policy considerations, such as the presence of fault, argue for preserving the debt, thereby benefiting, for example, a typically more honest creditor. See, *e.g.,* §§ 523(a)(2)(A), (a)(2)(B), (a)(6), (a)(9) (fault). See also, *e.g.,*

§§ 523(a)(1), (a)(7), (a)(14), (a)(14A) (taxes); § 523(a)(8) (educational loans); § 523(a)(15) (spousal and child support). In the absence of fault, it is difficult to find strong policy reasons favoring a broader exception here, at least in respect to those whom a scienter requirement will most likely help, namely *nonprofessional* trustees, perhaps administering small family trusts potentially immersed in intrafamily arguments that are difficult to evaluate in terms of comparative fault.

Fourth, as far as the briefs before us reveal, at least some Circuits have interpreted the statute similarly for many years without administrative, or other practical, difficulties. *In re Baylis*, 313 F.3d 9 (1st Cir.2002). See also *In re Hyman*, 502 F. 3d 61, 69 (2d Cir.2007) ("This [scienter] standard * * * also has the virtue of ease of application since the courts and litigants have reference to a robust body of securities law examining what these terms mean").

Finally, it is important to have a uniform interpretation of federal law, the choices are limited, and neither the parties nor the Government has presented us with strong considerations favoring a different interpretation. In addition to those we have already discussed, the Government has pointed to the fact that in 1970 Congress rewrote the statute, eliminating the word "misappropriation" and placing the term "defalcation" (previously in a different exemption provision) alongside its present three neighbors. The Government believes that these changes support reading "defalcation" without a scienter requirement. But one might argue, with equal plausibility, that the changes reflect a decision to make certain that courts would read in similar ways "defalcation," "fraud," "embezzlement," and "larceny." In fact, we believe the 1970 changes are inconclusive.

[*The Court remanded for application of the "heightened standard" it mandated.*]

It is so ordered.

Notes and Questions

1. Was it relevant that the debtor-trustee repaid the trust in full, principle plus interest? That he had no malicious motive?

2. Based on the facts set out in the opinion, how should the court decide the case on remand?

3. As we look at additional grounds for the nondischargeability of specific debts, think back to *Bullock* and consider whether it may have relevance to the interpretation of other subsections of § 523. Is *Bullock* also relevant to denial of discharge under § 727(a)?

4. "Recklessness" is pertinent in many other legal contexts, including criminal and securities laws. *Bullock* is likely to affect analysis of the level of scienter required for liability in those other contexts. That may be especially true given the Court's citation to *Hochfelder*—a securities case—and quotation from *Hyman*, which noted the availability of securities law precedents dealing with scienter.

5. SECTIONS 523(a)(5) AND (a)(15)—FAMILY-RELATED OBLIGATIONS

Section 523(a)(5)'s discharge exception for "domestic support obligations" (as defined in § 101(14A)) applies in all chapters. This reflects the importance Congress placed on such obligations as a matter of policy. The exception is designed to accomplish three goals:

> the protection of the spouse who may lack job skills or who may be incapable of working, the protection of minor children who may be neglected if the custodial spouse entered the job market, and the protection of society from an increased welfare burden that may result if debtors could avoid their familial responsibilities by filing for bankruptcy.

Shaver v. Shaver, 736 F.2d 1314 (9th Cir.1984). When family support obligations are at issue, the usual rule that discharge exceptions should be narrowly construed is turned on its head. Obligor-debtors do not win many of these cases. Think about it—how sympathetic is a court likely to be when a parent is trying to avoid paying for the support of his or her children?

Family-related obligations that are not for support—chiefly, divisions of property—were made nondischargeable in Chapter 7 cases by the addition of § 523(a)(15) in 1994. These obligations are also made nondischargeable in Chapters 11 and 12 by cross-references to § 523(a). See §§ 1141(d)(2) and 1228(a)(2). The rule is different in Chapter 13, however; obligations arising from property divisions are dischargeable in Chapter 13 cases. Thus, bankruptcy courts will be required to distinguish between support obligations, which are not dischargeable, and obligations arising under property settlements, which are. Generally speaking, bankruptcy courts do not reclassify as a dischargeable property settlement any payment identified as support in a marital dissolution decree or in the parties' separation agreement. But courts routinely recharacterize, as nondischargeable support obligations, payments the parties label a property settlement.

Subsection (a)(5), according to the court in *Werthen v. Werthen (In re Werthen)*, 329 F.3d 269 (1st Cir.2003), "rests on an unstable assumption"—namely,

> a supposed distinction between "support" payments for spouse and children * * * and other kinds of divorce awards—for example, a division of jointly owned property. * * *

> The underlying concept is easy to grasp: support payments are, roughly speaking, what is given to provide for the upkeep of the recipient spouse and children, while other divisions or payments serve different purposes. The central problem is that the two supposedly separate categories overlap because the need for ongoing support will often depend on how much property the less well-off spouse is given outright.

> * * *

> The larger problem remains that the present statute needs revision. It is no accident that the 1970 Commission on the Bankruptcy Laws of the United States recommended that the line-drawing approach between alimony and property division be abandoned. The competing interests are for Congress to sort out; but a more administrable solution is overdue.

Id. at 272-73, 274-75.

If § 523(a)(5) "rests on an unstable assumption," as charged by *Werthen*, the addition of § 523(a)(15) only compounded the difficulties. Nevertheless, domestic relations lawyers, who have long taken tax considerations into account when preparing settlement agreements in divorce cases, obviously need to know a little bankruptcy, too.

Sections 523(a)(5) and (a)(15) work in tandem with a slew of other Code provisions, some of which we have already seen: § 362-(b)(2), excepting from the automatic stay actions to establish paternity, to obtain or modify a support order, or to collect spousal or child support from nonestate property; § 507(a)(1), providing first priority for domestic support obligations; § 522(c), making exempt property liable for nondischargeable support obligations; § 522(f)(1)(A), barring avoidance of judicial liens that secure domestic support obligations; and § 547(c)(7), excepting payments for domestic support obligations from preference avoidance.

There are more: debtors must be current on domestic support obligations in order to confirm any reorganization plan, §§ 1129(a)(14), 1225(a)(7) & 1325(a)(8), or to receive a discharge in Chapters 12 and 13, §§ 1225(a) & 1328(a); information about pending bankruptcy cases must be sent to support claimants, as well as to state child support agencies, §§ 704(a)(10), 1106(a)(8), 1202(b)(6) & 1302(b)(6); and a debtor's failure to pay postpetition support obligations may constitute cause for conversion or dismissal of a case under Chapters 11, 12 and 13, §§ 1112(b)(4)(P), 1208(c)(10) & 1307(c)(11). (Did the Code's drafters miss anything?) Taken together, these provisions make support claimants the most favored creditors in bankruptcy.

6. SECTIONS 523(a)(6) AND 1328(a)(4)—WILLFUL AND/OR MALICIOUS INJURIES

Section 523(a)(6) excepts from discharge debts arising from "willful and malicious injury" to the person or property of another. This subsection applies to cases brought under Chapter 7 and, via incorporation by cross-reference, to cases under Chapters 11 and 12 as well. Chapter 13 has a similar provision—§ 1328(a)(4)—but it differs in three respects from § 523(a)(6). First, § 1328(a)(4) speaks of "willful *or* malicious" injury, raising the question whether a substantively different test was intended by use of the disjunctive. (Note § 522-(q)(1)(B)(iv), which caps the homestead exemption at $125,000 if the debtor owes a debt arising from, inter alia, "willful or *reckless* misconduct." Is this a *third* test?) Second, § 1328(a)(4) applies only to damages for personal injury (or wrongful death), and not to damages relating to property. Finally, it speaks of damages "awarded in a civil action," suggesting that these claims may be dischargeable if the debtor can manage to complete a Chapter 13 plan before entry of the civil judgment.

Most of the cases brought under § 523(a)(6) fall into two categories—allegations by a secured creditor that the debtor has sold encumbered collateral without authority, and personal injury caused by the debtor to another. The next two cases address these fact patterns.

C.I.T. FINANCIAL SERVICES, INC. v. POSTA
(IN RE POSTA)

United States Court of Appeals, Tenth Circuit, 1989.
866 F.2d 364.

PER CURIAM.

* * *

C.I.T. Financial Services, Inc. appeals the dismissal of its complaint objecting to the discharge in bankruptcy of a debt of Gregory Alyan Posta and Mary Jones Posta. CIT argues that the Postas' debt to CIT, secured by a mobile travel trailer, is nondischargeable under § 523(a)(6) of the Bankruptcy Code, because the Postas sold the trailer in violation of the terms of CIT's security agreement. In dismissing CIT's complaint, the bankruptcy court found that the Postas had not willfully disregarded CIT's rights by selling the trailer and that their debt to CIT was properly dischargeable. On appeal, the district court affirmed. We likewise affirm.

In 1983, the Postas purchased a mobile travel trailer from Washburn Enterprises in Lakewood, Colorado, financing $23,631 of the purchase price through CIT. The Postas executed a security agreement with CIT, granting CIT a security interest in the trailer. The agreement provided that the Postas could not sell, rent, or transfer the trailer, or move it from their home address unless CIT agreed in writing. The bankruptcy court found that neither Mr. nor Mrs. Posta read the security agreement before signing it.

Within a year after this purchase, payments on the trailer began to strain the Postas' finances. The couple determined that they would be unable to meet their other financial obligations and continue to make the payments on the trailer. Consequently, they moved the trailer from their home in Ridgeway, Colorado, to a dealership in Denver, attempting to lease it through the dealer. They also advertised the trailer for sale in Denver newspapers.

On October 7, 1984, the Postas were contacted by Mr. Ronald Swartz, who indicated that he was interested in buying the trailer. Mr. Swartz met with the Postas that day and, after some negotiation, agreed to purchase the trailer. That evening, the parties signed a sales agreement prepared by Mr. Swartz. As provided in the agreement, Mr. Swartz delivered $962.65 in cash to the Postas (representing their equity in the trailer plus the next monthly payment) and a promissory note for $22,245.00 (the remaining balance on their loan from CIT). To secure the note, Mr. Swartz executed a second deed of trust on certain condominium property located in Grand County, Colorado. He also purchased an insurance policy on the trailer, naming the Postas as additional insureds.

Mr. Swartz left that evening with the trailer. He returned the following morning to deliver a copy of the sales agreement and two football tickets which he had promised to Mr. Posta. After that morning, however, neither he nor the trailer were ever seen again. Mr. Swartz defaulted on his payments on the promissory note, and the Postas discovered that Mr. Swartz did not hold record interest in the property subject to the deed of trust securing the note. Despite their efforts, the couple was unable to locate Mr. Swartz at any of the addresses he had given them. They reported the incident to the appropriate authorities and to CIT, and unsuccessfully attempted to recover on the insurance policy covering the trailer. The Postas were then forced to default on their loan payments to CIT, and shortly thereafter they filed for bankruptcy.

CIT instituted the instant action in bankruptcy court on November 20, 1985, objecting to the discharge of the Postas' debt secured by the trailer. CIT alleged that, under § 523(a)(6) of the Bankruptcy Code, the debt was not dischargeable because the Postas had willfully and maliciously converted the travel trailer. * * * After a hearing on the matter, the bankruptcy court ruled that the Postas' sale of the trailer was merely a technical conversion. It found no evidence that the Postas' actions were taken in conscious disregard of the rights of CIT and held that the conversion was not malicious. The district court affirmed on appeal * * *.

* * * The only issue before us is whether the bankruptcy court properly construed the term "malicious" under § 523(a)(6) of the Bankruptcy Code. CIT argues that the Postas' intentional sale of the trailer in violation of the terms of the security agreement was, by its nature, malicious. We disagree.

We begin by examining the relevant provision of the Bankruptcy Code. Section 523(a)(6) of the Code excepts from discharge any debt "for willful and malicious injury by the debtor to another entity or the property of another entity." Such injury includes the conversion of property subject to a creditor's security interest. For a debt to be nondischargeable under this section, however, the debtor's conversion of property must be both "willful" and "malicious." The creditor objecting to the discharge has the burden of proving both of these elements by clear and convincing evidence.

The "willful" element is straightforward. It simply addresses whether the debtor intentionally performed the basic act complained of. "Willful" conduct is conduct that is volitional and deliberate and over which the debtor exercises meaningful control, as opposed to unintentional or accidental conduct. Thus, acts caused by the debtor's negligence or recklessness are not encompassed by this exception.

In this case, there seems to be little question but that the Postas voluntarily and intentionally sold the trailer; so their conduct was "willful." The issue is, instead, whether in doing so, they acted maliciously. CIT asserts that when a debtor intends to do an act which results in harm to his creditor, such conduct is "malicious." Consequently, because the Postas intentionally sold the trailer, and because the sale was in violation of the security agreement and ultimately harmed CIT, CIT contends that the "malicious" element is satisfied. We disagree.

Were we to accept CIT's argument, nearly any intentional conduct would fall within this exception to discharge, and the word "malicious" in this section would be rendered meaningless. Statutes should be construed to give effect to every word Congress has used. Although we agree that conduct which violates the rights of a creditor is wrongful, we refuse to infer that it is, by its very nature, "malicious." Instead, the focus of the "malicious" inquiry is on the debtor's actual knowledge or the reasonable foreseeability that his conduct will result in injury to the creditor, "not on abstract and perhaps moralistic notions of the 'wrongfulness' of the debtor's act." *In re Egan*, 52 B.R. 501, 507 n.4 (Bankr. D.Minn.1985). Thus, the Postas' sale of the trailer was not "malicious" simply because it violated the terms of the security agreement.

Under § 523(a)(6), the debtor's malicious intent can be shown in two ways. In the rare instances in which there is direct evidence that the debtor's conduct was taken with the specific intent to harm the creditor, the malice requirement is easily established. More commonly, however, malicious intent must be demonstrated by evidence that the debtor had knowledge of the creditor's rights and that, with that knowledge, proceeded to take action in violation of those rights. Such knowledge can be inferred from the debtor's experience in the business, his concealment of the sale, or by his admission that he has read and understood the security agreement.

We are not persuaded by CIT's argument that the bankruptcy court misconstrued the term "malicious" as to require actual malice, or a specific intent to harm the creditor. Rather, the court correctly looked to whether the Postas had willfully disregarded the rights of CIT in making the sale. The court noted that the Postas were relatively inexperienced in business matters, that they had difficulty in understanding business concepts, and that they had not read the security agreement. The evidence shows that, at all times, the Postas intended to fulfill their loan obligations to CIT by applying the proceeds of Mr. Swartz' note to the loan. They did not conceal the sale from CIT and, in fact, requested CIT's assistance when it appeared their arrangement with Mr. Swartz had gone sour. We agree with the bankruptcy court that, in light of these facts, at most, all that occurred was a "technical conversion." Technical conversions do not fall within the § 523(a)(6) exception to discharge.

CIT attempts to distinguish this case from other cases involving technical conversions by arguing that, because it did not acquiesce in any way in the Postas' sale of the trailer, the court may not excuse the Postas' disregard of the terms of the security agreement. This attempted distinction is illusory. The issue of a creditor's acquiescence comes into play only in those cases in which the debtor has knowledge of the creditor's limitations on the sale of its collateral but, because of some conduct by the creditor, is led to believe the sale would nevertheless be permissible. In this case, however, the threshold question, as noted above, is whether the Postas had *any* knowledge that the sale would violate the terms of the security agreement. The district court found that the Postas had no knowledge of such terms of the security agreement. It properly concluded that, because they did not knowingly violate CIT's rights by selling the trailer, the Postas' conversion of CIT's property was not "malicious." That CIT did not acquiesce in the sale was therefore irrelevant.

The order of the United States District Court for the District of Colorado is AFFIRMED.

Questions and Problems

1. Assume that the creditor in *Posta* had failed to perfect its security interest under state law. Would that render § 523(a)(6) inapplicable? See *Hardwick v. Petsch (Matter of Petsch)*, 82 B.R. 605 (Bankr. M.D.Fla. 1988).

2. Debtor is the president of a closely held corporation. Bank loaned money to the corporation, secured by the corporation's accounts receivable and backed by Debtor's personal guaranty. Proceeds of accounts receivable were supposed to be deposited into a special bank account and thereby made available to Bank to pay the loan. When the corporation encountered financial problems, however, Debtor diverted proceeds into another account and used the funds to try to keep the business running. Those efforts failed and both Debtor and the corporation ended up in bankruptcy. Can Bank, under § 523-(a)(6), block discharge of the amount Debtor diverted? See *Barclays American Business Credit, Inc. v. Long (In re Long)*, 774 F.2d 875 (8th Cir.1985).

3. Debtors borrowed $3,600 from Creditor and gave a security interest in personal property then worth $1,300. Debtors later sold the personalty at a rummage sale, without Creditor's permission, for $120. The fair market value of the property was then $865. If the court finds that Creditor has a nondischargeable claim under § 523(a)(6), what amount is nondischargeable—$120? $865? $1,300? $3,600? See *Friendly Financial Service Mid–City, Inc. v. Modicue (In re Modicue)*, 926 F.2d 452 (5th Cir.1991).

4. Debtor, an attorney, was sued for malpractice by a client, Creditor. The parties entered into a settlement agreement requiring Debtor to make designated payments to Creditor. Debtor later decided, on his own, that Creditor had no legitimate grounds for an assertion of malpractice, and Debtor stopped making payments. After Debtor's bankruptcy filing, Creditor sought to except the obligation from discharge under § 523(a)(6). Will Creditor succeed? See *Lockerby v. Sierra*, 535 F.3d 1038 (9th Cir.2008).

As indicated above, §§ 523(a)(6) and 1328(a)(4) also apply when the debtor has caused personal injury to another person. When injury results from an intentional tort, application of these provisions is straightforward. When the debtor's conduct was reckless or grossly negligent, however, courts have struggled with § 523(a)(6)'s phrase, "willful and malicious." (Will similar problems be encountered under § 1328(a)(4)'s formulation, "willful *or* malicious"?)

One of the early leading cases, *Perkins v. Scharffe*, 817 F.2d 392 (6th Cir.), *cert. denied*, 484 U.S. 853, 108 S.Ct. 156, 98 L.Ed.2d 112 (1987), arose out of "absolutely appalling" medical treatment rendered by a doctor in treating a patient's foot infection. The Sixth Circuit characterized the issue as whether § 523(a)(6) "requires an intentional act that results in injury or an act with intent to cause injury." The court concluded that " 'willful' means 'deliberate or intentional'" and that " 'willful' and 'malicious' requires the intentional doing of an act that necessarily leads to injury." *Id.* at 394. The court quoted

Collier's discussion of § 523(a)(6), in support of adopting the "looser standard":

> In order to fall within the exception of § 523(a)(6), the injury to an entity or property must have been willful and malicious. An injury to an entity or property may be a malicious injury within this provision if it was wrongful and without just cause or excessive, even in the absence of personal hatred, spite, or ill-will. The word "willful" means "deliberate or intentional," a deliberate and intentional act which necessarily leads to injury. Therefore, a wrongful act done intentionally, which necessarily produces harm and is without just cause or excuse, may constitute a willful and malicious injury.

Id., *quoting* 3 COLLIER ON BANKRUPTCY ¶ 523–111 (15th ed.1986). The Supreme Court finally took the issue, in a case with facts eerily similar to those in *Perkins*.

KAWAAUHAU v. GEIGER

United States Supreme Court, 1998.
523 U.S. 57, 118 S.Ct. 974, 140 L.Ed.2d 90.

JUSTICE GINSBURG delivered the opinion for a unanimous Court.

Section 523(a)(6) of the Bankruptcy Code provides that a debt "for willful and malicious injury by the debtor to another" is not dischargeable. The question before us is whether a debt arising from a medical malpractice judgment, attributable to negligent or reckless conduct, falls within this statutory exception. We hold that it does not and that the debt is dischargeable.

I

In January 1983, petitioner Margaret Kawaauhau sought treatment from respondent Dr. Paul Geiger for a foot injury. Geiger examined Kawaauhau and admitted her to the hospital to attend to the risk of infection resulting from the injury. Although Geiger knew that intravenous penicillin would have been more effective, he prescribed oral penicillin, explaining in his testimony that he understood his patient wished to minimize the cost of her treatment.

Geiger then departed on a business trip, leaving Kawaauhau in the care of other physicians, who decided she should be transferred to an infectious disease specialist. When Geiger returned, he canceled the transfer and discontinued all antibiotics because he believed the infection had subsided. Kawaauhau's condition deteriorated over the next few days, requiring the amputation of her right leg below the knee.

Kawaauhau, joined by her husband Solomon, sued Geiger for malpractice. After a trial, the jury found Geiger liable and awarded the Kawaauhaus approximately $355,000 in damages. Geiger, who carried no malpractice insurance,[2] moved to Missouri, where his wages were garnished by the Kawaauhaus. Geiger then petitioned for bankruptcy. The Kawaauhaus requested the Bankruptcy Court to hold the malpractice judgment nondischargeable on the ground that it was a debt "for willful and malicious injury" excepted from discharge by § 523-(a)(6). The Bankruptcy Court concluded that Geiger's treatment fell far below the appropriate standard of care and therefore ranked as "willful and malicious." Accordingly, the Bankruptcy Court held the debt nondischargeable. In an unpublished order, the District Court affirmed.

A three-judge panel of the Court of Appeals for the Eighth Circuit reversed, and a divided en banc court adhered to the panel's position. Section 523(a)(6)'s exemption from discharge, the en banc court held, is confined to debts "based on what the law has for generations called an intentional tort." On this view, a debt for malpractice, because it is based on conduct that is negligent or reckless, rather than intentional, remains dischargeable.

The Eighth Circuit acknowledged that its interpretation of § 523(a)(6) diverged from previous holdings of the Sixth and Tenth Circuits (citing *Perkins v. Scharffe*, 817 F.2d 392, 394 (6th Cir.), cert. denied, 484 U.S. 853 (1987), and *In re Franklin*, 726 F.2d 606, 610 (10th Cir.1984)). We granted certiorari to resolve this conflict, and now affirm the Eighth Circuit's judgment.

II

[The Court quoted § 523(a)(6).] The Kawaauhaus urge that the malpractice award fits within this exception because Dr. Geiger intentionally rendered inadequate medical care to Margaret Kawaauhau that necessarily led to her injury. According to the Kawaauhaus, Geiger deliberately chose less effective treatment because he wanted to cut costs, all the while knowing that he was providing substandard care.

---

[2] Although the record is not clear on this point, it appears that Dr. Geiger was not required by state law to carry medical malpractice insurance.

Such conduct, the Kawaauhaus assert, meets the "willful and malicious" specification of § 523(a)(6).

We confront this pivotal question concerning the scope of the "willful and malicious injury" exception: Does § 523(a)(6)'s compass cover acts, done intentionally,[3] that cause injury (as the Kawaauhaus urge), or only acts done with the actual intent to cause injury (as the Eighth Circuit ruled)? The words of the statute strongly support the Eighth Circuit's reading.

The word "willful" in (a)(6) modifies the word "injury," indicating that nondischargeability takes a deliberate or intentional *injury*, not merely a deliberate or intentional *act* that leads to injury. Had Congress meant to exempt debts resulting from unintentionally inflicted injuries, it might have described instead "willful acts that cause injury." Or, Congress might have selected an additional word or words, *i.e.*, "reckless" or "negligent," to modify "injury." Moreover, as the Eighth Circuit observed, the (a)(6) formulation triggers in the lawyer's mind the category "intentional torts," as distinguished from negligent or reckless torts. Intentional torts generally require that the actor intend "the *consequences* of an act," not simply "the act itself." Restatement (Second) of Torts § 8A, comment a, p. 15 (1964) (emphasis added).

The Kawaauhaus' more encompassing interpretation could place within the excepted category a wide range of situations in which an act is intentional, but injury is unintended, *i.e.*, neither desired nor in fact anticipated by the debtor. Every traffic accident stemming from an initial intentional act—for example, intentionally rotating the wheel of an automobile to make a left-hand turn without first checking oncoming traffic—could fit the description. A "knowing breach of contract" could also qualify. A construction so broad would be incompatible with the "well-known" guide that exceptions to discharge "should be confined to those plainly expressed." *Gleason v. Thaw*, 236 U.S. 558, 562 (1915).

Furthermore, "we are hesitant to adopt an interpretation of a congressional enactment which renders superfluous another portion of that same law." *Mackey v. Lanier Collection Agency & Service, Inc.*,

---

[3] The word "willful" is defined in Black's Law Dictionary as "voluntary" or "intentional." Black's Law Dictionary 1434 (5th ed. 1979). Consistently, legislative reports note that the word "willful" in § 523(a)(6) means "deliberate or intentional." See S. Rep. No. 95-989, p. 79 (1978); H. R. Rep. No. 95-595, p. 365 (1977).

486 U.S. 825, 837 (1988). Reading § 523(a)(6) as the Kawaauhaus urge would obviate the need for § 523(a)(9), which specifically exempts debts "for death or personal injury caused by the debtor's operation of a motor vehicle if such operation was unlawful because the debtor was intoxicated from using alcohol, a drug, or another substance." See also § 523(a)(12) (exempting debts for "malicious or reckless failure" to fulfill certain commitments owed to a federal depository institutions regulatory agency).[4]

The Kawaauhaus heavily rely on *Tinker v. Colwell*, 193 U.S. 473 (1904), which presented this question: Does an award of damages for "criminal conversation" survive bankruptcy under the 1898 Bankruptcy Act's exception from discharge for judgments in civil actions for "'willful and malicious injuries to the person or property of another'"? The *Tinker* Court held such an award a nondischargeable debt. The Kawaauhaus feature certain statements in the *Tinker* opinion, in particular: "[An] act is willful * * * in the sense that it is intentional and voluntary" even if performed "without any particular malice"; an act that "necessarily causes injury and is done intentionally, may be said to be done willfully and maliciously, so as to come within the [bankruptcy discharge] exception"; the statute exempts from discharge liability for "'a wrongful act, done intentionally, without just cause or excuse'" (quoting from definition of malice in *Bromage v. Prosser*, 4 Barn. & Cress. 247, 107 Eng. Rep. 1051 (K.B. 1825)).

The exposition in the *Tinker* opinion is less than crystalline. Counterbalancing the portions the Kawaauhaus emphasize, the *Tinker* Court repeatedly observed that the tort in question qualified in the common law as trespassory. Indeed, it ranked as "trespass vi et armis." Criminal conversation, the Court noted, was an action akin to a master's "action of trespass and assault * * * for the battery of his servant." *Tinker* thus placed criminal conversation solidly within the traditional intentional tort category, and we so confine its holding. That decision, we clarify, provides no warrant for departure from the current statutory instruction that, to be nondischargeable, the judgment debt must be "for willful and malicious *injury*."

* * *

---

[4] Sections 523(a)(9) and (12) were added to the Bankruptcy Code in 1984 and 1990 respectively.

Finally, the Kawaauhaus maintain that, as a policy matter, malpractice judgments should be excepted from discharge, at least when the debtor acted recklessly or carried no malpractice insurance. Congress, of course, may so decide. But unless and until Congress makes such a decision, we must follow the current direction § 523(a)(6) provides.

* * *

We hold that debts arising from recklessly or negligently inflicted injuries do not fall within the compass of § 523(a)(6). For the reasons stated, the judgment of the Court of Appeals for the Eighth Circuit is

Affirmed.

Questions

1. Given the Court's reading of "willful," what role is left for the additional requirement that the injury be "malicious"? What will be the significance of *Geiger*'s analysis in interpreting § 1328(a)(4)?

2. The Court quoted Comment a to Restatement (Second) of Torts § 8A, but it did not quote the text of that provision: "The word 'intent' is used throughout the Restatement of this Subject to denote that the actor desires to cause consequences of his act, *or that he believes that the consequences are substantially certain to result from it.*" (Emphasis added.) Is the Court's decision consistent with this provision?

3. Before § 523(a)(9) was enacted in 1984, arguments were sometimes raised that debts for injuries caused by the debtor while driving under the influence were nondischargeable under § 523(a)(6). Section 523(a)(9) was added to the Code largely because § 523(a)(6)'s application in drunk driving cases was uncertain. In light of that fact, is the Court's use of § 523(a)(9) a bit disingenuous?

4. Is § 523(a)(6) limited to tort cases? Can it ever be applied in the context of breach of contract? Recall the Court's reference to a "knowing breach of contract," and then look at *Williams v. International Brotherhood of Electrical Workers Local 520 (In re Williams)*, 337 F.3d 504 (5th Cir.2003).

7. SECTION 523(a)(7)—FINES PAYABLE TO GOVERNMENTAL UNITS

The legislative history to the 1978 Code suggests that § 523(a)(7) was primarily intended to deal with tax penalties. The provision also applies to criminal restitution obligations, however, as the next case demonstrates. It is the seminal decision dealing with § 523(a)(7).

KELLY v. ROBINSON

United States Supreme Court, 1986.
479 U.S. 36, 107 S.Ct. 353, 93 L.Ed.2d 216.

JUSTICE POWELL delivered the opinion of the Court.

We granted review in this case to decide whether restitution obligations, imposed as conditions of probation in state criminal proceedings, are dischargeable in proceedings under Chapter 7 of the Bankruptcy Code.

I

In 1980, Carolyn Robinson pleaded guilty to larceny in the second degree. The charge was based on her wrongful receipt of $9,932.95 in welfare benefits from the Connecticut Department of Income Maintenance. On November 14, 1980, the Connecticut Superior Court sentenced Robinson to a prison term of not less than one year nor more than three years. The court suspended execution of the sentence and placed Robinson on probation for five years. As a condition of probation, the judge ordered Robinson to make restitution to the State of Connecticut Office of Adult Probation (Probation Office) at the rate of $100 per month, commencing January 16, 1981, and continuing until the end of her probation.[2]

On February 5, 1981, Robinson filed a voluntary petition under Chapter 7 of the Bankruptcy Code in the United States Bankruptcy Court for the District of Connecticut. That petition listed the restitution obligation as a debt. On February 20, 1981, the Bankruptcy Court notified both of the Connecticut agencies of Robinson's petition and informed them that April 27, 1981, was the deadline for filing objections to discharge. The agencies did not file proofs of claim or objections to discharge, apparently because they took the position that the bankruptcy would not affect the conditions of Robinson's probation. Thus, the agencies did not participate in the distribution of Robinson's

---

[2] There is some uncertainty about the total amount Robinson was ordered to pay. Although the judge imposed restitution in a total amount of $9,932.95, five years of payments at $100 a month total only $6,000.

estate. On May 14, 1981, the Bankruptcy Court granted Robinson a discharge. See § 727.

At the time Robinson received her discharge in bankruptcy, she had paid $450 in restitution. On May 20, 1981, her attorney wrote the Probation Office that she believed the discharge had altered the conditions of Robinson's probation, voiding the condition that she pay restitution. Robinson made no further payments.

The Connecticut Probation Office did not respond to this letter until February 1984, when it informed Robinson that it considered the obligation to pay restitution nondischargeable. Robinson responded by filing an adversary proceeding in the Bankruptcy Court, seeking a declaration that the restitution obligation had been discharged, as well as an injunction to prevent the State's officials from forcing Robinson to pay.

After a trial, the Bankruptcy Court entered a memorandum and proposed order, concluding that the 1981 discharge in bankruptcy had not altered the conditions of Robinson's probation. The court adopted the analysis it had applied in a similar case decided one month earlier, *In re Pellegrino (Pellegrino* v. *Division of Criminal Justice)*, 42 B.R. 129 (Bankr.D.Conn.1984). In *Pellegrino*, the court began with the Bankruptcy Code's definitional sections. First, [§ 101(12)] defines a "debt" as a "liability on a claim." In turn, [§ 101(5)] defines a "claim" as a "right to payment, whether or not such right is reduced to judgment, liquidated, unliquidated, fixed, contingent, matured, unmatured, disputed, undisputed, legal, equitable, secured, or unsecured." Finally, [§ 101(10)] defines a "creditor" as an "entity that has a claim against the debtor that arose at the time of or before the order for relief concerning the debtor."

The *Pellegrino* court then examined the statute under which the Connecticut judge had sentenced the debtor to pay restitution. Restitution appears as one of the conditions of probation enumerated in Conn. Gen. Stat. § 53a–30 (1985). Under that section, restitution payments are sent to the Probation Office. The payments then are forwarded to the victim. Although the Connecticut penal code does not provide for enforcement of the probation conditions by the victim, it does authorize the trial court to issue a warrant for the arrest of a criminal defendant who has violated a condition of probation. Because the Connecticut statute does not allow the victim to enforce a right to receive payment, the court concluded that neither the victim nor the Probation Office had a "right to payment," and hence neither was owed a "debt" under the

Bankruptcy Code. It argued: "Unlike an obligation which arises out of a contractual, statutory or common law duty, here the obligation is rooted in the traditional responsibility of a state to protect its citizens by enforcing its criminal statutes and to rehabilitate an offender by imposing a criminal sanction intended for that purpose." The court acknowledged the tension between its conclusion and the Code's expansive definition of debt, but found an exception to the statutory definition in "the long-standing tradition of restraint by federal courts from interference with traditional functions of state governments." The court concluded that, even if the probation condition was a debt subject to bankruptcy jurisdiction, it was nondischargeable under § 523(a)(7) of the Code. That subsection provides that a discharge in bankruptcy does not affect any debt that "is for a fine, penalty, or forfeiture payable to and for the benefit of a governmental unit, and is not compensation for actual pecuniary loss."

The court also concluded that the purpose of the restitution condition was "to promote the rehabilitation of the offender, not to compensate the victim." It specifically rejected the argument that the restitution must be deemed compensatory because the amount precisely matched the victim's loss. It noted that the state statute allows an offender to "make restitution of the fruits of his offense or make restitution, in an amount he can afford to pay or provide in a suitable manner, for the loss or damage caused thereby." In its view, the Connecticut statute focuses "upon the offender and not on the victim, and * * * restitution is part of the criminal penalty rather than compensation for a victim's actual loss." Thus, the Bankruptcy Court held that the bankruptcy discharge had not affected the conditions of Pellegrino's probation. The United States District Court for the District of Connecticut adopted the Bankruptcy Court's proposed dispositions of *Pellegrino* and this case without alteration.

The Court of Appeals for the Second Circuit reversed. It first examined the Code's definition of debt. Although it recognized that most courts had reached the opposite conclusion, the court decided that a restitution obligation imposed as a condition of probation is a debt. It relied on the legislative history of the Code that evinced Congress' intent to broaden the definition of "debt" from the much narrower definition of the Bankruptcy Act of 1898. The court also noted that anomalies might result from a conclusion that such an obligation is not a debt. Most importantly, nondebt status would deprive a State of the opportunity to participate in the distribution of the debtor's estate.

Having concluded that restitution obligations are debts, the court turned to the question of dischargeability. The court stated that the appropriate Connecticut agency probably could have avoided discharge of the debt if it had objected under §§ 523(a)(2) or 523(a)(4) of the Code. As no objections to discharge were filed, the court concluded that the State could rely only on § 523(a)(7), the subsection that provides for automatic nondischargeability for certain debts. The court then looked to the text of the Connecticut statute to determine whether Robinson's probation condition was "compensation for actual pecuniary loss" within the meaning of § 523(a)(7). But where the Bankruptcy Court had considered the entire state probation system, the Court of Appeals focused only on the language that allows a restitution order to be assessed "for the loss or damage caused [by the crime]." The court thought this language compelled the conclusion that the probation condition was "compensation for actual pecuniary loss." It held, therefore, that this particular condition of Robinson's probation was not protected from discharge by § 523(a)(7). Accordingly, it reversed the District Court.

We granted the State's petition for a writ of certiorari. * * * We reverse.

II

The Court of Appeals' decision focused primarily on the language of §§ 101 and 523 of the Code. Of course, the "starting point in every case involving construction of a statute is the language itself." *Blue Chip Stamps* v. *Manor Drug Stores*, 421 U.S. 723, 756 (1975) (POWELL, J., concurring). But the text is only the starting point. * * * In this case, we must consider the language of §§ 101 and 523 in light of the history of bankruptcy court deference to criminal judgments and in light of the interests of the States in unfettered administration of their criminal justice systems.

A

* * *

Congress enacted the Code in 1978 against the background of an established judicial exception to discharge for criminal sentences, including restitution orders, an exception created in the face of a statute drafted with considerable care and specificity.

Just last Term we declined to hold that the new Bankruptcy Code silently abrogated another exception created by courts construing the old Act. In *Midlantic National Bank* v. *New Jersey Dept. of Environmental Protection*, 474 U.S. 494 (1986), a trustee in bankruptcy asked us to hold that the 1978 Code had implicitly repealed an exception to the trustee's abandonment power. Courts had created that exception out of deference to state health and safety regulations, a consideration comparable to the States' interests implicated by this case. We stated:

> "The normal rule of statutory construction is that if Congress intends for legislation to change the interpretation of a judicially created concept, it makes that intent specific. The Court has followed this rule with particular care in construing the scope of bankruptcy codifications. If Congress wishes to grant the trustee an extraordinary exemption from nonbankruptcy law, 'the intention would be clearly expressed, not left to be collected or inferred from disputable considerations of convenience in administering the estate of the bankrupt.'" *Id.* at 501 (quoting *Swarts* v. *Hammer*, 194 U.S. 441, 444 (1904)) (citations omitted).

B

Our interpretation of the Code also must reflect the basis for this judicial exception, a deep conviction that federal bankruptcy courts should not invalidate the results of state criminal proceedings. The right to formulate and enforce penal sanctions is an important aspect of the sovereignty retained by the States. This Court has emphasized repeatedly "the fundamental policy against federal interference with state criminal prosecutions." *Younger* v. *Harris*, 401 U.S. 37, 46 (1971). The Court of Appeals nevertheless found support for its holding in the fact that Connecticut officials probably could have ensured continued enforcement of their court's criminal judgment against Robinson had they objected to discharge under § 523(c). Although this may be true in many cases, it hardly justifies an interpretation of the 1978 Act that is contrary to the long-prevailing view that "fines and penalties are not affected by a discharge," 1A Collier on Bankruptcy ¶ 17.13, p. 1610 (14th ed. 1978).

Moreover, reliance on a right to appear and object to discharge would create uncertainties and impose undue burdens on state officials. In some cases it would require state prosecutors to defend particular state criminal judgments before federal bankruptcy courts. As JUSTICE BRENNAN has noted, federal adjudication of matters already at issue in state criminal proceedings can be "an unwarranted and unseemly duplication of the State's own adjudicative process." *Perez* v. *Ledesma*, 401 U.S. 82, 121 (1971) (opinion concurring in part and dissenting in part).

Also, as Robinson's attorney conceded at oral argument, some restitution orders would not be protected from discharge even if the State did appear and enter an objection to discharge. For example, a judge in a negligent homicide case might sentence the defendant to probation, conditioned on the defendant's paying the victim's husband compensation for the loss the husband sustained when the defendant killed his wife. It is not clear that such a restitution order would fit the terms of any of the exceptions to discharge listed in § 523 other than § 523(a)(7). Thus, this interpretation of the Code would do more than force state prosecutors to defend state criminal judgments in federal bankruptcy court. In some cases, it could lead to federal remission of judgments imposed by state criminal judges.

This prospect, in turn, would hamper the flexibility of state criminal judges in choosing the combination of imprisonment, fines, and restitution most likely to further the rehabilitative and deterrent goals of state criminal justice systems. We do not think Congress lightly would limit the rehabilitative and deterrent options available to state criminal judges.

* * * This Court has recognized that the States' interest in administering their criminal justice systems free from federal interference is one of the most powerful of the considerations that should influence a court considering equitable types of relief. This reflection of our federalism also must influence our interpretation of the Bankruptcy Code in this case.

III

In light of the established state of the law—that bankruptcy courts could not discharge criminal judgments—we have serious doubts whether Congress intended to make criminal penalties "debts" within the meaning of [§ 101(5)]. But we need not address that question in this case, because we hold that § 523(a)(7) preserves from discharge any condition a state criminal court imposes as part of a criminal sentence.

* * * On its face, § 523(a)(7) certainly does not compel the conclusion reached by the Court of Appeals, that a discharge in bankruptcy voids restitution orders imposed as conditions of probation by state courts. Nowhere in the House and Senate Reports is there any indication that this language should be read so intrusively.[13] If Congress had intended, by § 523(a)(7) or by any other provision, to discharge state criminal sentences, "we can be certain that there would have been hearings, testimony, and debate concerning consequences so wasteful, so inimical to purposes previously deemed important, and so likely to arouse public outrage," *TVA* v. *Hill*, 437 U.S. 153, 209 (1978) (POWELL, J., dissenting).

Our reading of § 523(a)(7) differs from that of the Second Circuit. On its face, it creates a broad exception for all penal sanctions, whether they be denominated fines, penalties, or forfeitures. Congress included two qualifying phrases; the fines must be both "to and for the benefit of a governmental unit," and "not compensation for actual pecuniary loss." Section 523(a)(7) protects traditional criminal fines; it codifies the judicially created exception to discharge for fines. We must decide whether the result is altered by the two major differences between restitution and a traditional fine. Unlike traditional fines, restitution is forwarded to the victim, and may be calculated by reference to the amount of harm the offender has caused.

In our view, neither of the qualifying clauses of § 523(a)(7) allows the discharge of a criminal judgment that takes the form of restitution. The criminal justice system is not operated primarily for the benefit of victims, but for the benefit of society as a whole. Thus, it is concerned not only with punishing the offender, but also with rehabilitating him. Although restitution does resemble a judgment "for the benefit of" the victim, the context in which it is imposed undermines that conclusion. The victim has no control over the amount of restitution awarded or over the decision to award restitution. Moreover, the

---

[13] * * *

It seems likely that the limitation of § 523(a)(7) to fines assessed "for the benefit of a governmental unit" was intended to prevent application of that subsection to wholly private penalties such as punitive damages. See H.R. Doc. No. 93–137, pt. 2, pp. 116, 141 (1973). As for the reference to "compensation for actual pecuniary loss," the Senate Report indicates that the main purpose of this language was to prevent § 523(a)(7) from being applied to tax penalties. S. Rep. No. 95–989 at 79, *reprinted in* 1978 U.S.C.C.A.N. at 5865.

* * *

decision to impose restitution generally does not turn on the victim's injury, but on the penal goals of the State and the situation of the defendant. * * *

This point is well illustrated by the Connecticut statute under which the restitution obligation was imposed. The statute authorizes a judge to impose any of eight specified conditions of probation, as well as "any other conditions reasonably related to his rehabilitation." Conn. Gen. Stat. § 53a–30(a)(9) (1985). Clause (4) of that section authorizes a judge to require that the defendant

> "make restitution of the fruits of his offense or make restitution, in an amount he can afford to pay or provide in a suitable manner, for the loss or damage caused thereby and the court may fix the amount thereof and the manner of performance."

This clause does not require imposition of restitution in the amount of the harm caused. Instead, it provides for a flexible remedy tailored to the defendant's situation.

Because criminal proceedings focus on the State's interests in rehabilitation and punishment, rather than the victim's desire for compensation, we conclude that restitution orders imposed in such proceedings operate "for the benefit of" the State. Similarly, they are not assessed "for * * * compensation" of the victim. The sentence following a criminal conviction necessarily considers the penal and rehabilitative interests of the State. Those interests are sufficient to place restitution orders within the meaning of § 523(a)(7).

In light of the strong interests of the States, the uniform construction of the old Act over three-quarters of a century, and the absence of any significant evidence that Congress intended to change the law in this area, we believe this result best effectuates the will of Congress. Accordingly, the decision of the Court of Appeals for the Second Circuit is

Reversed.

JUSTICE MARSHALL, with whom JUSTICE STEVENS joins, dissenting.

Petitioners failed to assert timely objections to the discharge of respondent Robinson's restitution debt, and the majority goes to considerable lengths to excuse this default. Respondent concedes that the restitution obligation would not have been discharged had petitioners objected in a timely fashion. * * *

The Court charitably attributes petitioners' inaction to the fact that from the start petitioners took the position they assert here. But their representations at oral argument suggest only that they failed to object because "state agencies were admittedly somewhat confused on how to handle it" and were "a little perplexed because this was the first time it happened." Petitioners seek a broad construction of the statute to excuse their confusion-induced waiver of the right to object and thereby guarantee that Robinson's restitution obligation would not be discharged. In my opinion, however, the statute cannot fairly be read to arrive at the result the majority reaches today.

The Court concludes that a criminal restitution obligation is nondischargeable under § 523(a)(7) because it is "a fine, penalty, or forfeiture payable to and for the benefit of a governmental unit, and is not compensation for actual pecuniary loss." I find unconvincing the majority's conclusion that the criminal restitution order at issue here is not "compensation for actual pecuniary loss."[2] While restitution imposed as a condition of probation under the Connecticut statute is in part a penal sanction, it is also intended to compensate victims for their injuries. * * * Were the restitution order purely penal, the statute would not connect the amount of restitution to the damage imposed. Tying the amount of restitution to the amount of actual damage sustained by the victim strongly suggests that the payment is meant to compensate the victim. This comports with the theory underlying restitution sanctions. Restitution is not simply a punishment that incidentally compensates the victim. Indeed, compensation is an essential element of a restitution scheme * * *.

Nor do I accept that we can avoid the consequences of respondent's discharge in bankruptcy by finding that the restitution obligation was not a "debt." First, the scope of debts under the Code is expansive. "Debt" is defined in [§ 101(12)] as "liability on a claim," and "claim" is

---

[2]   * * * The majority contends that "Congress enacted the Code in 1978 against the background of an established judicial exception to discharge for criminal sentences," and that Congress should not be deemed to abrogate judicially created law unless it makes explicit the intent to do so. But, far from abrogating judicially created law making fines and penalties nondischargeable as a general matter, Congress has codified that law *and* added the requirements of § 523(a)(7). The historical basis of the exception does not negate the additional limitations expressed in the statute.

defined in [§ 101(5)] as a "right to payment." The legislative history of the Code indicates that "claim" was to be given the "broadest possible definition." H.R. Rep. No. 95–595 at 309, *reprinted in* 1978 U.S.C.C.A.N. at 6266; S. Rep. No. 95–989 at 22, *reprinted in* 1978 U.S.C.C.A.N. at 5808. In light of the broad scope of "debt" under the Code, I agree with the Court of Appeals that the Probation Office had a right to payment, notwithstanding "that the right is enforceable by the threat of revocation of probation and incarceration rather than by the threat of levy and execution on the debtor's property. The right is not the less cognizable because the obligor must suffer loss of freedom rather than loss of property upon failure to pay."[4]

The definition of "debt" is intentionally broad not only to ensure the debtor a meaningful discharge but also to guarantee as many creditors as possible the right to participate in the distribution of the property of the estate. * * * As the Court of Appeals observed, a conclusion that the restitution obligation was not a debt "would produce the anomalous result that no holder of a right to restitution could participate in the bankruptcy proceeding or receive any distributions of the debtor's assets in liquidation. There is no evidence that Congress intended such a result." On the contrary, Congress plainly intended that fines, penalties, and forfeitures be deemed debts eligible to participate in the distribution of the bankruptcy estate, and the statute provides explicitly for that participation. See § 726(a)(4). The very fact that fines, penalties, and forfeitures are made nondischargeable under § 523(a)(7) indicates that they were deemed "debts"; if they were not debts, they would not be affected by discharge, see § 524, and there would be no need to make them nondischargeable.

* * *

Notes and Questions

1. Did *Kelly* put federalism concerns ahead of the Code's plain meaning?

2. Although the Court said it was unnecessary to decide whether criminal penalties are "debts," did the Court decide that question anyway?

---

[4] Though Connecticut does not permit the victim to enforce the restitution order as a civil judgment, other jurisdictions do. Under such statutes, it would be even more difficult to argue that a criminal restitution order does not create a "right to payment" and is consequently not a "debt."

3. What is the consequence in the context of *Kelly* if criminal restitution obligations are "debts"?

4. Read § 523(c)(1) and look again at §§ 523(a)(2) and (a)(4). Did the Court save the State when the State failed to take available steps to protect itself? Is the Court's explanation on this point convincing?

5. The Court decided in *Pennsylvania Department of Public Welfare v. Davenport*, 495 U.S. 552, 110 S.Ct. 2126, 109 L.Ed.2d 588 (1990), that restitution obligations, imposed by state courts as a condition of probation, are "debts" as defined by § 101(12), and thus are dischargeable in Chapter 13. Does this conclusion in *Davenport* undercut *Kelly*?

Congress legislatively overruled *Davenport* by enacting § 1328(a)(3), but that subsection does not affect *Davenport*'s interpretation of "debt."

6. Note that § 1328(a)(3) is much more absolute than § 523(a)(7): it leaves out any reference to tax penalties; it is not limited to debts owed to governmental units; and it does not except debts constituting compensation for pecuniary loss, thereby permitting them to be discharged. Did the Court in *Kelly* give sufficient attention to those elements of § 523(a)(7), instead reading the subsection as if it were written like § 1328(a)(3)?

8. SECTION 523(a)(8)—EDUCATIONAL LOANS

Congress had before it, in 1978, a few anecdotes about debtors who had incurred substantial loan obligations while attending medical or law school, and who had then discharged those obligations in bankruptcy immediately upon graduating and before commencing lucrative jobs. Section 523(a)(8) was included in the Code in order to deal with such cases, continuing the nondischargeability first enacted as part of the Higher Education Act of 1965. Ironically, the subsection does not seem to catch the high-flying debtors Congress had in mind. Rather, it applies most often when debtors have attended trade schools that either failed to equip their students with marketable skills or closed their doors before students completed the course of study.

Section 523(a)(8) has been repeatedly amended, and each change has made it more difficult for debtors to discharge educational loans. Originally, § 523(a)(8) barred the discharge only of governmentally-sponsored loans that had been outstanding for less than five years. Over the years, the subsection was amended to include educational loans from additional sources and to extend, and then eliminate, the time period. During that process, § 1328(a)(2) was also amended to incorporate § 523(a)(8), thereby making student loans nondischargeable in Chapter 13 as well.

Although the rule is now simply stated—educational loans are nondischargeable under § 523(a)(8) unless denial of discharge would present an "undue hardship" to the debtor or the debtor's dependents—the appropriate standard for determining "undue hardship" has been much debated. Most of the circuits follow the test set out in *Brunner v. New York State Higher Educational Services Corp.*, 831 F.2d 395 (2d Cir.1987). The next case explains it, as well as an alternative approach.

BRONSDON v. EDUCATIONAL CREDIT MANAGEMENT CORP. (IN RE BRONSDON)

United States Bankruptcy Appellate Panel, First Circuit, 2010.
435 B.R. 791.

LAMOUTTE, Bankruptcy Appellate Panel Judge.

This appeal arises out of an adversary proceeding filed by Denise Bronsdon (the "Debtor") seeking to discharge her student loan obligations to Educational Credit Management Corporation ("ECMC") on the grounds of undue hardship pursuant to § 523(a)(8). The bankruptcy court initially concluded that repayment of the student loans would impose an undue hardship on the Debtor and discharged the loans. On appeal, the U.S. District Court for the District of Massachusetts (the "district court") vacated the bankruptcy court's decision and remanded the matter to the bankruptcy court to consider the impact that participation in the William D. Ford Federal Direct Loan Program (the "Ford Program") would have on the undue hardship analysis. On remand, the bankruptcy court concluded that the Debtor's failure to participate in the Ford Program was insufficient to overcome a finding of undue hardship under § 523(a)(8), and again discharged the loans. ECMC appealed. For the reasons set forth below, we AFFIRM.

BACKGROUND

A. The Debtor's Personal Background

At the time of trial in January 2009, the Debtor was 64 years old and single. She did not have any dependents nor did she suffer from any disability or debilitating medical condition. In 1994, the Debtor, at the age of 50, received a bachelor's degree in English from Wellesley College. Thereafter, from 1996 until 2002, she worked at various jobs as a legal secretary until she decided to go to law school. She enrolled in Southern New England School of Law, and graduated in the top half of her class in December 2005. To finance her law school education, the Debtor took out the student loans now at issue, which at some point were assigned to ECMC. As of September 8, 2008, the loans totaled $82,049.45.

After law school, the Debtor failed the bar exam three times, each time by a significant margin. She does not plan to take the bar exam again because she has no money to pay for the exam fee or preparation materials, and because she has not come close to passing.

After graduating from law school, the Debtor worked briefly as a receptionist and as a temporary patent prosecution secretary at two different law firms. Although she continually went on interviews, made telephone calls, and spoke with employment agencies in an effort to find any kind of secretarial, receptionist, or contract manager work, she was unable to find employment. The Debtor pursued alternate means of earning income, but her attempts were unsuccessful.[5] At the time of trial, the Debtor's only income was a monthly Social Security payment of $946.00. She owned no real property and lived temporarily in her father's house.

B. Procedural History

The Debtor filed a chapter 7 petition in July 2007, and received a discharge in December 2007. Thereafter, the Debtor filed an adversary complaint seeking to discharge her student loan obligations to ECMC. At ECMC's request, the bankruptcy court took judicial notice of the Ford Program, 34 C.F.R. §§ 685.100, et seq. The Ford Program offers, among other things, a student loan consolidation repayment option known as the income contingent repayment plan (the "ICRP").

After a trial, the bankruptcy court issued an order and decision (the "First Decision") discharging the debts owed to ECMC. In the First Decision, the bankruptcy court applied a totality of the circumstances test to determine whether the Debtor would suffer an undue hardship. In applying this standard, the bankruptcy court found that, given the Debtor's lack of recent work history, narrow work experience, failure to pass the bar exam, age, unsuccessful attempts to find employment in a variety of fields, and unsuccessful attempts to sell a

---

[5] For example, the Debtor wrote a novel but was unable to find a publisher. She also applied for a patent on an invention to protect the privacy of hospital patients. At the time of trial, the Debtor had not received a response regarding the patent, and was considering writing another novel or starting a website that would feature commentary on current events.

novel and acquire a patent, the Debtor had no reasonably reliable future financial resources other than the Social Security payments.

The bankruptcy court also recognized that if the Debtor participated in the Ford Program, her current financial status would not require monthly payments. It rejected ECMC's argument that repayment would not cause the Debtor an undue hardship because the Debtor would not be required to make monthly payments under the program. The bankruptcy court stated that if the Debtor were to participate in the Ford Program, "the student loan forgiveness at the conclusion of her participation in the program would result in a tax liability that would subject the Debtor's Social Security benefits to garnishment," which would "promote a vicious cycle that could leave the Debtor in a financial state much more desperate than the one she is currently enduring." Additionally, the bankruptcy court referred to its reasoning in *In re Denittis*, 362 B.R. 57, 64-65 (Bankr. D.Mass.2007), in which it concluded that consideration of the Ford Program in the undue hardship analysis would, in effect, foreclose a conclusion of undue hardship whenever a debtor is eligible to participate.

On appeal to the district court, ECMC contested the bankruptcy court's factual findings regarding the Debtor's good faith efforts to find work and that she was not likely to earn income in the future. ECMC also argued that the bankruptcy court made errors of law concerning the ICRP. At the outset, the district court noted the two tests for determining undue hardship, but stated that the test to be applied was not a material issue in this case as the result was the same under both tests. The district court then determined that there was ample evidence supporting the bankruptcy court's factual findings and, therefore, that the findings were not clearly erroneous. It also concluded that the bankruptcy court had made a legal error by "giving no weight to the ICRP in the undue hardship analysis." As a result, the district court vacated the First Decision and remanded the matter to the bankruptcy court to consider the impact that participating in the ICRP would have on the undue hardship analysis.

On remand, the bankruptcy court concluded that "the Debtor's failure to participate in the ICRP [wa]s insufficient to demonstrate a lack of good faith (again assuming such finding is integral to the test under § 523(a)(8)) when weighed against this Debtor's efforts to try to improve her financial circumstance," and ordered that the student loans owed to ECMC were discharged. This appeal ensued.

* * *

DISCUSSION

I. The Appropriate Legal Standard

A. The Burden of Proof

Under § 523(a)(8), debtors are not permitted to discharge educational loans "unless excepting such debt from discharge * * * would impose an undue hardship on the debtor and the debtor's dependents." § 523(a)(8). The creditor bears the initial burden of establishing that the debt is of the type excepted from discharge under § 523(a)(8). Once the showing is made, the burden shifts to the debtor to prove that excepting the student loan debt from discharge will cause the debtor and her dependents "undue hardship."

B. The Tests for Determining Undue Hardship

The Bankruptcy Code does not define "undue hardship" and courts have struggled with its meaning. After several decades of case law interpreting this term, essentially two tests have emerged—the so-called *Brunner* test and the "totality of the circumstances" test. As the First Circuit has noted:

> [N]ine circuit courts of appeal [] have followed the Second Circuit's test set forth in *Brunner v. New York State Higher Educ. Servs. Corp.*, 831 F.2d 395 (2d Cir.1987) (per curiam). This is a tripartite test, requiring that the debtor show inability, at her current level of income and expenses, to maintain a "minimal" standard of living; the likelihood that this inability will persist for a significant portion of the repayment period; and the existence of good faith efforts to repay the loans.
>
> A facially different test is the Eighth Circuit's totality-of-circumstances test, which would have courts consider the debtor's reasonably reliable future financial resources, his reasonably necessary living expenses, and "any other relevant facts."

Nash v. Conn. Student Loan Found. (In re Nash), 446 F.3d 188, 190 (1st Cir.2006). Although the First Circuit acknowledged the two approaches in *Nash*, it declined to adopt formally a particular test for determining undue hardship, and it remains an undecided issue in this circuit.

* * * [T]he bankruptcy court applied the totality of the circumstances test to determine whether excepting the Debtor's student loan obligations from discharge would cause her undue hardship. The district court determined that the issue of the appropriate test was immaterial as the result would be the same under either test. On remand, the bankruptcy court again declined to endorse the *Brunner* test. On appeal, ECMC urges the Panel to formally adopt the so-called *Brunner* test.

C. Adopting a Test

As noted above, neither the plain language of § 523(a)(8) nor the First Circuit mandate a particular test for evaluating the dischargeability of student loans. The Panel has also declined to endorse a particular test. Most of the bankruptcy courts within the First Circuit have adopted the totality of the circumstances test over the *Brunner* test, although a few courts within this circuit have applied *Brunner* instead.

To determine the appropriate test, we first examine the differences between the *Brunner* and the totality of circumstances approaches. As the Panel noted in *Lorenz v. American Educ. Servs./Pa. Higher Educ. Assistance Agency (In re Lorenz)*, 337 B.R. 423 (BAP 1st Cir.2006), the distinctions between the two tests are modest, with many overlapping considerations:[12]

> The "totality of the circumstances" analysis requires a debtor to prove by a preponderance of evidence that (1) his past, present, and reasonably reliable future financial resources; (2) his and his dependents' reasonably necessary living expenses; and (3) other relevant facts or circumstances unique to the case, prevent him from paying the student loans in question while still maintaining a minimal standard of living, even when aided by a discharge of other prepetition debts. See *Hicks v. Educ. Credit Mgmt. Corp. (In re Hicks)*, 331 B.R. 18, 31 (Bankr. D. Mass.2005) (distilling so-called totality of the circumstances test to "one simple question: *Can the debtor now, and in the foreseeable future, maintain a reasonable, minimal standard of living for the debtor and the debtor's dependents and still afford to make payments on the debtor's student loans?"*). Courts

---

[12] Indeed, the Panel has stated that the only practical difference between the two tests is that under *Brunner*, the debtor must establish that she made a good faith effort to repay the loans. *Educational Credit Mgmt. Corp. v. Kelly (In re Kelly)*, 312 B.R. 200, 206 (BAP 1st Cir.2004).

"should consider all relevant evidence—the debtor's income and expenses, the debtor's health, age, education, number of dependents and other personal or family circumstances, the amount of the monthly payment required, the impact of the general discharge under chapter 7 and the debtor's ability to find a higher-paying job, move or cut living expenses."

The *Brunner* test differs, albeit modestly. *Brunner* requires a "three-part showing (1) that the debtor cannot, based on current income and expenses, maintain a 'minimal' standard of living for herself or her dependants if forced to repay the loans; (2) that this state of affairs is likely to persist for a significant portion of the repayment period of the student loans; and (3) that the debtor has made good faith efforts to repay the loans."

One can see readily that insofar as income and expenses are concerned, the tests take converging tacks. The "totality test" looks to past, present, and future "financial resources" and "necessary living expenses" and whether, taken together with other factors, the debtor has the ability to repay while maintaining a minimal standard of living. *Brunner* asks the same question looking to "current" income and expenses, then considers whether circumstances inhibiting repayment will endure.

Id. at 430-31.

Although the two tests do not always diverge in function, they do in form. As the *Hicks* court noted: "While under the totality of the circumstances approach, the court may also consider 'any additional facts and circumstances unique to the case' that are relevant to the central inquiry (*i.e.*, the debtor's ability to maintain a minimum standard of living while repaying the loans), the *Brunner* test imposes two additional requirements on the debtor that *must* be met if the student loans are to be discharged." Looking to the bankruptcy court's extensive analysis of the predominant tests * * * , the *Hicks* court agreed * * * that the *Brunner* test "test[s] too much."

At first blush, the second *Brunner* requirement—a showing that the debtor's "state of affairs is likely to persist for a significant portion of the repayment period of the student loan"—seems merely to resonate with the forward-looking nature of the undue hardship analysis. That is, under *any* undue hardship standard the debtor must show that the inability to maintain a minimum standard of living while repaying the student loans is not a temporary reality, but will continue into the foreseeable future.

Many courts interpreting and applying the second *Brunner* prong, however, place dispositive weight on the debtor's ability to demonstrate "additional extraordinary circumstances" that establish a "certainty of hopelessness." This has led some courts to require that the debtor show the existence of "unique" or "extraordinary" circumstances, such as the debtor's advanced age, illness or disability, psychiatric problems, lack of usable job skills, large number of dependents or severely limited education. * * * And, in the absence of such a showing, the court may conclude that the debtor has failed the second *Brunner* prong and the student loans will not be discharged. * * *

Requiring the debtor to present additional evidence of "unique" or "extraordinary" circumstances amounting to a "certainty of hopelessness" is not supported by the text of § 523(a)(8). The debtor need only demonstrate "undue hardship." True, the debtor must be able to prove that the claimed hardship is more than present financial difficulty. And the existence of any of the factors mentioned above may be highly relevant to a finding that the hardship will persist into the foreseeable future. But whether or not this Court subjectively views the debtor's circumstances as "unique" or "extraordinary" is, in a word, overkill.

331 B.R. at 27-28. We agree with this rationale and conclude that *Brunner* takes the test too far.

Furthermore, we agree that the "good faith" requirement of *Brunner* is "without textual foundation." *Id*. at 28. Ultimately, the debtor must establish by a preponderance of the evidence that her present and future actual circumstances would impose an undue hardship if her debts are excepted from discharge. Irrespective of the test, the decision of a bankruptcy court, whether the failure to discharge a student loan will cause undue hardship to the debtor and the dependents of the debtor under § 523(a)(8), rests on both the economic ability to repay and the existence of any disqualifying action(s). The party opposing the discharge of a student loan has the burden of presenting evidence of any disqualifying factor, such as bad faith. The debtor is not required under the statute to establish prepetition good faith in absence of a challenge. The debtor should not be obligated to prove a negative, that is, that he did not act in bad faith, and, consequently, acted in good faith.

Undue hardship is measured as of trial date, and is a forward-looking concept. Placing emphasis on prepetition failure to pay misconstrues the wording of the undue hardship requirement in the statute. As stated before, distilled to its essence, the finding of undue hardship under § 523(a)(8) following the totality of the circumstances test rests on one basic question: "Can the debtor now, and in the foreseeable near future, maintain a reasonable, minimal standard of living for the debtor and the debtor's dependents and still afford to make payments on the debtor's student loans?" *Hicks*, 331 B.R. at 31. Answering said question leads the bankruptcy court to discharge its task of making "a principled determination of the requirement's meaning and a careful review of the debtor's circumstances." *Kopf v. Department of Educ. (In re Kopf)*, 245 B.R. 731, 741 (Bankr. D.Me.2000).

Having considered the various tests used to determine undue hardship, the plain text of § 523(a)(8), and further recognizing that the majority of courts in the First Circuit adopt the totality of the circumstances test, the Panel declines to adopt the *Brunner* test as requested by ECMC. The Panel is persuaded that the totality of the circumstances test best effectuates the determination of undue hardship while adhering to the plain text of § 523(a)(8).

II. Consideration of the ICRP Under the Totality of the Circumstances Test

ECMC's primary argument on appeal is that the bankruptcy court failed to adequately consider the availability of the ICRP in its determination of undue hardship under the totality of the circumstances. As noted above, the totality of the circumstances test requires the bankruptcy court to consider "any other relevant facts and circumstances" unique to the particular case, such as the debtor's ability to repay her loans. Although courts applying the totality of the circumstances test have treated the ICRP differently, the weight of authority is to treat the ICRP as one of many factors to consider in evaluating the totality of the debtor's circumstances. Thus, a debtor's eligibility to participate in the ICRP may be considered by the court when applying the totality of the circumstances test, but it is not determinative. As set forth below, we conclude that the bankruptcy court properly considered the Debtor's eligibility for the ICRP as part of its examination of the totality of the circumstances.

The Ford Program allows student loans to be consolidated and payments on the consolidated loan to be adjusted based on a formula that takes into account poverty guidelines and a debtor's adjusted gross income. One of the consolidation options under the Ford Program is the ICRP. Under the ICRP, an eligible debtor's annual loan payment is generally equal to 20 percent of the difference between his or her adjusted gross income and the federal poverty guidelines for the debtor's family size, regardless of the amount of unpaid student loan debt. Repayments are made monthly. ICRP payments are recalculated annually based on changes to the debtor's reported household adjusted gross income. Unpaid interest is capitalized until the outstanding principal is ten percent greater than the original principal amount. If the borrower has not repaid the loan at the end of 25 years, the unpaid portion of the loan is cancelled.

Courts considering the ICRP as a factor under the totality of the circumstances test evaluate both the benefits and drawbacks of the program for the individual debtor within his or her unique circumstances. Although these courts acknowledge that the ICRP reduces the immediate debt burden of the student loan debtor, they are often concerned about the longer term debt and tax consequences of the program. They recognize that, although it may be appropriate to consider whether a debtor has pursued her options under the ICRP, participation in that program may not be appropriate for some debtors because of the impact of the negative amortization of the debt over time when payments are not made and the tax implications arising after the debt is cancelled. Because of these considerations, the ICRP may be beneficial for a borrower whose inability to pay is temporary and whose financial situation is expected to improve significantly in the future. Where no significant improvement is anticipated, however, such programs may be detrimental to the borrower's long-term financial health.

Central to this analysis is the idea that because forgiveness of any unpaid debt under the ICRP may result in a taxable event, the debtor who participates in the ICRP simply exchanges a nondischargeable student loan debt for a nondischargeable tax debt. Such an exchange of debt provides little or no relief to debtors. For example, in *Booth v. U.S. (In re Booth)*, 410 B.R. 672 (Bankr. E.D.Wash.2009), the bankruptcy court stated:

> Application of the ICRP does not result in a discharge of the debt nor relieve the debtor from personal liability on the debt. Further action may, and will, be taken to collect the obligation, even if that action is simply requiring the debtor to pro-

vide annual financial information to the Department of Education. The ICRP does not grant a discharge, but lapse of a period as long as 25 years may result in cancellation or forgiveness of the debt. There is no provision in the regulation for "partial" cancellation or forgiveness of the obligation. Unlike a discharge, cancellation or forgiveness of a debt results in a tax liability. As interest accrues during the 25 years or lesser repayment period, the amount of debt cancelled will be quite large. The resulting tax liability would not be subject to discharge in a later bankruptcy proceeding.

The focus of the ICRP is on deferral, not discharge, of debt. This is the antithesis of a fresh start. Congress has provided bankruptcy debtors relief which is not provided in the ICRP regulations. Compliance with ICRP regulations will not result in the same relief which can be granted by the courts under § 523(a)(8).

Id. at 675-76. In addition, many of these courts are concerned that the ICRP allows the Department of Education to substitute its administrative determination regarding undue hardship for the bankruptcy judge's statutorily mandated discretion under § 523(a)(8).

ECMC presented undisputed evidence that its loans to the Debtor were eligible for the ICRP. Based on the Debtor's adjusted gross income at the time of trial, the bankruptcy court found that her monthly ICRP payments would be $0.00. In its decision after remand, the bankruptcy court acknowledged that the Debtor was aware of the ICRP and her eligibility to participate, but stated that the fact that the Debtor would not be required to repay her student loan under the ICRP did not mandate a finding that her failure to participate in the program prevented a discharge of the debt. Acknowledging both the potential for significant tax liabilities under the ICRP and its concern that finding failure to participate in a zero payment ICRP is per se lack of good faith would be an abdication of the bankruptcy court's responsibility to determine dischargeability of student loans, it ultimately concluded that

shackling the Debtor to the ICRP would be * * * a pointless exercise. Although her current payments under the ICRP would be zero, interest would continue to accrue despite the fact that the Debtor's chances of ever repaying any portion of the loan are virtually non-existent. The Debtor is now 65 years old, has failed to pass the Massachusetts bar examination three times. She testified she has no plans to retake the exam, which is reasonable in light of her testimony that she lacks the funds to do so, has not come within "striking distance" of passing, and importantly had an adverse physical reaction during the third examination whereby she almost fainted. Moreover, as set forth in this Court's Memorandum of Decision, the Debtor has attempted unsuccessfully to find employment as a secretary and has sought to publish a novel. These efforts demonstrate her good faith despite her reluctance to be forced into the Ford Program. Nor are circumstances likely to improve for the Debtor. But for the ability to live in the den of her father's home, the Debtor, without some sort of financial aid, could easily become homeless. In view of her age and work history, her prospects for a better financial future are dim. To subject her to a meaningless repayment plan when she clearly does not have the ability to repay these student loans now or in the foreseeable future is not required by § 523(a)(8) and is inconsistent with this Court's role as the adjudicator of undue hardship.

2010 Bankr. LEXIS 71, at *5-6.

* * *

As set forth above, the Panel concludes that the bankruptcy court did not err in its legal conclusions after remand regarding the weight that the Debtor's eligibility to participate in the ICRP should have in the undue hardship analysis, as well as its conclusion that the totality of the circumstances warranted a finding of undue hardship. Therefore, we AFFIRM.

HAINES, Chief Bankruptcy Appellate Panel Judge, concurring.

I agree with the majority's conclusion that the judgment of the bankruptcy court should be affirmed; I write separately for several reasons.

* * *

I have no quarrel with the majority's conclusion that the debtor demonstrated undue hardship and, therefore, that her student loans should be discharged. This case, however, does not call for choosing between the totality of the circumstances test and the *"Brunner"* test, as employing either test would result in affirmance. The majority's rejection of the *Brunner* test is unnecessary to resolution of this appeal and, therefore, unwarranted. I am no fan of *Brunner*. The majority's criticisms of it are well-taken. I am disinclined to enshrine the majority's legal determination as a holding when it is of no consequence to this case.

Having lost below under the trial court's careful consideration of the totality of the circumstances touching on the debtor's case, the appellant begs us to "adopt" *Brunner*. But we need not respond (either "yes" or, as here, "no") when the answer is of no moment.

Having withstood one appellate assault, the bankruptcy court's factual findings are fixed. * * *

Taken together, these findings provide no basis to conclude that this debtor will ever have the financial resources to payoff (or even pay down) her student loan, on *any* terms.

One must ask, then, how could the failure to enroll in a program that would—as far as the judicial eye can see—require the debtor to pay *nothing*, be either a circumstance cutting against discharging the loan under the "totality" test or a lack of "good faith efforts" to pay under *Brunner*? Under either test, the court below was being asked to deny discharge of the loans on what basis? It could only be on the possibility that the debtor might win the lottery or that some equally improbable instance of financial good fortune could strike. Need it be said that, if such were a sufficient basis to deny discharge of a student loan, the prospect of ever discharging a student loan pursuant to § 523(a)(8) would become fantasy?

* * *

Given that the choice of test makes no difference in this case, and that to make the unnecessary choice here can only contribute to the confusion surrounding undue hardship analysis, I am left to concur in the majority's conclusion without joining it on the path it has taken to reach it.

Questions and Problems

1. Do you agree with the concurring opinion that this debtor could establish undue hardship, and thus discharge her educational loans, under either test? If so, why do you suppose the majority chose to discuss the tests at such length? Has the court "contribute[d] to the confusion surrounding undue hardship analysis," as the concurring opinion charged?

2. Which test makes more sense to you? Is it relevant that, when the *Brunner* test was formulated, the statute allowed the discharge of educational loans more than five years old?

3. The Supreme Court dealt with the discharge of educational loans in *United Student Aid Funds v. Espinosa*, 559 U.S. 260, 130 S.Ct. 1367, 176 L.Ed.2d 158 (2010). Debtor's Chapter 13 plan proposed that the debtor would repay the principal on his student loan debt, but the interest was to be discharged once the principal was repaid. The bankruptcy court confirmed the plan, although the debtor did not initiate the required adversary proceeding to establish undue hardship. The creditor received notice of the plan, but did not object either to its terms or to the debtor's failure to initiate the required proceeding. After the debtor repaid the principal and discharged the interest, the creditor sought to collect that interest.

The Supreme Court held that the bankruptcy court made a legal error by confirming the plan. The provisions of the Code imposing a finding of undue hardship and the initiation of an adversary proceeding are self-executing, so no action by the creditor was required. The bankruptcy court's clear legal error gave the creditor grounds for appeal, but it did not fall within Federal Rule of Civil Procedure 60(b)(4), which allows a party to seek relief from a final judgment that is "void."

The obvious lesson is that creditors with student loan debts cannot sit back and wait to receive notice of an adversary proceeding. Rather, they must read proposed plans and, if they dislike a provision, object to confirmation and, if necessary, take a timely appeal of the confirmation order.

The Court's decision should not be read as an invitation to debtors (and their attorneys) to include provisions in a Chapter 13 plan that are inconsistent with the Code. The Court said that "expanding the availability of relief under Rule 60(b)(4) is not an appropriate prophylaxis" in such cases, but that sanctions under Bankruptcy Rule 9011 are possible.

4. Debtor graduated from a state university with a degree in psychology, owing $25,000 in student loans. He looked for a position in employment relations, doing job placement testing, for six months but found nothing. Although Debtor can type, he has not looked for a secretarial position. When the university began pressing him to begin repayment, he scraped together a few hundred dollars. He then filed a bankruptcy petition, and he now seeks to discharge the balance of the loan obligation. What result?

5. Debtor borrowed $100,000 to finance her son's education at a fine private university. She maintained a repayment schedule for about a year, but encountered financial problems and filed bankruptcy. Assuming that Debtor cannot establish undue hardship, is there some other argument she might use to avoid nondischargeability under § 523(a)(8)? Compare *In re Pelkowski*,

990 F.2d 737 (3d Cir.1993), with *Northwestern University Student Loan Office v. Behr (In re Behr),* 80 B.R. 124 (Bankr.N.D.Iowa 1987).

9. ISSUE PRECLUSION

In *Grogan v. Garner*, 498 U.S. 279, 111 S.Ct. 654, 112 L.Ed.2d 755 (1991), the Supreme Court recognized that principles of issue preclusion, applicable in other cases, are also applicable in bankruptcy. In that case, Creditor sued Debtor in state court for fraud in connection with the sale of corporate securities, proved the case under a preponderance of the evidence standard, and obtained a judgment. When Debtor filed bankruptcy and sought to discharge the judgment, Creditor argued that collateral estoppel required a holding of nondischargeability under § 523. The issue in *Grogan* was whether the discharge exceptions must be established by a preponderance of the evidence, rather than by clear and convincing evidence. In the course of finding a preponderance standard appropriate, the Supreme Court recognized the applicability of collateral estoppel: "Our prior cases have suggested, but have not formally held, that the principles of collateral estoppel apply in bankruptcy proceedings under the current Bankruptcy Act [sic]. * * * We now clarify that collateral estoppel principles do indeed apply in discharge exception proceedings pursuant to § 523(a)." *Id.* at 284–85 n.11, 111 S.Ct. at 658 n.11, 112 L.Ed.2d at 763 n.11.

Issue preclusion requires that: 1) the issue under consideration be identical to that involved in a prior action; 2) the issue was actually litigated in the prior action; and 3) determination of the issue was necessary to the judgment entered in the prior action. See *Sheerin v. Davis (Matter of Davis)*, 3 F.3d 113 (5th Cir.1993). If these requirements are satisfied, then a state court judgment finding that the debtor, for example, obtained the debt by fraud or breached a fiduciary obligation, will preclude the debtor from contesting nondischargeability of the debt under the appropriate subsection of § 523. See *Bush v. Balfour Beatty Bahamas, Ltd. (In re Bush)*, 62 F.3d 1319 (11th Cir.1995) (holding debtor precluded from litigating the issue of fraud when "he engaged in dilatory and deliberately obstructive conduct" in earlier state court proceedings, but ultimately chose to suffer a default).

D. EFFECT OF DISCHARGE

Only the debtor's personal liability is affected by bankruptcy; liens that survive bankruptcy can later be enforced against the encumbered property. This doctrine, first established in *Long v. Bullard*, 117

U.S. 617, 6 S.Ct. 917, 29 L.Ed. 1004 (1886), is today reflected in at least two places in the Code. First, § 522(c) provides that liens may be enforced against exempt property after the case. Second, § 524(a) provides an injunction that bars the collection of prepetition debts "as a personal liability of the debtor." As enacted in 1978, § 524(a) provided that discharge enjoined efforts to collect a prepetition debt "as a personal liability of the debtor, or from property of the debtor." The latter phrase was dropped in 1984 to avoid any mistaken belief that discharge prevents postpetition enforcement of valid liens.

Problems

1. Creditor obtained a $5,000 judgment against Debtor on an unsecured loan obligation. Debtor filed a bankruptcy petition, listed the debt owed to Creditor on the schedules, and received a discharge under § 727. Debtor had no nonexempt assets, so Creditor did not file a claim. (See Rule 2002(e).) After the bankruptcy case was closed, Creditor brought suit to collect the debt in state court. Debtor appeared and moved for summary judgment, asserting the discharge. What result? Would the result change if Debtor had not appeared and a default judgment had been entered against Debtor by the state court?

2. Assume the same facts as in Problem # 1, except that Creditor argued in the subsequent state court proceeding that the loan had been procured by fraud and was therefore nondischargeable under § 523(a)(2). What result? See § 523(c)(1).

3. Creditor sustained injuries when Debtor's car jumped the curb and hit Creditor as she was walking on the sidewalk. Debtor filed a bankruptcy petition, listed the debt owed to Creditor on the schedules, and received a discharge under § 727. Debtor had no nonexempt assets, so Creditor did not file a claim. After the bankruptcy case was closed, Creditor sued in state court and argued that the debt was not discharged because Debtor had been intoxicated at the time of the accident. Debtor asserted the discharge injunction. What result?

4. Assume the same facts as in Problem # 3, except that Creditor wants to collect from Debtor's insurance carrier. Debtor, however, must be named as defendant under local rules. Does § 524(a) bar the filing of this suit postbankruptcy? See § 524(e).

5. Debtor, Eugene Andrus, discharged a $20,000 obligation owed to Stanley Stann, who lived two doors away. In a rage, Stann posted a sign in his front yard that read: "GENE ANDRUS IS A DEADBEAT! THIS IS A PUBLIC SERVICE ANNOUNCEMENT!" Has Stann violated § 524(a)? Is this protected speech? See *In re Andrus*, 189 B.R. 413 (N.D.Ill.1995).

6. Debtor wrote a check in payment for goods purchased from Seller. The check bounced and Seller filed a claim in Debtor's subsequent bankruptcy. Seller received a dividend of 10 cents on the dollar and, after closing of the bankruptcy case, filed a state criminal complaint against Debtor for writing a bad check. What result if the criminal statute makes repayment an affirmative defense to the crime? Would the result change if the statute includes no such affirmative defense but the local prosecutor as a matter of policy will not pursue a case if restitution has been made?

7. Can Creditor in Problem # 6 merely telephone Debtor and threaten to initiate criminal proceedings if the balance of the obligation is not paid?

8. Debtor, who was a major shareholder of a Hong Kong company, personally guaranteed the corporation's $24 million obligation to Hong Kong Bank. Debtor came to the United States and filed a Chapter 7 petition. Hong Kong Bank filed a proof of claim in the case and Debtor later received a discharge. Bank then sought to collect from Debtor in Hong Kong. Is that a violation of § 524? If so, what can the U.S. court do about it? See *Hong Kong & Shanghai Banking Corp., Ltd. v. Simon (In re Simon)*, 153 F.3d 991 (9th Cir.1998), *cert. denied*, 525 U.S. 1141, 119 S.Ct. 1032, 143 L.Ed.2d 41 (1999).

E. REAFFIRMATION

"Reaffirmation" is the making of a new agreement to repay a debt. Unlike redemption, which we encountered in Chapter 4, reaffirmation is consensual—both debtor and creditor must agree to it. Such an agreement is an enforceable contract under common law, despite the lack of fresh consideration to support the new promise to pay. Restatement of Contracts (Second) § 83. Thus, reaffirmation waives the discharge as far as that debt is concerned, and subjects the debtor to later collection efforts by the creditor if the debtor defaults.

Research done before enactment of the Code revealed that a large percentage of Chapter 7 debtors reaffirmed some debts: for example, 48% reaffirmed debts for appliances or furniture, and 30% reaffirmed debts for cars.

Congress believed that reaffirmations seriously threaten the fresh start bankruptcy is supposed to provide, and some efforts were made in 1978 to ban reaffirmations completely. Those efforts were unsuccessful, but a compromise was reached that surrounds reaffirmations with procedural safeguards. Note the extensive disclosures required by §§ 524(c), (d), and (k)–(m). Apply those sections to the following Problems.

Questions and Problems

1. You represent Debtor, who lives out in a rural area. Debtor's only source of income is disability benefits of $400 per month. Debtor wants to reaffirm a $5,000 debt owed to GMAC, which has a purchase money security interest in Debtor's car. It is Debtor's sole means of transportation to the doctor's office and grocery store. The car is currently worth only $3,500 and the monthly payment on the reaffirmed debt would be $220. Would you sign the affidavit required by § 524(c)(3)? Cf. *In re Delano*, 7 B.R. 72 (Bankr. D.Me.1980). If you refuse, what happens?

2. Debtor, who is represented by counsel, has signed an agreement reaffirming a debt. Debtor is notified of the reaffirmation hearing, but fails to appear. Is the reaffirmation enforceable? Compare *Sweet v. Bank of Oklahoma*, 954 F.2d 610 (10th Cir.1992), with *In re Fisher*, 113 B.R. 714 (Bankr. N.D.Okla.1990).

3. Debtor's car was subject to a security interest held by Credit Union, which had lent Debtor the money to purchase it. Debtor entered into a reaffirmation agreement with Credit Union, without assistance from her attorney, even though her disposable income was slightly less than the required payments on the obligation. (She was sure that she could economize on some of her expenses.) Does such an agreement require court approval?

4. Why did Congress not prohibit all reaffirmations? Can you see a reason for a debtor to reaffirm a debt owed an employer? A debt co-signed by a good friend? A debt nondischargeable under § 523(a)? A debt secured by a purchase money security interest in household goods?

Note on the Sears Reaffirmation Scandal

On November 14, 1996, Francis Latanowich sent a letter, handwritten on a yellow legal pad, to the bankruptcy court that had granted him a discharge in his Chapter 7 case the preceding April. He wrote:

> I took advice from a lawyer friend and he told me to keep some of my debts so I could start getting my credit back. * * * I have tried to meet the payment every month but it is keeping food off the table for my kids. I would like to know if you could reopen my case so I could get rid of all my debt forever.

Thus began a process that ultimately cost Sears almost half a billion dollars.

Latanowich owed Sears $1,161 when he filed bankruptcy. The obligation was secured by an automobile battery worth $75 and a television set worth $403. Sears told him he either had to return the items or reaffirm, and it offered to extend him an additional $200 in credit if he chose reaffirmation.

He signed. In the following seven months he charged purchases of $339 to his Sears card and made $375 in payments. With interest accruing on the prepetition debt, however, he owed Sears $160 more when he wrote the letter than he owed when he filed his bankruptcy petition.

The bankruptcy judge who got Latanowich's letter wanted to know why no reaffirmation to Sears was in the court's file. Dissatisfied with the proffered explanations, she ordered Sears to file a list of every case in the District of Massachusetts, from January 1, 1995 through January 29, 1997, in which Sears had obtained a reaffirmation agreement but had failed to file it with the court. Sears ultimately filed a list with an astonishing 2,733 cases on it. See *In re Latanowich*, 207 B.R. 326 (Bankr. D.Mass.1997). The ensuing investigation uncovered a nationwide, decade-long practice by Sears, as well as other retailers, of systematically and deliberately ignoring the requirements of § 524(c). As a result of these practices, Sears had improperly collected $110 million from 187,000 customers across the United States.

The company reacted by taking responsibility, cooperating with investigators, and making restitution to all affected customers. Almost $300 million went to debtors, both as refunds (plus interest) of $1.40 for every $1.00 improperly collected, and as forgiveness of debt for additional items they had purchased. Sears also paid over $40 million in civil penalties to the 50 states and $60 million to settle criminal bankruptcy fraud charges. In addition, the company settled a suit brought by shareholders who asserted that the scandal had hurt the value of their stock. Adding in legal fees and costs of researching its records, the scandal cost Sears approximately $475 million.

F. DISCRIMINATORY TREATMENT

The benefits of a discharge cannot be fully enjoyed if debtors are made to suffer various sorts of discrimination because of their resort to bankruptcy.

That understanding was at the heart of the Supreme Court's opinion in *Perez v. Campbell*, 402 U.S. 637, 91 S.Ct. 1704, 29 L.Ed.2d 233 (1971). *Perez* involved a statute that required debtors to pay tort judgments related to motor vehicle accidents, even if the judgments were discharged in bankruptcy, in order to retain their drivers' licenses. The Supreme Court invalidated the statute under the Supremacy Clause, holding that it frustrated bankruptcy's fresh start. Congress codified *Perez* in the 1978 Code, by enacting the prohibition against discrimination now found in § 525(a). Although the provision is narrowed by its limitation to governmental units and to discrimination *solely* on the basis of prior bankruptcy, the legislative history indicates that the section was not intended to be exclusive and that the courts should continue to develop the policy against discrimination.

Two subsequent additions to § 525 have made the Code some-what more protective of former debtors: subsection (b), added in 1984, which prohibits discrimination in private employment solely because of prior bankruptcy; and subsection (c), added in 1994, which prohibits denial of a student loan on the ground of bankruptcy. We begin with a case that discusses § 525(b).

BURNETT v. STEWART TITLE, INC. (IN RE BURNETT)

United States Court of Appeals, Fifth Circuit, 2011.
635 F.3d 169.

KING, Circuit Judge.

* * *

BACKGROUND

The facts of this case are straightforward. In September 2006, Shani Burnett filed a voluntary petition under Chapter 13 of the Bank-ruptcy Code. In July 2007, Burnett interviewed for prospective employment with Stewart Title, Inc. ("Stewart"), which made her an offer of employment contingent upon the results of a drug screening and background check. During the background check, Stewart dis-covered Burnett's bankruptcy and rescinded its offer on that basis.

Burnett filed suit against Stewart under § 525(b), asserting that Stewart unlawfully discriminated against her due to her bankruptcy status. Stewart filed a motion to dismiss under Rule 12(b)(6) for failure to state a claim. The bankruptcy court decided that § 525(b) does not prohibit private employers from engaging in discriminatory hiring on the basis of an applicant's bankruptcy status, and granted Stewart's motion to dismiss. The district court affirmed, and this appeal followed.

* * *

ANALYSIS

The single issue on appeal is whether a claim for discrimination is legally cognizable against a private employer that denies employment to an applicant solely on the basis of that person's status as a debtor in a bankruptcy proceeding. The governing statute is § 525, which provides two standards: one for government employers in § 525(a) and one for private employers in § 525(b). *[The Court quoted both subsections.]*

Burnett and amicus curiae contend that the act of denying employment to a person is to "discriminate with respect to employment against" that person, such that it is barred by the plain language of § 525(b). If § 525(b) were considered in isolation, Burnett's position may have merit. However, when interpreting the meaning of a phrase in a statute, the statute must be read as a whole * * * . In keeping with this rule, two basic canons of statutory construction guide our decision here.

First, "[w]here Congress includes particular language in one section of a statute but omits it in another section of the same Act, it is generally presumed that Congress acts intentionally and purposefully in the disparate inclusion or exclusion." *Russello v. United States*, 464 U.S. 16, 23 (1983) (citation and internal quotation marks omitted). Here, § 525(a) specifically states that a governmental unit may not "deny employment to, terminate the employment of, or discriminate with respect to employment against" a person on the basis of his or her bankruptcy status. Subsection (b), however, omits the prohibition against denying employment, stating only that a private employer may not "terminate the employment of, or discriminate with respect to employment against" such persons. Applying the *Russello* presumption, Congress's exclusion of the words "deny employment to" in subsection (b) was intentional and purposeful.

Second, when interpreting a statute, "it is a 'cardinal rule that a statute is to be read as a whole,' in order not to render portions of it inconsistent or devoid of meaning." *Zayler v. Dep't of Agric. (In re Supreme Beef Processors, Inc*.), 468 F.3d 248, 253 (5th Cir. 2006). To interpret the phrase "discriminate with respect to employment" to include the act of hiring would violate this canon by rendering superfluous the phrase "deny employment to" in § 525(a). Furthermore, if "discriminate with respect to employment" encompasses all employment-related actions, it would also render superfluous the phrase "terminate the employment of" in both § 525(a) and (b).

Applying these two canons of statutory construction to § 525(b), we conclude that Congress did not prohibit private employers from denying employment to persons based on their bankruptcy status. Our decision is in accord with the recent decision of our sister circuit in *Rea v. Federated Investors*, 627 F.3d 937 (3d. Cir. 2010), in which the Third Circuit held that "§ 525(b) does not create a cause of action against private employers who engage in discriminatory hiring." *Id.* at 938. We therefore reject the solitary view advanced in *Leary v. Warnaco, Inc.*, 251 B.R. 656 (S.D.N.Y. 2000), that Congress's omission of a specific reference to hiring in § 525(b), after expressly including it in § 525(a), was "simply because the scrivener was more verbose in writing § 525(a)," *id.* at 658. The view in *Leary* is contrary to overwhelming authority otherwise, and Burnett's reliance on it is misplaced. *See Rea*, 627 F.3d at 940 (collecting cases).

Nor are Burnett's other arguments convincing. Although § 525(b) was enacted six years after § 525(a), its language regarding employment discrimination is nearly identical to that used in § 525(a), implying that Congress modeled subsection (b) on subsection (a). Furthermore, Congress chose to place the two subsections directly adjacent to each other in the Bankruptcy Code, an unsurprising choice given that both subsections deal with the same subject: discrimination against debtors on the basis of their bankruptcy status. Finally, Congress is "presumed to have knowledge of its previous legislation when making new laws." *United States v. Zavala-Sustaita*, 214 F.3d 601, 606 n.8 (5th Cir. 2000) (citation and internal quotation marks omitted). Had Congress wished to bar private employers from discriminating against debtors in their hiring decisions, it could have done so by adding the phrase "deny employment" to subsection (b) when it amended § 525 in 1994 and again in 2005.

Burnett and amicus curiae also argue that application of the *Russello* presumption to this statute would "create an incoherent and inconsistent statutory scheme that would produce an untenable distinction between federal and private employers that would lead to the unreasonable result of allowing private employers to discriminate in an area that public employers could not." This is a policy argument best made to Congress, which intentionally and purposefully drew a line prohibiting governmental units, but not private employers, from denying employment to persons based on their status as debtors in bankruptcy proceedings.

CONCLUSION

The bankruptcy court and district court below properly held that § 525(b) does not prohibit private employers from denying employment to applicants based on their bankruptcy status. We therefore AFFIRM the judgment of the district court.

Questions and Problems

1. Do you agree with the court's reading of § 525(b)? Did the court give too little attention to the language stating that a private employer may not "discriminate with respect to employment"?

2. The other circuits seem to be falling in line with *Burnett*. In *Myers v. TooJay's Management Corp.*, 640 F.3d 1278 (11th Cir.2011), the debtor applied for a managerial position at a deli. He had an initial interview and then worked for two days, as an on-the-job evaluation, at half pay. During that time, he signed numerous forms and was given information about company policies. He was then scheduled to begin work with the deli. On the same day that he gave notice to his current employer, the deli sent a letter informing him that it was "necessary to rescind our previous offer of employment." He was later informed that the problem was a "financial matter"—namely, his prior bankruptcy filing—that the employer had discovered during the course of a credit check. He then sued, alleging, *inter alia*, a violation of § 525(b). The court found none, on reasoning similar to that of the Fifth Circuit in *Burnett*.

The cases are quite different factually, however, in that employment by the deli in *Myers* was a lengthy process. Myers had already worked at the deli—admittedly as part of the evaluation process—and had filled out numerous forms and been trained on company policies. Might principles of contract law permit a finding that Myers was already an employee? (As far as that is concerned, however, Burnett had already been offered employment and, presumably, had accepted.) If so, should that matter for purposes of § 525(b)?

A number of cases raise questions whether the rights asserted by the debtor constitute "a license, charter, franchise, or other similar grant." Not so in the following case, which involved the FCC's auction of licenses to use portions of the electromagnetic spectrum for personal communication services—that is, broadband PCS licenses. The parties conceded that a governmental unit had revoked a license granted to a debtor. That, however, was but the beginning.

FEDERAL COMMUNICATIONS COMM'N v. NEXTWAVE PERSONAL COMMUNICATIONS, INC.

United States Supreme Court, 2003.
537 U.S. 293, 123 S.Ct. 832, 154 L.Ed.2d 863.

JUSTICE SCALIA delivered the opinion of the Court.

In these cases, we decide whether § 525 of the Bankruptcy Code prohibits the Federal Communications Commission (FCC or

Commission) from revoking licenses held by a debtor in bankruptcy upon the debtor's failure to make timely payments owed to the Commission for purchase of the licenses.

I

[Acting under 1993 amendments to the Communications Act of 1934, requiring the FCC to disseminate spectrum licenses for broadband personal communications services to a wide variety of applicants, the agency held an auction for small businesses and allowed the winning bidders to pay over time. NextWave had the winning bid on two blocks of licenses, for just under $5 billion. It made a down-payment and signed promissory notes for the balance, executing security agreements that the FCC perfected. The licenses stated that they were "conditioned upon the full and timely payment of all monies due pursuant to * * * the terms of the Commission's installment plan as set forth in the Note and Security Agreement executed by the licensee," and that "failure to comply with this condition will result in the automatic cancellation of this authorization."

NextWave encountered difficulty in obtaining financing and the FCC agreed to restructure the payment obligations. When NextWave was unable to resume payments at the agreed-upon time, it filed Chapter 11 and proposed a plan to repay the remaining $4.3 billion obligation in a single lump-sum payment. The FCC objected to the plan on the grounds that the licenses had been automatically canceled when NextWave missed its payment deadline. NextWave argued that the FCC's cancellation of the licenses violated § 525.

The D.C. Circuit, ultimately, agreed with NextWave; the FCC appealed.]

II

The Administrative Procedure Act requires federal courts to set aside federal agency action that is "not in accordance with law"—which means, of course, *any* law, and not merely those laws that the agency itself is charged with administering. Respondent contends, and the Court of Appeals for the D.C. Circuit held, that the FCC's revocation of its licenses was not in accordance with § 525 of the Bankruptcy Code.

[The Court quoted § 525(a).]

No one disputes that the Commission is a "governmental unit" that has "revoked" a "license," nor that NextWave is a "debtor" under the Bankruptcy Act. Petitioners argue, however, that the FCC did not revoke respondent's licenses "solely because" of nonpayment, and that, in any event, NextWave's obligations are not "dischargeable" "debts" within the meaning of the Bankruptcy Code. They also argue that a contrary interpretation would unnecessarily bring § 525 into conflict with the Communications Act. We find none of these contentions persuasive, and discuss them in turn.

A

The FCC has not denied that the proximate cause for its cancellation of the licenses was NextWave's failure to make the payments that were due. It contends, however, that § 525 does not apply because the FCC had a "valid regulatory motive" for the cancellation. In our view, that factor is irrelevant. When the statute refers to failure to pay a debt as the sole cause of cancellation ("solely because"), it cannot reasonably be understood to include, among the other causes whose presence can preclude application of the prohibition, the governmental unit's *motive* in effecting the cancellation. Such a reading would deprive § 525 of all force. It is hard to imagine a situation in which a governmental unit would not have some further motive behind the cancellation—assuring the financial solvency of the licensed entity, or punishing lawlessness, or even (quite simply) making itself financially whole. Section 525 means nothing more or less than that the failure to pay a dischargeable debt must alone be the proximate cause of the cancellation—the act or event that triggers the agency's decision to cancel, whatever the agency's ultimate motive in pulling the trigger may be.

* * *

B

Petitioners contend that NextWave's license obligations to the Commission are not "debts that [are] dischargeable" in bankruptcy. § 525(a). First, the FCC argues that "regulatory conditions like the full and timely payment condition are not properly classified as 'debts' " under the Bankruptcy Code. In its view, the "financial nature of a condition" on a license "does not convert that condition into a debt." This is nothing more than a retooling of petitioners' recurrent theme that "regulatory conditions" should be exempt from § 525. No matter how the Commission casts it, the argument loses. Under the Bankruptcy Code, "debt" means "liability on a claim," § 101(12), and "claim," in turn, includes any "right to payment," § 101(5)(A). * * * In short, a debt is a debt, even when the obligation to pay it is also a regulatory condition.

Petitioners argue that respondent's obligations are not "dischargeable" in bankruptcy because it is beyond the jurisdictional authority of bankruptcy courts to alter or modify regulatory obligations. Dischargeability, however, is not tied to the existence of such authority. A preconfirmation debt is dischargeable unless it falls within an express exception to discharge. Subsection 1141(d) of the Bankruptcy Code states that, except as otherwise provided therein, the "confirmation of a plan [of reorganization] * * * discharges the debtor from *any debt* that arose before the date of such confirmation," § 1141(d)(1)(A) (emphasis added), and the only debts it excepts from that prescription are those described in § 523, see § 1141(d)(2). * * *

C

Finally, our interpretation of § 525 does not create any conflict with the Communications Act. It does not, as petitioners contend, obstruct the functioning of the auction provisions of 47 U.S.C. § 309(j), since nothing in those provisions demands that cancellation be the sanction for failure to make agreed-upon periodic payments. Indeed, nothing in those provisions even requires the Commission to permit payment to be made over time, rather than leaving it to impecunious bidders to finance the full purchase price with private lenders. What petitioners describe as a conflict boils down to nothing more than a policy preference on the FCC's part for (1) selling licenses on credit and (2) canceling licenses rather than asserting security interests in licenses when there is a default. Such administrative preferences cannot be the basis for denying respondent rights provided by the plain terms of a law. * * *

[JUSTICE BREYER, in a dissenting opinion, believed that the Government might have been able to show that revocation of the licenses had no relationship to the debt's dischargeability and would not otherwise interfere with the Code's fresh start goal. Thus, in JUSTICE BREYER's view, the judgment should have been vacated and the case remanded.]

Notes and Questions

1. Why would the FCC object to a plan under which it was to be fully paid? Might it have something to do with the current market value of the licenses?

2. Can the FCC's difficulties in this case be traced to its decision to act not only as a regulator, but also as a creditor? If so, was the FCC trying to obtain an advantage, through its regulatory authority, that would not be available to run-of-the-mill secured creditors?

3. Surely the regulatory motives argued by the FCC—to assure that licensees have the financial ability to provide the expected services to the public, and that the spectrum is used—are legitimate. Does this holding prevent the agency from fulfilling its duties in that respect?

4. NextWave could not reorganize without the licenses. Does that fact operate to highlight the conflict in this case between bankruptcy policies and the interests of the public at large? Is the Court sufficiently sensitive to the interests of the public?

5. Section 525's possible conflict with other statutory provisions—this time, another provision in the Bankruptcy Code—arose in *Stoltz v. Brattleboro Housing Authority (In re Stoltz)*, 315 F.3d 80 (2d Cir.2002). The first issue in the case—whether a debtor with a possessory interest in a residential lease has an "unexpired" lease that can be assumed under § 365—was resolved in the debtor's favor. She then confirmed a Chapter 13 plan permitting her to remain in possession of the premises and requiring payment of the rental arrearages over the course of several years. She defaulted two years later and requested conversion of her case to Chapter 7. The lease was deemed rejected, as required under of § 365(d)(1). BHA then sought relief from the automatic stay in order to evict Stoltz, arguing that § 525(a) does not protect a debtor from eviction when there is a payment default that would entitle nongovernmental landlords to relief from the stay. The court first held that a public housing lease is an "other similar grant" and that BHA was seeking to evict Stoltz "solely because" she failed to pay prepetition rent that was discharged in bankruptcy. The court then confronted the conflict between §§ 365 and 525(a):

> If we protect Stoltz from bankruptcy-based discrimination under § 525(a), we cannot allow BHA to evict her. If we do not allow BHA to evict Stoltz, however, then we cannot enforce the executory contract assumption requirements or the implications of rejection under § 365. Thus, we face a conflict between §§ 525(a) and 365 of the Bankruptcy Code. * * *

1. Specificity Analysis

Many courts have resolved this impasse by concluding that either § 525(a) or § 365 is the more specific provision and therefore trumps the other, more general provision. * * *

* * * Based on the text alone, without regard to each provision's meaning, § 365's claim to greater specificity, based on the invocation of the more specific word "lease" instead of the more general term "grant," seems no more compelling than § 525(a)'s claim to greater specificity, based on its use of the specific term "governmental unit," as compared to § 365's failure to discuss the public or private status of the grantor. Focusing on the meaning of §§ 525(a) and 365 in the housing context, however, makes plain that § 525(a) is the more specific provision. As discussed above, § 365 indicates that landlords (in general) may evict debtor-tenants for nonpayment of discharged prepetition rent. Section 525(a), on the other hand, specifically prohibits landlords who are also governmental units from evicting debtor-tenants solely because of nonpayment of discharged prepetition rent. Thus, these two sections dictate precisely opposite outcomes—except that § 365 applies to all landlords, whereas § 525(a) applies only to landlords which are also governmental units. Coupled with the district court's persuasive reasoning, our specificity analysis convinces us that § 525(a) is the more specific provision.

2. Sound Bankruptcy Policy

Our determination that § 525(a) should control on the basis of specificity is supported by sound public policy and the overarching goals of the Bankruptcy Code. The Code seeks to give debtors like Stoltz a fresh start. * * * Stoltz's fresh start would be thwarted if we were to permit BHA to evict her on the basis of nonpayment of debts discharged in bankruptcy.

* * *

Giving section 525(a) its full effect, however, will only marginally abbreviate the benefit BHA receives under § 365. It is undisputed that BHA, as a governmental unit, may not deny Stoltz a future public housing lease on the basis of the discharged prepetition rent. The only benefit BHA seeks, therefore, is eviction. Whether Stoltz remains in her apartment or is evicted and later readmitted to BHA's public housing, she is obligated to pay all postpetition rent. Neither Stoltz's discharge nor § 525(a) diminishes her obligation to pay postpetition rent, and the Code expressly prohibits Stoltz from receiving another discharge under bankruptcy for at least six years. § 727(a)(8). In the interim, Stoltz may be evicted if she breaches her lease by postpetition default. Therefore, all of BHA's creditor-interests are protected, regardless of whether Stoltz is evicted or not.

Given the serious harm posed to Stoltz's fresh start, and the minimal benefit BHA would receive, curtailment of BHA's state law remedy of eviction serves the sound public policy of granting debtors a fresh start and does the least mischief to the purposes underlying §§ 525(a) and 365 of the Bankruptcy Code. We therefore conclude that, when §§ 365(b) and 525(a) come "foot to foot" in the public housing context, § 365(b) must step aside and let § 525(a) pass.

Id. at 92-95.

Based on *NextWave* and *Stoltz*, do you think the courts are taking § 525 too far? Are governmental units now at an inappropriate disadvantage?

6. Colleges have, on occasion, refused to release copies of transcripts to students whose loans remain unpaid. Compare *In re Heath,* 3 B.R. 351 (Bankr.N.D.Ill.1980), with *Johnson v. Edinboro State College,* 728 F.2d 163 (3d Cir.1984). Transcripts, unlike new loan funds, have no intrinsic value to the college or university. What purpose other than collection could be furthered by refusing to release the transcript? Is that a basis for distinguishing cases in which debtors are seeking transcripts from cases in which debtors are seeking new loans? Does it matter, when debtors request copies of their college transcripts, whether the prior educational loan was discharged or was excepted from discharge?

7. May a state Board of Bar Examiners take a bankruptcy filing into account when assessing the fitness of an applicant to practice law? Cf. *Florida Board of Bar Examiners v. G.W.L.,* 364 So.2d 454 (Fla.1978); *Application of Gahan,* 279 N.W.2d 826 (Minn. 1979).

8. The General Services Administration, a federal agency, advertised used cars for sale. Small print at the bottom of the ad said "Credit terms available." When Michael Brown offered to buy a car, the GSA demanded cash because of Brown's recent bankruptcy. Has the GSA violated § 525?

9. Debtor is a sergeant in the armed forces with a top security clearance. If he is denied a transfer to the staff of the Joint Chiefs, solely on the grounds that he filed a bankruptcy petition, is § 525 violated? See *Applegate v. March (In re Applegate),* 64 B.R. 448 (Bankr. E.D.Va.1986).

Chapter 8

===

REORGANIZATION

A. INTRODUCTION

Chapter 11 is designed to accomplish the financial rehabilitation of, chiefly, business enterprises. (But individuals can take, and increasingly are taking, advantage of the benefits of Chapter 11. Remember *Toibb v. Radloff*?) Its underlying premise is that the assets of a particular enterprise are best used by being kept together so that the value of the going concern can be preserved. Given that premise, it may come as a shock to learn that most Chapter 11 cases do not culminate in the confirmation of a plan, much less its successful performance. One can only speculate as to why. Many of these firms, most likely, never belonged in Chapter 11 in the first place for one reason or another—they were bad business ideas from the beginning, or they were too far gone for resuscitation by the time bankruptcy was filed. Immediate liquidation, however, rarely serves a corporate debtor. Management personnel can remain in control as debtor-in-possession, preserving jobs for employees (and for themselves) while trying to reorganize, and they may also be able to preserve something for shareholders. Since many, if not most, Chapter 11 debtors are closely

731

held corporations, managers *are* shareholders. If the corporation is insolvent, the reorganization effort will be made with other people's money. The manager-shareholders will enjoy the upside benefit of a successful reorganization, but they may carry little of the downside risk. (Of course, the sole owner may have invested much of his or her personal wealth in the enterprise, and may have guaranteed the corporate obligations. In such a case, the shareholder-manager's financial future may be intertwined with that of the corporation.)

Another explanation, currently in vogue, for Chapter 11's fail-ure rate is that Chapter 11 is itself fundamentally flawed. The American Bankruptcy Institute's Commission to Study the Reform of Chapter 11 recently completed a two-year study of how well Chapter 11 is working, and how it might be improved in light of changes in the market and in practice. The Commission's purpose was to "propose reforms to Chapter 11 and related statutory provisions that will better balance the goals of effectuating the effective reorganization of business debtors—with the attendant preservation and expansion of jobs—and the maximization and realization of asset values for all creditors and stakeholders."

The Commission's final report detailed a number of specific principles, which were designed to:

- Reduce barriers to entry by providing debtors more flexi-bility in arranging debtor-in-possession financing, clari-fying lenders' rights in the chapter 11 case, disclosing additional information about the debtor to stakeholders, and providing a true breathing spell at the beginning of the case during which the debtor and its stakeholders can assess the situation and the restructuring alternatives;

- Facilitate more timely and efficient diligence, investi-gation, and resolution of disputed matters through an estate neutral * * * ;

- Enhance the debtor's restructuring options by eliminating the need for an accepting impaired class of claims to cram down a chapter 11 plan and by formalizing a process to permit the sale of all or substantially all of the debtor's assets outside the plan process, while strengthening the protection of creditors' rights in such situations;

- Incorporate checks and balances on the rights and remedies of the debtor and of creditors, including through valuation concepts that potentially enhance a debtor's liquidity during the case, permit secured creditors to realize the reorganization value of their collateral at the end of the case, and provide value allocation to junior creditors when supported by the reorganization value; and

■   Create an alternative restructuring scheme for small and medium-sized enterprises that would enable such enterprises to utilize chapter 11 and would enable the court to more efficiently oversee the enterprise through a bankruptcy process that incentivizes all parties, including enterprise founders and other equity security holders, to work collectively toward a successful restructuring.[a]

It remains to be seen whether any of the Commission's recommendations result in legislative changes to the Bankruptcy Code.

Since it was first enacted, Chapter 11 has provided relief to hundreds of businesses, and has brought us some remarkable (and sometimes successful) cases—A.H. Robins, Johns–Manville, LTV, Texaco and Eastern Airlines, just to name a few. Recall why these particular debtors filed bankruptcy and you will begin to appreciate the power and flexibility of Chapter 11: Robins and Manville were faced with enormous tort liabilities; LTV owed substantial environmental and pension plan obligations; Texaco could not afford the supersedeas bond necessary to stay Pennzoil's collection of its multi-billion dollar judgment during appeal; and Eastern had union troubles (among others). In cases such as these, Chapter 11 is theater, too.

B. AUTOMATIC STAY

Although you have already become familiar with the automatic stay, a few special applications arise in the context of a reorganization case, when the interests of the debtor are inextricably linked with the interests of various nondebtor entities. Those nondebtors may be individuals closely connected with the debtor, such as officers and directors. Or the nondebtor may be heavily involved in the bankruptcy proceeding as the insurer that issued a policy covering (arguably, perhaps) conduct by the debtor that forms the basis for extensive tort liability. In either case, continuation of legal process against those nondebtors may negatively impact the bankruptcy itself. The next case, which involved concerns of this type, illustrates the ways in which a bankruptcy court may be able to respond.

---

[a] www.commission.abi.org.

A.H. ROBINS CO. v. PICCININ

United States Court of Appeals, Fourth Circuit, 1986.
788 F.2d 994, *cert denied*, 479 U.S. 876, 107 S.Ct. 251, 93 L.Ed.2d 199 (1986).

RUSSELL, Circuit Judge.

Confronted, if not overwhelmed, with an avalanche of actions filed in various state and federal courts throughout the United States by citizens of this country as well as of foreign countries seeking damages for injuries allegedly sustained by the use of an intrauterine contraceptive device known as a Dalkon Shield, the manufacturer of the device, A.H. Robins Company, Incorporated (Robins) filed its petition under Chapter 11 of the Bankruptcy Code in August, 1985.

* * *

The filing of the Chapter 11 petition automatically stayed all suits against Robins itself under § 362(a) of the Bankruptcy Code, even though no formal order of stay was immediately entered. But a number of plaintiffs in suits where there were defendants other than Robins, sought to sever their actions against Robins and to proceed with their claims against the co-defendant or co-defendants. Robins responded to the move by filing an adversary proceeding in which it named as defendants the plaintiffs in eight such suits pending in various state and federal courts. In that proceeding, the debtor sought (1) declaratory relief adjudging that the debtor's products liability policy with Aetna Casualty and Insurance Company (Aetna) was an asset of the estate in which all the Dalkon Shield plaintiffs and claimants had an interest and (2) injunctive relief restraining the prosecution of the actions against its co-defendants. * * *

In his order granting the preliminary injunction, the district judge found (1) that continuation of litigation in the civil actions threatened property of Robins' estate, burdened and impeded Robins' reorganization effort, contravened the public interest, and rendered any plan of reorganization futile; (2) that this burden on Robins' estate outweighed any burden on the Dalkon claimants caused by enjoining their civil actions; and (3) that all remaining insurance coverage in favor of the debtor under its liability policy issued by Aetna was property of the Robins' Chapter 11 estate. The district judge then held that all actions for damages that might be satisfied from proceeds of the Aetna insurance policy were subject to the stay pursuant to § 362(a)(3) and enjoined further litigation in the eight civil actions, pursuant to § 362-(a)(1), (3) as supplemented by § 105.

Only the defendants Piccinin, the Mosas, and Conrad filed timely notices of appeal from the grant of the preliminary injunction. Their appeals, questioning the propriety of that preliminary injunction as against suits by Robins' co-defendants is the first of the issues now before this Court.

* * *

I

The initial question in the appeal of the first issue relates to the court's jurisdiction to grant a stay or injunction of suits in other courts against co-defendants of the debtor or of third parties; none of the parties herein contest the jurisdiction of the bankruptcy court to stay actions against the debtor itself in any court. Jurisdiction over suits involving co-defendants or third-parties may be bottomed on two statutory provisions of the Bankruptcy Act itself as well as on the general equitable powers of the court. The first of these statutory grants of jurisdiction is found in § 362. The purpose of this section by its various subsections is to protect the debtor from an uncontrollable scramble for its assets in a number of uncoordinated proceedings in different courts, to preclude one creditor from pursuing a remedy to the disadvantage of other creditors, and to provide the debtor and its executives with a reasonable respite from protracted litigation, during which they may have an opportunity to formulate a plan of reorganization for the debtor. * * *

Section 362 is broken down into several subsections, only two of which are relevant on this appeal. The first of such subsections is (a)(1), which imposes an automatic stay of any proceeding "commenced or [that] could have been commenced against the debtor" at the time of the filing of the Chapter 11 proceeding; the second is (a)(3), which provides similar relief against suits involving the possession or custody of property of the debtor, irrespective of whether the suits are against the debtor alone or others. We shall discuss the extent of jurisdiction given the bankruptcy court under these two subsections, beginning with (a)(1).

(a)

Subsection (a)(1) is generally said to be available only to the debtor, not third party defendants or co-defendants. * * * However, as the Court in *Johns–Manville Sales Corp.*, 26 B.R. 405, 410 (S.D.N.Y. 1983) remarked, * * * "there are cases [under § 362(a)(1)] where a bankruptcy court may properly stay the proceedings against non-bankrupt co-defendants" but, it adds, that in order for relief for such non-bankrupt defendants to be available under (a)(1), there must be "unusual circumstances" and certainly "'something more than the mere fact that one of the parties to the lawsuit has filed a Chapter 11 bankruptcy must be shown in order that proceedings be stayed against non-bankrupt parties.'" This "unusual situation," it would seem, arises when there is such identity between the debtor and the third-party defendant that the debtor may be said to be the real party defendant and that a judgment against the third-party defendant will in effect be a judgment or finding against the debtor. An illustration of such a situation would be a suit against a third-party who is entitled to absolute indemnity by the debtor on account of any judgment that might result against them in the case. To refuse application of the statutory stay in that case would defeat the very purpose and intent of the statute. * * *

(b)

But (a)(1), which stays actions against the debtor and arguably against those whose interests are so intimately intertwined with those of the debtor that the latter may be said to be the real party in interest, is not the only part of § 362 providing for an automatic stay of proceedings. Subsection (a)(3) directs stays of any action, *whether against the debtor or third-parties*, to obtain possession or to exercise control over property of the debtor. A key phrase in the construction and application of this section is, of course, "property" as that term is used in the Act. Section 541(a)(1) of the Bankruptcy Act defines "property" in the bankruptcy context. It provides that the "estate is comprised of all the following property, wherever located * * * all legal or equitable interests of the debtor in property as of the commencement of the case." * * *

Under the weight of authority, insurance contracts have been said to be embraced in this statutory definition of "property." * * * A products liability policy of the debtor is similarly within the principle: it is a valuable property of a debtor, particularly if the debtor is confronted with substantial liability claims within the coverage of the policy in which case the policy may well be, as one court has remarked in a case like the one under review, "the most important asset of [*i.e.*, the debtor's] estate," *In re Johns Manville Corp.*, 40 B.R. 219, 229 (S.D.N.Y.1984). Any action in which the judgment may diminish this "important asset" is unquestionably subject to a stay under this subsection. * * *

(c)

The statutory power of the bankruptcy court to stay actions involving the debtor or its property is not, however, limited to §§ 362-(a)(1) and (a)(3). It has been repeatedly held that § 105, which provides that the bankruptcy court "may issue any order, process, or judgment that is necessary or appropriate to carry out the provisions of this title," "empowers the bankruptcy court to enjoin parties other than the bankrupt" from commencing or continuing litigation. *In re Otero Mills, Inc.*, 25 B.R. 1018, 1020 (D.N.M.1982). In that case, the Court said:

> * * * Under the new Bankruptcy Code, the jurisdictional statute provides that the bankruptcy court shall have jurisdiction "of all civil proceedings arising under title 11 or arising in or related to cases under title 11." 28 U.S.C.A. § 1471. This broader jurisdictional statute, combined with § 105(a), grants the bankruptcy court power to enjoin parties from proceeding in state court against non-Bankrupts where the state proceeding is related to a case arising under Title 11.

In stating the same scope for § 105, the Court in *Johns–Manville Corp.*, 26 B.R. 420, 425 (S.D.N.Y.1983), * * * put the matter thus:

> * * *

> The exceptions to the automatic stay of § 362(a) which are set forth in § 362(b) are simply exceptions to the stay which protect the estate automatically at the commencement of the case and are not limitations upon the jurisdiction of the bankruptcy court or upon its power to enjoin. That power is generally based upon § 105 of the Code. The court will have ample power to enjoin actions excepted from the automatic stay which might interfere in the rehabilitative process whether in a liquidation or in a reorganization case.

Accepting that § 105 confers on the bankruptcy court power * * * to enjoin suits against parties in other courts, whether state or federal, it is necessary to mark out the circumstances under which the power or jurisdiction may be exercised. In *Otero Mills*, the Court approved a ruling that "to so enjoin a creditor's action against a third party, the court must find that failure to enjoin would effect [sic] the bankruptcy estate and would adversely or detrimentally influence and pressure the debtor through the third party." 25 B.R. at 1020. In *Johns–Manville*, the Court phrased somewhat fuller the circumstances when § 105 may support a stay:

> In the exercise of its authority under § 105, the Bankruptcy Court may use its injunctive authority to "protect the integrity of a bankrupt's estate and the Bankruptcy Court's custody thereof and to preserve to that Court the ability to exercise the authority delegated to it by Congress." Pursuant to the exercise of that authority the Court may issue or extend stays to enjoin a variety of proceedings [including discovery against the debtor or its officers and employees] which will have an adverse impact on the Debtor's ability to formulate a Chapter 11 plan.

40 B.R. at 226.

(d)

Beyond these statutory powers under § 362 and § 105 to enjoin other actions whether against the debtor or third-parties and in whatsoever court, the bankruptcy court under its comprehensive jurisdiction as conferred by 28 U.S.C. § 1334 has the "inherent power of courts under their general equity powers and in the efficient management of the dockets to grant relief" to grant a stay. *Williford v. Armstrong World Industries,* Inc., 715 F.2d 124, 127 (4th Cir.1983). In exercising such power the court, however, must "weigh competing interests and maintain an even balance" and must justify the stay "by clear and convincing circumstances outweighing potential harm to the party against whom it is operative." * * *

(e)

There are thus four grounds on which the bankruptcy court may enjoin suits against the bankrupt or its assets and property. In some instances only one of these grounds may be relevant; in an involved and complex case, several or even all of the grounds may require consideration. The present case is such an involved and complex case. It has a striking similarity to a Chapter 11 proceeding, initially begun in the bankruptcy court of the Southern District of New York, concerning the reorganization of the Johns–Manville Corporation. * * *

(f)

Johns–Manville, an asbestos producer, was beset by a mass of suits seeking large awards for damages sustained by reason of asbestos exposure much as has Robins in this case and, after suffering large and burdensome recoveries by plaintiffs and making substantial settlements in many of the cases, filed its Chapter 11 petition in the Southern District of New York in August, 1982. Such filing operated as an automatic stay of all proceedings against Johns–Manville. However, many of the thousands of cases named as defendants not only Johns–Manville but a number of other asbestos producers and dealers as co-defendants. Shortly after Johns–Manville filed its Chapter 11 petition, these co-defendants, charged in the complaints of the plaintiffs in the actions as joint tort feasors, sought judicial relief in the bankruptcy court, "inviting," that court by way of a declaratory judgment in the exercise of "its equitable powers" to enlarge the automatic stay provided by § 362 of the Act to include nondebtor defendants under the penumbra of § 362's protection" as well as under § 105, and to extend this stay throughout the nation to all asbestos litigation. The primary issue at this stage was stated to be whether this Court should take the unprecedented step of exercising its discretion pursuant to § 105 of the Code to extend the § 362 automatic stay so as to encompass the co-defendants herein." The bankruptcy court ruled, first, "that § 362 is limited in scope to the debtor and does not operate to stay actions against the co-defendants of this debtor." Secondly, it held that relief under § 105 is only available if found to be unnecessary or appropriate in order to achieve the goals of a Chapter 11 reorganization," and, even then, only after a finding that "a failure to enjoin would affect the bankruptcy estate and would adversely or detrimentally influence and pressure the debtor through that third-party," thereby justifying a finding of irreparable injury and likelihood of prevailing on the merits. None of these facts the court found present on the instant showing, but it added:

> In an appropriate case, where the proposed extension of the stay is designed to cover actions against entities that truly are inextricably interwoven with the debtor or which affect property of the debtor's estate, § 105 may be used. *In the instant case, such is not the situation as any liability of these co-defendants is not directly attributable to the debtor as it would be if these co-defendants were, for example, key employees of the debtor.*

Matter of Johns–Manville Corp., 26 B.R. 405, 418 (S.D.N.Y.1983) (italics in text). It concluded by declaring that there was "no basis [as shown by the record] to extend the § 362 stay to cover them [the appeals] by means of § 105."

A second action was begun shortly afterwards, this time by the debtor, to enjoin (1) the prosecution of "proceedings against Manville's employees, agents and others" and of discovery proceedings involving them in actions covering "the same issues and subject-matter as are involved in the stayed litigations against Manville," (2) " 'direct action' lawsuits against insurers and sureties of the debtor" since the coverage of such policies of insurance or suretyship "represented property of [the debtor's] estate which must be preserved for the benefit of all creditors," and (3) a suit brought by certain security holders against "various of the 'employees, agents and others' " in the district court of Colorado. *In re Johns–Manville Corp.*, 26 B.R. 420, 423 (S.D.N.Y.1983). It will be observed that this proceeding involved matters not litigated in the earlier proceeding; in fact, it involved actions against the debtor's employees for actions attributable to Manville, precisely the point which the court in the earlier case had said was not before it at that time. The bankruptcy court granted a temporary injunction against the continuance of either the suits or of discovery against present or future officers, employees and agents but refused a stay for past officers and employees. In reaching that conclusion it found that "in great measure the suits being pursued against Manville's officers and employees are in reality derivative of identical claims brought against Manville," which, if sustained against the officers and employees, would expose the estate "to claims for contribution and indemnification" and might result in collateral estoppel against the debtor "in subsequent actions." It accordingly held it proper to stay these actions and discovery "against [such] non-debtors which would frustrate the statutory scheme or impact adversely on a debtor's ability to formulate a plan or on the debtor's property." * * *

(g)

* * * In the three situations in which the defendants have challenged the injunction granted by the district judge [*i.e.*, the Mosa, Conrad and Piccinin cases], the only defendants other than the debtor, are the two Robins, Dr. Frederick A. Clark, Jr., Dr. Hugh J. Davis,[b] and the debtor's insurer Aetna. So far as the suits against the two Robins and Dr. Clark, those defendants were entitled to indemnification by the debtor under the corporate by-laws and the statutes of Virginia, the State of debtor's incorporation, and were, in addition, additional insureds under the debtor's insurance policy. Dr. Davis was the beneficiary of an express contract of indemnification on the part of Robins

---

[b] Dr. Davis was the principal developer of the Dalkon Shield, and Dr. Clark was the medical director for A.H. Robins Co. Eds.

and was, under a compromise agreement with Robins and Aetna, an additional insured under Robins' insurance policy. The Manville court had granted a preliminary injunction in favor of defendants in the same position as these defendants, as we have seen, on facts similar to those here, finding that the requirements of possible irreparable harm "had been satisfied by the showing * * * [that the suits against the defendants would represent] an immediate and irreparable impact on the pool of insurance assets, of the existence of sufficiently serious questions going to the merits," and of the tipping in the defendants' favor in the hardships in a balancing of the debtor's and the plaintiffs'. That court had previously disposed of the public interest being weighted in the debtor's favor: "Indeed, this Court finds the goal of removing all obstacles to plan formulation eminently praiseworthy and supports every lawful effort to foster this goal while protecting the due process rights of all constituencies." 26 B.R. at 428.

II.

The district court in this case * * * found, as had the *Johns–Manville* courts, that irreparable harm would be suffered by the debtor and by the defendants since any of these suits against these co-defendants if successful, would reduce and diminish the insurance fund or pool represented in Aetna's policy in favor of Robins and thereby affect the property of the debtor to the detriment of the debtor's creditors as a whole. The likelihood of success by the debtor under these circumstances appeared indisputable. The hardships which would be suffered irreparably by the debtor and by its creditors generally in permitting these plaintiffs to secure as it were a preference in the distribution of the insurance pool herein to which all creditors were entitled, together with the unquestioned public interest in promoting a viable reorganization of the debtor can be said to outweigh any contrary hardship to the plaintiffs. Such was the finding in the *Manville* cases and that finding does not appear unreasonable here.

* * *

Questions

1. The court justified the injunction vis-à-vis Aetna under § 362(a)(3), on the grounds that an insurance policy is property of the estate. Do you agree with that reasoning?

2. Whatever the merit of the court's reasoning regarding § 362(a)(3), it is inapplicable to the other defendants. What justifies an injunction as to Dr. Davis? As to Dr. Clark? In what way would continuation of the suit against

Drs. Davis and Clark "interfere with the rehabilitative process" (to use *Manville*'s phrase)? Did the court in *Piccinin* make such a finding?

3. What is the appropriate reach of § 105? Does a bankruptcy court not have power, under generally applicable law, to grant injunctive relief in a proper case in the absence of § 105?

4. Recall § 524(g), which codifies the trust device created in *Manville*, and the channeling injunction that effectuated it, for future asbestos cases. Even in such a case, the subsection would not be of assistance to nondebtor co-defendants seeking the benefit of the stay. The subsection supplements the injunctive effect of a confirmed plan, § 524(g)(1)(A), not the initial scope of the automatic stay. It expressly validates an injunction protecting third parties, but only third parties related to the debtor in specified ways, § 524(g)(4)(A). The relationship of co-defendant is not among those specified.

5. If courts are unduly stretching the automatic stay in cases like *Manville* and *Piccinin*, at least the bar is not permanent. Section 105, however, has been invoked not only to protect nondebtors under the automatic stay; it has also been relied upon by proponents of plan provisions that would release nondebtors and permanently enjoin any actions against them. A provision in the Continental Airlines reorganization plan, for example, enjoined shareholder suits against certain present and former directors and officers who were not themselves in bankruptcy. The bankruptcy and district courts upheld the provision, but the Third Circuit reversed, finding the provision legally and factually unsupportable. *Gillman v. Continental Airlines (In re Continental Airlines)*, 203 F.3d 203 (3d Cir.2000). The court recognized that other courts have "adopted a more flexible approach," notably in the Drexel, Manville and Robins bankruptcies, but the plans in those cases established trusts through which consideration was paid to the affected parties:

> A central focus of these three reorganizations was the global settlement of massive liabilities against the debtors and co-liable parties. Substantial debtor co-liable parties provided compensation to claimants in exchange for the release of their liabilities and made these reorganizations feasible.

* * *

* * * [T]he provision in the Continental Debtors' plan releasing and permanently enjoining Plaintiffs; lawsuits against the non-debtor D&O defendants does not pass muster under even the most flexible tests for the validity of non-debtor releases. The hallmarks of permissible non-consensual releases—fairness, necessity to the reorganization, and specific factual findings to support these conclusions—are all absent here.

Id. at 212-214 (footnote omitted). The court declined to take the opportunity to set out the circumstances under which such an injunction might be upheld.

———————

Single asset real estate cases (often called "SAREs," for short) are those in which the debtor's principal asset is a single piece of real property (frequently, a not-yet-completed development project) and the only large creditor is the undersecured mortgagee. Such debtors may have few, if any, employees, and only a small amount of unsecured debt. These debtors may be newly-created corporate entities, formed solely to act as transferee of the property at issue. Transfer of the property to a new corporation enables the transferor to insulate its other assets from bankruptcy and to obtain the benefits of the automatic stay for the troubled parcel. For this reason, these fact patterns have become known as the "new debtor syndrome." *In re N.R. Guaranteed Retirement, Inc.,* 112 B.R. 263, 273 (Bankr. N.D.Ill.), *aff'd,* 119 B.R. 149 (N.D.Ill.1990). Bankruptcy cases with this fact pattern are not new, but large numbers of them began to appear in the 1980s when the value of heavily encumbered parcels of land plummeted.

These cases raise questions that go to the heart of bankruptcy, chiefly because they do not present the "common pool" problem often identified as Chapter 11's fundamental jurisprudential justification. (Recall the Jackson excerpt in Chapter 2, Section A, of this casebook.) Instead, they involve the type of dispute between a debtor and one creditor for which state law remedies were designed. When these disputes are brought into bankruptcy, therefore, they raise serious questions regarding "good faith" and, ultimately, the appropriate function of bankruptcy. See, e.g., *Phoenix Piccadilly v. Life Insurance Co. of Virginia (In re Phoenix Piccadilly),* 849 F.2d 1393 (11th Cir.1988) (reprinted in Chapter 2, Section B.3 of this casebook); *Little Creek Development Co. v. Commonwealth Mortgage Corp. (Matter of Little Creek Development Co.),* 779 F.2d 1068 (5th Cir.1986).

Courts are particularly concerned that single asset real estate debtors, in order to avoid stay relief or dismissal, establish that a reorganization plan is feasible. Compare *In re 68 West 127 Street, LLC,* 285 B.R. 838 (Bankr. S.D.N.Y.2002) (refusing creditor's motion for relief from stay grounded on assertion of bad faith in case filed by debtor with no income and no employees hours before scheduled foreclosure of its only asset, an empty and derelict residential building, because debtor carried burden on key issue—that it could effectively reorganize in a reasonable time); with *In re JER/Jameson Mezz*

Borrower II LLC, 461 B.R. 293 (Bankr. D. Del.2011) (holding that Chapter 11 case commenced on eve of state court foreclosure proceeding, by single asset real estate debtor with few unsecured creditors other than attorneys and financial advisors, and with no reasonable prospect of reorganizing, had to be dismissed with prejudice on grounds of bad faith; "the inquiry of good faith is 'based more on an objective analysis of whether the debtor has sought to step outside the "equitable limitations" of Chapter 11 than the subjective intent of the debtor' ").

The court in the next case addressed the statutory requirements for a single asset real estate debtor.

IN RE OCEANSIDE MISSION ASSOCIATES

United States Bankruptcy Court, Southern District of California, 1996.
192 B.R. 232.

PETER W. BOWIE, Judge.

The senior secured creditor contends that this is a "single asset real estate" case and that the debtor must be held to the requirements of newly enacted § 362(d)(3).

* * *

The debtor, a limited partnership, owns undeveloped real property which generates no income. The property is subject to secured claims which exceed $4,000,000, but may be worth less than $4,000,000. The senior secured creditor has asked for relief from the automatic stay in part on the grounds that the property is "single asset real estate" and that the debtor has failed to comply with § 362(d)(3).

ANALYSIS

Section 218 of the Bankruptcy Reform Act of 1994 added two new subsections to the Bankruptcy Code to deal with the "single asset real estate" case. Section 101(51B) defines "single asset real estate" and § 362(d)(3) provides that the court shall grant relief from stay with respect to an act against "single asset real estate" unless the debtor has filed a plan or commenced interest payments within 90 days of the petition. It is undisputed that the debtor has failed to file a plan or commence payments within 90 days. The issue is whether the property is "single asset real estate."

[The court quoted § 101(51B).] The parties agree that the property is a "single property or project, other than residential real property with fewer than 4 residential units." The parties disagree as to whether § 101(51B) includes undeveloped or raw land that generates no income * * * .

1.   Must the Real Property Generate Income?

The definition of "single asset real estate" is limited to real property "which generates substantially all of the gross income of a debtor and on which no substantial business is being conducted by a debtor other than the business of operating the real property." Congress has obviously attempted to exclude certain debtors, but which ones? Section 101(51B) is clearly designed to exclude debtors that, although they own a single piece of property, have other income generating operations. The question is whether it is also meant to exclude debtors that own undeveloped land that generates no income. The language of the statute is, unfortunately, ambiguous.

Reading the first, or "gross income," clause to *include* raw land that generates no income is awkward but possible. If the debtor has no income, then substantially all of its income could be said to be generated by the property; i.e., substantially all of nothing is nothing. In addition to the awkwardness, this interpretation seems to render the second clause, "and on which no substantial business is being conducted by a debtor other than the business of operating the real property," superfluous. If the debtor has no "gross income," then the debtor is obviously not conducting "substantial business" on the property, or anywhere else for that matter. Conversely, a debtor operating a substantial business would not derive substantially all of its income from the property and would thus be excluded under either clause. It is well settled that statutes are to be interpreted so as to avoid rendering any portion superfluous. Thus, one might conclude that the two clauses are designed to exclude different types of property: the "gross income" clause to exclude property which generates no income and the "substantial business" clause to exclude restaurants, hotels, and the like. There are, however, problems with this interpretation.

Interpreting the statute to *exclude* raw land does not appear to serve the purpose of the statutory scheme. Sections 101(51B) and 362(d)(3) are designed to require debtors with "single asset real estate" to act in an expedited fashion. § 362(d)(3). The consequence of not acting quickly is that the automatic stay may be lifted without further ado. There is no apparent purpose for Congress to have excused debtors who own only raw land from this expedited program: If a debtor who owns an apartment complex is forced to act quickly why not a debtor who owns raw land? Legislative enactments are not to be construed as establishing statutory schemes that defeat the purpose of the statutes. Rather, appropriate statutory construction favors the more reasonable result. It is much more plausible that the "gross income" clause and the "substantial business" clause were both meant to exclude debtors who happen to own real property but who are also involved in income generating businesses in addition to ownership of the real property.

Since the language of § 101(51B) is unclear it is appropriate to look to the legislative history. With the Reform Act, Congress provided a "Section-By-Section Description" in which it paraphrased the definition of "single asset real estate":

Section 218. Single asset real estate

This section will add a new definition to the Code for "single asset real estate," meaning real property * * * which generates substantially all of the gross income of the debtor and has aggregate noncontingent, liquidated secured debts in an amount up to $4 million.

H.R. Rep. No. 835, 103rd Cong., 2d Sess. (1994), *reprinted in* 1994 U.S.C.C.A.N. at 3340. In describing the scope of "single asset real estate" Congress apparently found it unnecessary to use the "substantial business" clause. If the two clauses were meant to exclude different types of debtor, then the "substantial business" clause would have had to have been included in the paraphrase. Since it was not, one might conclude that both clauses were meant to exclude debtors with income generating operations beyond the real property. Other legislative history supports this conclusion.

Section 218 of the Reform Act can be traced back to § 211 of S. 1985 which provided:

"single asset real estate" means real property, other than residential real property with fewer than 4 residential units, which generates substantially all of the gross income of a debtor and on which no substantial business is being conducted by a debtor other than the business of operating the real property and activities incidental thereto * * * .

S. 1985, 102nd Cong., 2d Sess. § 211(a)(2) (1992). Senate Report 279 explained that "single asset real estate" was to be "limited to investment property of the debtor." S.Rep. No. 279, 102nd Cong., 2d Sess., May 7, 1992. Surely if any property is considered "investment property," raw, undeveloped land would be.

When faced with the task of interpreting "single asset real estate" the court in *In re Philmont Development Co.*, 181 B.R. 220 (Bankr. E.D.Pa.1995), found that the legislative history which accompanied the Reform Act was not particularly "illuminating." The court noted, however, that:

> The terms single asset case, or single asset real estate case, are well-known and often used colloquialisms which essentially refer to real estate entities attempting to cling to ownership of real property in a depressed market * * * rather than businesses involving manufacturing, sales or services. * * * The drafters of sections of (sic) 101(51B) and 362(d)(3) were aware of the colloquial use of the phrase "single asset real estate," and the Court believes that their intention in using that phrase grew out of its previous colloquial and common usage.

Id. at 223 (citations omitted.) It is well settled that where Congress uses terms that have accumulated settled meaning under the common law, a court should infer, unless the statute otherwise dictates, that Congress meant to incorporate the established meaning of these terms. In *In re KKEMKO, Inc.*, 181 B.R. 47 (Bankr. S.D.Ohio 1995), the court also looked to the history of the usage of the term "single asset real estate" and stated, albeit in dicta, that the definition in § 101(51B) did include raw land.

This Court has reviewed many of the cases that used the phrase "single asset real estate," and discovered several in which the phrase was applied to raw, undeveloped land.

If Congress intended to exclude raw land from the definition they would have done so specifically or at least explained in the comments that the definition was meant to exclude raw land. Without such an express exclusion this court does not believe that Congress meant for "single asset real estate" to mean less than it did before the sections were enacted. Although it requires a bit of a tortured reading, based upon the statutory purpose of the new sections, the limited legislative history, the usage of the term "single asset real estate" in prior case law and the fact that excluding raw land would simply not make sense, this

Court concludes that "single asset real estate" includes undeveloped real property which generates no income.

* * *

Notes

1. The cases seem to be in agreement with *Oceanside* that debtors whose only asset is raw land may nonetheless be subject to § 362(d)(3). See *In re Pensignorkay, Inc.*, 204 B.R. 676 (Bankr. E.D.Pa.1997) ("[T]he fact that the real property is currently undeveloped and not generating any income for the Debtor is of little consequence for purposes of the inquiry here, since the Court is satisfied that Congress did not intend to excuse from compliance with the revised statute the class of debtors who hold undeveloped tracts of land for future development."); *In re KKEMKO, Inc.*, 181 B.R. 47 (Bankr. S.D. Ohio 1995).

2. In addition to the special automatic stay provision for SAREs, found in § 362(d)(3), the Code also includes an automatic stay exception applicable only to small businesses—§ 362(n). A small business is one engaged in commercial or business activities (other than owning or operating real estate) with no more than $2 million in secured and unsecured debts owed to noninsiders and nonaffiliates. § 101(51D). The definition also requires either that the US Trustee has not appointed a creditors committee, or that the committee is not active enough to provide sufficient oversight.

Section 362(n)(1) provides that the automatic stay is inapplicable in four instances: (A) the debtor is a small business and has another case currently pending (which, one presumes, triggered an automatic stay); (B) the debtor is a small business and a prior case was dismissed in the preceding two years; (C) the debtor is a small business that had a plan confirmed in a prior case in the preceding two years; or (D) the debtor acquired the assets of a small business described in (A), (B) or (C). The automatic stay exception of § 362(n)(1) will not apply, however, to a noncollusive involuntary case, or if the second filing was necessitated by circumstances beyond the debtor's control and a court is likely to confirm a nonliquidating plan within a reasonable time.

C. CONTROLLING THE DEBTOR

Appointment of a trustee is unusual in a Chapter 11 case, as you already know. Ordinarily, the debtor becomes debtor-in-possession, exercising the powers of a trustee, § 1107(a), and the old managers stay in place. (Yes, the same folks who rode the corporation into bankruptcy in the first place.) Section 1104(a) sets out two grounds for appointment of a trustee, however—for "cause" and "in the interests of creditors" and other parties. Congress intended that a trustee be appointed only "if the protection afforded by a trustee is needed and the costs and expenses of a trustee would not be disproportionately higher than the value of the protection afforded." H.R. Rep. No. 595, 95th Cong., 1st Sess. 402 (1977). Cases interpreting § 1104(a) have not developed hard and fast rules; rather, courts look to the effect that appointment, or refusal to appoint, will have on the reorganization effort. Under that kind of standard, the outcome in the following case is unsurprising.

IN RE MARVEL ENTERTAINMENT GROUP, INC.

United States Court of Appeals, Third Circuit, 1998.
140 F.3d 463.

ALDISERT, Circuit Judge.

These expedited and consolidated appeals require us to decide if the district court properly exercised its discretion by appointing a trustee in the bankruptcy of Marvel Entertainment Group, Inc., because of the extreme acrimony between the debtor-in-possession and the creditors. * * * We will affirm the appointment of the trustee * * * .

I.

Marvel and various corporate affiliates filed chapter 11 petitions on December 27, 1996 and continued to run Marvel as debtor-in-possession. Approximately 1,700 creditors held $1 billion in claims against the Marvel estate.

Both before and after the filing of the petitions, Westgate International, L.P. and High River Limited Partnership, each controlled by Carl Icahn, (the "Icahn interests"), purchased at a discount a substantial number of pre-petition debt claims and bonds which had been issued by several holding companies owning all or substantially all of Marvel's stock. These holding companies, under the control of Ronald Perelman, had pledged their Marvel stock as security for the bonds. Two groups loomed large in the bankruptcy proceedings: one was an Official Bondholders' Committee and an indenture trustee, LaSalle National Bank, chosen to act primarily on behalf of the Icahn interests; the other, various creditors of Marvel, known as "the Lenders," who held over $600 million in debt claims at the time of the filings, secured by all of Marvel's assets.

From the start of the proceedings, disputes arose among the various parties, especially between the Icahn interests and the Lenders. The Icahn interests opposed an initial bankruptcy financing plan submitted by the Perelman holding companies, under which the holding companies would have infused $100 million into Marvel in return for priority recognition of the Lenders' debt claims. The Icahn interests contended that the Perelman-controlled Marvel debtors were favoring their "lender accomplices" to ensure that "Perelman re-acquires control of Marvel, without competitive bidding, for an obscenely low price." Notwithstanding the Icahn interests' objections, the bankruptcy court approved the financing plan.

From January through June of 1997, tension arose between the Lenders and the Icahn interests. The Icahn interests fought to take control of the Marvel board of directors. Substantial litigation went forward. On January 13, 1997, the Icahn interests moved the bankruptcy court to lift the automatic bankruptcy stay, § 362(a)(3), so they could foreclose on the holding companies' defaulted bonds and vote the pledged stock. Marvel sought a temporary restraining order from the bankruptcy court to enjoin the Icahn interests from voting the stock and replacing Marvel's board of directors. The bankruptcy court issued the order on March 24, 1997. On the same day, the Lenders moved the bankruptcy court for an order appointing a responsible officer to take control of the bankruptcy, or in the alternative a trustee. That same month, the Icahn interests took significant steps toward gaining control of Marvel. They offered to infuse $365 million into Marvel, partially for operation of its business but mostly to repay $300 million of its secured debt, in return for "exclusive" control of Marvel's operations. Through their agent Chase Manhattan Bank, the Lenders vigorously opposed this plan, explaining that the Icahn interests had presented no "concrete turn-around strategy * * * or a management team capable of executing one."

On May 14, 1997, the district court vacated the bankruptcy court's temporary restraining order, permitting the Icahn interests to vote the pledged stock. With the lifting of the restraining order, the litigation ended and the inevitable took place—on June 20, 1997, the Icahn interests took control of Marvel. Thus, an anomaly arose. The Icahn interests began to wear two hats—one as creditors of the holding companies that controlled Marvel; the other as the debtor-in-possession of Marvel.

Settlement negotiations proceeded throughout the summer of 1997. The new Icahn-controlled debtor-in-possession proposed a settlement in which the Icahn interests would control a newly-organized Marvel company merged with its affiliate Toy Biz, and would purchase the Lenders' claims at a substantial discount. To consummate the settlement, it was necessary to obtain the approval of two-thirds of all creditors as required under the Bankruptcy Code, § 1126(c). The Lenders were not successful in obtaining this approval.

The parties tried again. Another proposed settlement was attempted by the Icahn interests, this time with Chase directly as one of the Lenders. The terms were similar to those contained in the first effort, but this time Chase was required to sell its claims to the Icahn interests for even less than what was offered under the former proposal. Moreover, the settlement proposal required the creditors to support the Icahn interests' control of all Marvel entities and to agree to place High River's and Westgate's debt claims into a priority secured position. The necessary two-thirds approval not forthcoming, the settlement negotiations collapsed in October 1997.

On October 30, 1997, the Icahn-controlled debtor-in-possession commenced adverse litigation in the district court against the Perelman holding companies, the Lenders and other creditors in the Marvel bankruptcy (the "Perelman litigation"). It asserted 19 causes of action alleging breach of fiduciary duty, fraudulent conveyance, preferential transfer and breach of contract. The complaint sought to void the Lenders' claims or to subordinate them to the claims of High River and Westgate. The complaint described an alleged conspiracy between Toy Biz, the former Marvel board and the Lenders to "sabotage" the new Icahn-controlled debtor-in-possession's reorganization efforts. At the same time, the Icahn interests moved the district court for an order withdrawing the chapter 11 petitions and all related matters in the bankruptcy court and removing them to the district court to be heard in conjunction with the Perelman litigation. The Lenders opposed this withdrawal and renewed their motion before the bankruptcy court for the appointment of a trustee.

* * *

At a district court hearing on November 13, 1997, all parties agreed to the withdrawal of the Marvel cases from the bankruptcy court and their transfer to the district court. The district court then heard argument on whether a trustee should be appointed. The argument was summarized by the court:

In opposing the motion, the Debtors accuse the Lenders, and specifically Chase, of flip-flopping on positions throughout the life of this proceeding, whenever it suits their purposes. The Debtors describe the reorganization plan of the Lenders and Toy Biz as illegal, and claim that the Lenders have no desire that a neutral trustee be appointed. * * * They claim that the Lenders have put a strangle-hold on the Debtor's financing, and that the Lenders are responsible for failure of both the Settlement and the Second Settlement. They also repeat many of the allegations made in the Perelman litigation. * * *

The Creditors Committee describes the relationship between the Icahn interests and the Lenders as having reached an "impasse." * * *

In support of their motion, the Lenders accuse the Icahn interests of an elaborate scheme to take over Marvel at a discount price while diminishing the value of the Lender's claims on the company as creditors. They claim that the Perelman litigation is part of that scheme, and was brought, at least in part, as a weapon to punish the Lenders for not consummating the two Settlements. * * * The Lenders claim that the present board is incapable of neutrality, and is guilty of breaching its fiduciary duties to creditors.

On December 12, 1997, the district court granted the motion authorizing the United States Trustee to appoint a trustee. Appealing that order are Marvel and the Icahn interests which control it.

* * *

III.

Under the Bankruptcy Code, the district court was empowered to appoint a trustee: *[the court quoted § 1104(a)]*. The party moving for appointment of a trustee, in this case the Lenders, must prove the need for a trustee under either subsection by clear and convincing evidence. "It is settled that appointment of a trustee should be the exception, rather than the rule." *In re Sharon Steel Corp.*, 871 F.2d 1217, 1225 (3d Cir.1989). In the usual chapter 11 proceeding, the debtor remains in possession throughout reorganization because "current management is generally best suited to orchestrate the process of rehabilitation for the benefit of creditors and other interests of the estate." *In re V. Savino Oil & Heating Co.*, 99 B.R. 518, 524 (Bankr. E.D.N.Y.

1989). Thus, the basis for the strong presumption against appointing an outside trustee is that there is often no need for one: "The debtor-in-possession is a fiduciary of the creditors and, as a result, has an obligation to refrain from acting in a manner which could damage the estate, or hinder a successful reorganization." *Petit v. New England Mort. Servs.*, 182 B.R. 64, 69 (D.Me.1995) (internal quotations omitted). The strong presumption also finds its basis in the debtor-in-possession's usual familiarity with the business it had already been managing at the time of the bankruptcy filing, often making it the best party to conduct operations during the reorganization. The facts here, however, militate against invoking this presumption. The Icahn interests took control over Marvel's management six months after the chapter 11 filing. We are not confronted with a debtor who possesses extensive familiarity with the company's operations. It is therefore inappropriate to suggest that the usual presumption should be applied to a Johnny-come-lately debtor-in-possession, especially one that is also a substantial creditor.

The district court determined that the Icahn interests were "unable to resolve conflicts" with creditors of the estate. On the basis of this acrimony, it ordered the appointment of a trustee. We hold that the district court did not abuse its discretion because (A) this acrimony rises to the level of "cause" under § 1104(a)(1), and (B) a trustee would serve the best interests of the parties and estate.

A.

We have not heretofore addressed the question of whether acrimony between debtor and creditor in a bankruptcy case may rise to the level of "cause" necessitating the appointment of a trustee under § 1104(a)(1). Cf. *Sharon Steel*, 871 F.2d at 1228 (finding "cause" due to debtor-in-possession's gross mismanagement of estate and internal conflicts of interest). * * * A review of cases from other circuits, as well as the policies behind the appointment of a trustee, demonstrates that the district court here properly exercised its discretion by invoking § 1104(a)(1) to reach its conclusion.

It is significant that the language of § 1104(a)(1) does not promulgate an exclusive list of causes for which a trustee must be appointed, but rather provides that a trustee shall be appointed "for cause, including fraud, dishonesty, incompetence, or gross mismanagement * * * or similar cause." The Court of Appeals for the Fourth Circuit has recognized that "the concepts of incompetence, dishonesty, gross mismanagement and even fraud all cover a wide range of conduct," and courts must be given the discretion necessary to determine if the debtor-in-possession's "conduct shown rises to a level sufficient to warrant the appointment of a trustee." *Committee of Dalkon Shield Claimants v. A.H. Robins Co.*, 828 F.2d 239, 242 (4th Cir.1987) (internal quotation omitted). This discretionary authority is consistent with a "policy of flexibility" permeating the Bankruptcy Code's overall aim of protecting creditors while giving debtors a second chance. The Code itself, therefore, does not prohibit the appointment of a trustee based on a finding of acrimony between debtor and creditor, parties whose interests must be balanced and protected under the discretion of the courts.

Moreover, we are impressed by the persuasive reasoning in *In re Cajun Elec. Power Coop., Inc.*, 74 F.3d 599, 600 (5th Cir.) (adopting on rehearing the opinion of dissent in 69 F.3d at 751), *cert. denied*, 519 U.S. 808, 117 S.Ct. 51, 136 L.Ed.2d 15 (1996), in which the court upheld a trustee appointment based on a finding of acrimony. In that case, the debtor-in-possession's interests conflicted with those of its creditors to such an extent that "the appointment of a trustee may be the only effective way to pursue reorganization." The debtor-in-possession was a utility coop-erative whose board members were faced with a federal agency order lowering its utility rates. The debtor-in-possession's board members, themselves managers or members of the debtor-in-possession's individ-ual member utility companies, were required to decide whether to appeal the agency order, seeking to maintain the high rates charged to the individual member companies and thus to better enable the debtor-in-possession to meet its debt obligations to its creditors in bankruptcy, or to take no action and charge less to their individual companies. The court recognized that the debtor-creditor conflict went "beyond the 'inherent' conflicts under which all healthy cooperatives operate." 74 F.3d at 600 (adopting dissent at 69 F.3d at 751). The extent of this conflict alone provided sufficient cause for the appointment of a trustee under § 1104(a)(1).

In *Cajun Electric*, the court recognized that all cooperatives operate amidst certain "inherent" conflicts of interest, but rejected the notion that its holding created a "'per se rule' under which any coopera-tive seeking Chapter 11 protection would be automatically subject to the appointment of a trustee." Rather, the teachings of this case are that a district court may find cause to appoint a trustee for "acrimony" only on a case-by-case basis, when the inherent conflicts extend beyond the healthy conflicts that always exist between debtor and creditor, or as it found in that case, when the parties "begin working at cross-purposes."

We therefore adopt the reasoning in *Cajun Electric*, and apply its teachings to the case at bar. Here the district court found that "the

Debtors, as controlled by the Icahn interests, and the Lenders, take dramatically different stances on many issues." Citing (1) the debtor-in-possession's institution of several adversary actions, (2) the unconsummated settlements, (3) the U.S. Trustee's opinion "that the parties seem to be unable to reach a consensus" and (4) its observations that "the Debtors and the Lenders have flung accusations at each other, and have failed to demonstrate any ability to resolve matters cooperatively," the district court concluded that "there is no reasonable likelihood of any cooperation between the parties in the near future." As in *Cajun Electric*, the district court did not clearly err, based on its review of these events, when it found a deep conflict to exist between the Icahn-controlled debtor-in-possession and the creditors in bankruptcy. Also like *Cajun Electric*, "this is a large and messy bankruptcy that promises to get worse without a disinterested administrator at the helm."

We expressly hold that there is no per se rule by which mere conflicts or acrimony between debtor and creditor mandate the appointment of a trustee. In this case, rather, we are faced with circumstances in which the Icahn interests, themselves creditors of the Perelman holding companies, are currently in control of the debtor at the same time that the debtor proposes reorganization plans. In this position, although the Icahn interests are technically and officially fiduciaries to all creditors, they would also be placed in an awkward position of evaluating their own indenture and debt claims. Having found that this unhealthy conflict of interest was manifest in the "deep-seeded conflict and animosity" between the Icahn-controlled debtor and the Lenders and in the lack of confidence all creditors had in the Icahn interests' ability to act as fiduciaries, the district court did not depart from the proper exercise of discretion when it determined sufficient cause existed under § 1104-(a)(1) to appoint a neutral trustee to facilitate reorganization.

We reject the Icahn interests' argument that unhappy creditors involved in future bankruptcies could remove the debtors-in-possession by their obstinate refusal to cooperate. We are not impressed by this *argumentum ad terrorem*. In the view we take, it is within the district court's sound discretion to make a determination of cause, and this requires fact-finding and application of the facts to relevant precepts. The district court here determined that the Icahn interests were not entirely without blame for the breakdown of reorganization efforts with the Lenders * * * .

Finally, the policies behind the appointment of a trustee support our conclusion. The appointment of a trustee is the installation of a court officer charged with fiduciary duties. The district court's determination that cause existed to appoint an independent trustee based on the Icahn interests' actions is a recognition of their failure to assume these duties. When the chapter 11 petition was filed in this case, the debtor-in-possession assumed the same fiduciary duties as would an appointed trustee; the Icahn interests later stepped into this fiduciary position when they took control of Marvel. These obligations include "open, honest and straightforward disclosure to the Court and creditors." *See V. Savino Oil*, 99 B.R. at 526. The Icahn interests' actions surrounding the Perelman litigation fall short of this fiduciary benchmark. Also among the fiduciary obligations of a debtor-in-possession is the "duty to protect and conserve property in its possession for the benefit of creditors." *In re Ionosphere Clubs, Inc.*, 113 B.R. 164, 169 (Bankr. S.D.N.Y.1990). The intense and high-stakes bickering between the Icahn interests and the Lenders does not instill confidence that the Icahn interests could fairly negotiate with the creditors to whom they owe these duties, nor that reorganization will occur effectively.

As one bankruptcy court has noted:

The willingness of Congress to leave a debtor-in-possession is premised on an expectation that current management can be depended upon to carry out the fiduciary responsibilities of a trustee. And if the debtor-in-possession defaults in this respect, § 1104(a)(1) commands that the stewardship of the reorganization effort must be turned over to an independent trustee.

V. Savino Oil, 99 B.R. at 526. Here, the district court acted within the proper bounds of discretion in appointing a trustee under § 1104(a)(1) because of the Icahn interests' contribution to the acrimony with Marvel's creditors.

B.

Unlike § 1104(a)(1), which provides for mandatory appointment upon a specific finding of cause, § 1104(a)(2) "envisions a flexible standard." It gives the district court discretion to appoint a trustee "when to do so would serve the parties' and estate's interests." *Sharon Steel*, 871 F.2d at 1226. Here the court found that "deep seeded conflict and animosity between a debtor and its creditors" is at the heart of this bankruptcy case, thus "the selection of a plan, whatever its details, is in the best interests of all parties, and the best way to achieve that result is to appoint a trustee." Even if we were of the view that the appointment of a trustee was not mandated by the analysis required in § 1104(a)(1), we are satisfied that the district court's determination would come within proper exercise of discretion under the flexible § 1104(a)(2) standard. The level of acrimony found to exist in this case certainly makes the appointment of a trustee in the best interests of the parties and the estate.

* * *

We also reject the Icahn interests' arguments that the district court must apply a strict cost-benefit analysis when deciding to appoint a trustee. This is a case of profound financial magnitude, involving approximately $1 billion in claims against the estate. *See In re Sharon Steel Corp.*, 86 B.R. 455, 466 (W.D.Pa.1988) ("In a case of this magnitude, the cost of having a trustee in place is insignificant when compared with the other costs of administration and when compared with the enormous benefit to be achieved by the establishment of trust and confidence in * * * management.").

Neither did the court abuse its discretion by deciding not to appoint an examiner in the trustee's stead: "I'm just not convinced that an examiner is going to get done what needs to get done here. I think we need a decision-maker to come in and make some decisions." Under the Bankruptcy Code, a trustee is given all the powers of an examiner to analyze and report on the interests of the parties and actions of the debtor, but is also given the power to act on behalf of the estate, including the filing of a reorganization plan. §§ 1106(a)(5), (b). An examiner is not a substitute for a trustee. The district court need not have favored the appointment of an examiner here, especially after finding that a trustee is the more appropriate position.

Whether viewed from § 1104(a)(1) or (a)(2), the district court acted within appropriate bounds of discretion in appointing a trustee to act as a neutral and efficient fiduciary in this complicated bankruptcy under the circumstances of the strife-ridden history presented here.

* * *

Notes and Questions

1. Why did the court find that both §§ 1104(a)(1) and (a)(2) were satisfied? Do you understand the differences between the two subsections?

2. Is it so clearly correct that unhappy creditors could not obtain the appointment of a trustee "by their obstinate refusal to cooperate" with the debtor-in-possession? Consider the situation in the Eastern Airlines bankruptcy, described by the court in *In re Ionosphere Clubs, Inc.*, 113 B.R. 164 (Bankr.S.D.N.Y.1990). There, the creditors (including labor unions) became

disaffected with the leadership of Frank Lorenzo, who was in charge of Eastern, as huge operating losses were coupled with an inability to make operating projections and to formulate a long-range business plan. Some commentators might describe the stance taken by those creditors as an "obstinate refusal to cooperate"; others—including the creditors themselves—would no doubt take the position that ample reasons were presented. Where is the line between "obstinate refusal" and a good faith throwing in of the towel?

3. Why did Congress have such a strong preference for the retention of old management?

4. Old managers are not the only ones in control of the debtor-in-possession. The managers are themselves controlled by the corporation's board of directors. Board members, in turn, answer to the shareholders—*if* the shareholders are able to call a shareholders' meeting. In *Manville Corp. v. Equity Security Holders Committee (In re Johns–Manville Corp.)*, 801 F.2d 60 (2d Cir.1986), members of Manville's equityholders' Committee were cut out of negotiations that led to a plan diluting equity by 90%. They brought a state court action to compel Manville to call a shareholders' meeting, hoping to replace Manville's directors with individuals who would reconsider the proposed plan. Manville obtained a bankruptcy court injunction, by summary judgment, prohibiting the state proceeding on the grounds that it would obstruct the reorganization effort. The district court affirmed, but the Second Circuit reversed and remanded. The court held that shareholders' rights to govern a corporation—including the right to compel a shareholders' meeting for the purpose of replacing management—continue during bankruptcy and can be curtailed only for "clear abuse." The desire to obtain bargaining power, without more, is not such an abuse. Unless equityholders bargain in bad faith, demonstrating a willingness to risk the rehabilitation altogether in order to get a larger share, their interest in negotiating for a larger share is protected. Whether a shareholders' meeting would cause irreparable harm was a triable issue of fact and summary judgment should not have been awarded. The court remanded the case, over a dissent arguing that the lower courts had made the necessary findings the first time around.

On remand, and after trial, the bankruptcy court found—unsurprisingly—that a shareholders' meeting posed a "serious threat and real jeopardy" to Manville's reorganization. 66 B.R. 517, 534 (Bankr. S.D.N.Y.1986). The court found "that it has always been and still remains the *in terrorem* intent of [one shareholder group] to call a shareholders meeting, *with a full awareness of the devastating consequences to the fabric of the reorganization*, in order to elect a new Board of Directors *who will withdraw or substantially modify the present plan of reorganization*." *Id*. at 535. In light of doubt that new directors could achieve a consensual plan within a reasonable time, the court found that the call for a shareholders' meeting was a "clear abuse." *Id*. at 541. So perhaps the dissent was right—remand accomplished little more than requiring clarity in the bankruptcy court's order.

Notice, in *Marvel Entertainment*, that the Icahn interests took control after waging a battle—successfully, in that case—to call a shareholders' meeting.

5. The Second Circuit, in the course of its decision in *Manville*, suggested that a different result might be reached if a debtor were insolvent, "because the shareholders would no longer be real parties in interest." Why is that so?

The converse of efforts to replace current management are incentives designed to prevent them from being lured away by other, presumably solvent, enterprises. How better to do that than with money?

Prior to the enactment of BAPCPA, business debtors routinely utilized "key employee retention plans" or "KERPs" to compensate employees deemed essential to the business generally or to reorganization efforts in particular. Relying on §§ 105(a) and 363(b)(1), courts applied the deferential "business judgment" standard to assess these programs and approved plans found to be fair and reasonable. See, e.g., *In re U.S. Airways, Inc.*, 329 B.R. 793, 797 (Bankr. E.D. Va.2005); *In re Montgomery Ward Holding Corp.*, 242 B.R. 147 (D. Del.1999).

BAPCPA amended § 503(c), sharply restricting the incentives debtors can offer key employees. Specifically, § 503(c)(1) bans payment of retention bonuses to insiders as administrative expenses unless (a) payment is essential to retention of an employee who has received a bona fide job offer from another company at the same or greater rate of compensation; (b) services provided by the employee are essential to the survival of the debtor; and (c) the amount of the payment does not exceed either (i) 10 times the mean amount of similar transfers paid to nonexecutive employees for any purpose during the same calendar year, or (ii) if there are no such transfers, 25 percent of the amount of any similar transfer to the particular employee for any purpose during the preceding calendar year. Section 503(c)(2) prohibits severance payments except under narrow specified circumstances, and § 503(c)(3) prohibits payments outside the ordinary course of the debtor's business that are not justified by the circumstances of the case, including amounts paid to officers, managers or consultants hired after the commencement of bankruptcy.

KERPS have survived notwithstanding § 503's limitations, although debtors have been creative in characterizing the payments.

Clever debtors have designed their programs as "incentive" rather than "retention" plans. Arguably, incentive plans do not fall under the retention-based programs contemplated in §§ 503(c)(1) and (2), but are governed by § 503(c)(3)'s less restrictive provisions. Under § 503(c)(3), the payments merely need to be justified under the particular facts and circumstances. See, e.g., *In re Refco, Inc.*, Chapter 11 Case No. 05-60006 (Bankr. S.D.N.Y.2006) (payments to key staff); *In re Nobex Corp.*, Chapter 11 Case No. 05-20050 (Bankr. D. Del.2006) (permitting success fees to insiders); *In re Pliant Corp.*, Chapter 11 Case No. 06-10001 (Bankr. D. Del.2006) (approving management incentive compensation plan); *In re Calpine Corp.*, Chapter 11 Case No. 05-60200 (Bankr. S.D.N.Y.2006) (permitting payments to insiders).

Not all courts have elided the distinction between retention and incentive payments. In *In re Dana Corp. (Dana I)*, 351 B.R. 96 (Bankr. S.D.N.Y.2006), for example, the court refused to approve a compensation plan under which designated executives would receive a base salary, an annual incentive bonus and a "target completion" bonus. The latter had two components: a fixed component payable on the effective date of the plan, if the individual was still in Dana's employ at that time; and a variable component based on the debtor's enterprise value, measured six months after the effective date of the plan, but still payable even if that value had decreased by a certain percentage. The court found that the fixed component was within the prohibition of § 503(c)(1) because it was not incentive-based. Thus, the plan could not be approved, even under the sound business judgment standard: "If it walks like a duck (KERP) and quacks like a duck (KERP), it's a duck (KERP)." *Id.* at 102 n.3. The debtor then modified the plan to provide no guaranteed payments to executives other than base salary. The court found it a "substantial retreat" from the first plan and, because it was based on performance goals that would provide incentives to the executives, approved it under § 503(c)(1). *In re Dana Corp. (Dana II)*, 358 B.R. 567 (Bankr. S.D.N.Y.2006).

Interestingly, there appears to be no empirical basis for the argument that retention bonuses are an effective way of retaining key employees. Does that explain, perhaps, why Congress sought to limit the practice?

D. OPERATING THE BUSINESS

The effort to reorganize would halt in its tracks if the debtor-in-possession could not operate its business during the bankruptcy proceeding. That, however, requires money and the use of property in which creditors have an interest. Sections 363 and 364 address the debtor-in-possession's needs in this regard.

1. USE OF CASH COLLATERAL

"Cash collateral" is collateral (that is, property in which "an entity other than the estate [has] an interest") in a particularly liquid form ("cash, negotiable instruments, * * * deposit accounts, or other cash equivalents"). § 363(a). These assets are probably needed for daily operations and can very easily slip away from creditors. The Code prohibits the use of cash collateral without the creditor's consent or the court's authorization. § 363(c)(2). Is that sufficient protection for the creditor? (Note, too, that § 363(a) refers to cash collateral "whenever acquired." Thus, collateral that fits the description will be covered by these rules, even if acquired after the commencement of bankruptcy.)

MBANK DALLAS, N.A. v. O'CONNOR (IN RE O'CONNOR)

United States Court of Appeals, Tenth Circuit, 1987.
808 F.2d 1393.

JOHN P. MOORE, Circuit Judge.

* * *

The controversy under consideration evolves from a voluntary petition for reorganization filed by Mr. William Joseph O'Connor and Mrs. Jane Elizabeth O'Connor, husband and wife, (Debtors) pursuant to Chapter 11 of the Bankruptcy Reform Act of 1978 (Code). During administration of the case, the Debtors sought leave from the bankruptcy court to use certain cash on deposit in a court-controlled bank account to drill 3 gas wells in areas previously leased by a limited partnership in which Mr. O'Connor was the general partner. To protect creditors claiming interests in the subject cash, Debtors offered replacement liens on the well proceeds and on other unencumbered regular monthly income received by Mr. O'Connor. MBank Dallas, N.A. (Bank) asserted a security interest in the cash and objected to the Debtors' proposal.

After notice and a hearing at which the bankruptcy court took evidence regarding the value of the revenue that would be generated by the drilling project and the prospects for success, as well as the value of the monthly income offered as an additional replacement lien, the court made findings of fact and concluded it would be in the best interest of the estate to grant the leave requested. The court further concluded that the Bank would be adequately protected by the replacement liens offered by the Debtors.

The Bank appealed this decision to the district court which set bond and stayed the use of the cash. The district court ultimately reversed the bankruptcy court, concluding the bankruptcy court erred in finding the Bank would be adequately protected. Relying upon *Rader v. Boyd,* 267 F.2d 911 (10th Cir.1959), the district court concluded that the replacement liens were too speculative to provide the adequate protection required by § 363(e). * * *

The record indicates the Debtors had cash available from operations in the amount of $721,600. Since that cash represented proceeds from property on which the Bank claimed a security interest, it asserted the funds were subject to a proceeds lien and were "cash collateral" within the meaning of § 363. * * *

At the hearing before the bankruptcy court, the Debtors offered evidence that in the area in which Debtors proposed to drill, Mr. O'Connor's limited partnership had 150 proven wells, 148 of which were still producing. Mr. O'Connor testified that the 3 proposed wells would be drilled "on the inside of what we have already established as producing wells, therefore putting the risk down to a very nominal level." He also testified that purchasers of the gas to be produced were already available and that there was presently a ready market for that gas which would extend well into the future. The Debtors' expert testified that future cash flow could be expected from the project in the sum of $6,774,862 and that the O'Connor share of that expectation was $5,284,392. In the opinion of the expert, the Debtors' interest, discounted to present value, was worth $3,674,071 at the time of the hearing. Although the Bank offered contrary evidence, the bankruptcy court rejected the Bank's assertions.

On the basis of the disputed evidence, the bankruptcy court found that "future net revenues attributable to Debtors' interest in the wells will be $5.2 million and that the present value of those revenues is in excess of $2.8 million." The court further found that Debtors had additional unencumbered property with "a present value of $10,000 per month." The bankruptcy court concluded that the Bank was adequately protected by the replacement liens in the properties having these values and, as a consequence, "granting the motion would be in the best interest of the estate and its creditors."

In its appeal to the district court and in its brief here, the Bank has advanced many reasons why the bankruptcy court reached the wrong decision but gives only passing treatment to the issue of consequence; that is, whether the bankruptcy court's findings are clearly erroneous. We have not considered the issue before, but we are convinced that whether a creditor is adequately protected is a question of fact.

In recognition of the powers created in bankruptcy law to adjust debts and creditors' interests, Congress realized the need to protect creditors from unfair treatment. Hence, it codified the concept of adequate protection into the several aggressive remedies available to debtors and bankruptcy trustees. The whole purpose in providing adequate protection for a creditor is to insure that the creditor receives the value for which the creditor bargained prebankruptcy. * * * Since value is a function of many factual variables, it logically follows that adequate protection is a question of fact. As a question of fact, the bankruptcy court's determination that adequate protection exists or fails to exist can be reversed on appeal only if it is clearly erroneous. We have said that a clearly erroneous finding is one that leaves the reviewing court with the distinct and firm conviction that a mistake was made. We are left with no such conviction here.

* * *

The question of adequacy was examined and decided by the bankruptcy court on disputed but sufficient evidence. Mr. O'Connor testified that the wells were going to be drilled in a proven area in which all his previous attempts had been successful. He explained that he had drilled 150 wells and all were still producing except for 2 which had experienced mechanical failure. In addition, Debtors' expert witness testified that ready buyers existed to buy the product of the proposed wells in a quantity to provide a cash flow more than sufficient to protect the Bank's proceeds lien. * * *

In this case, Debtors, in the midst of a Chapter 11 proceeding, have proposed to deal with cash collateral for the purpose of enhancing the prospects of reorganization. This quest is the ultimate goal of Chapter 11. Hence, the Debtors' efforts are not only to be encouraged, but also their efforts during the administration of the proceeding are to be measured in light of that quest. Because the ultimate benefit to be achieved by a successful reorganization inures to all the creditors of the estate, a fair opportunity must be given to the Debtors to achieve that end. Thus, while interests of the secured creditor whose property rights are of concern to the court, the interests of all other creditors also have bearing upon the question of whether use of cash collateral shall be permitted during the early stages of administration.

The first effort of the court must be to insure the value of the collateral will be preserved. Yet, prior to confirmation of a plan of reorganization, the test of that protection is not by the same measurements applied to the treatment of a secured creditor in a proposed plan. In order to encourage the Debtors' efforts in the formative period prior to the proposal of a reorganization, the court must be flexible in applying the adequate protection standard. In doing so, however, care must be exercised to insure that the vested property rights of the secured creditor and the values and risks bargained for by that creditor prior to bankruptcy are not detrimentally affected.

Here, the creditor had a proceeds lien in cash worth $721,600. The Debtors proposed to use the cash thereby reducing the *value* of the creditor's security interest by $721,600, but in exchange, the Debtors proposed to give the creditor a *new* proceeds lien in property presently worth over five times that sum. The only distinction between the security interest the Bank had in the cash and the substitute security interest in the new wells is the risk inherent in drilling a dry hole.[6] Yet, the flexibility in judging whether that risk was significant or insignificant is what distinguishes this case from *Rader*.

The bankruptcy court found, in effect, that because the wells were to be drilled in proven areas, the risk to the Bank was not significant. That determination is supported by substantial evidence, and it is critical to the issue of adequate protection that exists in this case.

The Bank argued and continues to argue strenuously that granting the Debtors' motion was improper because the effect was contrary to the "reorganizational effect" of the plan it had proposed. The bankruptcy court found that the Bank's plan was nothing more than a program for liquidation of the Debtors' assets and concluded it was more

---

[6] This risk is set off somewhat, however, by the additional substitute lien in the $10,000 per month income received by Mr. O'Connor. There is nothing in the record indicating this income is speculative, and its present worth is more than half the value of the cash collateral Debtors wanted to use.

appropriate at that stage of the proceedings to allow the Debtors an opportunity to reorganize. We agree with that conclusion.

The judgment of the district court is REVERSED. The case is REMANDED * * * to the bankruptcy court for reinstitution of its order granting leave to use cash collateral.

Notes and Questions

1. In exchange for the use of $721,000 of its collateral, the creditor in this case was given an interest in the proceeds of a gas well, with a projected present value of $3,675,000, and an interest in the nonspeculative $10,000 monthly income of one of the debtors, with a present value of more than $360,000. Yet the creditor is arguing lack of adequate protection. Does this say anything to you about "the risk inherent in drilling a dry hole"?

2. An attorney representing the debtor-in-possession must pay attention to the use of cash collateral. In *Midwest Properties No. Two v. Big Hill Investment Co.*, 93 B.R. 357 (N.D.Tex.1988), the debtor-in-possession failed to establish a separate account and to account for cash collateral, in violation of § 363(c)(4). The bankruptcy court imposed sanctions on the debtor's president and on the corporation's attorney; if the sanctions were not paid by a specified date, the court imposed a 10% penalty and ordered that the parties be imprisoned until they made payment. The district court, on appeal, approved the imposition of sanctions, but reversed and remanded for more detailed findings on how the amounts were calculated.

2. PROTECTING THE INTERESTS OF NONDEBTORS

We already know that a creditor whose collateral is jeopardized in some way—such as use by the debtor-in-possession in its reorganization effort, or loss of priority to a postpetition lender—is entitled to adequate protection. Section 361 lists ways in which adequate protection can be given. Read it, and then answer the following Problems.

Problems

1. Debtor Corp. was in the business of hauling goods interstate. The trucks in its fleet were financed by Bank, which held perfected security interests in all of Debtor Corp.'s equipment. Debtor Corp. filed a Chapter 11 petition on February 1 and continued using the trucks while attempting to reorganize. Bank filed a motion for adequate protection on August 1 of the next year and it was heard on November 1. Bank presented very convincing evidence that the fleet of trucks had depreciated and continued to depreciate at the rate of $10,000 per month. Bank sought an order that Debtor Corp. pay $210,000 in adequate protection payments for the period since bankruptcy began, and

$10,000 every month until confirmation of a plan. Is Bank entitled to such an order?

2. Debtor, Inc. operated a retail store in an area of town suffering progressive urban blight. Debtor, Inc.'s premises were subject to a first mortgage for $350,000, owed to First Bank, and a second mortgage for $200,000, owed to Second Bank. The property was worth $450,000 when Debtor, Inc. filed a bankruptcy petition six months ago, but it is declining in value at the rate of about $1,000 per month. First Bank's loan accrues interest of $2,300 per month. Assuming that both First Bank and Second Bank act aggressively to preserve their interests, what amounts of adequate protection payments can each of them claim at the time of bankruptcy? Will those amounts change as the bankruptcy case progresses?

When an award of adequate protection ultimately proves to be inadequate, the creditor is entitled to a superpriority under § 507(b). The relationship between that subsection and § 503(b), however, has proved troublesome. As the court in *In re Callister*, 15 B.R. 521, 528, 529 (Bankr. D.Utah 1981), noted, the two subsections "may be at odds. One is keyed to preserving the estate, the other is designed to protect secured creditors. * * * If § 507(b) is faithful to one of these purposes, it may be untrue to the other." The following case addresses this issue.

FORD MOTOR CREDIT CO. v. DOBBINS

United States Court of Appeals, Fourth Circuit, 1994.
35 F.3d 860.

MICHAEL, Circuit Judge.

Chapter 11 debtors Rayfeal C. and Mary Ellen Dobbins appeal from a district court decision that was favorable in several respects to creditor Ford Motor Credit Corporation (FMCC) in its pursuit of a deficiency claim. The district court reversed the bankruptcy court (1) by granting FMCC a superpriority administrative expense under § 507(b) * * * . [W]e hold that the district court erred * * * in granting FMCC a § 507(b) superpriority * * * .

I. *Background*

[Debtors owned and operated a Lincoln-Mercury dealership in Roanoke, Virginia, with financing from FMCC, on premises they leased to the dealership (the "Melrose Avenue property"). Debtors personally guaranteed the dealership's debts, and the guaranty was secured by a

deed of trust on the Melrose Avenue property. The dealership en-countered financial problems and filed a Chapter 11 petition; debtors filed a personal Chapter 11 petition the same day. FMCC moved for relief from the stay in order to foreclose on the property, but the court found that FMCC was adequately protected by equity in the property and denied the motion.

Plans confirmed in both the debtors' and the dealership's bank-ruptcies called for sale of the Melrose Avenue property. When debtors were unable to sell, the court lifted the stay so that FMCC could do so. It finally sold the property for $375,000, and net proceeds of $301,124 were applied to FMCC's claim. FMCC sought a superpriority adminis-trative expense under § 507(b) for $322,720—the amount of the decrease in value of the property between the date of the adequate protection order and the date of sale.]

* * *

III. *§ 507(b) Superpriority*

FMCC contends that it is entitled to a superpriority administra-tive expense under § 507(b) because the value of the Melrose Avenue property declined after the adequate protection order, with the property eventually selling for less than the amount of FMCC's claim. In short, adequate protection proved to be inadequate. *[The court quoted § 507(b).]* It is apparent from the language of § 507(b) that a creditor must satisfy several requirements in order to trigger the superpriority. First, adequate protection must have been provided previously, and the protection ultimately must prove to be inadequate. Second, the creditor must have a claim allowable under § 507(a)(1) (which in turn requires that the creditor have an administrative expense claim under § 503(b)). And third, the claim must have arisen from either the automatic stay under § 362; or the use, sale or lease of the collateral under § 363; or the granting of a lien under § 364(d). For the reasons that follow, we conclude that FMCC is not entitled to a § 507(b) superpriority because it does not meet the second requirement above, *i.e.*, it does not have a claim allowable under § 507(a)(1).

A. *The requirement of a § 503(b) administrative expense*

"The presumption in bankruptcy cases is that the debtor's limited resources will be equally distributed among the creditors. Thus, statutory priorities must be narrowly construed." *In re James B. Downing & Co.*, 94 B.R. 515, 519 (Bankr. N.D.Ill.1988). Heeding this principle, we begin with the language of § 507(b), which allows a superpriority only to a claim otherwise allowable under § 507(a)(1). Section 507(a)(1), in turn, allows a claim for "administrative expenses allowable under § 503(b) * * * ." For our purposes, the administrative expenses allowable under § 503(b) are "the actual, necessary costs and expenses of preserving the estate * * * ." Thus, FMCC cannot receive a § 507(b) superpriority unless it can demonstrate that it has incurred postpetition an actual and necessary cost or expense of preserving the Dobbinses' estate.

"The modifiers 'actual' and 'necessary' must be observed with scrupulous care[,]" 3 L. King, *Collier on Bankruptcy* ¶ 503.04[1][a][i] at 503-24 (15th ed.1991), because

> [o]ne of the goals of Chapter 11 is to keep administrative costs to a minimum in order to preserve the debtor's scarce resources and thus encourage rehabilitation. In keeping with this goal, § 503(b)(1)(A) was not intended to "saddle debtors with special post-petition obligations lightly or give preferential treatment to certain select creditors by creating a broad category of administrative expenses."

General Amer. Transp. Corp. v. Martin (In re Mid Region Petroleum, Inc.), 1 F.3d 1130, 1134 (10th Cir.1993) (citations omitted).

Section 503(b) thus must be narrowly construed.

This * * * narrow interpretation requires *actual use* of the creditor's property by the debtor, thereby conferring a *concrete benefit* on the estate before a claim is allowable as an administrative expense. Accordingly, *the mere potential of benefit to the estate is insufficient* for the claim to acquire status as an administrative expense. The court's administrative expense inquiry centers upon whether the estate has received *an actual benefit, as opposed to the loss a creditor might experience by virtue of the debtor's possession of its property*.

In re ICS Cybernetics, Inc., 111 B.R. 32, 36 (Bankr. N.D.N.Y.1989) (citations omitted) (emphases added).

With this background in mind, we examine FMCC's argument, which essentially boils down to this: The Dobbinses used, and the Dobbinses' estate received a benefit from, the Melrose Avenue property in that the Dobbinses had the opportunity to market the property. We are presented with a close question here, but we do not believe that the mere opportunity to market collateral is the type of concrete, actual benefit contemplated by § 503(b)(1)(A). "Although this opportunity is advantageous to the [debtor-in-possession], it is not the type of benefit which is provided administrative expense protection because a benefit to the estate results only from use of the * * * property." *Mid Region Petroleum*, 1 F.3d at 1133 (creditor not entitled to § 503(b) administrative expense based on mere opportunity to maintain possession postpetition of leased railcars or opportunity to sell debtor's business with leases intact; "the railcars were never used postpetition"). As the Eleventh Circuit has observed:

> That which is actually utilized by a Trustee in the operation of a debtor's business is a necessary cost and expense of preserving the estate [under § 503(b)] and should be accorded the priority of an administrative expense. That which is thought to have some potential benefit, in that it makes a business more likely salable, may be a benefit but is too speculative to be allowed as an "actual, necessary cost and expense of preserving the estate."

Broadcast Corp. v. Broadfoot (In re Subscription Television), 789 F.2d 1530, 1532 (11th Cir.1986), *cert. denied*, 114 S.Ct. 1069 (1994) (creditor was obligated to keep broadcast signal available for trustee for sixty-day period, causing creditor to be deprived of signal's use; court held that creditor was not entitled to administrative claim for period of time during which the signal was available for, but not actually used by, the trustee).

In sum, there is a critical distinction between an actual benefit to the estate resulting from the actual postpetition use of collateral and a potential benefit to the estate resulting from a debtor's mere possession of collateral. This distinction, among others, separates the instant case from our decision in *Grundy Nat'l Bank v. Rife*, 876 F.2d 361 (4th Cir. 1989), upon which FMCC relies. *Grundy* involved the typical § 507(b) scenario: The debtor in possession actually used postpetition the collateral (two automobiles) in an effort to reorganize his business (vacuum cleaner salesman); the use of the collateral was essential to the reorganization of the debtor's business; and the use caused a decline in the collateral's value. Thus, *Grundy* involved an actual use by the estate, not a mere opportunity to benefit. See *id.* at 363 ("a debtor's estate is obligated to pay for collateral it controls and uses for the benefit of the estate"). The Eleventh Circuit's decision in *Broadcast Corp. v. Broadfoot (In re Carpet Center Leasing)*, 991 F.2d 682 (11th Cir.1993), upon which FMCC also relies, likewise is not on point because the debtor there "enjoyed more than mere potential post-petition use of collateral trucks. Rather than entertaining a speculative benefit, the Trustee actively used [the] collateral throughout its post-petition possession * * * . [The creditor was] entitled to an administrative expense priority because the Trustee actually used the collateral to the benefit of the debtor's estate."[7]

FMCC's theory is that a debtor's opportunity to benefit from the continued possession postpetition of collateral constitutes an actual and necessary cost of preserving the estate for purposes of § 503-(b)(1)(A). But every time a bankruptcy court denies a secured creditor's motion to lift the stay the debtor is given some "opportunity" to benefit from the continued possession of the collateral (e.g., to use, lease or sell it). Thus, were we to adopt FMCC's theory, we would be hard pressed to find a case where a creditor would not be entitled to a superpriority after adequate protection proved inadequate. In effect, FMCC would have us read out of § 507(b) Congress' requirement (in its cross-reference to § 503(b)) that the creditor must have incurred an actual and necessary cost of preserving the estate. This we decline to do * * *.

We appreciate that FMCC wants to be compensated for the delay and related opportunity loss occasioned by the Dobbinses' con-

---

[7] It may seem odd that a § 503(b) administrative expense can be created by a debtor's postpetition use (against the secured creditor's wishes) of collateral which the debtor had also used before going bankrupt. It seems odd because when we think of § 503(b) administrative expense claims, we think of claims "allowed for those who agree to extend postpetition credit to the bankruptcy estate as a loan or in the furnishing of goods or services." *In re Ralar Distrib., Inc.*, 166 B.R. 3, 8 (Bankr. D.Mass.1994) ("Congress granted this priority to offer an inducement for the postpetition extension of credit, in order to promote reorganization."). It may seem like somewhat of a stretch, then, to say that a creditor whose collateral is being used by the debtor against the creditor's wishes somehow is extending postpetition credit to the estate. But, as we said in *Grundy*, "what constitute actual and necessary costs and expenses of preserving the estate might well be opened to judicial construction." 876 F.2d at 364. It is this flexible judicial construction of § 503(b) which allows us to suggest that a creditor extends postpetition credit when in reality the creditor—who is forced to allow the debtor's continued use of collateral after the debtor slides into bankruptcy—extends no credit at all. But we will only stretch so far: Were we to allow a mere potential benefit to the estate to constitute an administrative expense claim, we would dilute § 503(b) to the point where it would become meaningless. To avoid that undesirable result, we interpret the terms "actual" and "necessary" with care and we require an actual use by (and therefore an actual benefit to) the estate for a creditor to have a § 503(b) claim.

tinued possession of its collateral. And we agree that in many cases "it would be inequitable to tax the creditor with the burden of the court's error if the judicially determined adequate protection later proves to be 'inadequate.'" *Cheatham v. Central Carolina Bank & Trust Co., (In re Cheatham)*, 91 B.R. 382, 387 (E.D.N.C.1988). However, it also strikes us as inequitable to tax unsecured creditors for a decline in the value of collateral when the decline does not result from a use that actually benefits the estate: "To prioritize * * * claims where they are not clearly entitled to such treatment, is not only inconsistent with the policy of equality of distribution but it also dilutes the value of the priority for the claims of creditors Congress in fact intended to prefer." *In re Chicago, M., St. P. and Pac. R.R.*, 658 F.2d 1149, 1163 (7th Cir.1981), *cert. denied*, 455 U.S. 1000 (1982).

B. *Conclusion*

We conclude that FMCC has not shown that its claim represents an actual and necessary cost or expense of preserving the estate and therefore the district court erred in granting FMCC a § 507(b) super-priority. Specifically, we hold that, in order to avoid rendering meaningless § 507(b)'s express requirement of a § 507(a)(1) administrative expense, § 507(b) requires something more than the mere opportunity of the debtor to market the secured collateral. We emphasize that our holding is narrow. We do not purport to provide a rigid definition of what constitutes an "actual benefit" to the estate for purposes of § 507(b); rather, that which constitutes an actual benefit must be determined on a case-by-case basis. Cf. *In re Callister*, 15 B.R. 521, 530 (Bankr. D.Utah 1981) ("[Section 507(b)] is a confederation of principles; it cannot be 'construed' to favor one at the expense of another; it should be interpreted to account for the merits of all. Hence, equitable considerations, arising from the facts of each case, should be examined.").

* * *

Questions

1. The Fourth Circuit distinguished its earlier holding in *Grundy*, and quoted that opinion's statement that "a debtor's estate is obligated to pay for collateral it controls and uses for the benefit of the estate." 876 F.2d at 363. Other language in *Grundy*, however, suggests that benefit is irrelevant: "We are persuaded that § 507(b) converts a creditor's claim where there has been a diminution in the value of a creditor's secured collateral by reason of a § 362

stay into an allowable administrative expense claim under § 503(b)." *Id.* at 363-64. So, is benefit relevant or not? Should it be?

2. Has *Dobbins* taken too narrow a view of § 507(b), rendering it less protective of secured creditors than Congress intended?

Adequate protection is, perhaps, the primary way in which the Code protects the interests of nondebtor parties caught up in a bankruptcy proceeding, but it is not the only way. The 2005 Amendments added a new type of administrative expense claim—one that applies to *prepetition* transactions with the debtor.[c] This provision, § 503(b)(9), gives a seller of goods an administrative expense for the value of goods received by the debtor in the ordinary course of business within the 20 days *before* the petition. This new provision, by itself, may substantially threaten the ability of certain debtors to reorganize. When it is combined with other provisions of the Code, its impact could be even greater. The next case discusses one of those interactions, and alludes to others.

CIRCUIT CITY STORES, INC. v. MITSUBISHI DIGITAL ELECTRONICS AMERICA, INC. (IN RE CIRCUIT CITY STORES, INC.)

United States Bankruptcy Court, Eastern District of Virginia, December 1, 2010.
2010 Bankr. LEXIS 4398, 2010 WL 4956022.

KEVIN R. HUENNEKENS, United States Bankruptcy Judge.

[Debtors were related corporations that operated as retailers of consumer electronics. They had 39,600 employees and more than 700 stores across the United States. Debtors filed Chapter 11 on November 10, 2008; by March 2009, they had completed going-out-of-business sales and, in August, confirmed a liquidating plan.

Mitsubishi asserted an administrative priority claim under § 503(b)(9), in the amount of $4,962,320.77, for the value of goods sold to Debtors during the 20 days before bankruptcy. Debtors requested that the court temporarily disallow the claim until the resolution of preference actions against Mitsubishi. Debtor sought a determination

---

[c] The Amendments added one other instance in which an administrative expense claim is available regarding prepetition transactions—back pay awards that fit the requirements of § 503(b)(1)(A)(ii).

of whether Mitsubishi could both receive payment of the administrative claim for the prepetition delivery of goods, and also use the same goods as the basis for asserting a new value preference defense under § 547(c)(4). With court approval, the parties established a fully funded reserve for Mitsubishi's exclusive benefit in an amount sufficient to pay the § 503(b)(9) claim.]

* * *

The purpose of the exception [in § 547(c)(4)] is fairly obvious and has been thus summarized:

> [T]he legislative history to § 547(c)(4) suggests that the subsequent new value defense was enacted to encourage creditors to replenish the estate by continuing to sell on credit to companies experiencing financial hardship. For trade creditors, who may ship goods to a debtor on a daily basis, the new value defense * * * is perhaps the best protection to the preference demand that inevitably will come once the debtor has filed its Chapter 11 petition. At the risk of grossly oversimplifying the defense, section 547(c)(4) permits creditors to reduce their preference exposure by essentially subtracting the value of the goods shipped subsequent to receipt of the preferential transfers but prior to the petition date from the aggregate preference demand amount.

Paul R. Hage & Patrick R. Mohan, *Is it Still New Value? Application of Section 503(b)(9) to the Subsequent New Value Preference Defense*, 19 J. BANKR. L. & PRAC. 4 (2010) (footnote omitted). The subsequent new value defense encourages lending to troubled debtors while also discouraging a "panic-stricken race to the courthouse." *Charisma Inv. Co., N.V. v. Airport Systems, Inc. (In re Jet Florida Sys., Inc.)*, 841 F.2d 1082, 1083 (11th Cir.1988). The subsequent new value defense is able to accomplish these dual goals and at the same time further the equal treatment of creditors because it applies only where "the bankruptcy estate has been enhanced by the creditor's actions." *TI Acquisition, LLC v. S. Polymer, Inc. (In re TI Acquisition, LLC)*, 429 B.R. 377 (Bankr. N.D.Ga.2010).

Mitsubishi has raised the § 547(c)(4) New Value Defense on account of goods it delivered to the Debtors subsequent to its receipt of the alleged Preferential Transfers. Mitsubishi has also made a claim for the payment of those same goods under § 503(b)(9) of the Bankruptcy Code. *[The court quoted § 503(b)(9).]* The Debtors' Motion places before the Court the issue of whether Mitsubishi can utilize a New Value Defense if it also receives payment for its § 503(b)(9) administrative claim where both its New Value Defense and its administrative claim are predicated upon that same recitation of value.

The parties agree that, subsequent to the alleged Preferential Transfers, the Debtors received goods valued at $4,962,320.77 from Mitsubishi in the twenty days prior to the Petition Date. Accordingly, the first element of § 547(c)(4) has been satisfied. The Debtors received subsequent new value from the creditor. The success of Mitsubishi's New Value Defense hinges upon the remaining provisions of § 547(c)(4) of the Bankruptcy Code. The critical provision in the issue before the Court is whether "the debtor did not make an otherwise unavoidable transfer to or for the benefit of such creditor" on account of the new value it received from the creditor. § 547(c)(4)(B).

In this case, the Debtors did make a "transfer to or for the benefit of [the] creditor" on account of the subsequent new value the Debtors received from Mitsubishi. Mitsubishi's argument to the contrary that no such transfer has occurred because it has not yet received payment of its § 503(b)(9) Claim is without moment. The statute does not by its terms require repayment of the new value but only a transfer on account thereof. Mitsubishi's § 503(b)(9) Claim was not denied. Allowance of the claim was merely deferred in order to enable this Court to consider the "double payment" concerns raised by the Debtors in the context of this preference litigation. The establishment of the reserve fund is absolute. The Debtors have parted with their interest in the monies that have been set aside in the reserve fund for the exclusive "benefit of" Mitsubishi. The stipulated settlement creating the reserve fund for the exclusive benefit of Mitsubishi guarantees that the total amount of Mitsubishi's § 503(b)(9) Claim, as ultimately allowed by this Court, will be paid in full. The creation of the reserve fund constitutes a "transfer" "for the benefit of" Mitsubishi within the meaning of § 547(c)(4)(B).

The Court must then apply the third and final element of the subsequent New Value Defense.[15] The use of the double negative in

---

[15] A recognized split has developed between the Circuits over the interpretation and application of § 547(c)(4)(B). Three of the Circuits that have dealt with this provision have concluded that § 547(c)(4)(B) of the Bankruptcy Code should be interpreted to mean that the new value must remain unpaid at the end of the preference period in order to be used to offset a creditor's preference exposure. *See generally* Noah Falk, *Section 547(c)(4): The Subsequent New Value Exception Defense to Preferences*, 2004 Norton Ann. Surv. of Bankr. Law Part I, § Q (Octo-

§ 547(c)(4)(B) does not render the plain meaning of that portion of the statute ambiguous. *Wahoski v. Am. & Efrid, Inc. (In re Pillowtex Corp.)*, 416 B.R. 123, 124 (Bankr. D. Del.2009); *Boyd v. The Water Doctor (In re Check Reporting Serv.)*, 140 B.R. 425, 434 (Bankr. W.D. Mich. 1992) ("Although [§547(c)(4)] does contain a double negative, this makes the statute *complicated*, not ambiguous. * * * Applying the statute requires several levels of analysis, but each step is clear and the process leads to a single result.") Rather, under what has been labeled the "subsequent advance" approach, § 547(c)(4)(B) simply requires a creditor to prove that the new value extended has not been repaid with an otherwise unavoidable transfer. *Id.* at 124. Under this approach, whenever a subsequent advance is made by a debtor to pay for new value extended after receipt of a preferential transfer, the New Value Defense is only available if the new value was repaid with a subsequent transfer that is itself avoidable.

The Fourth Circuit Court of Appeals adopted the subsequent advance approach in *Hall v. Chrysler Credit Corp. (In re JKJ Chevrolet, Inc.)*, 412 F.3d 545 (4th Cir.2005). There the Fourth Circuit held that:

> [a] creditor is entitled to offset preference payments through the extension of new value to the debtor so long as the debtor does not make *an otherwise unavoidable transfer* on account of the new value. Thus, even if [debtor] repaid all of the new value, under the plain terms of the statute whether those payments deprive [creditor] of its new value defense depends on whether the payments were *otherwise unavoidable.*"

*Id.*at 552.[16] Thus, under the holding of *JKJ*, the Transfer for the Benefit of Mitsubishi on account of its § 503(b)(9) Claim for the goods it

---

ber 2004). *See also Kroh Bros. Dev. Co. v. Cont'l Constr. Eng'rs Inc. (In re Kroh Bros. Dev. Co.)*, 930 F.2d 648, 653 (8th Cir.1991) (new value defense available unless creditor has been paid by the debtor for the goods and services that comprised the new value). * * *

[16] In its opinion in *JKJ*, the District Court for the Eastern District of Virginia relied upon Professor Countryman's explanation of § 547(c)(4)(B) of the Bankruptcy Code:

> If the debtor has made payments for goods or services that the creditor supplied on unsecured credit after an earlier preference, *and if these subsequent payments are themselves voidable as preferences* (or on any other ground), then under § 547(c)(4)(B) the creditor should be able to invoke those unsecured credit extensions as a defense to the recovery of the *earlier* voidable preference. On the other hand, the debtor's subsequent

supplied to the Debtors prepetition bars it from asserting a New Value Defense based upon the delivery of those same goods if the Transfer for the Benefit of Mitsubishi is an "otherwise unavoidable transfer."

The answer to the question whether the Transfer for the Benefit of Mitsubishi on account of its 503(b)(9) Claim is otherwise unavoidable turns on the provisions of the Bankruptcy Code governing the avoidance powers of a trustee. The applicable sections are §§ 544, 545, 547, 548, 549, 553(b) and 724(a). * * * In the instant Adversary Proceeding, the Court need not examine every facet of the various transactions between Mitsubishi and the Debtors in order to discern whether the transfer at issue is "otherwise unavoidable." The inquiry is confined to the Transfer for the Benefit of Mitsubishi on account of its § 503(b)(9) Claim.

The Court has analyzed the applicable avoidance provisions set forth in the Bankruptcy Code. Sections 544, 547, 548 and 553(b) of the Bankruptcy Code apply only to transfers made before the Petition Date. Those Bankruptcy Code sections are inapplicable to the satisfaction of administrative priority claims, which by definition are paid during the pendency of a bankruptcy case and not before its filing. Section 545 and 724(a) of the Bankruptcy Code are inapplicable because those sections apply only to the fixing of a lien. No lien is at issue in the instant Adversary Proceeding.

This leaves only § 549, which does apply to the avoidance of postpetition transfers. That section permits a trustee to avoid a transfer made after the petition date if the transfer was not authorized by the Bankruptcy Code or if the transfer was not authorized by the bankruptcy court. Here, establishment of the reserve fund for the exclusive benefit of Mitsubishi in order to facilitate payment of its § 503(b)(9) Claim is both authorized by the Court and by the Bankruptcy Code. Accordingly, the Transfer for the Benefit of Mitsubishi is not avoidable under § 549.

---

payments might not be voidable on any other ground and not voidable under § 547, because the goods and services were given C.O.D. rather than on a credit, or because the creditor has a defense under §§ 547(c)(1), (2), or (3). In this situation, the creditor may keep his payments but has no § 547(c)(4) defense to the trustee's action to recover the earlier preference. In either event, the creditor gets credit only once for goods and services later supplied.

312 B.R. at 804 n.2 (*quoting* Vern Countryman, *The Concept of a Voidable Preference in Bankruptcy*, 38 VAND. L. REV. 713, 788 (1985).

Because the Transfer for the Benefit of Mitsubishi to facilitate payment of Mitsubishi's § 503(b)(9) Claim is not avoidable through the use of §§ 544, 545, 547, 548, 549, 553(b) or 724(a), it is an "otherwise unavoidable transfer" that § 547(c)(4)(B) negates for qualification as new value. Mitsubishi can get credit only once for the goods it supplied to the Debtors in the twenty-day period preceding the Petition Date. As a matter of law, the Transfer for the Benefit of Mitsubishi on account of its § 503(b)(9) Claim precludes Mitsubishi from utilizing the value of the same goods that comprise the § 503(b)(9) Claim a second time as the basis for asserting a New Value Defense under § 547(c)(4).[18]

The result reached by this Court is similar to that reached by the Bankruptcy Court for the Northern District of Georgia in *TI Acquisition, LLC v. Southern Polymer, Inc. (In re TI Acquisition, LLC)*, 429 B.R. 377 (Bankr. N.D.Ga.2010). There the Chapter 11 debtor, a manufacturer of carpeting and textiles, had been supplied with materials within the twenty days prior to the petition date. The creditor that supplied the materials sought and received an order allowing its § 503(b)(9) administrative claim for the amounts due on account of the materials supplied within the twenty-day period. The court ordered that payment of the administrative claim should be deferred until the resolution of the debtor's preference action against the supplier. A fund was created to cover the amount required for the payment of the § 503(b)(9) claim.

In the preference action, the supplier sought to use the Bankruptcy Code's § 547(c)(4) New Value Defense. The debtor filed a motion for partial summary judgment to resolve the issue of whether the creditor was entitled to use the materials furnished as both the basis for an administrative claim and as a defense to the preference action. The court ruled that the creditor was not so entitled.

In reaching its conclusion in *TI Acquisition*, the court compared the interaction between §§ 547(c)(4) and 503(b)(9) to the interaction between reclamation claims and § 547. The seminal case, the court noted, was *In re Phoenix Restaurant Group, Inc. v. Proficient Food Co.*

---

[18] Mitsubishi also argues that this otherwise unavoidable transfer is inapplicable because it occurred postpetition. This argument is also without merit. The Fourth Circuit in *JKJ Chevrolet* clearly stated that "post-petition transfers may be considered under § 547(c)(4)(B)." 412 F.3d at 553 n.6. *See also Moglia v. Am. Psych. Ass'n (In re Login Bros. Book Co.)*, 294 B.R. 297, 300 (Bankr. N.D.Ill.2003) ("[B]oth the plain language and policy behind the statute indicate that *the timing of a repayment of new value is irrelevant*.") (emphasis added).

(In re Phoenix Restaurant Group), 373 B.R. 541 (M.D.Tenn.2007). In *Phoenix*, the district court ruled that the supplier had the right either to reclaim the goods or to have the reclamation claim given an "enhanced" priority status, but not both.[19] The bankruptcy court in *TI Acquisition* held that § 503(b)(9) claims (like reclamation claims that will be paid in full) should be treated in the same manner.[20]

The court in *TI Acquisition* concluded that the dual policy considerations underlying § 547(c)(4), of encouraging lending to troubled debtors and of promoting equality of treatment among creditors, were best fostered by allowing either a § 503(b)(9) claim or the use of § 547(c)(4)'s New Value Defense, but not both:

> The new value exception fosters these objectives because it limits the defense to the extent by which the bankruptcy estate has been enhanced by the creditor's actions. *See, e.g., In re Kroh Bros. Dev. Co.*, 930 F.2d at 654 ("The availability of the defense, then, depends on the ultimate effect on the estate"); and *In re Jet Fla. Sys., Inc.*, 841 F.2d at 1084 ("Thus, courts have generally required a transfer which fits within the subsequent advance exception to provide the debtor with a material benefit"). If the estate is not enlarged, no new value has been given. Thus, [supplier's] delivery of goods to Debtor pre-petition enlarged the Debtor's estate. Upon full payment to [supplier], the Debtor's estate is no longer enlarged by

---

[19] *Phoenix* was decided prior to the enactment of § 503(b)(9) and was based upon a seller's reclamation rights as provided in a previous version of § 546(c). In 2005 Congress made extensive changes to the Bankruptcy Code by enacting the Bankruptcy Abuse Prevention and Consumer Protection Act of 2005 ("BAPCPA"). Prior to BAPCPA, if a court denied a seller a valid right to reclaim its goods in a bankruptcy case, the court was required to provide the seller with an administrative claim or a junior lien. Among the many amendments made by BAPCPA, Congress deleted former subsection (c)(2) from § 546(c) and replaced that subsection with an entirely new provision. As a result, § 546(c) no longer expressly gives the court a choice between allowing reclamation or an administrative claim.

[20] The court in *TI Acquisition* noted that it did not agree with the analysis contained in *Commissary Operations v. DOT Foods Inc., (In re Commissary Operations)*, 421 B.R. 873, 877-79 (Bankr. M.D.Tenn.2010), in which the court found that reclamation claims and claims made pursuant to § 503(b)(9) were dissimilar and should be treated differently for purposes of § 547(c)(4) analysis. Additionally, the court in *TI Acquisition* distinguished critical vendor claims from § 503(b)(9) claims, whereas the court in *Commissary Operations* had analogized the two. This Court agrees with the analysis of the court in *TI Acquisition* in both of these regards.

the delivery. Therefore, [supplier] has no new value for which it has yet to receive full credit and should not be entitled to the new value defense.

429 B.R. at 384.

To allow a supplier of goods to a debtor to use the delivery of the same materials as the basis for both a § 547(c)(4) defense and a § 503(b)(9) administrative claim would not give equal treatment to all creditors. The supplier would be receiving, in essence, a double payment. The estate would be required to fund the administrative claim but would be unable to pursue the preference action.

Having reviewed the facts, the law, and the policy behind the law, the Court is persuaded that Mitsubishi may either (i) claim an administrative expense under § 503(b)(9) for the value of the goods received by the Debtors during the twenty days immediately preceding the Petition Date or (ii) utilize the value of those same goods as a § 547(c)(4) New Value Defense to a preference claim under § 547 of the Bankruptcy Code. However, Mitsubishi may not do both. * * *

Problems

1. Debtors—affiliated corporations in the paper industry—filed a Chapter 11 petition. Shortly thereafter, NewEnergy—the supplier of electricity to Debtors—filed a claim under § 503(b)(9) for $300,000, representing the cost of electricity supplied during the 20 days before bankruptcy. NewEnergy asserts that electricity is "goods" under § 503(b)(9). Is that right? See *In re Erving Indus., Inc.*, 432 B.R. 354 (Bankr. D. Mass.2010).

2. Debtor operated a chain of grocery stores. Its principal supplier, which sold between $2.5 and $3 million worth of goods to Debtor every week, held a security interest in most of Debtor's assets. Debtor filed Chapter 11 and the supplier filed a claim for an administrative expense priority in the amount of $6 million, pursuant to § 503(b)(9). Debtor resisted on the grounds that the supplier was a secured creditor and, therefore, ineligible under that provision. What result? See *Brown & Cole Stores, LLC v. Associated Grocers, Inc. (In re Brown & Cole Stores, LLC)*, 375 B.R. 873 (9th Cir. BAP 2007).

---

3. OBTAINING POSTPETITION CREDIT

Section 364 authorizes the debtor-in-possession to borrow postpetition on a series of terms, each more onerous and potentially detrimental to existing interests than the one before. Subsection (a) gives administrative expense priority to obligations incurred in the ordinary course of business (and obligations not in the ordinary course, but authorized by the court under § 364(b)).

If credit cannot be obtained on those terms, subsection (c)(1) permits the court to authorize a priority that trumps both § 503(b) administrative expense claims and those claims for inadequate adequate protection given a super-priority under § 507(b). That makes the § 364-(c)(1) claim a "super-super-priority."

If credit is still unobtainable, the court can authorize the granting of a lien on previously unencumbered property, (c)(2), or the granting of a junior lien in property already subject to encumbrance, (c)(3).

The last resort is § 364(d), which permits the court to authorize postpetition credit secured by a lien that is equal or senior in priority to an existing lien. Existing secured creditors are entitled to adequate protection of their interests.

A few creditors have seen a way to obtain collateral not only for their postpetition loans, but also for prepetition unsecured debts. The following case deals with this so-called "cross-collateralization."

SHAPIRO v. SAYBROOK MANUFACTURING CO. (IN RE SAYBROOK MANUFACTURING CO.)

United States Court of Appeals, Eleventh Circuit, 1992.
963 F.2d 1490.

Cox, Circuit Judge.

Seymour and Jeffrey Shapiro, unsecured creditors, objected to the bankruptcy court's authorization for the Chapter 11 debtors to "cross-collateralize" their pre-petition debt with unencumbered property from the bankruptcy estate. The bankruptcy court overruled the objection and also refused to grant a stay of its order pending appeal. The Shapiros appealed to the district court, which dismissed the case as moot under § 364(e) of the Bankruptcy Code because the Shapiros had failed to obtain a stay. We conclude that this appeal is not moot and that cross-collateralization is not authorized under the Bankruptcy Code. Accordingly, we reverse and remand.

I. FACTS AND PROCEDURAL HISTORY

Saybrook Manufacturing Co., Inc., and related companies (the "debtors"), initiated proceedings seeking relief under Chapter 11 of the Bankruptcy Code on December 22, 1988. On December 23, 1988, the debtors filed a motion for the use of cash collateral and for authorization to incur secured debt. The bankruptcy court entered an emergency financing order that same day. At the time the bankruptcy petition was filed, the debtors owed Manufacturers Hanover approximately $34 million. The value of the collateral for this debt, however, was less than $10 million. Pursuant to the order, Manufacturers Hanover agreed to lend the debtors an additional $3 million to facilitate their reorganization. In exchange, Manufacturers Hanover received a security interest in all of the debtors' property—both property owned prior to filing the bankruptcy petition and that which was acquired subsequently. This security interest not only protected the $3 million of post-petition credit but also secured Manufacturers Hanover's $34 million pre-petition debt.

This arrangement enhanced Manufacturers Hanover's position vis-à-vis other unsecured creditors, such as the Shapiros, in the event of liquidation. Because Manufacturers Hanover's pre-petition debt was undersecured by approximately $24 million, it originally would have shared in a pro rata distribution of the debtors' unencumbered assets along with the other unsecured creditors. Under the financing order, however, Manufacturers Hanover's pre-petition debt became fully secured by all of the debtors' assets. If the bankruptcy estate were liquidated, Manufacturers Hanover's entire debt—$34 million pre-petition and $3 million post-petition—would have to be paid in full before any funds could be distributed to the remaining unsecured creditors.

Securing pre-petition debt with pre- and post-petition collateral as part of a post-petition financing arrangement is known as cross-collateralization. The Second Circuit aptly defined cross-collateralization as follows:

[I]n return for making new loans to a debtor in possession under Chapter XI, a financing institution obtains a security interest on all assets of the debtor, both those existing at the date of the order and those created in the course of the Chapter XI proceeding, not only for the new loans, the propriety of which is not contested, but [also] for existing indebtedness to it.

Otte v. Manufacturers Hanover Commercial Corp. (In re Texlon Corp.), 596 F.2d 1092, 1094 (2d Cir.1979).

Because the Second Circuit was the first appellate court to describe this practice in *In re Texlon*, it is sometimes referred to as *Texlon*-type cross-collateralization. Another form of cross-collateralization involves securing post-petition debt with pre-petition collateral. This form of non-*Texlon*-type cross-collateralization is not at issue in this appeal. The Shapiros challenge only the cross-collateralization of the lenders' pre-petition debt, not the propriety of collateralizing the post-petition debt.

The Shapiros filed a number of objections to the bankruptcy court's order on January 13, 1989. After a hearing, the bankruptcy court overruled the objections. The Shapiros then filed a notice of appeal and a request for the bankruptcy court to stay its financing order pending appeal. The bankruptcy court denied the request for a stay on February 23, 1989.

The Shapiros subsequently moved the district court to stay the bankruptcy court's financing order pending appeal; the court denied the motion on March 7, 1989. On May 20, 1989, the district court dismissed the Shapiros' appeal as moot under § 364(e) because the Shapiros had failed to obtain a stay of the financing order pending appeal, rejecting the argument that cross-collateralization is contrary to the Code. The Shapiros then appealed to this court.

II. Issues on Appeal

1. Whether the appeal to the district court and the appeal to this court are moot under § 364(e) of the Bankruptcy Code because the Shapiros failed to obtain a stay of the bankruptcy court's financing order.

2. Whether cross-collateralization is authorized under the Bankruptcy Code.

* * *

V. Discussion

A. Mootness

We begin by addressing the lenders' claim that this appeal is moot under § 364(e) of the Bankruptcy Code. * * * The purpose of this provision is to encourage the extension of credit to debtors in bankruptcy by eliminating the risk that any lien securing the loan will be modified on appeal.

The lenders suggest that we assume cross-collateralization is authorized under § 364 and then conclude the Shapiros' appeal is moot under § 364(e). This is similar to the approach adopted by the Ninth Circuit in *Burchinal v. Central Washington Bank (In re Adams Apple, Inc.)*, 829 F.2d 1484 (9th Cir.1987). That court held that cross-collateralization was "authorized" under § 364 for the purposes of § 364(e) mootness but declined to decide whether cross-collateralization was illegal per se under the Bankruptcy Code. *See also Unsecured Creditors' Committee v. First National Bank & Trust Co. (In re Ellingsen MacLean Oil Co.)*, 834 F.2d 599 (6th Cir.1987), *cert. denied*, 488 U.S. 817 (1988).

We reject the reasoning of *In re Adams Apple* and *In re Ellingsen* because they "put the cart before the horse." By its own terms, § 364(e) is only applicable if the challenged lien or priority was authorized under § 364. *See* Charles J. Tabb, *Lender Preference Clauses and the Destruction of Appealability and Finality: Resolving a Chapter 11 Dilemma*, 50 OHIO ST. L.J. 109, 116–35 (1989) (criticizing *In re Adams Apple*, *In re Ellingsen*, and the practice of shielding cross-collateralization from appellate review via mootness under § 364(e)). We cannot determine if this appeal is moot under § 364(e) until we decide the central issue in this appeal—whether cross-collateralization is authorized under § 364. Accordingly, we now turn to that question.

B. Cross–Collateralization and § 364

Cross-collateralization is an extremely controversial form of Chapter 11 financing. Nevertheless, the practice has been approved by several bankruptcy courts. Even the courts that have allowed cross-collateralization, however, were generally reluctant to do so.

In *In re Vanguard Diversified, Inc.*, 31 B.R. 364 (Bankr. E.D.N.Y.1983), for example, the bankruptcy court noted that cross-collateralization is "a disfavored means of financing" that should only be used as a last resort. *Id*. at 366. In order to obtain a financing order including cross-collateralization, the court required the debtor to demonstrate (1) that its business operations would fail absent the proposed financing, (2) that it is unable to obtain alternative financing on acceptable terms, (3) that the proposed lender will not accept less preferential terms, and (4) that the proposed financing is in the general creditor body's best interest. This four-part test has since been adopted by other bankruptcy courts which permit cross-collateralization.

* * *

Cross-collateralization is not specifically mentioned in the Bankruptcy Code. We conclude that cross-collateralization is inconsistent with bankruptcy law for two reasons. First, cross-collateralization is not authorized as a method of post-petition financing under § 364. Second, cross-collateralization is beyond the scope of the bankruptcy court's inherent equitable power because it is directly contrary to the fundamental priority scheme of the Bankruptcy Code. *See generally* Charles J. Tabb, *A Critical Reappraisal of Cross–Collateralization in Bankruptcy*, 60 S. CAL. L. REV. 109 (1986).

Section 364 authorizes Chapter 11 debtors to obtain secured credit and incur secured debt as part of their reorganization. *[The court quoted §§ 364(c) and (d), emphasizing "may authorize the obtaining of credit or the incurring of debt."]* By their express terms, §§ 364(c) & (d) apply only to future—i.e., post-petition—extensions of credit. They do not authorize the granting of liens to secure pre-petition loans.

* * *

Given that cross-collateralization is not authorized by § 364, we now turn to the lenders' argument that bankruptcy courts may permit the practice under their general equitable power. Bankruptcy courts are indeed courts of equity, and they have the power to adjust claims to avoid injustice or unfairness. This equitable power, however, is not unlimited. * * *

Section 507 of the Bankruptcy Code fixes the priority order of claims and expenses against the bankruptcy estate. Creditors within a given class are to be treated equally, and bankruptcy courts may not create their own rules of superpriority within a single class. Cross-collateralization, however, does exactly that. As a result of this practice, post-petition lenders' unsecured pre-petition claims are given priority over all other unsecured pre-petition claims. The Ninth Circuit recognized that "[t]here is no * * * applicable provision in the Bankruptcy Code authorizing the debtor to pay certain pre-petition unsecured claims in full while others remain unpaid. To do so would impermissibly violate the priority scheme of the Bankruptcy Code." *Transamerica Commercial Finance Corp. v. Citibank (In re Sun Runner Marine, Inc.)*, 945 F.2d 1089, 1094 (9th Cir.1991) (citations omitted).

The Second Circuit has noted that, if cross-collateralization were initiated by the bankrupt while insolvent and shortly before filing a petition, the arrangement "would have constituted a voidable preference." *In re Texlon*, 596 F.2d at 1097. The fundamental nature of this practice is not changed by the fact that it is sanctioned by the bankruptcy court. We disagree with the district court's conclusion that, while cross-collateralization may violate some policies of bankruptcy law, it is consistent with the general purpose of Chapter 11 to help businesses reorganize and become profitable. Rehabilitation is certainly the primary purpose of Chapter 11. This end, however, does not justify the use of any means. Cross-collateralization is directly inconsistent with the priority scheme of the Bankruptcy Code. Accordingly, the practice may not be approved by the bankruptcy court under its equitable authority.

VI. Conclusion

* * * Because *Texlon*-type cross-collateralization is not explicitly authorized by the Bankruptcy Code and is contrary to the basic priority structure of the Code, we hold that it is an impermissible means of obtaining post-petition financing. The judgment of the district court is REVERSED and the case is REMANDED for proceedings not inconsistent with this opinion.

Notes and Questions

1. This sort of inquiry is exactly what § 364(e) was intended to prevent, is it not?

2. What relief is appropriate? Return of the new money and elimination of the new lien? Assuming that the debtor has spent a good bit of the new loan (a safe bet!), will the bank be forced to relinquish its new security interest and become unsecured for an additional $3 million?

3. As *Saybrook* recognized, courts are divided on the appropriateness of cross-collateralization. Which view is correct? If a debtor can make the showing required by *Vanguard*, why should cross-collateralization not be permitted?

4. CRITICAL VENDOR MOTIONS

Immediately upon filing a Chapter 11 petition, large corporate debtors commonly seek court approval on a variety of matters. Because these issues are raised quickly (and almost always *ex parte*), they are known as "first day" orders.

Arrangements for postpetition financing, such as we saw in *Saybrook*, are among the matters frequently covered. In addition, debtors routinely seek authority to pay prepetition obligations owed to certain creditors who, arguably, are important to the debtor's future prospects. These "critical vendors" are usually unsecured, so payments to them will not be in accordance with the Code's priority scheme. Should bankruptcy courts, nonetheless, permit such payments? The next case addresses that issue.

IN RE KMART CORP.

United States Court of Appeals, Seventh Circuit, 2004.
359 F.3d 866.

EASTERBROOK, Circuit Judge.

On the first day of its bankruptcy, Kmart sought permission to pay immediately, and in full, the prepetition claims of all "critical vendors." * * * The theory behind the request is that some suppliers may be unwilling to do business with a customer that is behind in payment, and, if it cannot obtain the merchandise that its own customers have come to expect, a firm such as Kmart may be unable to carry on, injuring all of its creditors. Full payment to critical-vendors thus could in principle make even the disfavored creditors better off: they may not be paid in full, but they will receive a greater portion of their claims than they would if the critical-vendors cut off supplies and the business shut down. Putting the proposition in this way implies, however, that the debtor must *prove*, and not just allege, two things: that, but for immediate full payment, vendors *would* cease dealing; and that the business will gain enough from continued transactions with the favored vendors to provide some residual benefit to the remaining, disfavored creditors, or at least leave them no worse off.

Bankruptcy Judge Sonderby entered a critical-vendors order just as Kmart proposed it, without notifying any disfavored creditors, without receiving any pertinent evidence (the record contains only some sketchy representations by counsel plus unhelpful testimony by Kmart's CEO, who could not speak for the vendors), and without making any finding of fact that the disfavored creditors would gain or come out even. The bankruptcy court's order declared that the relief Kmart requested—open-ended permission to pay any debt to any vendor it deemed "critical" in the exercise of unilateral discretion, provided that the vendor agreed to furnish goods on "customary trade terms" for the next two years—was "in the best interests of the Debtors, their estates and their creditors." The order did not explain why, nor did it contain any legal analysis, though it did cite § 105(a). * * *

Kmart used its authority to pay in full the pre-petition debts to 2,330 suppliers, which collectively received about $300 million. This came from the $2 billion in new credit (debtor-in-possession or DIP financing) that the bankruptcy judge authorized, granting the lenders super-priority in post-petition assets and revenues. Another 2,000 or so vendors were not deemed "critical" and were not paid. They and 43,000 additional unsecured creditors eventually received about 10¢ on the dollar, mostly in stock of the reorganized Kmart. Capital Factors, Inc., appealed the critical-vendors order immediately after its entry on January 25, 2002. A little more than 14 months later, after all of the critical-vendors had been paid and as Kmart's plan of reorganization was on the verge of approval, District Judge Grady reversed the order authorizing payment. He concluded that neither § 105(a) nor a "doctrine of necessity" supports the orders.

Appellants insist that, by the time Judge Grady acted, it was too late. Money had changed hands and, we are told, cannot be refunded. But why not? Reversing preferential transfers is an ordinary feature of bankruptcy practice, often continuing under a confirmed plan of reorganization. If the orders in question are invalid, then the critical-vendors have received preferences that Kmart is entitled to recoup for the benefit of all creditors. Confirmation of a plan does not stop the administration of the estate, except to the extent that the plan itself so provides. Several provisions of the Code do forbid revision of transactions completed under judicial auspices. For example, the DIP financing order, issued contemporaneously with the critical-vendors order, is sheltered by § 364(e) * * * . Nothing comparable anywhere in the Code covers payments made to pre-existing, unsecured creditors, whether or not the debtor calls them "critical." Judges do not invent missing language.

Now it is true that we have recognized the existence of a long-standing doctrine * * * that detrimental reliance comparable to the extension of new credit against a promise of security, or the purchase of assets in a foreclosure sale, may make it appropriate for judges to exercise such equitable discretion as they possess in order to protect those reliance interests. Thus once action has been taken to distribute assets under a confirmed plan of reorganization, it would take some extraordinary event to turn back the clock. These appeals, however, do not question any distribution under Kmart's plan; to the contrary, the plan (which was confirmed after the district court's decision) provides that adversary proceedings will be filed to recover the preferences that the critical vendors have received. No one filed an appeal, which means that it is appellants in this court that now wage a collateral attack on the plan of reorganization.

Appellants say that we should recognize their reliance interests: after the order, they continued selling goods and services to Kmart (doing this was a condition of payment for pre-petition debts). Continued business relations may or may not be a form of reliance (that depends on whether the vendors otherwise would have stopped selling), but they are not *detrimental* reliance. The vendors have been paid in full for post-petition goods and services. If Kmart had become administratively insolvent, and unable to compensate the vendors for post-petition transactions, then it might make sense to permit vendors to retain payments under the critical vendors order, at least to the extent of the post-petition deficiency. Because Kmart emerged as an operating business, however, no such question arises. The vendors have not established that any reliance interest—let alone any language in the Code—blocks future attempts to recover preferential transfers on account of prepetition debts.

* * *

Thus we arrive at the merits. Section 105(a) allows a bankruptcy court to "issue any order, process, or judgment that is necessary or appropriate to carry out the provisions of" the Code. This does not create discretion to set aside the Code's rules about priority and distribution; the power conferred by § 105(a) is one to implement rather than override. Every circuit that has considered the question has held that this statute does not allow a bankruptcy judge to authorize full payment of any unsecured debt, unless all unsecured creditors in the class are paid in full. We agree with this view of § 105. * * *

A "doctrine of necessity" is just a fancy name for a power to depart from the Code. Although courts in the days before bankruptcy law was codified wielded power to reorder priorities and pay particular creditors in the name of "necessity"—see *Miltenberger v. Logansport Ry.*, 106 U.S. 286 (1882); *Fosdick v. Schall*, 99 U.S. 235 (1878)—today it is the Code rather than the norms of nineteenth century railroad reorganizations that must prevail. *Miltenberger* and *Fosdick* predate the first general effort at codification, the Bankruptcy Act of 1898. Today the Bankruptcy Code of 1978 supplies the rules. Congress did not in terms scuttle old common-law doctrines, because it did not need to; the Act curtailed, and then the Code replaced, the entire apparatus. Answers to contemporary issues must be found within the Code (or legislative halls). Older doctrines may survive as glosses on ambiguous language enacted in 1978 or later, but not as freestanding entitlements to trump the text.

So does the Code contain any grant of authority for debtors to prefer some vendors over others? Many sections require equal treatment or specify the details of priority when assets are insufficient to satisfy all claims. E.g., §§ 507, 1122(a), 1123(a)(4). Appellants rely on §§ 363(b), 364(b), and 503 as sources of authority for unequal treatment. *[The court quoted § 364(b).]* This authorizes the debtor to obtain credit (as Kmart did) but has nothing to say about how the money will be disbursed or about priorities among creditors. To the extent that *In re Payless Cashways, Inc.*, 268 B.R. 543 (Bankr. W.D. Mo.2001), and similar decisions, hold otherwise, they are unpersuasive. Section 503, which deals with administrative expenses, likewise is irrelevant. Pre-filing debts are not administrative expenses; they are the antithesis of administrative expenses. Filing a petition for bankruptcy effectively creates two firms: the debts of the pre-filing entity may be written down so that the post-filing entity may reorganize and continue in business if it has a positive cash flow. Treating pre-filing debts as "administrative" claims against the post-filing entity would impair the ability of bankruptcy law to prevent old debts from sinking a viable firm.

That leaves § 363(b)(1) * * * . This is more promising, for satisfaction of a pre-petition debt in order to keep "critical" supplies flowing is a use of property other than in the ordinary course of administering an estate in bankruptcy. Capital Factors insists that § 363(b)(1) should be limited to the commencement of capital projects, such as building a new plant, rather than payment of old debts—as paying vendors would be "in the ordinary course" but for the intervening bankruptcy petition. To read § 363(b)(1) broadly, Capital Factors observes, would be to allow a judge to rearrange priorities among creditors (which is what a critical-vendors order effectively does), even though the Supreme Court has cautioned against such a step. See *United States v. Reorganized CF&I Fabricators of Utah, Inc.*, 518 U.S. 213 (1996); *United States v. Noland*, 517 U.S. 535 (1996). Yet what these decisions principally say is that priorities do not change unless a statute supports that step; and if § 363(b)(1) is such a statute, then there is no insuperable problem. If the language is too open-ended, that is a problem for the legislature. Nonetheless, it is prudent to read, and use, § 363(b)(1) to do the least damage possible to priorities established by contract and by other parts of the Bankruptcy Code. We need not decide whether § 363(b)(1) could support payment of some pre-petition debts, because *this* order was unsound no matter how one reads § 363(b)(1).

The foundation of a critical-vendors order is the belief that vendors not paid for prior deliveries will refuse to make new ones. Without merchandise to sell, a retailer such as Kmart will fold. If paying the critical vendors would enable a successful reorganization and make even the disfavored creditors better off, then all creditors favor payment whether or not they are designated as "critical." This suggests a use of § 363(b)(1) similar to the theory underlying a plan crammed down the throats of an impaired class of creditors: if the impaired class does at least as well as it would have under a Chapter 7 liquidation, then it has no legitimate objection and cannot block the reorganization. For the premise to hold true, however, it is necessary to show not only that the disfavored creditors *will* be as well off with reorganization as with liquidation—a demonstration never attempted in this proceeding—but also that the supposedly critical vendors would have ceased deliveries if old debts were left unpaid while the litigation continued. If vendors will deliver against a promise of current payment, then a reorganization can be achieved, and all unsecured creditors will obtain its benefit, without preferring any of the unsecured creditors.

Some supposedly critical vendors will continue to do business with the debtor because they must. They may, for example, have long term contracts, and the automatic stay prevents these vendors from walking away as long as the debtor pays for new deliveries. See § 362. Fleming Companies, which received the largest critical-vendors payment because it sold Kmart between $70 million and $100 million of groceries and related goods weekly, was one of these. No matter how much Fleming would have liked to dump Kmart, it had no right to do so. It was unnecessary to compensate Fleming for continuing to make deliveries that it was legally required to make. Nor was Fleming likely to walk away even if it had a legal right to do so. Each new delivery produced a profit; as long as Kmart continued to pay for new product, why would any vendor drop the account? That would be a self-inflicted wound. To abjure new profits because of old debts would be to commit the sunk-cost fallacy; well-managed businesses are unlikely to do this. Firms that disdain current profits because of old losses are unlikely to stay in business. They might as well burn money or drop it into the ocean. Again Fleming illustrates the point. When Kmart stopped buying its products after the contract expired, Fleming collapsed (Kmart had accounted for more than 50% of its business) and filed its own bankruptcy petition. Fleming was hardly likely to have quit selling of its own volition, only to expire the sooner.

Doubtless many suppliers fear the prospect of throwing good money after bad. It therefore may be vital to assure them that a debtor will pay for new deliveries on a current basis. Providing that assurance need not, however, entail payment for pre-petition transactions. Kmart could have paid cash or its equivalent. (Kmart's CEO told the bankruptcy judge that COD arrangements were not part of Kmart's business plan, as if a litigant's druthers could override the rights of third parties.) Cash on the barrelhead was not the most convenient way, however. Kmart secured a $2 billion line of credit when it entered bankruptcy. Some of that credit could have been used to assure vendors that payment would be forthcoming for all post-petition transactions. The easiest way to do that would have been to put some of the $2 billion behind a standby letter of credit on which the bankruptcy judge could authorize unpaid vendors to draw. That would not have changed the terms on which Kmart and any of its vendors did business; it just would have demonstrated the certainty of payment. If lenders are unwilling to issue such a letter of credit (or if they insist on a letter's short duration), that would be a compelling market signal that reorganization is a poor prospect and that the debtor should be liquidated post haste.

Yet the bankruptcy court did not explore the possibility of using a letter of credit to assure vendors of payment. The court did not find that any firm would have ceased doing business with Kmart if not paid for pre-petition deliveries, and the scant record would not have supported such a finding had one been made. The court did not find that discrimination among unsecured creditors was the only way to facilitate a reorganization. It did not find that the disfavored creditors were at least as well off as they would have been had the critical-vendors order not been entered. For all the millions at stake, this proceeding looks much like the Chapter 13 reorganization that produced *In re Crawford*, 324 F.3d 539 (7th Cir.2003). Crawford had wanted to classify his creditors in a way that would enable him to pay off those debts that would not be discharged, while stiffing the creditors whose debts were dischargeable. We replied that even though classification (and thus unequal treatment) is possible for Chapter 13 proceedings, see § 1322(b), the step would be proper only when the record shows that the classification would produce some benefit for the disfavored creditors. Just so here. Even if § 363(b)(1) allows critical-vendors orders in principle, preferential payments to a class of creditors are proper only if the record shows the prospect of benefit to the other creditors. This record does not, so the critical-vendors order cannot stand.

AFFIRMED.

Notes and Questions

1. Is the court condemning all critical vendor motions? Can a debtor ever succeed in making the requisite showing? (Recall the first-day context of these motions.)

2. The court mentioned in passing that the critical vendors were paid with money obtained from Kmart's postpetition financing, and that those lenders were entitled to a super-priority under § 364. Might such a fact be important when a future debtor tries to make the type of showing that the Seventh Circuit requires?

3. Kmart sent notice of its critical vendor motion to only 65 creditors, none of whom were among the 2,000 vendors "left high and dry." Is that important?

4. As the court suggests, critical vendor motions derive from the "doctrine of necessity" born in nineteenth-century railroad reorganizations. There, payments were justified in order to protect the public's interest in uninterrupted rail service. Now, critical vendor motions are, arguably, designed to protect the debtor's interest in reorganization. Has the doctrine been extended too far? Are the interests of employees and creditors sufficient to support the extension?

5. The particular critical vendor motion granted by the bankruptcy judge in *Kmart*, unlike the orders sometimes issued in other cases, did not list the particular vendors to be favored. Instead, it simply authorized the payment of hundreds of millions of dollars as Kmart saw fit, and, as the opinion reported, over $300 million was ultimately paid to "critical" vendors. That order has been described as "the bankruptcy equivalent of a writ from the king." Thomas J. Salerno, *"The Mouse That Roared" Or, "Hell Hath No Fury Like a Critical Vendor Scorned,"* AM. BANKR. INST. J., June, 2003, at 28 n.1. Would specificity have saved Kmart's motion? Should courts faced with more specific critical vendor motions distinguish *Kmart* on that ground?

6. The court in *Official Committee of Equity Security Holders v. Mabey*, 832 F.2d 299 (4th Cir.1987), held that the debtor, A.H. Robins, could not create a fund, before confirmation of a plan, to pay for reconstructive surgery or in vitro fertilization for Dalkon Shield victims, even though the passage of time might cost those victims any chance at fertility. The Fourth

Circuit reasoned that bankruptcy courts have to no equitable power under § 105(a) to approve such a fund.   Is such a flat rule too inflexible?   Is it possible to reconcile *Mabey* with approval of critical vendor motions?

7. If debtors are concerned about the willingness of vendors, holding prepetition unsecured claims, to continue providing goods and services, is there an approach other than making out-of-priority payments? Hint: think about § 362.   Need another hint?   See *Sportfame of Ohio, Inc. v. Wilson Sporting Goods Co. (In re Sportfame of Ohio, Inc.)*, 40 B.R. 47 (Bankr. N.D. Ohio 1984).

8. The 2005 Amendments made several changes that are protective of vendors: the seller of goods, in the ordinary course of the debtor's business, has an administrative expense claim for the value of goods received within 20 days of filing, § 503(b)(9); vendors may reclaim goods sold in the ordinary course of business while the debtor was insolvent, if they were received within 45 days of filing, § 546(c); and the trustee (or debtor-in-possession) has 120 days to move for authority to return goods to the vendor, with the vendor's permission, if return is in the best interests of the estate and the vendor agrees to offset the purchase price against any prepetition claim, § 546(h).

Will these changes reduce the perceived necessity for critical vendor orders?

5. SALE OF PROPERTY

Section 363 permits the trustee not only to use property in which a creditor has an interest, but also to sell or lease it. When the sale of such property is part of the debtor's ordinary course of business—as, for example, the sale of inventory from a store's shelves—§ 363(c) provides that no court authorization is needed. In that event, the creditor is protected by its interest in the proceeds. § 363(c)(2).

Sales outside the ordinary course of business, especially if free of claims and interests, are of more concern because of the possibility that the requirements for plan confirmation (including acceptance by interested parties and court approval) could be circumvented. Such sales must be approved by the bankruptcy court "after notice and a hearing," § 363(b)(1), which really only requires the *opportunity* for a hearing. § 102(1).

The next case addresses whether a significant portion of the debtor's assets may be sold outside of the plan.

INDIANA STATE POLICE PENSION TRUST v. CHRYSLER LLC (**IN RE CHRYSLER LLC**)

United States Court of Appeals, Second Circuit, 2009.
576 F.3d 108.

JACOBS, Chief Judge.

* * *

     In a nutshell, Chrysler LLC and its related companies (herein-after "Chrysler" or "debtor" or "Old Chrysler") filed a prepackaged bankruptcy petition under Chapter 11 on April 30, 2009. The filing followed months in which Chrysler experienced deepening losses, received billions in bailout funds from the Federal Government, searched for a merger partner, unsuccessfully sought additional government bailout funds for a stand-alone restructuring, and ultimately settled on an asset-sale transaction pursuant to § 363 (the "Sale"), which was approved by the Sale Order. The key elements of the Sale were set forth in a Master Transaction Agreement dated as of April 30, 2009: substantially all of Chrysler's operating assets (including manufacturing plants, brand names, certain dealer and supplier relationships, and much else) would be transferred to New Chrysler in exchange for New Chrysler's assumption of certain liabilities and $2 billion in cash. Fiat S.p.A agreed to provide New Chrysler with certain fuel-efficient vehicle platforms, access to its worldwide distribution system, and new management that is experienced in turning around a failing auto company. Financing for the sale transaction—$6 billion in senior secured financing, and debtor-in-possession financing for 60 days in the amount of $4.96 billion—would come from the United States Treasury and from Export Development Canada. * * *

     * * * Upon extensive findings of fact and conclusions of law, the bankruptcy court approved the Sale by order dated June 1, 2009. * * *

     * * * The Sale Order is challenged essentially on four grounds. First, it is contended that the sale of Chrysler's auto-manufacturing assets, considered together with the associated intellectual property and (selected) dealership contractual rights, so closely approximates a final plan of reorganization that it constitutes an impermissible "*sub rosa* plan," and therefore cannot be accomplished under § 363(b). We consider this question first, because a determination adverse to Chrysler would have required reversal. Second, we consider the argument by the Indiana Pensioners that the Sale impermissibly subordinates their interests as secured lenders and allows assets on which they have a lien to pass free of liens to other creditors and parties, in violation of § 363(f). We reject this argument on the ground that the secured lenders have consented to the Sale, as per § 363(f)(2). Third, the Indiana Pensioners challenge the constitutionality of the use of TARP funds to finance the Sale on a number of grounds, chiefly that the Secretary of the Treasury is using funds appropriated for relief of "financial institutions" to effect a bailout of an auto-manufacturer, and that this causes a constitutional injury to the Indiana Pensioners because the loss of their priorities in bankruptcy amounts to an economic injury that was caused or underwritten by TARP money. We conclude that the Indiana Pensioners lack standing to raise this challenge. Finally, we consider and reject the arguments advanced by present and future tort claimants.

* * *

The Indiana Pensioners characterize the Sale as an impermissible, *sub rosa* plan of reorganization. *See Pension Benefit Guar. Corp. v. Braniff Airways, Inc. (In re Braniff Airways, Inc.)*, 700 F.2d 935, 940 (5th Cir.1983) (denying approval of an asset sale because the debtor "should not be able to short circuit the requirements of Chapter 11 for confirmation of a reorganization plan by establishing the terms of the plan *sub rosa* in connection with a sale of assets"). As the Indiana Pensioners characterize it, the Sale transaction "is a 'Sale' in name only; upon consummation, new Chrysler will be old Chrysler in essentially every respect. It will be called 'Chrysler.' * * * Its employees, including most management, will be retained. * * * It will manufacture and sell Chrysler and Dodge cars and minivans, Jeeps and Dodge Trucks. * * * The real substance of the transaction is the underlying reorganization it implements."

Section 363(b) of the Bankruptcy Code authorizes a Chapter 11 debtor-in-possession to use, sell, or lease estate property outside the ordinary course of business, requiring in most circumstances only that a movant provide notice and a hearing. We have identified an "apparent conflict" between the expedient of a § 363(b) sale and the otherwise applicable features and safeguards of Chapter 11. *Comm. of Equity Sec. Holders v. Lionel Corp. (In re Lionel Corp.)*, 722 F.2d 1063, 1071 (2d Cir.1983).

In *Lionel*, we consulted the history and purpose of § 363(b) to situate § 363(b) transactions within the overall structure of Chapter 11. The origin of § 363(b) is the Bankruptcy Act of 1867, which permitted a sale of a debtor's assets when the estate or any part thereof was "of a perishable nature or liable to deteriorate in value." *Lionel,* 722 F.2d at 1066 (citing § 25 of the Bankruptcy Act of 1867) (emphasis omitted). Typically, courts have approved § 363(b) sales to preserve " 'wasting asset[s].' " *Id.* at 1068 (quoting *Mintzer v. Joseph (In re Sire Plan, Inc.)* 332 F.2d 497, 499 (2d Cir.1964)). Most early transactions concerned perishable commodities; but the same practical necessity has been recognized in contexts other than fruits and vegetables. "[T]here are times when it is more advantageous for the debtor to begin to sell as many assets as quickly as possible in order to insure that the assets do not lose value." *Fla. Dep't of Revenue v. Piccadilly Cafeterias, Inc.,* 554 U.S. 33, 57, 128 S.Ct. 2326, 2342, 171 L.Ed.2d 203 (2008) (BREYER, J., dissenting) (internal quotation marks omitted). Thus, an automobile manufacturing business can be within the ambit of the "melting ice cube" theory of § 363(b). As *Lionel* recognized, the text of § 363(b) requires no "emergency" to justify approval. *Lionel,* 722 F.2d at 1069. For example, if "a good business opportunity [is] presently available," *id.,* which might soon disappear, quick action may be justified in order to increase (or maintain) the value of an asset to the estate, by means of a lease or sale of the assets. Accordingly, *Lionel* "reject[ed] the requirement that only an emergency permits the use of § 363(b)." *Id.* "[I]f a bankruptcy judge is to administer a business reorganization successfully under the Code, then * * * some play for the operation of both § 363(b) and Chapter 11 must be allowed for." *Id.* at 1071.

At the same time, *Lionel* "reject[ed] the view that § 363(b) grants the bankruptcy judge *carte blanche*." *Id.* at 1069. The concern was that a quick, plenary sale of assets outside the ordinary course of business risked circumventing key features of the Chapter 11 process, which afford debt and equity holders the opportunity to vote on a proposed plan of reorganization after receiving meaningful information. Pushed by a bullying creditor, a § 363(b) sale might evade such requirements as disclosure, solicitation, acceptance, and confirmation of a plan. *See* §§ 1122-29. "[T]he natural tendency of a debtor in distress," as a Senate Judiciary Committee Report observed, is "to pacify large creditors with whom the debtor would expect to do business, at the expense of small and scattered public investors." *Lionel,* 722 F.2d at 1070 (quoting S. Rep. No. 95-989, 2d Sess., at 10 (1978), *as reprinted in* 1978 U.S.C.C.A.N. 5787, 5796 (internal quotation marks omitted)).

To balance the competing concerns of efficiency against the safeguards of the Chapter 11 process, *Lionel* required a "good business reason" for a § 363(b) transaction:

> [A bankruptcy judge] should consider all salient factors pertaining to the proceeding and, accordingly, act to further the diverse interests of the debtor, creditors and equity holders, alike. [A bankruptcy judge] might, for example, look to such relevant factors as the proportionate value of the asset to the estate as a whole, the amount of elapsed time since the filing, the likelihood that a plan of reorganization will be proposed and confirmed in the near future, the effect of the proposed disposition on future plans of reorganization, the proceeds to be obtained from the disposition vis-à-vis any appraisals of the property, which of the alternatives of use, sale or lease the proposal envisions and, most importantly perhaps, whether the asset is increasing or decreasing in value. This list is not intended to be exclusive, but merely to provide guidance to the bankruptcy judge.

722 F.2d at 1071.

After weighing these considerations, the Court in *Lionel* reversed a bankruptcy court's approval of the sale of Lionel Corporation's equity stake in another corporation, Dale Electronics, Inc. ("Dale"). The Court relied heavily on testimony from Lionel's Chief Executive Officer, who conceded that it was "only at the insistence of the Creditors' Committee that Dale stock was being sold and that Lionel 'would very much like to retain its interest in Dale,'" *id*. at 1072, as well as on a financial expert's acknowledgment that the value of the Dale stock was not decreasing, *see id*. at 1071-72. Since the Dale stock was not a wasting asset, and the proffered justification for selling the stock was the desire of creditors, no sufficient business reasons existed for approving the sale.

In the twenty-five years since *Lionel,* § 363(b) asset sales have become common practice in large-scale corporate bankruptcies. *See, e.g.,* Robert E. Steinberg, *The Seven Deadly Sins in § 363 Sales,* AM. BANKR. INST. J., June 2005, at 22, 22 ("Asset sales under § 363 of the Bankruptcy Code have become the preferred method of monetizing the assets of a debtor company."); Harvey R. Miller & Shai Y. Waisman, *Does Chapter 11 Reorganization Remain A Viable Option for Distressed Businesses for the Twenty-First Century?,* 78 AM. BANKR. L.J. 153, 194-96 (2004). A law review article recounts the phenomenon:

Corporate reorganizations have all but disappeared. * * * TWA filed only to consummate the sale of its planes and landing gates to American Airlines. Enron's principal assets, including its trading operation and its most valuable pipelines, were sold within a few months of its bankruptcy petition. Within weeks of filing for Chapter 11, Budget sold most of its assets to the parent company of Avis. Similarly, Polaroid entered Chapter 11 and sold most of its assets to the private equity group at BankOne. Even when a large firm uses Chapter 11 as something other than a convenient auction block, its principal lenders are usually already in control and Chapter 11 merely puts in place a preexisting deal.

Douglas G. Baird & Robert K. Rasmussen, *The End of Bankruptcy*, 55 STAN. L. REV. 751, 751-52 (2002) (internal footnotes omitted). In the current economic crisis of 2008-09, § 363(b) sales have become even more useful and customary. The "side door" of § 363(b) may well "replace the main route of Chapter 11 reorganization plans." Jason Brege, Note, *An Efficiency Model of Section 363(b) Sales*, 92 VA. L. REV. 1639, 1640 (2006).

Resort to § 363(b) has been driven by efficiency, from the perspectives of sellers and buyers alike. The speed of the process can maximize asset value by sale of the debtor's business as a going concern. Moreover, the assets are typically burnished (or "cleansed") because (with certain limited exceptions) they are sold free and clear of liens, claims and liabilities. *See infra* (discussing § 363(f) and tort issues).

A § 363 sale can often yield the highest price for the assets because the buyer can select the liabilities it will assume and purchase a business with cash flow (or the near prospect of it). Often, a secured creditor can "credit bid," or take an ownership interest in the company by bidding a reduction in the debt the company owes. *See* § 363(k) (allowing a secured creditor to credit bid at a § 363(b) sale).

This tendency has its critics. The objections are not to the quantity or percentage of assets being sold: it has long been understood (by the drafters of the Code, and the Supreme Court) that § 363(b) sales may encompass all or substantially all of a debtor's assets. Rather, the thrust of criticism remains what it was in *Lionel*: fear that one class of creditors may strong-arm the debtor-in-possession, and bypass the requirements of Chapter 11 to cash out quickly at the expense of other stakeholders, in a proceeding that amounts to a reorganization in all but name, achieved by stealth and momentum. *See, e.g., Motorola, Inc. v. Official Comm. of Unsecured Creditors and JPMorgan Chase Bank, N.A. (In re Iridium Operating LLC)*, 478 F.3d 452, 466 (2d Cir.2007) ("The reason *sub rosa* plans are prohibited is based on a fear that a debtor-in-possession will enter into transactions that will, in effect, short circuit the requirements of Chapter 11 for confirmation of a reorganization plan." (internal quotation marks and alteration omitted)); Brege, *supra*, at 1643 ("The cynical perspective is that [§ 363(b)] serves as a loophole to the otherwise tightly arranged and efficient Chapter 11, through which agents of the debtor-in-possession can shirk responsibility and improperly dispose of assets."); *see also* Steinberg, *supra*, at 22 ("Frequently, * * * the § 363 sale process fails to maximize value.").

As § 363(b) sales proliferate, the competing concerns identified in *Lionel* have become harder to manage. Debtors need flexibility and speed to preserve going concern value; yet one or more classes of creditors should not be able to nullify Chapter 11's requirements. A balance is not easy to achieve, and is not aided by rigid rules and prescriptions. *Lionel*'s multi-factor analysis remains the proper, most comprehensive framework for judging the validity of § 363(b) transactions.

Adopting the Fifth Circuit's wording in *Braniff*, commentators and courts—including ours—have sometimes referred to improper § 363(b) transactions as "*sub rosa* plans of reorganization." *See, e.g., Iridium*, 478 F.3d at 466 ("The trustee is prohibited from such use, sale or lease if it would amount to a *sub rosa* plan of reorganization."). *Braniff* rejected a proposed transfer agreement in large part because the terms of the agreement specifically attempted to "dictat[e] some of the terms of any future reorganization plan. The [subsequent] reorganization plan would have to allocate the [proceeds of the sale] according to the terms of the [transfer] agreement or forfeit a valuable asset." 700 F.2d at 940. As the Fifth Circuit concluded, "[t]he debtor and the Bankruptcy Court should not be able to short circuit the requirements of Chapter 11 for confirmation of a reorganization plan by establishing the terms of the plan *sub rosa* in connection with a sale of assets." *Id*.

The term *"sub rosa"* is something of a misnomer. It bespeaks a covert or secret activity, whereas secrecy has nothing to do with a § 363 transaction. Transactions blessed by the bankruptcy courts are openly presented, considered, approved, and implemented. *Braniff* seems to have used "*sub rosa*" to describe transactions that treat the requirements of the Bankruptcy Code as something to be evaded or subverted. But even in that sense, the term is unhelpful. The sale of assets is permissible under § 363(b); and it is elementary that the more assets sold that way, the less will be left for a plan of reorganization, or for liquidation. But the size of the transaction, and the residuum of corporate assets, is, under our precedent, just one consideration for the exercise of discretion by the bankruptcy judge(s), along with an open-ended list of other salient factors.

Braniff's holding did not support the argument that a § 363(b) asset sale must be rejected simply because it is a sale of all or substantially all of a debtor's assets. Thus a § 363(b) sale may well be a reorganization in effect without being the kind of plan rejected in *Braniff*. Although *Lionel* did not involve a contention that the proposed sale was a *sub rosa* or *de facto* reorganization, a bankruptcy court confronted with that allegation may approve or disapprove a § 363(b) transfer that is a sale of all or substantially all of a debtor's assets, using the analysis set forth in *Lionel* in order to determine whether there was a good business reason for the sale. *See Iridium*, 478 F.3d at 466 & n. 21 ("The trustee is prohibited from such use, sale or lease if it would amount to a *sub rosa* plan of reorganization. In this Circuit, the sale of an asset of the estate under § 363(b) is permissible if the 'judge determining [the] § 363(b) application expressly find[s] from the evidence presented before [him or her] at the hearing [that there is] a good business reason to grant such an application.'" (citing *Lionel*, 722 F.2d at 1071)).

The Indiana Pensioners argue that the Sale is a *sub rosa* plan chiefly because it gives value to unsecured creditors (*i.e.*, in the form of the ownership interest in New Chrysler provided to the union benefit funds) without paying off secured debt in full, and without complying with the procedural requirements of Chapter 11. However, Bankruptcy Judge Gonzalez demonstrated proper solicitude for the priority between creditors and deemed it essential that the Sale in no way upset that priority. The lien holders' security interests would attach to all proceeds of the Sale: "Not one penny of value of the Debtors' assets is going to anyone other than the First-Lien Lenders." Opinion Granting Debtor's Motion Seeking Authority to Sell, May 31, 2009, at 18. As Bankruptcy Judge Gonzalez found, all the equity stakes in New Chrysler were entirely attributable to *new* value—including governmental loans, new technology, and new management—which were not assets of the debtor's estate.

The Indiana Pensioners' arguments boil down to the complaint that the Sale does not pass the discretionary, multifarious *Lionel* test. The bankruptcy court's findings constitute an adequate rebuttal. Applying the *Lionel* factors, Bankruptcy Judge Gonzalez found good business reasons for the Sale. The linchpin of his analysis was that the only possible alternative to the Sale was an immediate liquidation that would yield far less for the estate—and for the objectors. The court found that, notwithstanding Chrysler's prolonged and well-publicized efforts to find a strategic partner or buyer, no other proposals were forthcoming. In the months leading up to Chrysler's bankruptcy filing, and during the bankruptcy process itself, Chrysler executives circled the globe in search of a deal. But the Fiat transaction was the *only* offer available.

The Sale would yield $2 billion. According to expert testimony—not refuted by the objectors—an immediate liquidation of Chrysler as of May 20, 2009 would yield in the range of nothing to $800 million. Crucially, Fiat had conditioned its commitment on the Sale being completed by June 15, 2009. While this deadline was tight and seemingly arbitrary, there was little leverage to force an extension. To preserve resources, Chrysler factories had been shuttered, and the business was hemorrhaging cash. According to the bankruptcy court, Chrysler was losing going concern value of nearly $100 million each day.

On this record, and in light of the arguments made by the parties, the bankruptcy court's approval of the Sale was no abuse of discretion. With its revenues sinking, its factories dark, and its massive debts growing, Chrysler fit the paradigm of the melting ice cube. Going concern value was being reduced each passing day that it produced no cars, yet was obliged to pay rents, overhead, and salaries. Consistent with an underlying purpose of the Bankruptcy Code— maximizing the value of the bankrupt estate—it was no abuse of discretion to determine that the Sale prevented further, unnecessary losses.

The Indiana Pensioners exaggerate the extent to which New Chrysler will emerge from the Sale as the twin of Old Chrysler. New Chrysler may manufacture the same lines of cars but it will also make newer, smaller vehicles using Fiat technology that will become available as a result of the Sale—moreover, at the time of the proceedings, Old Chrysler was manufacturing no cars at all. New Chrysler will be run by a new Chief Executive Officer, who has experience in turning around failing auto companies. It may retain many of the same employees, but they will be working under new union contracts that contain a six-year no-strike provision. New Chrysler will still sell cars in some of its old dealerships in the United States, but it will also have new access to Fiat dealerships in the European market. Such transformative use of old and new assets is precisely what one would expect from the § 363(b) sale of a going concern.

* * * For the foregoing reasons, we affirm the June 1, 2009 order of the bankruptcy court authorizing the Sale.

Questions

1. The court spoke of the "conflict" between § 363(b) and Chapter 11's "safeguards." What is the nature of that conflict?

2. According to the court, what factors are relevant in determining whether the debtor has a "good business reason" for the sale of assets?

———————————

Estate assets that are subject to sale are often encumbered by one or more liens. That, in itself, does not prevent the sale, as § 363(f) makes clear. But courts have sharply divided on the amount that must be realized, when property is overencumbered, in order to satisfy §§ 363(f)(3) and (f)(5). Is it enough that the sale produces the value of the property? Or must the sale produce an amount equal to the total of the claims held by creditors with an interest in the property? The following case addresses these questions.

CLEAR CHANNEL OUTDOOR, INC. v. KNUPFER (IN RE PW, LLC)

United States Bankruptcy Appellate Panel, Ninth Circuit, 2008.
391 B.R. 25.

MARKELL, Bankruptcy Judge.

This appeal presents a simple issue: outside a plan of reorganization, does § 363(f) of the Bankruptcy Code permit a secured creditor to credit bid its debt and purchase estate property, taking title free and clear of valid, nonconsenting junior liens? We hold that it does not.

* * *

The debtor in this case, PW, LLC ("PW"), owned prime real estate in Burbank, California. DB Burbank, LLC ("DB"), an affiliate of a large public hedge fund, held a claim of more than $40 million secured by PW's property. But problems large and small plagued PW's development plan. These problems ultimately led to PW's chapter 11 bankruptcy and to the appointment of Nancy Knupfer as PW's chapter 11 trustee ("Trustee").

DB, working with the Trustee, organized a campaign to consolidate all of PW's property and development rights and to sell this package, free and clear of all claims and encumbrances, at a sale supervised by the bankruptcy court. At the sale, DB was the highest bidder, paying its consideration by credit-bidding the entire amount of its debt.

The only problem was the existence of a consensual lien securing a claim of approximately $2.5 million in favor of a junior creditor, Clear Channel Outdoor, Inc. ("Clear Channel"). Relying solely on § 363(f)(5), the bankruptcy court confirmed the sale to DB free and clear of Clear Channel's lien. * * *

After reviewing applicable law, we conclude that § 363(f)(5) cannot support transfer of PW's property free and clear of Clear Channel's lien based on the existing record. We thus reverse that portion of the bankruptcy court's order authorizing the sale to DB free and clear of Clear Channel's lien, and we remand the matter to the bankruptcy court for further proceedings.

* * *

I. FACTS

Before filing for bankruptcy, PW owned and was attempting to develop real property in Burbank, California. It had a development agreement with the City of Burbank ("Development Agreement") that provided entitlements for a mixed-use complex of luxury condominiums and retail space. In order to realize the value of the entitlements, however, PW had to acquire an assemblage of eighteen parcels of real estate by February 2009. When it filed bankruptcy, PW owned only fourteen of the necessary parcels. It had, however, entered into an agreement to acquire the final four parcels, which were occupied by a church ("Church Property"). Closing this agreement and the final purchase of the Church Property was conditioned on the church's finding another suitable location for its activities.

[DB had a first priority lien on substantially all of PW's assets. DB began foreclosure proceedings and PW filed Chapter 11. DB's motion for appointment of a trustee was granted. Faced with the difficulty of obtaining the cure amount to acquire the church property and to implement the Development Agreement, the trustee began discussions with DB about a sale of the property. They reached an agreement under which DB would serve as stalking horse bidder and, if there were no qualified higher bids, buy the property for the "strike price" of

$41,434,465. The trustee moved to approve sale free and clear of liens under §§ 363(f)(3) and (f)(5). Clear Channel opposed the motion, asserting that (f)(3) was not applicable. The court approved the motion under (f)(5).

No qualified overbids were received, and DB bought the property by credit bid. Clear Channel received nothing. It appealed.]

III. DISCUSSION

* * *

B. *Statutory Interpretation of § 363(f)*

Our holding that the appeal is not moot requires us to consider whether § 363(f) permits the stripping of Clear Channel's lien. Sales free and clear of interests are authorized under § 363(f). *[The court quoted that subsection.]*

Of the five paragraphs that authorize a sale free and clear, three do not apply to this appeal. Paragraph (1) does not apply because applicable law—California real property law—does not permit a sale free and clear, and indeed would preserve Clear Channel's lien despite the transfer. Nguyen v. Calhoun, 105 Cal. App. 4th 428, 438, 129 Cal. Rptr. 2d 436, 445 (Cal. Ct. App. 2003) ("Real property is transferable even though the title is subject to a mortgage or deed of trust, but the transfer will not eliminate the existence of that encumbrance. Thus, the grantee takes title to the property subject to all deeds of trust and other encumbrances, whether or not the deed so provides.") (citations omitted). Paragraph (2) is inapplicable as Clear Channel did not consent to the transfer free of its interest. Paragraph (4) applies only if the interest is in bona fide dispute, and no one disputes the validity of Clear Channel's lien. As a result, we need only analyze the bankruptcy court's ability to authorize a sale free and clear of Clear Channel's lien under paragraphs (3) and (5).

1. Guidance on Interpretation

We first review case law on statutory interpretation because paragraphs (3) and (5) of § 363(f) present legitimate and difficult questions of statutory interpretation. Paragraph (3), for example, uses a nonstandard term to refer to the claims held by creditors secured by the property being sold. It refers to the "aggregate value of all liens" on the property. The Code, however, tends to refer not to the economic value of the property secured by liens but to the value of claims secured by those liens. See, e.g., §§ 506(a); 1129(b)(2). If § 363(f)(3) had been worded to refer to the "aggregate value of all claims secured by liens on such property," it would have been in the mainstream of other provisions of the Code, and no real question would be presented. But it was not. This variant locution requires us to decide whether the unusual construction should be given special interpretive significance.

Paragraph (5) presents an even greater conundrum: the competing constructions seem either to render it so specialized as never to be invoked, or all-powerful, subsuming all the other paragraphs of § 363(f). * *

2. Paragraph (3) and Sales for Less than the Amount of All Claims Secured by the Property

PW's property sold for less than the amount of claims secured by PW's property. DB and the Trustee contend that § 363(f)(3) authorizes the sale free and clear of the liens in this situation. The bankruptcy court found, and we agree, that § 363(f)(3) cannot be so used.

* * * The Trustee asserts that the "aggregate value of all liens" in this paragraph means the economic value of such liens, rather than their face value. This argument arises from § 363(f)(3)'s variance from general Code usage; that is, whether its reference to "value of all liens" is simply an unfortunate deviation from the Code's general preference to refer to claims, and not liens, or whether it has some other significance.

The Trustee and DB assert that, under conventional bankruptcy wisdom, supported by § 506(a), the amount of an allowed secured claim can never exceed the value of the property securing the claim.[14] Since a secured claim is a form of "lien," see § 101(37), some courts have found that an estate representative may use § 363(f)(3) to sell free and clear of the property rights of junior lienholders whose nonbankruptcy liens are not supported by the collateral's value. That is, there may be a sale free and clear of "out-of-the-money" liens. *See, e.g., In re Beker Indus. Corp.*, 63 B.R. 474, 476-77 (Bankr. S.D.N.Y.1986); *In re Terrace Gardens Park P'ship*, 96 B.R. 707 (Bankr. W.D.Tex.1989).

---

[14] This statement would not be true if a creditor could and did make the § 1111(b) election to have its allowed secured claim equal its total claim amount, § 1111(b), or, in a chapter 13 case, if the hanging paragraph of § 1325 applied, § 1325(a).

We disagree. This reading expands § 363(f)(3) too far. It would essentially mean that an estate representative could sell estate property free and clear of any lien, regardless of whether the lienholder held an allowed secured claim. We think the context of paragraph (3) is inconsistent with this reading. If Congress had intended such a broad construction, it would have worded the paragraph very differently.[15] For this reason, many courts and commentators have rejected this approach. See, e.g., Richardson v. Pitt County (In re Stroud Wholesale, Inc.), 47 B.R. 999, 1002 (E.D.N.C.1985), aff'd mem., 983 F.2d 1057 (4th Cir.1986); Scherer v. Fed. Nat'l Mortgage Ass'n (In re Terrace Chalet Apartments, Ltd.), 159 B.R. 821 (N.D.Ill.1993); In re Canonigo, 276 B.R. 257 (Bankr. N.D.Cal.2002); 3 COLLIER ON BANKRUPTCY ¶ 363.06[4][a] (Alan N. Resnick & Henry J. Sommer eds., 15th ed. rev. 2008).

But another reason, rooted in the text of the paragraph, exists to reject such an expansive reading. Paragraph (3) permits the sale free and clear only when "the price at which such property is to be sold *is greater than* the aggregate value of all liens." § 363(f)(3) (emphasis added). If, as DB and the Trustee assert, "aggregate value of all liens" means the aggregate amount of all allowed secured claims as used in § 506(a), then the paragraph could *never* be used to authorize a sale free and clear in circumstances like those present here; that is, when the claims exceed the value of the collateral that secures them. In any case in which the value of the property being sold is less than the total amount of claims held by secured creditors, the total of all allowed secured claims will *equal,* not exceed, the sales price, and the statute requires the price to be "greater than" the "value of all liens."

As a result, we join those courts cited above that hold that § 363(f)(3) does not authorize the sale free and clear of a lienholder's interest if the price of the estate property is equal to or less than the aggregate amount of all claims held by creditors who hold a lien or security interest in the property being sold.

3. Paragraph (5) and Sales for Less Than the Lienholder's Claim

The parties' main dispute lies over the proper application of § 363(f)(5). The bankruptcy court, supported by the Trustee and DB, found that the plain meaning of that paragraph permitted a sale free and clear of Clear Channel's lien. On appeal, Clear Channel argues that the paragraph's plain meaning does not support the bankruptcy court's

---

[15] Or it would have worded it as it worded § 1206. See *infra*.

construction. Clear Channel has the best of this argument. We thus reverse on this point. Because the meaning of paragraph (5) is anything but plain, we must carefully consider the statute's wording and the competing interpretations.

We start with the text of the statute. *[The court quoted § 363(f)(5).]* We parse this paragraph to contain at least three elements: that (1) a proceeding exists or could be brought, in which (2) the non-debtor could be compelled to accept a money satisfaction of (3) its interest.

Courts are divided over the interpretation of each of these elements. We analyze these components in reverse order. * * *

a. Lien as Interest

Clear Channel's primary contention is that the term "interest" must be read narrowly to exclude liens such as the one it holds. So read, § 363(f)(5) would be inapplicable, as a matter of law, to authorize the sale free and clear of Clear Channel's lien. Clear Channel asserts that to do otherwise renders the other subsections under § 363(f) mere surplusage.

We reject Clear Channel's argument. We believe that Congress intended "interest" to have an expansive scope, as shown by *United States v. Knox-Schillinger (In re Trans World Airlines, Inc.)*, 322 F.3d 283 (3d Cir.2003). In *TWA*, the Third Circuit held that there were two "interests" subject to § 363(f)(5): 1) travel vouchers issued in connection with settlement of a discrimination action and 2) discrimination claims made by the EEOC. The court reasoned that, if the debtor-airline had liquidated its assets under Chapter 7 of the Bankruptcy Code, the claims at issue would have been converted to dollar amounts, and the claimants would have received the distribution provided to other general unsecured creditors on account of their claims. Similarly, the EEOC discrimination claims were reducible to, and could have been satisfied by, monetary awards even if injunctive relief was sought.

Some cases, however, have adopted a restricted construction of "interest" in order to prevent needless overlap. In particular, cases such as *Canonigo*, 276 B.R. at 265, reason that the term "interest" must be read differently in (f)(5) from every other use of the term in § 363(f).

But the distinctions drawn by *Canonigo* are not supported by the plain reading we are required to give to the statute. It is telling that the introductory sentence to § 363(f) broadly refers to "any interest," and that four of the following paragraphs then refer back to "such interest." Within this group is § 363(f)(3), which explicitly states that it applies only if "such interest is a lien," making it apparent that Congress intended a lien to be a type of interest. Congress would not have, used the language it did in paragraph (f)(3), or at least would have included additional language in paragraph (5), if it had intended to exclude liens from paragraph (f)(5).

In addition, though the Code does not define "interest,"[17] it does define "lien." Clear Channel's reading contradicts that definition in which lien "means charge against or *interest* in property." § 101(37) (emphasis added). The definition of lien provides another inference consistent with the interpretation that a lien is but one type of interest. Clear Channel asserts that *Canonigo*'s interpretation promotes the statutory purpose of avoiding the use of § 363(f) as a means of escaping the rigors of the chapter 11 plan confirmation process.

Consistent with the plain reading of § 363(f) generally, and § 363(f)(5) in particular, we construe "interest" to include the type of lien at issue in this appeal.

b. Compelling Money Satisfaction

Clear Channel's alternative position is that if § 363(f)(5) does apply to authorize a sale free and clear of liens, then the bankruptcy court erred in holding that Clear Channel "could be compelled * * * to accept a money satisfaction" of its interest.

i. Compelling Satisfaction for Less Than Full Payment

The bankruptcy court found paragraph(f)(5) applicable when-ever a claim or interest can be, paid with money. We do not think that § 363(f)(5) is so simply analyzed. Although it is tautological that liens securing payment obligations can be satisfied by paying the money owed, it does not necessarily follow that such liens can be satisfied by paying *any* sum, however large or small. We assume that paragraph (5) refers to a legal and equitable proceeding in which the nondebtor could be compelled to take *less* than the value of the claim secured by the interest.

---

[17] Congress did refer to equity positions in partnerships as "interests," § 101(16)(B), and did define a "security interest" as a lien created by agreement. § 101(51).

Other courts agree and hold that it is not the type of interest that matters, but whether monetary satisfaction may be compelled for less than full payment of the debt related to, or secured by, that interest. *In re Terrace Chalet Apts.*, 159 B.R. at 829 ("By its express terms, § 363(f)(5) permits lien extinguishment if the trustee can, demonstrate the existence of another legal mechanism by which a lien could be extinguished without full satisfaction of the secured debt.". If full payment were required, § 363(f)(5) would merely mirror § 363(f)(3) and render it superfluous.

Under the view that full payment is not necessary, it is not the amount of the payment that is at issue, but whether a "mechanism exists to address extinguishing the lien or interest without paying such interest in full." *In re Gulf States Steel, Inc. of Ala.*, 285 B.R. 497, 508 (Bankr. N.D.Ala.2002). Other courts have required a showing of the basis that could be used to compel acceptance of less than full monetary satisfaction. *See In re Terrace Chalet Apts.*, 159 B.R. at 829.

Although this view leads to a relatively small role for paragraph (5), we are not effectively writing it out of the Code. Paragraph (5) remains one of five different justifications for selling free and clear of interests, and its scope need not be expansive or all-encompassing. So long as its breadth complements the other four paragraphs consistent with congressional intent, without overlap, our narrow view is justified.

Examples can be formulated that demonstrate this complementary aspect of a narrow view of paragraph (5). One might be a * * * case in which specific performance might normally be granted, but the presence of a liquidated-damages clause allows a court to satisfy the claim of a nonbreaching party in cash instead of a forced transfer of property. *See, e.g., O'Shield v. Lakeside Bank*, 335 Ill.App.3d 834, 781 N.E.2d 1114 (Ill.App.Ct.2002). Yet another might be satisfaction of obligations related to a conveyance of real estate that normally would be specifically performed but for which the parties have agreed to a damage remedy. *S. Motor Co. v. Carter-Pritchett-Hodges, Inc. (In re MMH Automotive Group, LLC)*, 2008 WL 725102 (Bankr. S.D.Fla., Mar. 17, 2008). In these cases, a court could arguably compel the holders of the interest to take less than what their interest is worth.

ii. Construction Consistent with §§ 363(f)(3) and 1206

While the bankruptcy court's reading is plausible if paragraph (5) is read in isolation, statutory interpretation requires a more detailed examination of the, context of the statute. Put another way, any interpretation of paragraph (5) must satisfy the requirement that the various paragraphs of subsection (f) work harmoniously and with little overlap. The bankruptcy court's broad interpretation does not do this.

Initially, if the Trustee's and DB's interpretation were accepted, paragraph (5) would swallow and render superfluous paragraph (3), a provision directed specifically at liens. The specific provisions of paragraph (3) would never need to be used, since all liens would be covered, regardless of any negative or positive relationship between the value of a creditor's collateral and the amount of its claim. A result that makes one of five paragraphs redundant should be avoided.

A more narrow reading is also suggested by Congress's addition of § 1206 to the Code in 1986. Pre-BAPCPA § 1206 provided that:

> [a]fter notice and a hearing, *in addition to the authorization contained in section 363(f)* the trustee in a case under this chapter may sell property under section 363(b) and (c) free and clear of any interest in such property of an entity other than the estate if the property is farmland or farm equipment, except that the proceeds of such sale shall be subject to such interest.

§ 1206 (emphasis added). Congress thus intended § 1206 to supplement an estate's rights. As a result, both § 363(f)(5) and § 1206 apply to sales of estate property in chapter 12.[23]

The interpretive challenge is to construe § 363(f)(5) in a way that complements § 1206. In this regard, the first difference between the two provisions is that, unlike § 363(f), § 1206 grants an absolute right to sell free and clear of an interest so long as the interest attaches to the proceeds. This absolute right does not exist in § 363(f)(5), requiring a more narrow interpretation.[24]

---

[23] Chapter 12 also permits confirmation over the dissent of a secured creditor, § 1225(a)(5), and thus § 1206's existence belies the effort to select cramdown as a type of legal or equitable proceeding to which § 363(f)(5) refers.

[24] A sale under § 363(f) is subject to § 363(e), which also conditions the sale on the provision of adequate protection. "Most often, adequate protection in connection with a sale free and clear of other interests will be to have those interests attached to the proceeds of the sale." H.R. Rep. No. 595, 95th Cong., 1st Sess. 345 (1977). With respect to a lien, then, § 1206 provides no more than § 363(f)(5) if the availability of nonconsensual confirmation under § 1225(a)(5) is sufficient as a legal and equitable proceeding to trigger a sale free and clear under § 363(f)(5).

Congress added § 1206 in 1986. Its purpose was "to allow family farmers to sell assets not needed for the reorganization prior to confirmation without the consent of the secured creditor subject to the approval of the court." H.R. Rep. No. 958, 99TH Cong., 2d Sess. 50 (1986). Significantly, Congress explicitly made it clear that an interest includes a lien. But § 1206 would be unnecessary with respect to liens if § 363(f)(5) already permitted a sale.

We follow this reasoning and hold that the bankruptcy court must make a finding of the existence of such a mechanism and the trustee must demonstrate how satisfaction of the lien "could be compelled." *In re Terrace Chalet Apts.*, 159 B.R. at 829-30. Here the bankruptcy court should not have explicitly dismissed the argument that any such finding or showing is required.[25]

c. Legal or Equitable Proceeding

Paragraph (5) requires that there be, or that there be the possibility of, some proceeding, either at law or at equity, in which the nondebtor could be forced to accept money in satisfaction of its interest. The bankruptcy court reasoned that there was no need to prove the existence or possibility of a qualifying legal or equitable proceeding when the interest at issue was a lien because all liens, by definition, are capable of being satisfied by money.

The language of § 363(f)(5) indicates that compelling a nondebtor to accept a monetary satisfaction cannot be the sole focus of the inquiry under that paragraph. The statute additionally requires that "such entity could be compelled, *in a legal or equitable proceeding,* to accept" such a monetary satisfaction. § 363(f)(5) (emphasis added). The question is thus whether there is an available type or form of legal or equitable proceeding in which a court could compel Clear Channel to release its lien for payment of an amount that was less than full value of Clear Channel's claim. Neither the Trustee nor DB has directed us to any such proceeding under nonbankruptcy law, and the bankruptcy court made no such finding.

The Trustee points out that courts have found that cramdown under § 1129(b)(2) is a qualifying legal or equitable proceeding. See, e.g., In re Gulf States Steel, 285 B.R. at 508; In re Grand Slam USA,

---

[25] The Trustee and DB attempt to resolve this dilemma by asserting that if (f)(5) is found to require full payment of the debt, then (f)(3) must require full payment of the economic value of the lien—the value of the property—rather than full payment of the debt itself. This interpretation, however, makes (f)(5) superfluous.

Inc., 178 B.R. 460, 462 (E.D. Mich. 1995); In re Healthco, 174 B.R. at 176; In re Terrace Chalet Apts., 159 B.R. at 829.

We disagree with the reasoning of these courts. As a leading treatise recognizes, use of the cramdown mechanism to allow a sale free and clear under § 363(f)(5) uses circular reasoning—it sanctions the effect of cramdown without requiring any of § 1129(b)'s substantive and procedural protections. 3 COLLIER ON BANKRUPTCY, *supra*, at ¶ 363.06[6]. If the proceeding authorizing the satisfaction was found elsewhere in the Bankruptcy Code, then an estate would not need § 363(f)(5) at all; it could simply use the other Code provision.

In addition, this reasoning undercuts the required showing of a separate proceeding. For example, it is correct that § 1129(b)(2) permits a cramdown of a lien to the value of the collateral, but it does so only in the context of plan confirmation. To isolate and separate the cramdown from the checks and balances inherent in the plan process undermines the entire confirmation process, and courts have been leery of using § 363(b) to gut plan confirmation or render it superfluous.

We thus hold that Congress did not intend under § 363(f)(5) that nonconsensual confirmation be a type of legal or equitable proceeding to which that paragraph refers. As a result, the availability of cramdown under § 1129(b)(2) is not a legal or equitable proceeding to which § 363(f)(5) is applicable.

In short, for the reasons outlined above, § 363(f)(5) does not apply to the circumstances of this case.

* * *

IV. CONCLUSION

* * *

2. The bankruptcy court did not apply the correct legal standard under § 363(f)(5), and it therefore did not make the findings required by that paragraph. We therefore reverse that part of the bankruptcy court's order that held that, under § 363(f)(5), the sale was free and clear of Clear Channel's lien.

3. Further, because of the bankruptcy court's incorrect interpretation of the statute, we remand this case for further proceedings consistent with this disposition. This will allow the parties to attempt to

identify a qualifying proceeding under nonbankruptcy law (if one exists) that would enable them to strip Clear Channel's lien and make the sale of PW's property to DB free and clear under § 363(f)(5).

* * *

Questions and Problems

1. Does an undersecured junior creditor have an incentive to block a sale, if possible, in every case in which the sale price will not be sufficient to pay that creditor's claim? If so, should this incentive influence a court in deciding whether to approve the sale?

2. What is "value"? "Amount"?

3. Does the disagreement among cases dealing with this issue arise from disagreement about the nature of secured creditors' rights in bankruptcy? That is, do courts that disagree with *Clear Channel* implicitly accept that a secured creditor is entitled to the value of its collateral and nothing more?

4. Debtor went broke while attempting to develop and market a subdivision comprised of 25 lots. The subdivision was subject to a blanket mortgage in favor of Developers' Bank, securing an obligation of $2 million. After filing a Chapter 11 petition, Debtor found buyers for two lots. Each of them was willing to pay $100,000 for a lot, but both required that Debtor deliver title free of Bank's lien. Bank will release its lien voluntarily only upon compliance with the terms of the note—that is, upon payment of $2 million. Can Debtor obtain a court order requiring Bank to release its lien on those two lots? See *Seidle v. Modular Paving, Inc. (In re 18th Avenue Development Corp.)*, 14 B.R. 862 (Bankr. S.D.Fla.1981).

5. Whittaker frequented bankruptcy sales, knowing that some wonderful bargains were sometimes available. Recently, Whittaker bought a luxury recreational vehicle from an individual's Chapter 11 estate, paying only about 60% of the retail price. The sale was authorized by the bankruptcy court and possession was given to Whittaker. An irate man, who introduced himself as Adams, visited Whittaker two weeks later. Adams claimed that the RV belonged to him and was merely parked for safekeeping at the debtor's home, while Adams was on an extended trip. Adams demanded possession. Must Whittaker hand Adams the keys? See *In re Sax*, 796 F.2d 994 (7th Cir.1986).

Another issue is whether sale of the debtor as a going concern can be made free and clear of successor liability claims—that is, whether the purchaser must assume the debtor's liabilities merely by having purchased its assets. The following case deals with that question in the context of Trans World Airline's third bankruptcy within ten years. (You may have noted that this case was cited by the court in *Clear Channel*.)

IN RE TRANS WORLD AIRLINES, INC.

United States Court of Appeals, Third Circuit, 2003.
322 F.3d 283.

FUENTES, Circuit Judge.

The issues in this bankruptcy appeal involve the doctrine of successor liability and arise out of the Bankruptcy Court's order approving the sale of the assets of Trans World Airlines ("TWA") to American Airlines ("American"). The primary question is whether the District Court erred in affirming the Bankruptcy Court's order, which had the effect of extinguishing the liability of American, as successor to TWA, for (1) employment discrimination claims against TWA and (2) for the Travel Voucher Program awarded to TWA's flight attendants in settlement of a sex discrimination class action. Because § 363(f) of the Bankruptcy Code permits a sale of property "free and clear" of an "interest in such property[,]" and because the claims against TWA here were connected to or arise from the assets sold, we affirm the Bankruptcy Court's order approving the sale "free and clear" of successor liability.

I. *Facts and Procedural Background*

We first review the factual background as it relates to the two types of claims under consideration here, the Travel Voucher Program and the Equal Employment Opportunity Commission ("EEOC") claims.

A. *The Travel Voucher Program*

[Two actions—one by the EEOC and the other by Linda Knox–Schillinger, representing a class of female flight attendants—were brought against TWA alleging that its former policy for maternity leaves violated the Civil Rights Act of 1964. In the settlement of both suits, TWA provided travel vouchers for each class member to be used by herself or her family at any time. Most flight attendants saved the vouchers for long trips to be taken after retirement.]

B. *EEOC Claims*

In addition to the claims arising out of the Travel Voucher Program, as of March 2, 2001, twenty-nine charges of discrimination had been filed against TWA with the EEOC or simultaneously filed with both the EEOC and a state or local Fair Employment Practices Agency. The charges alleged various violations of several federal employment discrimination statutes, including Title VII, the Americans with Disabilities Act, and the Age Discrimination in Employment Act. The appellants, the EEOC and the United States (collectively the "EEOC"), assert that they are unable to estimate the value, if any, of these claims, or the likelihood that the EEOC would commence litigation on the basis of any of these claims.

C. *American's Purchase of TWA's Assets*

On January 10, 2002, TWA filed a Chapter 11 bankruptcy petition.[2] Although it was the nation's eighth largest airline at the time, it had not earned a profit in over a decade. Months earlier, in the Spring of 2000, TWA determined that it could not continue to operate as an independent airline and that it needed to enter into a strategic transaction, such as a merger with, or sale of, TWA as a going concern to another airline. Throughout 2000, TWA held intermittent discussions with American concerning the possibility of a strategic partnership. On January 3, 2001, American contacted TWA with a proposal to purchase substantially all of TWA's assets. On January 9, 2001, American agreed to a purchase plan subject to an auction and Bankruptcy Court approval.

Though TWA's assets were being sold under a court-approved bidding process, as of February 28, 2001, the deadline for the submission of bids, TWA had not received any alternate proposals other than American's that conformed with the bidding procedures. Accordingly, TWA's Board of Directors voted to accept American's proposal to purchase TWA's assets for $742 million.

D. *Bankruptcy Court and District Court Approval of Sale*

The EEOC and the Knox–Schillinger class objected to the sale to American. After conducting an evidentiary hearing, the Bankruptcy Court approved the sale to American over the objections of the EEOC

---

[2] TWA had filed Chapter 11 petitions twice before, once in 1992 and again in 1995.

and the Knox–Schillinger plaintiffs. In approving the Sale Order, the Bankruptcy Court determined that there was no basis for successor liability on the part of American and that the flight attendants' claims could be treated as unsecured claims. In keeping with the Bankruptcy Court's conclusions, the Sale Order extinguished successor liability on the part of American for the Travel Voucher Program and any discrimination charges pending before the EEOC. Specifically, the Order provided that, in accordance with § 363(f) of the Bankruptcy Code:

> the free and clear delivery of the Assets shall include, but not be limited to, all asserted or unasserted, known or unknown, employment related claims, payroll taxes, employee contracts, employee seniority accrued while employed with any of the Sellers and successorship liability accrued up to the date of closing of such sale.

The Sale Order also enjoined all persons from seeking to enforce successor liability claims against American. The Court's order provided that:

> Pursuant to §§ 105(a) and 363 of the Bankruptcy Code, all Persons are enjoined from taking any action against Purchaser or Purchaser's Affiliates including, without limitation, TWA Airlines LLC, to recover any claim which such Person had solely against Sellers or Sellers' Affiliates.

Immediately after the Sale Order was entered, the EEOC filed a Notice of Appeal. On October 11, 2001, the District Court affirmed the Bankruptcy Court's decision, finding that TWA's assets were properly transferred free and clear of (1) the Travel Voucher Program and (2) the charges of employer misconduct filed with the EEOC. The District Court affirmed the Bankruptcy Court's holding that the claims against the debtor (TWA) were "interests in property" within the meaning of § 363(f), and therefore, the debtor's assets could be transferred free and clear of those claims. The District Court determined that the Bankruptcy Court's findings of fact were not clearly erroneous and that the Bankruptcy Court's legal conclusions were supported by the factual record. The District Court further noted that:

> there is record evidence supporting the bankruptcy court's conclusions that: (a) pursuant to a court-approved bidding procedure, debtors determined that American's offer was the highest and best offer for the purchase of substantially all of debtor's assets; (b) it was unlikely that debtors and American would

have consummated the sale if appellants' claims were not extinguished; (c) if the sale did not go forward, it was highly likely that debtors would have been liquidated with resulting material harm to creditors, employees and the St. Louis, Missouri region, as well as rendering debtors unable to satisfy its [sic] obligations under the Travel Voucher Program; and (d) the travel vouchers may be reduced to a monetary satisfaction.

On November 13, 2001, the Knox–Schillinger class filed a Notice of Appeal. On December 7, 2001, the EEOC also appealed the District Court's order. The appeals have been consolidated.

* * *

III. *Analysis*

The parties' dispute in this case concerns the meaning of the phrase "interest in such property" (hereafter "interest in property") as that phrase is used in § 363(f) of the Bankruptcy Code. This section "permits sale of property free and clear of any interest in the property of an entity other than the estate." S. Rep. No. 95-989, at 56 (1978). Appellants assert that the Travel Voucher Program and the pending EEOC charges are not interests in property within the meaning of this section and that, therefore, these claims were improperly extinguished by the Sale Order. They assert that interests in property are limited to "liens, mortgages, money judgments, writs of garnishment and attachment, and the like, and cannot encompass successor liability claims arising under federal antidiscrimination statutes and judicial decrees implementing those statutes." Appellants also assert that their claims are outside the scope of § 363(f), and therefore cannot be extinguished, because they could not "be compelled, in a legal or equitable proceeding, to accept a money satisfaction of [their] interest[s]." § 363(f)(5). The Airlines, on the other hand, argue that, while Congress did not expressly define "interest in property," the phrase should be broadly read to authorize a bankruptcy court to bar any interest that could potentially travel with the property being sold, even if the asserted interest is unsecured. They also assert that appellants' claims lie within the scope of § 363(f)(5), and therefore, can be extinguished because appellants can be compelled to accept a money satisfaction of their claims. We agree with the Airlines.[4]

---

[4] On appeal the Airlines also assert that the imposition of successor liability on American is not warranted under applicable nonbankruptcy law. * * * Here we decline to speculate as to whether there is a basis for successor liability and,

A. *Interest in Property*

The contentions of the parties require us to consider whether the claims in this case constitute an interest in property as understood within the meaning of § 363(f). *[The court quoted the provision, emphasizing "or" at the end of (f)(4).]* Some courts have narrowly interpreted interests in property to mean *in rem* interests in property, such as liens. However, the trend seems to be toward a more expansive reading of "interests in property" which "encompasses other obligations that may flow from ownership of the property." 3 Collier on Bankruptcy ¶ 363.06[1].

In *Folger Adam Sec., Inc. v. DeMatteis/MacGregor, JV*, 209 F.3d 252 (3d Cir.2000), we addressed the issue of whether certain affirmative defenses to a claim for breach of contract constituted an interest in property within the meaning of § 363(f). Specifically, we were asked to decide "whether the affirmative defenses of setoff, recoupment, and other contract defenses * * * constitute an 'interest' under § 363(f) of the Bankruptcy Code such that a sale of the debtors' assets in a consolidated Bankruptcy Court auction free and clear, extinguished such affirmative defenses * * * ." We observed that there was no support in the case law for the proposition that *a defense* may be extinguished as a result of a free and clear sale. Accordingly, we held that "a right of recoupment is a defense and not an interest and therefore is not extinguished by a § 363(f) sale."

In arriving at this conclusion, we explored the significance of the Fourth Circuit's decision in *In re Leckie Smokeless Coal Co.*, 99 F.3d 573 (4th Cir.1996). In *Leckie*, the Fourth Circuit held that, irrespective of whether the purchasers of the debtors' assets were successors in interest, under § 363(f), the Bankruptcy Court could properly extinguish all successor liability claims against the purchasers arising under the Coal Act by entering an order transferring the debtors' assets free and clear of those claims. The Fourth Circuit held that the two employer-sponsored benefit plans that sought to collect Coal Act premium payments from the debtors' successors in interest were asserting interests in property that had already been sold through the § 363 sale. The Fourth Circuit explained that:

> while the plain meaning of the phrase "interest in such property" suggests that not all general rights to payment are encom-

---

instead, assume for purposes of our analysis that but for the Sale Order, appellants could have asserted viable successor liability claims against American.

passed by the statute, Congress did not expressly indicate that, by employing such language, it intended to limit the scope of § 363(f) to *in rem* interests, strictly defined, and we decline to adopt such a restricted reading of the statute here.

Id. at 582. The Court explained that the employer-sponsored benefit plans had interests in the property of the debtors which had been transferred under § 363(f) in the sense that there was a relationship between their right to demand premium payments from the debtors and the use to which the debtors had put their assets. Importantly, in the course of our review of *Leckie*, we noted that "the term 'any interest' is intended to refer to obligations that are connected to, or arise from, the property being sold."

Here the Airlines correctly assert that the Travel Voucher and EEOC claims at issue had the same relationship to TWA's assets in the § 363(f) sale, as the employee benefits did to the debtors' assets in *Leckie*. In each case it was the assets of the debtor which gave rise to the claims. Had TWA not invested in airline assets, which required the employment of the EEOC claimants, those successor liability claims would not have arisen. Furthermore, TWA's investment in commercial aviation is inextricably linked to its employment of the Knox–Schillinger claimants as flight attendants, and its ability to distribute travel vouchers as part of the settlement agreement. While the interests of the EEOC and the Knox–Schillinger class in the assets of TWA's bankruptcy estate are not interests in property in the sense that they are not *in rem* interests, the reasoning of *Leckie* and *Folger Adam* suggests that they are interests in property within the meaning of § 363(f) in the sense that they arise from the property being sold.

Indeed, to equate interests in property with only *in rem* interests such as liens would be inconsistent with § 363(f)(3), which contemplates that a lien is but one type of interest. *[The court quoted § 363-(f)(3).]* In this regard, we find ourselves in agreement with Collier's observation that:

> Section 363(f) permits the bankruptcy court to authorize a sale free of "any interest" that an entity has in property of the estate. Yet the Code does not define the concept of "interest," of which the property may be sold free. Certainly a lien is a type of "interest" of which the property may be sold free and clear. This becomes apparent in reviewing § 363(f)(3), which provides for particular treatment when "such interest is a lien." Obviously there must be situations in which the interest is something other

than a lien; otherwise § 363(f)(3) would not need to deal explicitly with the case in which the interest is a lien.

3 Collier on Bankruptcy ¶ 363.06[1].

B. *Money Satisfaction*

In addition to asserting that their claims are not interests in property within the meaning of § 363(f), appellants also assert that their claims are outside the scope of § 363(f)(5) because neither the vouchers nor the EEOC claims are interests on account of which they could be compelled to accept money satisfaction. As noted above, under § 363(f), assuming the "interest in property" at issue falls within the meaning of the statute, a sale free and clear of such interest can occur if any one of five conditions has been satisfied. The Bankruptcy Court determined that, because the travel voucher and EEOC claims were both subject to monetary valuation, the fifth condition had been satisfied. We agree. Had TWA liquidated its assets under Chapter 7 of the Bankruptcy Code, the claims at issue would have been converted to dollar amounts and the claimants would have received the distribution provided to other general unsecured creditors on account of their claims. A travel voucher represents a seat on an airplane, a travel benefit that can be reduced to a specific monetary value. Indeed, TWA arrived at a valuation for tax purposes, as noted in the Annex to the settlement agreement. Likewise, the EEOC discrimination claims are reducible to, and can be satisfied by, monetary awards even if the relief sought is injunctive in nature.

C. *Other Considerations*

Even were we to conclude that the claims at issue are not interests in property, the priority scheme of the Bankruptcy Code supports the transfer of TWA's assets free and clear of the claims. The statutory scheme, § 507(a), defines various classes of creditors entitled to satisfaction before general unsecured creditors may access the pool of available assets. In *In re New England Fish Co.*, 19 B.R. 323 (Bankr. W.D. Wash.1982), the Bankruptcy Court held that the civil rights claims before it were *not* interests in property but decided that the claimants were general unsecured creditors and that the debtor's assets could be transferred free and clear of such claims.

In *New England Fish*, the issue was whether the Bankruptcy Court could extinguish the right to payment of claimants asserting civil rights claims in the Bankruptcy Court. The civil rights claims at issue in *New England Fish* were based on allegations of racial discrimination in employment. In that case, two class actions had been brought against the debtor by its employees. One of the suits went to trial and the plaintiffs obtained a damages award for job discrimination, housing discrimination and attorneys fees. In the other suit, there had been no determination of liability at the time of the bankruptcy filing.[6]

The Bankruptcy Court recognized the claimants holding a judgment as being general unsecured creditors with liquidated claims and recognized the other class of claimants as being general unsecured creditors to the extent they could prove liability. The prospective purchaser of the assets of the debtor and its trustee sought an adjudication that the assets of the debtor were transferred free and clear of the interests of the civil rights claimants. The prospective purchaser also sought a declaration that it did not qualify as a successor employer of the debtor, and, therefore, could not be held liable to the civil rights claimants.

In the course of discussing the civil rights claims in *New England Fish*, the Bankruptcy Court applied the Supreme Court's admonition in *Nathanson v. National Labor Relations Board*, 344 U.S. 25 (1952), that "if one claimant of the bankrupt's estate is to be preferred over others, 'the purpose should be clear from the statute.' " The Court reasoned that allowing the claimants to seek a recovery from the successor entity while creditors which were accorded higher priority by the Bankruptcy Code obtained their recovery from the limited assets of the bankruptcy estate would "subvert the specific priorities which define Congressional policy for bankruptcy distribution to creditors." 19 B.R. at 329.

Other courts have followed the rationale set forth in *New England Fish*. For instance, in *Forde v. Kee–Lox Mfg. Co., Inc.*, 437 F. Supp. 631 (W.D.N.Y.1977), the District Court dismissed a suit brought under Title VII by an employee of a bankrupt debtor against the purchaser of its assets on a successor liability theory. The Court rejected the civil rights claimant's assertion that the Court could not reduce his demand for reinstatement to a fixed amount of money that could be satisfied out of the proceeds of the sale of the assets of the debtor's bankruptcy estate. The Court explained:

---

[6] This parallels the status of appellants' claims here. The Knox–Schillinger class is comprised of general unsecured creditors whose claims have been liquidated by the Travel Voucher Program. The EEOC is a general unsecured creditor whose claims have not been liquidated.

There are two major difficulties with the plaintiff's position. First, the plaintiff would allow claimants such as himself to assert their claims against purchasers of the bankrupt's assets, while relegating lienholders to the proceeds of the sale. This elevates claims that have not been secured or reduced to judgment to a position superior to those that have. Yet the Bankruptcy Act is clearly designed to give liens on the bankrupt's property preference over unliquidated claims.

An additional difficulty with the plaintiff's position is that it would seriously impair the trustee's ability to liquidate the bankrupt's estate. If the trustee in a liquidation sale is not able to transfer title to the bankrupt's assets free of all claims, including civil rights claims, prospective purchasers may be unwilling to pay a fair price for the property, leaving less to distribute to the creditors.

Id. at 633-34.

* * *

We are sensitive to the concerns raised in *Forde*. We recognize that the claims of the EEOC and the Knox–Schillinger class of plaintiffs are based on congressional enactments addressing employment discrimination and are, therefore, not to be extinguished absent a compelling justification. At the same time, in the context of a bankruptcy, these claims are, by their nature, general unsecured claims and, as such, are accorded low priority. To allow the claimants to assert successor liability claims against American while limiting other creditors' recourse to the proceeds of the asset sale would be inconsistent with the Bankruptcy Code's priority scheme.

Moreover, the sale of TWA's assets to American at a time when TWA was in financial distress was likely facilitated by American obtaining title to the assets free and clear of these civil rights claims. Absent entry of the Bankruptcy Court's order providing for a sale of TWA's assets free and clear of the successor liability claims at issue, American may have offered a discounted bid. This is particularly likely given that the EEOC has been unable to estimate the number of claims it would pursue or the magnitude of the damages it would seek. The arguments advanced by appellants do not seem to account adequately for the fact that American was the only entity that came forward with an offer that complied with the court-approved bidding procedures for TWA's assets and provided jobs for TWA's employees.

The Bankruptcy Court found that, in the absence of a sale of TWA's assets to American, "the EEOC will be relegated to holding an unsecured claim in what will very likely be a piece-meal liquidation of TWA. In that context, such claims are likely to have little if any value." The same is true for claims asserted pursuant to the Travel Voucher Program, as they would be reduced to a dollar amount and would receive the same treatment as the unsecured claims of the EEOC. Given the strong likelihood of a liquidation absent the asset sale to American, a fact which appellants do not dispute, we agree with the Bankruptcy Court that a sale of the assets of TWA at the expense of preserving successor liability claims was necessary in order to preserve some 20,000 jobs, including those of Knox–Schillinger and the EEOC claimants still employed by TWA, and to provide funding for employee-related liabilities, including retirement benefits.

IV. *Conclusion*

After carefully considering the arguments discussed above and all other arguments advanced by appellants, we join the District Court in affirming the Bankruptcy Court's authorization of the sale of TWA's assets to American free and clear of the claims of the EEOC and the Knox–Schillinger class.

Notes and Questions

1. Successor liability arises, chiefly, in two types of cases—product liability and employee-related claims brought under federal statutes. This case, of course, involved the latter. Such claims are subject to successor liability as a matter of common law. See *Steinbach v. Hubbard*, 51 F.3d 843 (9th Cir.1995) (collecting cases).

2. Are TWA's flight attendants, and other possible victims of civil rights violations, bearing the brunt of this bankruptcy? Is this outcome any worse, from their point of view, than what cramdown might bring?

3. A bankruptcy court's power to permit sale of an entity free of claims and interests is clearer in the context of a plan, because of § 1141(c). That subsection provides that, after confirmation, "the property dealt with by the plan is free and clear of all claims and interests." Does this subsection suggest that such sales should be carried out only in accordance with a confirmed plan? Given this provision, why would a debtor not utilize the plan process, rather than the court-supervised auction seen in this case?

4. Before *Knox–Schillinger* was decided, some courts had questioned whether "any interest in such property" included not only liens and encumbrances, but unsecured claims as well. The Seventh Circuit was among those

courts. See *Zerand–Bernal Group, Inc. v. Cox*, 23 F.3d 159 (7th Cir.1994). The Seventh Circuit has since cited *Knox–Schillinger* for the proposition that the term "any interest in such property" should be interpreted expansively. *Precision Industries Inc. v. Qualitech Steel SBQ LLC*, 327 F.3d. 537, 545 (7th Cir.2003).

The issue in *Precision Industries* was one of first impression at the circuit level—namely, whether the sale of assets "free and clear" under § 363(f) cuts off rights of the debtor's lessee—here, Precision Industries—to use and possession of leased property included in the sale. The court held that it does, even though § 365(h)(1)(A) provides that rejection of a lease does not affect a nondebtor-lessee's rights:

> The district court, following the lead of other lower courts, concluded that the limitations imposed by § 365(h) vis-à-vis rejection of leases necessarily conflict with and override the debtor-in-possession's ability to sell estate property free and clear of a lessee's possessory interest. But for the reasons that follow, we conclude that the terms of § 365(h) do not supersede those of § 363(f).

> First, the statutory provisions themselves do not suggest that one supersedes or limits the other. Notably, §§ 363 and 365 both contain cross-references indicating that certain of their provisions are subject to other statutory mandates. But nowhere in either § 363(f) or § 365(h) is there a similar cross-reference indicating that the broad right to sell estate property free of "any interest" is subordinate to the protections that § 365(h) accords to lessees. The omission suggests that Congress did not intend for the latter section to limit the former.

> Second, the plain language of § 365(h)(1)(A) suggests that it has a limited scope. By its own terms, that subsection applies "if the trustee [or debtor-in-possession] *rejects* an unexpired lease of real property * * * ." (Emphasis supplied.) Here what occurred in the first instance was a sale of the property that Precision was leasing rather than a rejection of its lease. Granted, if the Sale Order operated to extinguish Precision's right to possess the property—as we conclude it did—then the effect of the sale might be understood as the equivalent of a repudiation of [lessee's] lease. But nothing in the express terms of § 365(h) suggests that it applies to any and all events that threaten the lessee's possessory rights. Section 365(h) instead focuses on a specific type of event—the rejection of an executory contract by the trustee or debtor-in-possession—and spells out the rights of parties affected by that event. It says nothing at all about sales of estate property, which are the province of § 363. The two statutory provisions thus apply to distinct sets of circumstances.

> Third, § 363 itself provides for a mechanism to protect the rights of parties whose interests may be adversely affected by the sale

of estate property. As noted above, § 363(e) directs the bankruptcy court, on the request of any entity with an interest in the property to be sold, to "prohibit or condition such * * * sale * * as is necessary to provide adequate protection of such interest." Because a leasehold qualifies as an "interest" in property for purposes of § 363(f), a lessee of property being sold pursuant to subsection (f) would have the right to insist that its interest be protected. "Adequate protection" does not necessarily guarantee a lessee's continued possession of the property, but it does demand, in the alternative, that the lessee be compensated for the value of its leasehold—typically from the proceeds of the sale. Lessees like Precision are therefore not without recourse in the event of a sale free and clear of their interests. They have the right to seek protection under § 363(e), and upon request, the bankruptcy court is obligated to ensure that their interests are adequately protected.

With these points in mind, it is apparent that the two statutory provisions can be construed in a way that does not disable § 363(f) vis-à-vis leasehold interests. Where estate property under lease is to be sold, § 363 permits the sale to occur free and clear of a lessee's possessory interest—provided that the lessee (upon request) is granted adequate protection for its interest. Where the property is not sold, and the debtor remains in possession thereof but chooses to reject the lease, § 365(h) comes into play and the lessee retains the right to possess the property. So understood, both provisions may be given full effect without coming into conflict with one another and without disregarding the rights of lessees.

We are persuaded that it is both reasonable and correct to interpret and reconcile §§ 363(f) and 365(h) in this way. It is consistent with the express terms of each provision, and it avoids the unwelcome result of reading a limitation into § 363(f) that the legislature itself did not inscribe onto the statute. Congress authorized the sale of estate property free and clear of "*any* interest," not "any interest *except* a lessee's possessory interest." The interpretation is also consistent with the process of marshaling the estate's assets for the twin purposes of maximizing creditor recovery and rehabilitating the debtor, which are central to the Bankruptcy Code.

Id. at 546-48.

The court noted that lessees are not without recourse, because they can seek adequate protection under § 363(e), "typically from the proceeds of the sale." But what would suffice for adequate protection of a possessory interest in real estate? Is the existence of § 365(h)(1) some evidence of a congressional conclusion that nothing will serve except continued possession? (Note use of the word "prohibits" in § 363(e).) If a monetary amount can provide adequate protection, what priority does that claim enjoy? Is it an administrative claim? If any adequate protection payment would come from sale proceeds, does that imply a secured claim?

5. Have courts like *Precision Industries* taken § 363(f) too far?

If the debtor's assets are to be sold, interested buyers must be located. This effort, which is of particular importance when the entire debtor enterprise is the subject of sale, sometimes requires the enticement of a "break-up" fee. The next case addresses the circumstances under which such a payment is permitted.

IN RE RELIANT ENERGY CHANNELVIEW LP

United States Court of Appeals, Third Circuit, 2010.
594 F.3d 200.

GREENBERG, Circuit Judge.

I. INTRODUCTION

This matter comes on before this Court on appeal from an order of the District Court entered on March 31, 2009, affirming March 18, 2008 and June 9, 2008 orders of the Bankruptcy Court in proceedings arising from the sale of a major asset of the Debtors' estate in this bankruptcy proceeding. The Bankruptcy Court denied the request of an unsuccessful bidder for the asset, Kelson Channelview LLC ("Kelson"), for disbursement of administrative expenses in the form of a break-up fee from the estate in the March 18, 2008 order, and then in the June 9, 2008 order approved the sale of the asset to Fortistar, LLC. Kelson appealed but the District Court affirmed the orders of the Bankruptcy Court. *In re Reliant Energy Channelview LP*, 403 B.R. 308 (D. Del. 2009). We will affirm the order of the District Court and, in effect, the order of the Bankruptcy Court of March 18, 2008.

II. BACKGROUND

The Debtors in the Chapter 11 proceedings, Reliant Energy Channelview LP and Reliant Energy Services Channelview LLC (together, the "Debtors"), decided to sell their largest asset, a power plant in Channelview, Texas. With the assistance of consultants with expertise in the energy industry, the Debtors contacted 115 potentially interested purchasers. This substantial effort was fruitful for 38 potential bidders executed confidentiality agreements with respect to a possible purchase, and 24 went further and conducted due diligence on the purchase. Ultimately 12, including Fortistar, made bids for the plant. Many of the bids, however, were contingent on the bidder obtaining financing, a difficult undertaking in the then prevailing business environment. Kelson, however, submitted a complete bid of $468 million not contingent on financing and was selected as the winning bidder. Consequently, Kelson entered into an Asset Purchase Agreement ("APA") with the Debtors for the power plant.

Inasmuch as the Debtors were in bankruptcy, consummation of the APA required the Bankruptcy Court's approval. Consequently, the APA provided that the Debtors immediately would seek an order from the Bankruptcy Court allowing the sale. Moreover, the Debtors agreed that they would seek an order approving certain "bid protections and procedures" for Kelson's benefit if the Court determined that there should be an auction for the plant before its sale. These proposed bid protections and procedures provided that Debtors could not accept a competing bid unless it exceeded Kelson's bid by $5 million. Furthermore, the proposed bid protections and procedures provided that if a competing bid was accepted, Kelson would be entitled to a $15 million break-up fee, about three percent of its bid, as well as reimbursement for expenses it incurred in the sale process up to $2 million. The practice of paying a break-up fee to an initial bidder for assets has developed in bankruptcy and other contexts to compensate the bidder for memorializing its interest in acquiring the asset, an interest which sometimes, as we will explain below, can be useful to the asset's seller even if the bid is not accepted.

As the APA required, the Debtors requested that the Bankruptcy Court authorize the sale of the plant to Kelson without conducting an auction. In that motion, the Debtors asserted that the Kelson bid "represents the highest and best offer available for the Debtors' assets and that further marketing of the assets will not result in a higher purchase price." The Bankruptcy Court delayed its decision on this motion when one of the Debtors' equity holders objected to the fast pace of the transaction.[3] Ultimately, however, the Court would not approve the sale to Kelson without an auction for the plant.

---

[3] The objector's claimed status as an equity holder was disputed at the time but we are not concerned with that dispute. We emphasize, however, that not all of the interested parties supported the original proposed sale, and the Bankruptcy Court, we think quite appropriately, acted with caution in considering this very substantial matter.

When the Court delayed the approval of the sale, the Debtors, with the support of their Creditors, asked the Court to authorize the bid protection measures that we have described. However, Fortistar, which previously had submitted a losing contingent bid, objected to this request and asserted that it was willing to enter a "higher and better" bid at an auction, but the $15 million break-up fee along with the $2 million reimbursement for expenses would be a deterrent to it doing so.

* * *

Ultimately the Bankruptcy Court entered its March 18, 2008 order approving the $5 million "overbid" requirement which required that bids competing with Kelson's bid must exceed it by $5 million. In addition, the Court approved the reimbursement to Kelson for expenses it incurred in the transaction up to $2 million. Finally, however, in the provision of its order at issue on this appeal, the Court refused to authorize payment of the $15 million break-up fee.

Kelson did not participate in the subsequent auction, and, in fact, argued that its offer was no longer available. Fortistar, however, submitted the winning, now fully financed bid, which topped Kelson's bid by $32 million. In accordance with the Bankruptcy Court's decision, the Debtors did not pay Kelson the $15 million break-up fee, although they did pay Kelson for its expenses.

After the Bankruptcy Court entered an order on June 9, 2008, approving the sale to Fortistar, Kelson appealed to the District Court from the order denying the payment of the $15 million break-up fee, arguing that the Bankruptcy Court abused its discretion by denying Kelson's request for the fee. Kelson also argued that it was a stalking-horse bidder entitled to a break-up fee as a matter of fundamental fairness and contended that the Debtors were estopped from opposing its appeal because they supported its request for the break-up fee in the Bankruptcy Court. The District Court rejected Kelson's arguments and affirmed the March 18, 2008 and June 9, 2008 orders of the Bankruptcy Court and thus the District Court did not allow the payment of the break-up fee. Kelson then filed this appeal * * * .

A. The *O'Brien* Standard

In *Calpine Corp. v. O'Brien Env't Energy, Inc. (In re O'Brien Env't Energy, Inc.)*, 181 F.3d 527 (3d Cir.1999) ("*O'Brien*"), we set forth the controlling legal principles applicable on this appeal. In *O'Brien*, the debtor, after considering bids from several interested buyers for certain of its assets, entered into an asset purchase agreement with Calpine Corporation, which conditioned its bid on the parties' ability to secure Bankruptcy Court approval of a $2 million break-up fee. The debtor, supported by many of its creditors, sought approval for the fee from the Bankruptcy Court. Nevertheless, the Court denied the application, stating that a break-up fee would complicate or even chill the bidding process. However, the Court gave Calpine permission to renew its application after an auction for the sale of the assets.

Notwithstanding Calpine's insistence that it would not make an offer without the assurance of a provision for a break-up fee, it did enter the bidding process. After a different bidder made the best offer, Calpine renewed its request for a break-up fee, but the Court denied the request after an evidentiary hearing. Calpine appealed and, after the District Court affirmed, Calpine appealed to our Court.

Calpine argued to us that it was seeking the fee under "applicable case law," but we rejected this contention. We held that courts do not have the authority to create new ways to authorize the payment of fees from a bankruptcy estate, and the methods of recovering fees from an estate are limited to the procedures established by the Bankruptcy Code. We concluded that a bidder must seek a break-up fee under § 503(b), which, so far as germane here, permits payment of postpetition administrative expenses for the "actual, necessary costs and expenses of preserving the estate." We also held that there was no "compelling justification for treating an application for a break-up fee and expenses under § 503(b) differently from other applications for administrative expenses under the same provision."

Therefore, we indicated that in considering requests for break-up fees, we would apply the general standard used for all administrative expenses—"the allowability of break-up fees, like that of other administrative expenses, depends upon the requesting party's ability to show that the fees were actually necessary to preserve the value of the estate." *Id.* Focusing specifically on break-up fees, we noted that it was permissible to offer a break-up fee and reimbursement for expenses to induce an initial bid, provided the allowance of the fee does not give an advantage to a favored purchaser over other bidders by increasing the cost of acquisition. We also indicated that a break-up fee is not "necessary to preserve the value of the estate" when the bidder would have bid even without the break-up fee. *Id.* (citing Bruce A. Markell, *The Case Against Breakup Fees in Bankruptcy*, 66 AM. BANKR. L.J. 349, 359 (1992)).

Applying this standard to the facts in *O'Brien*, we found that Calpine would have made its bid even without the assurance of a break-up fee, as it indeed did. For this reason, among others, we found that an award of a break-up fee was not necessary to preserve the value of the estate and we affirmed the order of the District Court and thus the order of the Bankruptcy Court denying allowance of the fee.

B. Application of *O'Brien* To This Case

Under *O'Brien*, we must decide whether an award of a break-up fee was necessary to preserve the value of the Debtors' estate. In this regard, we recognize that it could be argued that in either or both of two ways a break-up fee could have preserved the value of the estate. First, the opportunity to obtain a break-up fee could have induced Kelson to make its bid before the Bankruptcy Court ordered the auction, and second, the provision for a break-up fee may have been necessary to induce Kelson to adhere to its bid after the Court ordered the conducting of the auction.[9]

1. Was a break-up fee needed to induce the first bid?

Kelson's bid undoubtedly provided a benefit to the estate by establishing a minimum price and a complete set of offer terms and, in fact, the Bankruptcy Court required that any competing bid exceed Kelson's bid by at least $5 million. Indeed, it is plausible to believe that an initial bid, ordinarily or perhaps even always, will provide a benefit to an estate because it will establish a floor price for the assets to be sold. But we have to decide a different question, *i.e.*, was an award of a break-up fee necessary to produce this benefit and preserve the value of the estate?

We recognize that the first bidder in a bankruptcy sale necessarily takes a risk at least to the extent of investing the time,

---

[9] In its brief Kelson argues that the "APA was necessary to preserve the value of the estate, as it enabled the Debtors to resolve a dispute with the pre-petition secured lenders with respect to the use of cash collateral." While we do not doubt that a sale to Kelson would have resolved the cash collateral dispute inasmuch as all the Debtors' creditors were to be paid in full from the sale proceeds, the issue before us is quite different from the need to placate the Debtors' creditors, as we are concerned with whether the $15 million break-up fee was necessary to preserve the value of the estate, a matter relating to Kelson's bid rather than to the consequences of a sale of the plant such as the satisfaction of the Debtor's creditors. As we explain below, Kelson entered into the APA without the assurance that it would receive a break-up fee if it was unable to acquire the plant.

money and energy needed to produce its bid.[10] Nevertheless, while we understand that the first bidder may be motivated in part to submit its bid by the possibility that it will receive a break-up fee, it does not follow from that motivation that the bidder will withdraw its bid, pass up on the opportunity to acquire the asset to be sold, and nullify its work in preparing its bid if a court, when ordering that there be an auction of assets, declines to authorize a break-up fee to be paid to the initial bidder. Surely *O'Brien* makes that clear because even though Calpine had made its bid contingent on the award of a break-up fee, it competed at the auction after the Bankruptcy Court rejected the request for a break-up fee.

Here, however, Kelson argues that the provision of a break-up fee was necessary to entice it to bid, but the facts do not support this argument. We are satisfied that it is clear beyond doubt that Kelson did not condition its bid on the presence of a provision for a break-up fee, although it did condition the bid on the Debtors' promise to seek authority to pay it such a fee. * * * Accordingly, there is no escape from the fact that Kelson *did* make its bid without the assurance of a break-up fee, and this fact destroys Kelson's argument that the fee was needed to induce it to bid. Rather, the mere possibility of the payment of a break-up fee was sufficient for that purpose.

2. Was a break-up fee needed to preserve Kelson's bid?

The record suggests that although an assurance of a break-up fee may not have been needed to induce Kelson's bid, it nevertheless could have been useful to assure that Kelson adhered to its bid rather than abandoning its attempt to purchase the plant in the event that the Bankruptcy Court required an auction for its sale. A break-up fee certainly provides a benefit to an estate if a bidder remains committed to a purchase, though, as we have explained, we see no reason to believe that bidders who already have made a full and complete bid necessarily will abandon their efforts to obtain an asset without an assurance of a break-up fee. In this case, the Bankruptcy Court believed that the provision for the fee would deter other possible purchasers from bidding for the plant and would outweigh any possible benefit achieved for the estate by keeping Kelson committed to the purchase through the provision for the break-up fee.

---

[10] In this case, Kelson was compensated fully for its first-bid expenses when the Bankruptcy Court awarded it $1,210,257 for that purpose.

Clearly, the Bankruptcy Court was faced with a difficult choice. If the Court denied the break-up fee, then Kelson might abandon the purchase, as it supposedly did. If another suitable bid had not materialized and Kelson had walked away permanently from the purchase, the estate would have been harmed severely by the denial of a break-up fee. To avoid this result, the Court could have granted a break-up fee to secure Kelson's existing bid. Nevertheless, the Court decided that a $15 million break-up fee was not necessary for the protection of the estate. This decision, which we view from the Court's perspective on March 18, 2008, was justified by (1) Fortistar's assertion that it planned to continue bidding, (2) the binding language of the APA, and (3) the logical belief that Kelson would not abandon a fully negotiated agreement if no other bidder materialized. Though we do not decide the case on the basis of our knowledge of what happened after the Court denied the fee, as we decide the case on the basis of the record as of March 18, 2008, when the order from which Kelson appealed to the District Court was entered, there is no escape from the fact that the Bankruptcy Court's decision was shown to be correct when Fortistar placed a substantially higher bid for the assets.

3. Conclusion

We cannot say that the Bankruptcy Court abused its discretion in its application of the *O'Brien* standard. Though the allowance of a break-up fee might have benefitted the estate, Kelson made its bid before the auction knowing that it might not receive a break-up fee, and a retroactive grant of a break-up fee could not have induced a bid that Kelson already had made. Though, as we have made clear, the estate might have benefitted if on March 18, 2008, the Bankruptcy Court had provided for a break-up fee to secure Kelson's adherence to its earlier bid, the Court found that the potential harm to the estate that a break-up fee would cause by deterring other bidders from entering the bid process outweighed that benefit. We cannot say that the Bankruptcy Court abused its discretion in reaching its result.

C. Application of the Business Judgment Rule Instead of *O'Brien*

Kelson bases a substantial portion of its argument on the circumstance that none of the Debtors' creditors or equity holders objected to its request for a break-up fee. Kelson points out that the business judgment rule would have been applied to the Debtors' decision to support the award of a break-up fee if the Debtors had not been in bankruptcy. We agree that the Bankruptcy Court should not lightly dismiss such a consensus among the creditors, but we are not willing to conclude that the presence of unanimity among creditors should require the Court to decide the matter through the application of the business judgment rule. Clearly, § 503(b) does not give the Bankruptcy Court the authority to award fees solely because there is no objection to them from a party-in-interest. That section requires that for fees to be awarded they must be part of "the actual, necessary costs and expenses of preserving the estate," and does not suggest that that standard is met merely because there is no objection to the application for the fees. * * *

V. CONCLUSION

The Bankruptcy Court did not abuse its discretion when it concluded that an award of a break-up fee was not necessary to preserve the value of the estate and accordingly, we will affirm the District Court's order of March 31, 2009, to the extent that it affirmed the order of the Bankruptcy Court of March 18, 2008, denying authorization to pay the break-up fee

Notes and Questions

1. A break-up fee is, simply, a sum paid to the initial offeror in the event that a higher bidder ultimately purchases the assets. The payment is designed to reimburse the initial offeror for its expenses in conducting due diligence or negotiating an asset purchase agreement.

2. As you can gather from the case, some courts apply the business judgment rule drawn from corporate law. See, e.g., *In re 995 Fifth Avenue Associates, L.P.*, 96 B.R. 24 (Bankr. S.D.N.Y.1989). On the other hand, other courts find the business judgment rule inappropriate for the bankruptcy context. See, e.g., *In re Hupp Industries, Inc.*, 140 B.R. 191 (Bankr. N.D. Ohio 1992) (utilizing a factor approach in identifying the "best interests of the estate"). *O'Brien* rejected both, applying instead a test based on § 503(b), and *Reliant Energy* followed suit. Is that test more appropriate than the alternative approaches? Is it appreciably different from a "best interests" test?

3. What effect will *Reliant Energy* have on future auctions? Are bidders likely to bid more, or less? Are bankruptcy courts likely to approve future applications for break-up fees, under the authority of *Reliant Energy*?

4. In *Reliant Energy*, approval for the break-up fee was sought at the conclusion of the bidding process. In many cases, however, first-day motions include requests for approval of bidding procedures allowing break-up fees. Does *Reliant Energy* give any guidance to bankruptcy judges who have to decide whether to grant or deny motions such motions?

E. VALUATION OF THE FIRM

Valuation is a pervasive necessity in bankruptcy. A court may have to determine the going concern value of a reorganizing corporation in order to resolve several different issues—for example, whether a creditor is entitled to adequate protection or whether the proposed plan pays a particular creditor or group of creditors the minimum amount required by the Code. When the proposed plan is at issue, negotiations among the parties are carried out against the specter of cramdown, which offers the debtor substantial leverage.

The valuation method does not seem dependent upon the context of the issue to be decided. The following case arose from creditors' motions for relief from stay.

IN RE ASCHER

United States Bankruptcy Court, Northern District of Illinois, 1992.
146 B.R. 764.

JACK B. SCHMETTERER, Bankruptcy Judge.

Michael Brogan, Edward Long, and James Kelly (the "Movants") moved for relief from the automatic stay pursuant to § 362(d). They seek to remain in possession of the commercial laundry facility located in Harvard, Illinois, doing business as Royal Laundry Systems, in order to realize the value of their security interest. * * * The motion was opposed by the Debtor Walter Ascher ("Ascher") and the Chapter 11 Trustee David Grochocinski. * * *

FINDINGS OF FACT

1. All–American Laundry Service, Inc. ("All–American") was formed as a Corporation under Illinois law in 1988 for the purpose of acquiring the assets of Royal Laundry Systems ("Royal") and operating Royal's commercial laundry facility in Harvard, Illinois (the "Laundry"). Ascher was the president of All–American, and he also claims to be the company's sole shareholder.

Calculation of Movant's Secured Claim

[Bank lent All–American $668,000 to finance the purchase of Royal's assets. Bank perfected liens on all of Royal's real and personal property as security for the loan. As additional security, Ascher

pledged stock in All–American and Movants pledged stock in UPS. When the loan went into default 18 months later and Bank took steps to sell the UPS stock, Movants paid the balance due. Bank assigned the note and liens to Movants and their nominee, Laundry Credit Corp.

Movants ousted Ascher and took physical possession of the laundry. They were required to advance $41,357 in additional funds to cover payroll, accounting services and operating expenses. They also incurred $5,000 in legal fees recoverable under the terms of the note.

When the bankruptcy petition was filed, $625,000 in principal was due on the note. The parties disagreed regarding the applicable interest rate. If the contract postmaturity rate of 11% were used, as Movants advocated, $347,196 in interest had accrued as of bankruptcy. If the contract prematurity rate of 2% over prime were used, as the trustee argued, $184,417 in interest had accrued as of bankruptcy.]

* * *

14. Therefore, the total secured debt owed to Movants is either $855,774.12 or $1,018,553.43, depending on whether one accepts the Trustee's or the Movants' theory on which interest rate to apply to the balance due.

Calculation of the Laundry's Value

15. Expert testimony was offered as to the value of the Laundry. The net capitalized earnings (or discounted cash flow) is found to be the proper approach to determining value of the Laundry, because it is a going entity and is expected to remain as such by all the Parties to this litigation. Under this approach, the valuation is conducted by predicting the future earnings for the company, and then discounting those earnings by a capitalization (or discount) rate which is the rate of return required by a potential investor in order for his or her investment to be worthwhile. The following formula is applied to reach a prediction as to value:

$$\frac{\text{Predicted earnings per year}}{\text{Capitalization rate}} = \begin{array}{l}\text{Value of Company's future} \\ \text{net earnings to investors}\end{array}$$

16. The Laundry is currently controlled through the Laundry Credit Corporation which is an Illinois corporation wholly owned by Movants. Management and sales services are provided by Mr. John Eakes, a principal of Royal (the Laundry's former owner) and his subordinates through an agreement with Professional Laundry Service

Consultants, Inc., an Illinois corporation owned by Mr. Eakes. Mr. Eakes was hired because Movants' only business experience related to their jobs as executives at UPS, and they needed a person with experience in the commercial laundry industry to manage the Laundry. The management fees paid to Mr. Eakes and Professional Laundry Service Consultants are a reasonable and necessary component of the Laundry's expenses, and would be paid by a future investor.

17. The Movants also hired Mr. Brogan's son Steve to work at the Laundry as accounts payable and receivables clerk at a salary of about $36,000 a year. The Trustee and Debtor maintain that his salary is excessive and that his salary expenses cannot be attributable to the business in calculating its net profits. However, since these parties presented insufficient evidence by which the Court could judge the reasonableness of Steve's salary, this argument was not established.

18. The Management fees and Steve Brogan's salary shall be attributed to the business in calculating net profits. Management fees represent the costs of retaining competent management for the business, and Steve Brogan's salary represents the cost of keeping an owner's agent on the premises who has undivided loyalty to the owner. A future owner-manager might not need such agents, but owner-managers represent only a portion of the potential investors who could buy the Laundry. Thus, the assumption of management fees and on-site agent salary costs are necessary to find the real value of the laundry to potential investors.

19. Debtor further asks the Court to discount non-cash expenses, such as depreciation, when calculating the Laundry's net profits. The equipment used in the Laundry's operation wears down and needs to be replaced periodically, and depreciation accounts for this real cost of doing business. Thus, an accounting of profits without any provision for depreciation is, in effect, borrowing against the company's future. Since it is not rational to assume that any future investor would desire to run the business into the ground in an effort to maximize his first year's profits, Debtor's argument is rejected.

20. Annualizing the Laundry's net profits for the first half of 1992 (at $181,464) provides the most accurate basis for prediction of the Laundry's future earnings potential. This conclusion is made for several reasons:

a. In the first six months of 1992 the Laundry netted $90,732. The evidence shows that this figure is representative of the whole year.

b. The net earnings history of the Laundry is as follows: In 1990, the Laundry lost $58,754. In 1991, the Laundry lost $4,973. However, the Laundry was in a state of upheaval from 1989 to 1991. Management had changed hands several times, and several customers were lost. The business had only recovered to a stable condition in the latter half of 1991. Prior to the sale of the business in late 1988, the Laundry netted annual profits around $450,000.

c. Mr. Eakes testified that the Laundry is currently operating at or near capacity and that expenses have been reduced over the past year to an efficient level. Thus, earnings are not likely to increase, and expenses are not likely to decrease, beyond their current levels.

21. The Laundry's business consists of cleaning sheets, towels, and other washable items under contracts with hotels and hospitals. The business faces several risks in its operations:

a. All of the Laundry's business comes from five or six clients, and most of these clients have no contractual relationship with the Laundry itself. They have contracts with Mr. Eakes who then allocates the business to the Laundry. Over two-thirds of the laundry to be processed comes from these contracts with Mr. Eakes. Therefore, any new investor in the Laundry would be dependent on him until new business could be developed.

b. There is a dispute with the Internal Revenue Service over allegedly unpaid payroll taxes in the amount of $203,630. While this problem has not reached a critical stage, this threat of liability is apparently still outstanding.

c. The Laundry is likely to incur new expenses as a result of new regulations promulgated by the Occupational Safety and Health Administration which will require the laundry workers to wear protective clothing to prevent the spread of AIDS and hepatitis.

d. The local water supply contains a high iron content which occasionally causes rust-colored stains to appear on the processed laundry. An iron-removal system was installed by the Movants, but the problem has returned intermittently, and limits the Laundry's efforts to compete for certain clients. Related to this iron problem is a dispute over unpaid bills with the Village of Harvard which provides the water. An unpaid municipal water bill of $69,050 is currently outstanding. This dispute has not been formally settled, but Mr. Eakes reached an accommodation with the Village which defers the issue and may resolve it.

e. Workmen's Compensation insurance is likely to rise due to increased concern about AIDS and hepatitis. Mr. Eakes testified that the Laundry's current provider has demanded a significant increase in premiums in order to renew its policy.

f. The labor force of the business consists primarily of recent immigrants to this country. In August 1991, the Immigration and Naturalization Service paid the Laundry facility a visit, and half of its workers were taken away. This temporarily disrupted operations, but it did not cause any long term damage. The Laundry was able to replace lost workers quickly, but whether it has potential liability under federal law for hiring illegal aliens is unknown and was not addressed at trial.

g. Other risks may exist concerning environmental problems and possible competition between washable and disposable items. However, the potential liability for these speculative risks has not been quantified.

22. The estimate by the Trustee's expert for the required return for a putative equity investor in the Laundry is reasonable. Such an investor would require a 25% return on the equity investment in order to provide a reasonable profit and compensate for risks inherent in owning this business.

23. The Court further agrees with the Trustee's expert that an acquisition of the Laundry can partly be accomplished with debt financing. This expert found, and the Court agrees, that a lender would finance 45% of the purchase price. Based on this expert's testimony, the Court finds that the required return for this lender would be 12%. Thus,

a capitalization rate for this estimation of value would be 19% to 19.5%.[2]

24. Therefore, the Court applies an income estimate of about $180,000 a year and a capitalization rate of 19% to 19.5% to reach a finding of value in the range of $945,000 to $925,000.

25. The above valuation must be discounted by 10% to account for the broker costs, sales expenses, and risks inherent in selling the business. This leaves a net value to the owners, creditors, and estate of $850,500 to $832,500.

26. The Laundry's value is highly uncertain and there is no equity cushion over debt. Furthermore, the risk that the business value will fluctuate falls most heavily on Movants. Therefore, Movants are not adequately protected by equity cushion, and there is no suggestion that Movants will receive adequate protection payments.

27. Mr. Ascher filed for his petition for relief under Chapter 11 of the Bankruptcy Code on June 8, 1990. On August 1, 1990, he consented to entry of an Order by this Court for appointment of a Chapter 11 Trustee. Mr. David Grochocinski was subsequently appointed. No Plan of Reorganization was proffered at trial, nor is there any indication that a plan is in the offing, other than a liquidat[ing] plan.

* * *

CONCLUSIONS OF LAW

* * *

2. Section 362(d) of the Bankruptcy Code provides that the automatic stay may be modified to permit an action against debtor's property when the debtor has no equity in that property, and it is not necessary for an effective reorganization. § 362(d)(2).

---

[2]

Equity return (25%)	×	percentage of total investment (55%)	=	13.75%
Debt return (12%)	×	percentage of total investment (45%)	=	5.4%
		Capitalization Rate	=	19.5%

3. The Movants have the burden of proving by a preponderance of evidence that Debtor has no equity in the property. § 362(g). The parties opposing the motion have the burden of proof on all other issues. § 362(g). To establish that the property is necessary to an effective reorganization, Ascher and the Trustee must show that there is "a reasonable possibility of a successful reorganization within a reasonable time." *United Savings Assoc. v. Timbers*, 484 U.S. 365, 376 (1988).

4. The Movants have met their burden on the issue of Debtor's equity in the Laundry. The value of the Laundry business as a going entity to the Movants and to the estate is in the range of $850,500 to $832,500, and, even accepting the Trustee's theory on interest rates, the amount owed is $855,774.12. Therefore, Debtor has no equity in the Laundry.

5. Since the payments made by Brogan to fund the payroll and pay other expenses were necessary for the preservation of the Laundry as a going entity, Movants are entitled to recover these funds from the proceeds of the sale of the Laundry under § 506(c). With a super priority claim under § 506(c), Movants are entitled to payment of this claim ahead of any other claimant including the Trustee, and this claim may be recovered directly from the property. Therefore, the payments made by Brogan, as discussed in the Findings, are included in the calculation of Movant's secured claim against the Debtor's property.

* * *

7. The parties opposing [lifting] the stay have not met their burden to show that a plan of reorganization is reasonably in prospect or that the Laundry would be necessary for Debtor's reorganization. Therefore, Movants are entitled to judgment on the motion to modify the stay.

8. Relief from the stay may be granted by "terminating, annulling, modifying, or conditioning such stay." § 362(d). Therefore, the Court has considerable flexibility to fashion relief that protects the interest of the Movants, Debtor, and the estate.

CONCLUSION

The evidence is clearly in favor of the Movants on all issues in this case, and judgment will be entered in their favor on the motion to modify the stay. However, the actual value of the laundry remains uncertain and dependent on what offers the market will bring. In entering an order in this case, the Court has only modified the stay to allow the Movants to sell the Laundry, and several conditions are incorporated into the order to ensure that they make prompt and significant efforts to market and sell the property.

Notes

1. *Ascher* uses the "net capitalized earnings" approach to value the business. The court in *In re SM 104 Ltd.*, 160 B.R. 202 (Bankr. S.D.Fla.1993), characterized this approach as follows:

> This method gives recognition to the view that investors do not buy the bricks and mortar of a building. Rather, they buy the earnings the bricks and mortar will produce in the future. Measuring the fair market value of collateral under the income capitalization approach is a two-step analysis. First, the future net operating income of the property is estimated. Next, that income is divided by a capitalization rate ("capitalized") to obtain the fair market value of the property.
>
> The capitalization rate is computed by determining the annual rate of return a hypothetical investor would be looking for in deciding whether to buy the property. More specifically, the capitalization rate equals the risk-free interest rate available in the marketplace plus some risk premium the hypothetical investor would require to induce her to make the investment.

Id. at 211–12. (Another portion of the opinion in *SM 104* appears later in this chapter.)

2. Valuation on the basis of predicted future earnings is known as "going concern" or "enterprise" valuation. It requires either capitalization of the earning stream or a discounting of predicted future earnings back to present value.

The Supreme Court endorsed enterprise valuation in a decision under the 1898 Act, *Consolidated Rock Products Co. v. Du Bois*, 312 U.S. 510, 61 S.Ct. 675, 85 L.Ed. 982 (1941):

> As Mr. Justice Holmes said in *Galveston, H. & S.A. Ry. Co. v. Texas*, 210 U.S. 217, 226, "the commercial value of property consists in the expectation of income from it." Such criterion is the appropriate one here, since we are dealing with the issue of solvency arising in connection with reorganization plans involving productive properties. * * * The criterion of earning capacity is the essential one if the enterprise is to be freed from the heavy hand of past errors, miscalculations or disaster, and if the allocation of securities among the various claimants is to be fair and equitable. Since its application

requires a prediction as to what will occur in the future, an estimate, as distinguished from mathematical certitude, is all that can be made. But that estimate must be based on an informed judgment which embraces all facts relevant to future earning capacity and hence to present worth, including, of course, the nature and condition of the properties, the past earnings record, and all circumstances which indicate whether or not that record is a reliable criterion of future performance.

Id. at 526, 61 S.Ct. at 685, 85 L.Ed. at 993–94.

3. Two other valuation methods are also used on occasion. Under the "comparable sales approach," an appraiser compares recent sales prices of similar properties, adjusting for differences between comparable properties and the one at issue. The "replacement cost approach" determines the cost of constructing similar property. *SM 104,* which is quoted in note 1, also discusses these additional valuation methods.

F. CONFIRMATION OF THE PLAN

Section 1129(a) sets out requirements that a plan must meet in order to be confirmed, and we will deal with the most important of them in this section. Note as we proceed through these materials that many of § 1129(a)'s requirements are triggered only if a creditor does not consent to the plan.

The debtor-in-possession begins the process of plan negotiation with a fair amount of control because, in cases not involving small businesses, only the debtor may file a plan for the first 120 days after the order for relief. § 1121(b). In adopting an "exclusivity period," Congress was attempting to strike a balance between the power of debtors and creditors, and to address the imbalances under prior law.

Courts have been so willing to extend the exclusivity period, often for years, that §§ 1121(d)(2) and (e) were added to the Code in 2005. Section 1121(e) applies only to a small business debtor, which is defined in § 101(51D) as one with noncontingent liquidated debts of no more than the designated amount. Section 1121(e) is more generous than (b), giving an initial exclusivity period of 180 days rather than 120, but (e) permits an extension only if a plan is in the offing and the extension is approved before expiration of the existing deadline. As before, extensions are allowable only for "cause." Section 1121(d)(2), however, prohibits any extension beyond a designated period—18 months, in the case of the 120-day period from § 1121(b); and 20 months, in the case of the 180-day period applicable to small business debtors under § 1121(e). Thus, the 2005 Amendments eliminated bankruptcy courts' power to extend the exclusivity period indefinitely, and debtors cannot remain in long-term control of the reorganization process.

It remains to be seen how these changes will affect the balance of power between debtors and creditors as they negotiate plan provisions, but we may expect that some debtors will find reorganization much more difficult—if not impossible—to accomplish in a shortened time frame.

You should be aware that most Chapter 11 plans are consensual, often having evolved through protracted negotiation. Perhaps after our study you will see why the parties may have an incentive to avoid litigating these complicated issues!

We begin with classification.

1. CLASSIFICATION AND VOTING

Chapter 11 plans deal with creditors by classes. Section 1129(a) requires as a condition of confirmation that, if any class is impaired (a matter we will turn to momentarily), at least one impaired class has voted for the plan. § 1129(a)(10). Debtors often expend a great deal of effort to meet this requirement and no cases paint the issue more starkly than the single asset real estate cases. In order to follow the next two cases, however, you need an introduction to one of the most infamous sections in the Code—§ 1111(b).

Note on § 1111(b)

Section 1111(b) was enacted in response to the decision in *In re Pine Gate Associates, Ltd.*, 2 B.C.D. 1478 (Bankr. N.D.Ga.1976). The reorganizing debtor in *Pine Gate* owned an apartment project. Creditors holding an undersecured nonrecourse mortgage insisted that their debts be paid in full or that the property be turned over to them. The court, however, permitted the debtor to pay the appraised value of the collateral, rather than the full amount of the debt, and to keep the property free and clear of liens. Creditors were unhappy about *Pine Gate* because they could not bid in the amount of the debt, in the absence of a public sale, and they could not assert deficiency claims, when loans are nonrecourse.

Section 1111(b) addresses both of these complaints. First, it treats all liens as recourse, even though the obligation under state law can be asserted only against the debtor's property, thereby operating as an exception to the usual bifurcation rules of § 506(a). The consequence of this treatment is that the creditor, with no recourse under state law, will have in bankruptcy a secured claim measured by the value of the collateral and an unsecured claim for the deficiency. This unsecured claim will give the creditor "a voice in the Chapter 11 process" because the creditor may be able to "dominate the vote within the unsecured class." *In re 500 Fifth Avenue Associates*, 148 B.R. 1010, 1021 (Bankr. S.D.N.Y.1993).

Second, § 1111(b) permits an undersecured creditor to "elect" to have a secured claim measured by the amount of the debt rather than the value of the collateral. Thus, the creditor may waive its unsecured claim (whether it came by the claim as a recourse creditor under state law or as a nonrecourse creditor given the claim by § 1111(b)) and be treated as a fully secured creditor. A restriction, which will be applicable to a creditor completely under water, is that a creditor may not make the election if its interest in the collateral is of inconsequential value.

Be careful not to jump to the conclusion that an undersecured creditor would always choose to have an allowed secured claim in the amount of the debt. For one thing, as the court in *500 Fifth Avenue Associates* pointed out, the electing creditor gives up what may be a sizeable, and therefore influential, unsecured claim.

PHOENIX MUTUAL LIFE INSURANCE CO. v. GREYSTONE III JOINT VENTURE (MATTER OF GREYSTONE III JOINT VENTURE)

United States Court of Appeals, Fifth Circuit, 1991.
995 F.2d 1274, *cert. denied*, 506 U.S. 821, 113 S.Ct. 72, 121 L.Ed.2d 37 (1992).

[As amended on Petition for Rehearing, February 27, 1992.]

EDITH H. JONES, Circuit Judge.

This appeal pits a debtor whose only significant asset is an office building in the troubled Austin, Texas real estate market against a lender who possesses a multi-million dollar lien on the property. After obtaining bankruptcy relief under Chapter 11, Greystone III proposed a "cramdown" plan of reorganization, hoping to force a write-down of over $3,000,000 on the secured lender's note and to retain possession and full ownership of the property. Over the secured lender's strenuous objections, the bankruptcy court confirmed the debtor's plan. On appeal, the district court upheld the bankruptcy court's judgment.

For two reasons, we must reverse. First, the Greystone plan impermissibly classified like creditors in different ways and manipulated classifications to obtain a favorable vote. * * *

I.

Appellant Phoenix Mutual Life Insurance Corporation ("Phoenix") lent $8,800,000, evidenced by a non-recourse promissory note secured by a first lien, to Greystone to purchase the venture's office building. When Greystone defaulted on the loan, missing four payments, Phoenix posted the property for foreclosure. Greystone retaliated by filing a Chapter 11 bankruptcy reorganization petition.

At the date of bankruptcy Greystone owed Phoenix approximately $9,325,000, trade creditors approximately $10,000, and taxing authorities approximately $145,000. The bankruptcy court valued Phoenix's secured claim at $5,825,000, the appraised value of the office building, leaving Phoenix an unsecured deficiency of approximately $3,500,000—the difference between the aggregate owed Phoenix and its secured claim.

As filed, Greystone's Second Amended Plan of Reorganization (the "Plan"), the confirmation of which is challenged in this appeal, separately classified the Code-created unsecured deficiency claim of Phoenix Mutual, *see* § 1111(b), and the unsecured claims of the trade creditors. The Plan proposed to pay Phoenix and the trade creditors slightly less than four cents on the dollar for their unsecured claims, but it also provided that Greystone's general partner would satisfy the balance of the trade creditors' claims after confirmation of the Plan.

In a separate class, the Plan further provided for security deposit "claims" held by existing tenants of the office building. These claimants were promised, notwithstanding the debtor's eventual assumption of their leases, 25% of their deposits upon approval of the Plan and 50% of their deposits at the expiration of their respective leases. The Plan stipulated that the general partner would "retain its legal obligations and * * * pay the [tenant] * * * creditors the balance of their claims upon confirmation."

Finally, Greystone's Plan contemplated a $500,000 capital infusion by the debtor's partners, for which they would reacquire 100% of the equity interest in the reorganized Greystone.

Unsurprisingly, Phoenix rejected this Plan, while the trade creditors and the class of holders of tenant security deposits voted to accept it. On January 27, 1989, the bankruptcy court held a confirmation hearing at which the Debtor orally modified its Plan to delete the statements that the general partner would pay the balance of trade debt and tenant security deposit claims after confirmation. A Phoenix representative testified that the insurance company was willing to fund its own plan of reorganization by paying off all unsecured creditors in cash in full after confirmation. The bankruptcy court refused to consider this proposal and then confirmed Greystone's modified Plan. The district court upheld the confirmation.

Phoenix Mutual now appeals * * * .

II.

Phoenix first attacks Greystone's classification of its unsecured deficiency claim in a separate class from that of the other unsecured claims against the debtor. This issue benefits from some background explanation.

Chapter 11 requires classification of claims against a debtor for two reasons. Each class of creditors will be treated in the debtor's plan of reorganization based upon the similarity of its members' priority status and other legal rights against the debtor's assets. § 1122. Proper classification is essential to ensure that creditors with claims of similar priority against the debtor's assets are treated similarly. Second, the classes must separately vote whether to approve a debtor's plan of reorganization. § 1129(a)(8), (10). A plan may not be confirmed unless either (1) it is approved by two-thirds in amount and more than one-half in number of each "impaired" class, §§ 1126(c), 1129(a)(8); or (2) at least one impaired class approves the plan, § 1129(a)(10), and the debtor fulfills the cramdown requirements of § 1129(b) to enable confirmation notwithstanding the plan's rejection by one or more impaired classes. Classification of claims thus affects the integrity of the voting process, for, if claims could be arbitrarily placed in separate classes, it would almost always be possible for the debtor to manipulate "acceptance" by artful classification.

In this case, Greystone's plan classified the Phoenix claim in separate secured and unsecured classes, a dual status afforded by § 1111(b) despite the nonrecourse nature of Phoenix's debt. Because of Phoenix's opposition to a reorganization, Greystone knew that its only hope for confirmation lay in the Bankruptcy Code's cramdown provision. § 1129(b). The substantive impact of cramdown will be discussed later. Procedurally, Greystone faced a dilemma in deciding how to obtain the approval of its cramdown plan by *at least one* class of "impaired" claims, as the Code requires. § 1129(a)(10). Greystone anticipated an adverse vote of Phoenix's secured claim. If the Phoenix $3.5

million unsecured deficiency claim shared the same class as Greystone's other unsecured trade claims, it would swamp their $10,000 value in voting against confirmation. The only other arguably impaired class consisted of tenant security deposit claims, which, the bankruptcy court found, were not impaired at all.

Greystone surmounted the hurdle by classifying Phoenix's unsecured deficiency claim separately from the trade claims, although both classes were to be treated alike under the plan and would receive a cash payment equal to 3.42% of each creditor's claim. Greystone then achieved the required favorable vote of the trade claims class.

Phoenix contends that Greystone misapplied § 1122 by classifying its unsecured claim separately from those of trade creditors. The lower courts rejected Phoenix's argument in three steps. First, they held that § 1122 of the Code does not unambiguously prevent classification of like claims in separate classes. The only question is what types of class differentiations among like claims are acceptable. Second, Greystone's [sic] unsecured deficiency claim is "legally different" from that of the trade claims because it arises statutorily, pursuant to § 1111(b). Third, "good business reasons" justify the separate classification of these unsecured claims. We must address each of these arguments.

Section 1122 prescribes classification of claims for a reorganization * * *. We observe from this language that the lower courts' suggestion that § 1122 does not prevent classification of like claims in separate classes is oversimplified. It is true that § 1122(a) in terms only governs permissible *inclusions* of claims in a class rather [than] requiring that all similar claims be grouped together. One cannot conclude categorically that § 1122(a) prohibits the formation of different classes from similar types of claims. But if § 1122(a) is wholly permissive regarding the creation of such classes, there would be no need for § 1122(b) specifically to authorize a class of smaller unsecured claims, a common feature of plans in reorganization cases past and present. The broad interpretation of § 1122(a) adopted by the lower courts would render § 1122(b) superfluous, a result that is anathema to elementary principles of statutory construction.

Section 1122 consequently must contemplate some limits on classification of claims of similar priority. A fair reading of both subsections suggests that ordinarily "substantially similar claims," those which share common priority and rights against the debtor's estate, should be placed in the same class. Section 1122(b) expressly creates one exception to this rule by permitting small unsecured claims to be classified separately from their larger counterparts if the court so approves for administrative convenience. The lower courts acknowledged the force of this narrow rather than totally permissive construction of § 1122 by going on to justify Greystone's segregation of the Phoenix claim. Put otherwise, the lower courts essentially found that Phoenix's unsecured deficiency claim is not "substantially similar" to those of the trade creditors.

Those courts did not, however, adhere to the one clear rule that emerges from otherwise muddled caselaw on § 1122 claims classification: thou shalt not classify similar claims differently in order to gerrymander an affirmative vote on a reorganization plan. As the Sixth Circuit observed:

> [T]here must be some limit on a debtor's power to classify creditors in such a manner. * * * Unless there is some requirement of keeping similar claims together, nothing would stand in the way of a debtor seeking out a few impaired creditors (or even one such creditor) who will vote for the plan and placing them in their own class.

In re U.S. Truck Co., 800 F.2d 581, 586 (6th Cir.1986). We agree with this rule, and if Greystone's proffered "reasons" for separately classifying the Phoenix deficiency claim simply mask the intent to gerrymander the voting process, that classification scheme should not have been approved.

* * * We conclude that if § 1122(a) permits classification of "substantially similar" claims in different classes, such classification may only be undertaken for reasons independent of the debtor's motivation to secure the vote of an impaired, assenting class of claims. To those proffered reasons we now turn.

Greystone contends that the "legal difference" between Phoenix's deficiency claim and the trade creditors' claims is sufficient to sustain its classification scheme. The alleged distinction between the legal attributes of the unsecured claims is that under state law Phoenix has no recourse against the debtor personally. However, state law is irrelevant where, as here, the Code has eliminated the legal distinction between non-recourse deficiency claims and other unsecured claims.

The purpose of § 1111(b) is to provide an undersecured creditor an election with respect to the treatment of its deficiency claim. Generally, the creditor may elect recourse status and obtain the right to vote in the unsecured class, or it may elect to forego recourse to gain an allowed secured claim for the entire amount of the debt. If separate classification of unsecured deficiency claims arising from non-recourse debt were permitted solely on the ground that the claim is non-recourse under state law, the right to vote in the unsecured class would be meaningless. Plan proponents could effectively disenfranchise the holders of such claims by placing them in a separate class and confirming the plan over their objection by cramdown. With its unsecured voting rights effectively eliminated, the electing creditor's ability to negotiate a satisfactory settlement of either its secured or unsecured claims would be seriously undercut. It seems likely that the creditor would often have to "elect" to take an allowed secured claim under § 1111(b)(2) in the hope that the value of the collateral would increase after the case is closed.[6] Thus, the election under § 1111(b) would be essentially meaningless. We believe Congress did not intend this result.

As the bankruptcy court viewed this issue, the debtor's ability to achieve a cramdown plan should be preferred over the creditor's § 1111(b) election rights because of the Code's policy of facilitating reorganization. The bankruptcy court resorted to policy considerations because it believed Congress did not foresee the potential impact of an electing creditor's deficiency claim on the debtor's aspiration to cramdown a plan. We disagree with this approach for three reasons. First, it results here in violating § 1122, by gerrymandering the plan vote, for the sake of allegedly effectuating a § 1129(b) cramdown. "Policy" considerations do not justify preferring one section of the Code, much less elevating its implicit "policies" over other sections, where the statutory language draws no such distinctions. Second, as shown, it virtually eliminates the § 1111(b) election for secured creditors in this type of case. Third, the bankruptcy court's concern for the viability of cramdown plans is overstated. If Phoenix's unsecured claim were lower and the trade debt were higher, or if there were other impaired classes that

---

[6] In this case, for example, Greystone proposed to extinguish Phoenix's $3,500,000 deficiency claim by the promised payment of $140,000. Under the valuation process, it confined Phoenix's secured claim to $5.8 million. § 506(a). Phoenix obviously objects to this arrangement because, in the future, it might ultimately receive more than the written-down value of the office building in a liquidation following foreclosure. Yet, with its voting rights effectively eliminated by separate classification, Phoenix has no leverage to persuade the Debtor to consider a more reasonable settlement. Had this scenario triumphed, Phoenix's most realistic option might have been to take an allowed secured claim in the hope that eventually the market value of the office building will increase by more than $140,000 over the presently estimated value of the collateral.

favored the plan, a cramdown plan would be more realistic. That Greystone's cramdown plan may not succeed on the facts before us does not disprove the utility of the cramdown provision. The state law distinction between Code-created unsecured deficiency claims and other unsecured claims does not alone warrant separate classification.

Greystone next argues that separate classification was justified for "good business reasons." The bankruptcy court found that the debtor "need[s] trade to maintain good will for future operations." The court further reasoned:

> [I]f the expectation of trade creditors is frustrated * * * [they] have little recourse but to refrain from doing business with the enterprise. The resulting negative reputation quickly spreads in the trade community, making it difficult to obtain services in the future on any but the most onerous terms.

Greystone argues that the "realities of business" more than justify separate classification of the trade debt from Phoenix's deficiency claim. This argument is specious, for it fails to distinguish between the *classification* of claims and the *treatment* of claims. Greystone's justification for separate classification of the trade claims might be valid if the trade creditors were to receive different treatment from Phoenix. Indeed, Greystone initially created a separate class of unsecured creditors that could be wooed to vote for the plan by the promise to pay their remaining claims in full *outside the plan*. Greystone then changed course and eliminated its promise. Because there is no separate treatment of the trade creditors in this case, we reject Greystone's "realities of business" argument.

Even if Greystone's Plan had treated the trade creditors differently from Phoenix, the classification scheme here is still improper. At the confirmation hearing, none of the Debtor's witnesses offered any reason for classifying the trade debt separately from Phoenix's unsecured deficiency claim. There is no evidence in the record of a limited market in Austin for trade goods and services. Nor is there any evidence that Greystone would be unable to obtain any of the trade services if the trade creditors did not receive preferential treatment under the Plan. Thus, the bankruptcy court's finding that there were good business reasons for separate classification is without support in the record and must be set aside as clearly erroneous.

Phoenix's unsecured deficiency claim approximates $3,500,000, while the claims of the unsecured trade creditors who voted to accept the Plan total less than $10,000. Greystone's classification scheme, which effectively disenfranchised Phoenix's Code-created deficiency claim, is sanctioned neither by the Code nor by caselaw. The lower courts erred in approving it.

* * *

V.

For the foregoing reasons, the judgment of the district court affirming the bankruptcy court's confirmation of Greystone's plan of reorganization is REVERSED. The case is REMANDED for proceedings consistent with this opinion.

* * *

IN RE SM 104 LTD.

United States Bankruptcy Court, Southern District of Florida, 1993.
160 B.R. 202.

ROBERT E. GINSBERG, Bankruptcy Judge.

[Debtor owned and operated an office complex in Fort Lauderdale, Florida. At the time of bankruptcy, the property was worth $2.27 million. A first mortgage, securing a nonrecourse debt of $5.5 million, was held by EquiVest, Inc. Debtor's proposed plan classified EquiVest's deficiency claim, created by § 1111(b), in Class 3. Trade creditors, owed a total of $175,000, were placed in Class 5. Debtor gave no business reason to justify separate classification and proposed to pay both classes a dividend of 8.5%. EquiVest voted to reject the plan; Class 5 voted to accept it.]

* * * Given the size of EquiVest's § 1111(b) unsecured deficiency claim relative to the other unsecured claims and EquiVest's opposition to the plan, it is obvious the reason the Debtor seeks to separately classify EquiVest's § 1111(b) deficiency claim from the claims of other unsecured creditors is to satisfy the requirements of § 1129(a)(10); i.e., to get one impaired class to accept the plan. EquiVest claims that the Debtor's apparently manipulative motive is improper, and that EquiVest's unsecured deficiency claim should be placed in the same class as the claims of the general unsecured creditors. If the court accepts EquiVest's argument that it should be classified with the other general unsecured creditors in a single class and

EquiVest's argument that the Class 5 unsecured creditors were the only impaired class to accept the plan, such a joint classification would be the death knell for the Debtor's plan because the Debtor could no longer satisfy the requirements of § 1129(a)(10). EquiVest's deficiency claim would be large enough to overwhelm the claims of the other members of that single class, and, by voting no, EquiVest could prevent the plan from being accepted by two-thirds in amount of the total unsecured claims. *See* § 1126(c).

* * *

(2) May a plan classify an unsecured deficiency claim created by § 1111(b) separately from other general unsecured claims?[28]

In general, the proponent of a Chapter 11 plan has broad discretion to classify claims and interests in the plan according to the particular facts and circumstances of each case. The provision in Chapter 11 governing classification is § 1122 * * * .

Section 1122(a) expressly provides that only substantially similar claims may be placed in the same class. It does not expressly require that all substantially similar claims be placed in the same class, nor does it expressly prohibit substantially similar claims from being classified separately. Nevertheless, many courts, including five circuit courts of appeal, while recognizing that § 1122 does not explicitly forbid a plan proponent from placing similar claims in separate classes, have imposed significant limits on the ability of a plan proponent to do so. *See, e.g., Hancock Mutual Life Insur. Co. v. Route 37 Business Park Assoc.*, 987 F.2d 154, 159-60 (3d Cir.1993); *In re Lumber Exchange Bldg. Ltd.*, 968 F.2d 647, 649 (8th Cir.1992); *In re Bryson Properties XVIII*, 961 F.2d 496, 502 (4th Cir.), *cert. denied*, 113 S.Ct. 191 (1992); *Matter of Greystone III Joint Venture*, 995 F.2d 1274, 1278-79 (5th Cir.1991); *In re U.S. Truck Co.*, 800 F.2d 581, 586 (6th Cir.1986). The majority of lower courts have followed suit.

In *Greystone*, the Fifth Circuit held that "one clear rule" has emerged from the otherwise muddled § 1122 caselaw: "thou shalt not classify similar claims differently in order to gerrymander an affir-

---

[28] This section considers only the propriety of the separate classification of unsecured deficiency claims of nonrecourse creditors, which are created by § 1111(b). The court does not consider the propriety of separate classification of the unsecured deficiency claims of recourse creditors, which are created by contract.

mative vote on a reorganization plan." The court reasoned that if § 1122(a) were wholly permissive regarding the formation of different classes from similar types of claims, there would be no need for § 1122(b) to authorize a class of smaller, unsecured claims. The *Greystone* court then held that a broad interpretation of the powers to classify similar claims separately under § 1122(a) "would render § 1122(b) superfluous, a result that is anathema to elementary principles of statutory construction." Consequently, the *Greystone* court held that § 1122 must contemplate some limits on classification of claims of similar rights.

However, while *Greystone* and the other cases have paid lip service to principles of statutory construction and the language of § 1122, they have turned more on notions of basic fairness and good faith. Indeed, most courts seem to base their rulings less on the language of § 1122 than on their view that separate classification is usually done to manipulate the voting to insure that at least one impaired class of creditors accepts the plan, and thus that the plan meets the requirements of § 1129(a)(10).[32] Such manipulation is viewed as some sort of "abuse" of Chapter 11. As the Eleventh Circuit noted, "[t]here must be some limit on a debtor's power to classify creditors. * * * The potential for abuse would be significant otherwise." *In re Holywell Corp.*, 913 F.2d 873, 880 (11th Cir.1990). Courts subscribing to this view have rejected any plan where the classification scheme "is designed to manipulate class voting, or violates basic priority rights." *Id.* Under such an analysis, the courts in *Route 37*, *Lumber Exchange*, *Bryson*, and *Greystone* have held that separate classification of an unsecured deficiency claim created by § 1111(b) from general unsecured claims solely to gerrymander to create [an] impaired accepting creditor class (i.e. the general unsecured creditors) is impermissible.

Obviously, one premise for the rulings in *Route 37*, *Lumber Exchange*, *Bryson*, and *Greystone* has been that unsecured deficiency claims created by § 1111(b) are substantially similar to general unsecured claims. Indeed, if the claims are not substantially similar, § 1122(a) would bar them from being put in the same class. However, a few lower courts have rejected this conclusion and held that unsecured deficiency claims created by § 1111(b) are not substantially

---

[32] In fact, *Greystone* directly stated that separate classification was proper if "for reasons independent of the debtor's motivation to secure the vote of an impaired, assenting class." Indeed, separate classification for valid business reasons is uniformly accepted.

similar to other unsecured claims, and thus that separate classification of those claims is not only permissible, but mandatory.. *See In re D & W Realty Corp.*, 156 B.R. 140, 144 (Bankr. S.D.N.Y.1993); *In re Aztec Co.*, 107 B.R. 585, 587 (Bankr. M.D.Tenn.1989).[33]

These latter courts rely on two lines of reasoning to support their conclusion. First, some of these courts believe that general unsecured claims and unsecured deficiency claims created by § 1111(b) are legally distinct because the former are recourse claims cognizable under state law, while the latter exist only within the Chapter 11 bankruptcy case and are not cognizable under state law. The circuit courts have largely rejected this argument, holding that § 1111(b) has largely eliminated the legal distinction between nonrecourse deficiency claims for purposes of Chapter 11.

In addition, the minority of courts supporting the proposition that the separate classification of unsecured deficiency claims created by § 1111(b) is either proper or required often argue that separate classification is permissible on the grounds that the vote of such claims will be uniquely affected by the plan's proposed treatment of the secured claim held by the creditor. Thus, for example, the court in *Aztec* reasoned that the undersecured mortgagee would have "every incentive to vote its large deficiency claim to affect the treatment of its secured claim by defeating confirmation of any plan" if classified with other unsecured creditors. 107 B.R. at 587. Such a rationale is highly persuasive when viewed in light of the logic underlying § 1129(a)(10). Section 1129(a)(10) was intended not to give the real estate lobby a veto power, but merely to require "some indicia of creditor support" for confirmation of a proposed Chapter 11 plan.

* * *

Fortunately, this court does not have to sort out the validity of the various lines of reasoning enunciated by those courts considering separate classification of unsecured deficiency claims created by § 1111(b). Instead, this court believes that the lines of reasoning articulated by the circuit courts and the majority of district and bankruptcy courts have missed the forests for the trees. Section 1122(a) allows joint classification of claims *only* if the claims are substantially similar in terms of their legal rights. There are, however, significant differ-

---

[33] Because this court holds below that an unsecured deficiency claim created by § 1111(b) is not substantially similar to other general unsecured claims, this court need not address whether separate classification of substantially similar claims solely to gerrymander an accepting impaired class is permissible under the Code.

ences between the legal rights of a general unsecured claim and an unsecured deficiency claim created for the nonrecourse lender by § 1111(b). Thus, an unsecured deficiency claim created by § 1111(b) is not substantially similar to general unsecured claims, and, under § 1122(a), the two types of claims *cannot* be classified together.

The most obvious difference between a general unsecured claim and an unsecured deficiency claim created by § 1111(b) is that the former exists regardless of what chapter of the Bankruptcy Code the case is in, while the latter exists only so long as the case remains in Chapter 11. If the Chapter 11 case is converted to Chapter 7, the nonrecourse lender is confined to its collateral for recovery. It has no deficiency claim against the Chapter 7 estate. *See* § 502(b)(1). This distinction is significant.

One area in which the distinction between the rights of holders of general unsecured claims and the rights of § 1111(b) deficiency claimants can be seen clearly is in the application of the "best interests" test of § 1129(a)(7). Section 1129(a)(7) sets out the financial minimum that assenting creditors in an assenting class can impose on dissenting creditors within that class. * * *

Thus, the majority in a class can never force the minority in that class to take less in present value terms than the minority would receive in a Chapter 7 liquidation case involving the debtor.

The application of this standard to a class consisting of both general unsecured claims and § 1111(b) deficiency claims can lead to anomalous results. A simple example shows why. Suppose that an unsecured deficiency claim created by § 1111(b) is placed in the same class as the general unsecured claims, and that the plan provides for that class to receive a 25% payment of claims on the effective date of the plan. Suppose further that, in a Chapter 7 liquidation, the holders of general unsecured claims would be paid a 35% dividend. The plan would fail the best interests of the creditors test as to the general unsecured creditors, and the plan could not be confirmed unless each general unsecured claim voted for the plan. *See* § 1129(a)(7). This would be true even if a majority in number and two-thirds in amount of the claims in the class that voted on the plan voted to accept. *See* § 1126(c). On the other hand, the plan would propose to give the unsecured deficiency claim created by § 1111(b) more than it would receive in a hypothetical Chapter 7 liquidation: in a Chapter 7 case, the unsecured deficiency claim created by § 1111(b) would not exist and would not be paid at all.

All that is ever required to satisfy the best interests test as to a § 1111(b) nonrecourse deficiency claim is for the claimholder to receive the present value of the collateral.[36] Nevertheless, as long as joint classification is utilized, the holder of a § 1111(b) deficiency claim can hold out for a dividend equal to what the general unsecured claims are being paid to satisfy the best interests of the creditors test as to such creditors, even though the undersecured nonrecourse claim is never entitled to any payment in a Chapter 7 case for the amount by which the value of its collateral is less than it is owed. This is because § 1123-(a)(4) requires a plan to provide for the same treatment of all claims in a class, unless the holder of a claim agrees to less favorable treatment. Thus, in the hypothetical above, if the plan were amended to satisfy the best interests of the creditors test by giving the holders of general unsecured claims a 35% dividend, the holder of the § 1111(b) nonrecourse deficiency claim could, as long as the claims are jointly classified, insist on the same 35% dividend, or block confirmation of the plan. It would be hard to believe that the drafters of the Bankruptcy Code intended such an absurd result.

There are other significant disparities between the legal rights of the holder of a general unsecured claim and the holder of a § 1111(b) nonrecourse deficiency claim. For example, if the debtor is a partnership, the general partners are liable for the debts of the partnership in the event the case converts to one under Chapter 7. *See* § 723. If the Chapter 11 case shows signs of possible failure, the general unsecured creditors could seek equitable relief to prevent dissipation of the assets of the general partners pending resolution of the Chapter 11 case. It is unlikely that the holder of a § 1111(b) nonrecourse deficiency claim could pursue such relief, since the nonrecourse lender is confined to its collateral as a source of payment in Chapter 7. It has no deficiency claim against either the estate or the general partners.

It is clear that the legal rights of creditors holding unsecured deficiency claims created by § 1111(b) and general unsecured creditors are, for classification purposes, substantially dissimilar. Therefore, separate classification of unsecured deficiency claims created by § 1111(b) and general unsecured claims is not only permissible, but mandatory.

The conclusion that an unsecured deficiency claim created by § 1111(b) cannot be placed in the same class with general unsecured claims is further supported by the language of § 1111(b) itself. In fact,

---

[36] This result is made clear by § 1129(a)(7)(B) * * *.

the plain meaning of § 1111(b) clearly leads to the conclusion that the § 1111(b) claim must be placed in a class by itself or with only other § 1111(b) claims. The drafters of the Bankruptcy Code provided that the § 1111(b)(2) election is to be made not by the individual § 1111(b) claimants, but by "the class of which such claim is a part." *See* § 1111-(b)(1)(A)(i). If the § 1111(b) claim is placed in the same class as general unsecured claims, the literal language of the statute would afford the general unsecured creditors the opportunity to vote on whether their classmate, the § 1111(b) claimholder, should be permitted to make the § 1111(b)(2) election. *See D & W Realty*, 156 B.R. at 144. In fact, the general unsecured creditors could easily block the § 1111-(b)(2) election by denying the § 1111(b) creditor the approval of the election by a majority in number of claim holders in the class required by § 1111. Obviously, the drafters of the Bankruptcy Code did not intend such an absurd result. More importantly, the § 1111(b) election process makes perfect sense if § 1111(b) is read to require that an § 1111(b) unsecured deficiency claim must be placed either in a class by itself or in a class with only other § 1111(b) claims.

By the same token, § 1111(b)(1)(B) denies the right to make the election to "[a] class of claims" if, *inter alia*, the lien claims of the members of the class are of "inconsequential value." By definition, the general unsecured creditors have no lien claims. If the analysis is on a class-wide basis, as the statute clearly mandates, and the § 1111(b) claim and the general unsecured claims are placed in a single class, the general unsecured creditors theoretically could ride the § 1111(b) claimholder's coattails and participate in the § 1111(b) election process, since the collateral held by all of the members of the class collectively is not of inconsequential value. Again, such an absurd result can be avoided by simply reading § 1111(b) as its plain meaning provides; that is, by reading § 1111(b) to require that a § 1111(b) claim be placed in a class by itself or in a class with only other § 1111(b) claims.

Thus, this court rules that the Debtor's separate classification of EquiVest's Class 3 unsecured deficiency claim and the claims of the Class 5 general unsecured creditors is permissible. Indeed, such separate classification is required by § 1122(a). Since separate classification is required by § 1122(a), the Debtor's motive in separately classifying the § 1111(b) claim and the general unsecured claims is irrelevant.

* * *

Notes and Questions

1. *SM 104* was in a minority at the time it was decided. The court could cite only a few other cases also finding separate classification mandatory, and one of them, *In re D & W Realty Corp.*, 156 B.R. 140 (Bankr. S.D.N.Y.1993), was reversed on appeal, 165 B.R. 127 (S.D.N.Y.1994). In addition, the Second Circuit joined the majority, with its decision in *Boston Post Road Limited P'ship v. FDIC (In re Boston Post Road Limited P'ship)*, 21 F.3d 477 (2d Cir.1994). The Seventh Circuit, however, in *Matter of Woodbrook Associates*, 19 F.3d 314 (7th Cir.1994), criticized *Greystone* for its implicit proposition "that separate classification of a § 1111(b) claim is nearly conclusive evidence of a debtor's intent to gerrymander an affirmative vote for confirmation. The court gave a list of reasons, much like *SM 104*'s, why § 1111(b) claims are significantly different from general unsecured claims.

2. Do you see enough difference between an undersecured creditor's deficiency claim and other unsecured claims to justify a finding that they are not "substantially similar" under § 1122(a)? Does that difference exist only when the undersecured creditor's unsecured claim arises under § 1111(b)—that is, when the undersecured creditor has no recourse under state law?

3. Which case does a better job of interpreting the statute—*SM 104* or *Greystone*? Have the cases in the majority "turned more on notions of basic fairness and good faith" and "missed the forest for the trees," as *SM 104* charged? What, exactly, is the "fair" result in these single-asset real estate cases?

2. IMPAIRMENT OF CLAIMS AND INTERESTS

The Code only permits creditors whose interests are "impaired" within the meaning of § 1124 to vote on the plan by conclusively presuming that unimpaired creditors have accepted the plan, § 1126(f). Since only classes that reject the plan can obtain the protections of cramdown under § 1129(b), the concept of impairment is important.

A claim is "impaired" under § 1124 unless it fits within one of the listed exceptions. Read § 1124 and apply it to the following Problems.

Problems

1. Debtor owed $150,000 to Bank, secured by Debtor's inventory and accounts receivable. That collateral was worth $200,000 at the time of bankruptcy. Debtor's plan put Bank in a class by itself and provided that Bank would receive substitute collateral in the form of a second mortgage on Debtor's real estate. The real property was worth $750,000 and was encumbered by a first mortgage of $250,000. Is Bank's $150,000 claim impaired?

2. Debtor owed $300,000 to various trade creditors who had sold goods to Debtor on a net 30–day basis. The entire sum was past due as of the date of bankruptcy. Debtor's plan classified the trade debts together and proposed to pay 95% of the face amount of the debts, over the course of three years. Is the class of trade claims impaired?

3. Lender had a mortgage on Debtor's premises, worth $200,000, that secured a debt of $200,000. The parties' note entitled Lender to receive $2,500 per month, plus 8% interest, and 80 months remained in the loan term. Debtor was not in default at the time of bankruptcy, but made no payments to Lender during the 4–year pendency of the case. Debtor's plan separately classified Lender's claim and proposed to pay $2,500 per month, plus 8%, for a term of 80 months beginning the month after confirmation. Lender is upset about the four years during which nothing was paid on the loan and wants to vote against this plan. Is Lender's claim impaired?

4. Debtor, Inc., which was deeply insolvent, proposed a plan that would leave nothing for shareholders. Debtor, Inc. argued that the class of shareholders was not impaired because their interests were valueless at the time of bankruptcy filing. Will that argument be successful?

5. Debtor, which operated a retail shop on leased premises, closed its doors for several days in violation of a lease covenant requiring continuous operation. Debtor then filed bankruptcy and reopened its doors the same day. Debtor proposed a plan under which it would pay all prepetition rental arrearages to Lessor and assume the lease. Lessor pointed to Debtor's breach of the "going dark" clause and argued that its claim was impaired. Is Lessor correct?

3. BEST INTERESTS TEST AND FEASIBILITY

The so-called "best interests" test of § 1129(a)(7) is designed to protect individual dissenting creditors—not *classes* of creditors, but individual creditors—by requiring that each dissenting creditor receive under the proposed plan at least as much as that dissenter would have received in a Chapter 7 case. The protections of § 1129(a)(7) apply even though the dissenter is outvoted by other members of the class and, as a result, the class of which the dissenter is a part accepts the plan.

Subsection (a)(7) requires the court to conduct a hypothetical liquidation analysis and to compare the dissenter's hypothetical dividend with the plan's proposed payment. *In re Merrimack Valley Oil Co.*, 32 B.R. 485 (Bankr. D.Mass.1983), illustrates this process. Debtors in that case were in the business of selling oil. Their plan provided for a 35% dividend to unsecured creditors to be paid over three years, with an extra 5% to Belcher, their major supplier. The court, in determining whether the best interests test was met, began by listing and valuing the debtors' assets and liabilities:

The liquidation values are found to be as follows:

Cash	$ 310,900
Inventories	63,600
Real Estate—Business	100,000
Real Estate—Residential	340,000
Transportation Equipment	294,000
Furniture and Fixtures	10,000
Race Horses	173,000
Accounts Receivable	282,400
Other Assets	14,000
TOTAL NET REALIZABLE VALUE	$1,587,900

The value of goodwill and customer list is found to be highly speculative in the light of the restrictions and covenants required for their sale to be of any consequence.

The secured and priority claims are as follows:

Notes and mortgages	$126,100
Chapter 11 fees and expenses	157,500
Priority claims under Chapter 11	113,100
Post-filing debt	394,900
Estimated Chapter 7 expenses	160,000
TOTAL	$951,600

The net amount available on liquidation is therefore $636,000 or approximately twenty per cent (20%) of unsecured debt of $3,193,975.

The plan provides for thirty-five per cent (35%) to unsecured creditors and forty per cent (40%) to Belcher for its allowed claim. The present value of said payments is twenty-nine per cent (29%) (32% to Belcher). In liquidation, payment would not be made for at least six months of conversion to Chapter 7 because creditors have six months to file proofs of claims pursuant to Bankruptcy Rule 302(e). Secured creditors and administrative claimants are not impaired under the plan. Accordingly, I find that the debtors' plan which offers creditors 35% to 40% over three years, which amounts to a present value of 29% to 32%, is in the best interests of creditors, and complies with the requirements of § 1129(a)(7).

Id. at 487.

Section 1129(a)(11) imposes the so-called "feasibility" test, which we have seen before. It requires the court to make a finding that "the plan is not likely to be followed by the liquidation, or the need for further financial reorganization, of the debtor." According to *Merrimack Valley,* this obligates a court to determine, on a case-by-case basis, "that the plan offers a reasonably workable prospect of success and is not a visionary scheme." 32 B.R. at 488. Relevant factors include "(1) the adequacy of the capital structure; (2) the earning power of the business; (3) economic conditions; and (4) the ability of management." *Id.*

4. CRAMDOWN

a. Fair and Equitable Test

Section 1129(b)(1) requires that a plan be "fair and equitable" if it is to be confirmed over the objection of nonconsenting classes. This is "cramdown." Subsection (b)(2) elaborates the meaning of "fair and equitable" in three subsections, applicable respectively to secured classes, unsecured classes and classes of "interests" (that is, shareholders).

We will begin where § 1129(b)(2) does—with secured claims. To effect cramdown in the case of secured creditors, the plan can do one of three things. First, it can provide that the creditor retain its lien and receive payments that meet certain requirements. § 1129-(b)(2)(A)(i). Second, it can provide for sale of the property, subject to § 363(k), with the lien to attach to proceeds of the sale. § 1129-(b)(2)(A)(ii). Third, it can provide that the creditor receive the "indubitable equivalent" of its claim. § 1129(b)(2)(A)(iii). This alternative was derived from *In re Murel Holding Corp.*, 75 F.2d 941 (2d Cir. 1935), a well-known opinion written by Judge Learned Hand. (You may remember the Supreme Court's discussion of *Murel* in *Timbers*, which appears in Chapter 4, Section B of this casebook.)

For our purposes, the first of these alternatives is the most important—the creditor must retain its lien and receive a stream of payments that meets two criteria: 1) "deferred cash payments totaling at least the allowed amount of such claim"—a "principal amount" test;

and 2) "of a value, as of the effective date of the plan, of at least the value of such holder's interest in the estate's interest in such property"—a "present value" test. For example, assume that Debtor owes Creditor $25,000 and that the obligation is secured by a lien on collateral worth $10,000. Creditor's secured claim is measured by the value of the collateral under § 506(a)—$10,000. These tests require Debtor 1) to make a stream of payments having a face amount of at least the value of the secured claim ($10,000), and 2) to pay Creditor an amount equal to the present value of its collateral ($10,000 plus interest).

These tests look decidedly strange in light of § 506(a)(1) bifurcation. Why require that the face amount of the stream of payments be at least as much as the value of the secured claim *and* require that the creditor receive the value of the collateral plus appropriate interest? Satisfying the latter will necessarily satisfy the former, or so it seems. The key to understanding the statutory wording lies in § 1111(b).

The election under § 1111(b), rather than bifurcation under § 506(a)(1), determines the amount of the allowed secured claim for purposes of § 1129(b)(2)(A)(i)(II). Returning to our prior example, assume that Creditor, whose collateral was worth $10,000, elected to have a secured claim in the amount of the debt—$25,000. The tests now require Debtor 1) to make a stream of payments having a face amount of at least the value of the secured claim ($25,000), and 2) to pay Creditor an amount equal to the present value of its collateral ($10,000 plus interest).

Although this looks good for the undersecured creditor at first, be aware that the creditor need be paid no more, *in terms of economic value*, than an amount equal to the value of the collateral *even if the creditor makes the § 1111(b) election*. If payments are stretched out for a sufficient period of time, the present value of payments having a face amount equal to the debt ($25,000) can, in fact, be made to equal the value of the collateral ($10,000). Assume, for example, that Debtor's plan proposes to pay Creditor interest only, annually, at the rate of 10% for 15 years, with a balloon payment of $10,000 at the end of that time. If the court finds that 10% is the appropriate rate and confirms the plan, Debtor will make a stream of payments with a face amount of $25,000 ($1,000 per year for 15 years, plus a balloon of $10,000); the present value of that stream of payments as of the time of confirmation, however, is only $10,000.

Clearly, identification of the appropriate discount rate is critical in determining whether the "present value" test of § 1129(b)(2)(A)-(i)(II) is satisfied by a debtor's proposed plan. Recall *Till*, which appears in Chapter 4, Section F of this text. In that case, the Supreme Court adopted the formula approach in the context of § 1325(a)(5). Is there any reason to expect that a different approach should (or will) be applied in Chapter 11?

Payment, over time, of the present value of the secured claim is only one of the ways that a secured creditor's claim may be satisfied under the plan. One of the remaining alternatives—"realization by [the secured creditor] of the indubitable equivalent of" the claim, § 1129(b)-(2)(A)(iii)—has presented interpretive problems when a debtor has proposed transferring property to the secured creditor in satisfaction of the claim, but without exposing the property to a marketplace valuation. In *Arnold & Baker Farms v. U.S. (In re Arnold & Baker Farms)*, 85 F.3d 1415 (9th Cir.1996), for example, the debtor partnership proposed what is known as a "dirt for debt" plan. The debtor's obligation to the Farmers Home Administration (FmHA) was secured by a lien on 1,320 acres of land. The debtor proposed to convey 566.5 acres to FmHA as the "indubitable equivalent" of the obligation, on the basis of the bankruptcy court's finding that the land was worth $7,300 per acre. FmHA objected on the grounds that the land was only worth $1,381 per acre. This valuation was based, in part, on disagreement about the highest and best use of the land. In addition, the Resolution Trust Corporation had acquired several thousand acres near the debtor's property and was offering large parcels for sale at no more than $2,105 per acre.

The bankruptcy court confirmed the plan, but the BAP reversed. The Ninth Circuit affirmed:

> The bankruptcy court found the value of each acre to be $7,300, and thus the value of the 566.5 acres to be transferred to FmHA to be $4,135,450 ($7,300 × 566.5). We must decide, therefore, whether a distribution of land with an estimated value of $4,135,450 constitutes the indubitable equivalent of a $3,837,618 claim secured by 1,320 acres. Under the circumstances of this case, we conclude that it does not.

> The partial distribution of 566.5 acres to FmHA will not insure the safety of or prevent jeopardy to the principal. FmHA originally lent funds to Arnold and Baker secured by 1320 acres of land. If Arnold and Baker defaulted on the terms of the note,

FmHA bargained for the right to foreclose on the entire 1320 acres of land in order to satisfy the outstanding obligation. In this situation, the principal is protected to the extent of the entire 1320 acres held as security.

If FmHA subsequently sells the property for less than the value calculated by the bankruptcy court, FmHA has no recourse to the remaining collateral to satisfy the deficiency. As a result, the distribution to FmHA may not be "completely compensatory."

Id. at 1422, *quoting U.S. v. Arnold & Baker Farms (In re Arnold & Baker Farms*, 177 B.R. 648, 661-62 (9th Cir. BAP 1994). Under what circumstances would the Ninth Circuit approve a "dirt for debt" plan?

The preceding discussion has presumed that the debtor wants to keep the collateral. In many cases, however, the debtor wants to sell some of the assets—or, often, the entire business. We have already seen some of the issues surrounding sales of assets outside of a plan, pursuant to § 363. Related, difficult issues arise when the sale is governed by § 1129.

One of the protections for secured creditors whose collateral is to be sold, is the right to "credit bid." Credit bidding permits the creditor to bid the amount of the debt—money that it has already invested—and obtain possession of the collateral rather than accepting the proceeds of the sale. The effect of credit bidding in the bankruptcy context is the subject of some debate. On the one hand, it may provide a way in which the creditor can protect itself from an inadequate sales price. On the other hand, however, credit bidding may chill the bidding by third parties who have to bid with "real" money. In any event, creditors may very well want to decide for themselves, in a particular situation, whether to credit bid.

Questions arose in the courts regarding the circumstances under which a creditor has the right to credit bid. In *In re Philadelphia Newspapers, LLC*, 599 F.3d 298 (3d Cir.2010), the debtors sought court approval of bid procedures that would prevent secured lenders from credit bidding. The debtors proposed a plan under the "indubitable equivalent" prong of § 1129(b)(2)(A)(iii), whereby substantially all of the assets would be sold free of liens in a public auction. The Third Circuit held that the lenders had no right to credit bid. Subsection (iii), unlike subsection (ii), incorporates no reference to the right to credit bid created in § 363(k). Subsection (iii), therefore, plainly provides that secured creditors have no right to credit bid. The court noted that the Fifth Circuit had come to the same conclusion in *Bank of N.Y. Trust Co., NA v. Official Unsecured Creditors' Comm. (In re Pacific Lumber Co.)*, 584 F.3d 229 (5th Cir.2009).

Judge Ambro vigorously dissented. He began by recounting the "game the debtors are playing" and their efforts to obtain the assets "on the cheap" by favoring a stalking horse bidder composed of insiders. He read the Code to restrict plan sales free of liens to clause (ii), which mandates credit bidding. Clause (iii), he asserted, is not a "catch-all" "designed to supplant clauses (i) and (ii) where they plainly apply." He supported that reading with maxims of statutory interpretation and discussion of related provisions in the Code—specifically §§ 363(k), 1111(b) and 1123(a)(5)(D).

When the Seventh Circuit decided this issue in accordance with Judge Ambro's analysis, *River Road Hotel Partners, LLC v. Amalgamated Bank (In re River Road Hotel Partners, LLC)*, 651 F.3d 642 (7th Cir.2011), the decision was appealed to the Supreme Court. (There, the proceeding took the name of a related case that was separately administered, but raised identical issues.) In its decision, the Court gave us the last (?) word on credit bidding.

RADLAX GATEWAY HOTEL, LLC v. AMALGAMATED BANK

United States Supreme Court, 2012.
132 S.Ct. 2065, 182 L.Ed.2d 967.

JUSTICE SCALIA delivered the opinion of the Court.

We consider whether a Chapter 11 bankruptcy plan may be confirmed over the objection of a secured creditor pursuant to § 1129(b)(2)(A) if the plan provides for the sale of collateral free and clear of the creditor's lien, but does not permit the creditor to "credit-bid" at the sale.

I.

In 2007, petitioners RadLAX Gateway Hotel, LLC, and RadLAX Gateway Deck, LLC (hereinafter debtors), purchased the Radisson Hotel at Los Angeles International Airport, together with an adjacent lot on which the debtors planned to build a parking structure. To finance the purchase, the renovation of the hotel, and construction of the parking structure, the debtors obtained a $142 million loan from Longview Ultra Construction Loan Investment Fund, for which respondent Amalgamated Bank (hereinafter creditor or Bank) serves as trustee. The lenders obtained a blanket lien on all of the debtors' assets to secure the loan.

Completing the parking structure proved more expensive than anticipated, and within two years the debtors had run out of funds and were forced to halt construction. By August 2009, they owed more than $120 million on the loan, with over $1 million in interest accruing every month and no prospect for obtaining additional funds to complete the project. Both debtors filed voluntary petitions for relief under Chapter 11 of the Bankruptcy Code.

A Chapter 11 bankruptcy is implemented according to a "plan," typically proposed by the debtor, which divides claims against the debtor into separate "classes" and specifies the treatment each class will receive. See § 1123. Generally, a bankruptcy court may confirm a Chapter 11 plan only if each class of creditors affected by the plan consents. See §1129(a)(8). Section 1129(b) creates an exception to that general rule, permitting confirmation of nonconsensual plans— commonly known as "cramdown" plans—if "the plan does not discriminate unfairly, and is fair and equitable, with respect to each class of claims or interests that is impaired under, and has not accepted, the plan." Section 1129(b)(2)(A), which we review in further depth below, establishes criteria for determining whether a cramdown plan is "fair and equitable" with respect to secured claims like the Bank's.

In 2010, the RadLAX debtors submitted a Chapter 11 plan to the United States Bankruptcy Court for the Northern District of Illinois. The plan proposed to dissolve the debtors and to sell substantially all of their assets pursuant to procedures set out in a contemporaneously filed "Sale and Bid Procedures Motion." Specifically, the debtors sought to auction their assets to the highest bidder, with the initial bid submitted by a "stalking horse"—a potential purchaser who was willing to make an advance bid of $47.5 million. The sale proceeds would be used to fund the plan, primarily by repaying the Bank. Of course the Bank itself might wish to obtain the property if the alternative would be receiving auction proceeds that fall short of the property's full value. Under the debtors' proposed auction procedures, however, the Bank would not be permitted to bid for the property using the debt it is owed to offset the purchase price, a practice known as "credit-bidding." Instead, the Bank would be forced to bid cash. Correctly anticipating that the Bank would object to this arrangement, the debtors sought to confirm their plan under the cramdown provisions of § 1129(b)(2)(A).

The Bankruptcy Court denied the debtors' Sale and Bid Procedures Motion, concluding that the proposed auction procedures did not comply with § 1129(b)(2)(A)'s requirements for cramdown plans. The Bankruptcy Court certified an appeal directly to the United States Court of Appeals for the Seventh Circuit. That court accepted the certification and affirmed, holding that § 1129(b)(2)(A) does not permit debtors to sell an encumbered asset free and clear of a lien without permitting the lienholder to credit-bid. We granted certiorari.

II.

A.

A Chapter 11 plan confirmed over the objection of a "class of secured claims" must meet one of three requirements in order to be deemed "fair and equitable" with respect to the nonconsenting creditor's claim. [*The Court quoted § 1129(b)(2)(A).*]

Under clause (i), the secured creditor retains its lien on the property and receives deferred cash payments. Under clause (ii), the property is sold free and clear of the lien, "subject to § 363(k)," and the creditor receives a lien on the proceeds of the sale. Section 363(k), in turn, provides that "unless the court for cause orders otherwise the holder of such claim may bid at such sale, and, if the holder of such claim purchases such property, such holder may offset such claim against the purchase price of such property"—i.e., the creditor may credit-bid at the sale, up to the amount of its claim.[1] Finally, under clause (iii), the plan provides the secured creditor with the "indubitable equivalent" of its claim.

The debtors in this case have proposed to sell their property free and clear of the Bank's liens, and to repay the Bank using the sale proceeds—precisely, it would seem, the disposition contemplated by clause (ii). Yet since the debtors' proposed auction procedures do not

---

[1] The ability to credit-bid helps to protect a creditor against the risk that its collateral will be sold at a depressed price. It enables the creditor to purchase the collateral for what it considers the fair market price (up to the amount of its security interest) without committing additional cash to protect the loan. That right is particularly important for the Federal Government, which is frequently a secured creditor in bankruptcy and which often lacks appropriations authority to throw good money after bad in a cash-only bankruptcy auction.

permit the Bank to credit-bid, the proposed sale cannot satisfy the requirements of clause (ii). Recognizing this problem, the debtors instead seek plan confirmation pursuant to clause (iii), which—unlike clause (ii)—does not expressly foreclose the possibility of a sale without credit-bidding. According to the debtors, their plan can satisfy clause (iii) by ultimately providing the Bank with the "indubitable equivalent" of its secured claim, in the form of cash generated by the auction.

We find the debtors' reading of § 1129(b)(2)(A)—under which clause (iii) permits precisely what clause (ii) proscribes—to be hyperliteral and contrary to common sense. A well established canon of statutory interpretation succinctly captures the problem: "[I]t is a commonplace of statutory construction that the specific governs the general." *Morales v. TransWorld Airlines, Inc.*, 504 U.S. 374, 384 (1992). That is particularly true where, as in § 1129(b)(2)(A), "Congress has enacted a comprehensive scheme and has deliberately targeted specific problems with specific solutions." *Varity Corp. v. Howe*, 516 U.S. 489, 519 (1996) (THOMAS, J., dissenting).

The general/specific canon is perhaps most frequently applied to statutes in which a general permission or prohibition is contradicted by a specific prohibition or permission. To eliminate the contradiction, the specific provision is construed as an exception to the general one. But the canon has full application as well to statutes such as the one here, in which a general authorization and a more limited, specific authorization exist side-by-side. There the canon avoids not contradiction but the superfluity of a specific provision that is swallowed by the general one, "violat[ing] the cardinal rule that, if possible, effect shall be given to every clause and part of a statute." *D. Ginsberg & Sons, Inc. v. Popkin*, 285 U.S. 204, 208 (1932). The terms of the specific authorization must be complied with. For example, in the last cited case a provision of the Bankruptcy Act prescribed in great detail the procedures governing the arrest and detention of bankrupts about to leave the district in order to avoid examination. The Court held that those prescriptions could not be avoided by relying upon a general provision of the Act authorizing bankruptcy courts to " 'make such orders, issue such process, and enter such judgments in addition to those specifically provided for as may be necessary for the enforcement of the provisions of [the] Act.' " *Id.* at 206 (quoting Bankruptcy Act of 1898, § 2(15), 30 Stat. 546). The Court said that "[g]eneral language of a statutory provision, although broad enough to include it, will not be held to apply to a matter specifically dealt with in another part of the same enactment." 285 U.S. at 208. * * *

Here, clause (ii) is a detailed provision that spells out the requirements for selling collateral free of liens, while clause (iii) is a broadly worded provision that says nothing about such a sale. The general/specific canon explains that the "general language" of clause (iii), "although broad enough to include it, will not be held to apply to a matter specifically dealt with" in clause (ii). *D. Ginsberg & Sons, Inc.*, *supra*, at 208.

Of course the general/specific canon is not an absolute rule, but is merely a strong indication of statutory meaning that can be overcome by textual indications that point in the other direction. The debtors point to no such indication here. One can conceive of a statutory scheme in which the specific provision embraced within a general one is not superfluous, because it creates a so-called safe harbor. The debtors effectively contend that that is the case here—clause (iii) ("indubitable equivalent") being the general rule, and clauses (i) and (ii) setting forth procedures that will always, ipso facto, establish an "indubitable equivalent," with no need for judicial evaluation. But the structure here would be a surpassingly strange manner of accomplishing that result—which would normally be achieved by setting forth the "indubitable equivalent" rule first (rather than last), and establishing the two safe harbors as provisos to that rule. The structure here suggests, to the contrary, that (i) is the rule for plans under which the creditor's lien remains on the property, (ii) is the rule for plans under which the property is sold free and clear of the creditor's lien, and (iii) is a residual provision covering dispositions under all other plans—for example, one under which the creditor receives the property itself, the "indubitable equivalent" of its secured claim. Thus, debtors may not sell their property free of liens under § 1129(b)(2)(A) without allowing lienholders to credit-bid, as required by clause (ii).

B.

None of the debtors' objections to this approach is valid. The debtors' principal textual argument is that § 1129(b)(2)(A) "unambiguously provides three distinct options for confirming a Chapter 11 plan over the objection of a secured creditor." With that much we agree; the three clauses of § 1129(b)(2)(A) are connected by the disjunctive "or." The debtors contend that our interpretation of § 1129(b)(2)(A) "transforms 'or' into 'and.' " But that is not so. The question here is not whether debtors must comply with more than one clause, but rather which one of the three they must satisfy. Debtors seeking to sell their property free of liens under § 1129(b)(2)(A) must satisfy the requirements of clause (ii), not the requirements of both clauses (ii) and (iii).

The debtors make several arguments against applying the general/specific canon. They contend that clause (ii) is no more specific than clause (iii), because the former provides a procedural protection to secured creditors (credit-bidding) while the latter provides a substantive protection (indubitable equivalence). As a result, they say, clause (ii) is not "a limiting subset" of clause (iii), which (according to their view) application of the general/specific canon requires. To begin with, we know of no authority for the proposition that the canon is confined to situations in which the entirety of the specific provision is a "subset" of the general one. When the conduct at issue falls within the scope of both provisions, the specific presumptively governs, whether or not the specific provision also applies to some conduct that falls outside the general. In any case, we think clause (ii) is entirely a subset. Clause (iii) applies to all cramdown plans, which include all of the plans within the more narrow category described in clause (ii). That its requirements are "substantive" whereas clause (ii)'s are "procedural" is quite beside the point. What counts for application of the general/specific canon is not the nature of the provisions' prescriptions but their scope.

Finally, the debtors contend that the Court of Appeals conflated approval of bid procedures with plan confirmation. They claim the right to pursue their auction now, leaving it for the Bankruptcy Judge to determine, at the confirmation stage, whether the resulting plan (funded by auction proceeds) provides the Bank with the "indubitable equivalent" of its secured claim. Under our interpretation of § 1129-(b)(2)(A), however, that approach is simply a nonstarter. As a matter of law, no bid procedures like the ones proposed here could satisfy the requirements of § 1129(b)(2)(A), and the distinction between approval of bid procedures and plan confirmation is therefore irrelevant. We are speaking here about whether clause (ii) is a subset for purposes of determining whether the canon applies. As we have described earlier, after applying the canon—ex post, so to speak—it ceases to be a subset, governing a situation to which clause (iii) will no longer be deemed applicable.

III

The parties debate at some length the purposes of the Bankruptcy Code, pre-Code practices, and the merits of credit-bidding. To varying extents, some of those debates also occupied the attention of the Courts of Appeals that considered the question presented here. But nothing in the generalized statutory purpose of protecting secured creditors can overcome the specific manner of that protection which the text of § 1129(b)(2)(A) contains. As for pre-Code practices, they can be relevant to the interpretation of an ambiguous text, but we find no textual ambiguity here. And the pros and cons of credit-bidding are for the consideration of Congress, not the courts. The Bankruptcy Code standardizes an expansive (and sometimes unruly) area of law, and it is our obligation to interpret the Code clearly and predictably using well established principles of statutory construction. Under that approach, this is an easy case. Because the RadLAX debtors may not obtain confirmation of a Chapter 11 cramdown plan that provides for the sale of collateral free and clear of the Bank's lien, but does not permit the Bank to credit-bid at the sale, we affirm the judgment of the Court of Appeals.

It is so ordered.

Notes and Questions

1. Plan sales are common in current day Chapter 11 practice. The Supreme Court' blessing of credit bidding was roundly applauded by secured creditors. Do you see any parties to Chapter 11 cases who may be hurt by this decision?

2. Do you agree that this was an "easy case" with no "textual ambiguity"? Which common tools of statutory interpretation did the Court invoked?

3. What would have been the practical implications for secured creditors if they had to cash bid?

4. The Seventh Circuit, in the case that became *RadLAX*, recognized some significant policy reasons for denying a creditor its right to credit bid, such as the fostering of a competitive bidding process, and ensuring a successful reorganization. Did the Supreme Court entertain any such policy arguments?

5. Is an "unruly" bankruptcy law necessarily a bad thing?

b. Absolute Priority Rule

To effect cramdown in the case of unsecured creditors, a plan must comply with § 1129(b)(2)(B). That subsection provides two alternatives, the first of which is payment of the full amount of the allowed claim. That alternative is seldom chosen, given that the amount of the allowed unsecured claim is usually the full debt. A debtor who can pay that much is unlikely to need bankruptcy. The second alternative comes into play when debtors do not propose to pay their obligations in full. It provides that, if an unsecured class is not paid in full, then classes of claims or interests junior to the unsecured class will receive nothing. In other words, equity interests must be cut out completely if unsecured creditors are paid less than 100%. This is the absolute priority rule, and it is a substantial obstacle for shareholders who want to retain ownership.

An issue that continues to be hotly debated is whether a junior class—typically, the shareholders who were owners of the prebankruptcy firm—can contribute new value to the reorganized firm in order to retain some interest in it. (Section 1129(b)(2)(B)(ii)'s prohibition, after all, is only as to what a junior class may retain "on account of" their claim or interest.) This so-called "new value exception" to the absolute priority rule raises two interrelated questions. The first question—whether any such exception actually exists—is one that the Supreme Court has avoided time after time. The Court has, instead, presumed the existence of the exception and addressed the second question—what sort of contribution suffices as new value.

We will address the first question first, with a circuit-level case that decided the issue head-on. We will then turn to the Supreme Court cases that have discussed the sort of contribution that is necessary.

BONNER MALL PARTNERSHIP v. U.S. BANCORP MORTGAGE CO. (IN RE BONNER MALL PARTNERSHIP)

United States Court of Appeals, Ninth Circuit, 1993.
2 F.3d 899.

REINHARDT, Circuit Judge.

This case requires us to decide whether the new value "exception" to the absolute priority rule survives the enactment of the Bankruptcy Reform Act of 1978 (better known as the Bankruptcy Code), which replaced the Bankruptcy Act of 1898. The new value exception allows the shareholders of a corporation in bankruptcy to obtain an interest in the reorganized debtor in exchange for new capital contributions over the objections of a class of creditors that has not received full payment on its claims. Whether this doctrine is viable under the Bankruptcy Code has significant implications for the relative bargaining power of debtors and creditors in Chapter 11 cases. Although no circuit court has taken a definitive position on this question, *dicta* in several opinions demonstrate intra and inter-circuit disagreements. District and bankruptcy courts are sharply divided on the question, as are the commentators. The question will in all probability ultimately be decided by the Supreme Court. In the meantime, we conclude that the new value exception remains a vital principle of bankruptcy law.

I. Background

In 1984–85, Northtown Investments built Bonner Mall. The project was financed by a $6.3 million loan, secured by the mall property, from First National Bank of North Idaho, which later sold the note and deed of trust to appellant U.S. Bancorp Mortgage Co. ("Bancorp"). In October 1986 the mall was purchased by appellee Bonner Mall Partnership ("Bonner"), subject to the lien acquired by Bancorp. Bonner is composed of six partners, five trusts and one individual investor, and was formed for the express purpose of buying the mall. Unfortunately, the cash-flow from the mall was much smaller than Bonner expected. When Bonner failed to pay its real estate taxes to Bonner County, Idaho, Bancorp commenced a nonjudicial foreclosure action. After several unsuccessful attempts to renegotiate and restructure Bonner's debt, Bancorp set a trustee's sale for March 14, 1991.

[Bonner filed a petition under Chapter 11 on March 13, 1991 and proposed a plan that relied on the new value exception. Bancorp sought relief from the stay, arguing that the exception did not survive enactment of the Bankruptcy Code. The bankruptcy judge agreed with Bancorp and granted its motion for relief from the stay.]

On appeal, the district judge determined that the only issue before him was whether the Bankruptcy Code had eliminated the new value exception. He found that it had not. * * * Bancorp filed a timely appeal to this court. Like the district court, we resolve only the question whether the new value exception survives. * * *

III. Bonner's Plan, Confirmation, and the New Value Exception

* * *

The issue before the bankruptcy judge in deciding whether to grant Bancorp's motion for relief from the stay was whether Bonner's Plan had a reasonable possibility of confirmation in a cramdown, *i.e.*, whether the standards set forth in § 1129(b)(1) could feasibly be satisfied.

The resolution of this question turns on whether there is a reasonable possibility that a bankruptcy judge could find Bonner's Plan "fair and equitable." Section 1129(b)(2) of the Code defines "fair and equitable" as *including* several enumerated *requirements*. * * * Section 1129(b)(2)(B) is a two-part codification of the judge-made absolute priority rule, compliance with which was a prerequisite to any determination that a plan was "fair and equitable" under the Bankruptcy Act.

Here, each of the unsecured claims against Bonner will not be paid in full on the effective date of the Plan. As a result, § 1129-(b)(2)(B)(i) cannot be satisfied. Therefore, Bonner's Plan cannot be held to be "fair and equitable" unless it complies with the provisions of § 1129(b)(2)(B)(ii). If it fails to meet the requirements of that section it is unconfirmable as a matter of law. A critical area of dispute in this case is whether Bonner's Plan violates § 1129(b)(2)(B)(ii) and, in turn, the absolute priority rule and the "fair and equitable" principle.

Under pre-Code Bankruptcy Act practice, a plan that allowed stockholders in the business that had filed for bankruptcy protection (old equity) to receive stock in the reorganized debtor in exchange for contributions of added capital (new value) could under certain conditions satisfy the absolute priority rule and be considered "fair and equitable" even though a senior class was not paid in full. *See Case v. Los Angeles Lumber Products Co.*, 308 U.S. 106, 121 (1939). That set of conditions became known collectively as the "new value exception" to the absolute priority rule; the terms of that "exception" will be discussed below.

Although the question we must ultimately answer is whether the new value exception survived the enactment of the Bankruptcy Code, we should note, preliminarily, that the term "exception" is misleading. The doctrine is not actually an exception to the absolute priority rule but is rather a corollary principle, or, more simply a description of the limitations of the rule itself. It is, as indicated above, the set of conditions under which former shareholders may lawfully obtain a priority interest in the reorganized venture. The Supreme Court appeared to recognize as much in *Case v. Los Angeles Lumber* when it stated that if a new capital contribution satisfies certain conditions "the creditor cannot complain that he is not accorded full right of priority against the corporate assets." *Id.* at 122 (internal quotation omitted). More properly, the new value exception should be called something like the "new capital-infusion doctrine" or as one commentator has suggested, "the scrutinize old equity participation rule." Elizabeth Warren, *A Theory of Absolute Priority*, 1991 Annual Survey of American Law 9, 42.

The question whether the adoption of the Code served to eliminate the new value exception was before the Supreme Court in *Norwest Bank Worthington v. Ahlers*, 485 U.S. 197 (1988). While there is language in the opinion questioning the viability of the doctrine, the Court explicitly stated that it was not deciding the issue. Instead, the Court assumed that the doctrine existed but found that all of its requirements were not satisfied under the facts of that case. Since *Ahlers*, several court[s] of appeals have avoided a direct holding on the viability of the "exception" by using the same stratagem.

* * *

While there is a division in the district and bankruptcy courts of our circuit and nationwide, the majority of courts that have considered the question have held that the new value exception is alive and well. We share the view that the doctrine remains a vital legal principle. Accordingly, we hold that the Code permits the confirmation of a reorganization plan that provides for the infusion of capital by the shareholders of the bankrupt corporation in exchange for stock if the plan meets the conditions that plans were required to meet prior to the Code's adoption.

IV. The New Value Exception and the Code

Our explanation of why we hold that the new value exception survives will address several distinct but related issues. First, we determine that the Code provision codifying the absolute priority rule does not prohibit confirmation of a new value plan. Second, we decide that Congress' failure expressly to include the new value doctrine as a standard to be considered in applying the "fair and equitable" principle does not reflect an intent to eliminate the exception. Finally, we conclude that the new value exception is fully consistent with the structure and underlying policies of Chapter 11.

A. *The Codification of the Absolute Priority Rule Does Not Serve to Eliminate the New Value Exception.*

The parties take diametrically opposed positions as to the consistency of the new value exception with § 1129(b)(2)(B)(ii). Bancorp argues that * * * the plain meaning of § 1129(b)(2)(B)(ii) demonstrates that the new value exception did not survive the enactment of the Code. Bonner contends that: 1) the infusion of new capital from a source outside the bankruptcy estate, even if the source is a former equity holder, is an independent act that does not violate the absolute priority rule; and 2) § 1129(b)(2)(B)(ii) does not forbid confirmation of plans that meet the requirements of the new value exception.

In determining whether § 1129(b)(2)(B)(ii) abolishes the new value exception we apply the traditional tools of statutory construction. * * * Applying these familiar rules, we conclude that the plain language of § 1129(b)(2)(B)(ii) demonstrates that Bonner's, and not Bancorp's, reading of the provision is correct.

1. Because Qualifying New Value Plans Do Not Give Old Equity Holders Stock in the Reorganized Debtor "On Account Of" Their Prior Ownership Interests, They Do Not Violate § 1129(b)(2)(B)(ii).

Section 1129(b)(2)(B)(ii) requires that a plan provide that with respect to a class of unsecured claims that has not received full payment—

> the holder of any claim or interest that is junior to the claims of such class will not receive or retain under the plan *on account of such junior claim or interest* any property. (Emphasis added.)

In plainer English the provision bars old equity from receiving any property via a reorganization plan *"on account of"* its prior equitable ownership when all senior claim classes are not paid in full. The central inquiry in determining the reach of the prohibition is the meaning of the critical words "on account of."

We have no difficulty in reconciling the "on account of" language with the new value exception. Under Bankruptcy Act practice, old equity was required to meet several requirements in order to take advantage of that doctrine. Former equity owners were required to offer value that was 1) new, 2) substantial, 3) money or money's worth, 4) necessary for a successful reorganization[,] and 5) reasonably equivalent to the value or interest received. *Case v. Los Angeles Lum-*

ber, 308 U.S. at 121-22. Several courts have concluded that if a proposed plan satisfies all of these requirements, *i.e.* the new value exception, it will not violate § 1129(b)(2)(B)(ii) of the Code and the absolute priority rule. Such a plan, they reason, will *not* give old equity property *"on account of"* prior interests, but instead will allow the former owners to participate in the reorganized debtor *on account of* a substantial, necessary, and fair new value contribution. We agree with their analysis.

We recognize that in some larger sense the reason that former owners receive new equity interests in reorganized ventures is that they are former owners. But it is also true that in new value transactions old equity owners receive stock in exchange for the additional capital they invest. Causation for any event has many and varied levels. Here, the answer to the meaning of the phrase "on account of" lies in the level of causation Congress had in mind when it prohibited old equity owners from receiving property "on account of" their prior interests. A reading of the full text of § 1129(b)(2)(B)(ii) makes it clear that what Congress had in mind was direct or immediate causation rather than a more remote variety, and that it did not intend to prohibit persons who receive stock because they have provided new capital from becoming participants in the reorganized debtor simply because they were also owners of the original enterprise.[23]

Had Congress intended that old equity never receive any property under a reorganization plan where senior claim classes are not paid in full, it could simply have omitted the "on account of" language from § 1129(b)(2)(B)(ii). We would then be left with an absolute prohibition against former equity owners' receiving or retaining property in the reorganized debtor in such circumstances. The expansive reading of the phrase "on account of such junior claim or interest" suggested by Ban-

---

[23]   Professor Warren has stated:

> The Code does not prohibit old equity from becoming a post-petition financer of the business or a post-plan owner of the business. The Code leaves old equity in the same position as any other potential investor: it may offer to buy any of the assets of the estate on the same terms as any other buyer.

A Theory of Absolute Priority at 39. *Accord* Raymond T. Nimmer, *Negotiated Bankruptcy Reorganization Plans: Absolute Priority and New Value Contributions*, 36 EMORY L.J. 1009, 1051 (1987); Bruce A. Markell, *Owners, Auctions, and Absolute Priority in Bankruptcy Reorganizations*, 44 STAN. L. REV. 69, 96-102 (1991).

corp would lead to the identical result, thus rendering the disputed phrase superfluous. Under that interpretation any distribution to old equity would always be "on account of" its former interest in some sense. We decline Bancorp's invitation to nullify Congress' deliberate use of the term "on account of such junior claim or interest," particularly since nearly identical language can be found throughout the Code.[24] Congress must have intended the "on account of" language to have some significant meaning as well as some particular limiting effect.

We believe that Congress intended the "on account of" phrase in § 1129(b)(2)(B)(ii) to require bankruptcy courts to determine whether a reorganization plan that gives stock to former equity holders does so primarily because of their old interests in the debtor or for legitimate business reasons. The new value doctrine provides the means by which a court can discover whether a particular new capital transaction is proposed "on account of" old equity's prior ownership or "on account of" its new contribution. In other words, in evaluating whether a reorganization plan satisfies the requirements of the new value exception a court is in fact determining whether old equity is unjustifiably attempting to retain its corporate ownership powers in violation of the absolute priority rule or whether there is genuine and fair exchange of new capital for an equity interest.

Contrary to Bancorp's contentions, § 1129(b)(2)(B)(ii) does not by its terms eliminate, or even refer to, the new value exception. Rather, the language of that section and the requirements of the new value principle complement each other. Consequently, the fact that a reorganization plan provides for a new value transaction does not in and of itself violate § 1129(b)(2)(B)(ii) and the absolutely [sic] priority rule.

2. The "On Account Of" Language of § 1129(b)(2)(B)(ii) Does Not Bar Plans That Give Old Equity Alone the Opportunity to Acquire Stock for a New Capital Contribution.

As Bancorp notes, several courts have held that where a reorganization plan gives old equity *alone* the right to obtain an interest in the reorganized debtor in exchange for new value, as Bonner's Plan does, the old equity holders are given "property" *on account of their prior ownership interests* and the absolute priority rule is violated. * * * Under this analysis the "property" given to old equity in violation of

---

[24] For example, § 1129 alone uses a variant of the "on account of such claim or interest" language seven times.

the absolute priority rule is *not* the stock in the reorganized debtor received in exchange for a new value contribution. Rather "*[the] exclusive right* of [the] Debtor's existing partners to obtain equity interests in [the] Debtor itself constitutes property that the partners retain 'on account of' their existing interests." *In re Outlook/Century, Ltd.*, 127 B.R. 650, 654 (Bankr. N.D.Cal.1991) (emphasis added).

We disagree with this analysis. Even assuming that an exclusive opportunity is "property," it does not follow that such an opportunity is property received or retained "on account of" old equity's prior ownership interests in the debtor. A proposed reorganization plan may give old equity the exclusive opportunity to purchase stock in exchange for new capital for other reasons. Exclusivity may be given because the plan proponent may believe that the participation of old equity in the new business will enhance the value of the business after reorganization. It is possible the debtor will conclude that additional funding will be easier to obtain if the old owners, the most likely investors, know in advance that their partners will all be familiar faces. Even more important, it may be apparent to the proponents of the plan that there will be no other legitimate investors who would be willing to put substantial capital into a business that is just emerging from Chapter 11 protection. * * * The proponent of a plan may have good reason to believe that old equity would not participate without the incentive of an exclusive opportunity.

As stated earlier, whether a particular plan gives old equity a property interest "on account of" its old ownership interests in violation of the absolute priority rule or for another, permissible reason is a factual question. The answer depends upon whether the requirements of the new value exception are met. We believe that this same analysis applies whether a plan gives old equity an exclusive or non-exclusive right of participation in a new value transaction. What matters instead is whether the proposed transaction meets the criterion "necessary to the success of the reorganization". In other words, if an exclusive participation plan satisfies that requirement, then it allows the partners the sole right to participate in a new value transaction not because of illegitimate collusion between old equity and the plan proponent but because such participation is necessary for a successful reorganization and in the best interests of all concerned. Of course, any exclusive participation plan must also fulfill the new value doctrine's four other requirements as well.

In sum, where the strictures of the new value exception are met, there is simply no violation of the absolute priority rule, whether the plan provides for exclusive or non-exclusive participation, because old equity will not retain or receive property "on account of" its old owner-ship interests in violation of § 1129(b)(2)(B)(ii).

B. Congress' Failure to List the New Value Exception as a Specific Doctrine Permitted under the "Fair and Equitable" Principle Does Not Demonstrate an Intent to Eliminate It.

While the absolute priority rule clearly does not *prohibit* confir-mation of a new value exception plan in a cramdown, this does not necessarily mean that the "fair and equitable" provisions of the Code should be interpreted as *permitting* confirmation of such a plan. Ban-corp argues that Congress' failure expressly to provide for the continua-tion of the new value exception in the provision setting forth the requirements of the "fair and equitable" principle must be interpreted as an implicit statement that it did not intend the doctrine to survive the adoption of the Code. Recognizing that the Code does not unambig-uously allow for new capital contribution plans, Bonner argues that such plans are consistent with the "fair and equitable" principle and that despite the absence of an express provision, Congress intended to main-tain the new value exception.

Bonner relies upon "the normal rule of statutory construction * * * that if Congress intends for legislation to change the interpretation of a judicially created concept, it makes that intent specific." *Midlantic Nat'l. Bank v. New Jersey Dept. of Envtl. Protection*, 474 U.S. 494, 501 (1986) (citations omitted); *Kelly v. Robinson*, 479 U.S. 36 (1988). This rule is followed with particular care in construing the Bankruptcy Code. When Congress amends the bankruptcy laws, it does not start from scratch. The Bankruptcy Code should not be read to abandon past bankruptcy practice absent a clear indication that Congress intended to do so.

* * *

There is simply no question that the new value exception was an established pre-Code Bankruptcy practice of which Congress would have had (and did have) knowledge. First, several Supreme Court cases had mentioned the principle, albeit the last time in 1946. Second, several appellate court cases recognized the new value doctrine after 1946. Finally, a proposal to broaden the new value exception was put before Congress during the drafting of the Code. While the proposal was rejected, that action demonstrates that Congress knew of the doc-trine when it enacted the Code.

Once it has been shown that Congress was aware of a pre-Code practice, the remaining inquiry * * * is whether it has made clear its intent to change that practice. Bancorp argues that the codification of the formerly judicially-defined concept of "fair and equitable" without a reference to the new value exception shows Congress' clear intent to eliminate the doctrine. However, § 1129(b)(2) explicitly defines the term "fair and equitable" as merely *including* the general requirements listed in the Code and expressly leaves room for additional factors to be considered in applying the principle in other particular circumstances. *See* § 102(3) (defining "includes" as "not limiting"). There is nothing in the language of the Code that suggests that courts cannot continue to apply the requirements of the new value exception in determining whether a plan that affords old equity a property interest in exchange for a capital contribution is "fair and equitable." In any event, the text of § 1129(b)(2) does not evidence the clear intent necessary to support a conclusion that Congress decided to eliminate the new value doctrine; silence is not a sufficient basis from which we may infer such a purpose.

Where the text of the Code does not unambiguously abrogate pre-Code practice, courts should presume that Congress intended it to continue unless the legislative history dictates a contrary result. It does not do so here. If anything, the legislative history of the Code supports the continued existence of the new value doctrine. It contains statements by sponsors of the Code that although § 1129(b)(2) lists several specific factors interpreting "fair and equitable," others were omitted to avoid statutory complexity and because courts would independently find that they were fundamental to "fair and equitable treatment."[33] This legislative history is evidence that Congress enacted the Code with knowledge that other, judicially-created standards governing the application of the "fair and equitable" principle existed and that it failed to include such standards for reasons other than an intent to eliminate them.

* * * Congress rejected a proposal by the Bankruptcy Commission to expand the new value exception significantly. That proposal would have eliminated the "money or money's worth" requirement set forth in *Case v. Los Angeles Lumber* and permitted new "important" contributions, including contributions of management, to suffice. Congress' rejection of the Bankruptcy Commission's proposal shows only

---

[33] One example of a well-established component of "fair and equitable" that was not included was the concept that no senior class is to receive more than 100 percent of the amount of its claims. * * *

that it did not want to broaden the exception; it does not indicate rejection of the exception itself. Indeed, "the Commission's proposal presupposed the existence of the new value exception, and Congress's rejection of the modification could just as easily be construed as an endorsement of the status quo." *Snyder v. Farm Credit Bank of St. Louis (In re Snyder)*, 967 F.2d 1126, 1130 (7th Cir.1992).

* * * Given that there is no evidence of a clear intent on the part of Congress to eliminate the new value exception in either the statutory text or the legislative history, * * * pre-Code practice continues to apply.

C. Congress' Overhaul of the Reorganization Process Does Not Justify a Conclusion that the New Value Exception was Abolished.

Bancorp contends that where the Code totally revamps an area of bankruptcy law, pre-Code practice may appropriately be ignored. Bancorp relies on *Union Bank v. Wolas*, 112 S.Ct. 527 (1992), in support of this proposition. In *Wolas* the Court unanimously found that the text of the Code sharply limited the pre-Code practice at issue. * * * While the *Wolas* Court relied in part upon the major changes made to the statutory framework by the enactment of the Code, it did so only as a *confirmation* of its earlier conclusion that the plain text of the Code provision altered pre-Code practice. Here, and as shown above, the language of the text at issue, § 1129(b)(2), does not by its terms affect the new value exception in any respect.

* * *

Bancorp also contends that the Code meant to give creditors, not the bankruptcy court, the power to decide when to waive the absolute priority rule. It is true that § 1126(c) allows creditors to consent to confirmation of a plan that does not comply with the absolute priority rule. However, that section permits creditors to waive a priority *they* possess. The new value exception allows bankruptcy courts to afford a priority to *others* over the creditors. There is simply no logical analysis that would allow us to conclude that by permitting creditors to waive their own priority Congress demonstrated the intent to deprive bankruptcy courts of *their* power to afford investors of new capital a priority over an impaired class of creditors. Moreover, the very purpose of the Code's cramdown provision, § 1129(b), which had no direct equivalent under the Act, is to allow the court, and not the creditors, to decide whether a "fair and equitable" plan should be confirmed over creditor objections. While creditor autonomy is certainly an important aspect of the reorganization process, the argument that the new value exception impedes that autonomy is really a complaint against the practice of confirmation by cramdown. That grievance cannot be addressed here.

Finally, Bancorp argues that the Code's creation of the entity of the debtor-in-possession to run the business in lieu of a trustee would cause self-dealing by insiders if the new value exception were still allowed. However, the very purpose of the Code's creation of the debtor-in-possession was to increase the power of those in control of the debtor during the reorganization process. Bankruptcy law is very formalistic in that it treats the debtor, the debtor-in-possession, and old equity as legally distinct entities when in reality they may all be one and the same. The risk of self-dealing among these entities at the expense of creditors is a risk created by the Code itself. The stringent requirements of the new value exception are designed to mitigate that risk. The enactment in the Code of changes that aggravate the self-dealing problem constitutes good reason for courts to make certain that a proposed new value plan strictly adheres to the requirements of the exception. The modifications to the reorganization process are not, however, cause for us to ignore several decades of bankruptcy practice in determining Congress' intent with respect to the new value exception.

Despite all of the differences between the Act and the Code, the primary rationale for the new value exception has not been eliminated by any statutory alteration to the confirmation process. The new value exception is based on "practical necessit[y]," on the recognition that new money frequently could not be obtained for the reorganized debtor in the absence of that doctrine. *See Mason v. Paradise Irrigation Dist.*, 326 U.S. 536, 542 (1946). That practical necessity remains just as pertinent under the Code. * * *

D. The New Value Exception is Consistent with the Underlying Policies of Chapter 11.

In interpreting statutory language we are not confined to the specific provision at issue but may look to the structure of the law as a whole and to its object and policy. Chapter 11 has two major objectives[:] 1) to permit successful rehabilitation of debtors; and 2) to maximize the value of the estate. The new value exception, properly applied, serves both goals. By permitting prior stockholders to contribute new money in exchange for participation in the reorganized company, the debtor is given an additional source of capital. The new contribution increases the amount available for the estate to use both in its reorganization and in funding the plan and paying creditors. Without the inducement of participation in the reorganized debtor, the new money may be unavailable. All parties involved, including the creditors, benefit from an increase in the assets of the estate.

"Prior owners are a source of capital different in kind from new investors in that they have an ongoing role in the reorganization and a prior investment in the company." *Prudential Ins. Co. v. F.A.B. Indus. (In re F.A.B. Indus.)*, 147 B.R. 763, 769 n. 13 (C.D.Cal.1992) [internal quotations deleted]. Moreover, in many situations the new value exception allows control and management of the company to remain with the original owners, who arguably can best reestablish a profitable business. Old owners may have valuable expertise and experience that outside investors lack. Some studies demonstrate that reorganizations have been more successful when former management was allowed to use its expertise in running the business.

It has been argued that the new value exception allows old equity to repurchase the business at a bargain price, while superior creditors go unpaid, and that this result is contrary to the Chapter 11 policy of protecting creditor interests. We believe that this argument is incorrect in two respects. First, while the protection of creditors' interests is an important purpose under Chapter 11, the Supreme Court has made clear that successful debtor reorganization and maximization of the value of the estate are the primary purposes.[37] Chapter 11 is designed to avoid liquidations under Chapter 7, since liquidations may have a negative impact on jobs, suppliers of the business, and the economy as a whole. The ability of stockholders to remain in possession and control of operations, rehabilitate the business, and retain ownership through the new value exception encourages debtors to attempt Chapter 11 reorganization instead of simply liquidating their assets and starting over.

Second, we believe that if the new value exception's requirements are properly applied, creditors' interests will generally be benefited as well. The strictures of the new value doctrine provide creditors with significant safeguards against collusion between the proponent of

---

[37] From one perspective, the debate over the survival of the new value exception is a division between those who perceive the paramount objective of Chapter 11 to be successful reorganization of the debtor and those who believe it should be protection of creditors' interests.

the reorganization plan and the old equity owners.[38]   Although the new value exception has been criticized as a subversion of the absolute priority rule, its requirements actually enhance the rule.   As we noted earlier, they constitute guidelines by which a court can ensure that old equity will *not* acquire an interest in the reorganized debtor or other property *on account of* its old ownership interests.   In fact, the new value exception puts limits on the power of old equity to gain an interest in the reorganized business beyond that provided in the explicit language of the Code.   * * *

VI. Conclusion

Viewed properly, "the new value exception" may be seen as a rule of construction, or a rule that serves to define the meaning of the absolute priority rule and determine when it has been satisfied.   As such it is as pertinent today as it was under pre-Code bankruptcy practice. The arguments that Bancorp advances do not persuade us that Congress would have had any reason to disregard a beneficial rule of construction that assists courts in implementing an important bankruptcy doctrine at the very time it was incorporating that doctrine into the Bankruptcy Code.

Nothing in the text of the Code prohibits the confirmation of plans that properly employ the new value doctrine.   Nor does the legislative history demonstrate that Congress intended to abrogate this judicially created, pre-Code legal principle.   Therefore, we conclude that the new value "exception," with its stringent requirements, survives. We recognize that, if applied carelessly, the doctrine has the potential to subvert the interests of creditors and allow debtors and old equity to abuse the reorganization process.   The proper answer to these concerns is vigilance on the part of bankruptcy courts in ensuring that all of the requirements of the new value exception are met in every case.   Here, it is unclear whether Bonner's plan can meet all of the requirements of the doctrine and achieve confirmation.   Nevertheless, it may well be within the realm of potentially confirmable plans and thereby survive Bancorp's motion for relief from the automatic stay.   The bankruptcy court must make that determination initially.

---

[38] If old equity contributes a substantial amount of new capital to the business undergoing reorganization, then the risk of a later failure falls more heavily on stockholders than creditors.

The judgment of the district court is AFFIRMED and the case is REMANDED to the bankruptcy court for further proceedings consistent with this opinion.

Notes and Questions

1. The Supreme Court granted certiorari in *Bonner Mall*, but the parties reached a settlement soon thereafter. The issue on appeal to the Supreme Court then became whether the Ninth Circuit's opinion should be vacated. The Court held that mootness by reason of settlement does not justify vacatur. *U.S. Bancorp Mortgage Co. v. Bonner Mall Partnership*, 513 U.S. 18, 115 S.Ct. 386, 130 L.Ed.2d 233 (1994). Thus, the Ninth Circuit's opinion in the case retains precedential force. In addition, as the Ninth Circuit suggested, the question at issue—whether the new value exception survives in the Code—remained ripe for Supreme Court consideration.

2. Was the outcome in *Bonner Mall* driven by the rules of statutory interpretation that the court followed? Would other approaches to statutory construction have supported a different result?

3. Is the difference in opinion expressed by various courts on this issue "a division between those who perceive the paramount objective of Chapter 11 to be successful reorganization of the debtor and those who believe it should be protection of creditors' interests," as the court speculated in footnote 37?

4. As the court in *Bonner Mall* noted, the Supreme Court held in *Case v. Los Angeles Lumber Products Co.*, 308 U.S. 106, 60 S.Ct. 1, 84 L.Ed. 110 (1939), that the stockholder of an insolvent debtor may participate in the plan of reorganization if that participation is "based on a contribution in money or money's worth, reasonably equivalent in view of all the circumstances to the participation of the stockholder." *Id.* at 121-22. When asked in *Norwest Bank Worthington v. Ahlers*, 485 U.S. 197, 108 S.Ct. 963, 99 L.Ed.2d 169 (1988), to determine whether that "new value exception" to the absolute priority rule had survived in the Code, the Supreme Court declined to reach the issue. The Court held instead that the exception did not encompass a promise by the respondent-shareholders to contribute their future "labor, experience, and expertise" to the reorganized entity:

> *Los Angeles Lumber* itself rejected an analogous proposition, finding that the promise of the existing shareholders to pledge their "financial standing and influence in the community" and their "continuity of management" to the reorganized enterprise was "[in]adequate consideration" that could not possibly be deemed "money's worth." [308 U.S.] at 122. No doubt, the efforts promised by the *Los Angeles Lumber* equity holders—like those of respondents—had "value" and would have been of some benefit to any reorganized

enterprise. But ultimately, as the Court said in *Los Angeles Lumber*, "[t]hey reflect merely vague hopes or possibilities." *Id*. at 122–23. The same is true of respondents' pledge of future labor and management skills.

Viewed from the time of approval of the plan, respondents' promise of future services is intangible, inalienable, and, in all likelihood, unenforceable. It "has no place in the asset column of the balance sheet of the new [entity]." *Id*. Unlike "money or money's worth," a promise of future services cannot be exchanged in any market for something of value to the creditors *today*. In fact, no decision of this Court or any Court of Appeals, other than the decision below, has ever found a promise to contribute future labor, management, or expertise sufficient to qualify for the *Los Angeles Lumber* exception to the absolute priority rule. In short, there is no way to distinguish between the promises respondents proffer here and those of the shareholders in *Los Angeles Lumber*; neither is an adequate contribution to escape the absolute priority rule.

Id. at 204-05, 108 S.Ct. at 967, 99 L.Ed.2d at 178.

The Supreme Court had another chance, in the following case, to address the question whether the new value exception to the absolute priority rule survives in the Bankruptcy Code. Again, that question received no answer.

BANK OF AMERICA NATIONAL TRUST & SAVINGS ASSOCIATION v. 203 NORTH LASALLE STREET PARTNERSHIP

United States Supreme Court, 1999.
526 U.S. 434, 119 S. Ct. 1411, 143 L.Ed. 2d 607

JUSTICE SOUTER delivered the opinion of the Court.

The issue in this Chapter 11 reorganization case is whether a debtor's prebankruptcy equity holders may, over the objection of a senior class of impaired creditors, contribute new capital and receive ownership interests in the reorganized entity, when that opportunity is given exclusively to the old equity holders under a plan adopted without consideration of alternatives. We hold that old equity holders are disqualified from participating in such a "new value" transaction by the terms of § 1129(b)(2)(B)(ii), which in such circumstances bars a junior interest holder's receipt of any property on account of his prior interest.

I

Petitioner, Bank of America National Trust and Savings Association (Bank), is the major creditor of respondent, 203 North LaSalle Street Partnership (Debtor or Partnership), an Illinois real estate limited partnership. The Bank lent the Debtor some $93 million, secured by a nonrecourse first mortgage on the Debtor's principal asset, 15 floors of an office building in downtown Chicago. In January 1995, the Debtor defaulted, and the Bank began foreclosure in a state court.

In March, the Debtor responded with a voluntary petition for relief under Chapter 11 of the Bankruptcy Code, which automatically stayed the foreclosure proceedings, see § 362(a). The Debtor's principal objective was to ensure that its partners retained title to the property so as to avoid roughly $20 million in personal tax liabilities, which would fall due if the Bank foreclosed. * * *

The value of the mortgaged property was less than the balance due the Bank, which elected to divide its undersecured claim into secured and unsecured deficiency claims under § 506(a) and § 1111(b). Under the plan, the Debtor separately classified the Bank's secured claim, its unsecured deficiency claim, and unsecured trade debt owed to other creditors. See § 1122(a). The Bankruptcy Court found that the Debtor's available assets were prepetition rents in a cash account of $3.1 million and the 15 floors of rental property worth $54.5 million. The secured claim was valued at the latter figure, leaving the Bank with an unsecured deficiency of $38.5 million.

So far as we need be concerned here, the Debtor's plan had these further features:

> (1) The Bank's $54.5 million secured claim would be paid in full between 7 and 10 years after the original 1995 repayment date.

> (2) The Bank's $38.5 million unsecured deficiency claim would be discharged for an estimated 16% of its present value.

> (3) The remaining unsecured claims of $90,000, held by the outside trade creditors, would be paid in full, without interest, on the effective date of the plan.

> (4) Certain former partners of the Debtor would contribute $6.125 million in new capital over the course of five years (the contribution being worth some $4.1 million in present value), in exchange for the Partnership's entire ownership of the reorganized debtor.

The last condition was an exclusive eligibility provision: the old equity holders were the only ones who could contribute new capital.[11]

The Bank objected and, being the sole member of an impaired class of creditors, thereby blocked confirmation of the plan on a consensual basis. See § 1129(a)(8). The Debtor, however, took the alternate route to confirmation of a reorganization plan, forthrightly known as the judicial "cramdown" process for imposing a plan on a dissenting class. § 1129(b).

There are two conditions for a cramdown. First, all requirements of § 1129(a) must be met (save for the plan's acceptance by each impaired class of claims or interests, see § 1129(a)(8)). Critical among them are the conditions that the plan be accepted by at least one class of impaired creditors, see § 1129(a)(10), and satisfy the "best-interest-of-creditors" test, see § 1129(a)(7). Here, the class of trade creditors with impaired unsecured claims voted for the plan, and there was no issue of best interest. Second, the objection of an impaired creditor class may be overridden only if "the plan does not discriminate unfairly, and is fair and equitable, with respect to each class of claims or interests that is impaired under, and has not accepted, the plan." § 1129(b)(1). As to a dissenting class of impaired unsecured creditors, such a plan may be found to be "fair and equitable" only if the allowed value of the claim is to be paid in full, § 1129(b)(2)(B)(i), or, in the alternative, if "the holder of any claim or interest that is junior to the claims of such [impaired unsecured] class will not receive or retain under the plan on account of such junior claim or interest any property," § 1129(b)(2)(B)(ii). That latter condition is the core of what is known as the "absolute priority rule."

The absolute priority rule was the basis for the Bank's position that the plan could not be confirmed as a cramdown. As the Bank read the rule, the plan was open to objection simply because certain old

---

[11]   The plan eliminated the interests of noncontributing partners. More than 60% of the Partnership interests would change hands on confirmation of the plan. The new Partnership, however, would consist solely of former partners, a feature critical to the preservation of the Partnership's tax shelter.

equity holders in the Debtor Partnership would receive property even though the Bank's unsecured deficiency claim would not be paid in full. The Bankruptcy Court approved the plan nonetheless, and accordingly denied the Bank's pending motion to convert the case to Chapter 7 liquidation, or to dismiss the case. The District Court affirmed, as did the Court of Appeals.

* * *

We granted certiorari to resolve a Circuit split on the issue. The Seventh Circuit in this case joined the Ninth in relying on a new value corollary to the absolute priority rule to support confirmation of such plans. See *In re Bonner Mall Partnership*, 2 F.3d 899, 910-916 (CA9 1993), cert. granted, 510 U.S. 1039, vacatur denied and appeal dism'd as moot, 513 U.S. 18 (1994). The Second and Fourth Circuits, by contrast, without explicitly rejecting the corollary, have disapproved plans similar to this one. See *In re Coltex Loop Central Three Partners, L.P.*, 138 F.3d 39, 44-45 (CA2 1998); *In re Bryson Properties, XVIII*, 961 F.2d 496, 504 (CA4), cert. denied, 506 U.S. 866 (1992).[15] We do not decide whether the statute includes a new value corollary or exception, but hold that on any reading respondent's proposed plan fails to satisfy the statute, and accordingly reverse.

II

The terms "absolute priority rule" and "new value corollary" (or "exception") are creatures of law antedating the current Bankruptcy Code, and to understand both those terms and the related but inexact language of the Code some history is helpful. The Bankruptcy Act preceding the Code contained no such provision as subsection (b)(2)(B)(ii), its subject having been addressed by two interpretive rules. The first was a specific gloss on the requirement of § 77B (and its successor, Chapter X) of the old Act, that any reorganization plan be "fair and equitable." The reason for such a limitation was the danger inherent in any reorganization plan proposed by a debtor, then and now, that the plan will simply turn out to be too good a deal for the debtor's owners. * * * Hence the pre-Code judicial response known as the absolute priority rule, that fairness and equity required that "the creditors * * * be paid before the stockholders could retain [equity interests] for any purpose whatever." *Northern Pacific R. Co. v. Boyd*, 228 U.S. 482, 508 (1913).

---

[15]   All four of these cases arose in the single-asset real estate context, the typical one in which new value plans are proposed.

The second interpretive rule addressed the first. Its classic formulation occurred in *Case v. Los Angeles Lumber Products Co.*, in which the Court spoke through Justice Douglas in this dictum:

> "It is, of course, clear that there are circumstances under which stockholders may participate in a plan of reorganization of an insolvent debtor * * * . Where the necessity [for new capital] exists and the old stockholders make a fresh contribution and receive in return a participation reasonably equivalent to their contribution, no objection can be made * * * .

> "We believe that to accord 'the creditor his full right of priority against the corporate assets' where the debtor is insolvent, the stockholder's participation must be based on a contribution in money or in money's worth, reasonably equivalent in view of all the circumstances to the participation of the stockholder." 308 U.S. at 121-122.

Although counsel for one of the parties here has described the *Case* observation as "'black-letter' principle," it never rose above the technical level of dictum in any opinion of this Court, which last addressed it in *Norwest Bank Worthington v. Ahlers*, 485 U.S. 197 (1988), holding that a contribution of "'labor, experience, and expertise'" by a junior interest holder was not in the "'money's worth'" that the *Case* observation required. *Id.* at 203-205. Nor, prior to the enactment of the current Bankruptcy Code, did any court rely on the *Case* dictum to approve a plan that gave old equity a property right after reorganization. Hence the controversy over how weighty the *Case* dictum had become, as reflected in the alternative labels for the new value notion: some writers and courts (including this one, see *Ahlers*, supra, at 203, n.3) have spoken of it as an exception to the absolute priority rule, while others have characterized it as a simple corollary to the rule, see, *e.g.*, *In re Bonner Mall Partnership*, 2 F.3d at 906.

Enactment of the Bankruptcy Code in place of the prior Act might have resolved the status of new value by a provision bearing its name or at least unmistakably couched in its terms, but the Congress chose not to avail itself of that opportunity. In 1973, Congress had considered proposals by the Bankruptcy Commission that included a recommendation to make the absolute priority rule more supple by allowing nonmonetary new value contributions. Although Congress took no action on any of the ensuing bills containing language that would have enacted such an expanded new value concept, each of them was reintroduced in the next congressional session. After extensive hearings, a substantially revised House bill emerged, but without any provision for nonmonetary new value contributions. After a lengthy mark-up session, the House produced H. R. 8200, which would eventually become the law. It had no explicit new value language, expansive or otherwise, but did codify the absolute priority rule in nearly its present form.

* * *

The upshot is that this history does nothing to disparage the possibility apparent in the statutory text, that the absolute priority rule now on the books as subsection (b)(2)(B)(ii) may carry a new value corollary. Although there is no literal reference to "new value" in the phrase "on account of such junior claim," the phrase could arguably carry such an implication in modifying the prohibition against receipt by junior claimants of any interest under a plan while a senior class of unconsenting creditors goes less than fully paid.

III

Three basic interpretations have been suggested for the "on account of" modifier. The first reading is proposed by the Partnership, that "on account of" harks back to accounting practice and means something like "in exchange for," or "in satisfaction of." On this view, a plan would not violate the absolute priority rule unless the old equity holders received or retained property in exchange for the prior interest, without any significant new contribution; if substantial money passed from them as part of the deal, the prohibition of subsection (b)(2)(B)(ii) would not stand in the way, and whatever issues of fairness and equity there might otherwise be would not implicate the "on account of" modifier.

This position is beset with troubles, the first one being textual. Subsection (b)(2)(B)(ii) forbids not only receipt of property on account of the prior interest but its retention as well. See also §§ 1129-(a)(7)(A)(ii), (a)(7)(B), (b)(2)(B)(i), (b)(2)(C)(i), (b)(2)(C)(ii). A common instance of the latter would be a debtor's retention of an interest in the insolvent business reorganized under the plan. Yet it would be exceedingly odd to speak of "retaining" property in exchange for the same property interest, and the eccentricity of such a reading is underscored by the fact that elsewhere in the Code the drafters chose to use the very phrase "in exchange for," § 1123(a)(5)(J) (a plan shall provide adequate means for implementation, including "issuance of securities of the debtor * * * for cash, for property, for existing securities, or in exchange for claims or interests"). It is unlikely that the drafters of legislation so long and minutely contemplated as the 1978 Bankruptcy Code would have used two distinctly different forms of words for the same purpose.

The second difficulty is practical: the unlikelihood that Congress meant to impose a condition as manipulable as subsection (b)(2)(B)(ii) would be if "on account of" meant to prohibit merely an exchange unaccompanied by a substantial infusion of new funds but permit one whenever substantial funds changed hands. "Substantial" or "significant" or "considerable" or like characterizations of a monetary contribution would measure it by the Lord Chancellor's foot, and an absolute priority rule so variable would not be much of an absolute. Of course it is true (as already noted) that, even if old equity holders could displace the rule by adding some significant amount of cash to the deal, it would not follow that their plan would be entitled to adoption; a contested plan would still need to satisfy the overriding condition of fairness and equity. But that general fairness and equity criterion would apply in any event, and one comes back to the question why Congress would have bothered to add a separate priority rule without a sharper edge.

Since the "in exchange for" reading merits rejection, the way is open to recognize the more common understanding of "on account of" to mean "because of." This is certainly the usage meant for the phrase at other places in the statute, see § 1111(b)(1)(A) (treating certain claims as if the holder of the claim "had recourse against the debtor on account of such claim"); § 522(d)(10)(E) (permitting debtors to exempt payments under certain benefit plans and contracts "on account of illness, disability, death, age, or length of service"); § 547(b)(2) (authorizing trustee to avoid a transfer of an interest of the debtor in property "for or on account of an antecedent debt owed by the debtor"); § 547-(c)(4)(B) (barring trustee from avoiding a transfer when a creditor gives new value to the debtor "on account of which new value the debtor did not make an otherwise unavoidable transfer to * * * such creditor"). So, under the commonsense rule that a given phrase is meant to carry a given concept in a single statute, the better reading of subsection (b)(2)(B)(ii) recognizes that a causal relationship between holding the prior claim or interest and receiving or retaining property is what activates the absolute priority rule.

The degree of causation is the final bone of contention. We understand the Government, as *amicus curiae*, to take the starchy position not only that any degree of causation between earlier interests and retained property will activate the bar to a plan providing for later property, but also that whenever the holders of equity in the Debtor end up with some property there will be some causation; when old equity, and not someone on the street, gets property the reason is *res ipsa loquitur*. An old equity holder simply cannot take property under a plan if creditors are not paid in full.

There are, however, reasons counting against such a reading. If, as is likely, the drafters were treating junior claimants or interest holders as a class at this point, then the simple way to have prohibited the old interest holders from receiving anything over objection would have been to omit the "on account of" phrase entirely from subsection (b)(2)(B)(ii). On this assumption, reading the provision as a blanket prohibition would leave "on account of" as a redundancy, contrary to the interpretive obligation to try to give meaning to all the statutory language. One would also have to ask why Congress would have desired to exclude prior equity categorically from the class of potential owners following a cramdown. Although we have some doubt about the Court of Appeals's assumption that prior equity is often the only source of significant capital for reorganizations, old equity may well be in the best position to make a go of the reorganized enterprise and so may be the party most likely to work out an equity-for-value reorganization.

A less absolute statutory prohibition would follow from reading the "on account of" language as intended to reconcile the two recognized policies underlying Chapter 11, of preserving going concerns and maximizing property available to satisfy creditors. Causation between the old equity's holdings and subsequent property substantial enough to disqualify a plan would presumably occur on this view of things whenever old equity's later property would come at a price that failed to provide the greatest possible addition to the bankruptcy estate, and it would always come at a price too low when the equity holders obtained or preserved an ownership interest for less than someone else would have paid.[26] A truly full value transaction, on the other hand, would pose no threat to the bankruptcy estate not posed by any reorganization, pro-

---

[26] Even when old equity would pay its top dollar and that figure was as high as anyone else would pay, the price might still be too low unless the old equity holders paid more than anyone else would pay, on the theory that the "necessity" required to justify old equity's participation in a new value plan is a necessity for the participation of old equity as such. On this interpretation, disproof of a bargain would not satisfy old equity's burden; it would need to show that no one else would pay as much. No such issue is before us, and we emphasize that our holding here does not suggest an exhaustive list of the requirements of a proposed new value plan.

vided of course that the contribution be in cash or be realizable money's worth, just as *Ahlers* required for application of *Case*'s new value rule.

IV

Which of these positions is ultimately entitled to prevail is not to be decided here, however, for even on the latter view the Bank's objection would require rejection of the plan at issue in this case. It is doomed, we can say without necessarily exhausting its flaws, by its provision for vesting equity in the reorganized business in the Debtor's partners without extending an opportunity to anyone else either to compete for that equity or to propose a competing reorganization plan. Although the Debtor's exclusive opportunity to propose a plan under § 1121(b) is not itself "property" within the meaning of subsection (b)(2)(B)(ii), the respondent partnership in this case has taken advantage of this opportunity by proposing a plan under which the benefit of equity ownership may be obtained by no one but old equity partners. Upon the court's approval of that plan, the partners were in the same position that they would have enjoyed had they exercised an exclusive option under the plan to buy the equity in the reorganized entity, or contracted to purchase it from a seller who had first agreed to deal with no one else. It is quite true that the escrow of the partners' proposed investment eliminated any formal need to set out an express option or exclusive dealing provision in the plan itself, since the court's approval that created the opportunity and the partners' action to obtain its advantage were simultaneous. But before the Debtor's plan was accepted no one else could propose an alternative one, and after its acceptance no one else could obtain equity in the reorganized entity. At the moment of the plan's approval the Debtor's partners necessarily enjoyed an exclusive opportunity that was in no economic sense distinguishable from the advantage of the exclusively entitled offeror or option holder. This opportunity should, first of all, be treated as an item of property in its own right. While it may be argued that the opportunity has no market value, being significant only to old equity holders owing to their potential tax liability, such an argument avails the Debtor nothing, for several reasons. It is to avoid just such arguments that the law is settled that any otherwise cognizable property interest must be treated as sufficiently valuable to be recognized under the Bankruptcy Code. Even aside from that rule, the assumption that no one but the Debtor's partners might pay for such an opportunity would obviously support no inference that it is valueless, let alone that it should not be treated as property. And, finally, the source in the tax law of the opportunity's value to the partners implies in no way that it lacks value to others. It might, indeed, be valuable to another precisely as a way to keep the

Debtor from implementing a plan that would avoid a Chapter 7 liquidation.

Given that the opportunity is property of some value, the question arises why old equity alone should obtain it, not to mention at no cost whatever. The closest thing to an answer favorable to the Debtor is that the old equity partners would be given the opportunity in the expectation that in taking advantage of it they would add the stated purchase price to the estate. But this just begs the question why the opportunity should be exclusive to the old equity holders. If the price to be paid for the equity interest is the best obtainable, old equity does not need the protection of exclusiveness (unless to trump an equal offer from someone else); if it is not the best, there is no apparent reason for giving old equity a bargain. There is no reason, that is, unless the very purpose of the whole transaction is, at least in part, to do old equity a favor. And that, of course, is to say that old equity would obtain its opportunity, and the resulting benefit, because of old equity's prior interest within the meaning of subsection (b)(2)(B)(ii). Hence it is that the exclusiveness of the opportunity, with its protection against the market's scrutiny of the purchase price by means of competing bids or even competing plan proposals, renders the partners' right a property interest extended "on account of" the old equity position and therefore subject to an unpaid senior creditor class's objection.

It is no answer to this to say that the exclusive opportunity should be treated merely as a detail of the broader transaction that would follow its exercise, and that in this wider perspective no favoritism may be inferred, since the old equity partners would pay something, whereas no one else would pay anything. If this argument were to carry the day, of course, old equity could obtain a new property interest for a dime without being seen to receive anything on account of its old position. But even if we assume that old equity's plan would not be confirmed without satisfying the judge that the purchase price was top dollar, there is a further reason here not to treat property consisting of an exclusive opportunity as subsumed within the total transaction proposed. On the interpretation assumed here, it would, of course, be a fatal flaw if old equity acquired or retained the property interest without paying full value. It would thus be necessary for old equity to demonstrate its payment of top dollar, but this it could not satisfactorily do when it would receive or retain its property under a plan giving it exclusive rights and in the absence of a competing plan of any sort.[27] Under

---

[27] The dissent emphasizes the care taken by the Bankruptcy Judge in examining the valuation evidence here, in arguing that there is no occasion for us to consider

a plan granting an exclusive right, making no provision for competing bids or competing plans, any determination that the price was top dollar would necessarily be made by a judge in bankruptcy court, whereas the best way to determine value is exposure to a market. This is a point of some significance, since it was, after all, one of the Code's innovations to narrow the occasions for courts to make valuation judgments, as shown by its preference for the supramajoritarian class creditor voting scheme in § 1126(c), see *Ahlers, supra*, at 207 ("The Code provides that it is up to the creditors—and not the courts—to accept or reject a reorganization plan which fails to provide them adequate protection or fails to honor the absolute priority rule"). In the interest of statutory coherence, a like disfavor for decisions untested by competitive choice ought to extend to valuations in administering subsection (b)(2)(B)(ii) when some form of market valuation may be available to test the adequacy of an old equity holder's proposed contribution.

Whether a market test would require an opportunity to offer competing plans or would be satisfied by a right to bid for the same interest sought by old equity, is a question we do not decide here. It is enough to say, assuming a new value corollary, that plans providing junior interest holders with exclusive opportunities free from competition and without benefit of market valuation fall within the prohibition of § 1129(b)(2)(B)(ii).

The judgment of the Court of Appeals is accordingly reversed, and the case is remanded for further proceedings consistent with this opinion.

It is so ordered.

[The opinion of JUSTICES THOMAS and SCALIA, concurring in the judgment but taking great exception to the majority's approach to statutory interpretation, is omitted.

In a dissenting opinion, JUSTICE STEVENS stated that the majority had "wisely" rejected "the Government's 'starchy' position that an old equity holder can never receive an interest in a reorganized venture as a result of a cramdown unless the creditors are first paid in full." He believed, however, that the Court's interpretation of § 1129(b)(2)(B)(ii) was unsupported by the statutory text.]

---

the relationship between valuation process and top-dollar requirement. While we agree with the dissent as to the judge's conscientious handling of the matter, the ensuing text of this opinion sets out our reasons for thinking the Act [sic] calls for testing valuation by a required process that was not followed here.

Questions

1. Do you agree with the Court's interpretation of the confirmation procedures required by the Code?

2. What do you think the Court would do if confronted with a plan, reached through a process open to third parties, under which equity holders—the only bidders—were to contribute new value for new equity? In other words, *is* there a new value exception (or corollary) to the absolute priority rule?

Note on the Absolute Priority Rule in Chapter 11 Proceedings Involving Individual Debtors

Before 2005, most courts held that § 1129(b)(2)(B) applied equally to both individual and corporate debtors. Under that approach, the absolute priority rule would make it impossible for an individual debtor to retain his or her business unless unsecured creditors were paid in full. Changes to the Code made in 2005, however, have created questions regarding the continued viability of the absolute priority rule when the Chapter 11 debtor is an individual.

The 2005 Amendments added language to § 1129(b)(2)(B)(ii): "except that in a case in which the debtor is an individual, the debtor may retain property included in the estate under section 1115, subject to the requirements of subsection (a)(14) of this section." (Subsection (a)(14) requires, as a condition of plan confirmation, that all judicially-ordered post-petition domestic support obligations have been satisfied.) Section 1115, in turn, provides that, in individual cases, property of the estate "includes, in addition to the property specified in section 541," first, "all property of the kind specified in section 541 that the debtor acquires" during the case, and second, "earnings from services performed by the debtor" during the case.

The court in *In re Shat*, 424 B.R. 854 (Bankr. D. Nev. 2010), described the interpretive problem as follows:

> Section 1115 thus defines property of the estate for an individual chapter 11 debtor via a two-step process. Initially, § 1115 creates a baseline estate of all the property covered by § 541. It then adds to that one class of property excluded for other chapter 11's by § 541(a)(6): postpetition income from services.

> So far, so good. But other than postpetition income from services, what else, if anything, changes? That depends on what the meaning of the ambiguous phrase in § 1129(b)(2)(B)(ii) that an individual debtor may retain "property included in the estate under § 1115."

If "included" means only property which is added by § 1115, then § 1129(b)(2)(B)(ii) has a very narrow meaning: it refers only to postpetition income from services—and not to property originally specified in § 541. Section 1115, however, itself includes § 541(a) property. Thus, "included" could refer to all property § 1115 itself references, and this would then be a reference to the superset of § 541(a) property *and* the debtor's postpetition service income. Put another way, if § 1115 entirely supplants § 541 by specifically incorporating it and adding to it, the "included" has a very broad meaning, essentially exempting individuals from the absolute priority rule as to unsecured creditors.

Id. at 863.

Courts taking the "broad" view conclude that Congress intended abrogation, permitting the debtor to retain property owned at the time of the filing of the petition. That approach makes individual Chapter 11 cases parallel to Chapter 13, which has never had an absolute priority rule. See, e.g., *Shat*, *supra*; *In re Roedemeier*, 374 B.R. 264 (Bankr. D.Kan.2007). Under the "narrow" view, by contrast, courts read § 1129(b)(2)(B)(ii) to refer only to the additional property brought into the estate by § 1115, not to property that is already part of the estate under § 541. Those courts, therefore, permit the individual Chapter 11 debtor to retain only property acquired post-petition (unless, of course unsecured creditors are paid in full). See, e.g., *In re Walsh*, 447 B.R. 45 (Bankr. D.Mass.2011); *In re Maharaj*, 449 B.R. 484 (Bankr. E.D.Va.2011).

These issues are likely to arise with some frequency because a substantial number of Chapter 11 cases are filed by individuals. Early results from an ongoing empirical study, supported by the American Bankruptcy Institute, show that the debtors in nearly one-third of Chapter 11 cases are individuals. These debtors tend to have debts in excess of the Chapter 13 limits, and assets to match.

One of the principal questions being addressed by the study is whether Chapter 11, as currently structured, suits the needs of individual debtors.

c. Tax Claims

We end this Chapter where we began—with a debate about the limits of a bankruptcy court's power under § 105. The debate arose in the context of a Chapter 11 debtor's effort to allocate tax payments, first, to trust fund taxes. Five circuits considered this question before the Supreme Court granted certiorari. The process of appellate review provided sharp focus to the conflicting policies of the Internal Revenue Code, on the one hand—namely, to maximize the collection of revenue—and the Bankruptcy Code, on the other—to maximize a debtor's ability to reorganize.

Although the IRS is not a sympathetic character to many of us, perhaps general creditors stand to lose the most under the Supreme Court's holding.

UNITED STATES v. ENERGY RESOURCES CO.

United States Supreme Court, 1990.
495 U.S. 545, 110 S.Ct. 2139, 109 L.Ed.2d 580.

JUSTICE WHITE delivered the opinion of the Court.

In this case, we decide that a bankruptcy court has the authority to order the Internal Revenue Service (IRS) to treat tax payments made by Chapter 11 debtor corporations as trust fund payments where the bankruptcy court determines that this designation is necessary for the success of a reorganization plan.

I

The Internal Revenue Code requires employers to withhold from their employees' paychecks money representing employees' personal income taxes and Social Security taxes. Because federal law requires employers to hold these funds in "trust for the United States," these taxes are commonly referred to as "trust fund" taxes. Should employers fail to pay trust fund taxes, the Government may collect an equivalent sum directly from the officers or employees of the employer who are responsible for collecting the tax. 26 U.S.C. § 6672. These individuals are commonly referred to as "responsible" individuals.

This case involves corporations that have filed petitions for reorganization under Chapter 11 of the Bankruptcy Code. *[Both debtors, Newport Offshore and Energy Resources, proposed plans under which tax claims would be paid over time, with payments to be allocated first to satisfy trust fund taxes. The bankruptcy court confirmed Newport Offshore's plan, but the Rhode Island district court reversed. Newport Offshore appealed to the First Circuit. The IRS refused to apply Energy Resources's payments as the plan provided and the bankruptcy court ordered the IRS to do so. The Massachusetts district court affirmed and the government appealed to the First Circuit.]*

Consolidating the two cases, the First Circuit reversed in *In re Newport Offshore Ltd.* and affirmed in *In re Energy Resources Co.* The court first considered whether a tax payment made pursuant to a Chapter 11 reorganization plan is "voluntary" or "involuntary" as those terms are used in the IRS' own rules. IRS policy permits taxpayers who "voluntarily" submit payments to the IRS to designate the tax liability to which the payment will apply. The taxpayer corporations argued that tax payments within a Chapter 11 reorganization are best characterized as "voluntary" and therefore that the IRS' own rules bind the agency to respect the debtors' designation of the tax payments. Granting deference to the agency's interpretation of its own rules, the First Circuit accepted the IRS' view that payments made pursuant to the Chapter 11 plan are involuntary for purposes of the IRS' rules. The First Circuit concluded, however, that even if the payments were properly characterized as involuntary under the IRS' regulations, the Bankruptcy Courts nevertheless had the authority to order the IRS to apply an "involuntary" payment made by a Chapter 11 debtor to trust fund tax liabilities if the Bankruptcy Court concluded that this designation was necessary to ensure the success of the reorganization.

We granted certiorari because the First Circuit's conclusion on this issue conflicts with decisions in other Circuits. We affirm the judgment below, for whether or not the payments at issue are rightfully considered to be involuntary, a bankruptcy court has the authority to order the IRS to apply the payments to trust fund liabilities if the bankruptcy court determines that this designation is necessary to the success of a reorganization plan.

II

The Bankruptcy Code does not explicitly authorize the bankruptcy courts to approve reorganization plans designating tax payments as either trust fund or nontrust fund. The Code, however, grants the bankruptcy courts residual authority to approve reorganization plans including "any * * * appropriate provision not inconsistent with the applicable provisions of this title." § 1123(b)(5); see also § 1129. The Code also states that bankruptcy courts may "issue any order, process, or judgment that is necessary or appropriate to carry out the provisions" of the Code. § 105(a). These statutory directives are consistent with the traditional understanding that bankruptcy courts, as courts of equity, have broad authority to modify creditor-debtor relationships.

The Government suggests that, in this case, the Bankruptcy Courts have transgressed one of the limitations on their equitable power. Specifically, the Government contends that the orders conflict with the Code's provisions protecting the Government's ability to collect delinquent taxes. As the Government points out, the Code provides a priority for specified tax claims, including those at issue in this case, and makes those tax debts nondischargeable. See §§ 507(a)(7), 523(a)(1)(A). The Code, moreover, requires a bankruptcy court to assure itself that reorganization will succeed, § 1129(a)(11), and therefore that the IRS, in all likelihood, will collect the tax debt owed. The tax debt must be paid off within six years. § 1129(a)(9)(C).

It is evident that these restrictions on a bankruptcy court's authority do not preclude the court from issuing orders of the type at issue here, for those restrictions do not address the bankruptcy court's ability to designate whether tax payments are to be applied to trust fund or non-trust-fund tax liabilities. The Government is correct that, if it can apply a debtor corporation's tax payments to non-trust-fund liability before trust fund liability, it stands a better chance of debt discharge because the debt that is not guaranteed will be paid off before the guaranteed debt. While this result might be desirable from the Government's standpoint, it is an added protection not specified in the Code itself: Whereas the Code gives it the right to be assured that its taxes will be paid in six years, the Government wants an assurance that its taxes will be paid even if the reorganization fails—*i.e.*, even if the bankruptcy court is incorrect in its judgment that the reorganization plan will succeed.

Even if consistent with the Code, however, a bankruptcy court order might be inappropriate if it conflicted with another law that should have been taken into consideration in the exercise of the court's discretion. The Government maintains that the orders at issue here contravene § 6672 of the Internal Revenue Code, the provision permitting the IRS to collect unpaid trust fund taxes directly from the personal assets of "responsible" individuals. The Government contends that § 6672 reflects a congressional decision to protect the Government's tax revenues by ensuring an additional source from which trust fund taxes might be collected. It is true that § 6672 provides that, if the Government is unable to collect trust fund taxes from a corporate taxpayer, the Government has an alternative source for this revenue. Here, however, the Bankruptcy Courts' orders do not prevent the Government from collecting trust fund revenue; to the contrary, the orders require the Government to collect trust fund payments before collecting non-trust-fund payments. As the Government concedes, § 6672 remains both during and after the corporate Chapter 11 filing as an alternative collection source for trust fund taxes.

The Government nevertheless contends that the Bankruptcy Courts' orders contravene § 6672 because, if the IRS cannot designate a debtor corporation's tax payments as non-trust-fund, the debtor might be able to pay only the guaranteed debt, leaving the Government at risk for non-trust-fund taxes. This may be the case, but § 6672, by its terms, does not protect against this eventuality. That section plainly does not require us to hold that the orders at issue here, otherwise wholly consistent with a bankruptcy court's authority under the Bankruptcy Code, were nonetheless improvident.

III

In this case, the Bankruptcy Courts have not transgressed any limitation on their broad power. We therefore hold that they may order the IRS to apply tax payments to offset trust fund obligations where it concludes that this action is necessary for a reorganization's success. The judgment of the Court of Appeals is therefore

Affirmed.

JUSTICE BLACKMUN dissents.

Questions

1. What incentives has the Supreme Court created for individuals personally responsible for certain corporate taxes to look longingly at bankruptcy?

2. Does *Energy Resources* have any limiting principle? What solace can you offer a creditor who is concerned that corporate assets will be used, through a reorganization plan, to pay taxes for which corporate insiders are personally liable?

Index

References are to Pages